HOLOCAUST ENCYCLOPEDIA: UNCENSORED AND UNCONSTRAINED

Holocaust Encyclopedia

uncensored and unconstrained

Academic Research
Media Review
Education Group LTD

Holocaust Encyclopedia: uncensored and unconstrained.
Version 1.05, 28 November 2023
Published by: Academic Research Media Review Education Group LTD
86-90 Paul Street, London, EC2A 4NE, United Kingdom.

ISBN hardcover full-color edition: 978-1-911733-00-3
ISBN hardcover black-and-white edition: 978-1-911733-03-4
ISBN paperback full-color edition: 978-1-911733-04-1
ISBN paperback black-and-white edition: 978-1-911733-01-0
ISBN ePub edition (text only): 978-1-911733-02-7

© 2023 Academic Research Media Review Education Group LTD

https://NukeBook.org

The project *Holocaust Encyclopedia: uncensored and unconstrained* and its related products (videos, audio files and book, eBooks, print books, and the website www.NukeBook.org) are creations of the Academic Research, Media Review, Education Group, Ltd. Any copyrights and trademarks deriving from products created with this project are owned by Academic Research, Media Review, Education Group Ltd.

This encyclopedia was compiled by several scholars, with the assistance of numerous volunteers from various countries. Unless Western societies stop persecuting and prosecuting scholars and laypersons who peacefully voice their skepticism about aspects of the currently predominant Holocaust narrative, we will not disclose the identity of any of these individuals.

Table of Contents

Introduction 11

A

Absurd Claims 19
Adametz, Gerhard 20
Air Photos 21
Aktion 1005 23
Aktion Reinhardt 27
Aktion Reinhardt Camps 28
Amiel, Szymon 28
Auerbach, Rachel 29
Aumeier, Hans 30
Auschwitz 31
Auschwitz, Bombing of 34
Auschwitz Album 34
Auschwitz Death Books 38
Auschwitz Main Camp 39
Auschwitz Museum 47
Auschwitz Trials 49
Austria 50
Avey, Denis 51

B

Babi Yar 53
Bach-Zelewski, Erich von dem 57
Bacon, Yehuda 57
Bad Nenndorf 58
Bahir, Moshe 59
Baltic Countries 59
Bard-Nomberg, Helena 60
Bartel, Erwin 61
Barton, Russell 61
Baskind, Ber 61
Baum, Bruno 62
Becher, Kurt 62
Becker, August 63
Bednarz, Władysław 65
Beer, Abraham 65
Behr, Emil 65
Belgium 65
Belzec 65
Belzec Trial 71
Bendel, Charles S. 72
Bennahmias, Daniel 73
Benroubi, Maurice 73
Berg, Isai Davidovich 74
Bergen-Belsen 74
Bergen-Belsen Trials 76
Berger, Oskar 77
Berlyant, Semen 77
Bialek, Regina 78
Białystok 78
Bily, Henry 79
Bimko, Ada 79
Birkenau 80
Birobidzhan 89
Biskovitz, Ya'akov 89
Blaha, Franz 90
Blatt, Thomas 90
Blobel, Paul 91
Blyazer, A. 92
Bock, Ludwig 92
Böck, Richard 93
Boger, Wilhelm 94
Bomba, Abraham 95
Bone Mill 96
Boüard, Michel de 96
Brener, Hejnoch 97
Brest 97
British Radio Intercepts 97
Broad, Pery S. 98
Brodsky, Isaak 99
Bronnaya Gora 100
Buchenwald 100
Buchholcowa, Janina 101
Budnik, David 101
Buki, Milton 102
Bulgaria 103
BUNA 103
Bunkers 103
Burmeister, Walter 104

C

Camps 107
Carbon monoxide 107
Censorship 108
Chamaides, Heinrich 110
Chasan, Shaul 111
Chełmno 112
Chomka, Władysław 116
Christophersen, Thies 116
Chybiński, Stanisław 117
Code Language 117
Cohen, Leon 118
Commissar Order 119
Compensation 120
Concentration Camps 121
Construction Office 122
Convergence of Evidence 122
Corpse Photos 123
Corry, Joe 126
Cremation Propaganda 126
Crematoria 128
Criminal Traces 138
Crystal Night 139
Cykert, Abraham 140
Cyrankiewicz, Jozef 140
Czech, Danuta 141
Czechia 141
Czechowicz, Aron 141

D

Dachau 143
Dachau Museum 145

Dachau Trials	146
Daluege, Kurt	147
Damjanović, Momčilo	147
Davydov, Vladimir	148
Dawidowski, Roman	149
DDT	149
DEGESCH	150
Dejaco, Walter	150
Demjanjuk, John	151
Demography, Jewish	152
Denisow, Piotr	155
Denmark	155
Dibowski, Wilhelm	155
Diesel Exhaust	155
Długoborski, Wácław	156
Doessekker, Bruno	157
Doliner, Iosif	157
Dragon, Abraham	158
Dragon, Szlama	158
Dugin, Itzhak	160

E

Eberl, Irmfried	163
Edelman, Salman	163
Ehrenburg, Ilya	163
Eichmann, Adolf	163
Einsatzgruppen	165
Eisenschmidt, Eliezer	174
Eitan, Dov	174
Emigration	174
Engel, Chaim	177
Epstein, Berthold	177
Erber, Josef	177
Escapes, from Gas Chamber	177
Euthanasia	178
Evacuations, from German Camps	179
Evidence	179
Exaggerated Death Tolls	181
Excavations, of German Mass Graves	182
Execution Chambers	183
Exotic Murder Weapons	183
Explosives, as Murder Weapon	183
Explosives, to Erase Corpses	183
Extermination Camps	184
Extirpation (*Ausrottung, Vernichtung*)	184

F

Fabian, Bela	189
Faitelson, Alex	189
Fajgielbaum, Srul	190
Falborski, Bronisław	190
False-Memory Syndrome	190
False Witnesses	191
Family Camp, at Auschwitz	192
Farber, Yuri	193
Farkas, Henrik	194
Fat, Extracted from Burning Corpses	194
Feldhendler, Leon	195
Felenbaum-Weiss, Hella	195
Final Solution	195
Finkelsztein, Leon	196
First Gassing, at Auschwitz	197
Fischer, Bruno	198
Fischer, Horst	199
Flames, out of Crematory Chimneys	200
Fliamenbaum, David	200
Florstedt, Hermann	201
Flossenbürg	201
Fort IX	202
France	203
Frank, Anne	204
Frank, Hans	206
Franke-Gricksch, Alfred	207
Frankfurt Auschwitz Show Trial	208
Frankl, Viktor	210
Franz, Kurt	210
Freiberg, Ber	211
Friedman, Arnold	211
Fries, Jakob	212
Fritzsch, Karl	213
Frosch, Chaim	213
Fumigation Gas Chamber	213
Furnace	216

G

Gabai, Dario	217
Gabai, Yaakov	217
Gál, Gyula	219
Garbarz, Moshé	219
Gas Chamber	220
Gastight Doors	221
Gas Vans	222
Gaubschat Company	225
Generalplan Ost	225
Germany	226
Gerstein, Kurt	227
Gertner, Szaja	230
Geysers of Blood, from Mass Graves	230
Ghettos	231
Glazar, Richard	232
Globocnik, Odilo	233
Glücks, Richard	233
Goebbels, Joseph	234
Gol, Szloma	235
Gold Teeth	236
Goldberg, Szymon	236
Goldfarb, Abraham I.	236
Göring, Hermann	238
Göth, Amon	239
Grabner, Maximilian	239
Gradowski, Salmen	240
Gray, Martin	241
Greece	242
Grocher, Mietek	242
Grojanowski, Jakov	242
Gröning, Oskar	242
Gross-Rosen	243
Grossman, Vasily	243
Groundwater Level	243
Grüner, Miklós	245

Gulba, Franciszek	245
Gusen	246
Gypsies	246

H

Hähle, Johannes	249
Hair of Camp Inmates	250
Hanel, Salomea	250
Hartheim	250
Hassler, Johann	251
Healthcare	251
Hénocque, Georges	252
Herman, Chaim	252
Heydrich, Reinhardt	253
Himmler, Heinrich	254
Himmler Speeches	256
Himmler Visits	257
Hirszman, Chaim	258
Hirt, Joseph	258
Hitler, Adolf	258
Hitler Order, Final Solution (*Führerbefehl*)	261
Höfer, Fritz	262
Höfle, Hans	263
Holocaust, the	263
Holocaust Indoctrination	271
Holocaust Skepticism (Revisionism)	272
Holstein, Bernhard	273
Homicidal Gas Chamber	273
Homosexuals	276
Höss, Rudolf	276
Hössler, Franz	278
Höttl, Wilhelm	279
Hungary	279
Hydrogen Cyanide	281

I

I.G. Farbenindustrie AG	283
Instruments, of Extermination	283
Intentionality	284
International Military Tribunal (IMT)	284
International Tracing Service, Arolsen	290
Iron Blue	290
Isacovici, Salomón	291
Israel, Bruno	292
Italy	292

J

Jäger, Karl	295
Jäger Report	295
Jankowski, Stanisław	297
Janowska Camp	298
Jasenovac	299
Jehovah's Witnesses	299

K

Kaduk, Oswald	301
Kaindl, Anton	301
Kaltenbrunner, Ernst	302
Kammler, Hans	302
Kaper, Yakov	303
Karasik, Avraham	304
Karolinskij, Samij	304
Karski, Jan	304
Karvat, David	305
Kaufmann, Jeannette	306
Kaufmann Schafranov, Sofia	306
Kerch	306
Kersch, Silvia	307
Kertész, Imre	307
Kharkov	307
Klehr, Josef	309
Klein, Marc	309
Klooga	310
Koch, Ilse	312
Koch, Karl-Otto	312
Kon, Abe	312
Kon, Stanisław	313
Korherr, Richard	313
Korn, Moische	315
Kosinski, Jerzy	315
Kosów Podlaski	316
Kozak, Stanisław	316
Kramer, Josef	316
Kranz, Hermine	317
Krasnodar	318
Kraus, Ota	318
Kremer, Johann Paul	319
Krzepicki, Abraham	320
Kudlik, Aleksander	320
Kuklia, Vladislav	320
Kula, Michał	321
Kulka, Erich	322

L

Lampshades, of Human Skin	325
Langbein, Hermann	326
Langfus, Leib	327
Laptos, Leo	327
Larson, Charles	328
Lea, David	328
Lengyel, Olga	328
Lequeux, Maurice	329
Lerner, Leon	330
Lesky, Simcha	330
Lethal Injections	331
Lettich, André	331
Levi, Primo	332
Lévy, Robert	333
Lewental, Salmen	333
Lewińska, Pelagia	334
Lichtenstein, Mordecai	335
Lichtmann, Icek	335
Liebehenschel, Arthur	335
Limousin, Henri	336
Litwinska, Sofia	336
Lodz Ghetto	337
London Cage	338
Łukaszkiewicz, Zdzisław	338
Lumberjacks	338
Luxembourg	340

Lviv 340

M

Madagascar 341
Majdanek 342
Majdanek Museum 350
Majdanek Trials 351
Maly Trostenets 353
Mandelbaum, Henryk 354
Mansfeld, Géza 356
Manusevich, David 356
Marco, Enric 357
Marcus, Kurt 357
Marijampole 358
Maršálek, Hans 359
Mass Graves 360
Mauthausen 363
Mengele, Josef 364
Mermelstein, Melvin 365
Metz, Zelda 366
Microwave Delousing 366
Mogilev 367
Moll, Otto 368
Monowitz 369
Mordowicz, Czesław 369
Morgen, Konrad 370
Morgues 371
Motives 372
Mottel, Samet 378
Müller, Filip 378
Münch, Hans 381
Mussfeldt, Erich 382

N

Nadsari, Marcel 385
Nagraba, Ludwik 385
Nahon, Marco 386
Natzweiler 387
Nebe, Arthur 388
Netherlands 389
Neuengamme 389
Nisko Plan 390
Nordhausen 391
Norway 391
Nowodowski, Dawid 391
Nuremberg Military Tribunals 392
Nyiszli, Miklos 393

O

Oberhauser, Josef 395
Obrycki, Narcyz Tadeusz 395
Ochshorn, Isaac Egon 396
Office of Special Investigations 396
Ohlendorf, Otto 398
Ohrdruf 399
Olère, David 400
Open-Air Incinerations 401
Operation "Harvest Festival" 404
Oranienburg 406
Ostrovsky, Leonid 406
Ostrowski Company 407

P

Packing Density, inside Gas Chamber 409
Paisikovic, Dov 411
Pankov, Vassily 412
Pechersky, Alexander 412
Peer, Moshe 413
Pfannenstiel, Wilhelm 415
Phantom Extermination Camps 416
Phenol 416
Piazza, Bruno 416
Pilecki, Withold 417
Piller, Walter 417
Pilo, Aaron 418
Pilunov, Stefan 418
Pinsk 419
Pinter, Stephen F. 419
Plan, to Exterminate the Jews 420
Plucer, Regina 422
Podchlebnik, Michał 423
Podchlebnik, Salomon 424
Pohl, Oswald 424
Poland 426
Polevoy, Boris 427
Polish Underground Reports 428
Ponary (Paneriai) 429
Poswolski, Henryk 431
Pradel, Friedrich 431
Producer Gas 432
Pronicheva, Dina 433
Propaganda 434
Puchała, Lucjan 446
Putzker, Fritz 446

Q

Quakernack, Walter 449

R

Rabinowicz, Jakub 451
Rajchman, Chil 451
Rajgrodzki, Jerzy 452
Rajsko 453
Rajzman, Samuel (Shmuel) 453
Rascher, Siegmund 454
Rassinier, Paul 454
Rauff, Walter 455
Ravensbrück 456
Razgonayev, Mikhail 457
Red Cross 458
Reder, Rudolf 458
Reichssicherheitshauptamt 460
Religion, Holocaust as 460
Renard, Jean-Paul 461
Resettlement 461
Ringelblum, Emmanuel 463
Rogerie, André 463
Rögner, Adolf 463
Romania 465
Rosenberg, Alfred 465

Rosenberg, Eliyahu	467
Rosenblat, Herman	468
Rosenblum, Joshuah	469
Rosenblum, Moritz	470
Rosenthal, Maryla	470
Rosin, Arnošt	471

S

Sachsenhausen	473
Sackar, Josef	475
Sadowska, Rajzla	476
Saunas	476
Saurer Company	477
Schellekes, Maurice	477
Schelvis, Jules	478
Schindler's List, Movie	478
Schwarz, Deszö	479
Schwarzbart, Ignacy	479
Schwela, Siegfried	479
Sehn, Jan	480
Seidenwurm Wrzos, Mary	481
Self-Immolating Bodies	481
Semlin	482
Shanghai (China)	483
Sheftel, Yoram	483
Shoes of Deportees	483
Show Trials	484
Showers	486
Shrunken Heads, Myth of	488
Silberschein, Abraham	488
Simpson, Gordon	489
Six Million (Jewish Victims)	489
Skarżyński, Kazimierz	492
Slovakia	492
Soap, from Jewish Corpses	493
Sobibór	494
Sompolinski, Roman	500
Sonderkommando	501
Source Criticism	503
Soviet Union	506
Spanner, Rudolf	507
Special Treatment	507
Speer, Albert	510
Springer, Elisa	510
Srebrnik, Szymon	510
Stahlecker, Walter	512
Stahlecker Reports	512
Standing Upright, Dead Gassing Victims	513
Stanek, Franciszek	513
Stangl, Franz	513
Stark, Hans	514
Steiner, Jean-François	515
Stern, Ursula	515
Steyuk, Yakov	515
Strawczyński, Oskar	516
Streicher, Julius	516
Strummer, Adele	517
Stutthof	518
Suchomel, Franz	520
Sułkowski, Jan	521
Survivors	521
Süss, Franz	522
Swimming Pool	523
Szajn-Lewin, Eugenia	525
Szende, Stefan	525
Szlamek Report	526
Szmajzner, Stanisław	526
Szperling, Henike	527

T

Tabeau, Jerzy	529
Tauber, Henryk	530
Tesch & Stabenow	532
Tesch, Bruno	532
Theresienstadt	532
Thilo, Heinz	533
Tools, of Mass Murder	533
Topf & Söhne	534
Torture	535
Towels, Soap, Toothbrushes inside Gas Chambers	537
Trajtag, Josef	538
Transit Camps	538
Trawniki	540
Treblinka	541
Trubakov, Ziama	550
Turner, Harald	551
Turowski, Eugeniusz	552
Typhus	553

U

Uhlenbrock, Kurt	555
Ukraine	555
Uthgenannt, Otto	556

V

Vaillant-Couturier, Marie-Claude	557
van den Bergh, Siegfried	557
van Herwaarden, Maria	558
van Roden, Edward L.	558
Veil, Simone	559
Venezia, Morris	560
Venezia, Shlomo	561
Ventilation	564
Voss, Peter	568
Vrba, Rudolf	568

W

Wael, Monique de	571
Wannsee Conference	571
Wannsee Protocol	573
War Refugee Board Report	574
Warsaw Ghetto	574
Warszawski, Szyja	575
Watt, Donald	575
Wedding Rings	576
Weise, Gottfried	576
Weiss, Janda	577
Weissmandl, Michael Dov	578
Weliczker, Leon	578
Wennerstrum, Charles F.	580

Wentritt, Harry 580
Werner, Kurt 581
Wetzler, Alfred 581
Widmann, Albert 582
Wiernik, Jankiel (Yankiel) 583
Wiesel, Elie 584
Wiesenthal, Simon 586
Wijnberg, Saartje 587
Willenberg, Samuel 587
Wirth, Christian 588
Wirths, Eduard 588
Wirtschafts- und Verwaltungshauptamt 589
Wisliceny, Dieter 589
Witch Trials 590
Witnesses 591
Witnesses against Mass Murder 593
Wohlfahrt, Wilhelm 594
Wolff, Karl 594
Wolken, Otto 595
Wolzek 596

Y

Yad Vashem 599
Yugoslavia 599

Z

Ząbecki, Franciszek 601
Zaydel, Matvey 601
Zentrale Stelle 602
Zentralsauna, Auschwitz Birkenau 602
Ziereis, Franz 604
Żłobnicki, Adam 604
Zündel Trials 605
Żurawski, Mieczysław 605
Zyklon B 606
Zyklon-B Introduction Devices 609

Bibliography **613**

Index of Names **627**

Introduction

Why the Holocaust Matters

The Holocaust is a topic that everyone knows something about. It's a topic that none of us can avoid, like it or not. The reason for this is the fact that it is the single most-influential historical topic of the modern world. For sure, other modern-day genocides happened, and most people can probably name a few. But unless your country or ethnic group has been either a victim or a perpetrator of that genocide, these other, foreign genocides basically never play a role in domestic daily politics or social interactions. Most of them will never make it beyond a brief mention on a school's syllabus, if at all, and hardly any of them have dedicated museums and memorials. No one cares if we remember, forget, ignore or even deny these foreign events, or whether we pay tribute to their victims or disrespect them.

However, no one in any position of societal or political prominence can afford to ignore, disrespect or "deny" the Holocaust. If they did, they would not be prominent much longer. In fact, anyone can lose their job if violating this last taboo of Western societies. Many countries have made "denying the Holocaust" a crime, which means you can even end up in prison. Only one genocide in the history of mankind ever reached such prominence that it has a worldwide memorial day dedicated to it: January 27, which the United Nations has declared as the world's Holocaust Remembrance Day.

Therefore, the Holocaust matters. That being so, it is important that we understand what it was, and what it was not, lest we might be manipulated by people who want to take advantage of our ignorance. This includes extremists on both sides of the spectrum: those who deny what has been solidly demonstrated to be true, and those who want us to believe that which has been proven to be untrue.

If a topic has huge importance in society, then it is hugely important to understand it. The purpose of the present encyclopedia is to assist the reader in better understanding what exactly the Holocaust was. It is meant to serve as a reference book for all those who do not wish to search through stacks of books just to find one small piece of the larger puzzle.

Why an Encyclopedia on the Holocaust Matters

Nearly everyone knows something about this topic, and yet everyone's knowledge is also partial and incomplete. This is inevitable, given that the Holocaust is such a vast topic. It stretches over many years, encompasses almost an entire continent, and includes hundreds, if not thousands of individual locations and events, involving millions of people – perpetrators, victims and bystanders.

Even experts on this subject can be overwhelmed by the sheer amount of information available. The mere act of constructing an encyclopedia is a daunting task, requiring the combined expertise of many individuals. Then, the huge body of information has to be partitioned, edited, and simplified: What is important, and why? What can be left out? What can be relegated to notes or bibliographies? How much space should be allocated to each topic? And so on. Many difficult editorial decisions must be made.

But once done, the result is well worth the effort. Such a book captures the essential features of a major historical event, as we understand them at a given point in time. Certainly, things will change in the future; new information will come to light, new theories will be debated, and views will shift. But capturing and condensing so much research in a single volume as this provides an invaluable service for present and future researchers.

Other Holocaust Encyclopedias

This, of course, is not the first Holocaust encyclopedia that has been published. The first to appear was the huge 1,900-page, four-volume work titled *Encyclopedia of the Holocaust* published in 1990 by the Israeli Holocaust Remembrance Authority Yad Vashem, with Israeli scholar Israel Gutman as the lead editor. This was followed up ten years later by a 528-page, condensed, one-volume version. It has the same title, was edited by Robert Rozett and Shmuel Spector (two of Gutman's contributors), and was also published by Yad Vashem.

A year later, in 2001, Walter Laqueur and Judith Baumel-Schwartz published a 765-page volume titled *The Holocaust Encyclopedia*, which was in direct competition with the volume by Rozett and Spector. Had the two teams communicated, this double effort could have been avoided, and a combined, much-improved version could have been published instead.

A somewhat different approach was taken by Paul Bartrop and Michael Dickerman, who, in 2017, released a 1,440-page, four-volume work titled *The Holocaust: An Encyclopedia and Document Collection*. The first two volumes of this set, with their A-to-Z entries, resemble in style and content the other works mentioned. However, the third volume contains memoirs and testimonies of survivors and resistors, while the fourth volume contains reproductions of several documents pertinent to the topic.

All these encyclopedias have a central flaw: they compel the reader to adopt the conventional narrative. But we do not get a glimpse behind the scenes as to how this narrative came about. What kind of evidence is it based upon? Has the narrative changed over the decades, and if so, how, and why? Such questions are not even asked, let alone addressed. Even the basic question of *evidence* – what it is, and what makes it valid – is missing from these volumes.

So, what kind of information do we find in them, then? We have analyzed Gutman's and Rozett/Spector's works to find an answer to this question. Here, we only present the results for the more-complete Gutman version, but by and large it also applies to the trimmed-down, only slightly updated Rozett/Spector edition.

Gutman's encyclopedia consists of 898 entries. They can be divided into the following groups (with some entries falling into more than one group, hence the sum is larger than 898 entries or 100%):
– 214 entries (23.8%) are (usually short) biographies of Jewish individuals who were of some importance, either because they were prominent wartime figures, resistant fighters, chroniclers or martyrs.
– 75 entries (8.4%) are short biographies of gentiles who helped Jews in one way or another, many of them officially recognized by Israel as "righteous among the nations."
– 81 entries (9%) include descriptions of German organizations, individuals, concepts or terms that had nothing to do with the Holocaust, but get a negative mention anyway because during those years they played some role. For instance, German physicist Dr. Philipp Lenard had some peculiar views on "Jewish physics" versus "German physics," but had nothing to do whatsoever with the Holocaust. Or take Hans-Ulrich Rudel, a highly successful German fighter pilot who, after the war, voiced dissenting views on Third-Reich history, but had absolutely nothing to do with the Holocaust.
– 63 entries (7%) include descriptions of non-German organizations and individuals who had nothing to do with the Holocaust, but also get a negative mention because they were somehow aligned with, or supportive of, the Third Reich and its policies in general.
– 118 entries (13.1%) concern other historical topics or historical personalities having no bearing on the Holocaust. Take, for example, the Czechoslovakian Government in Exile or the British Home Army. They may be interesting historical topics, but they have no bearing on the Holocaust whatsoever.
– 85 entries (9.5%) concern locations such as cities, towns, regions and entire countries that have hardly any relationship to the Holocaust, if at all. For instance, take Katyn, Rome, Iraq or South Africa. None of them have any connection to the Holocaust.
– 35 entries (3.9%) are on camps, ghettos and prisons that have no connection with any Jewish extermination activities. If every kind of ghetto,

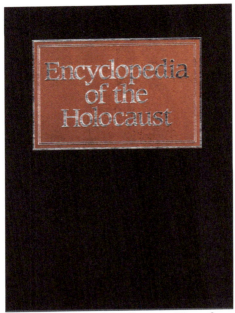

Front Cover of the library edition of Gutman's encyclopedia.

Israel Gutman (ed.), *Encyclopedia of the Holocaust*, Yad Vashem, Jerusalem/MacMillan, New York, 1990									
Total Entries	Holocaust	Hagiolatry		Gentile-bashing		Other Historical Topics	BS	non-Holocaust-Related Cities, Towns, Regions	non-Holocaust-Related Camps, Prisons, Ghettos
		Jewish	Gentile	German	non-German				
898	282	214	75	81	63	118	55	85	35
100%	31.4%	23.8%	8.4%	9.0%	7.0%	13.1%	6.1%	9.5%	3.9%

prison or camp were listed where, at some point, a Jew or political dissident was incarcerated during the war, then this would result in an encyclopedia of camps, ghettos and prisons. But that is not what this encyclopedia is about. In fact, there are dedicated encyclopedias that attempt to list all camps and ghettos.
- 55 entries (6.1%) are just plain nonsense. Take, for example, the entries on Austria's unification with Germany in 1938, or on the term *Blitzkrieg*, on Albert Einstein, on *Hitlerjugend*, on *Lebensraum*, Ernst Röhm, Horst Wessel Song, Third Reich, *Wehrmacht*, World War II, *Wehrwolf* (misspelled as Werwolf), *Parteitage*, Anthropology, Mauritius, Munich Conference, Nazi Party, Nazi-Soviet Pact, Prisoners of War. Why do they have an entry in an encyclopedia of the Holocaust?
- Finally, 282 entries (31.4%), hence not even a third, address topics related to the Holocaust in a strict sense.

Hence, roughly one third of this encyclopedia serves its declared purpose, another third is a celebration of the saints, heroes and martyrs of the Holocaust, while the last third is generally worthless. In other words, this *Encyclopedia of the Holocaust* is to no small degree a *Hagiography of the Holocaust*, meaning an uncritical, glorifying biography of the saints and martyrs of the Holocaust. Looking at the roster of more than 200 contributing authors, most of whom are Jews, and given the publishing organization (Yad Vashem), this probably had to be expected. Nevertheless, their book is designed more to *lecture* readers about the Holocaust than to help them *understand* it.

The trimmed-down version by Rozett and Spector deleted many of the less-relevant entries, but it also has several new entries, which show a stunning lack of good judgment. Of the 17 new entries, more than half should not be included in an encyclopedia on the Holocaust. For example:
- Neo-Nazism
- Heil Hitler
- Olympic Games 1936

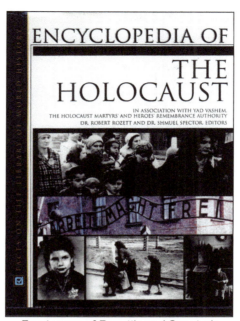
Front cover of Rozett's and Spector's encyclopedia.

- Leni Riefenstahl
- Swastika
- Doenitz (=Dönitz), Karl
- Priebke Trial
- Stauffenberg, Claus Schenk von
- Liberation

A Respectable Encyclopedia

If these sobering results disappoint us, the question to ask next is: What *should* we expect to find in an encyclopedia of the Holocaust?

We should find entries that tell us, first, *how* we know what we know, and then, what it is *that* we know. The "how" of our knowledge is based on one thing: evidence. We know, because we found material traces telling a story, or documents making clear statements, or someone claiming to be a witness who told us so. After all, we are dealing with one of the greatest murder cases in human history. To learn about and understand a murder case, you need to look at the evidence: the murder weapon (or traces thereof), the victims' bodies (or traces thereof), and traces of the perpetrators and the deed itself. This is standard procedure for every murder case. We should expect that the same standard applies here as well.

We begin by looking for a definition of the term "evidence." However, none of the encyclopedias discussed here have an entry on "evidence," so we are immediately at a loss.

Next, we turn to a certain subchapter of this murder case and want to learn:
- What material traces have been found and analyzed?
- What do documents tell us?
- What have witnesses said about it?

If we visit any entry in Gutman's encyclopedia that deals with an actual murder scene, such as an extermination camp or a mass-execution site, we find only a summary of the narrative as it has been published in more-or-less recent textbooks. In other words, we get a pre-packaged fast-food meal dished out. This entry does not include any information on *how* we know. We learn nothing about the evidence these claims rest on: no results of forensic investigations, no summary of the documented history, and also no hint regarding which witness testimonies were used.

There is also no entry explaining the basics of the murder weapons: What did the gas chambers, the gas vans, the crematoria and the huge outdoor pyres look like? And how did they work?

To make matters worse, the huge space allocated in these encyclopedias to celebrate Jewish martyrs, resistance fighters and survivors could have been used to give those among them who were "there" and have seen "it" an opportunity to testify. It should be expected that the testimonies of the most-important witnesses of the Holocaust are at least summarized in their respective entries.

But that is not what we find. Gutman's tome has only 21 entries on witnesses. Five of them are famous survivors, the rest are high-profile SS functionaries.[1] However, all these entries are merely biographic in nature. None of them summarize their testimonies, let alone discuss them.

The situation is essentially the same with all the other encyclopedias mentioned. While it is true that the one by Bartrop and Dickerman features an entire volume with long excerpts from numerous witness accounts, and another volume with document reproductions, this does not really help anyone to understand the issues at hand. First, such excerpts are always cherry-picked, raising the suspicion that we are fed a skewed version of history. Next, it is not the task of an encyclopedia to reprint entire collections of testimonies or documents. If a Holocaust encyclopedia wanted to reprint all testimonies ever made by the 300 most important witnesses, this would result in hundreds of volumes of text, much of which has been published already elsewhere. This is not helpful.

It is even worse with documents. Take the documents available from just one office of just one camp of the Third Reich, the Central Construction Office of the Auschwitz Camp. It has some 80,000 pages of documents. Imagine how many documents there are, if we cover *all* Auschwitz camp offices, and then *all* Third-Reich camps, and then *all* Third-Reich authorities dealing with these camps; there are literally millions of pages. So, what insight does the reader get from having a few randomly selected document reproductions thrown at them in a separate volume?

An encyclopedia needs to summarize and explain, using selected or representative information that is of greatest relevance, and not simply reiterate cherry-picked items that support a pre-established narrative.

There is a good reason why Gutman, Rozett/Spector, Laqueur/Baumel-Schwartz and Bartrop/Dickerman obscure essential issues from their readers, while flooding them with a celebration of Jewish and gentile martyrs, resisters, survivors and heroes. The "truth" that all these encyclopedias offer us has been sanitized, streamlined and cleansed of all inconvenient inconsistencies. They are hiding the evidence from us, rather than making it accessible and explaining it. But why would they do that?

If we could see with our own eyes the full picture of that which they call "evidence," we would understand their motives. This complete historical record consists of a huge amount of contradictory and, in many regards, physically impossible testimonies; documents that tell a completely different story than what witnesses claim; and forensic research results that, to some degree or another, collide with the versions spread by survivors. Add to this the trail of exaggerated or completely invented atrocity propaganda running like a red thread through the history of reporting about the Holocaust, and you end up with a historical concoction with almost no intellectual credibility. It is, in fact, an insult to serious and rational historiography.

But a true and honest encyclopedia will address all these issues. The Holocaust is not a straight-forward, simple event in history, as these other works want to make us believe. The actual story is much more contorted, conflicted and obfuscated than most people would ever have believed.

The Present Encyclopedia

This is where the present work comes in. We, the editors, hereby terminate the long history of bamboozling audiences into believing that Holocaust scholars have it all figured out. All we can do is lay bare the facts, provide some basic but essential explanations, and then let the readers make up their own mind.

First, we all ought to stop pretending to know what exactly the Holocaust is (or rather, was). No one knows for sure. Anyone claiming otherwise is

---

[1] In alphabetical order (survivors in italics): Erich von dem Bach-Zelewski (SS), Kurt Becher (SS), Paul Blobel (SS), Hans Frank (German politician), Kurt Gerstein (SS), Amon Göth (SS), Ernst Kaltenbrunner (SS), *Jan Karski*, Richard Korherr (SS), Josef Kramer (SS), *Primo Levi*, Arthur Liebehenschel (SS), Otto Ohlendorf (SS), *Alexander Pechersky*, Oswald Pohl (SS), Walter Rauff (SS), Alfred Rosenberg (German politician), Franz Stangl (SS), *Elie Wiesel*, *Simon Wiesenthal*, Dieter Wisliceny (SS).

either a fool or an impostor.

We all know about Auschwitz. But who knows what "Bunker 1" and "Bunker 2" were? Or how many furnaces with how many muffles existed in each Auschwitz crematorium?

Some may know about the extermination camps called Belzec, Sobibór and Treblinka, but who has ever heard of the extermination camps Semlin, Jasenovac, Maly Trostinets, Wolzek and Kosów Podlaski?

Most might know that Zyklon B was used to kill people, but how about murder by electrocution? By vacuum? By pneumatic hammers? By chlorine fumes? By brain-bashing machines? By atom bombs?

For everyone, there are always aspects of the Holocaust that we don't know or have never heard about before. For one thing, this is because we don't find much, if anything, about these "exotic" issues in the standard textbooks and encyclopedias. But they are important parts of the overall picture, and they need to be mentioned and explained in order to understand how today's narrative was shaped.

On the other hand, this topic is simply too huge to be grasped completely, even by the experts. There are simply too many details, too many sources, and too many technical matters to be sorted through, that no one person can be expected to grasp all the issues. Furthermore, we constantly forget, hence we are in constant need of reminders, and of easy access to them. This encyclopedia provides just such an assistance.

One option for the reader is to begin with the entry "Holocaust, the." It explains the many moving parts that make up the whole. From there, the reader can follow the various references to other entries, giving deeper insights into the relevant subtopics. This entry also has a flow chart explaining visually how the Holocaust narrative is organized – something not to be found in any other encyclopedia. This entry also has a text section explaining the main types of pertinent evidence forming the basis of our knowledge, and a chart explaining visually how this evidence is organized. The reader will find references pointing to entries dealing with the three major types of evidence:
1. Physical evidence, such as murder weapons and victims, technologies and forensic investigations.
2. Documents of a certain type, or pertaining to specific subchapters of the Holocaust.
3. Testimonies, organized by crime scene and by commonly made false claims, plus entries discussing factors influencing witnesses.

In contrast to the encyclopedias discussed earlier, which do not summarize and discuss witness testimonies at all, the present encyclopedia has nearly 300 entries dedicated to Holocaust witnesses. Each of these begins with only the most important biographic data, where available, but then summarizes and analyzes each person's statement(s). These testimonies are the bedrock upon which the Holocaust narrative rests. They are the core of the story. Any work on the Holocaust ignoring them has failed its mission.

The entry on "Witnesses" lists all the witnesses whose statements are summarized and discussed in this encyclopedia. In fact, this entry has numerous witness names listed which have not (yet) made it to an entry in this work. This demonstrates the necessary incompleteness of the issue; with millions of Holocaust survivors alive and kicking after the war, many thousands of testimonies must be expected to exist. However, we have tried to focus on the most essential witnesses: those who testified or deposited their memories early on, when memories were still fresh, and those who made detailed statements that can be verified or refuted.

These entries of critically reviewed witness testimony provide some of the most revealing truths about the Holocaust – in part because of their revelations, but often simply because of the contradictory, false or even absurd nature of the claims reviewed. Some false claims run like a red thread through many witness accounts. To help the reader locate witnesses who have chimed into commonly made false assertions, we have compiled entries that focus on these untrue claims. They summarize a claim, explain why it is untrue, and provide a list of the names of witnesses who claimed it. These entries include:
– Flames shooting out of chimneys.
– Fat extracted from burning corpses.
– Geysers of blood erupting from mass graves.
– Self-immolating bodies in cremation furnaces or on pyres, in need of no fuel.
– Explosives used to murder people, or to destroy their corpses.
– Soap, towels, and even toothbrushes issued to victims when walking into a gas chamber.
– Impossible packing densities of people squeezed into gas chambers.
– Dead gassing victims standing upright in gas chambers.

The Final Solution: Facts and Fiction	
DOCUMENTED FACT	**UNDOCUMENTED CLAIM**
25 Jan. 1942: Heinrich Himmler writes to Richard Glücks that the camps must prepare to accommodate up to 150,000 Jews; large-scale economic tasks would be assigned to them.	20 Jan. 1942: The total extermination of all Jews in the German sphere of influence is organized at the Wannsee Conference.*
30 April 1942: Oswald Pohl writes to H. Himmler that the main purpose of all camps would now be the use of inmate labor.	Feb. 1942: Beginning of mass gassings at Auschwitz-Birkenau. March 1942: Beginning of mass gassings at Belzec. May 1942: Beginning of mass gassings at Sobibór.
21 Aug. 1942: Martin Luther writes that the number of transported Jews would be inadequate to cover the shortage of labor, so that the German government asked the Slovakian government to supply 20,000 Slovakian Jews for labor.	23 July 1942: Beginning of mass gassings at Treblinka. August 1942: Beginning of gassings at Majdanek.
28 Dec. 1942: R. Glücks writes to all camp commandants that Himmler has ordered to reduce death rates in all camps by all means. The inmates have to receive better food.	End of 1942: Six "extermination" camps are active.
27 April 1943: R. Glücks writes to all camp commandants that Himmler has ordered all inmates physically unfit for work – even cripples, TBC patients and bedridden patients – to be kept alive and, whenever possible, assigned to do light work. "Bedridden prisoners should be assigned work that they can perform in bed."	March-June 1943: the new crematoria at Auschwitz-Birkenau become operational (fact); mass extermination of Jews unfit for labor unfolds inside them (undocumented claim).
26 Oct. 1943: Circular letter by O. Pohl to all camp commandants: All measures of the commanders must focus on the health and productivity of the inmates.	3 Nov. 1943: Some 42,000 Jewish factory workers are shot in Majdanek and several of its satellite camps. (Operation "Harvest Festival")
11 May 1944: Hitler orders the deployment of 200,000 Jews in the construction of fighter airplanes.	16 May 1944: Beginning of mass murder of several hundred thousand Jews from Hungary at Auschwitz-Birkenau.

* This claim is not confirmed by the protocol of this conference.

- Escape stories from gas chambers.
- The many ways poison gas is said to have been introduced into Auschwitz gas chambers.
- Exaggerated claims about cremation capacities.
- Unrealistic claims about the magnitude of outdoor corpse cremations on pyres, primarily revealed by their need for gigantic amounts of firewood.
- And last but not least an entry listing false witnesses, meaning persons who were caught having invented their entire wartime experiences.

This work moreover contains several entries dealing with forces that have an influence on how witnesses testified, and on how we perceive the Holocaust narrative today:
- Religion: in Western societies, the Holocaust has many features of a religion.
- False Memory Syndrome: explaining the many forces at work manipulating witness memory.
- Torture: demonstrating the systematic nature of third-degree interrogation methods used on arrested German officials by Allied investigators after the war.
- Witch trials: revealing the shocking similarities between medieval witch trials and postwar trials against alleged Holocaust perpetrators.
- Show Trials: defining the nature of a show trial, and revealing how this label fits for almost all postwar trials staged against alleged Holocaust perpetrators.

Finally, there are some nuggets of information that don't quite fit into any pattern, such as entries on the convergence of evidence, on criminal traces, on censorship to suppress what you are reading here, on Holocaust indoctrination of postwar generations, on propaganda activities of many governments, and on motives of all sides involved (the Holocaust perpetrator, the dogmatist, the skeptic, and the denier). We think they will prove enlightening and instructive.

One thing this encyclopedia does not have is a chronology of events. Other encyclopedias have one, typically including lots of political and war-related events unrelated to the Holocaust. This makes such chronologies impressive, but also inflated.

We, as editors, rarely consult these chronologies because they are typically deceptive, in that they also list events that are either entirely fictitious, or for which a precise date is unknown. In other words, such lists can be highly misleading. In order to explain this, consider the table we have reproduced here, taken from our entry on the "Final Solution," listing key events of the Holocaust. It has two chronological columns: One real and documented, and the other undocumented and fictional. Unfortunately, when there is a conflict between the two, as is clearly the case in these juxtaposed examples, orthodox encyclopedias will only list the undocumented events; clearly there is some bias at work.

We think, however, that all entries ought to be listed, and in cases of conflict explained. But this would quickly become unwieldy and almost useless. The orthodox Holocaust narrative simply isn't a straight-forward chronological series of events that can be squeezed into a calendar. Therefore, the reader will find no chronology here.

This encyclopedia also exists as an online version at www.NukeBook.org, which is accessible free of charge. In addition to the written text and the illustrations contained in the printed version, the online edition has all entries rendered as sound files, so you can listen to them rather than read them. A few entries also come with a video file, which presents the contents of an entry in a brief video documentary. We strive to produce more of these videos, but this will take some time.

This encyclopedia is a work in progress, and any progress made will be posted in real time online. The printed edition will expand and update with each new edition issued.

Now, the world finally has all the relevant information at its fingertips; no one can claim that they "could not know."

The Editors

A

ABSURD CLAIMS

Alleged victims, bystanders, and perpetrators have made a seemingly endless list of silly, bizarre, nonsensical, and outrageous assertions about their purported abuse, as part of the orthodox Holocaust narrative. The following is an incomplete list of some of the more ridiculous claims that they have made (where no sources or reference to other entries are given, see Rudolf 2019, pp. 124-127):

- a child survived six gassings in a gas chamber that never existed (M. Peer);
- a woman survived three gassings because Nazis kept running out of gas (see this and several other miraculous stories in the entry on Escapes, from Gas Chamber);
- to stay alive, gassing victim breathed through a keyhole in a gas chamber door at Flossenbürg Camp – where no homicidal gas chamber ever existed – and cursed the SS men when they opened the door, and then ran away (A. Friedman);
- Morris Hubert's fairy tale of a bear and an eagle in a cage at Buchenwald Camp, eating one Jew per day:

    "'In the camp there was a cage with a bear and an eagle,' he said. 'Every day, they would throw a Jew in there. The bear would tear him apart and the eagle would pick at his bones.'" (Ari L. Goldman, "Time 'Too Painful' to Remember," *The New York Times*, 10 November 1988)

- mass graves expelling geysers of blood (see the entry on Geysers);
- erupting (see the entry on Geysers) and exploding mass graves (K. Marcus);
- murder by shit: force Jews to lay down in an excrement pit, then force other Jews to defecate on their face until they suffocate (see the entry on Belzec);
- soap production from human fat with imprinted letters "RIF" – "*Reine Juden Seife*" (pure Jewish soap: see the entry on Soap, from Jewish Corpses);
- the SS made sausage in a crematorium out of human flesh ("RIW"– "*Reine Juden Wurst*"?; D. Olère);
- lampshades, book covers, driving gloves for SS officers, saddles, riding breeches, house slippers, and ladies' handbags of human skin (see the entry on Lampshades of Human Skin);
- pornographic pictures on canvasses made of human skin (*IMT*, Vol. XXX, p. 469);
- mummified human thumbs used as light switches in the house of Ilse Koch, wife of camp commandant Koch (Buchenwald Camp; Kurt Glass, *The New York Times*, 10 April 1995);
- production of shrunken heads from bodies of inmates (see the entry on Shrunken Heads);
- acid or boiling-water baths to produce human skeletons (M. Nyiszli, F. Müller; see Mattogno 2020a, pp. 106-110, 130, 142, 202 [Nyiszli]; 2021d, p. 63 [Müller]);
- muscles cut from the legs of executed inmates contracted so strongly that they made buckets jump about (F. Müller);
- an SS father skeet-shooting babies thrown into the air while his 9-year-old daughter applauds and shrieks: "Daddy, do it again; do it again, Daddy!" (See the section "Soviet Union" of the entry on Propaganda);
- Jewish children used by Hitler-Youth for target practice (Soviet propaganda, as above);
- "wagons disappeared into a depression in the ground" into an underground Crematoria at Auschwitz (such facilities never existed; K. Morgen);
- forcing prisoners to lick stairs clean, and collect garbage with their lips (Soviet propaganda, as above);
- injections into the eyes of inmates to change their eye color (Langbein 1985, pp. 383f.);
- artificially fertilize women at Auschwitz, and then gas them (*IMT*, Vol. V, p. 403);
- torturing people in specially mass-produced "torture boxes" made by Krupp (*IMT*, Vol. XVI, pp. 546, 556f., 561);
- torturing people by shooting at them with wooden bullets to make them talk;
- smacking people with special spanking machines (M.-C. Vaillant-Couturier);
- killing by drinking a glass of liquid hydrogen cyanide (which evaporates so quickly that it would endanger all those standing nearby);
- killing people with poisoned soft drinks (Soviet

propaganda, as above);
- killing prisoners during frost by spraying them with water, turning them into ice statues (*IMT*, Vol. 7, p. 433; Kaufmann, pp. 227f.);
- killing Dachau inmates with meat grinders (*20th Armored Division*, Spring 2000, p. 11);
- underground mass extermination in enormous rooms, by means of high-voltage electricity (see the entry on Belzec);
- blasting 20,000 Jews into the twilight zone with atomic bombs (see the entry on the Ohrdruf Camp);
- killing in a vacuum chamber, with hot steam, or with chlorine gas (see the entries on Belzec, Sobibór ad Treblinka);
- mass murder by tree-cutting: forcing people to climb trees, then cutting the trees down (Soviet propaganda, as above);
- killing a young man by forcing him to eat sand (R. Reder; see Mattogno 2021b, pp. 14, 40);
- gassing Soviet POWs in an open quarry (Soviet propaganda, as above);
- gas chambers on wheels in Treblinka, which dumped their victims directly into burning pits (see the entry on Treblinka);
- delayed-action poison gas that allowed the victims to leave the gas chambers and walk to the mass graves by themselves, before dying (also claimed for Treblinka);
- rapid-assembly portable gas chamber sheds (claimed by A. Eichmann);
- beating people to death, then conducting autopsies to see why they died (*IMT*, Vol. V, p. 199);
- introduction of Zyklon gas into the gas chambers of Auschwitz through showerheads (see the entry on showers) or from steel bottles (K. Gerstein);
- introduction of Zyklon gas into the gas chambers of Auschwitz via bombs (R. Bialek, M. Nahon, I. Ochshorn, J. Tabeau);
- mass murder with pneumatic hammers and in high-voltage baths (see the section "Polish Wartime Propaganda" of the entry on Birkenau);
- provisional gas chambers in ditches covered with canvas (O. Wolken);
- murdering millions of children at Auschwitz using wads soaked with hydrogen cyanide taken from vials (which never existed; K. Gerstein);
- electrical conveyor-belt executions (see the subsection "Soviet Propaganda" of the entry on Birkenau);
- bashing people's brains in with a pedal-driven brain-bashing machine while listening to the radio (Soviet propaganda, as above);
- cremation of bodies in blast furnaces (see the subsection "Soviet Propaganda" of the entry on Birkenau);
- cremation of human bodies using no fuel at all (see the entry on Self-Immolating Bodies);
- skimming off liquefied, boiling human fat from open-air cremation fires (see the entry on Fat, Extracted from Burning Corpses);
- mass graves containing hundreds of thousands of bodies, removed without a trace within a few weeks (see the entries on Cremation Propaganda and Lumberjacks);
- killing 840,000 Russian POWs at Sachsenhausen, and burning the bodies in four portable furnaces (see the entry on Sachsenhausen);
- eliminating corpses with explosives (R. Höss, V. Davydov);
- SS bicycle races in the Birkenau gas chamber;
- out of pity for a Jewish mother and her child (complete strangers), an SS man leaps into the gas chamber voluntarily at the last second in order to die with them;
- blue haze after gassing with hydrogen cyanide (which is colorless; R. Böck, Y. Gabai);
- a twelve-year-old boy giving an impressive and heroic speech in front of the other camp children before being "gassed" (Friedman 1946, p. 72);
- filling the mouths of victims with cement to prevent them from singing patriotic or communist songs (Soviet propaganda, as above).

ADAMETZ, GERHARD

Gerhard Adametz was in U.S. captivity after the war at Dachau, where he was interrogated, most likely using the customary torture applied by the Americans to many, if not most of their captives. (See the entry on torture.) He signed a 36-pages-long handwritten statement on 17 October 1945. However, that original has disappeared. All that survived is an alleged transcript of 12 pages. A Russian translation of it was given the document ID USSR-80 at the Nuremberg International Military Tribunal.

According to this transcript, Adametz claimed to have reached Kiev around 10 September 1943 with a group of 40 policemen called "Detachment 1005 b." There he was led "to an old cemetery about 5 km from Kiev," where he was led "into the adjacent field." There he saw about 100 inmates whose legs were shackled with a chain.

One hundred, later some 330 inmates, he claimed, were extracting corpses from mass graves and piling them up on stacks containing about 700 or even about 2,000 bodies each – with no wood in between. These bodies, merely placed "on a wooden base," were then surrounded by wood leaning against the finished pile, after which the whole pile was set ablaze. This work ended around 1 October 1943. All in all, about 100,000 bodies were exhumed and burned this way.

Rather than placing the mass graves and the resulting pyres in the ravine named Babi Yar, Adametz has this event take place in a field. He never mentions Babi Yar. This indicates that he was describing an event at a location he had never seen.

His description of the incineration technique allegedly used is technically impossible. His piles of corpses, allegedly two to three meters high, were merely sitting on a wooden base and then surrounded by wood leaning against the pile. The wooden base, covered by these large piles of corpses, would never have caught fire, and the wood leaning against the pile would have burned down without transferring any noticeable amount of heat to the bodies in the center.

The survivor witnesses who were interrogated by the NKGB after the war at least had their pyres built by alternating layers of wood and corpses, so in theory those could have worked. However, their calculated sizes would have made them technically impossible, too. (See the entries on Semen Berlyant, Isaak Brodsky, David Budnik, Vladimir Davydov, Iosif Doliner, Yakov Kaper, Vladislav Kuklia, Leonid Ostrovsky, Yakov Steyuk, Ziama Trubakov.)

The total number of 100,000 bodies allegedly cremated accidentally happens to coincide with the number of bodies allegedly buried at Babi Yar, according to the Extraordinary Soviet Commission.

Cremating an average human body during open-air incinerations requires some 250 kg of freshly cut wood. Cremating 100,000 bodies thus requires some 25,000 metric tons of wood. This would have required the felling of all trees growing in a 50-year-old spruce forest covering almost 56 hectares of land, or some 125 American football fields. An average prisoner is rated at being able to cut some 0.63 metric tons of fresh wood per workday. To cut this amount of wood within the five weeks (35 days) that this operation supposedly lasted would have required a work force of some 1,134 dedicated lumberjacks just to cut the wood. Adametz says nothing about huge piles of firewood, and where it came from.

In his affidavit, Adametz made statements about other locations where his unit supposedly guarded other inmate groups exhuming and burning corpses from mass graves. However, his claims as to where his unit went, and how long they stayed at which location, how many corpses were exhumed and burned are highly erratic and inconsistent. Moreover, his unit took extended breaks, recovery periods and furloughs. After having wrapped up Babi Yar, his unit was involved, from 16 October 1943 to 20 January 1944, in the exhumation and cremation of... 6,000 bodies! This is less than 62 bodies per day – a fraction of the hundreds of thousands of bodies that he allegedly just processed. It is also noteworthy that 40 to 50 inmate slave laborers were deployed at each location he mentions, no matter the number of corpses to be processed or the time available for it. In other words, his narrative was invented from scratch with no connection to reality.

The German text of Adametz's statement is riddled with anglicisms both by choice of words and by sentence structure. Hence, the original text of Adametz's statement was not written by a German in German, but in English, after which it was incorrectly translated into German by an inexperienced translator. Hence, even if Adametz handwrote this text, he did not write down his own words, but copied a poorly translated, originally English-language text. He would never have done this voluntarily. It therefore stands to reason that the American investigators cobbled together a text in English, translated it to German, softened up Adametz to make him cooperative, and had him sign it. This was probably done with assistance from the Soviets to make sure Adametz's story about Babi Yar aligned with the Soviet version, as the Soviets evidently planned to use it, and then indeed introduced it, as evidence. Hence, they may even have requested this affidavit from the Americans.

Finally, no person by the name of Gerhard Adametz is known to historiography in any other historical context. The whole thing may just have been made up from beginning to end by the Americans and Soviets.

(For more details, see the entry on Babi Yar, as well as Mattogno 2022c, pp. 542-546, 550-563, 598-600.)

AIR PHOTOS

In modern warfare, air superiority is crucial. It allows

one to know where the enemy is, what he is doing, and to attack him at will with minimal repercussions. Taking air photos to explore enemy territory was, therefore, a top priority during World War II. Many of these photos, however, disappeared after the war into secret Allied archives.

Air photos are prime evidence for investigating the Holocaust. Photos of alleged mass-murder locations, such as Auschwitz, Majdanek, Treblinka, Babi Yar etc., furnish insight into what did or did not happen there. Such photos can then be compared with what witnesses claim happened there, or with what should have been visible on those photos, if eyewitness statements are true. In fact, none of the photos taken of these locations corroborate commonly made claims.

In 1979, in the wake of the famous TV miniseries *Holocaust*, the CIA released a few air photos of the Auschwitz Camp in a brochure titled *The Holocaust Revisited*, claiming they prove that mass murder was indeed committed there at the time these photos were taken (Brugioni/Poirier 1979). Yet, a thorough analysis of the illustrations shows that their claims are partly unsubstantiated, and partly based on quite crude alterations of the original photos.

Additional air photos of the Auschwitz Camp have since been released, and photos from other suspected Holocaust crime scenes are accessible as well. Other sites of mass murder and destruction unconnected to the Holocaust, such as the bombing of German cities, the Soviet mass-murder sites at Katyn, Poland, and mass graves dug in Western camps (such as Bergen-Belsen) that were devastated by epidemics, give realistic reference points as to what to expect.

Auschwitz

During the time when the first Auschwitz air photos were taken – in May and June of 1944 – the mainstream narrative holds that, every day, ten thousand or more Jews deported from Hungary were killed and burned at Auschwitz-Birkenau, either in the cremation furnaces or, for the most part, on primitive outdoor pyres. The result of this gigantic mass-murder operation would have been (a) a dozen or more active pyres, (b) huge stockpiles of firewood, (c) widespread destruction of the surrounding ground vegetation by fire and heat, (d) large-scale movements of bodies, fuel and ashes, and most importantly (e) the area would have been covered under a thick layer of smoke.

Detail enlargement of an air photo of the Birkenau Camp of May 31, 1944, showing the area where huge pyres burning thousands of corpses daily were presumably located at that time.

*The same air photo as before but with **smoke added via Photoshop** to show how it would have had to look if the witnesses were telling the truth: massive formation of smoke.*

But the photos show nothing. Among the 10 known Auschwitz air photos during 1944, not one of them shows even a single crematorium chimney with smoke. Four of the photos show small, campfire-sized plumes from a single location, which cannot represent more than a few dozen corpse-burnings, at most. The logical conclusion is that the claimed destruction of the Jews deported from Hungary between mid-May and mid-July of 1944 simply didn't happen (Dalton 2020, pp. 234-243; Mattogno 2016b; Cox 2019, pp. 75-85).

Many witnesses claimed to have witnessed the burning of uncounted murdered Jews deported from Hungary on huge pyres outdoors at Auschwitz-Birkenau between mid-May and July 1944. This is a case of the "convergence of evidence" on a lie. It indicates that the origin of this claim is not personal experience, but black propaganda, rumor mongering, false-memory syndrome and/or coaching or even coaxing of witnesses by investigating judicial authorities. Here is a list of witnesses who made these false claims:

- Shaul Chasan
- Berthold Epstein
- Chaim Frosch
- Josef Kramer
- Olga Lengyel
- Maurice Lequeux
- Robert Lévy
- Salmen Lewental
- Pelagia Lewińska
- Henryk Mandelbaum
- Kurt Marcus
- Filip Müller
- Miklos Nyiszli
- Dov Paisikovic
- Joshuah Rosenblum
- Arnošt Rosin
- Josef Sackar
- Deszö Schwarz
- Henryk Tauber
- Morris Venezia
- Janda Weiss
- Elie Wiesel

Treblinka

At the Treblinka Camp, at least 700,000 corpses are said to have been cremated on pyres in a period of around 122 days (April – July 1943). Assuming the need of some 250 kg of fresh firewood to burn one corpse during open-air incinerations, this would have required some 175,000 metric tons of wood, or a corresponding number of trees. Witnesses claim they cut the tree from nearby forests. A 50-year-old spruce forest yields some 450 metric tons of wood per hectare (100 m × 100 m). This would mean that almost 390 hectares of forest were completely cut down (or 872 American football fields). This would have left a large area around this camp cleared of any forests. But there is not a trace of this on any Treblinka air photo (Rudolf 2020a, pp. 121-135; Kues 2009; Rudolf 2023, pp. 269-274).

Babi Yar

During the retreat of the German army from Kiev, the German air force took a high-resolution air photo of the area around Babi Yar. The photo was taken roughly a week after the 34,000 (or more) claimed victims of the Babi Yar mass murder are said to have been exhumed and cremated on huge pyres (Gutman, Vol. 1, pp. 113-115). However, this photo shows nothing indicating that any such human activity recently occurred. There is no disturbance of the soil from massive transports of fuels, no evidence that large mass graves were excavated, and no indication of the movement of soil, corpses, or ash remains. Furthermore, there is no sign of recent large pyres, and no indication of smoke in the vicinity. (Rudolf 2020a, pp. 153-156; Mattogno 2022c, pp. 523-579, 770-792.)

AKTION 1005

Orthodox Narrative

Sometime in 1942, SS chief Heinrich Himmler is said to have decided that the traces of atrocities committed by German units both in the various so-called extermination camps as well as during mass shootings outside of camps needed to be erased. To this end, mass graves were ordered to be opened, the corpses extracted and burned, the ashes scattered, and the graves backfilled and camouflaged by sowing grass and planting saplings on them. On the one hand, this concerned mass graves in the camps Auschwitz, Belzec, Chełmno, Sobibór and Treblinka. On the other hand, this operation concerned hundreds, if not thousands of mass graves scattered across millions of square miles mainly in the temporarily German-occupied Soviet territories, but also in Poland and Serbia. The code name for this operation was allegedly "*Aktion* 1005."

Paul Blobel is said to have been put in charge of this operation, sometime in the spring or summer of 1942. This was presumably due to the fact that he had gained some experiences with flamethrowers and incendiary bombs during the First World War. Blobel's first assignment was gaining experiences with the open-air incineration of corpses extracted from mass graves near the Chełmno Camp during summer 1942. The technique he allegedly developed consisted of setting a grate made of railway tracks on concrete or stone pillars up to one meter high. Underneath, firewood was placed, and the bodies on the grate.

Later, sometime in the summer of 1943, he established a *Sonderkommando* 1005. This unit was to roam the occupied eastern territories in search of mass graves. Randomly chosen Jewish inmates from local camps or ghettos were then forced to do the gruesome work: open the graves, extract the bodies, burn them on pyres, grind down any unburned bones, remove any valuables, scatter the ashes, backfill the graves, and camouflage them as mentioned earlier. A short while later, this *Sonderkommando* was split into 1005A, 1005B – in charge of processing mass graves in the Ukraine – and 1005-Center, with a focus on Belorussia. Other locations also had similar mass-grave-removal operations without any specific unit assigned to it, such as certain locations in the Baltic countries and Serbia.

Since there were allegedly no maps showing where all the hundreds or thousands of mass graves were, Blobel's units had to find out locally and by communicating with other German units where those mass graves were. As a means of communicating secretly about this, no written documents were supposed to be produced, and radio messages supposedly used a code language, such as giving the number of bodies in a grave as the cloud height in fake weather messages.

Critique of the Orthodox Narrative

Blobel was an alcoholic who was hospitalized from January 1942 for several months due to liver cirrhosis and stomach ulcers. Having handled flamethrowers and incendiary bombs a quarter century earlier did not make him a cremation expert. Germany had hundreds of real cremation experts, and Himmler's SS was working with many of them closely together building cremation facilities in many camps. Germany also had plenty of experiences with removing large-scale battle-field casualties with open-air incinerations during times of war (Franco-Prussian War 1870/71 and World War I). Scientific publications on these were readily available. Had Himmler wanted expert knowledge to build efficient field furnaces or simple pyres, that literature and Germany's many cremation experts were at his disposal.

Although a few documents exist mentioning a *Sonderkommando* 1005 formed due to a special Himmler order, it is unknown when this unit was formed, what its tasks were, and why it had the number 1005.

While in U.S. captivity in 1947, Blobel signed two affidavits, which are the basis for the orthodox narrative rather than the few extant documents. In these affidavits, Blobel made contradictory claims about what supposedly happened: He received the order either in March/April, in June or in fall of 1942. Blobel did not make any reference to any experiments conducted in Chełmno, and he never mentioned the term "*Aktion* 1005." Furthermore, Blobel also never mentioned any activities at the alleged extermination camps.

The timeline of "*Aktion* 1005" events is highly inconsistent and nonsensical. To start with, the alleged order of early/mid/late 1942 makes no sense. At that point, nothing foreshadowed a German defeat. Hence no one would have thought about having to remove evidence. Next, Blobel's alleged Chełmno experiments are based only on the testimony of Rudolf Höss, which were extracted with torture. Not even any Chełmno witness confirmed them. Furthermore, each alleged extermination camp is said to have received an order to erase traces of mass graves at a different point in time: they range from summer 1942 (Auschwitz, Chełmno, Sobibór) to November 1942 (Bełżec) to March 1943 (Treblinka). Moreover, the removal of mass graves at Auschwitz and Chełmno were triggered by hygienic concerns, not issues of secrecy. To make matters worse, Blobel formed his *Sonderkommando* 1005 only in summer 1943, hence roughly a year after allegedly receiving the order. Was he in a drunk delirium for an entire year? The time lost could not be recovered.

The entire operation contradicts existing documents. On 20 November 1942, Himmler issued an order to either cremate *or bury* all deceased inmates in SS custody. Hence, there was no order in place to cremate them all. Moreover, due to a 1942 order from central German authorities, all local authorities in the east were required to keep lists of all mass graves in their region, mark them conspicuously so local farmers didn't accidentally plow into them, for instance, and maintain them so groundwater does not get poisoned, and wildlife does not dig into them. In other words, lists of mass graves did exist, and the German authorities were doing the exact opposite of hiding them: they were clearly marking them for everyone to see. This attitude might have changed in 1943 when the Germans started retreating, and when the discovery of the Katyn mass graves in April of that year demonstrated the propagandistic value of discovering enemy mass graves.

The claim that fake weather reports were sent to disguise numbers of bodies cremated makes no sense. First, why would anyone insist on sending numbers of cremated bodies anywhere? But if it happened, where are they? There was no reason to destroy them, precisely because they were encoded. Yet not even one was ever found. If the reason for this is that they were indistinguishable from real weather reports, then how was the recipient to know what is real weather data and what is "corpse data"? That this claim is based solely on rumor and fantasy can be seen from other witnesses' claims that coded reports used water levels rather than cloud height, or even "watering holes" (whatever that meant). Every witness was making up stuff as they fibbed.

In addition, the *Einsatzgruppen* and associated units had created hundreds of documents describing in meticulous detail how many persons they executed, when and where. Hence, it would have made sense to create a list of priorities based on the figures mentioned in those documents, then start with the mass graves containing the most victims, and work down the list to smaller mass graves. But that is not what happened. The actual procedure was utterly random, often allegedly opening smaller graves while ignoring the big ones. Many locations of *Einsatzgruppen* executions were never mentioned by anyone as having had any "*Aktion* 1005" activities. Hence, all these mass graves must still be there, but no one ever looked systematically for them.

Moreover, while Himmler allegedly ordered the erasure of all traces of mass murder by cremating the bodies, no effort was made to destroy the meticulous documentation that the *Einsatzgruppen* had compiled and sent to Berlin. A complete set was discovered there by the Allies, who subsequently, during the *Einsatzgruppen* Trial at Nuremberg, relied on this vast documentation. They had no need whatsoever to locate and investigate any mass graves. So, what was the point of implementing a huge operation of cremating one million (or more) bodies all over Europe, when all the documents proving that they had been murdered in these locations were left intact?

Soviet Propaganda Claims

In many Soviet cities that the Red Army recaptured briefly during the German advance in 1941/42, or reconquered starting in 1943, investigative commissions were set up, which wrote reports about alleged atrocities of German units. Some of them were used during Soviet show trials, such as those in Krasnodar and Kharkiv. Witnesses were interrogated, a few of whom claimed to have survived a mass execution. Most witnesses, however, claimed to have been part of inmate units formed by the Germans who were forced to exhume and burn bodies from mass graves presumably containing the victims of German mass murder operations.

The number of victims most witnesses claimed to have assisted in exhuming and burning regularly exceeded the number of victims that were executed there, if we follow the figures listed in German wartime documents (reports of the *Einsatzgruppen*). These figures were then sometimes increased even more by the Soviet commissions when writing their reports.

On numerous occasions, the Soviets claimed to have found mass graves whose victims had not been burned, or only partially. Many of these graves were not exhumed and forensically investigated. If they were, often only a small fraction of the claimed number of victims was actually exhumed, while the rest – if they existed – were left untouched. In not a single case of these investigations were any foreign observers and experts, especially from neutral countries, invited to participate in these investigations, as the Germans had done when discovering the mass graves at Katyn and Vinnitsa.

In only a few cases were any photos taken or made publicly accessible. However, rather than showing thousands or tens of thousands of corpses, the photos usually show only a few bodies, a few dozen or at most a few hundred corpses. The latter quantity can be seen only on photos showing Soviet PoWs in their uniforms, but not civilians of all age groups stripped naked, as is said to have been the case where Jews were massacred.

One mass grave some 3 meters wide, 3 meters deep and some 30 meters long was filmed, and the footage used for the 1943 Soviet propaganda movie *The Battle for Our Soviet Ukraine*. However, here, too, the victims wear clothes, probably uniforms, so even these are either deceased PoWs or simply battle casualties.

The same type of Soviet commissions began to work here – some even with the same people in charge, who had compiled a completely forged and fake expert report on Katyn, with which they blamed these Soviet mass murders on the Germans. The same mendacity they proved to be capable of regarding Katyn they applied wherever else they went to work to prove German atrocities. In one case, they claimed to have found corpses allegedly killed in "gas vans" with carbon monoxide, whose skin, after many months of decomposition, miraculously was still "of bright pink color." In a similar case, they managed to prove the presence of carbon monoxide in severely decomposed tissue, an analytical feat which is impossible even today, after 80 years of technical progress!

Many mass graves the Soviets claimed to have located, however, presumably had no or hardly any bodies in them anymore, because the Germans allegedly had them all exhumed and burned, and their ashes and bones scattered by a team of inmate slave laborers. This convenient situation alleviated any needs for the Soviets to prove anything. The Germans had murdered, and then they had destroyed all the evidence for it. Hence, the lack of any evidence for mass murder proves that mass murder was committed!

Forensic Considerations

Blobel's alleged task to eliminate all traces of hundreds, if not thousands of mass graves containing a total of a million or more bodies was formidable. If Himmler had ordered this as a secret and important task, appropriate means would have been made accessible to Blobel: access to expert knowledge about open-air incinerations on pyres or field furnaces; access to the *Einsatzgruppen* reports listing the executions; access to the lists of mass graves prepared by local authorities; a team of hundreds of organizers, each with a team of hundreds of workers; orders by Himmler overriding the local forest authorities' jurisdiction regarding who is allowed to chop wood; and then an instant start of the operation in summer 1942. None of this happened.

Blobel waited a year without doing anything. He then formed only three teams, who traveled from one location to another, with no map or list, depending on guesses and speculations as to where they would find graves. Instead of taking a skilled and experienced group of lumberjacks, grave diggers and pyre builders with them, they allegedly killed off all workers after each job was done, then started from scratch with a new set of unskilled and untrained inmates.

Blobel's claimed cremation technique – rails on posts – is absurd. If bodies are to burn fast, they need to lie in the midst of the fire and glowing embers, not on top of a rack kept away from the heat. No matter how many witnesses confirmed this technique, it didn't happen this way.

The operations described by the witnesses – corpse extraction, pyre building, fire maintenance, processing of cremation remains – are at times ludicrous, and often technically impossible, but under any circumstances impossible to achieve with the minute labor teams allegedly involved, and within the short time frames claimed.

For instance, some witnesses claim that corpses were extracted from mass graves by fishing for them from the grave's edge using hooks on ropes. Many witnesses insist that the pyres they built were 4, 6, 8, even 10 meters high. This would have required cranes to build them. However, when set ablaze, such enormous stacks would have sooner or later collapsed, spilling burning wood and corpse parts all over the place. Others claimed that some workers stood right next to the blazing pyres, poking it with rods to make sure all bodies burned properly. In reality, however, they would have suffered severe burns within seconds, had they tried to stay close to these fires. Many witnesses also insisted that merely a few men sifted thousands of metric tons of ashes through handheld flour-type sieves, and that just as few men crushed unburned remains of inevitably enormous quantities with simple pestles within a few days or weeks. None of it is realistic.

However, most important is the observation that all witnesses, *without a single exception*, completely ignored or dramatically underestimated the quantity of firewood that would have been needed to cremate the number of bodies they claim to have processed. Thus, the self-proclaimed participants in these alleged operations never considered for a second the number of skilled, experienced and physically fit lumberjacks it would have taken to fell the trees that needed to be cut down and chopped up. They never imagined the large swaths of local forest that had to be denuded of all trees to get this wood. This issue is treated in detail in the entry on lumberjacks, where links to the individual witnesses or alleged crime scenes can be found, with further details on each witness's claims and orthodox tenets about these crime scenes.

The common hallmark of these witness accounts is that they were made in front of Soviet investigative commissions or, worse still, representatives of the Soviet terror organization NKGB. These have the reputation of orchestrating witness accounts and rigging their investigations along political demands of the Soviet Union's leadership. Hence, their claims cannot be trusted unless there is independent verification.

However, there is little to no evidence from independent sources, such as diary entries or photographs by the local populace, or air photos of Soviet or German planes. While the claimed crime scenes may not have been accessible to outsiders, the smoke which the claimed massive open-air incineration operations would have produced for weeks or even months could not have gone unnoticed by locals. Yet even in places near larger cities, such as Kiev, Minsk, Lviv and Kharkov, no one seems to have noticed anything unusual during those alleged long-lasting conflagrations.

A special case is Babi Yar, a claimed mass-murder location on the outskirts of Kiev. Just when the massive exhumation and cremation work allegedly carried out at that location was wrapped up, German reconnaissance planes took air photos of the region, revealing in high resolution that nothing claimed about this place ever happened: no smoke, no disturbed soil from recently opened mass graves, no trace of massive transports of fuel, or removal of ashes.

Other less prominent but equally instructive cases of Soviet atrocity propaganda that have entered history books due to orthodox credulity, and which have their own entry in this encyclopedia, are:
– Białystok
– Bronnaya Gora (near Brest)
– Janowska Camp (near Lviv)
– Maly Trostinets (near Minsk)
– Mogilev
– Ponary (near Vilnius)
– Semlin Camp (Serbia)

Proper forensic efforts to investigate mass graves were started only after the collapse of the Soviet Union in 1991. In a few cases, exhumations were made, but for the most part, mass graves were only located or at most exposed, but no bodies exhumed and examined. These efforts usually served only to locate graves and turn such sites into memorials. In all these cases, the mass graves had not been exhumed in 1943/44, and no bodies had been burned. Therefore, these graves evidently were not part of *Aktion* 1005. Hence, a few cases are discussed in the entry on the *Einsatzgruppen* instead.

(For many more examples and further details, see Mattogno 2022c, pp. 403-758.)

AKTION REINHARDT
Origin of the Term

The origin of the term *Aktion Reinhardt* (sometimes spelled *Reinhard*) is not clear. Some historians think it was named after German State-Secretary of Finance Fritz Reinhardt, but a majority of historians think that it was named after Reinhardt Heydrich (whose first name is often misspelled as Reinhard).

Orthodox Meaning of the Term

Mainstream historians insist that *Aktion Reinhardt* was an operation for the mass-murder of Jews in the General Government and the Białystok Region, mainly by sending them to the so-called pure extermination camps Belzec, Sobibór and Treblinka – the so-called *Aktion Reinhardt* Camps. Original wartime documents, however, prove that this operation had an entirely different background.

"*Generalplan Ost*"

After Germany's victory over Poland, and even more so after the invasion of the Soviet Union, Germany made grand plans to Germanize large areas in the east, to secure it with fortified settlements, and to improve the area's infrastructure. Large numbers of Soviet PoWs were to be deployed to that end. However, when those PoWs did not become available, the focus shifted to the Jews as an alternative labor pool.

Odilo Globocnik was in charge of the initial settlement and infrastructure projects. When the focus shifted to the Jews, he remained in charge as head of *Aktion Reinhardt*. However, if that new task was to exterminate without distinction all Jews, then Globocnik had been ordered by Himmler to fulfill two contradictory tasks: on the one hand he had to secure as large a Jewish labor force as possible for huge construction efforts in the East, and on the other hand he had to mass-murder all the Jews he could lay his hands on. Both cannot be true. The first objective is incontrovertibly proven by many documents and actual historical events, while the second rests almost exclusively on highly dubious witness testimony.

Documents on *Aktion Reinhardt*

The orthodoxy insists that *Aktion Reinhardt* entailed the murder of some 2.3 million Jews living in the General Government. Hence, this term would be another code word used for the extermination of the Jews, just like the term "Final Solution." But like the latter, this claim is not backed up by documents; in fact, existing documents refute it.

The earliest document mentioning the term "Reinhardt" is from June 1942, and is a simple request for "50 empty suitcases" – without any reference to murder. In an undated report by Globocnik, probably from 1943, we read (Nuremberg Document NO-057):

> "*The whole of Aktion Reinhardt can be split up into 4 areas:*
> *A) the deportation itself*

B) the use of the manpower
C) the use of objects
D) the securing of hidden values and real estate."

All other surviving documents about *Aktion Reinhardt* refer exclusively to the exploitation of material objects taken from the deported Jews. This includes a travel report by SS *Obersturmbannführer* Alfred Franke-Gricksch to several camps, which states explicitly that *Sonderaktion* "Reinhard" was about the seizure of all mobile Jewish property in the General Government. Furthermore, there are several documents about the Auschwitz Camp where that term is mentioned in conjunction with the storage and handling of inmate property.

Finally, the so-called Höfle telegram by Hans Höfle, listing arrival figures for *"Einsatz Reinhardt,"* lists deportation figures for a camp abbreviated with "L", which is generally assumed to mean Lublin, meaning the Majdanek Camp. This camp was therefore part of the *Aktion Reinhardt*, but today no serious historian claims that any kind of systematic mass-murder of Jews or anyone else occurred at that camp.

The choice of Heydrich's first name "Reinhardt" for this operation made sense, as it continued the task entrusted to him by Göring to resolve "the Jewish question by means of emigration or evacuation." (See the entry on Reinhardt Heydrich.)

Therefore, *Aktion Reinhardt* had nothing to do with mass murder. It aimed at deporting Jews, putting those fit for labor to forced labor, resettle the rest in the East, and loot their assets and properties.

(For more details, see Graf/Kues/Mattogno 2020, pp. 243-258.)

AKTION REINHARDT CAMPS

When writing about the *Aktion Reinhardt* Camps, orthodox historians commonly refer to the camps Belzec, Sobibór and Treblinka, which according to their narrative were pure extermination camps, but in fact served as mere transit camps for Jews deported to the East either for construction work or for resettlement. From a telegram sent by Hans Höfle, we learn that the Majdanek Camp near Lublin was also considered a camp of *"Einsatz Reinhard,"* as it is called in that document. Majdanek, however, was neither a pure extermination camp, nor was this even its secondary function. It was almost exclusively a labor camp – even in the current orthodox narrative. Right after the war, Soviet propaganda claimed that it was an extermination camp, but by 2005, this claim was all but abandoned by the orthodoxy.

Documents from other camps, such as Auschwitz, also on occasion mentioned *Aktion Reinhardt* as some aspect of their operation, although in no way connected with any murderous activities. Other documents about *Aktion Reinhardt* also clearly show that this operation had nothing to do with mass murder at all. See the entry on this term for more details.

AMIEL, SZYMON

Szymon Amiel was a Polish Jew living in the Białystok Ghetto. He claimed that some German authorities selected him in mid-May 1944 to participate in the exhumation of mass graves, and the cremation of the bodies contained in it. Amiel testified about this in late 1944 together with another member of this unit, Salman Edelman. Their tale was published, probably in an edited version, in the infamous Soviet propaganda book *The Black Book*. In October and November 1945, Amiel made two more depositions in front of a Polish judge.

There are several revealing differences between his testimonies, as well as many peculiar claims, among them:
- 1944: they were driven in a gas van to the worksite – without getting gassed.
  1945: it was an uncovered truck. In other words, he lied in 1944.
- 1944: corpses were put on top of a woodpile 2 meters high.
  1945: corpses were stacked up 5 meters high, without wood, then sprinkle with bitumen and gasoline and set on fire. However, these liquid fuels give off little heat to the bodies, and can merely char them superficially. In other words, he lied in 1945.
- 1944: The pyre was 3 meters tall.
  1945: the pyre measured 6 m × 7 m × 5 m, containing 1,000 bodies. Building such a pyre would have required a crane. Moreover, at a need of 250 kg of wood per body during open-air incinerations, burning 1,000 bodies would have required 250 metric tons of freshly cut wood. The density of green wood is roughly 0.9 tons per m³, and its stacking density on a pyre is 1.4 (40% for air and flames to go through). This means that the wood required to burn 1,000 bodies had a volume of some 390 cubic meters. However, Amiel's pyres only had a volume of 210 cubic meters. The wood alone would have stacked up to more than 9 meters in height.

Days	Bodies processed	Wood needed* [t]	Days needed†
12	5,000-6,000	1,250-1,500	46-55
7	4,000-4,800	1,000-1,200	37-44
9	14,000	3,500	129
11	5,000-6,000	1,250-1,500	46-55
18	12,000	3,000	111
57	40,000-42,800	10,000-10,700	369-395

* 250 kg fresh wood per body
† 0.63 metric tons of wood per worker and day, for 43 workers

Amiel's accounts contains other claims that are simply preposterous. For instance, he and Edelman claimed that corpses were extracted from mass graves by tossing "one or two hooks" tied to "ropes" into the uncovered pit; when one hook caught a corpse, it was pulled out – as if this was a child's angling game! The same absurd corpse-fishing game was described by Yuri Farber in a testimony also published in *The Black Book*. This is a case of convergence of evidence on a lie, probably because the witnesses contributing to this book had a chance to "learn" from one another.

Amiel seriously claimed that a Polish family that was shot and thrown onto a burning pyre was consumed by the flames within ten minutes! And that he could gauge the age of corpses by the lengths of their beard!

Amiel's inmate slave-labor unit supposedly contained 43 (1944) or 40 persons (1945). This team allegedly exhumed and cremated bodies at various locations in the area. In the table, the data in the left two columns is given by Amiel, while the data in the right two columns is calculated.

As can be seen, the time needed just to cut the wood, which would have been required for the claimed cremations, would have occupied the entire team in every single claimed case at least four times longer than they supposedly spent for all the rest of the work. This work allegedly included: uncovering mass graves, angling out bodies, building pyres, burning them down, sifting through the ashes, grinding down bones, filling up the mass graves.

If we look at the total claimed (last table row), we see that Amiel's team would have taken more than a year just to cut the wood needed to cremate all the bodies he claims they cremated. This would have required the felling of all trees growing in a 50-year-old spruce forest covering up to 24 hectares of land, or some 53 American football fields. To get this work done within the 57 days claimed would have required a work force of some 298 dedicated lumberjacks just to cut the wood.

This testimony relates to one of many events claimed to have been part of the alleged German clean-up operation which the orthodoxy calls *Aktion* 1005. The above data demonstrates conclusively that Amiel's entire scenario is completely detached from reality. It cannot be based on experience, but on mere imagination and delusion.

(For more details, see Mattogno 2022c, pp. 632-639.)

annihilation → **Extirpation**
anti-Semitism → **Motives, Section "Motives for National-Socialist anti-Judaism"**

AUERBACH, RACHEL

Rachel Auerbach

Rachel Auerbach (18 Dec. 1903 – 31 May 1976) was a Jewish Holocaust propagandist from Volhynia who spent the war years in the Warsaw Ghetto until March 1943, when she somehow moved to the non-Jewish side of Warsaw, thus surviving the war. For years after the war, she collected various witness accounts, with a focus on survivors of the Treblinka Camp, uncritically recording and repeating the most bizarre claims and assertions.

While still in the Warsaw Ghetto in 1943, she wrote a long manuscript, in which she claimed about Treblinka that mass murder was carried out there in "steam chambers." By 1946, Auerbach had access to a range of literature and testimonies about Treblinka, which she used to create her own spiced-up propaganda version of Treblinka in a long article. Here are several of her peculiar claims:

– Real showers in a nicely equipped "public bath" emitted not water but engine-exhaust gas. She took that from Abraham Krzepicki's story.
– She combined the vacuum chambers claimed by some Treblinka witnesses with the exhaust gas version claimed by others:
  "First, a suction pump was brought into play to draw the pure air from the chamber. Then the tank reservoir, where the engine's combustion gas is collected, is attached."
– The gassing victims were either white or blue and bloated. However, the victims of exhaust-engine gassings (with carbon monoxide as the active

toxin) are neither of these. If they are discolored, then they are reddish-pink.
- During the incineration of corpses on pyres, *"pans would be placed beneath the racks to catch the fat as it ran off, but this has not been confirmed. But even if the Germans in Treblinka or at any of the other death factories failed to do this, and allowed so many tons of precious fat to go to waste, it could only have been an over-sight on their part."*

However, extracting, collecting and using fat from corpses burning on a pyre would have been physically impossible for a number of reasons. (See the entry on the myth of fat extracted from burning corpses.)

We saved the best for last:

"In Treblinka, as in other such places, significant advances were made in the science of annihilation, such as the highly original discovery that the bodies of women burned better than those of men.

'Men won't burn without women.' […] [T]he bodies of women were used to kindle, or, more accurately put, to build the fires among the piles of corpses […]. Blood, too, was found to be first-class combustion material. […] Young corpses burn up quicker than old ones. […] [W]ith the help of gasoline and the bodies of the fatter females, the pile of corpses finally burst into flames."

Since blood is more than 90% water, it is safe to say that it is not a "first-class combustion material." Moreover, the human body (depending on its condition) is at least 65% water, it is also not good kindling material at all, but requires a lot of fuel to burn, particularly in open fires where heat losses are huge; for details on this, see the entry on open-air incinerations and self-immolating bodies. Auerbach moreover claimed that a total of 1,074,000 Jews died at Treblinka, which is at the high end of current orthodox estimates. (For more information, see Donat 1979, pp. 26f., 32-36; Mattogno/Graf 2023, pp. 23-25; Mattogno 2021e, pp. 147f.)

AUMEIER, HANS

Hans Aumeier (20 Aug. 1906 – 24 Jan. 1948), *SS Hauptsturmführer* at the time, was transferred to Auschwitz on 16 February 1942, and was head of the Protective-Custody Camp at the Auschwitz Main Camp until 15 August 1943. From October 1943 onward, he was commandant of the Vaivara Concentration Camp in Estonia, and in February 1945 became commandant of Mysen Concentration Camp in Norway, where he was arrested by the British on 11 June 1945.

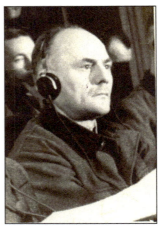

Hans Aumeier

In his first interrogation by British prison guards, dated 29 June 1945, he spoke quite naively of the crematories at Auschwitz, insisted that he had "no knowledge of gas chambers," and that during his time at Auschwitz "no detainee was gassed." Unsatisfied with this testimony, the interrogators demanded "exact data" on homicidal gassings, with full details, including the number of victims per day, total numbers, and a "confession of his own responsibility" and that of the other perpetrators and persons responsible for giving the orders. Aumeier was never asked whether there were any gassings or whether he participated; rather, he was effectively ordered to provide the details and make a confession. The result of this subsequent "confession" by Aumeier was then commented upon by his British jailers in a "Report on the interrogation of prisoner no. 211, *Sturmbannführer* Aumeier, Hans" on 10 August 1945:

"The interrogator is satisfied that the major part of the material of this report is in conformity with the truth as far as the facts are concerned, but the personal reactions of Aumeier and his way of thinking may change a bit when his fate gets worse."

Therefore, Aumeier was not interrogated to obtain true information, but rather to force him to confirm what the British already had decided was "the truth." The reference to "his fate getting worse" is a not-too-subtle hint at systematic torture, which applied to nearly all Germans in British or American captivity.

Aumeier's testimony on the alleged gas chambers of Auschwitz is full of untruths and is furthermore completely inconsistent with the chronology of events claimed by orthodox researchers. In order to say anything at all about the gassings, as demanded of him, he transposed all events by one year. Instead of fall/winter 1941 for the first experimental gassing of Soviet POWs, as the orthodoxy claims, Aumeier placed this event – with Jews as victims – in the fall/winter of 1942. Also, the initial mass gassings in dedicated facilities, usually alleged to have occurred in the Birkenau bunkers starting in March 1942, took place, according to him, in very early 1943. Since Aumeier came to Auschwitz only in early 1942, his claim to have first-hand knowledge of events that occurred earlier (according to orthodoxy) are necessarily invented and untrue. In other words, Aumeier made things up to please his tormentors, repeating what was given to him as a pre-established official "truth." Aumeier was eventually extradited to Poland, where he was executed in early 1948.

(For more details, see Mattogno 2016f, pp. 138-141.)

AUSCHWITZ

The Polish town of Oświęcim (German: Auschwitz) lies in a valley at the Sola River near its confluence with the Vistula River. Already during the time of the Austrian-Hungarian Monarchy, a military barracks existed southwest of the town on the left bank of the Sola River. After World War One, the facility was taken over by the newly formed Polish armed forces, using it as artillery barracks and horse stables. After Poland's defeat at the beginning of World War Two, the German Armed Forces took over the barracks.

Main Camp

During January and February 1940, the SS forces considered using these old barracks as a quarantine transit camp for Polish political prisoners, eventually to be sent to other camps. Due to lack of any sanitary installations, the facility was initially rejected. A change of mind followed in late February after suggesting some major upgrades. These were ordered in April, with a first detailed cost estimate following on 30 April 1940, listing numerous items to be constructed, such as: kitchen, laundry, water supply system, inmate bath, delousing facility. This facility would later be called Auschwitz Main Camp (German: *Stammlager*).

It is in this camp that the first gassing of inmates using Zyklon B is said to have occurred in late summer of 1941. This camp also saw the erection of cremation furnaces in a former munitions bunker, which was renamed to Crematorium I or "old crematorium," to set it apart from the new cremation facilities later built at Birkenau. The morgue of this old crematorium is said to have been misused for the mass-murder of inmates between late 1941 and early 1942. For a more detailed description of this camp, see its dedicated entry.

Birkenau

On 26 October 1941, the Auschwitz camp administration received a phone call informing them that the Berlin headquarters of the SS planned to set up

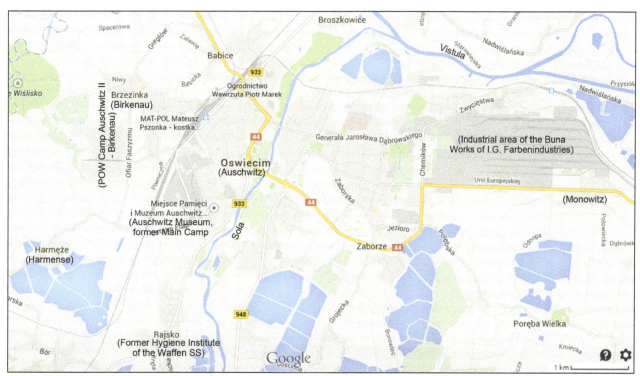
Google map of the region around Auschwitz, with black labels added.

near Auschwitz a separate PoW camp for some 60,000 Soviet PoWs, which would be an integral part of the Auschwitz Camp. The planned capacity was increased over time, and reached a maximum of 200,000 in September 1942, although that figure was never reached.

Planning and construction of the camp started immediately near the village of Brzezinka (German: Birkenau) two miles west of the town of Oświęcim. However, except for a few thousand PoWs arriving at Auschwitz in October 1941, the large wave of Soviet PoWs never arrived, so the camp's function changed from a PoW camp to a transit camp and forced-labor camp for Jews deported from numerous European countries.

On 22 November 1943, the PoW camp Auschwitz-Birkenau was separated from the Auschwitz Main Camp (then renamed to Auschwitz I) and became an independent concentration camp called Auschwitz II. However, on 25 November 1944, the Birkenau Camp lost its independence again, and was reintegrated in what was then simply called Auschwitz Concentration Camp.

For a more detailed description of this camp, see its dedicated entry.

Monowitz

Right from the beginning of the Auschwitz Camp's existence, so-call subcamps or satellite camps were established in its immediate vicinity as well as in the wider region. These camps served to lodge forced-labor inmates close to their workplace, which included various mining, manufacturing and farming enterprises. At its peak, there were 48 satellite camps attached to the Auschwitz camp complex. The larger and best-known among them were the camps near the villages of Monowitz, Harmense and Rajsko. The Monowitz Camp was by far the largest among them, accommodating thousands of inmates meant to work at the nearby BUNA plant of the I.G. Farbenindustrie. The Harmense Camp was agricultural in nature, whereas Rajsko housed the southwestern branch of the SS Hygiene Institute as well as a plant-breeding facility. On 22 November 1943, all satellite camps near Auschwitz were separated from the Auschwitz Main Camp and became an independent concentration camp called Auschwitz III, with the headquarters at the Monowitz Camp. On 25 November 1944, the name was changed to Monowitz Concentration Camp. For a more detailed description of this camp, see its dedicated entry.

Death-Toll Propaganda

The first exaggerated death-toll figure that gained international attention was spread by the War Refugee Board Report, published in late 1944. It contained a mendacious essay by Rudolf Vrba written in May 1944, in which he claimed that, between April 1942 and April 1944, 1,765,000 inmates had died, implying that many more had died throughout the camp's entire history.

The next notable event was a report issued by the Soviet Union after the Red Army had conquered the camp. The new figure was now four million victims. Not satisfied with this, the Polish court which tried former staff members of the Auschwitz Camp set the new mark at some five to five and a half million victims in 1947. There were other, higher figures bandied about right after the war, but they hardly received any attention (see the table at the end of this entry).

Several years after the war, after the hysterical propaganda dust had settled, the orthodoxy split into two schools. The western school of orthodox Holocaust scholars opined that the Auschwitz death toll was lower than the Soviet figure, but disagreed on the details. Their numbers ranged from just under a million (Reitlinger) up to three and a half million (Yehuda Bauer). Eastern scholars, on the other hand, had to comply with the Soviet four-million doctrine or suffer the consequences.

Many left-leaning western journalists and ideologues ig-

Old memorial plaque on the monument at Auschwitz-Birkenau with the "anti-fascist" propaganda number "four million" rendered into 19 languages (until 1990).

Since 1995: The new memorial plaque at the Auschwitz-Birkenau Memorial.

Number of Victims Claimed for Auschwitz	
NO OF VICTIMS	**SOURCE** (for exact references, see Faurisson 2003)
9,000,000	French documentary film *Nuit et Brouillard* (1955)
8,000,000	French investigative authority (Aroneanu 1945, pp. 7, 196)
7,000,000	Filip Friedman (1946, p. 14)
6,000,000	Tibère Kremer (1951)
5–5,500,000	Krakow Auschwitz trial (1947), *Le Monde* (1978)
4,000,000	Soviet document at the IMT
3,000,000	David Susskind (1986); *Heritage* (1993)
2,500,000	Rudolf Vrba, aka Walter Rosenberg, Eichmann Trial (1961)
1,5–3,500,000	Historian Yehuda Bauer (1982, p. 215)
2,000,000	Historians Poliakov (1951), Wellers (1973), Dawidowicz (1975)
1,600,000	Historian Yehuda Bauer (1989)
1,500,000	New memorial plaques in Auschwitz
1,471,595	Historian Georges Wellers (1983)
1,250,000	Historian Raul Hilberg (1961, 1985, 2003)
1,1–1,500,000	Historians I. Gutman, Franciszek Piper (1994)
1,000,000	J.-C. Pressac (1989), *Dictionnaire des noms propres* (1992)
800–900,000	Historian Gerald Reitlinger (1953 and later)
775–800,000	Jean-Claude Pressac (1993)
630–710,000	Jean-Claude Pressac (1994)
510,000	Fritjof Meyer (2002)
135,500	Carlo Mattogno (2023, Vol. 2, end of Chapter 3)
See also http://en.wikipedia.org/wiki/Auschwitz_concentration_camp#Death_toll	

nored the more-cautious numbers of western historians, and eagerly parroted the Soviet propaganda figure. Hence, the four million could often be heard in the West as well.

This schism was overcome only when the Soviet Union crumbled. In fact, it was Jews who started complaining in 1990. They accused the Poles of having rigged the numbers to make themselves look like the primary victims. They simply added to the more than one million Jews deported to Auschwitz two million Poles and other nationals. But most of them had been invented. Jews accused the Poles of "minimizing the Holocaust" by exaggerating the Auschwitz death toll. Yes: minimizing through exaggeration! They also demanded the primacy of their victimhood, as anything else would minimize their suffering. A commission was formed, which decided that two and a half million invented non-Jewish victims had to be removed. The old four-million memorial plaques were replaced with new ones commemorating the loss of 1.5 million lives – 90% of them Jews.

Leftist scholars were caught with their pants down. They admitted publicly that they had been lying about the Auschwitz death toll for decades, knowing full well that it was untrue. But they begged forgiveness, because they had done it for a good, anti-fascist cause. Wácław Długoborski, for decades the Auschwitz Museum's top historian under communist rule, excused his decade-long lies with the fact that "a prohibition against casting doubt upon the figure of 4 million killed was in force." He forgot to mention that this prohibition was only replaced with a new one a little later. Contesting the current orthodox narrative is now not just prohibited, it is actually a crime in Poland – and most other European countries. (See the entry on censorship.)

They lied in the past, they are compelled to lie now, and they will keep lying in the future – until all censorship laws have been rescinded, special statuses for minority groups have been revoked, and freedom and fair play finally reign.

The only number that is backed up by documental and material evidence is the last one in the table. Notably, it was presented by someone – Italian scholar Carlo Mattogno – who most certainly does not grovel before anyone's altar, does not pay homage to anyone's victim status, and does not get intimidated by governments threatening jail time in case of dissent.

(For more details, see Faurisson 2003; Rudolf 2023, pp. 123-128.)

AUSCHWITZ, BOMBING OF

In April 1944, the two Auschwitz inmates Rudolf Vrba and Alfred Wetzler escaped from the camp. They managed to flee to Slovakia, where they wrote down in May 1944 what they claimed was unfolding at Auschwitz. This report was sent in various versions and languages to several Jewish personalities. At the same time, the German authorities in Hungary started deporting the Hungarian Jews, many if not most of them via the Auschwitz Camp.

Since Vrba and Wetzler claimed that Jews were being mass murdered at Auschwitz, Jewish pressure groups concluded that the Hungarian Jews were brought to Auschwitz to be killed. They lobbied with the British and U.S. government to bomb the railway line leading to Auschwitz, and the Auschwitz camps themselves.

The U.S. government consistently and steadfastly refused to bomb targets not conducive to supporting the main goal of winning the war. While Britain's premier minister Winston Churchill agreed to have the camp bombarded, the Royal Air Force refused to carry out such a mission, claiming technical difficulties.

Allied airplanes could reach the Auschwitz region, beginning with the establishment of secure Allied airfields in Italy in early 1944. Reconnaissance flights were conducted regularly. The earliest known photos of the Auschwitz Camp were taken in May 1944, and from then on with some regularity every month. Furthermore, the British Government received all the intelligence information of the Polish underground with regularity. Therefore, the Allied governments and air forces knew exactly what was going on at Auschwitz.

Already in late summer of 1943, the chairman of the Allied Joint Intelligence Committee asserted their conviction that gas-chamber propaganda was untrue, and had been invented by Polish and Jewish agitators to rile up the Allies. (See the section on the United Kingdom in the entry on propaganda.)

Allied air photos of the Auschwitz camps confirmed this impression. These photos showed a peaceful camp. They refuted atrocity propaganda spread by the Polish and Jewish underground about huge open-air incinerations, smoking crematoria chimneys, and the entire area being blanketed in smoke. Therefore, the Allied air forces' decisions were correct to bomb the nearby I.G. Farben's BUNA factories at Monowitz instead, which were essential for Germany's war effort, and to not endanger the lives of innocent inmates in this forced-labor camp.

It goes without saying that no representative of the Allied governments back then and even today could ever admit that they considered the Polish and Jewish gas-chamber propaganda to be phony. As a result, Jewish organizations and orthodox Holocaust promoters accuse the Allies to this day of not having done anything to stop the slaughter at Auschwitz.

(See the section about Auschwitz in the entry on air photos.)

AUSCHWITZ ALBUM

During the deportation of Jews from Hungary to the Auschwitz-Birkenau Camp, the camp administration decided to document what was happening with these deportees at their camp with a series of photographs. Hence, on 26 May 1944, photographers Bernhard Walter and Ernst Hofmann took a series of photographs of the fate of Hungarian Jews who arrived on that day at Auschwitz. Some 200 of these photos were eventually put together into an album titled "The Resettlement of Jews from Hungary." The motivation for this is unclear. No other event or time period of the camp was ever documented with photos.

After the liberation of the Dora Camp by U.S. troops in early 1945, this album was accidentally found by the former Birkenau inmate Lili Jacob. She had been deported to Dora when Auschwitz was evacuated in January 1945. She claimed later to have found the album in the drawer of a nightstand in a former SS barracks at Dora, where she was recovering from illness.

Mrs. Jacob removed a few images allegedly showing relatives and acquaintances of hers, and then donated the album to Israel's Yad Vashem Center in 1980. An unchanged archival edition was published in 1980, and then in 1981 the first edition for the general public. The album currently has 193 photos; 188 of them were included in the 1981 and later editions of this album.

The orthodox Holocaust narrative, based on numerous witness statements, has it that, on arrival of a deportation train at Auschwitz-Birkenau, SS men were waiting for them with guns and rifles drawn or clubs, sticks and whips in hand, and with vicious German shepherd dogs ready to tear into any uncooperative inmate. The inmates are said to have been received with lots of threats and yelling, with beating and occasional wanton executions, all employed to intimidate the deportees and accelerate the procedure.

Arrival of a train of Jews from Hungary at Birkenau. In the background, two crematorium chimneys without smoke. On the ramp, many deportees, hardly any SS guards, nor dogs, no rushing, no urging, no threats. A sunny, cloudless and smoke-free day.

On the ramp, men at the left, women at the right side. A sunny, smoke-free day.

During the arrival of the Jews from Hungary from mid-May to early July 1944, the Birkenau crematoria are said to have been strained to the maximum, belching thick smoke and even flames uninterruptedly. Still unable to cope with the huge masses of inmates getting killed every day, huge ditches are said to have been dug inside the camp (near Crematorium V) and just outside of its perimeter to the west (behind the so-called *Zentralsauna*). In those pits, massive pyres were presumably set up in order to burn thousands upon thousands of murdered Jews. As a result, the entire area was covered in thick, nauseating smoke.

Once out of the train, the inmates are said to have been told to leave all their luggage behind on the ramp, and line up in order to get "selected." Those deemed fit for work were allegedly sent to one side, those unfit to the other. The latter group is said to have been directed immediately to one or several of the many claimed gas chambers.

The photos taken by the SS of the arrival and processing of a train full of deportees from the Carpa-

Peaceful, calm guards. A sunny, smoke-free day.

Woman with little children and luggage. A sunny, smoke-free day.

Mainly women and children waiting in the woods. A sunny, smoke-free day.

thian Mountains show the exact opposite. The sun is shining on all photos. There is no smoke in the skies, except near where the train's locomotive is (near the camp's main entrance, hence at the opposite end of where the smoke should be). Several photos show the chimneys of Crematoria II and III, the camp's largest cremation facilities. They do not emit any smoke, let alone flames. This impression is confirmed by many air photos taken at that time.

Most images show no SS men at all. If some are present, they are a minute minority within a sea of inmates. None of the SS men have whips, clubs or truncheons. None of them have any weapons drawn. There are no dogs visible anywhere. The SS men in-

Men (left) and women (right) fit for work, shorn, bathed, disinfested, with inmate clothes.

Shorn female inmates fit for work awaiting instructions. A sunny, smoke-free day.

teract normally with the inmates. There is no rushing, urging or threatening behavior visible in any of the photos.

The inmates lined up on the ramp in two groups: men and older boys on one side, women and smaller children on the other. Hence, the first selection on the ramp was by gender, not fitness. However, an entire section of the album shows groups of inmates divided into men fit and unfit for work, as well as women fit, and women with small children unfit for work. Hence, there evidently were two selections happening: One very superficial by gender on the ramp, and later another one according to physical fitness or the need to care for little children.

Several photos show old and young women with small children on their way from the ramp to unknown destinations along some camp road. Interestingly, some still have their luggage with them. Had they been slated to go to the next available gas chamber, they would not have been allowed to clog the mass-murder process by bringing along their sacks and bags and suitcases. Clearly, for these Jews unable to work, the journey wasn't over.

The album shows how these deportees gathered in a wooded area, sitting on the grass among trees, evidently relatively relaxed, recovering from the strenuous journey, calmly waiting for something to happen. The only wooded area inside the Birkenau Camp was in its western part near and around the Crematoria IV and V, put also near the camp's largest disinfestation facility, the so-called *Zentralsauna*. Hence, this is probably where these photos were taken.

Therefore, these deportees were either waiting to be gassed in the gas chambers claimed to have existed inside the two crematoria nearby, or they waited to be disinfested and showered in the *Zentralsauna* before continuing their journey elsewhere.

If the orthodox narrative were true, then these Jews evidently had to wait because the gas chambers weren't ready for them yet. The previous batch still had to be dragged from these chemical slaughterhouses. Hence, dramatic scenes of hundreds and thousands of gassed Jews being dragged out of these crematoria into the yard, to be burned on pyres, would have been visible to the Jews waiting outside for their turn to be slaughtered. Moreover, the flaming, smoking, crackling, stinking inferno caused by the gigantic pyres allegedly blazing behind Crematorium V and behind the *Zentralsauna* near the alleged Bunker 2 could not have gone unnoticed by anyone. It certainly would have caused panic among the waiting deportees, and inevitably would have left smokey traces on the photos. But none of it is visible on these photos.

The album also follows the path of those deemed fit for labor: they had their hair shorn, were disinfested, received prisoners' clothes, and were then assembled, probably to be told what awaited them next.

The editions of the *Auschwitz Album* available for purchase all have misleading comments and a rearranged sequence of photos. This was evidently done in an attempt to insinuate to the reader that what they see in the picture is not what happened. Rather, this album is allegedly part of just another evil plot by the SS to hide their intricate plans for the deportees' mass murder behind innocuous-looking photos.

(All photos taken from the Yad Vashem website; see Mattogno 2023c, Chapter 1.10; Faurisson 1983.)

AUSCHWITZ DEATH BOOKS

The Auschwitz Death Books (German: *Sterbebü-*

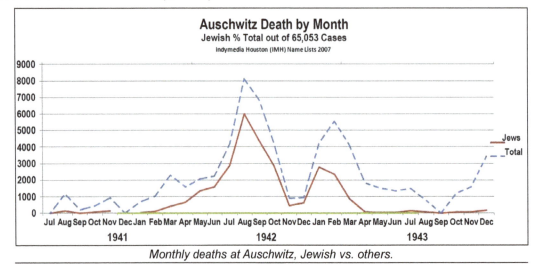
Monthly deaths at Auschwitz, Jewish vs. others.

cher) are death registers prepared under the responsibility of the Political Department of the Auschwitz Camp (comprising the Main Camp, Birkenau, and all the subcamps). These books contained the death certificates of the inmates who had been admitted and registered at the camp, and who subsequently died for whatever reasons, executions included. When a maximum of 1,500 of these single-sheet certificates had been issued, they were bound as hard-cover volumes. Three copies of each death certificate existed. One remained in the camp, while two others were sent to superior departments.

When the Auschwitz Camp was evacuated in mid-January 1945, these Death Books were taken to the Gross-Rosen Camp, where they were abandoned when the Germans retreated from that town. Soviet authorities found them there eventually. From a series of communications between Soviet agencies, we know that they found 80 volumes, which were sent to Moscow with all the other archival material captured. When the Soviet Union/Russia released the German wartime documents it still had in its archives during the early 1990s, only 46 of the original 80 volumes were left, covering the time from mid-1941 to the end of 1943 with some gaps. Considering the rampant corruption in post-collapse Russia, the remaining volumes might have been sold on the black market. One more volume was recovered elsewhere. The rest have not been recovered to this day.

The total number of deceased inmates registered in the available Death Books plus fragments of other volumes that were found elsewhere is 68,864. If all 80 volumes were filled, and all contained 1,500 or only slightly less death certificates, then this would indicate a total death toll among registered Auschwitz inmates of some 120,000 inmates. However, a thorough study of other documents that also registered deceased inmates shows that not all inmates who died at Auschwitz were registered in the Death Books. Adding those documented in other registries, the total death toll actually tallies to some 135,500 deceased inmates.

Some data of the available death certificates con-

Religious affiliations of victims listed in the Death Books of Auschwitz	
Catholic	46.8%
Protestant	3.4%
Greek Catholic	1.6%
Greek Orthodox	3.6%
Christian Total	55.4%
Jewish	42.8%

Ages of deceased registered Auschwitz inmates as documented in the Death Books (without fragments)		
AGE GROUP	NO.	%
>90	2	0.0
80-90	73	0.1
70-80	482	0.7
60-70	2,083	3.0
50-60	8,040	11.7
40-50	15,512	22.5
30-40	18,430	26.7
20-30	14,830	21.5
10-20	6,715	9.7
00-10	2,584	3.7
	68,751	99.6

tained in the Death Books was published in 1995 in a German study. Analyzing these data yields some interesting insights. For example, if we go strictly by the preserved death certificates, then more Christians (mostly Poles) died at Auschwitz than Jews (see the first table).

Furthermore, these volumes contain a considerable amount of very young and very old people, among them babies, even infants born in Auschwitz, and geriatrics 80 years and older. If we follow the orthodox narrative, such individuals should never have been admitted to the camp, but should have been slated for immediate gassing upon arrival (or birth). But that is evidently not what happened. The second table shows the relative representation of various age groups among registered Auschwitz inmates who died in that camp and found themselves duly documented as such.

The Death Books of Auschwitz also confirm that the death rate among inmates was catastrophically high in the summer and fall of 1942, and then again in early 1943, which coincides with the richly documented typhus epidemic during those times. All in all, there is no other German wartime camp that suffered from such a catastrophic inmate mortality. It was truly a "death camp" in terms of inmates dying like flies as a result of poor hygienic and sanitary conditions during long stretches of the camp's existence.

(For more details, see the entries on the Auschwitz Main Camp, Birkenau, healthcare, and France; see also Staatliches Museum 1995; Mattogno 2023, Part 2, pp. 163-170, 211; Kollerstrom 2023, pp. 87-90; Rudolf 2023, pp. 41-48, 242-245.)

AUSCHWITZ MAIN CAMP
Documented History

The first extant document of this camp, dated 30 April 1940, is a cost estimate totaling 2 million reichsmark to convert the former Polish barracks into a camp. It includes fences, walls, watchtowers, but also an inmate kitchen, a laundry, a water-supply system, an inmate bath, a delousing facility, and of course additional lodging buildings. Less than a

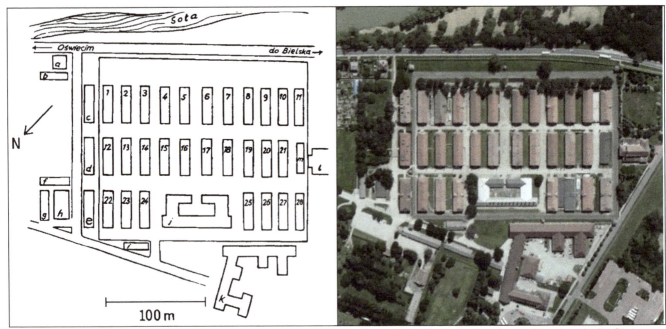

Auschwitz I/Main Camp (concentration camp). Left: map according to the information brochure of the Auschwitz State Museum in 1991. Right: Google Earth satellite image (2 Dec. 2016).

Block 1 – 28: inmate barracks; basement of Block 11: detention cells, location of the claimed first homicidal gassing, September 1941.
- a: commandant's house
- b: main guard station
- c: camp commandant's office
- d: administration building
- e: SS hospital
- f, g: political department (Gestapo)
- h: Crematorium I with claimed homicidal gas chamber
- i: guard station near camp entrance gate (block leader room)
- j: camp kitchen
- k: inmate admission building, showers, disinfestation (since June 1944: microwave)
- l: camp warehouse, theater building
- m: new laundry

month later, the Topf Company submitted an estimate for a double-muffle cremation furnace, to be built in the camp's former munitions bunker, to be converted into a crematorium (later called Crematorium I, or Old Crematorium). This furnace became operational on 15 August 1940, with two more following in March 1941 and March 1942, respectively. Many construction reports subsequently documented the steady expansion and improvement of the camp.

Hundreds of orders issued by the camp's headquarters over the years paint an inconspicuous picture, with nothing pointing at anything unusual going on. Radio messages sent by the camp to the SS headquarters in Oranienburg, which were intercepted and deciphered by the British between January 1942 and January 1943, speak of occasional inmate deaths due to executions or failed escapes, but indicate nothing unusual, such as mass murder. Various reports and documents of labor-deployment departments, infirmaries and other camp departments show a fluctuating camp population either deployed at work or idle mainly due to illnesses.

The mortality rate of the camp's registered inmate population grew steadily during the first few years, reaching dramatic proportions in the first half of 1942, and finally catastrophic dimensions in July 1942. This was primarily caused by a typhus epidemic. The situation was particularly bad at the Birkenau Camp due to a lack of sanitation facilities. The situation improved steadily during 1943 and into 1944 due to improved sanitation, hygienic and health facilities at the camp, before it deteriorated again toward the end of the war due to the general collapse of Germany's infrastructure resulting from Allied carpet bombings and invading armies.
(For more details, see Mattogno 2021, pp. 15-102; 2023, Part 1&2; Rudolf/Böhm 2020.)

Propaganda History

Note: Propaganda that cannot be allocated with certainty to the Auschwitz Main Camp or any of its satellite camps is addressed in the entry on Birkenau.

Camp Resistance

Right from the beginning of the camp's existence, inmates organized themselves in resistance groups. As the camp grew, so did the number of these groups and their members. Eventually, these groups integrated and coordinated their work. One aspect of their work was helping inmates to escape, but more

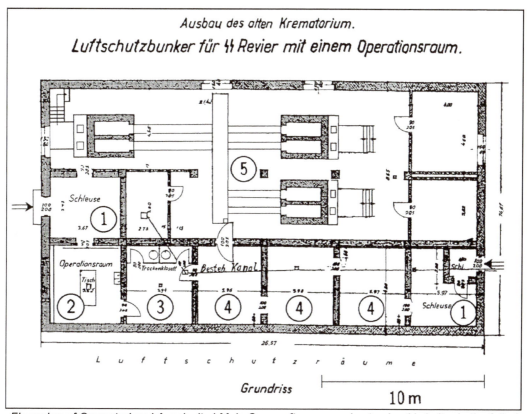

Floor plan of Crematorium I Auschwitz I Main Camp after conversion to air-raid shelter in the fall of 1944.
1: added entry door with air lock ("Schleuse"); 2: surgery room; 3: former washroom, now air-raid shelter with toilets; 4: air-raid shelter rooms; 5: former furnace room. Note that the swinging door, still shown in this plan, was removed and walled up during the conversion.

importantly to communicate to Polish civilians and members of the Polish underground outside the camp what was happening inside. After the war, leaders of this camp resistance, such as Hermann Langbein, Otto Wolken and Bruno Baum, bragged that they had members in all major inmate labor units, including the various so-called *Sonderkommandos*, and were always well-informed of what was transpiring in the camp. In fact, Bruno Baum bragged after the war that all the propaganda spread about Auschwitz during the war was created by these resistance groups.

First Gassing
With the camp resistance being so well-informed, their messages to the Polish resistance outside the camp should have reflected reality. However, the first reports about the alleged first gassing at Auschwitz, spread in late October 1941 and playing on gas-warfare fears, spoke of the testing of new war gasses on Soviet PoWs for later deployment at the eastern front. Later reports disagreed on who exactly – Soviet PoWs and/or Poles – and how many of them had become victims of this crime. After the story had circulated throughout the propaganda world for a year, liberated inmates testified all kinds of things about this event, creating an inextricable hodgepodge of mutually contradictory tales, but all of them replacing the claimed testing of war gases for the eastern front with the testing of Zyklon B for future mass-murder at Auschwitz. For more details on this mythological event refuted by documents, see its dedicated entry "first gassing, at Auschwitz."

Crematorium I
The Auschwitz resistance groups knew nothing about gassings supposedly carried out in the morgue of Crematorium I. Those mass-murder activities are said to have occurred between late 1941/early 1942 and early 1942/late 1942, depending on the anecdotal source. The most important among them is that of former Auschwitz Commandant Rudolf Höss. He claimed that, when a batch of Soviet PoWs arrived in late 1941, several holes were spontaneously hacked through the roof of the crematorium's morgue, so that Zyklon B could be thrown down on the Soviet PoWs locked up inside.

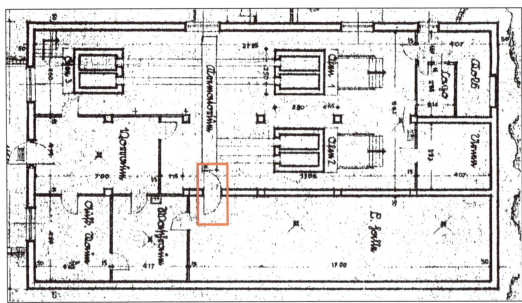
SS blueprint of Crematorium I drawn on 10 April 1942, while the morgue was allegedly equipped for usage as a homicidal "gas chamber." Grey box around door added, highlighting a swing door connecting the morgue ("Halle," bottom) and the furnace room with three double-muffle furnaces (top).

Today's orthodox narrative claims that there were only a few gassings in that building, and that they stopped once the first bunker near the Birkenau Camp was put into operation, which allegedly occurred in March 1942. The messages of the Polish resistance about Auschwitz, however, mention this building only once as a "poisoning site," and this in a report of November 1942, hence well after it ceased being used for gassings, if we follow the current orthodox narrative. However, had mass gassings really occurred there, then the Auschwitz resistance groups would have known about it and reported it early on with gory details and ferocious polemics. These messages would have been forwarded by the Polish underground to London, and there exuberantly exploited by the Polish government in exile and the British Political Warfare Executive. However, none of that happened, because no gassing happened.

The tale of gassings in Crematorium I was created by a Soviet investigative commission in February and March 1945, hence while the war was still raging. When the Soviets captured Auschwitz, all the buildings where mass-murders are said to have occurred were located at Birkenau but had all been demolished by the Germans before retreating (Crematoria II through V; plus the two bunkers, if they ever existed). Hence, they could not repeat a propaganda show similar to the one they had performed at the Majdanek Camp, where they had presented the local crematorium as a place of mass murder and mass cremation in July/August 1944. At Auschwitz, only the former Old Crematorium was still standing, because it had been converted to an air-raid shelter in 1944, hence was considered innocuous by the retreating Germans. Thus, Soviets went to work and presented this place as a mass-murder site, although clearly misunderstanding that, before its conversion to an air-raid shelter, this place had looked completely different.

Witnesses confirming this Soviet propaganda report were found only afterwards. A detailed analysis of their testimony shows that all of them are utterly untrustworthy:
– Stanisław Jankowski
– Erwin Bartel
– Filip Müller
– Hans Aumeier
– Rudolf Höss
– Pery Broad
– Maximilian Grabner
– Hans Stark

(For more information see Mattogno 2016c.)

Museum Propaganda

When the SS turned the Old Crematorium into an air-raid shelter in late 1944, they made changes to the building rendering it unsuitable as a museum exhibit of mass murder:
– they removed all cremation furnaces,
– tore down the cremation chimney,

HOLOCAUST ENCYCLOPEDIA – Auschwitz Main Camp

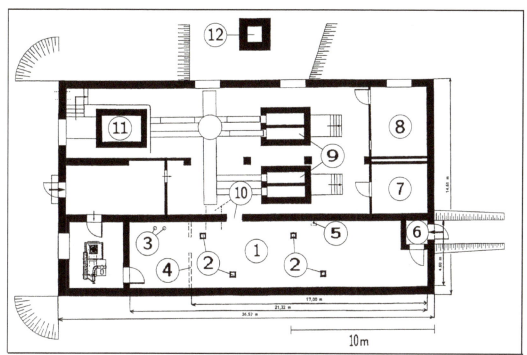

Floor plan of Crematorium I in Auschwitz I/Main Camp today, after the Polish manipulations of 1947.
1: "Gas chamber"; 2: fake Zyklon-B introduction holes, wrongly spread out to be somewhat evenly distributed in <u>today's</u> room; 3: toilet drains of former air-raid shelter; 4: former partition between morgue and washroom; 5: ventilation chimney of air-raid shelter; 6: air-raid shelter's additional entry door and air lock, until the end of the 20th Century wrongly referred to by the Museum as victim entryway; 7: urn room, 8: coke; 9: reconstructed furnaces;
10: newly broken-through entry way without any door connecting the alleged "gas chamber" with the furnace room; dashed line: original location of swinging door; 11: remains of the old furnace;
12: fake chimney.

- walled up the door connecting the morgue (the alleged gas chamber) with the furnace room,
- tore down a thin wall separating the morgue from the washroom next door, and another wall separating that room from the adjacent laying-out room,
- then added five thick, sturdy separation walls along the entire length of building, partitioning the air-raid shelter into six separate, almost square-shaped rooms,
- and added a pair of toilets with toilet-stall walls to one of the rooms.
- Furthermore, the SS added a feature that would have been essential for a homicidal gas chamber, but which did not exist originally: a door allowing access without having to walk through rooms filled with corpses. The entrance way they added features a sheet-metal-lined door with a peephole that leads into an air-lock. Such an air-lock is crucial for an air-raid shelter, but would be useless, in fact obstructive, for a homicidal gas chamber.

Understanding that a museum of National-Socialist atrocities at Auschwitz must absolutely feature a "gas chamber" in order to be convincing and attract visitors, the Polish postwar museum administrators went to work in 1946/47 to create the climax of their future museum tour: the "gas chamber." Without documenting either the state of the building before their changes, or the changes they were about to make, they

- built a new crematorium chimney, although it is not connected to any smoke duct;
- rebuilt two of the three furnaces, yet in a dysfunctional manner (they built the hearth in the ash chamber beneath the muffle rather than attached to the rear of the furnace);
- knocked a large, asymmetrical opening at the wrong spot through the wall connecting the former morgue with the furnace room, and "forgot" to put any door into it;
- knocked down all thick separation walls except for one, although they should have left one standing, meaning their new, larger room included what used to be the separate washroom;

- removed the toilet stall walls and the toilets, but left the toilet drains clearly visible;
- left the entrance to the air-raid shelter with its airtight door and air-lock standing, because without it there was no direct access for victims to the morgue, and this gas-tight air-raid-shelter door with peephole was a tempting (though fake) piece of evidence pointing to the room's alleged misuse as a homicidal gas chamber.
- As a climax of their criminal tampering with the evidence of a claimed crime scene, they crudely knocked four square-shaped holes through the ceiling, put some wooden boards around them and a wooden lid on top, and declared them to be Zyklon-B introduction shafts.

This grand plan of deception was and still is called to this day a "reconstruction" of the "original gas chamber," although there never was an original, and the mistakes made during the effort clearly qualify it as a forgery rather than a "reconstruction." Until the turn of the millennium, the Museum mendaciously told millions of visitors that this building was in its original state, although they knew better. Only later, beginning in the 1990s, did they admit having made some "mistakes" during their "reconstruction."

The only feature that "proves" that this room was a homicidal gas chamber are today's four Zyklon-B holes in the roof. The Museum claims that they made these holes in 1946/47 in spots where the old, "original" holes had been, which was allegedly visible by some concrete patches at the ceiling. Needless to say, the Museum did not document the existence of these patches, and they did not secure any witness testimony of the people involved in "reconstructing" these holes either. Moreover, the holes are located in spots clearly demonstrating that they were made to be equally spaced in the room as it exists *today* – with the air-lock of 1944 and a room that is much longer than the original. All the museum officials can present as evidence for their claim is the 1981 testimony of the former inmate and museum guard Adam Żłobnicki, who moreover made false claims about these Zyklon B introduction shafts (see the entry on him).

The many material and documented features that refute the claim that this morgue in its original state could have been a homicidal gas chamber are conveniently overlooked:
- The morgue was connected to the furnace room with a swinging door that could not be made airtight and could not be locked safely against a panicking crowd.
- The wall separating the morgue from the washroom was only 15 cm thick, hence one row of bricks. No massive, gas-tight and panic-proof steel door could have been anchored in such a thin wall.
- The room had no other door, hence the victims could not have entered it from the outside. They had to walk through rooms where corpses would have been piled up awaiting autopsies or cremation – an absurd thought.
- A powerful ventilation system for this room was delivered in late 1941, but it was never installed and rusted away in a warehouse. Instead, the SS made do with a much weaker makeshift solution, designed for a morgue, and installed at an earlier time when even the orthodox narrative concurs that no homicidal use was anticipated yet. In other words: the SS had no need for a powerful ventilation system. However, had they carried out mass gassings with powerful poison gasses, they certainly would have quickly installed the system delivered in late 1941.

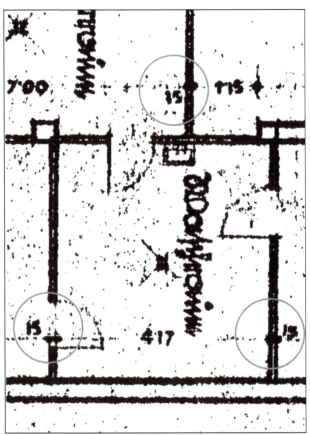

Section enlargement of the floor plan of Crematorium I of 10 April 1942, showing the washroom with adjacent walls with grey circles added to highlight the walls' width of 15 cm, unfit to hold a panic-proof massive steel door.

None of it ever happened, because no gassing happened. (For more information, see Mattogno 2016c; 2020, pp. 13-38)

Current Orthodox Narrative

The current orthodox Auschwitz narrative is based primarily on a series of articles by Polish historian Danuta Czech published in the late 1950s and early 1960s. They were republished in an expanded and slightly updated version as a book in 1989 (German) and 1990 (English). Czech's version is complemented by additional insights added by French historian Jean-Claude Pressac (1989, 1993), some of which the orthodoxy accepted, others not. The timeline of extermination events is as follows in this narrative (*set in italics*, followed by critical remarks):

1. *On 29 July 1941, Rudolf Höss, at that time the Auschwitz Camp's commandant, received an order from Himmler to turn Auschwitz into Germany's center for the annihilation of the Jews.* However, there is no proof of such an order, or Höss meeting Himmler. Höss insisted after the war that the meeting was either in May or June 1941, in any case before the war with the Soviet Union (before 22 June 1941). Höss repeatedly stated that Himmler chose Auschwitz, because the other camps killing Jews at that time – Belzec, Treblinka and Wolzek – could not cope with the task. Höss moreover claimed that he then visited Treblinka to learn how to improve things. However, the Belzec Camp was opened only in March 1942, the Treblinka Camp in July 1942, and no camp named Wolzek ever existed. In other words, the severely tortured Höss made it all up. (See Mattogno 2020b, pp. 184-204 for details.)

2. *Between 3 and 5 September 1941, the first (experimental) gassing using Zyklon B occurred in the basement of Block 11, which consisted of a series of prison cells. 600 Soviet PoWs and 250 sick Polish inmates were the victims.* However, the first Soviet PoWs arrived at Auschwitz only in early October 1941, and only more than a month later was a decision made that the fanatical communists among them – some 300 – were to be executed… by shooting. Furthermore, the multifarious witness accounts on this alleged event are extremely disparate, including the one by Höss, extracted with torture. Czech cherry-picked claims from various sources, discarded the majority of claims made, and constructed a completely fictitious event from it. (See the entry on the "first gassing" for more details.)

3. *On 16 September 1941, 900 Soviet PoWs were gassed in the morgue of the Main Camp's crematorium, presumably starting a phase of gassings in that building lasting until early 1942.* However, and again, Soviet PoWs arrived at Auschwitz only in early October, and a decision to execute some of them was made only in November. Czech relied on the confused and contradictory statements by Rudolf Höss. (For more on this, see Mattogno 2016c, pp. 54-57; 2020b, pp. 213-215.) Subsequent claims of gassings in that building (Czech has only one entry on 15 Feb. 1942) are based on testimonies by Rudolf Höss, Pery Broad and others (not listed by Czech). However, a detailed analysis of all the disparate claims made about this shows that not a single witness is trustworthy, and that the claims fly in the face of documental and material evidence as well as what was physically possible. (See the section on Crematorium I in the present entry for details.)

4. *On 20 March 1942, an old farmhouse near the newly established Birkenau Camp was converted into a gassing facility containing two gas chambers. In the spring of 1945, Polish judiciary christened this facility "Bunker 1." Subsequently, gassings are said to have been carried out only there, allegedly because gassings at the main camp were too conspicuous to be kept a secret. Thousands of deportees are said to have been gassed on arrival without being registered. The victims were allegedly buried in nearby mass graves.* However, a detailed analysis of all the disparate claims made about this shows that not a single witness is trustworthy, and that the claims fly in the face of documental and material evidence as well as what was physically possible. No evidence exists that a building in the claimed area was ever adopted by the camp administration and converted to anything. Instead, all extant buildings of Polish farmers were razed to the ground when the area was prepared for the camp's huge hospital section, Construction Sector III. Furthermore, all transports of Jews allegedly killed in this facility in the first half of 1942 were invented out of thin air. Up to early July 1942, all Jews of documented transports were registered. Hence, none of them were gassed on arrival. In spite of Himmler's alleged order to Höss of June 1941, no extermination policy of Jews existed. (For more details, see the entry on bunkers, as well as Mat-

togno 2016f.)

5. *On 30 June 1942, another old farmhouse near the growing Birkenau Camp was converted into a gassing facility containing four unequally sized gas chambers. In the spring of 1945, Polish judiciary christened this facility "Bunker 2." This facility is said to have been added to increase the mass-murder capacity. The victims were allegedly buried in nearby mass graves.* However, a detailed analysis of all the disparate claims made about this shows that not a single witness is trustworthy, and that the claims fly in the face of documental and material evidence as well as what was physically possible. Although a building existed in the claimed area, the ruin's foundation walls disprove all claims about the facility's appearance. (For more details, see the entry on bunkers, as well as Mattogno 2016f.)

6. *On 17 July 1942, Himmler attended a gassing at Bunker 2, and ordered the murder of all Jews unfit for work.* However, Himmler's diary and the lack of any incoming Jewish transports that could have been gassed prove that Himmler cannot have witnessed a gassing. (See Mattogno 2016d, pp. 16-25; 2020b, pp. 242-250.) Moreover, how can Himmler have ordered to kill all Jews unfit for work, if he had issued an order back in June 1941 to kill *all* Jews without exception? (See Mattogno 2020b, pp. 188-195.) Himmler's claimed gassing attendance plus the new order of "only" killing those unfit for work has been asserted only by the severely tortured Rudolf Höss, whose various postwar statements are riddled with contradictions, anachronisms and impossibilities.

7. *Between 21 September and 30 November 1942, some 107,000 corpses buried in mass graves near the bunkers of Birkenau were exhumed and burned on pyres in pits.* Air photos show that mass graves did indeed exist in Birkenau, but their size indicates that only the victims of the typhus epidemic can have been buried in them, which, due to a lack of cremation capacity, could not be cremated in the old crematorium in late spring and summer of 1942. Due to the high groundwater level at Birkenau, these graves were indeed exhumed, and their contents burned on pyres. (See the entry on mass graves.)

8. *Between 14 March and 25 June 1943, the four Birkenau crematoria, equipped with large homicidal gas chambers, became operational. Their claimed capacity was around 4,500 bodies per day* (Czech 1990, p. 429). *As a result, Bunker 1 was demolished tracelessly around that time, while Bunker 2 was temporarily retired.* However, a thorough technical study of these cremation facilities shows that their theoretical maximum capacity was "only" about 920 bodies per day. (See the section on Birkenau in the entry on crematoria.) Also note that Bunker 1 popped into existence without a trace, and vanished into oblivion without leaving a trace as well. Neither claim on Bunker 1 is supported by any documental or physical evidence.

9. *Crematoria II and III each had two underground morgues, one of which was used as the victims' undressing room, the other as a gas chamber. Zyklon B was poured into this room through four openings in the morgue's roof.* There is a long string of witnesses who testified about this, most of whom have made diverging, contradictory and frequently preposterous statements about these facilities and other topic concerning Auschwitz, lending them a very low credibility. (See section Auschwitz of the entry on witnesses.) Pressac (1989/1993) specialized in collecting so-called "criminal traces" in extant documents allegedly supporting the orthodox narrative. However, a detailed study of these documents and their context proves that none of them support any homicidal claim. (See more on those in the entry on criminal traces.) Moreover, several documents demonstrate that the crematoria's morgues were available 24/7 to store corpses of inmates who had died from numerous causes throughout the camp. They cannot have served both as gassing facilities and as corpse-storage facilities. While the latter fact is supported by documents, the former claim is not. (For more details on this, see the entry on morgues.)

10. *Crematoria IV and V each had a corridor and two rooms in an annex, whose purpose is not stated in any extant plan or document. The two rooms (and maybe also the corridor) were used as homicidal gas chambers. Zyklon B was poured into these rooms through hatches in the walls.* However, the situation here is similar to that described for Crematoria II and III. (See the entries on criminal traces and witnesses.). Moreover, the ventilation system ordered for both facilities was not installed, demonstrating that poison gas cannot have been used in them. A few documents show that a large shower facility was built in one of the

rooms, and a "gas chamber" in the other. In German pre-war and wartime documents, the term "gas chamber" always referred to fumigation chambers. Hence, the annex was probably planned to be a hygienic center, with inmate showers and a disinfestation facility. It may not have been finished to that effect due to other, better facilities becoming available (such as the *Zentralsauna* and the microwave delousing device.)

11. *On 9 May 1944, Bunker 2 was reactivated. Large pits were dug in its vicinity, and also north of Crematorium V, where thousands of Jews deported from Hungary were burned every day in open-air incinerations from mid-May until early July 1944, because the crematoria's capacity was insufficient for the great influx of Jews from Hungary. The whole area was blanketed in thick smoke.* However, German and Allied air photos of that time prove that to be wrong. There were no large pits anywhere, smoking or not, and the crematoria's chimneys didn't smoke either.

12. *On 26 November 1944, Himmler ordered the destruction of the Auschwitz crematoria, hence also the end of all gassing activities.* However, there is no such order. There is only a postwar affidavit by a person not involved – Kurt Becher – claiming that Himmler prohibited the extermination of Jews "sometime between mid-September and mid-October 1944." Crematoria are not mentioned. (See the entry on Kurt Becher for more details.) Czech shifted that date to end of November and changed the contents of that claimed order, so that, in her narrative, she could keep sending Jews to the gas chambers well after mid-September and mid-October 1944.

When it comes to mass-murder claims, both Danuta Czech's *opus magnum* and Jean-Claude Pressac's works mendaciously misrepresent the historical record in an astonishing way. (For more details, see the entry on Danuta Czech and on criminal traces.)

The entry on Auschwitz in Gutman's 1990 *Encyclopedia of the Holocaust*, written by two scholars (Shmuel Krakowski and Jozef Buszko) who had not specialized on Auschwitz, ignores Czech's studies and those published by other historians from the Auschwitz Museum (such as Franciszek Piper and Wácław Długoborski). As a result, this contribution contains many embarrassing omissions and mistakes, even from an orthodox point of view, some of which are (see Gutman 1990, pp. 107-119):

– The experimental "first gassing" of 3 September 1941 took place in a "relatively small gas chamber […] built in Auschwitz I," meaning the Main Camp, when in fact it allegedly happened in all of the prison cells of the already existing and unaltered basement of Block 11 in that camp.
– Subsequently, larger and permanent gas chambers were built in Birkenau. The alleged homicidal gas chamber inside the old crematorium at the Main Camp, the Auschwitz Museum's most prized exhibit to this day, is not given a single word.
– Starting in March 1942, Jews were unloaded at the railway ramp (the German word for which is misspelled as *rampa*; correct: *Rampe*) located *inside* the Birkenau Camp. However, the Birkenau railway ramp was finished only in early May 1944. Before that, all transports were unloaded at a railway ramp near Auschwitz Station, a mile away from Birkenau.
– The two "bunkers" of Birkenau are not mentioned at all.
– The Topf Company built the large Birkenau gas chambers. In fact, Topf built the cremation furnaces, one forced-draft device (which malfunctioned, so they had to take it back), and the ventilation systems for all crematoria. The Birkenau crematorium buildings were built by the Huta Company.
– "At least 1,600,000 people were murdered" in Birkenau alone. However, today's orthodox estimate is around one million.

This comes from the world's most exquisite collection of orthodox Holocaust scholars! (The 2000 *Encyclopedia of the Holocaust* by Robert Rozett and Shmuel Spector, both prodigious contributors to Gutman's 1990 encyclopedia, is basically a condensed version of Gutman's work, with so few details in its entry on Auschwitz – and anything else, for that matter – that it is completely devoid of any specific information about anything.)

AUSCHWITZ MUSEUM

Measured by yearly visitors, the Auschwitz Museum is the largest Holocaust-related Museum in the world, with a pre-COVID peak visitor number in 2019 of 2.3 million visitors.

The Auschwitz Camp Museum is also Poland's most-important foreign-policy asset, something that keeps the Jewish lobby happy and the Germans in a psychological stranglehold.

The main exhibit area of the Auschwitz Museum

consists of the almost completely preserved Main Camp. The Birkenau Camp has very few original structures remaining. The ruins of the four crematoria are presented more as symbols than as education about anything, least of all real cremation technology.

The so-called *Zentralsauna*, Birkenau's main shower and disinfestation facility, though largely intact, is not used to enlighten visitors much about the diverse and strenuous efforts of the German camp administration to improve the camp's healthcare services, sanitation facilities and hygienic conditions. This would evidently distract too much from the gas-chamber and cremation-furnace horror show that is the camp's main attraction.

The Museum's most-prized asset is no doubt the "reconstructed" – but actually phony – old crematorium. It has the ill-boding furnace room equipped with two – badly – reconstructed double-muffle furnaces, and the alleged homicidal gas chamber with four ominous Zyklon-B introduction openings in the ceiling/roof. That they were mendaciously inserted only in 1947, hence after the war, with no proven relation to any original, is hushed up. (For more on this building, see the subsection "Crematorium I" of the "Propaganda" section in the entry on the Auschwitz Main Camp.)

Another attraction is the basement area of Block 11, the so-called detention bunker. In its cells, the infamous "first gassing" with Zyklon B is said to have unfolded. No one explains to the million tourists that this entire event was invented from scratch. (For details, see the entry on the "first gassing, at Auschwitz.")

Other assets include showcases with what is presented as a pile of old shoes from murdered inmates. However, it is actually only a single layer of shoes of unknown origin fixed to an inclined plane. (For more on this show case, see the entry on shoes of deportees.) Piles of human hair, of spectacles, of luggage and other items that inmates may have brought along round off this collection of a German wartime camp's efforts to store, preserve and perhaps recycle its inmates' property. The Museum presents all this as evidence of mass murder. The average visitor is both spooked and impressed by these exhibits, although a pile of objects proves nothing about the fate of their former owners. This is as true for today's used-clothes collection drives as it is for the Auschwitz Camp. (For more information, see the entries on hair of camp inmates, on gold teeth, and on wedding rings.)

Showcase at the Auschwitz Museum, showing a layer of long fibers deposited on an inclined plane giving the false impression of a huge pile. These fibers all have the same color, whereas human hair would come in various colors: black, brown, auburn, red, orange, copper, blond, grey, salt & pepper, white. Moreover, the Museum claims that this is hair shorn off the heads of inmates after having been murdered at Auschwitz. However, every inmate admitted to the camp had their hair shorn. (See the illustrations in the entry on the Auschwitz Album.) If exceeding a certain length, this hair was collected, disinfested, bagged and submitted to companies for commercial use. No evidence exists whatsoever that this a) is human hair (it may just be flax), b) originates from murdered people.

Finally, Auschwitz has its bloody Black Wall, where thousands upon thousands of inmates are said to have been executed by shootings. As both wartime camp documents and British radio intercepts show, numerical claims in this regard are highly exaggerated as well. While executions did take place, they occurred as random events to the inmates, who had no insight into who had decided when to execute whom for what reason.

While death penalties during World War II were quite common among all belligerent parties, this does not mean that the Third Reich's executions were legal, legitimate, just or wise. In fact, due to a persistent lack of any due process within the SS camp system, not even most incarceration could be considered legal, let alone death penalties.

(Next to the other entries mentioned, see esp. Mattogno 2020, pp. 7-38.)

Auschwitz Protocols → War Refugee Board Report

AUSCHWITZ TRIALS

Overview

After the war, numerous trials were held in occupied Germany, in West Germany, East Germany, Austria and Poland, during which crimes allegedly committed at the former Auschwitz Camp were the main focus or at least an important factor. Among the first was the British Bergen-Belsen Trial against Josef Kramer and others. (See the entries on Josef Kramer and on the Bergen-Belsen Trials for more details.)

Poland conducted two trials, whose results set the propagandistic framework for all subsequent trials against defendants accused of having committed crimes there. East and West Germany both had several trials focusing on Auschwitz crimes, although only two of them had a major impact: The West-German first Frankfurt Auschwitz Trial, and the East-German trial against Horst Fischer. Two trials centering on Auschwitz crimes were conducted in Austria, with only the first of them against Walter Dejaco and Fritz Ertl having considerable impact.

Trial of Rudolf Höss

The first trial with a focus on events allegedly occurring at the former Auschwitz Camp was conducted in Warsaw, Poland's capital. The only defendant during that trial was Rudolf Höss, who was commandant of the Auschwitz Camp from the beginning until November 1943. This 17-session trial lasted from 11 March until 29 March 1947. The case for the prosecution was prepared by investigative judge Jan Sehn. He conducted his manipulative investigations with the clear aim of confirming the fraudulent propaganda version which the Soviets had created right after conquering the area, including the 4-million death-toll claim.

The trial itself was a typical communist show trial, where Höss's defense lawyer acted like an assistant prosecutor. Höss was sentenced to death and executed on 16 April 1947 by hanging at a gallows built for him near the former crematorium building of the Auschwitz Main Camp.

(For more information, see the entries on Jan Sehn, criminal traces, Roman Dawidowski, Rudolf Höss, and the section on Auschwitz of the entry on witnesses, many of whom either testified during the trial or at least made a deposition in front of Dr. Sehn.)

Trial of Members of the Camp Garrison

After the trial against the former Auschwitz camp commandant Rudolf Höss had cast the combined Soviet-Polish Auschwitz propaganda narrative into legal stone, the Polish authorities conducted a follow-up mass show trial against 40 defendants. They all had performed some official function at the camp during the war. Among the better-known defendants were:

– Arthur Liebehenschel, commandant of the Auschwitz Main Camp (death sentence, executed on 24 January 1948)
– Hans Aumeier, head of the Protective-Custody Camp (death sentence, executed on 24 January 1948)
– Maximilian Grabner, head of the Political Department, meaning the camp Gestapo (death sentence, executed on 24 January 1948)
– Erich Mussfeldt, labor unit leader, block leader, head of Crematoria II and III (death sentence, executed on 24 January 1948)
– Johann Paul Kremer, camp physician (death sentence, commuted to life, released early)
– Arthur Breitwieser, clothing chamber, head of disinfestation squad (death sentence, commuted to life, released early)
– Hans Münch, physician at the hygiene institute (acquitted)

As with the Höss Trial, Jan Sehn's manipulative pre-trial investigations also were the guidelines along which the trial was conducted. The hearings lasted from 24 November to 22 December 1947, ending with 23 death sentences, two of which were commuted to life imprisonments, both of which were released early. Furthermore, six life terms, seven 15-year prison terms, one 5-year and one 3-year prison term were imposed. Hans Münch was the only defendant who walked away as a free man.

(For more information, see here as well the entries on Jan Sehn, criminal traces, Roman Dawidowski, and the section on Auschwitz of the entry on witnesses, many of whom either testified during the trial or at least made a deposition in front of Dr. Sehn.)

Great Frankfurt Auschwitz Trial

The first West-German Auschwitz trial was conducted in Frankfurt against 22 defendants who were accused of having committed homicides at the Auschwitz Camp. It lasted 185 sessions from 20 December 1963 until 20 August 1965. It was the result of massive pressure from various lobby groups and from the German government itself, who insisted on accommodating national and international expectations. The historical framework was provided by the Polish authorities, as they had created it during their two communist show trials. Many of the 360 witnesses who testified during the trial came from Eastern-Bloc countries, foremost Poland, where they had been systematically manipulated to stick to the pre-ordained narrative during their testimonies at Frankfurt. The trial ended with four acquittals, six life sentences and a variety of prison terms. For more details, see the dedicated entry on the Frankfurt Auschwitz Show Trial.

Trial of Horst Fischer

Communist East Germany could not stay behind when its West-German rival state conducted a huge show trial aimed at improving West Germany's image in the world. Hence, East Berlin staged its own show trial with a focus on trying to smear West Germany's reputation. They found a scapegoat for this in Horst Fischer, who had been a camp physician at a forced-labor camp near Monowitz, a town near Auschwitz. The camp's inmates mainly worked at the local Buna factory of the *I.G. Farbenindustrie*. After the war, this conglomerate of German chemical corporations was disassembled into various independent chemical companies, all of which were conveniently located in West Germany. During this communist show trial, which lasted from 10 to 25 March 1966, Fischer willingly, at times even enthusiastically, embraced and accepted all accusations and even added new ones. Fischer was sentenced to death and killed on 8 July 1966 with a guillotine. On the absurdities of this trial and Fischer's various claims and confessions, see the entry dedicated to him.

Trial of Walter Dejaco and Fritz Ertl

Between 19 January and 10 March 1972, two Austrian architects were put on trial in Vienna, Austria, for their involvement in designing and constructing the crematoria at Auschwitz. On request of the judges, an expert report by a court-accredited architect was produced which concluded that, judged by the crematoria's original blueprints, these facilities could not have served as homicidal gas chambers. As a result, both defendants were acquitted. For more details, see the entry on Walter Dejaco.

Ausrottung → Extirpation

AUSTRIA

Austria had three roles within the context of the Holocaust:
1. Perpetrator
2. Crime Scene
3. Victim

With a few postwar Holocaust trials, it also had a minor role as a propagandist, which will not be covered here. However, see the last section in the entry on Auschwitz Trials in this regard.

Perpetrator

If one were to consider Austria as not being a part of Germany, then the main perpetrator of the Holocaust, Adolf Hitler, was originally Austrian, not German. It has also been observed that a higher number of Austrian nationals have been involved in the operation of the so-called extermination camps than would be expected from their share among all ethnic Germans.

Crime Scene

Only one of the camps that is said to have seen minor extermination activities was located on Austrian soil: Mauthausen. (See that entry for details.)

Victim

Austrian citizens of Jewish faith or descent (who in 1938 became German citizens until after the war) fell victim to the persecutorial measures of the German authorities during the war. On the details, see the section on demography below.

Demography

SS statistician Richard Korherr reported in his 1943 report that, by the end of 1942, 149,124 Austrian Jews had emigrated. When any further emigration was prohibited in late October 1941, some 50,000 to 60,000 were still present. Some 5,000 to 9,000 remained after the war.

The fate of the Austrian Jews between October 1941 and the end of the war was similar to that of the German Jews. For details, see the section on demography of the entry on Germany.

AVEY, DENIS

Denis Avey (11 Jan. 1919 – 16 July 2015) was a British soldier who was incarcerated at a PoW camp near the Auschwitz-Monowitz labor camp. In his 2011 memoirs titled *The Man who Broke into Auschwitz*, he claimed to have swapped places with a Jewish Monowitz inmate, so he could experience how the Jews were treated in their camp. He claimed that he wanted to report about this after the war. However, instead of doing this, he waited for 65 years. The tales he told then consisted mainly of clichés about the Auschwitz Main Camp and Birkenau, cobbled together in an incoherent narrative. If Avey spent some time at the Monowitz Camp, he could not have had any knowledge of what was unfolding in those other camps. Furthermore, the Jew he claimed to have swapped places with survived the war and was interviewed in 1995. Although he confirmed that some British soldier had helped him out, he said nothing about having swapped places with him.

Denis Avey

Holocaust skeptics blew the whistle on this fraud already in 2010, after Avey had given the BBC an interview in late 2009 (see Yeager 2010). A year later, investigative mainstream journalist Guy Walters exposed Avey's fairy tale along similar lines (see Walters 2011). However, that stopped neither the BBC nor the British government from piling praise and accolades on Avey for his alleged heroic deed (see Yeager 2011).

B

BABI YAR
Documented History

After German troops had occupied Ukraine's capital on 19 September 1941, Soviet partisans blew up several large buildings in the city center on 24 September, killing hundreds of German soldiers, mostly officers. The explosions caused a fire that eventually destroyed a square mile of Kiev's center, making some 50,000 persons homeless. Efforts to extinguish the fires were also sabotaged by partisans. The Germans found a Soviet mining map showing about 50 objects readied for remote-controlled detonation. Large quantities of mines, explosives and "Molotov Cocktails" were also discovered.

Several reports by the *Einsatzgruppen* and by other units mention the fatalities and destruction caused by the partisan activities. Since the Germans suspected Jews to have been the main participants in this disaster, the city's Jews were singled out for reprisal measures, officially by resettling them elsewhere to make room for the homeless. Posters in the city proclaimed that all of Kiev's Jews had to show up on 29 September at a certain street intersection near the city's cemeteries close to a ravine called Babi Yar.

The *Einsatzgruppen*'s Event Report No. 101 of 2 October 1941 states:

> *"In collaboration with Group Headquarters and two squads from the Police Regiment South, Sonderkommando 4a executed 33,771 Jews in Kiev on 29 and 30 Sept. 41."*

Later German documents repeated this number or a similar, rounded number as the death toll of this alleged blood bath, which allegedly found no opposition among the local non-Jewish populace, or was even supported by them. None of the documents indicate where exactly these executions took place.

Several photos taken by German military photographer Johannes Hähle in Kiev during those days show groups of several dozen people walking along streets; on other photos, numerous people are working with shovels in a ravine; several other photos show the bottom of a ravine littered with clothes and luggage, but with no people anywhere, dead or alive.

Although the radio messages sent by German SS units in Ukraine to Berlin were intercepted and deciphered by the British at that time, not a single reference to this event can be found.

Later *Einsatzgruppen* reports mention minor events in Kiev, such as the public hanging of three saboteurs or the shooting of a robber, but no large-scale execution.

Propaganda History

On 21 October 1941, the pro-National-Socialist Ukrainian newspaper *Krakiwski Wisti* wrote that the Jews of Kiev had been driven into barbed-wire enclosures, and from there by foot to an undisclosed destination.

On 4 November 1941, a certain Andrei I. Maremukha, a junior lieutenant in the militia, authored a report claiming that, on 23 September 1941, the Germans had killed a hundred Jews outside the city of Kiev by taken them to a pit that was mined.

On 13 November, a Polish underground radio station reported that Germans and Ukrainians had shot 35,000 Jews in Kiev.

On 16 November 1941, the *Jewish Telegraphic Agency* (JTA) published an article claiming that 52,000 Jews had been executed by the Germans in Kiev. On 31 December 1941, the JTA specified that "practically the entire Jewish male population of Kiev" had been executed as spies and partisans, and that the remaining Jews were killed by exploding mines, with any survivors getting machine-gunned. The report repeated the death-toll of 52,000 murdered Jews.

On 19 November 1941, the two Soviet newspapers *Pravda* and *Izvestia* reported that "the Germans in Kiev killed 52,000 Jews."

On 10 December 1941, the Soviet newspaper *Komsomolskaya Pravda* published the report of a regiment commissar about a massacre of Kiev's Jews, mentioning for the first time the name Babi Yar.

On 6 January 1942, the Soviet Union's Commissar for Foreign Affairs, Vyacheslav Molotov, reported the murder of a "large number of Jews" at the Jewish Cemetery of Kiev.

The JTA reported on 15 March 1942 that 240,000 Jews had been executed by the Germans in Ukraine, claiming that people were even buried alive, and that therefore the ground was "moving in waves."

On 20 July 1942, the Warsaw Ghetto's underground press agency claimed that all of Kiev's Jews had been drowned in the Dnjepr River.

On 28 October 1942, the JTA reported that Jews in Kiev were getting murdered, and their bodies dumped into the Dnjepr River.

On 29 November 1943, *The New York Times* reported that 50,000 Kiev Jews had been ordered to a ravine, where they had been machine-gunned, although the evidence for it was "sparse."

Late on 28 February 1944, Radio Moscow reported that the Germans had murdered "more than 195,000 Soviet citizens" in Kiev by torture, shooting and poisoning in gas vans. This was a preview of an expert report issued by a Soviet Extraordinary State Commission charged with investigating the claimed mass murder, burial, exhumation and cremation at Babi Yar, which was officially dated and issued the next day, 29 February 1944. (See the section on Forensic Findings below.)

To come to this conclusion, the NKGB interrogated several witnesses who either had witnessed the shootings in late September 1941, or who claimed to have worked on exhuming and burning the bodies of the murder victims.

Witness testimonies about the executions agree that the victims had to undress *at the top* of the ravine, meaning outside of it. Some stated that the victims had to walk naked to the edge of the ravine, where they were shot at point-blank range, thus falling into the ravine. Others claimed that the victims were shot with (sub)machine guns from the opposite side or from both side of the ravine (e.g., see the entry on Dina Pronicheva). Another witness claimed that the victims had to run through the ravine while getting shot at from the edges (Nadezhda T. Gorbacheva). Children were tossed alive into the ravine.

However, machine-gun fire from the other side of the ravine, up to 100 meters away, would have been very inaccurate, particularly when the targets were moving. Lots of ammunition would have been wasted this way. If shooting at victims standing at the ravine's edge from the opposite side, stray bullets could have hit any of the guards. Furthermore, if 33,771 Jews were all shot in one spot of the ravine's edge, they all would have been lying on one big heap that eventually would have reached the ravine's edge. Hence, someone had to drag away those corpses and spread them out in the ravine while all this wild submachine-gun shooting was allegedly happening. In other words, this most certainly did not happen.

German "perpetrator" witnesses who testified in the 1950s and 1960s (e.g., Fritz Höfer, Kurt Werner) insisted instead that the victims had to walk down into the ravine, then walk on the wobbly surface of wounded and dead victims already lying on the ground to a spot pointed out to them. There, they had to lay face down on the already executed victims below them, and then got shot at close range with a bullet from a submachine gun into the nape of their neck.

Of course, this would have required that all victims went like sheep to the slaughter. Furthermore, the photos taken by German military photographer Johannes Hähle show that people had deposited large amounts of clothes and personal belongings *at the bottom* of a ravine, hence inside, not at the top (outside). However, there are neither executed people visible on these photos, nor any other traces of a massacre. (See the entry on him.)

Within the so-called *Aktion* 1005, the mass graves are supposed to have been exhumed and the bodies cremated between mid-August and late September 1943 in order to erase all traces of this crime. Several witnesses, who all claimed to have been forced to do this work but managed to escape, testified about these alleged events. They all told a more-or-less consistent story:

Initially, some 100 inmates from the Syretsky Camp, 5 km from Kiev, were taken on or around 18 August 1943 to the ravine and put in shackles. There, they had to exhume bodies from mass graves, then pile them up on pyres in layers, alternating with layers of wood. These pyres contained some 2,000 to 3,000 bodies, rarely more. After they had burned down, bones in the cremation remains had to be crushed with pestles, and the ashes searched for valuables. After a while, this team of slave laborers was increased to some 320-330 men.

All in all, some 50,000 to 125,000 bodies were allegedly cremated, depending on the witness. On or around September 29, a revolt among the inmates broke out, and some of them managed to flee, among them the witnesses who testified. (See the entries on Semen Berlyant, Isaak Brodsky, David Budnik, Vladimir Davydov, Iosif Doliner, Yakov Kaper, Vladislav Kuklia, Leonid Ostrovsky, Yakov Steyuk, Ziama Trubakov.)

While these witnesses differ in several minor points, by and large they agree on what happened.

This is a classic case of the convergence of evidence. However, all these witness statements describe events that cannot have happened the way they are described (see the witnesses' entries for details):
- Almost all witnesses give approximate sizes of the pyres they built, and how many bodies they contained. Yet if we add to the bodies the wood that would have been required to burn these bodies, the resulting pyres would have reached absurd heights. Such pyres could never have been built, neither would they have been stable, toppling over already while getting built or at the latest when burning down.
- Sifting ashes with manual sieves and crushing unburned bones would have required that *all* the remains of a pyre had to be sifted. Wood-fired pyres burn unevenly and leave behind lots of unburned wood pieces, charcoal, and incompletely burned body parts, not just ashes and bones (80% of leftovers would have been from wood, not corpses). Incompletely burned wood and human remains could not have been crushed. If 100,000 bodies were burned, then several thousand metric tons of cremation leftovers had to be processed. Just this task would have required hundreds of men to complete in time. Any manual sieve – allegedly like flour sieves, hence with very small mesh sizes – would have clogged with the first load. Moreover, occasional inevitable rainfalls would have turned any burned-out pyre into a moist heap of highly alkaline, corrosive slush that could not have been processed this way at all. Any reasonable person facing this challenge would have employed industrial-sized strainers, loaded large quantities of cremation remains on them, flushed out all small parts with water, picked out any valuables, then dumped the rest onto a burning pyre for further cremation. The claim that a few inmates were sifting through thousands of tons of cremation remains with manual sieves is preposterous.
- Cremating an average human body during open-air incinerations requires some 250 kg of freshly cut wood. Cremating 100,000 bodies thus requires some 25,000 metric tons of wood. This would have required the felling of all trees growing in a 50-year-old spruce forest covering almost 56 hectares of land, or some 125 American football fields. An average prisoner is rated at being able to cut some 0.63 metric tons of fresh wood per workday. To cut this amount of wood within the five weeks (35 days) that this operation supposedly lasted would have required a work force of some 1,134 dedicated lumberjacks just to cut the wood. None of the witnesses mention any kind of wood-cutting team. They all state that everyone was busy digging out mass graves, extracting bodies, building pyres, sifting through ashes, crushing bones, and finally scattering the ashes and refilling the graves with soil. There was just no way to obtain that much firewood at such short notice for such a huge operation – especially not when the fighting front was getting dangerously close.

Hence, this is a classic case of the convergence of evidence on a lie. After all, these witnesses were interviewed not by some mild-mannered, serious prosecutor or judge, but by members of the Soviet state's terrorist organization NKGB.

Having several mutually consistent witness accounts in hand "confirming" the huge exhumation and cremation activities, the Soviet authorities neglected the other end of the equation: testimonies by locals. 25,000 metric tons of wood transported to the cremation sites with a typical 5-ton truck amounts to 5,000 truckloads. While there are a few witness statements of the local populace about the shootings claimed for the 29th and 30th of September 1941, there is not a single testimony or diary entry about the alleged cremation activities lasting five weeks, involving thousands of trucks driving in and out of Kiev, and smoke blanketing parts of the city.

Add to this the fact that a German report from early 1943 stated that it was impossible to provide Kiev's civilian population with sufficient firewood due to a lack of means to transport it. By August and September of the year, with the front near Kiev, the transportation situation was far worse. There simply was no wood and no huge truck fleet to haul them.

To bolster the case of mass murder at Babi Yar for presentation at the Nuremberg International Military Tribunal., U.S. and Soviet propagandists collaborated by extracting a coerced affidavit from an unknown (and maybe invented) German in U.S. captivity named Gerhard Adametz. His story has too many similarities with the NKGB-extracted testimonies to be independent, too many absurdities to be real, and too many anglicisms to have been written by a German. (See the entry on Gerhard Adametz.)

Once the Americans were on their own without any NKGB help to straighten out their stories, they faltered. In 1947, they extracted an affidavit, evidently by means of torture, from their captive Paul Blobel. Blobel is said to have been involved in both the murders and the clean-up action at Babi Yar. What he wrote about the clean-up operation, though, was physically impossible nonsense: bodies lying in mass graves burned right there and all by themselves, right to the bottom of the grave. (See the entry on Paul Blobel.)

When a show trial about Babi Yar was staged in Stuttgart, West Germany, in 1968/69, Soviet propaganda had long since been cast in stone. Gerhard Adametz's fake testimony played a central role even during that trial, which accepted the Soviet propaganda story. The four defendants played along with this charade, with one of them getting 4 years, another 2 and a half years in prison, while the other two were acquitted: 6.5 years for 50,000 murders, as the court claimed. That's 41 minutes for every Jewish life taken.

Soviet photo of Babi Yar taken in 1943, with no spectacular discoveries at all.

Forensic Findings

If 195,000 persons had been killed in and near Kiev, but only some 50,000 to 125,000 were exhumed and burned, as the witnesses claimed, where are the remaining 70,000 to 145,000 bodies? The Soviet Extraordinary State Commission investigating Kiev forced a few German PoWs to dig for them in several places, among them Babi Yar. But all they allegedly found were the remains of 150 Soviet citizens, and a few traces of burned remains. Even if that is true, who can reassure us that these weren't NKVD victims from before the war?

No tombstones, rails, iron racks or fences, presumably used to build pyres, were discovered in Babi Yar, although two witnesses insisted that they had been buried there. Lacking any hard evidence, the ravine was later used as a garbage dump by the city of Kiev.

In the late 1970s, the U.S. released German wartime air photos they had captured in Germany and brought to the U.S. after the war. Among them are photos of Kiev dated 26 September 1943, showing the Babi Yar ravine in high resolution. This is supposed to have been at the very end of the claimed daily burning of thousands of bodies. We should see the floor of the ravine and its surroundings mauled by hundreds of trucks delivering firewood for weeks; the ravine's walls massively damaged by people and vehicles going in and out; ramps allowing vehicles to drive in, unload fuel, and drive back out; large scorched areas of burned-down pyres, blackened by ashes and charcoal leftovers; the smoldering, smoking remnants of the last pyres.

Nothing of that sort can be seen on it, because nothing happened.

(For more details on Babi Yar, see Rudolf 2019, pp. 509-538; 2020a, pp. 153-156; 2023, pp. 317-324; Mattogno 2022c, pp. 523-579, 770-792.)

Repercussions

As mentioned at the beginning of this entry, several German wartime documents exist which mention the murder of 33,771 Jews in Kiev. The exactitude of this number itself is suspicious, because it is highly unlikely that any executioner would have kept such exact details.

If the huge exhumation and cremation in August and September never happened, the corpses should still be in the ground. But if so, why did the Soviets not find them after the war? However, none of these German documents mention Babi Yar. Could those Jews have been murdered and buried elsewhere? But if so, why were those mass graves never found or at least mentioned by anyone?

Maybe the death toll was vastly exaggerated, perhaps by accidentally (or deliberately) adding an extra

"3" or "7" – perhaps 3,371 were executed, or maybe even just 371.

Or worse, it is conceivable that the documents reporting this massacre are profoundly wrong simply because nothing ever happened. Or perhaps they were tampered with, or even forged. Anything is possible.

For more information on these issues, see the entry on Johannes Hähle, the *Einsatzgruppen* and on *Aktion* 1005.

BACH-ZELEWSKI, ERICH VON DEM

Erich von dem Bach-Zelewski (1 March 1899 – 8 March 1972) was SS *Obergruppenführer* during the war and served as Higher SS and Police leader (*Höhere SS und Polizeiführer*) in the central part of occupied western Russia, hence basically today's Belorussia. In this area, *Einsatzgruppe* B was charged with, among other things, fighting partisans and, according to the orthodox narrative, exterminating Jews.

After the war, Bach-Zelewski fell into the hands of the Western Allies, who threatened to extradite him to the Soviets. In reaction to this, he became a willing witness, making any statements that his captors desired. As a reward, he was neither extradited to the Soviets nor ever indicted for his deep involvement in the activities of the *Einsatzgruppen*.

Most famous is a lengthy report he wrote while in Allied captivity about an execution of roughly a hundred partisans on 15 August 1941, which Himmler is said to have attended. After the event, he purportedly gave a speech, allegedly explaining why it was necessary for the Nazis to kill inferior humans as vermin. The atrocious nature of that execution is said to have led Himmler to order the invention of a more humane killing method in the form of gas vans. Bach-Zelewski, however, did not mention this, but instead seriously claimed that the more "humane" method tried next on mental patients was explosives, with a predictably disastrous result.

The fictitious nature of Bach-Zelewski's story also shines through when claiming that the extermination of the Jews "was deliberately planned by Heinrich Himmler already before the war" and that "Himmler consistently worked towards the war in order to carry out his plans" – claims that have no justification at all. Furthermore, Bach-Zelewski declared that in 1943 some commission revealed the plan to him to establish a homicidal gassing facility at Mogilev. Since there were no Jews anymore in the Mogilev region in 1943, Bach-Zelewski concluded that there must have been a plan to exterminate the Slavic population next. Orthodox historian Richard Breitman concluded from this that there was a plan to establish a Mogilev extermination camp, but another orthodox historian, Christian Gerlach, demonstrated that German wartime documents show this project to have concerned a disinfestation chamber. (See Mattogno 2022c, pp. 293-302, 706-712.)

Bach-Zelewski told similarly preposterous nonsense during his testimony at the Nuremberg International Military Tribunal, where he claimed, among other things, that Himmler had announced in early 1941 that he planned "to decimate the Slav population by 30 million," and that fighting Soviet partisans was only a pretext to exterminate the Slav and Jewish populations (*IMT*, Vol. 4, pp. 482, 484-486).

BACON, YEHUDA

Yehuda Bacon (or Bakon, born 28 July 1929) was deported to Auschwitz in December 1943 at age 14. He was evacuated from there on 18 January 1945 and ultimately liberated at the Mauthausen subcamp Gunskirchen on 5 May 1945. In spite of his young age, he was not selected for gassing upon arrival, but was admitted to the camp.

Yehuda Bacon

Bacon testified during the Eichmann Show Trial in Jerusalem on 7 June 1961 and also during the Frankfurt Auschwitz Show Trial on 30 October 1964. He claims to have received privileged treatment at Auschwitz. He was allowed to wear long hair, he did not have to work initially, received better clothing and custom-made shoes, and he and his group of boys had a ping-pong table at their disposal.

In order to make it credible that he, as a 14-year old boy, could give a detailed description of the alleged gas chamber and its equipment, he claimed that, when it was cold outside, the nice SS allowed him and his group of boys to spend time in the gas chamber or the undressing room when not "in use," as this room was allegedly heated. He also stated that he loitered around the courtyard of Crematorium III, climbed onto the roof of the gas chamber, lifted the lid of the Zyklon-B introduction shaft, and studied its appearance. The SS was even more accommodating by allegedly giving him a tour of the inside of the crematoria, including the furnace hall!

It goes without saying that no 14-year-old inmate would have been allowed to do any of this, and that he most certainly did not get an inspection tour of any building, let alone any of the crematoria.

Without supervision and guards, he could have left neither his camp sector, which was surrounded by a barbed-wire fence, nor enter any of the four crematorium yards, which were also surrounded by barbed wire. No one would have allowed him to hang out in that yard and investigate this (alleged) crime scene.

Bacon apparently made it up in order to explain how he knew what the gas chamber looked like and how it was equipped. Hence, whatever he told about the appearance of this alleged room most certainly stems from what he read and heard elsewhere.

During his various statements, he described the alleged Zyklon-B introduction devices in various conflicting ways. They were pipes surrounded by four iron columns surrounded by strong wire, or simply pipes riddled with little holes. Ventilators were located below these pipes, which had holes in them for cleaning with water. He even saw these ventilators when the building was getting dismantled. However, the ventilators serving the basement rooms were installed in the building's attic, not in the basement, and most certainly were not below some introduction columns.

His description of these alleged introduction devices is a hodgepodge of features found in the descriptions by Michał Kula, Henryk Tauber and Miklós Nyiszli. He combined this with false ventilator claims like those made up by Janda Weiss.

Bacon also insists that he "saw" flames coming out of the crematoria's chimneys reaching "a height of four metres," although flame-spewing chimneys are technically impossible. He also asserted that inmates used the cremation ashes of their fellow inmates to sprinkle on the roads during winter, "so that people could walk on the road and not slip" – a handy use of your compatriot's leftovers.

(For more details, see Mattogno 2019, pp. 111f., 428-431.)

BAD NENNDORF

Bad Nenndorf is a German spa town some 15 km west of the northwest-German city of Hannover. After the end of the war, the town was part of the British Zone of Occupation. In violation of the Hague Convention of Land Warfare, the British occupiers hunted down civilians, especially the political leadership of the defeated country, which they prepared to prosecute during various show trials.

In preparation of this goal, at the beginning of August 1945, Bad Nenndorf's spa district located around the spa's mud bathhouse was declared a "civilian internment camp." Some 1,200 inhabitants of this area had to vacate their homes. The area was fenced in with barbed wire. The mud bathhouse was given a new purpose: interrogation center and prison for Germans who were to be tried as war criminals. In the bathing cabins, the fittings were removed, and the tubs embedded in the floor were filled with cement. Holding cells with tiled walls were created.

National-Socialist functionaries, SS members, officers from all parts of the German armed forces, diplomats and major industrialists were quartered in the cells as prisoners to be "prepared" here for the coming war-crimes trials. Also imprisoned were Soviet soldiers and other individuals who had fled west across the border from the Soviet Zone of Occupation. Although formally speaking, Britain and the Soviet Union were still allies at that point in time, neither side trusted the other.

The guards of this makeshift prison were members of a British penal squad who hoped to regain their revoked ranks through dedicated service. Many of them were ruthless rogues.

We have two testimonies of former inmates who were incarcerated in that detention center: The first is from Oswald Pohl, former head of the SS's Economic and Administrative Main Office (*Wirtschafts- und Verwaltungs-Hauptamt*, WVHA), which was in charge of the German wartime camps. The other is from a former official of the town of Bad Nenndorf, Heinrich Steinmeyer and his wife Marie. His report was published by the German weekly magazine *Quick* (9 March 1952, pp. 28-31; see also Heyne 2018).

Fortunately, we do not depend solely on their accounts to find out what happened inside that camp's interrogation center. In 2005, the British government finally released documents about this and other British wartime and postwar interrogation centers. Here is what British investigative journalist Ian Cobain wrote about it after he had studied the released documents:

"*Here* [in Bad Nenndorf]*, an* [British] *organisation* [...] *ran a secret prison following the British* *occupation of north-west Germany in 1945.*

[This organization], a division of the War Office, operated interrogation centres around the world, including one known as the London Cage, located in one of London's most exclusive neighbourhoods. Official documents discovered last month at the National Archives at Kew, southwest London, show that the London Cage was a secret torture centre where German prisoners who had been concealed from the Red Cross were beaten, deprived of sleep, and threatened with execution or with unnecessary surgery.

As horrific as conditions were at the London Cage, Bad Nenndorf was far worse. Last week, [British] Foreign Office files which have remained closed for almost 60 years were opened after a request by the Guardian under the Freedom of Information Act. These papers, and others declassified earlier, lay bare the appalling suffering of many of the 372 men and 44 women who passed through the centre during the 22 months it operated before its closure in July 1947.

They detail the investigation carried out by a Scotland Yard detective […]. Despite the precise and formal prose of the detective's report to the military government, anger and revulsion leap from every page as he turns his spotlight on a place where prisoners were systematically beaten and exposed to extreme cold, where some were starved to death and, allegedly, tortured with instruments that his [British] fellow countrymen had recovered from a Gestapo prison in Hamburg. Even today, the Foreign Office is refusing to release photographs taken of some of the 'living skeletons' on their release."

(For more details, see Cobain 2005a&b; Cobain 2013.)

BAHIR, MOSHE

Moshe Bahir was an inmate of the Sobibór Camp. In his 1950 memoirs, he claimed that he had received secret notes in empty buckets brought back from the camp's extermination sector that is said to have been cordoned off and invisible from the sector where Bahir worked and lived. These notes, allegedly written by inmates working at the gas chamber, described what was unfolding there. According to this, the gas was fed into the gas chambers through ordinary showers. After the murder, the floors opened, and the bodies were discharged into carts below, which brought them to mass graves. Bahir also claimed that, as of Himmler's visit in February 1943, the first million victims had already been disposed of.

Moshe Bahir

His claims are rejected as false by the orthodoxy, who insists that the gas was fed through pipes rather than showers. These chambers did not have collapsible floors with carts underneath either. The corpses were instead taken out of the chamber manually, sideways through a normal door. Furthermore, only about a quarter million victims are said to have died in the camp in total.

Here are some more peculiar contents of the secret notes that Bahir claims to have received from the inmates in the extermination sector:

– *"One note told of a bloodstain which could not, by any means, be cleaned or scraped from the floor of the gas chamber. Finally, experts came and determined that the stain had been absorbed into the chamber's floorboards after a group of pregnant women had been poisoned and one of them had given birth while the gas was streaming into the chamber. The poison gas had mingled with the mother's blood and had created the indelible stain."*

– *"Another note said that, one day, the workers were ordered to replace a few floorboards because several fragments of ears, cheeks and hands had become embedded in them."*

These are lurid fantasies, for sure, but they were certainly not part of the real world.

(See the entry on Sobibór for more details, as well as Graf/Kues/Mattogno 2020, pp. 32, 34, 72f., 82; Mattogno 2021e, pp. 85.)

ball mill → **Bone Mill**

BALTIC COUNTRIES

The three Baltic states Estonia, Latvia and Lithuania had four roles within the context of the Holocaust:
1. Perpetrator
2. Crime Scene
3. Victim
4. Propaganda Podium

Perpetrator

By the time World War Two began, the Baltic people had long-standing and deep cultural relationships with both Russia and Germany. However, while Russia had dominated, occupied and oppressed these countries for centuries, Germany had neither the imperialistic means nor intentions to conquer this area.

When the Soviet Union occupied the Baltic countries in the summer of 1940, many locals suffered terribly during the ensuing one-year long Stalinist terror. When the German armed forces moved in during the summer of 1941, they were initially welcome as liberators by many. However, Germany was also the country that abandoned the two northern Baltic states of Estonia and Latvia by handing them over to Stalin in a secret addendum to the Hitler-Stalin Pact.

Some inhabitants in the Baltic states were enraged enough to start pogroms against local Jews and any Soviet collaborator who had stayed behind. However, this sentiment was not nearly as widespread and deep-seated as in Ukraine. That country had a much longer and more dreadful history of suffering at the hands of Russian and Soviet imperialists than the Baltics.

The first Stahlecker Report mentions that instigating pogroms against collaborators and Jews wasn't as easy as had been hoped, and drastic actions had to be taken to carry things along. In the same vein, Baltic collaboration with Germans, while existing, was in general also not as pervasive as in Ukraine.

Crime Scene

Einsatzgruppe A had its main area of activities in the Baltic States. The two capitals of Latvia and Lithuania, Riga and Vilnius, as well as the Lithuanian city of Kaunas were also the largest crime scene of this formation. Ponary near Vilnius and Fort IX in Kaunas are local landmarks of wartime infamy, where huge massacres are said to have occurred. (See these entries for more details.)

Victim

With 240,410 recorded victims, *Einsatzgruppe* A has by far the most victims listed in these units' Event Reports. If we use these figures, then the second most murderous unit was *Einsatzgruppe* B with almost a hundred thousand recorded victims less: 142,359. If all this is true, then there was little left of the Baltic Jews after the German occupation was over, which lasted until the very last month of the war.

Riga ranks first in the list of *Einsatzgruppen* death tolls, with 46,662 victims – ahead even of Kiev and the alleged Babi Yar massacre. (For details, see the entry on the *Einsatzgruppen*.)

Propaganda Podium

The Baltic countries were reconquered by the Soviet Union only rather late in the war. By that time, the main thrust of Allied and in particular Soviet propaganda had shifted to Poland with its various claimed extermination camps (Belzec, Majdanek, Sobibór and Treblinka). Therefore, not nearly as much Soviet propagandist effort was made in the Baltic countries.

Several Jews claimed to have managed to escape from Fort IX and Ponary in Lithuania. They succeeded in reaching Soviet lines, and made depositions in this regard during the war, which the Soviets made maximum use of. (See the respective entries.)

At the Klooga Camp in northern Estonia, the Soviet staged a fake open-air incineration pyre at war's end in an attempt to take photographic evidence of mass cremations of murdered victims. However, the scenes photographed only show a few (living!) people on a small pile of fresh wood. (See the entry on Klooga.)

During the Soviet era, there was a general lack of official interest or political will to focus on local Jewish victims of World War Two in the Baltics. Therefore, the search for mass graves started seriously only after the renewed independence of the Baltic states in the early 1990s. The case of Marijampole is indicative of how this was more an event for commemorative culture than for scientific data-gathering to get the story straight. (See this entry for more details.)

BARD-NOMBERG, HELENA

Helena Bard-Nomberg (born in 1908) was a former inmate of the Auschwitz Camp who was interrogated by Polish authorities after the war.

In her deposition, she claimed that, while her fellow inmates were driven into the gas chamber, she simply decided to stay outside and hide under some pieces of clothes – which is highly unlikely. She then claimed that she (unwisely) came out of hiding before the gas chamber was closed and saw an SS man come out of the "bathroom" wearing a gas mask; this is absurd, because he would only have worn a mask after a gassing was over, not before, in order not to frighten the inmates. At that point, the SS man discovered her. However, instead of sending her into the gas chamber, he merely "kicked her in the behind" and led her back to her barracks – where she proceeded to tell everyone what had happened. All this is highly implausible.

Bard-Nomberg then claimed that the First Leader of the Protective Custody Camp, a high-ranking SS camp official, entered her block (unlikely), recognized her immediately among the hundreds of newly arriving inmates (impossible), praised her for her cunning ability to survive the gassing (which never would have happened), and then left her alone. Had she indeed been a witness of the claimed scene, however, she certainly would not have lived long. The only true part of her story is that she was, indeed, left alone – since she did survive. This proves that there never was a threat of her being 'gassed.'

This is a typical account of an inmate who, utilizing all of her vivid but deceitful imagination, wanted to be part of the post-World-War-II testimonial gas-chamber lore. (For details, see Mattogno 2021, p. 372.)

BARTEL, ERWIN

Erwin Bartel was a Polish Auschwitz inmate between 5 June 1941 and 26 October 1944, where he worked as a clerk in the Political Department under Hans Stark and Maximilian Grabner. In a deposition of 27 August 1947 in preparation for the Polish show trial against Grabner and other former Auschwitz staff members, Bartel merely confirmed that he saw Grabner on the roof of Crematorium I observing a homicidal gassing through one of the Zyklon-B introduction hatches. However, as the head of the Political Department, Grabner is unlikely to have crawled onto the roof, and even less likely to have jeopardized his life or that of others by keeping those alleged hatches open in order to observe what was going on inside, allowing Zyklon B fumes to reach him in the process. For observational purposes, a spyhole in the door is said to have existed, if we follow the orthodox narrative. Hence, this terse statement was clearly an attempt to frame his former boss Grabner.

Erwin Bartel

In preparation for the Frankfurt Auschwitz show trial, Bartel made another deposition in the late 1950s, but this time he targeted Hans Stark, who was among the defendants of that trial. Bartel merely stated that Stark was very interested in these gassings and saw him participate in them. He also claimed that Stark was responsible for the boxes of Zyklon-B cans, which were allegedly kept in the corridor next to the office where Bartel and Stark worked. However, anything connected with fumigations – Zyklon B, gas masks, test kits etc. – was the responsibility of the SS garrison physician and was stored in the SS infirmary. Furthermore, due to its dangerous nature, Zyklon B was certainly never kept in a corridor of a pencil-pusher office. (For more details, see Mattogno 2016c, pp. 35f.)

BARTON, RUSSELL

At the end of World War II, Russell Barton was an English medical student who spent a month in the Bergen-Belsen Camp shortly after the camp's liberation. While there, he investigated the reasons for the camp's disastrous conditions toward the end of the war, with thousands of dead inmates piling up everywhere when the British took over the camp (Barton 1975; cf. Kulaszka 2019, pp. 195-200):

> "German medical officers told me that it had been increasingly difficult to transport food to the camp for some months. Anything that moved on the autobahns was likely to be bombed. […]
>
> I was surprised to find records, going back for two or three years, of large quantities of food cooked daily for distribution. I became convinced, contrary to popular opinion, that there had never been a policy of deliberate starvation. This was confirmed by the large numbers of well-fed inmates. […] The major reasons for the state of Belsen were disease, gross overcrowding by central authority, lack of law and order within the huts, and inadequate supplies of food, water and drugs."

The piles of corpses found by the British, primarily caused by a rampaging typhus epidemic, was amply misused by Allied propaganda to portray Bergen-Belsen as a death camp where inmates were killed or left to die in masses on purpose.

BASKIND, BER

Ber Baskind was a survivor of the Warsaw Ghetto whose memoirs got published in France in 1945. In it, he retells stories about the Treblinka Camp he claims to have heard. According to these rumors, expensive toxic gases were used to kill within eight minutes. However, the current orthodox narrative has it that cheap engine-exhaust gases were used for the claimed mass murder. (See Mattogno 2021e, p. 185.)

BAUM, BRUNO

Bruno Baum (13 Feb. 1910 – 13 Dec. 1971) was a German-Jewish communist who was arrested in 1935 for disseminating "propaganda material hostile to the State," among other things. Baum was sentenced to 13 years for high treason in 1937. In April 1943, Baum was transferred to Auschwitz, where he worked as an inmate electrician. This allowed him access to almost all parts of the camp, inside and outside. In Auschwitz, Baum formed an underground group dedicated to spreading communist resistance propaganda, and became a leader of the Auschwitz camp partisans, who gathered espionage materials on German armaments operations and fabricated false atrocity stories, which were conveyed to Polish partisans outside the camp, who in turn radioed that material to the Polish government in exile in London. Other members of that group were Hermann Langbein (Austrian Communist Party, later Chairman of the Auschwitz Committee) and Jozef Cyrankiewicz (Polish socialist). After the war, Baum managed to get to communist East Germany, where he eventually became a leading communist official.

Bruno Baum

Three months after the end of the war, on 31 July 1945, Baum bragged in a communist newspaper that "All the propaganda that now began to circulate about Auschwitz in foreign countries originated with us [leading communist inmates], assisted by our Polish comrades." He continued by observing that the Auschwitz camp Gestapo's reaction to this propaganda was to improve the camp conditions to such an extent that "Auschwitz became a model camp in the end." In later books published about his experiences during the war, he repeated his claim that he and his communist comrades were the source of today's widespread propaganda about Auschwitz:

> "I believe it is no exaggeration if I say that the biggest part of Auschwitz propaganda, which was spread in the world around that time, has been written by us in the camp. […] We spread this propaganda to the public at large until the very last day of our stay in Auschwitz."

(Baum 1949, pp. 34f.; for details and sources, see Rudolf 2023, pp. 381-383; see also Polish underground reports.)

BECHER, KURT

Kurt Becher (12 Sept. 1909 – 8 Aug. 1995), SS *Obersturmbannführer*, was a member of the SS leadership office in very early 1944, from which he was assigned to procure horses and strategic goods in Hungary. In this connection, he was part of the famous negotiations between Himmler and Zionist organizations to exchange Jews for strategic goods (cf. Bauer 1994, starting on p. 220). For his involvement in the deportation of the Jews from Hungary, Becher was arrested by the Allies after the war and repeatedly interrogated. Due to his readiness to cooperate, he finally succeeded in being transferred to the "open wing" at Nuremberg instead of being treated like a possible defendant as before. As a reward for his cooperation, Becher was never charged with anything.

Kurt Becher

As is well known, there is no document ordering any extermination of the Jews (see the entry on the Hitler Order). But it is claimed that a document did exist which supposedly ordered an *end* to the extermination. In this way, the orthodoxy tries to circumvent the embarrassing lack of evidence that there was any order to systematically kill the Jews. However, no document ordering the end of exterminations has ever been produced either. Instead, as alleged proof of its existence, the Allies coerced Kurt Becher to write an affidavit and testify before the Nuremberg International Military Tribunal that he had obtained a Himmler order meant for Ernst Kaltenbrunner and Oswald Pohl "sometime between mid-September and mid-October 1944." With this order, Himmler is said to have prohibited "any extermination of the Jews, effective immediately" (IMT Document 3762-PS; *IMT*, Vol. 33, pp. 68f.). Becher repeated this claim in an affidavit deposited for the Eichmann Trial.

The true background of this coerced affidavit was revealed only some 50 years later, when Göran Holming, a major of the Swedish army who had befriended Kurt Becher, reported what Becher had told him in the 1990s. According to this, Becher stated that Himmler's order actually decreed that the German concentration camps should be surrendered in an orderly manner upon the approach of the enemy, without casualties. It had nothing to do with any "extermination" at all. Asked why he had lied in his affidavit, Becher replied that outsiders could not possibly understand the circumstances in Nuremberg at that time (Holming 2023; Rudolf 2023, pp. 398f.). This grand lie saved Becher his life and liberty.

BECKER, AUGUST

August Becker (17 Aug. 1900 – 31 Dec. 1967), at war's end an SS *Obersturmführer*, was a German Chemist who is said to have had a leading role in developing gas chambers for the Third Reich's euthanasia program. Later, he was presumably assigned to Office II D 3a of wartime Germany's Department of Homeland Security (*Reichssicherheitshauptamt*, RSHA), headed by Friedrich Pradel. This office was in charge of the Security Police's motor pool.

The only known document in this context bearing Becker's name is a letter dated 16 May 1942, presumably written by Becker. It is addressed to Walter Rauff personally, with no department or office mentioned. Rauff was the head of the RSHA's Office II D, and as such, Pradel's superior. Therefore, the address should have included exactly that information to reach its destination. However, that vital information is missing in that letter:

Reichssicherheitshauptamt, Amt II D.

This letter was presented by the prosecution during the International Military Tribunal as part of Document PS-501 (*IMT*, Vol. 26, pp. 102-105). The docket attached to it states that the letter was obtained from the British prosecution's office, but that its origins are unknown.

The letter pretends to be an inspection and maintenance report of gas vans used by *Einsatzgruppen* D and C in Ukraine to execute Jews. It is riddled with absurdities which prove conclusively that this is a fake report unrelated to any possible real-world events:

- The document identifies gas vans of a second series as Saurer vehicles. However, there is no trace of any "first-series gas vans" not being Saurer vehicles deployed by the *Einsatzgruppen*. All vehicles in extant documents that are (falsely) associated with gas vans have been Saurer vehicles.
- By the time the RSHA ordered Saurer vehicles, this company equipped all its trucks with Diesel engines. However, Diesel-engine exhaust is non-lethal in the short run, hence unsuited for homicidal gassing operations using its exhaust gasses as is claimed.
- The letter asserts that, after just half an hour of rain, none of the Saurer vehicles could be driven anymore. Hence, they could be used in absolutely dry-weather condition only. This is absurd.
- The document asserts that the vans were "camouflaged" from the local populace by painting little fake-windows on its side. This is puerile and absurd, as it would have attracted more attention, not less.
- The author mentioned a damaged combined hydraulic-air-pressure brake due to a sleeve having broken in several places. While the Saurer trucks had hydraulic brakes, there is no such thing as a combined hydraulic-air-pressure brake. Moreover, any sleeves on that system were made of rubber and could develop leaks, but they would not break.
- Using bribes, the author claims that he managed to have a dye manufactured to cast new sleeves. However, leaky rubber sleeves could be fixed with rubber repair patches. Casting new, exactly fitting rubber sleeves using caoutchouc and vulcanizing chemicals in a dye was impossible in the field. Clearly, the author did not know what he was writing about.
- Due to many off-road trips, the author complains about rivets of the cargo-box becoming lose, and cracks forming, which needed to be sealed to prevent gas leaks. However, no gas van could ever be "sealed," because the same volume of gas that was allegedly pumped into the cargo box as exhaust gas needed to escape from the box to prevent it from building up pressure and eventually exploding. Hence, little leaks would have been of little concern.
- The author suggests sealing small leaks by soldering them. However, that would have been futile, as soldering does not provide any firm connection of metal pieces. That would require welding. Again, the author exhibits his technical ignorance.
- The writer warns that the escaping exhaust gas might harm the executioners on the outside, so he warns everyone to stay away from the vehicle while gassing people. However, Diesel-engine exhaust gases escaping through various leaks of a cargo are of little consequence for people standing outside near the box. The Diesel-exhaust

Juxtaposition of the Becker and the Just documents	
BECKER DOCUMENT	JUST DOCUMENT
Reference to numerous flaws. No reference to openings for gas release.	Reports 97,000 executions, "without any defects in the vehicles becoming apparent."
In spite of the numerous flaws, no changes to the vehicles are requested.	Although no defects had occurred, seven changes are requested (internal contradiction).
Reference to difficulties of moving the vans: during moist and rainy weather, the vans are inoperable.	Reference to a highly reduced off-road capability while fully loaded, resulting in the need to reduce the load.
Emphasizes the importance of keeping the cargo box hermetically sealed; it is even considered to send the vans to Berlin for this purpose.	The first of the requested changes concerns two slits of 1 cm × 10 cm to avoid high internal pressure.
The vans were "camouflaged" without attaining a permanent deception about their purpose.	No attempts at camouflage were implemented.
Thoroughly addresses the danger of the operating personnel inhaling the gases – although the cargo box is hermetically sealed.	No reference to such a danger.
The author wants to ascertain that the victims do not die of suffocation but die a humane death through falling asleep.	No efforts are made to induce a painless death of the victims.

smell alone would tell people to stay away, for comfort's sake.

- The letter states that gassings are performed wrongly by giving full throttle. This resulted in the victims suffocating rather than falling peacefully asleep. However, hot, stinking, smoking engine-exhaust gases cannot, under any circumstances, lead to gassing victims falling asleep peacefully. This could be accomplished only with odor- and colorless carbon monoxide at room-temperature.

This so-called Becker Document is the second document allegedly proving the existence of gas vans. The other one – the so-called Just Document – is a clear forgery. (See the entry on the Gaubschat Company.) This Just Document also pretends to report about the operation of gas vans, allegedly written on 5 June 1942, not even three weeks after the Becker Document. A comparison of both documents' claims is revealing, as the table shows. Clearly, the forgers did not coordinate their efforts.

Becker was arrested by the West German judiciary in 1959 for his alleged role in the deployment of the gas vans. He made statements during several interrogations, among them:

- He claimed that as a Chemist, he had been put in charge of all the mechanical aspects of the gas vans. While that is what the Becker Document insinuates, the technical nonsense uttered in it also shows that whoever wrote it had no clue. Pradel, as motor-pool chief, never would have put a chemist in charge of vehicle mechanics.
- On the way to his gas-van inspection tour, Becker claims to have flown in Heinrich Himmler's personal plane from Mikolaev to Simferopol, Crimea. However, Himmler most certainly would not have lent his plane to a small second lieutenant (Becker was only an SS *Untersturmführer* at that time).
- Once done in Simferopol, Becker then presumably flew to Minsk in another plane together with SS *Hauptsturmführer* Rühl, who allegedly headed an extermination camp run by the *Einsatzgruppen* near Minsk. Rühl was so kind as to give Becker a tour of the camp and allow him to watch mass executions. If that refers to the Maly Trostinets Camp near Minsk, this was run not by the local *Einsatzgruppe*, but by the commander of the German Security Police Minsk. Moreover, SS *Hauptsturmführer* Felix Rühl was a member of *Einsatzgruppe* D which operated in southern Ukraine and the Caucasus area. He would not have flown to Minsk and would not have given Becker a tour of the camp. Nobody would have done that.
- Becker repeated the nonsense about the gas-van operators doing it all wrong, suffocating rather than gassing the victims. He thus proved that he had been an avid student of the document levied against him, internalizing it to the point where he

parroted its absurdities as his own memories. Becker was supposed to stand trial together with Harry Wentritt in 1966 for their role in designing, building and deploying the so-called gas vans. However, since Becker suffered several strokes by that time, he was declared unfit for trial and incarceration. Later attempts to use him as a witness against other defendants were futile, as he was unable to speak coherently.

(For more on this, see the entries on gas vans, the Gaubschat Company, and Alvarez 2023, pp. 42-57, 192-195.)

Becker Document → Becker, August

BEDNARZ, WŁADYSŁAW

Władysław Bednarz was a Polish investigative judge who, after the war, led the Polish judiciary's investigations into what transpired at the Chełmno Camp. He interrogated witnesses and supervised forensic excavations and sample-takings on the former campgrounds. He also investigated the wreck of a moving truck on the Ostrowski factory grounds, which some witnesses had claimed was a gas van used to kill deportees. To Bednarz's credit, he concluded that the truck was not a gas van, but he failed to confront the witnesses about their false statements. Rather, Bednarz cherry-picked from these statements what fit into the evidently preordained narrative of a mass-murder camp, and discarded what refuted it, was contradictory or blatant nonsense. Thus, he forced the discordant evidence he found into an artificially created "convergence of evidence" to make it look superficially convincing. (For more details, see the entry on the Chełmno Camp.)

BEER, ABRAHAM

In 1945, a former inmate of the Janowska Camp in Lviv, Abraham Beer, made a deposition about what is said to have unfolded there in the second half of 1943 within the context of what today's orthodoxy calls *Aktion* 1005. This deposition is characterized by the witness knowing a little bit about everything but not much about anything, making it impossible to assess it in any meaningful way. (For details, see Mattogno 2022c, p. 522.)

BEHR, EMIL

Emil Behr, a former inmate of the Auschwitz Camp, was one of many witnesses ignored by the Frankfurt Auschwitz Trial because he could not, or would not, confirm the usual atrocity stories about this camp. Together with the communist self-proclaimed propagandist Bruno Baum and the convicted compulsory liar and fraudster Adolf Rögner, Behr was a member of the Auschwitz Camp's inmate electricians. Although Behr must have experienced similar things as those other two witnesses, his recollection as recorded in early 1959, more than 15 years after he left Auschwitz, was much more realistic than the outrageous propaganda nonsense that Rögner spread at that time. During his interrogation, Behr stated repeatedly that he could not confirm the atrocities he was asked about, and that he knew about such things, if at all, only from hearsay (cf. Rudolf 2004c, p. 328).

Emil Behr

BELGIUM

Documents indicate that 25,437 Jews were deported from Belgium, with the Auschwitz Camp as their main destination. Few of these Jews reported back with the local authorities after the war. It is unknown how many returned without reporting back, and how many migrated elsewhere. The fate of the Jews deported from Belgium was probably very similar to that of the Jews deported from France. (See the entry on France, as well as the general entry on Jewish demography.)

BELZEC

Documented History

The Belzec Camp was initially one of a string of forced-labor camps set up along the eastern border of occupied Poland, meant to house prisoners, among them gypsies, Jews and Christian Poles, who were deployed to build roads and border fortifications. Living conditions in these camps were very bad, and mortality due to exhaustion, mistreatment and diseases was very high.

On 16 March 1942, Fritz Reuter, an employee of the Department of Population and Welfare in the office of the governor for the Lublin District, and SS *Hauptsturmführer* Hans Höfle, Odilo Globocnik's deputy chief of staff and delegate for Jewish resettlement in the Lublin district, decided that Jews slated to be sent to this district ought to be divided in those fit and those unfit for labor before being put on trains.

The former were to be collected in a camp for forced-labor, while the latter were to be sent through the outermost border station at Belzec "to cross the border [to the East] and never return to the Government General [occupied Poland]."

Very few official documents on deportations to the Bełżec Camp have survived. While they show a very harsh German attitude toward the Jews – "old, infected, frail, or untransportable Jews" were evidently on occasions shot – they do not confirm any extermination policy; for if every Jew was to be gassed at Belzec, why take the trouble of killing unfit Jews beforehand?

Some German documents report about problems with Jews who had been resettled, either because they tried to hide, left the resettlement location or fled from resettlement trains. Others indicate that, when the Belzec Camp was about to cease its activities, allegedly because all Jews in the region had been killed, German authorities were setting up large numbers of Jewish living quarters in the concerned districts.

A report of 7 April 1942 by Richard Türk, director of the Department for Population and Welfare in the office of the governor of the Lublin district (Reuter's boss) contains a paragraph on the "Jewish Resettlement Operation" listing the number of Jews from the west who had been settled in the area, and the number of Jews evacuated from the area to the East.

The history of the resettlement of Jews in the district of Lublin confirms fully the Höfle directive mentioned above. After the Bełżec Camp assumed its new function, many transports of western Jews arrived in the Lublin district and were settled there. There are documents showing that Jews left the Bełżec Camp and arrived in other camps, such as Majdanek. Many transport trains with western Jews were deported to the East without interrupting their journey at Bełżec or any other claimed extermination camp.

Several months after the Belzec Camp had been shut down, Höfle sent a telegram that was intercepted and decrypted by the British. Among other figures, it contained the number of persons who arrived at "B" (presumably Belzec) until the end of its operation: 434,508 individuals. Hence, if we take the extant documents at face value, this is the number of individuals transited through that camp, either on the way to other camps or to some resettlement destination, usually in the East.

(For more details, see Mattogno 2004a, pp. 97-108)

Propaganda History

The first report on Bełżec is from 8 April 1942, claiming that Jews were murdered there either by electrocution or by poison gas, after which the corpses were burned.

A text said to have been found after the war, allegedly buried on the former campgrounds by some inmate in 1942, claims that Jews were either killed by other Jews defecating on their heads until they suffocated in their excrements, or that they were electrocuted.

A report of the Polish underground from April 1942 stated that they didn't know how Jews were murdered at Belzec but listed electrocution (though there is no electricity at the camp), gases (though no gas effect has been observed), and vacuum.

This is followed by a string of reports in the second half of 1942 by such sources as the Jewish underground of the Warsaw Ghetto (Emmanuel Ringelblum's group), the Polish government in exile in London, and a Wehrmacht officer's diary entry.

On 30 August 1942, the Jewish Agency for Palestine issued a report claiming that the corpses of Jews murdered at Belzec were utilized for their fat.

On 15 November 1942, Ignacy Schwarzbart, a member of the Polish National Council, repeated claims that murder at Belzec occurred using either electrocution or lethal gas-chambers, but he described only the alleged electrocution process in some detail. His claims were spread by the *Jewish Telegraphic Agency* ten days later.

On 25 November 1942, Polish black-propagandist Jan Karski wrote a report claiming that Jews were killed inside deportation trains by putting a layer of chlorinated lime on the rail-car floors, and sprinkle it with water, which led to toxic fumes choking many inside. Those arriving alive at Belzec were electrocuted (here, Karski copied Schwarzbart's text). On 10 December 1942, the Polish government in exile in London repeated the claim that the floors of rail cars "were covered with quicklime and chlorine" to maximize transport casualties. Karski's report was also published in March 1943 by the newspaper *Voice of the Unconquered*. In his 1944 book *Story of a Secret State*, Karski has all victims die in the trains by quicklime eating the flesh off their bones; the electrocution chambers have disappeared.

On 20 December 1942, *The New York Times* endorsed those claims by writing executions at Belzec occurred using "electrocution and lethal gas," a story they repeated on 12 February 1944 with a detailed description of the electrocution process, claiming that the naked victims, standing on a metal platform, were lowered "into a huge vat filled with water," where they "were electrocuted by current through the water."

Also in 1944, Abraham Silberschein published two reports on the Bełżec camp, which both claimed that Jews executed were mass-murdered there by electrocution (or an "electric oven"), after which the corpses' fat was turned into soap.

Also in 1944, Stefan Szende claimed in a book that "5 millions people" were killed by lowering them on a huge metal floor-plate into a large water tank, where they were electrocuted, after which the water was drained, and the floor-plate turned into a gigantic electric furnace, cremating all victims.

When Ilya Ehrenburg and Vasily Grossman compiled the text for their *Black Book* starting in 1944, they wrote about the use of both gas and electric currents for mass murder at Belzec, and that the murdered Jews' fat was turned into soap.

In a deposition of 7 October 1944, Rozalja Schelewna Schier declared to know from hearsay that at Belzec people were killed with "gas and high-voltage electric current," after which the floor folded down, and the corpses fell into a pit, where they were burned.

On 26 April 1945, a deranged Kurt Gerstein signed one of his many affidavits in which he claimed that mass murder at Belzec was committed with Diesel-engine exhaust gasses, although these gases are so low in carbon monoxide that they are unsuited for mass-murder purposes.

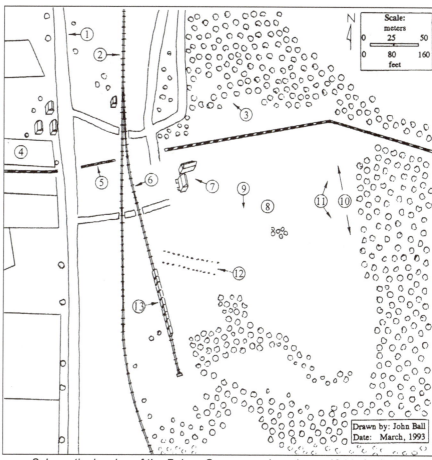

Schematic drawing of the Belzec Camp area, based on a 1944 air photo.
1 roads
2 main rail line passed through Belzec train station one kilometer (⅝ mile) north
3 trees
4 farms that were plowed and tilled in 1944
5 cleared line may have been a power cable
6 short railway spur
7 the lower building appears to have been a sawmill
8 the camp area between the ridge top and the railway spur of 240 m × 250 m (790 ft × 820 ft) was cleared by logging of all trees between 1940 and 1944.
9 site of the supposed 1942 homicidal gas chambers
10 hill-top ridge 30 m (100 ft) higher in elevation than the railway spur in the valley
11 location shown on alleged survivor's maps where more than 400,000 bodies were buried; it would have been cumbersome to transport the bodies uphill from the supposed gas chambers
12 heavily worn path in the soil appears to have been a skid for sliding logs downhill to the rail cars
13 rail cars

On 16 October 1945, a certain Jan G. declared to know from hearsay that the electrocution story was wrong. Rumors had it that the killing had been done with the exhaust gas of a 250-HP engine running in the camp. The witness confirmed the collapsible-floor rumor, although now to discharge the corpses into rail cars, bringing them to mass graves. On the same day, another hearsay witness, Michał Kuśmierczak, also peddled the 250-HP motor version.

Other 1945 publications insisted, though, that the electrocution claim was in fact correct, a theme elaborated on further by Simon Wiesenthal in a 1946 pamphlet, who added to that tale that soap had been made from Jewish bodies.

In preparation for the Nuremberg International Military Tribunal (IMT), the Polish War Crimes Office asserted in a 1945 report that Jews were killed at Bełżec in "special electric installations" by means of "electric current of high voltage." The same tale can be found in the Polish government's official report on Belzec accepted by the IMT as Document USSR-93 (see *IMT*, Vol. VII, pp. 576f.).

Interrogations of hearsay witnesses by the Polish judiciary in late 1945 and early 1946 resulted in a jumble of various methods of execution, with none prevailing: gas, electric current, vacuum. Only two witnesses who testified in this context claimed to have been inside the camp and have seen the mechanics of the alleged murder facility: Rudolf Reder and Stanislaw Kozak.

Reder described an absurdly complicated system with an engine, a fly wheel and glass tubes, insisted that he did not know how the killing was done, but was absolutely sure that the engine's exhaust gases were *not* used for murder but vented outside instead.

Kozak, who claimed to have been hired by the Germans in late 1941 to build three wooden chambers, described them as equipped with a furnace in each chamber and water pipes set along the chamber walls. In other words, he described either shower rooms or hot-steam disinfestation chambers, but certainly no mass-murder technology.

In spite of this Babylonian confusion, Eugeniusz Szrojt from the Central Commission for the Investigation of German Crimes in Poland wrote down a bold lie in a 1947 report that all except one witness had agreed that the murder was committed with engine-exhaust gases. This was repeated in 1948 in a report by the Polish government (which so far had endorsed the electrocution method). This move may have been induced by the traction that Gerstein's depositions had gained in the meantime with Western historians. From that point onward, all earlier false claims and lies about electrocution, trains of death, soap factories and fat exploitation, as well as collapsible floors, were forgotten and swept under the rug.

What crystalized as the orthodox "truth" from this was a first set of three wooden gas chambers as described by what Kozak claims to have built in late 1941/early 1942 (although he saw a hot-water or steam facility), and a second, later set of six brick-and-concrete chambers as described by Gerstein and Reder when they came to the camp in the summer of 1942. It mattered not at all that none of these witnesses were trustworthy, that their testimonies were internally and mutually contradictory, and that some of their claims were physically impossible.

For instance, Reder had "seen" a gas-chamber building measuring 100 m × 100 m containing six chambers, three on either side of a corridor 1.5 m wide. Therefore, the building's footprint was 10,000 square meters! Gerstein also saw six chambers, three each arranged on either side of a corridor, but the chambers measured 5 m × 5 m (or 5 m × 4 m). Hence, his building measured only some (3 × 5 m =) 15 m × (2 × 5 m + 2 m =) 12 m, resulting in a footprint of only 180 square meters! This is not even two percent of Reder's building! This is a clear-cut case of a *divergence* rather than convergence of evidence.

Mainstream historian Michael Tregenza revealed in 2000 that the camp's SS men and Ukrainian guards were socializing, even fraternizing with the local village population, with the latter supplying construction workers and employees, delivering food, and offering sexual services, all voluntarily and paid. Local villagers working inside the camp were allowed, even encouraged to take photographs of their SS friends inside the camp. In light of these interactions, it is inevitable that the Polish underground would have been informed right from the beginning of the camp's existence as to what exactly was unfolding there. Furthermore, the SS men's behavior clearly shows that they thought they had nothing to hide. Therefore, the confusion as to how mass murder was committed at that camp was *not* based on a lack of information, but on a lack of coordination among the black-propaganda liars.

By 1965, when the Bełżec Trial took place in Munich against several former members of the camp staff, the official narrative of death by engine exhaust had been so firmly established that the eight defendants, in the hope of minimizing their sentences, could not but accept it unconditionally and proffer painful "confessions." Seven of them saw their charges dropped in return, while the last defendant standing, Josef Oberhauser, received not even eight minutes of jail time for every single one of the 300,150 murders he was found guilty of having committed, resulting in a total of 4.5 years in prison. Jewish lives were still cheap in Germany at that time, but what mattered was that the dogma had been legally cast in stone.

(For more details, see the entry on the Bełżec Trial as well as Mattogno 2004a, pp. 11-47; 2021e, pp. 22-66)

Death-Toll Propaganda
- On 22 September 1944, Rudolf Reder claimed a death toll of 3 million.
- On 11 April 1946, a Polish prosecutor claimed a death toll of 1.8 million.
- In 1947, a Polish government commission claimed a death toll of 600,000.
- In 1965, the Munich Jury Court claimed a death toll of at least 300,000.
- German prosecutor Adalbert Rückerl, however, insisted that the Polish figure of 600,000 may even be too low.
- In 1999, historian Robin O'Neil claimed a death toll of some 800,000.
- In 2000, historian Michael Tregenza claimed a death toll of up to one million.

According to a telegram by Hans Höfle intercepted by the British and discovered in 2001, the total number of Jews *deported* to Belzec amounted to 434,508, with an unknown fate. (For more details, see Mattogno 2004a, pp. 47-50)

Forensic Findings

Before planning any forensic research, it should be clear at least to some degree what to expect. And this is where things already fall apart. Should we expect gigantic electrocution chambers? Gas Chambers? Collapsible floors? Mass-grave traces of 3 million people, or just 434,500, or maybe even much less?

The only witness who described the claimed second gas-chamber building made of brick and concrete (thus leaving durable traces), and who wasn't completely discredited – Rudolf Reder – insisted that this building had an incredibly large footprint of 100 m × 100 m. That's almost two football fields side by side.

Already in 1945, a few limited excavations were made by Polish investigators, revealing the presence of scattered ashes and human bones. However, these digs were too limited in scope and scale to draw any quantitative conclusion. This changed between 1997 and 1999, when Polish researchers systematically took soil core samples drilled from a network pattern of spots covering most of the former camp's area. The results were disappointing. First, no trace of any large former brick-and-concrete building coming anywhere near the expected size was found – except for the remains of a building that evidently was a vehicle garage.

The orthodoxy claims that virtually *all* Belzec victims were buried in mass graves, and only when the mass murder frenzy was over, did they start exhuming and burning these bodies on huge pyres. This presumably started in December 1942 and lasted until March 1943. However, the combined located volume of all disturbed soil found during the Polish investigations of 1997 and 1999 amounts only to some 21,000 m³. Yet in order to bury the minimum number of victims claimed by the orthodoxy for Belzec – 434,500 – at least some 72,000 m³ would have been needed at a packing density of 6 bodies per m³. This means that, in the volume of disturbed soil found, at most some 30% of the Jews deported to Belzec could have been buried. However, this is true only if we assume that *all* disturbed soil volume in fact was packed at this density from top to bottom. But that is certainly not the case, not the least also because some of the disturbed soil volumes located must have originated from the 1945 excavations, and from wild diggings by locals who turned the camp area upside down after the war in search of rumored Jewish treasures lost or hidden there.

Hence, not more than some 100,000 bodies can have been buried at Belzec, but probably fewer than that.

So, where are the other 300,000+ deportees?

Finally, only occasionally were ashes mixed with soil found, and only very rarely any human remains. Therefore, whatever was once buried there, if anything, must have mostly disappeared, if it ever existed in the first place.

There are no witness testimonies as to how exactly the bodies of these allegedly murdered Jews were made to disappear. The orthodoxy's narrative regarding Belzec was simply copied over from

The only remarkable forensic discovery at Belzec: the ruins of a former garage building.

Characteristics of Mass Graves and Mass Cremations at Belzec		
	CLAIMED	FOUND
no. of corpses	434,500 to 3 million	scattered remains
space required (@ 6 bodies/m³)	72,400 to 500,000 m³	at most 21,000 m³
claimed cremation time	Dec. 1942 – March 1943, ca. 120 days	
corpses cremated	3,620 to 25,000 per day	
green wood needed (@ 250 kg/body)	905 to 6,250 metric tons per day	
total green wood needed	108,625 to 750,000 metric tons	

claims made about the Treblinka Camp. As with this camp, the logistical problems that the perpetrators and their assistants would have faced would have been formidable. All the corpses claimed had to be burned with open-air incinerations on huge pyres, since the camp had no cremation furnaces. The table above shows some data about the claimed events.

The wood needed to cremate these corpses had to come from local forests, which would have led to large swaths of land around the camp getting denuded of any trees, but that evidently didn't happen. The space requirement for the many huge pyres, and the manpower needed – to exhume the bodies; fell, transport and chop tens or even hundreds of thousands of trees; build and maintain the pyres; extract and scatter the ashes – would have been formidable.

The maximum number of inmates, claimed by any witness, who were deployed at Belzec to cut trees and bring it to the camp as firewood was 60. Data based on experience with forced laborers such as PoWs shows that one man can fell some 0.63 metric tons of trees per day. This makes some 38 tons of wood for 60 inmates per day. Experiences with open-air incinerations show that it takes some 250 kg of freshly cut wood to cremate one average human corpse. Hence, the cremation of some 434,500 bodies would have required 108,625 metric tons of freshly cut wood. It would have taken these 60 inmates some 2,873 days of uninterrupted work to cut that much wood. This is almost eight years – while they had only 120 days to do it. Alternatively, to get the work done in time, it would have required 1,437 dedicated lumberjacks.

Add to this the fact that the Polish forests were tightly managed by the German occupational forces as precious resources for lumber and fuel. Hence, the SS couldn't send droves of inmates to adjacent forests and cut them down without getting permission to do so. Of course, there is no documental or material trace of any such massive tree-felling activity having been applied for, or granted, let alone occurred.

None of it has left a trace – either in witness statements, or in documents, or in the material and forensic record. Therefore, the most logical conclusion is that nothing of the claimed events actually happened.

To prevent any future research from messing with the orthodox narrative, the Polish authorities turned the entire area of the former Belzec Camp into a gigantic tomb covered with a huge concrete memorial and layers upon layers of rock.

(For more details, see Mattogno 2004a, pp. 71-96; 2021e, pp. 195-213, 273-295; Rudolf 2023, pp. 284-287)

Current Orthodox Narrative

Because Stanislaw Kozak's description of the alleged extermination building which he said he helped construct in late 1941 and early 1942 is completely different than what Rudolf Reder and Kurt Gerstein described seeing in the summer of 1942, the orthodoxy has split the camp's extermination activities into two stages (see Gutman 1990, pp. 174-179):

The first stage features Kozak's three wooden chambers, while hiding from the reader the fact that Kozak described a steam or water facility, not a homicidal gas chamber. Instead, they misleadingly write: "There were pipes in the chamber through which the gas was pumped," when Kozak had actually stated that water pipes were going along and up the wall and were connected to a heating furnace. They moreover posit the use of exhaust gases from a 250-HP diesel engine, although one witness who spoke about a 250-HP engine merely reported rumors from hearsay, and mentioned that the gas-chamber floors opened up, so the corpses would fall into carts below – a preposterous, false claim. Another witness, also reporting rumors from hearsay, nonsensically spoke of a 250-KW motor placed in a 3-m deep pit underground, 30 meters away from the gas-chamber building. Neither "witness" mentioned that it was a diesel motor. This claim relies on Gerstein's preposterous "confessions," ignoring that diesel-engine exhaust is unable to kill people within any reasonable timeframe. (See Mattogno 2004a, pp. 20, 46f.)

The claimed second stage of the camp, presumably initiated in the spring of 1942, features Reder's and Gerstein's six brick-and-concrete chambers, allegedly measuring 4 m × 5 m each (Gerstein's claim), while ignoring that Reder spoke of a *gasoline* engine whose exhaust was definitely *not* used for murder, and his gas-chamber building measured 100 m × 100 m, hence each of the six chambers would have been much larger than 4 m × 5 m. Gutman and colleagues claim that up to 1,200 people per batch were killed in those six chambers, resulting in an incredible packing density of 10 people per m². Yet they ignore that Gerstein, who gave the size of these rooms, had repeatedly insisted that 700 to 800 Jews were packed into *each* of these chambers, hence up to 40 people on a square meter – which would have been possible only if they all were ground to a pulp.

In other words, the orthodoxy selects claims from mutually contradictory and obviously preposterous sources in order to create a picture that looks superficially consistent and reasonable, while hiding from their readers the outrageous nature of the "evidence" all this is based upon.

BELZEC TRIAL

The West-German trial against defendants accused of having been deployed at the Belzec Camp is a typical case of a show trial where the facts of the case and a guilty verdict were a foregone conclusion. It was conducted by the same Munich court which had tried Himmler's chief of staff Karl Wolff just a year earlier – the scandalous circumstances of which were revealed ten years later by one of the jury members: The judges had pressured the jury to a guilty verdict with the argument that the whole world was watching and was expecting Wolff to be sentenced.

The same framework existed also during the Belzec Trial. The "facts" of what had transpired at Belzec had been cast in stone ever since the Allied postwar trials. Kurt Gerstein's various absurd postwar statements and their later "confirmation" by Wilhelm Pfannenstiel, who also testified in Munich in 1965, and perjured himself once again, set the stage, together with the only former inmate witness to testify, Rudolf Reder, who on that occasion systematically contradicted his own statements of the immediate postwar period. Most importantly, his claim of 1944/45 that definitely *no* exhaust gas was used to kill people, had turned around 180 degrees: yes, an engine's exhaust gas was pumped into the chambers to kill the people.

In a normal murder case, traces of the victim(s) and the weapon of crime are absolutely essential to open a criminal investigation, let alone to come to a conviction. But not so in this or any other similar Holocaust case. Neither the defense nor the court asked for any evidence confirming that the claimed crime happened. No forensic examination of the former campgrounds were requested, and no expert opinion was heard as to whether the claimed murder method could have worked. No one tried to compare Reder's or Pfannenstiel's earlier statements with their new ones to look for consistency or contradictions. No one critically scrutinized the testimonies submitted to the court by Polish authorities, which they had pulled from their archives. In other words: facts didn't matter. Everyone during that trial could just claim whatever they wanted, as long as the overarching dogma of mass-murder by engine-exhaust gas chambers was confirmed.

The defense played along with that game, and the court made it easy for them. Seven of the eight original defendants saw their charges dropped with the excuse that they were convinced they had acted under duress. In exchange for this tremendous favor, they all confirmed the dogma of mass murder by engine-exhaust gas chamber, repeating with brief and superficial statements the basic tenets of the dogma, which was well-known to the entire world by then. However, none of them contributed anything new or essential that would confirm first-hand knowledge of anything. Some uttered nonsense, such as normal barracks having been restructured into gas chambers. Others claimed to be unfamiliar with even the most basic data, such as how many gas chambers there were. No one challenged their statements by comparing them with other sources or with what was physically possible, and no one pressed them for more details, which they should have known, if mass murder really occurred. One of them – Karl Schluch – testified that, upon opening the gas chamber after the murder, the victims were standing upright, since they had no space to fall over. Here we have a detail enabling us to say that this certainly did *not* happen.

The last defendant standing was Josef Oberhauser. The court claimed that he was the liaison officer of the camp's commandant Christian Wirth, and hence could not claim to have acted under duress. During pre-trial interrogations, he offered some embarrassing statements, which led to the prosecution avoiding them during the trial. Among other things, he claimed that the first gas chamber (singular) initially used bottled carbon monoxide rather than engine exhaust.

Oberhauser was eventually found guilty of 300,150 cases of murder. However, instead of receiving 300,150 life sentences, he was sentenced to just 4.5 years imprisonment. Since his pre-trial detention was counted, and because he was released after serving only half his time, Oberhauser was a free man again a short while later. Clearly, in show trials, the defendant's fate does not matter. What matters is that the dogma is confirmed, and some version of "justice" is served.

(For more details, see the entry on Josef Oberhauser as well as Mattogno 2004a, pp. 62-69.)

BENDEL, CHARLES S.

Charles S. Bendel (born 1904) was deported to Auschwitz-Monowitz in late 1943. But he was transferred to Birkenau on 2 June 1944, where he was assigned to serve as a physician for the so-called "*Sonderkommando*" of the crematoria. He remained there until the evacuation from the camp in January 1945.

Charles S. Bendel

After the war, Dr. Bendel recorded at least six different testimonies on his alleged experiences in Auschwitz, all of which are riddled with implausibilities and outright lies. The most-extraordinary fact is that both Bendel and another Auschwitz inmate-physician, the Hungarian Jew Miklos Nyiszli, claimed independently from each other to have been the only *Sonderkommando* physician at the same location and during the same time span, and that they lived in the crematoria at Birkenau for the identical period of their stay at Birkenau. They were both chosen by, and worked under, the ineluctable Dr. Josef Mengele. Similarly, both claimed to be the only surviving *Sonderkommando* physician! But they were mutually unaware of each other's existence, described incorrect places, and offered mutually contradictory factual assertions.

Of the Birkenau crematoria, where he says he worked for many months, Bendel spread the following false claims:

– That thousands of inmates who worked on constructing these facilities (from the summer of 1942 through late spring 1943) died building them; no other witness has asserted that, there is no record of it happening, and Bendel wasn't even there when this supposedly happened.
– That Himmler personally attended the inauguration of the first completed crematorium in Birkenau in late January 1943 – when Bendel wasn't yet in Auschwitz – although Himmler's last visit to Auschwitz occurred in July of 1942.
– Bendel lifted wildly exaggerated claims about these facilities' cremation capacities straight from the War Refugee Board Report (claims by Alfred Wetzler and Rudolf Vrba).
– He repeated the absurd story of flames shooting "up to ten meters" out of crematory chimneys.
– He repeated the tall tale that fat, extracted from burning corpses on huge pyres, was collected with special conduits, leading to puddles of searing fat where some inmate "burned both his feet."
– That the cremation furnaces, being insufficient, were allegedly *shut down* and *replaced* by open-air incineration pits that could allegedly cremate 1,000 people per hour – a physical impossibility.
– In contrast to the mainstream narrative, which claims one homicidal gas chamber each for Crematoria II and III in Birkenau, Bendel insisted that each building had *two* such chambers, each with a capacity of 1,000 persons.
– Although he claims to have worked near these facilities for many months, Bendel got the size of these rooms terribly wrong, claiming that they measured only 10 m × 4 m or 10 m × 5 m, with an absurdly low height of only 1.5 m (too low for most people to even stand up). By contrast, orthodoxy claims that the gas chambers measured 30 m × 7 m, and were some 2.4 m high. The varied dimensions of the presumed four gas chambers inside Crematoria IV and V were just as incompatible with those asserted by Bendel. Moreover, squeezing 1,000 people into a room of barely 40 or 50 square meters, resulting in a packing density of 20 to 25 people per m², would have been an impossible feat.
– Without possible personal knowledge, Bendel parroted the Soviet propaganda figure of "more than four million" Auschwitz victims, 800,000-1,000,000 of which allegedly died during his stay at the camp.

This is only the tip of the iceberg of a much longer list of Bendel's lies and exaggeration. (For more details, see Mattogno 2020a, pp. 304-333).

BENNAHMIAS, DANIEL

Daniel Bennahmias (1923 – 22 Oct. 1994) was a Greek Jew deported to Auschwitz, where he arrived on 11 April 1944. After the war, he remained absolutely silent about his wartime experiences. Only toward the end of his life did he grant interviews to a writer who then wrote his alleged Auschwitz experience down as a third-person narration, published only a year prior to Bennahmias's death. The unreliability of an account of hearsay events some 50 years earlier is evident from the various false claims made:

- 3,000 people were killed in one batch in Morgue #1, the alleged gas chamber of Crematorium II, hence more than 14 people per square meter in this room of 210 m², which is an impossible packing density.
- After the gassing, the chamber was allegedly packed with corpses from "floor to ceiling," which means that people had been lying in layers on the floor and had reached, layer by layer, up to the ceiling! Assuming that three corpses fit onto a floor area of two square meters and that one layer was on average 25 cm high, and given the dimension of Morgue #1 of Crematorium II at Birkenau of (30 m × 7 m =) 210 m² × 2.4 m height, this results in (630 corpses per layer × 8 layers =) some 5,040 people, to reach a stacking height of just 2 meters. These 5,000 people would have had to walk into and stand in that room, which implies an utterly impossible packing density of 24 people on each square meter.
- When the door was opened, an SS man leaning against the chamber door, instead of wearing a gas mask, smoked a cigarette, which would have meant certain death.
- Bennahmias spreads the crudest black-propaganda anecdotes invented by the Auschwitz resistance movement, for instance, the claim that SS men randomly shot babies or tossed them onto the heads of the people crammed into the gas chamber awaiting their execution.
- He seriously claims that, after gassings, only one inmate was put in charge to shave the victims' hair, and another inmate to find and extract gold teeth. This process is supposed to have lasted eight hours for a batch of two to three thousand gassing victims. Under these conditions, those two inmates had between 10 and 14 seconds to "process" each victim.
- He states that the victims gouged the concrete walls of the gas chamber and left "bits of flesh" and blood all over it, requiring it to be washed and repainted after each gassing. It is impossible to gouge concrete with bare fingers, and there is also no way to have "bits of flesh" sticking to a wall. Furthermore, the walls of these rooms were never painted, and they are still covered with bare cement plaster to this day.
- Bennahmias (or rather his ghostwriter Rebecca Camhi Fromer) plagiarized claims from other sources, for example by taking events and numbers from Martin Gilbert's book *Auschwitz and the Allies*.
- In spite of the members of the *Sonderkommando* allegedly being killed off repeatedly to annihilate these "carriers of secrets," Bennahmias miraculously survived this culling process over and over again, like so many others of his colleagues.
- Bennahmias never mentions anything of relevance regarding the cremation furnaces, as if he had no knowledge about them at all.

An in-depth analysis of Bennahmias's account reveals many more untrue, impossible, and implausible statements (Mattogno 2022e, pp. 93-100).

BENROUBI, MAURICE

Maurice Benroubi (born 27 Dec. 1914) was a Greek Jew who had emigrated to France, from where he was deported to Auschwitz on 20 July 1942, arriving there three days later. He was assigned to a gravedigger unit. This unit had the horrific duty to bury thousands of victims of the typhus epidemic that had gotten out of control during that time. Since the camp's only crematorium had to be taken out of service for repairs around that time, there was not even any option to cremate these victims.

Sometime during the mid- to late-1980s, Benroubi was interviewed by French historian Jean-Claude Pressac, who published Benroubi's tale in 1989. Since this testimony was written down 40 years after the event, Benroubi's memory was possibly contaminated by forty years of exposure to the ubiquitous orthodox narrative. His brief testimony therefore has little probative value. Yet an analysis of this witness's claims is interesting all the same.

Benroubi claimed that he had been assigned to transport bodies to mass graves. He claims that there were ten open pits measuring 20 m × 3 m, 2.5 m deep, and that there were several older graves about 300 meters long which had been filled and covered recently. However, the mass graves visible on air photos show that Benroubi's dimensions are way off the mark. These graves were some 10 meters wide and 100 m long, and there were exactly four of them.

Benroubi also insisted that he had seen "trickles of light-colored decomposed fat mixed with blood" on the soil covering the mass graves. However, the bodies buried in there were mostly emaciated typhus victims, or if we follow the orthodox narrative, also gassing victims. Neither of them can spill blood after dying, and no corpse ever can spill fat.

Benroubi only briefly mentioned extermination facilities, which must be assumed to be the sources of the dead bodies he was transporting, although he was not explicit in this regard. The few details he mentioned about these facilities are all wrong:
- They were allegedly two concrete blocks measuring some 20 m × 20 m. However, the orthodox narrative has it that these were two old brick-and-mortar farmhouses (the so-called bunkers of Birkenau).
- They were located right next to each other. However, the orthodox narrative has it that they were located some 500 m apart.
- The building's doors were "of the rolling or sliding type." However, a sliding or rolling door could neither have been made gas tight nor secured against a panicking crowd.
- They had showerheads on the ceiling and clothes hooks at the walls. However, the orthodox narrative has it that the bunkers had bare rooms with nothing in them. Showerheads were claimed for the alleged gas chambers of the Birkenau crematoria, and clothes hooks presumably adorned the walls of the undressing basement rooms in Crematoria II and III. This shows how Benroubi's memory has been contaminated by claims about other facilities he must have heard or read about.
- In front of the bunkers, the *Sonderkommando* – with whom Benroubi insisted he had nothing to do – had piled up the victims, neatly sorted by gender and age: "One of men, one of women and one of children under ten." Benroubi had to load them on carts to be wheeled away. However, the orthodox narrative has it that the bodies were taken out of the bunker and loaded directly onto carts. Sorting them by age and gender certainly would not have happened. Moreover, the people doing the work of hauling the bodies from the bunkers to the graves were the very *Sonderkommando* members. Hence, if Benroubi tells the truth, then he was a member of that team, but he says he was not.

Benroubi's tale has a true core. From July to September 1942, the period of his experiences, the typhus epidemic in Auschwitz reached its catastrophic climax, with hundreds of victims per day. The camp's only crematorium at that time could not cremate them all. Hence, the just-mentioned four long mass graves were created, and Benroubi may have helped filling them up with bodies, spicing up his memories with disparate aspects taken from other sources.

(For more details, see Graf 2019, pp. 203-205; Mattogno 2016f, pp. 123-126.)

BERG, ISAI DAVIDOVICH

Isai Davidovich Berg (1905 – 1939), a Russian Jew and head of the economic department of the NKVD for the Moscow region, invented an actual method of executing people while being transported in prison vans. For this purpose, the highly lethal exhaust gases of Soviet-made, gasoline-engine vans were ducted into the rear cargo hold, where the prisoners inside subsequently died of carbon-monoxide poisoning. This method of executing unsuspecting prisoners was used by the NKVD from 1936 onward. In 1943, during the show trial of Kharkov, the Soviets started blaming this murder method on the German occupational forces, accusing them of having murdered thousands of unsuspecting innocent victims in so-called murder vans or gas vans.

(See the documentary *Monster: A Portrait of Stalin in Blood*, Part 2, *Stalin's Secret Police*, http://youtu.be/itPPRxy_AQ4; starting at 3 min. 21 sec.; Voslensky, pp. 28f.)

BERGEN-BELSEN

Documented History

The Bergen-Belsen Camp started out in the 1930s as a construction worker's camp for a nearby military training ground of the German armed forces. After World War Two broke out, the camp was repurposed and expanded as a PoW camp. In April 1943, several sections of this camp were taken over by the SS and served as a holding camp for Jews waiting for an exchange with German PoWs held by Allied forces. In early 1944, it became a hospital/rehab camp. In August 1944, a section was converted to a women's camp, which became noticeable during the British Bergen-Belsen Trial, where a considerable portion of the witnesses were former female camp inmates.

During the second half of 1944, with the begin-

Mass grave at Bergen-Belsen, dug by the British, filled by former German guards with camp inmates, mostly victims of diseases and starvation. To this day, these piles of dead bodies are falsely portrayed as the result of a deliberate German policy of extermination.

ning of evacuations of camps being overrun by advancing Allied forces, Bergen-Belsen started receiving an increasing number of inmates from other concentration camps. Overcrowding of the camp became catastrophic by the end of 1944. Around the same time, any supply of food, water, medicine and coke (for heating, cooking and cremations) became first unreliable, then ceased altogether as a result of Allied bombing.

A review of the camp's supply situation by a British medical student sent to Bergen-Belsen after its occupation by British forces revealed that the situation for the inmates was relatively good until late 1944, when it started deteriorating, first slowly, then catastrophically by the end of 1944.

As a result, all inmates starved, clean drinking water was no longer available, dirty well water led to dysentery and typhoid fever, lack of means to disinfest and wash closes and inmate housings led to the spread of fleas and lice, causing a typhus epidemic to break out. Any pharmaceutical or other means to provide medical treatment ran out. Inmates started dying rapidly, and so did the guards and SS men. Due to a lack of fuel, cremations could no longer be carried out, although the camp's one existing furnace would have been unable to cope with the thousands of inmates that were dying every week starting in February 1945, even if there had been enough fuel.

When British troops entered the camp on 15 April 1945, peacefully handed over by the Germans, they found an infernal scene. The campgrounds were littered with thousands of dead and dying inmates. The British Political Warfare Executive took advantage of this opportunity by recording these scenes, including the subsequent burial of thousands of deceased inmates in mass graves. Some bodies were hand-carried by SS men and women who had stayed behind, and were now forced by the British to clean up the mess, while other bodies were pushed into mass graves by bulldozers brought by the British.

(For details, see Stiftung Niedersächsische… 2010; Weber 1995a; Barton 1975; Kulaszka 2019, pp. 195-200.)

Propaganda History

The horrific scenes of a camp littered with emaciated dead and dying inmates, of hundreds, even thousands of victims thrown and pushed into mass graves, were integrated into Allied propaganda "documentaries." These were meant to prove to the world, and most importantly to "re-educated" Germans, the diabolical nature of National Socialism. Movies such as the

U.S. PsyOps documentary *Death Mills* and Alfred Hitchcock's *Memory of the Camps*, which misrepresent these veritable mountains of corpses as the result of a deliberate National-Socialist policy of extermination, are powerful tools of shock-and-awe social engineering to this very day, exactly because of the scenes recorded at Bergen-Belsen.

As a result, Bergen-Belsen misleadingly received the designation "death camp" by the Allies (e.g. in Nuremberg Document 036-USSR, *IMT*, Vol. 39, p. 277), which some took as a hint to push this propaganda envelope even further. For example, U.S. historian Francis Miller wrote in his 1945 *History of World War II* on page 868:

> "In Belsen, [camp commandant] *Kramer kept an orchestra to play him Viennese music while he watched children torn from their mothers to be burned alive. Gas chambers disposed of thousands of persons daily.*"

That same year, the Associated Press news agency reported about the testimony of a Jewish physician testifying during the Bergen-Belsen Trial that 80,000 Jews had been gassed or burned in that camp in just one night. Jewish historian Max Dimont wrote about gassings in Bergen-Belsen on page 383 of his 1962 book *Jews, God and History*, and so did a 1981 Polish book by Hrabar *et al.*, claiming that women and babies were "put to death in gas chambers" at Belsen. In 1995, one of the British soldiers who liberated the camp stated in an interview that he saw "the gas chambers" at Bergen-Belsen (Holland 1995). Moshe Peer, a Jew who at age 11 was in that camp, stated in 1993 that he survived six gassings in the Bergen-Belsen gas chamber, and former Bergen-Belsen inmate Elisa Springer also wrote about a gas chamber in her 1997 memoirs.

The problem with all these claims is that all historians now agree that the Bergen-Belsen Camp did not have any homicidal gas chamber at all. This example shows that gas-chamber claims are bound to pop up for any former National-Socialist Camp, no matter how far-fetched.

Death-Toll Propaganda

Although some sources have exaggerated the death toll of the Bergen-Belsen Camp, such as an article by the New York *Daily News* of 20 April 1985 (p. 30), which claimed that "probably 100,000 died at Bergen-Belsen," the more-common distortion is to add the victims of the PoW camp to the death toll of the later concentration camp, and to state that these inmates were killed, murdered or exterminated.

When it comes to individual suffering, it may not matter much how an inmate died, but there is a huge moral and legal difference between thousands of people getting mass-murdered, which did *not* happen at Bergen-Belsen, and people dying due to tragic, inescapable *force majeure* (effects of war), which was the main reason for some 37,000 inmates dying at that camp before the liberation – the vast majority of them between January and April 1945, and some 14,000 more victims under British rule, who initially struggled just as much to get this human tragedy under control.

(For more details, see Weber 1995a; Rudolf 2017; Barton 1975; Kulaszka 2019, pp. 195-200)

BERGEN-BELSEN TRIALS

The British conducted three trials on crimes allegedly committed at the Bergen-Belsen Camp. The first trial was staged between 17 September and 17 November 1945 against 45 SS men and women, some of whom had been transferred from Auschwitz to Bergen-Belsen toward the end of the war, just as were many inmates. Among them were Josef Kramer and Franz Hössler. Therefore, the charges concerned crimes allegedly committed at the Bergen-Belsen Camp as well as at Auschwitz.

In preparation of this trial, the 77 defendants arrested in this context as well as many other German members of the SS and other organizations were interrogated extensively in various British interrogation centers, such as Bad Nenndorf, which quickly gained the reputation of being torture centers. British investigation files declassified some 60 years later revealed that almost all prisoners in these centers had been tortured in the most bestial ways in attempts at extracting incriminating confessions from them, or simply for pure lust for vengeance.

The Bergen-Belsen Camp's last commandant, Josef Kramer, although severely abused in captivity, did not budge and told the tragic story of Bergen-Belsen's slide into chaos due to *force majeure* as it was (see his entry).

A special case is Pery Broad, an SS man deployed at Auschwitz who ingratiated himself with the British, and thus was exempted from prosecution, by volunteering an absurd "confession" about mass murder at Auschwitz which formed one of the bases from which they develop their Auschwitz narrative at the first Bergen-Belsen Trial (see his entry). Another mainstay of the British Auschwitz narrative are the "confessions" extorted from former camp commandant Rudolf Höss, who was not put on trial by the British but nevertheless enjoyed a particularly harsh torture treatment (see his entry). His later affidavit and testimony before the Nuremberg International Military Tribunal (IMT) played a pivotal role in convincing most defendants that the mass-murder charges must indeed be true.

On the other side of the trial were former Auschwitz and Bergen-Belsen inmates who, evidently inspired by a matching lust for revenge and a general anti-SS hysteria, made the most outrageous and nonsensical claims as to what transpired at Bergen-Belsen and/or at Auschwitz. No claim was preposterous enough to trigger any skepticism among the prosecution or the court, and none of these lies were ever challenged by the defense lawyers, all of them British nationals who were not much more than stooges of the prosecution making sure that the defendants did not revolt against this travesty of injustice.

Many of the perjuring inmate witnesses were women who had been transferred from Auschwitz to Bergen-Belsen and placed there in the women's camp. For a detailed analysis of these witnesses' mendacious tales, see the entries for:
– Charles Bendel
– Regina Bialek
– Ada Bimko
– Jeannette Kaufmann
– Hermine Kranz
– Sofia Litwinska
– Regina Plucer
– Roman Sompolinski

Twelve of the first Bergen-Belsen trial defendants, including Kramer, were executed, the rest was released within the next several years, no matter their prison terms. (On the official story of the first Bergen-Belsen trial with many witness testimonies, see Phillips 1949.)

The second Bergen-Belsen trial was staged between 13 and 18 June 1946, hence after the IMT. It was a small-scale repetition of the first show trial ending with four of the nine defendants getting executed, among them former SS *Oberscharführer* Walter Quakernack, once an official at the Auschwitz Political Department (camp Gestapo).

The third trial concerned only one defendant, Ernst Meyer, who was sentenced to life imprisonment for non-lethal abuse of inmates, but was pardoned on Christmas Eve of 1954.

BERGER, OSKAR

According to his own 1945 memoirs, Oskar Berger was deported from the Kielce Ghetto to Treblinka "in June 1942," therefore a month before the camp started operating in late July 1942. He managed to escape from the camp in September 1942.

Berger claims that, during the first weeks of his presence in the camp, deportees were machine gunned from the roof of a building. Imagine the panic among the deportees, how they start running chaotically, and how stray bullets are whizzing by everyone – deportees, guards, auxiliaries and SS men. It is an absurd picture. Both the wrong starting date and the machine-gunning claim were made by two more Treblinka survivors, Eugeniusz Turowski and Stanisław Kon, who were both interviewed by Polish judge Łukaszkiewicz on 7 October 1945. This is a clear case of "convergence of evidence" on a lie.

On one occasion, Berger claims, all deportees in a train were dead on arrival, so he suspected that they had been "killed by gas in the railway cars." He asserted that the victims' skin was "discolored bluish." This is a truly unique claim.

Later, he said, a gas-chamber building then under construction was used to kill the deportees. He and others were assigned to bringing the corpses in carts to "mass graves for burning," so he must have known this facility's design and mode of operation. Yet he neither describes this building nor says anything about how it operated. His reference to burning bodies in mass graves is anachronistic, if we take the orthodox narrative as a yardstick, which insists that all victims were merely buried in mass graves until early 1943; burning is said to have started only after that.

(See Mattogno 2021e, pp. 129f.)

BERLYANT, SEMEN

Semen Berlyant was a Ukrainian Jew working on a German-run farm near Kiev during the war. In early September 1943, he was taken from there to Babi Yar, a place where tens of thousands of Jews are said to have been shot and buried by the Germans in mass graves in late September 1941 (see the entry on Babi Yar). He was interrogated by the NKGB on 16 November 1943 about his alleged experiences at Babi Yar.

Among other things, Berlyant stated that he and some 320 other slave-labor inmates were put in chains and had to exhume mass graves and burn the extracted bodies on pyres. Those pyres had 300 corpses in one layer, alternating with layers of wood, with a total of 3,000 bodies per pyre. This results in ten layers.

Let's assume that a running meter of a pyre two meters wide can accommodate four corpses. Each corpse requires 250 kg of freshly cut wood (see open-air incinerations). The density of green wood is roughly 0.9 tons per m^3, and its stacking density on a pyre is 1.4 (40% for air and flames to go through). This means that the wood required to burn just one layer of corpses is some 0.75 meters high. Adding the body layer gets us to roughly a meter. Ten such layers result in a pyre ten meters high. It would have been impossible to build such a pyre, and also impossible to burn it down without it collapsing and spilling burning wood and corpses all over the place.

Berlyant claimed that in total 70,000 corpses were burned at Babi Yar. Cremating 70,000 bodies thus requires some 17,500 metric tons of wood. This would have required the felling of all trees growing in a 50-year-old spruce forest covering almost 39 hectares of land, or some 87 American football fields. An average prisoner is rated at being able to cut some 0.63 metric tons of fresh wood per workday. To cut this amount of wood within the five weeks this operation is said to have lasted (35 days) would have required a work force of some 800 dedicated lumberjacks just to cut the wood. Berlyant claims his unit consisted only of 320 inmates, all busy digging out mass graves, extracting bodies, building pyres, and according to other testimonies, also sifting through ashes, scattering the ashes and refilling the graves with soil. Berlyant says nothing about where the firewood came from.

Berlyant also asserted that people murdered in gas vans were brought to Babi Yar for cremation. However, considering that the front was getting very close to Kiev during September 1943, it is unlikely that anyone would have operated gas vans in Kiev's vicinity. All this apart from the fact that gas vans are a figment of Soviet atrocity propaganda (see the entry on gas vans).

(For more details, see the entry on Babi Yar, as well as Mattogno 2022c, pp. 533f., and 550-563.)

BIALEK, REGINA

Regina Bialek was a Polish Jewess deported to Auschwitz in July 1942 and later transferred to Bergen-Belsen. She participated in the British Bergen-Belsen Show Trial, for which she deposited an affidavit on 26 May 1945, which contains a remarkable string of lies (see Mattogno 2021, pp. 344f.):

– Following the pattern of common cliches about Auschwitz, she claimed to have been selected by Doctor Mengele to be gassed, because she had fallen ill with typhus.
– She insists to have been driven in a truck down a ramp straight into the gas chamber, where she and her fellow sufferers were allegedly unceremoniously dumped on the gas-chamber floor. In fact, there was no such building at Auschwitz allowing for such a procedure.
– Rather than Zyklon-B granules poured through some opening, as the orthodoxy asserts, for Bialek the lethal gas was piped into the room, hissing from a floor outlet in the middle of the room.
– She described the effects of the toxic gas by saying that people started "to bite their hands and foam at the mouth and blood issued from their ears, eyes and mouth and their faces went blue." She, too, claims to have suffered from all these symptoms. None of this can possibly have been the effect of hydrogen cyanide, the active ingredient in Zyklon B, which the orthodoxy insists was used in these chambers.
– Miraculously, just before dying, Dr. Mengele allegedly opened the gas chamber in mid-gassing, while full of toxic fumes, located her in the tangled mess of dying people, and led her from the chamber.
– Members of the inmate staff working in the gas chambers were killed in "a villa in the camp" by throwing in "gas bombs" through a window.

BIAŁYSTOK

At the beginning of the Second World War, the northeastern Polish city of Białystok was briefly occupied by German forces, but then handed over to the Soviets. After the outbreak of hostilities between Germany and the Soviet Union, Białystok was occupied by Germany within a few days. In early August 1941, all 50,000 Jews of that city and its surroundings were confined in a ghetto. In October, German authorities tried to move all Jews from Białystok to the town of Pruzhany, some 100 km south, turning it into a "*Judenstadt*" – Jewish town. However, the project failed and was abandoned.

In August 1943, the ghetto was to be dissolved, and its inhabitants to be sent to various labor camps. However, several Jews of the ghetto underground staged an uprising. The resulting heavy fighting lasted for five days, and ended with all resisting Jews getting killed. The remaining Jews were deported to various labor camps, some via Treblinka, although the orthodoxy insists that they were killed there.

Orthodox literature abounds with claims about several large-scale executions in the Białystok District between late June 1941 and the clearing of the ghetto in August 1943, with a total death toll of some 30,000 victims. There is no documental proof backing this up. The *Einsatzgruppen*'s Event Reports only list a total of a little more than 400 victims.

Anecdotal evidence deposited during Soviet investigations and Polish postwar show trials is limited mostly to Jews who claimed to have been forced in late spring and early summer of 1944 to exhume and burn the victims of these claimed large-scale executions. This includes Szymon Amiel, Salman Edelman and Avraham Karasik. Their claims of the number of corpses they presumably exhumed and burned forms the basis for orthodox assertions on execution figures. However, a critical analysis of these witnesses' testimonies does not instill confidence in their reliability.

Forensic efforts to locate mass graves of the expected size, or traces thereof, and to analyze any contents evidently have not taken place.

(For more details, see Mattogno 2022c, pp. 631-640.)

BILY, HENRY

Henry Bily was a former member of the crematorium stokers at Auschwitz, later falsely called the *Sonderkommando*. In 1991, his memoirs were published in a French periodical for former deportees (Bily 1991). However, in the next issue of that periodical, the editors retracted his contribution, as it had turned out that Bily had plagiarized the tall tales published by Hungarian Jew Miklos Nyiszli (Redaction 1991, cf. Faurisson 1992):

> "[Bily,] *without any references, took whole passages from Dr. Miklos Nyiszli's book* Médecin à Auschwitz, *especially chapters 7 and 28 […]. Unfortunately the errors made by Dr. Nyiszli were also copied: it concerns the detailed description of the activities of the Auschwitz-Birkenau Sonderkommando to which Henry Bily is said to have belonged. […] This analysis shows that the Henry Bily text cannot in any way be considered as an original personal eyewitness report.*"

BIMKO, ADA

Ada Bimko was a Polish Jewess who was deported to Auschwitz on 4 August 1943, and transferred to Bergen-Belsen on 23 November 1944. She signed two depositions for the British Bergen-Belsen Show Trial and took the stand during the trial itself. She claimed the following absurdities and falsehoods (Mattogno 2021, pp. 349-355):

- The SS allowed her to examine the (non-existing) camp records and concluded from her research that "about 4,000,000 persons" died and were cremated in Auschwitz.
- There were five crematoria in Birkenau that all looked similar – when in fact there were four, in two sets of two, with the first set (Cremas II and III) looking quite different than the second set (IV and V).
- When entering the gas chamber, the victims were issued a towel and a piece of soap. This most certainly would never have happened, considering the mess it would have created and the effort necessary to retrieve and clean these items afterwards. In addition, no one takes towels into a shower.
- She found a docile SS man who gave her a sightseeing tour through one of the crematoria, explaining to her how the poison-gas mass murder was perpetrated in those facilities.
- For her, the victim's undressing room was on the ground floor, and the gas chamber, camouflaged as a shower room, was directly adjacent, although no crematorium had that kind of room arrangement.
- She stated wrong dimensions for the gas chamber – "48 ft square and 10 ft high" – and claimed there were no drains in the floor, although that is untrue as well.
- She insisted that, from the other end of the gas chamber, a door led into a corridor which was equipped with railway tracks bringing the victims' corpses straight to the crematorium, a false claim probably plagiarized from the War Refugee Board Report.
- Near the entrance door to the undressing room, another door was located, behind which a set of stairs went into a room above the gas chamber; this room housed pipes and containers allegedly used to store and distribute the poison gas into the chamber below, where it exited through showerheads. In fact, none of the buildings said to have contained gas chambers had any rooms above them, let alone stairs leading to it, and the poison gas is said to have been administered by simply throwing in Zyklon-B granules through some

openings.

BIRKENAU
Documented History

After the victory over Poland, German officials developed the "*Generalplan Ost*," which aimed at Germanizing the territories annexed from Poland. In the summer of 1941, after the initial success in the war with the Soviet Union, Himmler expanded this plan to encompass the large conquered Soviet territories. He drafted ambitious plans for building a network of fortified German settlements throughout the Western Soviet regions connected with roads, and to improve the infrastructure of that region in general, bringing it up to German standards. Hundreds of thousands of workers were slated to work on these projects. Initially, the plan was to use Soviet PoWs for this effort. To this end, Himmler ordered huge PoW camps for more than 100,000 prisoners to be built in Lublin (Majdanek) and near Auschwitz next to the village of Brzezinka/Birkenau.

The Birkenau PoW Camp was conceived on 26 October 1941, when the Auschwitz camp administration received a call from the SS camp inspectorate in Oranienburg near Berlin, informing them of the plan to create a new PoW camp near Auschwitz for some 60,000 Soviet PoWs, which would become an integral part of the Auschwitz Camp. The first written document of 30 October 1941 has that capacity already increased to 125,000 prisoners, to be housed in 174 barracks. The first known camp drawing for the "PoW camp Auschwitz, Upper Silesia" is dated 7 October 1941, showing exactly 174 barracks. Three months later, another camp plan showed 282 barracks. A plan of 6 June 1942 had 360 barracks, and one dated 16 August showed 513, with the planned occupation given as 200,000 prisoners. (On the *Generalplan Ost*, its later expansion, and Birkenau's role in it, see Graf/Kues/Mattogno 2020, pp. 244-251.)

The first Soviet PoWs arrived at Auschwitz in early October 1941, but most of them were in such a very bad physical condition, and they may not have received the treatment they needed to recover, that most of them died in the subsequent months. The expected large number of Soviet PoWs never made it to western camps, hence Himmler's plans were not realized.

Since Auschwitz had in the meantime become the location of a major industrial project – the BUNA coal-liquefaction plant of the I.G. Farbenindustrie near the town of Monowitz – the Birkenau Camp's labor-supply focus shifted away from the *Generalplan Ost* to the local industrial enterprises. With no Soviet PoWs coming any time soon, the new Birkenau Camp was then slated to be filled with Jews deported from various European countries.

Since March 1942, when the Birkenau Camp was only in its initial construction phase, it was already filling up with deportees. At that time, only a few lodging barracks had been built in Construction Sector I, but no proper wash and toilet facilities yet, no inmate showers, and no operational delousing facilities at all. Jews "fit for labor" were deported from Slovakia and France, a total of some 16,000 by the end of June 1942. All of these Jews were registered and admitted to the camp. However, due to the deplorable sanitary situation, a typhus epidemic which had been lingering in the Main Camp already for many months, broke out inside the Birkenau Camp as well, and went out of control in July and August 1942, reaching a peak daily mortality of 542 on 19 August. It did not subside completely until well into the year 1943. Hence, during 1942 alone, some 47,000 inmates of the Auschwitz Camp complex (Main Camp, Birkenau and the satellite camps) died in 1942, most of them due to typhus, but also of dysentery and other diseases caused by the terrible sanitary conditions.

The Auschwitz SS reacted by putting the entire camp on lock-down and declaring the entire zone around Birkenau a dangerous, cordoned-off area. They order massive amounts of Zyklon B, and tried killing the millions of fleas and lice that had infested the camp and its inmates by fumigating all camp buildings and the inmates' clothes. They moreover implemented strict hygienic measures for the inmates themselves. Furthermore, from early July 1942 onward, many Jews deported to Auschwitz were taken off the train already at earlier stations, to be sent to one of the many satellite labor camps rather than to Auschwitz, where the epidemic made it very difficult to handle any new incoming inmates.

Due to the extreme load on the crematorium at the Main Camp caused by the huge demand, the crematorium's chimney and smoke ducts became damaged already in May 1942, and needed to be replaced. Hence, between June and mid-August 1942, the camp had no operating cremation facilities at all. But even at maximum capacity, the three double-muffle furnaces in this crematorium could cremate only one body per hour, which for a 20-hour workday amounted to a theoretical maximum daily cremation capacity of this facility of some 120 bodies, or 3,600 per month. The monthly mortality rate of the camp was higher than that between June 1942 and March 1943 (at which point the new Birkenau crematoria became successively operational). Hence, some 25,000 deceased inmates could not be cremated between June 1942 and March 1943.

Air photos of 1944 show four mass graves outside the camp perimeter at the northwest, with a potential capacity of some 10,000 to 20,000 bodies. Due to a possible contamination of the region's drinking-water supply, the bodies were again exhumed and cremated on pyres in open-air incinerations, probably starting in late summer 1942. Any new surplus corpses that the old crematorium could not handle were probably cremated on such fires right away. The atrocious work of burying, then exhuming and burning the corpses was performed by inmates. This is the true, horrific core of the horror tales told about Birkenau. However, those outdoor cremations ceased once the new Birkenau crematoria went into service starting in March 1943.

Plans to replace the old crematorium at the Main Camp with a new facility with five triple-muffle furnaces started in October 1941. At that point, the early planning stages for the Birkenau Camp provisioned that camp only with a small incineration hall with two triple-muffle furnaces. However, in early 1942, this project was cancelled, as it was decided to move the new crematorium to Birkenau, which required several structural changes due to the higher groundwater level and the access road being on the other side of the building. This was later called Crematorium II.

Heinrich Himmler visited Auschwitz on 17 and 18 July 1942, where he ordered the Birkenau's camp to be expanded to hold 200,000 prisoners. With the escalating typhus epidemic wreaking havoc, and with the prospect of many times more inmates to be housed in the camp, hence potentially even more victims of diseases, it was decided to increase the camp's cremation capacity. A second crematorium identical (but mirror-symmetrical) to the one planned so far (future Crematorium III), and two cheaper and smaller crematoria were added with one eight-muffle furnace each (the future Crematoria IV and V). For more details on these crematora, see that entry.

The first inmate showers with Zyklon-B delousing chambers at Birkenau became operational only in late 1942 (Buildings 5a and 5b). A larger facility with 50 inmate showers and a large hot-air disinfestation section, the so-called *Zentralsauna* (see this entry), together with many other project to drastically improve the camp's sanitary situation, was planned starting in October 1942. This was after Eduard Wirths, the camp's new garrison physician since early September 1942, had convinced the Berlin SS authorities that drastic measures needed to be taken to ensure the survival of the inmates and thus the camp's ability to function as a labor reservoir.

Wirths also successfully set in motion the construction of a huge inmate hospital in Construction Sector III of the Birkenau Camp, with more than 100 barracks to lodge and treat sick inmates, at the cost of hundreds of millions of dollars in today's currency. The construction of this hospital made steady progress throughout 1943 and 1944, but was halted and abandoned in late summer of 1944 due to the deteriorating war situation.

In the context of Dr. Wirths's attempt to have additional morgues set up in each infirmary, his superiors argued against it, arguing that all corpses by decree had to be brought to the crematoria's morgues twice a day, which means that those morgues were available 24/7 for the storage of corpses. We need to keep in mind that, according to the orthodox narrative, the morgues of Crematoria II and III were used as undressing rooms and homicidal gas chambers. However, morgues that were at all times partially filled with corpses of inmates who had died mainly of diseases elsewhere in the camp cannot also have served as homicidal gas chambers. (For more on this, see the entry on morgues.)

Since the *Zentralsauna*'s construction progress was slow, it was decided to equip all crematoria with inmate showers. Crematoria II and III had several showers built in one of their basement rooms, while Crematoria IV and V had one room in the rear of the building set up as a shower room, and another as a disinfestation gas chamber. It is not clear whether these facilities ever became functional, but if they did, they were probably taken out of service again, once the *Zentralsauna* became operational in late 1943.

In the same time frame, Birkenau also obtained a mobile microwave delousing facility. In early 1944, DDT was delivered to the camp for the first time. All this finally resulted in the typhus epidemic being brought under control. However, when most of the Jews deported from Hungary were transited through the Birkenau Camp on their way to forced labor camps in Germany, some of them were lodged in the still unfinished barracks of Camp Section III, which had been planned as a hospital camp. This unhygienic lodging situation led to a flare-up of typhus cases, and thus of the mortality rate.

On 22 November 1943, the PoW camp Auschwitz-Birkenau was separated from the Auschwitz Main Camp (now renamed to Auschwitz I) and became an independent concentration camp called Auschwitz II. However, in preparation for dissolving the entire camp complex, the Birkenau Camp lost its independence again on 25 November 1944, and was reintegrated in what was then simply called Auschwitz Concentration Camp. In that same time frame, the camp authorities dismantled and eventually blew up Crematoria II through IV, while Crematorium V was kept in reserve until the final days, when it, too, was dynamited. This was probably done in order to prevent the incoming Soviets from using them as staging grounds for atrocity propaganda, as they had done in late July and August 1944 with the crematorium of the Majdanek Camp.

The Birkenau Camp was the Third Reich's largest camp, both by surface area and by number of inmates housed in it, and transited through it, but it was also the camp with the largest death toll. Documents show that some 135,500 registered inmates died at the Auschwitz Camp Complex between 1940 and 1945, most of them in Birkenau. Last but not least, Birkenau was also the largest reservoir of witnesses of what transpired in the German camp system. During the years 1944 and 1945 alone, the Auschwitz authorities released or transferred to other camps some 280,500 inmates from the entire Auschwitz Camp Complex, most of them again from Birkenau. They all were ready to testify to the world what had happened there. A few hundred of them spread false atrocity stories, while some 200,000 witnesses remained silent.

(For details on the Birkenau's documented history, see Mattogno 2016a, 2019, 2023.)

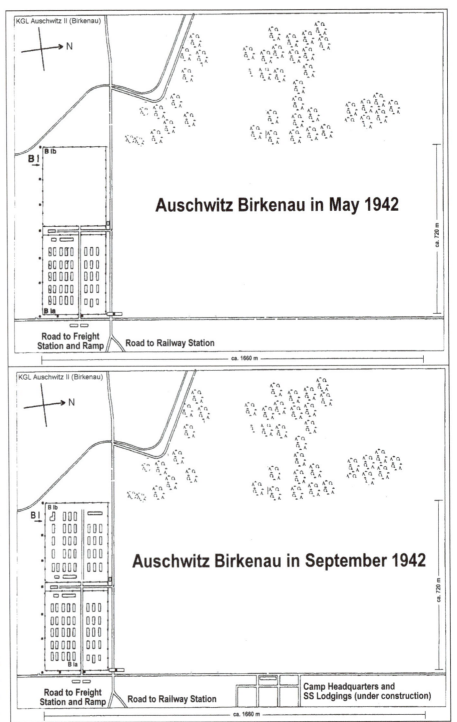

Propaganda History

Note: Propaganda that cannot be allocated with certainty to the Auschwitz Main Camp or any of its satellite camps is addressed in this entry.

Polish Propaganda

Polish Auschwitz propaganda is split into two sections: First, the information gathered, or disinformation invented, and then spread during the war by the Polish underground and the Polish government in British exile. Second, the misrepresentations created after the war by taking documents out of context, manipulating witness accounts, conducting show trials, and then writing a history of the Auschwitz Camp based on this skewed and misrepresented material, a process that continues to this day.

For details on claimed events specific for the Auschwitz Main Camp, see that entry.

Polish Wartime Propaganda

The Polish underground started spreading claims about systematic mass murder at Auschwitz in September 1942. The methods alleged were shootings, gassings, electrocutions and killings with a "pneumatic hammer" (*Hammerluft*). The latter two, freely invented methods were claimed until April 1943, but then disappeared from the agenda. These Polish reports frequently contain numerical claims about the number of inmates present in the camp, and how many inmates of each ethnic subgroup had been killed in which way. Most of these figures are inaccurate, and some freely invented, as documents about the camp's occupancy show.

References to gassings were usually without detail, and where details were mentioned, they were usually wrong. For example, a report of August 1942 and another one from that year's end mention two gas chambers with showers whose showerheads rained down gas instead of water, although that was impossible when using Zyklon B (which was not mentioned). Towels were allegedly issued to the victims before the gassing. However, considering the mess this would have cause, and also because no one takes towels into a shower, this most certainly would not have happened. The victims allegedly died while profusely bleeding from nose and mouth, which is not an effect of hydrogen-cyanide poisoning. Some 300,000 had presumably died this way by late August 1942, although the orthodoxy today insists on only 50,000 (35,130 of which are invented, and the rest misrepresented).

Two reports of October and November 1942 asserted that the first use of gas chambers happened in June 1941, but that the building converted to a gas chamber for this purpose proved too small. However, the orthodoxy insists that the *fictitious* first gassing occurred only in September 1941, and no building was converted for this event. The report continues that *five* new gassing facilities were built in Birkenau in April 1942, which were windowless, had a gas supply and ventilation. However, the orthodoxy in-

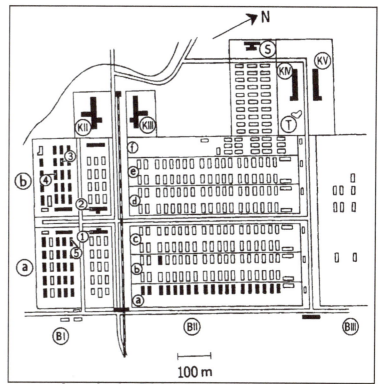

Auschwitz Birkenau in summer 1944
The shaded buildings still exist today, some of them, however, only in the form of ruins or foundations (Crematoria II-V), the rest having been torn down by Polish civilians for building materials and fuel after the war. According to the information brochure of the Auschwitz State Museum, 1991.

BI-III: Construction Sectors I to III
bIa/b: women's camp
BIIa: quarantine camp
BIIb: family camp
BIIc: Hungarian camp
BIId: men's camp
BIIe: gypsy camp
BIIf: inmate hospital
KII: Crematorium II with "gas chamber"
KIII: Crematorium III with "gas chamber"
KIV: Crematorium IV with "gas chɑ
KV: Crematorium V with "gas chɑ
S: "Zentralsauna," hot-air/steam
T: pond
1: Building 5a – Zyklon-B/hot-aɪ
2: Building 5b – Zyklon-B disinfɩ
3: Inmate Barracks no. 13
4: Inmate Barracks no. 20
5: Inmate Barracks no. 3

sists that only *one* gas-chamber building at Birkenau became operational in March 1942 – the so-called Bunker 1 – which allegedly had two chambers, little shuttered windows (hatches to pour in Zyklon B), and neither a gas supply nor any ventilation.

Two reports call the gas chamber a "*Degasungskammer*," which is a misspelled German word correctly spelled *Begasungskammer*, which means fumigation chamber. Hence, the Polish resistance was clearly getting its inspiration from disinfestation gas chambers, always equipped with ventilation systems, which did indeed exist at Auschwitz, and more were planned, which the camp's resistance was well aware of. A report of February 1943 even equates gassings with "so-called" delousings.

As soon as the first Birkenau crematorium became operational in March 1943, fantastic cremation capacities of 3,000 bodies per day were spread, while the real figure was about ten percent of that.

A report of April 1943 mentions mass graves *dug* by gigantic excavators, while another report from that month mentions cranes used to *exhume* bodies from graves; neither machine has ever been heard of.

Yet another report of that month tells of half-poisoned victims coming back to life inside the cremation furnaces, where they scratched the muffle walls and left bloody stains on them. Of course, no blood would withstand the high temperatures in such a furnace, and no one can possibly come back to life while lying in such a furnace. Anyone inhaling the hot gases inside such a furnace had his lungs burned instantly, leading to instant suffocation.

Auschwitz inmate Withold Pilecki escaped from Auschwitz. He claimed that he let himself get arrested on purpose in 1940 in order to gather intelligence on the camp from the inside. Yet what he told after he escaped from the camp in the spring of 1943, was a mixture of false claims – such as 1.5 million gassing victims by March 1943 alone – and a complete lack of any knowledge about any of the later orthodox tenets on mass gassings at Auschwitz. So, either he lied and did not gather any intelligence at all, or the orthodox narrative is untrue. (See his entry for more details.)

In the summer of 1943, escaped Auschwitz inmate Stanisław Chybiński wrote a report giving the first detailed – and absurdly wrong – description of the alleged gas-chamber setup and operation in Crematoria II and III, claiming that they had a capacity of 22 million bodies per year, ready to exterminate all Poles roaming the planet. (See his entry for more details.)

A report of February 1944 turned the Siemens mobile microwave disinfestation device sent to Auschwitz around that time into an electric furnace extracting fat from human corpses, adding that there

Former camp Auschwitz II/Birkenau, satellite image by Google Earth (Dec. 2, 2016).
1: Zentralsauna
2: ruins of Crematorium II
3: ruins of Crematorium III
4: ruins of Crematorium IV
5: ruins of Crematorium V
a: fire-fighting pools
b: sewage treatment plants
c: pond next to Crematorium IV
d: kitchen buildings
e: postwar memorial

was also a bone-glue factory at the camp.

A report of May 1944 described for the first time two peasant cottages turned into gas chambers at Birkenau (later christened "bunkers"), and it even mentions Zyklon B. The ceiling had fake shower-heads (not according to the current orthodox narrative, though), victims were given towels (not likely), the murder was instant (which is impossible), but before Zyklon could be used, another powder had to be thrown in first to "absorb the oxygen from the air," which is utter nonsense. After the deed, ventilators were turned on, but today's narrative has it that there were none. Transports destined for the gas chambers inside the crematoria allegedly arrived at the "'death ramp' at Rajsko," a small subcamp that had neither any ramp nor any crematoria.

A report of late May 1944 deals with the alleged mass gassing of Jews deported from Hungary, asserting that a total of 1,200,000 of these Jews were to be killed. It claimed that, due to insufficient cremation capacity, corpses were burned outdoors, blanketing the area in dense black smoke, while air photos taken at that time prove this to be invented. Later reports repeated the open-air incineration lie.

In June 1944, a Pole who had escaped from Auschwitz made it to Sweden, where he told a tall story of gassed Jews being transformed into grease for the "Auschwitz Lubricant Factory." The victims, equipped with towels and soap, were gassed, then loaded onto carts "which were carried to the grease factory on a mechanical conveyor." This, too, was freely invented.

(For more details, see Mattogno 2021, pp. 119-217.)

Polish Postwar Propaganda

Polish postwar propaganda about Auschwitz began with a combined Soviet-Polish group of "experts" created after the Soviet conquest of Auschwitz, which created an "expert report" proving with pseudo-technical arguments that the claimed extermination facilities at Auschwitz could (and thus did) exterminate four million people. A short while later, the Polish judiciary took over, with Investigative Judge Jan Sehn and "technical expert" Roman Dawidowski as the main actors. While Sehn interviewed a long list of witnesses with the clear goal of having the 4-million-victim dogma confirmed, he and Dawidowski sifted through SS documents left behind at Auschwitz in search for evidence of mass murder. Since none were found, they took innocuous documents out of context and gave them a criminal meaning they do not have, thus creating out of thin air a long list of "criminal traces" that would be used in decades to come by courts in Poland, Austria and Germany as evidence for the claimed exterminations.

The documental and anecdotal "evidence" created by Sehn, Dawidowski and their colleagues was then used for the Stalinist show trials against Rudolf Höss in Warsaw, and against other former members of the camp staff during another show trial staged in Krakow. The documentation of both trials is the richest source of information both about the Auschwitz Camp and about the way its historiography was distorted by these two trials. These trials shaped the Auschwitz narrative as it prevails to a large extent to this day.

The next stage of Polish Auschwitz propaganda was initiated with the creation of the Auschwitz State Museum, whose official task is the preservation of the orthodox Auschwitz narrative with all means necessary, including *lying* about the records in their archives, which is *required* by law in Poland, because Polish penal law expressly threatens any deviation from the orthodox narrative with severe prison terms. Another task of the Auschwitz Museum was influencing German historiography and in particular German judiciary by creating scholarly and pseudo-scholarly German-language material which misrepresents the historical records in order to ensure that German court proceedings involving Auschwitz led to the same conclusions as the two just-mentioned Polish postwar trials.

In order to secure a complete success of this operation, Polish authorities went to extremes during the 1964/65 Frankfurt Auschwitz Show Trial. They screened all the Polish witnesses about to travel to Germany for their political trustworthiness, interrogated them prior to leaving for Germany to make sure they know what to testify about, and then had them accompanied at all times by secret services agents, even inside the courtroom. As we know, this operation was a huge success. With the exception of the total death toll, which was reduced from four million to roughly one million in 1989 (see the entry on Auschwitz, section "Death-Toll Propaganda"), the Soviet-Polish propaganda version of Auschwitz is now required belief in Germany as well, with up to five years imprisonment for anyone voicing disbelief.

(For more details, see Mattogno 2019, pp. 29-32; 2020; 2020b; 2022b; Rudolf 2023, pp. 429f.)

British Propaganda

Between January 1942 and January 1943, the British were able to intercept and decipher radio traffic between German concentration camps and their Oranienburg headquarters (see the entry on British Radio Intercepts). Therefore, they were well informed as to what was unfolding in those camps, how many inmates they housed, how many died, and how many executions took place in them. Hence, when the Polish underground started sending reports about Auschwitz listing vastly exaggerated victim numbers and bizarre killing methods, the Brits knew it was all false. Yet they had to keep it a secret that they had cracked the German code, so they let the Polish account stand.

This situation changed, however, when the Germans discovered the mass graves at Katyn, and used that discovery for a massive, initially successful anti-Soviet propaganda campaign. The British had allied themselves with the Soviet mass murderers in the Soviet attempt to subjugate all of continental Europe, and in order to help Stalin in this endeavor, the British launched a counter-propaganda campaign with Auschwitz as its focus, picking up the Polish underground's propaganda themes.

For instance, the British distributed posters throughout Poland claiming that the German occupational government had ordered committees of all ethnic groups in Poland to witness how humanely – compared to the Soviet methods – the Germans were implementing the extermination of the entire Polish people at Auschwitz in gas, steam and electrocution chambers, with the local crematorium capable of handling 3,000 bodies each day.

The British Polish-language radio station *Sviet* broadcast similar invented counter-propaganda with the same claim of the crematorium at Auschwitz burning 3,000 people every day, which happens to be the same number of victims the Germans initially proclaimed to have found at Katyn. (For more, see Rudolf 2023, pp. 377f.)

The British became serious about Auschwitz propaganda only after the war, when they extracted "confessions" from many former SS men with bestial torture, and collected mendacious and vengeful "survivor" testimonies in preparation of their show trials against former staff members of the Bergen-Belsen Camp, some of which were also former staff members of the Auschwitz Camp. (For more details, see the entry on the Bergen-Belsen Trials.)

With the "incontestable" results of the first Bergen-Belsen Trial, the British then set out to prosecute the owner and some employees of the Hamburg pest-control company Tesch & Stabenow. This company had delivered large quantities of Zyklon B to the Auschwitz Camp, among other places. The British prosecutors mendaciously "demonstrated" that Tesch must have known that their deliveries were used for mass murder. However, the quantities of Zyklon B delivered to Auschwitz are perfectly explicable with the camp's enormous size and the various waves of a typhus epidemic devastating the camp between 1942 and 1944. (For more details, see the entry on Tesch & Stabenow.)

Some of the most-important contributions to the current Auschwitz narrative are the various confessions by former Auschwitz camp commandant Rudolf Höss, the first and most important of which he made after having been severely tortured by his British captors. Höss's testimony during the Nuremberg International Military Tribunal was a pivotal moment of the entire trial. Before that, none of the defendants believed the extermination claims, but Höss's testimony led to a moral collapse of the German defense, casting a spell of eternal condemnation on them.

(For details on Höss's torture, his various testimonies, and their bogus nature, see the entry on him, and Mattogno 2020b.)

U.S. Propaganda

U.S. media on occasion reported on claims spread by the Polish government in London exile, but the U.S. government did not get officially involved in Auschwitz propaganda until late 1944, when they published the War Refugee Board Report in late 1944, containing an edited version of the report by Rudolf Vrba and Alfred Wetzler, plus statements by Jerzy Tabeau and Arnošt Rosin. With this publication, the Auschwitz narrative peddled by these four witnesses became officially recognized by the Allies. (See the entry on the War Refugee Board Report for more details.)

Since the U.S. occupational zone was in South-West Germany with no connection to the Auschwitz Camp, none of the trials conducted by the U.S. in their zone of occupation had any bearing on extermination claims at Auschwitz. The Nuremberg Military Tribunal Case VI, "The Farben Case" (*NMT*, Vols. 7 and 8), concerned merely slave-labor charges against leading management members of the I.G. Farbenindustrie committed at the Monowitz Forced-Labor

Camp, but did not deal with extermination claims regarding Birkenau or the Auschwitz Main Camp.

Soviet Propaganda

For most of the war, the Soviets were preoccupied with German crimes allegedly committed on their own territory. Only in the second half of 1944 did the first Soviet reports on Auschwitz get issued. Two reports issued in August 1944, one of them based on numerous Soviet PoWs who managed to escape from the camp, mention gassings. The second goes into some detail, reflecting the knowledge gained by the plans smuggled out by Stanisław Chybiński and the description given in the Vrba-Wetzler Report, which was circulated widely at that point. The claimed cremation time for a batch of three to four bodies loaded at once into a muffle – 5 to 10 minutes – exposes the unrealistic, propagandistic nature of this report. The cremation furnaces at Auschwitz were designed for just one body per muffle at a time, and cremation took one hour for just one body. Loading more than two into them would have been physically challenging, if not impossible, and burning such a load would have lasted several hours. (See the entry on crematoria for details.)

When the Soviets captured Auschwitz, caution was cast to the winds. Soviet war corresponded Boris Polevoy wrote a propaganda report on Auschwitz, in which he claimed, among other things, that Auschwitz had a crematorium almost half a kilometer long equipped with shaft furnaces, and that victims were electrocuted, then loaded onto conveyor belts moving to the shaft furnaces. (For more details, see the entry on him.) Polevoy's lies were dutifully repeated by *Pravda* in its 2 February 1945 edition.

Another Soviet report of 26 February 1945 claimed that between 4.5 and 5 million people had been exterminated at Auschwitz in execution chambers holding 2,000-3,000 people each, and cremation furnaces of the same daily capacity. The chambers worked by first creating a vacuum, then throwing in hydrogen-cyanide gas bombs.

Of the more than 4,000 inmates the Soviets encountered at Auschwitz, 200 were interrogated, but only three of them claimed to have first-hand knowledge of what transpired in the alleged extermination facilities: Szlama Dragon, Henryk Mandelbaum and Henryk Tauber. As the entries on them amply demonstrate, all three of them bent over backwards to please their Soviet interrogators by confirming the most outrageous lies and exaggerations. Yet their tales became the framework of the orthodoxy's Auschwitz narrative.

Other witnesses did not want to be relegated to the backstage, so they invented their own stories full of preposterous propaganda, among them an appeal to the international public by four university professors (see the entry on B. Epstein for details), and a report by Hungarian Physician Gyula Gál.

Once the Soviets had surveyed the vast documentation the Germans had left behind at the Auschwitz Camp, had investigated its structures, and had interviewed the relevant inmates, a combined Soviet-Polish group of "experts" went to work and created an "expert report" that supposedly proved the vast extermination capacity of the Auschwitz crematoria, rigging their data in such a way that they could "prove" that, during their operational times, all the gas chambers and crematoria together could (and thus did) exterminate four million people.

This "expert report" was the technical basis for a document that was submitted and accepted by the Nuremberg International Military Tribunal as Document 008-USSR (see *IMT*, Vol. 39, pp. 241-261). Admitting to have heavily relied on the mendacious testimonies of Szlama Dragon and Henryk Tauber (see their entries), this document contains the following peculiar claims, among others:

- 3 to 5 bodies could fit into each cremation muffle, although the Auschwitz cremation furnaces were designed only for one body at a time, and its small doors would not have allowed for more than two to be inserted at once.
- Cremating a load of 3-5 bodies took 20-30 minutes, although in reality, the cremation of just one body took an hour.
- Death in the gas chambers occurred within 3-5 minutes, which would have been technically impossible. Zyklon B gives off its poison only slowly, and it dissipates through a large room only gradually, so any execution in the way described would be much slower than executions in U.S. gas chambers, which took on average ten minutes (see the entry on Zyklon B and on homicidal gas chambers).
- The Birkenau crematoria's daily capacity allegedly was 10,000 to 12,000 bodies, while their actual theoretical maximum daily capacity stood at some 920 bodies.
- The camp's total death toll amounted to some four million, while the current orthodox narrative insists on roughly one million, with only some

135,000 being documented.

To undergird this absurd death toll, the Soviets even coaxed the Polish railway employee Franciszek Stanek to "confirm" that five million people had been deported in some 2,000 trains to Auschwitz. (For more details, see Mattogno 2021, pp. 293-305.)

Forensic Findings

Between May 1945 and September 1946, the Polish investigating judge Jan Sehn and the Polish engineer Dr. Roman Dawidowski scoured the former camp's archives as well as material remains in search of evidence supporting mass-murder claims. They presented simple wooden doors and shutters as evidence for gas-tight doors used to kill humans. However, an objective study of these items demonstrates the opposite: Doors to homicidal gas chambers built to contain hundreds of human beings needed to be not just gastight, but most importantly panic-proof. Hence, they had to be made of massive steel, and had to be anchored solidly in thick, massive walls. Yet no such doors were ever ordered, let along delivered or installed at Auschwitz. (See the entry on gastight doors.)

In their search for evidence, Dawidowski's and Sehn's team attempted to get access to Morgue 1 of Crematorium II at Birkenau, which is said to have been a homicidal gas chamber. Since the building had been dynamited, the roof of that basement room had partly collapsed, and the entry area to it was blocked by rubble. Therefore, the Poles cut two openings through the roof to gain access to areas that hadn't completely collapsed. They removed wall samples, and asked a Polish lab to analyze them for cyanide residues. Such residues would have been deposited inside the wall's mortar and plaster, if the room had been filled repeatedly with hydrogen-cyanide vapors during gassings with Zyklon B. The resulting chemical compounds called Iron Blue are very stable, long-lasting pigments (see the entry on Iron Blue). However, the analytical report eventually submitted does not even mention those wall samples. Therefore, it stands to reason that the results were negative. The two openings cut through the collapsed roof were later mendaciously presented as Zyklon-B introduction holes, although they had been created only after the war by these Polish researchers.

In 1966, the Auschwitz State Museum had the Polish company Hydrokop take core samples from the soil at the former Birkenau Camp. The results were never published. From a terse footnote in an article by the Museum's director Franciszek Piper, we learn that, of the 303 core samples taken, 42 "contained traces of human ashes, bones, and hair." It is not known where these samples were taken, or what the quantity of the traces found was. It stands to reason that the positive samples were taken where four large mass graves can be identified on 1944 air photos, which contained thousands of typhus victims that could not be cremated in the summer of 1942. (See the entries on air photos and mass graves.)

In 1972, during the Vienna Auschwitz trial against Walter Dejaco and Fritz Ertl, the Austrian court asked Austrian accredited engineer Gerhard Dubin to determine, based on wartime construction blueprints of Crematorium II at Birkenau, whether that building's basement contained homicidal gas chambers, or could be modified to operate as such. In his expert report, Dubin concluded that, modified or unmodified, the rooms in question could not have served homicidal purposes.

In 1988, U.S. expert for execution technology Fred A. Leuchter wrote a report on his forensic findings about Auschwitz, among other things. His conclusion was that the rooms in question in the various crematoria could not have been used as homicidal gas chambers for several technical reasons. Leuchter also took numerous wall samples and had them tested for cyanide residues. Those taken from rooms alleged to have been used for mass murder with Zyklon B came back negative.

Between 1990 and 1992, German accredited chemist Germar Rudolf followed in Leuchter's footsteps by preparing a thorough expert report investigating many chemical, engineering and architectural aspects of the Auschwitz mass-murder claims. His conclusions were similar to those by Leuchter.

Between 1991 and 1994, in an attempt to refute Leuchter's and Rudolf's findings, the Auschwitz State Museum had a team of Polish forensic experts led by Jan Markiewicz take wall samples from various buildings at Auschwitz. Markiewicz's team chose an analytic method that could not detect long-term stable cyanide residues, hence exactly those that could have survived the 40 years since war's end. For that reason, all their samples – those taken from alleged homicidal gas chambers and from former fumigation chambers – yielded similar analytic results: close to zero. Markiewicz and colleagues concluded from this that samples from delousing chambers, where Zyklon B was indubitably used to fumigate clothes, showed similar results as samples taken from alleged homicidal gas chambers: close to zero. Therefore, this presumably proves the latter's exposure to Zyklon-B fumes on a similar level to fumigation chambers. Rudolf has expertly exposed this Polish fraud in all later, updated editions of his expert report.

After some 20 years of thorough archival and technical research, Italian historian Carlo Mattogno and Italian engineer Dr. Franco Deana published a three-volume historical, technical and forensic study on cremation technology in general, and on the history and technical features of the cremation furnaces installed at the Auschwitz and Birkenau Camps in particular. This study demonstrates the mundane nature of the Auschwitz furnaces. It proves that these furnaces and the fuel they were supplied with were barely able to cremate the number of inmates who died in that camp due to diseases and other non-homicidal reasons (some 135,500). It would not have been possible to cremate in them the additional roughly one million gassing victims claimed by the orthodox narrative.

(For more details, see Leuchter *et al.* 2017; Rudolf 2020; Mattogno/Deana 2021.)

Current Orthodox Narrative
For the current orthodox extermination narrative on the Birkenau Camp, see the respective (last) section of the entry for the Auschwitz Main Camp, which covers the orthodox narrative for both camps, as their history is intricately interwoven.

BIROBIDZHAN

In 1928, the Soviet Union created a Jewish Autonomous Oblast (JAO) in southeastern Siberia, with the newly created city Birobidzhan as its administrative center. The plan was to offer the Jews of the Soviet Union their own homeland as an alternative to Zionism, populate and develop the area, prevent Chinese and Japanese infiltrations, and exploit the area's resources.

The JAO reached a pre-war peak of some 20,000 Jewish inhabitants around 1937. After the German-Soviet pact of August 1939, Germany floated the idea with the Soviet Union to deport Jews from the German sphere of influence into that region. The idea found no takers among the Soviets, though.

It is possible that some of the Jews deported east by the Soviet Union during and after the Polish campaign in 1939 and while retreating from the Germans in 1941/42 ended up resettled or in labor camps in the JAO.

Interest among the Jews of Europe in the JAO was rekindled after the war, when many displaced Jews were looking for a new home. The area's Jewish population reached an all-time peak around 1948 with some 46,000 to 50,000 Jews. It may have grown even more in 1952/53, as Stalin initiated mass deportations of Jews to unknown locations in the Soviet Union's east, probably Siberian labor camps. (See *American Jewish Year Book*, Vol. 54, 1953, p. 331.)

After the creation of Israel, and due to liberal immigration policies for Jews in most western countries, the Jewish population in the JAO declined steadily. It basically collapsed in the years following the collapse of the Soviet Union, with most Jews emigrating to Israel, Western Europe and the U.S.

BISKOVITZ, YA'AKOV

Ya'akov Biskovitz (or Jacob Biskubicz) was a Polish Jew born in 1926. In his testimony of 5 June 1961 during the Eichmann Trial, he claimed that he had seen the workings of the gas chambers at Sobibór with his own eyes, even though he wasn't working in the presumably cordoned-off part of that camp (called Camp 3). He managed to peek inside that camp sector at an opportune moment anyway. At this opportunity, he saw how the floors of the gas chambers opened, and the bodies were discharged into a train below, which brought them to a pit for burning (State of Israel, Vol. III, p. 1184):

> *"Yes, that is the fire pit in which the victims who were brought out of the gas chambers were burned. After some time, a buzzing sound would be heard, the floor opened up, and the victims fell into the deep hollow below and were conveyed in this little train into the pit where the eighty men of Camp 3 were working, and they burned the bodies."*

Shortly thereafter he denied having seen the floors opening up, however, but he insisted having seen that, "underneath the gas chamber, there was a hollow which already contained bodies."

His claims are rejected as false by the orthodoxy, who insists that these chambers did not have collapsible floors with a train running underneath or through a "hollow." The corpses were instead taken out of the chamber manually, sideways through a normal door.

During his testimony on 9 November 1965 at the Sobibór Trial staged in Hagen, West Germany, he forgot all about collapsing floors and trains running underneath. Instead, he testified hearing engine noises instead.

(See the entry on Sobibór for more details, as well as Graf/Kues/Mattogno 2020, pp. 73, 77f.; Mattogno 2021e, pp. 89-91.)

BLAHA, FRANZ

Franz Blaha (or František Bláha) was a Czech physician who was deported to the Dachau Camp on 30 April 1941. He testified during the Nuremberg International Military Tribunal, and in that context claimed that he was ordered to investigate the result of a "test gassing" in the alleged homicidal gas chamber at Dachau, presumably supervised by camp physician Siegmund Rascher. However, Blaha was unable to describe how the facility is supposed to have worked. All he knew is that the gas used "smelled of chlorine," and that he was so horrified by what he saw that he simply ran out fast, because he "couldn't stand it in there."

Franz Blaha

However, no gas ever said to have been used during World War II smelled like chlorine. Furthermore, had Dr. Blaha really been put in charge by Dr. Rascher to check the result of a test gassing, he wouldn't have been allowed to simply run away from it because he disliked what he saw. In addition, the room he claimed to have been used for this experiment was unsuited for any gas experiments.

The suspicion that Dr. Blaha invented all this out of thin air is supported by the fact that no documentation at all exists on this or any other later test gassing, and also not about the gas chamber claimed to have been used. This stands in stark contrast to the voluminous documentation available about real medical experiments performed at Dachau by Dr. Rascher. Blaha himself confirmed that these experiments were the only kind performed at Dachau (*IMT*, Vol. 5, p. 185):

> "Well, Dr. Rascher made exclusively [sic] so-called Air Force experiments in the camp. He was a major in the Air Force and was assigned to investigate the conditions to which parachutists were subjected and, secondly, the conditions of those people who had to make an emergency landing on the sea or had fallen into the sea."

(For more details, see the entry on Dachau, as well as Mattogno 2022a, pp. 15-20.)

BLATT, THOMAS

Thomas (Toivi) Blatt was a Polish boy 15 years of age who was deported to Sobibór in early 1943. In the 1980s, he was an advisor for the 1987 movie *Escape from Sobibór*. Another ten years after that, and more than half a century after the events, he published two books titled *Sobibór: The Forgotten Revolt* and *From the Ashes of Sobibór: A Story of Survival*. In these books, he included all the clichés and wild stories spread for five decades in media, literature and trial verdicts about Sobibór. This only proves that Blatt had done his homework, because no inmate could have known everything from his own experience. Hence, Blatt has written a streamlined orthodox account of the camp's history, wrongly labeling it as his recollections. However, thusly contaminated by "information" from so many third-hand sources, his books are worthless as historical sources, as they cannot claim to be a source of exclusively first-hand knowledge.

Thomas Blatt

Here are several peculiar statements in his books:
- He was able to keep a diary, parts of which he managed to save, but that diary was never published. Instead, he claims to quote from it in his books.
- He found another diary of a Jew who allegedly had been transported to Sobibór from the Belzec Camp. That diary also survived Blatt's incarceration, but the person he entrusted it to afterwards (Leon Feldhendler) got killed a short while later, so this diary is now lost, too.
- He claimed that between 12,000 and 15,000 Jews were killed during an average working day. With such a daily capacity, Sobibór could have processed 5.5 million Jews in a year. Hence, there would not have been any need to have any other extermination camp; Sobibór could have handled them all!

(See the entry on Sobibór for more details, as well as Graf/Kues/Mattogno 2020, pp. 41-46, 93-98.)

BLOBEL, PAUL

Right before the beginning of the war against the Soviet Union, SS *Standartenführer* Paul Blobel (13 Aug. 1894 – 7 June 1951) was assigned head of *Sonderkommando* 4a within *Einsatzgruppe* C in Ukraine. According to the *Einsatzgruppen* reports, his men were involved in the mass execution of Jews, among them the claimed massacre at Babi Yar, which has since been refuted by air photos. Due to severe health problems resulting from excessive alcohol consumption, he was relieved of his duty in January 1942 and underwent extended health treatments in the following months.

Paul Blobel

He then is said to have been put in charge of implementing "*Aktion* 1005" in the eastern occupied territories, which allegedly was an – albeit technically impossible – grand-scale operation to eliminate all traces of *Einsatzgruppen* mass graves in Eastern Europe by exhumation and cremation. To this end, Blobel supposedly started out by conducting experiments with open-air incinerations at the Chełmno Camp, the results of which were allegedly implemented in the various extermination camps, such as Auschwitz, Belzec, Sobibór and Treblinka.

However, in his postwar depositions, Blobel never mentioned any cremation experiments conducted at Chełmno, and never mentioned the term "*Aktion* 1005" either. The tale of the Chełmno experiments was invented by former Auschwitz Camp Commandant Rudolf Höss in his postwar statements.

At the Chełmno Camp, a primitive field furnace was built, presumably for the cremation of dead deportees. (See the entry on that camp for details.) However, such a facility was neither erected in any other camp, nor during the alleged mass cremations of "*Aktion* 1005." Hence, if that field furnace was the result of experiments, neither Höss nor Blobel nor any other camp commandant adopted this cremation method.

Starting in early 1943, Blobel and his men allegedly roamed the huge area of still-German-occupied eastern territories in search of *Einsatzgruppen* mass graves, almost all traces of which he intended to eliminate by mid-1944. Apart from "confessions" by Blobel and his former associates made under duress while in Allied captivity, and numerous witness tales, there is no documentation to verify any of these claims.

Regarding attempts to eliminate the mass-murder victims buried at Babi Yar, Blobel claimed in an affidavit dated 18 June 1947 (NO-3947), that the bodies were eliminated by simply opening the mass graves, removing the top cover, drenching the exposed corpses with fuel, and set them on fire.

"It took about two days before the grave was burned down. I personally saw that the grave had smoldered through all the way to the bottom. After that, the grave was covered up, and with this all traces were as good as erased."

In other words, in Paul Blobel's world, bodies burned all by themselves after having been lit with some unspecified (evidently liquid) fuel. However, self-immolating bodies simply do not exist. Such bizarre statements are made only by people who have been coerced to make them, here probably by the customary torture that the Americans were inflicting on many if not most of their captives. (See the entry on torture.)

Blobel mentioned only one grave of a modest size ("55 m long, 3 m wide and 2½ deep") that could have contained around one to two thousand bodies. If 100,000 victims had been buried at Babi Yar, as most other witnesses and thus the orthodox narrative claim, then there would have been up to 100 of these mass graves, not just one.

Blobel's version stands in stark contrast to the claims made by alleged survivors among the inmates who claim to have been forced to exhume the bodies at Babi Yar. (See the entries on Semen Berlyant, Isaak Brodsky, David Budnik, Vladimir Davydov, Iosif Doliner, Yakov Kaper, Vladislav Kuklia, Leonid Ostrovsky, Yakov Steyuk, Ziama Trubakov.) They all agree that the corpses were extracted from the graves, and then burned on huge wooden pyres. Blobel made his statement while in U.S. captivity, whereas these survivor witnesses made their claims during interrogation by the Soviet terror organization NKGB (the successor of the NKVD and precursor of the KGB). In other words, while the Soviets could easily orchestrate the statements of the witnesses they interviewed (if need be, at gun point), Blobel was beyond their reach, so his statement was left unharmonized.

(For more details, see the entry on *Aktion* 1005 and Babi Yar, as well as Mattogno 2022c, pp. 541f., and 550-563.)

After a show trial, Blobel was executed in 1951

by the Americans.

blue wall discoloration → Iron Blue

BLYAZER, A.

A propaganda report by the Soviet terror organization NGKB dated 14 August 1944 about alleged German atrocities in the Ponary District of Lithuania contains an account by a certain A. Blyazer. The same witness was interrogated by a Soviet commission, whose report is undated, but probably from 1946.

According to these two documents, Blyazer claimed that he was to be executed with many other Jews in 1941 at a large pit near Ponary. However, when the shooting began, he let himself fall into the pit before getting hit. He subsequently was covered by many layers of other dead victims and a thin layer of sand. After lying there for four hours, he dug himself out and escaped into the woods. He was later captured, and in 1943 forced to assist exhuming and burning corpses from the mass graves he had escaped from two years earlier. He escaped from there as well at an unknown date and unknown circumstances.

Blyazer asserted that his team exhumed and burned altogether 68,000 corpses. He gives a breakdown of the number of inmates working on certain tasks, among them 15 persons felling and sawing trees or firewood. Cremating an average human body during open-air incinerations requires some 250 kg of freshly cut wood. Cremating 68,000 bodies thus requires some 17,000 metric tons of wood. This would have required the felling of all trees growing in a 50-year-old spruce forest covering almost 38 hectares of land, or some 85 American football fields. An average prisoner is rated at being able to cut some 0.63 metric tons of fresh wood per workday. To cut this amount of wood with just 15 persons would have lasted some 1,800 days, or almost five years.

According to Blyazer, only 2 (two!) inmates built the pyres, hence hauled 68,000 bodies and 17,000 tons of wood. Furthermore, only "[o]ne person with a two-meter poker constantly maintained the fire, adjusting the fire and clearing channels of the fire from ashes" – which would have burned him to a crisp.

If this tale has a real background, it can have been about at most a few thousand bodies, but certainly not 68,000.

This testimony relates to one of many events claimed to have been part of the alleged German clean-up operation which the orthodoxy calls *Aktion 1005*. The above exposition demonstrates that Blyazer's entire scenario is completely detached from reality. Its claimed dimension cannot be based on experience, but on mere propaganda, imagination and delusion.

(See also the similar accounts by Yuri Farber, Matvey Zaydel and Szloma Gol; for more details, see the entries on Ponary, on lumberjacks as well as Mattogno 2022c, pp. 677-679.)

BOCK, LUDWIG

Ludwig Bock (born 1942) is a German defense lawyer. During the West-German Majdanek Trial (1975-1981), he defended Hildegard Lächert, a former inmate supervisor at the Ravensbrück and Majdanek camps. While preparing the case for his client, Bock rightfully received access to the files of the prosecution, where he found the names and residential addresses of numerous witnesses, most of them in Poland and Israel. Bock subsequently visited many of these witnesses and recorded interviews with them about the case, without revealing that he was a defense lawyer.

During the trial, he juxtaposed the contents of his interviews with the statements the same witnesses made while in the witness stand. He demonstrated that these witness statements, which had been inconsistent and contradictory when he interviewed them years before the trial, in the meantime had been brought into mutual accord, and had been purged of their most unbelievable elements.

It turned out that the German Central Office for the Investigation of National-Socialist Crimes (*Zentrale Stelle*), following their general procedure, had submitted case-file binders to all witnesses containing already established "facts" about the case and about each defendant. Evidently, the judicial offices in the jurisdictions where the witnesses resided had collaborated with the German prosecutors to subsequently streamline and homogenize each witness's statement ahead of the trial.

When Bock revealed these systematic witness manipulations, there was a public outcry demanding that Bock be disciplined. Disciplinary steps were indeed initiated, but ultimately did not result in any penalty. However, the two nations where most witnesses resided, Poland and Israel, banned Bock for life from entering their countries again. (For sources, see Rudolf 2019, p. 106.)

In 1997, while defending Holocaust skeptic Günter Deckert in Germany (accused of "denying the Holocaust"), Bock filed a motion to hear several top officials of Germany's government as evidence that "primary massive political interests stand in the way of a breakthrough of the truth in connection with the Holocaust." Bock was subsequently prosecuted for this motion and sentenced to a fine for "inciting the masses." The case was confirmed by the German Supreme Court (*Bundesgerichtshof*, decision 6 KLs 503 Js 69/97.)

A second, similar case against German defense lawyer Jürgen Rieger, who filed a motion in 1996 to introduce forensic evidence challenging the orthodox Auschwitz narrative, initially ended with an acquittal. However, the German Supreme Court reversed that decision and, following the Bock precedent, demanded a guilty verdict for Rieger as well. (*Bundesgerichtshof*, decision 5 StR 485/01.) During the retrial, Rieger was found guilty and fined for "inciting the masses."

These two trials against defense lawyers created case law in Germany declaring it illegal to file motions for the introduction of evidence which challenge the orthodox Holocaust narrative. Ever since, it has been illegal for Holocaust skeptics to defend themselves in German courts of law.

BÖCK, RICHARD

Richard Böck (born 1906), SS *Unterscharführer*, served as a driver in the Auschwitz motor pool. Böck was a good friend of former Auschwitz inmate Adolf Rögner, a convicted fraudster and perjurer whose long series of lies was instrumental in initiating the investigations that later ended in the infamous Frankfurt Auschwitz Show Trial. Böck was interrogated twice by the fact-finding branch of the Public Prosecutors at the Frankfurt District Court. His description of a homicidal gassing that he claims to have witnessed is full of absurd, contradictory and technically-impossible statements; as such, it has been a source of mockery by Holocaust skeptics. (For more details, see Rudolf 2003d; 2023, pp. 457-459.)

– During the first interrogation, he claimed that the gassing took place in the summer of 1943, while in his second interrogation he moved the event to the winter of 1942/43.
– Although it was strictly forbidden for him as an unauthorized person to be present at the alleged gassings or during an execution in a gravel pit (that he also claimed to have witnessed), he

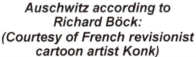

Auschwitz according to Richard Böck:
(Courtesy of French revisionist cartoon artist Konk)

The victims were pushed into the gas chamber.

The door was closed and Zyklon B introduced.

There was a wait of a few minutes.

And when the door was opened: "I was surprised that the inmate commando assigned to remove the bodies entered the chamber without gas masks, although this blue vapor floated over the corpses, from which I assumed that it was a gas."

THAT IS IMPOSSIBLE!
Everyone would have been dead! A room filled with Zyklon B gas has to be ventilated for hours (the manufacturer recommends 20 hours!)... Even with gas masks it would not have been possible.

claims that he simply drove to the gas chamber or accompanied SS men "a few meters behind" on their way to the execution.
- Ten minutes after the gas had been poured into the alleged gas chamber, the doors were opened. There was no ventilation, so the room would have been full of the colorless gas, but Böck saw "a bluish cloud floating over a gigantic pile of corpses," and, "this blue vapor floated over the corpses, from which I assumed that it was a gas." Since hydrogen-cyanide gas is colorless, this was nothing more than a product of his wild imagination, stemming from the (misleading) German name of hydrogen cyanide – *Blausäure* = blue acid.
- An unventilated room full of poison gas would have killed anyone trying to extract the corpses, and would also have endangered the lives of the SS men claimed to have supervised the process.
- Last but not least, Böck spread the well-worn lie that, from the crematorium located right next to the motor pool office, he "could see every day how the flames shot two meters high out of the chimney. It also smelled intensively like burned flesh." Yet the chimneys of cremation furnaces fired with coke, which burns almost flamelessly, cannot emit any flames, and a cremation furnace is not a barbecue grill but an incineration device operating at such high temperatures that the only scent would have been that of a normal coke-fueled fire.

Boelcke-Kaserne → **Nordhausen**

BOGER, WILHELM

Wilhelm Boger (19 Dec. 1906 – 3 April 1977), SS *Oberscharführer*, was employed at the Political Department of the Auschwitz Camp, where he investigated inmate escapes and theft, among other things. He was arrested on 19 June 1945, in Ludwigsburg, Germany, by U.S. service units. While in U.S. custody, he was "softened up," probably with the usual torture, to

Wilhelm Boger

such a degree that 16 days later, on July 19, he signed an utterly absurd, incoherent confession, in which he confirmed the Allied mass-murder propaganda about Auschwitz, down to the claim of four million victims. Such nonsense would never have come from an SS man voluntarily.

Boger was one of the main targets of convicted fraudster, serial liar and perjurer Adolf Rögner, who submitted an absurdly long list of outrageous accusations against Boger when trying to initiate West Germany's investigations into wartime-events at Auschwitz. Boger's own testimony of early 1959 was rather reasonable, except when it came to homicidal gassings, the existence of which he confirmed, yet claimed to have no personal knowledge at all. Considering that the Political Department was in charge of the crematoria that are said to have housed these gas chambers, this denial appears as a mere attempt to deny personal responsibility while confirming that which, for the judiciary, was irreversibly set in stone and which, after 15 years of propaganda, Boger may have come to believe himself.

Maryla Rosenthal, a Jewess, was one of Boger's secretaries in Auschwitz. As to her own statements, she refused to participate in the camp's rumor mill, and hence tried to rely only on what she had experienced herself. She was one of the first inmates interrogated in this context by West-German authorities in February of 1959, and had had no prior contact with other inmates or inmate organizations; thus she was largely uninfluenced. As such, she was unable to confirm either Rögner's raging accusations against her former boss, or the general allegations of cruelties in Auschwitz:

> *"Boger was polite to me, and I cannot complain about him with regard to my person. He even went so far as passing on to me parts of his food in his dishes on a regular basis, with the pretense that I should clean them. Apart from this, he organized clothes for me from the Birkenau camp. [...] He was also very polite to the other Jewish female prisoners, who worked in the Political Department, and we Jewesses liked him very much. I also remember that Boger had no distinct hatred against Jews. [...] To summarize it, I really cannot say anything bad about Boger in regard to my person and to the other female inmates of the Political Department."*

No one was inclined to believe Mrs. Rosenthal, though. (See Rudolf 2004b, c; 2023, pp. 368f., 384-386, 392-394)

Bohemia → Czechia

BOMBA, ABRAHAM

Abraham Bomba (9 June 1913 – 19 Feb 2000) was a Polish Jew who appeared as a witness in several postwar trials on Treblinka. Furthermore, he gave several interviews in later years. The first interview was conducted by Claude Lanzmann in September 1979. On 28 August 1990, Bomba gave an interview to the U.S. Holocaust Memorial Museum, and another one on 14 August 1996 to the University of Southern California's Shoah Foundation.

Abraham Bomba, 1979

Bomba claimed that he was deported to the Treblinka Camp on 30 September 1942. After having been there for about four weeks, he claimed to have been deployed, together with 16 other men, to cut the hair of naked women. For the first week or two, this shearing supposedly happened inside one of the camp's homicidal gas chambers, which was disguised as a shower room. After that, the shearing operation was allegedly moved to the undressing barracks.

Bomba claimed in 1979 that the alleged gas chamber was 12 ft × 12 ft in size. This fits the orthodoxy's description of the rooms inside the claimed first gassing building, which allegedly measured 4 m × 4 m (13 ft × 13 ft).

The room was allegedly furnished with benches. In addition to these benches and the 17 barbers, some 60 to 70 women came into the room to be shorn. Hence, a room of 144 or 170 square feet (13 or 16 m²) was occupied by a minimum of 77 people. Therefore, each person had about two square feet to stand on (five to six persons per square meter). To this, we must add the benches. This is clearly a physically impossible density of people in that small room. Shearing the hair of a sitting person requires at least a square meter of room for each sitting person and the barber.

There were only two reasons to shear off someone's hair: for hygienic reasons, to reduce risk of lice-borne diseases like typhus; or to collect the hair for later use (or both). The former practice was intended to improve inmate health and save lives. Hence, it is inconceivable in an extermination camp, but makes perfect sense in a transit camp. In the latter case, the hair obviously had to be collected afterwards. This means that the women had to leave the alleged gas chamber after the shearing, so the benches could be removed, and the hair collected. After that, the women (or other victims) would have reentered the same room for their execution – provided they could be convinced a second time to enter such a room.

Since this is a highly inefficient procedure, the orthodoxy claims that this shearing, if it happened at all, occurred elsewhere, but certainly not inside a gas chamber.

According to Bomba, the operation was moved to the undressing barracks only a week or two after he started this assignment. Because he arrived at Treblinka end of September, and started his barber job four weeks later, this means that the shearing operation was relocated in early to mid-November 1942. However, Treblinka had been active already since late July of 1942. Therefore, if we follow Bomba's timeline, the shearing inside the gas chamber had been done for almost four months, hence was a long-lasting routine. This is highly unlikely.

Bomba moreover asserted that he and his other fellow inmates worked and lived in the section of the Treblinka Camp where no extermination activities happened. They had no access to the other, prohibited part of the camp, presumably called Camp 2, where all the extermination activities allegedly unfolded. He even stated that this part of the camp was as distant and unreachable for them as Australia is for people living in the U.S. As a result, Bomba insisted that he never saw the results of a gassing; he knew no details about how the gas chambers operated; he had no first-hand knowledge about how the bodies were presumably removed from the gas chambers; and he had never seen how they were hauled to mass graves.

At the same time, however, he asserted that, for a week or two, he cut the hair of women right inside a gas chamber, hence evidently in the core of that very prohibited and inaccessible Camp 2.

He also insisted that he escaped from Treblinka before the large-scale open-air incinerations of bodies on pyres are said to have begun in the spring of 1943. Hence, he had no knowledge about this either.

In other words, Bomba's knowledge is limited to trivial maintenance operations of the camp, and how women had their hair shorn.

(The interviews mentioned are all accessible on YouTube and the website of the U.S. Holocaust Memorial Museum.)

BONE MILL

Four witnesses claimed that, at the Janowska Camp near Lviv, a machine was used to grind down bones that were left over from open-air incinerations of corpses, which are said to have been extracted from mass graves of German murder victims. These witnesses are: Heinrich Chamaides, Moische Korn, David Manusevich and Leon Weliczker.

Their claim was given a lot of attention and publicity by the Soviets, who had a team of experts examine and describe this device in detail, and photos were taken of it as well, one showing three of the aforementioned witnesses (Chamaides, Korn, Manusevich). The expert report does not indicate whether any samples of remnants in the mill's drum were taken to see whether it contained any traces of human bones. This device is today exhibited at a museum in Kiev with the usual orthodox claims about it.

A thorough 2013 investigation of all the documental and material traces of this device resulted in the following conclusions, among others:

1. The device was a standard "ball mill," manufactured by the Grusonwerk Company of Magdeburg, Germany.
2. The machine was found in an unknown location, but certainly not in the Janowska Camp. No photograph shows the machine against a recognizable background, and one photo, in which Moses Korn is depicted as standing right next to it, is a clumsy photo montage.
3. The Soviet commission's claim that the machine was designed specifically to grind human bone fragments is a lie. This type of ball mill was primarily designed to crush stones.
4. The mill was most likely used to crush gravel for roadwork on the German road-construction project *Durchgangsstraße* IV (Thoroughfare IV), linking Lviv to Taganrog with a highway 2,175 km in length. Another stretch linked the German city of Breslau (today's Wroclaw) to Lviv via Krakow. A German report of 22 June 1942 indicates that 18,365 Jews were working at road-construction projects, among them this large project.

Weliczker confirmed this connection when he spoke of a camp unit assigned to road construction, and of another unit "breaking up the tombstones and building the main road with the broken rock." The tombstones were therefore reduced to gravel, which required exactly a ball mill of the type found.

The witnesses who mentioned the machine probably really had something to do with it, but in the context of road construction. That three of them showed up side by side next to the ball mill in one photo proves that they met after the war, communicated with each other, and collaborated with the Soviet investigators as a group. Hence, their testimonies given to the Soviets were not independent, but rather most likely choreographed.

(For more details, see Schwensen 2013a; Mattogno 2022c, pp. 518-522.)

BOÜARD, MICHEL DE

Michel de Boüard (5 Aug. 1909 – 28 April 1989) was professor of history at the University of Caen since 1940. An active communist since 1942, he was eventually deported to the Mauthausen Camp. After the war, he wrote several articles about his wartime experiences. When confronted with Henri Roques's PhD thesis critiquing the so-called confessions of Kurt Gerstein, he changed his mind about the quality of the historical record on the German World-War-II camps (Lebailly 1988):

"I am haunted by the thought that in 100 years or even 50 years the historians will question themselves on this particular aspect of the Second World War which is the concentration camp system and what they will find out. The record is rotten to the core. On one hand, [we have] a considerable amount of fantasies, inaccuracies, obstinately repeated (in particular concerning num-

Wartime photo showing Heinrich Chamaides, Moische Korn and David Manusevich next to a ball mill used for road construction.

bers), heterogeneous mixtures, generalizations and, on the other hand, very dry critical studies that demonstrate the absurdity of those exaggerations."

BRENER, HEJNOCH

Hejnoch Bren(n)er was deported to the Treblinka Camp on 15 October 1942. He was interrogated by a Soviet investigative commission on 17 August 1944. Regarding the way people were allegedly killed at Treblinka, he stated merely that 5,000 people were killed at a time in the "bath."

During another interrogation by Polish judge Łukaszkiewicz on 9 October 1945, he claimed that Jews at Treblinka "were killed by pumping the air out with a motor located next to the chambers." However, creating a vacuum in a brick-and-mortar building is technically impossible (the external pressure would crush the walls), hence most certainly was not done.

Brener furthermore claimed to have been a barber cutting off women's hair. He claimed that this was done in one of the alleged vacuum chambers, so he knew exactly how they looked and operated. However, the orthodoxy insists that haircutting occurred in a separate building, not inside one of the gas chambers.

(See Mattogno 2021e, pp. 138, 155f.)

BREST

Brest, back then called Brest-Litovsk, is a Belorussian City close to the border to Poland. It belonged to Poland since 1921, but to Belorussia since 1939. After the German invasion of the Soviet Union, a ghetto for Jews was established in that city. According to German wartime documents, altogether almost 9,000 Jews from that ghetto were executed during several operations between July and September 1941.

In mid-October 1942, the ghetto's population of some 17,000 Jews was evacuated and resettled elsewhere, if we follow the terms used in German wartime documents. However, the orthodoxy insists that these were euphemisms for murder. The Jews were allegedly sent by train some 110 km northeast to the town of Bronnaya Gora, where they were supposedly executed and buried in mass graves. (See the entry on Bronnaya Gora.)

No railway documents about this evacuation have been located so far. Since there are plenty of German wartime documents in many other cases truly and verifiably reporting about relocations, evacuations and resettlement of Jews, the orthodoxy's claim of the use of "code words" or "camouflage words" is not credible. This is all the more so as the documents in question – *Einsatzgruppen* reports – mince no words when clearly speaking of executions and liquidations in hundreds of other cases, even with respect to Jews from the Brest Ghetto.

Regarding the mass graves of the almost 9,000 Jews from Brest allegedly killed in 1941, no cleanup activities by any *Aktion* 1005 are known, in terms of German units erasing traces of their alleged crimes by exhuming and cremating their victims. Hence, these graves should still be there. But no Soviet reports of their discovery are known either.

(See the entry on Bronnaya Gora, as well as Mattogno 2022c, pp. 742-755.)

BRITISH RADIO INTERCEPTS

In 1941, British Intelligence analysts cracked the German "Enigma" code used to encrypt radio traffic between German forces and their headquarters. This gave the British access to top-secret German data, among them for example the positions of German U-boats. This was an ingenious breakthrough which contributed considerably to Britain and the Western Allies winning World War II.

It is less-well known that these decrypts also contained a large amount of information about Germany's wartime camps, as well as the activities of various security and police forces in the East connected with the activities of the *Einsatzgruppen*.

The decrypts were kept as an enviously guarded state secret by Britain until the mid-1990s, when they were finally released to the public. Prior to this, only a few hand-picked members of the British intelligence community were allowed to view the files. One of them, British Intelligence analyst F.H. Hinsley, briefly lifted the lid in 1981 and let the public have a brief glimpse of what is contained in that secret stash of documents. He wrote in his book *British Intelligence in World War Two* (Hinsley 1981, p. 673):

> *"The return from Auschwitz, the largest of the camps with 20,000 prisoners, mentioned illness as the main cause of death, but included references to shootings and hangings. There were no references in the decrypts to gassings."*

During the International Military Tribunal, the British did not reveal that they had these intercepts, because their contents would have helped the case of the defense rather than that of the prosecution. The contents of these documents would have caused the Allies massive problems, just as much as it causes embarrassing questions for today's orthodox scholars. These intercepted radio transmissions contained communications among German top-level officials where they exchanged messages in clear language, assuming that their messages were unbreakably encrypted. These documents are the most authentic information anyone could possibly want about daily camp life under the National Socialists.

The problem is that they contain not the slightest trace of any "Final Solution" in terms of mass murder of Jews going on in those camps! Quite to the contrary, these messages confirm what we already know from the vast wartime documentation: Diseases and epidemics were the main killers in the camps, predominantly typhus, and in particular at Auschwitz. Those messages also chronicle the German authorities' desperate attempts to get those epidemics under control in order to maximize the labor output of their camp inmates.

Orthodox scholars scrambled to explain away this startling revelation. Unwilling to write history from the ground up based on the data available, as it should be done, and unwilling to rewrite their old, flawed narrative in the face of better and more reliable data, orthodox scholars decided to maintain their story line by forcing this new, round data into their square narrative holes. Their new mottos were: "The Germans used code language even in their encrypted radio messages!" and "The British Intelligence community was hoodwinked by the Germans double-encrypting their messages!"

However, if the Germans wanted to hide executions from any potential listener, then why did they neatly report all other executions in those radio messages? This even includes the shooting of thousands of Jews by the *Einsatzgruppen*. Some of these mass executions were reported to Berlin via radio, and then intercepted and deciphered by the British. Only those mass murders that are claimed to have occurred in gas chambers and gas vans are conspicuously missing.

The one final straw from the British decrypts to which the orthodoxy clings in their desperation to keep their scuttled narrative afloat is the so-called Höfle Telegram, sent to the Berlin headquarters of the SS by Hans Höfle. This radio message lists the number of Jews *arriving* at the various camps of *Aktion Reinhardt*. But on the orthodoxy's reading, "arrival" means "mass murder."

Ironically, while the British radio decrypts helped the United Kingdom win the Second World War, they help Holocaust skeptics to win the Holocaust Information War.

(For more details, see Kollerstrom 2023, pp. 104-118; Mattogno 2021, pp. 15-102; for important insights gained about the activities of the *Einsatzgruppen* through the British intercepts, see Mattogno 2022c, pp. 68f., 94, 122f., 142-144, 155f., 165, 218, 220f., 299, 303f., 309, 340, 366, 372, 374, 454, 456, 459f., 467, 567, 583, 589f., 706f., 725f.)

BROAD, PERY S.

Pery Broad

Pery Broad (25 April 1921 – 28 Nov. 1993), SS *Unterscharführer*, is one of the best-known SS witnesses who provided a detailed description of an alleged homicidal gas chamber at Auschwitz. Broad was a colleague of Wilhelm Boger at the camp's Political Department. Like Boger, Broad also penned a "confession" allegedly voluntarily written for the British, which was equally steeped in anti-fascist rhetoric parroting Allied wartime propaganda. Here an extract (Bezwinska/Czech 1984, pp. 143, 174):

> *"Auschwitz was an extermination camp! The biggest to exist in the history of the world. Two or three million Jews were murdered in the course of its existence. […]*
>
> *The first attempt* [= first gassing] *at the greatest crime which Hitler and his helpers had planned and which they committed in a frightening way, never to be expiated, was successful. The greatest tragedy could then begin, a tragedy to which succumbed millions of happy people, innocently enjoying their lives!"*

As the late French mainstream Auschwitz expert Jean-Claude Pressac put it (Pressac 1989, p. 128):

> *"But the form and tone of* [Broad's] *declaration sound false. His writings cannot be the faithful reflection of the thoughts of an SS man and indeed reading them gives the impression that they were written by a former prisoner. […] Lastly, who wrote (page 172): 'for <u>these SS monsters</u>, the spectacle of the suffering of ill-treated Jews constituted an amusing pastime!' […] P. Broad's tes-*

timony [...in] its present literary form is visibly coloured by a rather too flagrant Polish patriotism."

Although Broad never disputed that he wrote these or at least similar words, during the Frankfurt Auschwitz Show Trial, he claimed that he had merely repeated hearsay (Naumann 1965, p. 200).

Broad should have been extradited to Poland for his involvement in running the camp's Political Department, but his "confession" saved him because it secure convictions for other defendants during the Bergen-Belsen and Tesch Trials – and by extension for the German wartime leadership and nation as such. There is one tell-tale document supporting this assumption: In the documentation about the Tesch Trial, during which Broad testified as well, the following note by the British was found (Jansson 2015):

"Perry [sic] Broad has recently given much useful information. He should therefore receive as good treatment as is possible within ALTONA Prison."

Broad was neither extradited to Poland nor indicted by the British nor later by the West-German judiciary.

Broad's "report" is comprehensibly implausible, because his description of a gassing he claims to have witnessed is so rich in detail that he must have been omnipresent at all locations during the gassing, if it were a true account: on the roof of the gas chamber, in front of the closed gas-chamber door, and even inside the gas chamber during the execution. On the other hand, he insists to have experienced this only once while observing it from a considerable distance and from inside a different building. In other words: He must have invented all (or nearly all) of it (cf. Rudolf 2023b; 2023, pp. 445-457). This becomes clear when we consider his description of how the corpses were arranged in the gas chamber once the door was reopened after ventilation (Bezwinska/Czech 1984, pp. 174-177, here p. 177):

"The corpses, their mouths wide open, were leaning one upon the other. [...] It was difficult to tug the corpses from the mortuary, as their twisted limbs had grown stiff with the gas."

Corpses do not go stiff from inhaling hydrogen cyanide, and it takes hours for *rigor mortis* to set in, so anyone dying of gas poisoning in a standing position will fall or at least slump to the ground, not keep standing, no matter how tightly the people are packed.

Other implausibilities include (for more, see Graf 2019, pp. 273-281):

- The "unmistakable, penetrating stench of burnt hair," which allegedly emanated from the crematorium chimney, cannot come out of cremation furnaces.
- Broad reported flames shooting out of the crematorium chimney, which is technically impossible.
- Gassing victims of Zyklon B supposedly turned blue, although in fact they would have turned pink.
- Broad claims that the gassings were a secret, but all their circumstances make this a ludicrous claim.
- Broad mentioned six Zyklon-B insertion holes in the roof of the morgue of Crematorium I, while the orthodoxy insists on four (and revisionist research shows that there were in fact none).
- Broad claimed that 4,000 people were crammed at once into the 210-m²-sized Morgues #1 of Crematorium II and III, meaning an impossible packing density of 19 people per square meter.
- According to him, the cremation muffles could burn four to six bodies at once, even though they had been designed only for one body at a time, and the small doors would not have allowed introducing more than two bodies at once.
- He claimed that the Auschwitz Camp's records had been burned before the evacuation of the camp, when in fact some 150,000 documents were left intact, allowing us to reveal Broad's lies.
- Broad insisted that the exhumation of corpses in Auschwitz in 1942 began after the discovery of Soviet Mass Graves in Katyn, although those graves were discovered only in April 1943. His former superior Maximilian Grabner told the same lie.

This agreement on an impossible point in two independent testimonies, since it could not stem from the witnesses, demonstrates that it must have come from the interrogators who were questioning them. In other words, here, as in all the concordances and convergences that some orthodox scholars have found in independent testimonies, the information simply reflects all the commonplace facets of the propaganda "truth" about Auschwitz that were in circulation at the time.

BRODSKY, ISAAK

Isaak Brodsky was a Ukrainian Jew who claims to have been taken by German units in June 1943 to Babi Yar, a place where tens of thousands of Jews are said to have been shot and buried by the Germans in mass graves in late September 1941 (see the entry on Babi Yar). In an undated interview with the NKGB sometime in November or December 1943, he claimed that he was forced to exhume corpses from mass graves at Babi Yar and burn them on pyres. After that, the ashes were presumably sifted in search of valuables. He asserted that 70,000 bodies were burned at Babi Yar.

Brodsky's statement is very brief and devoid of any specifics, making it difficult to assess his claims. His dating is noticeably off, though, because other witnesses claim that exhumations and cremation started only in mid-August 1943, not in June.

His claim that the ashes were sifted for valuables is naïve and betrays a lie, that all the remains of a pyre had to be sifted for unburned remains. Wood-fired pyres burn unevenly and leave behind lots of unburned wood pieces, charcoal and incompletely burned body parts, not just ashes (80% of leftovers would have been from wood, not corpses). Any sieve would have clogged with the first load. Moreover, any occasional rainfall would have rendered any burned-out pyre into a moist heap of highly alkaline, corrosive slush that could not have been processed at all. If 70,000 bodies were burned, then several thousand metric tons of cremation leftovers had to be processed. Just this job would have required hundreds of men to complete in time.

Cremating an average human body during open-air incinerations requires some 250 kg of freshly cut wood. Cremating 70,000 bodies thus requires some 17,500 metric tons of wood. This would have required the felling of all trees growing in a 50-year-old spruce forest covering almost 39 hectares of land, or some 87 American football fields. An average prisoner is rated at being able to cut some 0.63 metric tons of fresh wood per workday. To cut this amount of wood within five weeks (35 days) that this operation supposedly lasted would have required a work force of some 800 dedicated lumberjacks just to cut the wood. Brodsky claims his unit consisted only of 320 inmates, all busy digging out mass graves, extracting bodies, building pyres, and according to other testimonies also sifting through ashes, scattering the ashes and refilling the graves with soil. Brodsky says nothing about where the firewood came from.

(For more details, see the entry on Babi Yar, as well as Mattogno 2022c, p. 534, and 550-563.)

BRONNAYA GORA

Bronnaya Gora is a Belorussian town located on the railway line from Brest to Minsk, some 110 km northeast of Brest. In mid-October 1942, the Brest Ghetto was evacuated and the roughly 17,000 Jews residing in it were officially resettled elsewhere according to German wartime documents. A Soviet investigative commission report, later published in the Soviet propaganda tome *The Black Book*, claimed instead that 30,000 Jews from that Brest region were taken between June and November to Bronnaya Gora, forced to strip naked, executed, and buried in mass graves 400 m northwest of the Bronnaya Gora train station.

Another Soviet report about Bronnaya Gora dated 15 September 1944 jacked up the death toll to 50,000, although the documented number of ghetto residence in October 1942 was just under 17,000. The Soviets described eight mass graves, but there is no evidence that photos were taken or any exhumations with forensic examination were made.

As a result, orthodox historians posit that the Jews from the Brest Ghetto were not resettled but rather killed at what they call the Bronnaya Gora extermination site. For instance, Israeli historian Yitzhak Arad claims that 48,000 Jews were killed at this site, and that their bodies were later exhumed and tracelessly burned during the so-called *Aktion* 1005, an operation of German units to erase the traces of their alleged atrocities. However, there is no documentation about that alleged erasure of traces either. But this claim conveniently explains why the Soviets evidently did not even try to exhume and examine the contents of any alleged mass graves.

The Brest Ghetto is only some 80 km away from the Sobibór Camp. If that camp was an extermination camp, as the orthodoxy insists, the question arises why the Jews of the Brest Ghetto weren't shipped there and process at this allegedly highly efficient death factory.

(For more details, see the entry on the Brest Ghetto, as well as Mattogno 2022c, pp. 742-755.)

BUCHENWALD

No historian has ever claimed or is currently claiming that any kind of systematic extermination of inmates by any technical means occurred at the Buchenwald Camp. Therefore, this camp would not have a place in an encyclopedia on the Holocaust, if it weren't for some witnesses having made claims to the contrary, and if the U.S. forces who occupied the camp at the end of the war had not abused this camp as a staging ground for their atrocity propaganda.

Among the witnesses who falsely claimed to have seen people being killed in gas chambers at Buchenwald, we find the French priest Jean-Paul Renard, who retracted it as soon as he was confronted about it. The French priest Georges Hénocque claimed to have closely inspected the Buchenwald gas chamber. Other witnesses reported from hearsay, so they will not be cited here.

After U.S. troops entered the Buchenwald Camp, Eisenhower's Psychological Warfare Division, tasked with recording material suited to reeducate the German population, set up a table inside the camp filled with various objects allegedly made of murdered inmates: soap, a table lamp, two shrunken heads, tattooed skin etc. Images of these objects are used for "educational" purposes to this day. All of these objects have since disappeared, and have never been subjected to forensic scrutiny as to their origin. (See Irebodd 2009, and the entry on lampshades, of human skin, for more details; see also Weber 1986.)

BUCHHOLCOWA, JANINA

Janina Buchholcowa was a Polish Jewess who signed a deposition sometime in 1945, where she asserted to have been deported to the Treblinka Camp. She claimed that, at the beginning of the camp's existence (at the end of July 1942), the gas chambers were not yet ready. Therefore, arriving deportees were killed with machine-gun fire right on the railway platform, as they climbed out of the train. This would have damaged the railway cars and threatened any SS guards as well, so it certainly did not happen.

She claimed an average daily "production" of some 12,000 corpses, with peak values up to 20,000 victims. Over the stretch of the camp's one-year existence, this would result in more than four million victims, which is one of the highest figures ever claimed about Treblinka. The orthodoxy currently has a death toll of just about 800,000.

The killing method presumably consisted in first "pumping out the air," and then "injecting into the chambers exhaust gas from a motor," and she asserted that "toxic 'cyklon' gas was also used instead." She clearly tried to cover all the bases with her deposition. (For a few more details, see Mattogno 2021e, pp. 146f.)

BUDNIK, DAVID

David Budnik was a Ukrainian Jew interned in the Syretsky Camp, 5 km from Kiev. On 18 August 1943, he was taken from there to Babi Yar, a place where tens of thousands of Jews are said to have been shot and buried by the Germans in mass graves in late September 1941 (see the entry on Babi Yar). He evidently was interviewed about his alleged experiences for the first time more than 20 years after the event on 14 February 1967. In 1980, during another interrogation in the Soviet Union – although not by court officials, yet by the KGB – Budnik repeated his terse description from 13 years earlier.

Among other things, Budnik stated that he and other slave-labor inmates were put in chains and had to exhume mass graves, and burn the extracted bodies on pyres. During his interrogations, he did not give any specifics about the pyres, other than that up to 2,000 bodies were placed on each of them. He asserted, however, that a total of 120,000 to 125,000 bodies were burned this way.

In a 1993 book containing an essay by Budnik, he describes the pyres used. They were built on an area of 10 m × 10 m, and were at least three meters high. However, this description was at least partially plagiarized from another witness, Ziama Trubakov, who testified in 1967:

"Tombstones and iron fences were brought from the Jewish cemetery, and then an area 10 x 10 m was planned, where they were laid in checker board pattern so that they formed an ash pan;"

In Budnik's 1993 essay, we read:

"These tombstones were laid on the site 10 meters across by 10 meters in width, like a chessboard. Rails and fences were laid on top of them."

On the pyre described by Budnik, some 20 bodies would have been placed per square meter. With some 250 kg of freshly cut word needed to burn one body, this would have amounted to 5 metric tons of wood. Fresh wood has a density of roughly 0.9 tons per m^3, and when stacked on a pyre, the gaps make up some 40% of the space (for air and flames to go through). Therefore, 5 metric tons of wood on a surface of one square meter stack up to a height of some 8 meters. Add to this the 20 to 25 bodies. This means that the pyres described by Budnik would have been at least ten meters high, not just "at least three meters." Such a huge pyre could have been built only with cranes. Once lit, it inevitably would have burned unevenly, hence would have toppled over and spilled burning wood and corpses all over the place.

Cremating an average human body during open-air incinerations requires some 250 kg of freshly cut wood. Cremating 120,000 bodies thus requires some 30,000 metric tons of wood. This would have required the felling of all trees growing in a 50-year-old spruce forest covering almost 67 hectares of land, or some 149 American football fields. An average prisoner is rated at being able to cut some 0.63 metric tons of fresh wood per workday. To cut this amount of wood within five weeks (35 days) that this operation supposedly lasted would have required a work force of some 1,360 dedicated lumberjacks just to cut the wood. Budnik didn't specify how many men were in his unit. The maximum number claimed by other witnesses was just over 300 men, all busy digging out mass graves, extracting bodies, building pyres, crushing bones, sifting through ashes, scattering the ashes and refilling the graves with soil. Budnik says nothing about where the firewood came from.

Budnik claimed that, after the pyres had burned down, unburned bones were ground down, the cremation remains sifted through sieves, and the powder scattered. However, wood-fired pyres burn unevenly and leave behind lots of unburned wood pieces, charcoal, and incompletely burned body parts, not just ashes and bones (80% of leftovers would have been from wood, not corpses). Incompletely burned wood and human remains could not have been ground. Any sieve would have clogged with the first load. Moreover, any occasional rainfall would have rendered any burned-out pyre into a moist heap of highly alkaline, corrosive slush that could not have been processed at all. If 120,000 bodies were burned, then several thousand metric tons of cremation leftovers had to be processed. Just this job would have required hundreds of men to complete in time.

Budnik also insisted that they had to throw bodies of people into the pyres who had been killed in gas vans. However, considering that the front was getting very close to Kiev during September 1943, it is unlikely that anyone would have operated gas vans in Kiev's vicinity. All this apart from the fact that gas vans are a figment of Soviet atrocity propaganda (see the entry on gas vans).

(For more details, see the entry on Babi Yar, as well as Mattogno 2022c, pp. 539f., and 550-563.)

BUKI, MILTON

Milton Buki (or Michal Majlech) was a former Auschwitz inmate. He signed two English-language depositions on 4 and 7 January 1945 while in Linz, Austria. In the first deposition, which is geared toward framing SS man Josef Erber, he did not mention any homicidal gassings. His second statement is geared toward framing Gestapo man Maximilian Grabner as one of the persons supervising homicidal gassings at Auschwitz. In it, he claimed to have been a member of the inmate unit dragging corpses out of the gas chamber (the so-called *Sonderkommando*, although Buki doesn't mention this term) from his arrival at Birkenau in 1942 until late 1944, when gassings presumably stopped. In this affidavit, Buki only mentions "the crematorium" in the context of alleged gassings, evidently ignorant of the fact that there were four of them, and that gassings in 1942 supposedly happened in separate facilities today referred to as "bunkers."

Milton Buki

Twenty years later, he testified during the Frankfurt Auschwitz show trial. While he knew nothing about any gassing facilities in little farmhouses (the bunkers) back in 1945, in 1965 he reported about his work at "little whitewashed" farmhouses, allegedly used for gassings before the crematoria were built. He gave a very terse description of a "little whitewashed" farmhouse and of a gassing taking place in it.

Some 15 years later still, on 15 December 1980, he signed a notarized statement, also not very long, but with a few more details. His statements contain a number of false claims and contradictions, revealing it all as mere fantasy:

– The only Auschwitz physician Buki mentioned by name who allegedly gave the order to pour Zyklon B into homicidal gas chambers is the ineluctable Dr. Josef Mengele.
– Zyklon B was inserted through a small chimney, to which one had to climb on a ladder, while the orthodoxy insists on a small wall opening, easily within reach and closed with a shutter. In his Frankfurt testimony, he had claimed that the gas was introduced through a window.
– Death occurred either within 6 to 8 minutes (his 1945 statement) or within some twenty minutes (his 1980 statement).
– Corpses in the gas chamber remained standing after their death – impossible.

– The room was only aired out between 20 to 30 minutes before Buki and his fellow inmates had to drag out the corpses – which would have led to their poisoning, as it would have taken at least a day to air out a facility devoid of any ventilation system and windows.
– The corpses are said to have had blue stains on their bodies, while hydrogen-cyanide poisoning leads to pink marks.

(For more details, see Mattogno 2016f, pp. 119-123.)

BULGARIA

Although Bulgaria was Allied with wartime Germany, no Jews were deported from that country or murdered there. Since Bulgaria was known as a relatively safe haven, several thousand Jews actually sought and found refuge there. (See the entry on Jewish demography for a broader perspective.)

BUNA

BUNA is an acronym formed from the two words BUtadiene and NAtrium (for sodium), denoting a method of polymerizing the chemical butadiene with the catalytic assistance of sodium to form artificial rubber. It was one of the methods used in wartime Germany to alleviate the rubber shortage due to the Allies' blockade of continental Europe. A new factory slated to produce artificial rubber, among other chemicals, was in the process of being erected near the town of Monowitz close to Auschwitz. The location was favorable due to its proximity both to the rich Upper-Silesian coal reserves and to the rivers Sola and Vistula, which could provide large amounts of process water. The plant was operated by the I.G. Farbenindustrie Trust, but due to labor shortage – induced not the least due to the raging typhus epidemics at the Auschwitz Camp – and general disruptions due to Allied bombardments, the plant never reached the state of producing any butadiene, let alone artificial rubber. Still, the Monowitz chemical factory is sometimes referred to as the BUNA works or factory (Rudolf 2020, pp. 57-62).

BUNKERS

Terms

Similar to the English term bunker, the German term *Bunker* can refer to three things:
1. A shelter facility protecting from projectiles, bombs, shrapnel or noxious gases in times of armed conflicts.
2. Bulk-item storage facilities, such as potatoes, coal or coke. The German language even has a verb for this: *einbunkern*, to store in bulk.
3. Facilities to incarcerate offenders, similar to a prison.

Within the context of the Holocaust, the term "bunker" plays a major role in the orthodoxy's narrative on mass gassings at the Auschwitz Camp.

All three uses of the term as listed above are documented in the archival material about the former Auschwitz Camp. The camp had a potato bunker; a former ammunition-storage bunker turned into a crematorium (Crematorium I of the Main Camp); many air-raid shelters referred to as bunkers; and finally, the Auschwitz Main Camp had a detention facility in the basement of its Block 11, often referred to as the "bunker," in which inmates who had committed some violation of the law or camp rules were locked up.

No documents exist on Auschwitz which refer to any mass gassings, hence no documents exist linking any facility called "bunker" to mass gassings either.

Left: May 2019 photo of a recently erected memorial constructed at an arbitrary location near the former Birkenau Camp marking the alleged location of "Bunker 1." No documental or material trace exists for this alleged building, and witness claims as to its location are contradictory. Right: 1992 photo of the ruins of a building west of the Zentralsauna, alleged to have been "Bunker 2."

That link was first made in late 1941 by propaganda reports sent by the Polish underground to London. These reports claimed that Soviet PoWs and Polish inmates had been gassed in early September 1941 in the basement detention cells of Block 11 at Auschwitz. This was the birth of the myth of the so-called "first gassing" at the Auschwitz Camp. (For more on this, see the entry dedicated to this event.) However, this is said to have been a singular event, and this detention bunker is not normally referred to when the "bunkers" of Auschwitz are mentioned. This term refers to two Polish farmhouses just outside the perimeter of the Birkenau Camp. All Polish civilian buildings in the area of that camp and its vicinity had been expropriated by the SS. Two of these buildings are said to have been converted to mass-gassing facilities.

Propaganda History

As two Zyklon-B delousing facilities were built at the Birkenau Camp in 1942, Polish underground reports started spreading the rumor that homicidal gassing facilities had been set up at Birkenau. In some reports, their description suspiciously resembled that of the new delousing facilities. In other reports, the mass-murder facilities were instead set up in a few cottages. This was possibly inspired by a delousing facility for the SS guards that had been set up in an old Polish building outside the camp. The term "bunker," however, was never used in any wartime report or testimony. Moreover, the various reports and testimonies were too disparate to make sense of them.

This changed only when the Soviets occupied the Auschwitz Camp and started interrogating former inmates. One of them – Szlama Dragon – proved particularly cooperative. In a statement of late February 1945, he gave very detailed descriptions of two alleged gassing facilities outside the Birkenau Camp. However, it took a second interrogation in May of that year, this time by Polish investigative judge Jan Sehn, to plant the term "bunker" for these alleged facilities into Dragon's mind. Thus, "Bunker 1" and "Bunker 2" were finally born.

Mainly based on Dragon's version, the story of the "bunkers" of Birkenau entered the orthodox narrative, and solidified in a story that was mainly shaped by Polish historian Danuta Czech in her *Auschwitz Chronicle*. She forced a "convergence of evidence" by cherry-picking from a range of contradictory witness statements those features that fit her preconceived notion, invented some data where none was available, while discarding everything that refuted her storyline or revealed her evidence as unreliable.

Dragon's two testimonies are partially contradictory, stand in contrast to other witness statements about these claimed facilities, have physically impossible and even absurd aspects, and are in conflict with extant physical evidence. (For more details on his testimony, see the entry on Szlama Dragon.)

Current Orthodox Narrative

The current orthodox narrative regarding the two bunkers of Birkenau is summarized and scrutinized in the entry on the Auschwitz Main Camp, section "Current Orthodox Narrative," Points 4, 5 and 11. The bunkers retain importance for the orthodox narrative because they were the alleged site of up to 230,000 gassing fatalities (60,000 total at Bunker 1, and 170,000 total at Bunker 2). And indeed, for the initial year of 1942, the two bunkers combined allegedly gassed some 140,000 Jews – far more than in Crematorium I (20,000). In fact, both bunkers individually allegedly gassed overall more people than either Crematorium I (20,000), Crematorium IV (30,000) or Crematorium V (50,000), a remarkable fact.

In reality, however, we have no reliable evidence that "Bunker 1" ever existed, while a building did exists where "Bunker 2" is said to have been, but its characteristics disprove all witness testimonies.

For other witnesses on the alleged bunkers and an assessment of their testimonies, see the section "Auschwitz" in the entry on witnesses, since most witnesses testifying about Auschwitz also had something to say about these alleged bunkers.

(For more details on the "Bunkers of Auschwitz," see Mattogno 2016f; 2021, pp. 119-217.)

BURMEISTER, WALTER

Walter Burmeister (14 Nov. 1894 – 23 Feb. 1980), SS *Oberscharführer*, is said to have served as a driver of one of the gas vans at the Chełmno Camp. Interrogated by Investigating Judge Władysław Bednarz after the war in Poland, he describes the vans as they appear in the extant authentic correspondence between Germany's Department of Homeland Security (*Reichssicherheitshauptamt*) and the Gaubschat Company, yet adding that exhaust gas was fed into the cargo box through a pipe, perforated with holes, which routed into a "metal spiral hose." Burmeister insisted that the vehicles he drove were "medium-weight Renault trucks with gasoline engine." However, there is no trace of any Renault truck ever used as a gas van, nor of the fanciful piping system, which Burmeister evidently made up when put under pressure by his Polish investigators to come up with something.

During an interrogation some 15 years later in Germany in preparation for the West-German Chełmno Show Trial at Bonn, Burmeister had learned enough about the orthodox narrative to adjust it to what was expected of him, no longer claiming a Renault, and simply feeding the gas into the cargo box through a hole in the floor via a flexible metal hose. Hence, Burmeister's knowledge had been "streamlined" over the years to fit the orthodox "truth." Despite his cooperation, he was sentenced to 13 years imprisonment for aiding in the murder of at least 130,000 people, hence, not even 53 minutes jail time for each life taken.

(For more details, see Alvarez 2023, pp. 149-151.)

CAMPS

In the context of the Jewish Holocaust of World War II, the camps of interest are those for which claims of mass extermination have been made. Although an argument could be made that the Soviet prisoners held in PoW camps in the temporarily German-occupied Soviet Union were subject to conditions that led to millions of them dying during the winter of 1941/42, this was not planned and premeditated mass murder. Had the Germans had enough transport capacity, temporary lodgings, clothing and food at their disposal during that winter in the East, one can expect that many if not most of these prisoners would have survived. However, this chapter of World War II, as tragic as it was, is not part of the *Jewish* Holocaust, so it will not be dealt with here, nor will any other PoW camp.

While there were many other categories of camps in German-controlled areas of World War II – voluntary labor camps, forced-labor camps, concentration camps – the orthodoxy, as a rule, does not claim any kind of systematic extermination at them. Therefore, these camps are not listed or discussed in this encyclopedia.

A condition for being included in this encyclopedia is a claim by either government authorities, historians, alleged perpetrators or witnesses that some kind of systematic extermination policy of Jews was implemented in a camp.

The orthodoxy splits camps in which systematic mass murder of Jews (as part of an alleged extermination policy) took place, into three groups of extermination camps:

1. Pure extermination camps, whose only purpose was to kill inmates deported there.
2. Mixed extermination and concentration/forced-labor camps.
3. Auxiliary extermination camps, which were mainly concentration or forced-labor camps, where exterminations took place only as an exception and on a relatively small scale.

There is a fourth category, however, which includes concentration or forced-labor camps for which the orthodoxy accepts that no extermination took place, but where some witnesses disagree. These camps we call:

4. Fraudulent or phantom extermination camps, because extermination claims about them are generally accepted to be either erroneous or fraudulent.

Holocaust skeptics contend that *all* extermination camps belong to the latter category, as a detailed analysis of claims about them demonstrates. For more details and a list of all four categories of extermination camps, see the entry on extermination camps.

CARBON MONOXIDE

Carbon monoxide (CO) is a colorless and odorless gas which is highly toxic to vertebrate animals, but not to non-vertebrates such as insects. CO clings more strongly than oxygen to the hemoglobin of vertebra blood, hence preventing oxygen transportation by the blood. Since the combination of CO and hemoglobin is more intensely red than the normal combination of oxygen with hemoglobin, and because CO is not consumed, and hence keeps accumulating, victims of CO poisoning are intensely pink; see the illustration.

For the average person, a CO concentration in air of some 0.4% becomes lethal within less than an hour (see the below table with more data). Healthy individuals with good cardio-vascular fitness can survive twice as long.

Toxic Effects of Carbon Monoxide (CO) (Henderson/Haggard, p. 168)	
CO in %/vol.	Physiological Effects
(0.01)	Permissible concentration for an exposure of several hours
(0.04 – 0.05)	Inhalation for up to 1 hour without appreciable effect
(0.06 – 0.07)	Appreciable effect after exposure of 1 hour
(0.10 – 0.12)	Indisposition but no dangerous effects after exposure of 1 hour
(0.15 – 0.2)	Dangerous concentrations for exposure of 1 hour
(0.4 and more)	Fatal in exposure of less than 1 hour

CO develops, for instance, during the combustion of carbon-containing fuels, if there is a lack of oxygen, preventing the complete combustion (transformation) of carbon into carbon dioxide (CO_2).

Pure CO in pressurized steel bottles is commercially available, and is said to have been used during the Third Reich's euthanasia killings. Because such bottles were allegedly too difficult to transport – although they were in fact more-easily transportable than any other device to produce this gas – it was allegedly decided to use other sources of CO for poison-gas murders; see the table:

CO sources of claimed extermination devices or locations	
CO Source	Device/Location
gasoline-engine exhaust, bottled CO	gas vans, Chełmno Camp
diesel-engine exhaust	gas vans, Einsatzgruppen
bottled CO*	Majdanek Camp
Diesel-engine exhaust	Bełżec Camp
(gasoline-)engine exhaust	Sobibór Camp
Diesel-engine exhaust	Treblinka Camp

* The steel bottles found at Majdanek contained carbon **di**oxide, which is not toxic!

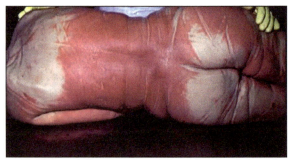

Pinkish-red discoloration of the skin of a victim of CO poisoning (Rudolf 2020, p. 229).

None of these claims are defensible; see the individual entries for more details. The following table gives an overview of existing CO sources in German-controlled areas during World War II, how easily they could have been made available, and what their possible CO-content was, meaning how lethal they were, if at all (cf. Rudolf 2019, esp. pp. 440-443).

Looking at this table, any potential mass murderer with technical knowledge common among specialists in wartime Germany would surely have made the correct and obvious choices:

– When choosing Auschwitz as an extermination center, erect facilities near the BUNA coal-liquification plant near Monowitz. The SS already had a forced-labor camp there. A small process-gas pipe from the factory to certain camp facilities could have been laid very easily.

– For any other location, the generator-gas technology was the obvious choice.
– Diesel engines are a bad choice, as they produce sufficient CO only when driven under heavy or full load. And even then, many fit and healthy victims will survive an exposure of half an hour or more, which was the alleged maximum gassing time.

A suicide inside a gasoline car carried out in the 1970s in the U.S. by a healthy 36-year-old man, who recorded his breathing noises, showed that it takes some 20 minutes for a healthy person to die in such a scenario. This gives a rough idea of the time required to kill with gasoline-engine exhaust gases piped into the interior of a vehicle. (See Rudolf 2023, pp. 265f.; Mattogno/Kues/Graf 2015, pp. 856-868.)

CENSORSHIP
Corporate Censorship

As long as plenty of companies compete with each other offering similar services, chances are high that

Availability and lethality of various CO sources			
CO Source	Availability	CO Content	Lethality
bottled CO	Commercially available, high price, easy to transport.	100%	extremely high
process gas	In large quantities available only near coal-liquefaction plants, such as at Auschwitz-Monowitz; requires gas-pipe hook-up.	30-100%	extremely to very high
city gas	Readily available in larger cities with coke processing; cheap, abundant, and with access to a large-scale infrastructure for adding and maintaining pipe networks.	±30%	very high
producer gas	From cheap fuel abundantly available (coke, coal, wood), generated in affordable producer-gas generator mounted mostly on commercial vehicles (vans, trucks, buses) and manufactured by the tens of thousands.	15-30%	very high
gasoline-engine exhaust	Readily available by the millions, although with fuel shortage.	1-7%	high
diesel-engine exhaust	Readily available by the hundreds of thousands, although with fuel shortage.	0.0 to 0.4%	Non-lethal within an hour under stationary conditions

someone will offer these services – even to individuals or groups whose views are rejected by many if not most in a society. However, the situation changes as shares in a certain market get more and more concentrated in the hands of a few players. If one player is absolutely dominant in a market or even has a total monopoly, censorship by that company – meaning refusal to offer services – can result in a censorship more effective than is even possible by governments with oppressive laws.

The following are some areas in which Holocaust skeptics face corporate censorship – in many cases severe enough to force them out of business:
– *Book printing*: large print-on-demand outlets, such as Ingram Spark/Lightning Source (Ingram Content Group), Lulu and CreateSpace (Amazon), have all banned material contesting the orthodox Holocaust narrative. Smaller print outlets drop Holocaust-skeptical works suddenly once "made aware" or put under pressure by leftist and/or Jewish lobby groups.
– *Media sales*: Amazon dominates the market of media sales in books, eBooks and audio books. In early 2017, after massive pressure primarily from Jewish groups, Amazon banned material contesting the orthodox Holocaust narrative, and so did Barnes & Nobles. Amazon's subsidiaries AbeBooks and The Book Depository followed a year later. Other major book sellers (like Walmart and Target) have done the same over the years.
– *Book distribution*: In the United States, book distribution is a monopoly by the Ingram Content Group. In early 2022, this firm banned all material contesting the orthodox Holocaust narrative. As a consequence, all books with skeptical contents disappeared from the U.S. book market *everywhere*, offline and online, except for small outlets buying directly from the publishers of such books.
– *Advertisement*: the entire mainstream media market is inaccessible to Holocaust skeptics worldwide. While ad campaigns could still be launched in the 1990s, massive Jewish lobby campaigns have since resulted in the implementation of zero-tolerance policies in most mainstream media for ads on skeptical material.
– *Social media*: YouTube banned material contesting the orthodox Holocaust narrative in the summer of 2019. Vimeo followed this example a year later. This cuts out the vast majority of the entire worldwide audience for streaming content video. Other mainstream social media, such as Twitter and Facebook, have increased their censorship behavior in this regard over the years as well.
– *Credit-card processing*: gateway providers, meaning the companies who connect a vendor's credit-card reading equipment of sales websites to banks, have systematically introduced zero-tolerance policies for content challenging the orthodox Holocaust narrative. There are today only a few tolerant providers left.
– *Banking*: PayPal, Wise, Square and other major players in the field of internet banks have all banned companies selling material contesting the orthodox Holocaust narrative. If caught violating this term, accounts are closed and responsible individuals banned for life. Brick-and mortar banks, particularly in Europe but also some in the U.S., even in countries where Holocaust skepticism is not a crime, frequently close bank accounts of Holocaust skeptics and companies selling such merchandise, refusing to do business with them.

(For more details, see Rudolf 2023a.)

Government Censorship
Government Contracts

Although the First Amendment of the U.S. Constitution prevents Congress from passing laws restricting free speech, laws exist on all levels of government that prohibit government agents or agencies from doing business with individuals or companies involved in spreading views contesting the orthodox Holocaust narrative – which is automatically considered to be "anti-Semitic" and thus discriminatory in nature.

Government Reaction to a Holocaust Skeptic's Book.

Executing the culprit of a thought crime.

Penal Law

The most barbaric form of censorship is via enacting laws which allow governments to incarcerate individuals for voicing peaceful dissent on any topic. In the present context, "peaceful" means an opinion that does not advocate, justify, promote or even condone the violation of anyone's civil rights.

In the wake of a rising number of skeptical voices on the mainstream narrative starting in the mid- to late 1970s, an increasing number of governments, particularly in Europe, have introduced new sections, or amended and reinterpreted older ones, enabling them to fine and incarcerate Holocaust skeptics. The first country to make this formal step from liberty to dictatorship was Israel in 1986. Here is a chronological list of countries that have followed this horrible example since then:

Year	Country	Max. Term
1986	Israel	5 years
1990	France	1 year
1992	Austria	20 years
1994	Germany	5 years
1995	Belgium	1 year
1995	Netherlands (conditional)	1 year
1995	Liechtenstein	2 years
1995	Switzerland	3 years
1997	Luxembourg	6 months
1997	Slovenia (conditional)	2 years
1998	Poland	3 years
2001	Slovakia	3 years
2001	Czechia	3 years
2002	Romania	5 years
2002	Australia (HRC)*	–
2007	European Union (recommendation)	3 years
2007	Portugal (conditional)	5 years
2010	Hungary	3 years
2011	Bulgaria	5 years
2012	Lithuania	2 years
2014	Russia	3 years
2014	Greece (conditional)	3 years
2016	Italy	6 years
2017	UK (conditional)	2 years
2021	Ukraine	5 years
2021	Bosnia	5 years
2022	Canada	2 years

conditional: only in conjunction with verbal abuses and/or threats.
* A Human Rights Commission can issue a cease-and-desist order. If ignored, it can lead to prosecution for ignoring a government order.

Holocaust skepticism is covered by the First Amendment to the U.S. Constitution. The Spanish Constitutional Court decided in 2007 that Holocaust skepticism is legal in Spain, while justifying acts of genocide is not.

CHAMAIDES, HEINRICH

Heinrich Chamaides was a Jew who claims to have been forced by German units in 1943 to exhume mass graves near the city of Lviv, and to burn the extracted bodies on pyres within the context of what today's orthodoxy calls *Aktion* 1005.

In a statement of 21 September 1944 to Soviet investigators, Chamaides claimed that some 120,000 bodies had been exhumed and burned by him and his unit, which is a figure assumed by the orthodoxy as correct.

Chamaides claimed that the pyres he built were 4 to 5 meters high, which is probably an exaggeration, as proper pyres for open-air incinerations are usually only up to 2 m high. Building and maintaining the burning of anything bigger is too challenging and impractical: Did the inmates have a crane to get bodies and wood onto layers more than 2 meters off the ground? And how did they prevent this huge pile, which inevitably burned unevenly, from toppling over, spilling embers, burning wood and partially burned body parts all over the place?

Chamaides moreover claimed that all bones were ground by a special mill. However, this alleged mill later turned out to have been a road-building device to crush gravel. Since most inmates from the Janowska Camp were deployed in building roads, this is what this machine was used for. A photo taken by a Soviet investigative commission shows Chamaides with two more witnesses (Moische Korn and David Manusevich) standing next to the claimed machine. This shows that at least these three witnesses knew each other and collaborated as a group with the Soviet commission, meaning that their testimonies were probably harmonized and orchestrated to some degree. (See the entry on bone mill.)

Furthermore, wood-fired pyres burn unevenly and leave behind lots of unburned wood pieces, charcoal, and incompletely burned body parts, not just ashes (80% of leftovers would have been from wood, not corpses). Those remains could not have been crushed or ground down in mills. If 120,000 bodies were processed, then several thousand metric tons of cremation leftovers had to be processed.

Cremating an average human body during open-air incinerations requires some 250 kg of freshly cut wood. Cremating 120,000 bodies thus requires some 30,000 metric tons of wood. This would have required the felling of all trees growing in a 50-year-old spruce forest covering almost 67 hectares of land, or some 149 American football fields. An average prisoner is rated at being able to cut some 0.63 metric tons of fresh wood per workday. To cut this amount of wood within the six month (160 days) that this operation supposedly lasted would have required a work force of some 300 dedicated lumberjacks just to cut the wood. Chamaides claims his unit consisted only of 126 inmates, all busy digging out mass graves, extracting bodies, building pyres, sifting through ashes, scattering the ashes, refilling the graves with soil, and planting them with grass seeds and saplings. He says nothing about where the firewood came from.

While there are a few numerical and temporal discrepancies between this account and the one by Leon Weliczker, the main witness on these alleged events, the more revealing aspect of Chamaides's is the following crude atrocity propaganda:

"As an eyewitness, I experienced how a violent German criminal, whose name I do not know, shattered an eight-year old boy and threw him into a fire. Several one- and two-year old children were thrown into the fire alive. The criminals gave the victims a glass filled with water to hold, and conducted their target practice by shooting at the glass: If they hit the glass, the victim was allowed to live. If they hit the victim's hand or arm, however, they went up to him, told him he was unfit for work, and as a result would have to be shot, after which they shot him right there on the spot. Small children were thrown into the air and shot while falling."

(For more details on Heinrich Chamaides, see Mattogno 2022c, pp. 513-515.)

CHASAN, SHAUL

Shaul Chasan was one of several Greek Jews deported to Auschwitz in April 1944 who all claim to have worked at Bunker 2 in Auschwitz-Birkenau, dragging gassing victims from the gas chamber(s) to the cremation pit(s). There are many issues with his testimony:

Shaul Chasan

- While orthodoxy maintains that Bunker 2 had four chambers of various sizes with one entry and one exit door each, and had several cremation pits nearby, Chasan mentions only one chamber and one door, with only one pit nearby.
- When a huge pyre with hundreds of corpses was already burning, he insists that inmates kept throwing in more corpses, although such a conflagration could not have been approached without getting severely burned.
- The pit was supposedly "about four meters deep," which would have quickly filled with water, preventing any fire to ever get ignited, considering that the groundwater level in that area was usually not much more than a meter beneath the surface – and during the rainy season of May and June even closer than that.
- Chasan insists that the pyre "burned day and night," although that was a violation of strict black-out order to protect from air raids. Furthermore, the air photos of that time prove that no large-scale pyres existed in the area where Bunker 2 is said to have been.
- Twice Chasan claimed to have observed that trucks backed up to the pit and dumped a load of old people straight into the pit to be burned alive. If the fire was blazing at that time, the truck would have caught fire. If it wasn't ablaze, then the people dumped into the pit wouldn't have burned. Either way, his tale is evident nonsense.
- According to Chasan, the gas-chamber door in Crematorium III was a "heavy door made of iron," but all gastight doors and other doors ever made and installed at Auschwitz were made of wood.
- He claimed that the gas chamber of Crematorium III could accommodate 2,500 people, hence a

packing density of 12 people per square meter, which is ludicrous.
– Chasan's description of the Zyklon-B introduction columns contradicts the orthodoxy's version, which insists that these columns went all the way to the floor, and that the pellets were retrievably lowered into that column in some container. Chasan insisted, however, that he knew it better:

> "*A latticework shaft came down from each opening.* […] *And the gas, in the form of little pellets, was thrown down the hollow shaft.* […] *A small space was left* [between the shaft and the floor] *so that you could clean there. We poured water on the floor and swept up what remained of the pellets. We always poured water there* […]*.*"

– After the gassing, instead of ventilating the gas before opening the door, he insists that the door was opened right away, and only then was the ventilation started. This was so dangerous, Chasan insists, that "we had to run for our lives."
– He claims that the dead gassing victim were "standing like statues," which is physically impossible.
– He insists that they used fat corpses to burn skinny ones, and that "every two or three days, we removed the bones from the furnaces," when in fact coke was used to burn corpses, not the body fat of well-nourished inmates. Furthermore, bones burn to ashes in cremation furnaces, so no one ever had to remove them, and the ashes of a cremation were removed after every single cremation.

This is only the tip of the iceberg of Chasan's fairy tales. (For more details, see Mattogno 2021, pp. 56-73.)

CHEŁMNO
Documented History
Only a few documents about the Chełmno Camp itself seem to have survived the war. The most important of them, dated 11 May 1943, refers to the earlier delivery of iron material to the Chełmno Special Unit. This delivery included a "water reservoir," "iron boiler pipes" with a total weight of 1,600 kg, as well as a disinfection oven weighing just over two metric tons. These items clearly prove that some major sanitary and disinfestation facilities were set up at some earlier point in that camp, probably to shower and disinfest Jews passing through (see Mattogno/Kues/Graf 2015, p. 877). Another document is an invoice for a used 18-HP stationary diesel engine, probably meant to drive an electricity generator (*ibid.*, p. 750; Mattogno 2017, pp. 45, 156).

Although the orthodoxy insists that the camp was opened on 8 December 1941, this is not even supported by witness testimony. The purpose of the camp alleged by the orthodoxy – extermination of all Jews deported to it, with the temporary exception of a few slave-labor Jews – is not documented either. It furthermore stands in stark contrast to the well-documented German policy to deport and resettle the Jews further East into the temporarily German-occupied western areas of the Soviet Union. (For more on this, see the entry on resettlement, as well as Mattogno 2017, pp. 23-31)

A document with an indirect reference to the Chełmno Camp is the so-called Korherr Report of early 1943 by SS statistician Richard Korherr. This document outlines the demographic trends of Jews in German-occupied Europe (NMT Documents NO-5193 to 5198). In it, we find one line about Jews "led through [*durchgeschleust*] the camps of the Warthegau……145,301." Since Chełmno was the only camp in that "Warthegau" area, this can be interpreted as indicating that 145,301 Jews had been *transited* through that camp by early 1943. (For more on this, see Mattogno 2017, p. 109; Graf/Kues/Mattogno 2020, pp. 311-330, esp. p. 315)

This is backed up by several German railway documents and also documents created by Jewish organizations in affected ghettos, showing that Jews – mostly those unfit for labor – were indeed deported throughout 1942 by rail. In these documents, these Jews are referred to as having been "resettled" ("*ausgesiedelt*"). Some documents indicate that the train went to Koło, the closest railway station to the Chełmno Camp (see Mattogno 2017, pp. 114-116)

A "document" which mentions Chełmno as a place where gas vans were allegedly deployed as a mass-murder weapon is the so-called Just Document, but this is clearly a forgery. (See the entry on the Gaubschat Company for more.)

Propaganda History
A report dated 25 March 1942 from the clandestine archive of the Warsaw Ghetto (also known as the Emmanuel Ringelblum Archive) claims that Jews from the areas around Chełmno were concentrated. Men aged 14 to 60 and women aged 14 to 50 were subject to a medical examination, evidently to ascertain fitness for work, after which they were trans-

ferred to an unknown location and not seen anymore. It contains no mass-murder or gas-van claims.

Another document, presumably of 1942, stems from an unknown author commonly referred to as "Szlamek," who supposedly escaped from Chełmno in late January 1942. Some orthodox scholars claim that the author was a man named Jakov Grojanowski, but others disagree. Whoever that person was, he wrote down his memories (or had them written down) after getting to Emmanuel Ringelblum in the Warsaw Ghetto. The text is structured like a diary, spanning some ten days in January 1942, is rich in detail, and even gives the exact time of events, although Chełmno inmates supposedly had to hand over all valuables on admission, including watches. It reports in detail about mass murder with gas vans, describes the two vehicles allegedly used, and reports about the work at the claimed mass graves. It stands to reason that this text was written after the one of 25 March, because the latter certainly would have included concrete information about mass murder, gas vans and mass graves, had that information been known to the Warsaw Ghetto underground.

The gassing vehicle supposedly operated as follows:
– A gas-developing apparatus was located in the driver's cab. However, the orthodoxy insists that the gas-developing apparatus was the truck's engine, which would have been located *beneath* the cab, with no access to it from the cab.
– The gas was piped directly from the driver's cab into the cargo box with two pipes. However, the orthodoxy insists that the engine's single exhaust pipe was connected to the cargo box, but certainly not by letting it run through the driver's cab and from there, routed into the cargo box.
– The gas was "switched on" by pushing a button in the driver's cab. However, the orthodoxy insists that the engine-exhaust was redirected into the cargo box by some mechanism located *outside* the vehicle, letting the exhaust gas flow either out into the open or through some metal-hose-connection into the cargo box.
– The victims supposedly looked normal, as if put to sleep. However, asphyxiation by carbon-monoxide poisoning would have resulted in corpses that would have had a very striking, distinctive pinkish-reddish complexion, something no real witness could have missed or forgotten.
– Initially there were two gas vans, but then, their number was increased to nine. However, the orthodoxy insists that there were only two or three such vans at Chełmno.
– The temperature in January was well below the freezing point. In fact, the diary mentions that it went as low as 20 degrees centigrade below zero (zero Fahrenheit). At the same time, it is claimed that inmates dug several deep pits with hoes and spades. However, the deeply frozen ground would have prevented any such endeavor.
– The rotting corpses in the grave allegedly gave off a strong smell. But at freezing temperatures, they certainly did not.

Hence, this "diary" clearly is a propaganda text made up from scratch by the Jewish resistance fighters of the Warsaw Ghetto.

In May of 1945, SS *Hauptscharführer* Walter Piller, the deputy commandant of the Chełmno Camp in 1944, wrote a "confession" in Soviet captivity. He listed freely invented deportation figures for the summer of 1944, and following the script of the 1943 Kharkov show trial (see the entry on gas vans for details), he claimed that the Chełmno gas vans were operated by the driver opening a valve during the ride, which killed the victims within 2-3 minutes. However, no such lever-operated gas-release from inside the cab existed, if we follow the orthodox narrative, and the speed of execution was impossible, considering that suicides with gasoline-engine exhaust gasses – prior to the age of catalytic converters – took some 20 minutes (see the entry on carbon monoxide).

Starting in June 1945, Polish investigative judge Władysław Bednarz interrogated a number of individuals who claimed or were suspected to have knowledge about events unfolding at the former Chełmno Camp. All of these testimonies are characterized by improbable or impossible claims, and many were apparently influenced by the judge himself, looking for information that he wanted confirmed:
– Walter Burmeister claimed that he drove and operated a Renault gas van with a fanciful, nonsensical piping system, none of which existed even according to the orthodox narrative. (See the entry dedicated to him)
– Bronisław Falborski asserted to have repaired the exhaust system of a gas van, yet his description of the system is absurdly nonsensical, and he falsely identified a harmless Magirus truck at the Ostrowski factory grounds as the gas van he repaired. (See the entry dedicated to him)
– Michał Podchlebnik also falsely identified a

harmless Magirus truck at the Ostrowski factory grounds as one of the gas vans he saw in operation, and made up a string of other absurd claims, such as that the inmates, before climbing in the gas van, were handed towels and soap – a reflection of gas-chamber rumors going rampant in postwar Poland. (See the entry dedicated to him)
– Szymon Srebrnik also misidentified a harmless Magirus truck at the Ostrowski factory grounds as one of the gas vans he saw in operation, and he filled his tale to the brim with absurd stories. (See the entry dedicated to him)
– Mieczysław Żurawski gave the fewest details of all witnesses, but where he made specific claims, they are clearly wrong. He insisted that the Magirus truck at the Ostrowski factory grounds was merely a disinfestation van, but later, during the Eichmann Trial in Jerusalem, he tried "correcting" this "mistake." Żurawski claimed that he was one among some 7,000 to 10,000 Jews deported from the Lodz Ghetto to Chełmno in the summer of 1944. In this regard, his testimony is pivotal for the orthodoxy's claim of a second phase of extermination activities at Chełmno. (See the entry dedicated to him.)

Compare this motley assortment of claims with Szlamek's detailed tale of a gassing device inside the cab, activated by push button, and you get the idea that everyone was just making up stuff as they pleased, or as they thought it pleased their interrogator.

Finally, Judge Bednarz interrogated the defendant Bruno Israel in late October 1945, who had been assigned to the Chełmno police in July/August 1944. Similar to Podchlebnik, Israel claimed that the victims were persuaded to climb into the gas vans by being told that they were taking a shower in it, and they were even given some soap. Just like Podchlebnik, Israel must have gotten his wires crossed here, confusing the claims about stationary gas chambers camouflaged as shower rooms with the gas vans. Moreover, no SS man would have wasted any soap on such a fool's errand of trying to convince inmates that they would take a shower inside the van's cargo box. But at least Israel got the gassing method straight: "the exhaust pipe went through the floor to the center of the vehicle," something the orthodoxy could later work with.

Months of postwar stories making the rounds in Poland about gas vans did not reach or convince everyone, though. On 27 October 1945, Polish veterinary surgeon Mieczysław Sekiewicz claimed that Jews rounded up in the Konin region near Chełmno were *not* brought to Chełmno and killed there in gas vans, but rather brought into some woods, placed inside a pit, and there killed by showering them first with water, then with boiling fresh lime, so they were cooked alive… (See Mattogno 2017, p. 49 for more.)

The propaganda about Chełmno ultimately solidified during the Chełmno Show Trial at Bonn, West Germany, in 1963 and 1965, where the final version of the orthodox narrative was cast in legal stone. Accused were eleven defendants who had been officials at the camp. None of the defendants denied the charges, while one of them tried to commit suicide when first confronted with them. They all claimed either that they had merely followed orders or that they acted under duress. One of the defendants argued that he was a philo-Semite, proving it by the fact that he had gotten engaged to a Jewess in Berlin in 1940. Yet still, he obediently followed the orders allegedly given him to kill all Jews. Another defendant stated that his father, an opponent of the NS regime who once had been tortured by the Gestapo, could not give him any advice either as to how to avoid this extermination activity. He got acquitted for the best theatric courtroom performance! The National Socialist's skills at making even their fiercest opponents follow their orders blindly was truly remarkable. (For more details, see Alvarez 2023, pp. 195f.; for details about Chełmno's propaganda history, see in general Mattogno 2017, pp. 47-72.)

Death-Toll Propaganda

As for almost all German wartime camps for which mass exterminations have been claimed, initial death-toll figures were grotesquely inflated, but were subsequently reduced step by step. Occasionally, media propagandists felt the need to promote somewhat higher figures:

Victim numbers claimed for Chełmno	
1,300,000	Polish postwar commission, May 1945
400,000	Claude Lanzmann, *Shoah*, 1985
350,000	Laqueur, Baumel-Schwartz 2001, p. 231
340,000	Polish judge Władysław Bednarz, 1946
310,000	Polish historical commission, 1979
≥152,000	Jury Court Bonn, 1963/65
For sources, see Mattogno 2017, pp. 107-111.	

Forensic Findings

Various Polish teams conducted forensic investiga-

One of the large areas near the former Chełmno Camp delineated by curbstones and covered with gravel, alleged to be former mass graves, because scattered human remains were found at a few spots in the area.

tions on the former campgrounds in 1945, 1951, 1986-1987 and in 2003-2004. During those investigations, the remnants of what appeared to have been a field furnace were found, measuring some 6 m × 5 m. It was described in some detail by Polish investigative judge Władysław Bednarz in 1946. Such field furnaces are known to consume some 1.45 kg of coal per kg of combusted organic tissue (usually livestock carcasses).

A few soil-core samples were taken at scattered locations, some of which revealed the presence of a few percent of human ashes and bone fragments, while others contained discarded objects, such as soles of shoes, prosthetic fittings, buckles, cutlery, handbags, suitcases, clothes pins and buttons, dentures, casings of rifle cartridges, pistols etc. No foundation of any major building was located. From the scattered findings of small amounts of human ashes and bone fragments, the Polish investigators delineated huge mass graves by simply drawing large rectangles to include most of these scattered findings.

Air photos as well as historical data of the surrounding forest show that roughly one hectare (100 m × 100 m) of the surrounding pine woods was replanted in 1942/43, hence was probably felled during the early phase of the camp's claimed existence. Since the woods in this area were only some 15-17 years old at that time, this hectare of pine wood could have yielded some 200 tons of *fresh* timber. Since fresh wood has only a third of the caloric content of coal, cremating an average body of 60 kg in the field furnace would have required some 260 kg of fresh wood. Hence, the 200 tons of fresh wood cut in the camp's surroundings would have sufficed for some 770 bodies – not 152,000 of them. There is no evidence – not even anecdotal – that vast amounts of wood were cut and transported to the camp by anyone from anywhere.

(For more details, see Mattogno 2017, pp. 83-89, 95-105.)

Current Orthodox Narrative

Since the primary sources (forensic findings, documents, witness reports) do not suffice to draw a comprehensive image of what exactly happened at Chełmno, Judge Władysław Bednarz resorted to creative writing when laying out the timeline of events, using cherry-picked statements from various witness testimonies to flesh out his narrative (see Bednarz 1946). This narrative was later adopted by the German judiciary and also by orthodox historians (see Gutman 1990, pp. 283-287). It claims the following:

The camp's first phase lasted from December 1941 to April 1943. During that phase, inmates were received at a mansion near Chełmno, where they had to undress and enter a gas van. That gas van was a Renault. (Other orthodox sources claim two small Diamond trucks and one Saurer truck, but there is no source pertaining to Chełmno sustaining that claim, except the fake Just Letter talking about a Saurer truck). The victims were then killed within ten minutes by the van's exhaust gases, after which the dead victims were driven to the so-called forest camp, where they were dumped into mass graves. In the summer of 1942, two crematoria were built to cremate the victims. At the end of this phase, the mansion was demolished, the crematoria destroyed, and the forest camp dissolved.

In April of 1944, the forest camp was reactivated. Two new crematoria were built in order to process Jews deported from the Lodz Ghetto, some of whose inhabitants were sent to Chełmno between late June and mid-July of 1944. In August 1944, in conjunction with *Aktion* 1005, the old mass graves were exhumed, and the corpses burned. The camp was abandoned in mid-January with the approach of the Red Army. The total death toll amounted to 320,000 Jews.

However, as stated above, forensic excavation located only the leftovers of not four crematoria but only *one* primitive field furnace with a very limited capacity, and the history of the woods surrounding the camp prove that the amount of wood felled during that time was not even enough to cremate 1,000 bodies.

Furthermore, the claim of a second phase of extermination activities – after the camp's infrastructure had been destroyed in 1943 – rests to a large degree on the unbelievable claims of the untrustworthy witness Mieczysław Żurawski (see the entry on him). His claim is simply implausible that skilled and experienced armament workers of the Lodz Ghetto were killed in Chełmno in the summer of 1944, rather than transferred to camps and labor sites in Germany, as documents clearly prove. (See the entry on the Lodz Ghetto.) In other words, there probably never was a second phase in the existence of the Chełmno Camp.

The claim that the gas van used at Chełmno was a Renault is unique to the testimony of Walter Burmeister, who gave a completely nonsensical description of its gas-piping system. Finally, ten minutes would not have sufficed to kill everyone in the van, as monitored suicides with carbon monoxide from gasoline-engine exhaust are proven to take some 20 minutes. Moreover, Walter Piller was the only witness who stated how long the gassings took: 2-3 minutes, not ten minutes, which is the value taken from the verdict of the Bonn Show Trial against former staff members of the Chełmno Camp.

In other words, the orthodoxy generously extrapolates beyond the little information contained in the few documental sources, cherry-picks what they need from divergent witness statements, hides from their readers the preposterous and nonsensical nature of these witness statements, and completely ignores the results of forensic studies.

CHOMKA, WŁADYSŁAW

Władysław Chomka was a railroad worker who maintained a track section from Małkinia up to two kilometers from Treblinka Station. Having talked to Jews working at the railway tracks, he claimed to know that "7,000-10,000 people were exterminated every day, but there were days when 30,000 were exterminated." Using the lowest figure, this yields a total of some 25 million victims for a year's worth of operation. This is yet another example of why testimonies from hearsay should never be permitted either in courts of law or in historiography. (See Mattogno 2021e, pp. 166f.)

CHRISTOPHERSEN, THIES

Thies Christophersen (27 Jan. 1918 – 13 Feb. 1997) was a German farmer who was put in charge of breeding efforts of a Russian type of dandelion producing a liquid similar to a natural rubber, like caoutchouc. The experiments were conducted at the village of Rajsko near Auschwitz, and inmates of the Auschwitz Camp were deployed by Christophersen for that project.

Thies Christophersen

In a brochure first published in Germany in 1973, he related his wartime experiences as a German army officer deployed at Auschwitz. "During the time I was in Auschwitz, I did not notice the slightest evidence of mass gassings," he wrote in his brochure titled, *Die Auschwitz-Lüge* (*The Auschwitz Lie*). Christophersen's first-hand account was a major factor in the growth and development of Holocaust skepticism. For this reason, the brochure was soon banned in Germany, but new editions were published abroad and in other languages.

Until the outbreak of war in Europe, Christophersen had worked as a farmer in Schleswig, northern Germany. Called to military service, he was badly wounded in 1940 while serving in the Western Campaign. After recuperating and undergoing some specialized agricultural training, he was assigned to a research center in German-occupied Ukraine. In the face of Soviet military advances, the center was transferred to the Rajsko labor camp, a satellite camp of Auschwitz. During the period he lived and worked there – from January to December 1944 – Christophersen was responsible for the daily work of inmate laborers. The young second lieutenant supervised about 300 workers, many of them Jewish, of whom 200 were women from the Rajsko Camp, and 100 were men from the nearby Auschwitz-Birkenau Camp. On a number of occasions, he visited the Birkenau Camp where, it is alleged, hundreds of thousands of Jews were systematically gassed to death in May-July 1944. Although he knew of Birkenau's crematoria, it wasn't until after the war that he first heard anything of "gas-chamber" killings or mass exterminations.

In March 1988, he testified for the defense during the so-called Second Zündel Trial. Due to ongoing persecution and prosecution for his views on Auschwitz, he left Germany and resided temporarily in Denmark, Belgium and Switzerland.

CHYBIŃSKI, STANISŁAW

Stanisław Chybiński was a Polish Auschwitz inmate who escaped from the camp on 20 May 1943, and subsequently wrote a report titled "Pictures of Auschwitz", which was submitted during the Polish show trial against former members of the Auschwitz Camp staff. The report had several copies of blueprints of Crematorium II of Birkenau attached with an extended legend. Here are some peculiar claims made by Chybiński:
- The building had nine triple-muffle furnaces (although it only had five, clearly visible from the plan).
- Four identical crematoria existed with altogether 36 such furnaces, although Crematoria IV and V were entirely different, with only one eight-muffle furnace each.
- Three bodies could be loaded into each muffle, although it was designed only for one body.
- The cremation of a load of three bodies took seven minutes. Compare this to the actual cremation time of one hour for a single body.
- The yearly capacity of two of these crematoria was more than 22 million bodies, which was designed to exterminate the entire Polish population of Poland. Jews are not mentioned in that report.
- The victims, upon entering the basement, got registered in the office, proceeded to a washroom for undressing, and from there to one of the three gas chambers. However, there was no "registration office" in that basement, and the orthodoxy insists that inmates were gassed without registration. The stairs allegedly used by inmates leading into that basement led directly into Morgue #2, presumably the undressing room. Furthermore, there was only one room in that building allegedly used as a gas chamber – Morgue #1.
- The gas chambers had a capacity of up to 2,800 persons. Applying this to Morgue #1 with its 210 m², this amounts to a physically impossible packing density of 13 people per square meter.
- Gas, not water, was blown into the room – through the lower air ducts! However, that was the ventilation system's air-*extraction* duct, which had nothing to do with water. Moreover, the orthodoxy insists that the gas was thrown in as Zyklon-B pellets through openings in the ceiling.
- Ventilation ensued after the gassing through the upper air ducts, when in fact these were the air-intake ducts.

It is clear that Chybiński, by looking at the plans in his possession, made up the entire story with no actual knowledge of the place. In fact, the plans he had were outdated. The actual basement layout looked different, but he didn't know that. So, he had the victims enter through the wrong door into the wrong area of the building. All subsequent descriptions were therefore nonsense.

His erroneous claim of nine muffles in four identical crematoria ended up in the even more preposterous report by Rudolf Vrba and Alfred Wetzler.

(For more details, see Mattogno 2021, pp. 171-174.)

CODE LANGUAGE

Facing an astounding lack of documents supporting the claim that a "Holocaust" was going on, orthodox scholars resort to the auxiliary hypothesis that the National-Socialist bureaucrats used code words when writing their documents. These code words stated one thing, when in fact something entirely different was meant.

The 1993 book *Nazi Mass Murder* is a classic example of an orthodox work created primarily to refute Holocaust skeptics. Before presenting their evidence, the editors of this volume "enlighten" their readers that they must read into this evidence something different than what these documents actually say. If a document states that people were "resettled" or "expelled," it really means that they were shot or gassed to death (Kogon *et al.* 1993, pp. 11f.).

However, the problems arising from this are insurmountable. For instance, there are many documents from the high-level bureaucracy of the German wartime government using words such as "emigration", "evacuation", "resettlement" or "deportation." Even orthodox scholars admit that, in many cases, these words did in fact mean what they say, hence were not code words at all. This is uncontested for all documents created until the alleged beginning of mass exterminations (mid- to late-1941). But even after that, there are many cases where it can be shown that a document using these innocuous words was telling the truth.

If that is so, then how was a recipient of a letter or an order supposed to know from which point onward, or in which particular cases, he was to do literally what he was told – evacuate, resettle, deport, relocate? And how was he to know in which cases he was to radically contravene orders given by *NOT* moving a set of persons, but rather killing them?

When words of central importance could arbitrarily and radically change their meaning in an instance, complete language chaos would have ensued. To avoid this, strictly defined and generally announced rules would have to be set and disseminated, explaining what each term means under which circumstances. It goes without saying that there is no trace of that ever having been done. Moreover, any such defined and disseminated rules would have undermined secrecy, and secrecy was the claimed reason for the alleged use of code words in the first place.

The utter absurdity of the code-word hypothesis becomes palpable within the context of the so-called "Aktion 1005." Here, secret reports of mass graves exhumed behind the retreating eastern front were supposedly sent as fake weather data, with the cloud height giving the number of corpses exhumed. Or maybe they were water-level reports, or watering-hole reports, depending on the witness. In any case, no such secret report was ever found.

Particularly blatant is the attempt to distort the historical record with code-word "explanations" when it comes to the Auschwitz Camp. This camp's documentation of comprehensive measures implemented to *save* inmates' lives, particularly during the phase when mass murder allegedly occurred (1942-1944), is vast and incontrovertible. In the face of this, claims that some documents containing the term "special" meant mass murder are ludicrous.

(For more details on this, see the entries special treatment, resettlement, healthcare, criminal traces, and the section "Documented History" of the entry on Birkenau.)

COHEN, LEON

The Greek Jew Leon Cohen was deported to Auschwitz and was registered there on 11 April 1944, although he claimed to have arrived "in late November [1943]." He claims to have been assigned to the so-called *Sonderkommando*, where he was deployed at what today is referred to as

Leon Cohen

"Bunker 2." He remained silent about his experiences until he was interviewed by Israeli historian Gideon Greif in early 1990. He also published a book about his experiences a few years later (Cohen 1996). His accounts are riddled with false and implausible claims:

– He incomprehensibly calls the SS guards "policemen."
– As has become fashionable among Auschwitz survivors, he claims to have been selected by Dr. Mengele on arrival.
– Sex sells, so he claimed something that is commonly associated with Ilse Koch, the wife of the former camp commandant of the Buchenwald Camp:

"*At [Mengele's] side, a very beautiful woman was leading two huge Alsatian dogs. This woman was reputed to be a nymphomaniac. She picked strong muscular men for one-night stands and when she had completely exhausted them, she killed them with her own hands and used their skin for lampshades or bookbindings. I sometimes wonder, is this madness, could it really have happened? To make it worse, at the Nuremberg trials, which was a complete farce, she only received a prison sentence and even managed a quick release as she was pregnant. [...] Or am I talking nonsense?*"

This proves that Cohen was lying, since his alleged personal experiences in fact came from

somewhere else.
- He claims to have carried gassing victims to pits 3 meters deep, although a pit this deep would have filled with water due to the high groundwater level in the area.
- He never mentions the term "bunker" in connection with the gassing facility and does not describe it either; instead, he calls the cremation pits "bunkers," yet does not indicate either their number or size (other than that they were 3 m deep).
- He claims that children's and women's bodies were put at the bottom of the pyre, as if they were used to ignite the wood and men lying on top.
- He claims that rail carts were used to transport corpses to the pits, although the orthodoxy insists that no such devices were used at Bunker 2 in 1944.
- He claims that, while the pyre was ablaze, men with long poles stood on either side stoking the fire, although those men would have been severely burned.
- He claims that, after the fire had died down, the pit had to be cleared of accumulated fat, although fat would have been the *first* thing to burn in a fire and could never have accumulated in it.
- He claims that, since the gas chambers didn't work fast enough, people were also gassed in "cattle trucks" parked in the fields – a unique and freely invented claim.
- His description of the crematoria has little resemblance to reality. (He attributed a capacity of 2,000 victims per batch to all crematoria's gas chambers, which would have resulted in an impossible packing density of 9.5 people per square meter for Morgue #1 of Crematoria II and III.)
- According to him, the gas made the victims turn "deep purple, nearly black," although cyanide poisoning turns the skin pink.
- He claims that a physically impossible number of two to five corpses were pushed into a cremation muffle designed for only one corpse.
- The cremation of these two to five corpses is said to have lasted half an hour, when in fact the cremation of just one corpse took roughly an hour.
- He repeats the myth that the fat of women's bodies was used to burn the men's bodies, hence that corpses burned by themselves, without the need for fuel. However, self-immolating bodies simply do not exist.

(For more, see Mattogno 2022e, pp. 74-92.)

COMMISSAR ORDER

Judging by the scale and scope of civil-rights violations and atrocities committed, the Soviet Union under Lenin and Stalin was a terrorist state second probably only to Pol Pot's Cambodia. The primary Soviet organization implementing and enforcing this rule of terror was the terrorist organization NKVD, later renamed to NKGB. Within the Red Army, the rule of terror against enemy soldiers and civilians as well as against Soviet soldiers of all ranks was monitored and enforced by the so-called Political Commissars.

Prior to and during the Second World War, the Soviet Union was not a signatory to any conventions of international law. This was by design, as it "allowed" the Soviet leadership to employ maximum terror and cruelty during warfare. Germany, on the other hand, was a signatory to these conventions. However, in case of a war between nations where some are signatories and others are not, Article 82 of the 1929 Geneva Convention on the treatment of PoWs states:

"Au cas où, en temps de guerre, un des belligérants ne serait pas partie à la Convention, ses dispositions demeureront néanmoins obligatoires entre les belligérants qui y participent."

This translates to:

"If, in times of war, one of the belligerents [= Soviet Union] is not a party to the Convention, its provisions shall nevertheless remain binding between the belligerents participating in it [the Convention]."

Therefore, Germany had to abide by the Geneva Convention during hostilities with all nations that were also signatories, but was *not* bound by them during hostilities with the Soviet Union as a non-signatory.

When German intelligence realized the aggressive intentions of the Soviet Union due to the massive Soviet troop buildup at its western border, Germany itself started preparing for war with an enemy that knew no mercy. On Hitler's initiative, "Guidelines for the Treatment of Political Commissars" were issued on 6 June 1941, which is today referred to as the Commissar Order (*Kommissarbefehl*). These guidelines declared the Red Army's Political Commissars as non-combatants acting outside of the rules of warfare. In today's parlance, they would be considered terrorists rather than soldiers, and they were to face the fate that all governments reserve for terrorists such as Osama bin Laden: "they are to be finished off."

While that Commissar Order was strictly speaking legal, it was certainly neither ethically defensible nor tactically smart. Although the German government tried to keep this Commissar Order a secret – it was to be conveyed only verbally – the Soviets quickly learned about it. They successfully used it to stiffen the resistance and increase the cruelty with which their commissars acted.

Realizing that this order was backfiring on the Germans, it met increasing resistance within the German military, whose leaders pressured Hitler to rescind it. It was finally rescinded on 6 May 1942.

Since the Soviets were both prosecutors and judges during the Nuremberg International Military Tribunal, the Commissar Order was declared illegal at this show trial. This nonsense is parroted to this day by most mainstream historians, who can either not read French, or lack any courage, or both.

The Commissar Order has no direct bearing on the Holocaust, as it does not mention Jews in any way. But that did not stop the late historian Raul Hilberg – during his lifetime one of the most prestigious orthodox Holocaust experts – to falsely portray it as Hitler's alleged first order to exterminate the Jews. In the 1961 first edition of his book *The Destruction of the European Jews*, Hilberg claimed that this order, "was given in the spring of 1941," and issued to the *Einsatzgruppen* (Hilberg 1961, p. 177). During his testimony at the 1985 trial against German-Canadian Holocaust skeptic Ernst Zündel, Hilberg specified that this referred to the Commissar Order, although it does not mention Jews at all. Hilberg removed this reference in later editions of his book.

(For more details, see Mattogno 2021c, pp. 57-62.)

COMPENSATION
Israel
After it had turned its Arab neighbors into lethal enemies with its genocidal war of 1948, Israel had to maintain huge armed forces to secure its spoils of war and prevent an Arab revenge. These armed forces were utterly disproportionate to Israel's financial and economic abilities. Hence, within a few years, Israel was in serious financial trouble. They needed money, lots of it, predictably and reliably.

As soon as the National Socialists managed to form a government in Germany in 1933, Jewish organizations called for economic and financial boycotts against Germany, and even declared war on Germany. The National Socialists reacted with their own boycott. From there on, things steadily escalated in threats and counterthreats. With National-Socialist Germany losing the war, all German anti-Jewish measures and threats also disappeared. However, with the alleged harm done to the European Jewish communities by National-Socialist wartime policies, Jews understandably continued their hostile attitude to anything German.

With the Cold War gaining traction in 1948, the United States of America needed West Germany to prosper economically, so that it could do its military share in the confrontation with the Eastern Bloc. This required, however, that West Germany forged trade agreements and got financial loans in order to rebuild its completely devastated economy. Most of its European neighbors were not pleased by the prospect of a resurging Germany.

In addition to her neighbor's resistance, Germany also faced Jewish opposition. Many influential Jews in media, finance, trade and politics did what they could to undermine any West-German attempts to rise from the ashes. West-German Chancellor Konrad Adenauer acknowledged that power when quipping in 1952 that "World Jewry is a great power!" Adolf Hitler had the same opinion, except that he drew radically different conclusions from it. It was left to Adenauer to rescue Germany from its postwar collapse. Against a majority of his own conservative party, he was looking for a way out by acknowledging the injustice done to Europe's Jews, and by paying for it – in return for Jews suspending their resistance to Germany's recovery efforts.

Israel's dependence upon the U.S. allowed the Americans to strongarm the Israeli government into negotiating with West Germany. After lengthy negotiations, the so-called Luxembourg Agreement was signed on 10 September 1952. It obligated West Germany to pay Israel 3 billion deutschmarks over a stretch of 12 years as compensation for Israeli expenses to accommodate Jewish refugees. In return, Israel agreed to use most of this money to buy goods and equipment from Germany to build, modernize and expand its infrastructure, among other things.

As a result of this agreement, large parts of Israel's postwar infrastructure were German-made. This gifted German infrastructure contributed significantly to stabilizing Israel's economy, and permitted it 15 years later, in 1967, to go on another imperialistic conquest against its Arab neighbors.

Germany, on the other hand, managed to pull off

its *Wirtschaftswunder* (economic miracle), meaning its phoenix-like rise from the ashes to an economic and financial powerhouse, once again dominating all of Europe. Although initially violently opposed by many Jews, particularly in Israel, who did not want to accept German "blood money," this agreement proved to be enormously beneficial for both sides.

Other Countries
Between 1959 and 1964, Germany signed compensation agreements with 12 western European nations relating to compensation payments to citizens of those countries for injustices suffered. Over the years, roughly one billion deutschmarks were paid out as a result of these agreements.

After the collapse of the Soviet Union, similar agreements were signed between Germany and Eastern European countries, although due to the late point in time, the inflation-adjusted payments were much lower.

Individuals
Right after the end of World War Two, the Allied occupational powers enacted laws and regulations in Germany for the compensation of National-Socialist injustice. These were later harmonized and accepted by West-Germany as German law in 1952 with the so-called Transition Treaty, granting West-Germany partial sovereignty.

Over the coming decades, this initial law was followed with a series of German laws allowing survivors of National-Socialist persecution to file claims against the West-German (and later reunified German) government for loss of property, damage to careers, as well as physical and mental injury and pain, among other things. Compensations were made either as one-time payments or as monthly pensions. Most but not all applicants were Jews or Jewish organizations.

When adjudicating applications for compensations of injuries suffered by the Third Reich, German postwar authorities instructed clerks to be generous, and not to question or doubt claims about events allegedly suffered.

During the Cold War, the Soviet Union prevented anyone in Eastern-Bloc countries from accepting compensation money from the West-German government. After Germany's reunification in 1990 and the collapse of the Soviet Union in 1991, a large, so-far untapped pool of individuals were entitled to compensation. Enticed by this renewed feeding frenzy at the troughs of a larger Germany, Jewish organizations threatened with calls for boycotts or multi-billion-dollar lawsuits against

– major German companies who had used forced laborers during the war;
– Swiss banks which presumably profited from dormant bank accounts of Holocaust victims;
– European insurance companies which allegedly had not paid out life insurances and other benefits to owners or beneficiaries listed in insurance contracts of victims and survivors;
– as well as the French and Hungarian governments for having aided and abetted in deporting Jews to Auschwitz.

The blackmail worked. Starting in the mid-1990s, billions upon billions were paid in return for these Jewish organizations waiving their right to file lawsuits. It is doubtful that much of the billions paid actually benefited any destitute survivor. Considerable amounts were also spent for Holocaust-indoctrination projects.

Next in line were demands to pay compensation to the "next generation of survivors," who suffer emotionally due to the resultant trauma from having to learn about their parent's horrific experiences. Hence, Germany was asked to pay for the consequences of Holocaust indoctrination. This demand has not been met so far.

As of late 2022, Germany has paid almost 82 billion Euros in compensation from all major agreements. And payments continue to grow: in mid-2023, Germany agreed to give another 1.3 billion Euros for calendar year 2024, and increasing for the following two years, despite declining numbers of survivors.

Compared to Germany's economy with an annual gross domestic product of some four trillion Euros, payments of 82 billion Euros spread out over 80 years is a relatively small amount. On the other hand, every billion given to Jews or Jewish organizations is one less billion for German needs. And every billion given away inevitably comes back to bite the West by further leveraging Jewish power or by further promoting Holocaust guilt.

(See the public data accessible on Wikipedia about compensation and *Wiedergutmachung* (literally: "making good again"); see moreover Finkelstein 2000, 2005.)

CONCENTRATION CAMPS

Concentration camps are prison camps for civilians incarcerated without due process. They were first created by the Spanish during the 1897 Cuban War of Independence. They were employed in subsequent years by the British (Boer War) and Americans (war against the Philippines).

Concentration camps made their first appearance in Europe with the 1918 Bolshevik revolution in Russia. While almost all inmates in the Soviet Union's camp system had been convicted after "due process," the trials were usually a mockery of justice, and in the case of political offenders, mere show trials.

The National-Socialist government in Germany, which to a considerable extent was a reaction against the Soviet Union's attempt to expand their reign of terror, set up concentration camps right at the beginning of their rule, with the claim to squash a possible communist insurrection.

Already before National-Socialist rule, German law permitted the state to keep criminal offenders in prison even beyond a court-imposed prison term, if the public's safety was at risk when releasing a usually hardened or repeat offender. That law exists to this day in Germany, but is now limited to severe felonies such as aggravated assault, rape and murder, and has many additional restrictions. This law could be applied more liberally in Germany's past, which was (mis)used abundantly by the Third Reich's police and SS authorities to keep dangerous criminals and political inmates incarcerated indefinitely. Camp admissions (without due process) increased over time, in particular during the war, and especially regarding the deportation of Jews.

In this encyclopedia, concentration camps are discussed only if any kind of extermination activity against Jews or against all inmates, irrespective of creed or ethnicity, has been claimed in them. This includes (see the respective entry, and the entry on extermination camps):

- Auschwitz
- Bergen-Belsen
- Buchenwald
- Dachau
- Flossenbürg
- Majdanek
- Mauthausen
- Natzweiler
- Neuengamme
- Nordhausen
- Ravensbrück
- Sachsenhausen
- Stutthof

CONSTRUCTION OFFICE

Every concentration camp of the Third Reich had a construction office (*Bauleitung*), which was in charge of building and maintaining the camp and its facilities. During the initial setup of a camp, this office was usually called a "new-construction office" (*Neubauleitung*). Larger camps (that had subcamps with their own construction offices) had one that organized all construction efforts in a "central construction office" (*Zentralbauleitung*).

At the Auschwitz Camp, the vast documentation of its central construction office survived the war almost completely. However, the Soviets removed the majority of that documentation, and transferred it to an archive in Moscow, where this material was kept hidden from the public until the final years of the Soviet Union. Only a fraction of the material was left in the archives of the former Auschwitz Camp, where it was meant to assist Polish investigative judge Jan Sehn to prepare the Polish show trials against Rudolf Höss and the Auschwitz camp garrison.

After the collapse of the Soviet Union in 1991, this material was made publicly available for the first time. It is today stored in the Russian State War Museum (*Rossiiskii Gosudarstvennii Vojennii Archiv*). It contains altogether some 88,200 pages of documents from the Central Construction Office.

Due to pressure from the German government, who did not want skeptical researchers using this highly informative material, access was restricted in 1998 to "officially accredited researchers."

A thorough analysis of this vast material reveals all the details of how this office was organized, operated, and what its responsibilities and activities were. Since this authority was responsible for the design and construction of every single camp facility and feature, it would also have been in charge of designing, constructing and maintaining any homicidal facilities. However, these 88,200 pages of documents do not contain a single shred of evidence pointing at the existence of homicidal gas chambers at Auschwitz. Better still, this archival resource reveals the huge efforts made and expenses incurred to improve the camps' hygienic, sanitary and healthcare facilities in desperate attempts to reduce inmate mortality and improve overall inmate health and fitness.

(For more details, see the Auschwitz section of the entry on healthcare; the section on "Documented History" of the Auschwitz Main Camp and the Birkenau Camp; see furthermore Mattogno 2015; 2019; 2023; Mattogno/Deana 2021.)

CONVERGENCE OF EVIDENCE

The "convergence of evidence" is a paradigm based on the observation that seemingly independent pieces of evidence all, or at least in their majority, point in the same general direction of an event or a perpetrator, even if they disagree on particulars. Historically, this paradigm was first applied by the judiciary during medieval witch trials. During those trials, it became quite evident that there was a total lack of physical evidence, and many witness assertions were often contradictory in nature, riddled with implausibilities about the existence of the devil and his claimed interaction with people. However, the courts overcame this obstacle by observing that the vast majority of witness statements all pointed in the same direction: the devil exists, and he interacts with malfeasant individuals (witches, wizards, sorcerers, warlocks etc.). In this way, convictions were obtained.

With regard to the Holocaust, this concept was revived by the Polish judiciary when investigating claims about German wartime camps on Polish soil. During the investigations by Polish investigative judges such as Jan Sehn (Auschwitz), Zdzisław Łukaszkiewicz (Majdanek, Sobibór, Treblinka) and Władysław Bednarz (Chełmno), many witnesses claimed that some kind of mass murder had happened. However, similar to the medieval witch trials, there was a distinct lack of physical and documental evidence to support these claims, and certain witness assertions about mass-murder claims were often contradictory in nature and riddled with implausibilities.

The Polish judiciary overcame this problem by highlighting the witnesses' common general extermination claims, picking the version that seemed most plausible, and sweeping all contradictions and implausibilities under the rug. In particular for the cases of Majdanek and Auschwitz, this was then propped up with cherry-picked documents ripped out of their proper context. This permitted their import to be distorted, often turning their meaning upside down. Such misrepresented documents were then presented as circumstantial evidence allegedly "converging" on the same conclusion: mass murder did occur. (See in this regard the judges and camps mentioned, as well as the entry on criminal traces.)

French historian Jean-Claude Pressac revived this mendacious method in his works of the late 1980s and early 1990s, and Jewish-Dutch cultural historian Robert van Pelt invented the term "convergence of evidence" for this method of fake historiography in his 1999 "expert report" as introduced during the 1999/2000 libel suit of British historian David Irving against Jewish-American theologian Deborah Lipstadt.

(For more details, see Mattogno 2019, pp. 389-440; Rudolf/Mattogno 2017, pp. 203-280.)

List of entries dealing with forced or real "convergence of evidence" – in truth or lies:
– Air Photos
– Amiel, Szymon
– Babi Yar
– Bednarz, Władysław
– Berger, Oskar
– Broad, Pery S.
– Bunkers
– Cremation Propaganda
– Criminal Traces
– Dragon, Szlama
– Falborski, Bronisław
– Farber, Yuri
– Fat, Extracted from Burning Corpses
– First Gassing, at Auschwitz
– Himmler Visits
– Kon, Stanisław
– Lequeux, Maurice
– Lichtenstein, Mordecai
– Łukaszkiewicz, Zdzisław
– Lumberjacks
– Morgen, Konrad
– Obrycki, Narcyz T.
– Pohl, Oswald
– Sehn, Jan
– Self-Immolating Bodies
– Showers
– Soap, from Jewish Corpses
– Standing Upright, Dead Gassing Victims
– Stanek, Franciszek
– Tauber, Henryk
– Towels, Soap, inside Gas Chambers
– Turowski, Eugeniusz
– Venezia, Shlomo
– Willenberg, Samuel
– Witch Trials
– Żurawski, Mieczysław

CORPSE PHOTOS

Photos of dead bodies said to have been taken inside German wartime camps are often used to bolster orthodox claims of a National-Socialist policy of extermination. The photos most frequently presented by scholars and in mass media were taken by armed forces of the Western Allies as they liberated those camps. Most prominent among them are photos from Bergen-Belsen, Nordhausen, Dachau and Ohrdruf.

All of these images show the devastating effect which Allied carpet bombing had on Germany. Germany's infrastructure completely collapsed, and no

In the majority, these are victims of an Allied air raid on the Boelke Barracks at Nordhausen. Among them are also victims of the camp's appalling hygienic, sanitary and healthcare conditions. This resulted from overcrowding and the inability of the German authorities to provide the inmates with anything due to Germany's complete collapse in the final months of the war. The bodies were lined up by U.S. soldiers for this photo and a corresponding film, to falsely portray these dead bodies as the result of a deliberate German policy of extermination.

Victims of an Allied strafing raid on an evacuation train full of camp inmates on the way to the Dachau Camp. U.S. troops who found that train misinterpreted the bullet holes in the rail cars and bullet wounds in the dead bodies as the result of a German massacre using machine guns. They subsequently executed all camp guards that had not already been lynched by the inmates.

Bodies piled up in front of the crematorium at the Dachau Camp. More corpses were piled up in the morgue inside. These victims were the result of diseases and exhaustion, resulting from overcrowding and the inability of the German authorities to provide the camp with anything due to Germany's complete collapse in the final months of the war. Due to a lack of fuel, these bodies could not be cremated. To this day, these piles of dead bodies are falsely portrayed as the result of a deliberate German policy of extermination.

Photo allegedly taken of the Polish resistance group at Auschwitz-Birkenau, presumably from one of the doors of Crematorium V. It shows a few dozen bodies on the ground in front of a smoking pit. However, several features reveal this clearly as a drawing, not a photo.

The second photo allegedly taken of the Polish resistance group at Auschwitz-Birkenau, also showing a few dozen bodies on the ground in front of a smoking pit. Several features of this image also reveal it as a drawing, not a photo.

one could receive anything – neither the civilian population in towns and cities, nor the inmates in prisons and camps. The camp administrations were powerless against malnutrition, hunger setting in, and vermin and diseases spreading. Drinking water supplies dried up or went bad, spreading dysentery and typhoid fever. Medical supplies and fuel were no longer available. Inmates died everywhere, as did the German civilian population in the bombed-out cities, and the millions of Germans expelled from their homes in Eastern Europe and East Germany.

Germany as a whole was, in effect, a rapidly growing pile of corpses. Today, we only tend to see the photos from the camps. We don't see the hundreds of thousands of bombed, burned and gassed civilians in the cities, or the millions of Germans starved to death, dead from exhaustion, or slain when driven from their ancestral homes in East Germany (Eastern and Western Prussia, Pomerania, Silesia), the Sudetenland, Czechia, Poland and from what once was Yugoslavia.

For more on this, see the documentary *Probing the Holocaust* (Rudolf 2017).

Famous photos published by the Soviets include one taken at Majdanek showing partial skeletons in front of cremation furnaces. (See the Majdanek section of the entry on crematoria.) Another prominent set of Soviet photos was taken at the Klooga Camp. They presumably show dead inmates piled up on an unlit cremation pyre, but this is actually a staged scene with living people. (See the entry on the Klooga Camp.)

Two images are said to have been taken by inmates from inside the Auschwitz-Birkenau Camp sometime in 1944. However, these images clearly are, at best, heavily retouched photographs, but more likely drawings. But even if they were real photos, they prove only that a few dozen bodies were once lying behind a crematorium, and that something was burning in the background. This is a far cry from the claim that thousands upon thousands are said to have been cremated in the open on huge pyres, darkening

Bodies of typhus victims at the Bergen-Belsen Camp being pushed by a British bulldozer into a mass grave. To this day, these piles of dead bodies are falsely portrayed as the result of a deliberate German policy of extermination.

the sky. (For more details, see Rudolf 2023, pp. 341-344, 540.)

CORRY, JOE

In 1990, British retiree Joe Corry published a book titled *Towards the Dawn* about his alleged wartime experiences. In it, he claimed, among other things, that he had assassinated a German scientist with a crossbow, watched D-Day from a house on the landing beaches, rescued the nuclear scientist Robert Oppenheimer from Holland, attached limpet mines to U-boats, was shipwrecked off Newfoundland, and had worked with the future James Bond author Ian Fleming. The climax of his book, however, is when he and his secret "Special Service Unit" discover a hidden German extermination camp in a Dutch forest.

The problem is that none of it is true. There never was a secret "Special Service Unit," Oppenheimer was in the U.S. throughout the war, there was no extermination camp hidden in any Dutch forest, and there were no British troops at the beach watching the invasion. (See Walters 2013 for more details.)

CREMATION PROPAGANDA

Imagining one's body burn is a veritable nightmare for us all. Hence, the cremation of the human body is a prime topic for propaganda stories, because it is easy to make an audience exposed to such stories shudder in horror. For this reason, the cremation of alleged victims of claimed German wartime atrocities is a prime target for distortions, exaggerations and inventions.

As the entries on crematoria and open-air incinerations document, cremations both in furnaces of various types and on outdoor pyres occurred indeed in German wartime camps, and maybe even outside of them. Hence, witness accounts of such events can have a real background. The challenge is to find documental, forensic and technical constraints that permit to separate the truth, or at least that which would have been possible, from distortions and exaggerations.

Open-Air Incinerations

Large-scale outdoor cremations are easily detectable in real time by the local populace, and they are clearly visible on air photos, either due to the smoke they develop, or due to the scorched earth they leave behind. As explained in the entry on air photos, such photos are available for two cases of claimed large-scale outdoor cremations: Auschwitz-Birkenau during late spring and summer of 1944, and Babi Yar near Kiev in September 1943. In both cases, these air photos demonstrate incontrovertibly that the claimed events cannot have happened.

Another way large-scale outdoor cremations can be verified is by forensic examinations of the traces they must have left behind. Large areas of scorched earth, inevitably mixed with ashes, charred wood, and incompletely burned human remains must have littered the area. For the scale of operations claimed, huge amounts of ashes and incompletely burned cremation remains must have been deposited somewhere.

These issues are discussed in the entries on the *Aktion Reinhardt* Camps (Belzec, Sobibór, Treblinka, but also Chełmno) and on *Aktion* 1005. The latter is said to have been the code name for the German's operation to erase the traces of their mass murders on temporarily occupied Soviet territories – by burning their victims' bodies on innumerable gigantic outdoor pyres. Many witness accounts about these events contain assertions that make them suspicious. For a list of witnesses with an entry in this encyclopedia discussing these issues, see the section "*Aktion* 1005" in the entry on witnesses.

The entry on open-air incinerations defines technical parameters for outdoor cremations. Based on this data, we can define how a large outdoor pyre would have looked like, and how much space, time, and fuel – here mostly firewood – would have been needed to operate it. For ease of building and maintaining such a pyre, as well as eventually clearing out its burned-out remains, they are best kept some two meters wide, and not higher than a man can reach.

While there is some flexibility regarding the shape and size of a pyre, other constraints are less flexible. One of them concerns claims that outdoor cremations were conducted in deep pits. If the area for which such pits are claimed had a high groundwater level, potentially intruding groundwater would have put a limit to the depth such a cremation pit could have had. This applies to the Birkenau Camp, where the groundwater level was quite close to the surface. Witnesses claiming cremation pits several meters deep certainly did not tell the truth. (See the entry on groundwater level for more details.)

Another inflexible constraint concerns the fuel needed to burn a body on a pyre. The entry on lumberjacks gives an overview of the firewood that would have been needed to burn the number of corpses alleged by witnesses or by the orthodox narrative for various claimed Holocaust crime scenes. The table contained in that entry also gives an idea of how many trees would have had to be felled to obtain that much wood, and how many dedicated lumberjacks would have had to be employed for this. The discrepancy between claims and material reality is striking.

One attempt at evading the insurmountable problem of a lack of fuel is the claim that the Germans found a way to burn corpses without any fuel. This myth is covered in the entry on self-immolating bodies, which also contains a list of witnesses who made such false claims.

Furnace Cremations

The list of witnesses asserting self-burning bodies also contains cases relating to furnace cremations in crematoria. However, witness statements about the amount of fuel (wood, coke or coal) required to cremate a certain number of bodies in a cremation furnace are otherwise virtually non-existent.

The situation is different regarding assertions as to how many bodies were inserted concurrently into a cremation muffle, and how long it took for such a load to burn to ashes. On the Auschwitz cremation furnaces, many witnesses have made claims in this regard. These assertions can be compared with verifiable data, thus giving us a yardstick to assess the

Cremation Claims for Auschwitz Crematoria

Witness claims on number of corpses cremated concurrently per muffle (#/muffle), per hour and muffle (#/hr), as well as minutes needed to cremate one corpse (min/#)

WITNESS	#/MUFFLE	#/HR	MIN/#
Reality	**1**	**1**	**60**
Charles Bendel	–	13*	4.5
Pery Broad (SS)	4-6	10*	6
Stanisław Chybiński	3	26	2.3
Leon Cohen	2-5	4-10	6-15
Roman Dawidowski (expert)	5	12	5
Szlama Dragon	3	9-12	5-6.7
Bela Fabian	–	13*	4.6
David Fliamenbaum	2	8	7.5
Dario Gabai	4	8-12	5-7.5
Yaakov Gabai	4	8	7.5
Rudolf Höss (SS)	–	13*	4.5
Stanisław Jankowski	3-12	16.7*	3.6
Jeannette Kaufmann	–	8	7.5
Ota Kraus/Erich Kulka	3	9	6.7
Olga Lengyel	3	6	10
Maurice Lequeux	6?	18	3.3
André Lettich	6	7.2	8.3
Henryk Mandelbaum	4-6	16-30	2-4
Kurt Marcus	2	4-8	7.5-15
Filip Müller	3	9	6.7
Erich Mussfeldt (SS)	3	6	10
Ludwik Nagraba	8-9	–	–
Miklos Nyiszli	3	9	6.7
Narcyz Tadeusz Obrycki	2	–	–
Dov Paisikovic	2-3	8-17	4-7
Aaron Pilo	–	10-19	3-6
Kurt Prüfer (Topf & Sons)	**1**	**1**	**60**
Fritz Putzker	3-4	27-31	2
Joshuah Rosenblum	4	24	2.5
Josef Sackar	–	22*	2.8
Karl Schultze (Topf & Sons)	**1**	**1**	**60**
Jan Sehn (judge)	3-5	6-10	6-10
Roman Sompolinski	? (bodies)	?	≤3
Soviet Expert Report (1944)	3-4	24-36	1.7-2.5
Soviet Expert Report (1945)	3-5	7-10	6-8
Franz Süss	–	22-26*	2.3-2.8
Henryk Tauber	4-5 (8)	3-12	5-18
Morris Venezia	1	3-4	15-20
Shlomo Venezia	2-3	6-9	20
R. Vrba/A. Wetzler (1944)	3	2	30
Rudolf Vrba (1963)	3	9	6.7
Alfred Wetzler (1964)	3	9	6.7

For sources, see each witness's entry, as well as Mattogno 2019, p. 288.
* Calculated from claimed daily capacity of all crematoria, at 20 hours of operation per day; Jankowski's value is based on the capacity claimed for Crematorium II.

trustworthiness of a witness. See the data listed in the table.

As is documented in the section "Simultaneous Cremation of Multiple Bodies" of the entry on crematoria, the muffles of the Auschwitz cremation furnaces were designed to accommodate and incinerate only one corpse at a time. This process moreover took roughly one hour. Although it would have been possible to insert two corpses concurrently, this would have lengthened the cremation time considerably, with little if any advantage compared to burning these two corpses consecutively instead.

As the table demonstrates, this is a striking case of a "convergence of evidence" on a lie. Across the board, witnesses have vastly exaggerated the Auschwitz crematoria's capacity by claiming physically impossible numbers of corpses stuffed into these small muffles concurrently, and by giving ludicrously short cremation times per body of only a few minutes.

The background of this convergence on a lie is the urge of most witnesses in the immediate postwar era to confirm the Soviet, in fact the victorious Allies' atrocity-propaganda claim that at least four million inmates were killed and cremated at Auschwitz. Instrumental in achieving this convergence was Polish investigative judge Jan Sehn, among others, who interrogated many of these Auschwitz witnesses at war's end. It stands to reason that he coached them to adjust their claims to match the expected "truth." (See the entry on Jan Sehn.)

Later witnesses simply copied what earlier witnesses had claimed. For instance, Filip Müller, who plagiarized Miklos Nyiszli's 1946 tales, copied Nyiszli's cremation figures as well.

The only exception from the rule are the two engineers of the Topf Company who had designed and built the furnaces. Although they were certainly not treated gently while in Soviet captivity in Moscow, they nevertheless both independently stuck to the truth in this respect when interrogated by Soviet officials. They confirmed what documents and technical data indicate: It took one hour to cremate one body per muffle in these furnaces.

CREMATORIA

Fire funerals were quite common in ancient times but were banned by the monotheistic religions.

Only with increasing population densities, a lack of cemetery space, hygienic concerns, and decreasing influence of religions did cremations make a comeback in the late 1800s. They have been on the rise ever since; see the data prior to World War II for Germany in the chart. When the war broke out, cremations were still rather rare in less-developed Eastern European countries, and were viewed with horror by members of orthodox Christian and Jewish communities. This is the background for many a horror story of former deportees confronted with, and utterly misunderstanding, the presence of crematoria in German wartime camps.

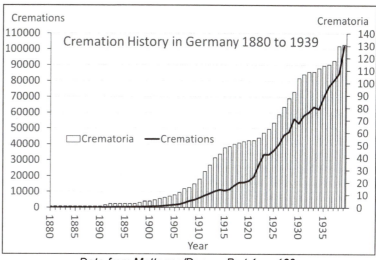

Data from Mattogno/Deana, Part 1, p. 139.

Considering the hygienic disaster common in crowded wartime camps, cremating the victims of those camps was a much better solution than burying them, which would have poisoned the drinking-water supply, thus further aggravating the hygienic situation.

Energetically speaking, the worst way of cremating corpses is on a pyre on the flat ground, because much of the heat gets lost due to radiation and convection. A better way is the incineration in relatively *narrow* trenches, where the earthen walls retain and reflect heat, and convection losses are limited (this advantage is lost when a pit is much wider than deep). Better still is combustion in so-called field furnaces, built in soil pits with stony walls and a ceiling of rocks. But all these methods are far surpassed by modern cremation furnaces. Such facilities not only reduce heat losses due to convection and radiation by encasing the combustion chamber with insulated material, but most of them also recover heat from the exhaust gases by way of heat exchangers or recuperators. The highest efficiency is reached by continuously operating furnaces used for incinerating animal carcasses and slaughter offal.

Many camps operated by German authorities before and during World War II were equipped with one or more cremation furnaces, usually (but not always) placed in a crematorium. Most of these furnaces followed standard civilian designs, although some were trimmed-down, cheaper and less efficient versions.

For that reason, all these furnaces were necessarily designed on the assumption that only one corpse is inserted and cremated at a time, as anything else was illegal, even by the rules promulgated by the SS authorities. Therefore, both the size of the muffle (and its corpse-introduction door) as well as the energy output of the fuel system (oil nozzles or coke hearths) were designed to cremate only one body at a time. Although two adult corpses and, if emaciated, maybe even three of them could be placed in a muffle at once with some skill and effort, such a procedure would have reduced the cremation speed considerably, as the furnace was not designed to evaporate the body water of several corpses at once. Hence, the muffle temperature would have dropped precipitously. On the other hand, once the body water had evaporated and the corpses started burning, they would have created much more heat and combustion gases than the system was able to handle. For more details on this, see the section "Simultaneous Cremation of Multiple Bodies."

Civilian Cremations

Civilian cremation expert state that the complete cremation process of a human body in their cremation furnaces takes between two to four hours. (See Kulaszka 2019, pp. 292f.; see also the statements on www.NationalCremation.com.) This complete cremation process includes:

– The burning of the coffin, which shields the body from the heat for an extended period, depending on the type of coffin.
– The main cremation phase, which is completed, when the body has disintegrated to such a degree that the main parts of it have fallen through the muffle grate into the post-combustion chamber underneath.
– The post-combustion phase, which usually takes place in a separate chamber, where bones and

smaller body parts burn out and turn to ashes.
- The cooling and cleaning phase after the combustion, when all the ashes get removed from the furnace, to prevent any (illegal) mixing of leftovers with ashes of subsequent cremations. The length of the cooling phase depends on how much heat the coffin added to the system, and also on the type of body cremated.

German Wartime Cremations

Cremations conducted in German wartime camps could be profoundly different than civilian cremations. If mass exterminations happened, the cremation procedure certainly did not abide by laws requiring that the ashes of cremated individuals be kept strictly separate. But the same is probably also true for emergency situations, such as catastrophic epidemics overwhelming a camp's cremation capacity. In that case, authorities were probably inclined to look the other way, as many lives were at stake, requiring the swift cremation of as many epidemic victims as possible.

The main differences between normal civilian cremations and those carried out in German wartime camps in the two scenarios mentioned are:
- Deceased camp inmates were usually cremated without a coffin. Hence, they were instantly exposed to the full heat of the furnace, which accelerated the cremation process.
- The cremation was considered finished, when the main cremation phase had come to an end, hence, when all major body parts had fallen through the muffle grate into the post-combustion chamber underneath. At that point, a new body could already be inserted, although the previous one was still burning and glowing underneath. This inevitably led to some mixing of the ashes of various individuals. However, since those ashes were not kept, but disposed of, it did not matter.
- Since no coffins were used, and most deceased inmates were lean or even emaciated – hence low in body fat – the furnaces actually needed more fuel than during civilian cremations. There was therefore no need for a cooling phase.
- Furthermore, cleaning the ash chamber could be done at any time, without any need to worry about a cremation coming to a complete end.

For these reasons, cremations in scenarios of mass extermination or epidemic emergencies are profoundly different than civilian cremations. As a result, the *net* cremation time needed to cremate a body – meaning the time between the subsequent insertion of two corpses – is considerably shorter.

The following sections will briefly discuss the cremation furnaces – or the lack thereof – in some of the more-prominent German wartime camps. Cremation times always refer to the shortest possible *net* cremation times as just explained, hence merely the time needed for the main cremation phase of a body inside the muffle, before its main parts have dropped into the post-combustion chamber underneath.

Aktion Reinhardt Camps

These three camps – Belzec, Sobibór, and Treblinka – are said to have been pure extermination camps, where Jews were slaughtered by the thousands every day. Any German engineer planning such a feat would have seen to it that large-scale, continuously operating carcass-incineration facilities were built in those camps. Yet mysteriously, *none* of these camps are said to have had *any* cremation facilities at all. Chełmno supposedly had a primitive field-furnace, but in Belzec, Sobibór and Treblinka, thousands of corpses at a time were allegedly burned on multi-story-high pyres placed in large pits, much wider and longer than deep, hence close to the worst possible solution (pyres on ground level). Surprisingly, in the summer of 1943, the SS Administrator at the Higher SS and Police Leader of the Government General (Poland) sent a letter to local camps stating that they have at their disposal – and have had for quite a while – a surplus of cremation furnaces, asking all camp headquarters to report if they needed any such device. There is no evidence that the *Aktion Reinhardt* Camps ever ordered or received any such devices, which most likely means they had no need for them.

Majdanek

The Majdanek Camp had two crematoria, built and operated sequentially. The first was erected as a provisional structure – a wooden barracks equipped with two commercially available mobile oil-fired cremation furnaces, one of which is today exhibited in the reconstructed crematorium building. Only one document exists about this structure, which operated only for about half a year (June 1942 to early 1943) and was shut down due to a lack of oil, and then dismantled. The second, proper crematorium became operational only in January of 1944 and was equipped with five cremation chambers (muffles) set in one large brick structure, fired by coke-fueled hearths in the rear of each muffle. There was a heat-exchange chamber between muffles one and two, and four and five, respectively, used to transfer heat from the flue gases to a system of coiled water-pipes providing hot water for inmate showers. The third center muffle was a reserve muffle, to be heated in case of emergency, with its exhaust gases fed alternatively to the heat-exchange chamber on either side. The size of the muffle was designed to accommodate one corpse at a time, and the size of the front doors (0.55 m × 0.65 m, with an arched top) was designed to insert corpses with only a small coffin or none at all. The capacity of the Majdanek coke-fired cremation furnaces was about one corpse per muffle and per hour. (See Graf/Mattogno 2012, pp. 99-116.)

The Majdanek Camp was overrun by the Red Army in late August 1944. The crematorium building itself was burned down around that time, but the furnaces themselves survived largely unscathed. Images of the cremation furnaces with partially cremated corpses – probably a staged scene, see illustration – were used to create a horrific impression in Allied mass-media reports. It was meant to lend credibility to the Soviet propaganda lie that up to two million inmates had been slaughtered and cremated in the Majdanek Camp. This abuse of images of a cremation device for the purpose of atrocity propaganda was probably the reason why the German authorities ordered that the Auschwitz crematoria be dismantled in late 1944 before the arrival of Soviet troops. (See the section on Auschwitz.)

Buchenwald

The Buchenwald Camp was equipped with two coke-fired triple-muffle furnaces of the company Topf & Sons, Erfurt, one of which had been adapted for optional use with oil. The other one was structurally identical to the furnaces installed in Crematoria II and III at Auschwitz-Birkenau. Since the Birkenau devices have been dismantled and destroyed, the Buchenwald cremation devices are important for the study of Auschwitz regarding capacity and fuel consumption. No outrageous cremation claims of note were made regarding the Buchenwald Camp's crematorium. (See Mattogno/Deana, Part 1, pp. 232f., 266-270.)

Mauthausen

The Mauthausen Camp was equipped with one coke-fired double-muffle furnace of the company Topf & Sons, Erfurt, which is identical to the three furnaces erected inside the crematorium ("Crema I") at the Auschwitz Main Camp. The Mauthausen furnace was erected only in early 1945 and was hardly used. To this day it is in an excellent state of preservation. This allows them to be studied in detail, since the equivalent devices in Auschwitz were dismantled in 1944, and were reassembled in a crude and flawed manner after the war by the Polish Auschwitz Museum, rendering them useless as objects of a technical study. (See Mattogno/Deana, Part 1, pp. 251-266.)

Gusen

The Gusen Camp, a satellite camp of the Mauthausen Camp, was equipped with one double-muffle coke-fired furnace of the company Topf & Sons, Erfurt. It has some structural differences compared to the three similar furnaces installed inside the crematorium at the Auschwitz Main Camp, making it superior to the Auschwitz devices. For instance, the gaps of the muffles' fire-clay grate were much larger than those of the Auschwitz furnaces (eight openings of some 30 cm × 25 cm in size in Gusen, compared to six slits of just 5 cm width in Auschwitz), so that large corpse parts could fall into the post-combustion chamber be-

Atrocity photo of the Majdanek cremation furnace taken by a Soviet photographer after conquering the Majdanek Camp.

neath the muffle, clearing the muffle faster for a new load (although adding a new corpse while parts of the old load were still burning in the post-combustion chamber would have been illegal, strictly speaking). Furthermore, the Gusen furnace had one dedicated forced-draft system, whereas at Auschwitz, the same type of system was handling the flue gases of three furnaces; the Auschwitz forced-draft system was completely removed in the summer of 1942.

Detailed documentation of the time and amount of coke it took to cremate a body has been preserved for the Gusen furnace. According to this, the average main-combustion phase of a single-corpse cremation took about 40 minutes and consumed some 30 kg of coke during continuous operation, and up to 48 kg/corpse during discontinuous operation (the difference is required to bring a cold furnace up to operating temperature). This allows for a realistic estimate of cremation times and coke consumption for similar devices, such as those installed at Majdanek and Auschwitz. (See Mattogno/Deana, Part 1, pp. 301-306, 311-314.)

Westerbork

The Westerbork transit camp in the Netherlands originally had an oil-fired cremation furnace of the Kori Company that was later refitted with a coke hearth. The camp's archives contain numerous cremation lists giving the number of corpses cremated, the duration of each cremation, and the total coke consumption. The average cremation duration of that furnace, which had a larger hearth than the Auschwitz furnaces and thus a larger heat output, was about 50 minutes per corpse. This allows for a realistic estimate of cremation times and coke consumption for similar devices, such as those installed at Majdanek and Auschwitz. (See Mattogno/Deana, Part 1, pp. 306-314.)

Auschwitz Main Camp

Step by step, three coke-fired double-muffle cremation furnaces manufactured by the company Topf & Sons were set up in a building that had once served as an ammunition bunker for a Polish artillery unit:
– first furnace operational on 15 August 1940
– second furnace operational on or around 1 March 1941
– third furnace operational in late March 1942

This building was subsequently called Crematorium

"Reconstructed" Crematorium I at the Auschwitz Main Camp during the 1990s.

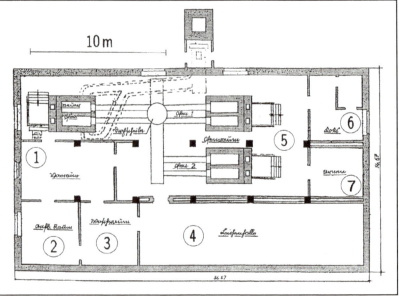

Floor plan of Crematorium I in Auschwitz I/Main Camp in its condition as of April 1942. The morgue is at that time said to have been equipped for usage as a homicidal gas chamber.
1: Vestibule; 2: laying-out room; 3: washroom; 4: morgue; 5: furnace room; 6: coke; 7: urns.

Furnace No.	Date Operational	Days in Existence
1	15 Aug. 1940	1066 days
2	22 Feb. 1941	511 days
3	31 March 1942	473 days

I or later, when the Birkenau crematoria became operational, simply "the old crematorium." It operated as such until 17 July 1943, when it was permanently shut down. See the data for each furnace in the table. Note that days *in existence* does not equal days *in operation*, as the first two furnaces had to be shut down and repaired several times during their existence. After the crematorium was retired, the furnaces were dismantled, and its parts stored. At that time, the chimney was also torn down.

In mid-May 1942, damage to the crematorium chimney and later also to the flue ducts was discovered. Hence, the crematorium had to be shut down completely in early June in order to build a new chimney and new smoke ducts. This work was finished on August 8. During the months June to August 1942, the typhus epidemic that had been lingering in the Auschwitz and Birkenau camps for months went completely out of control, causing hundreds of victims every day. This happened at a time when the camp had absolutely *no* cremation capacity. Hence, when the new chimney was completed, cremations were restarted at a furious pace, damaging the new, still wet chimney right away.

In the fall of 1944, this building was re-purposed to serve as an air-raid shelter for SS men of the nearby SS hospital. Among other things, a sheet-metal-clad door was added allowing access from the outside directly to the former morgue, then subdivided into several air-raid shelter rooms.

The changes made for that purpose were only partially undone by the Auschwitz Museum after the war, thus creating a confusing hybrid exhibit – shown to thousands of tourists every year – displaying some features of the original crematorium, some features of the later air-raid shelter, and some that were invented from scratch by the Museum, such as the Zyklon-B introduction shafts. Two of the three furnaces were also rebuilt using recovered original parts, although that reconstruction is highly flawed. For instance, the Museum did not add the coke hearth to the rear of the furnace, but built a small hearth un-

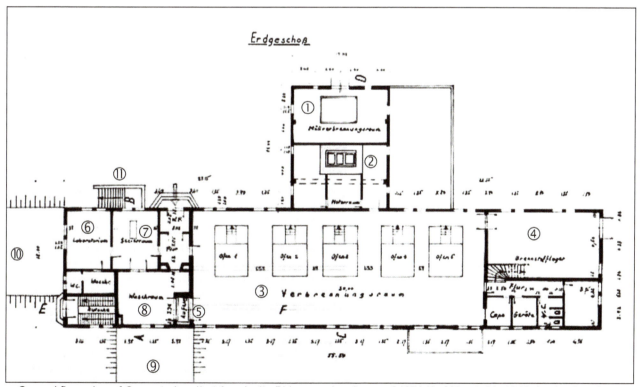

Ground floor plan of Crematorium II at Auschwitz-Birkenau; drawing no. 2197(p)I of March 20, 1943, by the Auschwitz Construction Office. Numbers here added: ① Garbage incineration room; ② chimney with three flues; ③ cremation room with five triple-muffle furnaces; ④ fuel storage room; ⑤ small freight elevator, only access to basement morgues from within the building; ⑥ laboratory; ⑦ dissecting room; ⑧ wash room; ⑨ semi-underground Morgue #1 (alleged homicidal gas chamber); ⑩ semi-underground Morgue #2 (alleged undressing room); ⑪ is an additional staircase to the underground area added later (not shown in the next older illustration).

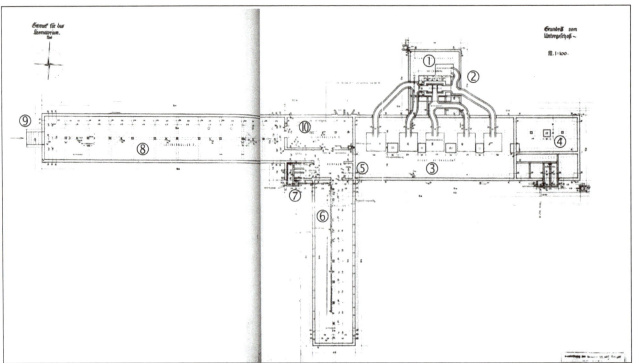

Basement floor plan of Crematorium II at Auschwitz-Birkenau; drawing no. 932 of January 23, 1942, by the Auschwitz Construction Office. Numbers here added: ① Garbage incineration room; ② chimney fed by six flues: five from the cremation furnaces and one from the waste incinerator; two flues merge together into one chimney flue; ③ cremation room with five triple-muffle furnaces; ④ fuel storage room; ⑤ small freight elevator, only access to basement morgues from within the building; ⑥ semi-underground Morgue #1, 7 m × 30 m (alleged homicidal gas chamber); ⑦ staircase from outside to the basement area; ⑧ semi-underground Morgue #2, 8 m × 50 m (alleged undressing room); ⑨ staircase from outside into Morgue #2; ⑩ Morgue #3, later subdivided into several rooms and equipped with a separate entry staircase from outside (see ⑪ in previous illustration).

derneath the muffle. A new chimney was also erected, although it is not connected to the former furnaces' smoke ducts. (See the entry on Auschwitz Main Camp, as well as Mattogno/Deana, Part 1, pp. 212-228; Mattogno 2016c.)

As late as the year 2000, the Auschwitz Museum lied to its millions of visitors by claiming that what they see is identical to the original state of the crematorium, including its alleged homicidal gas chamber. Then they changed their narrative, admitting some inaccuracies that happened during the "reconstruction" after the war, but they keep lying about several aspects of their mendacious post-war tampering with this important piece of evidence, in particular about their post-war fabricated Zyklon-B introduction shafts. (See Mattogno 2016c; 2020, pp. 7-38.)

Auschwitz-Birkenau

When plans were initiated for the construction of a huge PoW camp near the village of Birkenau, close to Auschwitz, a new, larger crematorium was planned as well, although it was initially planned to be constructed at the Auschwitz Main Camp. It was to be equipped with five coke-fired triple-muffle furnaces manufactured by the company Topf & Sons. By early 1942, the construction site had been moved to the Birkenau Camp. But when the typhus epidemic in Auschwitz got out of control in the summer of 1942, first a second crematorium of the same design (but mirror-imaged) was added (the later Crematorium III), then two further crematoria of a simplified design were added (the later Crematoria IV and V). The table below shows some features of these crematoria. (For this and many of the following data, see Mattogno/Deana, Part 1, pp. 228-251, 350f.)

The triple-muffle furnaces basically consisted of a double-muffle furnace with a third muffle inserted in the middle. The lateral muffles' combustion gases flowed through openings in the side wall into the center muffle, from whose rear end they flowed into the smoke duct. Hence, the center muffle was not equipped with a hearth, but rather used the heat contained in the lateral muffles' combustion gas to incinerate its load. Accordingly, the coke consumption of this furnace type was roughly 2/3 that of the double-muffle furnace (some 20 kg/corpse rather than 30

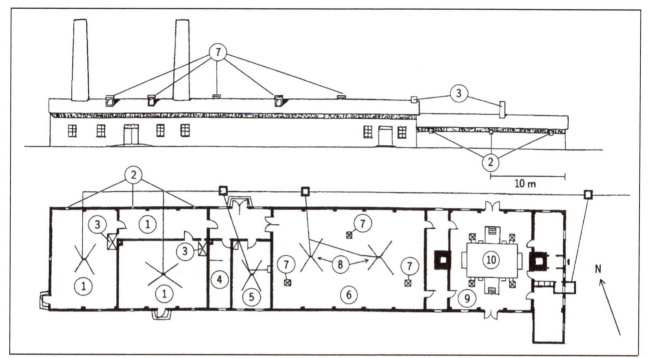

North lateral view (above) and floorplan (below) of Crematorium IV at Auschwitz-Birkenau (Crematorium V was its mirror image), based upon drawing no. 2036 of the Auschwitz Construction Office of Jan. 11, 1943. Numbers here added: ① Three annex rooms; one was probably merely a hallway, another a shower room, and the third was temporarily planned to serve as a disinfestation room; these three rooms (or sometimes only the two large ones) are said to have been homicidal gas chambers, but since there was no ventilation system installed, this was impossible; ② alleged Zyklon-B introduction hatches; since a metal grid was installed in those openings, they could not have served that purpose; ③ heating furnace, fueled from the hallway; ④ fuel storage room; ⑤ doctor's office; ⑥ morgue; ⑦ ventilation chimneys (note: the alleged homicidal gas chambers had no ventilation chimneys!); ⑧ drains (also in the doctor's office and the two large annex rooms); ⑨ cremation room; ⑩ four double-muffle furnaces are grouped into one large 8-muffle unit (Pressac 1989, p. 401).

kg/corpse), while the cremation time was somewhat longer because none of the Birkenau crematoria had any forced-draft devices to fan the hearth flames. The triple-muffle furnace's design was problematic, however, since twice as much combustion gas flowed through the center muffle as through each of the lateral ones, resulting in the gas flowing at twice the speed through the center muffle. That led to some of the combustion taking place in the smoke duct rather than the muffle, overheating and thus damaging the duct lining.

Hence, when Crematorium II was hastily put into operation in March 1943 due to a backlog of typhus victims in need of cremation, parts of the smoke ducts collapsed after only a few weeks, and the chimney lining was also damaged. This facility therefore operated at reduced capacity from early April 1943, and had to be shut down completely from mid-May until the end of August 1943 to rebuild the duct and chimney linings.

Crematorium IV fared even worse. Its furnaces and chimney were barely operational when incinerations began at a frantic pace. Since the fresh mortar and brickwork still contained much water, the resulting fast evaporation of this water damaged furnaces, ducts and chimney to such a degree that the entire facility became unusable within two months. The facility was never fully repaired afterwards and was abandoned as a cremation facility.

The coke-fired eight-muffle furnaces of Crematoria IV and V, also manufactured by the company Topf & Sons, consisted of a single-muffle furnace with an additional muffle attached to its side. The combustion gases of the first muffle were used to

#	Startup 1943	Shutdown	Furnaces	20-h Capacity	Coke per Corpse*	20-h coke*
II	14 March	Oct. 1944	5×3-muffle	300 corpses	20 kg	6,000 kg
III	25 June	Oct. 1944	5×3-muffle	300 corpses	20 kg	6,000 kg
IV	22 March	Oct. 1944	1×8-muffle	160 corpses	15 kg	2,400 kg
V	4 April	Jan. 1945	1×8-muffle	160 corpses	15 kg	2,400 kg

* for continuous operation; that value increases with increasing phases of furnace inactivity, up to twice that value and more.

The almost finished Crematorium II.   *The finished Crematorium III.*

The finished Crematorium IV.   *The finished Crematorium V.*

All photos were taken in the first half of 1943 by SS *Unterscharführer Dietrich Kamann.*

heat and incinerate the load of the second muffle. As a result, this furnace used roughly half the fuel per corpse compared to the double-muffle furnace, hence some 15 kg/corpse. Four of these furnaces were assembled to form a large block (two side-by-side, and two of these assemblies back-to-back), thus reducing heat losses due to convection and radiation.

In October 1941, the Birkenau Camp was planned to hold some 125,000 PoWs. In August of 1942, that number rose to 200,000 inmates. To this figure, we need to add the inmates held in the Auschwitz Main Camp and the various satellite camps. The project was huge and unparalleled. Initially, only 15 muffles (of Crematorium II) were planned, but by August 1942, with the camp's mortality reaching a catastrophic peak of some 8,600 victims per month, mainly of the raging typhus epidemic, the planned cremation capacity was increased from 15 to 46 muffles – hence 31 additional muffles. This may look excessive, but if we compare this with the ratio of monthly mortality to cremation muffles in other camps for which no one today claims any mass-extermination activities, the Auschwitz plans are not excessive at all; see the following table (cf. Rudolf/Mattogno 2017, pp. 164-171).

This clearly shows that the construction of four crematoria was dictated not by plans of mass extermination but rather by the catastrophic situation created by rampaging epidemics, combined with plans to massively increase the camp population.

By comparison: The distance a car can drive in its lifetime cannot be determined by multiplying its top speed by the hours contained in its lifespan of, say, ten years. At a top speed of 120 mph and a planned

Camp Mortality and Planned Cremation Capacity			
	Dachau	Buchenwald	Auschwitz
mortality during additional-furnace planning month:	66	337	8,600 (Aug. 1942)
planned number of additional muffles:	4	6	31*
ratio muffles/mortality:	6%	2.8%	0.4%
* 15 muffles in the future Crematorium III, and 16 muffles together in Crematoria IV and V			

Coke Deliveries to Auschwitz Cremas in 1943			
Month	coke [t]	Month	coke [t]
January	23	June	61
February	40	July	67
March	144.5	August	71
April	60	September	61
May	95	October	82
		Total:	704.5

lifetime of ten years, this would amount to more than ten million miles. A car cannot be operated at top speed round the clock for years on end, and neither can a cremation furnace. Hence, multiplying the number of muffles with the daily number of cremations possible at peak performance, multiplied with the days a facility existed, is deceitful at best.

The intensity at which the crematoria in Auschwitz and Birkenau were used can be gleaned from the coke deliveries to these facilities. Almost complete records of them have been preserved from early 1942 until October 1943; see the table to the right.

When considering all factors involved, such as the various furnace types operating at various times with various capacities, and the type of corpses requiring different amounts of fuel (emaciated victims of epidemics, low in body fat, require more fuel), the results show that the coke deliveries are fully compatible with the number of deaths recorded in the camp's documents, mainly due to the raging epidemics. The resulting average coke consumption per cremated body is furthermore quite similar to that at the Gusen Camp, for which detailed documentation on cremation activities has been preserved.

On the other hand, if the alleged but undocumented number of gassing victims are added to the documented deaths, the coke available for cremating each corpse would drop to an impossibly low amount of just some 2 to 3 kg. (See Mattogno 2019, pp. 272-275; 2021a, pp. 30-35.)

The vast documentation of the Birkenau crematoria includes many documents about repairs, but it does not include any trace of the muffle linings and refractory grates being completely replaced. These had a lifetime of about 2,000 cremations. This sets the maximum number of cremations to (46 muffles × 2,000 =) 92,000 for the Birkenau crematoria (see Mattogno/Deana, Part 1, pp. 348-350). Adding to this the maximum possible number of cremations performed in the old crematorium (6 muffles × 2,000 = 12,000), and the number of victims initially buried but then exhumed and cremated outdoors during open-air incineration (some ten to twenty thousand), this is in good agreement with the total number of actual victims of the Auschwitz camp complex – around 135,500 (see Mattogno 2023, Part 2, p. 211) – without the claimed one million gas-chamber victims, for whom there was no cremation capacity left at all.

Starting in late fall of 1944, in anticipation of a Soviet conquest of the area, the camp authorities started demolishing Crematoria II through VI. Crematorium V was dynamited only during the final days of the SS's presence at Auschwitz. This evidently was done to prevent the Soviets from staging atrocity photos, as they had done at the Majdanek Camp (Mattogno 2023, Part 1, pp. 481f.).

Dachau

The Dachau Camp initially had a mobile oil-fired double-muffle cremation furnace of the Topf Company, re-equipped (and immobilized) with two coke hearths, one on either side. The device was intensely used, showing clear signs of wear. It is located in a small building and can be inspected there to this day (see illustrations in Mattogno/Deana, Part 2, pp. 43-50). Two coke-fired double-muffle furnaces of the Kori firm were built in the new crematorium building, showing little sign of usage. (For a description, read Mattogno/Deana, Part 1, pp. 391f.)

Simultaneous Cremation of Multiple Bodies

In civilian crematoria, multiple cremations in the same muffle were prohibited by law and were never carried out. The furnaces set up in German wartime camps were built following civilian laws and regulations, so they, too, were designed to cremate only one body at a time. In fact, most furnaces set up in the camps were cheaper, trimmed-down versions. For one thing, their doors and muffles were usually

The five triple-muffle furnaces of Crematorium II. Photo taken by SS Unterscharführer Dietrich Kamann.

smaller than civilian ones, because the latter had to allow the occasional introduction of large coffins, while the camp furnaces either used only small caskets or none at all. This is particularly true for the furnaces of the companies Topf and Kori, the most-frequent camp furnaces.

The Topf furnace's doors were 60 cm (2 ft) wide and high. The lower approximately 10 cm of that height were taken up by the corpse-introduction stretcher resting on a pair of rollers, while the upper 30 cm consisted of a semi-circular arch. With human corpses being some 50 cm wide and 20 to 25 cm high, it was physically possible to enter two corpses stacked on top of each other through that door, but certainly not more. Once two corpses had been deposited on the muffle grate, introducing another set of two corpses, as for instance claimed by Henryk Tauber, would have required tipping the 45-cm-wide stretcher steeply upward to get it on top of the two corpses already in that muffle. Trying this would have made the corpses lying on the stretcher hit the muffle vault. There would have been no way of pushing the stretcher all the way into the muffle. Furthermore, with such an inclination, the two corpses lying on the stretcher might have slid backwards and off the stretcher.

In most camps, Auschwitz and Birkenau included, inmate bodies were cremated without a coffin. As a result, the muffle temperature dropped drastically when introducing a body, because the initial phase of evaporating the bodies' water requires a lot of heat. The coke hearth and the muffle wall's refractory material were designed to store only the heat needed to cope with one body's amount of water. Placing several bodies at once into such a furnace with several times the amount of water would have dropped the muffle temperature below the operational optimum. This would have slowed down the cremation process drastically. With many corpses in a muffle, the temperature would have dropped to a point where no cremation but only "charcoaling" would have occurred.

Placing several corpses at once into a muffle not designed for it leads to another problem: openings in the muffle grate and the side walls, through which the combustion gases travel, get obstructed, slowing down the evaporation phase even more.

However, once the water has evaporated and the bodies burn, the amount of heat produced would overwhelm the muffle walls' ability to store such heat, and the amount of combustion gasses developing would speed up the flow of overheated gases into the smoke ducts, which eventually would suffer heat damage.

In other words, burning several corpses at once in a muffle designed for only one body would not have sped up the cremation process but might have initially led to an almost standstill, while the latter combustion phase would have been so intense that the refractory lining of the muffles and smoke ducts would have been seriously damaged in the long run.

(For details, see Mattogno/Deana, Part 1, pp. 317-327.)

CRIMINAL TRACES

In preparation for the Polish show trial against former Auschwitz camp commandant Rudolf Höss, Polish engineer Dr. Roman Dawidowski and Polish Investigating Judge Jan Sehn rummaged through the documents left behind by the SS at Auschwitz. They were searching for evidence for the existence and operation of homicidal gas chambers. They found several documents with ambivalent expressions such as "gas chamber" or "gas-tight door," took them out of their documental and historical context, and submitted their biased interpretation as an "expert report" to the Polish Court.

French historian Jean-Claude Pressac, who discovered this report during his research in the Auschwitz Archives during the 1980s, also found a few more documents along the same line, and published them in 1989 together with his own skewed interpretation, rebranding them as "criminal traces."

A thorough analysis of these documents within their documental and historical context shows that not a single one of these documents proves the existence of homicidal gas chambers, but rather of very mundane facilities such as disinfestation chambers, inmate showers and ordinary mortuaries.

The most-commonly mentioned criminal traces can be grouped into the following categories, according to what the respective document mentions:

Gastight Windows or Doors, or Parts for Them
These documents are so numerous and concern so many doors, windows and buildings that it is clear that "gas-tight" was a generic term used for windows and doors made draft-proof with some felt strips. These were used in numerous places, not just rooms falsely claimed to have served as homicidal gas chambers. (For more details, see the entry on gastight doors.)

Gas(ing) Rooms

Due to the catastrophic hygienic situation at Birkenau in 1942 and early 1943, and the incessant need for more disinfestation capacities and inmate showers, the Auschwitz camp authorities made plans to include these in the Birkenau crematoria. At least some of these projects were fully implemented. Documents referring to gas chambers or gassing rooms in those buildings need to be seen in this context.

Undressing Rooms

The Auschwitz garrison physician Eduard Wirths requested in early 1943 that the new crematoria, where many corpses were delivered every day, had a designated undressing room. Many of these bodies were infested with fleas and lice, requiring occasional disinfestation measures. After that, the corpses could be safely undressed, and their clothes removed for treatment. Hence, during that time, one of the morgues was designated as such, to solve that problem.

Showers

Documents show that all crematoria acquired real working inmate showers – Crematoria II and III in one of their basement rooms, and Crematoria IV and V in one of the rooms alleged to have served as a homicidal gas chamber. These were not fake showers, but real ones. Once the *Zentralsauna* became operational, which was Birkenau's powerful and spacious inmate shower and disinfestation building, the inmate showers inside the crematoria were probably taken out of commission, resulting in a peculiar sight: showerheads in morgues partially filled with corpses. This was kindling for the fires that fueled the Auschwitz rumor machine.

The theory of "criminal traces" is a smoke-and-mirror show based on misunderstood or misrepresented documents that are ambivalent at worst, but usually utterly innocuous, if seen in their proper documental and historical context.

(For a full list and discussion of all the "criminal traces" ever brought up, see Rudolf 2016; Mattogno 2019, pp. 27-205; Rudolf 2019a.)

Croatia → **Yugoslavia**

CRYSTAL NIGHT

In October of 1938, the radically anti-Jewish Polish government decided that all Polish Jews living abroad who did not renew their passport in Poland by the end of October of that year would have their citizenship revoked. At that time, tens of thousands of Polish Jews were living in Germany, the majority of them in Berlin. Evidently, for them, Hitler's Germany was still the better place to be. However, the National-Socialist German government was not enthused by the threat of having tens of thousands of Polish Jews thrust upon Germany for good. Hence, they organized special trains and deported some 12,000 of these Jews to the Polish border, so they could cross into Poland and renew their passports. Although it was still October, and thus these Polish Jews, as Polish citizens, should have had the right to enter Poland, the Polish government closed the border for them. This resulted in a standoff between German and Polish border officials, with some 8,000 Jews caught in the middle. Many of them had to spend days stuck at the border zone. Eventually, the Germans caved in and let the Jews return home.

Enraged by this treatment of his fellow Jews, his parents among them, a Polish-German Jew living in Paris named Herschel Grynszpan went to the German embassy in Paris on 7 November and shot the German embassy official Ernst vom Rath. Two days later, vom Rath died of his wounds. When this news reached Germany, riots against Jewish individuals, synagogues, businesses and community centers broke out across Germany in the night from the 9th to the 10th of November 1938. It quickly developed into a full-fledged country-wide pogrom, during which roughly 100 Jews were killed, more than 200 synagogues were destroyed, and thousands of Jewish businesses were damaged to one degree or another. The financial damage went into the billions of reichsmarks. Due to the many Jewish shop windows broken during that night, this pogrom is commonly referred to as *Kristallnacht* in German – Crystal Night, the Night of Broken Glass.

It remains an open question to what degree the Third Reich's government and their paramilitary groups the SA and the *Stosstrupp* Hitler, instigated the actions. On the one hand, sanctioned anti-Jewish measures had been ramping up for some time, but acts of vandalism were frowned upon. For an extended defense against government involvement in Crystal Night, see Weckert 1991.

On the other hand, when actions were underway, the German government was happy to let it unfold, and even to fan the flames. In his diary entry of 10 November, Joseph Goebbels recounted events as they happened: "I bring the matter to the *Führer*. He decides: let the demonstrations continue. Withdraw the police... That's only right." Of the many fires at Jewish businesses and synagogues, Goebbels wrote, "We intervene only when necessary to save adjacent buildings. Otherwise, let them burn down."

Soon thereafter, the German government's reaction to this pogrom clearly shows that they thought the damage done wasn't enough. They passed a law, illegally applied retroactively, which prevented insurance companies from paying out any insurance payments to Jews who had coverage against vandalism. Next, they imposed a collective fine on all Jews of one billion reichsmarks, which amounted to a partial expropriation of German Jewry. It was an excessive collective punishment for the crime of one individual (Grynszpan), designed to drive the Jews out of Germany.

In the eyes of many observers abroad but also in Germany, the National-Socialist government made its ultimate step from civilization to barbarism with these acts. The Western powers used Crystal Night to accelerate their anti-German rhetoric and to become ever-more belligerent. The world geared up for war, which began not even ten months later.

cyanide gas → Zyklon B

CYKERT, ABRAHAM

Abraham Cykert

Abraham Cykert, a Jew from Łódź, Poland, was eventually deported, via the Belzec Transit Camp (according to his own statement), to Auschwitz, and later from there to the Buchenwald Camp. Had Belzec been an extermination camp rather than a transit camp, he would neither have seen Auschwitz or Buchenwald, nor have had any opportunity to testify after the war. However, incredibly, he survived all three camps. About Auschwitz, he told a completely invented, imaginary tale about his magic salvation while standing in line waiting to be gassed. (Mattogno 2021, pp. 343f.)

CYRANKIEWICZ, JOZEF

Jozef Cyrankiewicz (23 Apr. 1911 – 20 Jan. 1989) was a Polish socialist/communist politician who was active in the Polish resistance movement during the war. He was captured by the Germans and sent to the Auschwitz Camp, where he supposedly helped organizing the camp's resistance groups, although that is contested today. He was one of many communists influential in creating and spreading false anti-German wartime propaganda. For instance, in one message sent out to the Polish underground on 21 January 1943, he wrote:

Jozef Cyrankiewicz

"Gas. Entire transports are sent directly to the gas, without registering anyone at all. The number [of those murdered] in these transports already exceeds 500,000. Mostly Jews. Lately, transports of Poles from the Lublin Region are going directly to the gas (men and women). Children are thrown directly into the fire. Behind Birkenau the so-called 'eternal flame' burns – an open-air burning of corpses; the crematorium cannot cope."

At that time, however, only some 143,000 Jews had been deported to Auschwitz, of whom some 82,000 are said to have been killed in gas chambers (see Rudolf 2019b).

In early October 1944, Cyrankiewicz wrote in another message sent out to the Polish underground:

"The gassing never ends: 3,000 prisoners from Theresienstadt; 2,500 from Auschwitz I, II, and III; 6,000 Jewish women from Weimar; 500 male Jews from the ghetto in Lodz; 400 prisoners from Buchenwald. Selections from among the sick and the unhealthy for gassing continue unabated."

All of this is freely invented. In fact, the claim that 6,000 Jewesses from Weimar were gassed is so preposterous that Polish historian Danuta Czech changed that in her book *Auschwitz Chronicle* to read, "6,000 female Hungarian Jews" (Czech 1990, p. 724), but no documentation exists for that either. (For more details, see Mattogno 2022b, pp. 257, 266-271.)

After the war, Cyrankiewicz played a major role in the oppressive Polish-Communist postwar government.

Czechia → Protectorate

CZECH, DANUTA

Danuta Czech (1922 – 4 April 2002) was a Polish historian and deputy director of the Polish Auschwitz Museum. She was the lead historian of the Auschwitz Museum's project to write a day-by-day chronology of the Auschwitz Camp. This project got initiated when West Germany started its investigation against former members of the Auschwitz Camp's staff, which ended in the Frankfurt Auschwitz Trial. The results were published in a Polish periodical specifically established for that purpose, and shortly later in German translation (also in a periodical specifically established for that purpose), evidently in order to influence the West-German criminal investigations. This *Auschwitz Chronicle* was re-published in an updated version in 1989 in German and in 1990 in English (Czech 1989, 1990).

Danuta Czech

A detailed comparison of what Czechs claims about her sources with what they really state, and with the many sources she ignored, demonstrates that, when it comes to claims of mass exterminations, Czech's *Auschwitz Chronicle* is a mere jumble of conjectures, distortions, inventions and omissions. She used these mendacious methods to systematically draw a historical image depicting the defendants at that trial – and the German nation at large – as unfathomably perverted monsters. Czech even had the nerve to testify during the Frankfurt Show Trial and commit perjury by making blatantly false claims about the evidence she relied upon when writing her texts. (For details, see Mattogno 2022b; Rudolf 2019b.)

The entire operation was Poland's successful attempt at having the West-German judiciary accept and cast in stone the Polish-Communist Auschwitz narrative, which portrays the German nation as a monster, and instills in Germans an eternal feeling of guilt. This also had the effect of securing for all time the spoils Poland gained from the greatest ethnic cleansing mankind has ever seen – the Eastern German provinces of Pomerania, Silesia, West Prussia and southern East Prussia. (The northern part of East Prussia went to Soviet Russia, now the "Kaliningrad Oblast.")

CZECHIA

During the Second World War, the Sudetenland border areas of today's Czechia were part of Germany. The rest of Czechia itself was called Protectorate Bohemia and Moravia. Some 82,000 Jews were deported from that area. Most of them stayed temporarily at the Theresienstadt Ghetto, before being moved on to other places. Initially, many of them were sent to locations in the Baltics and to transit camps and ghettos in the Lublin District. Later, many of them ended up in the Auschwitz Camp. (See the entry on Jewish demography for a broader perspective.)

CZECHOWICZ, ARON

Aron Czechowicz was a Polish Jew who arrived at the Treblinka Camp on 10 September 1942 from the Warsaw Ghetto, but managed to flee a few weeks later. He was interviewed by a Polish investigator on 11 October 1945. He claimed that he saw a gas-chamber building with three chambers, where the killing occurred by a Ukrainian auxiliary pouring some liquid from a canister through "three openings surrounded by a tube in the shape of a small chimney" located in the roof over each chamber, while an engine ran. This killing method and the associated introduction chimneys are otherwise undocumented, and are rejected as false and invented by all historians and other witnesses. This is probably a reflection of claims made about Zyklon-B gassings at Majdanek, Auschwitz and Stutthof.

(For more details, see Mattogno 2021e, pp. 162f.; https://zapisyterroru.pl/.)

D

DACHAU

Documented History

The Dachau Camp enters the Holocaust stage in March 1942, when plans for a proper crematorium building were drawn up. The few documents that the conquering U.S. troops did not destroy show little unusual. However, on 9 August 1942, hence in the early stages of the planning and construction phase, Dachau camp physician Siegmund Rascher wrote a letter to SS chief Heinrich Himmler, in which he wrote that a facility equal to the one already existing at Linz is currently being built at Dachau. The reference to Linz probably pointed to Hartheim Castle near that Austrian city, which was one of the institutions where the Third Reich implemented its euthanasia program. Accordingly, Rascher mentions that invalids end up in certain chambers anyway, which is why he asked for permission to use these chambers in order to test Germany's new war gasses. The latter probably referred to the nerve gasses Tabun and Sarin, which had been discovered in Germany in 1936 and 1938, respectively; Tabun had gone into mass production in Germany in 1942.

At the time that Rascher wrote this letter, four Zyklon-B disinfestation chambers using the DEGESCH circulation method were under construction at the far end of the new crematorium building in Dachau. It stands to reason that Rascher was thinking about using those chambers for war-gas experiments.

Siegmund Rascher is known for his involvement in several (pseudo-)medical experiments using concentration-camp inmates as human guinea pigs. The documentation on low-pressure and cold-water experiments is vast, and was amply employed during the so-called "Medical Case," which was Case 1 of the U.S.-conducted Nuremberg Military Tribunals (*NMT*, Vol. I & part of Vol. II). However, there are no documents on experiments with toxic gases or the deployment of a gas chamber at Dachau. Therefore, it stands to reason that Rascher's request was turned down, assuming that the document is genuine.

Propaganda History

When U.S. troops closed in on the oldest and one of the most well-known German concentration camps in late April of 1945, they brought along a film crew from their propaganda division, the psychological warfare department. They did not only find the usual heaps of corpses in the camp, the result of Germany's catastrophic collapse at the end of the war, but they also found "the gas chamber." This was duly filmed, and that footage put to "good" use in the U.S. propaganda documentary *Nazi Concentration and Prisoner-of-War Camps*, which was shown during the Nuremberg International Military Tribunal (IMT) on 29 November 1945 (Document 2430-PS; see *IMT*, Vol. 30, p. 470). The narrator in that movie says:

> *"Dachau – factory of horrors. […] Hanging in orderly rows were the clothes of prisoners who had been suffocated in the lethal gas chamber. They had been persuaded to remove their clothing under the pretext of taking a shower for which towels and soap were provided. This is the Brausebad – the showerbath. Inside the showerbath – the gas vents. On the ceiling – the dummy shower heads. In the engineer's room – the intake and outlet pipes. Pushbuttons to control inflow and outtake of gas. A hand valve to regulate pressure. Cyanide powder was used to generate the lethal smoke. From the gas chamber, the bodies were removed to the crematory."*

Next, a commission of U.S. Senators and Representatives was quickly flown over to Munich to see with their own eyes not just the corpses, but the gas chamber itself. A U.S. investigation committee then wrote a report, which describes the ceiling of the gas chamber as being 3 meters high, although it is in fact only some 2.10 m high. It also asserts that the lethal gas was fed into the room through brass showerheads connected to two valves in the exterior wall. However, the room has only iron showerheads, and they are not connected to the large pipes in the rear of the room. Although factually wrong, this report was admitted in an edited version as Document 159-L during the IMT (*IMT*, Vol. 37, pp. 605-627; here p. 621).

Later reports by persons who tried to understand the design of this room and its purpose have concluded that this complex system of heat exchanger, pipes, valves, ducts, vents and a fan had one essential component missing: it had no means of adding or introducing any poison gas. It was an absurdly complicated and inefficient way of heating and ventilating this room. An internal expert report of the U.S. 3rd Army even called the room "a failure," as a result of which "no experimental work ever took place in it."

In support of the gas-chamber tale, one key witness testified during the U.S. Dachau show trial in late 1945 and also during the IMT in early 1946: Franz Blaha, who was the only witness to ever claim during a trial that a homicidal gassing happened at Dachau. However, his testimony is rather superficial and makes little sense, if any. (See the entry on Franz Blaha.) There were other witnesses whose claims about homicidal gassings at Dachau were recorded by U.S. investigators prior to their Dachau show trial, but in light of the internal U.S. expert report considering the gas chamber a "failure," and probably also due to the evidently hysterical and contradictory nature of these wild accusations, the prosecution decided to drop the charges in this regard and ignore those witness statements.

Today, the room in question has two openings in its outside wall that each can be closed with an iron hopper. Therefore, the orthodoxy changed tack and has claimed ever since that these hoppers were allegedly used to insert Zyklon B, and let it slide through the holes onto the chamber floor. However, this would have enabled every inmate outside to watch this operation, and it would have made it impossible to retrieve the Zyklon-B pellets after the deed, thus needlessly extending the required ventilation time.

More importantly, such a primitive "dump and forget" solution stands in stark contrast to the four advanced DEGESCH circulation fumigation chambers installed at the other end of the same building, only a few meters away. (See the entry on fumigation gas chamber). The Dachau camp authorities therefore knew perfectly well how to perform Zyklon-B gassings efficiently, swiftly and safely. Had they wanted to do the same inside the "gas chamber," they would have installed one of these devices in that room, allowing them to open a Zyklon-B can remotely, to develop its fumes swiftly, and to dissipate it rapidly throughout the room.

Death-Toll Propaganda
For re-education purposes, the U.S. occupational forces set up signs near the Dachau crematorium building to instruct the locals that some 238,000 had been cremated at this camp. That number never found entry in serious historian's narrative, though. Currently, a total death toll of some 28,000 to 32,000 is assumed, with almost half of them dying in the cat-

One of the two iron hoppers added later into the outside wall of the Dachau room claimed to have been a homicidal gas chamber.

astrophic last months of the war due to starvation and diseases.

Forensic Findings
The room in question has six large-size, fully functional floor drains with large sieve buckets underneath to catch hair and other items. One of the showerheads embedded into the ceiling has been removed. Underneath it, an object is visible that looks like a cut-open water pipe. If these showerheads are fake, then there is no other major water source in this room, other than one water pipe in the back wall. Hence, why are there six floor drains? Anyone seriously interested in resolving this riddle would open the ceiling and see what is behind it.

The outer brickwork and mortar around the two "Zyklon" openings in the outer wall show that these openings were not original but were added later, after the wall had been finished. This can also be seen on the inside, where the wall tiles around these openings were removed and "replaced" with plaster, merely made to look like tiles. If these openings were not present when the room was built in 1942/43, then there was no way of adding any poisonous substance.

Therefore, this room was *not* planned as a gas chamber.

It stands to reason that the two openings were added at a time when this room was no longer used as a shower room, but rather as an additional morgue, toward the later part of the war. These openings may have served simply to facilitate ventilating the room, by serving as fresh-air inlets. Alternatively, they may have been deliberately installed in order to align with the popular image of a "gas chamber."

Room in the crematorium building located on the grounds of the former Dachau Camp. It is said to have been a homicidal gas chamber. A sign on display in this room until the late 1990s stated, however, that this room was "never used as a gas chamber."

Current Orthodox Narrative

The orthodoxy cannot make up their mind whether this room was ever used for any gassing, or whether it was used only once, or rarely, or on occasion. Also, the question of whether this room was planned to serve a larger purpose of a future anticipated mass-murder facility is unresolved. For if this highly complex facility served to mass-murder people, then there must have been a plan to use it as such.

The whole issue disappears, once it is understood that this facility never has been and never was meant to be a homicidal gas chamber. Hence, in this case as well, we are dealing only with pure deception.

(For more details on this topic, see Leuchter *et al.* 2017, pp. 149-159, 173-193; Mattogno 2022a; Rudolf 2023, pp. 78-88.)

DACHAU MUSEUM

Measured by yearly visitors, the Dachau Museum is by far Germany's largest Holocaust-related museum, with a pre-COVID peak visitor number of just under a million tourists.

The Museum's most-prized asset, which is also the only one remotely connected to the Holocaust, is its alleged homicidal gas chamber, which is the main reason why most people come to the camp. As a detailed study of this room shows, however, it was anything but a homicidal gas chamber. (See the entry on the Dachau Camp for details.)

For many decades until the late 20th Century, the Dachau Museum had a (moveable) sign on display in that alleged gas-chamber room stating:

"GAS CHAMBER disguised as a 'shower room' – never used as a gas chamber."

That was a lie, as the room was not only never *used* as a homicidal gas chamber, it simply was never a homicidal gas chamber at all. Since one witness did in fact claim that the room was used once for gassing a few inmates (Franz Blaha), and no Holocaust witness may ever be accused of having fibbed, the statement that the room was never used had to disappear. Hence, this sign was eventually removed, and replaced with a longer text stating:

"Gas chamber – This was the center of potential [sic!] *mass murder. The room was disguised as 'showers' and equipped with fake shower spouts to mislead the victims and prevent them from refusing to enter the room. During a period of 15 to 20 minutes, up to 150 people at a time could be suffocated to death through prussic acid poison gas (Zyklon B)."*

Not a single witness has ever claimed the use of Zyklon B. But the orthodox scholars who concocted this text know that the room had this "potential"!

Dachau without a homicidal gas chamber is like an amusement park without rides. No one would come. Therefore, behold the gas chamber!

DACHAU TRIALS

The U.S. occupational authorities in postwar Germany conducted a series of trials against members of the German armed forces and of SS and Waffen SS. These were mainly about alleged crimes committed against inmates in the various concentration camps which had been liberated by the Americans, such as Dachau, Flossenbürg, Mauthausen, Nordhausen and Buchenwald, as well as alleged war crimes against downed Allied pilots and U.S. soldiers fallen into German captivity.

These trials stretched from August 1945 until December 1947, prosecuted 1,672 German defendants in 489 separate proceedings, and ended with almost three quarters of the defendants getting convicted; 297 death penalties and 279 life sentences were handed down. The investigations and hearings of these trials were conducted at the compounds of the former Dachau Concentration Camp. A few other, similar trials were held at Ludwigsburg (Württemberg), Darmstadt (Hesse) and Salzburg (Austria).

All highly questionable features that defined the International Military Tribunal (IMT) also applied to these trials, which were held under the same rules. (See the entry on the IMT for more details.) However, the framework of the Dachau Trials was much worse, due to the following features:

– The burden of proof was on the defense, meaning that a defendant was considered guilty until proven innocent.
– Any official of any Third Reich military or civilian authority was subject to "Automatic Arrest," meaning that he or she could be arrested and kept detained indefinitely without any court order or any recourse. Often, the only way out for a person in that situation was cooperation with the detaining authorities, often consisting of signing false affidavits meant to incriminate someone else.
– Charges against people in automatic arrest were cooked up by the prosecuting authorities using so-called "stage shows" or "reviews": The prosecuting authorities assembled former concentration-camp inmates and placed them in an auditorium of a theater or cinema. The persons in automatic arrest were placed on an illuminated stage, while the former concentration-camp inmates sat in a dark room and were allowed to make any kind of wild accusation. If – contrary to expectations – no accusations were made, or if the accusations weren't damaging enough, the prosecution "lent a helping hand," persuading the inmates to make accusations, often accompanied by the grossest intimidation and threats. This mockery of justice ended only when an American officer donned an SS uniform and appeared on the stage before the howling witnesses, who promptly incriminated him as a concentration-camp thug.
– "Second-degree" interrogation: interrogations lasting many hours or even days with little or no food, water, or any breaks; false incriminating statements of others; outright lies about existing incriminating evidence; threats of torture or extradition to the Soviet Union. These were the methods to obtain confessions or incriminating statements against others.
– From the records and transcripts of these interrogations, the prosecutors stitched together "affidavits," in which the exonerating passages were deleted, and the content was often distorted by rewording.
– Unsigned affidavits and "copies" of documents, as well as statements from hearsay were admitted as proof.
– Until the beginning of the trial, defendants lacked legal counsel.
– The court-appointed attorneys were often Allied citizens with poor, if any, command of the German language, and little interest in defending the defendants, sometimes even acting like prosecutors, threatening the defendants and advising them to make false confessions.
– Defense attorneys often received only partial and reluctant access to the files; conversations with defendants were only permitted shortly before commencement of the trial, sometimes even only during the trial, and only in the presence of the Allied prosecution personnel.
– Before the trial, the defense was often only informed of the main points of the indictment in terms of generalities.
– Motions to interrogate witnesses or to raise objections to evidence introduced by the prosecution – such as extorted statements – were usually rejected.

But worst of all were the interrogations of the "third degree." Here is what an extraordinary commission of the U.S. Congress, headed by Edward L. van Roden, former U.S. Chief of Military (Europe), and Gordon Simpson, justice at the Texas Supreme Court, had to say about this, among other things:

"Our investigators would put a black hood over the accused's head and then punch him in the face

with brass knuckles, kick him, and beat him with rubber hose. Many of the German defendants had teeth knocked out. Some had their jaws broken. All but two of the Germans, in the 139 cases we investigated, had been kicked in the testicles beyond repair. This was Standard Operating Procedure with American investigators."

"Evidence" gathered and verdicts rendered during these trials were then considered judicial "truths" that could not be challenged by the defense in other tribunals, such as the IMT and the subsequent Nuremberg Military Tribunals.

(For more details on this, see the entry on the IMT, on torture, on show trials, as well as Rudolf 2019, pp. 88-92; 2023, pp. 406-411.)

DALUEGE, KURT

Kurt Daluege (15 Sept. 1897 – 24 Oct. 1946) was the chief of the uniformed police in National-Socialist Germany. After Heinrich Himmler issued an order on 23 October 1941, stating "effective immediately, the emigration of Jews has to be prevented," Daluege issued a directive the next day, according to which "Jews shall be evacuated to the east in the district around Riga and Minsk" (3921-PS; *IMT*, Vol. 33, p. 535). This was the beginning of what is today called the "Final Solution of the Jewish Question." After the assassination of Reinhardt Heydrich in 1942, Daluege became deputy Reich Protector of occupied Czechia (the Protectorate of Bohemia and Moravia). As such, he was responsible for the retaliatory measures against the civilian population of the town of Lidice, after Heydrich had been assassinated. After the war, he was extradited to Czechoslovakia, tried in Prague during a typical Stalinist show trial, and subsequently executed.

DAMJANOVIĆ, MOMČILO

Momčilo Damjanović was evidently the only person to testify in front of a Yugoslavian war-crimes commission about the alleged exhumation and cremation of bodies from mass graves containing the victims of German atrocities in Serbia during World War II. His declaration is dated 7 February 1945, and contains the following peculiar claims:

– He claimed that 69,400 bodies were buried near the Semlin Camp, although the orthodoxy's current claim is that only some 12,000 bodies were buried there.
– Of the 12,000 buried bodies, 68,000 were supposedly exhumed and cremated by the time Damjanović managed to escape after 36 days of working on this task.
– He claimed that his team of some 100 inmates took 700 bodies out of a grave and piled them up like cordwood to a height of 2.5 meters. Only afterwards did they build a pile of wood half a meter high, and the bodies cremated on that. This clearly indicates that Damjanović had no experiences at all with building a pyre.
– Damjanović very clumsily described a device that, judging by the function he describes, would have been an excavator built on a railway car. It was supposedly used to transport two corpses at a time from a mass grave on rails to a burning pyre, onto which the two bodies were deposited. However, reaching with an excavator's shovel into a burning fire would have destroyed any hydraulics connected to it, so this is obviously mere fantasy. Again, this shows that Damjanović had no idea that one builds a pyre with alternating layers of wood and bodies first, and then sets it ablaze.
– Damjanović claimed that the location of the pyre was moved each time a new mass grave was opened. In other words, the railcar had to be moved as well, to a new set of tracks, via an intermediate set of moving tracks. No sane person would have used a railcar excavator for such a task.
– Damjanović claimed that this magical machine allowed them to burn 1,200 bodies a day. For this, the railroad excavator had to move 600 times forth and back between grave and pyre. For an 18-hour workday, this amounts to not even two minutes for an entire round trip.
– Cremating an average human body during open-air incinerations requires some 250 kg of freshly cut wood. Cremating 68,000 bodies thus requires some 17,000 metric tons of wood. This would have required the felling of all trees growing in a 50-year-old spruce forest covering almost 38 hectares of land, or more than 85 American football fields. An average prisoner is rated at being able to cut some 0.63 metric tons of fresh wood per workday. To cut this amount of wood within five weeks (36 days) that this operation supposedly lasted would have required a work force of some 750 dedicated lumberjacks just to cut the wood. Damjanović claimed his unit consisted only of some 100 inmates, all busy digging out mass graves, extracting bodies and building pyres. He said nothing about where the firewood came

from.

This testimony relates to one of many events claimed to have been part of the alleged German clean-up operation that the orthodoxy calls *Aktion* 1005. The above exposition demonstrates that Damjanović's scenario is detached from reality. Its claimed features and dimensions cannot be based on experience, but on mere propaganda, imagination and delusion.

(For more details, see Mattogno 2022c, pp. 701-705.)

DAVYDOV, VLADIMIR

Vladimir Davydov was a Ukrainian Jew interned in the Syretsky Camp, 5 km from Kiev, from 15 March to 16 August 1943. On 18 August, he was taken from there to Babi Yar, a place where tens of thousands of Jews are said to have been shot and buried by the Germans in mass graves in late September 1941 (see the entry on Babi Yar). He was interrogated at Kiev on 9 November 1943 by a local NKGB chief. During this interview, he stated, among other things:

- 100 inmates were picked out and taken to Babi Yar, where they were put in chains. Among them were even geriatrics. *However*, for the heavy labor awaiting them, geriatrics would not have been chosen. Why were they still alive anyway, if those unfit for labor were supposedly killed years ago?
- The exhumation and cremation work they needed to do was to be kept a secret, so no one was allowed to get closer to the ravine than 1 km. *However*, it would have been impossible to hide the fires and concomitant smoke.
- He claims there were two mass graves with about 50,000 bodies of Jews, plus another one farther away with about 20,000 bodies of Soviet PoWs. They built pyres with 2,000 to 3,000 bodies each, on stacks 10 to 12 meters high. *However*, this would have required cranes, and any pyre that high would have toppled over and spilled burning wood and body parts all over the place. Real pyres for open-air incinerations have only one large layer of fuel topped with bodies, together some 2 meters high.
- Unburned bones were pulverized with pestles on metal sheets, and the result thrown into the empty mass graves. *However*, for this to work, all the remains of a pyre had to be sifted for unburned remains. Wood-fired pyres burn unevenly and leave behind lots of unburned wood pieces, charcoal, and incompletely burned body parts, not just ashes and bones (80% of leftovers would have been from wood, not corpses). Incompletely burned wood and human remains could not have been crushed. If 70,000 bodies were burned, then several thousand metric tons of cremation leftovers had to be processed. Just this job would have required hundreds of men to complete in time.
- Three, later four of these pyres burned simultaneously. In total, some 75 of these pyres were built. *However*, if one pyre had at least 2,000 bodies, the total would have been 150,000 burned victims, not the roughly 70,000 bodies he claimed.
- When all bodies had been burned and one last pyre was built, the inmates figured that this one was for them, so some of them escaped during the night of 28-29 September.

Cremating an average human body during open-air incinerations requires some 250 kg of freshly cut wood. Cremating 70,000 bodies thus requires some 17,500 metric tons of wood. This would have required the felling of all trees growing in a 50-year-old spruce forest covering almost 39 hectares of land, or more than 87 American football fields. An average prisoner is rated at being able to cut some 0.63 metric tons of fresh wood per workday. To cut this amount of wood within five weeks (35 days) that this operation supposedly lasted would have required a work force of some 800 dedicated lumberjacks just to cut the wood. Davydov claims his unit consisted only of 100 inmates, all busy digging out mass graves, extracting bodies, building pyres, sifting through ashes, scattering the ashes and refilling the graves with soil. He says nothing about where the firewood came from.

More than 20 years after the events, on 9 February 1967, Davydov was interrogated by the German judiciary. In that statement, his pyres had shrunk from 10 meters in height down to 4 meters, but that still would have required a crane, and it still would have toppled over. The number of corpses burned had increased from 70,000 to 125,000, in line with other inmate claims. He moreover reduced the number of pyres from 75 to 55 or 60, so the math of 2,000 corpses per pyre fits to his total death toll. All this indicates that he had been instructed by Soviet officials in order to streamline his account.

In addition to merely grinding up unburned bones, Davydov also claimed in 1967 that all the leftovers of the burned-down pyres were run through sieves in search of valuables. That would have led to a drastic increase in workforce needed for this, apart from it being nearly impossible. If 125,000 bodies were processed, as Davydov claimed, then several thousand metric tons of ashes and unburned remains had to be processed this way by perhaps a few dozen inmates within just five weeks – in sieves that would have clogged with the first load. Moreover, any occasional rainfall would have rendered any burned-out pyre into a moist heap of highly alkaline, corrosive slush that could not have been processed at all.

In that German interview, Davydov must have figured out that his initial claim of just 100 working inmates was a little bit of a stretch, so he claimed that the Germans at some point "increased the number of prisoners to 330," and they allegedly also used "dynamiting techniques" – in order to achieve what? Scattering corpse parts all over the place? Explosives are not suitable tools for exhuming mass graves or destroying bodies.

For good measure, Davydov added to his 1967 testimony something that was unknown to him at war's end: that during his time at Babi Yar, the Germans killed people in gas vans, and threw them from the vans right onto the pyres. This late enrichment of his "memory" evidently also resulted from coaching sessions he had with Soviet authorities, who had claimed the use of gas vans in their 1944 expert report on Babi Yar.

(For more details, see the entry on Babi Yar, as well as Mattogno 2022c, pp. 527-530, and 550-563.)

DAWIDOWSKI, ROMAN

Roman Dawidowski

Prof. Dr. Roman Dawidowski was a Polish engineer who was one of four experts constituting a mixed Polish-Soviet expert commission tasked with investigating the Auschwitz crematoria. This Stalinist mock commission applied absurd technical parameters in order to come to the preordained conclusion that these crematoria had the capacity to cremate four million human bodies within just one and a half years of their existence.

Dawidowski later also served as the right-hand man of Polish investigating judge Jan Sehn in preparing the upcoming two Stalinist show trials against former camp commandant Rudolf Höss on the one hand, and against several former lower-ranking camp officials on the other. While sifting through the vast documentation left behind at Auschwitz by the German camp authorities, Sehn and Dawidowski cherry-picked ambivalent documents that included terms such as "gas," "gastight," and "gas chamber," or "*sonder*" and "*spezial*" (meaning separate or special), ripped them out of their documental and historical context, and mispresented them as circumstantial evidence allegedly proving that homicidal gas chambers existed at the former camp, and were actually used for mass murder.

Dawidowski and Sehn ignored and hid from the courts and the defense that the vast extant Auschwitz documentation actually proves the exact opposite of their narrative: terms such as "gas chamber" refer to disinfestation gas chambers meant to *save* inmate lives, not kill them. Furthermore, the camp authorities had gone to great length and enormous efforts and expenses in their desperate attempts at improving living conditions and thus survival chances for all inmates. (See the section "Documented History" of the entry on the Birkenau Camp and on healthcare for details.)

During the trial against Rudolf Höss, Dawidowski testified that the gas chambers at Auschwitz could exterminate 60,000 persons per day in total, hence 22 million per year or some 35 million during their entire existence. He pushed his testimony into the theater of the absurd when claiming that the Auschwitz crematoria could easily match this high productivity of corpses, as they had a capacity of 400,000,000 bodies! Yes: *four hundred million!*

Some so-called experts have made literally insane statements. Either they were grossly incompetent, or they should have been indicted for perjury. And the judges and prosecutors who played along were equally to blame.

(For more details, see Mattogno/Deana, Part 1, pp. 337-339; Mattogno 2019, pp. 453-455, 513-519; Mattogno 2020b, pp. 174f., 258.)

DDT

DDT (dichloro-diphenyl-trichloroethane), first synthesized in 1874 by Austrian chemist Othmar Zeidler, was discovered to be a formidable insecticide only in 1939 by Swiss Chemist Paul Müller, who won the 1948 Nobel Prize in Medicine for it. Due to its carcinogenic features and its devastating effects on birds' ability to reproduce, it was later banned.

In Germany, DDT was produced during the Second World War under license of the Swiss chemical company Geigy (later Ciba-Geigy; see Weindling 2000, p. 380), with the trade name Lauseto (for *Läusetod* = "lice death"). The Auschwitz Camp received DDT starting in 1944: 9 metric tons in April, 15 tons in August, and 2 tons in October (Setkiewicz 2011, p. 72). DDT, together with the new microwave delousing devices, allowed the Auschwitz camp authorities to bring the typhus epidemic in Auschwitz finally under control. These new technologies also made Zyklon B obsolete; hence, Zyklon B deliveries to Auschwitz declined significantly during the summer of 1944.

death marches → **Evacuations, from German Camps**
death tolls → **Exaggerated Death Tolls**
Defonseca, Misha → **Wael, Monique de**

DEGESCH

DEGESCH (*Deutsche Gesellschaft für Schädlingsbekämpfung*, German Association for Pest Control) was a limited-liability company specializing in the development of pesticides and pest-control technologies. It was established in 1919 as a subsidiary of the German chemical company Degussa (*Deutsche Gold- und Silber-Scheide-Anstalt*). In later years, the German chemical trust *I.G. Farbenindustrie*, Inc., held major parts of the shares as well. DEGESCH held the patent for Zyklon B, an insecticide based on hydrogen cyanide, and allowed other companies to produce and distribute it under their license. The company's first CEO was Nobel laureate Fritz Haber, but was made highly profitable in later years by German chemist Dr. Gerhard Peters; he (co)authored several articles and books on Zyklon B and other pesticides and their proper use for pest control, as well as on the best ways of designing fumigation facilities (Kalthoff/Werner 1998).

In 1986, DEGESCH was sold to Detia Freyberg Ltd. (today Detia-Degesch).

DEJACO, WALTER

Walter Dejaco (19 June 1909 – 9 Jan. 1978), SS *Untersturmführer*, was an architect employed by the Auschwitz Central Construction Office. As head of the planning department, he was deeply involved in the construction of the Auschwitz-Birkenau Camp, including the crematoria (see index entries in Mattogno 2023, Part 1).

On 16 September 1942, together with Camp Commandant Höss and the Head of the Concentration Camp Hössler, Dejaco visited a "experimental station for field incinerators *Aktion Reinhardt*" near Lodz operated by Paul Blobel, where it was decided to procure construction material for the erection of such a facility in Auschwitz (*ibid.*, pp. 155f.). It is unknown what this incinerator was for, but since the *Aktion Reinhardt* included looting the property of Europe's Jews deported by National-Socialist Germany, it is likely that these field furnaces served to burn useless or ruined Jewish property.

Mainstream historians assume that Blobel was conducting cremation experiments with victims of mass murder at the Chełmno Camp at that time, in the context of the so-called "*Aktion* 1005", which in itself is highly dubious. Moreover, Chełmno was some 60 km away from Lodz, so Dejaco went to the wrong place. Furthermore, there is no documental or anecdotal evidence that a field furnace was ever built at Auschwitz. Instead, both Crematoria II and III, which became operational in early 1943, were equipped with waste incinerators that allowed for the incineration of combustible material of all kinds (Mattogno 2017, pp. 73-81). In addition, if we follow (mostly implausible) witness statements, mass cremations at Auschwitz are said to have been conducted simply in pits on piles of wood, without the use of any construction material. See the entry on open-air incinerations for more.

In 1972, Dejaco was put on trial in Vienna, together with his former colleague Fritz Ertl, for their involvement in the construction of the Birkenau crematories, which are said to have been equipped with homicidal gas chambers. The court had court-accredited architect Gerhard Dubin evaluate the blueprints for these buildings, which had been drawn by Dejaco's department under his supervision. The

Walter Dejaco (left) and Fritz Ertl (right) in 1972.

result of this assessment was that the rooms in question could *not* have been homicidal gas chambers, and they also could *not* have been converted into such facilities. Not the least due to this expert report, which subsequently disappeared from the court files, the two defendants were acquitted. (Lüftl 2004; Faurisson 1991, pp. 59f.)

DEMJANJUK, JOHN

John Demjanjuk, 1993

John Demjanjuk (3 April 1920 – 17 March 2012) was a Ukrainian citizen who immigrated to the U.S. after the Second World War. He and many other Ukrainian immigrants were targeted by pro-Soviet groups in the U.S. for their alleged collaboration with German authorities during World War II. U.S. authorities cooperated with these pro-Soviet groups, stripped Demjanjuk of his U.S. citizenship, and deported him to Israel, where he was put on trial in 1987 for allegedly aiding in the murder of hundreds of thousands of Jews in the Treblinka Camp; he was found guilty as charged, and sentenced to death. That sentence was overruled by the Jerusalem Court of Appeals in 1993, which acquitted Demjanjuk for lack of evidence. He was subsequently repatriated to the U.S. and received his citizenship back.

However, in 2004, U.S. authorities again revoked his citizenship and deported him in 2009 to Germany, where he was put on trial for aiding in crimes allegedly committed at the former Sobibór Camp. He was sentenced to 5 years' imprisonment, but died while his appeal was pending.

Soviet-Russian Propaganda

For centuries, Russian authorities sought to undermine the credibility of independence-minded Ukrainian groups and individuals. During the Cold War, this meant among other things that pro-Soviet groups tried tarnishing Ukrainians' reputation by falsely implicating them in war crimes allegedly committed during World War II. In that context, the pro-Soviet weekly *News from Ukraine*, published in the U.S., defamed anti-communist nationalist-oriented Ukrainians living in U.S. exile, particularly by claiming that they had collaborated with the Germans during World War II. The Soviet Union's practice of combating opponents by means of disinformation using falsified evidence is generally known, but was ignored by U.S. authorities in Demjanjuk's case.

Western and Jewish Collaboration

The U.S. authorities charged with "hunting Nazis" in the U.S. – organized in 1979 as the FBI's heavily Jewish-dominated Office of Special Investigations (OSI) – collaborated closely with the pro-Soviet groups in the U.S. in their attempt to revoke the U.S. citizenship of Ukrainian immigrants and deport them. In Demjanjuk's case, Soviet, U.S., German and Israeli authorities all worked together to hide from judges and from the public the fact that evidence presented by the Soviets were plain forgeries, and that witness statements were utterly untrustworthy. Among them was an ID card forged by the Soviets allegedly proving that Demjanjuk had been a guard at the Sobibór Camp. However, the photo in that ID card had been taken from Demjanjuk's postwar immigration file to the U.S., meaning that the Soviets had U.S. collaborators for this framing operation. German authorities pressured one of their expert witnesses who had revealed this forgery to commit perjury in court in order to hide the rigged nature of the evidence presented by the Soviets and the OSI. As a result, Demjanjuk's citizenship was revoked, and he was deported to Israel in 1986 to serve as a sacrificial lamb on the altar of a typical show trial.

Public Outcry in the U.S.

When the scandalous pre-history and conduct of the Jerusalem show trial against Demjanjuk became apparent, two prominent U.S. personalities – U.S. Representative James Traficant (Democrat, Ohio) and U.S. presidential candidate Patrick Buchanan – spoke out on Demjanjuk's behalf, exposing not only his show trial and the corruption of the U.S. authorities collaborating with it, but the fraudulent nature of extermination claims about Treblinka in general.

Backfire

An expert on the reliability of witness testimonies called by the defense during the trial, as well as the director of Israel's Holocaust research center Yad Vashem, Shmuel Krakowski, agreed that many, if not most, of the witness statements made in court and found in archives in Holocaust matters are unreliable. In the end, the Jerusalem Court of Appeals agreed, threw out all witness testimony as unreliable, and acquitted Demjanjuk for lack of evidence. It was a resounding success of relentless lobbying by Holocaust skeptics behind the scenes. Later on, Demjanjuk was repatriated to the U.S., and his citizenship was restored.

Show Trial No. 2
From the late 1980s and throughout the 1990s and 2000s, Israel and several European countries implemented laws criminalizing dissenting views on the mainstream Holocaust narrative. (See the entry on censorship.) Consequently, societal pressure against dissidents increased dramatically, even in countries not outlawing historical dissent. Hence, when the OSI made a second attempt to revoke Demjanjuk's citizenship in 2002 based on the same forged evidence and similarly fraudulent witness statements, there was no second wave of official or underground support for Demjanjuk.

In German courts, the defense has no right to introduce evidence; if they motion the court to introduce evidence on their behalf which challenges the mainstream narrative, the court must, by law, reject that motion, and the prosecution must, by law, initiate criminal proceedings *against the defense lawyers* involved for having tried to deny the Holocaust in a public court proceeding. Furthermore, if a lawyer says anything challenging the mainstream narrative, he can be banned by the court from speaking any further in court, and be forced to make all submissions in writing instead.

With that German skill of perfect organization, Demjanjuk's second show trial in Germany went down without a hitch. The Soviet-forged ID card allegedly showing that Demjanjuk had been a guard at the Sobibór Camp was used again to "prove" that he had served in that camp. Although the prosecution did not succeed in proving that Demjanjuk had committed even a single murder himself, he was sentenced to five years in prison by the Munich District Court in 2011, just for having been *present* at the camp. Having enabled the operation of the camp in any way made Demjanjuk an accessory to murder.

When this verdict was upheld by the German Supreme Court in 2016, reverting 70 years of case law not holding bystanders responsible for murder, it opened the floodgates for the prosecution of any German ever involved in operating a German wartime camp.

Demjanjuk, however, died before the verdict could become effective.

(For details, see Brentar 1993; Jackson 2012; Rudolf 2023, pp. 116-123, 364-366, 432.)

DEMOGRAPHY, JEWISH

Six million Jews died in the Holocaust. This is a common assertion by the orthodoxy. However, the claim that six million Jews were threatened to perish, were in the process of perishing or had perished, is much older than World War Two. It appeared for the first time in the late 1880s – with respect to the Jews living in Russia. Hence, the six-million figure had been a feature of Jewish propaganda decades before Hitler came to power. (See the entry on Six Million for details.)

Claims about six million Jewish victims of *National-Socialist* persecution were made already toward the end of the Second World War. However, utter chaos prevailed in Europe since 1944. The political borders of many European nations in central and eastern Europe shifted dramatically. Ethnic cleansings of German and pro-German populations, as well as massive migration movements of ethnic and religious minorities, changed Europe's ethnic map as well.

For these reasons, it would have taken several years for these events to settle down, and for government authorities to get reestablished and organized. Only then would it have been possible to conduct any meaningful population statistics of any ethnic or religious group. Thus, anyone who claimed already in 1944, 1945 or 1946 to have secure knowledge in that matter cannot be trusted.

Furthermore, Jewish population statistics are more complex than those of other groups, precisely because this group is not largely confined to a certain geographic area as most other groups. Jews have always had the tendency of migrating faster and more easily around the globe than other groups. In addition, such migrations are not necessarily trackable, as being Jewish is very much a question of definition – and a very fluid one at that. Who counts as a Jew? Is it an ethnicity or a religious group? The answers often depend on who is asked those questions, and when.

Demographic Studies
The first encompassing demographic study on worldwide Jewish population developments before, during and after World War II was published in 1983 by Holocaust-skeptic demographer Walter N. Sanning (updated Sanning 2023). An orthodox study by several mainstream scholars was published in 1991, with Wolfgang Benz as lead editor. (German only.

Comparison of Methods Used by Sanning and Benz		
	Sanning 1983	Benz 1991
Sources used	few archival primary sources; secondary literature and media reports	rich archival primary sources
Claimed Jewish victims	ca. 300,000	ca. 6,300,000
Consistent country borders	Yes	No, leading to more than half a million victims counted twice
Regions covered	entire globe	countries at least under partial German control
Adjusting for emigration	Yes	inconsistently and incompletely
Adjusting for non-murder losses	Yes	No. All missing persons are counted as murdered

No translation was ever published.) Each contributing author covered a certain country that was at least partially controlled by National-Socialist Germany.

A thorough analysis of both studies reveals the characteristics and main differences as laid out in the table. Enjoying government support, Benz's collection of mainstream authors can boast excellent statistical source material, while Sanning used at times questionable sources. Whereas Sanning tried to take into consideration the massive Jewish exodus from Europe prior, during and right after the war, Benz's book arrives at its death toll basically by subtracting the earliest available postwar census data from the latest prewar census data. Hence, Benz overlooks a large chunk of the more than two million Jews who were not murdered in that time period, but who managed to emigrate to countries never under any German influence, such as Palestine/Israel, USA, Canada, Australia, England, South Africa and many Latin-American nations.

In addition to emigration, there can be many other reasons for the Jewish population of a country to shrink in size that have nothing to do with Holocaust murders, such as:
– Death due to Soviet deportation and imprisonment.
– Death due to pogroms by non-Germans, without German collaboration or sanction.
– Death due to effects of war (labor service, bombing victims, collateral combat casualties).
– Death as soldiers.
– Death as partisans (battle or execution).
– Natural excess of deaths over births.
– Religious conversions.
– Jews not identifying themselves as such in a census.

While Sanning has tried to adjust for these losses unrelated to Holocaust deaths, in Benz's book, all population reductions, no matter the cause, are counted as Holocaust victims.

The main numerical differences between the two studies result from very different data regarding just three countries: Poland, the Soviet Union and Hungary (wartime borders):

Country	Victims (Benz)	Missing (Sanning)
Hungary	550,000	71,000
Poland	2,700,000	516,511
Soviet Union	2,100,000	15,000
Total	6,277,441	1,113,153

Jewish losses on the territory of the Soviet Union primarily would be the result of the so-called *Einsatzgruppen*. Their reports indicate that up to a three-quarter million Jews may have been executed by these units, although this presumably includes Jews deported east from central and western European countries, so not all of these 750,000 victims were Soviet Jews. Furthermore, the numerical reliability of the *Einsatzgruppen* reports is highly questionable – potentially in both directions. (See the entry on the *Einsatzgruppen* for more details.)

Sanning evidently disregards these executions entirely, which is highly questionable. On the other hand, Benz and colleagues inflate that figure by expressly including in it all casualties among soldiers, partisans, and from Soviet mass deportations and incarcerations.

The numerical differences for Poland and Hungary have more-complex reasons. See the entries for these countries to learn more revealing facts.

In summary, the adjustments listed in the table at the top of the next page need to be made to the orthodox study by Benz and his colleagues.

Missing persons are not necessarily murdered persons. Hence, if defining the term "Holocaust victim" narrowly as a Jew murdered by National-Socialists, then that figure would be lower still.

The table at the bottom of the next page gives a

Corrections Needed for Benz

Benz's Figure	Minus	Reason
6.3 million	at least 1 million	unregistered post-war emigration
	at least 1.5 million	Jews not statistically registered in the Soviet Union
	at least 0.5 million	victims of war, partisan warfare and Soviet deportation
	0.7 million	statistically inflated no. of Jews in pre-war Poland
	at least 0.3 million	destruction of Hungarian Jews refuted
6.3 million minus at least 4 million → a maximum of 2.3 million missing persons		

rough overview on the Jewish pre-war and postwar population figures for all the countries involved. For each country, it gives an upper and a lower value as derived from either Sanning or Benz. While Benz usually declares the difference to be the victims, Sanning on occasion deducts birth deficits, emigrations (and for Bulgaria immigration) and other non-homicidal causes for reductions.

Prewar figures for France and the three Benelux countries are very difficult to assess, because tens of thousands of Jews migrated west and south as National-Socialist rule expanded, and as the German armed forces moved west. This migration continued even after France's defeat, with the migration route going from German-occupied territories to Vichy France, and from there to Switzerland, Italy, Spain, Portugal and overseas. When deportations started in 1942, two years of legal and grey-zone emigration efforts must have reduced the Jewish population considerably, but to an unknown level.

What can be said with certainty in the cases of France, Belgium and Luxembourg, and with some degree of certainty also for the Netherlands, is the number of Jews which were eventually deported – as documentation on this has been preserved, albeit evidently only with imprecise numbers for the Netherlands (see the next table):

Country	Deportees
France	75,720
Belgium	25,437
Netherlands	ca. 105,000
Luxembourg	512

Therefore, juggling wide estimates of prewar, postwar and emigration figures might be futile to a large degree. Trying to figure out how many of the known deportees were still alive after the war, and could be tracked to their unknown postwar whereabouts, may not be very promising either.

It is probably more elucidating to find out what exactly transpired at the locations where these Jews were deported. These were mostly the camps at Auschwitz and Sobibór, the latter particularly for Dutch Jews. See in this regard the entry on France, as the fate of the Jews deported from this country is similar to that of those deported from Belgium and Luxembourg, and to some degree also from the Netherlands.

Yad Vashem's Victim Database

The Jerusalem Holocaust Memorial and Research Center Yad Vashem has a database that tries to register all Jews who were reported as having died "during the Holocaust." Registering any person as a Holocaust victim does not require any proof or evidence. It does also not involve any verification process to

Europe	Prewar	Postwar	Difference
Belgium	52,000 – 85,000	23,482 – 61,000	20,000 – 28,000
Bulgaria	48,400 – 50,000	50,000 – 56,000	0 – +7,600
Czechoslovakia	251,745 – 254,288	40,000 – 82,000	160,000 – 202,000
Denmark	6,000	ca. 6,000	0
France	ca. 300,000	223,866 – 238,000	62,000 – 76,000
Greece	65,000 – 71,500	12,000 – 12,726	53,000 – 59,000
Italy	34,000 – 48,000	28,086 – 39,000	6,000 – 9,000
Luxembourg	1,500 – 3,700	500 – 2,450	1,000 – 1,200
Netherlands	105,000 – 160,820	36,500 – 64,020	70,000 – 95,000
Norway	1,700 – 2,000	ca. 1,000	700 – 1,000
Romania	465,242 – 466,418	ca. 430,000	35,000 – 36,000
Yugoslavia	68,000 – 82,000	12,000 – 16,000	56,000 – 65,000

prevent false entries and multiple listings. Hence, this database is largely worthless from a scholarly point of view. For more details, see the entry on Yad Vashem.

Survivors

During the frenzy of Jewish pressure groups trying to secure multi-billion-dollar compensation payments for Holocaust survivors in the 1990s and early 2000s, several mainstream institutions published figures on how many Jewish Holocaust survivors were still alive at that point in time: roughly a million at the turn of the millennium.

Life-expectancy data used by life insurers to calculate the longevity of certain populations permit calculating how many Jewish Holocaust survivors must have been alive in 1945 for one million of them to still be around in 2000. This number amounts to some four to five million Holocaust survivors in 1945. If there were eight million total under German control, then we have, at most, three to four million "missing" Jews, due to all causes. In no case does this support anything near the claimed six million deaths. It further demonstrates that the National Socialists utterly failed, if they were truly attempting to "exterminate" all the Jews under their control; they missed upwards of five million of them!

Among the orthodoxy, there is a tendency to maximize the Jewish death toll in order to maximize the Jews' status as the ultimate victims, which can be exploited in numerous political, societal and financial ways. However, there is also a tendency among the orthodoxy to maximize the number of Holocaust survivors in order to maximize potential payouts to them and the organizations claiming to represent them. (See Finkelstein 2000 for more details on this.) Hence, Jewish population statistics of any kind tend to be the subject of political manipulations for transparent reasons.

(For more details on Jewish population statistics, see each affected country's entry, the entry on survivors, as well as Rudolf 2019, pp. 175-206.)

DENISOW, PIOTR

Piotr Denisow was a Polish engineer who collaborated with the Germans to build the Majdanek Camp. After the war, he was eager to incriminate former German officials, among them primarily Erich Mussfeldt, who had been in charge of the camp's crematorium until May 1944. Denisow testified that a homicidal gas chamber was located inside the Majdanek crematorium, where Mussfeldt personally gassed people he had selected. However, even the Majdanek Museum concedes today that there never was a homicidal gas chamber in that building. Furthermore, the head of the crematorium had no right to select inmates for anything.

Denisow also claimed that one day Mussfeldt threw his own favorite, beloved dog "alive into the crematorium furnace, since he didn't want to give it to anyone else." (See Alvarez 2023a for details.)

deportation → Resettlement

DENMARK

The Jews living in Denmark were left unmolested by the German occupation forces until October 1943. Plans to deport them were leaked around that time, resulting in a large-scale rescue operation by Danish civilians, helping almost all Jews to escape to Sweden, where they were welcome. Some 500 Jews were arrested and deported to the Theresienstadt Ghetto, from where they were evacuated to Sweden shortly before the end of the war. There were hardly any casualties among these Jews, if any.

DIBOWSKI, WILHELM

Wilhelm Dibowski was an Auschwitz-Birkenau inmate from the winter of 1941/1942 until February 1943 because of his membership with the Communist Party of Germany. He was interrogated during the investigations leading to the Frankfurt Auschwitz Trial. Although an opponent of Germany's ruling regime, he insisted that he knew of mass-murder allegations only from hearsay and from what he learned after the war. He also knew two members of the SS staff after the war, one living as a neighbor; he could only "say good things about [them]."
(See Rudolf 2023, pp. 493f.)

DIESEL EXHAUST

Diesel-engine exhaust gases are claimed by numerous witnesses – including during the trial against John Demjanjuk in 1987 – to have been used to mass-murder Jews in the camps at Belzec, Sobibór and Treblinka, and in some of the so-called gas vans. However, diesel-engine exhaust gas is notoriously low in its most toxic component, carbon monoxide (CO), and relatively high in oxygen, as compared to gasoline-engine exhaust gas (ignoring the effect of catalytic converters, which didn't exist during World War II; see the chart).

While diesel-engine exhaust gases are lethal in the long run, they are unsuitable for killing within short periods of time, as claimed by witnesses. Experiments conducted with small mammals using exhaust from a diesel engine, rigged in the most extreme way to produce a maximum amount of CO, have demonstrated that it takes up to five hours of full exposure to the pure exhaust gasses in order to kill all individuals (Pattle *et al.* 1957). Since small mammals succumb to carbon-monoxide poisoning faster than humans, such a system could never have been used for mass murder.

German engineers were fully aware of the CO contents in exhaust gases of various engine types, and in particular of diesel engines, so they would have known which engine to pick, if they had intended to commit murder (Mattogno/Graf 2023, pp. 121-125). Due to their relatively innocuous nature, diesel engines were deployed in coal mines around the world, as their exhaust gases could be vented into the mines without doing much harm (Berg 2003; Rudolf 2019, pp. 453f.). As one report put it (Gilbert 1974, p. 403):

> "An examination of all safety records has revealed that no person has suffered any harmful effects either temporarily or permanently as a direct result of breathing any toxic gas emitted from any vehicle powered by a diesel engine."

More importantly, due to extreme shortage of any petroleum-based fuel in wartime Germany, the entire German road-transportation industry, incentivized by government decrees and subsidies, switched from liquid fuel to gas by installing so-called producer-gas or wood-gas generators on trucks, buses, vans and even tanks. These devices produce a gas rich in CO, which is then burned in the engine as fuel – unlike in a gasoline or diesel engine, where CO is a waste product. The CO gas is produced by partial combustion of various wet fuels (wood, coal, coke). Every German vehicle engineer knew about them during the war. They were easy to procure, cheap to operate, had endless fuel, and their gas would have been instantly lethal. In fact, the Germans even developed a method of exterminating warm-blooded vermin with this technology, which was very common to combat mouse and rat infestations of freight ships. But there are no reports of any of them ever having been misused for murder. (See the section "Carbon-Monoxide Fumigation" of the entry on fumigation gas chamber.)

Facing the impossibility of committing mass mur-

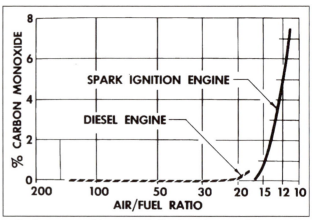

Carbon-monoxide content of exhaust gases from spark engines and diesel engines as a function of engine load (air-/fuel ratio)

der with Diesel-engine exhaust gases, some orthodox scholars now deny that any serious researcher still claims that any such gassings ever occurred (see e.g. Morsch/Perz 2011, p. 34), insisting instead that *gasoline* engines were used, although the evidence for Treblinka and Belzec clearly refutes that claim. Those camps likely did have stationary diesel engines, but they would have been used to drive electrical generators, not to kill people.

DŁUGOBORSKI, WÁCŁAW

Wácław Długoborski (3 Jan. 1926 – 21 Oct. 2021) was a partisan (civilian) fighter during World War II in Poland. He was arrested for this in 1943, and deported to the Auschwitz Camp. After the war, he became a professional historian in Communist Poland, and among other things was curator for research at the Auschwitz Museum. Together with Polish historian Franciszek Piper, he published a five-volume study of the Auschwitz Camp's history in 1999 that deals with extermination claims only superficially in its slim Volume 3 (English in Długoborski/Piper 2000).

Wácław Długoborski

In an interview with a German newspaper, he admitted in 1998 that, during the Communist time in Poland, historians had to lie about the history of Auschwitz:

> "Up until 1989 in eastern Europe, a prohibition against casting doubt upon the figure of 4 million killed was in force; at the memorial site of Ausch-

witz, employees who doubted the correctness of the estimate were threatened with disciplinary measures." (*Frankfurter Allgemeine Zeitung*, 14 September 1998)

This was the same year that "democratic" Poland introduced a law threatening any historical dissent in this regard with up to three years imprisonment, hence not just "disciplinary measures." Considering that Poland still has active "Holocaust denial" laws in place, it is reasonable to assume that current historians at the Auschwitz Museum continue to lie, and that, in the future, they will point to present-day laws in defense of their ongoing historical falsifications.

DOESSEKKER, BRUNO

Bruno Doessekker (born 12 Feb. 1941) is a Swiss national who invented from scratch the story of his alleged gruesome childhood spent at the Auschwitz and Majdanek Camps. It was published in 1998 as a book under the pen name Binjamin Wilkomirski (in English as *Fragments*), and was praised by the Holocaust orthodoxy for its gripping narrative, who bestowed honors and prizes on Doessekker. That same summer, a Swiss investigative journalist exposed the story as complete fiction, as it turned out that Doessekker had never left Swiss territory during the war years (*Weltwoche*, 27 August 1998, pp. 46f.; Mächler 2000, Ganzfried 2002). The reason why the entire Holocaust elite was so easily fooled by Doessekker was explained by Jewish mainstream author Howard Weiss:

Bruno Doessekker

"Perhaps no one was ready to question the authenticity of the [Doessekker] *account because just about anything concerning the Holocaust becomes sacrosanct."* (*Chicago Jewish Star*, 9-29 Oct. 1998; cf. Weber 1998.)

Holocaust dogmatist Deborah Lipstadt was ready to ignore this fraud by stating that this forgery "might complicate matters somewhat. But [the book] is still powerful" as a novel (*Forward*, 18 Sept. 1998, p. 1). And Jewish author Judith Shulevitz encouraged others to be more subtle with their forgeries so as to remain undiscovered (*Ottawa Citizen*, 18 Nov. 1998):

"I cannot help wishing Wilkomirski-Doessek[k]*er had been more subtle in his efforts at deception, and produced the magnificent fraud world literature deserves."*

Deborah Dwork, at that time director of the Center for Holocaust Studies at Clark University, Worcester, Massachusetts, insisted that Doessekker was not a perpetrator but rather *a victim*, "a deeply scarred man" exploited by his publisher (*New York Times*, 3 Nov. 1998). Israel Gutman, then director of the Yad Vashem Museum in Jerusalem, claimed it is irrelevant that Doessekker lied (Finkelstein 2000):

"Wilkomirski has written a story which he has experienced deeply; that is for sure. […] He is not a fake. He is someone who lives this story very deeply in his soul. The pain is authentic."

Such astonishing attempts to whitewash admitted lies is telling; Holocaust "witnesses" and "survivors" know they can lie with impunity, and that the orthodoxy will protect and cover for them, even when caught in the act. Such mendacity casts doubt on all survivors, putting all firsthand accounts into question. (See also the entry on false witnesses.)

DOLINER, IOSIF

Iosif Doliner was a Ukrainian Jew interned in the Syretsky Camp, 5 km from Kiev. On 18 August, he was taken from there to Babi Yar, a place where tens of thousands of Jews are said to have been shot and buried by the Germans in mass graves in late September 1941 (see the entry on Babi Yar). He was interrogated by the NKGB on 4 February 1943.

Among other things, Doliner stated that he and 99 other slave-labor inmates were put in chains and had to exhume mass graves and burn the extracted bodies on pyres. Those pyres were circular, two meters high, and 2-8 meters in diameter. Each contained up to 2,000 corpses.

A pyre of 8 meters diameter has a surface area of some 50 square meters. This means that there would have been 40 bodies per square meter. Each corpse requires 250 kg of freshly cut wood (see the entry on open-air incinerations). The density of green wood is roughly 0.9 tons per m³, and its stacking density on a pyre is 1.4 (40% for air and flames to go through). This means that the wood required to burn 40 bodies would have stacked up to a height of some 15 meters. Adding the bodies into this would have resulted in a height of some 20 meters – not two meters, as Doliner claimed. It would have been impossible to build such a tall pyre, and also impossible to burn it down without it collapsing and spilling burning wood and corpses all over the place.

After the pyres had burned down, the bones were

allegedly crushed to powder with pestles, and the resulting powder scattered. However, for this to work, all the remains of a pyre had to be sifted for unburned remains. Wood-fired pyres burn unevenly and leave behind lots of unburned wood pieces, charcoal, and incompletely burned body parts, not just ashes and bones (80% of leftovers would have been from wood, not corpses). Incompletely burned wood and human remains could not have been crushed. If 100,000 bodies were burned, then several thousand metric tons of cremation leftovers had to be processed. Just this job would have required hundreds of men to complete in time.

At the end of this alleged activity, Doliner claimed, the rails, bars and stones used to build the pyres were buried in the ravine. However, no such items were ever found at Babi Yar.

Cremating an average human body during open-air incinerations requires some 250 kg of freshly cut wood. Cremating 100,000 bodies thus requires some 25,000 metric tons of wood. This would have required the felling of all trees growing in a 50-year-old spruce forest covering almost 56 hectares of land, or some 125 American football fields. An average prisoner is rated at being able to cut some 0.63 metric tons of fresh wood per workday. To cut this amount of wood within five weeks (35 days) that this operation supposedly lasted would have required a work force of some 1,134 dedicated lumberjacks just to cut the wood. Doliner claimed his unit consisted only of 100 inmates, all busy digging out mass graves, extracting bodies, building pyres, sifting through ashes, crushing bones, and scattering the resulting powder. Doliner says nothing about where the firewood came from.

Doliner moreover claimed that every day "5-6 gas vans full of asphyxiated people" were brought, who were also burned. Often, these people were still alive, hence thrown into the fire still alive. However, considering that the front was getting very close to Kiev during September 1943, it is unlikely that anyone would have operated gas vans in Kiev's vicinity. All this apart from the fact that gas vans are a figment of Soviet atrocity propaganda (see the entry on gas vans).

(For more details, see the entry on Babi Yar, as well as Mattogno 2022c, pp. 535f., and 550-563.)

doors, gastight → Gastight Doors

DRAGON, ABRAHAM

Abraham Dragon, brother of Szlama Dragon, remained silent about his wartime experiences until 1993, when he and his brother met Israeli historian Gideon Greif. He not only parroted his brother's falsehoods as read from Szlama's Polish 1945 deposition, but added his own invention of homicidal railroad gassing cars (Mattogno 2016f, p. 134; 2022e, p. 161):

> *"They* [the SS] *had taken them* [other members of his labor unit] *to Lublin – locked* [them] *in a railroad car and somehow – I don't know how – pumped in gas."*

Such a claim is not only unique, it is also rejected as false by all historians, and it is clear that Dragon was in no position to have known anything about such a gassing train, as he wasn't part of this alleged transport.

DRAGON, SZLAMA

Szlama Dragon (19 March 1922 – 6 Oct. 2001) was a Polish Jew incarcerated at the Auschwitz-Birkenau Camp, where he claims to have served from 8 December 1942 until early 1944 at the so-called "bunkers" of Auschwitz, and since February 1944 in Crematorium V. His testimony is considered a key statement about the alleged extermination operations at these bunkers. His testimony consists of three statements: The first made to Soviet investigators on 26 February 1945, the second on 10 and 11 May 1945 to the Polish judge Jan Sehn in preparation of the show trial against former camp commandant Rudolf Höss, and a final one made in 1993 to the Israeli historian Gideon Greif (English in Greif 2005, pp. 122-180).

The two testimonies recorded at war's end are characterized by contradictions regarding the terms used to describe the facilities (the term "bunker" was unknown to any witness prior to March/April 1945), the number of doors it had, whether windows were made gastight or were bricked up, the locations of undressing barracks, how many cremation pits there were, and how far away these two bunkers were from each other. More important, however, are the following evidently false claims about these alleged facilities and their associated incineration pits (Mattogno 2016f, pp. 73-85):

– Dragon claimed that these facilities were packed with a physically impossible density of 20 to 25 victims per square meter.
– He claimed that he was selected at arrival on 7

December 1942 by Dr. Mengele, who was assigned to Auschwitz only on 30 May 1943. He also claimed that Mengele was in charge of homicidal gassings.
- He claimed that gassings were at times performed by an SS man called Schei[n]metz, but no person with this or a similar name was ever stationed at Auschwitz.
- Although he claimed to have worked at one of the bunkers only for a few days, he asserts that, on average, "17,000 to 18,000 persons were burned in 24 hours" in the trenches near the bunkers, which are said to have ceased operation at the end of March 1943. From 8 December 1942 to 31 March 1943 are 113 days, so in total some two million Jews would have been killed and burned just during those three and a half months – clearly impossible.
- At peak performance, he claimed a daily rate of 27,000 to 28,000 persons. With some 4,000 persons per batch as claimed by him, this amounts to around seven gassing batches per day, or one every three hours or so, around the clock; this is absurd.
- Dragon claimed that, at Bunker 1, with an average capacity of 7,000 to 8,000 corpses burned daily, only 28 inmates were in charge of procuring wood. Since open-air incineration of corpses require about 250 kg of freshly cut wood per corpse, some 1,750 to 2,000 tons of fresh wood would have been required *every day*, or 62 to 71 tons per inmate *every day*. However, an average prisoner is rated at being able to cut only some 0.63 metric tons of fresh wood per workday. Therefore, 2800 rather than 28 inmates would have been required to cut the wood needed.
- He described Bunker 1 and the events unfolding around it in detail, yet states at the same time that he never worked there.
- Dragon drew a sketch of "Bunker 2" showing four unequally sized parallel rooms. In his deposition, he claimed a capacity of each of the four rooms of 1,200, 700, 400 and 200-250 people, on an overall floor area of 100 m². All rooms had the same length (the width of the building), but different widths. Hence, their width ratio was roughly 12:7:4:2.5. Following his sketch, the building may have been some 8.5 m wide and 12 m long (not counting walls). In that case, the rooms had a width of roughly 5.5 m, 3.3 m, 1.9 m and 1.2 m. No competent person would have built

Abraham (left) and Szlama Dragon (right)

a "gas chamber" 8.5 meters long and just 1.9 or even 1.2 meters wide.
- This awkward division of the building, plus his description of the facility, contradict the description and sketches of that same building drawn by the other key witness for the bunkers, Dov Paisikovic (3 equally sized parallel rooms). Both Paisikovic's and Dragon's sketches and descriptions moreover radically contradict the foundation walls of this building, which still exist today (seven irregularly sized and arranged rooms, see the illustrations).
- Dragon claimed that liquid fat collected at the bottom of the cremation pits, and that it was collected by the SS and used to fuel the fire. The physically impossible fairy tale of fat extracted from burning corpses was often repeated by witnesses and proves their untrue, copy-cat nature.
- Dragon claimed that corpses pushed into the furnaces of Crematorium V caught fire immediately – which cannot be true, as human are not made of paper or wood – and that their limbs rose up, which is also physically impossible.
- He insisted that the cremation of three corpses in a furnace at Auschwitz lasted only 15 to 20 minutes, when in fact the cremation of just one corpse took roughly an hour.
- Dragon claimed that two corpses were inserted first, then another third corpse on top of it. However, this would have required tipping the 45-cm-wide stretcher steeply upward to get it on top of the two corpses already in that muffle, which would have meant hitting the muffle vault where it is 45 cm wide with the stretcher's end, rather than being able to insert it fully to unload the next two corpses – which might actually have slid

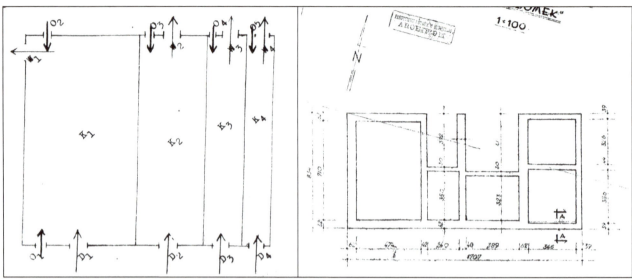

Left: floor plan of the alleged homicidal gassing facility called "Bunker 2," drawn in 1945 following Szlama Dragon's instruction (no measures given). Right: floor plan of the ruins of the only building located in the claimed area, drawn in 1985 on request of the Auschwitz Museum: some 17 m long and 8 m wide, with seven highly irregular rooms. (Taken from Mattogno 2016f, pp. 238.)

backwards and off the stretcher with such an inclination.

– Dragon asserted that they pushed in two corpses at once, then a third one, which had to be done quickly before the arms and legs of the first pair of corpses began to rise from the heat. However, dead people cannot raise their arms and legs, and neither can heat, which burns muscles, but does not contract them in a coordinated fashion, defying gravity. This statement resembles that of Henryk Tauber in this regard and shows a "convergence of evidence" for orchestrated lies.

– According to him, 300,000 Jews from Hungary were cremated just in Crematorium V, within two months in the spring of 1944, although that is the claimed total death toll of these two months for *all* crematoria and Bunker 2.

Dragon's testimony to Gideon Greif 50 years after the claimed events is characterized by him reading his own Polish deposition of 1945, from which he lifted passages at times almost verbatim. Therefore, the interview was a farce. Yet still, he added more absurdities to his tale, such as (*ibid.*, pp. 132-134; Mattogno 2022e, pp. 155-168):

– He claimed to have attempted suicide on the first day of being deployed at one of the bunkers, yet instead of being gassed as a dangerous witness unfit for work, he was nursed back to health, and his brother Abraham Dragon (also deployed at the bunker) was allowed to go with him to the infirmary and help him get better. Perhaps the SS men were kinder to the inmates than we have been led to believe; either that, or Dragon was lying.

– Dragon claimed that, when the inmates revolted due to ill treatment, the SS was nice and accepted all their demands.

– He claimed that all the other members of the *Sonderkommando* were killed as dangerous carriers of secrets, but that he was spared (and also his brother, and the many other *Sonderkommando* members who have since testified…). The reason for his miraculous survival: he got sick and was in the infirmary on that day. That claim is absurd, however, because *Sonderkommando* members who became unfit for work were supposedly killed instantly rather than nursed back to health. But that is evidently untrue as well.

– Dragon claimed to have put three corpses side-by-side on a stretcher to insert into a cremation furnace, although that stretcher was only 45 cm wide.

– He claimed that he could smell the "sweetish taste of the gas," although Zyklon gas does not smell sweetish. He moreover insisted to have worn a gas mask while smelling the gas, which would not have been possible. Had he ever been in a position to "smell" Zyklon gas, he would surely be dead.

DUGIN, ITZHAK

Itzhak Dugin, a Jew from Vilnius, was interviewed by Claude Lanzmann for his documentary *Shoah* sometime in the early 1980s, together with Matvey

Zaydel. They both testified about their alleged experiences during the war, when they claim to have been forced to exhume and burn corpses from mass graves near a Vilnius suburb called Ponary. For an analysis of their story, see the entry on Matvey Zaydel.

E

EBERL, IRMFRIED

Irmfried Eberl (8 Sept. 1910 – 16 Feb. 1948), SS *Obersturmführer* at war's end, was an Austrian-German physician who worked as medical director at two euthanasia institutes from February 1940 until late 1941. After this, he was transferred to *Aktion Reinhardt*. He served as the first commandant of the Treblinka Camp since 11 July 1942, but was replaced by Franz Stangl already in late August of that year, evidently due to Eberl's incompetence.

Irmfried Eberl

At the end of the war, he served in the German armed forces until the bitter end. In 1948, he was arrested, yet committed suicide before any trial could start. As far as is known, he did not make any deposition about his activities in Treblinka.

Eberl's correspondence was preserved and published in 2006. None of the letters sent by Eberl from Treblinka contains any reference to gassings of Jews. (See Grabher 2006.)

EDELMAN, SALMAN

Salman Edelman was a Polish Jew living in the Białystok Ghetto. He claimed that some German authorities selected him in mid-May 1944 to participate in the exhumation of mass graves, and the cremation of the bodies contained in it. Edelman testified about this after the war together with another member of this unit, Szymon Amiel. It was published, probably in an edited version, in the infamous Soviet propaganda book *The Black Book*. For a more-detailed discussion, see the entry on Szymon Amiel.

EHRENBURG, ILYA

Ilya Ehrenburg (26 Jan. 1891 – 31 Aug. 1967) was a Soviet-Jewish journalist and the Soviet Union's main war propagandist. He was put in charge of submitting daily articles to the Western Allies in order to foment "hate, hate, and more hate" against everything German, as Stalin put it. In fact, Ehrenburg ended up writing more than one article per day, sometimes up to five, inventing German atrocities in assembly-line fashion, and depicting Germans as subhuman monsters, calling upon his readers to kill every single German, wherever they may be found.

Ilya Ehrenburg

Together with another prominent Soviet-Jewish journalist, Vasily Grossman, Ehrenburg compiled a collection of Soviet atrocity stories on claimed German wartime crimes during the war, titled *The Black Book*. (See the entry on Grossman.)

Ehrenburg was also the first person to definitively and publicly announce that the Germans had killed six million Jews – at a time when the war wasn't yet over and no one could possibly have known the actual death toll: Ilya Ehrenburg in an article headlined, "Remember, Remember, Remember," *Soviet War News*, 22 December 1944 (pp. 4f.):

> *"In regions they seized, the Germans killed all the Jews, from the old folk to infants in arms. Ask any German prisoner why his fellow countrymen annihilated six million innocent people, and he will reply quite simply: 'Why, they were Jews.'"*

(Hoffmann 2001, pp. 156-168, 189, 402f.)

EICHMANN, ADOLF

Adolf Eichmann (19 March 1906 – 1 June 1962), SS *Obersturmbannführer*, was head of Sub-Department IV D4 of the *Reichssicherheitshauptamt* (wartime Germany's Department of Homeland Security) from 19 December 1939, charged with overseeing Jewish affairs and evacuation/deportation of the Jews. As such, he was responsible for the deportation of several million Jews to the various German labor, concentration and transit camps, as well as their evacuation to Polish ghettos and the eastern occupied Soviet territories. He was also involved in planning the deportation of Europe's Jews to Madagascar, a plan shelved in early 1942.

After the war, Eichmann went into hiding in Argentina and was eventually assumed either missing or dead. Therefore, during the Allied postwar tribunals, there was a tendency among German officials to use Eichmann as a scapegoat, blaming him not only for the deportation of the Jews, but falsely portraying him also as responsible for organizing their alleged wholesale slaughter. Two former German officials quoted Eichmann as having told them that the Jewish death toll was five or six million, respectively (Dieter Wisliceny and Wilhelm Höttl), although Eichmann later denied this. Furthermore, he would not have been in a position to know what happened to all the Jews whose deportation he organized, let alone to those millions he had nothing to do with. In fact, during his own trial, he stated that he himself "was kept in the dark as well as to how many or who would be killed." (See Heddesheimer 2017, p. 9; Rudolf 2023, pp. 400f.)

Adolf Eichmann

Eichmann's undoing was that, in Argentina, he started bragging about his wartime role, dramatizing his own involvement in the persecution of the Jews in interviews he gave to the Dutch journalist Willem Sassen, weaving into his narrative things he had read and heard about in the media, mixing his own memories with fact and fiction, with rumors and lies bandied about in the world's mass media. This led to his capture in Argentina by an Israeli Mossad team in May 1960, who transported him to Israel. The subsequent trial against him in 1961 was the role model of all later Holocaust show trials. The proceedings were broadcasted on Israeli TV, and many witnesses testified about the most horrific claimed events of the Holocaust, even though Eichmann, from his offices in Vienna and Berlin, had nothing to do with them. The quality of these witness accounts was similar to those later made during the Jerusalem trial against John Demjanjuk, with the difference that the Israelis did not allow any effective defense to be organized for Eichmann – or rather, Eichmann's lawyers decided not to challenge any of the dogmas surrounding the mainstream Holocaust narrative, trying only to minimize Eichmann's responsibilities in it (Rudolf 2019, p. 133).

Although Eichmann confirmed many of the orthodoxy's claims about the Holocaust during his trial, the following facts need to be considered:

– The Wannsee Memorial Museum has compiled a document containing various, at times contradictory, statements that Eichmann made during his trial.[2] This compilation inevitably gives the impression that Eichmann was confused.
– When asked about exterminations at Auschwitz, Eichmann qualified his memories about them:
  "I do not know whether I am only imagining that today, but I do not believe I am imagining it. I cannot recall exactly when and how he told me that and the location where he told me. Perhaps I read it and perhaps I am now imagining what I had read I heard from him. That is also possible."
  Eichmann had not only read a lot of literature on the topic before his capture, but was provided with even more material during his incarceration by his Israeli captors. Hence, his memories were inevitably altered by what he had read after the war.
– He made a number of nonsensical claims about alleged events: he insisted that the Germans had developed portable gas-chamber sheds that could be rapidly set up if, for instance, some Jews were found hiding somewhere in the woods (Rudolf 2019, p. 126).
– He seriously claimed that diesel engines taken from Soviet submarines were used in central Poland to gas Jews, never mind that diesel-engine exhaust gases are unsuited for mass murder, or that it is nearly impossible to take a submarine engine out of a captured Soviet submarine, transport it across Poland, and set it up and make it work in some remote camp (*ibid.*, p. 443, FN 57).
– Eichmann also repeated the cliché of mass graves expelling geysers of blood, a physical impossibility (*ibid.*, p. 124).

A full critical analysis of the 1961 Eichmann Show Trial is still pending, exposing its background and conduct rooted in fanaticism and mass hysteria. This trial defined the Holocaust as the most-important event for Jewish and Israeli identity, and the trial catapulted it into the center of worldwide public awareness, where it has continually grown in importance.

---

[2] www.ghwk.de/fileadmin/user_upload/pdf-wannsee/texte/eichmanns-testimony.pdf

EINSATZGRUPPEN

Historical Context

In Western and Central Europe, and in particular in Poland and Germany, it was well-known since 1918/1919 that the Bolshevists and their Red Army exhibited a savage bestiality during warfare and even in peacetime that was unparalleled in modern history. In addition, the Soviet Union rescinded any agreement of international law that Czarist Russia had agreed on, and refused to sign any new agreement, such as the Geneva Convention and the Hague Convention. The effects of this surfaced already during the war against Finland in the winter of 1939/1940. Hence, there could be no illusion as to how the Soviet Union would conduct a war, should it ever come to a clash with Germany or any other European nation.

The National Socialists perceived Bolshevism as an ideology of atrocities based mainly on Jewish support and participation. In fact, the extraordinarily over-proportionate participation of individuals with a Jewish background in the savage Bolshevist revolution and the subsequent bloody Soviet rule in the 1920s and early 1930s was one of the main pillars of National-Socialist anti-Judaism. (See the section on "Motives for National-Socialist anti-Judaism" in the entry on Motives for details.) National-Socialism saw itself as a revolutionary movement directed to no small degree at countering and undoing the Bolshevist revolution that Moscow was trying to spread around the globe.

This ideological confrontation set the stage for a war of annihilation between Germany and the Soviet Union, where Jewish-dominated Bolshevist atrocities during the 1920s and 1930s led to an irreconcilably hostile attitude of National Socialists toward Jews and Bolshevism. This in turn stoked Bolshevist and universal Jewish desire to wage a war of annihilation against anything German, which the National Socialists reciprocated in kind. The two largest European nations were gearing up for the ultimate confrontation.

Soviet Warfare

Right from the beginning of the invasion of the Soviet Union in 1941, German units encountered mass atrocities: In almost every town and city that the Soviets were about to retreat from, they murdered dissidents and potential opposition leaders by the hundreds. Wherever possible, they applied scorched-earth tactics, destroying critical infrastructure, industrial facilities and food supplies, burning down crops in the fields and on occasion even entire villages and towns before retreating. If by chance they captured German soldiers, these men were later found mutilated and savagely murdered. This stiffened and brutalized German responses.

Two decades of Soviet atrocities also led to retaliations by the local population against those whom they perceived as supporters of the savage Soviet rule. Hence, pogroms against Jews were a common occurrence during the opening days and weeks of the conflict. German units sometimes intervened to suppress those pogroms, but in many cases, they deliberately looked the other way or even encouraged mob violence.

Soon after the commencement of hostilities, Soviet partisans (civilian fighters) started their illegal warfare. The number of partisans acting behind German army lines rose steadily throughout the years, from a few thousands at the beginning, to some 100,000 in early 1942 to about half a million in early 1944. The defeat of the German armed forces in the East was to a large degree a result of this guerrilla warfare. Soviet Jews played a major part in these guerilla formations. The radical National-Socialist anti-Jewish stance gave Jews little choice as to which side to take, even if they opposed Stalin's cruel regime. Moreover, many of the Jews deported to the East by German resettlement operations decided to flee to the woods and join the partisans. Hence, Germany's resettlement and deportation policies to the East backfired on them.

The German reaction to the expected guerrilla warfare was extremely harsh from the outset: With the so-called "Commissar Order," Germany declared the Red Army's political commissars, who enforced the cruel Soviet warfare at the front lines, as non-combatants, hence as criminals who were to be executed when captured. In addition to that, reprisal shootings of civilians from the affected areas were conducted, which was in accordance with international law at that time, if kept within certain limits. However, in their rage, German units often exceeded those limits.

The Commissar Order, excessive reprisals, as well as mass execution of partisans, partisan suspects and those suspected of helping partisans backfired on the Germans. Recognizing this, the Commissar Order was rescinded in May 1942, and a little while later, in a unique act of gratuitous humanity, the German armed forces even recognized regular partisan groups as ordinary (legal) combatants.

Documented History
Polish Campaign

In preparation of the invasion of Poland in September 1939, Germany created special units named *Einsatzgruppen*, which literally translates to "deployment groups," but is usually translated as "task forces." Most of these units were divided into subunits called *Einsatzkommandos*. The *Einsatzgruppen* in Poland consisted of roughly two thousand members of various German police and intelligence units. In cooperation with the German military, these units' task was "to combat all elements hostile to the Reich and to Germans in enemy territory to the rear of the combat troops." Altogether eight *Einsatzgruppen* operated in distinct areas of occupied Poland during the German-Polish War. With combat operations ceasing in late October, the *Einsatzgruppen's* activities also largely ceased.

Only five wartime documents of these units have survived. They mention Jews only in the context of registering Jewish-owned enterprises, liquidating abandoned businesses of Jews who have fled, and implementing a policy of ghettoization and concentration, as well as emigration and expulsion of Polish Jews. This includes plans to resettle Jews to a "Jewish reservation" in southeastern Poland near the town Nisko. (See the entry on the Nisko Plan.) No documents refer to any executions or other extermination measures.

Orthodox authors tally the victims of executions in Poland to 16,336 victims for the time of military operations. Although there were Jews among the victims, they were not a specific target, and their share was not significantly higher than their percentage in acts of opposition to the German occupation.

Structure

When the German government prepared Germany's invasion of the Soviet Union, Germany's Department for Homeland Security, the *Reichssicherheitshauptamt* (RSHA), formed a new set of four *Einsatzgruppen* (EG), containing altogether some 3,000 men. They consisted each of several *Sonderkommando* subunits (SK), and were deployed in the rear of the operational area of certain German military formations as indicated in the table.

In addition to the *Einsatzgruppen*, the German occupational authorities also created police forces, which were also involved in combating individuals or groups hostile toward the German occupational authorities. They were organized in three groups, totaling some 8,000-9,000 men. These units were each commanded by a so-called Higher SS and Police Leader, as follows:

– Russia North and *Ostland* (Baltics), headed by Hans-Adolf Prützmann, later by Friedrich Jeckeln.
– Russia Central, headed by Erich von dem Bach-Zelewski;
– Russia South and Ukraine, headed by Friedrich Jeckeln, later by Hans-Adolf Prützmann.

Also occasionally involved in *Einsatzgruppen* activities were subunits of Himmler's personal SS formation called *Kommandostab Reichsführer* SS. It consisted of military units (infantry, cavalry, air-defense units) comprising altogether some 25,000 men.

Mission

The official mission statement for the *Einsatzgruppen* does not say anything about exterminating Jews. In the non-combat zone behind the German armies, they were to identify, capture and eliminate ideological and political enemies and those who committed hostile acts against German troops or the populations of the occupied countries, starting with the partisans.

Einsatzgruppen **Deployment Areas, Subunits and Successive Commanders**

EG	Deployed with (in)	SKs	Successive Chiefs
A	Army Group North (northern Russia)	1a, 1b, 2, 3	Walter Stahlecker, Heinz Jost, Humbert Achamer-Pifrader, Friedrich Panzinger, Wilhelm Fuchs
B	Army Group Central (Belorussia, central Russia)	7a, 7b, 8, 9, Advance Unit Moscow	Arthur Nebe, Erich Naumann, Horst Böhme, Erich Ehrlinger, Heinz Seetzen, Horst Böhme
C	Army Group South (northern + central Ukraine)	4a, 4b, 5, 6	Otto Rasch, Max Thomas, Horst Böhme
D	11th Army, Rumanian army (southern Ukraine, Crimea, Causcasus)	10a, 10b, 11a 11b, 12	Otto Ohlendorf, Walter Bierkamp

They moreover were tasked with gathering intelligence on a broad variety of areas, and informing the armed forces of the political situation. They assisted in the restoration of the administrative, social and economic structure of regions devastated by the combatants or by the Soviets' scorched-earth withdrawal. This also included the revival of the local populace's cultural and religious life. Meticulous reports on seizures and arrests were to be written, and records of their activities kept.

Two long reports by the first commander of *Einsatzgruppe* A, Walter Stahlecker, testify to the broad variety of the group's activities. The first of these so-called Stahlecker Reports (15 October 1941) has 143 pages and 18 appendices, while the second of February 1942 has 228 pages plus 19 appendices. Only very small parts of these reports deal with executions. The issues covered range from the civil population's morale via politics, culture and public health to religious and economic topics, to name only a few. (See the entry on the Stahlecker Reports from more details.)

Other summary documents created by the *Einsatzgruppen* testify to a similar diversity of activities, including description of an area's cultural life during the Soviet era and at the time of reporting, listing cultural institutions, theaters, cinemas, musical life, libraries, radio and museums. They explain issues of economy, trade, labor and social affairs, labor deployment, working morale and performance, as well as procurement of manpower into the Reich, to name but a few topics. The following table shows how many reports of which *Einsatzgruppe* dealt with which topic.

Number of *Einsatzgruppen* Reports Addressing a Given Topic

EG:	A	B	C	D
Propaganda	5	10	4	5
Economy	10	9	13	7
Churches	11	8	9	7
Education, Culture, Science	6	2	6	6
Press	4	/	/	/
Agriculture, Food	3	4	14	9
Jews, Jewish Question	4	5	/	6
Ethnic Groups	11	10	27	16

Being able to cover all these topics effectively required a staff that was highly educated. Hence, for a military formation, the *Einsatzgruppen*'s leading positions had an unusually high percentage of highly educated academics. About 40% of all EG commanders had PhDs.

The decision by the RSHA to recruit personnel with such a high degree of university training indicates that their primary task did not consist of extermination at all.

Reports

A huge set of documents related to the *Einsatzgruppen*'s activities was confiscated by the Allies in the Gestapo headquarters in Berlin on 3 September 1945. These consist largely of three sets of documents:
- 195 *Ereignismeldungen UdSSR* (EM; Event Reports USSR), which were created from 23 June 1941 until 24 April 1942 (almost 3,000 pages).
- 55 *Meldungen aus den besetzten Ostgebieten* (MO, Reports from the Occupied Eastern Territories) created between 1 May 1942 and 21 May 1943 (some 1,700 pages).
- 11 *Tätigkeits- und Lageberichte* (TL, Activity and Situation Reports) covering larger periods of time, the earlier of which are summaries of the events laid out in the EMs of that time.
- Three individual reports: two by the head of *Einsatzgruppe* A, Walter Stahlecker (15 October 1941 and February 1942; 143 and 228 pp.), and one by the head of *Einsatzkommando* 3 (of EG A), Karl Jäger (1 December 1941, 9 pp.).

The individual reports (EM and MO) therefore consist of some 4,700 pages of typed text. Not even 10% of these pages contain information about executions, while the rest deals with many other issues, such as intelligence, interrogation of PoWs, search of enemies and informants, creating ghettos and camps, isolating Jews, as well as eliminating people disturbing normal life and productivity.

The EMs and MOs were created in a convoluted way. A clerk of each *Einsatzkommando* (EK) drafted a handwritten account of his unit's activities. This was submitted to his unit's leader. He then created his own version of it and submitted it to the headquarters of his EG. There, the various reports of all EKs were summarized into one report, which was either mailed or communicated by radio or sometimes even by phone to the Berlin RSHA headquarters. In Berlin, those incoming reports from all EGs were again compiled into the final EM or later MO report. None of the original or various intermediary reports of this long chain have been preserved.

In Berlin, up to 77 copies of these reports were distributed to various recipients, most of them to various RSHA departments, but some also to a few outsiders. The set of EMs presumably found at the Gestapo headquarters should contain a complete set of all EMs intended for that office. However, it contains a mix of copies intended for disparate RSHA offices. Furthermore, an identical set of the same "originals" as stored in the German Federal Archives can also be found in the Russian State War Archives. Of course, both sets cannot be original. Either one or both are forgeries.

Even orthodox historians agree that the execution figures listed in these documents are highly unreliable. A thorough analysis reveals that some figures were evidently vastly exaggerated, while some events might have been invented altogether. The figures listed in various reports sometimes get repeated and counted twice. Other numbers and events claimed in one report contradict the data listed in others that should or do cover the same events.

More importantly, when a report gives a total number of executions carried out as of a given point in time, these figures usually do not agree with the individual executions reported, but are often vastly higher. For example, EM No. 88 of 19 September 1941 gives a total of 85,000 execution victims as of that date, but the individual figures only attest to some 15,000 victims, while only two executions are specifically mentioned in EMs with date/location, amounting to 4,300 victims. This is less than 6% of the claimed total.

Whenever execution figures run into the thousands or even tens of thousands per event, it is suspicious when these reports list victim counts down to the single digit, which would have required extremely accurate and meticulous bookkeeping during those claimed mass slaughters. For instance, one EM reports that within two days, 33,771 Jews were executed at Babi Yar in Kiev. All the evidence available in this case, including air photos taken in September 1943, points to this event not having occurred at all. It is quite obvious what the consequences are for the credibility of this EM, if not its authenticity.

Another red flag is the so-called Jäger Report, which lists the execution of 137,343 persons until late 1941, most of them Jews from Lithuania. However, most of the individual execution events mentioned cannot be found in the EMs of that time. In fact, the EMs "confirm" only some 2,900 of these alleged executions. That is barely over two percent! There are more issues with this report, which make its authenticity highly questionable. (See the entry dedicated to the Jäger Report.)

Death Toll

The EMs contain the main data about executions. The MOs contain hardly any information about executions, be it because the "job" had already been done by May 1942, or because this set of documents is actually authentic and gives a more-realistic figure of what was going on in the temporarily German-occupied Soviet territories.

The alleged death toll resulting from the various extant documents for each EG and other units are as follows:

Unit	Death Toll
Einsatzgruppe A:	240,410
Einsatzgruppe B:	142,359
Einsatzgruppe C:	134,260
Einsatzgruppe D:	114,449
Subtotal:	631,478
Other SS units:	120,307
Overall Total:	751,785

Of these claimed killings, 274,149, or more than a third, are listed in these reports without indication of when and where these alleged executions took place.

List of Execution Locations

The EMs list many locations in the temporarily German-occupied Soviet Union where executions are said to have occurred. Instead of dedicating an alphabetical entry to many of the major claimed mass-execution sites, as mainstream encyclopedias tend to do, it seems more appropriate to prepare a complete listing of all locations, with the total number of all victims presumably killed there, and the alleged perpetrator unit(s). Note that this list does *not* include non-Jewish victims, and it does not include the many killing events for which no specific location is given.

Executioners	Location	Victims
EG A	Ariogala	27
EG D	Babchintsy	94
EG A	Bakov	100
EG A, B	Baranovichi	2,388
EG C	Belaya Tserkov	68
EG B	Belovshchina	2,726
Rumanians	Beltsy (Balti)	45
EG C, HSSPF S	Berdichev	1,674
EG B	Berezna	8
BdS GG, EG z.b.V/EK Lemberg	Bialystok	490

EG B	Bobruisk	7,486
EG C	Boguslav	322
EG B	Borisov	962
EG B	Borovlyany	5
EG B	Bresk [?] Horsov [?]	?
EG z.b.V/EK Lemberg, OrPo, BdS GG	Brest-Litovsk	5,306
EG D	Buyuk Lambat and Alushta	30
EG B	Chausy	31
EG B, C	Chernigov	309
Rumanians	Chernovitsy	682
EG C	Chernyakov	156
EG A	Cherven	15,000
EG C	Chmielnik	229
EG A	Daugavpils	1,171
EG C, HSSPF S	Dnepropetrovsk	10,350
EG C	Dobromil	132
EG C	Dubno	100
EG C	Dymer	120
EG C	Fastov	312
EG D	Feodosia	16
Stapo Tilsit	Gargzdai	201
EG B	Gomel, Rogachev, Korma	2,468
EG B	Gorki	2,200
EG C	Gornostaipol	385
EG B	Gorodnia	21
EG B	Gorodok	446
EG B	Grodno	96
EG A	Ilya	520
EG C	Ivankov	195
EG B	Iviniec (Ivenets)	50
Pogrom	Jelgava	1,556
HSSPF S	Kamenets-Podolsky	23,600
Lithuanian Pogroms, HSSPF N, EG A	Kaunas	10,562 + Thousands
EG A	Kedainiai	93
EG C	Kharkov	305
EG B	Khislavichi	114
EG B	Kholopenichi	822
EG C, Pogrom	Khorostov	270
EG D	Khotin	150
EG C, A	Kiev	33,776
EG D	Kishinev	551
EG B	Klimov	27
EG B	Klimovichi, Cherikov	786
EG D	Kodyma	97
EG B	Komarovka	115
EG C, Ukrainians	Korosten	628
EG C	Korostyshev	40
EG C	Kozelets	125
EG C	Kozyatin Wezerajce [?]	22
EG C	Kremenets	130
Stapo Tilsit	Kretinga	214
EG B	Krichev	1,213
EG C	Krivoy Rog	284
EG B	Krugloye	31
EG B	Krupki	912
EG B	Kuyashiche [?]	32
EG A	Leningrad area	93
EG A	Liepaja	485
EG B	Lizny [?]	165
EG B	Logoysk	929
EG A	Loknya	38
EG C	Lubny	1,938
EG C	Lutsk	2,300
EG C, EG z.b.V/ EK Lemberg	Lviv	8,154
EG B	Lyubavichi	492
EG C	Makarov	14
EG A	Mariampole	103
EG B	Maryina Gorka	996
EG A, B	Minsk	14,212
EG C	Miropol	24
EG B	Mistislav [?]	900
EG B, Pol.Regt. Mitte	Mogilev	6,318
EG B	Monastyrshchina	46
EG B	Nevel	714
EG D	Nikolayev, Kherson	22,467
EG A	Novgorod	14
EG B	Novozybkov	1
EG B	Nowe Swieciany (Svencioneliai)	169
Rumanians	Odessa	10,000
EG D	Orel	?
EG B	Orsha	43
EG C	Oster	237
EG B	Ostrava	3
EG B	Ostrovno	169
EG B	Oszmiana (Oshmyany)	527
EG A	Pagiriai	1
Stapo Tilsit	Palanga	11
EG A	Panevezys	249
EG B	Patichi [?]	1,013
EG C	Pereyeslav	537
EG D	Pinsk	4,500
EG A	Plyussa	7
EG C	Poltava	1,538
EG C	Proskurov	146
EG C, Ukrainians	Radomyshl	2,057
EG A	Raseiniai	254
EG B	Rechitsa	216
Pogrom, EG A, HSSPF Riga	Riga	46,662
EG B	Roslavl, Shumyachi	510
EG C, HSSPF S	Rovno	15,240

EG C	Rudki	15
EG B, C	Rudnya	861
EG A	Salaspils	2
Pogrom	Sambor	50
EG C	Shepetovka	17
HSSPF S	Shepetovka-Rovno	1,643
EG B	Shidov [?]	627
EG B	Shklov	84
EG C	Shuealivka [?]	16
EG A	Siauliai	44
EG D	Simferopol	10,300
EG B	Sloboda, Polotsk, Bychikha, Bislatovo [?]	286
EG B	Slonim	1,159
EG B	Slutsk	1
EG B	Smolevichi	1,401
EG C	Stalino (Dontesk)	369
EG D	Mogilev-Podolsky	1,265
EG C	Starokonstantinov	439
EG B	Stolpce (Stolbtsy)	76
EG C	Stryi	11
EG B	Szuchari [Sukhari], Yasna	11
EG B	Talka	222
EG C	Tarashcha	109
EG C, Wehrmacht	Tarnopol	2,056
EG A	Tartu	50
EG B	Tatarsk	? + 3
EG D	Tighina	155
EG C	Troyanov	22
EG C	Tsybulov [?]	78
EG A	Ukmerge	296
EG C	Uman	1,412
EG A	Utena	251
EG A	Valka	10
EG A	Valmiera	25
EG A	Vandziogala	15
EG B	Velizh	1
EG A	Venden	3
EG A, B	Vileyka	302 + ?
EG A	Vilkaviskis	50
EG A, B	Vilnius	2,231
EG C	Vinnitsa	892
EG B	Vitebsk	7,750
EG B	Voroshilov	8
EG B	Vyazma CC	117
EG C	Yagotin	125
EG D	Yampol	9
EG B	Yanovichi	1,174
EG C	Yavorov	15
EG C	Yustungrad [?]	35
EG A	Zagare	250
Waffen SS	Zborov	600
EG C, D	Zhitomir	4,843
EG B	Zhlobin	31
EG B	Zlynka	27
EG C	Zolochev	3

Abbreviations:
- HSSPF: *Höherer SS- und Polizei-Führer*/Higher SS and Police Leader
- z.b.V: *zur besonderen Verfügung*/for special use
- OrPo: *Ordnungs Polizei*/regular police
- BdS GG: *Befehlshaber der Sicherheitspolizei Generalgouvernement*/commander of the Security Police, occupied Poland
- Stapo: *Staatspolizei*/state police

The next table lists the locations sorted by the number of victims claimed, from the highest down to 500. This gives an idea of the most important locations judged by the number of victims claimed.

Location	Victims
Riga	46,662
Kiev	33,776
Kamenets-Podolsky	23,600
Nikolayev, Kherson	22,467
Rovno	15,240
Cherven	15,000
Minsk	14,212
Kaunas	10,562 + Thousands
Dnepropetrovsk	10,350
Simferopol	10,300
Odessa	10,000
Lviv	8,154
Vitebsk	7,750
Bobruisk	7,486
Mogilev	6,318
Brest-Litovsk	5,306
Zhitomir	4,843
Pinsk	4,500
Belovshchina	2,726
Gomel, Rogachev, Korma	2,468
Lutsk	2,300
Vilnius	2,231
Gorki	2,200
Radomyshl	2,057
Tarnopol	2,056
Baranovichi	2,007
Lubny	1,938
Berdichev	1,674
Shepetovka-Rovno	1,643
Jelgava	1,556
Poltava	1,538
Uman	1,412
Smolevichi	1,401
Mogilev-Podolsky	1,265
Krichev	1,213
Yanovichi	1,174
Daugavpils	1,171
Slonim	1,159
Patichi [?]	1,013

Maryina Gorka	996
Borisov	962
Logoysk	929
Krupki	912
Mistislav [?]	900
Vinnitsa	892
Rudnya	861
Kholopenichi	822
Klimovichi, Cherikov	786
Nevel	714
Chernovitsy	682
Korosten	628
Shidov [?]	627
Zborov	600
Kishinev	551
Pereyeslav	537
Oszmiana (Oshmyany)	527
Ilya	520
Roslavl, Shumyachi	510

Extermination Order

There is no trace that the *Einsatzgruppen* ever received an order to systematically exterminate the Jews as they moved east into Soviet territory behind the German army. Otto Ohlendorf, head of *Einsatzgruppe* D, argued otherwise during the U.S.-staged *Einsatzgruppen* Trial at Nuremberg in 1947, but it turned out that he had devised this lie as a strategy to resort to the excuse of having received inescapable orders from higher up – which ultimately failed. (See the entry on Otto Ohlendorf.)

The documents tell a different story. The war diary of the Supreme Command of the German Armed Forces states in an entry of 3 March 1941, with regard to what Hitler had said about the coming invasion of the Soviet Union:

"The Jewish-Bolshevist intelligentsia, as the 'oppressor' of the people until now, must be eliminated."

A few lines later, the Supreme Command put the task ahead in its own words when stating "the necessity to render harmless immediately all Bolshevist warlords and commissars." Hence, when the Supreme Command interpreted Hitler's intention, the Jewish nature of Bolshevism was no longer mentioned.

When this task was put in legally binding form of a directive by the same Supreme Command on 13 March 1941, it was expressed even more generally, without any reference anymore to any elimination of rendering harmless of anyone:

"[T]he Reichsführer SS is receiving special tasks for preparation of the political administration [in the soon-to-be occupied territories] *by order of the Führer, which arise from the terminal struggle between two opposing political systems."*

Two red threads run through all German wartime documents:

1. Jews (and non-Jews) who are part of the Bolshevist intelligentsia or who actively oppose German efforts to win the war will be executed, and the remaining Jews will be concentrated in camps and ghettos, and put to work.
2. Later, after a successful conclusion of the war in the East, the Jews will be deported and resettled to some location outside of Europe. (See the entries on Hitler Order and resettlement.)

Even the *Einsatzgruppen* documents themselves point in that direction. On 6 August 1941, hence more than seven weeks into the invasion, Walter Stahlecker, head of *Einsatzgruppe* A, wrote in a document that the aim was to maximize the exploitation of the Jews as a labor force, and then to collectively relocate them to some "non-European Jewish reservation." Many references to executions of Jews listed in the EMs explain why these Jews were executed. Although some of the reasons given are far-fetched or sound like cheap excuses, if there had been a general order to exterminate all Jews, not a single entry about the killing of Jews needed to have an explanation. Yet there are numerous cases where even executions of a single Jew, or only a very few, are explained at great length.

Death Toll Propaganda

Since the mid- to late-1970s, source criticism by skeptical scholars has increasingly undermined the credibility of sources upon which the orthodoxy relies when claiming the existence of homicidal gas chambers in certain German wartime camps. (See in particular the cases of Majdanek and Auschwitz.) Therefore, a shift of focus away from these camps to the murders by the *Einsatzgruppen* and related units occurred since the 1990s.

Several orthodox scholars have claimed since that many more Jews fell victim to massacres perpetrated by various German units in the East. One prominent example is Daniel J. Goldhagen, who investigated the degree to which German police battalions contributed to the mayhem. Much of it is conjecture, and in many cases, their contribution probably did not consist in executions themselves, but in guard duties during execution or during simple deportations of unknown purpose. Here as well, the extant documentation is of little use in illuminating the affair. Hence, Goldhagen's speculations as to the ultimate death-toll figure in which these police battalions were complicit range from over a million up to three million. Such a range of death tolls is also reflected in claims made by various orthodox scholars, a few of which are listed in the next table.

Victim Numbers Claimed for *Einsatzgruppen* and Related Formations	
3,000,000	Solomon M. Schwarz (1951, p. 220)
≤ 2,624,500	Yitzhak Arad (2009, pp. 524f.)
2,200,000	H. Krausnick, H.H. Wilhelm (1981, p. 621)
2,100,000	Wolfgang Curilla (2006, p. 836)
1,300,000	Raul Hilberg (1985, p. 1219)

More recent studies are not much clearer either. Wolfgang Curilla, for example, managed to tally almost one million from various documents, but then claims a total of 2.1 million victims without indicating where he found the difference of over 1.1 million (Curilla 2006, p. 836). Yitzhak Arad claims up to 2.6 million victims, all based on rounded estimates for various regions of the Soviet Union (Arad 2009, pp. 524f.).

Forensic Findings

On 2 November 1942, the Presidium of the Supreme Soviet of the USSR decreed that investigative commissions had to be established which were to investigate crimes committed by the German occupants. Hence, as soon as the Soviets reconquered lost territory, they conducted investigations that included the interrogation of alleged witnesses as well as the exhumation of victims buried in mass graves. No international observers or experts from neutral countries were ever present during these investigations. Worse still, some of the experts involved in these commissions were identical to those who had fabricated the false Soviet expert report on the mass graves of Polish officers near Katyn.

Furthermore, in many cases, the Soviet authorities claimed, based on witness accounts, that the Germans had erased the traces of their massacres. This was allegedly done by inmates exhuming and burning hundreds of thousands of corpses from hundreds of mass graves all across the USSR. This vast effort is said to have been subsumed under the code name "*Aktion* 1005." (For more information on this, see the entry dedicated to this.) This relieved the Soviet authorities from having to search and identify the size and thus potential capacity of the claimed mass graves. They instead took at face value death-toll assertions made by witnesses who claimed to have helped with exhuming and burning the corpses.

In cases where intact graves were found, the Soviet commissions usually limited their efforts to exhuming a small part of a claimed mass grave. Then they extrapolated from the corpses found in a small area to the claimed total size of the mass grave(s). Photographic material was rarely prepared, and where it was, it usually showed only a small fraction of the number of corpses claimed.

The next table compares the data contained in the EMs with death-toll claims made about certain towns and cities across the Soviet Union by Soviet commissions or by witnesses they interviewed. The last column gives exaggeration factors. This gives the impression that the Soviets consistently exaggerated victim counts by one or more orders of magnitude, or invented them altogether.

EM Location	Documented Death Toll	Soviet and Witness Death-Toll Claims	Exagg. Factor
Babi Yar/Kiev	33,776	62,500 to 125,000	2-4
Białystok	490	42,800	87
Chernigov	309	52,453	170
Kaunas, Fort IX	16,013	70,000	4
Kramatorsk	none	812	∞
Kremenchuk	none	60,000	∞
Lviv	8,154	120,000 to 300,000	15-37
Mogilev	6,318	30,000	5
Novozybkov	1	2,860	2,860
Poltava	1,538	221,895	144
Ponary/Vilnius	2,231	38,000 to 80,000	17-36
Romny	none	3,000	∞
Rostov	none	15,000 to 18,000	∞
Rovno	15,240	102,000	7
Starokonstantinov	439	20,000	46
Sumy	none	5,000	∞
Vasilkov	none	1,000	∞
Vinnitsa	892	23,000	26
Voroshilov	none	1,901	∞
Zagare	250	2,402	10
Zaporozhie	none	43,000	∞

The activities of these Soviet commissions were evidently primarily propagandistic in nature. This even showed in the theatrical language used, where Germans were called "monsters," "hangmen," "cannibals," "German-Fascist invaders," etc., who always killed "peaceful" Soviet citizens for no reason at all. In such a context, there was no place for the truth, which might have been bad enough.

These Soviet reports were submitted during the

Nuremberg International Military Tribunal (IMT). Since they were reports issued by a government authority of one of the Allied powers, the IMT's statute demanded that they be accepted as true without any possibility for the defense to challenge them.

During the U.S.-American *Einsatzgruppen* Trial at Nuremberg, no witness accounts or Soviet commission reports were used by the prosecution to make their case. They relied entirely on the documents found at the Gestapo headquarters in Berlin. These documents make the alleged "*Aktion* 1005" look like a joke. What was the point of making this gargantuan effort of erasing the physical traces, if the documents chronicling the crimes in all details were left standing on the shelves?

During the existence of the Soviet Union, no serious efforts were made anymore after the initial postwar propaganda frenzy to locate, excavate and forensically investigate the contents of mass graves on Soviet territory. After all, it was far more likely to discover mass graves containing the tens of millions of victims of their own terror regime, and of the war itself, than it was to encounter mass graves containing the one or two million victims of claimed German atrocities.

Only one case of a serious excavation effort is known to this date. It was initiated by the Australian judiciary. They were looking for evidence regarding a claimed mass execution of hundreds of Jews in the town of Serniki in northwestern Ukraine in 1942. A forensic expert eventually found the grave. It measured roughly 40 m × 5 m × 2.5 m (ca. 500 cubic meters) and contained roughly 550 bodies. Most of them had been shot into the head. Rusty, German-made machine-pistol cartridges found in the grave, dating back to 1939 to 1941, pointed at the most likely killers. (Unless the killers used captured or imported German weapons and ammunitions, like the NKVD did in Katyn in 1940; see Margry 1996, p. 19.)

The town of Serniki is not mentioned in any German document. Hence, it is unfortunately not possible to compare the forensic results with documented claims. This comparative method would be the only way of establishing whether the figures listed in German wartime documents have any relation to reality. As it stands, the Serniki grave highlights once more that these documents are unreliable in every regard.

The packing density in this grave – only roughly 1.1 body per cubic meter – highlights that mass executioners usually do not climb into mass graves to neatly stack their victims in order to optimize the usage of grave space. If representative of most mass graves, this fact alone threatens to destroy the conventional narrative. At such low packing densities, astronomically huge graves would be required to hold all the claimed bodies.

Several efforts have been made by Jewish as well as government institutions throughout the territories of the former Soviet Union to catalog and, to some degree, locate mass graves containing the victims of the brief German wartime occupation. However, if any excavations were made in this context, they were limited to merely locating the graves and perhaps defining their perimeter. In none of these cases were any bodies exhumed and forensically examined as to their number, identity, cause of death or probable killers. (See the entry on Marijampole for one typical example.)

This is unfortunately also true for the huge efforts undertaken between 2002 and 2007 by the French priest Patrick Desbois (Desbois 2009). While he and his team located and opened 325 mass graves of various sizes throughout Ukraine, not in a single case did they even try to establish how many victims they contain, let alone who they were, how they died, and whether there is any trace enabling us to determine who or what killed them. In the end, all these efforts merely serve to create memorial sites for Jewish Holocaust victims.

The one thing these located mass graves prove for certain is that no effort was ever made by anyone to open these graves during the war, exhume the bodies, and burn them on pyres. Desbois's results furthermore proved that most of the mass graves he found are rather small, able to hold less than a hundred victims. Medium- and large-size mass graves potentially containing hundreds or thousands of victims were very rare.

If researchers were serious about finding out what exactly happened, a systematic effort needed to be made to locate, exhume, and forensically investigate as many mass graves as possible, in particular those recorded in German wartime documents. This would reveal to what degree these documents can be trusted, if at all, and it would silence doubters and dogmatists alike. But it will probably never happen.

There are very few memorial sites on mass graves containing the more than 20 million victims of Bolshevist terror. Most of them were not Jews, and their killers were not Germans. Emphasizing such victims and perpetrators is neither reputation-boosting nor career-advancing.

(For more details, see Mattogno 2015a; 2022c, pp. 11-445; Rudolf 2023, pp. 324-335.)

EISENSCHMIDT, ELIEZER

Eliezer Eisenschmidt (born 1920) was deported to Auschwitz, arriving there on 8 December 1942. He testified about his alleged experiences in Auschwitz only in 1993, when interviewed by Israeli historian Gideon Greif. Although he arrived at Auschwitz just two days after Szlama Dragon and claims to have worked at the same place and at the same time, his description of the labor units, of the buildings, and of the events diverge noticeably from Dragon's. Moreover, neither the Dragon brothers knew anything about Eisenschmidt, nor Eisenschmidt about the brothers.

Eliezer Eisenschmidt

Eisenschmidt furthermore also contradicts himself with two equally absurd claims about how the open-air incinerations of the corpses were carried out: first he says that the "fire was started before the bodies were thrown in," meaning that the corpses must have been hurled onto the conflagration by means of some catapults, as the heat would not have allowed anyone to get near the fires. But then he insists that "all the bodies were placed in the pits," after which the fire was lit, initially fueled by some wooden beams and gasoline – but once this fuel had been consumed, the bodies burned all by themselves: "the fat of the bodies would fuel the fire. In other words, the bodies themselves were the fuel. [...] Later on, the fire was fed by the fat of the bodies that remained in the pits." However, self-immolating bodies simply do not exist.

After the end of the bunkers' operation, Eisenschmidt claims to have been transferred to Crematorium V, where he and his teammates allegedly "let the fire billow up the smokestacks" during Allied bombing raids in 1944 in a futile attempt to attract the attention of the bombers overhead. However, the crematorium's long smoke ducts and stacks did not allow any flames to reach the outside.

Although Eisenschmidt never worked in Crematoria II or III, he claims to know how the corpses were brought from the elevator to the furnaces: they were loaded "onto [rail] carts," then moved from the carts onto stretchers, and then pushed with those stretchers into the muffle. While Crematorium II was initially equipped with a corpse-introduction cart – which brought the corpses from the elevator to the furnace *and* introduced them into the muffle – that system was dismantled at the end of March 1943 and replaced with simple stretchers. Hence, his tale is proof of his confusion caused by hearsay rather than his own experience. (For more details, see Mattogno 2022e, pp. 143-154.)

EITAN, DOV

Dov Eitan was an Israeli defense lawyer who led the successful defense team of John Demjanjuk during his show trial in Jerusalem in 1987. The day before Demjanjuk's appeal trial before the Jerusalem Court of Appeals was to start, Eitan jumped – or fell, or was thrown – to his death from the 20th floor of a high rise in Jerusalem. The story is recounted by Demjanjuk's second lawyer, Yoram Sheftel (Sheftel 1994, pp. 243-263).

EMIGRATION

Point 4 of the program of the National-Socialist Party states:

> "[German] *Citizen can only be who is a member of the people. A member of the people is who is of German blood, with no regard to the confession. No Jew can therefore be a member of the people.*"

When Hitler's party came to power in 1933, they worked steadily to deprive German Jews of their citizenship, and to incentivize them to leave Germany. Zionist Jews, at the same time, wanted Jews everywhere to immigrate to Palestine (not yet the nation of Israel). For this purpose, German authorities and Jewish-Zionist agencies worked closely together on this emigration. Jews interested in leaving received detailed advice and offers of help from both sides. Accounts of Jews fleeing Germany in secret by night across some border or straits are simply untrue; on the contrary, the German government was only too happy to have Jews live elsewhere – at least until well into the war, when emigrating Jews started to work for the Allies.

Pre-war Emigration from Germany

Zionists among German Jews aimed at winning over primarily young Jews for emigration to Palestine. They realized early on that working together with the National-Socialist regime was the only promising course for them. Hence, from the time Hitler became chancellor of Germany in 1933, an ever-closer and *positive* relationship between Zionists and the National Socialists developed prior to the war, as German institutions were also desirous of completing the emigration as quickly as possible.

In Germany, three Jewish emigration agencies had operated since the beginning of the century: the Aid Association for German Jews (*Hilfsverein für deutsche Juden*) focused on emigration assistance to all parts of the world except Palestine; the Palestine Office (*Palästinaamt*) focused on emigration to Palestine; and the Main Office for Jewish Migration Welfare (*Hauptstelle für jüdische Wanderfürsorge*), initially with a focus on relocating Jews within Germany, which later assisted non-German Jews with their emigration efforts.

Two principal agreements were implemented by the National-Socialist government to promote the emigration of its unwanted Jewish citizens: the 1933 "Haavara" Agreement, and the 1939 "Rublee-Wohlthat" Agreement. Both agreements were practically in force until 1941, when the German government moved to ban the emigration of Jews from its realm on 23 October 1941 (see the entry for Kurt Daluege). The Haavara banking connection, however, ceased to function in December 1941 with America's entry into the war.

Haavara Agreement
Already in February 1933, Palestinian representatives of the citrus-growing company Hanotea Ltd. approached the German government to explore ways of realizing their mutual interests: for the Germans, the emigration of Jews; for the Jewish Palestinians, the immigration of Jews. German authorities accepted the Jewish proposals, and in May 1933 the first accords on economic policy were signed, forming the basis of the Haavara (=Transfer) Agreement. The agreement allowed Jews who wished to migrate to Palestine at some point to deposit money into an account of Jewish banks in Germany. This money could be used to benefit Jewish individuals or companies in Palestine by investment, or to pay for medical insurance up to ten years in advance. This allowed Jews to circumvent existing German laws preventing capital flight abroad.

With a voucher system, the agreement also allowed German Jews to travel to Palestine without having to obtain heavily regulated and expensive British Pounds, and once they emigrated, they could obtain the minimum amount needed for this, demonstrating their ability to support themselves. This exception was made by Germany's government exclusively for the benefit of the Jews. Emigrating Jews were also exempted from the so-called "Reich Escape Tax" (*Reichsfluchtsteuer*) which every non-Jew leaving Germany had to pay. Funds in the Haavara bank accounts could be used to pay for purchases in Palestine and several neighboring areas, and Jews in Palestine could pay into the Haavara accounts to help Jews in Germany – a transnational banking approach that was revolutionary at the time. Furthermore, Jews could transfer all their social-benefit and pension funds from Germany to Palestine.

The influx of German Jews, businesses and capital to Palestine starting in 1933 changed that area from a backward agricultural society to an increasingly highly educated and rapidly developing industrial and merchant region. Those people formed the basis of what would become the population of Israel after the war.

Emigration and the SS
Until late 1941, the SS and its agencies were very supportive of any activity encouraging Jewish emigration. They promoted the idea of a Jewish national and ethnic identity, and helped to establish and finance retraining centers in Germany (and later also in Austria) meant for young Jews willing to learn agricultural and trade skills, in order to prepare them for a new life in Palestine. The SS even provided the land on which such camps could be established.

Rublee-Wohlthat Agreement
The Rublee-Wohlthat Agreement was initiated after the pogrom of 9 and 10 November 1938 (*Kristallnacht*), when both NS Germany and many foreign countries felt the need to have as many Jews leave Germany as possible. As with Palestine, other countries also required proof of the immigrant's financial self-sufficiency, which caused considerable problems for Germany. The German Reichsbank was forced to provide large amounts of already-scarce foreign currency for this emigration. In addition, many countries refused to accept Jewish immigrants at all.

The agreement seeking a financial solution to this problem was named after the two main negotiating personalities: the U.S. lawyer George Rublee, director of the Intergovernmental Committee on Refugees, formed in mid-1938 by 30 countries concerned about Germany's anti-Jewish policies, and the German political scientist Helmuth Wohlthat, a subordinate of Hermann Göring in charge of foreign trade and foreign currency regulation.

The agreement established trust funds comprising 25 percent of the wealth belonging to Jews in Germany. Jewish emigration would be financed through foreign loans, for which both the UK and the U.S. pledged to raise considerable funds. Each Jewish emigrant would receive the requisite amount of cash for entry, plus a minimum amount of capital necessary to establish himself. Jews over 45 years of age were to be able to remain in Germany and be protected from discrimination. Residential and work restrictions for these Jews were to be lifted. Hitler wholeheartedly assented to the agreement, while the 30 governmental representatives of the Intergovernmental Committee merely promised to do everything to facilitate the emigration of Jews from Germany. Based on that agreement, Germany established the Reich Center for Jewish Emigration in January 1939, headed by Reinhardt Heydrich, to simplify the emigration process, but the success was limited, again because most countries (other than Palestine) refused to accept Jewish immigrants.

Emigration from German-Controlled Areas during the War

With the outbreak of war, emigration diminished, mainly due to the Royal Navy blocking previously used sea routes. Palestine was furthermore practically closed to immigration due to severely tightened British requirements for entry. Hence, Jewish emigration continued mainly over land, and was possible due to international Jewish connections and German bureaucratic assistance, but also due to an organization that was later to play a completely different role – the Jewish underground organization *Mossad le Aliyah Bet*, which later turned into Israel's secret-service agency (the Mossad).

Even after Germany's official policy changed from emigration to deportation and resettlement to the East, Adolf Eichmann, the SS official in charge of Jewish affairs and deportation, collaborated closely with the Mossad to support "illegal" emigration of hundreds of thousands of European Jews. SS units even escorted Jewish emigration groups across the border to ensure their safe passage. (For details, see Weckert 2016; Black 1984; Nicosia 1985.)

Final Solution

As emigration became increasingly difficult after the outbreak of the war, a different approach to the problem was required – not the least because of Germany's conquest of Poland, and the victory over France, the Netherlands, Luxembourg and Belgium, in which millions more Jews came under German influence. Therefore, on 24 June 1940, Heydrich approached the German Foreign Minister for a ministerial meeting regarding the "final solution of the Jewish question," where he wanted to discuss new approaches to solving the Jewish problem not by emigration, but by finding a dedicated territory under German control where all European Jews could be resettled.

This initiative resulted in the so-called Madagascar Plan, meaning the transfer of this French colony in a peace treaty from France to Germany, and the establishment of a Jewish autonomous region on that island under German auspices. (See the entry on Madagascar for more details.) Other plans were briefly discussed as well, such as relocating Jews to the Soviet Jewish autonomous region of Birobidzhan – but was rejected by the Soviet Union (see that entry for more details).

When it became clear that there would be no peace in the West, and when Germany had large initial successes during its invasion of the Soviet Union, which the Germans expected to eventually collapse, plans for this Final Territorial Solution shifted toward the newly occupied territories in the East.

For more details on the German policy of deportation and resettlement to the East from late 1941 until 1943, see the entries on resettlement and Final Solution.

| Emigration of Jews from German-Controlled Territories, acc. to Richard Korherr |||
Territory	From… to 31 Dec. 1942	Emigration
Old Reich (with Sudeten Jews)	31 Jan. 1933 (29 Sept. 1938)	382,534
Ostmark [Austria]	13 March 1938	149,124
Bohemia & Moravia [Czechia]	16 March 1939	25,699
Eastern territories (with Bialystok)	September 1939 (June 1940)	334,673
General Government (with Lemberg)	September 1939 (June 1940)	427,920
Total		1,319,950

Emigration Figures

In April 1943, Dr. Richard Korherr, the SS's head statistician, wrote a report titled "The Final Solution of the Jewish Question in Europe," in which he reported the data listed in the table for emigrations of Jews from German-controlled territories (Nuremberg Document NO-5193, short version).

Therefore, the German National-Socialist government allowed and supported the emigration of more than 1.3 million Jews out of German-controlled territories.

ENGEL, CHAIM

Chaim Engel was an inmate of the Sobibór Camp. In a deposition of 19 July 1946, he claimed that the gas was fed into the gas chambers through showerheads, and that, after the murder, the floors opened, and the bodies were discharged into a space below. He claimed a total of some 800,000 victims for the camp.

His claims are rejected as false by the orthodoxy, who insists that the gas was fed through pipes rather than showerheads. These chambers did not have collapsible floors either. The corpses were instead taken out of the chamber manually, sideways through a normal door. Furthermore, only about a quarter million victims are said to have died in the camp.

(See the entry on Sobibór for more details, as well as Graf/Kues/Mattogno 2020, pp. 71, 109; Mattogno 2021e, p. 81.)

Ertl, Fritz → Dejaco, Walter

EPSTEIN, BERTHOLD

Berthold Epstein was a professor of medicine from Prague, who was incarcerated at the Auschwitz Camp until it was captured by the Soviets on 27 January 1945. Together with three other European professors – Bruno Fischer, Henri Limousin and Géza Mansfeld – and coached by their Soviet conquerors, he signed an appeal on 4 March 1945 "To the International Public," which contained many untrue propaganda clichés about Auschwitz:

– On arrival at the railway ramp, selections of inmates for the gas chambers were conducted by the ineluctable Dr. Josef Mengele while whistling a tune.
– The gas-chamber doors were opened after only four minutes ventilation time. This would have never sufficed for any of the claimed gassing facilities at Auschwitz.
– Gigantic open-air incineration pyres operated during the time when transports with Jews deported from Hungary arrived in May-July 1944. However, air photos prove that no such pyres existed at Auschwitz during that time.
– Oils and fats were extracted from corpses to assist in their cremation, thus saving other fuel. However, fat catches fire and burns as soon as it comes into contact with fire or embers, so no fat can be extracted from a corpse on a pyre.
– The corpses were processed to obtain technical oils, machinery grease and laundry soap.

(See Mattogno 2021, pp. 296f.)

ERBER, JOSEF

Josef Erber (16 Oct. 1897 – 31 Oct. 1987), SS *Oberscharführer* at war's end, was an ethnic German from Bohemia. He was deployed to the Auschwitz Camp in November 1940, where he served first as a guard, then in the armory, and finally from mid-1942 in the Political Department of the Auschwitz Camp (camp Gestapo).

After the war, Erber was one of the defendants during the Frankfurt Auschwitz Show Trial. He was sentenced to life imprisonment for contributing to the murder of 70 people while serving at the Political Department, but released early in 1986.

While in prison, he gave an interview to German journalist Ebbo Demant (1979), during which he made statements indicating that he had learned by heart the orthodox Auschwitz narrative, including its various absurdities. For example, he stated that the "gas chambers" of the Crematoria II and III at Birkenau (their Morgue #1) had a capacity of 3,000 people. This room had a surface area of 210 m². Hence, the packing density would have amounted to more than 14 people per square meter, which is physically impossible.

"Erntefest" → Operation "Harvest Festival"

ESCAPES, FROM GAS CHAMBER

Numerous self-declared eyewitnesses of homicidal gas chambers have declared that they miraculously escaped from a gas chamber when they were just about to get gassed. The following individuals made such claims:

– Regina Bialek (Auschwitz)
– Arnold Friedman (Auschwitz)
– Mietek Grocher (Majdanek)
– Sofia Litwinska (Auschwitz)

– Filip Müller (Auschwitz)
– Moshe Peer (Bergen-Belsen)
– Mary Seidenwurm Wrzos (Majdanek)

Estonia → **Baltic Countries**

EUTHANASIA

On the day Germany's armed forces invaded Poland, Hitler signed an order permitting the "mercy killing" of severely mentally disabled persons in what is called Germany's Euthanasia Program. In charge of the program was Viktor Brack, a high official in the Reich's Chancellery. The program was also called *Aktion* T4, an acronym for the Berlin address of Brack's office, Tiergartenstrasse 4. In the course of this program, some 100,000 mental patients are said to have been killed in various euthanasia centers throughout Germany. Technically, it is said to have been implemented by gassing inmates in small gas chambers using bottled carbon monoxide. However, no document survived the war substantiating these claims. Due to public protests, Hitler ordered the termination of the euthanasia program in late August 1941.

The program was extended in 1940 to encompass inmates in concentration camps. Within the bureaucracy of Germany's Department of Homeland Security (*Reichssicherheitshauptamt*), the program was called "Special Treatment 14 f 13." This department had developed a code system for all kinds of events. 14 f referred to any kind of death cases, while the figure attached behind it identified the type of death. For example, 14 f 14 were executions, while 14 f 13 referred to euthanasia.

There are several documents giving instructions on how to implement "Special Treatment 14 f 13," none of which single out Jewish inmates or deportees. Inmates subjected to the program had to be permanently unfit for labor. They underwent a preliminary selection by camp doctors, and afterwards another selection by doctors of the Euthanasia Program. If selected, the inmates were then killed in institutions of the Euthanasia Program. This implies, of course, that none of the camps involved had any means of killing such inmates in their "own" gas chambers.

Due to the Third Reich's increasingly desperate manpower situation, Himmler amended the prerequisites for inmates subject to euthanasia by stipulating on 27 April 1943 that

"in the future, only mentally ill prisoners may be processed by the medical boards created for Program 14 f 13. All other prisoners unfit for work (tuberculars, bedridden, crippled, etc.) are in principle exempt from this program. Bedridden prisoners should be assigned work that they can perform in bed."

The rich documentation preserved from the Auschwitz Camps shows that neither mentally ill inmates nor those irrecoverably or permanently unfit for work were killed, let alone inmates merely temporarily sick. It seems that Program 14 f 13 shifted over time from a program of special treatment by euthanasia to one of special treatment by special care.

After the general Euthanasia Program had been discontinued by Hitler in the summer of 1941, most SS staff members involved in it were eventually reassigned to the camps of "*Aktion Reinhardt*," as these became operational over time. The orthodoxy concludes from this continuity of *staff* a continuity of *purpose*. If the Euthanasia Program consisted of mass murder in gas chambers using carbon monoxide, then the same must have happened in the camps of the *Aktion Reinhardt* (Belzec, Sobibór, Treblinka).

However, we need to consider the assignments which the staff of the (former) Euthanasia Program received after this program had ended. First, during the winter of 1941/42, a large detachment of former personnel was sent to the eastern front as physicians and nurses to help wounded soldiers. This is the opposite of a killing program. Then, after most camps of *Aktion Reinhardt* had been closed in late 1943, a major part of their SS staff was transferred to the Adriatic coast of northern Italy, where they were mainly engaged in fighting partisans, but to a minor degree also in arresting and deporting Jews to labor camps. This means that continuity of staff did not prove a continuity of purpose.

Furthermore, if there really was a mass-murderous system involved in the camps of *Aktion Reinhardt* and the other claimed extermination camps (Chełmno, Majdanek, Auschwitz), then why was the development of the alleged gassing facilities so disparate for all these camps? At Auschwitz, Zyklon B as a murder weapon was discovered "accidentally," gas vans – also "accidentally" discovered by Arthur Nebe – were used at Chełmno, whereas the Belzec, Sobibór and Treblinka camps are said to have used engine exhaust. However, these are all merely unsubstantiated claims by today's orthodoxy, which fly in the face of the actual evidence exhibiting far more disparate claims by alleged witnesses. In addition, none of this is supported by documental, material or forensic evidence. (For more details, see the entries on all these camps.)

To make matters even more inconsistent, consider the fate of the chemist Helmut Kallmeyer. During the "Medical Case" of the Nuremberg Military Tribunals, he was singled out as "the technical expert on operation of the gas chambers in the euthanasia stations." Therefore, when the extermination camps are said to have been planned, he should have been the most important expert to be assigned to them, to advise on how best to build and operate homicidal gas chambers. However, he never got involved in any of this in any way. Instead, at every camp, the local SS units were fending for themselves, having to reinvent the wheel every time.

(For more details, see Graf/Kues/Mattogno 2020, pp. 270-281; Mattogno 2016a, pp. 87-91.)

EVACUATIONS, FROM GERMAN CAMPS

Toward the end of the war, as Allied forces approached German concentration camps, orders were issued to evacuate all inmates capable of walking. Lublin (Majdanek) and Auschwitz were among the first camps to be subjected to this order. In anticipation of future events, many inmates had already been transferred to other camps earlier.

However, during the final months of the war, Germany's infrastructure had mostly collapsed under the relentless carpet-bombing campaign of the Anglo-American bomber fleets. Rail transportation was sketchy and unreliable, with frequent stops and reroutings due to disrupted and damaged rail lines. Rolling stock was damaged or inadequate, leading to open freight cars also getting used for hauling inmates in wintertime through the frigid cold. Fuel for vehicles was almost non-existent.

Hence, large groups of inmates were forced to walk long distances, for lack of any other means of transportation. Vehicle convoys on roads as well as trains were frequently strafed by Allied airplanes. A train with evacuated inmates in open cars running from Buchenwald to Dachau suffered that very fate. It arrived at Dachau with many inmates dead, both due to Allied bullets and general exhaustion and exposure to the cold. (See the entry on Dachau.)

Many inmates who survived the death marches reported on violent excesses of the German guards. As Germany collapsed, fronts retreated, and all German troops faced getting captured and potentially killed, their nerves were increasingly frayed. Under such circumstances, acts of violence were increasingly likely. However, considering the generally unabated tendency to exaggerate stories of German wartime atrocities, it stands to reason that these stories, too, should be taken with a grain of salt.

It also needs to be kept it mind that Germany in general was in a state of mass death at that time. As Soviet troops entered German territory in East Prussia, they unleashed an unheard-of wave of violence. This in turn triggered massive German evacuations of the entire local populace of more than a million people. All these German civilians went on a "death march" far greater in quantity and loss of lives than the death marches unfolding from the various German camps. Panicked by actual and rumored Soviet atrocities, millions more Germans fled west from other eastern German territories. Many thousands of them found temporary shelter in Dresden, for instance, where many of them died in the Allied firebombing campaign of 13-15 February 1945.

Stories of Soviet atrocities spread throughout Germany from the outbreak of the German-Soviet war, and were also known to most camp inmates. Hence, when given the choice to either wait for the arrival of the Red Army or evacuate west with the Germans, many inmates chose to leave with the Germans. Considering the violent purges which the Red Army inflicted on the populations they conquered, these inmates had good reasons for their fear. (See Rudolf 2023, pp. 479-481 for details.) However, had they known the chaotic and catastrophic circumstances of the evacuations awaiting them, many might have reconsidered their choice. Furthermore, the German authorities should have known the logistical impossibility and complete uselessness of these evacuations, and should never have ordered them. But many of them were in utter denial of Germany's impending collapse and defeat, and of realistic and humane options left to them.

In 1945, Germany in general was a rapidly growing, gigantic pile of corpses, figuratively speaking. Inmates in prisons and camps always fare worst under such circumstances, and in particular with a government hell-bent on fighting to the last man.

EVIDENCE

Technically speaking, *evidence* is an object or piece of information aiming to prove the veracity, or at least high probability, of a particular claim. Not all pieces of evidence are created equal. In science as well as in jurisprudence, there exists a general hierarchy of the types of evidence, ranked by their ability to prove the truthfulness of a claim. Traditionally, there are five categories of evidence – listed below, from strongest to weakest.

1. logic
2. physical evidence
3. documental evidence
4. witness evidence
5. party testimony

1. Logic

This concerns mainly rules of argument, among them the proper application of mathematical rules, but also more basic rules. For instance, we agree that two contradictory claims cannot be true at the same time, hence at least one must be false (and both could be false). This is called the Law of Non-Contradiction, and it has been accepted as valid since the time of Aristotle.

Another important logical rule is this: we are not allowed to posit a hypothesis that is defined in such a way that it is impossible to verify or refute. Therefore, anything we claim must, in principle, be open to verification or refutation. For instance, claiming "The Nazis murdered six million Jews and destroyed all the evidence" is a hypothesis that is immune to verification or refutation because the claim includes the assertion that there is no evidence; in other words, it is a self-serving or self-validating assertion, which is therefore meaningless. Worse, someone could make such a claim and then, when confronted with a lack of evidence (for the Six Million, for example), they may say, "Yes, this is exactly what my hypothesis claims, and thus it is true!" But this is nonsense. The claim is logically meaningless.

2. Physical Evidence

Physical evidence consists of material traces, objects, or physical remains supporting a claim. Apart from rules of logic, this type of evidence is generally regarded as the most reliable evidence, superior to all others. Speaking of crimes, this includes traces of victims (bodily remains), perpetrators, crime weapons and of the events and actions connected to a crime. Such traces often require the analysis and interpretation of experts, commonly involving advanced technical methods. While analytical data produced by technological means can be considered reliable, choosing the best method of analysis and interpreting the results properly depends on human judgement, where errors and malfeasance can come into play.

3. Documental Evidence

Documental evidence concerns information of any kind recorded on some physical medium. It consists of a physical part – the data carrier (paper, film, magnetic or electronic devices etc.) – and an information part, encoded in some form (writing, numbers, digital code etc.). A document is more reliable if fewer people were involved with creating it, or if it is less susceptible to manipulation. For instance, an automatically recorded footage on emulsion film has barely any human factor involved and is difficult to manipulate (in contrast to digital recordings), thus probably records events accurately, whereas a text typed on paper written by a human can contain just about anything, independent of the truth.

The physical part of the document can be subjected to analysis like every piece of physical evidence, whereas the informational part requires proper interpretation. Before a document can acquire probative value, it must be proven that the document is genuine and its contents factually correct. In order to establish this, factual evidence is again required to establish the authenticity and accuracy of the document. Moreover, a document has a higher probative value if it was created at a time when a contentious issue was not yet in dispute. This is particularly true for written bureaucratic documents during wartime.

4. Witness Testimony

A claim cannot be its own evidence. If a person claims that an event took place and claims also that s/he witnessed it, this does not make it evidence; it merely makes it a set of two claims, each of which still needs to be demonstrated to be true. In courts of law, however, witness testimony is often accepted as evidence *for itself*, which has led to countless travesties of justice worldwide for as long as courts have existed.

Witness testimony is a very unreliable way of trying to prove anything for numerous reasons, not the least because human memory is unreliable and easily manipulated, and because the tendency of humans to tell only half-truths or lie outright is legendary. The more a person is emotionally involved in a claimed event, the more likely it is that his or her testimony will be unreliable. Furthermore, the more an event is made the object of discussion in mass media and society at large, the more likely it is that genuine memory is replaced with later impressions from these secondary sources. There is currently no subject where these outside influences are stronger than when it comes to events of the Holocaust, because it is the most-thematized historical subject worldwide. Moreover, it is the only event where dissent from a given narrative commonly leads to massive societal pressure, if not outright persecution, and even prosecution in numerous countries.

5. Party Testimony

If a person is a party in a dispute – such as an (alleged) victim or perpetrator – s/he should not even be considered a witness but merely a party. Party testimony, which is a subset of witness testimony, usually is the most unreliable kind of testimony, and should be seen at best as circumstantial indicators, since parties have an interest in incriminating the other party and exonerating themselves – all the more so during or after an atrocious war. In case of dogmatic societal or judicial situations, where the event in question is considered "self-evident" by the general public and/or the courts – as with the Holocaust – party testimonies from alleged perpetrators become almost worthless, as these are very often made not for reasons of honesty, but in order to gain advantages or benefits. This is especially true for claimed events of the Holocaust, where the alleged crime is cast in stone, the circle of possible perpetrators is determined beforehand, and only guilt and punishment remain to be meted out. In such a situation, contesting the reality of "self-evident" claims would only lead to an aggravated punishment.

Therefore, admitting the general, non-contestable historical charge as true while attempting to incriminate others and simultaneously trying to exonerate oneself is quite common. Such admissions of the general veracity of the overarching claims are therefore no evidence of their truth, but only hallmarks of corrupted legal procedures within a close-minded, intolerant society. The bottom line is that, with the Holocaust, claims by members of any victim group on the one hand, and of any perpetrator group on the other hand, are the weakest and most dubious forms of evidence.

See the list of witnesses in that entry. For a general overview of Holocaust evidence, see Section 5 "Evidence" in the entry on the Holocaust.

Source Criticism

Evidence needs to be evaluated as to its reliability, accuracy and authenticity. Furthermore, those who create, maintain or interpret evidence need to be evaluated for their trustworthiness. To learn more about the principles of source criticism and its impact on Holocaust studies, see the entry dedicated to this topic.

EXAGGERATED DEATH TOLLS

Right after the war, wild numbers of inmates killed at various German wartime camps circulated in the media and among historians, often initiated by unsubstantiated or fraudulent claims made by witnesses or official "expert reports." The following table lists several of the better-known German camps. The second column gives the number of victims claimed immediately after the war by certain sources, the third column an approximation of the numbers claimed by the orthodoxy today, and the fourth column the post-war-exaggeration multiple.

This is followed by a column giving the death toll that results from extant documents for the camps where such documents are available (Auschwitz, Majdanek, Mauthausen, Sachsenhausen, Dachau), or the maximum possible death toll considering forensic findings for camps, for which we have no documentation at all (Belzec, Chełmno, Sobibór, Treblinka). These findings give only rough upper limits of what was physically possible, but do not yield actual death-toll figures. The last column gives the exaggeration factor between the initial orthodox death-toll figure on the one hand, and the documented or maximum possible figure on the other hand.

The numbers for Belzec, Sobibór and Treblinka are based on disturbed soil volume found, with the assumption that this volume was once densely packed with corpses. However, this is only one forensic constraint that can be applied. Another constraint – the amount of firewood available to burn the corpses as claimed by the orthodox narrative – results in much lower values for the maximum possible numbers. However, we currently have reliable data to calculate this only for the Chełmno Camp.

This is the reason why Chełmno comes out on top as the winner in this contest, with an exaggeration factor of 1,300 – between what the orthodoxy claimed at war's end, and what forensic evidence allows, based on trees felled in the camp's vicinity. If we took this firewood constraint into account for the other camps, the numbers for Belzec, Sobibór and

Treblinka would be quite similar to the numbers for the Chełmno Camp.

Currently, skeptical Holocaust scholars give only rough estimates as to the probable death tolls in those camps. For instance, they estimate about 10,000 fatalities for Sobibór, which is a factor of 200 lower than the initial orthodox estimate for that camp. For Belzec, Mattogno (2004a, p. 91) argues, based on the actual evidence, for a death toll of "several thousands," or at most, "some tens of thousands" – thus, perhaps 40,000 or 50,000. Regarding Treblinka, Thomas Kues has informally suggested a range of 20,000 to 30,000.

For Majdanek, Graf and Mattogno (2012, page 265) document a toll of nearly 28,000 Jews among the camp's total death toll of some 42,200 inmates. And for Auschwitz, we have a documented total death toll of about 135,500.

When considering these exaggeration factors, we must keep in mind that 'honest' errors, which do occur in historiography all the time, are generally random, in the sense that a numerical error could equally be too high or too low. However, with the Holocaust, it seems that there are no 'honest errors'; in fact, *all* initially reported death tolls, for *all* the camps, have proven to be significantly too high. This strongly suggests that the initial estimates were deliberately and systematically distorted, likely for political or ideological reasons.

We find a similar pattern when looking at the claimed mass executions by the *Einsatzgruppen* behind the German-Soviet front. A comparison of the execution numbers recorded in the *Einsatzgruppen*'s Event Reports with the death tolls claimed by witnesses or Soviet investigative commissions reveals that witnesses and commissions consistently inflated the numbers, often grotesquely beyond the probable death toll. (See the section "Forensic Findings" in the entry on the *Einsatzgruppen*.)

(For details, see the entries for each of the camps listed; for an overview of the various camps, see Dalton 2020; for death-toll claims of other claimed crime locations and events, see their respective entry.)

EXCAVATIONS, OF GERMAN MASS GRAVES

The excavation of mass graves containing victims of mass murder committed by German forces during World War II can be divided into two groups:

1. Excavations presumably carried out by German units during the war in attempts to erase traces of their crimes. This is said to have happened during a large-scale operation nowadays referred to as *Aktion* 1005. These excavations are covered extensively in the entry on this topic.
2. Excavations by groups inimical to the Third Reich with the aim to expose National-Socialist mass atrocities. These were carried out already during the war by the Soviets, as they reconquered their territory. In subsequent years, Polish and other judicial authorities, forensic investigators and historical researchers continued this work well into the 2000s.

The reports of Soviet commissions claiming to have excavated German mass graves on Soviet territory are discussed in the entry on *Aktion* 1005. Polish, Soviet, Israeli, Serbian and British forensic research into mass graves at the various claimed extermination camps are discussed in the respective entries for these camps (Belzec, Chełmno, Maly Trostenets, Semlin, Sobibór, Treblinka). No systematic forensic research on possible (former) mass graves at Auschwitz seems to have been conducted, or at least their results have not been made publicly accessible. Latter-day forensic examination of *Einsatzgruppen* mass graves are discussed in the section "Forensic Findings" of the *Einsatzgruppen* entry.

Death-Toll Figures of Selected German Wartime Camps

Camp	Orthodox Death Toll		Factor	Actual or Max. Toll	Factor
	Initial	Today			
Auschwitz	4 to 8 million	1 million	4 to 8	135,500	30-60
Bełżec	3 million	600,000	5	<100,000*	>30
Chełmno	1.3 million	150,000	9	<1,000‡	1,300
Dachau	238,000	41,000	6	27,800	9
Majdanek	2 million	78,000	26	42,200	47
Mauthausen	1 million	100,000	10	86,200	12
Sachsenhausen	840,000+	30,000	28	20,600	41
Sobibór	2 million	200,000	10	80,000+†	±25
Treblinka	3 million	800,000	4	<143,000*	>21

* based on disturbed soil volume found; † enough disturbed soil volume was found to accommodate the claimed 80,000 buried victims, but more are said to have been killed later without being buried; however, tracelessly burning those bodies would have been nearly impossible with the means and the time at the camp's disposal; the latter is also true for Belzec and Treblinka; ‡ based on number of trees felled in the camp's vicinity. If taking this as a measure, the numbers for Belzec, Sobibór and Treblinka would be quite similar to Chełmno's numbers.

EXECUTION CHAMBERS

Witnesses have claimed all kinds of methods allegedly used in certain facilities to mass murder people at German wartime camps. Nowadays, the orthodoxy only recognizes claims as valid which posit the use of toxic gases, hence homicidal gas chambers (see that entry for details). However, during the war and in the immediate postwar years, when memories were still fresh, witnesses also claimed other murder methods that had nothing to do with toxic gases at all, such as:

- *Vacuum*, which can be found in accounts on Belzec and Treblinka, and rarer also for Auschwitz, but only as a first stage to gassing. See also the following entries: Rachel Auerbach, Hejnoch Brener, Vasily Grossman, Abe Kon, Aleksander Kudlik, Mordecai Lichtenstein, Henryk Poswolski, Chil Rajchman, Samuel Rajzman, Kazmierz Skarżyński, Oskar Strawczyński.
- *High,-voltage electricity*, which was frequently claimed for the Belzec Camp, but also on rarer occasions for Auschwitz, Treblinka and Sobibór. See also the following entries: Srul Fajgielbaum, Boris Polevoy, Jakub Rabinowicz, Abraham Silberschein, Stefan Szende.
- *Steam*, a claim quite common for the Treblinka Camp. See also the following entries: Rachel Auerbach, Jakub Rabinowicz, Abraham Silberschein, Vasily Grossman, Eugenia Szajn-Lewin.
- A *"dark substance,"* which was claimed for the Sobibór Camp by Alexander Pechersky.

It was all fraudulent, though. Embarrassed by these indicators of witness mendacity, the orthodoxy today sweeps these propaganda falsehoods under the carpet.

EXOTIC MURDER WEAPONS

Many of the commonly claimed murder methods allegedly used during the Holocaust are exotic in nature by objective standards, but due to incessant exposure to tales about them, we have become calloused as to their peculiar nature, and have accepted them as "normal." This includes homicidal gas chambers as well as gas vans, which both have their own entry.

In the present context, "exotic" refers to murder methods that have been claimed by one or more sources, but which are rejected by the orthodoxy as false rumors or propaganda lies. The entry on Tools of Mass Murder, Point 4 of its section on "Murder Weapons," contains a list of such methods. See also the entry on Absurd Claims.

EXPLOSIVES, AS MURDER WEAPON

Albert Widmann, a German scientist employed at Germany's top crime lab, claimed that experiments to kill innocent civilians with explosives were made during World War Two. He came up with this nonsense when conjuring up a fairy tale in the 1960s in an attempt to "explain" how gas vans were invented.

Erich von dem Bach-Zelewski, a high-ranking SS official, made similar claims in an absurd postwar deposition, probably extracted by torture. He claimed that Himmler had watched the execution of 100 partisans in the summer of 1941, after which he ordered a new, more humane method to be devised. This new method, Bach-Zelewski claimed, was blowing up people with explosives.

No rational person would ever have implemented such an idea. It is obvious that blowing up people with explosives leads to

- objects in the vicinity getting damaged and destroyed;
- the victims' body parts strewn around the area,
- and deep craters in the ground, which need to be filled in afterwards.

Other witnesses have claimed that explosives were used when trying to destroy the corpses of mass-murder victims. See the next entry on this.

EXPLOSIVES, TO ERASE CORPSES

Only two witnesses have suggested that dynamite was used to assist in the removal of traces of mass murder. One of them was Rudolf Höss, the former commandant of the Auschwitz Camp. During a postwar interrogation, he claimed that Paul Blobel had tried to destroy the corpses of inmates killed at the Chełmno Camp by blowing them up with explosives, "but their destruction had been very incomplete," Höss explained. After his capture by the British, Höss had been tortured and abused for days before he started "confessing." (See the respective entries for details.)

A similarly ludicrous corpse-removal technique was claimed by Vladimir Davydov. He asserted that the SS used unspecified "dynamiting techniques" at Babi Yar when trying to erase the traces of their alleged mass murder.

Such "techniques" merely would have scattered body parts all over the place, but would not have made them disappear in any way. Therefore, it can be excluded with certainty that these claims relate to real events.

Other witnesses have claimed that explosives were used as a murder weapon. See the previous entry on this.

extermination → **Extirpation**

EXTERMINATION CAMPS

In the context of the Jewish Holocaust, the term "extermination camp" refers to camps established by the German authorities or any of their allies with the claimed exclusive, main or auxiliary purpose of exterminating inmates in masses, either by mass execution (shooting) or by mass gassings in stationary gas chambers or mobile gas vans. In addition, there are those camps for which some witnesses have claimed exterminations of inmates, although all historians agree that these claims are false, erroneous or fraudulent. Hence, we have three categories of extermination camps:

1. Pure extermination camps, whose only purpose was to kill inmates deported to them.
2. Mixed-purposed camps, which had characteristics of both an extermination and concentration/forced-labor camp. These range from camps whose extermination aspect was its main purpose, to those where extermination was only an auxiliary purpose, sometimes even only a minor aspect.
3. Phantom extermination camps, because extermination claims about them are universally accepted to be either erroneous or fraudulent.

The table lists extermination camps claimed by orthodox historians, plus those only by witnesses, opposing learned mainstream opinion. Of these, the majority of alleged deaths by all causes, according to the current orthodox narrative, occurred in just six camps:

– Auschwitz – ca. 1,000,000 victims.
– Treblinka – ca. 800,000 victims.
– Belzec – ca. 434,000 victims.
– Sobibór – ca. 200,000 victims.
– Chełmno – ca. 150,000 victims.
– Majdanek – ca. 80,000 victims.

For details, see the entries for each individual camp.

LOCATION	CLAIMED TYPE	ALLEGED MURDER WEAPON(S)
Auschwitz	mixed/main	gas chambers
Belzec	pure	gas chambers
Bergen-Belsen	phantom	gas chamber
Buchenwald	phantom	gas chamber
Chełmno	pure	gas vans
Dachau	mixed/auxiliary	gas chamber
Flossenbürg	phantom	gas chamber
Gross-Rosen	phantom	gas chamber
Gusen	mixed/auxiliary	gas chamber
Kosów Podlaski	phantom	gas chamber
Lviv	phantom	gas chamber
Majdanek	mixed/auxiliary*	gas chambers, executions
Maly Trostenets	pure	executions
Mauthausen	mixed/auxiliary	gas chamber
Mogilev	phantom	gas chamber, executions
Natzweiler	mixed/auxiliary	gas chamber
Neuengamme	mixed/auxiliary	gas chambers
Nordhausen	phantom	massacres
Pinsk	phantom	gas chamber
Ravensbrück	mixed/auxiliary	gas chamber
Sachsenhausen	mixed/auxiliary	gas chamber
Semlin	mixed/main	gas vans
Sobibór	pure	gas chambers
Stutthof	mixed/auxiliary	gas chamber
Trawniki	phantom	gas chamber
Treblinka	pure	gas chambers
Wolzek	phantom	gas chamber

* Until 2005, mass murder in gas chambers was supposedly the camp's main purpose, but then the museum switched to exterminations mainly by executions and only rarely by gassings, and merely as the camp's auxiliary purpose.

EXTIRPATION (*AUSROTTUNG, VERNICHTUNG*)

One of the most contentious issues about the Holocaust is the alleged "language of genocide," that is, the claim that Hitler, Goebbels, Himmler and others used explicit language in their speeches and writings that called for the mass murder of Jews. Indeed, this is often cited as "proof" of genocidal intention, and as "proof" that the Nazis were, or would soon, embark on a program of mass murder. But as with many aspects of the Holocaust, this simplistic distortion of reality obscures deeper truths. In reality, the language of the leading Germans is far more suggestive of a program of removal and ethnic cleansing than it is of mass murder.

Much hinges on the German words used, the context and the corresponding English translation. The two most contentious words are *Vernichtung* and *Ausrottung*, but other verbs suggestive of murder include *liquidieren, eliminieren* and *auslöschen*. Here we will focus on the first two. *Vernichtung* (verb form *vernichten*) translates to "annihilation" or "extermination." The root of this word is *nichts*, "nothing," which in Latin is *nihil*, which in turn is the root of the Latin verb *an+nihilare*. In verb form, *vernichten* means "to bring to nothing." This, in fact, is the same meaning as "annihilate." Similarly, the English word "exterminate" derives from Latin *ex+terminare*, which means to "push something beyond the borders" or to totally remove it. Again, this need not have fatal implications.

Ausrottung (verb form *ausrotten*) is a synonym of *Vernichtung*, and standardly translates to "extermination" or "eradication." The latter derives from *e[x]+radicare*, to root out, which derives from the Latin word *radix*, meaning "root." The German verb *aus+rotten* derives from a word similar to the English "root," although it has lost that direct connection in modern German, where root is now "*Wurzel*." Yet still, the original meaning of *ausrotten* literally was to "root out" or "uproot." The Oxford German-English dictionary translates the phrase "root out" simply to *ausrotten*.

As with the English words "annihilate" and "exterminate," which are inherently ambiguous and have a wide range of meanings, the same is true with *Vernichtung* and *Ausrottung*. In English, it is standard usage for sports figures and politicians to speak of "destroying," "annihilating," or "obliterating" their opponents; this is just "tough talk," for rhetorical effect. In German language, the German dictionary website DWDS includes the following actual (and benign) usages of *Vernichtung*:

- "A hurtful political style, if not aimed at the personal destruction (*Vernichtung*) of the opponent…"
- "[T]he critic… slammed the novel *Beyond Love*, up to the perceived destruction (*Vernichtung*) of the author Walser…"
- "A genealogy of critical destruction (*Vernichtung*) runs through the history of German literature…"
- "He was seen as a politician who does not seek the annihilation (*Vernichtung*) of political opponents…"

Furthermore, and importantly, one can destroy or extirpate a *collective* – a group, an organization, an institution – without killing or even harming any members of that collective. A group can be disintegrated, defunded and banned, and thus "destroyed," without any direct effect on the individual people in that group. Naturally, killing them would also destroy the group, but that is far from required or implied.

Thus, when leading Germans spoke of "destroying" or "annihilating" or "exterminating" the Jews, they in no sense were mandating or suggesting mass murder. Based on all contextual discussion and on actual events as they occurred, it is clear that the Germans wanted the social and economic power of Jewry destroyed, and the Jewish people removed from the territory of the Reich. In some cases, it may have meant limited or targeted killings. But in no case does it mean or imply mass murder of all Jews.

The same point was made by Alfred Rosenberg, the Third Reich's chief ideologist, during his cross-examination at the Nuremberg International Military Tribunal (see the entry on him).

There are many points in favor of the "non-fatal" interpretation of such words. First, the alleged German plan to murder all European Jews did not exist until mid-1941 at the earliest, according to the orthodoxy. Therefore, any usage of such terms prior to mid-1941 cannot have meant mass murder.

For example, in Volume One of *Mein Kampf*, dating to 1925, Hitler uses variations on *Ausrottung* 14 times, and *Vernichtung* 37 times. He speaks of rooting out (*ausgerottet*) German influence in Austria (Sec. 4.1), rooting out a doctrine (5.9), the destruction (*Vernichtung*) of "Prussian militarism" (7.1), the wish to destroy (*vernichten*) the world (10.22) – none of which have fatal implications. When he applies the term to Jews, it is more ominous, perhaps fatal in some cases, but far short of genocide: he wants to root out (*auszurotten*) the Jewish agitators (5.7) and the Jewish pestilence (5.8); left to themselves, Jews would exploit and uproot (*auszurotten*) one another (11.9); Jews in power try to root out non-Jewish intelligentsia (11.22); and the international Jewish poisoners must be rooted out (*ausgerottet*; 12.4).

World media, especially American media, initially took such words in their non-fatal senses, such as when *The New York Times* (NYT) reported on the National-Socialist party's accession to power in 1933. In March of that year, the NYT reported on a speech by Rabbi Schulman in which he decried Hitler's "economic persecution [that] aims at the extermination of the Jewish people" (13 Mar., p. 15). The following month, we again read of the Nazis' "deliberately calculated [plan] to accomplish the economic extermination of the Jews" (6 Apr., p. 10). Such reports were correct; they drew upon Hitler's harsh but nonlethal use of the words *ausrotten* and *vernichten*.

But already by June of 1933, the NYT began to drop the economic descriptor. Hence, we read simply that "Hitler's program is one of extermination" (29 June, p. 4). And in August, the ominous final message is clear: "600,000 [German Jews] are facing certain extermination" (16 Aug., p. 11). Thus, we can see the rapid evolution from a plan of economic dismantling and removal (reality) to a distorted vision implying outright murder (fiction). None of this, of course, was explained to the reading public.

In a 1933 speech, Joseph Goebbels declared that the global conspiracy against Germany "would not lead to our destruction (*Vernichtung*)," but he never contemplated the mass-murder of Germans. In a 1935 speech, Hitler's deputy Rudolf Hess said,

"[The fact that] *Jewry is not, for example, being ruthlessly exterminated (ausrotten) in National-Socialist Germany is proven by the fact that, in Prussia alone, 33,500 Jews are active in industry and crafts, 98,900 in trade and transport – and is further proven by the fact that, with a proportion of 1% of the population of Germany, 17.5% of all lawyers are still Jewish.*" (Hess 1935)

Clearly, in 1935, Hess was referring to eliminating Jewish power and influence, not mass killing – and he denied even this!

By the late 1930s, top Germans were admitting, publicly and privately, that they were indeed "rooting-out" and "destroying" the Jews – none of which meant mass murder. But they also used this kind of language in other, non-Jewish contexts.

In a 1936 memo on the Four-Year Plan, for example, Hitler remarked that the Wehrmacht and the German economy had to be ready within four years for a war with the Soviet Union. Because if the Soviet Union ever managed to conquered Germany, he reasoned, that would mean the annihilation of the German people (Treue 1955, p. 187). Naturally, Hitler did not mean that the Soviets would kill 80 million Germans, but that they would eliminate Germany as an independent political factor.

On 10 November 1938, Hitler stated during a press conference that there was a need to annihilate the class of German intellectuals (Treue 1958, p. 188). Here as well, he cannot have meant a physical extermination of the intellectuals, but merely trimming back their influence.

In January 1939, Hitler received the Czech Foreign Minister, criticizing, among other things, the liberal Czech attitude toward the Jews. He referred to the Jewish policy of his government with the words "In Germany, they are being annihilated" (Billig 1977, p. 51). It is obvious that he cannot have meant a physical annihilation of the Jews, since nothing of the sort is alleged to have been going on at the time.

Then came Hitler's infamous Reichstag speech of 30 January 1939. He said:

"Today I will once more be a prophet: If the international Jewish financiers in and outside Europe should succeed in plunging the nations once more into a world war, then the result will not be the Bolshevization of the earth, and thus the victory of Jewry, but the annihilation (Vernichtung) of the Jewish race in Europe."

This is the most frequently cited passage of Hitler's alleged intention to commit genocide. And yet, it cannot have meant this, since there was utterly no plan for such a thing at that time. And even if there was, it is absurd to think that Hitler would expose that plan in a major public speech.

War came in September of 1939, but even then, there was no plan for Jewish mass murder, according to the experts. The next month, Goebbels wrote in his diary, "This Jewry must be annihilated (*vernichtet*; 17 Oct.)," clearly referring to the collectivity and to the annihilation of their power and influence. We find another diary entry in mid-1940, referring to Jewish press as "riff-raff that must be rooted out (*ausgerottet*; 6 Jul.)." In late 1940, Himmler's personal attendant, Felix Kersten, quoted Himmler as saying "We must wipe out (*ausradieren*) the Jews," and again in April 1941, "The Jews will be annihilated (*ausrotten*) by the end of the war." (Bauer 1994, p. 273, n. 10.) Again, all this *prior* to the earliest possible plan or decision to commit genocide. All these cannot have meant mass murder.

And yet, suddenly, after mid-1941, the experts expect us to believe that *exactly* the same words, in *exactly* the same contexts, now are "proof" of genocidal intention. This is nonsense, baseless and utterly lacking in substantiation.

We should note here that the German language has no lack of words that mean explicit killing: *morden, ermorden, töten, umbringen, erschlagen, erschiessen*, and so on. The Germans had no shortage of such words, if they wished to use them. Instead, and even in the most private of settings, they used nonlethal terms.

Consider these 1941 passages from Hitler's *Table Talk* – private discussions among his most trusted colleagues:

– "If any people has the right to proceed to evacua-

tions [of Jews], it is we... We consider it a maximum of brutality to have liberated our country from 600,000 Jews" (8 Aug. 1941).
- "The Jew, that destroyer [of culture], we shall drive out (*setzen wir ganz hinaus*)" (17 Oct. 1941).
- "I prophesied to Jewry that, in the event of war's proving inevitable, the Jew would disappear from Europe (*aus Europa verschwinden*)... Let nobody tell me that, all the same, we can't send them to the [Russian] swamps!" (25 Oct. 1941).
- "This sniveling in which some of the [German] bourgeois are indulging nowadays, on the pretext that the Jews have to clear out (*auswandern müssten*) of Germany, is typical of these holier-than-thou's. Did they weep when, every year, hundreds of thousands of Germans had to emigrate... ?" (19 Nov. 1941).

The same language continues into 1942:
- "One must act radically. When one pulls out a tooth, one does it with a single tug, and the pain quickly goes away. The Jew must clear out of Europe (*Der Jude muss aus Europa heraus*)... For my part, I restrict myself to telling them they must go away (*Ich sage nur, er muss weg*)... But if they refuse to go voluntarily, I see no other solution but extermination (*Ausrottung*)." (25 Jan. 1942).
- "The Jews must pack up, disappear from Europe (*Der Jude muss aus Europa hinaus*)! Best if they go to Russia." (27 Jan. 1942).
- "[The Jew] bears in mind that, if his victims suddenly became aware of [the damage he causes to society], all Jews would be exterminated. But this time, the Jews will disappear from Europe (*aus Europa verschwinden*)." (3/4 Feb. 1942).
- "We shall regain our health only by eliminating (*eliminieren*) the Jew." (22 Feb. 1942).
- "Until Jewry... is exterminated (*ausrottet*), we shall not have accomplished our task." (30 Aug. 1942).

If Hitler had truly wanted to kill the Jews, he would have said so – more than once, and in no uncertain terms. Instead, we find repeated reference to evacuation, expulsion, and the like. Goebbels's diary shows more of the same:
- "[The Lithuanian Jews] must somehow be rooted out (*ausrotten*)"; 2 Nov. 1941.
- "The World War is here, and the destruction (*Vernichtung*) of Jewry must be the necessary consequence"; 13 Dec. 1941.
- "Jewish terrorism must be rooted out (*ausgerottet*) from all of Europe... [The Jews] will experience their own destruction (*Vernichtung*) along with the destruction (*Vernichtung*) of our enemies"; 15 Feb. 1942.
- "The Jewish race... must be rooted out (*ausgerottet*), stump and stem"; 18 Feb. 1942.
- "Jewry has to pay for triggering a new world war with the complete uprooting (*Ausrottung*) of their race"; 29 Apr. 1942.
- "[Hitler] threatens the Jews with destruction (*Vernichtung*), so far as they run into our area... We must completely remove the Jews from the Reich"; 1 Oct. 1942.

Again, we must ask why Goebbels chose such ambiguous language in his own personal diary. Why not say, "We are killing the Jews," "We are gassing them," "We have shot hundreds of thousands so far," etc.? And yet, nothing like this appears. Instead, all talk is of deportation, ghettoization, removal and forced evacuation.

In sum, nearly all English translations of leading Germans are highly tendentious; one must exercise due caution, and ideally seek out the German original, in order to understand the words in their proper context. Even the most ominous-sounding phrases may well have far more benign meanings.

(See Dalton 2019, 2023; also the entries on Adolf Hitler and Joseph Goebbels as well as on Alfred Rosenberg.)

F

FABIAN, BELA

Bela Fabian was a Hungarian politician deported to Auschwitz, where he was employed in the camp's records office. He was evacuated to the West at war's end and managed to escape, reaching American lines. In an interview given to a U.S. official, he testified that, based on his experience with camp records, "up to June 1944, five million people had been gassed and burned" at Auschwitz. He also claimed to have seen flames billowing from the crematorium chimneys, which was technically impossible. This witness also claimed that the Auschwitz crematoria burned 12,000 corpses daily on average, hence some 4,380,000 per year – a lie matching his lie about five million gassing victims. He furthermore spread the rumor that the Gypsies at Auschwitz were killed in August of 1944, a claim clearly refuted by documental evidence (see the entry on Gypsies). His final imaginary contribution concerns a selection among inmates at the camp's infirmary in late October 1944, leading to all seriously sick inmates being gassed and burned; this claim is unsupported by any document or any other witness story, and is refuted by rich documentation showing the life-saving healthcare that seriously-ill inmates received at Auschwitz. (For more details, see Mattogno 2021, pp. 389f.)

FAITELSON, ALEX

Alex Faitelson was a Lithuanian Jew who was incarcerated at Fort IX near Kaunas, Lithuania. This was a 19th-century fortress used by the Soviets and the Germans as a prison. Faitelson claims to have escaped from this fortress on 25 December 1943. A day later, he signed a declaration together with ten other escapees. In it, the signatories stated that they had been involved in the exhumation and cremation of some 12,000 bodies from several mass graves, which presumably contained some 40,000 bodies altogether. However, German documents of the *Einsatzgruppen* report "only" some 16,000. Therefore, 4,000 bodies should still be there, but evidently they were not discovered so far.

One of the other ten signatories, a certain Makar Kurganov, wrote an affidavit on 12 May 1959, in which he claimed that they had been "forced to unearth and burn on pyres hundreds of thousands of shot Soviet citizens."

Every pyre they built allegedly measured 4 m × 4 m in length and width, and contained 300 bodies. The density of green wood is roughly 0.9 tons per m³, and its stacking density on a pyre is 1.4 (40% for air and flames to go through). Assuming a requirement of 250 kg of green wood per body for open-air incinerations, the required wood would have a volume of some 117 m³. Laid out on a square measuring 4 m × 4 m, the resulting pyres would be more than 7 meters high, reaching 8 meters when adding the bodies. It would have been impossible to build such a pyre, and also impossible to burn it down without it collapsing and spilling burning wood and corpses all over the place.

In 1996, an autobiography by Faitelson appeared. It is full of references to other sources, hence obviously a mixture of memories propped up or replaced with tenets of the orthodox narrative. He even has a bulldozer clear out cremation remains, although such vehicles did not exist in eastern Europe during the war. Here are some more peculiar claims in his book:

- "A narrow ditch was dug around the fire, into which the fat and fuel from the bodies would drip." However, fat catches fire and burns as soon as it comes into contact with fire or embers, so no fat can be extracted from a corpse on a pyre.
- The pyres were allegedly lit by placing "mines under the lowest layer of wood." This would have blown the pyre apart and scattered corpse parts all over the place. A similar story by as certain Dmitrii Gelpern was published in 1948 in the Yiddish periodical *Der Emes* published in Moscow. Faitelson may have plagiarized this nonsense directly or through some intermediate source.
- The 64 inmates involved had to haul dry firewood from Fort IX to the cremation site every day. However, burning 300 bodies per day, as Faitelson claimed, would require almost 40 metric tons of wood. Therefore, every inmate had to carry some 600 kg of wood.
- The inmates filled up the stash of firewood at Fort IX by collecting branches on the way back to the fort – 600 kg of *branches* every day.

The only event that is backed up by documents is the

escape of 63 Jews from Fort IX on 25 December 1943. However, the rest of Faitelson's testimony, which relates to one of many events claimed to have been part of the alleged German clean-up operation which the orthodoxy calls *Aktion* 1005, is not backed up by anything. The above-critiqued peculiar claims indicate that Faitelson's entire scenario is completely detached from reality. It cannot be based on experience, but on mere imagination and delusion.

(For more details, see Mattogno 2022c, pp. 656-665.)

FAJGIELBAUM, SRUL

Srul Fajgielbaum was an inmate of the Sobibór Camp. In a deposition of 5 November 1945, he claimed to have been involved in building the (one) gas chamber at Sobibór. The room's ceiling, floor and walls were allegedly lined with iron plates, and the execution was carried out with electricity "produced inside the chamber by means of a special motor and machine."

His claims are rejected as false by the orthodoxy, who insists on several gas chambers operating with engine-exhaust gas. The chambers moreover were not lined with iron plates.

(See the entry on Sobibór for more details, as well as Mattogno 2021e, pp. 76f.)

Fajnzylberg, Alter → Jankowski, Stanisław

FALBORSKI, BRONISŁAW

Bronisław Falborski was a Polish car mechanic who claims to have repaired a gas van's exhaust system near the Chełmno Camp. Interrogated by the Polish judiciary on 11 June 1945, Falborski described the van as a converted moving truck, which at the time of his interview was parked at the Ostrowski factory grounds in Koło, near Chełmno. However, that vehicle was investigated in detail by the Polish judiciary and turned out *not* to be a gas van at all. The way he describes the repair he did to this "gas van's" exhaust system confirms that the witness was lying:

Bronisław Falborski

- According to him, this truck's exhaust pipe went all the way to the end of the chassis. However, truck exhaust pipes exit overhead behind the driver's cabin or on the side behind the motor. They don't go on for many more meters to the rear. That's done with passenger cars only.
- Falborski's description and sketch of the switching system for the exhaust from venting to piping into the cargo box was inconsistent and pointlessly complicated.
- He asserted that the Germans did not allow him and his seven Polish colleagues to investigate the design of the vehicle, but they let him repair the lethal and most compromising part of it! If the Germans wanted to keep anything a secret, they wouldn't have let Poles do the repair work.
- Two of Falborski's colleagues – Jozef Piaskowski and Bronisław Mańkowski – confirmed the awkward, nonsensical setup of the alleged exhaust system, showing that they all were under the same spell of wanting to deliver a coherent story, even if it meant agreeing on nonsense. This is a clear-cut case of the "convergence of evidence" on a lie.

Hence, Falborski's and his colleague's statements were meant to corroborate the intended claim by the Polish Investigative Commission that the moving truck found in the courtyard of the former Ostrowski Company had been a homicidal "gas van." That, however, backfired on them and their testimonies.

When Falborski was interviewed for Claude Lanzmann's 1985 documentary *Shoah* 40 years after the war, he suddenly knew everything about the gas vans' operation and even about the entire program of exterminating the regional Jews, something he could not possibly have known in 1945, nor did he claim it back then. To top it off, Falborski tells the tall tale that, on one occasion, the gas van tipped over, the doors burst open, and out came tumbling 50 living Jews, which were then shot by one single German using a pistol. Since that weapon had at most eight bullets, he had to reload seven times – from what ammunition stash is unclear. All the while, all the tumbling Jews needed to sit patiently and await their turn to be shot, and not be tempted to run away into the woods. Clearly, the scene is absurd. Falborski made it up, and Lanzmann swallowed it completely.

(For more details, see Alvarez 2023, pp. 151-156.)

FALSE-MEMORY SYNDROME

Scientific research shows that even mildly manipulative interviewing techniques, repeated multiple times, succeed in implanting false memories into roughly one third of all average adults, making them firmly believe that they experienced events that never happened (Loftus 1994, 1997, 2003). It has also been demonstrated that the human memory is more easily manipulated when questioning takes place under more emotional circumstances and when the alleged experiences are more emotional. Even emotional media reporting can lead to massive distortion of memory. It is therefore possible to make people "remember" traumatic events that never occurred, such as sexual abuse during childhood, abduction by extra-terrestrials, etc. (cf. Bjorklund 2000, Dineen 1996, Goldstein/Farmer 1993, Ofshe 1996.).

Furthermore, it has been proven that it is easier to manipulate memory if the event that you want to insert or distort includes aspects that the subject actually does remember; these aspects thus act as an anchor point for the untrue implant.

Memories about events allegedly experienced by former inmates of German wartime camps are particularly prone to be false, for numerous reasons:

1. They are usually recalled many years or even decades after the claimed event, when human memory inevitably has deteriorated.
2. They concern events that happened in a framework of traumatic persecution and oppression, and of emotional distress, and the claimed horrors increase these sensations to an extreme degree, even years after the claimed events.
3. Stories surrounding the (alleged) misdeeds of Germans against the Jews during World War II have been spread through all possible channels of society for decades: schools, colleges and universities, judiciary, politics and all media. In fact, there has never been a propaganda campaign on a historical issue so intense, so long-lasting, and so one-sided as with the Holocaust. Many memes have become clichés that many survivors then "recall" and repeat.
4. Witnesses are under enormous pressure to "remember" what everyone expects them to – gas chambers, piles of dead bodies, evil Germans, and so on. Witnesses who cannot remember certain details may be accused of betrayal, denial and even anti-Semitism. Therefore, many witnesses "recall" incidents that they read or heard from others, rather than things they personally experienced. Loyalty to their fellow survivors is often given precedence over honesty and truthfulness.
5. Failing to confirm certain events or clichés about the Holocaust can not only lead to societal persecution, but even to legal prosecution in many countries. (See the entry on censorship.) Not since the time of the medieval witch trials has there been a topic where entire societies dogmatically enforce certain facts and versions of history, using all means at their disposal.

Therefore, there has never been an event in history where more false memories may be expected to occur, from many or even most witnesses. Outright deceit was likely most pervasive right after the war, when actual memories were fresh but anti-German sentiments were still raw. In more recent times, however, legitimate memories have been systematically rewritten and replaced by a relentless, media-driven form of propaganda. Holocaust skepticism, therefore, serves as an important corrective to the many false memories that witnesses may honestly believe and continue to promote. (Cf. Rudolf 2023, pp. 363-374.)

FALSE WITNESSES

A false witness is a person who falsely claims to have witnessed an event, when in fact he was not physically present at the time of the event. It is therefore irrelevant what such a person claims about the given event, as he cannot have any personal knowledge of it. This stands in contrast to a person who *was* at a given location to witness an alleged event, but who gives false *testimony* about the event – meaning that the event did not happen at all or not the way the person claims. Such a person is a 'true witness,' but one who has given false testimony.

In the context of the Holocaust, over the decades since the end of World War II, numerous persons have been exposed as false witnesses – people who were never at a given location at the time in question. These cases have become so frequent that the German-language section of Wikipedia dedicated a specific page to them, calling it Wilkomirski-Syndrome, after one of the most prominent cases. Cases that reached public notoriety have become more frequent since the 1990s.

However, to this day, it is very risky to scrutinize "survivor" testimony and expose false witnesses, as many lobby groups – the Jewish lobby foremost of all – demand that anyone doubting survivor stories be ostracized, shunned, excluded from good society, and even prosecuted where possible. After all, some 20 countries in the world have made it illegal to question or refute the orthodox Holocaust narrative, yet proper source criticism necessarily requires questioning every aspect of what a witness claims – especially once a witness's credibility has collapsed due to proven mistakes, exaggerations, distortions and falsehoods.

Here is a certainly incomplete list of acknowledged cases of false witnesses:
– Denis Avey
– Joe Corry
– Bruno Doessekker (aka Binjamin Wilkomirski)
– Martin Gray (aka Mieczyslaw Grajewski)
– Marie Sophie Hingst
– Joseph Hirt
– Bernard Holstein
– Magdolna Kaiser
– Rosemarie Koczy
– Jerzy Kosinski
– Enric Marco
– Alfred Mende (aka Isaac Lewinson)
– Karin Mylius
– Wolfgang Seibert
– Axel Spörl
– Otto Uthgenannt
– Irena Wachendorff
– Monique de Wael (aka Misha Defonesca)
– Donald Watt
– Laurel Rose Willson
– to be completed

(See each entry as well as Vice 2014a&b and, as long as it exists, https://de.wikipedia.org/wiki/Wilkomirski-Syndrom)

FAMILY CAMP, AT AUSCHWITZ

Starting on 6 September 1943, Jews from the Theresienstadt Ghetto in what is today Czechia were deported in large numbers to the Auschwitz-Birkenau Camp and lodged there in the so-called Family Camp. More such transports arrived in December 1943 and May, September and October 1944.

On 10 and 11 July 1944, some 7,000 Jews quartered in that camp section are said to have been murdered in gas chambers. Even earlier, a number of these Jews were allegedly gassed, and most Jews of the transport arriving after that date are said to have suffered the same fate.

To support the mass murder claim, two main witness accounts are quoted:

– The demonstrably false report authored by Rudolf Vrba and Alfred Wetzler, a version of which was later included in the so-called War Refugee Board Report.
– The testimony of Otto Wolken, which is littered with demonstrably false claims.

The orthodoxy's claim that inmates regularly registered at Auschwitz and admitted to the camp could at some point be killed without leaving a documental trace is simply wrong. Once people were part of the camp bureaucracy, extensive paperwork was produced, and many entries in various logs were created if the status of an inmate changed, including and especially in cases of death, for any reason.

In addition, inmates arriving at the Auschwitz Camp were usually placed in a six-week quarantine (some claim six *months*), and Jews coming from Theresienstadt were no exception to that rule. During that time, they could not leave their camp section; hence even Jews otherwise fit for labor were considered "useless eaters" during that time. But most importantly, the mere fact that there was a quarantine period demonstrates that Jews were expected to survive and work; why have a quarantine, only to later send them to gas chambers? It would have been wasteful and pointless.

Unfortunately, documentation about the inmates deported from the Theresienstadt Ghetto is incomplete. From the extant documents, one can conclude, however, that a wanton killing of these Jews, which would have affected many fit for labor, is highly unlikely. As a group, their fate can be deduced as having been altogether innocuous. Many more were transferred to other camps than previously assumed, and even those inmates considered "unfit" for anything – infants, young children and geriatrics – were generally left unharmed.

In July of 1944, the Family Camp was dissolved, and its inmates transferred to other camp sectors or away to other camps. That space gave way to an urgently needed transit camp for female prisoners, which temporarily housed Jewesses deported from Hungary. After going through quarantine, they, too, were eventually transferred to other labor and concentration camps throughout Germany, as a part of at least 280,500 Auschwitz inmates who can be demonstrated to have been transferred away from Auschwitz in 1944/45. And that list is almost certainly incomplete.

(For details, see Mattogno 2016a, pp. 144-167; 2023, Part 2, pp. 289-310.)

FARBER, YURI

Yuri Farber was a Jewish PoW in German captivity. A propaganda report by the Soviet terror organization NKGB dated 14 August 1944 about alleged German atrocities in the Ponary District of Lithuania contains a long account of an unnamed Soviet PoW written with the intention to "assist in the crushing defeat of [the] Hitlerite gangs." A very similar account by Yuri Farber was published in the infamous *Black Book*. It is evidently an edited and rearranged version of this NKGB propaganda report.

In these two accounts, Farber claimed to have been transported to an abandoned Soviet construction site in the woods near a Vilnius suburb called Ponary on 29 January 1944. Together with 79 other prisoners, he was allegedly forced to exhume and burn bodies buried in mass graves at that location, while their legs were shackled with chains.

He tells how he eventually managed to escape on 15 April 1944: They were lodged inside a circular pit, four meters deep, 24 meters in diameter, whose walls were lined with concrete. Three days after their arrival, the inmate started digging an escape tunnel starting from inside their shelter pit.

Within 68 days, they dug out a tunnel 200-250 m long, 0.7 m wide, and 0.65 m high (*Black Book*; the NKGB version speaks only of a 30-m upward slope, evidently at the tunnel's end, but not how long it was before the slope started). The soil of the tunnel roof was propped up by boards resting on poles (7–8 boards and 14–16 poles per meter). These boards and poles were made from firewood using saws. Tools and materials needed for this construction were retrieved from the corpses, which implies that the execution victims had neither been searched for weapons nor stripped before the execution, and carried with them an entire armory of construction tools. Since the workers depleted all oxygen in the tunnel, candles wouldn't burn, so they installed electric light in the tunnel.

However, Farber does not explain how they managed to get the tools needed to dig through their pit's concrete wall, and then through 200+ meters of soil filled with tree roots; where the supplies for the electric lighting inside the tunnel came from; where the electricity for the light came from; what they did with the excavated soil (at least some 90 cubic meters for 200 m of tunnel); how they managed to do hard labor in a tunnel depleted of oxygen; and how they could have hidden all this frantic construction activity from their guards.

Moreover, since there was room only for one worker lying on his belly, this prostrate worker had to dig almost (200m/68 days=) three meters a day. Since all inmates had to work during the entire day on exhuming and cremating corpses with all the concomitant work (chopping wood, hauling wood and corpses, crushing bones etc.), they all would have been utterly exhausted in the evening. Hence, no one would have had any energy left for such intense digging work performed under low-oxygen conditions.

Another witness of the same event, Szloma Gol, was more realistic, or perhaps only less imaginative, by claiming that they dug the tunnel with their bare hands. A further witness, Matvey Zaydel, asserted that, after a while of digging with bare hands, they switched to using a tablespoon.

Farber claims that the corpses were extracted from the graves by a person outside the grave by throwing a hook down into the grave, and if by chance a corpse or body part got hooked, he pulled it out. The same absurd corpse-fishing game was described by Szymon Amiel and Salman Edelman in a testimony also published in *The Black Book*. This is a case of convergence of evidence on a lie, probably because the witnesses testifying for the NKGB – which were *The Black Book*'s sources – had a chance to "learn" from one another and from their interrogators.

Farber's description of the pyres they built is peculiar. Each had an outer scaffold of wooden logs, and in its center a chimney(?) made of pine trunks – for some unknown purpose. He asserted that 3,500 bodies were placed on a pyre measuring 7 m × 7 m, and was some four meters high. If the pyre had a cuboid shape, its volume would have been (7 m × 7 m × 4 m =) 196 cubic meters. If we assume for each heavily decomposed body a volume of only 26 liters (hence a mass of 26 kg), 3,500 of them, stacked with 40% gaps in between, would have occupied (3,500 bodies × 0.026 m^3/body × 1.4 =) around 127 cubic meters, leaving less than 70 m^3 for the wood. However, Farber claimed that his pyres were pyramidal in shape. In that case, there would have been *no* space left for any wood. Clearly, his pyres would not have burned, let alone reduced the corpses to ashes.

The alleged pyramidal shape of the pyre with a wooden chimney at the top was also claimed by Szloma Gol, who testified 2 years after Farber.

Farber moreover claimed that one prisoner was standing right next the burning pyre with a spade, stoking the wood and bodies "to make sure that the fire did not die out." That person would have burned to a crisp, if such a pyre had burned so hot that it reduced all wood and bodies to ashes, as he claims it did.

Cremating an average human body during open-air incinerations requires some 250 kg of freshly cut wood. Cremating 38,000 bodies thus requires some 9,500 metric tons of wood. This would have required the felling of all trees growing in a 50-year-old spruce forest covering 21 hectares of land, or some 47 American football fields. An average prisoner is rated at being able to cut some 0.63 metric tons of fresh wood per workday. To cut this amount of wood within 75 days would have required a work force of some 200 dedicated lumberjacks just to cut the wood. Yet Farber's entire slave-labor unit of 80 men were merely busy digging out mass graves, extracting bodies, building pyres, crushing bones, sifting through ashes, scattering the ashes and refilling the graves with soil. The firewood needed was just magically there.

Here are some contradictions in Farber's tale:
– The pyres were built "near the excavation," but at the same time 400 m away.
– They managed to process up to 800 bodies a day, but lit a pyre with 3,500 corpses within a couple of days, or every three days (*Black Book*).
– If they processed 800 bodies per day during Farber's stay of 76 days, this results in some 60,000 bodies; if assuming 3,500 bodies every three days, that's some 90,000 bodies; yet in his NKGB statement, he claimed that "only" 38,000 were processed during his time, of his estimate of a total of 80,000 buried bodies; hence, 56,000 were still there. Still, he claimed that in mid-April they learned that their "work on the corpses was coming to an end." Yet the Soviets claimed that this work continued for months after Farber's escape.

If Farber's tale has any real background, it would have been on a much smaller order of magnitude than what he claimed.

This testimony relates to one of many events claimed to have been part of the alleged German clean-up operation which the orthodoxy calls *Aktion 1005*. The above exposition demonstrates conclusively that Farber's entire scenario is completely detached from reality. It cannot be based on experience, but on mere propaganda, imagination and delusion. (See also the similar accounts by A. Blyazer, Matvey Zaydel and Szloma Gol; for more details, see Mattogno 2022c, pp. 670-677.)

FARKAS, HENRIK

Henrik Farkas was a Hungarian Jew deported to Auschwitz on 15 June 1944. After the war, he made a deposition which was published in a 1945 collection titled, "Data on the Martyrdom of Hungarian Jewry during the 1941-1945 War." Farka's chapter on the "gas chambers" was plagiarized from the 1944 report by Rudolf Vrba and Alfred Wetzler, repeating almost every (often false) detail, but claiming to have received this information from some unnamed Jewish engineer. (For more, see Mattogno 2021, pp. 242.)

FAT, EXTRACTED FROM BURNING CORPSES

The lowest temperature at which mammalian animal fat, including fat from human tissue, emits sufficient vapor in air to cause ignition upon contact with a flame or spark – the so-called flashpoint – is 184°C (or 363°F; Perry 1949, p. 1584.). This means that, in the presence of fire or embers, human fat ignites at that temperature or above. While small wood fires (such as campfires) may burn at temperatures as low as 315°C (600°F), large wood fires, such as major pyres, easily reach temperatures of 1,000°C and more (some 2,000°F). Therefore, burning wood inevitably ignites any fat exuding from animal carcasses or human corpses lying in such a fire. This effect is familiar to anyone who has ever barbecued a steak and saw fat drip from their meat into the burning charcoal; the grill is quickly ablaze because the fat burns instantly, ferociously and completely. Any witness claiming that, during open-air incineration of corpses on pyres fueled by wood, liquid fat collected at the bottom of a cremation pit, in any shape, is inventing a physically impossible story (Mattogno 2014a).

Witnesses who have claimed this include (where no source is given, see the entry for that person for details):
– Charles S. Bendel
– Leon Cohen
– Szlama Dragon
– Eliezer Eisenschmidt
– four distinguished university professors: Berthold Epstein, Prague; Bruno Fischer, Prague; Henri Limousin, Clermont-Ferrand; and Géza Mansfeld, Budapest
– Alex Faitelson
– Rudolf Höss
– Stanisław Jankowski

- Henryk Mandelbaum
- Kurt Marcus
- Filip Müller
- Joshuah Rosenblum
- Henryk Tauber
- Shlomo Venezia

This agreement of so many witnesses on something physically impossible is a striking case of a "convergence of evidence" on a lie.

Similarly impossible is the claim made in a report sent to London by the Polish underground in May 1944, which stated that at Auschwitz, during "the demolition of the [crematorium] chimney, a true and proper layer of unburnt human fat several centimeters [thick] was found in the soot on the bricks" (Mattogno 2021, p. 183).

The first "historian" to take this nonsense seriously and include it in his description of Auschwitz was the Polish-Jewish writer Filip Friedman in his pamphlet *To jest Oświęcim!* (*This Is Auschwitz!*; cf. Mattogno 2021, pp. 409-415, here p. 412).

Feinsilber, Alter → Jankowski, Stanisław

FELDHENDLER, LEON

Leon Feldhendler

Leon Feldhendler was an inmate of the Sobibór Camp. In a 1946 book, he is quoted as having testified that, in the sector where he was employed, the living conditions for the Jews were agreeable: "The [Jewish] tradesmen were living very nicely, in their workshops, they had comfortable quarters." He claimed that the gas chambers at Sobibór used chlorine gas for the murder, but that "other gases were continuously tested."

His claims are rejected as false by the orthodoxy, who insists that living conditions for Jews were hellish, and that an engine produced lethal exhaust gas for the murder.

(See the entry on Sobibór for more details, as well as Graf/Kues/Mattogno 2020, pp. 43, 59, 71; Mattogno 2021e, p. 84.)

FELENBAUM-WEISS, HELLA

Hella Felenbaum-Weiss

Hella Felenbaum-Weiss was an inmate of the Sobibór Camp. In a deposition probably recorded in 1946, she claimed that inmates were gassed using chlorine inside the train during transit on the way to Sobibór. This claim is rejected as false by the orthodoxy, who insists that inmates were gassed only after their arrival at the camp in stationary gas chambers using engine-exhaust gas.

(See the entry on Sobibór for more details, as well as Graf/Kues/Mattogno 2020, pp. 32f., 72; Mattogno 2021e, pp. 85.)

FINAL SOLUTION

The term "final solution" (German: *Endlösung* – end/terminal/final solution) within the context of what National Socialists called the "Jewish Question" first appeared in a letter written on 24 June 1940 by Reinhardt Heydrich, head of Germany's Department of Homeland Security (*Reichssicherheitshauptamt*), to Joachim von Ribbentrop, German Minister of Foreign Affairs. In this letter, Heydrich asserted that, after conquering Poland with its three million Jews, the Jewish problem could no longer be solved "by emigration," as was done so far. Now, "a territorial final solution" was required, which implied that some territory was to be put aside for the Jews as a kind of homeland or reservation. (For more, see the entry on Reinhardt Heydrich.)

The quantitative challenge got exacerbated after Germany invaded the Soviet Union in June 1941. Many more million Jews living in the Soviet Union were expected to be soon under German control. For that reason, Hermann Göring expanded Heydrich's role in a letter dated 31 July 1941. Reinhardt Heydrich's task now encompassed all of Germany's area of influence in Europe. Heydrich was to submit a draft plan to implement this final solution of the Jewish question. In this document, Göring used the terms *Gesamtlösung* (total or comprehensive solution) and *Endlösung* (end or final solution) synonymously. (See the entry on Hermann Göring for more details.)

The orthodoxy insists that the term "final solution" ultimately meant the total physical extermination of Europe's Jews. The two documents mentioned here prove this to be untrue. A long string of

The Final Solution: Facts and Fiction	
DOCUMENTED FACT	UNDOCUMENTED CLAIM
25 Jan. 1942: Heinrich Himmler writes to Richard Glücks that the camps must prepare to accommodate up to 150,000 Jews; large-scale economic tasks would be assigned to them.	20 Jan. 1942: The total extermination of all Jews in the German sphere of influence is organized at the Wannsee Conference.*
30 April 1942: Oswald Pohl writes to Heinrich Himmler that the main purpose of all camps would now be the use of inmate labor.	Feb. 1942: Beginning of mass gassings at Auschwitz-Birkenau. March 1942: Beginning of mass gassings at Belzec. May 1942: Beginning of mass gassings at Sobibór.
21 Aug. 1942: Martin Luther writes that the number of transported Jews would be inadequate to cover the shortage of labor, so that the German government asked the Slovakian government to supply 20,000 Slovakian Jews for labor.	23 July 1942: Beginning of mass gassings at Treblinka. August 1942: Beginning of gassings at Majdanek.
28 Dec. 1942: Richard Glücks writes to all camp commandants that Himmler has ordered to reduce death rates in all camps by all means. The inmates have to receive better food.	End of 1942: Six "extermination" camps are active.
27 April 1943: Richard Glücks writes to all camp commandants that Himmler has ordered all inmates physically unfit for work – even cripples, TBC patients and bedridden patients – to be kept alive and, whenever possible, assigned to do light work. "Bedridden prisoners should be assigned work that they can perform in bed."	March-June 1943: the new Birkenau crematoria become operational; mass extermination of Jews unfit for labor unfolds inside them.
26 Oct. 1943: Circular letter by Oswald Pohl to all camp commandants: All measures of the commanders must focus on the health and productivity of the inmates.	3 Nov. 1943: Some 42,000 Jewish factory workers are shot in Majdanek and several of its satellite camps. (Operation "Harvest Festival")
11 May 1944: Hitler orders the deployment of 200,000 Jews in the construction of fighter airplanes.	16 May 1944: Beginning of mass murder of several hundred thousand Jews from Hungary at Auschwitz-Birkenau.

* This claim is not confirmed by the protocol of this conference.

documents created after these two documents also point to the fact that "final solution" did not refer to any physical extermination, but to a program of ruthless ethnic cleansing by deporting the Jews to some territory reserved for them.

Furthermore, many other documents addressing the question of what to do with the inmates in Germany's various camps confirm that no policy of physical extermination was in place.

For more information on this, see the table presented here with its references, as well as the entries on the Nisko Plan, on Madagascar, and on resettlement.

FINKELSZTEIN, LEON

Leon Finkelsztein was a Polish Jew deported to the Treblinka Camp on 22 July 1942, who escaped during the uprising on 2 August 1943. On 28 December 1945 he was interrogated by Polish judge Łukaszkiewicz. Here are some pertinent claims from his deposition:

- Deportees were killed in the trains in transit with chlorine sprinkled in the railway cars (this probably refers to chlorinated lime). This is a clear echo of the black propaganda spread by Jan Karski, and also claimed by Abraham Goldfarb.
- When he arrived, the camp was not yet fenced in. This is unlikely.
- The gas-chamber building consisted of three rooms and an engine room, whose exhaust gases were used for the murder. If it failed, chlorine was used instead.
- Sometimes people were still alive after chlorine gassings, but were buried alive anyway.
- Finkelsztein insisted that the chamber floors were not collapsible, which means that he must have had access to other witness testimonies, in this case that of Henryk Poswolski, who is the only witness known to have claimed such floors for Treblinka.
- Although Finkelsztein claimed to have been in Treblinka from the first day to the last, the only thing he knew about the alleged second gassing facility was that it had ten chambers and also worked with engine exhaust.
- He claimed that the camp had 21 pits, each containing 200,000 victims, which would result in 4.2 million victims. That is also near the upper limit of deportees he claimed arrived at Treblinka (the lower limit being just over a million).

- Finkelsztein claimed that, after some experiments, the Germans found a way of building a cremation grate that "was lit with a small amount of wood or rags soaked in gasoline, and then the corpses burned by themselves." However, self-immolating bodies do not exist.
- He claimed that, due to inmate sabotage, large quantities of bodies were never burned, but such large numbers of unburned corpses have never been found.

(For details, see Mattogno 2021e, pp. 160-162; https://zapisyterroru.pl/.)

FIRST GASSING, AT AUSCHWITZ

Rumors about the "first gassing" at the Auschwitz Main Camp originated in propaganda spread by inmate resistance groups there in October of 1941. This propaganda claimed that the Germans were testing toxic gases on Russian PoWs in preparation for chemical warfare at the Eastern front. Similar claims of the preparation of weapons of mass destruction have been used by war propagandists ever since to incite their people to support a war, or to justify escalations in an ongoing war.

In later reports of resistance groups, as disinfestation at Auschwitz using Zyklon B became commonly known, the theme gradually shifted by mentioning this pesticide as the killing agent, and by placing the event in the basement of Block 11 of the Auschwitz Main Camp. The normal removal of corpses of registered detainees who had died in the camp for various reasons, from the morgue of Block 28 to the camp's crematorium, was then used to progressively enrich the story.

After the war, in preparation for the two Polish show trials – one against former camp commandant Rudolf Höss and the other against several other leading members of the former camp staff – Polish Investigating Judge Jan Sehn set out to "historicize" the utterly contradictory accounts of a plethora of witnesses ready to accuse the Germans of anything. Among the widely varying data claimed by the witnesses, Sehn decided *ex cathedra* which ones were "correct": the number and types of victims as well as the various phases of the gassing; but he did not decide on the event's date. That was done only in 1959 by the Auschwitz Museum's lead historian Danuta Czech by way of aggressively manipulating the sources. She resurrected and augmented Jan Sehn's already cherry-picked tale, and drew from a hodgepodge of contradictory testimonies a purely fictitious

Auschwitz Main Camp, Block 11, wall facing south-southwest, close-up of concrete screens around the window wells of the basement detention cells presumably used for the "first gassing."

"convergence of evidence," and attributed to it a precise but completely invented date.

According to this narrative, the very first gassing concerned 250 sick Polish inmates and 500 Soviet PoWs. The event started on 3 September 1941, took place in the basement of Block 11 of the Auschwitz Main Camp, and supposedly lasted 15 hours, followed by another two days of ventilation and removal of the corpses.

However, if we look at *some* of the claims made by the various witnesses, a completely different picture emerges. According to this, depending on the witness, the notorious event occurred either
- in the spring of 1941
- immediately after the invasion of Russia (late June/early July 1941)
- or in August 1941
- or on August 14, 1941
- or on August 15, 1941
- or on September 3-5, 1941
- or on September 5-6, 1941
- or on September 5-8, 1941

– or on September 13, 1941
– or in the fall of 1941
– or in September or (early) October
– or on October 9, 1941
– or during October/November 1941
– or in November 1941
– or in winter of 1941(/1942)
– or at the turn of 1941 to 1942
– or in early 1942
– or in March 1942
– or in December of 1942.

The location was either
– the old crematorium
– or one room…
– or a gas chamber looking like a bathroom
– or all rooms…
– or even all rooms plus the hallway of the basement of Block 11
– or somewhere at Birkenau.

The victims were either
– Soviet PoWs
– or partisans
– or political commissars
– or Poles
– or Soviet PoWs and sick Polish detainees
– or Soviet PoWs and Polish officers

There were either
– 100, or 200, or 300, or 350, or 470, or 500, or 600, or 696, or 700, or 800, or 850, or 850-900, or 880, or 900, or 980, or 1,000, or more than 1,000, or 1,400, or 1,663, or 2,000 victims.

The poison gas was administered either by
– SS *Hauptscharführer* Palitzsch (*Rapportführer*)
– or by Tom Mix (an invented person)
– or by "the strangler" (another invented person)
– or by SS *Unterscharführer* Breitwieser, head of the inmate clothing department.

either into the corridor or into the cells of the basement of Block 11, a total of three cans or perhaps two cans into each cell, either
– through the door
– or through a ventilation flap
– or through openings above the doors to the cells.

The victims either died immediately, or perhaps stayed alive for 15 hours. The corpses were removed either
– the following day
– or the following night
– or one to two days later
– or three days later
– or on the 4th day
– or after 4 or 5 days
– or the 6th day.

The work took either
– a whole day
– or a whole night
– or two nights
– or three nights.

The bodies of the victims were either
– cremated
– or buried in mass graves (in Birkenau)
– or partly cremated and partly buried.

In fact, however, this alleged event left no trace in any extant documents. Its implementation is full of technical absurdities, contradicting all well-known and generally practiced safety procedures for fumigations using Zyklon B. The majority of the alleged victims – Soviet PoWs – arrived at Auschwitz only starting in late October 1941; a Gestapo commission arrived in November and started interviewing the inmates, sifting out those who were fanatical communists – some 300 – and marked them for execution. Yet those were not gassed, but rather executed by shooting in smaller groups over time. And there is also no trace of sick Polish inmates murdered in masses – they are all accounted for.

One mainstay of the orthodox narrative about this defining moment in the history of the Auschwitz Camp are the various statements made by Rudolf Höss after the war (see his entry). However, these are themselves riddled with a plethora of absurdities, contradictions and chronological as well as technical impossibilities, rendering them historically worthless. They serve only as an instructive example of what several days of torture followed by months of abuse can do to a man.

(For details on the First Gassing, see Mattogno 2022f.)

FISCHER, BRUNO

Bruno Fischer was a professor of medicine from Prague, who was incarcerated at the Auschwitz Camp until it was conquered by the Soviets on 27 February 1945. Together with three other European professors, and coached by their Soviet conquerors, he signed an appeal on 4 March 1945 "To the International Public," which contained many untrue propaganda clichés about Auschwitz. See the entry on Berthold Epstein for details.

FISCHER, HORST

Horst Fischer (31 Dec. 1910 – 8 July 1966) was a wartime physician and SS *Hauptsturmführer*. From 6 November 1942 until 1944 he was deployed as camp physician at the labor camp Auschwitz-Monowitz and at the worksite of the nearby Buna branch of the German chemical giant *I.G. Farbenindustrie*.

Horst Fischer

In September 1944, he became deputy garrison physician for the entire camp complex, subordinate to Dr. Eduard Wirths. While in Monowitz, he decided, among other things, which seriously sick or wounded inmates would be transferred to the inmate infirmary at Auschwitz-Birkenau.

In the wake of the Frankfurt Auschwitz Show Trial of 1964-65, communist East Germany staged its own Auschwitz Show Trial by trying Fischer for his decision to have sick and injured inmates transferred to Birkenau, for allegedly supervising gassings, and for ordering deliveries of the insecticide Zyklon B. The trial's focus was not so much Fischer's personal guilt but the attempt to incriminate *I.G. Farbenindustrie*, the predecessor of numerous West-German chemical companies, in the claimed genocide committed at Auschwitz.

During the trial, which lasted from 10 to 25 March 1966, Fischer acted like almost all defendants during Stalinist show trials: he willingly, at times even enthusiastically, embraced and accepted all accusations and even added new ones. His defense lawyer was one of East Germany's top political lawyers. (Dirks 2006, 2011; Leide 2019, pp. 167-177)

Fischer's description of a makeshift facility near the Birkenau Camp where he claims to have supervised some 12 gassing actions clashes violently with the orthodox narrative. Fischer never uses the by-then officially ordained term "bunker" but rather calls the building a "sauna," a term not used by any other witness, and probably inspired by the so-called *Zentralsauna*, Birkenau's large hygiene building with inmate showers and hot-air disinfestation devices.

Fischer claims that the building had only one room with two doors, and one opening to introduce Zyklon B, while the orthodoxy insists that both alleged bunkers had several rooms, each with doors and Zyklon-B introduction hatches. After a homicidal gassing, the chamber, not equipped with any ventilation system, was presumably opened after just 15 minutes. Another quarter hour, Fischer claimed, was enough for "the poison gas to escape from the gas chamber." After that, inmates went in and dragged out the bodies using 2-meter-long poles with hooks at one end. This absurd extraction technique is Fischer's invention.

What completely destroys Fischer's credibility, however, is his claim that a room packed with bodies and sprinkled with Zyklon-B pellets could be aired out successfully through just two opened doors. The pellets would have released their poison for up to two hours, and unless there was a howling wind blowing through the room, ventilating such a room would have taken many hours – up to a day or even two. (For details, see Mattogno 2016f, pp. 156-159.)

Further undermining Fischer's credibility are his assertions about the speed at which Zyklon-B gassings allegedly worked. He seriously claimed that the gas led to unconsciousness already after a few seconds, and that breathing stopped altogether after just a few minutes. (See Rudolf 2020, p. 259.) However, Zyklon B gives off its poison only slowly, and it dissipates through a large room only gradually, so any execution in the way described would by necessity be much slower than executions in U.S. gas chambers, which took on average ten minutes (see the entry on Zyklon B and on homicidal gas chambers).

Fischer furthermore described Morgue #1 of Crematorium II, the alleged gas chamber, completely wrong. He stated that it measured 10 m × 10 m (it was 30 m × 7 m), and had a second door in the opposite wall for removing the bodies, although the room had only one door. Fischer stated that Zyklon B was dumped into the room through chimney-like objects in the roof, which runs contrary to the orthodox narrative that insists on Zyklon B not having been poured into the room itself, but into some Zyklon-B introduction devices. Furthermore, he claimed to know from hearsay that the bodies were put into a corpse elevator which deposited them directly into the furnaces, which is a unique and false claim. (See Rudolf 2020, pp. 395f.)

In reality, Fischer was one of many physicians deployed at Auschwitz desperately trying to improve health care for the inmates and the sanitary conditions. Fischer was sentenced to death and beheaded on 8 July 1966 with a guillotine. (See Mattogno

2016a, and the many health-related entries in Mattogno 2023, Part 1, for details).

FLAMES, OUT OF CREMATORY CHIMNEYS

All crematorium furnaces in German wartime camps, including Auschwitz and Birkenau, were fired by coke (which is a purified, high-carbon form of coal). Even those furnaces initially equipped with oil burners were retro-fitted with coke hearths during the war, due to lack of oil. Coke is a fuel that burns clean and develops only very short flames, if any. Such flames are hardly able to leave the hearth of a cremation furnace, let alone traverse the length of a cremation muffle. They certainly could neither reach the smoke ducts nor enter the chimney, let alone exit from it.

The only other source of flames in a coke-fired cremation furnace is therefore the corpse burning inside of it. However, as shown in both controlled experiments and civilian crematoria, flames could never travel the entire length from the muffle through the smoke ducts and the chimney stacks – a distance of some 21 to 26 meters (70 to 85 feet) in case of Birkenau Crematoria II and III – unless an enormous amount of fat were released and burned in the muffle in a very short period of time. This happens only during the cremation of severely obese people, whose cremation can indeed lead to an entire cremation building catching fire. Since severely obese people were virtually nonexistent among the impoverished Jewish masses deported to Auschwitz during the war, and because the small muffle doors would not have allowed the introduction of severely obese people in any case, such a scenario can safely be excluded.

Another possible scenario is a brief flaming-out of thick layers of soot deposited on the inside of a chimney duct, but it takes years of operation for so much soot to deposit – and a lack of chimney maintenance by chimney sweeps. Since the Auschwitz crematoria existed only for a few years, they did not have enough time to accumulate significant amounts of soot for such chimney fires to occur.

Any flames exiting a crematorium chimney would have meant that the entire system of ductwork was exposed to extreme heat, given that such flames create temperatures easily beyond 1,000 °C. Neither ducts nor chimneys were designed to resist such temperatures and would have quickly cracked and collapsed, leading to the affected facility being incapacitated for weeks or months. Hence, if any flame had ever been observed exiting from a cremation chimney, it would have alarmed all those trying to keep those facilities operational, and preventative measures would have been implemented instantly. (For details, see Mattogno 2004b; Mattogno/Deana, Part 1, pp. 382-387.)

For some reason, claims of flame-belching chimneys are limited almost exclusively to the cremation facilities of Auschwitz and Birkenau. The following witnesses have testified about this (see the person's entry for sources, if none is given here):

– anonymous women from Szolyva, Hungary (Mattogno 2021, p. 198)
– Yehuda Bacon
– Charles S. Bendel
– Ada Bimko
– Pery Broad
– Eliezer Eisenschmidt
– Bela Fabian
– Viktor Frankl
– Arnold Friedman
– Chaim Frosch
– Hungarian Auschwitz inmate I.M. (Mattogno 2021, p. 380)
– Pelagia Lewińska
– Filip Müller
– Miklos Nyiszli
– David Olère
– Anany S. Petko & Vladimir Y. Pegov (Mattogno 2021, p. 211)
– Henryk Tauber
– Marie-Claude Vaillant-Couturier
– Siegfried van den Bergh
– Shlomo Venezia
– Janda Weiss
– Albert Widmann
– Elie Wiesel

A review of mainly French literature has found more examples, among them (see Plantin 2023):

– Lucie Adelsberger
– Adolf Bartelmas
– Margarete Buber-Neumann
– Henry Bulawko
– Gilbert Debrise
– Fania Fénelon
– Nelly Gorce
– Nadine Heftler
– Denise Holstein
– Oswald Kaduk
– Annette Kahn

- C. Kalb
- Sylvain Kaufmann
- Primo Levi
- Renée Louria
- Françoise Maous
- Edmond Michelet
- Liana Millu
- Pierre Nivromont
- Elisa Springer
- Paul Steinberg
- Georges Straka
- Germaine Tillion
- Béatrice de Toulouse-Lautrec

FLIAMENBAUM, DAVID

David Fliamenbaum (born 1924) was incarcerated in Auschwitz-Birkenau, where he was encountered by Soviet troops upon their occupation of the area. During an interview conducted on 1 March 1945, he claimed to have witnessed various atrocities. Fliamenbaum claims to have been made an apprentice in a masons' school with 600 other boys and young men. Within a short period of time, two thirds of all apprentices were allegedly slain by the teacher. However, a detailed study of the rich extant documentation of that school proves Fliamenbaum's story to be utterly fictitious (Jastrzębska 2008). Neither the claimed mass murder of its apprentices, nor the names of the people he accuses as the perpetrators, nor the deployment of these apprentices at various construction sites has anything to do with reality.

Fliamenbaum's description of Crematorium II, which he claims to have helped construct, is superficial, and his description of the extermination process – from undressing through gassing to cremation of the victims – is filled with inaccuracies and false claims, making it clear that he cannot have this knowledge from personal experience. For example, he claimed that two bodies were inserted into each cremation muffle, which then burned to ashes within just 15 minutes. However, these furnaces could cremate only one body within an hour.

It is furthermore inconceivable that a teenage mason's apprentice who may have been involved in laying bricks during the initial construction phase was allowed to be inside the building after its completion, so that he could witness the gassing of a batch of 2,000 Jews from beginning to end, as he claims, including the issuance of towels and soap to the victims – a wasteful practice that most certainly would not have happened.

Although Fliamenbaum could not possibly have any knowledge about cremation capacities, the number of arriving deportation trains, or the number of deportees in each of them, he nevertheless made statements about it as if he were running the camp. His statements included absurdly exaggerated cremation capacities, and inflated numbers of Jews allegedly gassed during the months for which he claimed to have intimate knowledge:

> "In June, July, August and September [1943], an average of 3 to 6 transports arrived per day. Each transport contained from 1,000 to 1,500 people, of whom no less than 85-90% went to the crematorium."

This would amount to between 360,000 and one million Jews killed during those four months alone. Meanwhile, orthodox Polish propaganda-historian Danuta Czech claims only some 52,000 gassing victims for that time period (Czech 1990; for details, see Mattogno 2021d, pp. 230-235).

Fliamenbaum is the typical case of a witness who, from his perspective as a simple working deportee who had little insight into what was unfolding around him, could not have known much at all, but could not resist the urge to claim to know everything, and that he partook in all relevant events that Polish and Soviet propaganda were claiming at that time.

FLORSTEDT, HERMANN

Hermann Florstedt (18 Feb. 1895 – 5 April 1945), SS *Standartenführer* since 1938, served in the Sachsenhausen Camp from 1940 until 1942, when he was transferred to the Majdanek Camp, becoming its third commandant.

Florstedt was soon investigated by the SS-internal court system for suspicion of embezzling inmate property and murdering inmates to cover up his crimes. He was arrested but never tried due to the ongoing war. He is said to have been executed by the SS on 5 April 1945, just prior to the collapse of the Third Reich.

FLOSSENBÜRG

Stephen Pinter, the U.S. chief investigator preparing the prosecution against former staff members of the Flossenbürg Camp after the war, came to the conclusion that no homicidal gas chamber ever existed at that camp. Today, all historians agree with that conclusion. That didn't stop former inmates from making gas-chamber claims, though, as it was fashionable for "witnesses" during the first few decades after

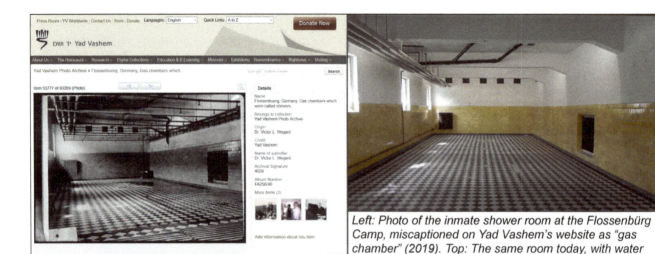

Left: Photo of the inmate shower room at the Flossenbürg Camp, miscaptioned on Yad Vashem's website as "gas chamber" (2019). Top: The same room today, with water pipes removed, and with large windows shown.

the war to claim gas chambers for every camp. One such person was Arnold Friedman, who, in his 1972 book *Death Was Our Destiny*, wrote that the SS tried to gas him at Flossenbürg, but that he managed to survive by breathing through the door's keyhole – as if homicidal gas-chamber doors are locked with simple keys… (See the entry on Arnold Friedman for an excerpt.)

For the longest time, even the Yad Vashem Archives had a photograph of the Flossenbürg inmate shower room, mendaciously and maliciously mislabeled as follows:

"*Flossenbürg, Germany, Gas chambers, which were called showers.*"

It used to have Archival Signature 4029, Album No. FA256/40 (retrieved online in 2019), but it seems to have been removed since. Had this photo been taken from a different angle, showing the many windows in this real, once-working shower room (see the illustrations), no skeptical mind would have ever believed it.

FORT IX

The city of Kaunas, Lithuania, has nine 19th-century fortresses surrounding the entire city. Some of them were used as NKVD prisons after the Soviet Union's invasion of the Baltic states in 1940. During the German occupation of the area, these prisons served to detain and presumably kill Jews from the Kaunas Ghetto and deported from Germany.

While the reports by the *Einsatzgruppen* mention the execution of 10,562 plus "thousands" more at Kaunas, Fort IX is not explicitly mentioned in them. The Jäger Report of early December 1941, however, tallies 3,420 Jews executed at Fort IV, 3,238 Jews at Fort VII, 16,013 at Fort IX, and 534 Jews killed at an unspecified fort. Some 5,000 of the Jews executed at that fort are said to have been German Jews sent to Kaunas allegedly for "resettlement," but who were instead all killed on arrival, if we are to believe the orthodox narrative. The other victims are all said to have been Jews from the local ghetto.

The Jäger Report has several problematic features, among them that its data are not corroborated by the *Einsatzgruppen's* Event Reports. Witness testimonies on the alleged exhumation and burning of corpses from the claimed mass graves of this execution site are highly problematic. They make a string of claims that are technically impossible. This is particularly true for the testimony of Alex Faitelson (see this entry for more details).

German wartime documents confirm that during the night from 25 to 26 December 1943, 63 Jews escaped from Fort IX. On 26 December 1943, eleven of them signed a declaration written in the classical style of Soviet propaganda. In it, they claimed that their group of initially 72 prisoners, shackled with steel chains, had been forced to exhume and burn some 12,000 bodies from 4½ mass graves between 1 November and 25 December 1943. Some 5,000 of them were German Jews, while 7,000 were from Kaunas. How they could know this is unknown. The signatories estimated that 9½ more mass grave had not yet been processed when they fled. Hence, a total of some 40,000 victims were presumably buried in all graves taken together – not the 16,013 listed in the Jäger Report.

Cremating an average human body during open-air incinerations requires some 250 kg of freshly cut wood. Cremating 12,000 bodies thus requires some

3,000 metric tons of wood. This would have required the felling of all trees growing in a 50-year-old spruce forest covering some 7 hectares of land, or some 15 American football fields. An average prisoner is rated at being able to cut some 0.63 metric tons of fresh wood per workday. To cut this amount of wood within 55 days would have required a work force of some 87 dedicated lumberjacks just to cut the wood.

Yet these eleven witnesses claim that their team of 72 prisoners had their legs chained together and merely removed corpses from graves, built pyres with wood, piled bodies onto the wood piles, burned them down, ground the cremation remains to powder, and mixed it with the soil. The firewood needed was just magically there.

One witness provided a description of the pyres allegedly used for these outdoor cremations. Around 300 bodies are said to have been placed on a pyre measuring 4 m × 4 m, hence covering a surface area of 16 m². This pyre was lit using explosive charges – which would have scattered body parts and wood all over the area.

Assuming a requirement of 250 kg of green wood per body, an average specific weight of 0.9 for the wood, a stacking density of the pyre of 1.4 (40% of free space for air and flames to go through), the volume of the wood would have been (250 kg/body × 300 bodies ÷ 900 kg/m³ × 1.4 =) approximately 117 m³; plus another 8 m³ for the bodies (average weight due to severe decomposition: 26 kg), the pyre would have been (125 m³ ÷ 16 m² =) almost 8 meters high!

A Soviet investigative commission was not satisfied with the death toll claimed by the eleven signatories, hence they increased it to 70,000 in their report.

(For more details, see the entries on the Jäger Report, Alex Faitelson, as well as Mattogno 2022c, pp. 656-668.)

FRANCE

France's role in the Holocaust was twofold. First, during the German occupation of northern France, the French government in southern France collaborated with the German authorities and agreed to have those Jews living in France deported to Auschwitz who either had no French citizenship or who had obtained it only recently. The deportation lists have been preserved and were published in 1978 by Serge Klarsfeld. They contain 75,720 names.

The second aspect of France's role unfolded after the war, when French prosecutors and investigators sought to bolster the case of Allied prosecutors that horrendous crimes against humanity had been perpetrated by German forces and officials during the war. This aspect of France's contribution to postwar propaganda is discussed in detail in the section on France of the entry on propaganda. Hence, the following will focus on the fate of the Jews deported from France.

The French police recorded the names, birth dates and birth places of all Jews deported toward Auschwitz. At Auschwitz, those Jews who were registered in the camp were recorded with the same data – at least theoretically. Practically, some variations in the way names and towns are spelled do occur, but for the most part, these differences still allow an identification. If a person registered in the camp died, the Auschwitz camp authorities registered that death in a number of documents, most prominent among them in the Death Books (*Sterbebücher*; see the entry on the Auschwitz Death Books). Forty-six volumes of these Death Books have survived the war, covering all of 1942 and most of 1943.

A person-by-person comparison of the deportation lists with all entries in the Death Books and some other extant documents on deceased Auschwitz inmates reveals the fate of those deportees who were admitted into the camp.

Altogether 45 transports with Jews from France were deported to Auschwitz in 1942, almost all of which contained roughly 1,000 deportees. All deportees transported with the first six trains leaving for Auschwitz between March and mid-July 1942 were admitted and properly registered in the camp. Then things started changing due to the typhus epidemic raging at Auschwitz, which led to a complete lockdown of the camp on 23 July 1942. Of the next seven trains arriving in late July 1942, the majority of inmates was still admitted to the camp, but a few were not. All later transports of 1942 had only a minority of usually a few hundred inmates or less registered at the camp.

Initially, the orthodoxy claimed that the inmates deported but not registered were killed on arrival in the "gas chambers." However, later research has revealed that an unknown number of deportees was taken off the train prior to its arrival at Auschwitz. The German authorities evidently decided to admit them to various labor camps in the larger region of Upper Silesia rather than exposing them to the unsafe conditions prevailing inside the Auschwitz Camp.

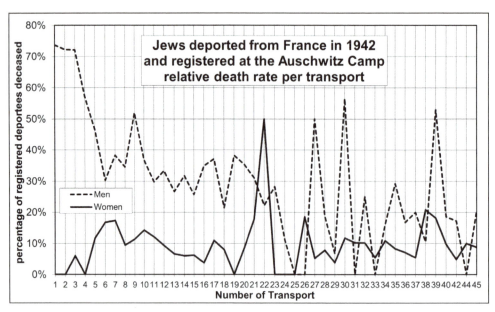

Other inmates may have stayed at Auschwitz only briefly, to be deported further east to other camps or ghettos. The documentation on this is very incomplete (see Rudolf 2019b).

The orthodoxy claims that those deemed unfit for labor were killed on arrival. However, up to mid-July, everyone was registered, even the very old and very young. From transports arriving later, many if not most adults in the prime of their working years (20 to 50 years of age) were *not* registered at Auschwitz – precisely because the stepped off the train elsewhere.

The data also shows that the mortality of the French Jews deported during the first four transports was shockingly high: between 50 and 70% of them died within the first two years of having been admitted to Auschwitz. The survival rate of deportees admitted later, on the other hand, was considerably better, although still catastrophic by any decent standard. (See the chart.) Women in general fared much better than men.

The highest death rate among the deportees from France occurred in August 1942 with 1,782 casualties. This coincides with the peak of mortality for the entire camp of 8,507 deceased inmates during that month, mainly due to the raging typhus epidemic. The available, incomplete documentation shows that almost half of all Jewish men deported from France and admitted to the camp died there, and some 10% of all admitted women. Since many later volumes of the Death Books are missing, the total number is most likely higher, although the mortality in general subsided considerably in late 1943 and in 1944 – only to escalate again toward the end of the war due to the generally catastrophic circumstances in collapsing Germany.

The orthodoxy considers only those Jews deported from France as survivors who returned to France after the war and registered there as a survivor. Precisely 2,566 of the originally deported 75,720 Jews did exactly that. However, most Jews deported from France were not French citizens but rather refugees from central and eastern Europe, and those who had French citizenship had obtained it only recently. Therefore, it stands to reason that many of them, displaced as they were, decided to emigrate elsewhere instead (Israel, USA etc.). But even if they returned to France, many may have distrusted French authorities and decided not to register with them. It is impossible to estimate how many might have made such a decision.

Either way, the Jews deported from France did indeed experience a *shoah* – catastrophe – at Auschwitz. However, this catastrophe did not occur in homicidal gas chambers, but rather due to the catastrophic hygienic and sanitary conditions.

(For more details, see Aynat 2023; Mattogno 2022b, pp. 101-105, 109, 116-118, 129.)

FRANK, ANNE

Despite her status as perhaps the most famous Holocaust victim, the story of Anne Frank has little direct bearing on the larger Holocaust narrative. In one sense, she was just one more Jewish victim of the evil Nazis. And yet, there is so much controversy around her famous diary that it threatens to expose deeper and more troubling aspects of what might be termed "Holocaust propaganda." These troubling aspects suggest much about how the conventional Holocaust story is marketed and promoted. Indirectly, then, Anne's story has value for understanding the present-day phenomenon of the Holocaust.

The basics of Anne's life story are relatively clear. She was born Annelies Marie Frank, in Frankfurt, Germany, on 12 June 1929. She was the youngest of the two Frank girls, her older sister Margot having been born in 1926. Anne's parents, Otto and Edith, lived a fairly conventional middle-class life in Frankfurt – Otto was a small businessman – until the rise of Adolf Hitler's National-Socialist party in 1933, at which time they decided to flee to the Netherlands. Anne and her family moved to Amsterdam in February 1934 when she was four years old. There she attended school, becoming quite fluent in Dutch, which became the primary language of the Frank family. Germany invaded the Netherlands in May 1940, putting new pressure on Dutch Jews, all of whom now had to adopt a low-profile existence. Eventually, the Frank family, along with another Jewish family of three and a dentist, went into hiding in an "annex" of her father's office building in central Amsterdam. They lived in hiding, more or less continuously, for around two years.

Sometime in mid-1944, perhaps early August, the Frank family was exposed, apprehended, and deported to the Westerbork transit camp, and soon thereafter on to Auschwitz in the south of present-day Poland. At Auschwitz, Otto was separated from the three female members of his family. He stayed in the camp until its liberation in January 1945, but the two Frank girls were shipped on to Bergen-Belsen Camp in October 1944. (Edith died in Auschwitz.) Like many camps late in the war, Bergen-Belsen had a large outbreak of typhus. Apparently, both girls contracted the disease and died in February or March 1945. Anne's body was never found. She was 15 years old.

Unfortunately, these few sketchy details are about all that we can say with certainty about Anne/Annelies Frank. Everything else that we think we know about her is in doubt: what she wrote, how much she wrote, what she did during her 10 years in Amsterdam, what life was like during her two-year "hideout" in the annex of her father's office building, and so on. Most importantly, we literally do not know how much, if any, of the famous diary was written by her. And if Annelies was not the author of the diary – then who was? When did they write it? And why?

Annelies Frank

For many years, the most prominent critic of the Anne Frank diary was a French professor of text and testimonial critique, Dr. Robert Faurisson – see in particular his 1982/1985 essay "Is the diary of Anne Frank genuine?" With his passing in 2018, new scholars have taken up the challenge. Among the most important of recent studies is *Unmasking Anne Frank* (2022) by Japanese scholar Ikuo Suzuki. He cites the following problems and anomalies:

– The rewritten ("B") version contains numerous trivial and arbitrary changes from the "original" A-version. There is no obvious explanation for this.
– The version made public is a highly edited version of the "B" draft, now called the "C"-version.
– Another Jewish writer, Meyer Levin, got involved with Anne's father Otto very early on; there is good reason to suspect that he in fact was the author.
– Translations into other languages make arbitrary and factually incorrect translations of many words and phrases.
– There are many irreconcilable problems with eight people living in an attic for two years: food, bathing, trash disposal, toilets, etc.
– Anne includes many highly-mature passages about human sexuality, her own sexual organs, and so on – very unlikely for a 13- or 14-year-old girl.
– Despite being a virtual "genius writer," Anne wrote nothing more between her deportation in mid-1944 and her death in March 1945, despite many clear opportunities to do so.
– The Germans transferred Anne away from Auschwitz, presumably a "gas-chamber" camp, to Bergen-Belsen, which had no gas chambers.

For Suzuki, all this is evidence that (a) the diary cannot possibly be the actual transcriptions of a teenage girl in wartime Amsterdam, (b) someone – likely Anne's father Otto and Meyer Levin – conspired to foist upon the world a bogus story of an innocent young girl and her death, and (c) large portions of the Holocaust story itself were likely also edited, embellished, altered and rewritten, as the need arose.

Holocaust critics sometimes like to refer to the "ballpoint pen" issue: "significant" portions of the diary were allegedly written in such a pen, even though it did not exist until after the war. They use this claim as evidence of fraud. In reality, there are only two attached notes written in ballpoint, and clearly distinct from the diary itself. Hence, no serious scholar today cites the ballpoint-pen claim. But orthodox scholars will still bring it up, only to shoot it down, in strawman-like fashion, as a way of distracting from the many other, very serious issues with the diary.

FRANK, HANS

Hans Frank

Hans Frank (23 May 1900 – 16 Oct. 1946) was governor of occupied Poland (called General Government) during the war. Four of the so-called extermination camps – Belzec, Majdanek, Sobibór and Treblinka – were on the territory he governed. (The territories where Auschwitz and Chełmno were located had been annexed by the Third Reich). Therefore, Hans Frank should have known what was transpiring in these camps.

He was a defendant during the Nuremberg International Military Tribunal (IMT). During his testimony at the IMT (Vol. 12, pp. 7-45), he claimed that he had not been informed at all as to what happened in those camps. He asserted that he had conducted his own investigation in this regard, because he had heard rumors spread by enemy media about the camps at Majdanek, Belzec and Auschwitz. He testified that his inquiries did not confirm the rumors (*ibid.*, pp. 17-19).

Frank kept a massive service diary, which in the end comprised 43 volumes of grandiloquent verbosity. Passages from it were introduced by the prosecution during the IMT. Here are a few of his pertinent statements (*IMT*, Vol. 29, starting at p. 354):

– On 12 July, and again on 25 July 1940, he reports that occupied Poland will no longer be the destination for more transports of Jews. He reveals that, after a pending peace treaty, all Jews will be deported "to an African or American colony. The talk is of Madagascar." (pp. 378, 405)
– On 20 December 1940, he mentioned that he "could not drive out all lice and Jews within just one year." (p. 416)
– 22 January 1940: Frank states during a speech that he doesn't care whether the Jews end up in Madagascar or anywhere else, but he would prefer it if they shuffle back to Asia where they came from. (p. 469)
– 13 October 1941: During a meeting with Alfred Rosenberg, minister for the occupied eastern territories, Frank suggests expelling Jews from the Government General into the occupied territories. Rosenberg stated that this was already in process, but would take some time. (Rudolf/Mattogno 2017, pp. 269f.)
– 17 October 1941: As a result of a governmental meeting, it is stated that a final clarification of the "Jewish Question" will be possible only once the complete deportation of all Jews can be accomplished. (*IMT*, Vol. 29, p. 494)
– 20 November 1941: Frank announces that the Polish Jews would ultimately be transferred further east. (Kulischer 1943, pp. 110f.)
– 16 December 1941: With reference to Hitler's "prophetic" speech of 30 January 1939 (see the entry on Adolf Hitler), Frank states during a governmental meeting that "we have to do away with the Jews," and continues:

"[…] *if the Jewish tribe in Europe survives the war, while we have sacrificed our best blood in the protection of Europe, then this war will only have been partly successful. Basically, therefore, with regard to the Jews, I must simply assume that they are to disappear. They will have to go. I have initiated negotiations for the purpose of deporting them to the east. In January, there will be a big conference on this matter in Berlin* [Wannsee Conference], *to which I will send State Secretary Dr. Bühler. This conference will be held in the Reich Security Main Office of SS Obergruppenführer Heydrich. A great Jewish migration will set in at any rate.*

But what is supposed to happen to the Jews? Do you think they are going to be housed in settlement villages in the eastern territories? They've told us in Berlin: What's all the fuss? We cannot do anything with them, either in the eastern territories or in the Reich Commissariat [occupied Ukraine], *liquidate them yourselves!* […]

We must destroy the Jews, wherever we find them, in order to maintain the overall structure of the Reich here. […]

Currently there are in the Government General [occupied Poland] approximately 2½ million, and together with those who are kith and kin and connected in all kinds of ways, we now have 3 ½ million Jews. We cannot shoot these 3 ½ million Jews, nor can we poison them, yet we will have to take measures which will somehow lead to the goal of annihilation, and that will be done in connection with the great measures which are to be discussed together with the Reich. The territory of the General Government must be made free of Jews, as is the case in the Reich. Where and how this will happen is a matter of the means which must be used and created, and about whose effectiveness I will inform you in due time." (IMT, Vol. 29, pp. 502f.)

Hence, according to Frank, it was *not* possible to shoot or poison these Jews at a time when – if we follow the orthodox narrative – Jews were *already* being poisoned in so-called "gas vans" at the Chełmno Camp, and shot in masses by the *Einsatzgruppen*. This means that Frank was either clueless, he lied to his audience, or it didn't happen. Of course, the Wannsee Conference anticipated by Frank decided upon deporting the Jews and/or putting them to forced labor, not to shoot or poison them.

There are other references to Jews in Frank's diary, always with reference to evacuation, emigration or deportation (18 March 1942, 15 January 43, 18 November 1943; pp. 571f., 629, 644f.). On 4 March 1944, however, with the war going badly for Germany, he got again more radical when polemicizing (p. 687):

"The Jews are a race that must be effaced. Wherever we catch one, he is coming to an end."

FRANKE-GRICKSCH, ALFRED

Alfred Franke-Gricksch (30 Nov. 1906 – 18 Aug. 1952), SS *Obersturmbannführer*, was an SS bureaucrat. He was arrested by the Soviets in 1951 in East Berlin, and after a show trial in Moscow, he was sentenced to death and executed for his alleged propaganda, espionage and counter-revolutionary activities, but not for any involvement in mass-murder activities. In 1995, the Russian legal authorities, after reviewing his case, rehabilitated him (Roginskij *et al.*, pp. 158f.).

His importance to the Holocaust derives from his participation in an inspection trip to several German wartime camps in Poland, Auschwitz among them. Franke-Gricksch wrote a report about it, which unfortunately has been lost. We know of it only due to an English translation prepared by the British and kept in the British National Archives. It contains a long description of the Auschwitz camp complex that is completely innocuous. The report also contains a brief definition of the *"Aktion Reinhardt,"* here called "special enterprise REINHARD":

"This branch has had the task of realising all mobile Jewish property in the Gouvernement Poland."

The British analysts of this document concurred when writing in their summary:

"Sonderaktion 'Reinhard'.
This special unit deals with the seizure of Jewish property."

We recall that the three Reinhardt camps – Belzec, Sobibór, and Treblinka – were allegedly pure extermination camps; but this report suggests that they were rather about confiscating Jewish property and then deporting the affected individuals.

An alleged "supplement" to the innocuous travel report also exists. It has no letterhead, date, signature, stamp or any element that links it either to Franke-Gricksch or to the claimed trip. It describes the alleged extermination procedure of Jews at Auschwitz by way of mass gassings inside one of the Auschwitz crematoria. The text contains numerous architecturally, chronologically and technically impossible claims, as well as victim numbers and cremation capacities that contradict even the orthodox narrative. It is highly likely that this document was based on false figures found in atrocity reports spread by the Polish underground during the war.

The first version of this "supplement" was typed – in faulty German – by Eric Lipmann, an American Jew employed by the U.S. occupational authorities to collect German documents useful for indicting German wartime leaders. His text was then retyped in an improved version, a carbon copy of which was then placed in a German archive. This "document" was never used in any trial, and could not have been used either, since it has no identifying hallmarks and because an original evidently does not exist. This mockery of a document has been used by mainstream historians since 1982 in support of their claim regarding mass gassings at Auschwitz.

(See Renk 1991; Mattogno 2019, pp. 97-205; Mattogno 2021a, pp. 101-119.)

FRANKFURT AUSCHWITZ SHOW TRIAL

Background

Before the investigations for the great Frankfurt Auschwitz trial started, the German government was reluctant to evaluate the contents of eastern European archives. Offers by communist countries were conceived as attempts to destabilize West Germany with propaganda, potentially falsified evidence and manipulated witnesses. This resistance, however, collapsed under the lobbying of various pressure groups interested in a West-German Auschwitz trial, among them foremost the International Auschwitz Committee. This organization, which was headed by the communist former Auschwitz inmate Hermann Langbein, was initially headquartered in Polish – *i.e.*, Stalinist-ruled – Krakow. Therefore, it clearly was a communist organization with political objectives.

Langbein used Adolf Rögner, another former Auschwitz inmate, as a pawn to initiate the West-German investigations on Auschwitz. During the late 1950s, Rögner, an incorrigible, pathological liar with multiple convictions for swindling, forgery, and perjury, was in prison, serving time for his crimes. Due to his record of false accusations, his right to testify as a witness had been revoked permanently.

Langbein provided Rögner with literature and documents on Auschwitz. With plenty of time on his hands, Rögner consumed this material and cooked up an avalanche of wild accusations against numerous former members of the SS camp staff, claiming to have knowledge of thousands of crimes committed.

The prosecutor handling the case correctly assessed Rögner's submissions as the dishonest statements of a sick and vindictive mind. However, he was eventually ordered by his superiors to press charges anyhow, because "it concerns an important investigation case, in which the Ministry of Justice is very interested." Hence, the German political class made a U-turn from rejecting communist atrocity propaganda to embracing it uncritically. The case was eventually assigned to the Frankfurt judiciary, where Jewish public prosecutor Fritz Bauer took charge of the criminal investigations.

Langbein and his organization were subsequently pivotal in liaising between the German judiciary and the communist propagandists in Poland's Department of Justice, as well as the Auschwitz State Museum. Langbein and his organization were also helpful in locating and motivating former camp inmates to testify. After the trial, both prosecutors and judges thanked Langbein and his organization in a letter for their invaluable support in preparing and conducting the trial.

During the pre-trial investigations, some 1,400 persons were interrogated. Only those statements that confirmed the imputed crimes were considered relevant. Any witness unable to confirm atrocities, mass gassings or murder, was usually ignored. After all, a person who has not witnessed anything is not a witness. With that logic, any claim about any event is automatically considered true, since anyone stating that it did *not* happen simply is not a witness.

The Polish government was particularly active with preparatory measures in the background. As Langbein was stirring up Rögner to harass public prosecutors, the Polish Auschwitz State Museum was busy writing the camp's official history. This history, written by the museum's historian Danuta Czech, was published in the Auschwitz Museum's own periodical *Zeszyty Oświęcimskie* starting in 1958, and with a little delay also in the museum's German-language periodical *Hefte von Auschwitz*. Considering that Poland showed genocidal hostility toward anything German in those immediate postwar years, the choice of the German language for this periodical points to the real target audience: the German judiciary, enlightened about all this thanks to the liaison work by Hermann Langbein. And in fact, the distorted narrative presented in these publications was to form the framework, into which the Frankfurt judges would force all evidence to come.

The Polish efforts to write an "official" version of Auschwitz history had another aspect: They needed a uniform script which the witnesses could learn before going to Frankfurt to testify. During the trial, the defense found out that the witnesses who had traveled to Germany from countries of the eastern Communist Bloc, had all been interrogated for their political trustworthiness by various communist authorities prior to their journey. On that occasion, the testimonies of these witnesses were also streamlined to bring them in line with the script developed by the Auschwitz Museum. When travelling to Frankfurt, those witnesses were accompanied at every step by officials of the same communist authorities, even inside the courtroom, in order to make sure that no one would deviate from the official party line. Unfazed by this scandal, Germany's Supreme Court later brushed off these facts as no reason to declare a mistrial. Political interests were more important than justice.

Organizations of former inmates supplemented this by providing "information material" to all witnesses, and by organizing meetings in Frankfurt for all arriving witnesses prior to their testimony. During those meetings, they could exchange stories, "learn" from others about what was expected to be remembered, and adjust their upcoming testimonies to ensure that "justice" could be served.

Conduct

During the Frankfurt Auschwitz trial, 22 defendants were accused of homicides. All other alleged crimes had by then exceeded their statute of limitations, hence could no longer be prosecuted. Among the more-prominent defendants were:
- Wilhelm Boger, investigator of the camp's Political Department (camp Gestapo).
- Arthur Breitwieser, head of the inmate clothing department.
- Pery Broad, clerk at the camp's Political Department (camp Gestapo).
- Victor Caspesius, head of the camp pharmacy.
- Josef Klehr, male nurse
- Oswald Kaduk, *Rapportführer*.
- Hans Stark, clerk at the camp's Political Department (camp Gestapo).
- Robert Mulka, adjutant of the camp commandant.
- Karl Höcker, another adjutant of the camp commandant.

The trial lasted 185 sessions, from 20 December 1963 until 20 August 1965. In order to accommodate 22 defendants and their defense lawyers, but foremost to allow hundreds of members of the public to attend the proceedings, the hearings were conducted not in a normal courtroom, but, revealingly, in large-size assembly halls.

The defendants were treated by the prosecution, the witnesses, the audience and the media with insults, contempt, derision and mockery, without the court intervening. In fact, the judges joined the mob by displaying a similar attitude. Filming and photographing the defendants in the courtroom were unlawfully permitted, resulting in the defendants being besieged like zoo animals. During their statements, defense lawyers and defendants were interrupted by insults and even threats from courtroom spectators, again with no court intervention. In a public exhibition, the defendants were presented as already guilty.

The defense faced an accusatory body organized on a worldwide scale that had been operating uninterruptedly for 20 years, receiving exclusively incriminating evidence from all over the world. A defense against this deluge of accusations was basically impossible. This gross inequality of means is the reason why, under German law, the prosecution is also obligated to search and present exonerating evidence. But this *never* happened.

If a witness had something exonerating to say, it was usually turned on its head by the judges. For instance, former Jewish Auschwitz inmate Maryla Rosenthal had only positive memories of her time as a typist at the camp's Gestapo office. She knew of no atrocities. The judges talked her into believing that her experiences must have been so traumatic that she must have suppressed all memories of it. With that logic, any exonerating evidence can be – and was – turned into incriminating evidence.

The defense lawyers in this court case failed catastrophically. None of the 360 witnesses who testified during the trial were ever cross-examined about the veracity of extermination claims made. No defense lawyer, let alone judge or prosecutor, ever asked for any material confirmation of the crimes claimed; for any expert report on cremation technology; on fumigation technology; on the toxicology of hydrogen cyanide; on the chemistry of Zyklon B; on homicidal gas chambers such as they exist in the United States; on forensic evidence from corpses examined; on exhumations of claimed mass graves; on an expert assessment of blueprints provided; or on getting unlimited access to the camp authorities' wartime files as stored in the Auschwitz Museum's archives.

In the verdict, the judges themselves admitted that they had none of the usual evidence present at a murder trial. The court

> *"lacked the bodies of the victims, autopsy records, expert reports on the cause of death and the time of death; it lacked any trace of the murderers, murder weapons, etc. An examination of the eyewitness testimony was only possible in rare cases."*

But that was so only because no one ever tried.

Defense lawyer Laternser, who had defended clients both during the IMT and the Frankfurt Auschwitz trial, characterized the atmosphere during the latter as having been much worse than that which prevailed during the Nuremberg trials. In fact, a comparison of this trial's features with that of the medieval witch trials reveals shocking parallels. (See the entry on witch trials.)

Repercussions

The Great Frankfurt Auschwitz Trial was a watershed event in German history, similar to the 1961 Eichmann Show Trial in Israel. During this trial, the German mass media for the first time managed to direct massive public attention to alleged National-Socialist mass-murder crimes within what is today called "the Holocaust." With this trial, the German authorities full-heartedly joined the efforts of Jewish (and non-Jewish) pressure groups, as well as the governments of East and West alike, to face the ugly German past, learn from it, atone for it, and hold the National-Socialist criminals accountable.

Such a show trial on this topic is very much in line with the tradition of all of Germany's occupying powers, including Israel. Hence, nothing was learned from history – other than that show trials are useful for distorting the historical record.

The superficial conclusions of this trial regarding mass-murder allegations with Zyklon-B gas chambers at Auschwitz are based almost exclusively on false witness testimony. Yet still, these conclusions are the foundation upon which the German judiciary subsequently based its dogma that everything about Auschwitz is self-evident, common knowledge, and in no need to be proved again. Attempts at challenging the fraudulent Auschwitz narrative cast into legal stone at Frankfurt were later made illegal. In this regard, history itself is dictated *by penal law* in Germany and many other nations.

This act of totalitarian thought-control is far beyond even what the National-Socialist German government ever dreamed of imposing on its people.

(For more information, see the entry on show trials, as well as Rudolf 2019, pp. 99-120; 2023, pp. 414-434.)

FRANKL, VIKTOR

Viktor Frankl (26 March 1905 – 2 Sept. 1997) was an Austrian Jew and Psychiatrist. In 1942, he and his family were deported to the Theresienstadt Ghetto. On 19 October 1944, he was deported to the Dachau subcamp Kaufering III, where he arrived on 25 October, after a brief layover of three days in the transit-camp section at Auschwitz.

After the war, he wrote a book about his experiences in the concentration camps. The English translation of this book, titled *Man's Search for Meaning*, became a huge bestseller in the U.S. In this book, Frankl gave the false impression that he spent considerable time at Auschwitz, when in fact he was never even admitted to the camp itself. He also claimed to have been liberated at Auschwitz in the spring of 1945, hence half a year after having been deported there, although Auschwitz was captured by the Red Army already on 27 January 1945.

Viktor Frankl

On the one hand, he reported about medical care that injured and sick inmates received at Auschwitz, but on the other hand, he also reported to have seen jets of huge flames shooting out of the crematorium chimneys. Because this was technically impossible, this is simply a lie. (See the entry on Flames, out of Crematory Chimneys.)

Frankl mentioned twice that he was pleased, in fact delighted, to see water really come out of the showerheads. Thus, he cleverly implied that, sometimes, gas must have come out through the showerheads – although he never explicitly wrote this.

In this book, Frankl often mixes his actual experiences with rumors, assumptions and insinuations, and wraps it all in a language of doom and gloom. It is the typical work of a psychiatrist whose life work is manipulating other peoples' minds.

Interestingly, the transport by which Frankl and his family were deported is mentioned in Danuta Czech's *Auschwitz Chronicle*. Only a few of the 1,500 Jews in this transport were admitted to that camp. The rest, Czech insists, were "killed in the gas chamber of Crematorium III." As usual, she does not provide any proof for this homicidal claim (Czech 1990, p. 736). Therefore, either Frankl was one of the miraculous and lucky few, or… no one was gassed at all. (For more details, see O'Keefe 2001; Schepers 2023.)

FRANZ, KURT

Kurt Franz (17 Jan. 1914 – 4 July 1998), SS *Oberscharführer*, was deployed as a guard at the Buchenwald Camp, and later as a cook at several institutions of the Third Reich's euthanasia action. In April 1942 he was assigned as a guard to the Belzec Camp. In September 1942, he became deputy commandant of the Treblinka Camp under Franz Stangl. When Stangl left in August 1943, Franz is said to have become camp commandant until the dissolution of the camp in November 1943. Franz, however, denied this, since he was an NCO, unable to take such a leadership position.

Kurt Franz

Together with nine other defendants, Franz was put on trial in 1964/65 for his involvement in the alleged gas-chamber mass murders at Treblinka, and sentenced to a life-long prison term. Throughout his trial and imprisonment, and even after his release due to poor health in 1993, he insisted that he was innocent and never killed or contributed to killing a Jew. Like the Demjanjuk Show Trial, the Düsseldorf Show Trial against Franz was characterized by some 100 Jewish witnesses telling the most absurd stories, none of which were ever challenged by the defense, and all of which were swallowed completely by the court, and as such entered the court record. The trustworthiness of these witnesses, or the lack thereof, can be assessed by the critical analysis of their testimonies as summarized in the respective entries. (See the section "Treblinka" of the entry on witnesses.)

This verdict established the legally-sealed "self-evident" truth about Treblinka. At the core, the verdict of the Düsseldorf Court states (Mattogno/Graf, pp. 162-169):

> *"The gas chambers, in which the Jews were killed by means of exhaust fumes of a diesel engine, formed the center of the death camp."*

But Diesel engine exhaust gases have such low toxicity that they are unsuited for the claimed mass murder.

Franz is a typical example of many alleged NS perpetrators who are said to have been sadistic beasts of epic proportion, but seemed absolutely harmless to anyone who ever met them afterwards, showed no signs of remorse or insight, and also exhibited no signs of post-traumatic stress behaviors, as would be expected for men involved in the brutal slaughter of hundreds of thousands of innocent victims. German public prosecutor Helge Grabitz once suggested that the conundrum of the defendants' strange behavior could be reasonably explained *only* by assuming that they were indeed innocent – but he immediately rejected this "seductive" explanation as cynical and as flying in the face of the evidence (Grabitz 1986, p. 147). This "evidence," however, consisted of nothing more than wild, unverified claims by hysterical witnesses testifying in a frenzied public atmosphere of lust for revenge and retribution, and of an obsessive tendency for self-denigration and a self-chastising guilt complex among the Germans.

FREIBERG, BER

Ber (or Berisch) Freiberg was an inmate of the Sobibór Camp. In three depositions of 10 and 18 August 1944 and 27 July 1945, he claimed that executions at Sobibór happened in just one gas chamber. A gas, perhaps chlorine, was produced by an electric machine, from where the gas was piped into gas tanks or cylinders, and from there through hoses or pipes into the chamber. The gassing was observed by an SS man through a roof window. After the murder, the floors opened, and the bodies were discharged into carts below, which brought them to mass graves.

All his claims are rejected as false by the orthodoxy, who insists on several gas chambers; on an engine producing lethal exhaust gas; on this gas being piped directly into the chambers; on no observation windows in the roof; and on no collapsible floor with carts underneath. The corpses were instead taken out of the chamber manually, sideways through a normal door.

Freiberg claimed in his 1945 deposition that he had no access to the camp sector where the gas chamber was allegedly located. However, in statements made in 1960 and 1965, he claimed to have been employed as a barber who cut off the hair of naked women "in a barracks in front of the gas chamber," which means he was employed in that very camp sector.

(See the entry on Sobibór for more details, as well as Graf/Kues/Mattogno 2020, pp. 79f., 94f., 105-107; Mattogno 2021e, pp. 73-75.)

FRIEDMAN, ARNOLD

Arnold Friedman was arrested during a raid in Slovakia and deported to Auschwitz in the spring of 1944, but survived his stay there. When the Auschwitz Camp was evacuated, Friedman ended up in the Flossenbürg Camp in northeastern Bavaria. Although all historians agree today that this camp had no facilities to mass murder inmates, in particular no homicidal gas chamber, Friedman disagreed with them by writing the following story in his 1972 book

Death Was Our Destiny (pp. 49f.):

> "*I stayed in the hospital* [at Flossenbürg Camp] *for three days and had good food and a rest.* […] *Then one evening, a lot of S.S. walked into the room and they ordered us to follow them. They ordered us into a room and locked the door. I heard a noise like a snake hissing, and then I heard the slave laborers shouting, 'They are gassing us!' I smelled an awful odor. Some of the men dropped dead. The rest of us ran around the room cursing the Nazis.*
>
> *I couldn't take it much longer and ran to the door and took hold of the knob and tried to open it. The door was locked. The smell of the gas got stronger. I coughed, and choked, and put my face to the keyhole and kept inhaling a little air from the outside.*
>
> *We had been in the room for about five minutes when I heard them outside the door talking in German. 'Let's see if some of them are still alive.' I went away from the keyhole and the door opened. For some reason which I could never figure out, God had saved me from the gas chamber. The S.S. shouted for us to go out. There were only five of us still alive; sixty lay behind, dead.* […]
>
> *Why hadn't the S.S. murderers finished the job in the gas room? No, I couldn't figure these things out.*"

Arnold Friedman

He couldn't figure it out because he made up the whole story. That wasn't the last time Friedman was caught lying. In 1985, he agreed to testify about his Auschwitz experiences at the first Zündel Trial. He and another testifier, Rudolf Vrba, were the only Holocaust witnesses ever to be cross-examined in a court of law by a skilled and skeptical interrogator. During his testimony, Friedman claimed the following, among other things (Rudolf 2020b, pp. 68, 69, 81):

> "*There was smoke belching from the crematories, and it gave us a constant smell – the crematories being close enough and low enough for the smoke to be dispersed through the camp rather than go straight up.* […] *Well, there was – the building that I described as a crematorium is a cottage-type low building with a short chimney protruding from it. At nighttime you saw the flames shooting above the chimney about a meter or two meters, depending on the particular time. There was smoke coming out,* […] *Well, it was the odour of burning flesh, and the flames were changing colours from yellow to a deep red on various occasions.* […] *We were discussing various things and this was part of the discussion of the guesswork we kids had in guessing that these were Hungarian transports because they have these type of flames, and these are Polish transports, they're very skinny,* […]"

Asked by the defense lawyer upon cross-examination whether he testified under oath that "skinny people" have "a different coloured flame" coming out of the crematorium chimney "than the fatter people," Friedman confirmed, "That was an opinion, yes, an opinion we formed" (*ibid.*, p. 82). A bit later, he added (*ibid.*, p. 88):

> "*I remember we distinguished them* [the skinny from the fat people], *that this is a clear yellow flame as opposed to a vermilion or pink type of flame, and the odour and so on.*"

Here we have doubly impossible nonsense that, first of all, no flames can come out of a crematorium chimney, and second, that the color of the flame with which people burn does not depend on their national origin or body weight. During cross-examination, when confronted with the fact that crematorium chimneys emit neither flames nor much smoke, Friedman eventually admitted that he didn't really know any of that from personal experience, but that he had simply repeated what others had told him (*ibid.*, p. 87):

> "*I don't know if I would have listened to you. Some time I would have listened to other people, maybe I would have attached more credibility to your portion than theirs, but at the time I accepted theirs.*"

When asked whether he ever heard rumors while in Auschwitz, Friedman answered: "Constantly" (*ibid.*, p. 78), which means that he, as so many other witnesses, likely converted rumors and stories that he had heard into events that he claimed to have witnessed himself.

FRIES, JAKOB

Jakob Fries was incarcerated at Auschwitz as a "professional criminal." When he was interrogated after the war in 1959 in preparation of the Frankfurt

Auschwitz Show Trial, he was still in prison, serving a 14-year prison term. At Auschwitz, Fries was foreman of all inmate labor units at the Auschwitz Main Camp. As such, his immediate superior was SS *Hauptsturmführer* Aumeier, head of the protective-custody camp and assistant commandant of Auschwitz. Fries therefore was likely much better informed than the average inmate about events unfolding in Auschwitz; yet even then, he could not confirm the usual atrocity stories about the camp, which he claims to have learned about only after the war through media reports (see Rudolf 2023, pp. 489f.).

FRITZSCH, KARL

Karl Fritzsch (10 July 1903 – 2 May 1945), SS *Hauptsturmführer*, was the head of the Protective-Custody Camp at the Auschwitz Main Camp from 14 June 1940 until 1 February 1942. Later he had that same role at the Flossenbürg Camp.

Karl Fritzsch

According to the demonstrably false postwar confessions of former Auschwitz commandant Rudolf Höss, Fritzsch supposedly invented the gassing of inmates using Zyklon B in late summer of 1941 while Höss was away on a business trip. During that so-called "first gassing" at Auschwitz, several hundred Soviet PoWs and a few hundred sick Polish inmates are said to have been gassed in the basement detention cells of Block 11 at the Auschwitz Main Camp, if we follow the current orthodox narrative. However, Soviet PoWs arrived at Auschwitz only in the fall of 1941.

This false story is nothing more than a character assassination by the perjurious Höss, who had been tortured into the submissive role of a confessing, contrite defendant by the British.

Fritzsch's date of death is only estimated, as he went missing at the end of the war.

(For more details, see the entries on Rudolf Höss and the first gassing at Auschwitz.)

FROSCH, CHAIM

Chaim Frosch, who claims to have been deported to Auschwitz on 30 April 1942, recorded a rather brief and terse undated account of his alleged experience in that camp, probably shortly after the war, which is now archived at the Yad Vashem Center in Jerusalem. He admitted having knowledge of extermination activities mainly – in other words, virtually entirely – from hearsay. His descriptions are both superficial and inaccurate. (Among other things, he claimed an unlikely capacity of 2,000 victims for the gas chambers of Crematoria II and III, hence some 10 people per m².) He is exposed as, at best, a mere rumormonger when describing the huge pyres allegedly set up in Birkenau in the spring and summer of 1944 for the open-air incineration of hundreds of thousands of Jews deported from Hungary allegedly murdered at that time. Air photos of the camp from that time provide irrefutable proof that this event has been invented from scratch. (For details, see Mattogno 2021, pp. 378f.)

Führer Order, *Führerbefehl* → Hitler Order

FUMIGATION GAS CHAMBER

When the link between infectious diseases, bacteria and bacteria-carrying pests (like insects or rodents) was discovered during the second half of the 19th Century, it quickly became apparent that this was a pivotal event in the history of human healthcare. Some of these pests were the vectors of major epidemic diseases, such as the body louse for typhus bacteria, and fleas for the plague.

While the plague was very much under control in the 20th Century, typhus was not. This often-lethal disease was still widespread (endemic) in Eastern Europe, where sanitary equipment was often very primitive, if it existed at all, and thus hygienic conditions were poor, treated water was unknown, sewage systems did not exist, and primitive outhouses were the standard everywhere. Lice and flea infestation was therefore quite common for all populations that could not (or would not) bathe, did not wash their clothes and bed linens regularly, and where there were no means of exterminating pests.

By the time of World War One, Germany's and Austria-Hungary's eastern borders were also the borders that separated hygienically advanced Central and Western Europe from areas where primitive hygienic conditions allowed diseases such as typhus to persist. It was in the first decades of the 20th Century that Germany started equipping its eastern border railway stations with large rail-car fumigation chambers, allowing the disinfestation of rail-cars coming in from Eastern Europe.

The increased and often uncontrolled traffic of

soldiers, civilians and merchandise between Central and Eastern Europe during both world wars led to hygienic crises in Germany, as lice infested with typhus bacteria were reintroduce in masses in Germany. Hot spots of those infestations were the various camps (refugee, labor, PoW, concentration, transit camps etc.) where people were housed in close quarters under poor hygienic conditions.

After World War One, a newly established German company, DEGESCH, became a leader in developing disinfestation gases and fumigation chambers, and issued licenses for their production and distribution. Among the various disinfestation methods used were hot steam, hot air, T-Gas, Areginal, Tritox, carbon monoxide produced by producer-gas generators, and Zyklon B. In German camps of the Second World War, hot steam and hot dry air, as well as Zyklon B, were commonly used for disinfestation purposes in a desperate attempt to control typhus epidemics. While hot steam and hot air also act as a *disinfectant*, meaning they also kill bacteria, Zyklon B does not; it merely kills the pests, such as lice or mice, that carry the bacteria. However, hot air and steam can damage fumigated objects, hence they are not suitable for all applications. In many cases, Zyklon B was the preferred method. Toward the end of the war, new techniques like DDT powder and microwave delousing facilities were introduced for pest-control at the Auschwitz Camp.

In principle, any enclosed or closable space can serve as a fumigation chamber, if the acting gas can be released in it in sufficient quantities during the gassing procedure. If the acting gas is poisonous to humans, and if the fumigated space is not air- or gastight, safety precautions must be taken to keep unprotected people away from the space by warning signs, physically-isolating the gassing facility (fences, walls, etc), and possibly by guards.

Carbon-Monoxide Fumigation

Already before World War One, the German medical professors Bernhard Nocht and Gustav Giemsa developed a fumigation method using carbon monoxide produced by a producer-gas generator. This device burned wood, coal or coke with limited amounts of oxygen, thus producing a gas that contained high amounts of carbon monoxide (CO). Since insects are not sensitive to carbon monoxide, this method is only suitable to kill warm-blooded pests, such as mice and rats. Before, during and after World War One, it was a very common method to combat mice and rats in freight ships.

Due to extreme shortage of any petroleum-based fuel in Germany during World War Two, the entire German road-transportation industry, incentivized by government decrees and subsidies, increasingly switched from liquid fuel to gas by installing mass-produced versions of producer-gas generators similar to those used for the Nocht-Giemsa fumigation method. In fact, these industrial models produced a gas that contained even more CO than the models used for fumigation, hence they were even more lethal. These devices were installed on trucks, buses, vans and even tanks. Their CO-rich gas was fed into the engine as fuel. Every German vehicle engineer knew about them during the war. They were easy to procure, cheap to operate, had endless fuel, and their gas would have been instantly lethal. In fact, specialists for fumigation and disinfestation, among them those who developed, produced, sold and applied Zyklon B, most likely knew these devices from the Nocht-Giemsa method. But there are no reports of any such device ever having been misused for murder, although they would have been the logical choice. (For details, see Rudolf 2019, pp. 463-467.)

Zyklon-B fumigations

Fumigations using the pesticide Zyklon B (hydrogen cyanide) became one of the most-commonly used methods of pest control between the two world wars. Initially, fumigation chambers were nothing more than ordinary rooms with sealed doors and (perhaps) windows, a heat source for the room, and equipment for some means of ventilation. The Zyklon-B carrier material – a chalk-like gypsum in the form of small

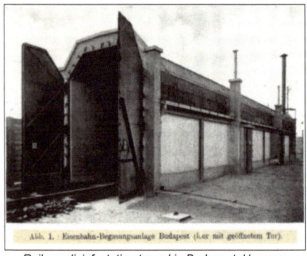

Railway disinfestation tunnel in Budapest, Hungary. (Peters 1938, pp. 98f.)

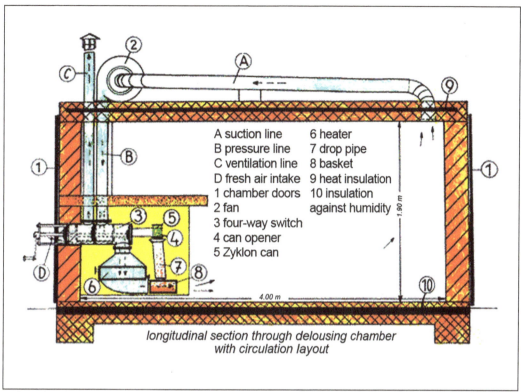

Longitudinal section through a Degesch Normal Gas Chamber with circulation layout (Gassner 1943).

pellets – soaked with liquid hydrogen cyanide, was simply spread out on the floor by a fumigation expert wearing a gas mask, who then retreated and locked the door. The gassing process could take many hours, even up to a day or two, depending on the size of the room, the type and density of materials placed in it, the room temperature, and the gas concentration reached with the applied quantity.

If there were any leaks in the chamber, or the heating system extracted any air (and thus also gas) from the chamber, concentrations could sink over time and reduce the efficacy of this method. Also, since the gas had to diffuse into the target objects, thick or dense objects might never become fully saturated, and thus complete success was never guaranteed.

Due to the many safety risks, German wartime regulations prescribed certain safety measures for these types of fumigation chambers:
- Whenever a person wearing a gas mask entered a fumigation chamber containing, or about to contain, poison gas, a second person had to remain outside behind the closed door, also wearing a gas mask, so that he could rush to help in case of an emergency.
- That second person had to observe the other entering the chamber through a window or (better) a peephole in the door.

Furthermore, since clothes were typically brought into these chambers hanging on metal racks on wheels, which might bang against the door, the peepholes were to have a metal protection grille on the inside to protect the glass pane from getting cracked by the metal racks. Multiple doors found in Auschwitz used to enclose fumigation chambers had such grille-protected peepholes. (See the entry on gastight doors.)

This haphazard and dangerous nature of Zyklon-B gassings was overcome only when DEGESCH introduced their so-called Normal Gas Chamber. In such a chamber, the room was sealed hermetically, heated electrically, and allowed remote opening of a Zyklon-B can and the dispersal of its pellets. Additionally, a heating device blew warm air over the pellets to evaporate and dissipate the gas quickly, and circulated the air in the chamber constantly to accelerate the procedure. Finally, there were ventilation mechanisms for quickly and safely evacuating the poison gas; see the construction drawing of a Normal Gas Chamber in the illustration.

The fumigation chambers at Dachau included similar systems, which still exist to this day. Nineteen such chambers were planned for the Auschwitz reception building, but they were never installed because the building construction proceeded quite slowly, and because an even newer and more-advanced system, based on microwaves, soon emerged, causing the camp administration to delay installation of any new Zyklon chambers.

(For further information, see the entry on microwave delousing, as well as Berg 1986, 1988; Rudolf 2020, pp. 68-90; 2019a, pp. 18-26.)

FURNACE

The term 'furnace' is commonly used for any industrial heating device used for the high-temperature processing or burning of material objects. The term 'oven,' in contrast, is commonly used for food-processing and -heating devices not intended to burn the food but rather to cook or heat it. Hence, a corpse cremation device is a *furnace*, while a microwave food-heating device is an *oven*.

A cremation furnace is a closed space heated by some heat source to an operating temperature of around 800-1000°C, rarely more, in order to completely burn organic tissue of either humans or animals. Such a furnace can have one or more spaces into which the organic tissue, or body, is placed, and which is usually called a 'retort' or a 'muffle.'

Cremation furnaces can have a wide variety of heat sources (wood, coke, oil, gas, electricity). Wood and coke-fired furnaces get their heat from heating spaces separate from the muffle, called a hearth or gas generator, since the incomplete burning of coke and wood in them produces a highly combustible gas rich in carbon monoxide that, when forced hot into the muffle, burns there upon contact with air or oxygen. This technology was widespread in Europe during World War II, and was also the technique used in the crematoria built in German wartime camps.

The term 'gas oven' is sometimes used in mainstream literature on the Holocaust. This refers both to cremation furnaces (using the wrong term "oven") as well as to homicidal gas chambers, but illegitimately mixes the two concepts. Strictly speaking, there is no such thing as a "gas oven" in terms of an oven in which people are gassed to death. Gas chambers and cremation furnaces are two separate devices that, technically speaking, have nothing to do with each other. One can construct a crematorium without any homicidal gassing capability, and one can construct a homicidal gassing facility without any cremation capacity. In fact, given the combustible nature of many gasses claimed to have been used most commonly for homicides in the Holocaust (carbon monoxide and hydrogen cyanide), it would be highly dangerous and foolhardy to construct a homicidal gassing facility using these gasses too close to a cremation facility. And yet, this is precisely what has been claimed of the Germans in case of Crematorium I at the Auschwitz Main Camp.

G

GABAI, DARIO

Dario Gabai (or Gabbai, 2 Sept. 1922 – 25 March 2020) was a Greek Jew deported to Auschwitz in March 1944. Possibly incentivized by his brother's interview with Israeli historian Gideon Greif a few years earlier (see the entry on Yaakov Gabai), Dario started giving his version of

Dario Gabai

events in numerous media venues, soon after his brother's death. Among these was an interview with the Shoah Foundation of the University of Southern California in late 1994. This interview, as many similar others, is characterized by the interviewer letting the subject ramble on with few interruptions by asking only occasional, superficial and often leading questions. Therefore, Gabai's statements typically include only fleeting remarks with few details, making it difficult to assess the reliability of what he claims.

During his interview with the Shoah Foundation, Gabai claimed that the SS forced between 2,500 and 3,000 inmates at once into the alleged gas chambers of Crematoria II and III (210 m²), a physically impossible packing density. Just 4 to 5 minutes after the gas had been applied, everyone was supposedly dead – a highly unlikely speed of execution (see Zyklon B). Only 15 to 20 minutes later, the doors were opened, after which the ventilation system of the room could not possibly have removed all the poisonous gas. When the doors were opened, all the dead victims were standing upright, mothers still with babies in their arms, which is physically impossible, because when dying, everyone would have slumped down and collapsed, no matter how densely they were packed. The victims were black and blue from the gas, Gabai claimed, although the allegedly used poison gas hydrogen cyanide turns victims pink, not black and blue.

When talking about the cremation of the victims, Gabai claimed that they put four corpses into every muffle, and that it took 20 to 30 minutes to cremate them. These figures are physically impossible (see the entry on crematoria) but they do match those that his brother had claimed during his interview with Greif. This suggests that Dario was simply expanding the web of lies begun by his brother.

In an interview segment included in the 2005 PBS documentary *Auschwitz: Inside the Nazi State*, Gabai is quoted as claiming that the inmates locked in the gas chamber of Crematoria II and III "scratched the walls." These walls were plastered with very hard cement mortar, multiple times harder than fingernails. It is therefore physically impossible for any person to scratch these walls.

– For excerpts from the Gabai interview with the Shoah Foundation, see Skorczewski 2015; video excerpts at https://youtu.be/jgrJ0jvy_sA;
– For a transcript of *Auschwitz: Inside the Nazi State*, see www.pbs.org/Auschwitz/transcripts.html.

GABAI, YAAKOV

Yaakov Gabai (or Gabbai, aka Ya'akov, Jaacov, Jacob; born in Athens in 1912) wrote a brief text about his alleged experiences in Auschwitz in 1983, almost four decades after the events, when asked to do so by Erich Kulka. Some ten years later, he was interviewed by Israeli historian Gideon

Yaakov Gabai

Greif. He arrived at Auschwitz from Greece on 11 April 1944.

Gabai's testimony given to Greif is riddled with claims and data about events that he, as a simple member of the crematoria stokers, could not possibly know, such as which transport arrived at Auschwitz from where, with how many inmates, how many people were presumably killed in all claimed killing facilities at Auschwitz, and what the overall capacity of these facilities were. Where his claims can be verified by wartime documents, Gabai's assertions turn out to be false, including:

- the distance from the railway ramp to the Birkenau Camp (3 km claimed by Gabai, versus 500 m according to maps.);
- the number of inmates working as stokers (750 claimed by Gabai, 315 according to documents);
- the number of Hungarian Jews cremated daily in mid-May (24,000 murdered and cremated claimed by Gabai, yet only some 5,000 Jews unfit for work arrived daily according to documents);
- the start of mass murder of Hungarian Jews (for Gabai the murder started in late April, but Hungarian Jews started arriving at Auschwitz only in mid-May 1944);
- the end of mass murder of Hungarian Jews (August for Gabai, yet the last train with Hungarian Jews arrived on 11 July);
- the percentage of inmates deemed "fit for labor" (Gabai claimed this was arbitrary, giving wildly divergent figures, while documents show that these assessments were made thoroughly);
- the names and ranks of SS men in charge of the crematoria (Gabai gave names and assigned SS ranks that are completely invented);
- the fate and date of the last transport from Greece (Gabai has it arrive at Auschwitz in late June 1944, with not a single inmate being registered, while the last transport from Greece in fact arrived on 16 August 1944, and the only one in June had more than 600 inmates getting registered);
- the number of transports arriving in August (almost none according to Gabai, but eight major transports arrived from the Łódź Ghetto);
- the month of the claimed Gypsy mass murder (June 1944 for Gabai, August for the orthodoxy, but the event is refuted by documentation);
- the murder of 2,500 Jews arriving on Yom Kippur, 4 October 1944 (there is no record of any such arriving transport);
- the event and number of victims of an inmate uprising (Gabai has Crema IV detonated and some 850 casualties, while Crema IV was only set on fire, and the orthodoxy claims 451 casualties);
- the sleeping arrangement for crematorium stokers (Gabai gave them all private rooms in the crematorium's attic, while blueprints show only one large common dormitory);

Interestingly, just like many other inmates interviewed by Greif (J. Sackar, S. Chasan, L. Cohen, E. Eisenschmidt), Gabai insisted that pits dug at Birkenau to burn the gassing victims by means of open-air incinerations were called "bunkers." He evidently had no knowledge of the make-shift gassing facility called "Bunker 2" which the orthodoxy claimed was in full operation during Gabai's time at Auschwitz. He insisted instead – and contrary to the orthodox narrative – that the victims gassed in the crematoria were dragged out into the fields next to the camp to be cremated there in pits.

Gabai moreover paid homage to the lore of human fat serving as fuel that "kept the fire going," although he added that firewood was used, too, and repeated the widespread but untrue claim that the crematoria spread a "stench of scorched human flesh." He repeated the standard figure of 2,000 victims fitting into the alleged gas chamber of Crematoria II and III, which at a packing density of almost 10 people per square meter would have required the utmost discipline and cooperation of all inmates in order to make it happen.

According to Gabai, the poison gas was introduced by throwing in "blue cubes" through "four openings in the ceiling of each gas chamber," which were "glass windows protected with iron bars," causing "blue vapors" to spread through the chamber. This claimed way of introducing the poison is in stark contrast to the commonly claimed but equally fictitious wire-mesh introduction columns. While Zyklon B gypsum cubes may have a pale turquois hue, they certainly were not "blue cubes," their hydrogen-cyanide vapors were not blue but colorless, and they also did not cause "immediate asphyxiation," as Gabai has it. Absent any means to force a swift evaporation and dissipation of the gas, the process would have taken many minutes, even hours.

For Gabai, the chamber was ventilated by opening the non-existing iron-barred glass windows in the ceiling, while he seems to have been ignorant of the room's ventilation system with many vents in the side walls. (Although he referred to it in his 1983 text.)

For Gabai, the victims of a gassing were full of blood due to "internal hemorrhages that burst in the gas chambers. The gas made blood vessels break open." This is utter nonsense, as hydrogen cyanide has no such effect at all. Claiming to have worked in such a gas chamber for eight months, he should know that victims of cyanide poisoning have a pinkish skin color but are otherwise unaltered.

Gabai claimed that four corpses were placed at once in a cremation muffle (designed and sized to hold only one corpse), and that it took only half an hour to cremate them – compared to an hour for each corpse in reality (see the entry on crematoria). Hence, he exaggerated the maximum theoretical capacity by a factor of 8. He also claimed that the triple-muffle furnaces of Crematoria II and III had two introduction doors at the front and one in the rear, although they were all at the front, side by side. He insisted that, when loading the muffles with fresh corpses, it took them three minutes to load 60 corpses, with two corpses being introduced in one batch, two batches per muffle. With 30 batches, this amounts to just 6 second per batch – impossible.

Gabai claimed that, during the cremation, they turned over the bodies with pitchforks to get them "near the flames," but assuming they managed to accomplish the impossible feat to get four bodies into the narrow muffle, there would not have been any space left to turn them over. Furthermore, cremation muffles do not have a "flame" to which the corpses need to be exposed. The entire muffle glows red-hot, giving off heat from all around, and the combusting coke gas streams throughout the muffle. Cremation muffles are not barbecue grills, where the burger needs to get flipped once in a while to make it equally done on all sides!

Gabai insisted that, once the furnaces had been lit, the cremation process required no fuel at all, because "the human fat fueled the flames" – although self-immolating bodies simply do not exist, and it is well-documented that the type of furnace he worked with had a fuel requirement of at least 20 kg of coke per corpse under perfect conditions. Gabai also claimed that the ash-extraction door was located at the furnace's rear, when in fact it was also located at the front.

Summarizing, it is clear that Gabai either had his real memories almost completely replaced with what he heard and memorized – often incorrectly – from other sources over the decades, or that he never actually had any real memories and made up the whole thing.

Gabai's earlier statement made in Jerusalem on 20 June 1983 is considerably shorter than his interview with Greif. It contains numerous contradictions to his interview claims, some of them minor, but others quite blatant. For a detailed study of them, and for a deeper analysis of Gabai's Greif interview, see Mattogno 2022e, pp. 31-55.

GÁL, GYULA

Gyula Gál was a Hungarian physician who was deported to Auschwitz, where he stayed until the camp was conquered by the Soviets. Not quite two months later, he wrote a report about Auschwitz, which contains the following peculiar statements, among others:

– The camp's total death toll was 5 million persons, 3½ million of them Jews, and the rest Poles and Russians. Compare this with the orthodoxy's current death-toll claim of roughly one million victims.
– Before entering the gas chambers, the victims were given towels and soap. This most certainly would never have happened, considering the mess it would have created and the effort necessary to retrieve and clean these items afterwards. In addition, no one takes towels into a shower.
– Zyklon B killed within two minutes. This would have been physically impossible, considering that there was no device heating and dissipating the toxic fumes, which would have evaporated from the gypsum pellets only slowly.
– Gál wrote specifically of only *one* crematorium (instead of four), which he claims had a daily extermination capacity of 15,000 people! In other words, he had no clue what he was talking about.

(For more details, see Mattogno 2021, pp. 297f.)

GARBARZ, MOSHÉ

Moshe Garbarz (born on 28 Dec. 1913) was a Polish Jew who emigrated to France in 1929. He was deported from there to the Auschwitz Camp on 17 July 1942. In 1945, he was evacuated to Buchenwald, where he was liberated by U.S. troops in April.

Moshe Garbarz

In 1983, an autobiographic book titled *Un Survivant* (*A Survivor*) was published that had been written together with his son Elie. Within the context of the Holocaust, Moshe Garbarz's claims about his activities during his stay at the Birkenau Camp are of interest. Since this testimony was written down 40 years after the event, the author's memory was possibly contaminated by forty years of exposure to the ubiquitous orthodox narrative. It is also likely that this book was edited or to some degree possibly even ghostwritten by his son. In other words, this book has little if any probative value. Yet an analysis of this witness's claims is interesting all the same.

Moshe Garbarz claims to have been employed at

Birkenau as an inmate electrician. One morning in September 1942, he had to report with his colleagues to a new worksite, where he said he had to move floodlights on poles from one spot to another.

During that work, he claimed to have seen from a distance a hay barn closed on three side but open on the fourth, and in its vicinity three or four "pretty little country houses." Garbarz's subsequent narrative is a variation of claims about the so-called bunkers of Birkenau. Hence, before delving into Garbarz's tale, an explanation is due. The two so-called bunkers of Birkenau were allegedly located outside the camp itself. However, these facilities did not consist of a collection of three or four country houses with a hay barn near them. If we follow the orthodox narrative, Bunker 1 and Bunker 2 were isolated houses half a kilometer away from each other. They supposedly had two undressing barracks near them, but if they could compare to anything Garbarz was familiar with, these would have been the kind of standard barracks he himself lived in while in Birkenau. His description is therefore completely invented, with no relation to either reality or the orthodox narrative.

After spotting these non-existing buildings, Garbarz next claimed that he saw completely naked people walking in groups of twenty, led by four men in white and two SS men. These twenty people entered one of the houses. Once inside, the door was shut. An SS man came with a can that looked like a pot of paint. Then he first heard a bang of some shutter, then a Hebrew prayer being said, and then very faint cries.

This scene has been freely invented as well. The orthodox narrative has it that men and women undressed in said barracks by the hundreds, not in groups of twenty. Then they walked from the barracks to the "bunker," although not led by four people "in white," but rather surrounded by a ring of guards. Finally, if Garbarz heard the dying people cry only very faintly, he most certainly would not have been able to hear someone saying a prayer. Imagine several persons who are locked inside a massive house, with all panic-proof and gastight, hence massive doors, windows and shutters bolted. Now these persons are saying a prayer. How much of it could be heard when standing a hundred meters away? Nothing. Again, Garbarz made this up.

Later, he claimed, he saw how dead bodies were carried on a cart running on tracks from the little house to a mass grave of some 2,000 cubic meters in volume. This grave had been dug overnight by a team of some 200 inmates. In other words: this massive grave appeared overnight out of nowhere. Again, this is highly unlikely. In addition, the mass graves visible on air photos show that the dimensions Garbarz gave – 20 to 30 m wide and 50 to 60 m long – are way off the mark. These graves were some 10 meters wide and 100 m long.

While Garbarz did his job of relocating the lamp post, he insisted that he waded in the victims' blood, which had saturated the soil. Unfortunately for Garbarz, gassing victims do not bleed, and buried bodies do not saturate the soil with blood. Once more, we catch Garbarz making things up.

Finally, he claimed that bodies buried in mass graves had to be exhumed during the winter using pickaxes, since the ground was frozen, so they could be burned in the first crematorium becoming operational. However, the first crematorium at Birkenau became operational in March 1943. At that point in time, all mass graves filled in the summer of 1942 had long since been emptied. If we follow the orthodox narrative, that activity ended in early December 1942, and those bodies were cremated on pyres, not in cremation furnaces.

Garbarz's tale has a true core, though. In August and September of 1942, the period of his experiences, the typhus epidemic in Auschwitz reached its catastrophic climax with hundreds of victims per day. During that time, the above-mentioned mass graves were created, and Garbarz may have witnessed some of it, spicing up his memories with disparate aspects taken from other sources.

In a video interview of 20 August 1991, Garbarz told of the practically non-existent hygiene facilities in Birkenau at that time, about the hopeless infestation of the detainees by lice, and that every day numerous corpses were dragged out of each barracks.[3] Most of them were typhus victims, although Garbarz did not mention this important fact. Had he stuck to this ugly truth, we for once would have had a credible witness.

(For more details, see Graf 2019, pp. 205-210; Mattogno 2016f, pp. 117-119.)

GAS CHAMBER

A gas chamber is an enclosed space or room to expose items to a chemically active gas in order to achieve certain effects. There are three main types of

---

[3] Jewish Family and Children's Services of San Francisco, Interview with Moishe Garbarz 8/20/1991; USHMM Oral History Archive, RG-50.477.0909; https://collections.ushmm.org/search/catalog/irn516926.

Typical advertisement of the firm Degesch for the use of their various fumigation gases in "Gaskammern" = "gas chambers" for disinfestation. (Der praktische Desinfektor, Vol. 33, No. 2, 1941, inside cover)

gas chambers:
- Training/testing gas chambers: used by military and civilian-defense agencies to test gas-protection equipment and to train personnel in their use.
- Disinfestation or fumigation gas chambers, used to kill vermin that have infested portable items, such as lice, fleas and bedbugs in clothes, mattresses and bed linens.
- Execution gas chambers, subdivided into those for animals, used by veterinaries and animal-control units, and homicidal gas chambers, used for the legal implementation of capital punishment or for illegal murder.

Before and during World War II, the term "gas chamber" in German literature and bureaucratic documents (*Gaskammer*) referred exclusively to fumigation chambers, as the concept of killing humans by gas was unknown in Europe. The only country in which human beings were ever killed with poison gas in specifically built homicidal gas chambers was the U.S., where several states built such devices to implement capital punishment, starting in the 1920s. See the entries homicidal gas chamber and fumigation gas chamber for more.

Although there are several documents, including some created by the Auschwitz Camp authorities, that use the term "gas chamber" or similar terms, they always expressly refer to fumigation devices, if these documents are put in their proper historical and bureaucratic context. See the entry criminal traces for more details.

GASTIGHT DOORS

A series of wartime documents from the Auschwitz Camp authorities mention terms such as 'gastight door' or 'gastight window.' Polish investigators right after the war, and subsequently many orthodox scholars, have claimed that this so-called "criminal trace" points at the existence of homicidal gas chambers at Auschwitz.

However, a thorough analysis of these documents shows that most of them were destined to be installed in delousing chambers, while others were used for completely innocuous rooms. There are only a few documents where neither their contents nor their contexts allow determining what they were used for.

Homicidal gas chambers holding tens, hundreds or even thousands of victims need more than just gastight closure, though. Most of all, their doors need to be secured against a panicking crowd. This requires a massive wall into which a panic-proof door frame can be set, as well as the frame and the door itself. The door would have to be made of steel to prevent buckling and

Wooden door of a delousing chamber at the Auschwitz Camp with peephole and metal grill. As required by law, this peephole allowed observation from the outside when someone was inside spreading Zyklon B. The grill protected the glass during collisions of the door with clothes racks. Note the paper strips to "seal" the gaps between the wooden boards. Note also the flimsy latches to close the door, which would not have withstood a panicking crowd. This was the sturdiest and most "airtight" gas-chamber door ever installed and found after the war at Auschwitz – used for a disinfestation chamber.

splintering from a crowd of people banging, kicking and pushing against it.

Doors that would have suited this purpose were mass-produced in Germany before and during the war as air-raid-shelter doors. While they were not built to keep people and noxious gases inside, but rather to keep out falling debris and noxious, hot gases, they would have served the purpose.

Several other camps received such air-raid-shelter doors and used them for their delousing chambers, such as Majdanek, Stutthof and Dachau. Auschwitz, however, never received any such door. The camp administration requested an estimate for a set of such doors in 1942. These were to be installed in its planned Zyklon-B delousing chambers inside the Main Camp's administration building. However, since these chambers were never finished – they were eventually substituted by a microwave delousing facility – the doors offered by an air-raid-shelter company were never ordered, let alone delivered.

All doors and windows at the Auschwitz Camp were manufactured by the camp's own inmate workshop using wooden planks and boards. These boards were held together by iron bands on both sides, bolted together through holes in the wood and bands. The doors leaked through the wood, through the cracks between the boards, through the bolt holes, and also between door and frame through the primitive felt seals. If used for delousing chambers, the gaps between the boards were "sealed" with paper strips, which was not a good seal at all. (See the illustration.) These doors may have been free of any draft, but certainly not gastight. All the doors and shutters found by Polish investigators after the war were manufactured this way, without exception. In

Massive steel door of a professionally designed delousing chamber (DEGESCH circulation procedure) at Dachau Concentration Camp. (Technology from the 1930s.)

Massive steel door of the execution gas chamber of the Mississippi State Penitentiary at Parchman, Miss., USA. (Technology from the 1930s.)

particular, these doors would not have withstood a panicking crowd for long.

Even the door installed in late 1944 at the entry to the Main Camp's air-raid shelter was made of simple wooden boards, upon which pieces of sheet metal had been nailed to make it somewhat fire- and gasproof. That air-raid shelter was installed in what used to be the morgue of the former crematorium building, before it was shut down in the summer of 1943.

This morgue is said to have been a homicidal gas chamber in 1941/1942. Therefore, the door leading into that morgue from the adjacent washroom – the only access way into the morgue from the outside – must have had a massive, panic-proof steel door. However, the building's original blueprints show that the walls separating the morgue from the washroom next door was only 15 cm thick, which is the thickness of a normal brick. While this was enough for a normal door frame, such a thin, one-brick-row wall could not have accommodated the long and wide anchors of the frame for a heavy steel door. Hence, this room could not have had a homicidal-gas-chamber door installed, even if the camp had ever obtained any.

While there were doors, windows and shutters at Auschwitz that were draft-resistant, neither truly gastight doors ever existed at that camp, nor a single door that could have been used for a homicidal gas chamber.

(For more details, see Rudolf 2019, pp. 317-329; Mattogno 2016d, pp. 47-52; 2019, pp. 65f., 141f., 154f.; Rudolf 2020c.)

GAS VANS

A gas van is a large-capacity truck or van allegedly used to murder passengers in the rear cargo hold via engine exhaust gas.

Soviet Gas Vans

In the mid-1930s, Isai Davidovich Berg – a Russian Jew and head of the economic department of the NKVD for the Moscow region – had the idea of using prisoner-transfer vans to kill inmates locked inside by piping the engine exhaust gases into the enclosed coachwork box. These vans were powered by a gasoline engine produced in the Soviet Union under a licensed from the Ford Company, so their exhaust gas was highly lethal. This invention was in fact built, and from 1936, these vans were used to murder prisoners during transit without them even suspecting it. (Grigorenko 1981, pp. 275f.; *Monster: A Portrait of Stalin in Blood*, Part 2: "Stalin's Secret Police," youtu.be/itPPRxy_AQ4, starting at 3 min, 21 sec.; Voslensky pp. 28f.). This fits well into the framework of the Soviet Union's (and Russia's) secret services' long tradition of using poison to kill dissidents and anyone it considered an obstacle to their ambitions, as has been amply documented (Volodarsky 2009).

British Gas-Van Accusations

The first mention of mobile gas chambers in the context of World War II occurred in 1942. The British newspaper *Daily Telegraph* – which, back in World War I, spread the atrocity lie that Austrian forces had murdered 700,000 Serbians by gassing them (22 March 1916, p. 7) – resurrected the same atrocity lie once more, when announcing on 25 June 1942 (p. 5) that the Germans had murdered 700,000 Jews in "Travelling Gas Chambers" in Poland.

Soviet Gas-Van Accusations

The Soviets – actual inventors of the homicidal gas van – levelled the same charge against Germany during their Krasnodar Show Trial, which was staged in July of 1943 against Soviet citizens accused of having collaborated with their German liberators. (See Bourtman 2008 for an assessment of this trial.) During the trial and in its portrayal in Soviet mass media, "Hitler's murder vans" were a prominent topic, although the defendants were not accused of having partaken in their use. These vans were said to have killed using the exhaust gases produced by their diesel engines which supposedly "contained a high concentration of carbon monoxide," "causing the rapid poisoning and death from asphyxiation of the prisoners." The German word and concept of *diesel* engines evidently was meant to instill particularly anti-German horrors and disgust – except that it backfired, because diesel exhaust gas is notably unsuited for the claimed purpose, due to its low toxicity, contrary to the court's and its experts' mendacious claims.

This travesty of justice was repeated a few months later, when the Soviets staged a show trial in Kharkov mainly against captured German soldiers who were accused, among other things, of having operated these diesel-driven gas vans, although the Soviets never claimed that Jews were the victims.

No material traces of such a gas van were ever presented. On some occasions, mis-captioned photos showing irrelevant vehicles were at times erroneously or mendaciously presented as evidence for their existence. (See the entry on the Ostrowski Company for more details.)

Gas Vans at the Nuremberg Trials

Gas-van claims played only a minor role during the International Military Tribunal after the war. Whenever they were mentioned, these claims were based on allegations made by the Soviet prosecutors, who used the same kind of "evidence" to prove their claim as had been presented during the Krasnodar and Kharkov show trials. Attempts by the defense to have this propaganda material rejected as impermissible was denied by the court, since the IMT's statute clearly stated that any records and findings of any court of the Allied nations, including the Soviet Union, were considered admissible, self-evident and true. This way, the claims made during Stalinist travesties of justice became legally binding "truths" for all Allied and (later) German courts.

Witness testimonies by German officials regarding these vans are characterized either by their lack of any concrete knowledge about them, if their existence was admitted, or by an outright denial that such devices ever existed. The IMT protocols mention at least 63 affidavits affirming that no such vans ever existed in German units. None of these affidavits submitted to the IMT seem to have survived.

Documents produced in preparation of the IMT aiming at substantiating gas-van claims – not all of which were submitted as evidence – exhibit clear hallmarks of crude manipulations and forgeries.

(For more details, see then entries on Gaubschat Company (Just Document); Becker, August; Turner, Harald.)

Gas Vans in West-German Trials

While East-German, communist show trials – where gas-van accusations played a role – faithfully followed in Stalinist propagandist footsteps, West-German trials also used the results of Allied post-war trials as a starting point and dogmatic basis for their proceedings. None of the German trials ever questioned whether gas vans really existed in the first place. None of the usual requirements for a murder trial was ever requested – neither by the prosecution, nor by the judges, *nor by the defense*: namely, traces of the murder weapon or of the murder victims.

The Soviet show-trial claims, puffed up by numerous "witness" claims along the same line, and hence of very dubious provenance, were simply taken as historical dogma. While several defendants still insisted in earlier trials that they had no knowledge of gas vans, the same defendants "remembered" increasingly more about them the more often they were dragged into court over the years, either as defendants or as witnesses. Thus, by way of constant bombardment with "self-evident" propaganda "facts," false memories were created even among the defendants.

Gas Vans and the *Einsatzgruppen*

Gas vans are said to have been developed mainly to aid the *Einsatzgruppen* in Russia mass-murdering Jews behind the German-Russian front line. The documentation about the activities of the *Einsatzgruppen* is vast, but among the hundreds of documents, not a single one mentions the use of gas vans for any murderous activities. Not even the Soviet show trials mentioned them in the context of mass-murdering Jews.

Laqueur and Baumel-Schwartz (2001, p. 231) claim that as many as 350,000 Jews were killed in vans by the *Einsatzgruppen*; this is the highest mainstream estimate.

Gas Vans and Mainstream Historians

Since no documents exist giving any indication as to how, when, where or by whom the gas vans were conceived, developed, produced, deployed, maintained and then made to disappear without a trace, historians have developed a unique narrative in this regard. It is full of inconsistent, implausible and at times outright absurd claims, supported by similar claims made by defendants during post-war proceedings. These are the same defendants who faced the alternative of either endorsing the unchallengeable dogma or being mercilessly persecuted, prosecuted and punished.

The current orthodox narrative has it that the invention of gas vans was initiated by Himmler, upon allegedly witnessing a mass execution in mid-August 1941 together with Erich von dem Bach-Zelewski, after which Himmler supposedly ordered a more-humane method to be developed. Rumors (!) have it that the idea to use engine exhaust to kill people in vehicles presumably occurred to Arthur Nebe when he accidentally gassed himself in a car. Other historians claim that initially bottled carbon monoxide (CO) was used, an idea allegedly copied from the euthanasia centers. This gas was presumably pumped into a trailer pulled by a tractor, but that idea was later abandoned, not because of Nebe's accidental drunk-gassing event, but because CO steel bottles were allegedly difficult to obtain outside of Germany, and also difficult to transport. Once engine-exhaust gases had been "discovered" as the better source of toxic fumes, some vehicles were then allegedly developed and tested by the Germans, and then eventually deployed, first at the Chełmno Camp, and then later also behind the Eastern front – and in one case even in occupied Serbia. None of this is documented.

Gas vans at Chełmno remain significant to the overall Holocaust narrative, however, due to their alleged large number of fatalities. Chełmno vans supposedly killed up to 350,000 Jews (Laqueur/Baumel-Schwartz 2001, p. 231). This, combined with the 350,000 allegedly killed in vans by the *Einsatzgruppen*, puts the van total at 700,000 (*ibid.*; also Gutman 1990, p. 544; Rozett/Spector 2000, p. 230) – a substantial portion of the "6 million."

Real Gas Vans

Mainstream historians tend to interpret German wartime documents containing terms such as "special (*sonder-*) vehicles" or simply "S-vehicles" as references to homicidal gas vans, when in fact every vehicle produced for the military was called a "special vehicle," including every type of *Panzer*. Some of these special vehicles were, indeed, veritable gas vans – mobile fumigation vehicles used behind the front lines to disinfest soldiers' clothes of lice.

Furthermore, due to Germany's lack of reliable supplies of liquid fuels during the war, German authorities mandated that Germany's entire rolling transportation fleet be switched gradually to producer gas as a fuel source. Vans and trucks equipped with such producer-gas devices were truly lethal gas vans that could easily kill its operators, if they weren't careful, because producer gas consists of 18-30% of highly flammable and toxic carbon monoxide. These poison-gas generators were known to every vehicle engineer in Germany, were mass-produced by the tens of thousands, and were easy to fuel and operate. Yet, amazingly, not a single source or witness has ever claimed that they were used to commit mass murder, although they would have been the logical and indeed ideal choice of any aspiring mass murderer.

(For details, see Alvarez 2023; Mattogno 2017, pp. 9-16, 32-45; Mattogno 2022c, pp. 293-380.)

GAUBSCHAT COMPANY

The company Gaubschat Fahrzeugwerke Ltd. was a Berlin coachwork manufacturer mainly known for producing bus coachworks. During the war, the company also built custom-made coachworks (bodies) for trucks.

In April 1942, the German Department of Homeland Security (*Reichssicherheitshauptamt*, RSHA) approached Gaubschat with the intent to equip the cargo boxes of special vehicles ordered *but not yet manufactured* by Gaubschat with a device to accelerate their unloading. A series of unclassified letters resulting from it, stretching from late April to September 1942, speaks of "*Sonderfahrzeuge*," the common German bureaucratic term for all non-mass-produced non-civilian vehicles. The term is internally consistent and completely innocuous. The technician charged with implementing the changes testified after the war that he was told these vans were used to transport typhus victims, hence corpses.

One highly contested document was added to the archival file of this series which is not part of the series: it is dated (in handwriting) 5 June 1942, and contains a number of suspicious characteristics. This document

– has a different reference number,
– is marked "top secret" on every page,
– does not give a sender (although a mere signature at the end suggests "Willy Just"),
– uses a different term "*Spezialwagen*," rather than "*Sonderfahrzeuge*,"
– requests changes not mentioned in any of the other letters; most of these changes are utterly nonsensical,
– also insists that vehicles already delivered be changed,
– nonsensically begins with the sentence "For example 97,000 were processed..." without indicating what this refers to,
– expressly refers to homicidal use,
– and anachronistically refers to a consultation between the RSHA and Gaubschat that took place only 11 days later, on 16 June 1942.

This suspicious document seems to have been intended to replace a similar, yet innocuous document of the genuine series dated June 23. Both letters have their arguments listed in seven numbered paragraphs and talk about suggestion on how to make changes, and both refer to a consultation between the RSHA and Gaubschat, yet only the real document mentions the date (16 June 1942). That the creator of this suspicious document had problems dating it, results from the fact that the space for the date was left empty when that letter was typed, and filled in manually only later – by someone who didn't pay attention to the genuine letters' chronology.

This so-called "Just Document" of 5 June 1942 is a clear-cut example of a document forgery, probably committed by German-speaking collaborators of the Allied occupational forces in Europe.

Another document also used to "prove" the existence of homicidal gas vans is the so-called Becker Document, presumably authored by August Becker. For a discussion of this document as well as a juxtaposition with the Just Document, see that entry.

(For more on this, see the entries on gas vans, August Becker, and in general Alvarez 2023, pp. 66-86.)

GENERALPLAN OST

After Germany's victory over Poland and the annexation of West Prussia and the Warthe Region in early 1940, German officials developed a plan called "*Generalplan Ost*" ("General Plan East") that aimed at Germanizing these regions and resettling those parts of the population that they thought could not be integrated, including all Jews. These people were to be resettled into the remaining Polish territories (the General Government).

On 17 July 1941, hence some three weeks after the invasion of the Soviet Union, Chief of the SS Heinrich Himmler charged Odilo Globocnik, at the time head of SS and police in Lublin, with installing SS and police agencies in the "new eastern region," with the aim of securing more space for the settlement of Germans in the East. To this end, Himmler planned on employing vast numbers of masons and bricklayers – in fact, hundreds of thousands of workers, some of them to be taken from concentration camps and also from PoW camps. He also planned on acquiring huge quantities of construction material for gigantic projects to improve the infrastructure in the conquered eastern territories. In this context, the Majdanek Camp was created, initially meant to house more than 100,000 Soviet PoWs. In late 1942, that camp was ordered to establish "a transit support camp," which was to supply the various agencies involved in construction projects in the eastern territories.

Parallel to this and with the same background, the Auschwitz-Birkenau Camp was created, equally initially planned to house more than 100,000 Soviet PoWs, soon to be increased to 200,000. The Stutthof Camp was also integrated into this *"Generalplan Ost"* as a tool to secure a vast labor force. In total, some 375,000 Soviet PoWs and camp inmates were expected to be deployed for construction work.

Due to the catastrophic conditions at the eastern front, however, most Soviet PoWs never made it west. The focus therefore shifted to the Jews as an alternative labor pool for *"Generalplan Ost"* in early 1942, as is clear from the protocol of the Wannsee Conference, among other documents. Consistent with this, only Jews fit for labor were initially sent to Auschwitz.

In this context of the shift away from Soviet PoWs to Jews, Globocnik is also said to have been made head of *Aktion Reinhardt*. The orthodoxy insists that this was an operation with the goal to exterminate without distinction all Jews of occupied Poland. However, if that was so, then Globocnik had been ordered by Himmler to fulfill two contradictory tasks: on the one hand, he had to secure as large a Jewish labor force as possible for huge construction efforts in the East, and on the other hand, he had to mass-murder all the Jews he could lay his hands on. Both cannot be true.

As the war against the Soviet Union went from bad to worse, *"Generalplan Ost"* was eventually abandoned, and Jews as well as other forced laborers were no longer deployed in infrastructural projects in the East but in war-related industries in and around Germany (production of weapons and ammunitions etc.).

A detail analysis of evidence regarding *Aktion Reinhardt* shows that this operation was about the deportation of Jews, their deployment for forced labor, and the looting of their property and assets – not mass murder.

(For more details on *Generalplan Ost*, see Graf/Kues/Mattogno 2020, pp. 244-251.)

generator gas → **Producer Gas, Carbon Monoxide**

GERMANY

Germany had four roles within the context of the Holocaust:
1. Perpetrator
2. Crime Scene
3. Victim
4. Propagandist

The last role is discussed in detail in the section on Germany of the entry on propaganda, so it will not be covered here.

Perpetrator

If we consider Austria as not being a part of Germany, then the main perpetrator of the Holocaust, Adolf Hitler, was originally Austrian, not German. It has also been observed that a higher number of Austrian nationals was involved in the operation of the so-called extermination camps than would be expected from their share among all ethnic Germans. Of course, considering the involvement of the vast majority of all German officials and government agencies in actively supporting, advocating, promoting, implementing, carrying out or at least condoning the persecution of the Jews – whatever that might have entailed – there is no way around the fact that it was, at its main core, a German affair.

Crime Scene

Orthodox scholars state that no extermination camp was erected on German soil. However, the German government of the time surely saw that differently, because both the areas around the Chełmno Camp (in the Warthegau) – and Auschwitz (eastern Upper Silesia) had been annexed by Germany after the invasion of Poland. Hence, these camps were on German territory in the eyes of Third-Reich officials. The same is true for the Natzweiler Camp. It was located in the Alsace region, which was annexed by Germany after France's defeat in 1940. However, that camp was only the claimed location of one minor gassing incident.

To this must be added the many claimed minor extermination crime scenes by gassings at several other camps. All of them were on German (or Austrian) soil, such as Mauthausen, Neuengamme, Ravensbrück, Sachsenhausen and Stutthof, plus others not supported by orthodox historians. (See the entry on extermination camps.)

Victim

German citizens of Jewish faith or descent fell victim to the persecutorial measures of the German authorities during the war. On the details, see the section on demography below.

Demography

SS statistician Richard Korherr reported in his 1943 report that, by the end of 1942, 382,534 German Jews had emigrated from the territory of the "Old Reich" (not including Austria, the Sudetenland and any later gains). On the other hand, when any further emigration was prohibited in late October 1941, the Reich Association of Jews in Germany reported to the German government that 164,000 Jews were still present in Germany at that time. Even as late as May 1942, Goebbels was complaining in his diary that there were "40,000 Jews still in Berlin" alone (entry of 24 May 1942). Mainstream figures for Jews still present in Germany after the war was around 25,000.

Deportation figures resulting from extant documents show that the differential between the two estimates (164,000 and 25,000) were people largely deported to various camps in the East, or "for resettlement" to the East, mainly to Kaunas and Minsk. Orthodox scholars insist that many if not most of them were killed there on arrival by mass executions. (See the entries on Fort IX and Maly Trostenets.) However, if the intention was to kill these deportees to the East, trips to Auschwitz, Chełmno or any of the other alleged extermination camps would have been shorter and cheaper. These camps are also said to have been better prepared to cope with the deportees, as they were allegedly equipped with sophisticated mass-extermination facilities. But that is not what happened.

Furthermore, there is abundant documentation that a real resettlement indeed took place. (See the entry on resettlement.) If so, it is difficult to assess how many of these Jews sent east and placed there in ghettos, camps or settlements managed to survive the war. Many may have been executed by the *Einsatzgruppen* for the slightest transgressions, as reprisal victims or during simple massacres. Others may have starved to death or succumbed to diseases. Again others joined partisan forces, some of whom perished in this context. Some became collateral damage when the front moved through with heavy gunfire and artillery shelling. At war's end, some may have gotten deported to Siberia by Stalin, and some may have migrated west and emigrated to Israel, the U.S. and other countries without ever getting registered as such.

(For details on demographics, see Rudolf 2019, pp. 178f.)

GERSTEIN, KURT

Kurt Gerstein (11 Aug. 1905 – 25 July 1945), SS *Obersturmführer*, was a mining engineer by education, and from early 1942, head of the technical disinfection services of the hygiene department of the Waffen-SS's health services. In that role, he was involved in supplying the Auschwitz Camp with the pesticide Zyklon B. He also inspected the Belzec and Treblinka Camps' hygienic situation in 1942, together with Dr. Wilhelm Pfannenstiel, professor at, and director of, the Hygienic Institute at the University of Marburg and hygienic adviser to the Waffen-SS.

Kurt Gerstein.

Gerstein suffered from type-one diabetes, which likely contributed to his emotional instability and resulted in several delirious events throughout his adult life. He also was an opponent of the NS regime. He was sentenced to prison several times for spreading anti-government propaganda, but at the same time he repeatedly affirmed his loyalty to the *Führer* and the NS state, asking unsuccessfully not to be expelled from the party, and later to be readmitted. He joined the Waffen-SS in early 1941. Considering his police record of multiple thought-crime offenses due to his opposition to the regime, he most certainly would not have been allowed to assume a position within the Waffen-SS hierarchy that gave him access to top-secret matters, let alone go on trips to visit the active annihilation of the Jews at the so-called extermination camps Belzec, Sobibór and Treblinka.

At the end of the war, Gerstein wrote several texts – some in French, some in German – which claim to describe his visit to the Belzec Camp, among other things. Gerstein was held captive by the French for three months, at which point he (allegedly) committed suicide in 1945 at the age of 40. His text was brought to public attention only in 1953, when a German government-sponsored historical periodical published one version of it, praising it as a reliable first-hand account of the claimed extermination activities at the Belzec Camp (Rothfels 1953). Gerstein's "confessions" had an enormous impact on the orthodoxy, in particular with its dramatization in Rolf Hochhuth's play *The Deputy*.

Because Gerstein's various texts are riddled with contradictions and historically as well as technically impossible statements, they are no longer taken seriously by mainstream historians. In plagiarized form, however, Gerstein's claims live on in countless texts and movie scenes, which is why a wide range of evidently untrue claims are exposed here (for more details, see Roques 1989; Mattogno 2021b):

– On 8 June 1942, Gerstein received an order to procure 100 kg – or perhaps 260 kg – of hydrogen cyanide (HCN) – or perhaps *potassium* cyanide (KCN) – for an extremely secret mission.
– The quantity of substances to procure was either specified *to* him or set *by* himself.
– The destination of this secret mission was known only to his driver, but Gerstein gave Prof. Pfannenstiel ("more by accident" than on-purpose) a ride along this secret mission to an unknown place.
– Gerstein decided himself (or was ordered) to drive from Berlin to Kolin near Prague in order to pick up the above substances, then drive them to a secret place in Poland.
– In Kolin, he did not pick up 100 (or 260) kg HCN (or KCN), but rather 44 steel bottles of liquid HCN. Gerstein never mentions Zyklon B, even though he actually bought tons of it and had it delivered to the Auschwitz Camp, among others.
– When Gerstein finally went on his trip in August 1942, he stopped over in Lublin to see Odilo Globocnik, commander "of the four extermination camps," who revealed to him and Pfannenstiel the Reich's greatest secret, which was so secret that anyone revealing it to outsiders would be shot on the spot – and thus Globocnik, in revealing this to the accidental hitchhiker Pfannenstiel and the regime's opponent Gerstein, should have been immediately executed. (He was not).
– Gerstein arrived in Lublin with 44 steel bottles of HCN in his vehicle, although the Lublin Camp received large supplies of Zyklon B on a regular basis for pest control, and hence all Gerstein had to do to get HCN was ask Globocnik for some, rather than haul 44 steel bottles across Europe.
– Gerstein has Globocnik claim that the Belzec Camp so far (March through August 1942) had killed on average 11,000 Jews daily, hence some $(150 \times 11,000 =)$ 1.65 million Jews – while only some 434,500 Jews were deported to or through Belzec during its entire existence until the end of 1942.
– Gerstein has Globocnik claim that the latter didn't know where the Sobibór Camp was located, but that he knew that there, on average, some 20,000 Jews were killed daily since June 1942, hence after some two and a half months of operation, around $(75 \times 20,000 =)$ 1.5 million Jews, while today's orthodox death-toll figure for the entire time of the camp's existence stands at "only" some 300,000.
– For Treblinka, Globocnik allegedly claimed 13,500 daily killings on average, also since June of that year, thus some $(75 \times 13,500 =)$ one million for just that short period of time, while the orthodoxy claims a total death toll of 700,000 to 900,000 victims for the entire time of the camp's existence. But more importantly: the camp opened only at the end of July 1942.
– Gerstein has Globocnik claim that textiles confiscated from the Jews processed in his camps so far amounted to some 400,000 to 800,000 tons, meaning that every Jew had carried with them clothes weighing about one metric ton.
– Gerstein has Globocnik claim that Hitler and Himmler had recently visited the camps Belzec, Sobibór and Treblinka, requesting that the process be accelerated – although neither of them ever set foot in these camps.
– Gerstein claimed that his secret mission was to convert the existing gas chambers operating with Diesel exhaust gases to something better and faster, such as hydrogen cyanide. Gerstein later described the gassing operation at Belzec with a Diesel engine. As a mining engineer, Gerstein certainly could recognize a diesel engine, and knew that their exhaust gases were relatively harmless and useless for murder.
– Gerstein also met Christian Wirth in Lublin, the commandant of the Belzec Camp. He drove in Wirth's car to Belzec, yet when getting there, Wirth was either already there to receive him, or Wirth was not present at all; and the 44 steel bot-

- tles were in the vehicle, but Wirth's car was a passenger car, while the transport of 44 steel bottles requires a large truck. Globocnik also came along, as only he could grant entry into the camp for outsiders.
- When arriving at the Belzec Camp together with his accidental hitchhiker Pfannenstiel, Gerstein hid the 44 HCN steel bottles *from Wirth and Globocnik* some 1,200 meters away from the camp, although he had traveled in Wirth's car, presumably with Wirth, and accompanied by Globocnik. (And how does one hide a pile of 44 steel bottles?) Or, if we follow another version of the text, Gerstein (with or without Wirth?) parked the vehicle with the bottles 1,200 meters away from the camp and walked the rest of the way – or, according to yet another version, Gerstein took the bottles into the camp.
- Gerstein convinced Commandant Wirth not to use the HCN steel bottles, but to stick to his Diesel-exhaust system, which Wirth gladly accepted as "satisfactory."
- Gerstein saw a 500-m long train pull into the Belzec Camp spur, which was only 260 m long.
- Gerstein saw a gargantuan pile of shoes 35 or 40 meters high (or 25 m in another version).
- 700-800 people were crammed into a room of only 25 square meters, or 28-32 persons per square meter in a room only 1.8 m high – which is both nonsensical and a physically impossible packing density. To this blatant nonsense, orthodox historians reacted either by hushing it up, falsifying the numbers claimed by Gerstein – Neumann (1961, p. 192) *reduced* the number of people, while Poliakov (1979, p. 223) *increased* the room size – or by absurdly declaring that this "error" "reinforces the credibility and good faith of the story" (Adam 1985, Note 85, p. 260).
- During an alleged gassing event, the Diesel engine wouldn't start, and so the victims had to wait almost three hours in the closed gas chambers before the gassing commenced. At that point, all victims were still alive, according to one version, yet if we follow another, all were already dead. In fact, hardly anyone would have survived being jammed into a sealed room for three hours.
- The gassing took 32 minutes (or perhaps one hour).
- Either the victims fell as they died, or they remained standing like "columns of basalt" due to a lack of space to fall over – but no matter the packing density, any dying person slumps down.
- After Gerstein had abandoned the 44 steel bottles and had convinced Wirth not to switch from Diesel to Zyklon B, Globocnik still allowed him and his accidental hitchhiker Pfannenstiel go on to see the Treblinka Camp, although Gerstein's mission of switching Diesel for Zyklon B had become moot.
- At Treblinka, Gerstein saw another mountain of clothes 35-40 meters high.
- Although Gerstein never returned to any of these camps, he claimed to know that "later" all corpses buried in mass graves were exhumed and burned using "gasoline and Diesel oil" – a physically impossible technique, since liquid fuels only singe superficially; sprinkling gasoline on a corpse and setting it afire will not even begin to totally consume the body.
- Although the victims had not been counted exactly, Gerstein claimed to know that the total death toll of those camps amounted to 25 million (or perhaps 20 million) "according to my secure documents"! This is an outrageously high figure, far above anything ever claimed for the Holocaust.
- Gerstein was not asked to, and did not report to anyone about his top-secret mission initiated by Hitler and Himmler personally, and ultimately did nothing to implement the requested changes to "speed up the process" by replacing the Diesel engines with some Zyklon-B procedure.
- When he found out that large quantities of hydrogen cyanide had been ordered by German authorities, he claimed to know that a plan existed to kill vast numbers of people in "reading or club rooms," so he made sure that this pesticide disappeared. Documents show, however, that those orders were meant for lice disinfestations, and that they were all delivered.
- Gerstein claimed that the German pest-control company DEGESCH produced HCN "in vials" for killing people. No such vials ever existed.
- He also insisted that "millions of people have disappeared" in the Mauthausen Camp "in gas chambers and gas cars (mobile chambers)," which no mainstream historian takes seriously.
- "In Auschwitz, millions of children alone were killed by holding a swab of hydrogen cyanide under their noses." This is ridiculous and utterly without confirmation.
- "Attempts have also been made with compressed

air: people were put into cauldrons, into which compressed air was pressed by means of the usual asphalt-road compressors." Even more ridiculous than above.

By all accounts, Gerstein was either delusional and in need of serious mental-health assistance, or he was tortured and coerced into writing nonsense. It is tragic that his testimony is the main basis upon which the myth of the Belzec extermination camp rests. There is only one other witness who made detailed statements about Belzec, Rudolf Reder, whose testimony is similarly unreliable, although for other reasons.

GERTNER, SZAJA

Szaja Gertner was a Polish Jew who was deported to Auschwitz from Łódź, Poland, on an unknown date. His testimony was published in a Polish book in 1945. Right after his arrival, he claims to have been assigned to the so-called *Sonderkommando*. There he claims to have witnessed things that are absurd or demonstrably impossible:

- Each person received a receipt for the clothing they left behind when undressing to be gassed, which is a unique and nonsensical claim.
- They all received a piece of soap and a towel to take with them to the "shower," a useless waste of resources, plus no one takes towels into a shower.
- Rather than calming the victims to make them cooperative, the Germans began to beat the inmates to cause confusion.
- The panicking victims "threw themselves on top of each other, and fled from each other," a completely senseless way of acting.
- Then, the victims were driven from the showers into "the chamber," meaning that the shower room was clearly *not* the gas chamber. So, they had actual showers? And then the freshly-cleaned Jews were gassed?
- The gas was thrown in through a window, though that room had no window, and the orthodoxy insist of the poison having been introduced through ceiling holes by way of some special Zyklon-B introduction device.
- After the gassing, ventilation through mere opening of doors and windows took only five minutes, an impossibly short time.
- The *Sonderkommando* inmates dragging out the corpses put "cotton plugs" into their mouth to protect against the gas that "escaped from the bodies as soon as they were moved," although cotton plugs offer no protection at all against hydrogen-cyanide vapors.
- "Railway tracks ran from the door of the gassing room to the furnace," where the rail carts carrying 40 corpses each dumped this load onto a huge grate. No crematorium in Auschwitz had railway tracks going from any room to the furnace room.
- The cremation grate was heated with a strong electric current, turning the corpses to ashes within just 10 minutes. But no electrically heated furnace was ever erected in any German wartime camp. Cremations of *single corpses* in such furnaces take as long as those in other furnaces, hence around an hour.
- The witness moreover fantasized about a large fan blowing the cremation ashes into a separate pit, where a worker "filled a barrel with ashes, and a winch pulled it up." No document, no material trace and no other witness tale substantiates this unique claim.

Some parts of this testimony echo aspects of atrocity propaganda spread by the Polish underground during the war, which indicates the likely source of this witness's claims. (For more details, see Mattogno 2021, pp. 307f.)

GEYSERS OF BLOOD, FROM MASS GRAVES

Some witnesses have claimed that mass graves filled with murdered Jews emitted geysers of blood. It ought to be unnecessary to provide scientific proof for this to be physically impossible. Among those who claimed this are:

- Adolf Eichmann
- Kurt Marcus
- Elie Wiesel
- Rudolf Reder

Related, but not quite as extreme, are claims that the victims buried in mass graves had soaked the soil with so much blood that one waded through bloody mud (Moshe Garbarz), that an entire lake of blood had formed (David Manusevich), or that the blood rose to a grave's surface and ignited there, as if it were oil (Chil Rajchman). Albert Hartl, an official of Germany's Department of Homeland Security (*Reichssicherheitshauptamt*), claimed the following about a huge mass grave he once claimed to have seen (Sereny, p. 97):

"At one moment – we were driving along a long ravine. I noticed strange movements of the earth:

clumps of earth rose into the air as if by their own propulsion – and there was smoke: it was like a low-toned volcano; as if there was burning lava just beneath the earth."

When Hartl was interrogated by U.S. investigators after the war, they added a remark to his file stating that Hartl "is known as a boaster of the highest order." (See Mattogno 2021c, pp. 69f.). He was not the only one. The sad thing is that witnesses telling such tall tales are still taken seriously by orthodox scholars.

GHETTOS

At least since the time of Raul Hilberg's initial work in the early 1960s, orthodoxy has partitioned the claimed 6 million Jewish fatalities into three major categories: camps, shootings and ghettos. Under the headings "German controlled ghettos" and "Theresienstadt," Hilberg allots "over 700,000" Jewish deaths – on his way to a total figure of 5.1 million (the lowest estimate of any major orthodox scholar, incidentally; Hilberg 1985, pp. 1219f.; 2003, pp. 1320f.). Unfortunately, Hilberg provides no substantiation whatsoever for his ghetto figure; it seems as if some such number was required, simply in order to approach a total of 6 million.

For those who would defend the standard 6-million figure, then, the total number of ghetto deaths must be scaled up, to at least 850,000, and perhaps as high as 1 million. It would be helpful to compare such numbers to other conventional estimates, but sadly, and remarkably, no other estimates exist. One can peruse standard works on the Holocaust, and conventional websites, but one will not find any total figure for "ghetto deaths" – which is amazing, given that it is one of the three major death categories. This fact alone is highly revealing.

It will be helpful to establish some context for this topic. Ghettos were generally small sections of cities that were designated as Jewish-only areas. They began to be formed in early 1940, and most were established by the end of 1941 – more than 1,000 in total, so we are told. There were some two dozen large ghettos (over 10,000 people), but the vast majority were quite small, holding 1,000 people or less. From early 1943, they began to be dismantled; hence the average ghetto life was about two years.

Contrary to popular belief, ghettos were not prisons. Many were completely open, and Jews could come and go as they pleased – they were only required to live and do business there. Oftentimes the ghetto was marked only by a sign. Clearly, they were never intended as a means of mass killing. Peter Longerich (2010, p. 166) evidently agrees:

"The establishment of the ghettos was carried out so haphazardly and slowly that it would be wrong to see it as a systematic policy ultimately aimed at the physical annihilation of the Jews."

Ghettos were, however, the logical first step in a program of exclusion, removal and expulsion. If the Nazis indeed wished to ethnically cleanse the Reich, and later also other areas under their control, they would have begun by rounding up Jews, confining them to specified areas, and then methodically transporting them out. And this is precisely what happened. For example, the two largest ghettos – Łódź (200,000 Jews) and Warsaw (400,000-590,000) – were established in February and November 1940, respectively. Jews were confined there until new areas opened in the East, upon which time the deportations commenced.

But despite clear and well-documented histories of the ghettos, we are sorely lacking in death statistics, both overall and for individual locations. Consider the largest and most-examined ghetto: Warsaw. Here we theoretically know everything, and in great detail. So, we may pose a simple question: *How many Jews died in the Warsaw Ghetto?* But we come away empty-handed. No conventional source provides even a plausible estimate of this essential number.

Incredibly, our experts cannot even clearly answer the simpler question: How many Jews were *in* the Warsaw Ghetto? Friedman (1954, p. 79) says 420,000 to 500,000. Corni (2003, p. 195) says 400,000. Dean (2010, p. 342) says "some 450,000." Longerich (2010, p. 167) says 410,000 to 590,000. If we don't know how many people we have to start with, we certainly can't answer the follow-up questions regarding deaths and deportations. And if we can't answer those questions for one of the three major Holocaust categories, then the entire picture is up in the air.

One reason for the reluctance to establish an overall death toll may be the obvious lack of evidence – that is, absence of victims' bodies. Based on Corni's data, the Warsaw Ghetto yielded nearly 130 corpses per day, on average, for two or more years. What did they do with the bodies? They could not bury them, since they were in the middle of a large city. They had neither crematoria nor wood to build pyres. So – what happened to the bodies? And are there any remains that we might examine today in order to confirm things?

Unsurprisingly, none of the orthodoxy's ghetto experts addresses this thorny issue. At best we find mere passing comments in other sources. For example, in a 1942 article in *The New York Times* (*NYT*) we read that the Warsaw Jews "have no means for funerals, so the dead are put into the street, where they are collected by the police." (7 Jan., p. 8). The same article, incidentally, claims that 300 per day were dying, mostly due to typhus – the very disease that the Germans were trying so hard to forestall. If the police collected the bodies – 4,000 or 5,000 per month – what did they do with them? Bury them? If so, where? Did they even count them? More unanswered questions.

Without such answers, we cannot really trust any information from orthodox sources. In reality, the actual numbers could have been quite low. If there were (say) 400,000 Jews in the Warsaw Ghetto, this would imply around 4,000 natural deaths per year, or about 11 per day. With this relatively low number, we can well understand how the bodies may have disappeared without a trace. But Corni and others tell us that some 130 Jews died every day – ten times the natural rate. The *NYT* said 300 per day, or 30 times the natural rate. These are much harder to explain.

Or maybe it was much worse than we presume. In one striking 1943 report in the *NYT*, we read that "approximately 10,000 people are killed daily in Warsaw alone by different means; the cruelest and most inhuman instruments, which only the black satanic spirit of Hitlerism can invent, are employed" (7 Feb., p. SM16). Ten thousand deaths per day, in an area barely over one square mile, is sheer fantasy. Obviously, the writer – "noted novelist" Sholem Asch – was engaging in some extreme hyperbole.

We must always keep in mind the natural death rate. If, say, 3 million Jews were confined to "1,000 ghettos," we then would expect some 30,000 deaths per year – or nearly 100 per day – due strictly to natural causes. One hundred deaths per day, spread over several countries and some 1,000 different locations, could easily vanish amidst a major war. But this would yield only some 100,000 deaths in total – a mere 10 percent of the claimed figure of one million.

To summarize: The ghetto system ran essentially for three years: 1941-1943. Over this time period, we are told that up to 1 million ghetto deaths occurred; hence almost 28,000 per month, on average, or about 925 per day. Every day, somewhere in the system, as many as 925 bodies were either buried or burned. Somewhere, in total, are the remains of perhaps 1 million people, on the orthodox view.

And yet we have no record of any such bodies whatsoever – no mass graves, no crematoria, no open-air pyres, no 'dumping in the river' stories. Not even the natural deaths are accounted for, which causes us to suspect that the total number of interned Jews was perhaps much smaller than claimed.

These are relevant questions that skeptics ask. Lacking good answers, they conclude that far fewer ghetto deaths actually occurred than claimed. Perhaps the Warsaw Ghetto saw only a couple of hundred, rather than thousand, deaths per month. This, at least, would be easier to explain. But then the total deaths in the ghetto would amount to something on the order of 10,000, rather than 100,000 (or more).

Finally, consider this easily overlooked point: Well over 1,000,000 Jews were eventually transported out of the ghettos – most to death camps, it is claimed. (Holocaust skeptics insist, however, that these Jews went either to forced labor camps or to transit camps further east.) Either way, these clearly cannot count as "ghetto deaths," since the orthodoxy later counts them again as "extermination-camp deaths." Here is an opportunity ripe for double-counting. But without the most basic details, we simply don't know how the deaths are being counted. This is not too much to ask, surely, for "the most well-documented event in history."

(For more details, see Dalton 2020, pp. 83-89.)

GLAZAR, RICHARD

Richard Glazar (29 Nov. 1920 – 20 Dec. 1997) was a Czech Jew who waited 49 years before having his alleged memories of his stay at the Treblinka Camp published in a book titled *Trap with a Green Fence* (the German edition, *Die Falle mit dem grünen Zaun*, appeared in 1992). Although the orthodox narrative claims that slave-labor inmates at this camp were killed after several weeks or a few months, Glazar insists that he spent ten months in that camp, from October 1942 until August 1943. The account of his "memories" is a hodgepodge of claims that can be found in the tales of other Tre-

Richard Glazar

blinka survivors. One main source is the tall tale by Samuel Willenberg, which appeared in English three years before Glazar's tall tale:

Willenberg 1989, pp. 104f.:	Glazar 1995, pp. 89, 93
"A slightly strange crowd spilled out – people with dark faces, curly, raven-black hair, and a foreign tongue on their lips. […] Every last one of them exited the cars in a state of total calm. [… The SS man] Mitte found three Greeks with a command of German and drafted them as interpreters."	"People climb calmly out of the cars, […] Their faces look healthy, and they have an unusual dark complexion. Black hair – all I see black to pitch-black hair. […] I can hear that the people are speaking a completely foreign language." "Three were chosen from this transport. […] They can speak a little, a very little German. Through them the others were informed […]."

Glazar's major blunder is his claim that his unit, a group of 25 men called the "camouflage unit," was the only unit in the camp that was doing real work: they had to climb up trees in the surrounding woods to break off branches, carry those back to the camp, and weave the branches into the fences to hide from outsiders what was going on inside the camp. This claim has three insurmountable problems:

1. This feeble attempt at camouflaging what was going on in the camp would have been futile, because anyone could have climbed up a tree to look over the fence, and the huge pyres sending tall flames into the sky would have been multiple times the height of any fence.
2. The gigantic fires allegedly burning and certainly spreading flying embers in close proximity to those fences would have quickly dried out and set ablaze the branches, making the camouflage unit's work pointless.
3. It is claimed that some 700,000 to 900,000 corpses were cremated on huge pyres in Treblinka between April and July of 1943 (some 120 days). Assuming the need of some 250 kg of fresh firewood to burn one corpse during open-air incinerations, this would have required at least some 175,000 metric tons of wood. That would have been about a thousand trees per day. They all came with branches that had to be cut off – tens of thousands of branches every day. Hence, why was there a need to climb on trees and cut off additional branches? And if Glazar's tree-climbing gang was the only unit doing real work around the camp, then who felled, debranched, cut up and transported the 1,000 trees needed *every day*? And this is not to mention that freshly cut trees make very poor firewood.

This all shows that Glazar was telling outrageous lies. If we follow him, however, all that was required to burn up to a million corpses within four months was to put "a lot of kindling in among the corpses, and then douse the whole thing in something very flammable." Once lit, the corpses apparently burned by themselves. However, self-immolating bodies simply do not exist. (See Mattogno/Graf, pp. 38-40; Kues 2009)

GLOBOCNIK, ODILO

Odilo Globocnik (21 April 1904 – 31 May 1945), SS *Gruppenführer*, during the war SS and Police Leader of the General Government (occupied Poland), and in charge of implementing the *Aktion Reinhardt*. After the war, he was arrested by a British unit, who interrogated him, possibly with the help of their customary torture, after which he committed suicide.

Odilo Globocnik

GLÜCKS, RICHARD

Richard Glücks (22 April 1889 – 10 May 1945), SS *Gruppenführer*, head of Office Group D of the SS Economic and Administrative Main Office (*Wirtschafts- und Verwaltungs-Hauptamt*), and as such head inspector of the concentration camps. Glücks's office was responsible for organizing

Richard Glücks

the German concentration camps and making sure that they were optimized to deliver a maximum in capable forced-inmate laborers to Germany's war industries.

Starting in 1942, and due to wartime needs, Glücks's main focus was on changing the principal role of Germany's concentration camps from political "reeducation" and oppression to a reliable source of forced labor for the war industries. To this end, he repeatedly ordered all camp commandants to *improve* the inmates' living conditions, to do anything in their power to *reduce* inmate mortality, and to implement extremely costly *improvements* of sanitary and healthcare conditions, particularly for the Auschwitz Camp. Such measures were obvious, given Germany's increasingly urgent need for labor. And they are completely at odds with any alleged mass-murder scheme in the camps. (See Mattogno 2016a, esp. pp. 13-72.)

On 10 May 1945, 10 days after Hitler and Goebbels committed suicide, Glücks did the same.

GOEBBELS, JOSEPH

Joseph Goebbels (29 Oct. 1897 – 1 May 1945) was the National-Socialist leader of the Berlin district as well as the Third Reich's Minister of Propaganda from its very beginning to the bitter end, when he committed suicide.

Joseph Goebbels

Goebbels was meticulous in keeping a diary with almost daily entries. In addition, his list of speeches and articles published in various Third-Reich periodicals is long. He voiced his opinions on many things. Jews were only one of them. Still, putting all his elaborations – public and private – together in which he addressed the "Jewish Question" fills an entire book of its own.

The earliest entry in Goebbels's diary about the impending fate of the Jews after the beginning of the war with the Soviet Union is dated 19 August 1941. In it, he remarked that "the *Führer* promises me he'll deport the Berlin Jews to the East as soon as possible, when the first means of transport are available." Referring to Hitler's infamous prophecy during his *Reichstag* speech on 30 January 1939, Goebbels states that "[i]n the East, the Jews must pay the price" for presumably having caused the current war.

On 7 March 1942, Goebbels records in his diary his reaction on reading the Wannsee Protocol outlining the project of removing Europe's Jews to the East. He wrote that the Jews

"will have to be concentrated first in the East; perhaps later after the war, an island can be assigned to them, such as Madagascar. In any case, there can be no peace in Europe until the last Jews are totally excluded from the European territory."

Twenty days later, on 27 March 1942, Goebbels calls the deportation of the Jews "from the General Government [occupied Poland] to the east" "a somewhat barbaric procedure," during which those unable to work (some 60% according to his estimate) "will have to be liquidated." No doubt, according to common ethical standards, the forced resettlement of entire families to the economically barren east was "barbaric," but his numerical estimates are not based on any known data or documents.

On 30 May 1942, Goebbels wrote that

"the Führer does not want the Jews to be evacuated to Siberia. […] He would much prefer to resettle them in central Africa. […] In any case, the Führer's goal is to make Western Europe completely Jew-free. They can no longer have their homeland here."

On 21 August 1942, one month into the evacuation of the Jews from the Warsaw Ghetto, Goebbels was informed by officials involved as to what was going on. The orthodox narrative has it that these Jews were sent to the Treblinka Camp, where they were all killed on arrival. But here is what Goebbels wrote in his private diary:

"The responsible Higher-SS leader reports to me on the conditions in the [Warsaw] *ghetto. The Jews are now in large part evacuated and established in the East. This proceeds quite generously."*

No word of mass murder on arrival at Treblinka. Rather, they have been deported and resettled to the East.

Goebbels's diaries have a total of 123 passages where he talks about the Jews and their fate under National-Socialist rule. Except for two entries, they consistently refer only to expulsion and deportation, not to extermination.

One exception occurred on 7 October 1943, the day after Heinrich Himmler had given a long speech about his activities to the top leadership of the Third

Reich. In this speech, he spoke about how he was in the process of making the Jews "disappear from the earth." Goebbels wrote about it:

> "As to the Jewish Question, [Himmler] gives a very frank and candid picture. He is of the opinion that we can solve the Jewish Question for all of Europe by the end of this year. He advocates the most radical and harshest solution, namely, that the whole of Jewry will be exterminated [*auszurotten*]. This is surely a consistent, if brutal, solution."

Owing to the ambiguity of the German verb *ausrotten* (see the entry on extirpation), this could mean anything from forced evacuation to mass murder. In any case, Himmler's boastful claims stand in stark contrast to the facts on the ground. Himmler was bragging and fibbing, in the face an increasingly deteriorating war situation. (See the entry on Himmler speeches.)

The second entry is dated 14 March 1945, where we read:

> "The Jews are reemerging. Their spokesman [...] is now arguing in the American press that under no circumstances should Germany be given lenient treatment. Anyone with the power to do so should kill these Jews like rats. In Germany, thank God, we have already thoroughly attended to this. I hope the world will take this as an example."

It is unclear whether Goebbels refers here to Jews advocating a harsh punishment for Germany, or to all Jews in general.

Except for these two entries, and to some degree his entry on 27 March 1942, Goebbels's diaries offer no support for the orthodox view that a plan of mass extermination was being carried out. Did Goebbels systematically lie to himself in his own private diary? Or was he unaware of the mass killing that was allegedly happening? Neither of these are plausible. And why did he never mention the key camps (Auschwitz, Treblinka, etc.) in any discussion of the Jews? And why would he use "code words" *in his own diary?* It makes no sense. The only reasonable explanation is that Goebbels was accurately recording a German program of mass evacuation and deportation.

(For more on Goebbels on the Jews, see the entry on extirpation, as well as Dalton 2019.)

GOL, SZLOMA

Szloma Gol was a Jew from Vilnius. On 10 August 1946, he signed an affidavit. He claimed in it that he was part of a team of 80 prisoners who were shackled by the legs. They were then forced to exhume and burn corpses from mass graves near a Vilnius suburb called Ponary from December 1943 for six months (hence until May 1944). He escaped from there by digging a tunnel out of the pit they were housed in.

This escape story resembles that of Yuri Farber, deposited two years earlier. While Farber described a sophisticated construction operation with pole supports and roof boards propping up the tunnel that was lit by electric lights, all made possible with tools and supplies miraculously found in the mass graves, Gol was more down to earth. His team simply dug the tunnel with their bare hands, broke their chains – evidently also with their bare hands – and ran away.

Their pyres were built over trenches 7 meters long, were pyramidal in shape, and had a wooden chimney sticking out at the top used to pour fuel down. The pyramidal shape and the weird wooden chimney also show up in Farber's testimony. Hence, it looks like Gol plagiarized Farber's account. However, Faber had his team of 80 people work only from late January 1944 until mid-April.

The pyres presumably consisted of 14 layers of alternating firewood and bodies. Cremating an average human body during open-air incinerations requires some 250 kg of freshly cut wood. With such pyres, a layer of a running meter of a pyre that is as wide as the bodies are tall can accommodate some four to five bodies. Four bodies require a ton of freshly cut wood. The density of green wood is roughly 0.9 tons per m^3, and its stacking density on a pyre is 1.4 (40% for air and flames to go through). This means that the wood required to burn four bodies would have had a volume of some 1.55 m^3. Spread out over 2 square meters, this wood would have stacked up to a height of some 0.8 meters, together with the corpse to about 1 meter. A pyre with 14 such layers would have been 14 meters high. Of course, a pyre two meters wide can never be 14 meters high; it would collapse at a far shorter height. While the shape of the pyre can be changed (for instance 7 m × 7 m, as other witnesses claimed, although that makes it much more difficult to build, burn and dispose later), this would not affect the height, if it had 14 layers.

Gol asserted that his team exhumed and burned a total of 80,000 bodies. Cremating 80,000 bodies requires some 20,000 metric tons of wood. This would have required the felling of all trees growing in a 50-

year-old spruce forest covering almost 45 hectares of land, or some 100 American football fields. An average prisoner is rated at being able to cut some 0.63 metric tons of fresh wood per workday. To cut this amount of wood within six months (180 days) would have required some 176 dedicated lumberjacks doing nothing else but felling and cutting up trees. Gol's prisoner unit allegedly consisted of 80 inmates, with most of them busy digging out mass graves, extracting bodies, building pyres, sifting through ashes, crushing bones, and scattering the resulting powder.

If Gol's tale has any real background, it would have been on a much smaller order of magnitude than what he claims.

This testimony relates to one of many events claimed to have been part of the alleged German clean-up operation which the orthodoxy calls *Aktion 1005*. The above exposition demonstrates that Gol's scenario is detached from reality. Its claimed dimension cannot be based on experience, but on mere propaganda, imagination and delusion.

(See also the similar accounts by Yuri Farber, A. Blyazer and Matvey Zaydel; for more details, see Mattogno 2022c, pp. 680-682.)

GOLD TEETH

Among the vast documentation of the Auschwitz Camp are documents showing that the camp's dentistry collected and submitted to the camp's Political Department, on regular intervals, gold and other precious metal alloys originating from tooth fillings.

The orthodoxy presents these as proof of the claim that members of the *Sonderkommando* had to extract gold teeth from inmates murdered in homicidal gas chambers.

All inmates who died at Auschwitz were slated for cremation. Before cremating a body – whether in a concentration camp or in a civilian crematorium – all removable metal parts, such as metal tooth fillings, metal dentures and prostheses, had to be removed, as they do not burn and can damage the refractory lining. Especially amalgam fillings, which were the vast majority of all fillings during those years, had to be removed, because such fillings contain mercury, which would evaporate during the cremation process and poison the environment.

Of course, for this procedure to be legal, any (rare) gold filling or any other precious metal would have to be handed over to the deceased person's surviving family members. In the cases at hand, it stands to reason that the Third Reich authorities kept any gold collected this way for themselves.

The amount of precious-metal fillings documented does not support the claim that up to a million people were murdered and robbed of their dental gold. Furthermore, since the deportees presumably gassed on arrival at Auschwitz are said to have been killed without registration, gold extracted from them would not have been neatly registered by the camp's dentistry either. If we follow the witnesses' tale, the gold was collected and smelted right next to the gas chamber, and then sent directly to the SS headquarters in Berlin, without the dentistry getting involved. Hence, there is no documental evidence supporting this alleged dental gas-chamber robbery.

(For more details, see Mattogno 2020, pp. 129f., 191f.)

GOLDBERG, SZYMON

Szymon Goldberg was a former inmate of the Treblinka Camp. He claimed that Jews were killed in masses at Treblinka by three methods:

1. First, by pumping the air out of the gassing cabins, then introducing the exhaust gas of some vehicle – rather than from a stationary engine, as the orthodox narrative claims today.
2. Ether was burned, and this vapor was used.
3. Chlorine was also used as a poison gas.

None of these methods are defended today by the orthodoxy. This demonstrates that Goldberg was telling his story based on hearsay and rumors, rather than his own experience. Goldberg also claimed that victims were bleeding from their mouths, which was possible in case of chlorine mass murder, but not with engine exhaust.

(Cf. Mattogno/Graf 2023, pp. 66f.; Mattogno 2021e, pp. 158f.)

GOLDFARB, ABRAHAM I.

Abraham Goldfarb was deported from his hometown Międzyrzec Podlaski on 18 or 25 August 1942 to the Treblinka Camp. On 21 September 1944, a Soviet investigative commission interrogated him. The resulting testimony was later submitted by the Soviets during the Nuremberg International Military Tribunal (Document USSR-380). A second, undated deposition by Goldfarb, published in a 1987 book, was made in the context of the Jerusalem show trial against John Demjanjuk, hence probably dates to the mid-1980s.

There are a few differences between both statements. Most notably, in his later deposition, he claimed that the railway cars going to Treblinka were sprinkled with chlorine (probably referring to chlorinated lime), while no such reference is in his 1944 account. Here are some notable claims from Goldfarb's statements:

- When he arrived, there was only one gassing building with three chambers, each measuring 5 m × 4 m, and 2 m high.
- A tractor engine located in an annex was used both to generate electricity, and to gas victims with its exhaust gases. This stands in contrast to the current orthodox narrative of a tank engine used for gassing, and a separate motor used to generate electricity. Engine-generator devices were rather complex. Running 24/7, they needed to be reliable and easy to maintain. Hence, devices specifically designed for that purpose were used, not some engine taken from some vehicle, rigged in some awkward way to a dynamo.
- The victims' corpses bled from their mouths. Killings with chlorine could have that effect, as it destroys the lungs, but engine exhaust does not lead to bleeding.
- A new gas-chamber building was built between late August and late November 1942, with 2 × 5 rooms, each measuring 6 m × 6 m, and 2 m high.
- There were windows in the roof and round spy windows in the corridor walls to observe the gassings. Neither of this is part of the current orthodox narrative. Roof windows were frequently claimed for the Sobibór gas chambers, while spy holes in the wall are Goldfarb's unique invention.
- Each gas chamber had gas-escape openings in the roof. These, too, are Goldfarb's unique contributions to the tale.
- The engine in a room next to the last chamber was too small; it could only feed exhaust gas into two of the ten chambers. Therefore, between late November 1942 and April 1943, when a larger engine was installed, the victims were killed *not* with exhaust gases, but instead with moistened chlorinated lime, killing people within 24 hours. This is an echo of Jan Karski's black-propaganda story of Jews getting killed during transit with chlorinated lime spread out inside deportation trains. A similar claim was made by Leon Finkelsztein and Szyja Warszawski.
- Victims crammed together so tightly that they kept standing upright after death (from his 1985 deposition). However, people dying slump down, no matter how tightly they are packed.
- On average 5,000 victims per day, which would result in 1.8 million during the camp's operational span of roughly a year, which would be twice the amount claimed by today's orthodoxy.

In his 1944 account, Goldfarb mentions Jankiel Wiernik and also the latter's book, which means that he probably read the book, and possibly other accounts as well. This suspicion becomes a certainty when comparing Goldfarb's 1944 account with Wiernik's booklet: Goldfarb took essential elements of his story from Wiernik's account, such as the first 3-chamber and the second 2×5-chamber building with similar measures. He also included one pivotal aspect that Wiernik had dragged through his evolving story. This enables us to identify this plagiarism. In his earliest, handwritten text, Wiernik wrote:

"On the roof [of the gas-chamber building] *– a safety hatch used in the case of killing people with chlorine. After throwing the appropriate amount of chlorine, the hatch closes hermetically."*

In Wiernik's later typewritten text of what was soon to be published as his booklet, chlorine is no longer mentioned, but rather engine-exhaust gas. Therefore, the roof hatches had lost their function. But they hung around nonetheless. Wiernik included them in his typed text anyway, without giving any explanation of what they were used for:

"On the roof, an outlet with an airtight closure."

In the published English translation, this turned into:

"The outlet on the roof had a hermetic cap."

Goldfarb fell into that trap when copying Wiernik's roof outlets to his first gas-chamber building:

"Each chamber had an opening in the ceiling, which was covered with a net."

The orthodox story knows nothing about such openings.

When describing the new, larger gassing facility, Goldfarb included openings here as well, assigning a new function to them:

"There were special openings in the roof for the gas to flow out of the chamber."

Considering that large amounts of exhaust gas were allegedly pumped into those chambers, these rooms had to have some gas-release opening, or else the gas would have forced its way out during a gassing by bending or breaking something. Hence, Goldfarb's literary evolution of Wiernik's chorine-introduction hatches was actually smart – if that's what Goldfarb meant by that, rather than a simple ventilation opening used after the gassing.

However, for some inscrutable reason, Goldfarb reverted to the chlorine murder with his unique claim that, due to an insufficient engine, chlorinated lime was used for four months. He also described victims bleeding from their mouths, which could be cause by chlorine, but not by exhaust gases.

Goldfarb added features to his plagiarized story to make it sound like his own story, which are all unheard of, far-fetched and in conflict with the narrative ultimately accepted by the orthodoxy.

(For more details, see Mattogno 2021e, pp. 141-145, 178-181.)

GÖRING, HERMANN

Hermann Göring (12 Jan. 1893 – 15 Oct. 1946), *Reichsmarschall*, was the second-most powerful man in the Third Reich after Adolf Hitler. During World War One, he was a decorated war pilot, becoming something of a national hero. During the Second World War, his main responsibilities lay in organizing Germany's economy and its air force.

Hermann Göring

Göring's role in the persecution of Europe's Jews was very limited, but decisive. On 31 July 1941, he expanded Reinhardt Heydrich's task to solve the Jewish question in Germany by emigration and evacuation, as decreed back on 24 January 1939, to encompass all of Germany's area of influence in Europe. Göring also ordered Heydrich to submit a draft plan to implement this comprehensive or total solution of the Jewish question. In this document, Göring used the terms *Gesamtlösung* (total or comprehensive solution) and *Endlösung* (end or final solution) synonymously.

This document has been maliciously misinterpreted as Göring conveying Hitler's order to switch from a policy of emigration and evacuation to one of homicidal annihilation. However, the text says expressly that Heydrich's new task was a *supplement* (*Ergänzung*) of the old task of emigration and evacuation from Germany, not its *replacement* (*Ersatz*) with something different. In January 1939, Germany was still at peace, and its influence was limited to its own territory. By the end of July 1941, however, Germany's government expected the swift collapse of the Soviet Union, which would have resulted in Germany ruling all of Europe, except for a few neutral countries and Britain, which they hoped to appease after the collapse of Soviet Russia. Therefore, Heydrich's authority to act within Germany had to be extended and supplemented to encompass all of Germany's areas of influence in Europe.

Furthermore, the challenge of getting rid of the Jews via emigration and evacuation had become much larger, not only due to the vast territories now in Germany's sphere of influence, but also because of the huge number of Jews (mainly in Eastern Europe) coming under German direct or indirect rule. Hence, a comprehensive solution of the Jewish question through emigration and evacuation required a completely new approach, for which Göring asked Heydrich for a comprehensive draft (*Gesamtentwurf*). (See Document 710-PS, *IMT*, Vol. 26, pp. 266f.).

When this document was introduced by the prosecution during the International Military Tribunal (IMT) on 20 March 1946, the translation twice used the term "final solution." In the first instance, "comprehensive solution" was the clear meaning; in the second case, "final solution" is ambiguous and could have had a lethal interpretation. Göring noticed the prosecution's attempt to misrepresent this document's meaning and protested instantly, also pointing out that Heydrich's original task had been decreed during peace time. (*IMT*, Vol. 9, p. 519)

When the U.S. prosecutor Thomas Dodd, introduced the documentary movie *The Nazi Concentration Camps* on 29 November 1945 (*IMT*, Vol. 2, pp. 431-434; transcript in Vol. 30, pp. 462-472), Göring reportedly commented off the record that this must be a forgery (or so Wikipedia claims in his entry). What was shown on that day was real footage showing the disastrous impact of Germany's total collapse, primarily mass death due to starvation and disease (common everywhere in Germany, inside and outside the camps). Yet the narrator of this film, working under the direction of the U.S.'s secret service O.S.S. – the CIA's predecessor – misrepresented the scenes as resulting from a premeditated German extermination policy. (See Irebodd 2023, Rudolf 2017). Therefore, Göring wasn't far off the mark with his alleged comment.

Göring also, and correctly, refused to believe the 4-million death toll for Auschwitz claimed during the IMT (Vol. 9, p. 611), as well as the total claimed death toll of "something like 10,000,000 people [who] have been done to death in cold blood" (*ibid.*, p. 612). Göring kept insisting that a "policy of emigration, not liquidation of the Jews," had been implemented, and that he had no knowledge of any extermination policy (*ibid.*, p. 619). Göring remained skeptical even after Rudolf Höss had testified at Nuremberg, asking him in a private note (see Mattogno 2020b, p. 117):

> *"How is it technically possible in the first place to exterminate 2 1/2 million people within 3 1/2 years?"*

Hermann Göring was the world's first Holocaust skeptic, with an astonishing ability to anticipate future research results.

GÖTH, AMON

Amon Göth (11 Dec. 1908 – 13 Sept. 1946), SS *Hauptsturmführer*, was in charge of constructing and then heading the Płaszów Camp. As such, he ended up getting prosecuted by the SS-internal court system for looting inmate property and selling it on the black market. He was arrested in early 1945, but due to the war situation, could

Amon Göth

not be tried. He was eventually arrested by the Americans and later extradited to Poland, who put him on a Stalinist show trial, where his guilt was predetermined and where former inmates of his camp were encouraged to testify against him. Göth denied all charges and challenged the credibility of all incriminating testimonies – unsuccessfully. He was hanged in Krakow on 13 September 1946.

Amon Göth was made known to a wider audience through Steven Spielberg's move *Schindler's List*, in which Göth is shown committing various atrocities, including randomly shooting inmates from his home balcony overlooking the camp. This, however, was physically impossible in reality, because Göth's house was at the bottom of a hill and the camp on top of it. This alleged incident was thus yet more "artistic license" by the Jewish director Spielberg.

(See the entry on *Schindler's List*, as well as Rudolf 2019, pp. 253f.)

GRABNER, MAXIMILIAN

Maximilian Grabner (2 Oct. 1905 – 24 Jan. 1948), SS *Untersturmführer*, was a detective with the Vienna police, and later with the State Police at Kattowitz. In June 1940, he was transferred to Auschwitz to become head of that camp's Political Department. In December 1943, he was arrested for unlawful appropriation of inmate property (embezzlement) and sentenced to 12 years' imprisonment by an SS tribunal.

Maximilian Grabner

The Political Department was in charge of the camp's cremations in its crematoria. Since these buildings were also claimed to be the location of gas-chamber mass murder, Grabner logically was accused of bearing co-responsibility for them, organizing and supervising the alleged homicidal gassings. After the war, he made the following incriminating statements in this regard:

– *Starting in early 1942, several gassings were carried out in the basement cells of Block 11.* The orthodoxy insists, however, that only one such gassing took place in this building, in early September 1941, although that fictitious event is refuted by genuine wartime documents.

– *300,000 dead inmates were buried in 1941 and 1942 due to lack of cremation capacity.* The orthodoxy insists on some 100,000 buried inmates, but wartime air photos set the figure closer to 10,000 to 20,000. (See Rudolf 2020a, p. 119.)

– *In order to erase the traces of this mass murder, orders came from Berlin in 1942, after the discovery of the Katyn mass graves, to unearth and burn the corpses.* However, Katyn was discovered only in April of 1943. (His former subordinate Pery Broad told the same lie, suggesting that these false ideas were planted by their interrogators.)

Grabner further testified against his fellow camp officers, "confessing" the most absurd charges:

– He affirmed three times that the Auschwitz death toll during his presence at the camp (to the end of 1943) amounted to "at least three million." (Orthodoxy insists on 1 million, for the entire life of the camp.)

– At another interrogation, he set that figure even

higher: "some 3 to 6,000,000 people."
- He blamed it all on the former camp commandant Rudolf Höss, whom Grabner described as a merciless and blood-thirsty man.
- Grabner claimed to have sabotaged the mass murder wherever he could, in one case by damaging the two large Birkenau crematoria by pouring "used engine oil into the chimney" – But imagine the camp's top Gestapo officer secretly clambering up the 25 iron steps of the 15m-high chimney, single-handedly, while holding a large can of used engine oil in one hand... (without that oil doing anything to the furnaces at the other end of the smoke ducts...)
- On another two occasions, he claimed to have poured oil into the smoke duct where it meets the chimney (although there is no opening to allow this to happen), and the second time he did that, the chimney blew up, together with the furnaces! Engine oil is not explosive, however.
- Grabner seriously claimed that Auschwitz had been set up as an extermination camp already in April 1940 "by an order from Berlin."

We will likely never know the conditions that compelled him to testify thusly. Physical and psychological torture were commonplace, as were vague (and false) promises of acquittal. Oftentimes, the Allied (often Jewish) interrogators would draft their own version of a "confession" statement and then pressure the accused to sign it. This is implied here, based on Grabner's own words, written while he was in a prison of the occupation force in Austria:

"The signatures on the reports drawn up in the course of these investigations are in my own hand, but in the formulation of the content of these reports I had no influence, because I had to sign them as a result of the methods employed during my interrogations."

Grabner ended up as one of the most prominent among the defendants during the Polish show trial against members of the former Auschwitz camp garrison. Despite his cooperative testimony, he was sentenced to death on 22 December 1947, and subsequently hanged. (For details, see Mattogno 2016c, pp. 63-67; 2022f, pp. 117-126.)

GRADOWSKI, SALMEN

Salmen Gradowski is the name that can be found on a set of handwritten documents – one of which is known today as a "diary" – that were allegedly found inside an aluminum container by a Soviet investigative commission on 5 March 1945, near the ruins of the former Crematorium II at Birkenau. The texts, said to be in Yiddish, are stored at the Museum of Military Medical Service in St. Petersburg, and were deciphered and translated by Polish professor Bernard Mark.

One of the documents, a letter dated 6 September 1944, mentions twice that millions of people were exterminated at Auschwitz, and that at the time when this letter was written, "tens of thousands of Jews from the Czech and Slovakian regions" were being murdered. However, the only mass murder of Jews from the region of former Czechoslovakia in the summer of 1944 was the alleged elimination of the Theresienstadt Family Camp (affecting some 7,000 people), which is said to have happened on 10 and 11 July, if we follow the orthodox narrative of events (Czech 1990, pp. 662f.); but this is a mere figment of two witnesses' vivid yet mendacious imagination (see the entry on the Family Camp). The next such alleged event was the murder of Jews deported from the Theresienstadt Ghetto, but they arrived at Auschwitz only on 29 September 1944 (Czech 1990, p. 718). Hence, the letter cites exaggerated victim numbers along the line of Soviet post-war propaganda, plus an imaginary event.

The "diary" has Gradowski's deportation train pass through "the well-known Treblinka train station." While this camp with its train station was probably well-known to the Soviet investigators who "discovered" the diary, it would have been completely *unknown* to Gradowski during his alleged deportation in late 1942, and there is no reason why his train would have passed through this station's minor railway line at all.

About the alleged murder weapon which Gradowski is said to have helped operate (as a member of the *Sonderkommando*), the diary only fleetingly mentions "the gas chamber," nothing more. If these homicidal gas chambers had been real, any diary would be full of references to this object of horrors, with detailed descriptions.

Another manuscript attributed to Gradowski, also in Yiddish, is also said to have been dug up near the ruins of one of the former Birkenau crematoria by some unnamed, probably Polish civilian. The partly damaged text was eventually deciphered, translated and then published in Israel. The text exudes a sugary rhetoric of sentimental lyricism, often bordering on the ridiculous. At the beginning, the text, in an attempt to prevent being dismissed as "atrocity propaganda," appeals to future information that will confirm the "terrible secret," although that very text of an alleged member of the *Sonderkommando* should by all means *be* the primary source of such information to confirm this "terrible secret." However, the text contains nothing of substance. Quite to the contrary, it tells one whimsical anecdote after another, like a novel authored by an omnipresent person, seeing, hearing, feeling everything that was happening, and describing at great length and in great detail the vicissitudes of male and female inmates, sounding out their innermost thoughts and emotions, like an all-seeing eye capable of peering through the barrack walls. Here is a list of peculiarities:

- The text tells a gripping tale of the presumed annihilation of the Jews from the family camp, an event that has been refuted as atrocity propaganda.
- The cremation furnaces allegedly were kept hot for three days without anything getting burned – a waste of fuel that would not have happened.
- This text (like other false testimony) used the term "bunker" to refer to the basement morgues of Crematoria II and III allegedly misused as gas chambers, rather than for the makeshift gassing facilities outside the camp perimeter.
- In celebration of a mass gassing, all members of the camp's Political Department allegedly lined up in a room in front of the gas chamber – which is not only obvious nonsense but was also impossible, because there was no room that could have accommodated all these members.
- The text describes in gripping detail the interaction of a husband and wife inside the gas chamber, for which the author must have stood right next to them. The moment the toxic gas was released, the husband instantly solidified into an immovable statue.
- After a gassing, two doors with four bolts were opened, but the room in question only had one single-leaf door and no bolts.
- The opened gas chamber had the "atrocious stench of death," meaning that the inmates of the *Sonderkommando* did not wear gas masks (which would have been fatal), but freshly asphyxiated people do not exude much of any smell.
- The gas turned the pink faces "reddish, purplish or black" – while a hydrogen-cyanide poisoning would have turned faces from a normal to a pinkish hue.
- Cremating three corpses (two adult and one child) took "a few minutes" (or later, "20 minutes"), when in fact the cremation furnaces at Auschwitz took one hour to cremate *one* body (see the entry on crematoria).
- 2,500 people were crammed into the morgue (aka gas chamber) of 210 m², hence a packing density of 12 per square meter, which, if at all possible, would have required training, discipline and the victims' willing cooperation.
- A gassing scene contains enough pro-Soviet resistance rhetoric to fill a Stalinist propaganda movie.
- The victims even sing Israel's national anthem and predict the country's resurrection – which hints at this entire fairy tale having been concocted *after* the founding of the state of Israel (in 1948), and possibly in Israel itself.

Some descriptions of the equipment used inside Crematorium II are rather accurate, which indicates that the author of this text had some reliable knowledge in this regard and may indeed have been a member of the crematorium stokers.

(For details, see Mattogno 2021, pp. 248-259.)

GRAY, MARTIN

Martin Gray (27 April 1922 – 24 April 2016), born Mieczyslaw Grajewski, was a Polish Jew who claimed to have been deported to the Treblinka Camp, from where he managed to escape. He then joined the Soviet NKVD and helped break up the Polish anti-communist underground. He initially immigrated to the United States in 1946, then to France in 1960. In 1970, he had a ghostwriter named Max Gallo write an "auto"-biography for him in French titled *For Those I Loved* (*Au nom de tous les miens*), which covers his alleged experiences at Treblinka. However, Gitta Sereny, a mainstream Holocaust scholar with a good knowledge of Treblinka's history, had this to say about Gray's book, written in an article titled "The Men Who Whitewash Hitler," published by the *New Statesman* (Vol. 98, No. 2537, 2 Nov. 1979, pp. 670-673):

> "*During the research for a* Sunday Times *inquiry into Gallo's work, M. Gallo informed me coolly that he 'needed' a long chapter on Treblinka because the book required something strong for pulling in the readers. When I myself told Gray, the 'author', that he had manifestly never been to, or escaped from Treblinka, he finally asked despairingly: 'But does it matter? Wasn't the only thing that Treblinka did happen, that it should be*

written about, and that some Jews should be shown to have been heroic?'"

Something similar could well have motivated many witnesses when testifying or writing their memoirs.

GREECE

In early March 1943, the Bulgarian authorities arrested and handed over to the Germans some 4,000 Greek Jews from the Bulgarian zone of occupation. These Jews are said to have been deported to the Treblinka Camp. In the spring and summer of 1943, some 40,000 Jews from Greece were deported by German forces to Auschwitz. After Italy had surrendered to the Allies in September 1943 and Germany had moved into the formerly Italian occupation zone, some 1,800 more Greek Jews were deported to Auschwitz in 1944. (See the entry on Jewish demography for a broader perspective.)

GROCHER, MIETEK

Mietek Grocher was a Polish Jew who claims to have been incarcerated at the Majdanek Camp during the war. After the war, he immigrated to Sweden. After he had retired, he went on a mission to tell his wartime memories to school children. According to an interview published on 8 December 2004 in the Swedish local newspaper *Östgöta-Correspondenten*, Grocher managed to sneak out of a gas chamber at Majdanek:

> *"When I was in there, I understood what was awaiting me and the others inside that space. Instinctively, I started to move a little backwards, without really thinking that I would manage to escape. By chance, I managed to do it. An officer started talking to another officer and moved away a few steps. During that moment, I managed to sneak away and reunite with my parents in the camp."*

According to another article about Grocher published in the local *Katrineholms-Kuriren* on 15 May 1998, the guard discovered young Mietek sneaking out of the chamber and fired all six shots of his revolver at him, missing the escapee but hitting six other Majdanek martyrs. So much for German marksmanship! Mr. Grocher remarked about this:

> *"I would say I'm the only one who managed to do that."*

There are others, however, who have experienced the same good luck, see the entry on escapes, from gas chamber.

GROJANOWSKI, JAKOV

Some orthodox scholars claim that Jakov Grojanowski is the name of a Polish Jew who wrote a report in 1942 about his alleged experiences at the Chełmno Camp. The report itself is only signed with the name "Szlamek," and the identity of its author is uncertain. Other scholars claim that it was a certain Szlojme Fajner, but it is all just speculation. An analysis of the text, written in a diary style, reveals that it is a propaganda text written by the Jewish resistance fighters of the Warsaw Ghetto.

(For more details, see the entry on the Chełmno Camp, as well as Mattogno 2017, pp. 51-59.)

GRÖNING, OSKAR

Oskar Gröning

Oskar Gröning (10 June 1921 – 9 March 2018), SS *Unterscharführer*, was deployed from late September 1942 in the department that stored and administered inmate valuables at the Auschwitz Camp. Although several criminal investigations were initiated after the war, all were eventually shelved.

He volunteered to give an interview for the 2005 BBC atrocity-propaganda movie *Auschwitz: Inside the Nazi State*. During that interview, he stated that he wanted to speak out also in order "to oppose the Holocaust deniers," and then he exclaimed (see the German Wikipedia entry on Gröning):

> *"Weil ich den Leugnern sagen will: Ich habe die Krematorien gesehen, ich habe die offenen Feuerstellen gesehen. […] Ich war dabei."*
>
> *"Because I want to tell the deniers: I have seen the crematoria, I have seen the open fireplaces. […] I was there."*

That wasn't good enough for the BBC, though, who falsified that sentence and added gas chambers into the mix by translating as follows (underscore added; see the PBS transcript):

> *"Because I want to tell those deniers: <u>I have seen the gas chambers</u>, I have seen the crematoria, I have seen the burning pits. […] I was there."*

Gröning was a minor bureaucrat in an office at the Auschwitz Main Camp handling inmate valuables. He would not have been allowed to walk into any of the crematoria or to the so-called "bunkers" in order to "see" the gas chambers or watch a gassing, so the BBC once again made a fool of themselves with this forgery. Furthermore, Gröning was evidently entirely oblivious of what the "deniers" claim. He was fighting a "straw denier." As can be seen from the entries on crematoria and open-air incinerations, no one denies the existence of crematoria and "open fireplaces" at Auschwitz. In fact, the latter were probably blazing at their highest intensity when Gröning arrived in late September 1942. This must have left quite an impression on the young man. But his legitimate seeing of crematoria buildings and open-air burnings does not prove any mass-extermination claim.

Considering the fallibility of human memory, and in particular the issue of false memories planted by 60 years of incessant one-sided propaganda, expecting an 83-year-old geriatric, utterly unfamiliar with actual revisionist research, to "refute" them is irresponsible at best, if not utterly ridiculous.

Due to his media appearances resulting from his BBC interview, Gröning was eventually indicted in Germany for aiding in the murder of at least 68,000 persons. After a show trial descending into a theater of the absurd in 2015, with a 94-year old defendant suffering from dementia reading from a script prepared for him, and accused by similarly old and demented "witnesses" (see Winter 2015), Gröning was sentenced to four years imprisonment. In 2018, at age 97, he was ordered to serve his time, but he died before setting foot in prison.

GROSS-ROSEN

The Gross-Rosen Camp, located near a town of that same name in Lower Silesia, was initially a labor subcamp of the Sachsenhausen Camp, but became an independent concentration camp in 1941. Its relevance for the Holocaust is strictly limited to the unique and false claim by former Gross-Rosen inmate Isaac Egon Ochshorn, that this camp had a homicidal gas chamber, in which some 150,000 Soviet PoWs were allegedly murdered. All historians agree that Gross-Rosen had no such facility, and that only some 3,000 Soviet PoWs died in that camp throughout its existence. Hence, Gross-Rosen is a phantom extermination camp, existing only in Ochshorn's lurid fantasies.

GROSSMAN, VASILY

After Ilya Ehrenburg, the Jewish journalist Vasily Grossman (12 Dec. 1905 – 14 Sept. 1964) was probably the second most-impactful Soviet atrocity propagandist of the Stalinist era. His two most-important works of propaganda are his booklet on the Treblinka Camp, titled *The Hell of Treblinka*, and the collection of Soviet atrocity stories on claimed German wartime crimes, titled *The Black Book*. This book was announced in the U.S. media already in November of 1944 as a tome that would document "the German massacre of approximately six million European Jews" (Shapiro 1944), clearly showing that the six-million death toll was not a figure established after the war, but predetermined beforehand. However, Stalin must have changed his mind, for the project was put on ice, and the book was published only posthumously in 1980 (Ehrenburg/Grossman 1980). The book is filled with the most outrageous atrocity lies ever spread about the Germans, all based on "witness" accounts, many of which are summarized in the present work.

Vasily Grossman

In his brochure on Treblinka, Grossman did not quote "witness" statements but decided to streamline – meaning manipulate – them into a coherent narrative. Grossman claimed, among other things, that the death toll of this camp was 10,000 victims a day, for a total of three million victims (more than triple the amount claimed by today's orthodoxy). These victims were allegedly murdered by gassing, scalding with hot steam, and suffocation by means of vacuum pumps. The latter two versions are admitted by today's orthodox historians as having been freely invented. As to the gassing, Grossman specified that this was allegedly done using "exhaust gases of a heavy armored tank engine, which served the power station of Treblinka" – hence probably a Diesel-powered electric generator, which would have been useless for mass murder, as diesel exhaust is relatively harmless. (See Mattogno/Graf 2023, pp. 19-23, and throughout the book)

GROUNDWATER LEVEL

Many alleged Holocaust crime sites are said to have included pits of various depths. These would have been dug for one of two reasons: either to bury (temporarily or permanently) victims' bodies, or to use as "burn pits" to dispose of the corpses. In the second case, the burnings allegedly occurred either immediately after their murder, or much later, after their corpses had been first buried but then exhumed again in order to erase evidence of these crimes. The latter is true for almost all claimed crime sites connected with the *Einsatzgruppen* shootings and the so-called *Aktion* 1005, and with most victims purportedly killed in the camps of the *Aktion Reinhardt*: Belzec, Sobibór and Treblinka, plus Chełmno.

A special case is Auschwitz Camp, where some 100,000 victims of diseases and mass murder are said to have been first buried, but then, starting in September of 1942, exhumed again and burned on pyres in deep pits. These pits are said to have been used until March/April 1943, when the Birkenau crematoria started coming into operation. Furthermore, during the deportation of Jews from Hungary to Auschwitz between mid-May and early July 1944, new pits are said to have been dug and used to cremate many, if not most, of the claimed murdered Jews.

Air photos of Birkenau show no signs of large pits during the spring and summer of 1944 – as would have been required for the claimed open-air incineration. But the claims made about deep pits run into further problems, because the Auschwitz-Birkenau Camp was located in the vicinity of the confluence of three rivers: the Sola, the Vistula and the Przemsza River. Therefore, depending on the water level of these rivers, the groundwater level in the area of the Birkenau Camp could be as high as just a few inches below the surface, or even right up to the surface – turning the entire area into a swamp.

Under these circumstances, it was physically impossible to dig pits deeper than about one meter

Small pond just outside the outer fence of the Birkenau Camp, showing the groundwater level (1997).

Depth of Claimed Auschwitz Cremation Pits		
Witness	Depth	Location
Charles Bendel	1.5 m	near Crematorium V
Shaul Chasan	4 m	near "Bunker 2"
Leon Cohen	3 m	near "Bunker 2"
Szlama Dragon	3 m	near Crematorium V
Stanisław Jankowski	2 m	near Crematorium V
Kurt Marcus	4 m	near "Bunker 2"
Filip Müller	2 m	near Crematorium V
Miklós Nyiszli	3 m	near "Bunker 2"
Joshuah Rosenblum	2 m	unspecified

Source: Mattogno 2016b, p. 28; for more details, see the entry on open-air incinerations.

(three feet) without groundwater swiftly filling them in. For this reason, the construction pits for the three buildings at Birkenau which had a basement – Crematoria II and III as well as the so-called *Zentralsauna* – had to have intruding groundwater continuously pumped out. Many documents about the hours spent for this work have been preserved.

Equally preserved are several documents addressing the high groundwater level and the problems resulting from it for the area's various camps and for the entire area, primarily worries about contaminating the drinking water.

During the construction of Birkenau, drainage ditches were dug to lower the groundwater level inside the growing camp. However, the large pits said to have been operated near the so-called "bunkers" were located outside the camp perimeter, hence would not have been included in this system of drainage ditches. The depth of the cremation pits claimed for that area is said to have been between two and four meters, depending on the witness (see the table). At that depth, these pits would have filled up with groundwater quickly, foiling any attempt at initiating or maintaining open-air incinerations in them.

For similar reasons, mass graves dug in the vicinity of the Birkenau Camp could not have been much deeper than a meter – not only because they would, again, have filled quickly with water, but more importantly, submersing corpses in groundwater contaminates it. Bacteria and viruses diffuse from corpses soaked in water, and would very adversely affect the health of all those drinking water in the region.

Air photos show that mass graves existed indeed, but probably only very shallow graves, and only for a very limited time (see the entry on air photos). Due to the danger of contaminating the drinking water, these bodies were probably exhumed again in late

1942, and incinerated on pyres. The atrocious scenes that must have accompanied this activity probably formed the true core of the rumors about mass murder at Auschwitz. (For details on the groundwater level at Auschwitz and its relevance to Holocaust claims, see Gärtner/Rademacher 2003, Mattogno 2003a; Mattogno 2016b, pp. 97-127)

GRÜNER, MIKLÓS

Nikolaus Michael Grüner

Nikolaus Michael (aka Miklós) Grüner was a Hungarian Jew who claimed that he knew Elie Wiesel from their time together at the Auschwitz Camp, but that the person who claimed to be Elie Wiesel after the war and became famous as the best-known Holocaust "survivor" is a different person.

Documents prove that a Lazar Wiesel, born in 1913, was deported to and registered at the Auschwitz Camp. He was deported together with his 13-year older brother Abraham. Elie Wiesel claims to have been born in 1928, hence 15 years after Lazar Wiesel, that he had received Lazar's inmate number (and was tattooed with it), and that Abraham was actually his father. However, his father's first name was Shlomo, who was six years older than Abraham Wiesel. There is no trace in the Auschwitz records or anywhere else of any other person with the last name Wiesel (or any spelling derivative of it) with the biographical data of Elie Wiesel. The documents suggest, therefore, that Elie Wiesel is not identical with Lazar Wiesel. Thus, there is no proof that Elie Wiesel was ever interned at Auschwitz. (For details, see Grüner 2007; Routledge 2020, pp. 377-418.)

GULBA, FRANCISZEK

Franciszek Gulba was deported to Auschwitz on 11 February 1941. In November 1944, he was transferred to the Buchenwald Camp. Twenty-five years after the war, on 2 December 1970, he signed a lengthy affidavit in Polish at the Auschwitz Museum. Four years later, on 30 December 1974, he wrote a letter to the International Auschwitz Committee at Warsaw, where he made some more statements. Here are some of his pertinent claims:

– In August of 1942, he allegedly saw a steamroller ready to prepare an access road to a new gassing facility outside the camp's perimeter, the so-called Bunker 2. However, no such heavy equipment has ever been claimed to have been used at Auschwitz for such gravel-road projects. (In his 1974 letter, the gravel road had mutated into a road with "solid pavement" – although no such road ever existed.)
– He claims that they built the road by first putting down a layer of bricks, then a layer of gravel, topped with a layer of – sand!
– They also allegedly built a drainage ditch next to this road "with vertical brick walls to sustain it." Gulba clearly knew nothing about road and drainage construction. He invented this entire scenario, so he had a "reason" to claim how he ended up witnessing a gassing.
– A large excavator was used to dig deep trenches, presumably to serve as mass graves. However, the orthodoxy insists that mass graves were dug manually by inmates.
– Red firs were planted to hide the mass graves. However, air photos of 1944 show that the mass graves had not been hidden, and that no stand of young fir trees existed anywhere.
– The gassing facility allegedly consisted of a corridor, from which entry doors into individual gas chambers opened to the left and right. The chambers' exit door led directly to the mass graves. However, the orthodoxy insists that Bunker 2 had no corridor at all. Each door led directly into and out of one of several parallel gas chambers. The design described by Gulba is said to have existed in the latter-phase gas-chamber buildings at Belzec, Sobibór and Treblinka.
– Gulba claimed that the ceiling of the old farmhouse had been replaced with a massive concrete slab, but the straw roof had been kept in place nonetheless. This claim is unique among all witnesses. However, replacing the ceilings across the entire building with a concrete slab would have required removing the roof – and putting it back later. That's not likely to have happened.
– The gas was thrown in through openings in the ceiling. However, the orthodoxy insists that Zyklon B was poured in through hatches in the side walls. Openings in the ceiling are claimed for the gas chambers posited to have existed inside Crematoria I through III.
– The gassing he claimed to have witnessed in August 1942 in Bunker 2 was, in his opinion, the first to have occurred in the Birkenau area. However,

the orthodoxy insists that gassings in that area had occurred much earlier – since March 1942 in the so-called Bunker 1, some 500 meters to the north, and since early July 1942 in Bunker 2. Because Gulba had been in the camp since early 1941, and claims to have been lodged in Birkenau since April 1942, earlier mass gassings nearby could not have evaded his attention.

– In 1970, he did not yet know the term "Bunker." In 1974, however, after the International Auschwitz Committee had sent him an article on the "bunkers," he named the facility he claimed to have seen "Bunker 2," but insisted that he knew nothing about "the other farmhouse" (Bunker 1).

This is how cross-pollination, or rather cross-pollution, of witness memory works.

(For more details, see Mattogno 2016f, pp. 113-116.)

GUSEN

When the Mauthausen Camp became overcrowded in 1939, subcamps were established to house inmates near to their worksites. Eventually, three such camps near the creek Gusen were established, named Gusen I through III.

Of particular interest for Holocaust historiography is the cremation furnace established at the Gusen I Camp, which was almost identical to the furnaces set up at the Auschwitz Main Camp. Extant records of the Gusen furnace's operation allow insights into those at Auschwitz. (See the entry on crematoria.)

Gusen is also of interest to Holocaust historians due to claims that one of the three Gusen camps supposedly had a homicidal gas chamber. This tale is exclusively based on eyewitness claims of the late 1960s. Orthodox historians claim that a few improvised homicidal gassings allegedly occurred either in some barracks, or that the camp's fumigation chamber was used for it, although it had windows which would have been shattered by hypothetical victims. (For more, see Mattogno 2016e, pp. 143f.)

This gassing facility was supposedly set up during the final months of the war, hence after the Himmler order in late 1944, alleged by Kurt Becher, that no more exterminations should happen. It is more likely that inmates evacuated from Auschwitz to Mauthausen and Gusen brought along Auschwitz rumors of gas chambers, and that these rumors were then also spread at and about the Gusen Camps.

Politically speaking, Gusen *must* have had a homicidal gas chamber, because every memorial site or museum about a German wartime concentration camp demands such a prime tourist attraction. Furthermore, no inmate testifying about homicidal gas chambers can ever be accused of being untruthful, or else prosecutors in many European countries turn their attention to the skeptic.

GYPSIES

"500,000 Gypsies were murdered by the Third Reich." This accusation has been made by Gypsy organization for decades. They demanded that Germany recognizes this as a genocide, and that compensations be paid to these Gypsy organizations. These claims were disseminated by all major news media, German and international. The German government quickly caved in, and its highest representatives have since repeatedly acknowledged both the genocide as such and the alleged death toll of half a million victims (which some inflated to one million).

However, if requested to provide any kind of documentation supporting these charges, no one seems to be able to provide any – neither these media outlets, nor any Gypsy organizations, nor historians specializing in the field, nor the International Red Cross's Tracing Center of victims of Third-Reich persecution, nor any other governmental or non-governmental historical organization.

In the late 1980s, Michael Zimmermann, a German history student, wrote a thesis on the issue. He came to the conclusion that not half a million Gypsies had died but "only" 50,000. That's only 10% of the claimed figure, and only some 5% of the Gypsies then roaming continental Europe. Clearly, there was no systematic attempt at wiping them off the face of the earth.

However, since Zimmermann was a German and not a Jew, some politically correct readers could question his motives. Moreover, both his 1989 thesis and his 1996 book on the topic were written in German and have never been translated, and thus they are inaccessible to most people. Hence, a few years after that, a German Jew came to the rescue: With his 2001 book *The Nazi Persecution of the Gypsies*, Günther Lewy drove home basically the same message as Zimmermann had done. Everyone can read and quote Lewy's English book without fear of being accused of anything, except maybe philo-Semitism.

The Jewish community could breathe a sigh of relief, as their exclusive primacy of victimhood was restored.

Some documentation exists about the arrest and deportation of Gypsies by German authorities during the Second World War. Thousands of them were sent to the Auschwitz Camp. Here is where the story of the gypsy genocide in gas chambers has its roots.

When rummaging through thousands of wartime documents in the archives of the Auschwitz Museum, Polish historian Danuta Czech stumbled over documents indicating that on 2 August 1944 the number of Gypsies registered in a certain section of a particular sector of the Birkenau Camp dropped by 2,897. Hence, she concluded in her *Auschwitz Chronicle* that they must have been killed in gas chambers! She backed up that claim with witness accounts by Stanisław Jankowski, Otto Wolken and a certain Jakub Wolman. Jankowski's and Wolken's credibility can be assessed by their claims as a whole. (See the entries dedicated to them.) Jakub Wolman's only terse remark in this regard was that, of the almost 3,000 Gypsies gone missing on 2 August 1944, *18,000* were gassed – hence six times more than allegedly went missing.

Had Czech thoroughly checked all the records of all the other camp sectors and of transfers to other camps, she would have found those missing Gypsies. They were not murdered but simply relocated. Comparing hundreds, even thousands of wartime camp documents with long lists of occupancy numbers for several camp sections is an ungrateful and tedious job, but there's no other way of getting the story straight. Yet with her gas-chamber obsession, she jumped straight to false conclusions of wishful thinking.

Czech has another entry in her *Auschwitz Chronicle*, on 23 March 1943, where she claims that on this day some 1,700 unregistered, hence undocumented, Gypsies were gassed at Auschwitz. However, there is not the slightest trace in the documentation that these Gypsies existed in the first place, such as a document showing their deportation or arrival at Auschwitz. This claim is based exclusively on one imprecise witness account.

The Polish Resistance Movement at that time was well-informed about the Gypsy Sector, which had been set up in the Birkenau Camp just a month earlier. They knew and reported about the typhus epidemic wreaking havoc in this sector, but they knew nothing about a mass gassing of the Gypsies. Such an event would have been much-more newsworthy than any epidemic.

In other words, even the claim that 50,000 Gypsies died during the Third Reich, let alone that many thousands of them were murdered in gas chambers at Auschwitz, is untenable. However, Günther Lewy and his like-minded fellow historians will not challenge those gassing stories, as this would undermine the very foundation upon which the uniqueness of Jewish victimhood is erected. Toppling the Gypsy gassings would make the other gassings come tumbling down as well.

(For more details, see Lewy 2001; Müller 2004; Schirmer-Vowinckel 2004; Mattogno 2003c; 2014; 2022b, pp. 157f., 224-231.)

H

HÄHLE, JOHANNES

Johannes Hähle is said to have been a German military photographer with the 637th Propaganda Company of the German Sixth Army. Between 29 September and 1 October 1941, a series of photographs were taken in Kiev, which are attributed to Hähle.

The photos of interest in the current context can be divided into two groups. One group of photos shows from several dozen up to a few hundred persons gathered at or walking along city roads. The other group shows various aspects of a ravine, with one set showing several dozen men doing some earthwork with shovels mostly at the ravine's bottom, while the other set shows a large collection of items placed at the bottom of the ravine. The items evidently consist mostly of clothes, bedding and

Various photographs presumably taken by Johannes Hähle at Kiev between 29 September and 1 October 1941.

bags.

The orthodoxy claims that the first group of photos shows Jews on the way to their execution, while the second group shows the Babi Yar ravine near Kiev, where 33,771 Jews are said to have been executed on 29 and 30 September 1941.

The orthodox narrative of Babi Yar asserts that the Jews had to leave their belongings, including their clothes, before approaching the ravine. They were then either shot while standing at the ravine's edge, then falling into it, or they had to climb down to the bottom of the ravine and were shot there. Either way, they presumably all ended up naked and dead at the ravine's bottom, where they were then covered with soil.

Hähle's photos refute that narrative. First, none of his photos show an assembly of people coming anywhere close to 33,771 people. Next, while it is unknown who the owners of the items were that had been placed at the bottom of the ravine, it is clear that these items cover the bottom of the ravine. Hence, the owners did not leave these items outside it. It is, of course, conceivable that the owners of the items left them in one part of the ravine and were shot in another part.

However, the photos showing ongoing earthworks in a ravine have no signs of any corpses being covered. The bottom of the ravine is flat and largely undisturbed. Hence, it does not consist of huge mass graves that had just been covered. Therefore, this work is evidently unrelated to mass executions. This is supported by the fact that there are very few German soldiers visible, and in one of the photos, one soldier is casually talking to two evidently local women.

None of this harmonizes with the assumption that this is the crime scene of the mass execution of 33,771 local Jews.

(For more details, see Mattogno 2022c, pp. 574-578, 783f., 788-792.)

HAIR OF CAMP INMATES

During the Second World War, all inmates admitted to any kind of camp of the Third Reich had to have their hair shorn and kept trim during the entire time of their incarceration. Exceptions were granted only in special cases. This is graphically demonstrated by the so-called Auschwitz Album showing shorn male and female inmates after their admission into the camp.

This life-saving procedure, considered humiliating for many women, became necessary due to the persistent presence and spread of lice in the German war-time camps. Lice glue their eggs (nits) onto human hair, thus vitiating attempts at eradicating them by merely disinfesting clothes and washing the inmates.

During the war, most everything was recycled and reused in Germany, as the country was increasingly cut off from any foreign supplies. Hair was no exception. From a certain length onward, hair was collected and submitted to various companies specializing in turning them into industrial products. Before such hair was sent out, it had to be disinfested to make sure no lice and nits were spread with it, and thus potentially typhus, which is transmitted by lice.

There is no evidence that hair found at Auschwitz or elsewhere upon capture by Allied armies originated from inmates who had been gassed. Even if chemical analysis showed the presence of cyanide resulting from the exposure to Zyklon B (hydrogen cyanide), this merely proves that the hair was disinfested before getting bagged and stored, but not that it was exposed to hydrogen-cyanide gas while still on the head of an inmate.

(For more information, see Rudolf 2020, pp. 47f.; Mattogno 2021, pp. 98f.; 2023, pp. 153, 162, 371.)

HANEL, SALOMEA

Salomea Hanel was an inmate of the Sobibór Camp. In a deposition published in 1945, she claimed that chlorine was the gas used at Sobibór in "the chamber" to kill inmates. This claim is rejected as false by the orthodoxy, who insists on several gas chambers and on an engine producing lethal exhaust gas.

(See the entry on Sobibór for more details, as well as Graf/Kues/Mattogno 2020, pp. 71f.; Mattogno 2021e, pp. 84f.)

HARTHEIM

Hartheim Castle near Linz, Austria, was one of National-Socialist Germany's euthanasia centers. It entered the Holocaust stage with two affidavits containing claims attributed to Franz Ziereis, the former commandant of the Mauthausen Camp. Both affidavits are written by former Mauthausen inmates, one of it by Hans Maršálek. Both contain the claim that Ziereis allegedly confessed on his death bed to the murder of 1 to 1½ million people at Hartheim Castle. (See the entry on Hans Maršálek for more details.) Of course, no historian has ever taken that claim seriously. However, less excessive claims by other inmates or profile-neurotic historians can be found in the pertinent orthodox literature, claiming various figures of inmates from the Mauthausen camp complex to have been murdered/gassed at Hartheim Castle, and describing the location and design/setup of its alleged gas chamber in multifarious ways. (See Leuchter *et al*. 2017, pp. 168-171, for an overview.) Since none of the victims are claimed to have been Jews, no further elaboration is required here.

"Harvest Festival" → Operation "Harvest Festival"

HASSLER, JOHANN

Johann Hassler, SS *Unterscharführer*, testified some 16 years after the war that he once operated a gas van for the *Einsatzgruppen* near Minsk. The vehicle he drove had a complex system of piping exhaust gases into the cargo box: to the exhaust pipe, a "connecting piece with a thread"

Johann Hassler

had been added, onto which "a metal hose could be screwed" leading into the cargo box. "Behind the connecting piece," evidently suspended in mid-air "was a slider, which closed the exhaust pipe opening to the rear." This is pure nonsense, since the metal hose screwed to the end of the exhaust pipe already redirected the gases, so nothing could get into any detached rest of the exhaust pipe anymore. Closing this detached rear end of the exhaust pipe with a slider was just as pointless as the existence of that rear end itself. In addition, adding a slider into an exhaust pipe to close it would have required quite a contraption.

Not even the claim of adding a connecting piece with a thread to the exhaust pipe makes sense. Exhaust pipes are made of rather thin steel; hence they cannot have threads. Adding a thick metal piece to its end with a thread would have been a complicated operation, yet flexible metal hoses allegedly attached to it did not come with threads. Furthermore, the extreme temperature difference between cold and hot exhaust pipes would have led to massive expansion and contraction of the metals involved, causing problems with the thread.

Hassler's story makes no sense and contradicts all other claims about how these vans' exhaust system were allegedly designed. In other words: he made it up on the fly to contribute something to the tall tale of gas vans.

(For more details, see Alvarez 2023, pp. 156-158.)

HEALTHCARE

Healthcare provided by the SS in German concentration camps is said to have been of very low quality, if it existed at all. Inmates too sick or injured to be cured quickly are said to have been killed in order to get rid of "useless eaters." But like so many aspects of the orthodox Holocaust story, this is mostly a myth.

Then as now, most skilled physicians either have their own practice or find attractive employment in larger medical practices or hospitals. A prison or detention camp is the least-likely place anyone would voluntarily work at, as the quality of working atmosphere and clientele are the worst imaginable. As a result, the quality and dedication of physicians working there is the lowest, and so is the quality of care. This is true for all societies. In a war, when camp populations soar but staff cannot be increased due to many physicians and nurses having to care for wounded soldiers and civilians, the quality of care inevitably declines even further.

In that situation, Germany's camp authorities attempted to let the inmates organize camp life by themselves, supervised only by a few officials. This included healthcare, for which inmate physicians and nurses were frequently used. However, as French camp veteran Paul Rassinier has aptly described for the wartime camps at Buchenwald and Dora, lack of SS supervision and corruption led to unscrupulous criminal prisoners and scheming political inmates filling favorable positions on the basis of connections and favors, rather than according to skill. Therefore, inmates who had been physicians in their civilian lives often ended up doing menial labor, while criminals and political fanatics ended up playing doctors; they accepted patients by their importance in the pecking order or by how much they could pay, rather than by who was most in need of help. The results were catastrophic. (See Rassinier 2022.)

Auschwitz

While there is reason to believe that the situation at the Auschwitz camps was similar to that reported by Paul Rassinier, the extant documentation on medical service provided at those camps is vast. It irrefutably proves that the SS policy was at all times to do anything they could in order to preserve and reinstate the health of all inmates, and to care even for those inmates who were incurably sick.

For instance, at least 25 x-ray books have been preserved containing the names of 34,876 inmates who were x-rayed in order to diagnose diseases or injuries, very frequently followed by all kinds of surgeries. Frequent reports of the Auschwitz inmate hospital listed surgeries performed, among other things. Daily reports on inmate deployment showed, at times, a staggering number of inmates lodged in the camp who were unfit for labor, none of whom was ever killed. Patients suffering terminally from tuberculosis were nursed for months on end, with daily records of the disease's progression, until they eventually died. None of them was killed.

The SS established a branch of its hygiene institute in Rajsko, a village near Auschwitz. Tens of thousands of inmates who contracted typhus were admitted to the inmate infirmary and nursed back to health. The Rajsko institute did tens of thousands of tests on stool and blood samples of these inmates to make sure they were indeed cured, before they were released back to the normal camp population.

When Eduard Wirths became SS garrison physician of Auschwitz in September 1942, the camp saw its first truly dedicated physician determined to make a difference for the welfare of all inmates. He set in motion not only a huge project to improve the camp's sanitary infrastructure, but also the construction of a huge inmate hospital in Construction Sector III of the Birkenau Camp. This was to have more than 100 barracks, at the costs of hundreds of millions of dollars in today's currency, where the sick inmates of all camps of the entire wider region were to be admitted and treated with the most modern equipment. The construction of this hospital made steady progress throughout 1943 and 1944, but was ultimately halted and abandoned in late summer of 1944 due to the deteriorating war situation.

A relatively honest description of the healthcare and sanitary conditions at the Monowitz Camp was co-authored in 1946 by the Italian physician Primo Levi who had been incarcerated in that camp since early 1944. As well-equipped as the Monowitz hospital was according to his description, if an inmate required more care than this facility could provide, he was transferred to Birkenau, where the facilities were even better.

In summary: the Birkenau Camp cannot have been *both* a camp where tens of thousands of sick and injured inmates, unfit for labor, were cared for with great effort in order to cure them, *and* a camp where hundreds of thousands of the inmates unfit for labor were slaughtered wholesale. While the first claim can be substantiated with a rich documentation and with many witness accounts of survivors who were treated in the infirmaries, the second claim is substantiated only by claims that contradict themselves, contradict the extant documentation, contradict material traces, and contradict technical possibilities.

(For more details, see Mattogno 2016a, esp. pp. 42-72; Mattogno 2023, Part 1, all entries on health-related issues, the improvement of sanitary facilities, and the presence of inmates unfit for labor.)

HÉNOCQUE, GEORGES

Georges Hénocque (13 Oct. 1870 – 23 March 1959) was a French priest and member of the resistance. As such, he was eventually caught by German occupational forces and deported to the Buchenwald Camp. In his 1947 book *Les Antres de la Bête* (*The Caves of the Beast*), he described in detail the alleged homicidal gas chamber at the Buchenwald Camp (pp. 115f.). However, all historians agree that no homicidal gas chamber existed there. Some aspects of Hénocque's description resemble features of the room inside the crematorium at the *Dachau* Camp, which today is presented as a homicidal gas chamber. Hénocque may have seen U.S. American footage taken after the war and shown in various propaganda movies, such as *Nazi Concentration Camps*.

However, Hénocque added a conveyor belt continuously transporting corpses from the room next to the gas chamber right into the cremation furnaces. Such a device never existed anywhere. He furthermore claimed to have seen flames eight to ten meters tall coming out of the *furnaces* (rather than chimneys). Of course, cremation furnaces are closed and don't emit any flames. If opened to insert a body, the chimney's draft sucks air inside through the open door, preventing any hot gasses from coming out.
(A partial English translation of Hénocque's text is in Rudolf 2019, pp. 297.)

HERMAN, CHAIM

Chaim Herman was a Jew deported from Drancy, France, to Auschwitz, where he arrived on 4 March 1943 and was assigned inmate number 106113. He is said to have written a secret letter hidden in a bottle that poked out of a pile of ashes at the railway siding near the crematoria ruins at the former Birkenau Camp, where a Polish medical student is said to have found it after the war. The student then supposedly traveled all the way to Warsaw to hand over the item to the French mission, from where it traveled to France. Three years later, the French government handed it over to the Auschwitz Association at Paris, which gave the Auschwitz Museum a photocopy in 1967 – a tangled history, to say the least.

The letter itself was written intending to be concealed from the SS, hence one would expect some decisive revelation. But in it, we only read:

> "20 months have already passed since then [his arrival at the camp], it seems like a century, it is perfectly impossible to write you all the proofs of what I experienced there, if you live, you will read many of the works written with regard to this sonder kommando [sic], but I must ask you never to judge."

What sane writer would refuse to tell his story in a secret letter, instead pointing to literature yet to come? This would only make sense if the writer had nothing to tell from his own experience, and knew already of that postwar literature, because it had already been published by the time the letter was written.

The letter also contains a reference to a transport of 200 members of the *Sonderkommando* in early 1944 to Majdanek, where these people were then supposedly "exterminated a few days later." Sitting in Auschwitz, isolated from the rest of the world, the author of this letter could not possibly have known what happened to such people. By all reasonable accounts, this letter is a blatant postwar forgery. (See Mattogno 2021, pp. 245-248.)

HEYDRICH, REINHARDT

Reinhardt Heydrich (7 March 1904 – 4 June 1942), SS *Obergruppenführer*, has been the head of the National-Socialist Party's Security Services (*Sicherheitsdienst*) since its inception in 1931. As Heinrich Himmler's deputy, he was head of the Security Police and the Security Services, which were merged in 1939 into Germany's equivalent of the Department of Homeland Security, the Reich Security Main Office (*Reichssicherheitshauptamt*, RSHA). Heydrich headed the RSHA until he died on 4 June 1942 after an assassination orchestrated by the British.

Prior to the war against Poland, Heydrich was tasked with forming the so-called *Einsatzgruppen* of the Security Police and the SD, whose task was to pacify the occupied Polish territories. These *Einsatzgruppen* were then also deployed on the temporarily German-occupied Soviet territories.

Reinhardt Heydrich

The orthodox narrative has it that Heydrich's role in organizing and carrying out the so-called Holocaust was crucial in many regards. Here are the documented decisions that Heydrich made or implemented with regard to the "Jewish Question":

– On 24 January 1939, Heydrich was appointed by Göring as head of the Reich Center for Jewish Emigration in Berlin (*Reichszentrale für jüdische Auswanderung*).
– On 15 July 1939, Heydrich ordered Eichmann to set up a Central Office for Jewish Emigration in Prague (*Zentralstelle für jüdische Auswanderung*).
– On 24 June 1940, Heydrich wrote to Joachim von Ribbentrop, German Minister of Foreign Affairs, saying that the Jewish problem could no longer be solved "by emigration" but required "a territorial final solution;"
– On 20 May 1941, Heydrich prohibited the emigration of Jews from France and Belgium in an effort to render the emigration of "Jews from the Reich territory" easier.
– On 31 July 1941, Heydrich was entrusted by Hermann Göring with the task of making preparations "for a comprehensive solution of the Jewish question within the German sphere of influence in Europe" in "addition" to the tasks Göring had given him on 21 January 1939, viz. to resolve "the Jewish question by means of emigration or evacuation."
– On 18 September 1941, Himmler ordered Heydrich to implement the *Judenwanderung* (Jewish migration) via Łódź.
– On 10 October 1941, Heydrich declared in Prague that plans were drawn up to deport 50,000 Jews from the Protectorate to Minsk and Riga between 15 October and 15 November, where they were to be housed "in the camps for communist detainees in the operational territory."
– On 20 January 1942, Heydrich headed the Wannsee Conference on the policy of Jewish emigration.

He reported that, as a result of the Third Reich's policy of emigration, some 537,000 Jews had emigrated from the Reich territory by 31 October 1941. He also stated that Himmler had "forbidden any further emigration of Jews in view of the dangers posed by emigration in wartime and the looming possibilities in the East." He added that, "as a further possible solution and with the appropriate prior authorization by the *Führer*, emigration has now been replaced by evacuation to the East." This conference resulted in a slew of correspondence between various government agencies, with the main contentious subject being a possible mass sterilization of certain groups of Jews. However, no such mass-sterilization program was ever initiated, let alone implemented. None of these documents hints at any kind of extermination.

Heydrich was therefore indeed the chief planner of the final solution in Europe, but as all these and other documents show, this term actually designated the evacuation of the Jews from Europe to the temporarily German-occupied Soviet territories.

Heydrich's first name was probably the namesake for "*Aktion Reinhardt*" – the vast program of expropriation and deportation of Jews for resettlement or forced-labor deployment. See the entry on *Aktion Reinhardt* for details.

(For more details on Heydrich's role, see Graf/Kues/Mattogno 2020, pp. 201-225, 255f.)

HIMMLER, HEINRICH

Heinrich Himmler (7 Oct. 1900 – 23 May 1945) was *Reichsführer* SS, meaning national leader of the SS, and head of the German police. As such, he gave the orders to his subordinates as to what to do with the Jews within Germany's reach: He ordered the police to arrest them; to deport them; to detain them in ghettos and camps; he told the SS what to do with them in the various camps; to deploy them at forced-labor tasks; and he decreed to the leaders of the Security Police and the Security Service, including their *Einsatzgruppen*, how to handle them in the temporarily German-occupied eastern territories. Hence, Himmler was second only to Hitler when it came to implementing the "Final Solution of the Jewish Question."

Heinrich Himmler

Interestingly, the order to prepare the "Final Solution of the Jewish Question," as an extension of prior efforts to make Jews emigrate from Europe, was issued on 31 July 1941 by Hermann Göring to Himmler's subordinate Reinhardt Heydrich. Himmler was circumvented.

Himmler's statements regarding the treatment of the Jews within his reach can be divided into two distinct and separate sets:

First, Himmler's various speeches, during which he lectured to high German government and military officials throughout the war. (See the dedicated entry on Himmler speeches.) Starting in late 1943, he was very blunt in several of his speeches as to the ongoing project of annihilating the Jews within the German sphere of influence.

Second, his orders to his subordinates as to how he wished the Jews to be treated. These documents paint a different picture than what he stated in some of his 1943 speeches. Not annihilation, but maximum exploitation of the Jews' labor force was increasingly at the top of Himmler's priorities.

Here is a list of orders and other documented statement by Himmler:

– In a memorandum of May 1940, Himmler rejected "the Bolshevik method of physical annihilation of a people [...] as un-Germanic" with regard to the Jews, and Hitler commented upon this by writing in the margin, "Quite correct."

– On 18 September 1941, Himmler wrote a letter to *Gauleiter* Arthur Greiser. The document states explicitly that the Jews from Germany and the Protectorate (Czechia) will be deported to eastern areas as a first step. In spring 1942, they were to be moved still further east.

– On 23 October 1941, Himmler ordered a stop to all Jewish emigration. A day later, his subordinate Kurt Daluege, chief of the German police force, issued a directive according to which "Jews shall be evacuated to the east in the district around Riga and Minsk."

– On 25 January 1942, five days after the Wannsee Conference, Himmler wrote to Richard Glücks, Concentration Camp Inspector:

"You will make preparations to receive 100,000 Jews and up to 50,000 Jewesses in the concentration camps in the coming weeks. Large scale economic tasks will be assigned to the concentration camps in the coming weeks."

- On 29 January 1942, Himmler issued his "Guidelines on the Treatment of the Jewish Question." They stipulated that all measures aimed at solving the issue for all of Europe do so by way of the expulsion of Jewry and by using the Jews for forced labor at "road, railway and canal construction, agriculture, etc." Jewish workers should be pooled "in purely Jewish enterprises under supervision."
- On Apr. 30, 1942, Oswald Pohl, chief of the SS Economic and Administrative Main Office, reported (129-R; *IMT*, Vol. 38, pp. 364f.):
    > "1. The war has brought about a visible structural change in the concentration camps and their tasks regarding the employment of inmates. The increase in number of prisoners detained solely on account of security, re-education, or preventive reason is no longer in the foreground. The primary emphasis has shifted to the economic side. The total mobilization of inmate labor, first for wartime tasks (increase of armaments) and then for peacetime tasks, is moving ever more to the forefront.
    > 2. From this realization arise necessary measures which require a gradual transformation of the concentration camp from its original, exclusively political form into one commensurate with its economic tasks."
- On 17/18 July 1942, Himmler ordered the expansion of the Auschwitz Camp to house 200,000 mainly Jewish prisoners for labor deployment.
- On 16 September 1942, one day after his meeting with Armaments Minister Albert Speer, Oswald Pohl, head of the SS's Economic and Administrative Main Office reported to Himmler that all prisoners of the Reich were to be conscripted for armaments production:
    > "The Jews destined for eastern migration therefore will have to interrupt their journey and work at armaments production."
- 28 December 1942: Glücks conveyed Himmler's order to all camp commandants that death rates in all camps must be reduced by all means. The inmates have to receive better food.
- On 20 January 1943, Glücks elaborates in more detail about Himmler's order by giving detailed instructions on how to improve living conditions in the camps.

The rich surviving documentation on the Auschwitz Camp proves beyond doubt that a) there was no order to kill Jews, and b) that there were many orders to save the lives and improve the health and survival chances of all inmates in that camp. Hence, the just-mentioned orders to reduce death rates in all camps by all means were not just on paper. (For details, see the entry on Auschwitz, on healthcare, and on the Birkenau Camp.)

Himmler's service calendar is also revealing, as it has only one entry about this matter, dated 18 December 1941: "Jewish question | to be exterminated as partisans." It is unclear what this referred to, but it is likely that this concerned the growing partisan activities in the East, which was heavily supported and contributed to by Jews. Hence, if Jews were encountered as partisans, they were to be exterminated. Other than that, this calendar contains absolutely nothing indicating that Himmler was in any way concerned with how best to exterminate six million innocent civilians. There is also no trace in this calendar of Himmler discussing with any of the alleged main executors of the Holocaust any pertinent issues: Adolf Eichmann, Rudolf Höss, Odilo Globocnik, Christian Wirth and Paul Blobel are all conspicuously absent. In his meetings with Reinhardt Heydrich and Adolf Hitler, Himmler never broached the Jewish question.

As with the missing Hitler Order, there is also no Himmler Order for the extermination of Europe's Jews. To circumvent this "problem," American interrogators managed to "convince" German mid-level official Kurt Becher that he once saw an order issued by Himmler in late 1944 to *stop* the extermination. (See the entry on Kurt Becher.) However, no such order has ever been found either, so it stands to reason that Becher made it up in order to receive favorable treatment from his Allied captors.

After the end of the war, Himmler tried to escape from northern Germany in civilian clothes, but was captured by the British. He was interrogated for a while, then died. The British claimed that he committed suicide by taking a cyanide pill he is said to have hidden in a hollow tooth. However, the capsule photographed as evidence is far too big to be hidden in a tooth. Moreover, a high-level British government document discovered in the early 2000s shows that orders had been given to the arresting British unit to kill Himmler and let his body vanish. Others claim that he was buried in an unmarked grave somewhere near Lüneburg. (See Allen 2005; Kollerstrom 2014.)

(For more details, see Mattogno/Graf 2023, pp. 194-196; Rudolf 2023, pp. 168-173, 197f., 352-360;

Mattogno 2022c, pp. 74-76, 157-165.)

HIMMLER SPEECHES

Heinrich Himmler, chief of the Third Reich's SS and police forces, had an obsession with delivering endless speeches. Many if not most of his speeches were delivered in front of non-public audiences usually consisting of high-profile personalities of politics and military. The topics Himmler covered reach from the mundane to the top secret. Surprisingly, many of these speeches were recorded and have been preserved, both as sound recordings and as transcripts. It is as if Himmler did not want to keep top secret issues a secret, but rather have them eventually announced to the world.

When it comes to the treatment of the Jews, Himmler's attitude underwent a remarkable shift from late 1942 to late 1943. In 1942, he was talking about the National-Socialist policy of deportation and resettlement. For instance, in a speech of 23 November 1942, he stated:

> "The Jewish question in Europe has completely changed. The Führer once said in a Reichstag speech: If Jewry triggers an international war, for example, to exterminate the Aryan people, then it won't be the Aryans who will be exterminated, but Jewry. The Jews have been resettled outside Germany, they are living here, in the east, and are working on our roads, railways etc. This is a consistent process, but is conducted without cruelty."

Not even a year later, Himmler gave two speeches in the West-Polish city of Poznan (German: Posen) where he gave a completely different picture of what his forces were in the process of committing. On 4 October 1943, he said in a brief passage of his long sermon in front of the gathered leadership of SS and police the following:

> "I am thinking now of the evacuation of the Jews, the extermination of the Jewish people. It is one of those things that is easy to say: 'The Jewish people will be exterminated,' says every Party comrade, 'that is quite clear, it is in our program: deactivation [Ausschaltung] of the Jews, extermination; that is what we are doing.' And then they all come along, these 80 million good Germans, and every one of them has his decent Jew. Of course, it is quite clear that the others are pigs, but this one is one first-class Jew. Of all those who speak this way, not one has looked on; not one has lived through it. Most of you know what it means when 100 bodies lie together, when 500 lie there, or if 1,000 lie there. To have gone through this, and at the same time, apart from exceptions caused by human weaknesses, to have remained decent, that has made us hard. This is a chapter of glory in our history which has never been written, and which never shall be written; since we know how hard it would be for us if we still had the Jews, as secret saboteurs, agitators, and slander-mongers, among us now, in every city – during the bombing raids, with the suffering and deprivations of the war. We would probably already be in the same situation as in 1916/17 if we still had the Jews in the body of the German people.
>
> [...] We had the moral right, we had the duty to our own people, to kill [umzubringen] this people which wanted to kill us [umbringen]."

Here, Himmler uses the term "evacuation" and "deactivation" as equivalent with "extermination." However, the National-Socialist's program he refers to nowhere mentions extermination, but only rescinding the Jew's citizenship, hence pushing them out of Germany. So, was "extermination" a word for "evacuation," or vice versa?

This speech was not only recorded, but at war's end, the Allies found a stash of shellac disks with that speech. In other words: Himmler had seen to it that his "secret" speech – containing stuff no one should ever talk about – was multiplied!

Just two days later, on 6 October 1943 and in that same city, Himmler was at it again, this time in front of the political elite of the Third Reich. In a brief excerpt from his long speech, we read the following (Smith/Peterson 1974, pp. 169f.):

> "I ask of you that that which I say to you in this circle be really only heard and not ever discussed. We were faced with the question: what about the women and children? – I decided to find a clear solution to this problem too. I did not consider myself justified to exterminate the men – in other words, to kill them or have them killed and allow the avengers of our sons and grandsons in the form of their children to grow up. The difficult decision had to be made to have this people disappear from the earth. For the organization which had to execute this task, it was the most difficult which we had ever had. [...] I felt obliged to you, as the most superior dignitary, as the most superior dignitary of the party, this political order, this political instrument of the Führer, to also

speak about this question quite openly and to say how it has been. The Jewish question in the countries that we occupy will be solved by the end of this year. Only remainders of odd Jews who managed to find hiding places will be left over."

The following day, Joseph Goebbels wrote in his diary about Himmler's speech, stating that Himmler had claimed, quote, "that the whole of Jewry will be exterminated," thus corroborating what Himmler had stated (see the entry on Joseph Goebbels).

But it is all wrong. Great efforts were being made at that time to save the lives of the Jews incarcerated at Auschwitz, for example. The Jews in Hungary had not been touched, and no plans existed in October 1943 to change that. In Poland, nobody had yet been deported from the large ghetto of Lodz, and many other ghettos were still around as well. None of them had been "eliminated" by the end of 1943. In France, three quarters of the Jews remained unmolested until the end of the war. And in any case, it would have been technically impossible to kill and vaporize the 1.5 million or so Jews remaining under German control, in just under three months.

In truth, Himmler was something of a babbler who loved to hear himself talk tough. Despite all the talk about not spreading the word about what he was about to say, he had it all recorded for posterity to read and hear! It is clear that Himmler was a security liability for the Third Reich. Hitler wised up to him only toward the end of the war, when he had the secretive Heinrich Müller take over for Himmler.

While Himmler's orders to his subordinates demanded ever-increasing efforts to *save* the lives of the Jews and to put everyone to productive work, in his speeches he ranted about having killed, by the end of 1943, each and every single Jew in the German sphere of influence his henchmen could lay their hands on. Himmler was a grandiloquent liar! Or perhaps just a typical politician.

He showed a little more restraint in a speech two and a half months later, on 16 December 1943, delivered to the commanders of the German Navy. In it, he mentioned the killing of partisans and political commissars, including their families, but not of all Jews within reach. That was closer to the truth, even though the order to execute the Red Army's political commissars had been rescinded in May 1942 (see the entry on the Commissar Order), and since 1943, partisans weren't shot automatically anymore either, if they operated as recognizable units.

(For more details, see Rudolf 2023, pp. 356-360.)

HIMMLER VISITS

Himmler's service calendar proves that he visited Auschwitz on 17 and 18 July 1942, in order to follow up on the implementation of plans to expand the Birkenau Camp. The orthodoxy claims that, on this occasion, Himmler attended the gassing of an incoming transport of Jews. However, Himmler's service calendar, showing that he was busy doing something else during his entire visit, and the lack of any incoming Jewish transports that could have been gassed, demonstrate that Himmler cannot have witnessed a gassing. (See Mattogno 2016a, pp. 16-25; 2020b, pp. 242-250.)

The next day, 19 July 1942, Himmler briefly visited the Sobibór Camp, which he visited again in early 1943. (See Graf/Kues/Mattogno 2020, pp. 58-60; Mattogno 2021e, pp. 150f.)

There is no evidence showing that Himmler visited the Auschwitz Camp a second time, or that he ever visited any of the other alleged extermination camps (Belzec, Chełmno, Treblinka).

Despite these facts, several witnesses claimed that Himmler visited the Treblinka Camp in early 1943, issuing an order to exhume and burn all buried victims. Many Auschwitz survivors claimed that Himmler visited Auschwitz in early 1943, on occasion of a claimed festive inauguration of the first Birkenau crematorium (or on a later date for a crematorium inspection). No such inauguration party ever happened.

These false testimonies are a "convergence of evidence" on a lie. This indicates that these claims are not based on personal experience but on black propaganda, rumor mongering, false-memory syndrome and/or coaching or even coaxing of witnesses by investigating judicial authorities. Here is a list of witnesses who made these false claims:
– Charles S. Bendel (Auschwitz)
– Henryk Mandelbaum (Auschwitz)
– Isaac Egon Ochshorn (Auschwitz)
– Lucjan Puchała (Auschwitz)
– Arnošt Rosin (Auschwitz)
– Franz Süss (Auschwitz)
– Rudolf Vrba (Auschwitz)
– Alfred Wetzler (Auschwitz)
– Rudolf Reder (Belzec)
– Stanisław Kon (Treblinka)
– Henryk Poswolski (Treblinka)
– Lucjan Puchała (Treblinka)
– Samuel Rajzman (Treblinka)
– Jankiel Wiernik (Treblinka)

See also the entry on Erich von dem Bach-Zelewski for the claimed Himmler visit of an *Einsatzgruppen* execution.

HIRSZMAN, CHAIM

Chaim Hirszman was a Polish Jew presumably deported to the Belzec Camp in September 1942, where he stayed until the camp was dissolved. On 19 March 1946, he made a deposition about his alleged experiences there in front of a Jewish historical commission. His text is very short and merely claims that deportees were killed in "the gas chamber." He does not describe it in any more detail. Hirszman was murdered a short while later, hence could not testify in any more detail. Here are a few peculiar claims in his short text:

Chaim Hirszman

- He mentions having led deportees "to the furnaces," although Belzec never had any furnaces. He did not mention anything about the burning of corpses on pyres.
- The door (singular) of the gas chamber (singular) allegedly closed automatically, although no automatic mechanism is mentioned by anyone else for the claimed three, and later six, gas chambers.
- The corpses were only shorn after the execution, although everyone else insists that this happened before the execution.
- He claims to have found his wife among the murdered victims, and had to cut off her hair, yet his wife testified after the war, after he had been murdered, reiterating what her husband had allegedly told her.

Hirszman's wife Pola had little to add from hearsay to her former husband's account, among them the unique atrocity claim that children up to three years of age were buried alive in a pit.

Therefore, these two meager testimonies merely echo the black propaganda circulating about Belzec at that time.

(For more, see Mattogno 2021e, pp. 58-60.)

HIRT, JOSEPH

Joseph Hirt (born 1925) was a school psychologist at Chester County, Pennsylvania, until his retirement in 1993. Starting in 2001, he gave hundreds of presentations at churches, schools and other organizations about his alleged experiences during the war as an Auschwitz inmate. After attending one of Hirt's presentations in April of 2016, history teacher Andrew Reid realized that some of Hirt's claims could not be true. He subsequently did some research into Hirt's claim and came up with a long list of essential claims in Hirt's story that were wrong:

Joseph Hirt

- The Auschwitz database of inmates shows that Hirt was never at Auschwitz.
- The number he tattooed on his arm belonged to another person.
- Hirt claimed to have encountered Josef Mengele before his escape from Auschwitz in March 1942, but Mengele was posted to Auschwitz only in 1943.
- The photo Hirt presented as showing him shortly before his escape from Auschwitz actually shows a Dachau inmate photographed by a U.S. soldier.

Other central claims in his story of megalomania were just as false, such as his claim, that he saw Hitler refuse to shake Jesse Owens's hand during the 1936 Olympics – a non-event that never happened – and that he had a close friendship with Eleanor Roosevelt, through whom he managed to have President Roosevelt intervene personally, so Hirt's entire family could immigrate to the U.S.

Exposed as a liar and fraud, Hirt first denied any wrongdoing, but when his nephew confirmed that his entire Auschwitz story is a lie, Hirt eventually backed off and confessed to having made it all up, but claimed to have had "good intentions."

(For details, see Scott 2016.)

HITLER, ADOLF

Adolf Hitler (20 April 1889 – 30 April 1945) is the central figure in the Holocaust narrative. Considering the monolithic nature of Hitler's dictatorship, his decisions, orders and decrees are what should have caused, started and shaped the progress of the Holocaust. Yet when we look at the historical records, all we have are some general threats uttered during polemic speeches which Hitler used to shape public opinion.

In Hitler's political manifesto *Mein Kampf* (*My Struggle*), one notable statement about the Jews is the following:

"In defending myself against the Jew, I am fighting for the work of the Lord." (Vol. 1, 2.27)

This evidently referred to passages in the New Testament, according to which Jesus made critical remarks about the Jewish political, religious and financial elite of his time. (See Matthew 12:34, 23:33, 27:25; Luke 16:14; John 8:44)

The worst threat Hitler ever uttered in public happened during his address to the German parliament (the *Reichstag*) on 30 January 1939:

"Today I will once more be a prophet: If the international Jewish financiers in and outside Europe should succeed in plunging the nations once more into a world war, then the result will not be the Bolshevization of the earth, and thus the victory of Jewry, but the annihilation [Vernichtung] *of the Jewish race in Europe, for the time when the non-Jewish nations had no propaganda is at an end. National-Socialist Germany and Fascist Italy have institutions which enable them when necessary to enlighten the world about the nature of a question of which many nations are instinctively conscious, but which they have not yet clearly thought out.*

[…] If this [Jewish] *nation should once more succeed in inciting the millions which compose the nations into a conflict which is utterly senseless and only serves Jewish interests, then there will be revealed the effectiveness of an enlightenment which has completely routed the Jews in Germany in the space of a few years. The nations are no longer willing to die on the battlefield so that this unstable international race may profiteer from a war or satisfy its Old Testament vengeance."*

Hence, Hitler predicted the annihilation of the Jewish race in Europe, not by bullets or gas, but by way of enlightening the world with propaganda about the true nature of the Jew. Genocide by propaganda!

On 30 January 1941, during another address to the Reichstag, Hitler explained his prophecy of 1939 as follows:

"And I should like to repeat the warning that I have already once given, on 1 September 1939 [correct: 30 January 1939], *in the German Reichstag: namely, the warning that, if Jewry drives the world into a general war, the role Jewry plays in Europe will be over!"*

Adolf Hitler

Here we have the annihilation of the Jews by way of ending Jewry's influential role in economy, politics, and culture.

On 25 October 1941, two days after Himmler had stopped all Jewish emigration, allegedly because Hitler gave the (oral) order for the Holocaust, we have the following statement from Hitler. It was uttered during a private dinner with his closest co-conspirators and top executors of the Holocaust, SS chief Heinrich Himmler and the head of Germany's Department of Homeland Security (*Reichssicherheitshauptamt*), Reinhardt Heydrich:

"In parliament [30 January of 1939 and 1941], *I prophesied Jewry that the Jew will disappear from Europe if war is not avoided. This criminal race has to account for two million deaths in World War I, and now again hundreds of thousands. Don't anybody tell me that we cannot send them into the morass! Who cares about our people? It is good if the terror precedes us that we are exterminating Jewry. The attempt to create a Jewish state will be a failure!"*

This time, it is extermination by letting Jews disappear from Europe by way of sending them into the morass – which was a reference to the Belorussian swamps, one focus of Germany's planned resettlement projects.

No trace of a written order by Hitler to start the murder of the Jews has ever been found. (See the next entry on the Hitler Order.) Worse still, not a single hint at an ongoing slaughter of millions can be found in any of Hitler's utterances made when dining with his closest friends and confidants. These monologues were meticulously recorded for years by his secretaries, but they leave us baffled as to their complete silence about the presumably ongoing Holocaust. Here in short sequence are a few more of Hitler's statements during his private dinners with his friends (emphases added):

19 November 1941, after Hitler had supposedly issued the oral genocide order, as some orthodox historians claim:

"If today some citizens cried because Jews have

to <u>emigrate from</u> Germany, then this throws a light on these types of self-righteous philistines."

12 January 1942, when mass exterminations had presumably started at the Chełmno Camp:

"The Jews are the chosen dumbest people: they should, for God's sake, never have instigated this war. They will disappear from Europe. All because of a few fools!"

25 January 1942, hence shortly after the Wannsee Conference:

"If I <u>extract</u> the Jew today, then our bourgeoisie becomes distressed. What happens to him? But did the same people care what happened to those Germans who had to <u>emigrate</u>? […] The Jew <u>must leave Europe</u>. Otherwise we won't come to a European understanding. […] At the end of it: I don't know, I'm being so colossally humane. At the time of the papal reign in Rome, Jews were maltreated. […] I simply say: <u>they must go</u>. If he goes phut in the process, I can't help it. I see only one thing: <u>absolute extermination, if they won't go voluntarily</u>."

27 January 1942:

"The Jews must <u>get out of Europe</u>! It is best they <u>go to Russia</u>. I don't have any pity on the Jews."

4 April 1942, after mass extermination allegedly started at Auschwitz and Belzec:

"It is therefore indicative that the upper classes, who never cared for the hundreds of thousands of German <u>emigrants</u> and their hardship, now feel pity on the Jews, although the Jews have their accomplices throughout the entire world and are the most climate-resistant species there is. Jews thrive everywhere, even in Lapland and Siberia."

15 May 1942, after mass extermination allegedly started at the Sobibór Camp:

"Our so-called bourgeoisie laments over the same Jew who stabbed us in the back in the past when he is <u>deported to the East</u>. […]

If a pronounced population parasite is rendered harmless on behalf of the state by slaying him, for instance, then the entire bourgeoisie screams that this is a brutish state. […]

Not a single one of those who shed crocodile tears at the <u>deportation of the Jews to the east</u> considers that the Jew as a parasite is the most climate-resistant individual on the planet who, in contrast to the German, gets accustomed to Lapland as much as to the tropics."

29 May 1942:

"All of western Europe must be freed of the Jews within a given period. […] It is therefore not recommendable to <u>deport them to Siberia</u> because with their climate-resistance, they would only become even more hardened. It is better – as the Arabs don't want them in Palestine – to <u>transport them to Africa</u> and thus submit them to a climate which impairs every person of our resilience, thereby eliminating all points of common spheres of interest with the European part of humanity."

24 July 1942, when mass extermination is said to have just started at the Treblinka Camp:

"<u>After the end of the war</u> he [Hitler] will rigorously take the position that he will destroy one city after another, if the Jews don't come out and <u>emigrate to Madagascar</u> or some other Jewish homeland."

Other documents clearly show that Hitler wanted the "solution of the Jewish question" postponed until after the war. For example, a memo of the Reich Chancellery dating from March or April of 1942 states that Hitler had repeatedly informed Lammers, the head of the chancellery, "that he wanted to postpone the solution of the Jewish question until after the war." Therefore, all wartime measures were to be only temporary in nature.

Here is how German mainstream historian Joachim Fest, in his vast biography on Hitler, summarized Hitler's baffling Holocaust denial in his many private statements to his alleged main accomplices, but also in other contexts (Fest 1973, p. 931; 1975, p. 681):

"For in the table talk, the speeches, the documents or the recollections of participants from all those years not a single concrete reference of [Hitler] to the practice of annihilation has come down to us. No one can say how Hitler reacted to the reports of the Einsatzgruppen, whether he asked for or saw films or photos of their work, and whether he intervened with suggestions, praise, or blame. When we consider that he ordinarily transformed everything that preoccupied him into rampant speechmaking, that he never concealed his radicalism, his vulgarity, his readiness to go to extremes, this silence about the central concern of his life – involving, as it did in his mind, the salvation of the world – seems all the stranger."

In his book *Hitler's War*, British historian David Irving concluded that Hitler didn't know what Himmler and Heydrich were doing behind his back – which seems quite unbelievable. It appears more appropriate to conclude that Hitler had to fight a war against the entire world. The skirmish against the Jews, small in comparison, simply wasn't important enough for him to care too much.

(See also the entry on extirpation; for more details, see Werner 2019, pp. 25-31; Dalton 2023; Graf/Kues/Mattogno 2020, pp. 209-226.)

HITLER ORDER, FINAL SOLUTION (*FÜHRERBEFEHL*)

The former commandant of the Auschwitz Camp Rudolf Höss, after having been coerced to sign various absurd "confessions" dictated to him by the British after severe torture, testified on 15 April 1946 at the Nuremberg International Military Tribunal. Among other things, he claimed that Heinrich Himmler had told him in the summer of 1941 about an order issued by Adolf Hitler to exterminate the Jews of Europe (*IMT*, Vol. XI, p. 398). This alleged *Führerbefehl* immediately became the cornerstone of orthodox Holocaust historiography. And for sure, if "it" happened, it must have been ordered by Hitler, and there must exist traces of this order.

During his lifetime, Raul Hilberg was considered by many as the world's leading orthodox Holocaust scholar. In the first, 1961 edition of his book *The Destruction of the European Jews*, he wrote that Hitler actually issued *two* separate orders for the extermination of Europe's Jews: one for the *Einsatzgruppen* in the spring of 1941, and another one for the extermination centers shortly after Germany's invasion of the Soviet Union. When Hilberg testified as a witness for the prosecution at the first Zündel Trial in 1985, he had to admit during cross-examination that he could not produce any document for either of these orders. He stated instead that he was really referring in the first case to the so-called "Commissars' Order." However, this order merely demanded the execution of Jewish-Bolshevik commissars, hence of certain fanaticized Soviet apparatchiks. (See the entry on that order.)

In the *second*, 1985 edition, Hilberg deleted any reference to a Hitler order to exterminate all Jews. He replaced it with a reference to musings of a German general on having to render harmless "all Bolshevik chieftains and commissars" in the Soviet Union. A second source he quoted is an order eventually issued which mentions *nothing* about killings. (For details on this, see Mattogno 2021c, pp. 57-62.)

Other historians have been more straight forward to admit that no order for the extermination of the Jews written or authorized by Adolf Hitler has ever been discovered. Popular media frequently suggest that there is a significant amount of material in Hitler's hand that ordered a vast extermination program. The historical evidence is just the opposite, as the entries on emigration and resettlement clearly demonstrate.

The result of this situation is that many historians presume that the order was transmitted orally or through "winks and nods." Hilberg, contradicting what he wrote in the first edition of his book, also led the charge in this regard. During a public discussion in 1983, Hilberg tried to explain how this vast program of extermination, spanning an entire continent, encompassing six million victims, and lasting some four years, could have evolved with no order from the very top, and more still: without a centrally developed plan, and without a budget (De Wan 1983):

"But what began in 1941 was a process of destruction [of the Jews] *not planned in advance, not organized centrally by any agency. There was no blueprint and there was no budget for destructive measures. They* [these measures] *were taken step by step, one step at a time. Thus came about not so much a plan being carried out, but an incredible meeting of minds, a consensus mind reading by a far-flung* [German] *bureaucracy."*

In other words, "Holocaust by mind-reading." That this is ridiculous in the extreme requires no explanation.

Here are several other historians' takes on the central issue of the missing "Hitler order":

"What became known in high Nazi circles as the Fuehrer Order on the Final Solution apparently was never committed to paper – at least no copy of it has yet been unearthed in the captured Nazi documents." — William Shirer (1960, p. 1256)

"For in the table talk, the speeches, the documents or the recollections of participants from all those years not a single concrete reference of [Hitler] *to the practice of annihilation has come down to us. No one can say how Hitler reacted to the reports of the Einsatzgruppen, whether he asked for or saw films or photos of their work, and whether he intervened with suggestions, praise, or blame. When we consider that he ordinarily transformed everything that preoccupied him into rampant speechmaking, that he never concealed his radicalism, his vulgarity, his readiness to go to extremes, this silence about the central concern of his life – involving, as it did in his mind, the salvation of the world – seems all the stranger."*
— Joachim Fest (1975, p. 681)

"The process by which total extermination replaced resettlement in Madagascar or 'the East' as the so-called final solution of the Jewish question remains unclear. No written order by Hitler for the extermination of the Jews has been discovered, and the evidence of an oral order is only indirect. The chronology of the development of the extermination program is also confused." — Jeremy Noakes, Geoffrey Pridham (1988, Vol. 2, p. 1136).

"No written document containing or reporting an explicit command to exterminate the Jews has come to light thus far. This does not of course mean that such direct evidence will not appear in the future. In the meantime, the presumption must be that the order or informal injunction to mass-murder Jews was transmitted orally." — Arno Mayer (1990, pp. 235f.)

"For the want of hard evidence – and in 1977 I offered, around the world, a thousand pounds to any person who could produce even one wartime document showing explicitly that Hitler knew, for example, of Auschwitz. My critics resorted to arguments ranging from the subtle to the sledgehammer (in one instance, literally). They postulated the existence of Fuehrer orders without the slightest written evidence of their existence. […] Of explicit, written, wartime evidence, the kind of evidence that could hang a man, they have produced not one line." — David Irving (1991, pp. 19f.)

The confusion among orthodox historians facing the fact that no extermination order by Hitler exists, and also no document from any of his subordinates referring to such an order, was demonstrated during two international conferences organized in Europe during the 1980s. At these conferences, the most competent mainstream experts on the Holocaust wrestled aimlessly and unsuccessfully with this issue. Each one of them came up with another "explanation" of when and how "the decision" was made. However, all of them merely pointed at hints and clues, but none of them were able to demonstrate it convincingly to their like-minded colleagues, let alone to skeptics.

The issue has flared up repeatedly in later years, leading to an ever-growing diversity of opinions on the fact that there is still nothing concrete to talk about. It all resembles the fruitless discussion among medieval scholars of Christian theology as to how many angels can dance on the head of a pin.

It is clear that, for virtually all orthodox scholars, the Hitler Order is an element of faith; despite the fact that we cannot find it, it "must" be there. A rational person would apply Occam's Razor here – simply put, that the simplest answer is most likely the correct one: The reason why there is no trace of a Hitler order to exterminate Europe's Jews is: *Hitler did not order it!*

(See Graf/Kues/Mattogno 2020, pp. 227-243; Mattogno 2021c, pp. 230-254; 2022c, pp. 123-132, for detailed discussions of this important topic.)

HÖFER, FRITZ

During the war, Fritz Höfer was a truck driver for German units. On 27 August 1959, he testified during West-German investigations on the alleged mass shooting of Kiev Jews at Babi Yar. He claims to have driven a truck to the ravine in order to get loaded up with items left behind by the Jews when walking up to their execution. According to him, the Jews left their clothes on the high plateau above the Babi Yar ravine in such a fashion that every item of clothing had its own pile. Hence, the items were presorted by types, such as shoes, coats, trousers etc.

However, the photos taken by Johannes Hähle presumably showing the items left behind by the executed Jews are all at the *bottom* of the ravine, and they were dumped randomly onto the ground. There are no piles, and most certainly no piles of presorted items.

Höfer claimed that the Jews – men, women and children – had to walk down into the ravine through two "entrance ways" and lay down on already executed Jews, where they themselves were then shot. Only two men did all the shooting, while one man made sure the Jews arranged themselves conveniently for the shooter to kill them. The shooter walked across the wobbly surface of already shot Jews from one pre-arranged Jew to the next.

This version is in stark contrast to claims by witnesses who were interrogated by the NKGB after the German retreat from Kiev. They insisted that the victims were either shot while standing at the upper edge of the ravine, then falling down into the ravine dead or wounded. Alternatively, they had to run along the ravine and were shot at while running by men standing at the ravine's edge. Children were tossed alive into the ravine.

It is moreover unlikely that only two men did the shooting. In order to kill 33,771 Jews within two days of 12 hours of daylight, as is claimed for Babi Yar, every shooter had to kill 8,443 victims during a full 12-hour workday of uninterrupted shooting. That amounts to 703.5 Jews per hour, or some 12 per minute, or one every 5 seconds.

And if Höfer was loading up clothes outside and away from the ravine, how would he have known the particulars of the shootings?

Another German witness, Kurt Werner, who claims to have shot victims at Babi Yar, stated that there were 12 shooters. That would have reduced the workload per shooter to one per minute.

(For more details, see the entry on Babi Yar, as well as Mattogno 2022c, pp. 572f.)

HÖFLE, HANS

Hans Höfle (19 June 1911 – 21 Aug. 1962), SS *Sturmbannführer*, was Odilo Globocnik's deputy chief of staff. As delegate for Jewish resettlement in the Lublin District, he was deeply involved within the *Aktion Reinhardt* in organizing the deportation of Jews from German-occupied Poland to the Majdanek Camp and through the camps at Belzec, Sobibór, and Treblinka, and in the looting of Jewish property and valuables.

Hans Höfle

Most famously, Höfle is the author of a telegram sent on 11 January 1943 to the commander of the security police in Krakow. This telegram was intercepted and deciphered by the British, who documented and archived it. The telegram gives the reported numbers of arrivals (*Zugang*) within "Operation (*Einsatz*) Reinhar[d]t" for the last two weeks of 1942, and totals as of end of 1942 for locations abbreviated with L, B, S, and T, which are commonly interpreted as Lublin (Majdanek), Belzec, Sobibór and Treblinka. The figures are:

Location	Last fortnight 1942	Totals
L[ublin]	12,761	24,733
B[elzec]	0	434,508
S[obibór]	515	101,370
T[reblinka]	10,335	713,55[5]
Total		1,274,166

If we deduct the single totals of L, B and S from the overall total, the resulting figure for T is 713,555 rather than 71,355 as given in the telegram, so the figure for T is probably missing a "5."

Nothing in this document indicates that the Jews *deported* to these locations were *killed* there. In fact, even mainstream historians agree that Jews sent to Lublin-Majdanek in 1942 were not subjected to wholesale mass murder there, so the word "*Zugang*" used by Höfle to describe what happened to the Jews sent to these camps means just that: they *arrived* there.

The total reported by Höfle in this telegram was later used by SS statistician Richard Korherr in his report about the fate of Europe's Jews as of the end of 1942, where these Jews are listed under the category of "Transport of Jews from the Eastern provinces to the Russian East." This category has two entries, one for the Chełmno Camp (145,302 Jews), and one for Jews processed "through the camps in the General Government," listing precisely Höfle's figure: "1,274,166 Jews." Such figures are compatible with deportations of Jews, but we have no evidence at all for the murder of such numbers of people at those camps. (See Mattogno 2004a, p. 127; Graf/Kues/Mattogno 2020, pp. 311-330)

Höfle was captured by the British in 1945, who handed him over to Austria in 1947, where he was soon released. He was arrested again in 1961 for allegedly organizing the deportation and murder of more than a million Jews. However, because Höfle evidently not only refused to "confess" but must have thrown quite a few monkey wrenches into the investigations, the Vienna prosecutors had problems compiling a formal indictment, in spite of the substantial material they had accumulated. On 21 August 1962, just prior to the opening of the trial, Höfle is said to have hanged himself in prison.

The truth is that the Austrian judiciary could not afford a trial against a defendant who knew everything that really had happened, who knew he could expect no mercy no matter how hard he tried to please the court, and who therefore most likely was going to speak the truth. Austrian officials could not allow this, and thus there is a fair chance that they "encouraged" his suicide. (See Graf/Kues/Mattogno 2020, pp. 197f.)

HOLOCAUST, THE

The word holocaust originates from the two Greek words *hólos* (whole) and *kaustós* (burnt). It used to refer to a religious sacrifice whereby an animal carcass is completely consumed by fire (burnt offering).

Starting in 1903, the term was occasionally used

in articles of *The New York Times* referring to the persecution of Jews in Czarist Russia (16 May 1903, 20 May 1903, 10 and 13 Nov. 1905). The term reappeared in a 1942 edition of that same newspaper with reference to the alleged mass murder of Jews by National-Socialist Germany (13 December 1942, p. 21):

> "*The slaughter of a third of the Jewish population in Hitler's domain and the threatened slaughter of all is a holocaust without parallel.*"

The term "the Holocaust," with a capital H and the definitive article, became universally accepted as referring to the claimed National-Socialist mass-murder of Europe's Jews after the tremendous success of the U.S. TV mini-series *Holocaust* in 1978.

A common definition of *the Holocaust* consists of three main characteristics (see for instance Shermer/Grobman 2000, p. xv; Berenbaum 1993, p. 1):

1. An intention and plan to commit the crime.
2. The tools with which the crime was committed.
3. The type and number of victims: Six Million Jews.

Another feature commonly attributed to the Holocaust is its alleged uniqueness; that it is "without parallel." Pogroms and persecutorial measures against Jews in the past were never based on an overall plan designed to comprehensively kill every Jew within reach. But this is said to be exactly what happened during the Holocaust, moreover with the sophisticated technical and logistical means at the disposal of a highly industrialized nation. This sets this event apart from anything else in the history of mankind.

From this perspective of a singular event, there are aspects of the National-Socialists' actions against the Jews which are not unique at all, and which, as such, are not part of the unique Holocaust in its more-narrowly defined sense:

– Discrimination against Jews, such as the Nuremberg Laws or other measures implemented later by the Third Reich, are not unique in Jewish history or the history of mankind. We need only recall the biblical Exodus, which is said to have occurred around 1200 BC.
– Ghettos for Jews were a frequent feature of many European societies in ancient and medieval time, and in Eastern Europe even up to the dawn of the 20th Century. For example, the famous Venetian ghetto was created in 1516.
– Wholesale incarceration of Jewish civilians. Concentration camps for the wanton wholesale incarceration of civilian populations were set up by the Spanish, the British, the Americans and the Soviets since the late 1800s.
– Occasional massacres, even widespread excesses of violence, have accompanied Jews throughout European history, for instance during the crusades. Perhaps the first major massacre was of the Jews in Jerusalem by the Romans in 70 AD.

Therefore, for an event to qualify as part of *the Holocaust* in the strict sense, it needs to be part of a plan to wholesale kill all Jews reachable, with the sophisticated technical and logistical means at Germany's and her allies' disposal.

Following the above common definition, an analysis of the Holocaust can be divided into four major units: (1) intentionality, (2) instruments of murder, (3) number of victims, and (4) manipulation. See the chart. The following text will briefly address each of these four areas. This entry closes with a short look at the concept of evidence.

1. Intentionality

For any crime, intention matters. In this case, we are dealing with a hierarchical state where opinions were formed, decisions were made, and orders flowed strictly from the top to the bottom, or so we are told. The entries in the present work on the top officials of the National-Socialist government – Adolf Hitler, Heinrich Himmler, Joseph Goebbels, Hermann Göring – as well as lower-ranking officials in charge of dealing with Jewish issues – Reinhardt Heydrich, Ernst Kaltenbrunner, Hans Frank, Oswald Pohl, Richard Glücks, Rudolf Höss, Adolf Eichmann, Odilo Globocnik – lay out which opinions they voiced prior to and during the war as to how they intended to treat the Jews.

Since opinions and intentions do not always translate into concrete plans and actions, it is important to look at a wide range of documents produced during the war dealing with Jewish issues. They show which plans were conceived, and what orders were issued or received to implement these plans. In this regard, see the entries on emigration and resettlement.

Ultimately, the story starts at the very top, so the issue of whether Hitler ever issued an order to murder Europe's Jews is at the center of this debate. (See the entries on Adolf Hitler himself and on the debate around the Hitler Order.)

2. Instruments of Extermination

Instruments of extermination can be divided into two groups: organizational instruments, which include institutions and organizations, and physical instruments or tools, which includes the actual murder

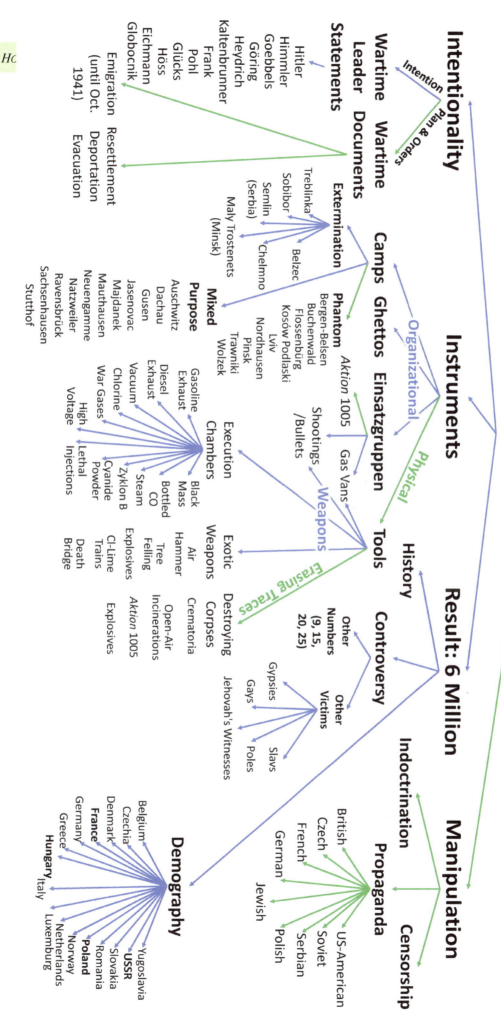

weapon and tools to erase any traces of murder.

a. Organizational Instruments
Camps and Ghettos
Since neither the establishment of Jewish ghettos nor of concentration camps is a unique feature of the Holocaust, they will not be considered as a tool here, unless it is claimed that measures or facilities were put in place in a ghetto or camp to accomplish a planned mass extermination. Such claims are made by the orthodoxy for many camps, but not for any ghettos. Camps which, according to the orthodox narrative, had at least some features of an extermination camp, can be divided into three categories (see the entry on extermination camps for details):

1. Pure extermination camps, set up for the exclusive purpose of killing all arriving deportees, if we follow the orthodox narrative.
2. Mixed-purpose camps, where some inmates were allegedly killed on arrival, while the rest was – at least temporarily – spared to perform slave-labor tasks. This includes a wide variety of camps. It ranges from those where murder is said to have been the main purpose, while slave labor was only a side show (Auschwitz), to those where mass murder only is said to have been planned, but not implemented (Dachau), and anything in between.
3. Phantom extermination camps, which are camps for which extermination activities have been claimed, but which are universally rejected by all historians as erroneous or fraudulent. Since they are important to understand the trustworthiness of witness accounts, these cases deserve to be discussed.

Einsatzgruppen
The *Einsatzgruppen* were a task force set up by Germany to "pacify" the territories conquered in the east. According to the mainstream narrative, the main goal of these units was the mass murder of Jewish civilians in the temporarily German-occupied areas of the Soviet Union. This mass murder is said to have been implemented mainly by mass shootings, and to a smaller degree also by way of asphyxiation in so-called gas vans.

Once the German armed forces were retreating out of the Soviet Union, the *Einsatzgruppen* are said to have organized a grand scheme to exhume all the bodies in thousands of mass graves scattered throughout the occupied Soviet territories, and to burn the remains on pyres in order to erase the traces of these crimes. The Holocaust orthodoxy refers to these activities as "*Aktion* 1005."

b. Physical Instruments, or Tools
Murder Weapons
The primary physical instruments or tools of the Holocaust were the actual weapons presumably used. While bullets used during executions of the *Einsatzgruppen* and associated units hardly need any discussion as to their mode of operation, other weapons deserve a lot of attention, as some of them are themselves unique to the Holocaust, while others have technical features often misunderstood or misrepresented.

The murder weapons fall into four main categories:
1. Bullets
2. Gas Vans
3. Execution chambers. These come with a wide variety of claimed murder methods, such as engine-exhaust gases, vacuum, chlorine, high-voltage electricity, and of course Zyklon B, to name a few. This variety points at a random, chaotic approach, rather than central coordination and planning.
4. Finally, there are "exotic weapons," most of which are not seriously considered to be true by most historians, such as pneumatic hammers, explosives or quick lime. These claims reinforce the impression of chaos rather than a plan.

For details, see the entry on Tools, of Mass Murder.

Tools to Erase Murder Traces
Secondary physical instruments of the Holocaust are tools and methods used to erase any traces of mass murder, meaning primarily the destruction of the victims' bodies. The tools to erase the traces of the crime come in three flavors:

1. Cremation furnaces. These should be expected to have existed foremost at the pure extermination camps, but none of them had any crematoria.
2. Open-air incineration on pyres. These were allegedly used virtually at every location, for which large numbers of victims are claimed, including during the *Einsatzgruppen*'s *Aktion* 1005.
3. Explosives. This method was primarily claimed by Rudolf Höss; Vladimir Davydov made related claims.

Hence, especially regarding the tools to commit and afterwards hide the murder, we find chaos and anarchy rather than a plan and a systematic approach.

For more details on the murder weapons allegedly used, and the tools to erase claimed murder traces, see the entry Tools, of Mass Murder.

3. The Victims: Six Million Jews

a. History

The claim that six million Jews are threatened with extermination, are dying or have died, was spread for the first time in the 1890s by *The New York Times* in reaction to anti-Jewish measures of Czarist Russia. Ever since, the theme of Six Million Jews in danger, dying or dead has run like a red thread through the media. It became a standard feature during and right after the *First* World War, when Jewish organizations in the U.S. were raising funds to support Jewish communities and projects in Eastern Europe, in particular in the fledgling Soviet Union. The number became popular again in the years running up to World War Two, although this time levied against Germany. The Six-Million claim really took off during the final years of the war, and was firmly implemented in the public mind as well as in court proceedings right afterwards.

b. Controversy

Six Million, however, is not the only figure claimed. Right after the end of World War Two, claims of more than six million victims of NS persecution were published – 9, 15, 20, even 25 million victims. These figures include Jews and non-Jews. The controversies these higher death-toll claims have triggered shed a revealing light on some political issues involved in "creating" victim numbers. (For details on the history and controversy of that figure, see the entry on Six Million.)

While "the Holocaust" is exclusively about the Jews, there are other victim groups who have been portrayed by orthodox scholars as having been the target of systematic extermination as well. These include Gypsies, homosexuals and Jehovah's Witnesses, but also Slavs in general and Poles in particular. While these aspects of claimed National-Socialist persecution are not part of the Holocaust in the narrow sense, the way scholars, media and the public at large have dealt with these often-controversial side topics is very instructive to the overarching topic. For this reason, these issues are covered to some degree in the respective entries.

c. Demography

The actual Jewish death toll of World War Two requires a thorough study of demographic developments on a worldwide scale, starting in the pre-war years and ending many years after the war. In the present work, an entry on demography gives an overview of the challenges involved, and the studies published so far. Furthermore, each entry on a country where Jews are said to have been murdered within the Holocaust contains a section on demography and/or on the fate of the Jews deported from that country. Central to our understanding of what happened during those years is the fate of the Jews in mainly four countries: The Soviet Union, Poland, Hungary and France.

4. Manipulation

One major aspect of what we today consider to be *the Holocaust*, but which is never mentioned by orthodox Holocaust scholars, is the manipulation of public discourse by various means:

a. Propaganda

Truth is always the first victim of any war, and the victors never write an unbiased history of any war. The same is true for World War Two, of which the Holocaust is an integral part. There was never a war where propaganda and psychological warfare have played such an important role. To believe that propaganda had no effect on our concept of "the Holocaust" is naïve at best.

For this reason, the propaganda activities of all major nations involved in the writing of Holocaust history are dealt with in sections of the entry on Propaganda:
– Czechoslovakia
– France
– Germany
– Poland
– Serbia
– Soviet Union
– United Kingdom
– United States

Jewish contributions do not fit into that national pattern, yet still, they have their own section.

b. Indoctrination

While adults can choose which media products to consume or refuse to consume, students in a growing number of countries around the globe are forced to learn the orthodox Holocaust narrative, with no option or encouragement to demonstrate critical thinking. This way, impressionable young minds are taught that dictatorial intolerance and suppression of opposing views is acceptable. More about this ultimate tool to breed totalitarian societies can be found in the entry on Indoctrination.

c. Censorship
In many nations around the globe, anyone voicing views deviating from the orthodox Holocaust narrative is maligned, excluded from public discourse, and censored on both societal and legal levels. Today, censorship laws prohibit the public dissemination of such dissenting views under threat of incarceration in most Western countries. Read more about this ultimate tool of oppression in the entry on Censorship.

5. Evidence
The most important question to ask about any topic of deliberation is: How do we know? Knowledge is based on evidence. There are various types of evidence, which vary with regard to their reliability. For a more detail discussion of the theory of evidence in general, see the entry dedicated to this. As for any historical topic, we are concerned mainly with three types of evidence:
1. Physical evidence
2. Documents
3. Testimonies

a. Physical Evidence
This includes material traces of an object or the object itself. In a murder case, this primarily includes the bodies of the victims and the murder weapon – or parts or traces of them – as well as any physical trace a perpetrator may have left behind. It also includes scientific methods to analyze and correctly interpret such traces.

Each crime scene of the Holocaust must have had a weapon and victims, and some if not most had some way of disposing of the victims' bodies. Just as any other murder investigation, investigations into Holocaust crime scenes also must primarily concern themselves with finding and assessing material evidence of weapon and victim.

In the present work, several entries address the material and technical aspects of claimed murder weapons – homicidal gas chambers, gas vans, diesel exhaust, carbon monoxide, producer gas, Zyklon B and hydrogen cyanide, Zyklon-B introduction devices, Iron Blue, gastight doors, ventilation, morgues, and explosives. Other entries address tools to erase the crime's traces – crematoria, cremation propaganda, open-air incinerations, groundwater level, lumberjacks, and again explosives.

Furthermore, each major crime scene claimed for the Holocaust discusses material traces that were presumably found during forensic investigations, or if nothing else, it elaborates on physical traces that should be expected. These are discussed in the entries dedicated to the claimed extermination camps at Belzec, Chełmno, Semlin, Sobibór and Treblinka.

The entry on the *Einsatzgruppen* has a section discussing forensic findings claimed by Soviet authorities about *Einsatzgruppen* massacres. The entry on *Aktion* 1005 has a similar section that discusses material claims made by witnesses in connection with large-scale outdoor corpse cremations.

Some of the evidence presumably gathered by Soviet investigators in this context were presented during the show trials at Krasnodar and Kharkov, and are discussed in these entries.

Two entries discuss forensic examinations conducted by Allied investigators in camps in western Germany and France. One is dedicated to Charles Larson, a U.S. pathologist who conducted autopsies of victims in camps liberated by U.S. forces, and the other looks into alleged gassing victims at the Natzweiler Camp.

Several entries discuss items that were allegedly manufactured from the dead bodies of murder victims, or property presumably taken from the victims:
– Hair, cut off from the victims, and slated for industrial use.
– Two shrunken heads allegedly found at the Buchenwald Camp.
– Soap manufactured from the body fat of victims.
– Lampshades and other objects made from the skin of camp inmates.
– Gold teeth pulled from the victim's corpses.
– Collected wedding rings,
– and mountains of shoes.

Images of these items are used to this day to achieve the greatest possible horror effect. But are they genuine? And if so, what do they really prove?

b. Documents
From an evidentiary standpoint, a document is any information recorded in any way that contains data which can help us understand what happened. This includes photos, film footage, letters, diaries, bureaucratic documents, computer data, etc. The most reliable documents are generally those that are least prone to human manipulation and human error. Conversely, the more that human manipulation has an influence on the creation of a document, the less re-

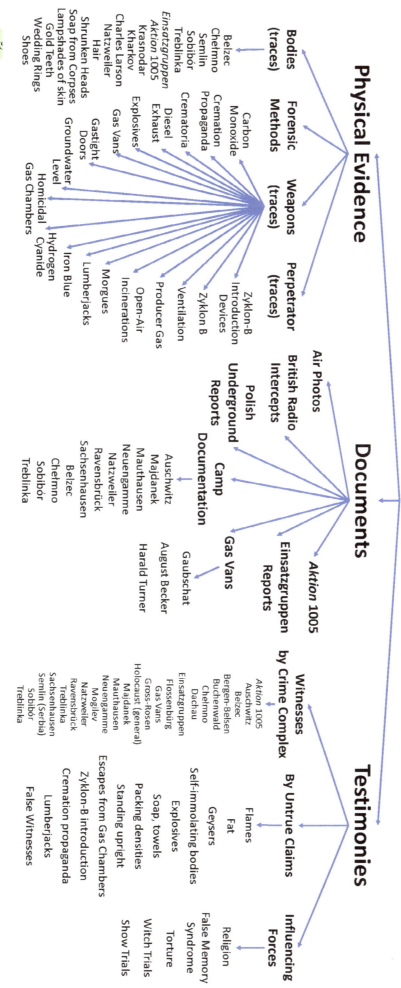

liable it usually is.

Regarding the Holocaust, air photos are probably the most reliable documents, and are summarized in that very entry. These are followed closely by radio messages the SS sent through what they thought were secure channels, but which were secretly intercepted and deciphered by the British. See the entry on British Radio Intercepts for a summary. Another set of interesting documents are propaganda messages prepared by the Polish underground, and sent to the Polish Government in Exile in London. These are discussed in the entry on Polish Underground Reports.

Documents created by a wartime bureaucracy oblivious of their later historical significance are also quite trustworthy. This includes the vast extant documentation of various camp administrations, such as Auschwitz and Majdanek, but also other camps of minor importance. However, for the claimed pure extermination camps, very few documents have survived the war, but some of them are very revealing. The documented history of each major camp is summarized in a specific section of its respective entry.

Documents on the activities of the *Einsatzgruppen* are quite abundant, and they paint a disturbing picture. However, contradictions and inconsistencies raise issues that can be resolved only by forensic investigations.

In contrast to the killing activities of the *Einsatzgruppen*, there is almost no documental trace of any attempt to erase the mass graves of these massacres, as is said to have happened during the so-called *Aktion* 1005. See that entry for details.

There are very few documents mentioning the existence of homicidal gas vans. They are summarized in an entry dedicated to these vehicles. A more thorough discussion is contained in the entry on the Gaubschat Company that presumably built these vehicles, and in entries of two individuals, who both are said to have written a letter mentioning gas vans: August Becker and Harald Turner.

c. Testimonies

In lieu of material traces of murder weapons and victims, and due to the scarcity of documents proving the existence and operation of mass-murder facilities such as gas chambers and gas vans, the orthodox Holocaust narrative mainly rests on witness testimonies. Witnesses are the evidentiary bedrock upon which the orthodox account rests.

In order to understand the historical and societal framework within which these testimonies were made, it is important to understand that testimonies are not given in an atmosphere of neutral objectivity. In fact, powerful forces were, and in some respects still are, at work that influence people's memories, or at least what they are willing to testify. The entries on religion, false memory syndrome, torture, witch trials and show trials address some of these forces.

The present work contains more than two hundred entries on the most important witnesses who testified about pivotal aspects of the Holocaust. The vast majority of these testimonies were recorded during the war or in the first few years after the war, when memories were still fresh. These witness entries summarize a witness's statement(s) and assess veracity and reliability. The entry on witnesses lists them all, sorted by the claimed crime complex about which a witness testified.

Several entries contain a discussion of verifiably untrue claims made by a series of witnesses on certain issues, as well as a list of witnesses who made claims to that effect. These entries are:
– Flames shooting out of crematory chimneys.
– Fat extracted from burning corpses.
– Geysers of blood erupting from mass graves.
– Self-immolating bodies in cremation furnaces or on pyres, not needing any fuel.
– Explosives used to murder people, or to erase their traces.
– Soap, towels and even toothbrushes issued to victims when walking into a gas chamber.
– Packing densities of victims in gas chambers that are physically impossible.
– Standing upright: as a result of these impossible packing densities, gassing victims allegedly kept standing straight up after dying.
– Escapes from gas chambers.
– Zyklon-B introduction devices: the many contradictory ways, poison gas is said to have been introduced into Auschwitz gas chambers.
– Cremation propaganda: claims of technically impossible cremation speeds and capacities.
– Lumberjacks: this entry documents the gigantic amounts of firewood needed to cremate the number of victims claimed for most Holocaust crime scenes, and the number of lumberjacks needed to procure that wood.

A separate entry on false witnesses deals with individuals who falsely claimed to have witnessed an event, when in fact they were not even present at the time of the claimed event.

HOLOCAUST INDOCTRINATION

School Education

Many genocides were committed during the history of mankind. The worst of recorded history is probably the auto-genocide perpetrated in Cambodia by the Khmer Rouge between 1975 and 1979. Up to a third of the entire Cambodian population is said to have been slaughtered during that time.

In absolute death-toll figures, the genocide against the indigenous peoples of what later became the United States of America rivals that of the trans-Atlantic slave trade of sub-Saharan Africans, also committed mainly by post-Columbian invaders of North America.

However, there is only one genocide that is compulsory teaching at high-school level in many countries around the world: "the Holocaust" against the Jews by Third-Reich Germany. It is not only taught as part of history lessons on the Second World War, but also as a topic of literature studies. Books such as Elie Wiesel's *Night* or *The Diary of Anne Frank* are compulsory readings in many middle- and high-school classes around the globe.

While teaching history is fine, teaching skepticism and scrutiny is even better. However, student skepticism and scrutiny of the orthodox Holocaust narrative would get many students in trouble, and in many countries even in conflict with the law. Teachers supporting such mature behavior face disciplinary measures. Teachers voicing any dissent themselves are removed from their position and become unemployable in every country where the orthodoxy holds any sway. In many countries, they even face criminal charges for "denial."

Forcing lessons down students' throat under threat of punishment for any dissent is not called teaching. This is indoctrination, plain and simple.

Museums and Memorials

Wikipedia lists 84 Holocaust Memorials and Museums across the United States of America. While there are many historical sites and museums dealing with slavery and the fate of indigenous peoples, there is no such thing as a memorial or museum in the U.S. or any other Western country dedicated to any genocide committed abroad: Cambodia, Ukraine's Holodomor of the 1930s, or any other large-scale massacre, such as the Bolshevist revolution in Russia and its aftermath, or Mao Zedong's "cultural revolution."

None of these massacres took place in the United States, or were contributed to in any meaningful way by that country. Therefore, it stands to reason that it is not in the center of the country's commemorative activities. But the same is true for "the Holocaust." The situation is no different in other Western countries not involved in "the Holocaust," such as the UK, for instance. But there as well, the Holocaust has taken commemorative center stage.

The reason for this is that neither Ukrainians, Russians, Chinese, Cambodians nor any other ethnic

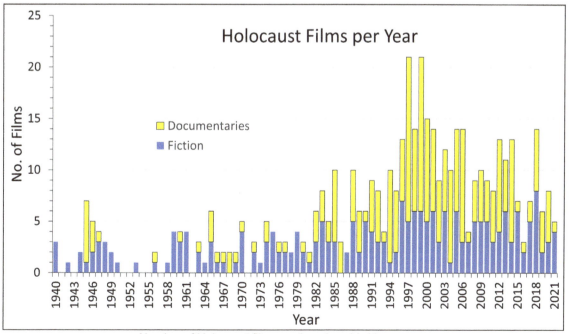

Number of Holocaust films produced worldwide per year.
(acc. to https://en.wikipedia.org/wiki/List_of_Holocaust_films, as of 7 June 2022)

group which suffered a genocide has any powerful lobby group in the U.S. or any other western country that successfully managed to impose its own historical perspective and priorities onto its host nation. Only Jewish lobby groups have managed to accomplish this feat – by way of vast wealth, political corruption and incessant indoctrination.

Media, Movies and Literature

The number of media articles, news reports, book and movie releases dealing with the Holocaust in one way or another is simply staggering. Throughout the years since the turn of the millennium, on average more than four new books on the Holocaust were released every single day! The situation is not much different when it comes to movies. The screening of so-called documentaries peaked during a time when Jewish lobby groups were pushing hard to get compensation payments mainly from German and Swiss companies. The trend seems to have been receding a little after that (see the illustration). There is no historical topic about which so many movies have been made as on the Holocaust. Some are documentaries, but most are fictional movies presumably based on real stories.

The cultural dominance of the Jewish historical perspective and priority in all Western countries is absolutely mind-boggling. For all those who jump onto this band wagon, there's truly no business like Shoah business.

For everyone else, it is a steady indoctrination of non-Jews, imposing Jewish perspectives and priorities upon them. In effect, it washes any thought of dissent or resistance out of the consumer's mind. Instead, it recruits them to welcome and embrace denying the dissidents any space to voice their views. It makes the brain-washed mind accept any restrictions of civil rights deemed necessary to suppress those who disagree. It solidifies and perpetuates Jewish cultural dominance.

After all, where would we end up if we allowed anyone to oppose "the Jews"? (Whatever that means.) Well, it is claimed, the Jews would ultimately end up, once again, in an Auschwitz-like gas chamber. Thus, anything is warranted to prevent that from recurring: burn the books, jail the dissidents, and throw away the key.

(One small problem: There were no gas chambers at Auschwitz…)

(For more details, see the entry on censorship, as well as Dalton 2020, pp. 279-286.)

HOLOCAUST SKEPTICISM (REVISIONISM)

Hermann Göring was the first person to express skepticism about the Holocaust narrative imposed upon the world by the prosecution during the Nuremberg International Military Tribunal (see the entry on him). The next person to voice his skepticism was the Frenchman Paul Rassinier. He had been incarcerated at the Buchenwald and Dora Camps due to his activities within the French resistance. Yet when he read the distortions and lies spread after the war by some of his former co-inmates, he tried setting the record straight – first only about Buchenwald and Dora (see Rassinier 2022), but later also on a much broader scale regarding the Holocaust in general. Since Rassinier did not have the means to access primary sources in various archives, however, his later works were necessarily somewhat superficial.

Throughout the 1960s and early 1970s, the writings of Holocaust skeptics were more anecdotal and journalistic in nature, lacking academic stringency. That changed between 1975 and 1983 with the well-researched and -argued writings of Arthur Butz, Robert Faurisson, Wilhelm Stäglich and Walter Sanning. With this, Holocaust skepticism matured to a historical school that soon exceeded most orthodox studies in mastery of source material and stringency of argumentation. (See Mattogno 1988 for an overview of early revisionist works.)

Works of profound source criticism followed, which sent shockwaves through the orthodox establishment, as they undermined the very basis on which their narrative was based: Henri Roques's PhD thesis on Kurt Gerstein (Roques 1989) and Carlo Mattogno's papers on the first gassing of Auschwitz (Mattogno 1989) as well as on the testimonies of Miklós Nyiszli (1988a), Ada Bimko and Charles S. Bendel (1990), Filip Müller (1990a), and last but not least Rudolf Vrba and Alfred Wetzler (1990b). As a result, the orthodoxy did not review their own work to consider whether they made any mistakes, but rather demanded that the iconoclastic skeptics be censored and punished. Roques, for example, lost his PhD title as a result of the ensuing witch hunt.

The Second Zündel Trial in 1988 made it fashionable to apply common forensic methods to the claimed murders within the Holocaust. In addition, the collapse of the Soviet Union suddenly made vast archival resources in Eastern Europe accessible, which allowed deep insights into the documented history of many camps. Both trends resulted in a swiftly growing list of thorough forensic and archival studies about many alleged crime scenes of the Holocaust, which coalesced in the series *Holocaust Handbooks*. As of 2023, this series contains 51 monographs of mostly extremely thorough and detailed studies of various aspects of the Holocaust, putting orthodox studies on the same topics to shame.

The orthodoxy's reaction to this development was the introduction of laws in most European countries as well as Israel, Canada and Australia that mandate the writing of history by penal law, thereby threatening any dissidents with prison terms of up to twenty years (this in Austria). This dictatorial approach to academic questions on such a broad, international scale has not been seen in the world since the Catholic Church's Holy Inquisition. The supposedly "free" West is not so free after all. (See the entry on censorship.)

One typical strategy used by the orthodoxy is to refuse to cite, or even *mention*, any of the major skeptical or revisionist scholars. If pressed, they will cite 40- or 50-year-old publications, or mention only marginal, inactive or deceased revisionists. But they will assiduously avoid mention of the most-recent sources and the most-important revisionist scholars.

A litmus test for any work on the Holocaust is whether or not it mentions any of the more than 50 pertinent monographs and papers by Carlo Mattogno. This Italian historian is so dangerous to the establishment that they don't even dare to say or write his name. The same holds, to only a slightly lesser extent, regarding such men as Jürgen Graf, Thomas Kues, Germar Rudolf, Thomas Dalton, Nick Kollerstrom and others who present a solid, academic case for Holocaust skepticism.

HOLSTEIN, BERNHARD

In 2004, the Australian writer Bernard Brougham, alias Bernard Holstein, published a book recounting his time at Auschwitz, titled *Stolen Soul*. It turns out that the book was a complete fraud. In October of that year, the publisher, University of Western Australia Press, discovered the many lies in it and pulled copies of the book from bookshops after a private investigator probed the author's background. Brougham had claimed that, as a nine-year-old Jew at Auschwitz, he was subjected to medical experiments, that he belonged to the resistance, and that he had fled and was caught and tortured. Upon investigation, his adopted family reported to the publisher that Brougham was neither born in Germany nor was he a Jew. The detective discovered that Brougham was born in Australia and baptized a Roman Catholic in 1942 (Madden/Kelly 2004).

There have been many such Holocaust frauds over the years, and the reaction to revelations here was typical (Singer 2004):

"*Publisher Judy Shorrock […] was still 'shocked' by the revelations and fears the incident may incite Holocaust denial. 'I have spent three years working on this book. I am devastated… that it could damage the credibility of the Holocaust – that just makes me feel sick,' she said.*"

HOMICIDAL GAS CHAMBER
U.S. Execution Gas Chambers

Between 1924 and 1999, the U.S. states of Arizona, California, Colorado, Maryland, Mississippi, Missouri, Nevada, New Mexico and North Carolina have employed hydrogen-cyanide gas in homicidal gas chambers in order to kill persons sentenced to death (capital punishment). For safety reasons of everyone involved – prison warden, technicians and witnesses – these chambers had to be absolutely gastight, the gas had to be safely evacuated afterwards by powerful fans through a high stack, and the door(s) had to be made of massive steel not only to seal in the gas, but also to prevent an inmate from breaking out who might succeed in breaking or untying the straps holding him to the execution seat.

In 1999, American executions in gas chambers were terminated because they were found to be a form of cruel punishment. Executions in them lasted on average some ten minutes, but could last as long as 20 minutes, while the victim was visibly and audibly suffering extreme pain. The toxin employed was hydrogen cyanide, which was produced right beneath the execution chair by pouring semi-concentrated sulfuric acid into a bowl containing potassium cyanide. From this, hydrogen-cyanide gas developed rapidly and rose in a mist to engulf the victim within seconds. The concentrations used were around 0.3% (3000 ppm), and the average execution time was around ten minutes. In order to prevent accidental poisoning of the individuals removing the corpse afterwards, the corpse (and the chamber equipment) had to be treated chemically to neutralize any hydrogen cyanide adhering to surfaces.

(See Rudolf 2020, pp. 15-19; Christianson, 2010; Leuchter *et al*. 2017, pp. 193-224)

Euthanasia in Germany

During the euthanasia program initiated in Germany at the beginning of World War II, gas chambers using bottled carbon monoxide as the toxin are said to have been used. There is little if any extant documentation about this, however. See the entry on euthanasia.

Claimed German Wartime Gas Chambers

Gas chambers for the mass murder of inmates in German wartime camps are said to have existed in many camps. The way these gas chambers are said to have been contrived and designed, as well as their claimed methods of execution, are inconsistent and highly illogical, suggesting that these claims originated not in reality but rather in wartime atrocity propaganda and rumors. Strikingly, there exists absolutely no documentation whatsoever for any of these gas-chamber claims. In many cases, there doesn't even exist any physical trace; and where such traces do exist, their interpretation by the orthodoxy is highly questionable. Here are the *orthodoxy's* claims for each camp (for details, see the camp's entry):

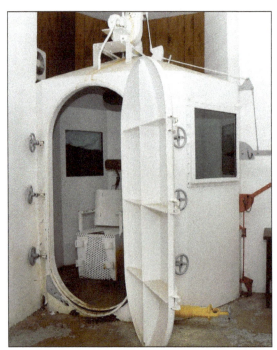

Execution gas chamber of the State Penitentiary in Jefferson City, Missouri, USA. Note the heavy steel door.

Auschwitz

Prior to the beginning of the German-Soviet war in June 1941, Himmler allegedly ordered Auschwitz Camp Commandant Rudolf Höss to establish in this camp the main center for the extermination of the Jews. Höss furthermore claimed that Adolf Eichmann was tasked with finding a suitable poison gas but was unsuccessful for several months. In early September 1941, Höss's deputy Karl Fritzsch supposedly discovered the method of extermination by chance, while Höss was away on a business trip: He performed the "first gassing" haphazardly in some basement rooms using Zyklon B. After that, several rooms in other buildings at the Auschwitz Main Camp and at Birkenau are said to have been haphazardly retrofitted over time, so they could serve as homicidal gas chambers.

Chełmno

Here, mobile gas chambers, so-called gas vans, are said to have been deployed since late 1941, after the method had been discovered accidentally by Arthur Nebe when he almost gassed himself in his car. The vans' engine exhaust was ducted into the cargo hold, which was filled with up to a hundred or more victims.

Belzec, Sobibór, Treblinka

When the "Final Solution" of the Jewish question was implemented with the creation of these three "pure extermination camps" – allegedly starting in October of 1941 – predominantly SS men who previously served at various euthanasia institutions were deployed to these three camps. Yet, instead of applying the methods used at those institutions, they are said to have used completely different murder methods. For Belzec were claimed: unslaked lime, high-voltage electricity, vacuum and diesel-engine exhaust gas. For Sobibór were claimed: chlorine gas, engine-exhaust gas, high-voltage electricity or a black liquid. For Treblinka were claimed: unslaked lime, hot steam, high-voltage electricity and diesel-engine exhaust gas. Today, only engine exhaust is claimed for all three camps.

Mauthausen

A gas chamber using Zyklon B heated with "a hot brick" is said to have started operating in May 1942 with the murder of Soviet PoWs.

Majdanek

Although the Majdanek Camp – like Belzec, Sobibór and Treblinka – was also part of *Aktion Reinhardt*, the decision to have gas chambers built there was taken only sometime in early 1942, and the methods used were allegedly both Zyklon B and bottled carbon monoxide. There were no exotic methods claimed, such as those for the other Reinhardt camps.

Dachau

Camp physician Dr. Siegmund Rascher supposedly

requested permission in the summer of 1942 to use some facility under construction at Dachau as an experimental gas chamber for the testing of war gases using inmates. The only witness to such a gassing claims to have smelled chlorine, but Zyklon B is today claimed as the toxin used.

Neuengamme
In the fall of 1942, nonsensical modifications were made to a room at that camp, allowing homicidal gassings with Zyklon B. Two gassings with 100 to 200 victims each are said to have occurred there.

Sachsenhausen
Since March 1943, a small Zyklon-B disinfestation cubicle, similar to the DEGESCH fumigation gas chamber, was allegedly used to mass murder inmates, although the use of a non-existing liquid "Zyklon A" is also hypothesized.

Natzweiler
A makeshift gas chamber was jury-rigged in that camp in the summer of 1943 using a cyanide powder, over which some liquid was poured in order to release toxic hydrogen-cyanide fumes. This method was only used once for the killing of a batch of inmates, allegedly in order to retrieve their skeletons for some museum collection. Additionally, the war gas phosgene was tested in some facility of that camp.

Stutthof
In this camp, an existing Zyklon-B disinfestation chamber is said to have been used for homicidal purposes starting in the summer of 1944, when Soviet troops were closing in on Germany.

Ravensbrück
This gas chamber was allegedly put into operation absurdly late, in early 1945, after Himmler presumably had prohibited all inmate murders in late 1944. (See the entry for Kurt Becher.)

The Chain of Command
If there were in fact an intention by the Germans to implement mass gassing as a central policy of the Third Reich, there certainly would have been a clear and consistent chain of command, from the highest levels. Instead, we see disparate, disconnected and decentralized (alleged) chains – or no organizational structure at all. Looking at just the larger camps where homicidal gas chambers are said to have existed makes this clear. According to current orthodox Holocaust historiography, which is based almost exclusively on anecdotal evidence, there were at least three different chains of command for these camps:

1. Hitler → *Führer* chancellery → The technical services of the German FBI (*Kriminaltechnisches Institut*): carbon monoxide in steel bottles (euthanasia centers, Majdanek) or gas vans (Chełmno, *Einsatzgruppen*);
2. Hitler → Himmler → Eichmann (or Fritzsch) → Höss: Zyklon B (Auschwitz, Majdanek);
3. Himmler → Globocnik → Höfle → Wirth: exhaust gases of diesel and/or gasoline engines (Bełżec, Sobibór, Treblinka).

Any of the other minor camps could have had some other chain of command, but there is not even enough anecdotal evidence in these cases, let alone any documents, and so it is futile to draw similar lines of command.

Changing Murder Methods
Today, the orthodoxy claims *only one* murder method for each of the alleged extermination camps. But during the war and in the immediate aftermath, many different methods were claimed, which were

Camp	Once-Claimed Methods	Still-Claimed Method
Auschwitz	war gases, high-voltage, gas showers, gas bombs, pneumatic hammer, conveyor belt	Zyklon B
Treblinka	mobile gas chamber, stunning gas, vacuum, unslaked lime, hot steam, high voltage	Diesel-engine exhaust gas
Bełżec	subterranean murder chamber, unslaked lime, high voltage, vacuum	Diesel-engine exhaust gas
Sobibór	chlorine gas, a black liquid, high voltage, collapsible gas-chamber floor	engine exhaust gas
Majdanek	Zyklon B	bottled carbon monoxide

later relegated to the dustbins of historiography, swept under the carpet by mainstream historians too embarrassed to ever mention these absurdities. Unfortunately for them, the remaining methods are no less absurd. The following table lists in the center column all the methods quietly dropped, while the right column lists what is still claimed by the orthodoxy to this very day:

HOMOSEXUALS

The growing political influence of the LGTBQ+ movement has led to efforts to publicize the victim-status of homosexuals in National-Socialist Germany, who were said to also be targeted for systematic extermination. Following the general pattern of Holocaust hagiography, the number of homosexuals alleged to have died in National-Socialist concentration camps has been extremely exaggerated over time, with some claiming as many as 500,000 victims or even more. Today, some researchers are reluctantly acknowledging figures as low as 5,000 victims – a reduction of 99%.

In prewar Germany, and also in postwar Germany for more than two decades, homosexuality was a crime, as it was in many other countries – such as, for example, Great Britain and the USSR. Between 50,000 and 60,000 homosexual males were sentenced by German courts between 1933 and 1944. After having served their prison term, a minority of these – some 10,000 to 15,000 – were kept in "preventive custody" in concentration camps. These were mostly repeat offenders, male prostitutes, transvestites and pedophiles. Considering the high mortalities in some of the wartime camps, homosexuals fell victim to these conditions at similar rates as other inmates, rather than to a policy specifically targeting them. (See Wickoff 2023 for details.)

HÖSS, RUDOLF

Rudolf Höss (25 Nov. 1901 – 16 April 1947), SS *Obersturmbannführer*, served at the Dachau Concentration Camp from December 1934 until 1938, then at the Sachsenhausen Camp until May 1940, when he was charged with setting up the new Auschwitz Camp, where he became commandant in October of that year. As head of Office Group DI at the SS Economic and Administrative Main Office (*Wirtschafts- und Verwaltungs-Hauptamt*), Höss then became deputy inspector of concentration camps in November 1943, but returned to Auschwitz in early May 1944 as "camp eldest" to help organize the deportation and processing of some 400,000 Jews from Hungary deported to various labor camps throughout Germany via the Auschwitz Camp. Höss's last assignment was to the women's camp at Ravensbrück.

After he had been discovered by the British in March of 1946, he was severely and uninterruptedly tortured for three straight days, at the end of which he signed a "confession," the contents of which he stated he did not even know. In this "confession," in numerous subsequent interrogations, in his autobiographic notes while in Polish custody, and in his testimonies at the Nuremberg International Military Tribunal and in Warsaw, he made numerous claims that are impossible, historically wrong, and contradictory. This situation renders his entire testimony worthless from a historiographic point of view. In his detailed monograph on Höss's various postwar statements, Mattogno has exposed and explained a total of 53 falsehoods, inconsistencies and contradictions (Mattogno 2020b). Here is a brief list of the more striking examples:

– Höss insisted repeatedly that he received the order to turn Auschwitz into an extermination center from Heinrich Himmler in May or June 1941, before the war against the Soviet Union. Höss's entire timeline of subsequent extermination events depends on that date: the first gassing of September 1941, the use of the Main Camp's crematorium morgue for gassings in late 1941/early 1942, and the rigging of two former farmhouses ("bunkers") as makeshift gassing facilities in early and mid-1942. In fact, the timeline of the entire orthodox Auschwitz narrative depends on it. And yet, it cannot have happened. Höss insists that the order came *after* other extermination camps had already been active for some time. He names Belzec and Treblinka several times, and even claims to have visited Treblinka to see how extermination was done there. However, the Bełżec Camp became operational only on 17 March 1942, and the Treblinka Camp on 23 July 1942. Furthermore, mainstream historians insist that a decision to start the Final Solution was made by Hitler in October of 1941 at the earliest, hence four to five months after Höss's imaginary meeting with Himmler.

– When referring to the extermination centers already in operation when Himmler gave him the order, Höss mentioned a camp near Lublin named "Wolzek" in four statements. Such a camp never

existed, and as the former deputy inspector of concentration camps, Höss knew which camps existed in Poland, and what their names were. This was no accident. Having been tortured and constantly facing physical and emotional abuse by his captors, the only plausible explanation is that he injected this fictional camp as a message to the world: "What I am saying here is nonsense."
– Höss contradicted himself, claiming first that Himmler ordered him to exterminate all Jews without distinction, but then claiming that only those unable to work had to be killed. He flip-flopped between those two mutually exclusive statements numerous times. The documents show, however, that every single Jew deported to Auschwitz was registered there and admitted to the camp until July of 1942, so no extermination order can have existed at all until that date.
– Höss made conflicting and altogether false statements about who headed the other alleged extermination camps.
– Höss claimed that Auschwitz was developed as an extermination center because the other camps had such low and limited capacities, whereas at Treblinka, the orthodoxy claims that some 700,000 were killed within just half a year – a much higher rate than Auschwitz is said to have ever accomplished.
– Höss claims that, when he visited Treblinka in 1941, the Jews from the Warsaw Ghetto uprising were just being processed, and the corpses buried earlier in mass graves were being unearthed again and burned on pyres. However, the Warsaw Ghetto uprising happened in the summer of 1942, and the exhumation of mass graves with subsequent burning of the bodies' remains is said to have started only in early 1943. Höss creates a mess, chronologically speaking, by mixing all kinds of (alleged) events that don't belong together into one big stew.
– Höss claims that Adolf Eichmann was looking for a suitable agent to commit the planned gas murder, but according to Höss, his deputy Karl Fritzsch took matters in his own hands by using Zyklon B to kill some Soviet PoWs, thus solving the "problem." This is the famous first gassing of Auschwitz. Yet in another statement, Höss has Eichmann continue looking for a gas, although it had already been found.
– Höss stated on the one hand that Fritzsch's "first gassing" took place while he was absent on a business trip, but only a few paragraphs later, he said – probably to impress his readers/listeners – that he vividly experienced that first gassing himself by looking into the gas-chamber door while wearing a gas mask.
– He stated that, already in 1941, Slovakian Jews were killed in gas chambers, but documents clearly show that Slovakian Jews started arriving at Auschwitz only in late March of 1942, and that they were all registered and admitted to the camp.
– Höss claimed that, during his rule of the camp, some three million inmates died or were murdered – a figure reminiscent of the Soviet propaganda number of four million victims in total. In order to make this number appear realistic, he also exaggerated the numbers of Jews living in various European countries by an approximate factor of ten.
– Höss also repeated the fairy tale of collecting human fat during open-air incinerations and pouring it on the flames.

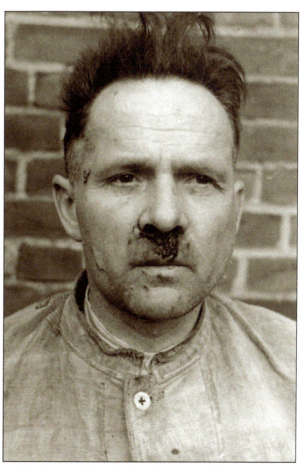

The tortured, bloody Rudolf Höss in British custody 1946.

- He stated that, at the Chełmno Camp, Paul Blobel had attempted to get rid of corpses with "explosives, but their destruction had been very incomplete." But this is irrational; explosives scatter body parts all over the landscape but do not make them disappear.
- Höss insisted that, after a gassing was completed, the doors were opened immediately, and the inmate corpse-removal team started working on this instantly, even eating food items they found. This means they did not wear any gas masks, which would have been swiftly fatal. He even expressly stated on another occasion that gas masks were not worn and not needed.

Höss's testimony, filled with blatant nonsense, has nonetheless been one of the most influential witness accounts. His appearance even impressed most German defendants at the Nuremberg International Military Tribunal, who, until then, did not believe their accusers' mass-murder claims. Only Hermann Göring remained skeptical, sending Höss in his Nuremberg prison cell a few questions (through the prison psychologist) regarding how the claimed mass murder was technically possible.

What Höss really thought about Auschwitz can be gleaned from a speech he gave on 22 May 1943 in Auschwitz. It was a meeting of high SS officials discussing the progress and future plans of the Auschwitz Camp. The main target of this speech was Hans Kammler, head of Office Group C (Budget and Construction) of the SS Economic and Administrative Main Office. As such, he was in a key position to make construction decisions. Here is what Höss had to say about the camp's history and purpose:

> "In the year 1940, the Auschwitz Camp came into existence in the estuary triangle between the Vistula and Sola rivers after the evacuation of 7 Polish villages, through the reconstruction of an artillery-barracks site and much construction of extensions, reconstructions and new structures, utilizing large quantities of material from buildings that had been demolished. Originally intended as a quarantine camp, this later became a Reich camp and thereby was destined for a new purpose. As the situation grew ever more critical, its position on the border of the Reich and G.G. [Government General, occupied Poland] proved especially favorable, since the filling of the camp with workers was guaranteed. In addition to that, the solution of the Jewish question was added recently, which required creating the means to accommodate 60,000 prisoners at first, which increases to 100,000 within a short time. The inmates of the camp are predominantly intended for the growing large-scale industries in the vicinity. The camp contains within its sphere of interest various armament firms, for which the workers are regularly provided."

The "solution of the Jewish question" thus required no extermination or cremation facilities, but instead construction measures to accommodate 100,000 prisoners. The supposed homicidal function of the camp was not only no priority, it was utterly absent from Höss's speech. (See Mattogno 2016d, pp. 52f., 138.)

HÖSSLER, FRANZ

Franz Hössler (4 Feb. 1906 – 13 Dec. 1945), SS *Obersturmführer*, started his career at the SS as a cook at the Dachau Camp. He assumed that same role when transferred to Auschwitz in June 1940, then became Labor Service Leader in early 1941 at the Auschwitz Main Camp, and eventually leader of the women's protective-custody camp at Birkenau in August 1943. After a short stint at a subcamp of the Natzweiler Camp, he returned to Auschwitz in June 1944, and was there leader of the Main Camp's protective-custody section. After the evacuation of Auschwitz, he first served in the same role at the Dora Camp, and then ended up at the Bergen-Belsen Camp, where he was arrested by the British.

Franz Hössler

After the usual treatment by the British – commonly involving torture – Hössler compliantly wrote an affidavit, in which he pledged full cooperation with his captors. Hössler was incriminated by one of his former SS colleagues, Pery Broad, and by two former inmates (Michał Kula, Zygmunt Smużewski) of having organized the gassings at the old crematorium at the Main Camp (see Mattogno 2016c, pp. 58f.; 2022f, pp. 61, 63). In his affidavit, Hössler denied any responsibility for gassings, and explicitly stated that he knew of gassing only because "everyone […] knew about it" or because he had learned about it "through conversation with the doctors." (See Phillips 1949, p. 714.)

Hössler was a defendant during the Bergen-Belsen Show Trial, where he was sentenced to death, despite his cooperation, and subsequently hanged.

HÖTTL, WILHELM

Wilhelm Höttl (19 March 1915 – 27 June 1999), SS *Sturmbannführer*, was a German official working at the espionage section of the Germany's Department of Homeland Security during the war (*Reichssicherheitshauptamt*). At the end of the war and afterwards, he was involved with U.S. intelligence services in various activities.

Wilhelm Höttl

Together with Dieter Wisliceny, Höttl was instrumental in "establishing" for the Nuremberg International Military Tribunal that six million Jews had died as a result of National-Socialist persecution and extermination policy. Höttl claimed in an affidavit that he had heard that number from Adolf Eichmann. Eichmann, so Höttl claimed, was allegedly asked by Himmler to prepare a report, because the latter wanted to know how many Jews had been killed. Based on the report he had then prepared, Eichmann supposedly concluded that some 4 million Jews had been killed in various extermination camps, while two million more had died otherwise, most of them by execution behind the Eastern front (*IMT*, Vol. 31, pp. 85f.). Höttl's affidavit is quoted to this day as "proof" for this 6-million claim, although Adolf Eichmann denied having had any knowledge of the total number of Jewish victims during his own trial at Jerusalem in 1961, and there is no trace of any such Eichmann report.

From March of 1944, Höttl served at the German embassy in Budapest under Edmund Veesenmayer, who at that time was spearheading Germany's efforts to have some 400,000 Jews from Hungary deported to German forced-labor camps via Auschwitz. This action is said to have led to most of these Jews being exterminated there. As such, the Allies could have easily indicted Höttl for his collaboration in these efforts, but probably due to the pro-American espionage services he rendered (or promised) at that time, and because of his service "proving" the six-million figure, Höttl was never indicted for anything.

In his 1997 autobiography, Höttl tried to worm his way out of his Nuremberg lie by writing as follows (Höttl 1997, pp. 412f.):

"I do not know where Eichmann got this figure, [...] which today belongs to the iron stock of historiography and which to doubt is forbidden by law. One can only assume: Eichmann also listened, as he confessed to me, to 'enemy radio stations,' in whose broadcasts this number certainly also appeared, and repeated it as his 'official' knowledge. The notorious chief of the Auschwitz Concentration Camp Höss also operated with numbers in the millions which were incorrect. Were these statements all just 'hunter's lore'?"

However, his Nuremberg affidavit explicitly refers to a report Eichmann had prepared for Himmler. That wasn't just regurgitated enemy propaganda. Clearly, Höttl lied at Nuremberg in order to save his own life. (See Rudolf 2023, pp. 23f.).

Houstek → Erber, Josef

HUNGARY

Between 1938 and early 1941, Hungary took control of considerable swaths of territory of its various weak or disintegrating neighboring countries, but lost them all again after the war. With these new territories also came many additional Jews. While Hungary proper had some 400,000 Jews, that number swelled to 725,000 with the new territories, plus thousands of war refugees streaming in from Poland in late 1939.

While Hungary had an independent government, its Jews, though subject to discrimination, were largely safe from more-severe measures, such as ghettoization and deportation. This changed in early 1944, when the Hungarian government, foreseeing the defeat of the Axis Powers, tried to pull out of the war. As a reaction, German forces invaded the country, and installed a puppet government. Anti-Jewish measures swiftly followed, including plans of mass deportations.

Documented History

A series of transcribed telegrams sent by the German plenipotentiary in Hungary Edmund Veesenmayer to the Foreign Office in Berlin report the daily number of Jews that had been deported from Hungary. The last report of July 9 mentions 437,402 deportees. However, these reports do not indicate the destiny of these transports. A report by Eberhard von Thadden, an expert on Jewish issues at the German Foreign Office, mentions that about a third of the Jews deported from Hungary were fit for work, and that they would be made available "immediately after their arrival at the Auschwitz Camp," to various government agencies for forced-labor deployment. Other documents also mention that roughly a third of all deported Jews from Hungary were able to work, and numerous sources show that many, if not most or even all, of these Jews were deployed in a variety of locations throughout Germany and Austria.

A wide variety of documents permits a somewhat complete reconstruction of the number of Jews deported from Hungary and admitted to the Auschwitz Camp, either with or without registration. This results in a total of some 128,700 Jews, or some 30% of all deported Jews. Almost all of them were eventually transferred to other labor camps and worksites, mostly in Germany or Austria.

Interestingly, the age of some of those who were registered shows that "fit for work" was, at times, a very generously applied concept, because quite a few of them were children, and some of them persons well over 60 years of age. Of the 578 Hungarian Jews who were encountered alive at the Auschwitz Camp by the Soviets on 27 January 1945, 29 were ten years old and younger.

Another set of documents shows that the Hungarian Jews temporarily lodged at Birkenau were given medical treatment to keep them alive and well, as best as was possible under the bad circumstances of an overcrowded, overwhelmed camp. For example, a medical report of 28 June 1944 informs us that 1,426 surgical interventions for serious medical issues were performed on some of these Hungarian Jews.

While currently known documents do not permit any conclusion about the fate of the Jews deemed unfit for work, both the analysis of air photos and of ground photos prove that their fate was probably innocuous.

Two SS men at Auschwitz were charged with documenting the processing of the Hungarian Jews, as they streamed into Auschwitz. They took photos, which were later put together into an album, today referred to as the Auschwitz Album. It was discovered after the war, and has since been published in numerous editions. Gutman's 1990 *Encyclopedia of the Holocaust* uses many of its photos to illustrate its article on the Auschwitz Camp (pp. 112-118). It shows how those fit for work were shorn, deloused and given prison clothes, while those unfit for work kept their clothes and belongings and were sent elsewhere. These photos prove that the arriving Hungarian Jews were not slaughtered irrespective of their fitness, and that those unfit for labor could even keep their belongings. (See the entry on the *Auschwitz Album*.)

Moreover, some of these photos show the chimneys of Crematoria II and III, and they all show sections of the sky. Like the air photos of Auschwitz taken in May, June and July 1944, these photos, too, demonstrate that there was no smoke coming out of the crematoria's chimneys, that no gigantic open-air incineration pits burned thousands of murdered Jews every day, and that no smoke was blanketing the sky. (See the entry on Air Photos.)

Most of the German officials primarily responsible for the deportation of the Jews from Hungary got off lightly after the war:

– Kurt Becher, representative in Hungary of the SS *Führungshauptamt* (and thus Himmler's right-hand man), served the prosecution at the Nuremberg International Military Tribunal by signing an affidavit and testifying that he received from Himmler an order in September or October 1944 prohibiting "any extermination of the Jews." No such order ever existed. (See the entry on Becher for details.)

– Edmund Veesenmayer got indicted during Case 11 ("Ministries Case") of the U.S.-conducted Nuremberg Military Tribunals (NMT), where he was sentenced to 20 years imprisonment, but was pardoned two years into his prison term.

– Eberhard von Thadden, an expert on Jewish issues at the German Foreign Office and Eichmann's contact person, testified for the prosecution during NMT Case 11 and confirmed everything they wanted, after one of the Allied interrogators had threatened him with extradition to the French, who were eager to sentence him to death. Von Thadden was never prosecuted for his involvement in the deportation of Jews from Hungary.

– Horst Wagner, a member of the personal staff of Germany's foreign minister Joachim Ribbentrop, and von Thadden's superior as head of Department *Inland II*, also testified for the prosecution during NMT Case 11. Several attempts to prosecute him in West Germany went nowhere.

– Several other officials of the German foreign office whose names, signatures or initials can be found on documents pertaining to the deportation of Jews from Hungary – Geiger, Wissberg, Hencke, Reichel, Mirbach – were never indicted or prosecuted for their involvement either.

The two big exceptions are Adolf Eichmann and one of his deputies, Dieter Wisliceny. Eichmann was missing after the war and served as a scapegoat for everyone else during the various Nuremberg trials, while Wisliceny's deal with the Allies – to be let off the hook for testifying as requested – evidently went sour. He was eventually extradited to Czechoslovakia, where he was tried and hanged in 1948.

Current Orthodox Narrative

The orthodoxy insists that almost all Jews deported from Hungary to Auschwitz were killed on arrival in the various homicidal gas chambers at Birkenau. In fact, so many Jews were allegedly killed every day between 17 May and end of June 1945 that not even the vastly exaggerated cremation capacity of the Birkenau crematoria could keep up with the mass-murderous frenzy. Therefore, large cremation pits are said to have been operated, both in the yard north of Crematorium V as well as in the vicinity of the so-called Bunker 2 just outside the camp to the west. As a result, the crematoria chimneys were smoking heavily, and the entire area was blanketed in smoke coming from the blazing pits burning thousands of corpses daily.

However, as mentioned before, neither the photos taken by the SS and put together as the so-called *Auschwitz Album* nor the various air photos taken by German and American reconnaissance aircraft show any trace of smoking crematorium chimneys or of any large pits from which smoke is billowing, covering the area in smoke.

Gutman's 1990 *Encyclopedia of the Holocaust* shows one of these air photos (26 June 1944). However, it covers the entire Auschwitz region, and the Birkenau Camp is too small to recognize details. Furthermore, the area around Crematorium V and the alleged Bunker 2, where the billowing smoke would be, is conveniently cut off at the top (p. 120). Van Pelt reproduces the same photo, plus one of 31 May 1944, without any smoke visible anywhere, and no explanation provided for the reader as to what is and is not visible on it (van Pelt 2002, pp. 91, 449).

(For more details on this, see Mattogno 2023c, Part 1; 2016b, esp. pp. 57-79; Butz 2015, pp. 205-227; for demographic deliberations on the Hungarian Jews, see Rudolf 2019, pp. 183-185.)

HYDROGEN CYANIDE

Hydrogen cyanide (HCN) is the active toxic ingredient in the pesticide Zyklon B. It has no effect on microbial lifeforms at prescribed levels. It is lethal above certain concentrations to multi-cellular lifeforms, such as insects and mammals. This chemical blocks a cell's ability to use oxygen for its metabolism, and hence suffocates it on a cellular level. As a result, the blood stays rich in oxygen, becoming over-saturated with it as the poisoning progresses. The visible hallmarks of cyanide poisoning are therefore a distinct pink complexion, and pinkish-red rather than purple-bluish death marks (*livor mortis*).

Most witnesses falsely described victims of Zyklon-B poisoning as black, blue, green or purple (e.g. Michał Kula, Filip Müller, Milton Buki, Pery Broad, Walter Petzold, Jan Wolny, Józef Weber, Aleksander Germański, Tadeusz Kurant, Wiesław Kielar, Ludwik Banach, Josef Klehr). Since a pinkish-red discoloration of the skin is not what people expect to see when confronted with victims of suffocation – be it by means of poison gas or simple oxygen deprivation – the sight of such pinkish-red corpses should have left a distinct impression in the memory of basically all those who claim to have witnessed it. Yet the rule is that almost all witnesses making statements about this followed the beaten path of a false cliché. This is just one piece of evidence that suggests that mass homicidal gassings with hydrogen cyanide never occurred.

Insects – and in particular insect eggs – are considerably less sensitive to hydrogen-cyanide poisoning than are warm-blooded animals. This is due, first of all, to their greater resistance (slower metabolism). Additionally, in order to reach insects, their larvae, pupae and eggs, lethal concentrations of the gas must penetrate into every hem and seam of, for example, clothing and bedding. Consequently, it also penetrates into every crack, crevice, and gap in a gassing facility. Warm-blooded animals, by contrast, are rapidly exposed to high concentrations of the gas, not only because of their size, but above all due to their continuous breathing through lungs.

Lethal Concentration

Lethal doses of cyanide can be ingested orally, inhaled, or absorbed through the skin. Oral poisoning (for example with potassium cyanide, KCN) is very painful due to muscular convulsions (cramps) caused by cell suffocation. Inhalation poisoning induces unconsciousness faster, but can still cause painful convulsions, depending on the circumstances.

A dose of 1 mg cyanide per kg body weight is generally considered lethal for humans. Non-lethal doses of cyanide are quickly decomposed and excreted by the body.

Absorption through the skin is especially likely when the skin has become moist, for example, as a result of sweating. Thus, it is generally advised to avoid sweating during the handling of hydrogen cyanide. For poisoning through the skin, concentrations from 6,000 parts per million (0.6% by volume) constitute a health hazard, while 10,000 parts per million (1% by volume) can cause a lethal poisoning within just a few minutes.

Lethal concentrations of HCN given in today's literature are based on experiments conducted with rabbits before World War One. More recent tests have shown that humans are *less* susceptible to HCN poisoning than small mammals such as rabbits (McNamara 1976). Furthermore, when considering the intention of killing *all* individuals exposed to HCN (such as in a large gas chamber with multiple victims), different standards must be used than those given in toxicological literature, which are not only based on inapplicable animal models, but moreover keep lethal threshold levels intentionally low to protect sensitive individuals. However, healthy and fit individuals can survive higher doses of toxins than weak or sick individuals.

Calculations and extrapolations from more-realistic animal models have resulted in a concentration, lethal within ten minutes for 100% of all individuals, of some 4,400 mg of hydrogen cyanide per m³ of air, or some 0.4%. This is close to the concentration that used to be applied during executions in U.S. gas chambers, where the average time until death was reportedly about 10 minutes, with extreme cases up to

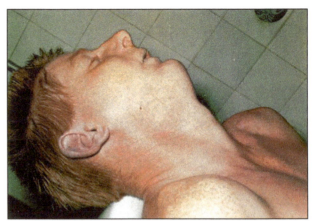

Pinkish discoloration of the skin of a victim of cyanide poisoning by ingesting calcium cyanide.

almost 20 minutes.

Hence, in order to kill all individuals in a hypothetical gas chamber within ten minutes, an average concentration during those ten minutes of some 0.4% would have to be applied. Faster execution times would require proportionally higher concentrations, with a time of five minutes requiring almost 1% of HCN in the air, which is a commonly used concentration during fumigations, also in disinfestation chambers, in order to kill pests such as fleas and lice. (See Rudolf 2023, esp. pp. 227-236.)

Chemical Traces

When coming in contact with material containing iron oxide (rust), hydrogen cyanide can form durable components under certain circumstances. These components are bluish in color. They can withstand decades of exposure to the elements, hence lend themselves as an indicator of previous exposure to hydrogen cyanide. See the entry on Iron Blue for more details on this.

I

I.G. FARBENINDUSTRIE AG

The trust *Interessen-Gemeinschaft Farbenindustrie AG* (in short, I.G. Farben) was a conglomerate of German chemical and pharmaceutical companies, including Bayer, BASF, Hoechst and AGFA. It was established in 1925 and dissolved at the end of World War Two. After the war against Poland in late 1939, the I.G. Farben soon made plans to set up a new chemical plant in the vicinity of Auschwitz near the town of Monowitz for the synthesis of chemical raw materials out of coal. One of the intended final products was rubber made from a process called BUNA, which also became the name of this plant. This plant took ample advantage of the slave-labor force provided by the SS running the nearby Auschwitz Camp, which established a separate labor subcamp nearby (see the entry on Monowitz).

I.G. Farben was moreover a major shareholder of the DEGESCH pest-control company, which held the patent for Zyklon B, and developed and patented a standard fumigation gas chamber that was mass-produced during the war years.

Due to this entanglement with the slave-labor camp system and the German war effort, 23 of the top representatives of I.G. Farben were prosecuted by the U.S. occupational forces, who organized an entire trial at Nuremberg against them, the so-called "I.G. Farben Case" (NMT, Vols. 7f.). Ten of the defendants were acquitted, and 13 received prison sentences between 1½ and eight years (NMT, Vol. 8, pp. 1206-1209).

indoctrination → Holocaust Indoctrination

INSTRUMENTS, OF EXTERMINATION

The tools which the orthodoxy claims National-Socialist Germany used to accomplish the extermination of Jews (and also other victim groups) fall into two groups:

1. Organizational Instruments

a. Ghettos. Orthodox historians claim that the Third Reich forced Jews to live in ghettos, not just to separate them from the non-Jewish population and to keep them under tight control, but also to subject them deliberately to conditions whereby many of them would inevitably die. See the entry on ghettos for more details.

b. Camps. Concentration camps and labor or PoW camps are not a unique feature of the Holocaust. Therefore, they are not included in this work, unless it is claimed that measures or facilities were put in place to accomplish a planned mass extermination. Such claims were made by many witnesses for numerous camps. Most of them were accepted by orthodox historians as true, while a few were rejected as erroneous or fraudulent. For a list of these camps, see the entry on extermination camps.

c. *Einsatzgruppen.* These German military units operated in eastern occupied territories with numerous tasks. The orthodoxy insists that their main task was to round up and murder Jews. The main methods to accomplish this were mostly mass executions by shootings, with gas vans used as a secondary murder weapon. When German armed forces started retreating from the Soviet Union, special units within the framework of the so-called *Aktion* 1005 are said to have roamed the temporarily German-occupied territories in order to empty mass graves containing *Einsatzgruppen* victims, and to burn all bodies.

2. Physical Instruments, Tools

These are the material tools used during and after the murder. They are divided into the actual murder weapon on the one hand, and tools to destroy the victims' bodies on the other hand:

a. Murder Weapons. This includes a wide array of claimed murder methods, such as bullets, various toxic gases in stationary and mobile gas chambers, electricity, vacuum, steam, war gases etc., but also some exotic methods, such as tree felling, death bridges, explosives, pneumatic hammers, etc. For a closer discussion, see the entry on tools of mass murder.

b. Tools to erase the traces of the murder. These include crematoria, open-air incinerations as well as alleged attempts to remove corpses with explosives (see the respective entries for details).

For more details on this, see the entry on tools of

mass murder.

INTENTIONALITY

In the context of the Holocaust, intentionality refers to leading National-Socialist functionaries having had intentions to physically annihilate the Jews within their reach, plans they devised to that effect, and orders they issued to make it happen.

Intentions can be gleaned from public and private statements of leading National-Socialist politicians. See in this regard the entries on:
– Adolf Hitler
– Heinrich Himmler
– Himmler Speeches
– Joseph Goebbels
– Hermann Göring
– Hans Frank
– Alfred Rosenberg

Whether any plans existed that were devised to turn such a potential intention into reality, is furthermore discussed in the following entries:
– Plan, to Exterminate the Jews.
– Hitler Order, Final Solution.

Which orders were actually issued, is discussed in the following entries:
– Final Solution
– Emigration
– Resettlement
– *Einsatzgruppen*, section "Extermination Order"

Other entries on mid-level functionaries also cover some aspects of this overarching topic, such as:
– Rudolf Höss
– Otto Ohlendorf
– Kurt Becher
– Reinhardt Heydrich
– Richard Glücks
– Oswald Pohl

INTERNATIONAL MILITARY TRIBUNAL (IMT)

The Origins

With victory over National-Socialist Germany in May of 1945, the Allied forces consolidated their gains, moved to take control of German territory, and accelerated plans to hold leading Germans legally accountable for the war.

Initially, Stalin suggested rounding up the top 50,000 or even 100,000 top German war leaders and executing them without further legal ado, as they had done in 1939/40 with the Polish elite. At first, the British and U.S. administrations agreed to this proposal. Shortly afterwards, the British backpedaled and instead suggested handing over for further processing the smaller war criminals to the countries where they had committed their crimes, while arresting and executing the Axis's top 50 or 100 war leaders.

It was Stalin, of all leaders, who opposed this plan, insisting instead on a trial – no doubt the Soviet mock style – before executing these leaders. It took Roosevelt to die and Truman to take office for the U.S. administration to agree with Stalin and bring the British around. Stalin, however, dragged his feet when it came to organizing this mock trial. Hence, Truman had the U.S. take the lead, installed Justice Robert H. Jackson of the U.S. Supreme Court to be the chief prosecutor of all Allied Nations, and made sure that the upcoming trial was firmly under U.S. control.

Jackson, however, disagreed that he or anyone ought to lead the entire prosecution, as he foresaw that the Soviets would submit evidence which no one else wanted to take responsibility for. Hence, in the end, all four Allies had their own prosecutors. Jackson won the support of the Office of Strategic Services (O.S.S.), the CIA's predecessor, to prepare the U.S.'s case. Since the O.S.S. was involved in spreading black propaganda about Germany, among other things, this did not bode well for what was to come. The O.S.S. in turn collaborated closely with the Soviet NKVD to prepare their case. Fine bed fellows indeed.

In June 1945, barely one month after Germany surrendered, all four Allies agreed to have their top legal experts convene in London to hammer out a framework for the upcoming show trial. The Soviets insisted on a trial with a swift verdict based on what was already "known" to be the defendants' guilt. Evidence and arguments were quite superfluous. However, eventually, the Soviets agreed to an Anglo-American proposal of a more formal trial, which was then signed by all four Allies on 8 August 1945 as the London Agreement, which set out the framework and procedural rules of the upcoming International Military Tribunal (IMT).

The Illegality and Illegitimacy

The IMT was technically illegal for three reasons:
1. Up to the creation of the IMT, no international court had existed. Therefore, any such court could have had jurisdictions over the citizens of a certain country only if that country had agreed to ac-

cept the jurisdiction of that court. The German post-Hitler government under Admiral von Dönitz was not asked to accept the court's jurisdiction.

Under international law, only German courts of law could have legally prosecuted German war crimes. In fact, Dönitz's government offered just that on 15 May 1945. He authorized Germany's Supreme Court in Leipzig to conduct a German trial against suspected German war criminals. Dönitz's request to Eisenhower for permission to go ahead with that trial resulted in U.S. and British forces arresting all members of the German government on 23 May 1945, hence more than two months prior to the creation of the IMT. Therefore, there could not have been any consent by any German government in accepting the jurisdiction of the IMT.

2. In no court of the world would it be legal to put those who claim to have been wronged in the position of being both the prosecutor and the judge. At a minimum, the judges should have been chosen from countries not part of the conflict, such as Switzerland or Sweden.
3. Four laws were invented for this trial under which the German war criminals were to be prosecuted:
   a. Conspiring to commit crimes against peace
   b. Waging wars of aggression
   c. Committing war crimes
   d. Committing crimes against humanity

   While points b) and c), if following earlier precedents of international law, could be seen as a mere reframing of old laws, points a) and d) were completely new and unheard of. These new laws were then applied *retro-actively* on acts allegedly perpetrated *before* these laws existed. This is a violation of one of the most basic principles of law.

The farcical nature of the entire setup becomes clear when considering that this "international" court by its statute was only allowed to prosecute suspected war criminals of the Axis powers. Any truly international court would have charged whoever committed war crimes, not just those of the vanquished. During the IMT, any argument by the defense to demonstrate that the Allies had done no better, or even worse, was rejected as invalid.

During the IMT, the German leaders on trial were accused of:

1. having waged wars of aggression or invading peaceful countries – when the Soviet Union had waged wars of aggression against Poland and Finland in 1939, had invaded Romania and the Baltics in 1940, and was conspiring to overrun all of continental Europe in 1941; the British had conspired to invade neutral Norway and Sweden; the U.S. had invaded neutral Iceland and Iran.
2. having incarcerated hundreds of thousand without due process – while simultaneously the Allied nations had incarcerated hundreds of thousands of Americans of Japanese descent, Italians and Germans without due process, not to mention the millions who were incarcerated in the Soviet Union without due process;
3. having exploited hundreds of thousands as slave laborers – while at the same time the Soviets were deporting hundreds of thousands of Germans and anyone who had collaborated with them during the war to slave-labor camps;
4. letting hundreds of thousands die of neglect in ghettos and camps – while during those very months of the IMT, German "disarmed enemy forces" were dying by the hundreds of thousands in American, Canadian, Polish, French and Russian camps, not to mention the millions who had disappeared and were still disappearing in the Soviet Union's GULag;
5. having ethnically cleansed hundreds of thousands of Poles from their centuries-old homesteads in the "Warthegau" – while concurrently some ten million German civilians in East Germany and all over eastern Europe were ethnically cleansed from their centuries-old homesteads, with more than two million of them dying in the process;
6. having mass-murdered innocent (Jewish) civilians by the millions – when more than two million innocent German civilians had been burned alive and blown to pieces during Allied carpet-bombing campaigns, and were being mass-slaughtered in East Germany and eastern Europe in the biggest ethnic-cleansing campaign the world had ever seen.

The worst hypocrisy of all was reserved for Justice Jackson. As a representative of the very nation which instantly mass-murdered hundreds of thousands of innocent civilians by dropping nuclear bombs on undefended cities of a country that was ready to surrender (Japan), he seriously – and falsely – accused German leaders during the IMT of having mass-murdered 20,000 innocent Jewish civilians with a nuclear blast! Here is the United States' chief prosecutor Jackson talking during the IMT (*IMT*, Vol. 16, pp. 529f.):

"And certain experiments were also conducted and certain researches conducted in atomic energy, were they not? [...] Now, I have certain information, which was placed in my hands, of an experiment which was carried out near Auschwitz [...]. The purpose of the experiment was to find a quick and complete way of destroying people without the delay and trouble of shooting and gassing and burning, as it had been carried out [...]. A village, a small village was provisionally erected, with temporary structures, and in it approximately 20,000 Jews were put. By means of this newly invented weapon of destruction [= nuclear bomb], *these 20,000 people were eradicated almost instantaneously, and in such a way that there was no trace left of them;"*

(But see also the entry on Ohrdruf.)

During the IMT, Jackson aptly described what this trial was essentially all about:

"As a military tribunal, this Tribunal is a continuation of the war effort of the Allied nations. As an International Tribunal, it is not bound by the procedural and substantive refinements of our respective judicial or constitutional systems [...]."
(*IMT*, Vol. 19, p. 398)

This mockery of international justice found its stage at the Nuremberg Court House, where the show unfolded from November 1945 to October 1946.

The Structure

By mid-1945, the Allies had designated 24 Germans, among the hundreds captured, as "major war criminals." These would be subject to the IMT's unprecedented brand of justice. Of the 24, the two highest-ranking men were Hermann Göring, Reichstag president (1932–1945) and head of the *Luftwaffe*, Germany's air force (1935–1945), and Martin Bormann, chief of the Reich Chancellery (1941–1945). Since Bormann was missing but believed to be alive, he was tried *in absentia*. Both men were sentenced to death, but Göring committed suicide before his execution. The remaining 22 men, all held in custody, were, in alphabetical order (see *IMT*, Vol. 22, pp. 524-587 for the verdicts, and pp. 588f. for the sentences):

- Karl Dönitz, head of the *Kriegsmarine* (German Navy, 1943–1945): ten years imprisonment.
- Hans Frank, head of the General Government in occupied Poland (1939–1945): death sentence.
- Wilhelm Frick, Minister of the Interior (1933–1943), Reich Leader (1933–1945), Protector of Bohemia and Moravia (occupied Czechia, 1943–1945): death sentence.
- Hans Fritzsche, popular radio commentator and head of the Nazi news division: acquitted.
- Walther Funk, Minister of Economics (1938–1945), Reichsbank president (Germany's Central Bank, 1939–1945): life imprisonment.
- Rudolf Hess, Hitler's Deputy (1933–1941): life imprisonment.
- Alfred Jodl, Chief of Operations Staff of the Wehrmacht's *Oberkommando* (Supreme Command, 1939–1945): death sentence.
- Ernst Kaltenbrunner, Chief of the *Reichssicherheitshauptamt*, Germany's Department of Homeland Security (1942–1945) and highest-ranking SS leader to be tried: death sentence.
- Wilhelm Keitel, head of the Wehrmacht's *Oberkommando* (Supreme Command, 1938–1945): death sentence.
- Gustav Krupp von Bohlen und Halbach, major industrialist; found medically unfit for trial.
- Robert Ley, head of *Deutsche Arbeitsfront* (DAF, German Labor Front, 1933–1945): committed suicide three days after being indicted.
- Erich Raeder, Commander in Chief of the *Kriegsmarine*, Germany's navy (1935–1943): life imprisonment.
- Joachim von Ribbentrop, Minister of Foreign Affairs (1938–1945): death sentence.
- Alfred Rosenberg, leading racial theorist and Minister of the Eastern Occupied Territories (1941–1945): death sentence.
- Fritz Sauckel, *Gauleiter* (district leader) of Thuringia, and General Plenipotentiary for Labor Deployment (1942–1945): death sentence.
- Hjalmar Schacht, Reichsbank president (Germany's Central Bank, 1933–1939) and Minister of Economics (1934–1937): acquitted.
- Arthur Seyss-Inquart, Reichskommissar of the occupied Netherlands (1940–1945): death sentence.
- Albert Speer, architect, and Minister of Armaments (1942–1945): twenty years imprisonment.
- Julius Streicher, *Gauleiter* of Franconia (1929–1940) and publisher of the weekly tabloid newspaper *Der Stürmer*: death sentence.
- Baron Konstantin von Neurath, Minister of Foreign Affairs (1932–1938): fifteen years imprisonment.
- Franz von Papen, Chancellor of Germany (1932) and Vice-Chancellor (1933–1934): acquitted.

- Baldur von Schirach, Head of the Hitler Youth (1933–1940), Reich Leader of Youth Education (1940-1945), and *Gauleiter* of Vienna (1940–1945): twenty years imprisonment.

Each of them could be charged with any one, or any combination, of the above-listed four charges. Twelve men were in fact indicted on all four counts. Verdict was then rendered for each man on each individual count. A guilty verdict on even one count was sufficient for the death penalty.

In order to implement the tribunal, each of the four powers supplied one judge and one leading prosecutor, along with a support team of many individuals. These leading men were as follows:

	Judge	Lead Prosecutor
Britain:	Geoffrey Lawrence	Hartley Shawcross
US:	Francis Biddle	Robert Jackson
France:	Henri de Vabres	François de Menthon
USSR:	Iona Nikitchenko	Roman Rudenko

British Judge Lawrence would also serve as president of the IMT. The American team was extensive, and included such men as Telford Taylor, Thomas J. Dodd, William Walsh and Walter Brudno. On the British side, Shawcross was supported by David Maxwell-Fyfe, John Wheeler-Bennett and Mervyn Griffith-Jones.

Notable, though, was the extensive Jewish presence on both the American and British teams from the very beginning. Roosevelt's close confidant Samuel Rosenman "crafted... the founding document of the IMT," together with Jackson (Townsend 2012, pp. 173f.). British Jews at the trial itself included Maxwell-Fyfe, Benjamin Kaplan, Murray Bernays, David Marcus and Hersh Lauterpacht. Jewish-American prosecutors or advisors were far more numerous; they included William Kaplan, Richard Sonnenfeldt, Randolph Newman, Raphael Lemkin, Sidney Alderman, Benjamin Ferencz, Robert Kempner, Cecilia Goetz, Ralph Goodman, Gustav Gilbert, Leon Goldensohn, Siegfried Ramler, Hannah Wartenberg and Hedy Epstein.

The striking Jewish presence was noted at the time by the (non-Jewish) American Thomas Dodd. In a letter to his wife of 20 September 1945, he explained his concerns about Jewish dominance:

"The staff continues to grow every day. Col. [Benjamin] Kaplan is now here, as a mate, I assume, for Commander [William] Kaplan. Dr. [Randolph] Newman has arrived and I do not know how many more. It is all a silly business— but 'silly' really isn't the right word. One would expect that some of these people would have sense enough to put an end to this kind of a parade. [...Y]ou will understand when I tell you that this staff is about 75% Jewish." (Dodd 2007, p. 135)

Dodd clearly felt that this undermined the integrity of the trials:

"[T]he Jews should stay away from this trial—for their own sake. For—mark this well—the charge 'a war for the Jews' is still being made, and in the post-war years it will be made again and again. The too-large percentage of Jewish men and women here will be cited as proof of this charge. Sometimes it seems that the Jews will never learn about these things. They seem intent on bringing new difficulties down on their own heads. I do not like to write about this matter [...] but I am disturbed about it. They are pushing and crowding and competing with each other, and with everyone else. They will try the case I guess." (Ibid., pp. 135f.)

Who had decided that it was appropriate to have dozens of Jews on the prosecution? Who believed that anything like 75% representation was acceptable, from a nation that had, at best, 2% Jews? And why?

The trial itself was conducted from 14 November 1945 until 1 October 1946.

Structural Problems

Mounting a defense for the defendants during the IMT was borderline impossible for many structural problems that the Allies had put in place either deliberately or as an inevitable result of their occupational policies.

Finding Representation

The best defenders would have been German lawyers familiar with the details of the German government and military, and sympathetic to their cause. However, most of these lawyers were barred from practicing law because they had been involved in German official affairs or were members of organization deemed criminal in nature by the Allies. This left lawyers of lower tiers with less experience who were likely unsympathetic to the defendant's cause.

Paying Representation

The defendants' properties, funds and assets had largely been confiscated, and what was left was usually devalued by the collapse of the Reichmark's value at war's end. Hence, the defendants could not afford hiring large legal teams, and they most certainly could not hope to get support by the German government, which no longer existed, or by any group of sympathizers, who would have been disbanded and arrested by the Allies, had they dared make a public appearance.

Access to Prosecution Files

The Allies confiscated tons of documents from all over Germany. Much of it was brought to the Allies' document center in Paris, where a large team of hundreds of legal clerks sifted through the material in search of incriminating material. Thousands of documents were eventually cherry-picked by the prosecution to bolster their case. However, none of the defense lawyers was ever granted access to this pool of documents. No defense team can prepare any legal case without access to the files of the prosecution. The only material that the defense lawyers ever saw were the thousands of pre-selected incriminating documents. If they wanted to find exonerating documents, they were on their own. However, with no noteworthy financial resources or manpower at their disposal, such a search for any left-over documents not confiscated and hidden by the Allies had little chance of success.

Impediments

To make matters worse, German lawyers couldn't just travel through Germany in search of documents or witnesses. The Allies had carved up Germany into occupational zones, and traveling through them and across zone borders was restricted. Furthermore, many potential witnesses for the defense were either arrested and inaccessible to defense lawyers, or they would put themselves in acute danger of getting arrested, should they agree to testify on behalf of the defense. Here is a concise list of challenges the defense faced during the IMT:
- Defendants: threats and psychological torture; prolonged interrogations; confiscation of personal property.
- Witnesses for the defense: intimidation, threats, even arrests; withholding of defense witnesses; forced testimonies.
- Evidence: "proof" based on hearsay; documents of arbitrary kinds; disappearance of exonerating evidence; distorted affidavits; tendentious translations; twisted meaning of documents.
- Procedure: dishonest simultaneous translations; arbitrarily rejected motions to introduce evidence; confiscation of files; refusal to provide defense access to documents; systematic obstruction of the defense's efforts by the prosecution.

Rules of Procedure

The IMT started out with every prosecutor and judge assuming that all defendants were considered guilty unless proven innocent. The very nature of the IMT demanded relatively rapid verdicts for a large number of people, which effectively prohibited time-consuming but essential phases of evidence-collection and refutation, on-site visits, expert reports, and the like. However, the prosecution did not intend to spend time on this, and the defense could not afford it due to financial and manpower restrictions. Time-cutting measures were even integrated into the very rules of the IMT. Article 19 of the London Statute, for example, states:

"The Tribunal shall not be bound by technical rules of evidence. It shall adopt and apply to the greatest possible extent expeditious and non-technical procedure, and shall admit any evidence which it deems to have probative value." (*IMT*, Vol. 1, p. 15)

In other words, testimony did not have to be confirmed with material or forensic evidence. The IMT could accept virtually any statement as fact: opinion, hearsay, rumor, inference, belief. The top priority was "expeditiousness."

Furthermore, any facts that the court chose to take as "common knowledge," no matter how they were obtained or how improbable they were, required no proof or evidence at all. This was known as "judicial notice." Hence, we have Article 21:

"The Tribunal shall not require proof of facts of common knowledge, but shall take judicial notice thereof. It shall also take judicial notice of official governmental documents and reports of the United Nations, including the acts and documents of the committees set up in the various Allied countries for the investigation of war crimes, and the records and findings of military or other Tribunals of any of the United Nations." (*Ibid.*)

This "common knowledge" included any alleged "fact" established by any authority or commission of any Allied country, whether in documents, verdicts, acts, reports, or other records. Once the court had taken judicial notice of something, it stood as an established fact and could not be challenged. If the defendant happened to disagree, he had no recourse.

Some of the "facts" which the IMT accepted as

common knowledge were fraudulent reports written by Soviet investigative commissions about alleged atrocities committed at places such as Auschwitz, Majdanek and Treblinka. Other "facts" were those created by verdicts of Allied show trials prior to the IMT, such as those staged by the Soviet Union in Krasnodar and Kharkov, where accusations of mass murder with so-called gas vans were levied; or those that unfolded under British and American aegis in West Germany, where it has been solidly documented that both American and British investigators systematically tortured German defendants to extract false confessions. (See the entry on torture for details.)

Therefore, the IMT was a highly problematic event consisting of criminal actions against helpless detainees, and "confessions" obtained under the worst conditions imaginable. Little surprise that it found prominent critics, even among Westerners. American jurist Harlan Fiske Stone served on the U.S. Supreme Court from 1926 until his death in 1946. In his final year, he described the situation as follows (in Mason 1956, p. 716):

"[Chief U.S. prosecutor] Jackson is away conducting his high-grade lynching party in Nuremberg. I don't mind what he does to the Nazis, but I hate to see the pretense that he is running a court and proceeding according to common law. This is a little too sanctimonious a fraud to meet my old-fashioned ideas."

He was not speaking metaphorically; eleven of the 23 men were ultimately sentenced to death, and nine of them executed by hanging. Göring committed suicide shortly before his scheduled execution, while the eleventh death sentence against Bormann was only declamatory in nature, since he was not present.

U.S. judge Charles Wennerstrum, who presided over the seventh of the 12 later NMT trials, the "Hostages Trial," stated the obvious: "The victor in any war is not the best judge of the war crime guilt." The whole system was "devoted to whitewashing the Allies and placing sole blame for World War II upon Germany." (For more extracts, see the entry on Charles Wennerstrum.)

The reflections of lawyer and U.S. senator from Ohio Robert Taft are also pertinent. Though not directly involved in the trials, Taft took an interest in events happening in postwar Europe, and he was generally appalled at the brutality and harshness of the victorious Allies. Just after the conclusion of the IMT on 1 October 1946, Taft offered a stinging indictment of the entire trial process based primarily on the principle that one cannot, after the fact, create laws by which individuals can then be prosecuted:

"I believe that most Americans view with discomfort the war trials which have just been concluded in Germany and are proceeding in Japan. They violate that fundamental principle of American law that a man cannot be tried under an ex post facto statute. The hanging of the 11 men convicted at Nuremberg will be a blot on the American record which we shall long regret.

The trial of the vanquished by the victors cannot be impartial, no matter how it is hedged about with the forms of justice. I question whether the hanging of those who, however despicable, were the leaders of the German people, will ever discourage the making of aggressive war, for no one makes aggressive war unless he expects to win. About this whole judgment there is the spirit of vengeance, and vengeance is seldom justice." (Taft 2003, p. 200)

Overall, The IMT was a highly flawed and tendentious mock trial aimed not at truth or justice but at revenge, punishment and ideological hegemony.

Documenting the Trials

Documentation on the IMT is extensive. The full proceedings, mostly in the form of transcripts and documents submitted as evidence, were published shortly after the trials. In hard-copy format, it comprises 42 volumes, each running to 500 or 600 pages. Only the largest research universities have actual copies, but fortunately it is now available for free online. The work, published in 1947, appears under two titles: *The Trial of German Major War Criminals*, and *Trial of the Major War Criminals before the IMT*. It is also referred to as the "Blue Series" or the "Blue Set" due to the blue cloth these 1947 volumes were bound with. The full series is online at the US Library of Congress website:

www.loc.gov/rr/frd/Military_Law/NT_major-war-criminals.html

However, a comparison of the trial's original sound recordings with the published transcripts has revealed, that the transcripts are not always accurate. Some passages have been excised (see the case of Julius Streicher). Some statements made in foreign languages were inaccurately translated. This mostly concerns the defendants' German testimonies. Furthermore, even the spoken English words were at times misrepresented.

(For details, see the entry on show trials, as well as von Knieriem 1953; Irving 1996; Rudolf 2019, pp. 94-98; 2023, pp. 411-414.)

INTERNATIONAL TRACING SERVICE, AROLSEN

Already in 1944, the British government organized a Central Tracing Bureau for the registration and tracing of missing people resulting from Axis persecution. In 1955, after several reorganizations and relocations, the center ultimately was named International Tracing Service (ITS) and established with its permanent archives in the West-German town of Arolsen. It was put under the aegis of the International Committee of the Red Cross (ICRC), with a governing commission of representatives of 11 countries (Belgium, France, Germany, Greece, Israel, Italy, Luxembourg, Netherlands, Poland, UK, USA).

The ITS's purpose was limited to collecting documents on the fate of the victims of persecution by National-Socialist Germany, and assist survivors in filing compensations claims against Germany. Its archival material was not publicly accessible due to privacy and safety concerns for the former persecutees.

In 2007, the ITS opened its archives to the public, and extended its purpose to research and education. It moreover prepared copies of its archival material for each governing country. In 2012, the Red Cross withdrew from the ITS's management. In 2019, the ITS started posting its archival material online, with the aim of making everything accessible online eventually.

Until 1993, the ITS sent out lists of registered deaths in National-Socialist camps on request, consisting of data contained in their archives. The total death toll of their victim lists steadily rose over the years as their documentation became more complete. It reached a value just short of 300,000 victims in 1993. This includes both Jews and non-Jews.

This figure stands in stark contrast to exclusively Jewish Holocaust death-toll figures of six million. However, the ITS lists only cases where a death can be ascertained by official documents, such as camp records documenting the death of an inmate. Most victims of the Holocaust are said to have been murdered in the so-called extermination camps or by the *Einsatzgruppen* without ever having been registered or documented in any way. Hence, there is hardly any relationship between the ITS's death-toll list and the claimed death toll for the Holocaust.

Furthermore, many of the documents preserved in Eastern European archives were not yet accessible to the ITS by 1993, let alone analyzed and integrated into their database. Therefore, the ITS's data was highly incomplete, even for documented cases of camp deaths. This can be seen especially in the case of Auschwitz, where wartime camp documents show some 135,500 victims, whereas the ITS had data for only 60,056 of them in 1993.

As of this writing, the ITS's archival material is accessible in a format that virtually prevents any user from tallying up victim numbers. This was probably done by design. However, once all the ITS documents have been made accessible and analyzed, it is likely that a more accurate overall death toll of documented victims will become available. That still leaves out the uncounted multitude of those whose fate might never be known.

Notably, there has never been a similar archival tracing of the victims of persecution by other participants in the Second World War, such as the roughly 12 million ethnic Germans expelled from East Germany and Eastern Europe toward the end and after the war, or the many victims of purges in territories reconquered or liberated from the German armed forces. These victims evidently don't count.

(For more details, see Rudolf 2019, pp. 292-295; 2023, pp. 46f.; Kollerstrom 2023, pp. 91-96.)

IRON BLUE

Iron Blue is the standard name for a broad variety of pigments formed of iron and cyanide that can exhibit a variety of hues, ranging from dark blue to greenish turquoise. It is formed of a mixture of bi- and tri-valent iron cations in the presence of cyanide anions. Other names frequently used are Prussian Blue, Turnbull's Blue and Berlin Blue. As long as it is not subjected to alkaline, reducing or oxidizing environments that disturb its balance of bi- and tri-valent iron, the pigment is very stable and insoluble, and as such non-toxic, despite its high cyanide content.

Iron Blue can form within masonry material if it is exposed to hydrogen cyanide (HCN), such as during fumigations or homicidal gassings using Zyklon B, with its active ingredient of HCN. The formation of this pigment inside masonry when exposed to HCN occurs most readily when the wall – made of plaster, mortar, cement or concrete – is moist and cool, and ideally, not fully set. Since almost all types of cement and sand contain considerable amounts of tri-valent iron (as rust), and because cyanide itself is a powerful reducing agent in unset (alkaline) mortar and cement, and easily capable of reducing some tri-valent iron to bi-valent iron, the formation of Iron Blue in relatively fresh masonry is well documented. This is true both for former German wartime fumigation chambers, and for accidental damages during the 1970s, in which structures that had been freshly replastered were then fumigated with Zyklon B.

The camps at Auschwitz (Main Camp), Birkenau (two structures), Majdanek (two structures) and Stutthof all contain Iron-Blue-stained walls within fumigation chambers, both on the interior and exterior surfaces, and within the walls themselves; these have survived to the present day (see the many color illustrations in Rudolf 2020). The two civilian structures damaged in the 1970s concern the churches at Untergriesbach and Meeder-Wiesenfeld, both in Bavaria.

Importantly, none of the remaining masonry in rooms alleged to have been homicidal gas chambers at Auschwitz exhibit any discoloration due to Iron Blue. Wall samples analyzed for cyanide residues show no significant traces of cyanide above the detection limit either.

Since the physical conditions of some of these walls (cool, damp basement morgues of Crematoria II and III in Birkenau, made of long-term alkaline cement plaster and mortar) were more conducive to forming the pigment than the walls of the Auschwitz *fumigation* chambers (warm, dry, above-ground rooms made with only briefly alkaline lime mortar), the lack of any cyanide traces can be explained only by the lack of any significant exposure to HCN fumes. Consequently, such rooms can never have

Outside wall of fumigation chamber BW 5b, Birkenau.

Inside wall of fumigation chamber BW 5a, Birkenau.

Inside wall of fumigation chamber, disinfestation annex, Majdanek.

Inside walls of fumigation chamber, Building #41, Majdanek.

Inside walls of fumigation chamber, Stutthof.

been used for the mass-gassing of people using Zyklon B. (For details, see Rudolf 2020, esp. pp. 27-29, 181-226, 299-361.)

ISACOVICI, SALOMÓN

In the 24 July 1998 issue of the U.S. newspaper *Forward*, a case of a possible Holocaust forgery was reported. The "hero" in this bizarre tale was Salomón Isacovici, a Romanian Jew who settled in Ecuador at the end of the Second World War. The account of his alleged wartime fate in Europe under German rule was published in Mexico in 1990 in the book *Man of Ashes* (*Hombre de Cenizas*). The book describes Isacovici's life, but its core consists of many typical, well-known clichés about the camps Auschwitz, Gross-Rosen, Javorsno, etc., where Isacovici served or claims to have served time. What sets this book apart from the others is not so much the content but the fact that it was written by a Jew residing in Latin America, which has hardly ever happened before. The publication of the book's English edition was delayed because, when big money was at stake, the Jesuit priest Juan Manuel Rodríguez claimed that *he* was actually the co-author of the book, and that this story was not Isacovici's autobiography but a novel that he wrote all by himself on the basis of events reported by Isacovici. Isacovici himself could no longer be questioned about this, as he died in 1995.

However, in a letter shortly before his death, Isacovici claimed that he was the legitimate author of this book, and that Rodriguez had merely helped him with structure and writing issues. The English edition book was published in 1999 with Rodríguez listed as the co-author.

Rodriguez claimed that Isacovici had only completed 40 pages of his book when he joined the project. Isacovici had instructed him to put his transcript into good Spanish, which he refused to do because he was not an editor. He then borrowed the first pages and produced the first complete chapter from them that same night. When he showed the result to Isacovici, the latter agreed with the procedure. Thus, based on Isacovici's manuscripts and oral reports, the book was completely written by Rodriguez, including the title. Rodriguez stated verbatim:

Salomón Isacovici

> "I used my memories of the Iberian countryside as inspiration. […] When I showed the result to Salomón, he was thrilled at how much I knew about his past. This went so far that I invented passages and details, and he subsequently believed that he had really experienced it. For him, the book is an autobiography. For me, it's a lovely novel."

Rodriguez repeatedly referred to this book as a novel, even though this designation is not found in the book itself. Instead, it states that it is a horrific and true testimony about the German concentration camp.

This case proves how easily "Holocaust survivors" can be talked into believing that they have genuinely experienced all sorts of events, whenever they are confronted with a trusted source and when events follow typical, well-trodden paths.

ISRAEL, BRUNO

Bruno Israel was an ethnic German police officer with a Polish background. He was assigned to the Chełmno police in July/August 1944. Due to his cooperation with the German authorities during the war, he was arrested by the Poles after the war.

On 29 and 30 October 1945, he was interrogated by Polish investigative judge Władysław Bednarz. Evidently due to his cooperative attitude and Polish background, he was released shortly after his interrogation.

With regard to the Chełmno Camp, Israel stated that during his brief stay at the camp, two transports with 700-800 Jews arrived from the Łódź Ghetto at the Koło train station. Then the story gets bizarre. Israel asserted that the Jews were eventually gassed in gas vans, but the way this was done is utterly irrational:

- The Jews were picked up with trucks at the Koło train station and driven to the Chełmno Camp. At this point, if a plan to kill them in gas trucks existed, one would think that exactly these trucks were used for the transit from the train station to the camp. But no, these were normal trucks. Lots of fuel was spent to get the Jews alive to the camp, and the exhaust gas produced along the way was wasted.
- Once in the camp, the Jews were made to undress in a shack sporting a sign with the inscription "transit camp" ("*Durchgangslager*"). They were then told that they would take a shower *inside a truck*. Evidently to deceive them, they were all given a piece of soap, and then made to climb into a "special vehicle." How anyone could believe such a tale is unfathomable.
- For Israel, the exhaust pipe went directly into the cargo box. The orthodox narrative insists instead that a flexible metal hose was used to connect the exhaust pipe to the cargo box.
- The victims inside the vehicle were gassed during transit to "the furnaces." Once there, the dead bodies were thrown into the furnaces, where they burned "quickly." However, forensic excavations have revealed the remains of only one field furnace at Chełmno. Furthermore, the cremation of bodies in such a primitive device takes many hours, which is the opposite of "quickly."
- Israel insisted that the furnaces were demolished in late 1944, and all bricks and concrete debris removed. However, as just mentioned, plenty of concrete debris of one furnace was left in place.
- Israel mentioned that the Chełmno Camp had two gas vans plus "a third vehicle that was used to fumigate clothes." He identified the photo of a damaged moving truck found on the grounds of the Ostrowski Company in Koło as being the fumigation truck. However, that truck was simply a moving truck, as Judge Bednarz himself concluded.

(For more details, see the entry on the Chełmno Camp, on gas vans as well as Mattogno 2017, pp. 60f.)

ITALY

After the Italian surrender to the Allies in September 1943 and Germany's partial occupation of northern and central Italy, German forces tried arresting and deporting all Jews to labor camps. However, due to advanced warnings and lack of cooperation by the local Italian authorities, not quite 7,000 Jews could be apprehended, plus 1,800 in the Italian zone of occupation in Greece. Most of them were deported to Auschwitz, but a few also to other camps, such as Buchenwald, Ravensbrück and Flossenbürg. (See the entry on Jewish demography for a broader perspective.)

J

JÄGER, KARL

Karl Jäger (20 Sept. 1888 – 22 June 1959) was an SS *Standartenführer* since 1940. He joined the SS in 1932, and the German Security Service (*Sicherheitsdienst*) in 1938. Prior to the invasion of the Soviet Union, he became commander of *Einsatzkommando* 3a of *Einsatzgruppe* A. His unit operated mainly in Lithuania. Jäger is said to be the author of the so-called Jäger Report, which lists all the executions of Jews by his unit up to late November 1941, totaling some 130,000. However, several issues with this report make its authenticity questionable. (See the entry dedicated to the Jäger Report.)

Karl Jäger

At the end of the war, Jäger lived normally in Germany under his real name, while hiding the fact that he had been an SS member. As a result of West-German investigations into *Einsatzgruppen* murders, he was arrested on 10 April 1959. The minutes of his interrogations between the 16th and 19th of June fill 29 pages. He committed suicide in his prison cell on 22 June 1959.

As to an alleged order to execute Jews in the East, Jäger was ambivalent. On the one hand, he claimed that, during a leadership meeting of Germany's Department of Homeland Security (*Reichssicherheitshauptamt*) in Berlin a few weeks before the invasion of the Soviet Union, Heydrich had declared that the Jews in the East had to be shot. On the other hand, when all heads of the *Einsatzgruppen* and *Einsatzkommandos* met a week or two before the invasion of the Soviet Union, "nothing was said about shootings of Jews." And this, although these leaders were exactly those who would have had to implement such an order. Jäger was quite sure that neither an oral nor a written order was ever issued to this effect. Still, he considered Heydrich's earlier oral remark as a binding order.

Jäger asserted that his superior, the head of *Einsatzgruppe* A, Walter Stahlecker, presumably justified the execution of Jews by declaring that "the Jews are the carriers of Communism. They furthermore orchestrate acts of sabotage and thereby endanger the front. In order to protect the front, the rear areas and the homeland, they must be annihilated."

Jäger insisted that he regularly sent event reports about his unit's activities to his superior, detailing all activities, including executions. He remembered that, upon his unit's arrival in Kaunas, Lithuanian militias had taken matters in their own hand by executing some 3,000 Jews. Jäger recalled executions at the Lithuanian towns of Raseiniai, Olita, Siauliai, Mariampol, Ukmerge, Vilnius, Aglona and Daugavpils (the latter two are in Latvia).

Jäger's postwar testimony contradicts some of the statements found in the "Jäger Report." Since that report was made available to the West-German judiciary by Soviet authorities only in 1963, Jäger could not be confronted with them.

(For more details, see Mattogno 2022c, pp. 199-202.)

JÄGER REPORT

The so-called Jäger Report was presumably authored in early December 1941 by Karl Jäger, then commander of *Einsatzkommando* 3a of *Einsatzgruppe* A. This unit operated mainly in Lithuania.

This document was allegedly discovered by the Soviets in Lithuania after the reconquest of Lithuania by the Red Army in 1944. For inscrutable reasons, they hushed up the existence of this document until 1963, when it was made available to the West-German *Zentrale Stelle*, the country's central organization investigating National-Socialist crimes.

The document lists 95 executions of a total of 137,348 persons until late 1941, most of them Jews from Lithuania. However, most of the individual execution events mentioned cannot be found in *Einsatzgruppe* A's Event Reports (*Ereignismeldungen*, EM) of that time. In fact, the EMs "confirm" only eleven of these alleged executions with a total of some 2,900 victims, hence just over two percent. However, EM 8 of 30 June 1941 mentions "thousands" executed in Kaunas on 28 June, and EM 48 of 10 Aug. 1941 lists a total for Kaunas and Riga of

28,000 victims, without giving any specifics.

The following table contains the total number of victims listed in the Report for each location, in comparison to the number of victims found in the Event Reports of *Einsatzgruppe* A.

Location	Victims	EM
Aglona	544	27
Alytus	2,231	
Ariogala	700	
Babtei (Babtai)	91	
Butrimonys	740	
Carliava	247	
Cekiake	146	
Dagda and Kraslawa	216	
Darsuniskis	99	
Daugavpils	9,606	1,150
Eysisky	3,446	
Georgenburg	412	
Girkalnis (Girkalinei)	6	
Herkine	854	
Jahiunai	575	
Jasvainai	282	
Jesuas	144	
Jonava	2,108	
Joniskis	355	
Kaisiadorys	1,911	
Kaunas, total, of which	23,205	209†
Fort IV	3,420	
Fort VII	3,238	
Fort IX	16,013	
Kedainiai	2,201	93
Krakes	1,125	
Lazdijai	1,535	
Leipalingis	155	
Mariampole	5,328	103
Nemencing	403	
Novo-Vileyka	1,159	
Obeliai	1,160	
Panevezys	8,837	249
Pasyalis	1,349	
Petrasiunai	125	
Pleschnitza, Bicholin, Scak, Bober, Uzda	3,050	
Pogrom	4,000	
Pravenischkis	253	
Prienai	1,078	
Rasainiai District	3,603	254
Rieza	1,767	
Rokiskis	99	
Rumsiskes and Ziezmariai	784	
Seduva	664	
Seirijai	953	
Semeliskes	962	
Seredsius	193	
Simnas	414	
Svenciany	3,726	
Trakai	1,446	
Ukmerge	6,356	296
Utena and Moletai	4,609	251
Uzunalis	43	
Vandziogala	305	15
Varena	831	
Velinona	159	
Vilnius	21,169	*
Wilkia	402	
Wilkowiski	115	
Zagare	2,236	250
Zapiskis	178	
Zarasai	2,569	
Totals	137,348	2,897

† Plus "thousands" on 28 June; total for Kaunas & Riga in EM 48 of 10 Aug. as 28,000.
* A total of 2,231, but all at other (mostly later) dates.

In addition to this December Jäger Report, an earlier version of it also exists, which is dated 10 September 1941. It lists a total of 76,355 victims of executions, over 13,000 more than are listed in the December Jäger Report as of that date. An update requested on 6 February 1942 by the commander of the Security Police and Security Service in Kaunas lists a total of 138,272 victims, 136,421 of them Jews. If we follow Jäger, these massacres were committed by a squad of just 10-11 SS men from *Einsatzkommando* 3 with the assistance of 50 to 100 Lithuanian collaborators.

The December Jäger Report has several odd features which make it suspicious:

– Although Jäger was to submit regular reports to his superior Stahlecker, the document in question has as its (rubber-stamped) letter head Stahlecker's official position. However, there is neither an addressee or address on this report, nor a sender.

– If connecting on a map the claimed execution locations in chronological order, then a completely erratic pattern of chaos and disorganization emerges of a team going around in circles and crisscrossing Lithuania back and forth. Some listings even exclude one another chronologically.

– Some entries claim death tolls for single-day executions that are difficult to believe for a team of just some ten men plus auxiliaries:
  – 9,200 on 29 October 1941
  – 7,523 persons on 23 August
  – 5,090 on 1 September
  – 3,782 on 29 August.

– EM 88 of 19 September 1941 reports that *Einsatz-*

kommando 3, together with their Lithuanian auxiliaries, had executed a total of 46,692 Jews. However, the Jäger Report reports 78,305 persons shot as of this date, which is 68% more.
– Although Jäger had reported Lithuania free of Jews in his report, except for some 35,000 "labor Jews and their families," later data show that there were more Jews alive in these areas than the Jäger Reports would have us believe.
– The Jäger Report mentions the wholesale slaughter of some 5,000 Jews deported from Germany to Kaunas (at Fort IX) in five deportation trains in November 1941. However, numerous other German wartime documents, among them also EMs, clearly demonstrate that these Jews were accommodated in camps and ghettos, and deployed at forced labor wherever possible.

On the corroborative side, a letter written by the medical examiner of Trakai County to the district commissar Vilnius dated 8 July 1942 lists mass graves in that area, including their size. With a few exceptions, their location and size by and large agree with the number of executions mentioned in the Jäger Report for these locations – provided that these mass graves indeed contain executed Jews, which the letter does not mention.

Hence, if this Jäger Report is a genuine document – and this is highly dubious – its claims are questionable, to say the least. Ultimate certainty about the veracity of claims made in this document could be gained only with thorough forensic examinations of mass grave located at the claimed locations. However, considering the present *zeitgeist* of accepting any atrocity claim against German wartime units at face value, such investigations seem highly unlikely.

(For more general information, see the entries on the *Einsatzgruppen* and on *Aktion* 1005; for more details, see Mattogno 2022c, pp. 198-242, 641-646.)

JANKOWSKI, STANISŁAW

Stanisław Jankowski (23 Oct. 1911 – 20 Sept. 1987) – also known as Alter Fajnzylberg, Alter Feinsilber and Stanisław Kaskowiak – was a Polish Jew incarcerated at the Auschwitz Camp from March 1942 to January 1945. In April 1945, he testified in front of an investigator of a Polish commission, and he also testified during the 1947 trial against Rudolf Höss. In 1980 and then once more in 1985, he made two more depositions. His testimonies contain a large number of implausible or impossible claims, including:
– He claims that his train arrived at Auschwitz on March 27 at 10 am after a five-day journey, with many detainees having died *en route*; while documents show that the train arrived on March 30 at 5:33 am after not even three days, with all inmates alive, well, and properly registered at Auschwitz.
– He claims to have witnessed how the SS executed inmates using machine guns inside the morgue of the old crematorium. Machine guns would be utterly unsuitable and highly dangerous to the gunners inside a building.
– According to his 1947 testimony, the only gassing inside the old crematorium known to him took place in November or December 1942. In 1985 he claimed that a gassing he witnessed concerned inmates who had exhumed and cremated corpses in Birkenau, which would place that event also in late 1942. However, the orthodoxy assumes that gassings in the old crematorium took place only between late 1941 and March 1942, when gassings were allegedly moved to Bunker 1 near the Birkenau Camp.
– According to his brief 1980 statement, the morgue had a ventilator in the ceiling, but nothing else of note. In his 1985 statement, he mentioned two Zyklon-B "gas-feed holes," but could not remember any ventilator. The orthodoxy, however, insists on four Zyklon-B introduction hatches.
– He stated that three corpses were placed into a cremation muffle designed for just one corpse. Moreover, the small furnace door would not have allowed more than two corpses to be pushed into the muffle.
– At the end of the shift, ten to twelve corpses were supposedly crammed into each muffle to burn overnight, which is utterly impossible.
– The cremation of a load of five corpses – which would not have fit into the muffle – allegedly took half an hour (6 minutes each), although the Auschwitz cremation furnaces needed one hour to cremate a single corpse. (See the entry on crematoria.)
– "When the furnaces were properly heated, the corpses burned by themselves for weeks on end." However, self-immolating bodies simply do not exist.
– In outdoor burning pits, male corpses were stacked alternatingly with females, because the fatter women helped to burn the men; but this has utterly no scientific justification.
– In those pits, drainage channels for human fat had been dug, although he thinks that no fat was col-

- lected, as the corpses burned completely.
- 1,500-2,000 people were crammed into the larger chamber of Crematoria IV and V, which, at a size of not quite 100 m², would mean an impossible packing density of 15 to 20 people per m².
- Following the postwar cliché, Jankowski claimed that the ineluctable "Mengele gave the order" to pour Zyklon B into the gas chamber.
- In the smaller gas chamber of Crematoria IV and V, the gas was "poured in through the door" – which is totally at odds with the orthodox account that insists that Zyklon pellets were poured in through hatches in the wall (even though these hatches had iron bars that would have prevented anyone from sticking a Zyklon can in them).
- Although these gas chambers had no ventilation, the airing out of the room "lasted a short time" only, "about 5 minutes," after which the inmates of the *Sonderkommando* started removing the corpses without wearing gas masks. This would have meant working in an almost undiluted, highly toxic atmosphere. Yet Jankowski claimed that this only caused "lightheadedness."
- He mentions a large number of transports from various countries arriving after he was transferred to Birkenau in July 1943, yet the documented transports show that he is wrong about many of his claims, including the total number of inmates arriving at Auschwitz, and those allegedly gassed on arrival, which is not even confirmed by (unfounded) orthodox claims.
- In April 1945, he claimed "a few million" as the total death toll for Auschwitz, parroting Soviet propaganda at the time. (The orthodoxy today insists on one million.)

(For details, see Mattogno 2021d, pp. 160-179)

JANOWSKA CAMP

In mid-October 1941, a camp was set up at Janowska Road in Lviv to house transports of Austrian and Czech Jews deported for resettlement to the east. It was to serve as a transit as well as forced-labor camp, and started operating in November of that year. Its relevance for the Holocaust starts in the summer of 1943. According to witness statements of five Jewish inmates of the camp, they were forced to exhume mass graves of murdered Jews in and near this camp, and burn them on huge pyres.

Most of these witness statements were made to a Soviet investigative commission researching alleged crimes committed by the Germans in the Lviv region. In their report of 23 December 1944, they described their findings, claiming that "in the Janov[ska] Camp the fascists shot more than 200,000 peaceful Soviet people." They also claimed to have found "three pits with the bodies of Soviet citizens," but did not state how many bodies they contained, and whether any were exhumed and examined. The rest of the report is full of claims evidently not based on accurate forensic findings, but on conjectures extrapolated from a few local impressions, and from the witness accounts gathered.

An analysis of these inmate accounts indicates that they were probably orchestrated. Death-toll numbers range from 100,000 to 300,000, resulting in insurmountable logistical problems for the claimed activities to exhume, burn and erase all traces of these claimed victims in the context of the so-called *Aktion* 1005. Hence, these claims are probably highly exaggerated, if not invented. See the entries on lumberjacks and for the five witnesses: Abraham Beer, Heinrich Chamaides, Moische Korn, David Manusevich, Leon Weliczker. See also the entry about the bone mill allegedly used in that camp to grind down unburned bones.

The Soviet report's comparison on how the Germans allegedly tried to cover up their crimes is revealing:

> *"In that manner, the Hitlerite murderers in Lvov Region stuck to the same methods of concealing their crimes which they began earlier, by killing the Polish officers in a forest near Katyn. The commission of examiners has established full identity of the burial sites located in Lisenitsy with the same type of masking* [=camouflaging, as used for] *the graves of the Polish officers killed by the Germans in Katyn."*

However, the mass murder of Polish officers near Katyn, and the subsequent concealment of the graves, had been perpetrated by *Soviet* forces in 1940, and discovered in early 1943 by the Germans. The Soviets prepared a fake expert report about Katyn after the German retreat, blaming their own crime on the Germans. This shows the mendacity in which all Soviet "expert" reports were steeped at war's end. It cannot even be ruled out that some of the mass graves and human remains allegedly discovered in fact originated from Soviet murders committed in the two decades before the German invasions. After all, Ukraine has always been a hot spot of anti-Russian and anti-Soviet resistance, and thus also of Russian and Soviet mass atrocities against

Ukrainians.

(For more information on the Janowska Camp, see Mattogno 2022c, pp. 485-522.)

JASENOVAC

The Jasenovac Camp in wartime Croatia was established in August 1941 near a village of the same name. It was operated by the Croatian wartime regime. It consisted of five separate camps, two of which were short-lived, but the other three – Ciglana, Kozara and Stara Gradiska – operated until April 1945.

The purpose of the camp is disputed; some claim it was strictly a detention and labor camp, whereas orthodox historians assert it was an extermination center. However, the camp had no technical equipment that could be re-interpreted as execution facilities. Therefore, murder is said to have happened haphazardly by ubiquitous random violence using knives, hammers, axes and simple shootings. The victims were mostly Serbs, but also Jews, Gypsies and Croatian dissidents.

Death-toll estimates vary wildly. Individuals sympathetic to Croatian independence, like former Croatian President Franjo Tudjman, gave figures of just 3,000 to 4,000 in total. Such numbers date back to the first forensic examinations of the camp in 1947. But by the 1970s and 1980s, the numbers were rising; the 1990 *Encyclopedia of the Holocaust* claims that some 600,000 people were murdered at Jasenovac (p. 740). Over the years, Western media articles have claimed death tolls up to one million. Serbian publications of the 1990s cited figures as high as 1.2 million. If true, this would make Jasenovac the bloodiest extermination camp of the Second World War. Wikipedia currently sets the total death toll to 77,000 to 100,000, up to 20,000 of them with a Jewish background. This shows that many accounts about this camp are rife with wartime atrocity propaganda twisted by ethnic prejudice and hyperbole.

The problem with Jasenovac is that it had no technical equipment or infrastructure to achieve anything on a large scale – neither mass murder itself nor the destruction of the bodies. There isn't even anecdotal evidence of the destruction of tens or even hundreds of thousands of bodies by way of large-scale open-air incinerations, as exists for many of the claimed major German crime scenes. Hence, if there was no mass cremation of the victims, where are their bodies?

During the 47-year rule of the communist Yugoslavian government over Jasenovac, they never bothered even once to try and locate any of the missing remains. Nothing has changed in this regard to this day; more than 30 years of Croatian self-rule, and still no attempt at locating mass graves or remnants thereof.

In contrast to the rest of the Holocaust, Jews have only a minor stake in Jasenovac. They are the minority among the victims. Hence, even if Jasenovac falls, it won't affect them, or so they might think. Therefore, occasional Jewish voices can be heard admitting that Jasenovac is "the only wartime concentration camp without any verifiable data" confirming the claimed mass slaughter. But that is a self-delusion. The evidentiary situation isn't much better for the claimed extermination camps whose primary victims are said to have been Jews. If Jasenovac falls, that may well have a domino effect.

(For more details, see Dalton 2021.)

JEHOVAH'S WITNESSES

Jehovah's Witnesses are conscientious objectors by principle. Hence, in any country that goes to war and becomes intolerant toward individuals refusing to serve in their armed forces, Jehovah's Witnesses will get in trouble. In Canada, for example, male Jehovah's Witnesses refusing to serve in the military were incarcerated in camps during World War II, sometimes together with their entire family. In the U.S., a 1940 Supreme Court decision against the Jehovah's Witnesses about their refusal to salute the U.S. flag resulted in lynch-mob attacks against some 1,500 Witnesses across the USA by the end of 1940, some of whom were killed or castrated.

In the Third Reich, Jehovah's Witnesses were sentenced to prison terms due to their refusal to serve. Some of them served their time in concentration camps, where some of them died due to the prevailing unfavorable conditions.

While there were occasional claims of the Third Reich having pursued a policy of physically exterminating Jehovah's Witnesses, these claims neither stood up to scrutiny, nor were they backed by their own organizations. They are, for the most part, honest and truthful Christians who are uninterested in public attention and financial extortion schemes against the German government and people.

Whatever their flaws, they have one real virtue: If all men and women had the same attitude toward war as the Jehovah's Witnesses, wars would no longer be possible.

Just Document → Gaubschat Company

K

KADUK, OSWALD

Oswald Kaduk

Oswald Kaduk (26 Aug. 1906 – 31 May 1997), SS *Unterscharführer* at war's end, was a German soldier who, after having been wounded several times, was transferred to the Auschwitz Camp in July 1941, where he served as a *Rapportführer* until the camp's evacuation in January 1945.

Kaduk was arrested by the Soviets in 1946, sentenced to 25 years forced labor, yet released early in 1956. He moved to West Germany afterwards, where he was again arrested in 1959 and put on trial in 1965 during the Frankfurt Auschwitz Show Trial. From the interview Kaduk gave some ten years later to German journalist Ebbo Demant (1979), it becomes clear that Kaduk had a very simple mind.

During the trial, he was badgered by witnesses and judges so dreadfully that he suffered a nervous breakdown. Confused and desperate, he even tried to refute testimonies in his favor. He eventually simply gave up, recognizing that he had been considered a murderer right from the outset, with no chance of any defense, and that no one would believe him anyway. He was sentenced to life imprisonment for allegedly contributing to the murder of over 1,000 people.

Kaduk's confusion lasted well into his prison time, as is demonstrated by Demant's interviews with him, during which Kaduk expressed his outrage at the boundless lies of the witnesses who had incriminated him. Reading this interview with compassion makes this scandalous travesty of justice palpable for the attentive reader.

Kaduk was released early in 1989 at the age of 83. (For references, see Rudolf 2019, p. 116.)

KAINDL, ANTON

Anton Kaindl (14 July 1902 – 31 Aug. 1948), SS *Standartenführer*, was the last commandant of the Sachsenhausen Camp from 1 September 1942 until 22 April 1945. Together with 15 other defendants, he was put on a typical Stalinist show trial staged in Berlin by the Soviet occupational authorities from 23 October to 1 November 1947. The trial assumed as given that the National-Socialist regime worked out "a plan for the mass extermination of political opponents of Nazism," in fact, "for the mass destruction of men" in general, of which the Sachsenhausen Camp allegedly was one of many camps for this plan's implementation. Kaindl's defense lawyer acted and argued like a second prosecutor. The defendants willingly or even enthusiastically embraced and confirmed even the most outrageous charges against them, including that Sachsenhausen was a death camp equipped with homicidal gas chambers. For instance, Kaindl repeatedly started answering questions put to him about executions and mass murder with "Yessir!"

Anton Kaindl

Kaindl "confessed" not only that gas chambers (plural) as a mass extermination site were introduced by him personally – although a Soviet investigative commission found only *one* "gas chamber" in the camp, and it was a tiny fumigation cubicle – but also that, under his command, about 42,000 inmates were killed and some 8,000 more died of starvation, although documents show that during the camp's *entire* existence since 1936, a little less than 20,000 inmates died altogether. (The Soviets claimed a total death toll of 100,000 for this camp, half of it during Kaindl's time, which began in August 1942.)

The absurdity of the charges levied against Kaindl and his co-defendants during that show trial become crystal clear when he was asked whether he received orders to destroy the camp in order to erase the traces of his crimes. Here is Kaindl's frenzied, enthusiastic response:

"Yessir! On 1 February 1945, I had a conversation with the head of the Gestapo, Müller. On that occasion he conveyed to me the order to destroy

the camp by artillery fire and air attack or by gassing."

None of it happened, of course, but not because it was impossible to implement, as Kaindl claimed, but because such utterly insane methods would not even have occurred to a fool. Or take his "confession" to another Soviet-invented "planned crime," which also didn't happen, not the least because it was unfeasible:

"On April 18 [1945], I received orders to load them [the remaining Sachsenhausen inmates] on barges and bring them along the channel of the river Spree into the Baltic Sea or the North Sea and to scuttle them there in the open sea."

Needless to say, there is no trace of such an insane scuttling order ever having been given.

Stalinist methods to make any defendant enthusiastically embrace and confirm any accusation are legendary, and the transcript of this show trial confirms this clearly. Sadly, orthodox historians take this trial's claims and conclusion seriously.

Kaindl was found guilty, shipped off to the GULag, and died there after just six months.

(For more details, see Mattogno 2023d; 2016e, pp. 150-180.)

KALTENBRUNNER, ERNST

Ernst Kaltenbrunner (4 Oct. 1903 – 16 Oct. 1946) was Higher SS and Police Leader in Austria from 1938 until early 1943. On 30 January 1943, after Reinhardt Heydrich had been assassinated the previous summer, Kaltenbrunner replaced him as chief of Germany's Department for Homeland Security (*Reichssicherheitshauptamt*, RSHA).

Ernst Kaltenbrunner

However, all matters concerning the SS and its vast network of forced-labor industries and labor as well as concentration camps were integrated under the SS's Economic and Administrative Main Office headed by Oswald Pohl (*Wirtschafts- und Verwaltungs-Hauptamt*). Therefore, Kaltenbrunner had nothing to do with the Third Reich's camp system.

In addition, the activities of the *Einsatzgruppen* in terms of mass executions also petered out around the time of Kaltenbrunner's appointment. As a result of all this, Kaltenbrunner's name is completely absent from the entire documentation in the context of the so-called Holocaust. Orders on concentration-camp matters went directly from Himmler to Pohl or Richard Glücks. Kaltenbrunner was simply not involved.

In spite of all this, with Hitler, Himmler and Heydrich dead, Kaltenbrunner became the Allies' scapegoat during the Nuremberg International Military Tribunal (IMT). Kurt Becher framed him by falsely claiming that Himmler had issued a "stop extermination" order to Kaltenbrunner. Such an order implies that a prior "start extermination" order must have existed, and that Kaltenbrunner had the power to start and stop such a program.

Kaltenbrunner was also framed by former Mauthausen inmate Hans Maršálek, who made outrageous claims about Kaltenbrunner in a postwar affidavit.

During Kaltenbrunner's defense at the IMT, his lawyer tried in vain to take advantage of the false affidavit and testimony of Rudolf Höss, the former commandant of the Auschwitz Camp. Höss had claimed that he had received an extermination order orally from Himmler directly in June of 1941, hence a year prior to Kaltenbrunner's promotion to chief of the RSHA. Höss also claimed that he had been told by Himmler to keep this order a secret even from any superiors. However, since Kaltenbrunner's appointment to chief of the RSHA, SS matters were no longer within the RSHA's jurisdiction. (For more on this, see Mattogno 2020b, index entries on Kaltenbrunner; see also *IMT*, Vol. 11, esp. pp. 231-386 [Kaltenbrunner's testimony], 396-422 [Höss's testimony].)

It was all to no avail. Kaltenbrunner was sentenced to death for war crimes and crimes against humanity. He was hanged on 16 October 1946, at the age of just 43.

KAMMLER, HANS

Hans Kammler (26 August 1901 – unknown), SS *Obergruppenführer*, was deputy chief of the SS Economic and Administrative Main Office (*Wirtschafts- und Verwaltungs-Hauptamt*) directly under Oswald Pohl. Kammler was in charge of Office C, overseeing all construction efforts at all the Third Reich's camps.

After the Auschwitz Camps' newly appointed garrison physician Eduard Wirths had lobbied for massive improvements of the hygienic, sanitary and healthcare facilities at Auschwitz-Birkenau, Kammler ordered and supervised a massive "special construction program" to turn Birkenau into a huge and modern hospital camp for tens of thousands of sick inmates.

Hans Kammler

After the British had bombed the Third Reich's rocket testing and production facilities in Peenemünde in August 1943, Kammler was put in charge of moving rocket production underground at the new Dora Camp near Buchenwald. The living and working conditions at the Dora forced-labor camp were horrific. Hence, Wernher von Braun's team of rocket engineers at one point went on strike in protest against the SS's inhumane treatment of their inmate co-workers. As a result, von Braun and his team were arrested and kept in detention until they decided to quit their protest.

Kammler later also assumed responsibility for all other "secret weapon" construction efforts.

At the end of the war, Kammler offered the United States his services to transfer all knowledge and expert teams of Germany's advanced-weapons research to the United States. The U.S. accepted, gave him a new identity, and let him immigrate to the U.S. His whereabouts and final destiny there are unknown.

Had there been any homicidal gas chambers at Auschwitz or in any other camp, Kammler would have been the person centrally responsible for ordering, financing and overseeing their design, planning and construction. The U.S. secret services evidently either thought otherwise or considered modern-weapons technology to be more important than prosecuting a high-level mass murderer.

(For more details, see Brauburger/Sulzer 2019.)

KAPER, YAKOV

Yakov Kaper was a Ukrainian Jew interned in the Syretsky Camp, 5 km from Kiev. In August 1943, he was taken from there to Babi Yar, a place where tens of thousands of Jews are said to have been shot and buried by the Germans in mass graves in late September 1941 (see the entry on Babi Yar). Kaper evidently was interviewed about his alleged experiences for the first time more than 20 years after the event by German court officials on 13 February 1967. In 1993, a book was published containing an essay by Kaper, which repeated with different words what he had stated in his 1967 testimony.

Among other things, Kaper stated that he and more than 300 (or exactly 330) other slave-labor inmates were put in chains and had to exhume mass graves and burn the extracted bodies on pyres. He does not give any specifics about the pyres, other than that they consisted of many layers of wood and bodies and were 2.5 or 3 meters high. This makes it difficult to assess his claims. He asserted, however, that a total of 120,000 bodies were burned this way.

In his 1993 essay, Kaper mentions the evil SS officer Topaide, who was invented in 1944 by the Soviet commission investigating the alleged events at Babi Yar. This little detail hints at what the actual source of Kaper's "information" is.

Kaper claimed that, after the pyres had burned down, unburned bones were ground down, the cremation remains sifted through sieves, and the powder scattered. However, wood-fired pyres burn unevenly and leave behind lots of unburned wood pieces, charcoal and incompletely burned body parts, not just ashes and bones (80% of leftovers would have been from wood, not corpses). Incompletely burned wood and human remains could not have been ground. Any sieve would have clogged with the first load. Moreover, any occasional rainfall would have rendered any burned-out pyre into a moist heap of highly alkaline, corrosive slush that could not have been processed at all. If 120,000 bodies were burned, then several thousand metric tons of cremation leftovers had to be processed. Just this job would have required hundreds of men to complete in time.

Kaper also insisted that they had to throw onto the pyres bodies of people who had been killed in gas vans, some by gas, some by getting shot. Often, the allegedly gassed people were still alive, hence thrown into the fire still alive. However, considering that the front was getting very close to Kiev during September 1943, it is unlikely that anyone would have operated gas vans in Kiev's vicinity. All this apart from the fact that gas vans are a figment of Soviet atrocity propaganda (see the entry on gas vans).

Cremating an average human body during open-air incinerations requires some 250 kg of freshly cut wood. Cremating 120,000 bodies thus requires some 30,000 metric tons of wood. This would have required the felling of all trees growing in a 50-year-old spruce forest covering almost 67 hectares of land, or some 149 American football fields. An average prisoner is rated at being able to cut some 0.63 metric tons of fresh wood per workday. To cut this amount of wood within five weeks (35 days) that this operation supposedly lasted would have required a work force of some 1,360 dedicated lumberjacks just to cut the wood. Kaper claimed his unit consisted only of 300+ inmates, all busy digging out mass graves, extracting bodies, building pyres, crushing bones, sifting through ashes, scattering the ashes and refilling the graves with soil. Kaper says nothing about where the firewood came from.

(For more details, see the entry on Babi Yar, as well as Mattogno 2022c, pp. 536f., and 550-563.)

KARASIK, AVRAHAM

Avraham Karasik was a Polish Jew who testified in 1961 during the Eichmann Show Trial. He stated that, during the war, he had been incarcerated in the prison of Białystok. Together with some 40 other inmates, he was taken from there in May 1944 to various places (Białystok, Augustów, Grodno) to exhume and burn bodies from mass graves. He claims to have kept exact records, hence knew that 22,000 bodies had been exhumed and burned by the time this operation ended on 13 July 1944.

Karasik claims to have been present at the same operation as another witness, Szymon Amiel. However, while Karasik claimed for Augustów 15 or 17 mass graves measuring 8 m × 2 m, with 250-300 bodies each, Amiel had allegedly worked on three large graves, 15 meters long, and one small one, 5-6 meters long. The total number of bodies exhumed and burned in the entire region is also contradictory: 22,000 according to Karasik, but at least 40,000 for Amiel.

If we assume that Karasik's team started working on this project in mid-May 1944 (as Amiel had claimed), then they would have had some 57 days to chop the wood needed to cremate these 22,000 bodies. Cremating an average human body during open-air incinerations requires some 250 kg of freshly cut wood. Cremating 22,000 bodies thus requires some 5,500 metric tons of wood. This would have required the felling of all trees growing in a 50-year-old spruce forest covering more than 12 hectares of land, or some 27 American football fields. An average prisoner is rated at being able to cut some 0.63 metric tons of fresh wood per workday. To cut this amount of wood within 57 days would have required a work force of some 153 dedicated lumberjacks just to cut the wood. Karasik claimed his unit consisted only of some 40 inmates, all busy digging out mass graves, extracting bodies, building pyres, crushing bones, sifting through ashes, scattering the ashes and refilling the graves with soil. Karasik said nothing about where the firewood came from.

This testimony relates to one of many events claimed to have been part of the alleged German clean-up operation which the orthodoxy calls *Aktion 1005*. The above data demonstrate conclusively that Karasik's entire scenario is completely detached from reality. It cannot be based on experience, but on mere imagination and delusion.

(For more details, see Mattogno 2022c, p. 639.)

KAROLINSKIJ, SAMIJ

Samij Karolinskij was a former Auschwitz inmate who claimed to have seen a gas chamber once. He was interrogated by a Soviet investigator on 22 February 1945 in Auschwitz, but there is little of essence to this deposition. Karolinskij was cutting up wood for the cremation furnaces and "the fires," but entered a crematorium only once during a downpour, when he was allegedly permitted to find shelter from the rain "in the gas chamber." There he met inmates of the "*Sonderkommando*," who told him about "the crematorium" while allegedly being completely unsupervised by any guards. Such an event could have happened only if the inmates in that building were involved in completely innocuous activities. (See Mattogno 2021d, pp. 235f.)

KARSKI, JAN

Jan Karski (aka Jan Kozielewski, 24 April 1914 – 13 July 2000) was an agent of the Polish government in exile, whose task was to invent and spread "black propaganda" – meaning atrocity lies – in German-occupied Poland (Laqueur 1998, p. 230). During World War Two, the Polish government in exile maintained

Jan Karski

close relations with the resistance movement in occupied Poland, which, in addition to sabotage activities, had a dense network of agents, couriers and propagandists. These propagandists, for example, sent atrocity stories about Auschwitz to London on a regular basis. (Cf. Mattogno 2021, pp. 105-289.)

In November 1942, Karski created a story he handed to the Polish government in London about Jews being deported *en masse* in trains whose floors were covered in moist lime and chlorine, resulting in half the deportees dying before arriving at their destination Treblinka, Belzec and Sobibór, where they were mass murdered "by firing squads, electrocution and lethal gas-chambers." For Belzec, Karski specifically insisted on an "electrocution station" consisting of a huge metal plate as a floor, as was *en vogue* at the time. That text about Belzec is identical to an earlier text by Ignacy Schwarzbart, hence was simply copied. Karski's text was subsequently published in England.

Two years later, in 1944, a book appeared authored by Karski and titled *Story of a Secret State*, where the story changed from trains of torture driving *to* Belzec, where those who had survived were electrocuted, to a new story line in which people arriving at Belzec got loaded into trains with floors covered with quick lime. This chemical ate away the flesh from the deportees' bones, killing them in the process. These trains actually drove *away* from Belzec, then stood in some field for days waiting for the chemical to finish them all off. Then their load of corpses was dumped, burned, and the ashes buried (Karski 1944, pp. 339-351). How could he "know" any of this? Because he claims to have gotten smuggled, disguised as an Estonian guard, in and out of the Belzec Camp, which he described as being located on a, quote, "large flat plain," unquote. In that camp, he was allegedly shown around by a "real" Estonian guard. The problem is that the Belzec Camp was located on the side of a hill, not a plain, and that no Estonian ever served there in any function.

In a 1987 interview, he even tried to bail out of the orthodox narrative completely by stating that he had thought during the war "that Bełżec was a transit camp," and that he found out about its real role only after the war. (See Jansson 2014.)

The historical framework of Karski's story is also invented, as he claims that his mission was to see what happened to Jews deported from the Warsaw Ghetto, and that the Jews present in Belzec had all come from the Warsaw Ghetto; but after the Warsaw Ghetto uprising, the ghetto Jews were all deported to Treblinka, not to Belzec.

True to his job description, Karski merely spread "black propaganda" about Belzec. This is now also recognized increasingly by mainstream historians who disregard his "testimonies" as "unreliable." (For details, see Mattogno 2004a, pp. 22-33.)

Karski was the Polish government's agent who brought the world's attention to the mass murder allegedly committed at Belzec by the Germans. While his story is now disregarded, transmogrified versions of his themes live on, and Karski himself is still revered as a hero.

The black propaganda spread by Karski and his many colleagues has served, does serve, and will continue to serve to instigate wars, sustain wars, and escalate them to fiercer levels. A world that makes "heroes" of such people can only be a darker world.

KARVAT, DAVID

David Karvat was a Czech Jew who claimed to have been a member of the Auschwitz *Sonderkommando* for an entire (unspecified) year. In January 1947, he deposited an account in Italy about his alleged experiences. However, his description is both short and devoid of any details. He neither describes the "gas chambers," the crematoria, the furnaces, nor the gassing or cremation procedure, although he claims to have worked there a full year. He does not even mention which of the four crematoria he worked in, or how many there were.

He claims that not all of the claimed 500-600 Italian victims whose gassing he purports to have experienced were gassed at once – which makes no sense, as the chambers presumably in existence could have easily accommodated the entire batch. Instead, they were split into two groups, one of which had to wait in a (non-existent) place separated by "a wall and some buildings." The claimed criterion to select the victims is also purely fictitious: The SS killed young, strong men "because they were immediately qualified as lazy in character and therefore unfit for work." However, Karvat knew better, because he had a buddy among the SS who told him the real reason: they were killed because they were Jews loyal to the Italian king – who was also a Jew – and who planned to overthrow Mussolini. None of it was real.

After "experiencing" this gassing, Karvat was… not killed as a year-long witness to mass murder, but merely transferred to a different job. That's also why he could not tell more stories like this, despite his one-year membership in the *Sonderkommando* club.

Since he gave this interview to an Italian historian, the whole story, which focuses entirely on one transport of Italian Jews deported to Auschwitz, was not based on facts and memory, but evidently geared toward pleasing and satisfying the interviewer and his audience. (See Mattogno 2022e, pp. 180-182.)

KAUFMANN, JEANNETTE

Jeannette Kaufmann was an Austrian Jew deported from Vienna in early 1941 and passed through several labor camps before getting transferred to Birkenau on 1 August 1944. In the fall, she was assigned to the crematorium demolition squad dismantling equipment in Crematoria II and III and tearing them down. Then she was evacuated and ultimately ended up in Bergen-Belsen. In a deposition of 21 April 1945 and in a second undated text, she declared:
- The cremation capacity was 20 bodies every 10 minutes – when in fact it was fifteen corpses (in 15 muffles) in an hour.
- A light railway line ran into it for conveying sick persons too ill to walk (first text), or to remove the dead from the gas chamber (second text) – no such thing ever existed.
- The "bathroom" – aka "gas chamber" – had a very big door like that of a bank safe – all normal-looking doors at Birkenau were made of simple wooden planks.
- The showerheads were connected to gas pipes instead of water pipes – while the morgues of Crematoria II and III had real showers, and the gas was supposedly supplied by throwing in Zyklon-B pellets.
- Gas may have penetrated into the room through "boxes with little holes in them which looked like electric fuse boxes."
- The "bathroom" (Morgue #1, 210 m²) could process 2,000 people within 15 minutes – a packing density of some ten people per square meter, which would have required discipline, training and cooperativeness.

This is a typical witness who was not in a position to know, but had to rely on hearsay and (dis)information she perceived during and after the war in order to make sense of what she saw when helping to demolish these buildings. It is a classic case of a testimony deformed by third-party input. (For more details, see Mattogno 2021, pp. 355-357.)

KAUFMANN SCHAFRANOV, SOFIA

Sofia Kaufmann, married name Schafranov, was a Persian Jewess of Russian origin who lived in Italy. She was arrested on 2 December 1943, and later deported to Auschwitz, where she arrived on 6 February 1944. On 18 January 1945, she was evacuated, and ultimately ended up in Mauthausen Camp. Her testimony was published in 1945. In it, she claimed to have heard about gas-chamber killings from another inmate who had managed to escape. Therefore, she could have learned this from him only after her camp was liberated, hence after the war. Her hearsay story includes the following claims:
- The deportees employed in the gas chambers were killed every two months – whereas many of them miraculously survived to testify.
- The victims were given towels and soap when sent into the "fake shower bath." This most certainly would never have happened, considering the mess it would have created and the effort necessary to retrieve and clean these items afterwards. In addition, no one takes towels into a shower.
- The chamber had a low ceiling – when in fact it was 2.40 meters high.
- The chambers could hold 25 or 30 persons – a hundredth of the amount otherwise claimed.
- Showerheads on the ceiling sprayed poison gas instead of water – while the morgues of Crematoria II and III had real showers, and the gas was supposedly supplied by throwing in Zyklon-B pellets.
- The Germans were stingy, so gas was applied only sparingly, as a result of which the people did not die, and therefore "were thrown into the furnaces while still alive." Imagine the scene: a few Jewish inmates of the *Sonderkommando* needed to somehow throw tens, hundreds or even thousands of undead Jews into the furnaces.

(For a few more details, see Mattogno 2021, p. 373.)

KERCH

Kerch is a port city in the east of the Crimea Peninsula. Soviet media reported that German formations had committed a massacre outside of this city, near the village of Bagerovo. Photos of dozens of dead civilians littering the landscape were published alongside small pits with a few dead bodies, yet still it was claimed that 7,000 victims had been executed in an anti-tank ditch two kilometers long. Joseph Weingartner, who claimed to have survived the execution, claimed that the victims had to undress before the execution, yet all the photos show fully dressed persons.

During the Nuremberg International Military Tribunal, the Soviets presented an "expert report" on this alleged massacre, in which they added that the Germans killed school children with poisoned pies, or by smearing a quick-acting poison onto their lips. While there is no way of verifying or refuting this story, its improbability points at the pure propaganda nature of this report. Yet because the report came from one of the Allied governments, the Tribunal had to accept it as incontestable evidence.

No German document attests to any massacre in Kerch, and certainly not of the claimed magnitude. In 1944, the Soviets compiled a list of wartime victims of the city of Kerch. It contains just over 1,200 names. Even if true, these would include victims of all causes – starvation, diseases, armed conflict, partisan activities etc.

This case shows how Soviet media and investigators turned wartime atrocity propaganda into legally incontestable evidence, thus polluting the historical record with forgeries.

(For more details, see Mattogno 2022c, pp. 715-720.)

KERSCH, SILVIA

Silvia Kersch was deported from Grodno to Treblinka on 18 January 1943. On 12 December 1945, she wrote to her relatives in the United States a letter, which eventually found its way into the Yad Vashem Archives (archival reference O.33-2117, p. 4). In this letter, Kersch stated:

> *"Tremblika* [sic] *was called the people's factory, where thousands of people perished every day. There were '4 big furnaces' in which people were thrown alive for cremation. The sight was terrible. In a dense forest, a red ground-level building and 4 tall chimneys."*

This is a completely unique description that goes against everything the orthodox narrative currently claims about Treblinka, which is said to have had two gassing facilities, but no crematorium at all, hence also no chimneys.

KERTÉSZ, IMRE

Imre Kertész (9 Nov. 1929 – 31 March 2016) was a Hungarian Jew who, at the age of 14, was deported to Auschwitz in 1944. After the war, he wrote a novel – and he insisted that it is a novel, not an autobiography! – titled *Fatelessness*. It was first published in 1975 in Hungary, and is only very loosely based on basic data of his own life, such as his brief presence at Auschwitz – where he presumably stayed only four days before being transferred on to Buchenwald (rather than being gassed on arrival, as was the fate of all other kids his age, or so the orthodoxy claims). Kertész received the Nobel Prize in Literature for this book in 2002.

Imre Kertész

A detailed analysis of the book shows that Kertész plagiarized platitudes from other texts, such as Elie Wiesel's mendacious book *Night*. Vice versa, a scene described in the fictitious novel *Fragments* by Binjamin Wilkomirski (aka Bruno Doessekker) about an SS man wielding a whip was probably inspired by a passage in Kertész's novel. In Kertész's novel, we read, among other things:

- A "real firework of flames and sparks" escaped from the Auschwitz crematorium chimneys – although that was technically impossible.
- The crematorium chimneys also spread an unpleasant smell – which is also impossible, unless they were operated at such low temperatures that the bodies were not cremated but merely fried.
- Poison gas streamed out of showerheads onto the victim's heads – the morgues of Crematoria II and III had real showers, and the gas was supposedly supplied by throwing in Zyklon-B pellets.
- Soap was handed out to those going into the gas chamber – which most certainly would not have happened.

What is the Nobel Prize in Literature worth if it is awarded to purveyors of lies *exactly because* they wrote a cock-and-bull story? And what about a civilization that celebrates such a literary fraud? (For more, see Springer 2004.)

KHARKOV

The northwestern Ukrainian city of Kharkov (today spelled Kharkiv) had some 700,000 inhabitants, when it was occupied by German forces in late October 1941. The city changed hands three times in 1943, and was ultimately reconquered by the Soviets in late August 1943.

In a repeat performance of what had been staged earlier in Krasnodar, the Soviets prepared another Stalinist show trial, this time against three captured German soldiers and one local Soviet citizen accused of having collaborated with the Germans. The charges were, among other things, that these defendants

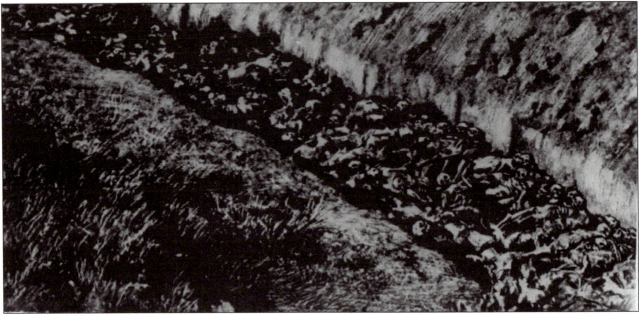
Drawing of bodies allegedly found at the Drobitsky Ravine near Kharkov, presented by the Soviets as a photo.

had been involved in hanging, shooting and asphyxiating "many tens of thousands" Soviet civilians. The latter was said to have been committed by the use of so-called gas vans.

The trial itself took place between 15 and 18 December 1943. The conditions of the Kharkov Trial were basically identical to that of the Krasnodar Trial. It was a stage show following a preordained script, where every actor played a theatric role. The defendants had been abused and tortured so much that, during the trial, they were either completely apathetic, or they enthusiastically embraced their charges. Defense lawyers were additional prosecutors.

In addition to teaching all Soviet citizens a lesson that collaborating with the Germans will be punished severely, this show trial had the additional purpose of portraying the Germans as the much worse butchers than the Soviets. After the German discovery and propagandistic exploitation of the mass graves of Soviet mass-murder victims at Katyn and Vinnitsa earlier that year, the Soviets felt a keen need to get back at the Germans.

While the prosecution claimed only some 7,000 civilian victims in total for Krasnodar, that death toll was significantly increased during the Kharkov Trial to 30,000. As during the Krasnodar Trial, here, too, the prosecution and its coached witnesses asserted that the asphyxiation occurred in trucks with carbon monoxide emitted by Diesel engines. However, that exhaust gas is unsuited for executions due to its lack of toxicity.

Just as in the case of Krasnodar, the prosecution repeated its claim that they had exhumed and forensically investigated the remains of the victims extracted from mass graves. They claimed that their forensic experts had established the presence of carbon monoxide in the victims' blood. However, after a year or two of decomposing in mass graves, it can be safely ruled out that anyone was able to establish anything about remnants of carbon monoxide in severely rotten tissue samples.

The three German defendants were groomed to make all kinds of absurd statements. Among them, what Hitler supposedly ordered (how would they know?), and how gassings at Auschwitz were being carried out: by suddenly switching showers spouting water to emit gas instead. This preposterous nonsense demonstrates once more the ludicrous nature of these Stalinist show trials.

Kharkov is mentioned only once in the reports by the *Einsatzgruppen*. In mid-December 1941, 305 Jews are said to have been executed in this city by *Einsatzgruppe* C. In addition to this, Jews in Kharkov are mentioned in three *Einsatzgruppen* reports of early 1942. However, these only report about the registration of all Jews, the preparation of new accommodations for them, and their relocation to these new accommodations.

Two images exist claiming to be photos of a mass grave near Kharkov allegedly taken by the Soviets during some exhumation work. However, these are clearly drawings. Also, if those bodies were in the process of getting exhumed, there would be soil among and on top of some of the bodies. However, these bodies have been drawn with no soil anywhere. (See the illustration.)

There is also a certainly genuine film footage showing the exhumation work of a Soviet commission at a mass grave of maybe a few hundred bodies. However, orthodox sources contradict one another as to what this footage shows. Most of them insist that these are victims at Babi Yar, although the visible landscape shows no resemblance with that ravine near Kiev. Some close-up frames suggest that these victims wore uniforms when killed, hence may simply be battle casualties or deceased PoWs.

Therefore, just as in the case of Krasnodar, there is no independent evidence that could reliably verify the inflated death-toll claims made by the Soviets regarding Kharkov.

(For more details, see the entry on gas vans, as well as Bourtman 2008; Alvarez 2023, pp. 122-129; Mattogno 2022c, pp. 725-737.)

KLEHR, JOSEF

Josef Klehr (17 Oct. – 23 Aug. 1988), SS *Oberscharführer* at the end of the war, was an SS guard at the Buchenwald Camp from 1939 for a year. He then served as a medical orderly at the Dachau Camp, until he was transferred to Auschwitz in early 1941, where he fulfilled that same role. In addition to this duty, he also became the head of the camp's disinfestation unit in 1943. As such, he organized and supervised delousing operations and disinfestation facilities operating with various methods (hot air, Zyklon B, later also DDT and microwave ovens).

Josef Klehr

During the Frankfurt Auschwitz show trial, Klehr was framed by former Auschwitz inmates, as well as by historians of the Auschwitz Museum, for the invented crime of lethal injections with phenol. He was also implicated as one of the main actors during the invented "first gassing" at Auschwitz. Klehr's function as head of the camp's disinfestation unit further exposed him to mendacious claims by vengeful witnesses of having supervised the use of Zyklon B for mass gassings.

Klehr was sentenced to life imprisonment for 475 counts of murder and 2,730 counts of assisting in murder. After almost 20 years of imprisonment, Klehr was interviewed by a German journalist fishing for confessions. He was successful, but only in general terms by getting Klehr to declare that "people were gassed." No details were ever asked of him, and neither did he volunteer any (Demant 1979, p. 114).

How can anyone cope with having to spend the rest of one's life in prison for a crime that never happened, when the entire world insists it did? In such a situation, where any relief is impossible, insisting on one's innocence only leads to feelings of total senselessness, abandonment, desperation and depression, and ultimately suicide. Some went that route, such as Ilse Koch; but Klehr chose to accept the court-imposed "truth," and to adjust his recollection accordingly.

(For more information, see the index entries on Klehr in Mattogno 2022f; 2016a, pp. 99f.)

KLEIN, MARC

Marc Klein (1905 – 1975) was a professor of biology at the University of Strasbourg. In May 1944, he was arrested by the Gestapo and sent to the Auschwitz Camp, then later to Buchenwald. After the war, he wrote in his memoirs under the headline "Auschwitz I Main Camp" (Faculté… 1954, p. 453; similar in Klein 1946; see also Faurisson 2001):

> *"During Sun- and holidays, when most commandos had the day off, working hours were different. The roll call took place at noon; during the evening one relaxed or dedicated his time to a selection of athletic or cultural activities. Soccer, basketball, and water ball games (in the outdoor pool that had been built by inmates within the camp) attracted the spectator masses. It should be noted that only the fit and well-nourished inmates, who were spared from hard labor, could get engaged in such games that attracted the vivid applause of the masses of the other inmates."*

Of course, as with all such swimming pools, its water could also be used to help extinguishing fires in case of emergency. In fact, Marc Klein writes in his article that at the Auschwitz Camp "there were firemen with very modern equipment." Among those things he had not expected to find when he arrived in June 1944, "at a camp whose bad reputation was known

to the whole world thanks to Allied radio broadcasts," were:
- "a hospital with specialist wards together with the most modern hospital practices" for the inmates,
- "a spacious and well-equipped washhouse together with communal toilets built according to modern hygiene principles,"
- "a microwave delousing plant that had just been erected,"
- "a mechanical bakery,"
- legal aid for prisoners,
- the existence of a "diet kitchen" for some of the sick with "special soups and even special bread,"
- "a library where a rich reference literature, classical books and periodicals could be found,"
- the daily passing, just past the camp, of the "Krakow-Berlin express train," making any claim that anything could be kept a secret at Auschwitz a farce,
- a cinema,
- a cabaret,
- an orchestra.

Marc Klein also reports on the horrible aspects of camp life and on all the rumors, including the "terrible stories" about gassings, but in this connection, he mentions that his knowledge comes largely due to testimonies during the "various war crimes trials," hence this is postwar knowledge.

Anyone who ever has been in any kind of prison or internment camp knows that usually only the very first period of such imprisonment is truly horrible. As an inmate settles in, he learns how to arrange life, get little privileges, make friends, and how to meet basic needs. Each time an inmate gets transferred elsewhere, all this has to start over, and this is very unpleasant. Hence, transfers are usually considered bad news.

On the other hand, anyone who has ever been in a situation where one's life is constantly threatened and hangs on a thread, the choices look very different: It is either fight or flight. One constantly looks for possibilities to either escape, no matter the cost, or, if caught, to fight until death. If Auschwitz had been a place where death by wanton murder and wholesale mass slaughter was a common occurrence, the reaction of the vast majority of individuals exposed to this would have been clear: fight or flight, no matter what.

Here is how Prof. Dr. Marc Klein described his reaction when he had a chance to "get the hell out of" the place commonly described as Hell on Earth:

"It was always an unpleasant menace to be transported [away from Auschwitz], because one instantly lost all material advantages, the big ones and the little ones, which one had gained in a camp in the long run. It was a departure to the unknown, paired with the burden of the travel and the difficulties of the new environment in a different camp. Despite all, at least for the Jews, who were always threatened by massive Jewish gassings, a transport could sometimes be a path of rescue. […] One day a transport left for Natzweiler/Struthof. I was intensely tempted to be a part of it, because that would get me home to the Alsace. But from a safe source [giving false information] I had learned that this would be a certain death assignment, so that I renounced."

Evidently Auschwitz was not quite the "hell on Earth" that has been portrayed. All it takes is one honest witness to show.

KLOOGA

The Klooga Labor Camp was a satellite camp of the Vaivara Camp in northern Estonia. It was set up in the summer of 1943, and at its peak housed up to 3,000 Jewish men and women, mainly from the Vilnius and Kaunas Ghettos. Toward the end of the German rule in this area, most inmates were transferred to the Stutthof Camp near Danzig.

In late September 1944, the Soviets captured the camp. Interrogating 85 inmates who the Germans had left behind, they concluded that, during the last days of their reign, the Germans had shot some 2,400 inmates, most of them Jews, plus 100 Soviet PoWs. Not having enough time to bury the slain, the Germans presumably prepared large pyres to burn them, but for some reason did not find the time to light the pyres.

In order to document this atrocity, the Soviets took several photos showing piled-up tree trunks with people on and in between them. In total, these photos show maybe a few dozen people on pyres, but certainly nowhere near 2,400.

Note that none of these pyres had been lit, indeed. All people on them are perfectly dressed; they all lie straight and face down; many are wearing caps; and some have put their hats/caps between their faces and the log below, evidently as padding, so they would not get hurt by the rough wood underneath. Had these been massacred persons, their clothes would be ragged; they would lie randomly face up, face down, twisted and contorted; none of them would wear caps; and most certainly none of them would use their hats as padding to make themselves comfortable. Moreover, these victims are said to have been killed more than a week earlier. Had that been the case, they would by now be massively bloated due to decomposition gases forming subcutaneously.

In other words: these are staged images. The real reason why these pyres weren't lit is because they are fake pyres with living people on them staging a scene. This proves incontrovertibly that the Germans did not commit any massacre at Klooga. Had they done it, the Soviets would have found traces of it: 2,400 bodies either lying around or buried, or dozens of partly or completely burned pyres with hundreds of partly burned corpses in each. None of this was found.

Gutman 1990, p. 807

Yad Vashem, archival reference 19B07

Yad Vashem, archival reference 16F01

Yad Vashem, no archival reference given

Klee/Dressen, p. 158

St. George, pp. 64f.

These fake propaganda images can be found in orthodox publications to this day as evidence for these mendacious Soviet propaganda claims. (See for example St. George 1967, pp. 64f.; Klee/Dressen 1988, p. 158; and Gutman's 1990 *Encyclopedia*, p. 807.)

KOCH, ILSE

Ilse Koch (22 Sept. 1906 – 1 Sept. 1967) was the widow of former Buchenwald commandant Karl-Otto Koch, who had been executed by the SS for murdering inmates and embezzling inmate property at the Buchenwald Camp.

Ilse Koch

Ilse Koch was the only civilian indicted by U.S. troops during the infamous Dachau Trials, in preparation of which many defendants were subject to brutal torture, and which were characterized by an atmosphere of hysteria, propaganda and mass-hypnosis. Frau Koch was accused, among other things, of having had inmates killed because of their attractive skin tattoos, then to have those tattooed skin areas surgically removed and turned into household items such as lampshades, book bindings, gloves etc.

When a review of this set of show trials later found out about the circumstances, Frau Koch was pardoned and released from prison. However, the West-German authorities put her on trial again for the same type of freely invented offenses, and with yet another show trial dominated by hysteria, propaganda and mass-hypnosis, where any former Buchenwald inmate could tell any lie he wanted, Koch was sentenced to serve the entire rest of her life in prison. Having exhausted all means of getting legal remedies to this travesty of justice, she eventually committed suicide in her West-German prison cell.

In an interview Konrad Morgen granted the British historian John Toland years after the war, he insisted that the stories about Ilse Koch using tattooed human skin for lampshades and other objects were unfounded legends, since he had searched the Koch household himself without finding any such objects. (See Toland 1976, pp. 845f.).

In sum, the trials against Ilse Koch are the "modern" equivalent to medieval witch trials. (See Smith 1983, which unfortunately has never appeared in an English edition; see also Rudolf 2023, pp. 94-97.)

KOCH, KARL-OTTO

Karl-Otto Koch

Karl-Otto Koch (2 Aug. 1897 – 5 April 1945), SS *Standartenführer*, first headed the Esterwegen Camp in 1936, then became the first commandant of the Sachsenhausen Camp. In 1937, he was put in charge of the Buchenwald Camp, and in 1941 of the Majdanek Camp. In August 1942, Koch was arrested by the SS-internal police for crimes committed in Buchenwald. He was charged and eventually sentenced by an SS court in 1945 for having embezzled large amounts of inmate property, and for having killed three inmates who were about to become whistleblowers. Koch was executed by an SS firing squad one week before the camp was occupied by the U.S. Army. Karl Koch had already been sentenced to a prison term for embezzlement in 1930. (See the entry on Konrad Morgen and his testimony, *IMT*, Vol. 20, pp. 500f.)

Karl Koch's wife Ilse Koch supposedly was involved in her own set of crimes while at the Buchenwald Camp – among them the murder of inmates for the sake of retrieving human skin with fancy tattoos, with the aim of manufacturing certain objects of them. See the following entry on her.

Kommissarbefehl → **Commissar Order**

KON, ABE

Abe Kon, a former Treblinka inmate who claimed to have arrived there on 2 October 1942, made the following claims on 17 August 1944 during an interview conducted by Soviet investigators (see Mattogno/Graf 2023, esp. pp. 64f.; Mattogno 2021e, pp. 136f., 154f.):

– There were 12 gas chambers in one building, each measuring 6 m × 6 m, which accommodated 400 inmates at a time – which amounts to an unlikely 11 people per square meter. The orthodoxy insists that only a building with three gas chambers existed when Kon arrived there, and that a second

building with 10 more chambers was added later.
- The victims were killed by a machine that pumped the air out of the chambers, suffocating the people within 6 to 15 minutes. However, creating a vacuum in a brick-and-mortar building is technically impossible (the external pressure would crush the walls), hence most certainly was not done.
- In a deposition five days later, he replaced the vacuum murder method with gas: "The gas was turned on."
- Three batches of people were gassed every day, which resulted not in (12 × 600 × 3 =) 21,600 victims, but according to Kon, in 15,000 to 18,000 victims daily.
- This went on for two months, with (60 × 15,000 to 18,000 =) 900,000 to 1,080,000 victims, plus probably more before his arrival and then afterwards. This death toll for just two months is already more than the camp's total death toll usually claimed by the orthodoxy of some 800,000.
- A "specially manufactured furnace" could burn up to 6,000 bodies at once, using gasoline or petroleum as fuel – which might be good for lighting a fire, but would only singe the bodies superficially.
- The cremation lasted up to an hour – when in fact open-air incinerations of that type easily burn an entire day or two.
- Those unable to walk were led to the edge of a blazing pit, shot in the neck and made to fall into the fire – while the proximity to this conflagration would have fatally burned the executioner as well.

In an interview with Polish investigating judge Łukaszkiewicz on 9 October 1945, Kon reverted again to the vacuum murder method, which he claimed he learned from a bricklayer who had been involved in building the facility.

Kon furthermore asserted that the largest inmate labor group was the one sorting the deportees' clothes and valuables, while there was also a group that "went into the woods to collect branches in order to make fences." However, the largest group should have been the lumberjacks felling trees, debranching, sawing and transporting them to the camp for the cremation activities. That would have made the collection of branches unnecessary. Kon also claimed in this otherwise terse statement that SS generals inspected the camp often, which is an oft-repeated but unsubstantiated myth. (See his complete Polish statement at https://zapisyterroru.pl/.)

KON, STANISŁAW

Stanisław Kon was a former Treblinka inmate who told a Soviet investigator on 18 August 1944 that some three million people were killed in Treblinka. In a Polish testimony of 7 October 1945 taken by Polish judge Łukaszkiewicz, he testified that he had learned only from hearsay how inmates were allegedly killed at this camp: the killing began in June 1942 – although the camp opened only end of July that year.

Initially, arriving inmates were allegedly killed with machine guns, because the execution chambers weren't ready yet. But this is an absurd claim: SS men gunning down crowds of newly arrived inmates, with bullets flying everywhere. Still, both the wrong starting date and the machine-gunning claim were mentioned by another Treblinka survivor, Eugeniusz Turowski, who was interviewed by Polish judge Łukaszkiewicz on that same day. This is a clear case of "convergence of evidence" on a lie. Oskar Berger also claimed this early starting date combined with machine-gun killings.

Once the execution chambers were ready, they killed "by means of pumping out the air or by introducing engine-exhaust gases," meaning he didn't know and wasn't sure – just as Abe Kon had changed the method from one to the other within just five days (see Abe Kon) thus switching to exhaust gases, which has been accepted by the orthodoxy as the "truth."

For Kon, excavators dug up buried corpses and dumped them onto a pyre that was constantly burning, meaning that the excavator was evidently fireproof, and the corpses burned without fuel all by themselves. However, self-immolating bodies simply do not exist. Kon also claimed that the camp was inspected by SS generals, and that Himmler had visited the camp in early 1943, which is devoid of any historical reality. (See Mattogno/Graf 2023, pp. 67, 141; Mattogno 2021e, pp. 138f., 154; https://zapisyterroru.pl/.)

KORHERR, RICHARD

Dr. Richard Korherr (30 Oct. 1903 – 24 Nov. 1989) was a statistician, and from late 1940, the head of the SS's statistical office. In early 1943, Himmler ordered him to compile a report on the trends of European Jewish population developments since the National Socialists' rise to power. After several discussions and some correspondence with Himmler, Korherr submitted a 16-page long version for Himmler (Nuremberg Document NO-5194), and a 6½-page short version meant for Hitler (NO-5193).

These two reports and a few accompanying letters are seen by the orthodoxy as a smoking gun for the Holocaust. They claim that these documents prove that some two million Jews had been murdered as of early 1943. The subsequent discussion will focus on the long version.

The data used by Korherr to compile these statistics were provided to him by various SS offices. For instance, the number of Jews listed in the long version (p. 9, Point 4) as "passed through the camps in the General Government," meaning occupied Poland, is identical with the number given by SS official Hans Höfle in a radio message sent in early 1943 to the SS headquarters. Höfle listed this number as a total of individual "arrival" figures ("*Zugang*") of all the camps located in that area: Belzec, Lublin (meaning Majdanek), Sobibór and Treblinka. While Höfle had the inmates arrive at these camps, Korherr listed them as "passed through" ("*durchgeschleust*"), suggesting that these camps served as transit camps.

An earlier draft of Korherr's report used the term "special treatment of the Jews" here ("*Sonderbehandlung der Juden*"). In a letter, Himmler asked Korherr not to use that expression anywhere, and to headline Point 4 of page 9 instead: "Transportation of Jews from the Eastern provinces to the Russian East." Some 35 years later, in a letter to the editors of the German news magazine *Der Spiegel* (No. 31, 1977, p. 12), Korherr explained that he was perplexed by the term special treatment, hence had inquired about it with the German Department of Homeland Security (*Reichssicherheitshauptamt*). He was told that it referred to resettlements. That phone call probably triggered Himmler's letter giving instructions on what term to use instead. This supports Korherr's postwar statement that these camps had been presented to him as transit camps for Jews getting resettled.

Korherr's report also has 145,302 Jews "passed [...] through the camps in the Warthegau" (*ibid.*). However, there was only one camp in that area: Chełmno. This figure gives a maximum number of Jews deported to that camp. While the orthodoxy claims that they were all killed there in gas vans, Korherr's report again suggests a mere transit camp.

The orthodoxy claims that the original term used (special treatment) was a euphemism for murder

Richard Korherr

(through gassing). However, the largest of all claimed mass-murder centers – Auschwitz – is not included in that number. Most Jews deported to Auschwitz are instead listed in the next entry of that list ("Evacuations of Jews from other countries," Point 5, pp. 9f.), which evidently never had the term "special treatment" attached to it, hence was in no need of any changes. Therefore, if special treatment meant murder, then Jews evacuated to Auschwitz were not murdered according to the Korherr Report.

On the other hand, Höfle's radio message proves that the "camps in the General Government" included the Majdanek Camp. In this case, the rich extant documentation allows us to ascertain that Jews sent to this camp were not murdered there. (See the entry on that camp). Hence, "special treatment" did not mean murder in this case. By analogy, it may not have meant murder for Jews sent to the other three camps either (Belzec, Sobibór, Treblinka).

When summing up all evacuation figures on page 10 (for which Himmler had not requested any change), all single items are tallied, "including special treatment." That instance of this term's use had been overlooked by Himmler and Korherr. It was a back reference to Point 4 on page 9, but after its text had been changed, this reference pointed nowhere.

We know from numerous Auschwitz documents that the evacuation of Jews to and through Auschwitz was indeed labeled "special treatment." (See the entry on that term.) However, this referred not to murder, but to the special treatment Jews were getting in comparison to all other groups of people who were arrested, incarcerated and/or deported by the Third Reich. Everyone else had to have committed – or be suspected of having committed – some infraction to get arrested. The Jews, however, got arrested and deported simply because they were Jews. That was their special treatment.

Furthermore, the report lists a little over 1.6 million Jews who are said to have been evacuated or transported from Germany, the Protectorate (occupied Czechia) and the eastern provinces to "the East" or the "Russian East" (meaning the then-occupied

Soviet territories; p. 9, Points 2 and 4.). It then states that these "evacuations […] are counted here as part of the decrease" (p. 15), although mere transfers to the European part of Russia, strictly speaking, did not remove them from Europe, which is what this report was all about. However, if they had been killed in the East, they would not just count as decreases, but be irreversible population declines.

Hence, in this regard as well, Korherr believed – or wrote as if he believed – that mass relocations to Russia happened, and that these relocated Jews were very much alive and kicking. Not a single word, expression or inkling in this document indicates that mass murder was being perpetrated against the Jews.

The orthodoxy insists that all this is a game of smoke and mirrors, where euphemisms are used to hide the ugly truth of genocide. The problem is that this report was not meant to be published or spread. It was for Himmler's and Hitler's eyes only. So why use lies, euphemisms and code language in top-secret documents to be seen only by the nation's top leaders? Who was Korherr or Himmler trying to dupe?

(For more details, see Graf/Kues/Mattogno 2020, pp. 311-330.)

Korherr Report → Korherr, Richard

KORN, MOISCHE

Moische Korn was a Jew who claims to have been forced by German units in 1943 to exhume mass graves near the city of Lviv, and to burn the extracted bodies on pyres within the context of what today's orthodoxy calls *Aktion* 1005. He escaped from that unit on 10 October 1944.

In a rather generic statement of 13 September 1944 to Soviet investigators, Korn made claims that are partially at odds with those made by the other two witnesses to this alleged event, Heinrich Chamaides and Leon Weliczker.

Korn claimed that the pyres he built measured "10 x 10 x 10 meters," which can be dismissed safely as a vast exaggeration, as proper pyres for open-air incinerations are usually only one body-length wide and up to 2 m high. Building and maintaining the burning of anything bigger is too challenging and impractical: Did the inmates have a crane to get bodies and wood onto layers more than 2 meters off the ground? And how did they prevent this huge pile, which inevitably burned unevenly, from toppling over, spilling embers, burning wood and partially burned body parts all over the place?

Korn says nothing about where exactly this event occurred nor how many bodies were "processed." If we assume the number claimed by the orthodoxy (based on Heinrich Chamaides's account), then 120,000 had to be burned on pyres. Cremating an average human body during open-air incinerations requires some 250 kg of freshly cut wood. Cremating 120,000 bodies thus requires some 30,000 metric tons of wood. This would have required the felling of all trees growing in a 50-year-old spruce forest covering almost 67 hectares of land, or some 149 American football fields. An average prisoner is rated at being able to cut some 0.63 metric tons of fresh wood per workday. To cut this amount of wood within the six month (160 days) that this operation supposedly lasted would have required a work force of some 300 dedicated lumberjacks just to cut the wood. Korn claims his unit consisted only of 120 inmates, all busy digging out mass graves, extracting bodies, building pyres, sifting through ashes, scattering the ashes, refilling the graves with soil, and planting them with grass seeds and saplings. He says nothing about where the firewood came from.

Korn moreover claimed that all bones were ground by a special mill. However, this alleged mill later turned out to have been a road-building device to crush gravel. Since most inmates from the Janowska Camp were deployed in building roads, this is what this machine was used for. A photo taken by a Soviet investigative commission shows Korn with two more witnesses (Heinrich Chamaides and David Manusevich) standing next to the claimed machine. This shows that at least these three witnesses knew each other and collaborated as a group with the Soviet commission, meaning that their testimonies were probably harmonized and orchestrated to some degree.

(See the entry on bone mill; for more details, see Mattogno 2022c, pp. 515f.)

KOSINSKI, JERZY

Jerzy Kosinski (born Jozef Lewinkopf, 14 June 1933 – 3 May 1991) was a Polish Jew, whose family managed to get through the war by assuming the fake Catholic name "Kosinski." He emigrated to the U.S. in 1957. In 1965, his first novel, *The Painted Bird*, appeared, which he claimed for many years was autobiographic in nature. It describes a boy during World War II separated from his parents, roaming through Poland from one temporary shelter to another, where he experiences all sorts of cruelties to him and others. Elie Wiesel praised the book, and it opened Kosinski's path into U.S. high society.

In 1994, Polish journalist Johanna Siedlecka exposed the book as pure fiction by proving Kosinski's real, rather mundane wartime experiences in Poland. This was later confirmed in a Kosinski biography written by James P. Sloan (see Sloan 1997).

Jerzy Kosinski

KOSÓW PODLASKI

The Polish underground "Memorandum on the Situation in the Country for the Period July 16 –August 25, 1942" claimed four death camps in existence in German-occupied Poland: Bełżec, Treblinka II, Sobibór and one at "Kosów Podlaski." (See Mattogno 2021e, p. 97, for the source.)

No such town exists, but there is a town called Sokołów Podlaski some 80 km east of Warsaw. All historians agree, however, that no such camp with any mass-murder facility ever existed in or near this or any similarly named town. This phantom extermination camp is a creation of black-propaganda sources.

KOZAK, STANISŁAW

Stanisław Kozak was a Polish civilian from the village of Belzec hired by the Germans in October 1941 to help build the facilities inside the Belzec Camp. When interrogated on 14 October 1945 by Regional Investigative Judge Czeslaw Godzieszewski, Kozak described a building made of wood with three chambers, each one equipped with a heavy coke furnace. Water pipes connected to those furnaces entered the room and ran along the walls. Kozak did not indicate whether this set up was used to kill people, and if so, how that was supposed to work. His description indicates that, what he was involved in constructing, were either shower rooms or hot-steam disinfestation chambers, but certainly not any facilities to mass murder anyone. (For more, see Mattogno 2004a, pp. 44-46.)

KRAMER, JOSEF

Josef Kramer (10 Nov. 1906 – 13 Dec. 1945), SS *Hauptsturmführer*, started his SS career as a guard at Dachau, then served at the Sachsenhausen and Mauthausen Camps, and became Rudolf Höss's adjutant in 1940 during the initial set-up phase of the Auschwitz Camp. In April 1941, he was made commandant of the Natzweiler Camp, Alsace, where he supposedly set up a rudimentary gas chamber in 1943 in order to kill several Jews whose skeletons were meant to be added to a ghoulish anatomical collection at the University of Strasbourg. (See the entry on Natzweiler for details.)

Josef Kramer

On 8 May 1944, he was transferred to Auschwitz as commandant of the Auschwitz II-Birkenau Camp, where he stayed until November. He then was transferred to the Bergen-Belsen Camp as that camps' last commandant until its catastrophic end in April 1944. (See the entry on that camp and on the Bergen-Belsen Trials for details).

When the British took over the Bergen-Belsen Camp, Kramer was arrested. In the early days of his arrest, he wrote a lengthy affidavit that reacted to numerous questions put to him (Phillips 1949, pp. 721-737). Among them was what he knew about experiments conducted on inmates for a professor at Strasbourg. He insisted that he had no knowledge about any such thing, but if this had occurred, he would have known about it. About his time at the Auschwitz-Birkenau Camp, he stated in that affidavit (*ibid.*, p. 731):

> "No prisoners were flogged; there were no executions, shootings or hangings in my part. […] During my inspections I never saw prisoners who had died through physical violence. […] All efforts were made by these doctors to keep the prisoners alive. Medical supplies and invigorating drugs were applied. […] It was never reported to me that prisoners had to be treated for dog bites. […]
>
> I have heard of the allegations of former prisoners in Auschwitz referring to a gas chamber there, the mass executions and whippings, the cruelty of the guards employed, and that all this took place either in my presence or with my knowledge. All I can say to all this is that it is un-

true from beginning to end."

Then Kramer underwent, for weeks on end, the kind of torture that almost all SS prisoners in British custody had to endure. A member of the French Resistance present during some of this mistreatment described with glee how Kramer was locked up an entire night in a refrigeration chamber. (Fréjafon 1947, p. 22). As Montgomery Belgion reported in his 1949 book *Victor's Justice*, at the end of this treatment, Kramer and many other SS men and women begged their British tormentors to please let them die (Belgion 1949, pp. 80f., 90). After that treatment, he "confessed" to French interrogators about a ridiculously primitive gassing he claims to have performed at Natzweiler Camp (see that camp's entry, as well as Phillips 1949, pp. 174f.). He suddenly also "remembered" what he was asked to state about Auschwitz, writing it down in a later, shorter affidavit (*ibid.*, p. 738):

> "The first time I saw a gas chamber proper was at Auschwitz. It was attached to the crematorium. The complete building containing the crematorium and gas chamber was situated in Camp No. 2 (Birkenau), of which I was in command."

Actually, the orthodox narrative has it that there were five buildings at Birkenau with altogether 12 gas chambers (one each in Crematoria II and III, three each in Crematoria IV and V, and four in Bunker 2). So, Kramer had yet to learn some lessons. What he did understand, though, was a way to yield to what his captors forced him violently to confess, while at the same time trying to dodge responsibility for the claimed gas-chamber mass murders by stating (*ibid.*; also p. 175):

> "[…] *I received a written order from Hoess, who commanded the whole of Auschwitz Camp, that although the gas chamber and crematorium were situated in my part of the camp, I had no jurisdiction over it whatever. Orders in regard to the gas chamber were, in fact, always given by Hoess* […]."

During the trial, Kramer's "defense" lawyer played the prosecution's game by asserting (*ibid.*, p. 150):

> "The gas chamber existed, there is no doubt about that."

In his testimony, Kramer repeated his nonsense about the gas chamber(s) not having been any of his business, and asserted that he had lied in his first affidavit because he still felt bound by some "word of honor" to Hitler and Himmler to keep the chambers a secret (pp. 157, 174). This at a time when the whole world was talking about this "secret" already. He uttered no word about his torture, meaning that he was mortally afraid that, as soon as he returned to his prison cell, the tormenting would continue. One can feel the tension in the air with every terse answer he gave, usually consisting only of a mere "Yes" or "No." This man's spirit had been utterly broken.

When asked whether burning ditches existed in his Birkenau Camp in the summer of 1944, he again answered "Yes" (*ibid.*, p. 175), but air photos show that they did not exist. Here we have prime evidence of which of his affidavits was a lie, and which was true, and there is no hesitation to point out why.

In the end, Kramer was sentenced to death, and hanged on 13 December 1945, at the age of just 39.

KRANZ, HERMINE

Hermine Kranz was a Slovakian Jewess deported to Auschwitz towards mid-1942. She testified during the British Bergen-Belsen Show Trial, and signed a deposition on 9 May 1945, in which she declared as having personally seen when visiting the "gas chamber," or having been told by inmates working there, that:

- There were altogether six such crematoria – there were four in Birkenau and one at the Main Camp.
- The victims entered the gas chamber through an iron door – all doors at Auschwitz were made of simple wooden planks.
- Three thousand persons could be dealt with at a time – with a room of 210 m², that amounts to a packing density of some 14.5 people per square meter, which is physically impossible.
- Towel and soap were given to each person entering the gas chamber – that would not have happened. Imagine 3,000 towels and pieces of soap between three thousand corpses. Retrieving and cleaning them would have been a huge task, but ditching them would have been a huge waste.
- The gas chamber was also used as an anatomical research laboratory – actually, the laboratory was upstairs near the furnace room.
- The gas chamber had a very pretty tiled floor – nowhere in any of the crematoria were any floor tiles used.
- In the gas chamber, there were benches all around – why in the world would anyone put benches into a gas chamber? The orthodoxy claims that these were located in the undressing room instead.
- In the gas-chamber floor there were trap doors which opened after the gassing. Under these were

trucks, into which the bodies fell. They were then driven to the furnace. This is a wild fantasy conclusively proving that Kranz made it all up.

Repeating the clichés, she moreover stated: "Dr. Mengele was always present."

(For details, see Mattogno 2021, pp. 361f.)

KRASNODAR

Krasnodar is a city northwest of the Caucasus Mountains, today with over a million inhabitants, but much less during the Second World War. It was occupied by German forces in August of 1942. After the defeat during the Battle of Stalingrad in early 1943, German forces withdrew from the Caucasus area in order to avoid getting cut off.

The Soviets subsequently reoccupied the area and prepared a Stalinist show trial against eleven local Soviet citizens accused of having collaborated with the Germans, among other things by assisting them in killing civilians "by hanging, mass shootings, and use of poison gases." The latter was said to have been committed by the use of so-called gas vans.

The trial itself took place between 14 and 17 July 1943. The conditions of the Krasnodar Trial were of the worst kind imaginable. It was a stage show following a preordained script, where every actor played a theatric role. The defendants had been abused and tortured so much that, during the trial, they were either completely apathetic, or they enthusiastically embraced their charges. Defense lawyers were additional prosecutors, and the entire trial was geared toward teaching all Soviet citizens a lesson that collaborating with the Germans, which happened on a grand scale throughout the war, would be punished with the death penalty or decades-long jail time in Siberia.

The prosecution claimed that more than 6,000 civilians were poisoned in trucks with carbon monoxide using their Diesel-engine exhaust gas, although that exhaust gas is unsuited for executions due to its lack of toxicity. A certain witness Kotov claimed to have survived a gas-van gassing by ripping off his shirt, peeing on it, and holding that urine-soaked rag to his mouth and nose. However, carbon monoxide does not get absorbed by moisture, urine or not, so it wouldn't have had any effect. This all shows that these charges have been freely invented and backed up with fraudulent arguments and testimonies by perjurious witnesses.

The prosecution claimed moreover that they had exhumed and forensically investigated the remains of the victims extracted from mass graves. The Soviet forensic experts allegedly managed to prove the presence of carbon monoxide in the victims' blood. However, after several months of decomposing in mass graves, it can be safely ruled out that anyone was able to establish anything about remnants of carbon monoxide in severely rotten tissue samples.

Krasnodar is not mentioned in any report by the *Einsatzgruppen*. The only proof the Soviets could come up with was a series of photographs allegedly showing exhumed victims near Krasnodar. However, the photo with the most bodies visible shows perhaps 100 to 150 bodies arranged haphazardly on the ground.

Therefore, there is little if any proof that there was any kind of massacre in that city during the brief German occupation.

(For more details, see the entry on gas vans, as well as Bourtman 2008; Alvarez 2023, pp. 20-22, 111-122; Mattogno 2022c, p. 731.)

KRAUS, OTA

Ota Kraus

Ota Kraus (7 Sept. 1909 – 10 July 2010) was a Czech Jew who was arrested in 1940 for distributing resistance magazines. He was interned at Auschwitz from November 1942 until October 1944, when he was transferred to Sachsenhausen Camp. In Auschwitz, he headed the inmate metalworking shop together with the Czech Jew Erich Kulka. After the war, they both wrote a book titled *The Death Factory*, which was translated into German and published by a Communist East-German publisher in 1957. See the entry about Erich Kulka for more.

During the Krakow trial against some of the former Auschwitz camp staff, Kraus testified succinctly that the Birkenau Camp was "the extermination camp of all peoples. The Jews came first, then the Poles and Czechs had to follow." According to Kraus's "calculations" – but actually based on tales he claims to have received from "people who worked in the so-called 'Kanada' and the '*Sonderkommando*' and from the secretaries at the Political Department", because he knew them all – roughly 2 million Poles, "150,000 Czechs, 500,000 Hungarians, 250,000 Germans, 90,000 Dutch, 60,000 Belgians, 80,000 Greeks and several ten thousand Yugoslavs, Italians and others died in the gas chambers," plus "about 400,000 people who were political prisoners." This neatly summed up with the Soviet propaganda lie of 4,000,000 victims. (See Mattogno 2021d, pp. 77f.)

KREMER, JOHANN PAUL

Johann Paul Kremer

Johann Paul Kremer (26 Dec. 1883 – 8 Jan. 1965), professor of medicine at the University of Münster, West Germany, substituted for a convalescing camp physician at the Auschwitz-Birkenau Camp from 30 August to 18 November 1942. During that time, he added numerous entries to his diary. He also wrote a letter on 21 October 1942, in which he wrote:

"Though I have no definite information yet, nonetheless I expect that I can be in Münster again before December 1 and so finally will have turned my back on this Auschwitz hell, where in addition to typhus, etc., typhoid fever is now mightily making itself felt."

His diary contains several entries displaying his opposition to the civil-rights violations going on in Germany, mocking the Third Reich's theory of a "German Science" and comparing censorship in Germany to the Holy Inquisition of Galileo's time. Yet in spite of this opposition, his diary does not contain a single entry about any kind of mass murder going on at Auschwitz. The only reference to gassing refers to fumigating "a block with Zyklon B against the lice."

Assuming that the Third-Reich authorities would have allowed a non-initiated, independent-minded professor to experience the darkest secret of the nation for two months, then let him go back to his civilian life as if nothing had happened, is simply preposterous. It is similarly preposterous to assume that this professor did nothing to somehow convey his knowledge of this terrible secret to anyone.

He only "confessed" and confirmed all the orthodox accusations of mass murder when he faced charges at a Polish Stalinist kangaroo court in 1947. During that trial, truth was no defense, or rather "truth" had been cast in stone by political powers hell-bent at paining the defeated Third Reich in the worst light possible, in order to justify the various Allied crimes committed against humanity, including against Germans. Among these crimes looms large the greatest ethnic cleansing in the history of mankind then wrapping up: the mass murder and expulsion of some 12 million Germans from Eastern Europe and East Germany, in which Poland was the primary culprit.

Western mainstream historians contributed to this distortion of history by mistranslating Kremer's diary entries. For example, in the context of the terrible death toll caused by the typhus epidemic raging during those months at Auschwitz, Kremer, quoting his physician colleague Heinz Thilo, called the camp the "anus mundi" and a veritable "camp of annihilation", which the Auschwitz Museum twisted into "extermination camp" while omitting the context of the epidemic. Kremer repeatedly mentions "special operations from Holland," which clearly referred to the arrival and admission of deportees coming from Holland, but historians mistranslated that as a "special operation *with a draft* from Holland" or as a "special operation *on people coming* from Holland," thus hiding from the reader the fact that the deportation of Jews from Holland *itself* was the special operation, not what was supposedly done *with* or *on* them at Auschwitz.

There are many more entries in Kremer's Diary where words such as "special" are used, none of which mean anything ominous, if seen in the proper historical and documental context, but all of which are distorted by the mainstream to support their cause of trying to demonstrate mass homicide.

Like so many of his co-defendants, Kremer was sentenced to death in Krakow, but had the luck of getting pardoned and released early after having served a little over ten years. Scarcely had he returned home, when the German authorities put him right back on the next show trial, with truth being no defense. Kremer had learned his lessons well, and meekly confirmed once more the unchallengeable orthodox narrative. He was sentenced to ten years, yet walked away as a free man, counting the time served in Poland. Again standing in court a few years later, this time as a witness during the Auschwitz Show Trial at Frankfurt, he wisely abstained from rocking the boat, and once more submissively repeated all the lies which, by that time, he actually might have believed himself. He died shortly afterwards. (For details, see Mattogno 2016d, pp. 82-95; Rudolf 2023, pp. 451-453; Faurisson 1980, pp. 55f.; 1981.)

Kristallnacht → **Crystal Night**

KRZEPICKI, ABRAHAM

Abraham Krzepicki was a former inmate of the Treblinka II Camp. He was deported to Treblinka on 25 August 1942, but managed to escape just 18 days later. Shortly afterwards, he wrote two different texts about his alleged experience, a shorter one with little information, and a longer, much more detailed one. The originals were presumably written in Yiddish, and atrocity propagandist Rachel Auerbach is said to have translated those originals into Polish, which seems to be all that has survived; thus, we have to take Auerbach's word for her claim that she produced accurate translations. Krzepicki died during the Warsaw Ghetto Uprising in April 1943. Here are the oddities in his account:

Abraham Krzepicki

– He consistently speaks only of "the gas chamber" or "the bath hall", in the singular, when there supposedly were three of them at the time he was there.
– He describes the facility he inspected in detail, but mentions no engine room with a "gas generator", nor any ducts or openings allowing the introduction of gas.
– He mentions pipes on top of the roof, as if describing water pipes feeding the showerheads in the room's ceiling, which he mentioned, whereas ducts feeding in exhaust gas would have come through wall openings, not first led from the engine room outside onto the roof, then back inside again through the roof.
– He claims to have worked on constructing a crematorium building at Treblinka, although no such facility was ever conceived, let alone built.

(For details, see Mattogno 2021e, pp. 122-124; https://zapisyterroru.pl/.)

KUDLIK, ALEKSANDER

Aleksander Kudlik was a former inmate of the Treblinka II Camp, who arrived there on 12 October 1942 from Częstochowa. He signed an affidavit on 10 October 1945, in which he stated that he had no first-hand knowledge of how exterminations were carried out at Treblinka, but instead relied on the tales told by inmates who claimed to know, primarily Jankiel Wiernik. At that camp, he claimed to have been allowed to *sort fountain pens* for six months straight.

In deviation from Wiernik's account, Kudlik claimed that the killing was done by first pumping air out, and then pumping exhaust fumes in, a nonsensical procedure that is a compromise between some claiming the use of exhaust gasses and others insisting on vacuum as the murder method. However, creating a vacuum in a brick-and-mortar building is technically impossible (the external pressure would crush the walls), hence most certainly was not done.

Kudlik also reduced the packing density in the gas chamber to a value that is at least theoretically possible, from Wiernik's 1,000 to 1,200 per chamber of some 50 m² (20 to 24.5 people per m²) to just 5,000 people in all ten chambers, without giving a chamber size. But if we take Wiernik's claim, then this results in 10 people per m².

Kudlik insisted that, during his time at the camp from mid-October to around Christmas (some 70 days), on average three transports arrived per day with 60 rail cars of 120 deportees each, hence in total 1.5 million Jews just in that time span – almost twice the number of all Jews ever deported to or through Treblinka.

(For details, see Mattogno 2021e, p. 165; https://zapisyterroru.pl/.)

KUKLIA, VLADISLAV

Vladislav Kuklia was a Ukrainian Jew interned in the Syretsky Camp, 5 km from Kiev. On 22 August 1943, he was taken from there to Babi Yar, a place where tens of thousands of Jews are said to have been shot and buried by the Germans in mass graves in late September 1941 (see the entry on Babi Yar). He was interrogated by the NKGB on 4 February 1944 about his alleged experiences at Babi Yar.

Among other things, Kuklia stated that he was shackled and forced to exhume and burn corpses buried in mass graves. He asserted that 70 to 80 pyres, each measuring about 10 meters long and 5 meters wide, and with 2,000 to 4,000 and even more bodies on them, were built, burning a total of 95,000 to 100,000 bodies. In an interview on 1 March 1944, Kuklia specified that each layer of bodies on the pyre contained 250 bodies, alternating with layers of wood, until the pyre contained two to four thousand bodies. In other words, a pyre contained between 8 and 16 layers of wood and bodies. Each layer had a surface area of 50 m², meaning that 5 bodies were lying on every square meter.

Since each corpse requires 250 kg of freshly cut wood (see open-air incinerations), this means that each layer of wood under a layer of bodies had to contain 1.25 metric tons of wood. The density of green wood is roughly 0.9 tons per m³, and its stacking density on a pyre is 1.4 (40% for air and flames to go through). This means that the wood required to burn just one layer of corpses would have stacked up to a height of almost 2 meters. Adding the body layer gets us beyond 2 meters. 8 to 16 such layers result in a pyre 16 to 32 meters high. It would have been impossible to build such a pyre, and also impossible to burn it down without it collapsing and spilling burning wood and corpses all over the place. Kuklia actually stated that the pyres they built were only as high as a normal room. In fact, that would have been the height of just the bodies stacked up – without any wood.

Kuklia claimed that, after the pyres had burned down, unburned bones were ground down, the cremation remains sifted through sieves, and the powder scattered. However, wood-fired pyres burn unevenly and leave behind lots of unburned wood pieces, charcoal, and incompletely burned body parts, not just ashes and bones (80% of leftovers would have been from wood, not corpses). Incompletely burned wood and human remains could not have been ground. Any sieve would have clogged with the first load. Moreover, any occasional rainfall would have rendered any burned-out pyre into a moist heap of highly alkaline, corrosive slush that could not have been processed at all. If 100,000 bodies were burned, then several thousand metric tons of cremation leftovers had to be processed. Just this job would have required hundreds of men to complete in time.

Kuklia also insisted that they had to throw bodies of people into the pyres who had been killed in gas vans. However, considering that the front was getting very close to Kiev during September 1943, it is unlikely that anyone would have operated gas vans in Kiev's vicinity. All this apart from the fact that gas vans are a figment of Soviet atrocity propaganda (see the entry on gas vans).

Cremating an average human body during open-air incinerations requires some 250 kg of freshly cut wood. Cremating 100,000 bodies thus requires some 25,000 metric tons of wood. This would have required the felling of all trees growing in a 50-year-old spruce forest covering almost 56 hectares of land, or some 125 American football fields. An average prisoner is rated at being able to cut some 0.63 metric tons of fresh wood per workday. To cut this amount of wood within five weeks (35 days) that this operation supposedly lasted would have required a work force of some 1,134 dedicated lumberjacks just to cut the wood. Kuklia claimed his unit consisted only of 122 inmates, all busy digging out mass graves, extracting bodies, building pyres, sifting through ashes, scattering the ashes and refilling the graves with soil. Kuklia says nothing about where the mountain of firewood came from, other than: "firewood, twigs." One wonders how many "twigs" it takes to burn 100,000 bodies.

(For more details, see the entry on Babi Yar, as well as Mattogno 2022c, pp. 534f., and 550-563.)

KULA, MICHAŁ

Michał Kula was a Polish inmate incarcerated in Auschwitz, where he was deployed at the inmate metalworking shop, the communication hub of the Auschwitz resistance. Kula made three statements about his alleged experiences in Auschwitz, one in preparation of the Polish show trial against Rudolf Höss, one while taking the stand during that trial, and then again during the Polish show trial against former members of the Auschwitz camp staff. Here are several of Kula's claims from those three depositions:

– There were two homicidal gas chambers in each Birkenau Crematorium II and III, a smaller and a larger one. Every other witness and, based on this, every orthodox scholar insists, however, that only one of the basement rooms of these buildings was used as such.
– 2,500 people were pushed into the larger chamber (later he reduced that to 2,000), and 1,500 into the smaller – resulting in a packing density of either $(2,500/2,000/1,500 \div 210 m^2 =)$ 12, 9.5 or 7 people per square meter, where only the last figure is realistic.
– People entered the gas chamber by being unloaded from a truck via a tipping mechanism, throwing them onto a concrete ski jump, on which the victims slid down straight into the gas chamber. A corpse chute in between two flights of stairs existed in these crematoria, connecting the

ground floor to the basement, but trucks could not get access to the door leading into this staircase containing that chute, and if they had been able to drive up to it (across an extended lawn), tipping the truck's load bed would have made the victims fall into the entry area at most, but not down the chute. Finally, the chute ended in a hallway, not the morgue that supposedly served as a gas chamber. (See the similar testimony by Sofia Litwinska.)
- There were fake showerheads in the "gas chamber," when in fact documents show that these showerheads were real and operational.
- All members of the *Sonderkommando* were exterminated every three months at some gas chamber "in the vicinity of Gleiwitz." The myth of a frequent killing of *Sonderkommando* members is refuted by the many (often merely self-proclaimed) survivors of this labor unit. No other inmate has ever claimed the existence, let alone use, of a gassing facility near Gleiwitz (today's Gliwice), nor is there any documental or material trace for it.
- The gassing victims he once claimed to have seen looked greenish, when in fact the victims of hydrogen-cyanide poisoning look pinkish, not greenish.
- His metalworking team allegedly manufactured Zyklon-B introduction columns for the Crematoria II and III. However, in two separate depositions, he gave entirely different dimensions for them. The first description made them too large to fit into the claimed space, and the second version made them so small and narrow that they could not have functioned as he claimed. Finally, there is no material or documental trace of these columns. For example, had they been installed, they had to have been bolted to the concrete floors of these morgues, yet no traces of any such anchoring points can be found in the floors.
- The vast documentation of orders submitted to the metalworking shop has no trace of such columns ever being manufactured. As a reason for this, Kula claimed that orders prepared for the crematoria were not recorded due to their secrecy. Yet the extant documentation contains a plethora of orders for the crematoria which the metalworking shop received and properly fulfilled.
- Kula's description of these Zyklon-B introduction columns contradict those of other witnesses, some of whom claimed to have worked for a long time inside the "gas chamber," seeing those columns for months on end, and even cleaning them out.

(For details, see Rudolf 2020, pp. 148-162, 229.)

KULKA, ERICH

Erich Kulka

Erich Kulka (aka Schön, 18 Dec. 1911 – 13 July 1995) was a Czech Jew who was arrested due to his communist resistance activities, and spent time at the Theresienstadt Ghetto and in the camps at Dachau, Neuengamme and Auschwitz. In Auschwitz, he headed the inmate metalworking shop together with the Czech Jew Ota Kraus. This workshop was a communications hub for the Auschwitz resistance groups, providing Kraus and Kulka with the most recent information, rumors, lies and black-propaganda plans. (See also the entry on Michał Kula.)

After the war, they both wrote a book titled *The Death Factory*, first published in Czechia in 1946 (as *Továrna na smrt*), which contained a good deal of this (dis)information. A German translation was published by a Communist East-German publisher in 1957, and an English translation in 1966. In the book, the authors attempt to justify the Soviet propaganda lie of the four million Auschwitz victims by inventing mass deportation transports: in total, they claimed mass transports of unregistered Jews allegedly gassed on arrival for a total of 3,500,000 persons, adding 320,000 more victims who allegedly died at the camp for other reasons, and another 15,000 who allegedly died during the evacuation of the camp, thus arriving at a figure close to the Soviet propaganda lie of four million victims.

When it comes to extermination claims, their book is entirely based on hearsay and rumors, hence has little value. The only identifiable person they mention as a source of their information is a certain František Feldmann, a "dentist" among the *Sonderkommando* inmates. However, they did publish separately a long statement by their long-term friend Filip Müller in their book about his alleged experiences at Auschwitz as a *Sonderkommando* member. If Müller really had been a long-term member of this unit involved in dragging gassing victims out of the gas chambers and cremating them in the furnaces, one would have expected Müller to have informed them about many details. However, this is utterly absent from their account, and where it does contain details, they are often wrong.

This lack of their knowledge becomes particularly apparent when they describe the cremation furnace at Crematoria II and III as a "three-stage furnace," where air was presumably blown in at the bottom level, fuel was burned on the center level, and the corpses were placed – "two or three at a time" – at the top level. In fact, the furnaces were triple-*muffle* furnaces, not triple-*stage* furnaces, whose fuel was burned in their rear, air was blown in through openings in the muffle vault, and the corpses were placed in the muffle. Embers and ashes fell into the ash chamber beneath. Furthermore, the muffles were designed to accommodate only one corpse, not three. Müller should have known this and should have corrected his friends' faulty description – but he didn't.

Here are some more lies spread by Kraus and Kulka:
- There were fake showers in the gas chamber – when, in fact, they were real showers.
- Two iron pillars served to feed in the gas – while there is no trace of any such pillar, although the orthodoxy insists that there were *four* of them, not two.
- All four crematoria had the same capacity of 2,000 people for one gassing batch – although the Crematoria IV and V had a completely different layout, and in any case, 2,000 people on 210 m² (Morgue #1 of Crematoria II and III) would have led to an unrealistic packing density of some 9.5 people per m².
- They claimed a cremation speed of three corpses at once within 20 minutes – in muffles designed to burn just one corpse within an hour.
- They claimed that the Germans operated an inmate sauna inside the Birkenau Camp in order to torture inmates. The sauna was real, and the treatment which Kraus/Kulka described is a normal sauna procedure, thoroughly misunderstood by the uneducated authors. (See the entry on saunas.)

This book is a typical Jewish-communist propaganda work of the Stalinist era.

A few years after writing his book, Kulka also testified as a witness during the Polish show trial against members of the former Auschwitz camp staff. He claimed there that a commission of senior figures from the Reich, including Eichmann and Pohl, arrived at Auschwitz in February 1943, which is pure fiction, and that "often entire medical commissions of technicians and scientists came from Berlin" to study the gassings, which is just another preposterous lie. He also repeated from his book the wild story about the alleged fate of the inmates lodged in the Auschwitz family camp, and although there is not a documental shred to back it up, his tale found official recognition by way of entry in Danuta Czech's *Auschwitz Chronicle* (see Mattogno 2016a, pp. 160-164).

(For details, see Mattogno 2019, pp. 522f.; 2021d, pp. 78-88; in Mattogno 2021, see entries for Kulka in the index of names.)

Kulka dedicated much of his time after the war to interviewing other Auschwitz survivors, with a focus on former alleged members of the *Sonderkommando*. He cooperated closely with the young Israeli historian Gideon Greif, who continued these efforts, and has published two books on the *Sonderkommando* so far (see Mattogno 2022e).

Kulmhof → Chelmno

L

LAMPSHADES, OF HUMAN SKIN

There are plenty of photographs and film footage of tattooed human skin, allegedly taken from deceased or murdered inmates of German wartime camps. Especially famous is film footage recorded by U.S. troops after liberating the Buchenwald Camp. They had set up a table there, onto which they had arranged all kinds of objects which were allegedly made of dead or murdered inmates: soap, a table lamp, two shrunken heads, tattooed skin etc. The local population was forced to walk by this table for "educational purposes." It was an operation staged by the United States' psychological warfare department (see Irebodd 2009). The scenes were filmed and later used to further "reeducate" the German populace by showing this footage all over the country in cinemas. If Germans did not watch these "documentaries," the Allied authorities would deny them food stamps, which for many were pivotal for survival in the immediate postwar years.

This "documentary" and the objects, as well as an expert report by a pathologist of the U.S. Army of May 1946, served later as evidence during the Dachau show trial against the staff of the Buchenwald Camp, and during the trials of Ilse Koch, the wife of the former camp commandant of the Buchenwald Camp. She is supposed to have selected living prisoners in the camp according to their tattooing and designated them for killing in order to have household objects produced from their skin.

In an interview that SS judge Konrad Morgen granted the British historian John Toland years after the war, he insisted that the stories about Ilse Koch using tattooed human skin for lampshades and other object were unfounded legends. He had searched the Koch household himself during the war when investigating crimes committed by Ilse's husband Karl-Otto Koch, former commandant of the Buchenwald Camp, without finding any such objects. (See Toland 1976, pp. 845f.)

In a detailed study, U.S. mainstream author Arthur L. Smith determined that the objects identified as human skin by a U.S. examination, after they were sent to the International Military Tribunal at Nuremberg, disappeared without a trace (Smith 1983, pp. 103, 138, 153, 164). According to the statement of General Clay of the U.S. Army, the alleged human-skin lampshades are supposed to have consisted of

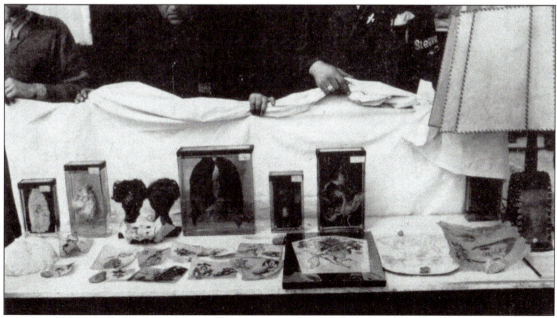

Collection of objects allegedly found in Buchenwald Camp, here at war's end on display on a table outdoors in the Buchenwald Camp. The local civilian German population was forced to file by this table, with U.S. officials making atrocious claims about these objects. At the very right: a lamp with a shade allegedly made from human skin. At the left, two shrunken heads.

goatskin (*ibid.*, p. 227; but see also the Buchenwald Museum at www.buchenwald.de, citing two "trustworthy" witnesses for the existence of such a lamp, although they claim that it was conveniently destroyed without a trace already in late 1941). All other objects found later were either made of synthetic leather, animal leather, textile or cardboard.

The story may have had a real background, though, as Smith reports. There evidently was a medical student from the University of Jena during the war period who was doing his medical dissertation on the correlation between skin tattooing and criminality (Smith 1983, pp. 127f.), which then was briefly touched upon in yet another PhD thesis some 65 years later on the history of forensic medicine at the University of Jena (Bode 2007, pp. 106f.).

The trials against Ilse Koch were the worst examples of the many show trials conducted after World War Two against alleged "Nazi criminals," which have a shocking resemblance to medieval witch trials.

(For more details, see Rudolf 2023, pp. 94-97; see also the entry on Hans Maršálek.)

LANGBEIN, HERMANN

Hermann Langbein

Hermann Langbein (18 May 1912 – 24 Oct. 1995) was an Austrian communist who fought during the Spanish Civil War with the Stalin-supported International Brigade. Due to his opposition to the National-Socialist regime, he was incarcerated at the Dachau, Auschwitz (from 21 August 1941 until 25 August 1944) and Neuengamme Camps. At Dachau and Auschwitz, he served as a clerk for the camp's garrison physician, hence had access to a lot of information. After the war, he co-founded and headed the International Auschwitz Committee, which initially had its headquarters in Stalinist Poland (Krakow). Later, the headquarters were moved to Langbein's hometown Vienna.

Not content with the Soviet lie that 4 million people had been killed at the Auschwitz Camp, Langbein declared in a deposition of 8 August 1945 meant to incriminate Maximilian Grabner that 5 million people had been gassed. Interestingly, Langbein knew nothing about the "first gassing" at Auschwitz, although that event is said to have occurred just two weeks after he had arrived at the camp, so it certainly would have left quite an impression, had the event really occurred.

Knowing that his former boss at Dachau *and* Auschwitz, Dr. Eduard Wirths, with whom he stood on very good terms and who Langbein respected tremendously as a kind, humane physician, could not defend himself anymore due to his suicide at the end of the war, Langbein committed perjury when he testified the following atrocity propaganda during the Frankfurt Auschwitz show trial:

"In 1944, children were thrown alive into the huge fires that were burning near the crematoria. We heard about this at the main camp, and I informed the garrison surgeon. Dr. Wirths refused to believe me. He went to Birkenau to find out. When I went to him the next day for dictation, he simply said 'that was an order of camp commandant Höss. It was issued because there was no more gas.' From that time on, Dr. Wirths believed anything I told him."

This apparently included Langbein's claim that 5 million people were killed, most of them under Wirths's auspices. Furthermore, the Auschwitz Camp never ran "out of gas." That's an auxiliary lie meant to shore up the master lie.

Langbein worked closely together with his communist buddy and multi-convicted liar, fraudster and perjurer Adolf Rögner, in trying to get the criminal investigations launched that ultimately led to the Frankfurt Auschwitz show trial. Langbein worked closely together with prosecutors and judges to compile so-called "perpetrator files," which contained names and photos of all possible defendants, and a list of all the crimes alleged against them. These files were then given to all possible witnesses, so they could "identify" the perpetrators and "remember" their crimes. (See the entry on the *Zentrale Stelle*.)

Langbein also worked closely together with the Polish authorities, who influenced their witnesses in an even more blatant way, coaching the witnesses to get them to agree on the official version of what happened at Auschwitz. Then some police or secret-service agent accompanied them to West Germany, and even into the court room, to make sure none would deviate from the official narrative (or tried to seek asylum in the West). When this manipulation was revealed during the appeals procedure, but rejected by the court of appeals as a reason for declaring a mistrial, Langbein boasted about him and his communist and Polish cronies having gotten away with their mega-fraud.

(For more details, see Rudolf 2023, pp. 383-385, 422f., 430; Mattogno 2016a, pp. 220-224; 2016f, pp. 97f.; 2022f, pp. 126, 180.)

LANGFUS, LEIB

In November 1970, a resident of the city of Auschwitz handed over a manuscript in Yiddish that he claimed to have found in a glass jar within the ruins of Crematorium III. Since that building was completely obliterated in late 1944 when the Germans blew it up, it is safe to say that a glass jar located inside of it would have been shattered to pieces. Hence, this glass jar was placed inside the ruins after the building had been dynamited.

The manuscript – with a total of 111 pages written in fountain pen – was first published in a German translation in 1996. It is attributed to a certain Leib Langfus. The first 99 pages contain a verbose account of the background to the deportation, and the deportation from the Polish town of Mława itself. The related transport is said to have arrived at Auschwitz on 6 December 1942. Then, when it should get interesting, the text of the following pages (100-105) is suddenly "illegible." Page 106 has the description of a claimed homicidal gassing of unknown victims at an unknown location on an undisclosed date, evidently based on the knowledge of someone who was there but somehow didn't get killed in the gassing, but stood aside instead, so he could later write a superficial, meaningless account whose only distinctive features are all wrong:

– Gas was allegedly thrown into this *one small* room through just *one* small hatch in the *ceiling*. However, if we follow the orthodox narrative, in December 1942, the *large* morgue inside the old crematorium at the Main Camp was no longer used for homicidal gassings; the orthodoxy claims that it had *four* hatches in its ceiling; the so-called bunkers near the Birkenau Camp supposedly had *several* rooms each, not just one; they are said to have had hatches only in their *side walls*, not in the ceiling; and the new crematoria at Birkenau were all still under construction.
– Langfus's ghost writer could even see through walls, for he was able to observe the victims' death struggle, who, rather than falling over dead, decided to arrange themselves neatly in piles of corpses stacked up to a meter high.
– Moreover, the ghost writer saw that some of the victims "turned quite blue under the influence of the gas," while poisoning by hydrogen cyanide (the active ingredient in Zyklon B) turns victims pink, not blue.
– Since not all victims could fit into the gas chamber, some allegedly had to wait in a hut until the next day for their turn, although at that time there were allegedly *two* gassing bunkers in operation, each with several chambers, so plenty of capacity and no need to wait.
– Langfus uses the term "bunker" for this makeshift gassing facility outside the Birkenau Camp. However, that term has not been used by any wartime source or witness, and was invented only toward the end of the war, meaning that this text was probably written long after the Auschwitz Camp was occupied by the Soviets (see Mattogno 2016f).
– Langfus's ghost writer has the victims thrown by some inmates onto a gigantic blazing pit fire – who would have gotten burned to a crisp themselves, had they dared approach it. Furthermore, Langfus talks only about one pit, when in fact there were many, if we were to believe other witnesses and the current orthodox narrative.
– Finally, the ghost writer claims that all that was left of the entire transport after this conflagration had died down was "a small pile of burnt bone" that was simply "thrown aside," although burning, say, a thousand people would have left a veritable mountain of human and wood ashes, including many partially burned body parts and charcoaled wood pieces, probably some 10 cubic meters in all.

(For details, see Mattogno 2021, pp. 259-261; see also the entry on Salmen Lewental.)

LAPTOS, LEO

Leo Laptos was an Auschwitz inmate, who worked at Birkenau as a pharmacist. After his transfer to the Dutch camp of Vught, he reported that at Auschwitz people were killed in gas chambers equipped with showerheads emitting gas rather than water. However, the product allegedly used at Auschwitz, Zyklon B, contains liquid hydrogen cyanide absorbed on gypsum pellets. The liquid poison evaporates slowly, and the developing gas is not under pressure, hence cannot be ducted through pipework. Laptos also claimed that, after the murder, the gas-chamber floors were allegedly tipped up, making the victims fall onto a conveyor belt, which transported them to the crematorium. No tipping-floor facility or conveyor-belt system ever existed at Auschwitz. (See Mattogno 2021, p. 295.)

LARSON, CHARLES

Charles P. Larson was a U.S. forensic pathologist, among other things working for the U.S. Army's Judge Advocate General during and after World War II. After the war, Larson was put in charge of determining the reasons for the mass deaths occurring in German wartime camps. Larson performed autopsies on hundreds of victims in some twenty former concentration camps. He concluded that they had died from famine and disease, largely typhus, and that there was no evidence for any systematic, mass cyanide gassing (McCallum 1979).

In 1980, he stated during a newspaper interview which bore the telling title "Concentration Camp Conditions Killed Most Inmates, Doctor Says," (Floerchinger 1980; reprinted in Kollerstrom 2023, p. 47):

> "What we've heard is that six million Jews were exterminated. Part of that is a hoax. [...There] never was a case of poison gas uncovered."

Latvia → Baltic Countries
Lauseto → DDT

LEA, DAVID

David Lea was a Greek Jew deported to Auschwitz on 9 May 1943, where he claims to have been assigned to the *Sonderkommando*, but on 6 September 1943, he was transferred away from Auschwitz. When he was interviewed in Paris in August 1946, he made disconnected and at times contradictory statements in words that are difficult to comprehend. Where his statements make sense, they frequently contain propaganda clichés, at times about events that supposedly happened when he wasn't even in the Auschwitz Camp anymore.

When his statement was published in 2016, the editor tried to excuse all this with language barriers between Lea and his interpreter, but also by claiming that Lea must have mixed up his own memory with tales he had heard from others he had been in touch with while residing at the displaced-persons camps near Paris. While it is possible that he declared as his own knowledge what he knew only from hearsay, it is unlikely that he could not distinguish hearsay from his own experiences so shortly after the war. On the other hand, some of his statements leave the distinct impression that he was simply demented rather than confused, which, using Occam's Razor, seems to be the simplest and thus most likely explanation for his bizarre ramblings. (For more details, see Mattogno 2022e, pp. 132-142.)

legislation, against Holocaust skepticism → Censorship
Lemberg → Lviv

LENGYEL, OLGA

Olga Lengyel

Olga Lengyel (19 Oct. 1908 – 15 April 2001) was a Hungarian Jewess deported to Auschwitz in the spring of 1944. After the war, she wrote a book which appeared in an English translation in 1947 with the title *Five Chimneys* or *I Survived Hitler's Ovens*, depending on the edition. In it, she claimed regarding the alleged extermination facilities and their activities, among other things:

– Before entering the gas chambers, the victims were given towels and soap (Lengyel, p. 68). This most certainly would never have happened, considering the mess it would have created and the effort necessary to retrieve and clean these items afterwards. In addition, no one takes towels into a shower.
– A *cylinder* of Zyklon B was released through a roof whole closed with a glass pane (*ibid.*, p. 69). However, the current orthodox narrative has it that the content of a *can* of Zyklon B was poured into some Zyklon-B introduction device closed with a wooden or concrete lid.
– Babies were put into the furnaces first, "as kindling" (*ibid.*, p. 70), as if human bodies were fuel capable of cremating one another. However, the tale of self-immolating bodies is a mere myth.
– Human fat extracted during cremation was gathered in immense casks, making her suspect that this is the reason the camp's soap smelled peculiar (*ibid.*). However, fat catches fire and burns as soon as it gets in contact with fire or embers, so no fat can be extracted from a corpse on a pyre or inside a cremation furnace.

- Each of the four Birkenau crematoria had one gas chamber – although the orthodoxy insists that two of the four had two or even three such facilities (Crematoria IV and V).
- Each crematorium had one chimney – although Crematoria IV and V had two chimneys each.
- Each crematorium had "nine fires" – meaning furnaces. This number was evidently lifted from the War Refugee Board Report. In fact, Crematoria II and III had five triple-muffle furnaces, while Crematoria IV and V had one 8-muffle furnace.
- There were altogether 120 "openings" (muffles) – although there were actually (twice 5×3 and twice 8 =) 46 muffles.
- Three corpses fit into each muffle – while they were designed only for one, and could at best accommodate two, but without gaining any advantage in speed.
- 720 corpses could be cremated within an hour – while the cremation of a single corpse lasted actually an hour, hence a maximum of 46 corpses per hour could be cremated by all facilities.
- The "death pits" could destroy 8,000 bodies a day – although air photos clearly prove that those pits never existed.

From this it is clear that Lengyel took a little information from the War Refugee Board Report, but then freely invented and further inflated the cremation capacity to preposterous dimensions. From the flawed way she described the crematoria, it is clear that she had neither first-hand knowledge nor reliable hearsay information.

With regard to the number of victims, Lengyel's figures are identical to those mentioned in a report allegedly written by an unnamed Jew deported from France (possibly Maurice Lequeux, who was with her in Lublin in early 1945), so either Lengyel copied it from there, or vice versa: the French Jew copied her figures. Either way, the numbers mentioned are obviously mendacious: 1,314,000 Jews just for the period from May 1944 to late July 1944, more than the orthodoxy currently claims for the entire existence of the camp.

In her book, Lengyel was simply incorporating the usual clichés, rumors and atrocity lies that filled survivor chatter, show-trial frenzies and sensationalistic media reports of the time, spicing it up with her own inventions, exaggerations and lies.

(For details, see Mattogno 2021, pp. 385-387; Langer 2021, pp. 169-195.)

LEQUEUX, MAURICE

In early 1945, when impressions were still fresh of the alleged atrocities uncovered by the Soviets after they had occupied first the Majdanek Camp in August 1944 and then the Auschwitz Camp in January 1945, Paddy Costello, an official at the embassy of New Zealand in Moscow, was at Lublin and visited the Majdanek Camp. He was evidently invited by the Soviets to become a witness of the alleged German atrocities. In Lublin, this official met a certain Maurice Lequeux and Olga Lengyel, who both claimed to have been interned at Auschwitz in 1944. A while later, on 4 May 1945, Costello wrote a report on both the Majdanek and the Auschwitz Camps. For the latter, he relied mostly on the tales told by Lequeux, which were allegedly confirmed by Mrs. Lengyel.

Since this report is from hearsay, it will not be analyzed here in detail, as inaccuracies and errors may be the New Zealand official's fault. A similar report, this time allegedly directly from a certain "Lequeu" (without the ending 'x'), was included in a 1946 French book edited by Eugéne Aroneanu, which contains many outrageous claims about Auschwitz. This French report was later translated to English, and received a document number during the U.S.-conducted Nuremberg Military Tribunals (NO-1960). This document claims that the author had been deported from Compiègne to Auschwitz, but the lists of all transports from Compiègne to Auschwitz, which have survived the war, do not contain a Lequeu or Lequeux. Both the New Zealand and the Lequeu report have distinct features making it likely that they stem from the same person, indeed, whoever that was.

Interestingly, the report by the New-Zealand official contains monthly victim numbers for the Auschwitz Camp for the months from May to July 1944, which are identical with those published by Olga Lengyel, totaling 1,314,000 murdered Jews. This is a prime example of the "convergence of evidence," here identical but false claims by evidently not independent witnesses. The total death toll of the Auschwitz Camp according to Lequeux (as reported in that New Zealand report) was allegedly six million, rather than the still-exaggerated total of around one million, as currently claimed by the orthodoxy.

While the New Zealand official might have misunderstood certain things and reported others inaccurately, one would think that he did not invent the following preposterous claim allegedly uttered by Lequeux:

"Lequeux saw one parade of 2,000 women stark naked marching 'to the gas' with the German band at their head playing tangos and fox-trots."

The report ends with the following remark:

"The above sounds like the invention of an insane mind. [Who could disagree? But…] *I am convinced that Captain Lequeux was telling the truth* [Which underscores once more that at war's end almost the entire world was in an insane anti-German hysteria]. *Captain Lequeux was anxious to return to Paris to deliver a full report on this subject."*

Turning to this "full report," or rather its English translation (NO-1960), we can see from it that the author was familiar with some internal features of the Birkenau Crematoria II and III, but that his inclination to tell the truth was highly compromised. He claimed:

– Crematoria II and III had two gas chambers with a capacity of 1,500 to 1,600 victims each, and they were called "Bunker." Although there were two large basement morgues in these facilities, the orthodoxy insists that one was used for undressing, not gassings. The term "Bunker," is said to have referred to makeshift homicidal gassing facilities outside the Birkenau Camp, not to the basement morgues.
– Before the gassing commenced, some 90% of the victims had already suffocated due to the extreme packing density. This is a unique claim.
– A gassing lasted only 5 minutes, after which glass openings in the ceiling and the doors were opened. However, no glass opening in the ceiling existed, and any homicidal gassing using highly toxic gases would have required an extended ventilation time before any doors would have been opened.
– The dead victims kept standing upright on their feet. People dying slump down, no matter how tightly they are packed.
– The cremation of a batch of corpses – 36 in six furnaces (six bodies per muffle (?) in a muffle build for just one!) – took just 20 minutes. The Birkenau furnaces were designed to cremate a *single* body within *one* hour.
– Zyklon B was filled in through "a [=one] square, grated column of 30 cm on each side with a glass opening on the top," instead of the four wire-mesh introduction columns with wooden or concrete lids currently claimed by the orthodoxy.
– Once the furnaces were heated up, the bodies burned all by themselves without the need of fuel. However, self-immolating bodies simply do not exist. The furnace type used inside Crematoria II and III needed at least some 20 kg of coke for a normal (unemaciated) corpse under ideal conditions. However, the inmate force-laborers did not operate the furnaces under ideal conditions, and at Auschwitz, most corpses were underweight or even emaciated, with little or no body fat to fuel any fire.
– The total daily cremation capacity of all crematoria was 10,400 on average, whereas the *maximum theoretical* (not practical average) capacity for a 20-hour workday (4 hours daily for letting the hearths burn out, clean and reheat them) was (46 muffles × 20 hours × one corpse per hour =) 920 bodies. Hence Lequeux exaggerated the theoretical maximum by more than a factor of ten.
– 12,000 to 14,000 bodies were burned daily on huge pyres, especially during the Hungarian transports from mid-May through July 1944. Air photos prove, however, that no large-scale pyres at all burned during that time.

As the New Zealand official correctly put it:

"The above sounds like the invention of an insane mind."

(For more details, see Mattogno 2021, pp. 369-372, 382-385.)

LERNER, LEON

Leon (Jehuda) Lerner was deported to Sobibór in the summer of 1943. In his deposition recorded in Haifa on 16 December 1959, he claimed that the Sobibór gas chambers operated by an SS man throwing in Zyklon-B gas. This claim is rejected as false by the orthodoxy, who insists on engine-exhaust gasses as the toxic agent used to kill at Sobibór.

(See the entry on Sobibór for more details, as well as Mattogno 2021e, p. 91.)

LESKY, SIMCHA

In 1946, the "eyewitness account" of Simcha Lesky about his brief stay at the Treblinka Camp was published in a Jewish historical journal. Lesky arrived there at the end of July 1942, and managed to escape just four days later. According to this, inmates in a hidden part of the camp were killed with machine guns during the night. The next day, the victims were put on a pyre and burned.

However, no sane person would kill people at night with machine guns. Imagine the panic among the deportees, how they start running chaotically, and how stray bullets are flying everywhere. And all this in the darkness of the night, when aiming was all but impossible.

The cremation of corpses in late July-early August 1942 is also completely anachronistic, as the orthodox narrative insists that cremations started only in March of 1943. (See Mattogno 2021e, pp. 185f.)

LETHAL INJECTIONS

The chemical phenol has been used in the past as a wound and instrument disinfectant in hospitals all over the world. It was also used to this end by the inmate infirmary of the Auschwitz Camp. The camp's documentation contains several orders of phenol by employees of the infirmary (see Mattogno 2023, Part 1, pp. 140, 194, 249, 264, 282).

A book called Morgue Registry was kept at the morgue of the Auschwitz Main Camp. It contained the data of deceased inmates, whose corpses were stored in that morgue temporarily prior to burial or cremation. There is nothing suspicious about this document. However, inmates active for the camp's underground resistance made a copy of this Morgue Registry. Behind some of its entries, they added the term "szpila" in their copy, which is a misspelled version of the Polish word "szpilka," which means pin or awl (as in a sewing needle).

During the Frankfurt Auschwitz show trial, Danuta Czech, a Polish historian employed by the Auschwitz Museum to chronicle the history of the Auschwitz Camp, testified wrongly that these words can be found in the original of the document up to mid-December 1942. She furthermore claimed that these words referred to an injection syringe, although the Polish word for the needle of a syringe is "igła."

Danuta Czech's perjury served to lend credence to many mendacious testimonies by former Auschwitz inmates who had claimed that seriously sick inmates, who had been admitted to the camp's infirmary but had little prospect of a speedy recovery, were picked out by camp doctors during so-called selections, and then murdered with an injection of phenol into the heart.

Danuta Czech further manipulated the record by claiming that even after mid-December 1942, when no "szpila" was added anymore by some inmate resister, killings by injections occurred. She based this claim on the simple fact that some inmates had died in Block 28, which was the inmate infirmary's central ward and outpatient clinic. However, the word "szpila" added by the inmate resisters was added only to two entries of inmates who had died there, while 58 were added to the names of inmates who had died in other blocks. Hence, there is no meaning and pattern behind those entries of this non-word that doesn't even mean syringe. Still, Czech decided that, from mid-December 1942 onward, any inmate who died at Block 28 was a victim of phenol injections.

However, the vast documentation about the healthcare at the Auschwitz Camp clearly shows that inmates, no matter how sick, were cared for with great effort, including complicated surgeries and long-term care for terminally ill patients. Furthermore, the camp's frequent statistics of the deployment status also show that inmates unfit for work were not killed at all.

The primary victim of this grand lie was SS *Oberscharführer* Josef Klehr, a medical orderly at Auschwitz and later the head of the disinfestation unit. Klehr was framed for this invented crime by witnesses such as Withold Pilecki. However, a detailed analysis of his testimony reveals Pilecki as an untrustworthy liar.

(See also the entry on healthcare, as well as for more details Mattogno 2016a, esp. pp. 97-102; 2022b, esp. pp. 40-45.)

LETTICH, ANDRÉ

André Lettich was a French Jew deported to Auschwitz on 20 July 1942. Between September 1942 and March 1943, he claims to have served as an inmate physician for members of the so-called *Sonderkommando*. In 1946, he wrote a memorandum, in which he claimed the following about the alleged exterminations at Auschwitz, among other things:

– He was unaware of the term "bunker" allegedly used for the makeshift gassing facilities outside the Birkenau Camp, mentioned only one of the two which the orthodoxy claims existed, called it simply a "cottage," and placed it two kilometers away from the camp, although both are said to have been only a few hundred meters away from the camp's perimeter fences. Lettich also placed the related undressing hut a ludicrous 500 meters away from the "cottage."

– Inmates were handed towels and soap before entering the chamber, something that most certainly would never have happened, considering the mess it would have created and the effort necessary to retrieve and clean these items afterwards.

– Showerheads not connected to pipes were at the

cottage's ceiling, which is a feature claimed, according to the current narrative, for the underground morgues aka gas chambers of Crematoria II and III, but not for the bunkers. (And also for early gas-chamber claims, according to which gas actually came out of those showerheads…)

– In addition to a sky light for dumping in Zyklon B, the "cottage" had windows that were opened for ventilation, which runs contrary to the current orthodox narrative, according to which those facilities had only hatches with shutters in the wall to supply the poison.
– Some elements Lettich plagiarized from the War Refugee Board Report, such as the claim that, after the gas-chamber doors had been closed, there was a waiting period to make sure the temperature in the chamber was high enough.
– The (wrong) number of muffles in two of the crematoria was also lifted from the War Refugee Board Report, (nine, instead of 15), while Lettich claims six muffles for the other two crematoria (instead of the correct number: eight).
– He also repeats the myth spread by the War Refugee Board Report of a commission of German high officials coming to Auschwitz from Berlin in early 1943 on occasion of the first crematorium's inauguration, monitoring the first gassing there through "little skylights" which did not exist in these facilities, and neither does any trace of such an absurd commission.
– Each muffle allegedly could accommodate six bodies at a time, which burned in fifty minutes, resulting in 180 bodies cremated in all crematoria within an hour. In fact, those muffles were designed only for one corpse, to burn within an hour, resulting in a maximum of 46 corpses per hour.
– A fable he plagiarized probably from Miklós Nyiszli, is his claim that powerful blowers fanned the furnaces' flames, when in fact these furnaces had only small blowers to duct combustion air through openings in the muffle vault (this cold air actually cooled the muffle and did not fan any flames).
– Lettich repeats Miklós Nyiszli's legend that the members of the *Sonderkommando* were killed every 3-4 months, yet the many survivors claiming to have been part of that unit prove otherwise. He even contradicts his own claim by stating that he had no difficulty getting transferred to the Gypsy Camp in March 1943.
– To crown this insipid regurgitation of wartime atrocity propaganda, he claims that the total death toll of the Auschwitz Camp was 4 or 5 million, "without exaggeration," although he was in no position to know.

As is evident, even after "almost three years" in Auschwitz (although only six months as a *Sonderkommando* physician), Lettich evidently knew close to nothing of the crematoria's internal structure and alleged gas chambers, and he copied lavishly from what he had heard and read elsewhere. Lettich himself called his testimony "the most-precise" – which is a laughable claim, in light of the facts..

(For details, see Mattogno 2016f, pp. 100-103; 2021, pp. 317-321.)

LEVI, PRIMO

Primo Levi (31 July 1919 – 11 April 1987) was an Italian Jewish chemist who, due to his activities as a partisan fighter, was deported to Auschwitz, where he ended up in the Monowitz labor camp, deployed at the BUNA factories. Under international law, partisan fighters could be executed, and as a Jew, Levi should have been in

Primo Levi

double jeopardy, but the Germans evidently had no intention of killing him.

Shortly after the war, in 1946, he co-authored a report on healthcare at the Monowitz Camp, which paints a rather favorable picture of the situation. Both this report and his later books certainly contain the usual references to exterminations and gas chambers, but Levi never claimed to have witnessed any of it personally. Instead, he relied on the accounts of others and on what he learned elsewhere. In fact, the reference to mass gassings in his 1946 report neatly repeats all the mistakes made by Vrba and Wetzler in their 1944 report that was included in the widely disseminated U.S. War Refugee Board Report, meaning that Levi had copied it from there. (See Mattogno 2021, pp. 242f.)

In a 1976 appendix to his book *Se questo è un uomo* (*If This Is a Man*), Primo Levi clarified this (Levi 1984, p. 233):

"I have not quoted the figures of the Auschwitz massacre, nor have I described the details of the gas chambers and crematoria. In fact, I did not know these things when I was in the camp, and I only learned about them later, when the whole world learned about them."

In his book *Survival in Auschwitz*, the last entry of 17 January 1945 reveals what Levi really felt when he was in Auschwitz. At that time, he was at the inmate infirmary, too sick to be evacuated with the other inmates. Yet he describes how he would have liked to follow common instincts and would have joined the other inmates who fled with the SS, had he not been so sick (Levi 1986, p. 154):

"It was not a question of reasoning: I would probably also have followed the instinct of the flock if I had not felt so weak: fear is supremely contagious, and its immediate reaction is to make one try to run away."

Note: Levi writes here about running away with the Germans from the Red Army approaching Auschwitz. Had he believed in the extermination stories, he would have welcomed anyone liberating him from this veritable hell, hence would have been happy to stay and wait. Therefore, Levi did not fear his evidently relatively harmless German prison guards, but rather the Soviet "liberators." After all, the Red Army never liberated anyone.

LÉVY, ROBERT

Robert Lévy was a French-Jewish professor of medicine from Strasbourg deported to Auschwitz in September 1942, where he was deployed as a surgeon working at the Auschwitz inmate hospital. In a 1947 article, he reported about his experiences in Auschwitz. He claimed no direct knowledge of the alleged extermination procedure, but summarized what he had heard elsewhere. In this article, he regurgitated a string of clichés, among them the legend – refuted by air photos – that gigantic open-air incinerations took place in the summer of 1944. He moreover invented a new extermination method by stating that the victims "went into an immense freight elevator, where they were gassed; thanks to this system, the bodies were transported to the furnaces without wasting time." It is needless to say that no such thing ever existed. This only proves that, no matter your academic title, you should limit yourself to writing about things you are well-familiar with, or else you might look like a fool and do your own cause a huge disservice by discrediting witness statements in general.

(Mattogno 2021, p. 395.)

LEWENTAL, SALMEN

The story of Salmen Lewental resembles that of the manuscript allegedly written by a certain Leib Langfus. In this case, two containers were found in 1961 and 1962, respectively, both near the ruins of Crematorium III at Birkenau. The first find contained a diary of an unknown author kept in the Lodz Ghetto, plus six pages of comments on it by Lewental, who claims to have found the diary in Auschwitz. However, Lewental's comments say nothing about any ongoing extermination activity, which is peculiar, especially in light of the second find, which presumably reports in detail about such activities. This consists of two set of manuscript from different authors, one by Lewental, the other one from an unknown author.

Since the manuscript of this second find was badly damaged, deciphering it was partly impossible, and partly required a lot of interpolations to bridge illegible passages. As a result, different translators have prepared divergent translations and interpretations, which drastically reduces the source value of these texts. From what is claimed about the texts' contents, we can glean the following oddities:

– His transport of 2,300 Jews arrived at Auschwitz on 10 or 12 December 1942 with only 500 of them deemed fit for admission, while the rest was allegedly killed in a gas chamber. The train of this transport is said to have come via the rail line passing by Małkinia, which is right next to the Treblinka Camp. If the majority of these Jews indeed had been slated for extermination, then why were they hauled all across Poland, if most of them could have been dispatched right there at Treblinka?

– Although the passage describing a gassing scene is severely damaged, and only parts of it are barely legible, the scant information given of the makeshift gassing facility outside the Birkenau Camp resembles Langfus's description. Like Langfus, the building described had only one gas-introduction opening, hence only one chamber, whereas the orthodoxy insists that the facilities in question each had several gas chambers and gas-introduction ports.

– Since not all victims could fit into the gas chamber, just as Langfus had claimed, some allegedly had to wait in a hut, although at that time there were allegedly *two* gassing bunkers in operation,

- each with several chambers, so plenty of capacity and no need to wait.
- Lewental, like Langfus, claims that there was only one pit for the cremation of the victims' bodies, when in fact there were many, if we take other witnesses' claims and the current orthodox narrative for granted. Furthermore, the pit was presumably 800 meters away from the gas chambers, which is highly unlikely.
- The gassing procedure allegedly lasted only "a few minutes." Considering that there was no way of forcing the swift evaporation and dissipation of the gas in these makeshift facilities, this is highly improbable.
- Lewental then explains that he was admitted to the camp and deployed with various labor units, even one at the Buna-Monowitz Camp, and that he was transferred to the Birkenau *Sonderkommando* only on 25 January 1943. If that is so, how could he have become an eyewitness to the above-reviewed gassing of the 1,800 non-admitted Jews of his transport on 12 December 1942? The author must have made it up.
- Lewental, like Langfus, uses the term "bunker" for the makeshift gassing facility outside the Birkenau Camp. However, that term has not been used by any wartime source or witness, and was invented only toward the end of the war, meaning that this text was probably written long after the Auschwitz Camp was occupied by the Soviets (see Mattogno 2016f).
- A separate essay contains a dramatized description of the gassing of 3,000 registered female inmates in Crematorium III "at the beginning of 1944," by throwing Zyklon B through "small upper doors." There is no trace of such an event, and not even orthodox historians claim otherwise.
- Lewental claims that "we shall then have to burn a million of Hungarian Jews" and later that "half a million Hungarian Jews were burned in the meantime," which are not only more than were ever deported, but moreover air photos refute the claim that massive open-air incinerations took place during the deportation of Jews from Hungary to Auschwitz.
- Lewental claims that the *Sonderkommando* members informed the Auschwitz resistance in detail of what was going on, but complains that they were not credited for having helped the resistance. This reveals this manuscript as a postwar fraud, because the resistance, throughout the war, disseminated the most-outrageous false and conflicting claims about Auschwitz, clearly showing that either they were *not* informed of what later was established to have happened (hence Lewental lied), or they *ignored* Lewental's "facts," and replaced them with lies (which is inconceivable), or nothing sinister was going on, and Lewental and his *Sonderkommando* friends reported nothing that could serve as atrocity propaganda. While we have a choice here, we have none for the next conundrum: How could Lewental know that he and his fellow *Sonderkommando* members were not credited for their cooperation to reveal the "truth"? That was only possible by reading what eventually reached the Polish government in exile in London, and what of it they published/archived. Lewental could have verified this only after his release/liberation, that is to say, after the war.

Just as the manuscript assigned to Langfus, this set of manuscripts evidently is also a postwar forgery. (For details, see Mattogno 2021, pp. 119-217, 276-283.)

LEWIŃSKA, PELAGIA

Pelagia Lewińska was a Polish Jewess admitted to the Auschwitz Camp on 28 January 1943. After the war, she wrote a short book that was published in Polish and French in 1945. Here are some revealing claims made by Lewińska about the claimed exterminations:

- In 1944, the number of crematoria at Auschwitz was increased to 14. In fact, the number planned in 1942 and built in 1942/43 – four – was not increased at all.
- Deep pits were dug for burning alive all children under the age of 14 to save "gas." The mainstream narrative has it that pits were dug because either there were no crematories in Birkenau (early 1942 to early 1943) or because their capacity was insufficient (May to July 1944). Shortage of gas was never said to have been a problem. However, air photos prove that at least in 1944, these pits did not exist.
- For months on end, flames shot uninterruptedly from the crematorium chimneys. However, flames cannot shoot out of crematorium chimneys.
- Dense clouds of smoke covered Auschwitz and the surrounding area. Air photos of the area show this to be untrue.

– Inside the homicidal gas chambers, toxic gas came out of the showers, although this was technically impossible when using Zyklon B.

It is evident that this witness's narrative is based exclusively on false rumors and clichés, not on her own recollection. (For details, see Mattogno 2021, pp. 388f.)

LICHTENSTEIN, MORDECAI

Mordecai Lichtenstein wrote a report in 1945 in London about his alleged experiences at the Auschwitz Camp, where we read, among other things:

- Sometimes those entering the gas chamber were given a towel and a piece of soap. This most certainly would never have happened, considering the mess it would have created and the effort necessary to retrieve and clean these items afterwards.
- First, the air was pumped out with electric motors, then Zyklon B was thrown in through one hatch in the ceiling. The claim that a vacuum was created first before adding toxic gas is technical and toxicological nonsense. Creating a vacuum in a brick-and-mortar building is technically impossible (the external pressure would crush the walls), hence most certainly was not done. Vacuum claims are frequently found in statements about the Treblinka Camp. There were supposedly four Zyklon-B introduction columns going through the ceiling, not one hatch.
- The corpses were taken to the crematoria on little carts. None of the crematoria had tracks with carts. This tale may have been plagiarized from the War Refugee Board Report, which spread the same untruth – a convergence of lies.
- Cremation was carried out "by an electrical current of 6,000 volts." In fact, all cremation furnaces in German wartime camps were heated with coke.
- If the SS wanted to hurry things up, the victims were killed in their clothes. However, after the gassing, the *Sonderkommando* members supposedly had to undress corpses, which most certainly took much longer than had the living inmates undressed themselves beforehand.
- This witness's "very careful estimate" of the Auschwitz death toll amounts to 3 million Jews plus one million non-Jews, which happens to coincide with the Soviet propaganda lie of four million Auschwitz victims, a convergence of lies.

From this hodgepodge of untrue statements, it is clear that the witness had no first-hand knowledge about any of it, but relied on false rumors and clichés. And yet, the Jewish Central Information Service in London, which collected this statement, stated this about the report:

"We have carefully checked our informant's identity and reliability, and are certain that his report is true in every detail."

(For details, see Mattogno 2021, pp. 387f.)

LICHTMANN, ICEK

Icek (or Itzhak) Lichtmann was an inmate of the Sobibór Camp. In a deposition of 18 December 1945, he located the (meaning one) gas chamber at a distance of 200 m away from the camp. After the murder, the floors opened, and the bodies were discharged into carts below, which brought them to mass graves. In total, about a million people were allegedly killed at Sobibór.

His claims are rejected as false by the orthodoxy, who insists on several gas chambers in a building *inside* the camp, which did not have collapsible floors with carts underneath. The corpses were instead taken out of the chamber manually, sideways through a normal door. Furthermore, only about a quarter million victims are said to have died in that camp.

(See the entry on Sobibór for more details, as well as Mattogno 2021e, p. 78.)

LIEBEHENSCHEL, ARTHUR

Arthur Liebehenschel (25 Nov. 1901 – 24 Jan. 1948), SS *Obersturmbannführer*, served initially at the Lichtenburg Camp, but since 1937 at the Inspectorate of Concentration Camps, at the SS headquarters in Oranienburg. He became commandant of the Auschwitz Main Camp on 11 November 1943. Hermann Langbein describes him as a relatively humane commandant who abolished numerous draconian measures, such as arbitrary shootings (Langbein 1995, pp. 59-61), if those ever happened. In preparation for the arrival of the Jews from Hungary, Liebehenschel was replaced by Richard Baer, and was transferred to serve as

Arthur Liebehenschel

commandant of the Majdanek Camp.

After the war, he was extradited to Poland, where he was tried during the Warsaw show trial against former members of the Auschwitz Camp's staff. He was sentenced to death, and eventually executed.

Since the three camps Auschwitz I (Main Camp), II (Birkenau) and III (Monowitz and other satellite camps) were organizationally independent, and because no extermination activities are claimed for the Main Camp for the few months Liebehenschel was in charge of it, he reasonably could not have been accused of having contributed in any way to any atrocities. Of course, that didn't stop the Polish judiciary from framing him anyway. His undoing was the fact that, during his time at the Inspectorate in Berlin, he had signed several permissions for the Auschwitz Camp to pick up Zyklon B at the manufacturer for the sake of combating lice, which to this day is misrepresented as orders to fetch poison gas to mass murder Jews. (See Mattogno 2016d, pp. 42-47, 58, 77f., 135, 145; 2019, pp. 193-197.)

LIMOUSIN, HENRI

Henri Limousin was a professor of medicine from Clermont-Ferrand (France), who was incarcerated at the Auschwitz Camp until it was conquered by the Soviets on 27 January 1945. Together with three other European professors, and coached by their Soviet captors, he signed an appeal on 4 March 1945 "To the International Public," which contained many untrue propaganda clichés about Auschwitz. See the entry on Berthold Epstein for details.

Lithuania → Baltic Countries

LITWINSKA, SOFIA

Sofia Litwinska was a Polish Jewess incarcerated at Auschwitz from mid-1942 until November 1944. She was later transferred to Bergen-Belsen. She signed an affidavit on 24 May 1945 and took the stand on 24 September 1945. Her noteworthy claims are:
– Together with some 300 other inmates, she was taken by "'Tipper-type' lorries [meaning a dump truck] to the gas chamber chute," where they were dumped down the chute straight into the "gas chamber." A corpse chute between two flights of stairs did exist in Crematoria II and III at Birkenau, connecting the ground floor to the basement; but trucks could not get access to the door leading into this staircase containing that chute, and if they had been able to drive up to it (across an extended lawn), tipping the truck's load bed would have made the victims fall into the entry area at best, but not down the chute. Finally, the chute ended in a hallway, not the morgue that supposedly served as a gas chamber. (See the similar testimony by Michał Kula.)
– The "gas chamber" had showers, towels, soap, mirrors on the wall, and benches for comfort's sake, as well as small windows near the ceiling. Since they had been dumped straight into the gas chamber, issuing towels and soap would have been pointless. The mirrors are a unique statement of this witness, not to be found elsewhere, and not in need of further comment. Furthermore, if we follow the orthodox narrative, benches are said to have been located in a separate undressing room, but certainly not in the "gas chamber." Finally, there were allegedly four Zyklon-B introduction columns in those basement rooms, but certainly no windows near the ceiling.
– She saw "fumes coming in through a [non-existing] window," although hydrogen-cyanide gas is invisible.
– The toxic gas allegedly used caused eyes to water, coughing, pain in chest and throat, and foaming around the mouth. While the latter can occur when ingesting cyanide salts orally, poisoning with hydrogen-cyanide gas (the active ingredient in allegedly used Zyklon B) would not have caused any watering eyes or coughing.
– After two minutes, an SS man wearing a respirator opened the gas-chamber door and called out Litwinska's name. For this to have happened, everyone in the room had to be absolutely silent – no coughing – so she could hear her name called *through a respirator*. She raised her arm, and then some strong man, unaffected by the gas and totally selfless, picked her up and threw her out of the room. For this to have happened, the other inmates respectfully must have made room, so her hero could walk with her in his arms to the door, and then they had to allow the SS man to shut the door again, so they all could carry on with their important task of dying in the name of future atrocity propaganda.
– She was then taken on a motorcycle, wrapped up in blankets, to the hospital to recover, which took six weeks of receiving special treatment from… Dr. Mengele. Of course!

The audacious density of preposterous lies in this testimony leaves the critical observer speechless. (For details, see Mattogno 2021, pp. 345-348.)

LODZ GHETTO

The Lodz Ghetto was the second largest Jewish ghetto in Poland during World War Two, after the Warsaw Ghetto. It was established in February 1940. By the end of that year, it already had 160,000 inhabitants. Due to the enormous quantities of commodities of all kinds produced there, especially textiles, the ghetto soon became a highly important production center for the German economy.

The percentage of Jews working was always very high: for example, in the period from 6 to 12 October 1942, a total of 74,735 Jews were employed, which is almost 84% of a total population of approximately 89,200. Even children from the age of 9 were used for light work. Because of its great economic importance, the ghetto remained in existence until 1944. It was evacuated only in the summer of that year in the face of the threatening Soviet advance.

The last known statistics on the population of the ghetto date from 1 March 1944, when a total of 77,679 Jews lived there, of whom over 5,500 were 14 years old and younger, and more than 1,000 Jews were over 60 years old.

According to the orthodox version of history, the Jews of this ghetto were all murdered between the end of June and mid-September 1944. About 7,000 are said to have been gassed in gas vans at the Chełmno Camp, the rest in the Auschwitz Camp. This claim rests mainly on the implausible testimony of the untrustworthy witness Mieczysław Żurawski. (See the entry on him and on the Chełmno Camp.)

Although there are ten transport lists of a total of 7,170 Jews from the Lodz Ghetto in the period from 23 June to 14 July 1944, the documents indicate that these Jews were transferred "for work." The documents do not state where they were sent. The age of the deportees indicated on the lists shows that almost all of them were of working age. Of the young children and adults over 60 living in the ghetto at that time, hardly anyone was transferred. The few young children who were transferred were children of mothers who were also transferred. The intention was evidently not to break up families. If the purpose of the transfer had been to exterminate Jews who were unfit for work, the thousands of very young and very old ghetto residents would have been the primary ones transferred.

There is therefore no evidence that any Jews of this ghetto were transferred to Chełmno. The evidence for Auschwitz is somewhat better, although no deportation lists appear to have survived. Here the assertions of various orthodox authors contradict each other as to the dates and extent of the deportations. The Polish Auschwitz historian Danuta Czech originally claimed that 15 transports of Jews from Lodz arrived at Auschwitz between 15 August and 18 September. Precisely 3,076 of them were registered and admitted to the camp. In each case she claims, without any proof, that there was an undetermined "remainder" of deportees unfit for work in these transports, who were gassed on arrival, namely a total of about 67,000.

The number of registered prisoners, including the assigned registration numbers, is derived from Auschwitz registration lists which were copied by prisoners and smuggled out of the camp. The number of deportees left as the alleged "remainder" is derived from the testimony of former Auschwitz inmate Miklós Nyiszli. He had claimed in his book that 95% of the 70,000 Jews deported from Lodz to Auschwitz were gassed on arrival, apparently because they were unfit for work.

If one considers that, when the Jews were deported from Lodz, almost all of them were assigned to work, meaning they were very much fit for work, one wonders how some 95% of ghetto dwellers fit for work could suddenly turn into 95% of deportees unfit for work. However, as one can see from the entry about Miklós Nyiszli, this proven impostor and serial liar lacks any credibility. Using him as a source undermines Czech's own credibility.

In later years, it turned out that many Jews sent from the Lodz Ghetto were sent to other camps, above all the Stutthof Camp, to which 11,464 Jews were transferred and registered, including many children under the age of 14. In addition, it turned out that the Auschwitz registration numbers assigned to Jews from the Lodz Ghetto since 7 September had been issued to those who had arrived at Auschwitz earlier. They had spent some time there in the Birkenau transit camp rather than being instantly admitted and registered. It may be assumed that many more Jews from Lodz passed through this transit camp, but were ultimately sent to other camps without getting registered in Auschwitz.

A letter from Georg Lörner, the head of the administration of the concentration camps in the Economic and Administrative Main Office (*Wirtschafts- und Verwaltungs-Hauptamt*), dated 15 August 1944, finally provides clarity. It states that 60,000 Jews were just in the process of getting transferred from Lodz to various concentration camps in Germany for labor deployment.

Camp	Peak Claimed Death Toll	Łukaszkiewicz's Death Toll	Today's Orthodox Death Toll	Probable Death Toll
Treblinka	3 million	800,000	~800,000	25,000?
Sobibór	2 million	250,000	170,000-250,000	10,000?
Majdanek	2 million	360,000	78,000	ca. 42,000
Stutthof	1.3 million	65,000	65,000	26,100

Since there was not enough prisoner clothing available for them, a special quota of spinning material was requested. Czech mentions that letter, but hides the passage on the Jews from Lodz. If a mass murder of these deportees fit for labor deployment had been planned, such a letter would never have been written.

(For more details, see Mattogno 2023a&c; on Czech's mispresentations, see Mattogno 2022b, pp. 236-238, 241-243, 246f., 257.)

LONDON CAGE

In 2005, the British government released several hitherto secret files from the immediate time after World War Two. In this context, several documents came to light revealing that a division of His Majesty's War Office operated secret interrogation centers all over the world. One of them was located in London itself and was nicknamed the "London Cage." The released documents show that this was a secret torture center where German prisoners were systematically tortured in order to extract confessions to be used either to blackmail other prisoners to similar confessions, or as evidence during upcoming trials in Germany against so-called war criminals.

After the German Wehrmacht had surrendered, German prisoners of war lost this status, and many were rebranded as "disarmed enemy forces," which did not enjoy the protection of the Geneva Convention, or so the Western Allies falsely claimed. In fact, when a war is over, PoWs are supposed to go home, not be stripped of all their rights, misused and tortured.

Many former staff members of former German wartime camps who fell into British hands suffered horrific tortures either in London or in any of the other British torture centers. One of the most infamous among them was the British torture center at Bad Nenndorf, some 25 km west of Hanover. (For more details, see the entries on torture, on Bad Nenndorf, and in general Cobain 2005a&b, 2013.)

Lublin → Majdanek

ŁUKASZKIEWICZ, ZDZISŁAW

Zdzisław Łukaszkiewicz was a Polish judge who, at the end of the Second World War, became a member of the Stalinist Main Commission for the Investigation of German Crimes in Poland. As such, he issued reports and wrote books on several of the German wartime camps in Poland, among them the Majdanek Camp (Graf/Mattogno 2012, pp. 80-89), the Stutthof Camp (Graf/Mattogno 2016, pp. 39f.), the Treblinka Camp (Mattogno/Graf 2023, esp. pp. 82-109) and the Sobibór Camp (Graf/Kues/Mattogno 2020, pp. 25f., 150).

Łukaszkiewicz was probably the most influential individual in that commission. When it comes to the orthodox narrative of extermination claims in German camps on Polish and East-German territory, his writings had one of the greatest impact. Within the framework of the commission he was working for, he interviewed many witnesses. Out of the often contradictory and preposterous claims, he artificially created a superficially consistent narrative by cherry-picking from each testimony what fit into the image he considered most convincing.

In the case of Sobibór Camp, he in fact discarded all witness testimony, and created a completely new narrative from scratch. He also completely sanitized the testimonial anarchy reigning among early Treblinka witnesses, by deciding to accept one witness's account (that of Jankiel Wiernik) and to discard almost all the rest.

Along the way, Łukaszkiewicz also trimmed down the outrageously inflated death-toll claims of the immediate postwar era to a level that seemed credible, at least to the uninitiated observer. Most of these figures, as well as the murder methods, have been accepted largely by mainstream historians to this day, with the exception of the Majdanek Camp, where further radical downward revisions have been made since. (See the table above.)

LUMBERJACKS

Several German wartime camps claimed to have been the site of mass murder, such as Auschwitz,

Majdanek and Stutthof, had coke-fueled cremation furnaces which steadily burned the remains of inmates who had died for whatever reason. However, several other camps which supposedly were pure extermination camps, such as Belzec, Sobibór and Treblinka, had no cremation facility at all. Furthermore, no cremation devices were at the disposal of the German *Einsatzgruppen* and other units who are said to have mass-murdered thousands of Jews in the temporarily German-occupied Soviet territories. Due to the lack of cremation options in these cases, the victims of German atrocities are said to have been initially buried.

However, when the tide of war changed, the German authorities allegedly decided to exhume and burn the victims in order to erase the traces of their crimes. This operation presumably bore the code name "*Aktion* 1005" (see the entry on this.) In order to burn these corpses with open-air incinerations on pyres, a certain amount of wood had to be available.

Most witnesses reporting about the alleged activities of exhuming and burning the victims buried in mass graves did not mention where the wood came from. They seem to have assumed that the wood was simply there. If witnesses gave a breakdown of how many inmates did which job, felling trees and chopping them up is usually not included. Very few inmates mentioned that some of their teammates were tasked with getting firewood, yet the number of inmates having done this is hugely inappropriate for the gigantic task they would have faced.

In the upper part, the following table gives an overview of data claimed by several witnesses regarding corpse-burning scenarios at various alleged crime scenes of the Holocaust. The lower part adds five crime scenes with data following the current orthodox narrative.

The second column lists the claimed number of bodies allegedly cremated on open-air pyres. The third column list the amount of freshly cut wood (in

Witness/Location	Bodies	Wood Needed [t]	Hectares[*]	Football Fields[*]	Days	Lumberjacks[†]
Gerhard Adametz/Babi Yar	100,000	25,000	56	125	35	1,134
Szymon Amiel/Białystok	42,800	10,700	24	53	57	298
Semen Berlyant/Babi Yar	70,000	17,500	39	87	35	800
A. Blyazer/Babi Yar	68,000	17,000	38	85		15, ca. 5 years
Isaak Brodsky/Babi Yar	70,000	17,500	39	87	35	800
David Budnik/Babi Yar	120,000	30,000	67	149	35	1,360
Heinrich Chamaides/Lviv	120,000	30,000	67	149	160	300
Momčilo Damjanović/Semlin	68,000	17,000	38	85	36	750
Vladimir Davydov/Babi Yar	70,000	17,500	39	87	35	800
Iosif Doliner/Babi Yar	100,000	25,000	56	125	35	1,134
Yuri Farber/Ponary	38,000	9,500	21	47	75	200
Szloma Gol/Ponary	80,000	20,000	44	100	180	176
Yakov Kaper/Babi Yar	120,000	30,000	67	149	35	1,360
Avraham Karasik/Białystok	22,000	5,500	12	27	57	153
Moische Korn/Lviv	120,000	30,000	67	149	160	300
Vladislav Kuklia/Babi Yar	100,000	25,000	56	125	35	1,134
David Manusevich/Lviv	200,000	50,000	111	249	160	500
Leonid Ostrovsky/Babi Yar	62,500	15,625	35	78	35	700
Stefan Pilunov/Mogilev	30,000	7,500	17	37	16	744
Yakov Steyuk/Babi Yar	50,000[‡]	12,500	28	62	35	567
Ziama Trubakov/Babi Yar	125,000	31,250	69	156	35	1,417
Leon Weliczker/Lviv	300,000	75,000	167	374	160	750
Matvey Zaydel/Ponary	80,000	20,000	44	100	150	211
Babi Yar	100,000	25,000	56	125	35	1,134
Belzec	434,500	108,625	241	541	120	1,437
Majdanek (Harvest Festival)	≥17,000	4,250	9	21	45	150
Sobibór	≥170,000	42,500	94	212	365	185
Treblinka	≥700,000	175,000	389	872	122	2,277

[*] On average, a 50-year-old spruce forest yields some 450 metric tons of wood per hectare (100 m × 100 m) or 201 tons per American-Football field. Fell all trees of such a forest of this size to obtain the required amount of wood.
[†] Number required for the time span claimed, which varies from case to case. Blyazer gave the number of lumberjacks in his team (15), who would have finished their work sometime in 1948.
[‡] In a later interview, Steyuk doubled the number of bodies burned. See the values listed for Adametz, Doliner, Kuklia.

metric tons) that would have been necessary to cremate these bodies, based on an average need of some 250 kg of fresh wood per body. The fourth column gives the surface area of an average 50-year-old spruce forest that would have had to be completely felled and chopped up in order to obtain the amount of wood required, based on an average yield of 450 metric tons of wood per hectare for such a forest, which equals some 201 metric tons of wood growing on an area the size of an American-Football field. The fifth column is intended to help the reader visualize the vast forest area needed.

The sixth column has the number of days which each open-air incineration event is said to have lasted. The last column lists the number of dedicated inmate lumberjacks, working seven days a week, who would have been required to fell and chop up that wood, assuming a daily performance of 0.63 metric tons of wood per inmate.

Note that the inmate team size supposedly involved in these exhumation and cremation activities of the upper part of this table rarely reached 100, and most if not all of them supposedly were (or would have been) busy opening mass graves, extracting bodies, building pyres, sifting through ashes in search of valuables and unburned remains – with handheld flour-type sieves! – and crushing unburned bones with pestles. No one would have had time to get firewood.

In case of the three pure extermination camps listed in the lower part of the table, the number of inmates involved in acquiring wood is also said to have been well below 100 persons in each case.

For Auschwitz, witnesses have made disparate statements about the features of outdoor cremations, thus making calculations difficult. These claims are discussed in the section "Holocaust Scenarios" of the entry on open-air incinerations.

Note that self-immolating bodies are not part of the scientific literature, as none have ever been discovered during single-body or large-scale cremations. Therefore, the scenarios described by these witnesses, or agreed upon by orthodox scholars, are simply technically impossible.

For details, see the entry for each of these witnesses and places, as well as the entries on open-air incinerations and *Aktion* 1005.

LUXEMBOURG

Documents indicate that 512 Jews were deported from Luxembourg, with the Auschwitz Camp as their main destination. Few of these Jews reported back with the local authorities after the war. It is unknown how many returned without reporting back, and how many migrated elsewhere. The fate of the Jews deported from Luxembourg was probably very similar to that of the Jews deported from France. (See the entry on France, as well as the general entry on Jewish demography.)

LVIV

An extermination camp equipped with homicidal gas chambers was allegedly located in the western Ukrainian city of Lviv (Lemberg in German). On 18 May 1943, the British received a "Memorandum" from Stockholm containing the statements of two Belgian prisoners of war who had escaped from Germany on 28 April and arrived in Sweden on 5 May 1943. They had been kept in the penal camp at Rawa Ruska, where they claim to have heard how "the Germans themselves boasted that at Lemberg they had specially constructed gas chambers where the Jews were systematically killed and buried. The total number was said to exceed 80,000." (See Mattogno 2021e, p. 98, for the source.)

All historians agree that no such facility ever existed, let alone that 80,000 Jews fell victim to it. This phantom extermination camp is a creation of black-propaganda sources.

Lwow → Lviv

M

MADAGASCAR

Madagascar is a large island (almost 600,000 sq km) located off the coast of southeast Africa. Currently it is an independent nation of some 28 million people, but from 1897 through World War Two, it was a colony of France.

For at least two centuries prior to the war, German critics of the Jews had discussed the option, and the need, to physically remove the allegedly troublesome German Jews from German territory. In 1885, German writer Paul de Lagarde offered some specific suggestions: the Jews should be transferred "to Palestine or, better still, to Madagascar" ("*nach Palästina oder noch lieber nach Madagaskar*"). Evidently, the island was both large enough to accommodate well over a million Jews, and of sufficiently benign climate to allow them to survive and prosper. It was also far enough away to make any return to Europe implausible. It would be a permanent mass relocation, not a death sentence.

Some time in the early 1930s, German National Socialists picked up on this idea and began to seriously promote it. By the late 1930s, leading Germans began to discuss the concept of a negotiated transfer solution with France. In April 1938, Goebbels first referred to the idea in his diary:

> *"Long discussion at breakfast, on the Jewish Question. The Führer wants the Jews completely squeezed out (*herausdrängen*) of Germany. To Madagascar, or some such place. Right!"* (11 April 1938)

The onset of war in September 1939 temporarily sidelined plans, but within a year, when it became clear that the French government would soon fall, the idea reemerged. In a May 1940 memo, Himmler wrote to Hitler of the need for "massive immigration of all Jews to Africa or some other colony," implicitly referring to Madagascar. In June, Franz Rademacher was tasked with developing a formal proposal for a "Madagascar Plan" for the Jews, which he completed on 3 July:

> *"The approaching victory gives Germany the possibility, and in my view also the duty, of solving the Jewish Question in Europe. The desirable solution is: all Jews out of Europe. ... France must make the island of Madagascar available for the solution of the Jewish Question... The island will be transferred to Germany under a mandate. ... Apart from this, the Jews will have their own administration in this territory: their own mayors, police, postal, and railroad administration, etc... Moreover, the Jews will remain in German hands as a pledge for the future good behavior of the members of their race in America."*

In July and August, Goebbels again briefly remarked on the plan in his diary:

> *"The big plan for the evacuation (*Evakuierung*) of the Jews from Berlin was approved. Additionally, all the Jews of Europe are supposed to be deported (*deportiert*) to Madagascar after the war."* (26 July 1940)

> *"Later on, we want to ship (*verfrachten*) the Jews to Madagascar. There they can build their own state."* (17 August 1940)

We see here, in private and personal documents, a remarkable lack of animosity; the Jews simply needed to leave the Reich, and a new home had been found for them. Clearly there was no plan to kill them because, "after the war," they would be relocated. And in any case, the Jews were worth more alive than dead; they would serve as insurance against belligerence by the potent American Jews.

Due to developments in the war, however, the plan never moved beyond this stage. There was little discussion in 1941, and by early 1942, some in the National-Socialist hierarchy were ready to abandon it completely. But Goebbels, at least, still considered it a viable option, as late as March 1942:

> *"I read a detailed report from the SD and police regarding a final solution of the Jewish Question. Any final solution involves a tremendous number of new viewpoints. The Jewish Question must be solved within a pan-European frame. There are 11 million Jews still in Europe. They will have to be concentrated later, to begin with, in the East; possibly an island, such as Madagascar, can be assigned to them after the war. In any case, there can be no peace in Europe until the last Jews are shut off (*ausgeschaltet*) from the continent."* (7 March 1942)

This is a highly significant statement: that the "final solution of the Jewish Question" is still, in March

1942, a territorial solution – first concentration in the East, and then deportation after the war. Still, there is no talk of mass murder; and this at a date when, if we follow the orthodox narrative, the camps at Chełmno, Belzec and Auschwitz had already begun their homicidal gassings.

By May of 1942, the British had begun their invasion of Madagascar in order to take it out of the hands of the Vichy French government. The Brits completed their takeover in November of that year, effectively ending all German talk of a Madagascar Plan for the Jews.

(For details, see Jansen 1997; Brechtken 1998; Graf/Kues/Mattogno 2020, pp. 204-218; see also the entry on resettlement.)

MAJDANEK
Documented History

The decision to set up a concentration camp for 25,000 to 50,000 inmates near the Polish city of Lublin was made on 20 July 1941. It was meant to supply a slave-labor force for Himmler's ambitious *Generalplan Ost* aiming at the colonization, development and Germanization of territories in Eastern Europe. After the initial success in the war against the Soviet Union, large numbers of Soviet PoWs were meant to occupy the camp. The first plan for the camp, labeled a PoW camp and meant to hold 125,000 inmates, dates from 7 October 1941. The camp's nickname "Majdanek" – never used in official German documents – can be traced back to the nearby Lublin city district Majdan Tatarski.

Construction work began in October 1941 using Jewish-Polish and Soviet PoWs. The camp was huge.

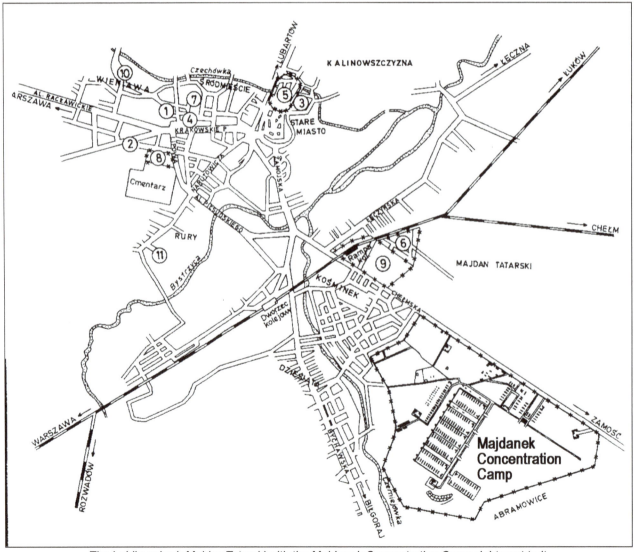

The Lublin suburb Majdan Tatarski with the Majdanek Concentration Camp right next to it.

The first layout provided for ten camp sectors with a total of 236 barracks, 207 of them for lodging inmates. These plans changed repeatedly over time, and in the end, of eight planned camp sectors, only five were finalized, with just over a hundred barracks. One reason for the constant changes in plans was that the camp's planned purpose changed as well. It started out as a PoW camp, received dual-purpose status of both PoW camp and concentration camp in April 1942, and was converted to a mere concentration camp a year later.

Similar to most other German concentration camps, living conditions in the camp were very harsh at the beginning, as everything had to be built from the ground up, meaning initially inmates had to sleep in the open, and there were no sanitary facilities or anything else. While private civilian companies, many of them Polish, did the detailed planning and provided skilled labor, inmates made up the unskilled labor force. The large presence of Polish civilians on the camp's construction sites made it easy for the inmates – and for the resistance movement in particular – to communicate with the outside world.

For many months, the city administration of Lublin refused to connect the camp to the local drinking water, city gas and sewer system. This was resolved only after top officials from Berlin intervened. It still took until early 1943 for the camp to be connected to the sewer system, and the drinking water system in the camp was finalized only in the fall of that year. Before that, well water infested with bacteria was used, and during winter, snow was melted to obtain water. The camp's first laundry facility was available only in early 1943. As a consequence, the camp's hygienic conditions remained dreadful for a long time, resulting in persistently appalling living conditions. With the outbreak of epidemics (typhus, dysentery, tuberculosis), this led to catastrophically high death rates, far worse than in any other camp of the Third Reich (except maybe Auschwitz during its cataclysmic typhus epidemic from mid-1942 to mid-1943). Medical care was almost non-existent initially, and then improved only with the slowly improving sanitary conditions. A careful study of the extant documentation results in a total death toll due to "natural" (non-homicidal) reasons of some 42,200 during the camp's entire existence. Some 20,000 inmates were released, hardly any of whom ever made any mass-murder claims.

Logistical problems prevented the mass transfer of Soviet PoWs from Russia, so only relatively few of those, mostly transferred from other PoW camps

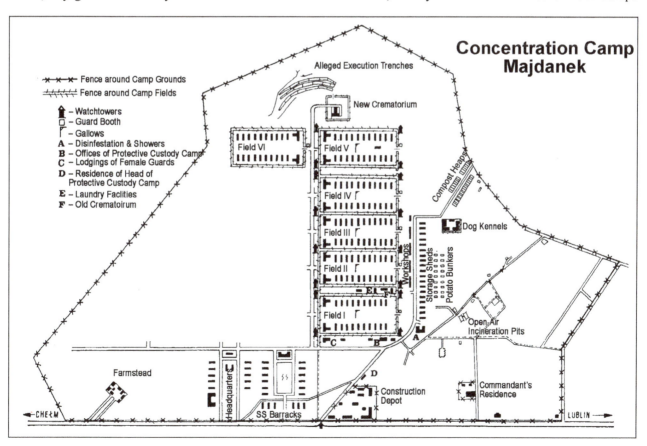

in the region, were lodged in Majdanek. Bottlenecks in transporting the required construction materials eventually led to a downgrading of Himmler's ambitious *Generalplan Ost* project. Rather than for PoWs, the camp was then used to incarcerate Polish inmates who had resisted the German occupational forces, as well as Polish Jews and Jews deported from Western and Central European countries. Once the basic camp infrastructure was set up, the camp's inmates were increasingly employed in various local industries, in particular several SS-owned operations set up inside or right next to the camp, with a focus on manufacturing or recycling clothes and shoes for the German armed forces.

In the context of the Holocaust, four buildings are of interest: the crematorium, and the two disinfestation barracks "Bath & Disinfection I" and "Bath & Disinfection II," together with the fumigation facility next to them.

The crematorium was planned as early as October 1941, but became operational only in January of 1944, hence operated only for six months before the Soviet conquest of the camp. It was equipped with five single-muffle cremation furnaces set in one large brick structure. To have any cremation options at all during the early phase of the camp, two mobile oil-fired furnaces were installed in a shed in 1942, but due to a lack of oil, they operated only for six months, and were then dismantled. (For details, see the Majdanek section of the entry on crematoria.)

According to a construction-progress report of the Majdanek Camp's Central Construction Office dated 22 October 1942, the buildings "Bath & Disinfection I" and "Bath & Disinfection II," in the camp's num-

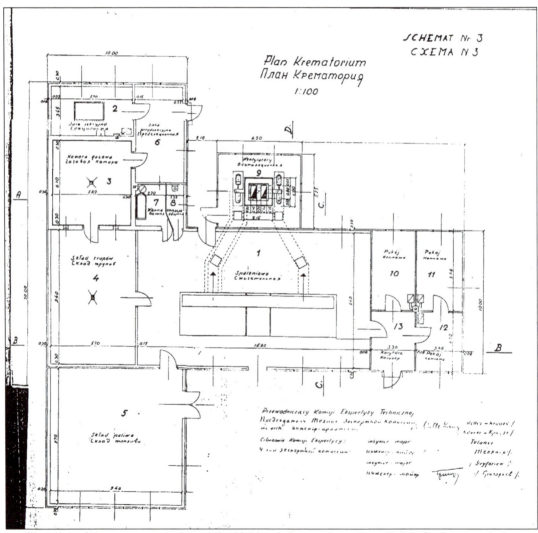

Floor plan of the new crematorium at the Majdanek Camp, drawn by a Polish-Soviet commission. Room 3 is labeled as "gas chamber" ("komora gazowa") although the room had two wall openings to Room 4 (morgue) that could not be closed, and it had no means of ventilating it: no fan, no window, no door to the outside. This homicidal-gas-chamber claim was dropped around the year 2000.

bering systems Barracks No. 41 and 42 (or Buildings XII^A and XII in a different system), were the only delousing and bath facilities for inmates at that time. In fact, initially only "Bath & Disinfection II" was equipped with a delousing facility. Construction work to convert one of the rooms of "Bath & Disinfection I" into a fumigation chamber (called "gas chamber" in the documents) started only in late 1942 by adding two ventilation chimneys in its roof.

Numerous documents exist, starting in May 1942, for the construction of a separate Zyklon-B disinfestation facility next to "Bath & Disinfection I," which was to be used for delousing clothes of the "Fur and Clothing Works" of Lublin. The original plan provided for two parallel rooms in a brick-and-mortar/concrete building, set beneath a large pole-support roof. Each room was to have two gastight steel doors. With a few modifications, this building was finished in late October 1942.

Several other projects to add more disinfestation facilities existed between 1941 and 1943, but it seems that few of them, if any, were carried out.

Propaganda History

Anything going on inside the Majdanek Camp was easily visible from nearby towns and roads. Furthermore, due to the ease with which information (and disinformation) could travel out of the camp as described before, the Polish resistance movement must have been well-informed about what was going on inside the camp, and most certainly communicated it (and the disinformation) to the Polish government in exile in London.

The first reference to a "gas chamber and a crematorium" at Majdanek were published by Polish periodicals in the UK in late 1942, and that wasn't even wrong, if "gas chamber" here means "fumigation gas chamber." Until May 1943, in 25 reports about Majdanek, not a single one mentions homicidal gassings, although one report claims mass murder of inmates by way of lethal injections. One long report of February 1943 – half a year after mass gassings are said to have started – describes the camp and its living conditions rather correctly, but without any references to gassing. It demonstrates the accuracy and completeness of information accessible to the Polish underground.

After the Auschwitz camp resistance had spread gas-chamber propaganda beginning in September 1942, the Polish underground reciprocated for Majdanek in May of 1943, when homicidal gas-chamber claims were made on a few occasions in reports about that camp. This may have been triggered by a general increase in Allied and Polish gas-chamber propaganda after the German discovery of the mass graves of the Soviet's murder victims in Katyn. The rare reports about gassings at Majdanek, however, remained without any specific details. Not even the type of gas was mentioned. One report mentioned painted gas-chamber windows to hide from the outside what was going on inside, but homicidal gas chambers most certainly would not have had any windows, or else the gassing victims would have smashed them before their demise.

In 1944, an account of an unnamed inmate was published who is said to have escaped from the camp in 1943. His description includes the claim that those unfit for work were killed in gas chambers, but his description of the alleged murder facility is a chaotic jumble of different parts of separate facilities that have nothing to do with one another. The facilities that were later "identified" as homicidal gas chambers are not mentioned at all. This witness's claim

Majdanek's new crematorium, once alleged to have been a homicidal gas chamber. Note the wall openings leading to Room 4, a morgue. Top right: hole in the ceiling, see below.

Majdanek's new crematorium, alleged Zyklon-B introduction hole knocked through the concrete ceiling of Room 3. However, this was done at war's end by the Polish-Soviet commission in order to rig the room as a fake homicidal gas chamber.

that thousands were gassed every day, and that two million had been killed by the end of 1943 alone, put this account safely in the category of atrocity propaganda.

The propaganda tune changed completely after the Soviets had conquered the camp in late July 1944. First, the Soviets joined the Poles, formed an "expert commission" they called *Polish-Soviet Extraordinary Commission for Investigating the Crimes Committed by the Germans in the Majdanek Extermination Camp in Lublin*, and finalized their report on 23 August. This document was later also submitted to the Nuremberg International Military Tribunal (IMT) as Document USSR-29 (see *IMT*, Vol. VII, p. 590). This report claimed a total of 1,500,000 victims of the Majdanek "extermination" camp. It described in detail six alleged homicidal gas chambers, and mentioned in passing a seventh chamber located in the crematorium building. The report also mentions gas vans – one witness spoke of a gas bus, another of a gas truck. As one proof for their mass-murder claim, the Soviets presented photographs of mountains of shoes which they had found in the shoemaker's workshop. It was admitted only decades later that these shoes did not belong to murdered inmates but had been sent to Majdanek by various German authorities in order to have their material recycled there.

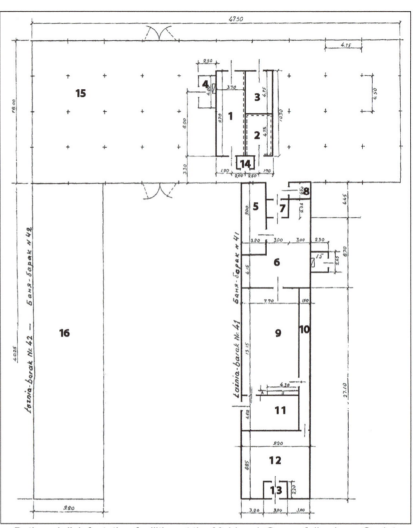

Bath and disinfestation facilities at the Majdanek Camp, following a Soviet-Polish map prepared in 1944. 1-4, 14: Detached disinfestation wing under pole-support roof (15). 1: Zyklon-B and hot-air disinfestation chamber, with blue wall stains from hydrogen-cyanide exposure. 4: Hot-air furnace and blower. Dotted lines: perforated steel pipes along wall, connected to CO_2 bottle in Room 14.
5-13: Shower and delousing facility Barracks No. 41. 6: Fumigation room with two air vents in ceiling, and blue wall staining from hydrogen-cyanide exposure; until 2000, misrepresented by scholars and the Majdanek Museum as homicidal gas chamber. 9: Shower room, sometimes misrepresented in the media as a homicidal gas chamber. 11: Boiler room.
16: Inmate shower and delousing facility Barracks No. 42.

With this "expert report" in hand, the Soviets started a propaganda blitz the world had never seen before. At its center were the burned-out ruins of the Majdanek crematorium with its five furnaces. Photos taken by the Soviets showed the furnaces with partly burned human corpses inside and human skeletons lying on the ground in front of them. Media representatives of all Allied nations were invited and given a camp tour. During a press conference on 25 August 1944, the Soviets told the gruesome tale of Majdanek having been a death factory where "rough-ly two million innocent people" had been murdered by the Germans "by every method of mass murder."

Furthermore, the Polish-Soviet Commission also appointed a committee of "experts" who wrote a report on the alleged capacity of the five cremation furnaces found at the Majdanek Camp. They claimed that this furnace, built by the Kori Company, operated at a temperature of 1,500°C, that four bodies were stuffed into each muffle concurrently, and that it took a mere 12 minutes to cremate such a load, resulting in a daily capacity of just under 2,000 bodies.

For the six months that this facility operated, this would amount to a maximum capacity of some 360,000 bodies.

That was still not enough, though, because the Polish-Soviet commission claimed in its report submitted to the IMT that 600,000 bodies had been cremated in that facility – plus 400,000 on pyres, 80,000 in the old crematorium with its two oil-fired furnaces, and 300,000 corpses had been buried in mass graves.

It is a fact, however, that the Kori furnace's muffle had been designed to accommodate only *one* body at a time, which took roughly *one* hour to cremate. It could also not operate safely beyond a temperature of some 1,000°C. At higher temperatures, the refractory material becomes soft and starts to slowly flow (sinter), among other things also fusing with bones placed on it. Since the furnaces show no signs of sintering to this day, it is clear that they never operated at temperatures beyond 1,000°C. Their actual theoretical daily capacity of a 20-hour operating day was thus 100 bodies, or some 18,000 for half a year. (For more details on this furnace, see the entry on crematoria).

An analysis of witness testimony collected by Polish authorities between 1945 and 1947 shows that they are mostly based on hearsay, and rarely contain any specifics that would allow any critical assessment. A few witnesses who gave at least a modicum of information located "the" gas chamber either inside the crematorium or next to the inmate shower room, two locations which today are ruled out even by the Majdanek Museum. (See Alvarez 2023a for that overview.)

To this day, orthodox sources sometimes erroneously present the shower room inside Barracks 41, equipped with large windows, as "the gas chamber." Most prominent in this regard are Alain Resnais's 1955 documentary *Nuit et Bruillard* (*Night and Fog*, starting at 22 min 35 sec), the 2013 BBC documentary *Treblinka: Inside Hitler's Secret Death Camp* featuring British archeologist Caroline Sturdy Colls (starting at 19 min 18 sec), and the 2000 *Encyclopedia of the Holocaust* by Robert Rozett and Shmuel Spector. They use a photo of this room to illustrate their entry on "gas chambers," of all things (p. 230), while images of the rooms actually claimed to have been homicidal gas chambers at Majdanek are abundantly available. Rozett and Spector also mendaciously present a 1945 Soviet photo of a pile of shoes as belonging "to victims of the Majdanek camp" (p. 312).

Majdanek, disinfestation wing, Room 14, photo showing condition at war's end: contraption to hook up steel bottles to pipes leading into adjacent rooms, yet without any bottles.

Steel bottle containing non-lethal carbon dioxide hooked up to the above contraption for the last several decades. A museum fraud.

Majdanek, disinfestation wing, Room 1 with steel pipe running along wall. And blue wall staining from hydrogen-cyanide exposure, particularly along the pipe. This indicates that the gas escaping from the pipe cooled down the wall drastically, making it moist, which boosted blue-pigment formation. This can be achieved with long-term use of non-toxic carbon dioxide for cooling purposes, but not with toxic carbon monoxide used during occasional short-term homicides.

While film directors such as Resnais and journalists of the BBC may claim ignorance, leading ortho-

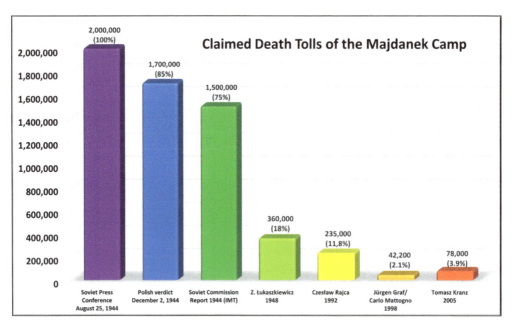

dox Holocaust scholars such as Rozett and Spector don't have that excuse. If incompetence is ruled out, all that is left is malice. This impression gets supported by the fact, that the 1948 death-toll figure of 360,000 is repeated in their Majdanek entry three times (pages 312 and following), even though Polish historian Czesław Rajca had reduced the death toll in 1992 to 235,000 (see the next section).

Comparing this entry to the one in Gutman's 1990 encyclopedia reveals that Rozett and Spector copied parts of the Majdanek text from Gutman. They took time and effort to rephrase the text, but this time would have been spent better by updating this entry to the state of orthodox knowledge prevailing in 2000.

Death-Toll Propaganda

While the Soviets mentioned a death toll of "roughly two million" during their August 1944 press conference, the Polish-Soviet commission reduced that number slightly to 1.5 million. During the Polish show trial against six former Majdanek camp guards, staged at Lublin in late 1944, this number was increased again to 1.7 million, which the Polish government submitted as a court-proven fact during the Nuremberg IMT (*IMT*, Vol. VII, p. 214).

Once the hysterical anti-German frenzy of the war's last phase and the immediate postwar years had somewhat subsided, Polish investigative judge Zdzisław Łukaszkiewicz took a second look at the Majdanek Camp, and concluded in 1948 that "only" some 360,000 inmates had died in that camp.

Once the Soviet Union collapsed, thus freeing Poland from its communist propaganda shackles, two more death-toll reductions followed. The first by Polish historian Czesław Rajca from the Majdanek Museum set the new number at 235,000 in 1992.

In the meantime, Western historians published all kinds of claims about Majdanek's death toll, ranging from some 1.4 million by Lucy Dawidowicz in 1979 down to "tens of thousands" by Raul Hilberg in 1961, which gives the impression of a bunch of bungling schoolchildren rather than scholars doing proper research. Basing itself on this, the verdict of the Düsseldorf Majdanek Show Trial announced in 1981 a death toll of at least 200,000 victims.

Thirteen years later, the Majdanek Museum's new director, Polish historian Tomasz Kranz, reduced that death toll much more radically to just 78,000, and he also threw overboard five of the seven gas chambers which the Soviets had originally claimed in their report. Hence, according to the narrative *en vogue* since 2005, allegedly only two homicidal gas chambers ever existed at Majdanek.

Therefore, of the "roughly two million" victims of the Majdanek Camp claimed in 1944, not even four percent were left in 2005.

Forensic Findings

The Polish-Soviet Commission's attempt to substantiate the magnitude of their mass-murder claims with forensic findings were a dismal failure. In mass graves at the claimed location, they found the remains not of the claimed 300,000 victims, but only of 733 bodies. Instead of finding ashes of the burned bodies of over a million people, they only found an amount corresponding to some 3,000 victims.

The first government-independent forensic investigation was made in early 1988 by Fred Leuchter, then the U.S.'s only expert for execution technologies. Since it was carried out in a rush with a narrow deadline for an ongoing trial (the Second Zündel Trial), it was inevitably superficial. That same year, French historian Jean-Claude Pressac tried remedying this by providing a more-detailed discussion of the material aspects of the seven claimed homicidal gas chambers of the Majdanek Camp. While he made a few mistakes himself, he confirmed that most of the seven claimed homicidal gas chambers could not have operated as such.

Further research by skeptical scholars Jürgen Graf and Carlo Mattogno revealed in 1998 that *all* gas-chamber claims are untenable for numerous technical reasons, and that *all* actual gas chambers exclusively served as disinfestation chambers, as is also shown by documents.

Current Orthodox Narrative

Cornered by the results of skeptical forensic and archival research, orthodox historians have in the meantime abandoned five of the originally claimed seven homicidal gas chambers, but resurrected the gas-van rumors, with nothing but disparate witness statements to back it up with.

In addition, they keep insisting that in early November 1943, when all efforts of the Third Reich were focused on recruiting as many slave laborers as possible for the war effort, and to keep them fit for work, the Majdanek camp authorities allegedly decided to murder some 18,000 Jews. The claimed mass shootings within just one day raise insurmountable logistical issues that the orthodoxy assiduously avoids. (For more details on this, see the entry on Operation "Harvest Festival".)

Here is the current orthodox stance with regard to the various homicidal gas-chamber claims of the past:
- The alleged gas chamber inside the crematorium is a windowless room in the center of that building. It has no ventilation system, two wall openings to a neighboring room that could not be closed, and a crudely broken-through hole in the concrete ceiling, with reinforcement bars left where they were, allegedly representing a Zyklon-B introduction hole. Evidently, this room could neither be closed nor ventilated. Hence, it could not have served as a gas chamber, homici-

Majdanek, disinfestation wing, ceiling of Room 2: crude hole knocked through the ceiling by Soviet or Poles, with rebars not removed, in order to fake a Zyklon-B introduction shaft – just like in the new crematorium.

Majdanek, disinfestation wing, ceiling of Room 3: as before. Claims that Rooms 2 and 3 served as Zyklon-B homicidal gas chambers were dropped around the year 2000, because neither room has any ventilation system.

Majdanek, disinfestation wing, wall opening between Room 1 and Room 14 with steel bottles. The opening has no window pane, and no sign that it ever had one. In other words, poison gas could not have been used without the "observing" SS man dying himself.

dal or not. Therefore, this room was silently rebranded in the early 2000s as a morgue (which it was according to wartime blueprints), and the embarrassing fake Zyklon-B hole in the ceiling, probably added by the Poles to sell this room as a gas chamber, is never mentioned at all.

– The two alleged gas chambers next to the camp's laundry, which have always been mere drying facilities, were quietly dropped. No one talks about them anymore.

– The Zyklon-B disinfestation chamber next to the inmate shower room of Barracks 41 ("Bath and Disinfection I"), once the main "gas-chamber" tourist attraction of the camp, is now declared as what it was: a place to delouse clothes. The two openings in its roof, formerly mislabeled as Zyklon-B introduction holes, are now properly named ventilation shafts. This room's window no longer causes embarrassing questions by visitors: "Wouldn't the victims have smashed that in?" And neither does the fact that the room's entry and exit doors open inward, hence would have been blocked by dead bodies during homicidal gassings. Furthermore, the doors had no locking mechanism, and the northern door is made of thin wooden boards that would have been unable to withstand a panicking crowd.

– All that is left standing is the disinfestation building next to "Bath and Disinfection I," and here only two of the three rooms. These two rooms have a pipe running along the wall, allegedly to feed in carbon monoxide. Since carbon monoxide is harmless to insects, the purpose was not to kill these pests. However, the only gas bottles ever found in the camp contained carbon *DI*oxide, which is not toxic to humans. Furthermore, both rooms allegedly also served to kill with Zyklon B. However, the larger one of the two has *no* means of inserting it. The two smaller rooms have crudely knocked out holes in the concrete ceiling, a similarly botched job as that in the crematorium. While one of these two rooms allegedly served to kill (either with carbon monoxide through the pipe or with Zyklon B through the hole), the other has been dropped. But if the ceiling hole in that room does *not* prove homicidal use (or in the crematorium room), then why does it prove such use in the other room?

The reason why the orthodoxy maintains these ludicrous gas-chamber claims is very simple: If they followed where the evidence inevitably leads, they would have to concede that all government reports, all court decisions, and all witness testimonies claiming otherwise were profoundly wrong. And if they were profoundly wrong about Majdanek, why should anyone believe that they were more accurate regarding gas-chamber claims about other camps?

And indeed, why should we? To prevent a disastrous de-holocausting domino effect, they desperately cling to some semblance of homicidal gassings.

What they do not realize is that the difference between the initially claimed 1.5 to 2 million victims and the current death toll of just 78,000 already completely eviscerates their credibility. The game is already over. The reason why this house of cards hasn't collapsed yet is that, due to the ongoing disinformation campaign combined with threats of prosecution, the public at large hasn't been informed about this orthodox disaster yet. Only a propagandistic window dressing keeps up the illusion.

(For details on Majdanek, see Graf/Mattogno 2012; Rudolf 2023, pp. 18-21, 295-303; as well as Alvarez 2023a.)

MAJDANEK MUSEUM

If a museum were to put on display how its own storyline has changed over the decades, the Majdanek Museum would be the most interesting Holocaust-related museum in the world. One massive reduction of the camp's total death-toll figure chased the previous one, and gas-chamber claim after gas-chamber claim ended up in the dustbins of history. (See the entry on the Majdanek Camp for details.)

Of course, such a juxtaposition of former camp narratives would expose the Museum's tradition of uninterrupted mendacity, after which no visitor would believe anything anymore – not even the story told today. That skepticism instilled in the average tourist would both be very healthy and very much appropriate, because to this day, the lying continues without interruption.

Here are the most strident examples:

1. The morgue in the crematorium building, until the end of the 20th Century stubbornly presented as a homicidal gas chamber by the museum, is no longer presented as such. Now they tell us that the morgue was – a morgue. Unfortunately, the hole in this room's ceiling, once labeled as a Zyklon-B introduction hole to kill people, is still there. The museum officials hush it up, because they cannot possibly admit that this fake hole was added only after the war. If they did that, many tourists would rightly ask: If

that hole is a Polish-Soviet fraud, then what about the same type of crude Zyklon-B introduction holes visible in two rooms of the disinfestation building still presented as homicidal gas chamber today? They must be frauds, too! And indeed, they are.

2. The delousing facility and the bath and disinfection building number 1, although located close to each other, were originally separate structures with no connection. Wartime blueprints and air photos clearly prove this. That was not good enough for the museum officials, however. They wanted to sell their visitors the grand lie that inmates once walked from the bath and disinfection building number 1 stark naked to the delousing facility, so they could be gassed there. But it is not credible that naked people walked through an open area where hundreds of inmates and the local civilian population could have seen them. Hence, the Museum added a wooden structure connecting both facilities (see the illustration). Even during the remodeling of the building in 2020/21, this fraudulent structure was kept in place. Although the Museum admits now in its publications that this is a postwar addition, their forgery still prevents visitors from detecting this absurd gassing claim.

3. Last but not least, we have the ongoing mendacious way the Museum presents the thousands of old shoes found in the camp upon Soviet occupation. They allegedly prove, insists the Museum, that their former owners were mass murdered. That is just as true and logical as the claim that any other collection of recycled shoes proves that their former owners were mass murdered. For some reason, tourists fall for this kind of obvious nonsense, because they are accustomed to be mere spectators rather than critical thinkers. Yet still, this was a shoe storage area of the shoemaker shop next to it, which made new shoes and refurbished old ones arriving from many sources. (For more details, see the entry on shoes of deportees.)

Clearly, it is time for Museum authorities to admit the truth and stop lying to millions of tourists. But of course, if they did that, Majdanek would be stuck without any homicidal gas chambers; this would be bad for the tourism business, and they know it. And this is not to mention that an admission of mendacity here would raise the same questions at the other camps, threatening to topple the entire orthodoxy. This must be avoided at all costs.

(For illustrations, see the entry on Majdanek.)

MAJDANEK TRIALS

Several trials were orchestrated by both Poland and Germany with a focus on crimes alleged to have been committed at the Majdanek Camp during the war.

Soviet-Polish Show Trials

The first show trial in Poland was conducted by a mixed staff of Soviet and Polish officials. It was staged at Lublin from 27 November to 2 December 1944. Four members of the SS camp staff and two *Kapos* (inmate foremen) captured by the Soviets when overrunning the camp were accused of murder and abuse of prisoners. The proceedings were a typical Stalinist show trial, where the focus was not on the individual defendant's alleged crimes, but on painting a horrific picture of alleged German atrocities committed in Poland in general, and in Majdanek in particular.

For example, one prosecutor claimed that half a million Germans had been involved at Majdanek in the "well-organized machinery for killing defenseless people." Another prosecutor made a witness confirm that the Germans had planned "the extermination of the Slavic peoples in Majdanek." Another

Left: bath and disinfection building no. I at Majdanek Camp. Right: disinfestation building containing Rooms I-III. In a white box: structure fraudulently added after the war connecting the two buildings.

As above, but with postwar structure removed, showing how it would have looked like during the war (minus a pole-support roof spanning the larger area to allow spreading out fumigation clothes for airing).

had a defendant describe in detail how children were gassed in an unspecified gas chamber. The witness saw how the children's lungs burst due to the gas, making them bleed out of mouth and nose. However, none of the gasses claimed to have been used at Majdanek – carbon monoxide and hydrogen cyanide – have such an effect. Therefore, it is undeniable that this show trial was carefully orchestrated.

The methods used to make the defendants cooperative can be gleaned from the fact that one of the defendants committed suicide during the trial. The defense lawyers didn't help either, as they acted like auxiliary prosecutors who expressed their revulsion at their client's alleged crimes, and their unwillingness to defend them.

The prosecution's atrocity claims were based substantially on the bogus conclusions of a mixed Soviet-Polish investigative commission. They asserted the existence of seven homicidal gas chambers inside the Majdanek Camp, claimed that over a million bodies of mass-murder victims had been cremated in the camp's cremation furnaces, and that mass graves contained a further 300,000 bodies. All this flies in the face not only of documented and material facts, but also stands in stark contrast to today's orthodox narrative. In its verdict, the Soviet-Polish judges determined that 1.7 million victims had died at the Majdanek Camp. (For more details, see the section "Propaganda History" of the entry on Majdanek.)

All remaining defendants were sentenced to death and hanged one day after the verdict was announced. They were sacrificed on the altar of Soviet-Polish atrocity propaganda designed to crush the German spirit during that final phase of the war, and to justify the targeting of all Germans. (For more details, see Graf/Mattogno 2012, pp. 229-233.)

This initial show trial was followed by a series of minor Polish trials against a long list of German defendants. These defendants were extradited to Poland step by step by the Allied occupational authorities in West and Central Germany. These trials took place at various locations between 1946 and 1948. They all followed the strict propaganda script predefined by the first Majdanek Trial of 1944. Therefore, the prosecutions' arguments and the courts' decision were effectively pre-ordained. It was a conveyor-belt conviction machine, with sentences ranging from 2-year imprisonments to death sentences.

German Majdanek Trials

The first two German trials on crimes committed at the Majdanek Camp were carried out during the war by the SS-internal court system against two former camp commandants, Karl-Otto Koch and Hermann Florstedt. They were accused of having embezzled valuables confiscated from camp inmates. Both Koch and Florstedt were found guilty as charged, and were executed just prior to Germany's military collapse.

West Germany conducted one major show trial on crimes allegedly committed at the Majdanek Camp, and one single-defendant trial some 20 years later.

The large-scale Majdanek Show Trial was staged in Düsseldorf between 26 November 1975 and 30 June 1981. In the dock were 15 former members of the camp staff, including six women. One defendant died a year into the proceedings, while another's case was shelved due to the defendant's unfitness for imprisonment. Four defendants were acquitted four years into the trial. Of the remaining nine defendants, one was acquitted, one was imprisoned for life, while the rest received prison terms between 2 and 12 years.

The trial was characterized by large-scale manipulations of witnesses by the *Zentrale Stelle* and by Polish judicial authorities, which was revealed by defense lawyer Ludwig Bock. Hence, many witness accounts had been streamlined and harmonized prior to the trial, so they would support the camp's narrative prevalent at the time.

This trial gained much public attention in West Germany and abroad. The judges found themselves under massive pressure from domestic and foreign media, anti-fascist organizations as well as foreign governments and their own West-German government. Every early acquittal of some of the defendants resulted in a flood of protests. The atmosphere during the trial was in many ways similar to that prevailing during the Frankfurt Auschwitz Show Trial. Hence, radically revising the prevalent Majdanek narrative – as documental, physical and forensic evidence would have required – was not a politically acceptable option.

During the Majdanek Trial (as during the Frankfurt Auschwitz Show Trial), neither judges nor prosecution nor any of the defense lawyers ever tried to support or verify any of the death-toll or gas-chamber claims with documents from the Majdanek Museum's archives. They never asked for any forensic evidence of mass graves; or requested expert opinions on cremations in furnaces or during open-air incinerations; or whether the alleged gas chambers could have operated as claimed. No one involved in this mass-murder trial was interested in examining the claimed murder weapons or any traces of the alleged victims.

The court's utter ignorance of documental evidence is reflected in its claim that the term "delousing facility" was only a code word to hide homicidal facilities. If the judges had studied the surviving German documents, they would have found many documents detailing the planning, design, construction and operation of real delousing facilities. The reality of delousing operations is even apparent from many witness reports.

The court's verdict reflects the orthodox narrative of that time, with bogus gas-chamber claims, an exaggerated death-toll figure of "a minimum of 200,000 victims," and the story of mass-executions of some 17,000 inmates during the so-called Operation "Harvest Festival," all taken uncritically at face value.

It is one of the many travesties of justice, of which the German political class and judiciary are particularly proud, as major events of "moral cleansing."

A late sequel to the Düsseldorf Majdanek Trial was staged in 1989 against Karl-Friedrich Höcker. During the war, Höcker made a career as adjutant of several camp commandants at various camps, among them Auschwitz and Majdanek. In 1989, the Bielefeld District Court sentenced him to four years in prison for having ordered a total of 3.6 metric tons of Zyklon B for the Majdanek Camp between May 1943 and May 1944.

However, Höcker's purchase of Zyklon B was used for disinfestation purposes. Hence, it probably saved the lives of thousands of inmates. Yet Höcker fell into the trap that the British had laid during their Bergen-Belsen Trials and particularly during the Tesch Trial. During those trials, the British used flawed arguments and bogus evidence in order to turn any Zyklon-B order, used to save inmate lives, into evidence for mass murder.

(In addition to the entries on *Zentrale Stelle*, Ludwig Bock, Operation "Harvest Festival," the Bergen-Belsen Trials and Tesch & Stabenow, see Graf/Mattogno 2012, pages 233-245, for more details.)

MALY TROSTENETS

Maly Trostenets (also spelled Trostinets) was a village in the suburbs of Belorussia's capital Minsk. Near it is located the so-called Blagovshchina Forest of roughly 2.5 square kilometers in size (one square mile). According to Russian sources of the 2000s, this forest was the execution site of choice for the local branches of the Soviet secret service NKVD in the Minsk region prior to World War II. Up to 270,000 people fell victim to the NKVD terror, many of which were buried in the Blagovshchina Forest.

The estate of a state-run farm near that same village is also the location of the so-called Maly Trostenets Camp. It was run by the commander of the German Security Police Minsk. A series of documents exists showing that, between May and October 1942, 16 trains arrived either at Minsk or directly near Maly Trostenets. These trains came mostly from Vienna and the Theresienstadt Ghetto, but one each came from Cologne and Königsberg. Each of them brought roughly 1,000 deported Jews (two of them only some 500). That is where the certainty about what unfolded there ends.

After the reconquest of Minsk by the Soviets in July 1944, they established their usual commission to investigate alleged German crimes. Nikolai N. Burdenko headed the commission. This was the same man who had overseen the commission which, only a short while earlier, had written the fake report that blamed the Soviet massacre of thousands of Polish officers near Katyn on the Germans. Now it was Burdenko's task to redeclare the tens if not hundreds of thousands of NKVD victims buried in the Blagovshchina Forest as victims of German terror. Witnesses were interrogated, who told terrible tales of massacres on hundreds of thousands of innocent Soviet citizens. Those murders were said to have been committed by mass shootings and with "murder vans." Here, Burdenko followed the script developed during the Krasnodar and Kharkov show trials held in 1943. (See those entries for details.)

Thirty-four mass graves with a total volume of some 25,000 m³ were allegedly found by the Soviet commission in the forest, but merely five of them were only "partly opened." The claimed death toll of this German atrocity was said to be between 200,000 and 546,000. The victims were all Soviet citizens. Jews were not mentioned, let alone victims from other countries.

In 1963, the West-German judiciary staged a trial against eleven former members of the Security Police Minsk, where the alleged events at Maly Trostenets played a major role. Basing itself on the above-mentioned 16 railroad transports to Maly Trostenets, the court ruled that most of the deportees were killed on arrival. The same fate is said to have befallen the majority of the 25,000 Jews of the Minsk Ghetto, with an initial focus on those unfit for labor, hence the very young, very old and the sick and fragile. No one at this trial requested to look for any physical evidence for that massacre.

Documents show, however, that many children and elderly people still lived in the Minsk Ghetto in 1943, and that thousands of Jews were still alive in the ghetto in late 1943. Furthermore, there is anecdotal evidence showing that, starting in September 1943, numerous railway transports with Jews were sent from Minsk westward via the Sobibór Camp, which indeed served as a transit camp. Hence, many if not most of the Jews presumed shot or gassed were very much alive.

Other documents proffered by historians to support the claimed massacre are highly dubious. For instance, there are four documents by a certain Arlt, a Waffen SS sergeant who headed a squad of nine riflemen. None of the documents have an address. Each has an "Arlt" signature with a distinctly different handwriting. The writer of these documents could not even get basic German military terms right. And last but not least, the documents were "discovered" around 1964 in an archive of the Communist eastern bloc. All these documents say is that Jews deported from Germany were "led to the pits" or "handed over to the soil." The reports described in rich detail the fight against partisans, but how a unit of ten men managed to kill a thousand Jews is not explained.

Another absurd "document" claims that the three gas vans used near Minsk are not enough to process the Jews, so another one is needed. However, around the same time, the three alleged gas vans at the Chełmno Camp, presumably of the same type as those deployed near Minsk, are said to have had no problem at all to process many more victims in a much shorter period of time.

This entire scenario becomes even more absurd when considering that the Jews deported from Vienna and Theresienstadt traveled huge distances to reach Minsk, passing by places such as Treblinka, Sobibór and/or Auschwitz along the way without stopping to get "processed" there. If the intention had been to murder them, and if these camps located along the way had indeed been extermination camps, then the journey of these Jews would have been much shorter. Sending them to Minsk made sense only if the intention was *not* to kill them but to keep them alive, for whatever purpose.

In the larger orthodox picture of the Holocaust, the events said to have transpired at Maly Trostenets can be seen as part of the mass murders by shooting or gas vans that were presumably perpetrated by the *Einsatzgruppen* and associated units. Because this alleged mass-murder site had some rudimentary features giving it a temporary presence, such as a provisional railway station, an assembly square and several barracks, orthodox historians tend to call it an extermination or death camp. This sets it apart from mere execution sites such as Babi Yar. In several respects, Maly Trostenets resembled the Chełmno Camp.

Witnesses, Soviet "experts" and orthodox historians have mentioned death-toll figures ranging from 40,000 up to 546,000, thus repeating the pattern found elsewhere of basing these claims more on wild guesses than thorough research.

Maly Trostenets Death-Toll Claims	
Source	Victims
Soviet Report of 25 July 1944	546,000
Mira Zaretskaya	500,000
Lev Lansky	299,000
Soviet Report of 22 Sept. 1944	206,500
Isak Grünberg	45,000
Christian Gerlach	40,000 to 60,000

As with all other mass-extermination scenes of the Holocaust, here the victims are said to have been buried at first, but then, in the context of the so-called "*Aktion* 1005," it is said that they were all exhumed and tracelessly burned on huge pyres. This operation is said to have lasted only some seven weeks, from end of October until mid-December 1943.

However, when assessing the various witness testimonies about this alleged operation to remove criminal traces, they turn out to contradict one another, and some of their claims are technically untenable. Furthermore, most of them describe utterly unworkable, even ridiculous scenarios bordering on the absurd, as to how these pyres were built and burned. This clearly leaves the impression of a badly orchestrated atrocity propaganda campaign.

(For more details, see Kues 2011a&b, Mattogno 2022c, pp. 330-333, 600-610.)

MANDELBAUM, HENRYK

Henryk Mandelbaum (15 Dec. 1922 – 17 June 2008) was a Polish Jew who was deported to Auschwitz in late April 1944. He claims to have been assigned to the *Sonderkommando* in June, and supposedly worked there until January 1945. Mandelbaum was interrogated by Soviet investigators in late February 1945, then again in preparation for the Höss Show Trial by Polish investigators in late September 1946. He testified both at the Krakow Show Trial against Rudolf Höss and at the Warsaw show trial against former members of the Auschwitz Camp's staff. Almost 60 years later, he was repeatedly interviewed by employees of the Auschwitz Museum, who published these interviews in a book. From all these depositions, we can glean the following regarding Mandelbaum's claims on exterminations at Auschwitz:

Henryk Mandelbaum

- Unsurprisingly, many of his claims in his various statements differ in many details, which makes it difficult to extract a consistent storyline.
- In 1945, he claimed that during his work at the *Sonderkommando*, 1.5 million people were killed, more than the orthodoxy today claims for the camp's entire existence.
- Not satisfied with the Soviet propaganda claim of 4 million victims, he increased that total during the Höss Trial to more than 4.5 million.
- Selections of inmates at the railway ramp were conducted by the ineluctable Josef Mengele, as if no other SS physician ever worked at Auschwitz.
- He claimed that up to 3,000 people went into the underground morgue of Crematoria II and III, which would have led to an impossible packing density of $(3,000 \div 210 \text{ m}^2 =)$ just over 14 people per m².
- Against all other witnesses and the mainstream's current claim, he insisted that the alleged homicidal gas chamber inside Crematorium V was equipped with false showerheads. He confused this with the basements of Crematoria II and III, which had real showers – declared false by many witnesses.
- The intended victims were issued towels, soap and *toothbrushes* (that is unique!) before entering the gas chamber of Crematorium V. This most certainly would never have happened, considering the mess it would have created, and the effort necessary to retrieve and clean these items afterwards.
- Mandelbaum claimed that Zyklon B needed to get wet to release its poison, whereas the opposite is true: moisture severely impeded the release of hydrogen-cyanide vapors from the carrier material.
- The gassing lasted half an hour, or maybe only seven minutes, and then the room was briefly aired out by opening doors "on both sides", although none of the gas chambers had doors on both sides, and the ventilation of a room stuffed full of people and without a forceful mechanical ventilation would have taken many hours, if not days. The *Sonderkommando* members worked in the chambers almost right away, and often succumbed to the gas, but did not die – when in fact they would not have lived for long.
- In Crematoria II and III, the gas was inserted through "windows," "4 gas injection devices," or some "columns with screens"; yet once all victims had died after 7 minutes, "gas was still released," meaning that the Zyklon pellets could not be retrieved. This clashes with the current orthodox narrative of a retrievable Zyklon container.
- The victims were so tightly packed that they kept standing up straight even after they died – which is physically impossible.
- Four to six corpses were placed into each cremation muffle – designed and sized to hold only one body.
- The cremation of such a physically impossible load lasted 12 to 15 minutes, when in fact the cremation of just one body took an entire hour.
- The crematorium he worked in had ten furnaces – while Crematoria II and III each had five triple-muffle furnaces, and Crematoria IV and V had one 8-muffle furnace each.
- He claimed that 3,000 people had to be cremated per shift, and that just two persons loaded these 3,000 bodies into the elevator. Hence, they lifted some $(3,000 \times 60 \text{ kg} \div 2 =)$ 90 metric tons during one shift, which is impossible to accomplish even for a strong, fit man.
- He insisted that during arrival of large transports from Hungary, the crematoria were shut down and pyres used instead, because the corpses allegedly burned better in them. But that is patently absurd; why develop cremation furnaces in the first place, if simple pyres worked so well? And why were cremation furnaces built in so many German concentration camps, at great expense? Later, however, he claimed that "the trunks and thighs" did not burn in the pits, hence had to be fished out

of the ashes, and thrown into another blazing pit… Air photos prove, however, that no open-air incineration pits existed in Birkenau during the deportation of the Hungarian Jews.
- Mandelbaum made up a non-existing visit to the crematorium by Himmler and army generals in late summer of 1944, and spoke of other, equally non-existing commissions visiting from Berlin.
- He insisted that one of those conjured-up commission members stated that the Jews "burned like paper." That was Mandelbaum's preposterous false claim.
- Mandelbaum claimed that corpses were thrown on top of an already blazing, gigantic pyre, which would have been all but physically impossible, considering the heat of such a large fire.
- He also repeated the tall tale that highly combustible fat did not burn but rather dripped out of the burning corpses, ran along gutters at the pit's bottom, was collected in special pans in holes, retrieved from there, and poured right back onto the pyre. He even expressly stated: "So the deceased in the pits fried rather than burned."
- In 1942 alone, when Mandelbaum wasn't even at Auschwitz, he insisted that 25 railway cars full of victims' spectacles were hauled out of Auschwitz.

The last statement is typical for this witness, who had very little first-hand knowledge of anything, yet still regurgitated whatever rumor, cliché and black propaganda he had heard, made it his own, and wrapped it in a story that changed with every testimony he gave. (For details, see Mattogno 2021d, pp. 179-216.)

MANSFELD, GÉZA

Géza Mansfeld was a professor of medicine from Budapest, who was incarcerated at the Auschwitz Camp until it was conquered by the Soviets on 27 February 1945. Together with three other European professors, and coached by their Soviet captors, he signed an appeal on 4 March 1945 "To the International Public," which contained many untrue propaganda clichés about Auschwitz. See the entry on Berthold Epstein for details.

MANUSEVICH, DAVID

David Manusevich was a Jew who, from November 1942 to May 1943, was interned in a camp at Brody some 100 km northeast of Lviv. From there, he was sent to Bełżec Camp. He somehow managed to escape, but got arrested again. He ultimately ended up in the Janowska Camp, allegedly to be executed. Instead, he was assigned in June 1943 to exhume mass graves near the city of Lviv, and to burn the extracted bodies on pyres within the context of what today's orthodoxy calls *Aktion* 1005.

He gave a statement on 13 September 1944 to Soviet investigators, which was later introduced as evidence during the Nuremberg International Military Tribunal (Document USSR-6(c), *IMT*, Vol. 7, p. 391). Here are some of Manusevich's peculiar claims:
- In the Bełżec Camp operated a human soap factory producing "soap from human bodies," which is a propaganda lie (see the entry on Belzec). He added that persons were sent for extermination to Belzec from Italy and France – which is untrue as well.
- At Bełżec, "2 million people were exterminated," which is almost five times the amount assumed by today's orthodoxy.
- Manusevich claimed that the pyres he built were 4 to 5 meters high, which is probably an exaggeration, as proper pyres for open-air incinerations are usually only up to 2 m high. Building and maintaining the burning of anything larger is too challenging and impractical: Did the inmates have a crane to get bodies and wood onto layers more than 2 meters off the ground? And how did they prevent this huge pile, which inevitably burned unevenly, from toppling over, spilling embers, burning wood and partially burned body parts all over the place?
- He claimed that all cremation ashes were sifted through a "special sieve," undoubtedly to separate unburned remains from the ashes. If 100,000 bodies were processed, as the orthodoxy claims, then several thousand metric tons of ashes and unburned remains had to be processed this way by a few dozen inmates within a few months – in sieves that would have clogged with the first load. Moreover, any occasional rainfall would have rendered any burned-out pyre into a moist heap of highly alkaline, corrosive slush that could not have been processed at all. Hence, Manusevich's tale is pure fiction.
- He moreover claimed that all bones were ground down in a "specially constructed grinding machine." However, this alleged mill later turned out to have been a road-building device to crush gravel. Since most inmates from the Janowska Camp were deployed in building roads, this is

what this machine was used for. A photo taken by a Soviet investigative commission shows Manusevich with two other witnesses (Heinrich Chamaides and Moische Korn) standing next to the claimed machine. This shows that at least these three witnesses knew each other and collaborated as a group with the Soviet commission, meaning that their testimonies were probably harmonized and orchestrated to some degree. (See the entry on bone mill.)
- He claimed a total death toll of some 200,000 for the areas he worked on – in contrast to the 120,000 assumed by the orthodoxy today (based on Heinrich Chamaides's claim).
- Due to these gargantuan mass shootings at the Janowska Camp, "an entire lake of blood has formed, measuring 4 x 5 meters and 1 meter deep."
- Other units of the German Security Service were sent to Janowska Camp to learn the trade of mass executions and take "training courses in cremation." There is no trace of any other units, or of any training course of this kind.
- Cremating an average human body during open-air incinerations requires some 250 kg of freshly cut wood. Cremating 200,000 bodies thus requires some 50,000 metric tons of wood. This would have required the felling of all trees growing in a 50-year-old spruce forest covering 111 hectares of land, or some 249 American football fields. An average prisoner is rated at being able to cut some 0.63 metric tons of fresh wood per workday. To cut this amount of wood within the six month (160 days) that this operation supposedly lasted would have required a work force of some 500 dedicated lumberjacks just to cut the wood. Manusevich stated that his unit consisted only of 126 inmates, all busy digging out mass graves, extracting bodies, building pyres, sifting through ashes, scattering the ashes, refilling the graves with soil, and planting them with grass seeds and saplings. He says nothing about where the firewood came from.

(For more details, see Mattogno 2022c, pp. 516-518.)

MARCO, ENRIC

Enric Marco (12 April 1921 – 21 May 2022) once was the president of the Spanish association of former inmates of the Mauthausen Camp, *Amical de Mauthausen*. Marco had claimed since the late 1970s to have been incarcerated in the German camps of Mauthausen and Flossenbürg during the war. During the 60th anniversary of the liberation of Auschwitz on 27 January 2005, he even addressed the Spanish parliament on occasion of the International Holocaust Remembrance Day. But these were all lies, as Spanish mainstream historian Benito Bermejo found out in early 2005. During the war, Marco actually volunteered in 1941 to work in a German navy dockyard, from where he returned to Spain in 1943. He never saw any German camp from the inside (Tremlett 2005; Badcock 2015; Cercas 2018).

MARCUS, KURT

Enric Marco

A certain Kurt Marcus authored a German essay whose title translates as "Auschwitz-Birkenau. The largest Extermination Camp of the World." It was introduced into evidence during the Warsaw show trial against Rudolf Höss. No inmate by that exact name is known, although there were two inmates whose last name was spelled with a "k," but it is unknown whether one of them was the author. This essay has one of the highest densities of preposterous nonsense ever found in any account, such as:
- SS members assured Marcus in the spring of 1945 (!) – when Auschwitz had already been evacuated by the Germans – that they had planned to build 34 more crematoria!
- The entire population of Poland "and other nations of the East, and perhaps also of the West," were next in line to be exterminated, "exactly like the Jews."
- Even Africans had been brought to Europe with transport aircraft and taken to Auschwitz.
- From mass graves, geysers of water and blood squirted up to 3 m high, and "corpses, sprinkled with chlorine, were thrown up to 1 meter into the air."
- Although the "area was extremely swampy" – which is true, due to the high groundwater level – he dug pits four meters deep, in which to burn the corpses – although these pits would have quickly filled with water.
- Bodies were stacked up in open ditches, drenched with crude oil, and burned – without any firewood, although open-air incinerations of this type

require vast amounts of fuel.
- In fact, "no wood needs to be added if average or well-nourished human bodies burn." However, self-immolating bodies are simply a myth.
- Fat running to the bottom of the pit was scooped up by inmates with iron ladles on long handles, and poured right back onto the burning bodies.
- Before entering the alleged gas chamber, everyone received a towel and soap. This most certainly would never have happened, considering the mess it would have created and the effort necessary to retrieve and clean these items afterwards.
- The chamber was equipped with showers, towel holders, soap dishes and bath mats. No other witness has ever claimed that, and there are no traces on the remaining wall ruins of anything having been fixed to these walls.
- Zyklon was introduced by sprinkling it through a hole onto a net hanging beneath the ceiling. That is probably a misunderstood interpretation of the wire-mesh Zyklon-B introduction columns claimed by the orthodoxy.
- The execution lasted only 3 to 5 minutes, and the doors were opened after only some 15 minutes, and only then were fans turned on to ventilate the place. In fact, the place would have had to be ventilated for several hours before it could have been opened.
- The cremation of two bodies in each muffle took 15 to 30 minutes – when in fact the cremation of one single body took an entire hour.
- If another transport was already waiting, the corpses were laid out in front of the crematorium for everyone to see, "or they drove the men into the gas chamber on top of the corpses of their gassed wives and children" – because there was plenty of room to spare, and every intended gassing victim would have willingly agreed to climb on the heap of dead bodies to be killed next…
- When transports from Hungary started arriving in May 1944, cremations were carried out in the crematoria and in the open ditches. "For months on end, the sky over Birkenau glowed night and day in the fiery glow of the burnt corpses." Air photos show, however, that nothing of that sort ever happened.
- 800,000 Hungarian Jews were killed at Auschwitz – although documents show only a little more than 400,000 Jews having been *deported* from Hungary in total.
- The total Auschwitz death toll amounted to 5 million – rather than the one million claimed by today's mainstream historians.

It is telling that a Polish court accepted this blatant nonsense as evidence. This means that the entire proceedings were just that. (For details, see Mattogno 2021, pp. 395-401.)

MARIJAMPOLE

Marijampole is a Lithuanian city some 120 km west of Vilnius. According to a German document from 1 September 1941, 5,090 persons were killed there by German *Einsatzgruppen* units. In the summer of 1996, Marijampole's city administration decided to erect a Holocaust Memorial on top of the presumed mass graves, whose locations were not exactly known. Archeological explorations at the spot indicated by witnesses initially failed, but a mass grave was eventually found some 100 m farther away. However, since the reason for this exploration was only to locate the grave, no efforts were made to exhume and forensically examine the victims in order to establish their number, their likely identity, or the perpetrators.

In 2008, Lithuanian newspapers reported about a mass grave located beneath the buildings of a former Red-Army barracks, some of it underneath a large, one-meter-thick concrete slab. Excavation was stopped, as it would have required heavy machinery to remove this slab. No efforts were made to exhume and identify any of the bodies found, or who their killers were.

It is unclear whether this site is identical with the one explored in 1996, which was located near an already existing, older memorial. It is hard to believe that the Soviets would have built a military barracks on top of one or more mass graves containing Jewish victims killed by their former enemies. If they did, was their intention to cover up their former enemy's crimes?

This case highlights a general problem with excavations of mass graves allegedly containing victims of German mass atrocities. The Germans are considered to have killed up to two million civilians in the East, most of them Jews. However, some 20 million civilians were murdered by the Soviets since the Bolshevist Revolution, and a similar number of people are said to have died in the Second World War. Therefore, any mass grave found on the territory of the former Soviet Union is more likely to contain victims of war and Soviet atrocities than victims of German atrocities. It is therefore not at all superfluous to ask for confirmation of the victims' identity and their likely murderers. But such efforts are rarely if ever made. Today's Germans are happy to take any blame for anything, and neither money nor fame can be gained by pinning a mass grave onto the Soviets. It is actually a crime in Russia; they have declared illegal any attempts to denigrate the commemoration of the Great Patriotic War.

(For more details, see Mattogno 2022c, pp. 694-699.)

MARŠÁLEK, HANS

Johann Karl Maršálek

Johann Karl (aka Hans) Maršálek (19 July 1914 – 9 Dec. 2011) was an Austrian communist of Bohemian descent. He got caught in 1941 organizing acts of sabotage, for which he ended up incarcerated at the Mauthausen Camp. He was deployed there as a clerk, and used his position to organize the camp's inmate resistance group and carry out acts of sabotage. After the war, he was employed by the Austrian government as a special agent to hunt down alleged war criminals. He had a leading role in organizing an association of former Mauthausen inmates.

Maršálek played a key role in the formation of atrocity lies about the Mauthausen Camp when he signed an affidavit on 8 April 1946 claiming to have interrogated the former Mauthausen commandant Franz Ziereis, and summarizing the contents of that alleged interrogation (3870-PS, *IMT*, Vol. 33, pp. 279-286). In this affidavit, Maršálek claims that Ziereis had been shot by U.S. troops on 22 May 1945 when trying to flee, and was bleeding to death from three gunshot wounds. In that state, during the night from 22 to 23 May, he supposedly made the confession that Maršálek then summarizes. Among other things, it contains the following absurd claims:

– Ziereis had personally executed 4,000 inmates.
– At the Gusen Subcamp, pieces of human skin with tattoos on them were tanned and turned into book bindings, lampshades and purses.
– Himmler allegedly ordered all inmates of the camps at Mauthausen and Gusen killed by herding them into a mining tunnel, then dynamiting the exit, thus burying them alive.
– The Mauthausen Camp had a gassing facility camouflaged as a bathroom.
– A gas van shuttled between the Mauthausen and Gusen Camps, gassing inmates along the way, and it was driven by Ziereis himself.
– Between 1 and 1½ million people were killed at the euthanasia center at Hartheim Castle near Linz.

A key feature of this "confession" is that Maršálek has Ziereis incriminate the entire roster of leading SS personalities: Heinrich Himmler, Reinhardt Heydrich, Ernst Kaltenbrunner, Heinrich Müller, Richard Glücks and Oswald Pohl, among others. As such, the document was then used during the Nuremberg tribunals.

A second version of this "confession" exists, presumably authored by two Polish inmates working at the Mauthausen hospital where Ziereis lay dying. This document is longer, was written during the night of 23 to 24 May 1945, and contains elements not included in Maršálek's version, but which makes even more-absurd claims, such as

– a total of four million victims of the camps of the Mauthausen complex;
– ten million victims from the areas of Warsaw, Kaunas (Kowno) and Libau;
– a homicidal gassing at the Gusen Subcamp, although the entire orthodoxy agrees that this camp had no such facility;
– an undocumented Himmler visit to Mauthausen during which he ordered the inmates working at the quarry to carry rocks weighing more than 50 kg (110 lbs) up a steep hill;
– Ziereis getting summoned to Berlin – of which no trace exists – because the 3% mortality at his camp was considered much too low – while documents prove that Berlin always strove to *reduce* camp mortalities;
– An invented meeting of camp commandants at the Sachsenhausen Camp, where they were allegedly shown an installation for neck-shooting inmates.

Maršálek has admitted indirectly that his entire story of having interrogated Ziereis was invented: In the second, 1980 edition of his book on the history of the Mauthausen Camp, we read that Ziereis was arrested on 23 May 1945, hence a day *after* he claims to have interviewed him. Furthermore, the book does not contain any reference to his alleged Ziereis interview anymore, but tellingly states in its preface that "all statements that cannot be documented [...] have been deleted" – including any reference to his 1946 affidavit.

Maršálek thus became one of the most-influential historians of the Mauthausen Camp's history. (For details, see Mattogno 2016e, pp. 133-150; Alvarez 2023, pp. 144-147.)

MASS GRAVES

The orthodox Holocaust narrative contains a plethora of claims about mass graves of Jewish victims which are said to have been emptied out later, when the order was allegedly issued to erase the traces of these mass crimes, by exhuming the corpses and burning them using large open-air incinerations. (See the entry for *Aktion* 1005.) For this reason, in many cases, the mass graves themselves cannot be investigated, but merely the area or volume where they are supposed to have been located. In order to establish how many corpses a certain volume of an alleged mass grave could have contained, it is important to know what the possible and most-likely packing density of such mass graves were – meaning how many bodies could or were commonly buried per given space, usually given as "bodies per cubic meter."

Packing Density

Mass graves of known and well-documented cases of mass death or murder, such as those created in Hamburg after the Allied bombing in 1943, in the Bergen-Belsen Camp by the British to bury typhus victims, the mass graves of Polish officers exhumed at Katyn, or of Jewish victims of German mass shootings behind the Eastern front, show that the density with which bodies are commonly packed in them lies only between 1 to 2.5 bodies per cubic meter. (See Dalton 2020, pp. 29f.; Rudolf 2019, p. 264.) While higher density are physically possible, easily up to 6 or even 8 bodies per cubic meter, such values are rarely achieved, since usually layers of bodies get covered with soil before a new layer is added, and because graves are usually not filled higher than up to one meter beneath the surface in order to avoid accidental exposure of body parts – be it by weather and erosion, by wild life and human landscaping, or by horticultural and agricultural activities. Another limiting factor is the depth of a grave, which can be limited due to a location's groundwater level; digging a pit deeper than that level would result in it filling up with water even during the digging process, and depending on the nature of the soil, may prevent the digging of deeper pits, as the side walls may become increasingly unstable.

Auschwitz

Outside the Birkenau Camp, some 160 meters north of where Crematorium V was later located, air photos taken in 1944 show elongated rectangles that have a distinctively lighter color than the surrounding vegetation. All of these rectangles were some 10 meters wide, with two of them measuring 100 meters in length, two others some 130 meters.

It may be assumed that these rectangles are the visible remains of former mass graves containing the victims of the typhus epidemic raging in the Auschwitz Camp since mid-1942, some of which could not be cremated in 1942 due to a lack of cremation capacity.

Documents show that some 48,500 detainees died at Auschwitz during 1942. The documented coke supplies to the main-camp crematorium indicate that only some 12,000 could have been cremated by that facility. Hence, some 36,500 corpses had to be cremated using open-air incinerations, although many of them were probably first buried in mass graves.

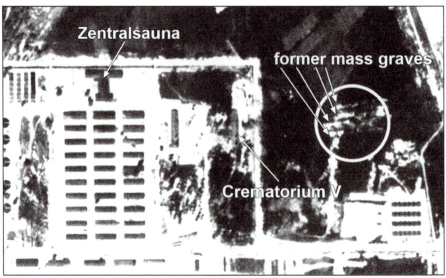

Section enlargement of a German air photo of the Auschwitz-Birkenau Camp of 31 May 1944, showing four elongated rectangular shapes north (right) of Crematorium V, probably the traces of former mass graves.

However, due to the high groundwater level in this area not drained by any ditches, these mass graves could not have been deeper than one or two meters at most. If we assume a net usable depth of one meter to bury corpses, and a common packing density of 1 to 2.5 corpses per cubic meter, this would result in (2×[100m×10m×1m] + 2×[130m×10m×1m]=) 4,600 m³ of usable space, with room for some 4,600 to 11,500 corpses. If we assume an extreme and unlikely packing density of some 8 corpses per m³, this would make room for 36,800 bodies. Either way, these numbers are compatible with the documented numbers of excess deaths of registered inmates who died mainly of diseases and whose bodies could not be cremated in the Main Camp's crematorium.

The orthodoxy claims that, between early 1942 and late September 1942, up to 107,000 bodies were buried in mass graves – victims of the typhus epidemic *plus* those allegedly gassed in the so-called bunkers. However, the space that can be identified in air photos as possible mass graves could not have accommodated this many bodies. No systematic attempts to locate and excavate/investigate alleged mass graves or their remnants have been made at Auschwitz (or if they were made, the results have not been published). Starting in late September 1942, the mass graves are said to have been reopened, and the human remains they contained extracted and burned on huge pyres. (See Rudolf 2020a, p. 119; Mattogno 2016b, esp. pp. 35f., 56, 123.)

"*Aktion Reinhardt*" Camps

At the Chełmno Camp, mass graves are said to have been filled with the victims of mass-murder since late 1941. In the summer of 1942, the decision was made – either for hygienic reasons or on Himmler's order – to exhume and burn the remains of these buried victims. Several attempts were made to locate those claimed mass graves, but only in 2003-2004 were investigators able to locate some spots containing human ashes and bones. However, the spots where drilling core samples were taken were so far apart that no conclusion could be drawn about the shape and size of any (former) mass burial sites associated with these sampling locations. Therefore, the possible size and contents of potential former mass graves near that camp are unknown. (For details, see Mattogno 2017, esp. pp. 73f., 95-105.)

In the Sobibór Camp, some 80,000 victims of mass murder are said to have been buried in mass graves, which were supposedly exhumed and cremated with open-air incinerations starting in October of 1942.

In the Belzec Camp, all 441,000 deportees to this camp (presumably murdered there) are said to have been buried in mass graves, which were supposedly exhumed and cremated with open-air incinerations starting in January of 1943.

In the Treblinka Camp, some 764,000 of the Jews deported to this camp (presumably murdered there) are said to have been buried in mass graves, which were supposedly exhumed and cremated with open-air incinerations starting in April of 1943.

Modern archaeological research by mainstream scholars was done on all three camp areas since 1999. The effective volume of mass graves located in those camps, the claimed number of corpses once buried in them, and the resulting packing density is summarized in the following table:

Camp	claimed no. of buried corpses	effective grave volume [m³]	no. of bodies per m³ of grave	no. of victims at 3 bodies/m³
Bełżec	441,000	~ 18,565	~ 23.8	~ 56,000
Sobibór	80,000	~ 13,275	~ 6.0	~ 40,000
Treblinka	764,000	~ 14,300	~ 53.4	~ 43,000

From this, we see that there simply wasn't enough space in the Belzec and Treblinka camps to bury anywhere near the number of corpses claimed. Even the resulting packing density for Sobibór is at the high end. If we assume a more-realistic packing density for all camps of 3 bodies per cubic meter, the resulting numbers of victims possibly buried are given in the last column. But even if we push the packing density to the physical extreme of 10 bodies per cubic meter, still only some 40% of all deportees sent to Belzec and only 20% of those deported to Treblinka could have been buried there. Where are the remaining bodies?

However, the grave-volume figures given by the mainstream researchers are inflated, because they did *not* detect mass graves, but rather regions with disturbed soil. This includes soil regions disturbed by previous archeological digs and by many years of wild diggings by local residents, some of which were not done in areas of former mass graves. Therefore, the true figures of total mass-grave volume must have been even smaller than this. (For details, see Mattogno 2021e, pp. 274-278.)

Soviet Union

The Eastern-European Theater of World War Two

had been a region of many mass murders and deaths ever since the outbreak of World War One. War casualties during the First World War were complemented by civilian deaths due to epidemics. The war transitioned into a bloody revolution that cost the lives of millions on the battlefield, due to Red Terror and White counter terror, starvation and more epidemics. After the victory of the Red Terror, Leninist and then Stalinist terror led to mass executions of dissidents and citizens resisting forced collectivization.

Ukraine was hit particularly hard with all this, and it escalated in the 1930s with Stalin's attempt to subdue the Ukrainians with a starvation policy, leading to the death of millions in the ensuing famine called the Holodomor. The ongoing Stalinist terror leading to more and more mass graves of killed (alleged) dissidents and opponents transitioned straight into the mass slaughter of World War Two, with millions of military deaths on both sides, with hundreds of thousands of non-combatants killed by both sides, and with subsequent violent ethnic and political cleansings in areas re-conquered by the Red Army. Hence, the soils of Ukraine, Belarus, the Baltic countries and Western Russia are littered with mass graves altogether containing tens of millions of corpses from all these conflicts and disasters.

Einsatzgruppen

Somewhere among these mass graves are those of Jews killed for whatever reasons by German units such as the *Einsatzgruppen*.

Considering that a large amount of mass graves in these areas contain victims of Soviet terror and oppression, it cannot surprise anyone that the Soviet Union and today's Russia have never had any interest in systematically searching for mass graves, then exhume and forensically investigate their contents to determine the nature of the victims, their cause of death and their perpetrators. However, as the Red Army advanced in previously German-occupied territories since 1943, Soviet investigators did locate numerous alleged mass graves presumably containing victims of German mass executions, carried out exhumations and forensic excavations, and eventually published some of the results.

Unfortunately, none of these investigations were conducted with the involvement of international observers, as the Germans did when investigating the Katyn and Vinnitsa mass graves. In fact, the commissions had a similar composition and setup as the one that committed the Soviet fraud of pinning the Katyn Massacre on the Germans toward the end of the war. Hence, the credibility of these commission reports about mass graves with alleged victims of presumed German atrocities is rather low.

Very few forensic investigations have been conducted after the collapse of the Soviet Union, because both Jewish organizations and modern Russia oppose them, as neither have much, if anything, to gain from a revision of the current narrative. After all, both groups managed to establish their narrative of what happened under German occupation as the "truth" without the need of any kind of forensic proof. This narrative, which for the most part is based merely on anecdotal evidence, is even enforced by penal law in many countries, Israel and Russia included. Hence, there is little prospect, if any, of any relevant forensic research being conducted in the foreseeable future.

The mass graves containing victims of German mass executions are said to have been opened, and any human remains burned almost tracelessly, starting in the summer of 1943, presumably due to a Himmler order to efface all evidence. For more on this operation dubbed "*Aktion* 1005," see the entry on this.

(For details on mass graves in the former Soviet Union and their investigation, see Mattogno 2022c, Part 2.)

Inconsistencies

Note the inconsistent and irreconcilably different times at which the exhumations and cremations of mass graves of claimed German atrocities are said to have begun, although Himmler's order was allegedly issued in early 1942:

Location/Unit	Claimed start of mass-grave exhumation
Chełmno	summer 1942
Auschwitz	late September 1942
Sobibór	October 1942
Belzec	January 1943
Majdanek	February 1943
Treblinka	April 1943
Einsatzgruppen	July 1943

Note also that none of this is based on any documents. The one document by Himmler that speaks of what to do with the bodies of deceased Jews dates from 20 November of 1942 and clearly specifies that the bodies of deceased Jews have to be *either* cremated *or* buried. Hence, still in late 1942, no order existed to exhume and cremate all buried bodies. (See Mattogno 2022c, p. 450.)

MAUTHAUSEN

On 9 August 1938, a new concentration camp near the Austrian town of Mauthausen near the city of Linz was established. The camp was mainly populated by political prisoners, later also Soviet PoWs and partisans from southeastern Europe. The camp served as a reservoir of slave labor for several enterprises, foremost a company for construction material employing inmates in a large granite quarry. Jews became a sizable part of the camp population only when other camps filled with Jews started to evacuate their inmates westward toward the end of the war.

Although Mauthausen has the reputation of having been one of the most brutal camps of the Third Reich, it enters Holocaust history due to the alleged presence of facilities to mass murder inmates with toxic gasses. The first propaganda reports about alleged mass murder in a homicidal gas chamber at the Mauthausen Camp were published in a Jewish periodical in the United States already in November 1941 – at a point in time when orthodox historians insist that no such facility yet existed. In fact, no documents exist at all which support the orthodoxy's claim that a homicidal gas chamber existed at the Mauthausen Camp.

Not satisfied with one utterly unsupported claim, the orthodoxy added another related hypothesis: the Mauthausen Camp also had a gas van in which inmates were murdered with exhaust gas. Both claims ultimately rest on an affidavit written by third persons about what the commandant of the Mauthausen Camp, Franz Ziereis, supposedly stated while lying on his death bed, bleeding to death from gunshot wounds. Rather than providing medical care, several former inmates allegedly interrogated him in that state, and then concocted an "affidavit," not signed by Ziereis, but by the inmates. (See the entry on Hans Maršálek.)

One of the claims put into Ziereis's mouth via this "affidavit" concerns an alleged meeting of all concentration-camp commanders at the SS headquarters in Oranienburg – or rather the Sachsenhausen Camp attached to these headquarters. During that meeting, these commanders were allegedly shown an automatic shoot-in-the-neck device for the conveyor-belt execution of Soviet commissars. No evidence exists for this meeting nor for the existence of a shoot-in-the-neck device during the war.

Orthodox historians take this invented meeting as their basis to claim that, upon his return from this meeting, Ziereis initiated the construction of a homicidal gas chamber at Mauthausen. But the "affidavit" about Ziereis's alleged death-bed confessions claims that the homicidal gas chamber was constructed either on the initiative of the SS garrison physician of the Mauthausen Camp, Eduard Krebsbach, or on orders of Richard Glücks, chief inspector of concentration camps. Apart from this "affidavit," there is not a shred of evidence to support any of this.

During the Soviet Show Trial against former staff members of the Sachsenhausen Camp, the claim about the meeting of camp commandants in that camp for the sake of inspecting the above-mentioned execution device was "confirmed" by witness testimony.

Also "confirmed" by witness testimony during a later West-German show trial were claims of mass murder by gassings perpetrated at the Mauthausen Camp. The location allegedly used for that was a

"Gas chamber" of Mauthausen, with real showerheads of the real inmate shower at the ceiling, and a radiator on the wall. (Photo of 1990.)

real(!) shower room of just 13.3 square meters of floor area, located in the basement of the camp's inmate hospital. This room was supposedly "retrofitted" with a metal box and a fan in an adjacent room. A hot brick was supposedly put into the box, then shreds of Zyklon-B wood-fiber disks were presumably put onto that brick, the box was closed, and the fan turned on. The fan blew the evaporating fumes through a pipe into the shower room.

This procedure was not only primitive, but also highly dangerous. Putting shreds of wood fiber soaked with hydrogen cyanide onto a hot brick would result in the instant release of cyanide vapors, like water hitting a hot surface. Before the box could have been closed, these vapors would have spread throughout the room, which was not ventilated. To make matters worse, mixtures of 5.4% and more of hydrogen cyanide in air are explosive. If the brick had been pre-heated a little too much, the whole thing could have blown up into the face of whoever was trying to put those fiber shreds into the box.

Keep in mind that, at the same time, and in contrast to this nonsense, it is documented that a professional Austrian pest-control company set up proper DEGESCH circulation fumigation chambers at the Mauthausen Camp, which were designed to prevent any dangerous situation. That same company is said to have been involved in rigging the homicidal gas chamber with a "brick" heater. Hence, instead of equipping the homicidal chamber with the safe technology known and available to them that would have allowed the claimed crimes to be perpetrated professionally, this company supposedly used an utterly ridiculous setup for the homicidal gas chamber: a "preheated" brick was put into a box… That is a sure sign of delusions conjured up by incompetent witnesses.

After the war, as the Mauthausen Camp was prepared to serve as a museum, the shower room was "reconstructed." As was the case at the Auschwitz Main Camp's crematorium, neither the original state nor the "reconstructions" performed during that phase were recorded. The claimed gas-introduction box with pipes disappeared, and the two original doors were replaced with two air-raid-shelter doors made of steel and with peepholes. This way, the room now looks menacing to the uninformed visitor. The original doors have totally disappeared.

Unlike Auschwitz, where the Museum admits at least some of the fraudulent post-war changes, visitors of the Mauthausen Museum are misled to this day to believe that the room is in its original condition, when in fact it is a post-war forgery. If the original doors to this room could have convincingly serve as "gas chamber" doors, they wouldn't have been replaced by air-raid-shelter doors.

Speaking the truth – this room *is* a postwar forgery – is punishable with up to ten years imprisonment in Austria.

(For more details, see Mattogno 2016e, pp. 130-150.)

MENGELE, JOSEF

Josef Mengele (16 March 1911 – 7 Feb. 1979), SS *Hauptsturmführer*, had two PhD titles, one in anthropology, and the other in medicine. From mid-1940 to mid-1942, he served as a medical officer behind the front line. Due to serious injuries incurred in mid-1942, he was declared unfit for military duty. After his recovery, he was assigned to the Auschwitz Camp on 24 May 1943. He arrived there on 30 May, and took over the position of camp physician at the Gypsy Camp on 17 June of that year (Auschwitz-Birkenau, Sector BIIe).

Josef Mengele

On 13 December 1943, Mengele was successfully recommended to receive the War Merit Cross 2nd Class, with the following reasons given:

"He has particularly distinguished himself in the fulfillment of the [tasks] assigned to him and, beyond his service, has still been active with urgent scientific problems in the research of the racial affiliation of the Gypsies. In addition, he has regularly collaborated in the completion of special tasks. In the course of his medical duties in combating the severe typhus epidemic in Auschwitz CC, he became infected himself and contracted a very severe typhus disease, after he had already contracted severe malaria in June/July 1943, also in the course of his duties at Auschwitz CC." (See Mattogno 2023, Part 1, p. 375.)

On 19 August 1944, his boss, the garrison physician of the Auschwitz Camp, Dr. Eduard Wirths, wrote a professional evaluation of Mengele, in which he stated:

"Dr. Mengele has an open, honest, firm character. He is absolutely reliable, upright and straight. In his appearance he shows no weakness

of character, opinions or addictions. He acquired his knowledge during his work in Auschwitz CC practically and theoretically as a camp physician in the fight against serious epidemics. With prudence, perseverance and energy he fulfilled all the tasks assigned to him, often under the most difficult conditions, to the complete satisfaction of his superiors, and showed himself ready to face any situation.

In addition, as an anthropologist, he has eagerly used the short time he had left off duty to further his own education, and has made a valuable contribution to anthropological science in his work by evaluating the scientific material available to him on the basis of his official position. His achievements are therefore to be described as outstanding. […] He is catholic. […] In the most conscientious performance of his medical duties, he contracted typhus while fighting the epidemic in Auschwitz. […]

In addition to his medical knowledge, Dr. M. possesses special knowledge as an anthropologist. He appears quite suitable for any other assignment and also for the next higher assignment. He has no criminal record. As an SS doctor, he is popular and respected everywhere [even among inmates…].*" (Ibid., p. 447)*

Israeli historian Efraim Zuroff discovered that Mengele's image among former Auschwitz inmates who were interviewed right after the war was rather harmless. His image as the "Angel of Death," who is said to have committed unspeakable atrocities, particularly on twin children, has evolved only slowly over the decades (Zuroff 1994, pp. 127f.). In the same vein, the German professional "Nazi hunter" Adalbert Rückerl mentioned once in passing that witnesses in Australia, where media and educational campaigns about the Holocaust had been virtually non-existing for the first three decades after the war, could no longer remember any details of what happened in the camps during the war, quite in contrast to witnesses in Europe, the USA, and Israel where the Holocaust had always been a topic of public discourse (Rückerl 1984, pp. 258f.). The *Times of Israel* wrote about historians realizing that something is wrong when almost every Auschwitz survivor testifying in later years was convinced that it was Mengele who selected them for this or that fate (Mark 2020).

In other words, witnesses testifying many years or even decades after the war about Mengele and alleged events associated with him are rarely truthful, but at best suffering from false memory syndrome, repeating clichés that have grown increasingly imposing over the decades, as step by step the entire globe embraced the orthodox horror tales about Auschwitz.

Research into the fate of the twin children who were the object of Mengele's anthropological studies at Auschwitz shows that most of them actually survived the war unharmed. In fact, the survival rate among these twins was much higher than that of the average Auschwitz inmate. In other words, Mengele protected these children and made sure they had a good chance of survival. (For details, see Mattogno 2020a, pp. 383-407.)

After the war, Mengele fled to Argentina, and later lived in Paraguay and Brazil. He drowned while swimming in the ocean at the age of 67, thus managing to escape the show-trial fate of many of his colleagues. Perhaps in part for this reason, Mengele has become the victim of the greatest campaign of character assassination the world has ever seen.

The following is a list if witnesses discussed in this encyclopedia who claimed to have encountered Mengele at Auschwitz:

– Charles Bendel
– Regina Bialek
– Milton Buki
– Leon Cohen
– Szlama Dragon
– Berthold Epstein and three other professors
– Joseph Hirt
– Stanisław Jankowski
– Hermine Kranz
– Sofia Litwinska
– Henryk Mandelbaum
– Filip Müller
– Miklós Nyiszli
– Dov Paisikovic
– Rajzla Sadowska
– Shlomo Venezia
– Franz Süss
– Henryk Tauber
– Janda Weiss
– Elie Wiesel
– Otto Wolken

MERMELSTEIN, MELVIN

Melvin Mermelstein (25 Sept. 1926 – 28 Jan. 2022) was a former Auschwitz inmate who tried to take advantage of the Institute for Historical Review (IHR), located in California. This organization had had offered a reward of $50,000 to anyone who could present "provable physical evidence for the extermination of Jews in gas chambers." Mermelstein demanded that the reward be paid to him, yet the IHR refused payment, as Mermelstein merely offered his testimony but no provable physical evidence. Mermelstein subsequently sued the IHR for this sum. The judge dealing with the case determined on 9 October 1981 that the Holocaust and the killing in gas chambers with Zyklon B are indisputable facts, thus denying the defense to prove the opposite. So, the IHR grudgingly had to pay the reward plus expenses (Weber 1982). The mainstream mass media to this day celebrate this as a victory over Holocaust skepticism, although not a single argument was exchanged during that trial, let alone refuted or confirmed.

Melvin Mermelstein

This case moreover had an important aftermath, which could have easily resulted in the financial ruin of the IHR. Four years after the above trial, Bradley R. Smith published an article in the IHR's newsletter, in which he called Mermelstein a liar. Mermelstein sued the IHR again, but this time for eleven million dollars of damages. During the ensuing trial in 1991, the IHR was able to substantiate its claim that Mermelstein had indeed lied in a plethora of cases. Hence, Mermelstein met a crushing defeat, and his motion for an appeal was eventually denied (Piper 1994, O'Keefe 1994 & 1997).

METZ, ZELDA

Zelda Metz was an inmate of the Sobibór Camp. In a deposition published in a 1946 book, she claimed that executions in that camp happened in one gas chamber with chlorine. The gassing was observed by an SS man through a small window. After the murder, the floors opened, and the bodies were discharged into carts below, which brought them to mass graves.

Zelda Metz

Metz also claimed that Himmler visited the Sobibór Camp in late summer of 1943, and that, on that occasion, 7,500 "beautiful young girls were brought" to Sobibór and executed in front of him. Metz claimed that in total some two million Jews were killed at Sobibór.

All her claims are rejected as false by the orthodoxy, who insists on several gas chambers; on an engine producing lethal exhaust gas; on no observation windows; and on no collapsible floor with carts underneath. The corpses were instead taken out of the chamber manually, sideways through a normal door. Himmler visited the camp indeed, but in March 1943. However, it is preposterous to think that he spent his time watching the execution of 7,500 Jewesses. Furthermore, the orthodoxy currently claims a death toll of only some 10% of what Metz claimed.

(See the entry on Sobibór for more details, as well as Graf/Kues/Mattogno 2020, pp. 59, 71, 109, 187f.; Mattogno 2021e, p. 84.)

MICROWAVE DELOUSING

The 1936 Berlin Olympic Games were the first event in history which were transmitted live on TV. The powerful radio transmitters built for this had a frequency spectrum that was rather broad, so a minor amount of its energy was emitted in the frequency range now known as microwaves. When this transmitter was operated, it was found that insects present in the transmitter's room had died. Further investigation revealed that radiation in the microwave spectrum quickly heats water to such a degree that living creatures exposed to it would quickly be burned or boiled to death. This included not only insects, but also microbes. Thus, it quickly became apparent that this could be a highly effective, efficient and rapid method not only for disinfestation (against vermin), but also for disinfection (against germs).

When the war broke out in 1939, the importance of pest control, particularly for soldiers at the front, was once more accentuated, since infectious diseases were the second greatest cause of casualties among German soldiers. Hence, the Siemens Company, which had manufactured the TV transmitters, set out to develop a microwave device to kill pests, with a primary focus on killing lice as the carriers of epidemic typhus. The aim was to overcome the long exposure times and frequent ineffectiveness of older methods, such as hot air or toxic gasses, and to find a way of killing not just the insects, their eggs and larvae, but also the dangerous microbes they carried.

Together with the Reich Biology Institute in Berlin-Dahlem, two subsidiaries of Siemens were involved in the development of the first microwave device the world has ever seen. When the device was demonstrated to civilian and military authorities at

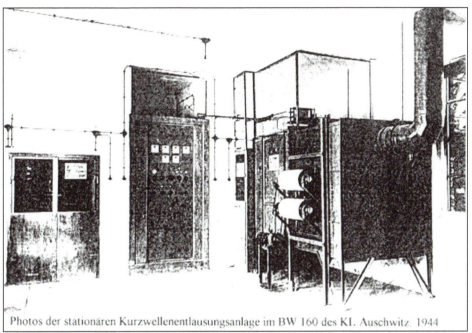
Microwave delousing device in the reception building of the Auschwitz Main Camp, summer 1944.

the beginning of the war, achieving not only a great throughput in a very short treatment time, but also absolute certainty in killing off lice, nits and microbes, the interest of the *Reichsführung* of the SS – Himmler's office – was aroused. His personnel and material support greatly facilitated the further development of microwave devices.

Initially, these facilities were supposed to be used for front-line troops, for which purpose they were mounted onto a trailer. Ultimately, however, a stationary model was given preference. To operate the device, only a 380-Volt outlet or an electric generator with that output was needed, as well as some water to moisten the items to be treated (which were not allowed to contain any metal objects).

While the conservative Wehrmacht (army) was reluctant to order these new devices, the SS was very enthusiastic and ordered an initial five devices. After the first mobile version, which was deployed in Lublin, had demonstrated phenomenal efficiency and effectiveness in 1943, five more stationary devices were ordered.

The first camp to obtain a stationary microwave disinfestation device was Auschwitz. Its delivery had been promised for May 1943, hence the construction of some of the initially planned delousing facilities using other techniques was shelved. However, the delivery was repeatedly delayed due to problems with the development, not the least because the Siemens factories in Berlin had been bombed by Allied planes. As a result, epidemic control at the Auschwitz Camp was compromised, costing the lives of many inmates in 1943 and 1944.

The first microwave device, a mobile unit, was delivered and put into operation in early 1944 at the Birkenau Camp. A second, stationary device was installed in the reception building of the Auschwitz Main Camp a few months later and became operational in June 1944. Together with the first deliveries of the insecticide DDT to the Auschwitz Camp in April 1944, this revolutionarily effective new technology heralded the end of the need for Zyklon B and its associated fumigation gas chambers.

Adjusted for inflation, the stationary microwave delousing facility cost some two million U.S. dollars (value as of 2023). Interestingly, instead of utilizing this new technology at the eastern front to protect the lives of German soldiers, Germany's wartime leaders decided to use it in Auschwitz to protect the lives of the inmates, most of whom were Jews. When it came to protecting lives threatened by infectious disease, the Germans gave priority to the Auschwitz prisoners. Since they were working in the Silesian war industries, their lives were evidently considered comparably important to the lives of German soldiers on the battlefield.

(For details, see Weber 1999; Rudolf 2019, pp. 311-317.)

MOGILEV

Mogilev is a city in eastern Belorussia. It was the location of a German PoW transit camp, where many Soviet PoWs were held captive. Due to the high death rate among them, a crematorium with several wood-fired 8-muffle cremation furnaces of the Topf Company from Erfurt, Germany, was slated to be built there. However, that project was eventually cancelled, and some of the material for these furnaces was sent to Auschwitz instead.

German wartime documents indicate that, between August and October 1941, a total of 6,434 persons were executed at Mogilev by the *Einsatzgruppen* and associated formations. Most of them were Jews. The whereabouts of their mass graves is unknown.

Mogilev is also the location of phantom extermination-camp claims. They are based on false postwar statements by Erich von dem Bach-Zelewski, who during the war was Higher SS and Police leader in this area, with his headquarters at Mogilev. In his eagerness to please his American captors, Bach-Zelewski claimed among other things that a civilian commission revealed to him a plan in 1943 to set up a homicidal gassing facility at Mogilev. Because Bach-Zelewski claimed that the region no longer had any Jews at the time, he concluded from this that the German government planned to exterminate the area's indigenous Slavic population.

Orthodox historian Richard Breitman swallowed this nonsense completely, but tried to rebrand it as an extermination camp for Jews. He tried to back it up with German wartime documents that, at closer inspection, had nothing to do with homicidal gassings at all, as another orthodox historian, Christian Gerlach, demonstrated. Despite this, Gerlach proceeded to label this camp a "death camp" anyway, based on the fact that several mass executions of partisans and Jews occurred in the Mogilev area, and that another 4,000 Jews were allegedly killed in the camp in 1942, although he could not back this up with any reliable evidence.

Stefan Pilunov, a self-proclaimed witness of alleged German mass cremations of murder victims in 1943 within the context of the so-called *Aktion* 1005, claimed in an affidavit to Soviet investigators in 1944 that he helped exhume and burn 48,000 bodies using a ludicrous cremation technique.

(For more details, see Mattogno 2012; 2022c, pp. 706-712.)

MOLL, OTTO

Otto Moll

Otto Moll (4 March 1915 – 28 May 1946), SS *Hauptscharführer* at the war's end, was employed as a gardener at the Sachsenhausen Concentration Camp until May 1941. Then he was transferred to Auschwitz, where he served in the same role. According to his own statement during postwar interrogations, he was deployed to excavate mass graves at Auschwitz in 1942. After that, he was transferred to the Monowitz Camp in late 1942, where he remained until early 1944. He was then transferred to the Gleiwitz Subcamp, were he remained until the evacuation in January 1945.

After the war, he was arrested by U.S. forces and held in Dachau, where imprisoned defendants were systematically tortured, as the U.S. commission led by van Roden and Simpson determined later.

Charles S. Bendel testified during the British Bergen-Belsen show trial that Moll had been in charge of an inmate unit deployed at the gassing "bunkers," where these inmates buried and later burned corpses during the summer and fall of 1942. Bendel moreover asserted that, during the deportation of Jews from Hungary between May and July 1944, Moll was put in charge of all Birkenau crematoria. These claims entered the court's verdict, and thus became legally indisputable "facts." An analysis of Bendel's various claims demonstrate, however, that he lied through his teeth on multiple issues, hence is untrustworthy. Other witnesses who made similar claims about Moll are Stanisław Jankowski, Henryk Tauber, Szlama Dragon and Filip Müller. (See their respective entries for an assessment of their trustworthiness.)

Due to these unchallengeable facts, Moll was sentenced to death on 13 December 1945 after a show trial staged by the U.S. in Dachau. Before he was executed, U.S. investigators interrogated him several times, probably to get "confessions" with which they could prosecute other former German officials, who were still awaiting their trial. During those interrogations, Moll accepted the claim that he was head of the crematoria during the claimed extermination of the Jews deported from Hungary. However, whenever he was asked for any details about the crematoria and about gassings supposedly taking place in them, he displayed a striking ignorance of the most basic (claimed) features of these facilities, clearly showing that he had never set a foot into these facilities, let alone managed their operations for two months.

When asked about the operations at the so-called Birkenau bunkers, he insisted that he did not know what the interrogator was talking about. Moll did not even change his mind when the interrogator pointed out to him that he was already a dead man, and that they would let him live only as long as he was willing to talk and confess. Moll insisted on his innocence and asked to be confronted with his former boss, the former Auschwitz camp commandant Rudolf Höss.

The Americans actually made this happen. They let both men talk in the presence of an interrogator and recorded the exchange. Höss, however, had been tortured by the British so severely that his spirit had been broken. He repeated any kind of historical nonsense his captors demanded him to confirm. During the confrontation with Moll, Höss betrayed him; step by step, Höss and the U.S. interrogator tried coercing Moll into confirming all Höss was claiming about him. Moll fought valiantly and desperately, but ultimately in vain. He was hanged twelve days later.

(For more details, see Mattogno 2020b, pp. 80-104, 229-231.)

The I.G. Farbenindustrie chemical plant in Auschwitz-Monowitz in winter 1944/45.

MONOWITZ

Monowitz is the German spelling of the Polish town Monowice located some 5 km east of the city of Auschwitz. East of that town, the German chemical trust *I.G. Farbenindustrie* constructed a large chemical plant starting in 1940, which was meant to convert the regional coal into liquified chemicals.

The nearby Auschwitz Camp was to provide some of its inmates as slave laborers for the construction and eventual operation of this chemical factory. To this end, the SS authorities established a labor camp right next to the chemical plant, which was also called Auschwitz-Monowitz. On 22 November 1943, all satellite camps near Auschwitz were separated from the Auschwitz Main Camp and became an independent concentration camp called Auschwitz III, with the headquarters at the Monowitz Camp. On 25 November 1944, the name was changed to Monowitz Concentration Camp.

The camp's living conditions were harsh, and so were the conditions on the I.G. Farben construction site. Many inmates got sick, and physical abuse by I.G. Farben personnel was widespread. Inmates who became unfit for work were transferred to Birkenau, which increasingly became the holding camp for inmates unfit for work. One of the camp physicians of the Monowitz Camp, Horst Fischer, was eventually tried during a show trial in communist East Germany for his role in transferring inmates from Monowitz to Birkenau. The orthodoxy claims falsely that these transferred inmates were gassed at Birkenau, when in fact Birkenau was being converted into a huge hospital camp. The Italian chemist Primo Levi described after the war the sophisticated healthcare system in place at the Monowitz Camp, of which Horst Fischer was a part.

The Monowitz Camp itself came into the focus of Holocaust claims only once, during the testimony of former SS judge Konrad Morgen, who erroneously claimed that mass exterminations of Jews were not carried out at the Auschwitz Camp but rather in "a separate extermination camp near Auschwitz, called 'Monowitz.'" No such claims have ever been made before this or afterwards by anyone.

Moravia → Czechia

MORDOWICZ, CZESŁAW

Czesław Mordowicz (2 Aug. 1919 – 28 Oct. 2001) was a Polish Jew incarcerated at the Auschwitz Camp. He managed to escape on 27 May 1944 together with Arnošt Rosin. They both wrote a report about their alleged experiences at Auschwitz, which was included in the War Refugee Board Report. (For more details, see the entries on Arnošt Rosin and the War Refugee Board Report.) After his escape, Mordowicz participated in a partisan uprising against the Slovak wartime government. He was arrested and again sent to Auschwitz, where he survived.

Czesław Mordowicz

MORGEN, KONRAD

Georg Konrad Morgen (8 June 1909 – 4 Feb. 1982), SS *Sturmbannführer*, was a judge of the SS-internal court system. In that function, he investigated numerous allegations of crimes committed in various concentration camps by members of the SS staff. Morgen testified during the International Military Tribunal (IMT) at Nuremberg and also during the Frankfurt Auschwitz show trial. The trustworthiness of this witness results from the various statements he made during the IMT. Right after swearing an oath to tell the truth, he claimed that he had been forced into the SS and was drafted into the Waffen SS at the beginning of the war. However, no one was ever forced to join the SS, and membership in the Waffen SS was strictly voluntary and limited to qualifying individuals until the later phase of the war. Having started his testimony with committing perjury in order to make himself look like a victim, Morgen then mixed true statement with tendentious claims and outrageous lies:

Georg Konrad Morgen

During his investigations of crimes committed by SS staff members in various concentration camps, he lived at the Buchenwald Camp starting in July of 1943, which he initially described rather favorably:

"The installations were clean and freshly painted. There was much lawn and flowers. The prisoners were healthy, normally fed, sun-tanned, working. […] The installations of the camp were in good order, especially the hospital. The camp authorities, under the Commander Diester, aimed at providing the prisoners with an existence worthy of human beings. They had regular mail service. They had a large camp library, even books in foreign languages. They had variety shows, motion pictures, sporting contests, and even had a brothel. Nearly all the other concentration camps were similar to Buchenwald."

Morgen amended his statement the next day, since he "did not mean to say that the concentration camps were sanatoria, or a paradise for the prisoners." He then explained:

"The prisoner could not contact the public freely, and so his observations were not made known to the public. By this isolation in the concentration camp he was practically under the sway of the camp. This meant that he had to fear that at any time crimes could be committed against him. I did not have the impression from these facts that their purpose was to produce a system of crimes; but, of necessity, individual crimes were bound to result from these conditions."

After describing how he investigated illegal killings of camp inmates by some SS staff members, among other offenses, which had occurred on a scale similar to that in the armed forces, he recounted what Christian Wirth, the head of the *Aktion Reinhardt* Camps (Belzec, Sobibor, Treblinka), allegedly had told him about the exterminations going on in his camps, presumably set in motion by a (non-existing) *Führer* order. Here is where Morgen's credibility collapses, as none of it is part of any other witness account and thus not part of today's orthodox narrative:

– In order to win the voluntary cooperation (!) of the Jews to help exterminate their fellow Jews, they were given every freedom and the right to plunder the wealth of the victims.
– Wirth even organized a huge Jewish wedding with 1,100 guests, during which "gluttonous consumption of food and alcoholic drinks occurred, and even some SS members of the camp guard joined in this revelry."
– At the extermination camps' train stations, Potemkin villages were built that made the arriving Jews think they had come to a real village or city.
– Fake cloakrooms were set up, and at various stations inside it, people had to hand in first their hats, then at the next station their coats, their shirts, etc.
– "As soon as death had set in, the ventilators were

started." None of the claimed homicidal gas chambers of these camps are said to have been equipped with fans.
- Morgen's claim about how the bodies were destroyed, however, concurs with many witness accounts in a convergence of lies about self-immolating bodies:

   "By means of a special procedure which Wirth had invented, they were burned in the open air without the use of fuel."

   However, self-immolating bodies simply do not exist.
- To develop this magical system, Wirth allegedly "received no aid, no instructions, but had to do it all by himself." The mainstream narrative claims, however, that Paul Blobel was the magician who pulled off this trick.
- Morgen also misrepresented the killing of incurable mental patients as having happened in an institution that Wirth had set up, who is said to have deceived the mental institutions sending patients to him about their impending fate, when in fact Wirth merely had advisory functions at several of the mental institutions carrying out the euthanasia program.

Morgen next described accurately the condition leading to high mortality rates at many camps, caused by *force majeure*, such as the outbreak of epidemics despite the strictest and most comprehensive measures to prevent and combat them; high fluctuations of inmates, bringing in at times more prisoners than could be accommodated; air raids destroying food, water and pharmaceutical plants and logistics, so supplies could not reach the camps anymore; and evacuations from the East leading to catastrophic overcrowding.

When reporting about Auschwitz, he got off the truth track again when claiming that exterminations in that camp were not committed at the Auschwitz Concentration Camp but rather in "a separate extermination camp near Auschwitz, called 'Monowitz,'" hence the forced-labor camp near the BUNA plant of the I.G. Farbenindustrie, where no extermination activities are said to have happened at all.

Two decades later, when testifying during the Frankfurt Auschwitz Show Trial, he lied by claiming that incoming "wagons disappeared into a depression in the ground" when driving into the underground crematoria. (See Czech 1990, p. 819.)

Morgen also claimed that the extermination of the Jews started in Christian Wirth's extermination camps, and that Auschwitz only followed later. Wirth supposedly taught the former commandant of the Auschwitz Camp Rudolf Höss how to do it, yet allegedly called Höss his "untalented student." This echoes the anti-chronological timeline which Höss gave in his various testimonies extracted by torture. Höss claimed that he learned the extermination trade by visiting Treblinka in the summer of 1941, although that camp did not become operational until late July 1942. The first gassing test at Auschwitz, however, is said to have been carried out already in September 1941, followed by more-or-less regular mass killings. Here we clearly see a convergence of a lie. Morgen was either given Höss's false affidavit(s), or he was otherwise convinced to repeat Höss's lies.

(For Morgen's Nuremberg testimony, see *IMT*, Vol. 20, pp. 487-503; his affidavits in Vol. 42, pp. 551-565.)

In an interview Morgen granted the British historian John Toland years after the war, he insisted that the stories about Ilse Koch using tattooed human skin for lampshades and other object were unfounded legends, since he had searched the Koch household himself without finding any such objects. In that context, Morgen also mentioned that he was threatened with physical violence and was physically mistreated by his U.S. interrogators, which confirms the systematic nature of physical violence used against any German official in Allied captivity after the war (see Toland 1976, pp. 845f.; see also the entry on torture).

MORGUES

Morgues, also called mortuaries, serve to temporarily store human corpses awaiting identification, autopsies and burial or cremation. To slow decay, they are usually chilled to temperatures close to the freezing point, and they are equipped with efficient ventilation systems to remove gases resulting from decomposition.

In the context of the Holocaust, it is worthwhile knowing that German architectural expert literature prior to and during World War Two recommended that morgues be equipped both with a cooling and a heating system. The later served during winter times to prevent any freezing temperature, which could lead to the corpses bursting open. Ventilation systems are recommended to carry out some five air exchanges per hour, but up to ten air exchanges in cases of intensive use. (See Mattogno 2019, pp. 46, 105.)

The only morgues of interest in connection with Holocaust mass-murder claims are the morgues of the old crematorium at the Auschwitz Main Camp and the underground morgues of Crematoria II and III at Auschwitz-Birkenau.

The morgue of the old crematorium was located right next to the furnace room, from which it was separated by a double-layered wall for insulation purposes. The room always worked with only a make-shift ventilation equipment. A properly designed powerful ventilation system was delivered in late 1941, but it was never installed.

Crematoria II and III at Birkenau had two large basement morgues each. In blueprints, these rooms are labelled as such (*Leichenkeller* = corpse cellar). The buildings were planned for a PoW camp with an expected high mortality rate due to infectious diseases, as they were quite common in these type of camps during wartime. The rooms were equipped with ventilation systems with a capacity of some ten air exchanges per hour, as would be expected for intensely used morgues. (See the section "Morgues" in the entry on ventilation for more details.)

Due to their underground construction, these morgues were kept naturally cool throughout the year. A heating system was not provided, although during construction it was contemplated to add one for Crematorium II, but that project did not come to pass. As a result, there are witness statements reporting about problems with corpses stored in those morgues having frozen together.

Since these rooms were the only large basement rooms in the entire Birkenau Camp, German building code required that they be built in such a way as to serve as auxiliary bomb shelters. Hence, they were built with massive reinforced concrete ceilings and sturdy support columns. Weakening those ceilings by later jack-hammering crude holes through the roof – allegedly for inserting Zyklon B, as the orthodoxy insists (see the entry on Zyklon-B introduction devices) – would not have been permitted by the responsible architects and engineers. (See Lüftl 2003.)

The Auschwitz Camp did not just suffer from a persistent typhus epidemic spread by lice. The camp was also infested with fleas, and rats multiplied throughout the camp. Among other things, they feasted on the bodies of inmates who had died in one of the camp's many inmate infirmaries, or in other places, and whose bodies had not yet been removed to solidly built morgues (inside the crematoria). Fearing that the plague might also break out, Auschwitz garrison physician Eduard Wirths lobbied from July 1943 until May 1944 for the construction of brick-built mortuaries in each camp sector, or at least in each infirmary, where bodies could be stored safely before getting removed to the crematoria. His request was repeatedly rejected by his superiors with the argument that, by regulation, corpses had to be picked up twice a day in the entire camp and brought to the crematoria morgues for storage. In other words, those crematoria morgues were available 24/7 for the storage of corpses, which is what they were built for. There was neither time nor space to use any of these morgues as homicidal gas chambers. (For more details on this, see Mattogno 2004c; 2016b, pp. 93f.)

MOTIVES

Regarding the Holocaust, we may identify four separate groups, each with a distinguished attitude toward the Holocaust, and propelled by different sets of motives:
1. Holocaust dogmatism
2. Holocaust skepticism
3. Holocaust denial; and
4. National-Socialist anti-Judaism.

1. Motives for Holocaust Dogmatism
War Propaganda
Leaders of a warring nation need to override the natural inhibition of their soldiers to kill, murder, even slaughter members of their own species. This is best accomplished by portraying the enemy as barbaric, savage, subhuman, inhuman, bestial. Therefore, it has been common practice in war to do exactly this. Modern media have intensified this kind of propaganda, while modern total warfare that lays waste to entire countries and kills not only soldiers but also systematically butchers civilians has intensified the need to dehumanize the enemy.

World War Two was the most atrocious war fought so far in the history of mankind. Therefore, the need for atrocity propaganda has never been as great, and its use never been as widespread and intense as in this war. Each allied nation fighting against Germany had their own motives for the propaganda they spread and sustained, ultimately leading to the orthodox Holocaust narrative as it coalesced in the first few years after the war. Each country's contribution to this, and its reasons to maintain the propaganda narrative to this day, is discussed in more detail in their respective section of the entry on propaganda.

Ideological Fanaticism

The strongest motive among the orthodoxy not to tolerate any doubt, let alone revision, of their narrative is ideological in nature. For secular and reformed Jews, who are the majority among Jews, the Holocaust has become the most-important aspect of their identity. Anything undermining the Holocaust dogma is seen as an attack on their identity, if not on their existence. Drastic revisions to the Holocaust narrative are portrayed as an assassination of memory. The attempt to destroy the commemoration of what (allegedly) happened is seen as a first step to repeating the Holocaust. Hence, many if not most Jews perceive Holocaust skepticism as an existential threat. The more radical among them consider it even justified to murder Holocaust skeptics as an act of preventing that "it" happens again.

National Socialism, with its ultimate crime, the Holocaust, is generally perceived as the ultimate evil emanation of right-wing extremism – although strictly speaking, Hitler's Germany was a socialist welfare state, with the benefits reserved to ethnic, non-Jewish Germans not opposing the regime. However, with its mass incarceration of communists, socialists and social democrats during its reign, as well as its war against the communist Soviet Union, Hitler's Germany is seen as a mortal enemy of everything on the political left. National Socialism is a convenient historical example that presumably demonstrates what right-wing politics leads to if left unopposed. Therefore, the historical horror image of National Socialism is the ultimate ideological weapon for everyone on the political left to fight and destroy anything considered right-wing. Revising this horror image will arouse fierce resistance from the left.

Internationalist and globalist movements – including international finance, globally acting corporations and NGOs – strive to dissolve ethnic, cultural and religious identities. Ultimately, one common, worldwide market with only one type of consumer maximizes profits for corporations and high finance, and results in maximum power and influence by globalist NGOs and politicians. Any movement that opposes this by trying to preserve and protect ethnic, cultural and religious identities may find itself attacked for allegedly harboring exclusivist, right-wing, even racist ideas. If the ethnic and cultural identities at stake are European in nature, or worse still, German, then the attacks become greatly facilitated by linking these movements to Hitler's attempt to preserve and protect the German, European, or Aryan ethnic, cultural and religious identities. Here again, the historical horror image of National Socialism is the ultimate ideological weapon of internationalist and globalist movements to undermine, weaken and ultimately destroy any identity movement. Contesting this image meets their utmost opposition.

Moral absolutism – setting something as morally absolute, and deriving everything else from it – is another ideological fanaticism that motivates people to treat the Holocaust as an immutable dogma. To a large degree, because of the commonly accepted orthodox Holocaust narrative, Hitler and National Socialism are seen as evil incarnate, the absolute moral evil, by which everything else must be judged morally. If there has ever been a historical figure commonly portrayed as the devil incarnate, it is Adolf Hitler. What the devil was to the Church and the Christian masses during the medieval witch hunts, Hitler is to modern-day, "enlightened" people. Already during the medieval witch trials, one of the worst offenses possible was to disbelieve in the evil machinations of the devil: "*Haeresis est maxima, opera maleficorum non credere.*" ("The worst heresy is disbelief in the evil deeds.") Consequently, any doubt or revision of these evil deeds claimed within the Holocaust is met with reflexive moral outrage by many – and with the call for the police and prosecutors in several countries. Social conditioning with Holocaust propaganda has reached such intense, subconscious levels that many react to violations of this ultimate taboo with mere Pavlovian reflexes. Their moral outrage completely incapacitates their critical thinking. (See the entry on witch trials.)

Self-Preservation

The Holocaust is the ultimate "third-rail" topic.[4] Even in countries with free-speech absolutism such as the United States, doubting the veracity of the orthodox Holocaust narrative leads to social ostracism and career destruction, and consequently often to financial ruin. The more people have to lose, the more they will think twice whether they should step into the quagmire of Holocaust skepticism. Hence, the more influential people are, the less likely they are to violate the taboo. It is better to pay lip service to the beast than to become a free-speech martyr, sacrificed

---

[4] The "third rail" refers to the high-voltage rail used in some urban electric-railway systems to power the trains' electric systems. Touching that rail and simultaneously one of the two traction rails leads to instant death by electrocution.

on the altar of political correctness. In many countries, breaking the West's last taboo will even get you indicted for "denial," against which there is no defense, as "truth" and accuracy are irrelevant in the ensuing trials. All that matters is that you have "denied."

As a result of this situation, most of those who harbor private doubts about certain aspects of the orthodox narrative will publicly prop up the dogma for mere reasons of self-preservation, just as everyone during the medieval witch trials happily confessed to believe in the devil and his evil machinations.

The Holocaust has become a profitable business, not just for "survivors," for Jews in general, for their country and for their multitude of organizations, but also as a safe career path for historians and academicians, as a morally profitable reporting venue for journalists, and as a power tool for politicians. All these people have backed themselves into a corner with their dogmatism. If they admitted having supported and profited from a grotesque historical misrepresentation, this would badly undermine their self-image. Which Holocaust historian would ever admit having built a career on a pack of lies? Which journalist could confess to have bamboozled their audience for decades? Which politician could still be elected who has climbed the ladder by kowtowing to a false mammon? Who of them could still face themselves in the mirror each morning? Therefore, they are stuck; they cannot back out. They need to keep pushing the envelope and do everything possible to suppress any information that might reveal them as frauds.

Political and Social Pragmatism
Trust in the integrity of politicians and mainstream media is low in most countries. If Holocaust skepticism were to become acceptable, if not to say widely accepted, not only would trust in mainstream politicians and media collapse, but also trust in the judiciary, which has largely created the current orthodox Holocaust narrative with hundreds of evidently rigged trials.

Furthermore, any ideological movement disadvantaged or suppressed by the repercussions of the orthodox Holocaust narrative inevitably will surge to one degree or another. Hence, the social and political situation in countries affected by this – mostly within the Western world – could become unstable, or at least start to move in a direction undesirable to currently dominating societal groups. Hence, even if these groups had to concede behind closed doors that Holocaust skepticism has its merits, they would not, and could not, give it free reign for fear of serious societal changes.

The post-World-War-Two world order rests to no small degree on the psychological power derived from the "lessons" learned from the Holocaust: The influence of Jewish power lobbies in politics, academia and media; the international pecking order of countries in the world; the power to wage unconditional and, if need be, eternal war against any new "Hitler" that allegedly shows up at the horizon; and the rule of political correctness in many Western societies, usually running parallel to leftists and globalist ideologies. Holocaust skepticism threatens to unsettle this world order of "eternal war for eternal peace" by destroying the very pseudo-moral foundation it is erected on. At this juncture, all relevant power players worldwide have a mutual interest in not letting that happen, no matter whether the skeptics have a point or not.

2. Motives for Holocaust Skepticism
Truthfulness, Scholarly Ethics
The orthodoxy had to admit in the past repeatedly that they were wrong. See in this regard particularly the dramatic revisions of the orthodoxy's narrative on the Majdanek Camp. There are many other areas of Holocaust studies where similar corrections are due, if evidence matters. Truth and accuracy should be the primary ethical guidelines of all scholars. However, anyone deviating from the orthodox narrative will experience some form of political and societal pressure, up to threats of criminal persecution. This knowledge injects motives of self-preservation into Holocaust historians which collide head-on with the demand to be truthful and accurate. No historian in the world can openly voice his dissent in this field without severe repercussions. Therefore, it must be expected that they all, to one degree or another, "adjust" their research results, or at least the published versions of it, in order to stay out of trouble. Hence, we ought to be skeptical whether historians feel encouraged by their social environment to lie and twist the facts in cases where those don't confirm the orthodox narrative. That should make any person skeptical about the accuracy and truthfulness of their public statements.

Civil-Rights Idealism
The suppression of Holocaust skepticism and the

persecution and prosecution of skeptics is one of the biggest hypocrisies of Western societies. While they declare freedom of speech to be one of their highest values, they systematically strive to deny this civil right to anyone who voices skeptic remarks about the Holocaust, in many countries even with the help of penal law. (See the subsection "Penal Law" in the entry on censorship.) This goes against the very grain of our humanity. In fact, the ability to doubt our senses, to search for the truth, and to communicate to others what we have found, is the only thing that sets us apart from animals. Whoever denies us the right to doubt, to search, and to communicate is denying us the core of our humanity. These human-rights deniers must be opposed by every true humanitarian.

A long series of resolutions by the United Nations General Assembly against Holocaust skepticism demonstrates that, regarding the Holocaust, almost all governments of the world agree to dictate the writing of history by all means at their disposal, and to suppress peaceful dissidents wherever they can. In that sense, the United Nations is an assembly of dictatorial governments inimical to free speech. These resolutions squarely pit the world's governments against humanity itself.

As described in the section on the Motives for Holocaust Dogmatism (above), Holocaust dogmatists use the Holocaust as a tool to deny ethnic, cultural or religious identity movements a level playing field, particularly those of European background. In many cases, the Holocaust is even used, directly or indirectly, to deny such movements and their adherents certain civil rights. Even to those who do not agree with such identity movements, such discrimination obviously violates the ideal of an open market of ideas, where arguments count rather than political and moral blackmailing.

There may be some who delude themselves that a society is better off when the political "right" (whatever that means) is permanently suppressed by Holocaust guilt trips. But careful consideration should make them realize that, just as no airplane can fly with just a left wing, no society can prevail with just a left wing. Where one ideology forces absolute hegemony over all others by moral blackmail and penal laws, it creates a sterile atmosphere of an incestuous monopoly where alternatives do not exist, and societal deformations and fateful mis-developments remain unchecked, ultimately leading to catastrophe. It does not matter whether you enforce a dictatorship by physical or by mental concentration camps.

Where the human mind is not free, societies will ultimately fail.

It is wrong to discriminate against Jews, just because they are Jews. That is true for any other group of people as well. But it is also wrong to discriminate *to the advantage* of Jews, just because they are Jews. That statement is also true for any other group of people. The fact is, however, that Jews, as an ethnic or religious group, are in a privileged position in many regards. Belonging to the group that was the target and the victim of the Holocaust conveys a special status in today's society. As understandable as this reaction is, it is neither just nor justifiable. Every person ought to be judged by his or her personal merits, not by the group to which he or she belongs.

Some are motivated by taking away that special victim status which Jews enjoy today, by reducing the National-Socialist persecution of the Jews to its actual historical dimension, thus depriving it the special status of uniqueness. Without that unique status, other victims of human catastrophes in history ascend to the same moral level as the Jews, and the Jews' privileged position in society becomes untenable. They become as human as everyone else.

Last but not least, many Holocaust skeptics are motivated by the outrageous treatment of the Palestinians and other Arabs by many Israelis in particular and Jews in general. This oppression is ultimately justified to a large degree by the orthodox Holocaust narrative. This narrative allegedly justified the creation of the State of Israel, and it is used as a justification for the oppression and ethnic cleansing of Palestinians from their homeland. Particularly in the Arab world, many see Holocaust skepticism not as an honest research effort, but as a means to subvert Jewish power or even to discriminate against Jews. While the former is understandable, the latter is wrong. Holocaust skepticism is an attitude, not a political tool. While the results of historical research will ultimately have an impact on affected societies, they should never become a tool to curtail anyone's civil rights.

Pacifism

World War II is often called the "good war," as it was fought against the absolute evil of Adolf Hitler, National Socialism and the Holocaust. This black-and-white image has been used ever since to justify more wars. Leaders portray their enemies as Nazis and their enemies' leaders as a new "Hitler," out to commit a new holocaust. Once this comparison sticks, tanks roll, and bombs are dropped. This pattern of psychological warfare against the public at large has worked for eight decades now.

Pacifists with deep insights into history understand that the orthodox Holocaust narrative plays a key role not only in justifying the horrors of World War II in retrospect, but also in justifying new wars to prevent new "holocausts." The U.S. war against Iraq is a striking example. Saddam Hussein was turned into a new Hitler, out to mass murder his Kurdish minority, and to use weapons of mass destruction allegedly at his disposal to wipe the Jews off the middle-eastern map in a new Holocaust. It was all a lie.

Holocaust skepticism is teaching a historic lesson about being skeptical of our governments' historical and political lies, which are conceived for ulterior motives. A profound skeptical, critical attitude toward government-sponsored narratives is key to understanding that governments have lied, are lying, and will always lie to us, particularly when they want to justify wars and the mass atrocities resulting from them. Holocaust skepticism is also key to understanding what power elites in modern "democratic" governments are willing to do in order to suppress ideas which threaten their nefarious ways.

Ultimately, Holocaust skepticism, if embedded in a general skepticism toward any kind of government-sponsored narrative, is one key to world peace, albeit of course not the only one.

(For more on this, see Mattogno 2019, pp. 9-14.)

Anger

Most people get angry when they find out that they have been lied to by their teachers, and by countless historians, politicians and journalists – in fact, by entire societies. Such emotions can be a powerful motivator for an initial boost of involvement in Holocaust skepticism. The initial anger usually tapers off with time, although it can be rekindled with every new lie that is encountered in media, politics or academia. This motivation is potentially dangerous, as it can lead to destructive overreactions by individuals with anger-management issues. Being righteously angry is fine, but this anger needs to be managed and channeled to constructive acts of finding and revealing the truth, rather than lashing out against perceived liars – who may simply be misguided fools, as all skeptics were before their own conversion.

If anger is not managed, it can overreact: "If they were wrong in these cases, then they must be wrong with everything." This conclusion is untenable. If that step is taken, skepticism turns into outright denial (see the next entry), which then often gets associated with dangerous hostile emotions. But we need to always keep in mind: Just because some aspects of the orthodox narrative are wrong, doesn't change the immutable fact that Jews were victims during World War II who suffered terrible fates, no matter the details of that fate.

3. Motives for Holocaust Denial

Denying aspects of the Holocaust narrative, even when they are solidly confirmed by documental and forensic evidence, is usually motivated by hostile feelings (see the previous entry) or ideological fanaticism. The ideological motives involved are commonly a mirror image of the ideological motives for Holocaust dogmatism. While the dogmatists use and abuse the Holocaust narrative to suppress certain ideological movements – mainly those of the "right" – Holocaust deniers are motivated by the prospect that a broader acceptance of Holocaust skepticism or even denial may reduce the suppression of their favorite ideology, or may even lead to the suppression of what they consider to be hostile ideologies. Facts matter little in this concept, hence skepticism toward the orthodox narrative is often replaced with outright rejection of all aspects of it, irrespective of the evidentiary situation.

In reality, however, any association with Holocaust skepticism unfailingly leads to more persecution for these ideology-driven deniers than what they already experience due to their controversial ideological views. Hence, emotional denial does not mix well with intellectual skepticism.

4. Motives for National-Socialist Anti-Judaism

Philo-Gentilism

Conflicts between ethnocentric Jews and the new globalist Jewish sect called Christianity arose right from the start, as one can read in the New Testament. Initially, ethnocentric Jews persecuted what they perceived as heretics. Once Christianity had been made the state religion of the Roman Empire in the 4th Century, those heretics returned the favor. In subsequent centuries, organized Christianity itself turned into a persecutorial ideology, step by step converting, subjugating and terrorizing many areas of Europe and later also the Americas. Simultaneously, the Vatican found moral offense in certain passages of the Jewish law book called *Talmud*, because it showed hostility toward gentiles in general and Christians in particular. Therefore, the *Talmud* was on Rome's list of banned books for centuries.

Specifically German criticism of Jewish anti-Gentilism started with Martin Luther's 1543 polemic booklet *On the Jews and Their Lies* (*Von den Jüden und iren Lügen*). This started a controversy in Germany which erupted into a major exchange of polemics during the second half of the 19th century. During this so-called "Quarrel about anti-Semitism" (*Antisemitismusstreit*), critics of the Jewish religion attacked immoral passages in *Talmud* and the *Shulchan Aruch*, which is a condensed version of the *Talmud*. On the other side, defenders of Judaism denied the existence or relevance of these immoral passages.

One late-comer to this quarrel, Theodor Fritsch, took what he believed to be the essentials of this quarrel, spiced it up with pseudo-Darwinian racial claims about the evil nature of Jews as a race, and published it all in the late 19th Century in a *Handbook on the Jewish Question* (*Handbuch zur Judenfrage*). Over the following decades, this book was printed in hundreds of thousands of copies. It became somewhat of a bible for all German opponents of Jews and the Jewish religion, National Socialists included.

The "Quarrel about anti-Semitism" was settled in the late 1920s, when Dr. Erich Bischoff, a German expert on Jewish religious texts, wrote an expert report with a focus on how non-Jews are portrayed in the *Shulchan Aruch*. It was a resounding intellectual victory for the philo-Gentiles, which exposed the defenders of Talmudic Judaism either as immoral perverts or as mendacious anti-Gentiles. Fritsch incorporated references to Bischoff's treatise in new editions of his *Handbook*. Once National Socialism took power in Germany, many German intellectuals were swayed by Bischoff's type of arguments to view Judaism as an immoral anti-Gentile ideology worthy of opposition.

During the wave of the Allies' postwar book burnings in Germany, they tried to ban and burn all the books ever published in Germany about this controversy, among many other books. Ever since the end of World War Two, philo-Gentile arguments against anti-Gentile attitudes in Jewish religion were seen as outrageous at best in almost all countries around the globe. In Germany and Austria, they were even made a criminal offense.

In 1994, Prof. Dr. Israel Shahak, an Israeli Jew and Holocaust survivor, followed in Bischoff's intellectual footsteps by pointing out the same kind of anti-Gentile laws in Talmudic Judaism. He exposed the devastating impact of this Jewish anti-Gentilism throughout 3,000 years of Jewish history in his book *Jewish History, Jewish Religion: The Weight of 3,000 Years*. Four years later, he followed up on this topic with another book, *Jewish Fundamentalism in Israel* (co-authored with Norton Mezvinsky). In this book, he demonstrates how fundamentalist Jews in Israel are practicing the same immoral anti-Gentilism as their Jewish ancestors in their pursuit of an Israel ethnically cleansed of all non-Jews.

This is the rational, perfectly justifiable moral core of National-Socialist anti-Judaism, which is why, in the eyes of anti-Gentiles, this ideology had to be portrayed as absolute evil, lest anyone touch this topic ever again.

Racism

After the publication of Charles Darwin's *On the Origin of Species*, evolutionary and hereditary explanations for differences in human behavior became popular. Many opponents of the Jewish religion sought to explain the persistent anti-Gentile attitude of Talmudic Jewish religion with racial (meaning genetic) differences. National Socialism eventually incorporated these ideas.

DNA, the carrier of genetic information within all terrestrial life forms, was discovered only after the Second World War. Serious studies of identical twins, which can point at genetic causes of human behavior, were only just beginning. Therefore, during the 1930s and 1940s, any theory trying to explain behavioral differences of various human subgroups as genetic in nature could only be speculative.

The results of decade-long studies of identical twins conducted after the Second World War indicate that much of our individual behavior is indeed driven by genetics. However, despite mass sequencing of millions of human genomes, science has made little progress, if any, with attempts at linking complex social behaviors to genetic causes. It is therefore still undecided whether behavioral differences of human subgroups are caused by genetic differences between that subgroup and other subgroups.

For that reason, giving the impression that something which is mere speculation is a proven fact is wrong. Using this speculation as a basis for policy decisions with far-reaching consequences seems, moreover, irresponsible. Nevertheless, some feel that the persistent Jewish hostility toward non-Jews stretching over thousands of years can only have genetic causes. The National Socialists were among them.

Anti-Bolshevism
Czarist Russia (1547 to 1917) was an autocratic regime that oppressed most of its population, both Christian and Jewish, but it had a specific anti-Jewish aspect to it. While the Christian rural masses, many of them trapped in servitude, had little education and put up little resistance, Jews were more urban, more educated, better organized, and for many decades spearheaded reform as well as revolutionary movements. They were supported in this by their Jewish brethren abroad, particularly in the United States, as can be seen from many supportive articles in *The New York Times* starting in the mid-1800s.

When the communist/Bolshevist revolution broke out in Russia in 1917/18, Jews dominated the movement, and U.S.-American Jewish groups were not only verbally supportive, but openly organized huge fund drives to finance it with millions of dollars. Since the bloody, atrocious Bolshevist revolution was visibly a Jewish revolution, Jewish voices in the West trembled that, if Soviet Russia were to collapse, bloody anti-Jewish purges throughout Russia, of hitherto unheard-of proportions, would be inevitable. Jews also dominated communist parties of other countries, trying to conduct similar revolutions there. The Soviet Union's publicly voiced plans for world revolution, which many feared would be accompanied by massacres against any opposing force, therefore gave the impression of being an entirely Jewish affair.

In hindsight, as an American Jew expressed it, the revolutionary Jews spearheaded Bolshevist massacres between the world wars, and Jews in general consequently paid the price in anti-Jewish massacres during the Second World War.

It should be mentioned, however, that Stalin himself carried out a hidden anti-Jewish cleansing during the "Great Purge" of 1937 and 1938. During those years, the percentage of Jews employed in the upper echelons of the Soviet terror apparatus NKVD dropped from some 40% down to 4%. That percentage rose again during the war, when Stalin used the Jews' fear of National Socialist anti-Judaism to entangle them in the Soviet war and propaganda machine, only to ditch them again after the war.

Throughout the existence of National Socialism as a movement, it insisted that the root cause of communism and the inevitably accompanying horrors of Bolshevist reign were Judaism and its teachings. They could not know what the non-Jews Mao Zedong and Pol Pot had in store for the world.

(For more details on this, see Heddesheimer 2017, pp. 17-26; Rudolf 2023, pp. 39f., 333-336.)

Anti-Usury
Throughout medieval times until well into the 19th century, legislation and rules in many countries prevented Jews from joining certain professional trades. On the other hand, Christian and Muslim laws forbade the taking of interest on financial loans. In contrast to this, Jewish law only forbids taking interests from fellow Jews, but permits taking interest from non-Jews. With such a system in place for centuries, it was inevitable that some Jews became very successful in the West's finance world, and amassed huge wealth and influence.

Modern times have seen an almost-global legalization of interest, and even of usury. (2% monthly interest rates on credit-card loans is normal, which amounts to almost 27% annual interest, which is usury by any standard.) Hence, the financial playing field for plundering the masses has been level for quite a while. Jews, however, are still massively overrepresented in that field in many Western countries.

National Socialists saw this overrepresentation, with its accompanying wealth and political leverage, as a hallmark of Jewish malice toward the general non-Jewish masses.

MOTTEL, SAMET
Samet Mottel was an inmate of the Sobibór Camp. In a deposition of October 1945, he claimed that there was one "death chamber" at the camp, without providing further details. He furthermore claimed that his comrades had calculated that "about two and a half million people had been liquidated at the camp."

His claims are rejected as false by the orthodoxy, who insists on *several* gas chambers, and on a death toll of only some 10% of what Mottel claimed.

(See the entry on Sobibór for more details, as well as Mattogno 2021e, p. 76.)

MÜLLER, FILIP
Filip Müller (3 Jan. 1922 – 9 Nov. 2013) was a Slovakian Jew deported to Auschwitz in April 1942. His first deposition was published in 1946 in a Czech

book. He next testified first at the 1947 Krakow show trial against former staff members of the Auschwitz Camp, then in October 1964 during the Frankfurt Auschwitz show trial. In 1979, a book was published in English and German listing him as an author, but it was basically written by his German ghostwriter Helmut Freitag. Finally, Müller agreed to be interviewed by French-Jewish activist Claude Lanzmann between 1978 and 1981 for his 9-hour documentary *Shoah*. Sections of it are featured in that movie.

Filip Müller

There is a conspicuous difference between the two earlier and all later statements. While his narrative in the two earlier statements is focused almost exclusively (1946) or entirely (Krakow) on his alleged experiences at the old crematorium of the Auschwitz Main Camp, his later statements have their focus predominantly on his alleged activities with the *Sonderkommando* of Birkenau.

It is striking that Müller's focus of claimed activities shifted with the focus of the audience he was addressing. The Krakow Trial had its focus on defendants who had been in charge of activities in the Main Camp, whereas during the Frankfurt trial, Müller was called to testify against Hans Stark, who had been active at the Birkenau Camp. Since most of the atrocities claimed for Auschwitz are said to have happened at Birkenau, this main attraction was also the focus of Müller's statements both in his interview with Lanzmann and in his book.

Already during his statement in Frankfurt, he hinted at the fact that he had a collection of literature on this topic from which he drew some of this knowledge. A thorough analysis of his book reveals that he (or rather Freitag) plagiarized entire passages and episodes from other sources, mainly from Miklós Nyiszli's narration that had been serialized by a German magazine in 1961. He reused blueprint drawings of the Birkenau Crematoria II and III from the Czech book where his initial statement had appeared, and used elements of the testimonies by Stanisław Jankowski and Rudolf Höss as well as claims published by Polish historian Danuta Czech in her German-language articles on the chronology of Auschwitz.

The most blatant plagiarism is his detailed description of a gassing scene in Crematorium II that was copied in almost all its details from Nyiszli's narration, although he reworded them to make it difficult to track. One might think that maybe both witnesses simply viewed the same or very similar scenes. That explanation fails, however, because when Nyiszli wrote his story, he assumed and claimed wrongly that the poison gas used at Auschwitz was some type of chlorine, a gas much heavier than air which would have spread along the floor. Nyiszli describes, how the victims tried to get away from the floor, attempting to reach higher toward the ceiling to avoid breathing in this gas as long as possible. In the process, they trampled on and climbed on top of each other, ending up lying dead in huge piles reaching toward the ceiling. All this proves is that Nyiszli has never seen a gassing with Zyklon B, because its active ingredient hydrogen cyanide is slightly lighter than air and is also invisible (chlorine is yellowish), so no victim would have seen it, and there would have been no point for anyone to climb anywhere. Müller made the mistake of using different words to describe the same scene, thus demonstrating that he, too, had never seen the results of a gassing with Zyklon B (and neither did Freitag, evidently).

Müller's various narrations contain many self-contradictions and contradictions to the claims made by other witnesses, which we will ignore here for brevity's sake. They are moreover full of many improbable and impossible claims as well as slip-ups indicating that his source of information was not his original memory, such as:

– In his book, he describes the furnaces at the Auschwitz Main Camp's crematorium in the faulty, incomplete state, as they had been rebuilt by the Auschwitz Museum after the war.

– Three corpses were place in a muffle and cremated within 20 minutes – although the muffles were designed only for one corpse, and its cremation took an hour.

– He invented a physically impossible story of a "fire" caused by leaving air blowers on too long, claiming that they had fanned the flames too much, when in fact the fans of these furnaces fed *cold* air into the muffle, hence leaving them on too long would have *cooled* the furnace down, not led to a "fire."

- He claimed that flames shot out of the smoke duct when it partly collapsed, yet the smoke duct works with a negative pressure due to the chimney's draft, hence cracks in its masonry would have led to cold air getting sucked in rather than hot air (or even flames) being able to escape.
- He then claimed that the fire was extinguished by throwing water on it, which most certainly would not have been done, because pouring water on red-hot refractory bricks would have severely damaged most of them.
- He claimed that the chimney was rebuilt at one point (correct), but that cremations continued at the same time, which is incorrect and would have been physically impossible.
- He insisted that he worked in that facility from early May until June of 1942, and in this context described the results of an alleged homicidal gassing of Slovakian Jews in the old crematorium's morgue in early May. However, the orthodox narrative has it that, with the first of the two Birkenau bunkers having become operational in March 1942, gassings at this crematorium were discontinued in April of 1942 at the latest, hence Müller cannot have experienced any gassing there. Moreover, the first transport of Slovakian Jews that allegedly resulted in some of them getting gassed (in the bunkers) arrived on July 4, hence after Müller had left the old crematorium. Yet still, he repeatedly claimed that gassings in the old crematorium and in his presence were very common, causing some 10,000 victims overall.
- The inmates of that invented gassing kept standing upright after they had died. While this is a common cliché, it is also physically impossible.
- Müller seriously claimed that these imaginary gassing victims not only had not undressed before getting gassed, but that they had even taken their luggage into the chamber!
- The chamber was equipped with six openings in the ceiling to introduce Zyklon B, while today's orthodox narrative claims four, due to the Poles having built four such openings after the war, which are in place to this day.
- Müller could smell the poison gas in the gas chamber when entering it to clean it out – in other words, he did not wear a gas mask, in a room evidently full of toxic gas! (Hydrogen cyanide has only a faint smell, hence to notice it, it has to be present in considerable and dangerous amounts!)
- He claimed during the Frankfurt Auschwitz trial that he managed to get out of the Main Camp's *Sonderkommando* by paying some other inmate "a lot of dollars" – not Reichsmarks, but US dollars! US dollars were a coveted currency in Eastern-Bloc countries during the Cold War – which is where Müller lived when he testified in Frankfurt – but they were virtually non-existent and mostly useless in Europe during the war.
- He claimed that sick inmates unable to work were killed, but when *he* got sick, he was taken to the Birkenau inmate hospital and treated to full recovery.
- After his transfer to Birkenau, whenever there was a dramatic event happening at any of the crematoria there, he happened to have been transferred precisely to that building. It is clear that he used that as a literary device to explain his omnipresence and omniscience.
- During an inmate uprising in October 1944, he claimed to have hidden inside the smoke duct of Crematorium IV, while the building was set on fire by inmates. He claimed to have entered the duct through a cast-iron cover. However, the ducts of this crematorium had no access ports (with or without covers) for anyone or anything to crawl into them.
- Müller claimed that the cremation furnaces were fed with seven times more coke than they were able to contain and burn.
- Out of the crematoria's chimneys, "raging flames rushed into the open air" – which was technically impossible.
- For Müller, "once they had caught fire, the dead would continue to burn without any further coke being required." The legend of self-immolating bodies is simply physically impossible.
- The ventilation of the gas chambers in Crematorium V took only "a few minutes." This facility wasn't even equipped with *any* ventilation system. Ventilation by draft through opened doors and wall openings would have taken many hours, if not days. But even if there had been a ventilation system, it still would have taken several hours, all the more so because the Zyklon-B pellets, allegedly dumped on the inmates' heads, would have given off its deadly fumes for up to an hour or two, so even the strongest fans could not have expelled all the gas, until that time had passed.
- Inmates entered this unventilated room right away, without gas masks!

- Since mid-May 1944, huge pyres in five large pits behind Crematorium V and four more near the "bunker" were blazing every day, to burn thousands of murdered Hungarian Jews, yet air photos clearly show that no such thing ever happened. (Müller called the bunker "Bunker 5," a term used only by Rudolf Höss in his published memoirs and by Dov Paisikovic in his various unpublished statements.)
- Two naked women and an SS man stood at the edge of a blazing pit, until the SS man shot the women. The scene is plagiarized from a drawing by David Olère, yet physically impossible, as the heat of the blazing pit would not have allowed anyone to step close to it without getting burned.
- While a cremation pit was already ablaze, additional corpses from the gas chamber were continually thrown in – which would have led to the throwers getting burned up themselves.
- Fat dripping from burning corpses flowed through channels in the pits' bottom toward collecting pans, from which the "sizzling fat was scooped out with buckets on a long, curved rod and poured all over the pit, causing flames to leap up amid much crackling and hissing." If the fat poured back caused a massive blaze, why didn't it cause the same blaze and burn off when exiting the corpses? And how could the person, standing right next to the fire while scooping and pouring out the fat onto the fire, avoid getting burned himself?
- One SS man loved flinging babies into the boiling human fat at the bottom of the pits – except that no such pool of fat could have existed.
- The ineluctable Dr. Mengele was often present when inmates were shot whose thigh muscles were to be used "for various [medical] purposes."
- Thigh and calve muscles from freshly executed inmates were cut out and placed in buckets. The muscles' convulsion made the buckets jump about. However, not only do cut-out muscles from dead people not convulse. But even if they did, they could not make the buckets jump.
- Being suicidal, Müller tried to gas himself by joining a batch of Jews to be gassed. However, two naked, sexy young girls convinced him that he needs to live to tell the tale, so they pushed him out of the chamber while they died.

Filip Müller's book has been one of the most influential to cement the public perception of the Auschwitz Camp. In this book, Müller uses the word "perverse lust" to describe the motive of the SS man allegedly tossing babies into boiling human fat. However, these words only describe the author himself (and his ghostwriter) in concocting this preposterous web of lies.

(For details, see Mattogno 2021d, pp. 13-131.)

MÜNCH, HANS

Hans Münch

Hans Münch (14 May 1911 – 27 Jan. 2002), SS *Untersturmführer*, was a physician who in June 1943 was assigned to the southeastern branch of the Hygiene Institute of the Waffen SS at Rajsko, a village near Auschwitz. In that role, he was involved in testing thousands of blood and stool samples of Auschwitz inmates to verify whether they had contracted typhus and/or whether they had cleared the typhus bacterium out of their system, hence could be released from the hospital. Münch was the only defendant who walked away with an acquittal from the Krakow show trial against former members of the Auschwitz camp staff.

Münch then testified at the Frankfurt Auschwitz Show Trial, and appeared as a "good SS man" during many a media event, convention and meeting. He confirmed the orthodox narrative of what was going on at Auschwitz, although he was never deployed there. He always maintained that he had kept a clean sheet.

In 1994, Münch was interviewed at length by a skeptical scholar. Here are some of the claims Münch made during that interview (for details, see Rudolf 2023b):
- Crematoria II and III were camouflaged as barns, and their chimney was detached from the building, standing separately, However, these buildings were neither camouflaged nor did they looked like barns, and their chimney was part of the building, not standing separately.
- The victims' entry into the gas chamber, located on the ground floor, was through a large sliding barn door. However, the gas chamber is said to have been in the building's basement, and access to it was through a normal-sized hinged door via

a few steps.
- The victims entered the gas chamber through a door on one side, and were taken out dead through a different door at the opposite side. However, the alleged gas chamber of these buildings, their Morgue #1, had only one door.
- The victims were given towels and soap before entering the gas chamber. This most certainly would never have happened, considering the mess it would have created and the effort necessary to retrieve and clean these items afterwards. In addition, no one takes towels into a shower. When this was pointed out to Dr. Münch, he agreed, and stated that he never actually saw it anyway.
- The maximum capacity of this alleged gas chamber was 3,000 people. However, in this room of 210 m², that would have resulted in a physically impossible packing density of more than 14 people per square meter.
- Zyklon B was inserted through shafts by an SS man climbing onto a ladder to pour in the granules. However, in those buildings, insertion columns are said to have protruded only a little over the room's roof, which was almost at ground level. Hence, no ladder would have been required.
- The victims' bodies were put on rail carts running on tracks that left the chamber, ran through an outdoor space, and then entered into the crematorium. However, Morgue #1, the alleged gas chamber, was a basement room *inside* the crematorium. It was connected to the furnace room, not by rail tracks running partly outdoors, but by a freight elevator.
- During outdoor cremations, corpses were placed on large grates which had been brought from Treblinka or Majdanek. However, the orthodox narrative has it that no grates were used at Auschwitz during open-air incinerations at all. Bodies were simply put in pits and burned.
- The fuel used for open-air incinerations consisted of diesel or gasoline. However, liquid fuels can merely ignite other, solid fuels (such as wood or coke) and at most singe corpses, but can never incinerate them to ashes. The orthodoxy has it that wood was used as fuel.
- Münch confused Crematoria II and III with Crematoria IV and V,
- He claimed that he saw the *Sonderkommando* clean out the gas chamber, and later he denied ever seeing it.
- He said that he looked once into a gas chamber during a gassing; or maybe several times; or maybe he never saw anything.
- When pressed to give details about anything of what he reportedly experienced, he avoided any concrete answers, and ultimately admitted that he doesn't know.
- When he was confronted with the many internal contradictions of his claims, and with the help of blueprints was made to understand that his description of the crematoria and gas chamber is completely wrong, he had to admit that he cannot remember anything reliably; that he gets everything mixed up; and that he is unable to distinguish his wartime impressions from what he has learned later.

To counter the devastating effect of this interview, the German news magazine *Der Spiegel* conducted their own rather brief and superficial interview with Münch, trying to entrap him with provocative statements (Schirra 1998). Starting with this interview, Münch increasingly displayed historical and personal confusion, making increasingly erratic and provocative statements leading to various prosecutions. (See Wikipedia for a detailed documentation on this.)

murder weapons → **Tools, of Mass Murder**

MUSSFELDT, ERICH

Erich Mussfeldt

Erich Mussfeldt (18 Feb. 1913 – 24 Jan. 1948), SS *Oberscharführer*, was deployed to the Auschwitz Main Camp in August 1940 as a labor unit leader, and then as a block leader. In November of 1941, he was transferred to the Majdanek Camp, where he was put in charge of cremations, after the provisional crematorium at Majdanek, with two mobile oil-fired furnaces, became operational in June 1942. Until then, deceased inmates had been buried in mass graves.

Starting in February 1943, Mussfeldt is said to have been put in charge of exhuming and cremating the bodies in these mass graves by way of open-air incinerations within the context of the so-called *Aktion* 1005.

In May 1944, he was transferred to the Auschwitz-Birkenau Camp, and there put in charge of Crematoria II and III.

After the war, he was arrested by U.S. troops and, during one of the infamous Dachau show trials, sentenced to life imprisonment. After this, he was extradited to Poland, where he was one of the 40 defendants during the Krakow show trial against former members of the Auschwitz camp staff. He was sentenced to death and subsequently executed.

While in Polish captivity, Mussfeldt signed various statements. Having suffered through one of the U.S. American Dachau trials, where SS defendants were routinely severely tortured to extract confessions, and having been subjected to Polish imprisonment using gentler, but no less effective Stalinist means of softening up defendants, Mussfeldt showed some resilience by insisting, for instance, that the furnaces he operated at Majdanek could cremate only one corpse per muffle and would take an hour to do so (Graf/Mattogno 2012, p. 112). However, when asked about the more-primitive cremation furnaces at Auschwitz, he stated that they could cremate three bodies per muffle within half an hour, hence six times of what was physically possible (Mattogno 2019, p. 287).

On the other hand, he compromised with his oppressors by giving them a detailed description of a mass shooting at which he claims to have been a mere forced observer: the alleged execution of some 17,000 Jews at the Majdanek Camp within just one day, 3 November 1943, in what was later dubbed Operation "Harvest Festival." This was a completely made-up event whose mainstream narrative rests predominantly on Mussfeldt's physically and organizationally impossible account. Mussfeldt claims to have subsequently supervised the burning of the victims with open-air incinerations.

It goes without saying that it can be excluded with certainty that any superior would have ordered, hence forced, Mussfeldt to be present at the presumably 10-hour-long mass shooting of 17,000 camp inmates. What would have been the point of this, except terrorizing a subordinate?

Mussfeldt was basically forced to confirm and flesh out atrocity claims that had been circulated by the Polish resistance movement since late 1943. (See the entry on Operation "Harvest Festival," as well as Graf/Mattogno 2012, pp. 212-228.)

N

NADSARI, MARCEL

Marcel Nadsari (or Nadjari) was a Greek Jew who was deported to Auschwitz in April 1944. He survived the war, and in 1947 wrote down some memoirs. In 1980, a thermos bottle was found near the ruins of Crematorium III at Birkenau containing several handwritten pages in Greek which are signed with Nadsari's name. In 1991, twenty years after Nadsari's death, a text was published as a book that presumably stems from him as well. Nadsari never testified at any trial or made any other public statement, as far as is known.

Among all the manuscripts allegedly found in Auschwitz, Nadjari's account comes closest to the final version of the orthodox narrative on exterminations at Auschwitz-Birkenau, although his descriptions are very terse and superficial, and contain exaggerations and false claims common to many false testimonies:

- He claimed an impossible packing density of 3,000 people in the alleged gas chamber, Morgue #1 of Crematoria II and III, which had 210 m², resulting in more than 14 people per square meter.
- Rather than showers, he mentioned only pipes on the ceiling, which is true, as there were real showers in that room requiring pipes at the ceiling.
- Men and women undressed separately, which contradicts the orthodox narrative, but makes perfect sense.
- The victims allegedly took soap into the gas chamber. This most certainly would never have happened, considering the mess this would have created and the effort necessary to retrieve and clean these soap pieces afterwards (or the waste to just throw them away).
- The gas was poured through openings into the room. His text does not contain any reference to any Zyklon-B introduction devices, as claimed by the current orthodox narrative.
- The execution time was implausibly short: 6 or 7 minutes. Executions in U.S. gas chambers, using the same poison, took on average some ten minutes. However, in those cases, the poison was released instantly and completely right beneath the victim. In Auschwitz, the gas had to slowly evaporate, and dissipate throughout a large room, without any means to accelerate this process. (See the entry on homicidal gas chambers.)
- The doors were opened after only half an hour, but that would not even have been enough for all hydrogen cyanide to evaporate from the Zyklon-B carrier, let alone for the ventilation of a room filled with poison gas and jammed with people preventing any efficient air exchange. In fact, Nadjari doesn't even mention any ventilation. Hence, it looks like he didn't even think it was necessary.
- The bodies were cremated in the furnaces, "without the use of fuel, because of all the [body] fat they have," although self-immolating bodies simply do not exist.
- Each body allegedly produced only some 640 grams of ashes (or a little less than 1½ pounds), which is less than a fifth of the actual amount of ashes resulting from cremating an average body weighing 70 kg (3.5 kg, or some 5% of the original body mass).
- He claimed that 1,400,000 victims were gassed, a figure 40% higher than what the orthodoxy assumes, but all he could have known is how many people were "processed" during the time he was there.

(For more details, see Heliotis 2018; Mattogno 2021, pp. 283-289.)

NAGRABA, LUDWIK

Ludwik Nagraba was a former Auschwitz inmate who testified during the Höss show trial on 22 March 1947. In September 1947, he made a deposition in preparation of the Krakow show trial against former members of the Auschwitz camp staff.

Nagraba claimed to have been admitted to the Auschwitz Camp on 15 February 1941, where he stayed until October 1944, when he was transferred to Buchenwald. At Auschwitz, he was deployed at various innocuous jobs until July 1942, when he contracted typhus. After the Germans had nursed him back to health with great efforts, he was assigned to work inside Crematorium III – which started up only in June 1943, hence 11 months after he had become sick. He worked there until the building was demolished in late 1944. Here are some peculiar claims

Nagraba made with his two statements:
- Eight or nine people were put into one muffle at once – although the muffles were designed to cremate only one corpse at a time.
- 2,850,000 deportees were gassed, and Nagraba knew this because the transports were recorded, and the numbers conveyed from the "transport commandant" to the camp commandant, which he managed to somehow intercept. However, many more than that perished, because many victims allegedly went straight to their death without being counted. Perhaps the witness was aiming at the Soviet's 4-million death-toll number.
- Even German soldiers arriving in uniforms were killed in the gas chambers (though shot, not gassed), plus "large number of civilians, professors, priests." This is clearly absurd.
- He called the first Birkenau crematorium "the modern 2-furnace crematorium," although that building had five furnaces.
- He claimed that there were 18 cremation pits for open-air incinerations, each burning 8,000-10,000 corpses per batch (every other day?), hence a total capacity of 144,000 to 180,000 corpses per batch, or roughly a million corpses within just two weeks (assuming one batch every other day).
- Once lit with some flammable substances, the corpses burned all by themselves. However, self-immolating bodies simply do not exist.
- German "*Gasmeisters*" – a term Nagraba invented – carried Zyklon-B cans around in their backpacks. That runs not only contrary to the orthodox narrative, which maintains that Zyklon-B cans were transported by a red-cross vehicle, but it was also against all safety rules.
- Nagraba claimed that he had to collect the emptied Zyklon-B cans and transport them back to the Main Camp in a cart. No SS man in his right mind overseeing a mass murder with Zyklon B would ever have allowed an inmate to get anywhere near containers that might still have toxic residues in them.
- He also claimed that *Sonderkommando* members of Crematorium IV were gassed in a disinfestation chamber at the inmate-property warehouse, whose corpses he claims to have removed and then cremated. The orthodoxy insists, however, that the SS did that dirty job themselves. Furthermore, no *Sonderkommando* member ever would have voluntarily set a foot into the fumigation chamber, if they had observed homicidal gassings for months on end.

(For details, see Mattogno 2021d, pp. 216-222.)

NAHON, MARCO

Marco Nahon was a Greek Jew who was interned at the Auschwitz Camp from May 1943 until October 1944. Toward the end of his stay, when SS surveillance allegedly slacked, he claimed to have been able to talk to some members of the *Sonderkommando*. He presented his narration of an inspection of a crematorium and a description of what was happening inside in the first person, thus giving the false impression of a first-hand report. Here are Nahon's peculiar hearsay remarks:

- The intended victims were trucked to the crematorium, entered the undressing room and undressed, but then it was discovered that 1,400 were not enough, so they all went back to their barracks. Only two days later, with 2,000 inmates, did the process get completed. Of course, that would never have happened. On the one hand, 1,400 was more than "enough," and on the other, it might have been a smart idea to count the intended victims before picking them up on trucks and carrying them some place. The SS were hardly so foolish.
- Above the door to the gas chamber was a clock and a window. We don't know about a clock (no other inmate has ever mentioned it), but we know that there was no window above any door leading to any room ever alleged to have served as a homicidal gas chamber.
- Zyklon B was stored in metal containers similar to vacuum flasks or thermos bottles. Actually, it was stored in tin cans, some 15 cm in diameter and of variable heights.
- An SS man threw such a bottle through the window above the door into the gas chamber. On impact, it detonated. First, there was no such window. Next, Zyklon-B cans were not bombs that exploded on impact. And finally, they were certainly not themselves thrown in, but at most their contents.
- "The walls of the gas-chamber tremble under the incredible impact and the desperate knocking of those being asphyxiated." The heavy double-brick walls built into the ground most certainly would not have trembled.
- Nahon described what the gassing victims experienced: "All of us are pale, our hair stands up on

our heads, a cold sweat forms in drops over our foreheads… The blood drains from our bodies." Remember this is an account from hearsay! Hydrogen cyanide, Zyklon B's active ingredient, does not drain anyone's blood.
- The execution lasted only 3-5 minutes, which is both a common claim and also physically impossible with the claimed setup.

Statements such as these are the reasons why testimonies from hearsay should not be admissible in court – they are admissible in many countries! – or in historiography. (For details, see Mattogno 2021, pp. 376-378.)

NATZWEILER

The Natzweiler Camp, located in Alsace, operated from May 1941 until September 1944. It is also sometimes referred to as the Struthof Camp. It was a concentration and forced-labor camp. Within the framework of the Holocaust, this camp entered the scene in 1942, when the macabre topic of a collection of human skeletons involving the anatomical institute at the University of Strasbourg was brought up. In the summer of 1943, preparations were made to transfer 115 inmates from Auschwitz to Natzweiler, presumably to have them killed and turned into skeletons for that collection.

The orthodox narrative has it that a room originally used as a refrigeration cubicle was rigged to serve as a homicidal gas chamber in order to "process" these 115 transferred inmates. There is documental and anecdotal evidence pointing to this room having served as a training gas chamber for soldiers to practice wearing a gas mask. Other evidence points to this room also having been used on a small scale to conduct experiments on inmates with antidotes to the war gas phosgene. The western Allies were stockpiling this war gas at that time in North Africa, evidently with the intention to carpet-bomb German cities with it, or so the Germans must have feared.

The assertion that this refrigeration room was indeed used as a homicidal gas chamber rests mainly on three affidavits and the trial testimony of Natzweiler's former commandant Josef Kramer. Kramer later served for a brief period as commandant of the Birkenau Camp, and then at the end of the war as commandant of the Bergen-Belsen Camp. He was captured there by British occupational forces, who subsequently put him on trial. During that trial, Kramer initially denied any knowledge of homicidal gassings at Auschwitz or Natzweiler. It was only after prolonged torture by the British that Kramer broke down and started "confessing." (See the entry on Josef Kramer for details.)

Kramer's two longer, signed affidavits describing the alleged gassings contradict each other on various points:
- Either the gas chamber existed already when Kramer received the order from Berlin, or it did not.
- Either Kramer observed the killing process through the peephole, or he was content with only "listening."
- Both affidavits give different numbers of inmates killed, different numbers of batches the victims were split into, how many and what kind of victims each batch contained, and also when they were allegedly killed.
- The gassing was carried out either by pouring some hydrogen-cyanide-generating "salts" into a pit inside the gas chamber, then pouring water on this which flowed from the outside through a funnel and a pipe. Or "salts" and water were mixed outside the chamber, then poured through the funnel to flow through the pipe into the chamber.
- After the act, either the gas-chamber door was opened and at the same time the fan turned on, or the door was opened only fifteen minutes after the fan had been switched on.

These contradictions aren't even the crucial issue, though. The claimed method itself was technically impossible, as pouring water onto any cyanide salt could not have resulted in the swift release of lethal amounts of toxic gases under any circumstances. If

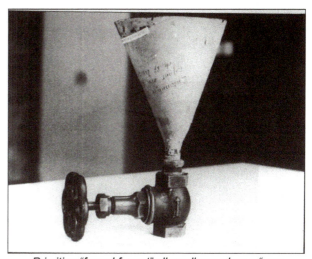

Primitive "funnel faucet" allegedly used as a "gas introduction device" for the claimed homicidal gas chamber at the Natzweiler Camp. (Pressac 1985, p. 66)

some method had been found that quickly releases toxic fumes, then Kramer's second gassing method – mixing water and salt on the outside – would have been suicidal, as the gasses would have hit his face right away. (He claimed to have worn no gas mask.)

The Natzweiler Camp had a Zyklon-B fumigation chamber, hence the camp authorities had access to Zyklon B and knew how to use it. Had there been an intention to kill with hydrogen cyanide, this insecticide would have been used. To accomplish this, staff trained and licensed to use Zyklon B would have been ordered to carry out the gassings. It is absurd to think that the camp commandant himself would have carried out all the steps of the gassings, as Kramer claimed.

At the end of the war, numerous corpses were recovered which were allegedly those of the inmates transferred from Auschwitz. A toxicological autopsy of these corpses by French toxicologist Dr. René Fabre revealed that they had *not* died of cyanide poisoning. Hence, if they were murdered for the sake of enriching some macabre skeleton collection, then this happened some other way.

Desperate to conjure up a homicidal gas chamber for "their" camp, in order to compete with their co-Allies' propaganda success with their various gas-chamber claims, the French bungled it badly. Yet still, modern-day orthodox historians cling desperately to this delusion, for admitting that "confessions" were extracted with torture, and that lies were spread deliberately, could lead to a cascade collapse of other gas-chamber claims.

If, on the other hand, we took seriously Kramer's ludicrous description of the Natzweiler homicidal gas chamber, then this would prove that, in mid-1943, the German concentration-camp commandants had no idea how to build and effectively operate them. This implies, of course, that there were no such operating facilities in existence at that time, whether at Auschwitz, Belzec, Birkenau, Majdanek, Sachsenhausen, Sobibór, Stutthof, Treblinka or elsewhere.

Either way, logic spells disaster for the orthodox propagandists.

(For more details, see Faurisson 1999, pp. 247-255; Mattogno 2016e, pp. 205-222.)

NEBE, ARTHUR

Arthur Nebe (13 Nov. 1894 – 21 March 1945), SS *Gruppenführer*, became head of Germany's Criminal Police in 1936. In 1939, one of Nebe's subordinates, Christian Wirth, got involved in supervising the so-called euthanasia action, which is said to have consisted of killing severely mentally disabled patients with bottled carbon-monoxide gas. Hence, Nebe was probably aware of what methods were used to quickly carry out this "mercy killing."

Arthur Nebe

In June 1941, he volunteered to head *Einsatzgruppe* B, which he led from its inception just before the beginning of the war against the Soviet Union until October 1941, hence for some four months. As such, he approved several *Einsatzgruppen* reports sent to Berlin which documented the execution of thousands of Jews in the deployment area of his *Einsatzgruppe* B.

The current orthodox narrative has it that Nebe played a central role in the invention of gas vans in the second half of 1941. After Himmler had allegedly witnessed a mass execution in mid-August 1941 by Nebe's unit, he is said to have ordered a more-humane mass-execution method to be developed, although no documental evidence exists either for Himmler attending such an execution or for him issuing such an order, other than a bogus postwar affidavit by Erich von dem Bach-Zelewski.

A rumor spread by Albert Widmann has it that the idea to use engine exhaust to kill people in vehicles occurred to Arthur Nebe when he allegedly gassed himself by accident in his car after having driven home drunk. However, since remote-controlled garage doors didn't exist back then, he or someone else must have closed that door, or else no accidental gassing could have occurred. Therefore, either Nebe wasn't alone, then no accidental gassing could have occurred, or he was alone, but then had to get out of the car while leaving the car running, then close the garage door, then get back in the car and fall asleep with the car still running. This is hardly a credible scenario. Furthermore, considering that Nebe was familiar with the euthanasia killings and how they operated, and the toxicity of gasoline-engine exhaust was certainly known to this head of Germany's criminal police, the claim that it took an accidental self-gassing while drunk to come up with this idea is also preposterous. Because Nebe died before the end of the war and never made a statement about any of this,

this entire story is moreover based only on hearsay claims and thus completely unfounded.

After the war, the myth was created with a number of manipulative maneuvers by postwar investigators: that Nebe, together with Albert Widmann, a chemist at the German Institute for Criminological Technology in Berlin (*Kriminaltechnisches Institut*), went on a trip from Berlin to Minsk in order to do some tests to find out how best to mass-murder people. The two are said to have traveled a thousand kilometers east with 400 kg of explosives in their car to test whether it was feasible to blow up mentally ill people with dynamite. The story is so outrageously absurd that it boggles the mind why it ever found credence. Since this story is closely linked to investigations related to Albert Widmann, the issue is discussed in more detail in the entry dedicated to him.

(For more details, see also Alvarez 2023, pp. 219-225; Mattogno 2017, pp. 10–16; 2022, pp. 293-302.)

NETHERLANDS

Between the summer of 1942 and September 1944, some 105,000 Jews were deported from the Netherlands, mainly to Auschwitz and Sobibór, but some also to Theresienstadt, with the ultimate destination again being Auschwitz. The first set of transports between July 1942 and February 1943 went to Auschwitz. Their fate there was probably similar to that of the Jews deported there from France and Belgium around the same time frame. The second set of transports from March to July 1943 went to Sobibór, where the orthodoxy insists they were murdered on arrival, while skeptics suspect that this was a transit camp for destinations farther east. All transports leaving the Netherlands after this until the summer of 1944 once more went to Auschwitz. (See the entry on France, as well as on Jewish demography for a broader perspective.)

NEUENGAMME

The Neuengamme Concentration Camp was established in 1938 near a village of the same name in the southeast of Hamburg. Its relevance for Holocaust historiography lies in claims about a few select homicidal gassings in that camp. There is no wartime source for this. No documents confirm any witness claim in this regard, and the building where most witnesses claimed these events occurred was destroyed in 1949 or 1950, leaving only the foundations. In other words, everything depends on claims, and nothing is supported by evidence. However, if the building that allegedly served as a homicidal gas chamber really had the claimed features, it would have been a prime piece of evidence, and the most important exhibit for any future museum. In other words: it would have been preserved at all costs. But it wasn't.

The first testimonies about homicidal gassings at Neuengamme were deposited in the context of British postwar investigations. They were embedded in the British preparations for their Bergen-Belsen Show Trials, their show trial against Bruno Tesch, and of course the Neuengamme show trial itself. Confessions from some SS men allegedly involved in those crimes were extracted in the context of pervasive threats and torture.

Quite a few witnesses interrogated 25 years later by West-Germany's judiciary knew nothing about homicidal gassings, or could tell only hearsay stories, so they were ignored. Testimonies of former camp inmates who confirmed gassing claims were ac-

Undated photo of the outside of the detention bunker at Neuengamme Camp. Its five detention cells were allegedly used to kill inmates in one or two claimed gassing events.

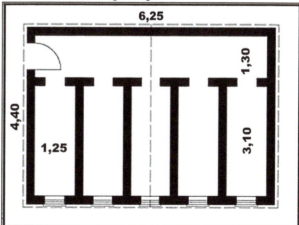

Floor plan of the detention bunker at Neuengamme Camp.

cepted at face value, no matter what they stated. Here is a summary of those claims:
- either one or two gassings took place;
- the first gassing occurred either in late 1941 to early 1942, spring or summer 1942, July 1942, September 1942, late September to early October 1942, October 1942, late October to early November 1942, fall 1942, winter 1942-1943, or January 1943;
- the gassing took place either early in the morning, late in the morning, in the afternoon, or in the evening, and lasted either 10 minutes, 20 minutes, 30 minutes, an hour, two hours, or at least four hours;
- either 80, 156, 180-200, 190, 193, 197, 200, 200-250, 250, 251 or as many as 1,400-1,500 altogether fell victim to the first gassing;
- no one witnessed the alleged second gassing or knew anything specific about it, but it allegedly happened either between late 1941 to early 1942, in November 1942, or fall 1942, and it had either 95, over 100, 150, or 251 victims;
- the victims were Soviet PoWs (although maybe Poles for the second gassing), who came either from Lüneburg, from Fallingbostel or from the Göring Factories;
- the building where the crime supposedly unfolded was retrofitted with six or seven pipes in the roof for pouring in Zyklon B, measuring either 8, 10-15, 15 or 38 cm in diameter; the facility's heating was provided by either a radiator, heating coils, or by electric heating wires, which were located beneath the ceiling or on the walls.
- after the murder, the corpses were loaded either onto a "trailer of a lorry," also called "car trailer" and "truck trailer," or "on an open tarp cart," or onto 3 "transport carts," or onto "2 or 3 carts," or onto "four trolleys," or onto a "car trailer" and "carts" together; the work was carried out by the "corpse-recovery unit" or by the "roll commando";

If accounts from later, West-German investigations were included in this list, the claims would be even more disparate.

If reading this list in parallel with a similar list of what has been claimed about the alleged first gassing at the Auschwitz Camp, the similarities are striking, down to minute details. Considering that several transports of Auschwitz inmates arrived at the Neuengamme Camp since early 1943, it becomes apparent that the black-propaganda story spread among Auschwitz inmates was simply transplanted to Neuengamme.

The one unique feature setting the claimed Neuengamme gassing(s) apart from all other gassings is the claim that the event is said to have taken place in plain view of the *entire* camp. Three witnesses even claimed that all camp inmates had to line up for roll call and sing a song while the victims of the gassings were carted by them. This was allegedly a demonstration by the SS of their omnipotence. However, if that tale were true, there would be hundreds, if not thousands of witnesses confirming this. But we only have three, who furthermore contradict one another in other aspects of their claims.

It can be safely assumed that no homicidal gassing at Neuengamme – or anywhere else, for that matter – would have taken place in plain view of the entire camp, or would even have been celebrated by the SS in the presence of all inmates. This claim merely highlights the preposterous nature of this tale and seals the untrustworthiness of the witnesses.

Furthermore, no camp administration would have troubled themselves to convert a normal building into a homicidal gas chamber just for the sake of executing one or two small batches of Soviet PoWs.

As in the case of Auschwitz, orthodox historians aided and abetted the fraudsters in British and West-German judiciary by subsequently transforming this disparate tale of wartime atrocity propaganda into "history" by cherry-picking from the mishmash of claims those that appear conducive to their agenda, while papering over all the cracks in the story in order to hide them from their unsuspecting readers.

Neither the encyclopedia by Gutman (1990) nor that of Rozett/Spector (2000) mentions gassings or a gas chamber in their entry on Neuengamme, although Gutman quotes as his sources two books which very much mention them, while Rozett/Spector have copied from Gutman, as usual, without giving sources.

(For more details on this, see Mattogno 2022.)

NISKO PLAN

As soon as Germany had defeated Poland in late September 1939, Reinhardt Heydrich, head of Germany's Department of Homeland Security (*Reichssicherheitshauptamt*, RSHA), issued directives on how to handle the "Jewish question" in the occupied territories. One of these directives was the so-called Nisko Plan, which foresaw the creation of a Jewish reservation in southeastern Poland near the town

Nisko. The plan was possibly initiated by Adolf Eichmann, the RSHA's expert on Jewish issues. Between 20 October 1939 and 12 March 1941, 6,615 Jews from Austria were indeed resettled to Nisko and other towns in the General Government. However, this plan for a resettlement of the Jews within Europe ultimately failed and was soon abandoned. It was superseded by the Madagascar Plan, which was also later abandoned. (For more details, see Goshen 1981; Mattogno 2022c, pp. 33f.)

NORDHAUSEN

The Dora-Mittelbau Camp was the nucleus of a network of forced-labor camps in and around the Harz Mountains in Thuringia, Central Germany. It served primarily to provide a slave-labor force to factories of Germany's defense industries. Among them featured most prominently the underground production facilities of the so-called V Weapons (*Vergeltungswaffen*, retaliation weapons), meaning the V-1 cruise missiles and the V-2 ballistic missiles.

As former Dora inmate Paul Rassinier has aptly described, the living and working conditions in that camp were at times horrific (Rassinier 2022). This is particularly true for the final months of the war, when SS men were increasingly unnerved by Germany's impending collapse, and when neither Germany's civilian population nor any camp population could be provided with appropriate food, shelter, clothing, medical care, drinking water etc. The scenes well-documented on film and photo about the Bergen-Belsen Camp were not much different in many other camps, Dora included.

In that context, on 8 January 1945, the SS took control over a military barracks of the German air force, the Boelcke-Kaserne in the city of Nordhausen near the Dora factories. It subsequently served as a holding facility for all inmates of the Dora camp system who were no longer fit for work. The barracks were soon overcrowded, and the sick, injured and dying inmates could neither be treated medically, nor was there enough food, clothing, shelter or even drinking water or sanitary facilities. Like Belsen, the Boelcke Barracks were a place of mass dying, with no one able to stop it.

To turn disaster into catastrophe, the British Royal Air Force flew two massive bombing raids against the city of Nordhausen on the 3rd and the 4th of April 1945. Large parts of the city were destroyed, and so were the Boelcke Barracks. Some 1,500 inmates lost their lives during that raid. Law and order in the city and inside the camp completely collapsed. The survivors among the SS staff fled, leaving the sick and dying inmates behind in the rubble. Any inmate who could walk fled as well.

A week later, the city with the barracks were occupied by U.S. troops, meeting no resistance. These soldiers discovered the inferno which their genocidal warfare against Germany had caused: Some two thousand inmates were dead and dying amidst the rubble of the former barracks buildings. The Americans mistook this as evidence for a National-Socialist policy of extermination against these inmates. In their rage, some U.S. soldiers went into the devastated city of Nordhausen. Wherever they found German civilians who had survived the bombing raid, they killed them in their lust for revenge. (On this, see Mauriello 2017, p. 35.)

U.S. troops pulled the dead inmates out of the destroyed buildings, and lined them up on the barrack's square. They took photos to document all this, and they recorded these Dantesque scenes on film. Some of that footage was used in the movie *The Nazi Concentration Camps* as evidence for German mass atrocities. On 29 November 1945, during the early phase of the Nuremberg International Military Tribunal, this movie was shown by the prosecution as alleged evidence for Germany's genocidal intent against its vast concentration-camp population (*IMT*, Vol. 2, pp. 431-434; transcript in Vol. 30, pp. 462-472: Nordhausen on p. 467). Photos showing the lined-up dead Nordhausen inmates have been reproduced in many publications as evidence for a premeditated German extermination policy, starting with *Life* magazine in its edition of 21 May 1945, and climaxing in the booklet accompanying the movie *Schindler's List*. See the photo reproduced in the entry on corpse photos.

(For more on this, see Rudolf 2023, pp. 314f., as well as the documentary Rudolf 2017, starting at 1:08:38.)

NORWAY

Some 800 Jews were deported from Norway, with the Auschwitz Camp as their main destination. Few of these Jews reported back with the local authorities after the war. Most of them have gone missing, and their fate is unclear. (See the entry on Jewish demography for a broader perspective.)

NOWODOWSKI, DAWID

Dawid Nowodowski was one of the first witnesses to

testify about the Treblinka Camp. He was deported there on 18 August 1942, but managed to escape after just a few days. On 28 August 1942, hence before any propaganda or alleged witness accounts about this camp started spreading, he wrote a "Report of the stay at the extermination camp of Treblinka." However, it does *not* contain any reference to mass extermination or killing chambers. The only terse and uninformative allusion to it reads: "2 executions after 15 minutes up to 40 minutes." (See Mattogno 2021e, p. 121.)

NUREMBERG MILITARY TRIBUNALS

During the International Military Tribunal (IMT) in Nuremberg, the Allied victors tried 24 major German war criminals. However, already during the preparation of this tribunal, the victorious powers agreed that many more suspected war criminals needed to be prosecuted. But since it had proven very difficult to get all four Allied powers to agree on conducting one trial together, plans to conduct a series of mutual follow-up trials against lesser alleged war criminals did not materialize. The U.S. decided therefore to organize such a series of trials all by themselves. At the end, twelve of them were conducted between late October 1946 and April 1949. These trials were called "Trials of War Criminals before the Nuernberg Military Tribunals," and are often simply called Nuremberg Military Tribunals (NMT). Summaries of the proceedings were published in 15 volumes. Some pertinent data of these trials are listed in the table, including the sentences imposed. The case numbers of tribunals relevant to Holocaust claims are set in bold face.

The NMTs were conducted by the U.S. following the same principles and statutes as used for the IMT. Therefore, these tribunals were plagued by the identical problems, minus the grotesque absurdities at times exhibited by the Soviet prosecutors during the IMT. In some regards, the NMTs were actually worse than the IMT, because the NMTs attracted much less public attention. As a consequence, both prosecution and judges felt that they could get away with more violations of proper legal procedures. Hence, they exhibited a tendency to treat the defendants and their defense lawyers more harshly than during the IMT. Some judges even had defense lawyers temporarily arrested for insisting on their client's right to be properly defended.

For more details and references, see the entry on the International Military Tribunal.

Case	U.S. versus	When (dd/mm/yyyy)	Vol.	Sentences
1	Karl Brandt *et al.* (Medical Case, physicians)	25/10/1946 – 20/8/1947	I & II	7 death, 5 life, 2×20, 15, 10 ys
2	Erhard Milch (air force, medical experiments)	13/11/1946 – 17/4/1947	II	life
3	Josef Altstotter *et al.* (Justice Case)	4/1/1947 – 4/12/1947	III	4 life, 4×10, 7, 5 ys
4	Oswald Pohl *et al.* (WVHA, concentration camps, gas chambers)	13/1/1947 – 3/1/1947	V	2 death, 4 life, 2×20, 15, 6×10 ys
5	Friedrich Flick *et al.* (Industrialists, slave labor)	8/2/1947 – 22/12/1947	VI	7, 5, 2½ ys, 3 acquittals
6	Karl Krauch *et al.* (I.G. Farben Case, slave labor, DEGESCH, Zyklon B)	3/5/1947 – 30/7/1948	VII & VIII	2×8, 7, 2×6, 5, 4, 3, 3×2, 2×1½ ys
7	Wilhelm List *et al.* (Hostage Case, reprisals)	10/5/1947 – 19/2/1947	XI	2 life, 2×20, 15, 12, 10, 7 ys, 2 acquittals
8	Ulrich Greifelt *et al.* (RuSHA, ethnic cleansing)	1/7/1947 – 10/3/1948	IV & V	1 life, 2×25, 20, 3×15, 10 ys, 5 releases, 1 acquittal
9	Otto Ohlendorf *et al.* (*Einsatzgruppen*, mass shootings, gas vans)	3/7/1947 – 10/4/1948	IV	14 death, 2 life, 3×20, 2×10 ys
10	Alfried Krupp *et al.* (Industrialists, slave labor)	16/8/1947 – 31/7/1948	IX	3×12, 2×10, 2×9, 7, 2×6, 2 ys
11	Ernst von Weizsäcker *et al.* (Ministries, NS policies, anti-Jewish measures)	4/11/1947 – 13/4/1949	XII-XIV	25, 2×20, 3×15, 2×10, 6×7, 6, 2×5, 4 ys, 1 release
12	Wilhelm von Leeb *et al.* (German High Command)	28/11/1947 – 28/10/1948	X, XI, XV	2 life, 3×20, 2×15, 8, 7, 5, 3 ys, 2 acquittals

NYISZLI, MIKLOS

Miklos Nyiszli (17 June 1901 – 5 May 1956) was deported from what was Hungary to Auschwitz in the context of the wholesale deportation of Hungary's Jews. He arrived at Auschwitz on 29 May 1944. He spent two weeks at the Monowitz Camp, but due to the fact that he was a physician, he was then transferred to Birkenau to make use of his medical knowledge. This much is documented.

After the war, Nyiszli wrote a number of texts that claim to report in detail what he experienced while incarcerated at Auschwitz. This includes a declaration of July 1945; a book published in 1946; an affidavit written in Nuremberg in 1947 where he went in an – ultimately failed – attempt to be accepted as a witness during any of the Military Tribunals; and a fictitious, serialized text of 1948 claiming to be Nyiszli's testimony when he took the stand at Nuremberg.

The contents of the last text mentioned will not be discussed here, as it is entirely fictitious. However, it is important to note that Nyiszli insisted that this is indeed a true and accurate protocol of his testimony in Nuremberg. This shows that Nyiszli had the criminal energy to make up an entire story about his appearance as a witness in Nuremberg, and then invent his testimony, including questions asked by prosecutors and his answers to them. But none of it ever happened. In other words: Nyiszli's credibility as a witness is zero. Having said this, let's look into the claims he made in his declaration and affidavit, and most importantly in his book, which also claims to describe exactly what he experienced.

Nyiszli's criminal energy shows up again in his book, where he minutely describes a scene he claims to have witnessed after an alleged homicidal gassing in the basement Morgue #1 of Crematorium II at Birkenau, and the way he explains it. To begin with, Nyiszli wrongly assumed in his 1945 statement and in his book that Zyklon B is a product that, upon contact with air, released toxic chlorine gas. Since chlorine gas is roughly 2.5-times heavier than air and has a distinct yellowish color, upon release it tends to fill up a closed space like water, from the bottom up.

With that assumption in mind, Nyiszli describes in his book in lavish detail how the victims in the gas chamber, evidently seeing the yellowish vapors crawling up on their feet and legs, tried to get away from the floor and to reach higher up toward the ceiling to avoid breathing in this gas as long as possible. In the process, they trampled onto each other and ended up climbing on top of each other, so that at the end of the gassing, the corpses were stacked in huge piles reaching toward the ceiling rather than lying scattered around the entire room.

Miklos Nyiszli

The problem is that Zyklon B's active ingredient is not chlorine but hydrogen cyanide, which is released by evaporation, no matter whether air is present or not. It is moreover slightly lighter than air and also invisible, so it would attack people seemingly from out of the blue. This proves irrefutably that Nyiszli did not know what Zyklon B was. Had he been the witness of many gassings with this product, he would have known. He moreover has never seen a gassing with Zyklon B, because the scene he describes would be utterly inconceivable with it.

In his book, Filip Müller (or rather his ghostwriter Helmut Freitag) copied almost every aspect of Nyiszli's gassing scene, except Müller did not claim that Zyklon B was chlorine. With this act of plagiarism, Müller provided incontrovertible proof that he, too, had never seen a gassing with Zyklon B.

Another extraordinary fact is that Nyiszli and Charles S. Bendel, another Auschwitz inmate physician, both claimed independently from each other to have been the only *Sonderkommando* physician at the same location and during the same time span, and that they lived in the Birkenau crematoria for an identical period of their stay in that camp. Similarly, both claimed to be the only surviving *Sonderkommando* physician! But they were mutually unaware of each other's existence, and described incorrect places and mutually contradictory factual assertions. However, while Nyiszli's description is at least close to reality – which means that he did see the building or at least a blueprint of it – Bendel described a fantasy place that has no resemblance to reality.

Yet still, Nyiszli's description of Crematorium II is filled with exaggerations, inaccuracies and invented rooms that never existed. For instance, he claimed that tens of thousands of inmates were employed to build the Birkenau crematoria, whereas documents demonstrate that on average some 70 inmates worked at each of the four crematoria's constructions site at any given time. Morgue #1 of Crem-

atorium II, the alleged homicidal gas chamber, as well as its furnace room, were both 30 m long, but Nyiszli claimed that they were 150 m long. The other morgue, almost 50 m long, he described as 200 m long. While there was one small freight elevator in that building, he turned this into four large elevators. Nyiszli also invented the following non-existing places:
- a changing room for the *Sonderkommando* members next to the gas chamber
- an entire carpentry shop
- a gigantic storeroom for clothing & toiletries
- an SS office
- lodgings for SS guards
- a kitchen

He moreover incorrectly described the cremation furnaces and the way they supposedly operated, adding a corpse-introduction device to his narrative that had existed only in the Auschwitz Main Camp's crematorium, but by the time Nyiszli arrived at Auschwitz, this facility had been decommissioned for almost a year.

Nyiszli's most extreme deviations from the orthodox narrative concern the alleged bunkers outside the Birkenau Camp. While mainstream historians insist that these were makeshift homicidal gassing facilities, Nyiszli insisted that people were not gassed there, but used it only as an undressing facility. They were then all shot standing at a cremation pit's edge. Nyiszli never used the term "bunker."

Nyiszli filled his narrative with the usual lies, exaggerations and camp rumors:
- Flames were shooting out of the crematoria chimneys (six times in his book!), although that was technically impossible.
- Three bodies were cremated at once in each muffle within 20 minutes – although these muffles were designed only for the cremation of one corpse at a time within one hour.
- He assigned to all crematoria the same capacity of 5,000 corpses per day, hence 20,000 per day together, when in fact their total theoretical maximum daily capacity was just under 1,000 bodies.
- 2,000 or even 3,000 people were gassed in the 210 m² "gas chamber" – an impossible 9.5 to 14.5 people per square meter.
- Zyklon B was thrown into "tinplate pipes" rather than the wire-mesh Zyklon-B introduction devices of the current orthodox version.
- The gas murder lasted only 2 to 5 minutes, which is impossibly fast for the slow-evaporating hydrogen cyanide, Zyklon B's active ingredient, especially in a large room jammed with people and with no means of forced convection.
- Gigantic pyres burned day and night outside the Birkenau Camp, covering the area with thick smoke – while air photos of the area clearly show that no such thing ever happened.
- SS men stood lined up at the edge of the blazing pits, ready to shoot some 5,000 to 6,000 Jews daily, as they streamed naked out of the undressing hut – except that the SS men would have quickly gotten badly burned, and their ammunition would have been at risk of exploding.
- Auschwitz allegedly had a murder rate of at least 25,000 people per day, which comes to at least some 750,000 per month, hence a preposterous three million during the four months of extermination activity he claims to have experienced.
- Nyiszli's entire story is centered around Auschwitz physician Josef Mengele. He mentioned him 124 times in his novel, whose original title translates to "I Was Dr. Mengele's Forensic Pathologist in the Auschwitz Crematorium." Therefore, with his mendacious story, Nyiszli created Josef Mengele's diabolic postwar reputation, which was then copied by many later witnesses. (See the entry on Josef Mengele.)

Another key feature of Nyiszli's testimonies is his claim that the members of the so-called *Sonderkommando* – the inmates allegedly in charge of pulling the corpses out of the gas chambers and burning them in furnaces or on pyres – were killed by the Germans every four months, and replaced with new inmates, in order to leave no witnesses of the crime behind. This claim has been repeated by many other self-proclaimed members of the *Sonderkommando*. However, if that were true, the world wouldn't be awash in Holocaust survivors claiming to have been a member of such a *Sonderkommando*, and to have worked in it much longer than just four months, with no SS man ever attempting to murder them as "carriers of a terrible secret." Hence, even mainstream historians acknowledge today that Nyiszli made this up.

Nyiszli's narrative contains many more false claims. To cover them all would require writing a thick book, which is exactly where all the details about this masterful liar can be found: see Mattogno 2020a.

O

OBERHAUSER, JOSEF

Josef Oberhauser (21 Jan. 1915 – 22 Nov. 1979) was an SS *Untersturmführer* at war's end. From 1939 until August 1941, he was responsible at various locations for cremating the bodies of persons who had been killed during the so-called Euthanasia Program.

Josef Oberhauser

From November 1941 until August 1942, Oberhauser served as the head of the Belzec camp guards, and is said to have overseen the development of the camp, including the construction of its facilities. Toward the end of the war, Oberhauser and many others of the remaining SS staff were transferred to Triest, Italy, to fight partisans.

In 1948, he was sentenced to 15 years imprisonment for his involvement in the Euthanasia Program, but got amnestied in 1956.

In 1963, he was put on trial in Germany during the Belzec Show Trial staged in Munich. Oberhauser refused to testify during the trial itself, but he had agreed to pre-trial interrogations. During those interviews, he added some new "information" never heard before from anyone else: According to him, the first set of gas chambers at Belzec consisted only of one "small chamber" used "to determine technically how gassings could be carried out." This test chamber was allegedly used only for maybe 7-9 transports with only some 150 Jews each. However, the orthodoxy asserts that there were three chambers in the first gas-chamber building, not just one, and that they were used at maximum capacity for several months, resulting in mind-boggling victim counts.

Oberhauser moreover insisted that the first four transports were killed with "bottled gas" (presumably carbon monoxide) rather than engine exhaust gas. An engine is said to have been added only later. This is a strident deviation from the pre-ordained historical script, which insists that engine-exhaust gasses were used in *all* claimed Belzec gas chambers at *all* times.

With such a deviation, Oberhauser's statements were useless to the court, so they were ignored. However, they are the most important ones of all the statements made during that trial, since they clearly indicate that Oberhauser was making up things on the fly, exactly because he evidently had no first-hand knowledge of gas-chamber mass murders at all. He evidently had not read or internalized the exact details of the dogma then already in place.

While the charges against all other defendants were dropped, with claims of acting under duress, Oberhauser's case was the only one ending with a conviction. He was sentenced to a prison term of 4½ years for aiding in the murder of at least 300,150 Jews. That is eight minutes for every life taken. As a first-time offender with no risk of relapsing, and due to his excellent conduct in prison, Oberhauser was released after serving only half his time. Since his pre-trial detention was made to count, he walked out of prison only a short while after the trial had ended. Had he insisted that the orthodox narrative is all wrong, he might have risked a much longer prison term due to denial and lack of remorse.

(For more details, see Mattogno 2004a, pp. 62-69.)

OBRYCKI, NARCYZ TADEUSZ

The Pole Narcyz Tadeusz Obrycki was deported to Auschwitz on 13 May 1943. In December 1946, he signed an affidavit about his time there. In it, he described the structure of Crematoria II and III rather accurately. But there are some peculiarities of his testimony, for which he relied exclusively on camp rumors:

– The victims were given towels and soap before entering the gas chamber. This most certainly would never have happened, considering the mess it would have created and the effort necessary to retrieve and clean these items afterwards. In addition, no one takes towels into a shower.
– He claimed the alleged gas chamber was equipped with fake showers, when indeed there were real showers in that basement room.
– The poison gas was allegedly administered by launching a cartridge from the outside – rather than by pouring a can of it through some opening,

as the orthodoxy has it.
- There were five furnaces with five openings each – although Crematoria II and III had five *triple*-muffle furnaces.
- Two corpses were loaded into one muffle at a time – whereas these muffles were designed for only one corpse. Although loading two would have been physically possible, it wouldn't have had much of an advantage, if any.
- Five million Jews were cremated in the crematoria and on the pyres – one million more than the Soviets' atrocity lie, and four million more than today's mainstream narrative.
- The crematorium staff was liquidated every three months – this is the echo of a rumor proven false by the many survivors of this staff.
- These crematorium staff members slated for murder were gassed at a facility in Gleiwitz (today's Gliwice), where no such facility existed. That's a lie invented by Michał Kula, and as such we see here another "convergence of evidence" on a lie.

(For details, see Mattogno 2021, pp. 393-395.)

OCHSHORN, ISAAC EGON

Isaac Egon Ochshorn was an inmate in a long row of German camps: Buchenwald, Dachau, Gross-Rosen, Auschwitz-Birkenau, Warsaw. He signed a deposition about his alleged experiences, which was filed by the United Nations War Crimes Commission in September 1945. He documented in it the most-preposterous nonsense, such as:

- In Buchenwald, 20,000 Polish Jews were scheduled to be killed every month – whereas this camp was a mere labor camp with no Jewish camp population to speak of.
- Half the Jews arriving at Buchenwald were murdered on arrival, the rest put into cages, where they were given neither food nor water and were "bestially mishandled." Buchenwald's orthodox history has no knowledge of this at all.
- At the Dachau Camp, "Jews were thrown alive into huge concrete mixers where they were milled into pulp. This material served as street plaster; hence, these streets were commonly called 'Juden-Strassen' (Jew-roads)." This is an unheard-of fairy tale, nothing more.
- At Gross-Rosen, 500 to 600 Soviet PoWs were gassed every day for eight months straight, hence altogether some 150,000 victims, although that camp didn't have any gassing facility even according to the orthodox narrative, and the actual number of Soviet PoWs who died there amounted to some 3,000.

Regarding the Auschwitz Camp, Ochshorn claimed that he had an opportunity to see every step of the extermination process. From the unloading at the ramp to the handing out of soap and towel inside the undressing room, every sentence starts with "I saw…" He then switched back to the outside to see the SS throw in gas bombs through a roof hole into the homicidal gas chamber – rather than pouring in Zyklon-B granules. He even had x-ray vision, as he could see from a distance that the people inside the gas chamber looked like a beehive. Furthermore:

- The crematoria had many hundreds of furnaces – while all crematoria together had just 12 furnaces with together 46 muffles.
- He stated that, in September 1943, a commission headed by Himmler arrived at Auschwitz to enlarge the extermination capacity of the crematoria from 8,000 to 40,000 per day. However, the theoretical maximum cremation capacity of the Birkenau crematoria stood at 920 per day, and there is no trace whatsoever of any commission or any other entity planning more cremation facilities.
- The new (invented) facilities were to be used to genocide the Poles and Czechs, since there were no Jews left.

Ochshorn moreover tells a tale how he allegedly heard the camp commandant say that the reality was so terrible that anyone revealing it to the world would be considered "a fantastic liar" – evidently a Freudian slip made by "a fantastic liar."

(For details, see Mattogno 2021, pp. 366-369.)

OFFICE OF SPECIAL INVESTIGATIONS

After the Second World War, as the Cold War was gearing up, both the U.S. and the Soviet Union competed to secure the spoils of war in occupied Germany. For instance, with "Operation Paperclip," the U.S. transferred many German rocket scientists to the U.S., first as privileged prisoners, but later as voluntary immigrants willing to assist the U.S. in the ensuing space race. Parallel to this, the U.S. government also let German individuals of the Third Reich's military and security sector immigrate under false IDs in order to assist with the transfer of "secret weapons" technology and with the cleansing of U.S. society from pro-Soviet spies and collaborators (later known as McCarthyism).

On a broader scale, many Soviet citizens who had fought in pro-German units or who otherwise had collaborated with the Germans, fled West at war's end. Many of them later immigrated to the U.S., with the immigration services welcoming them as staunch anti-communists, turning a blind eye to some of these immigrants' questionable past. Among them were many Ukrainians, since many if not most non-Jewish Ukrainians had collaborated with the Germans, which they saw as liberators from Stalinist terror and Russian domination.

Some of these Ukrainians in exile formed Ukrainian nationalist associations and lobby groups in the U.S. The Soviet Union reacted to this by forming Soviet-loyal groups, feeding them with material undermining the reputation and credibility of the Ukrainian independence movement. Central in these efforts were accusations of collaborations with Germans during World War Two. In that context, the most effective Soviet propaganda weapon consisted of assertions that certain Ukrainian immigrants had been involved in war crimes. Specifically, this concerned members of auxiliary forces who were (mis)used by the Germans for guarding and running concentration, labor and alleged extermination camps. Furthermore, some of them are said to have assisted during mass executions of Jews by the *Einsatzgruppen* and other German units. This kind of accusation secured the support of Jewish pressure groups in the U.S., such as the Anti-Defamation League and the Simon Wiesenthal Center. While treasonous pro-Soviet groups could never turn Congress into a tool for the Soviet Union's imperialistic policies in Ukraine, Jewish pressure groups could – and did.

While Germany caved in to Jewish and international pressure already in 1958 by creating a special investigative office in charge of collecting incriminating material against suspected National-Socialist war criminals (see the entry on the Zentrale Stelle), the U.S. Congress, not being susceptible to international pressure, caved in only after Jewish pressure had mounted drastically in the 1970s. This was partly due to an increased Soviet campaign against nationalist Ukrainian immigrants. Another contributing factor was that the memories of the Apollo Moon-Landing Program were fading. As a result, the hero status of Wernher von Braun, who had died in 1977, and of his team of German scientists and engineers was declining. This exposed them increasingly to accusations of having contributed to the inhuman treatment of slave laborers in the Third Reich's factories of its "V weapons," meaning rockets. Finally, the Holocaust itself moved onto societal center stage with the airing of the TV mini-series *Holocaust* in 1978.

All this taken together led to the formation of a special branch within the FBI, the so-called Office of Special Investigations (OSI). It was formed on 4 September 1979 to enforce Public Law 95-549 passed by Congress on 30 October 1978. Its purpose was to identify individuals residing in the U.S. who might have committed war crimes while serving the Axis powers during World War Two. The OSI then had to collect incriminating evidence against them in order to enable the U.S. Immigration Services to either deport them to their country of origin, if they had no U.S. citizenship, or to revoke their citizenship and deport them afterwards.

The OSI was staffed mainly with fanatical Jewish lawyers. Leading among them was staunch Zionist Neal Sher, who headed the OSI from 1983 until 1994, after which he headed the Jewish lobby group AIPAC until 1996. He then headed a commission aiming at making Holocaust-era insurance claims (because it's all about the money), from which he resigned in 2002, after it had been discovered that he had misappropriated some of the commission's funds. For this, he was disbarred as a lawyer in 2003.

One of the first and most prominent targets of the OSI was German-born rocket engineer Arthur Rudolph. He had developed the Third Reich's ballistic V-2 rockets, managed the U.S.'s ballistic Pershing Rocket program, and was project director of the Saturn-V rocket program that brought Americans to the moon. With the late Wernher von Braun no longer able to protect the members of his German rocket team, Rudolph agreed in 1983 to leave the U.S. and renounce his U.S. citizenship rather than face a long and expensive litigation. (See Tarter 1992/2000 for more details.)

The case which had the largest impact, though, was that of Ukrainian-born John Demjanjuk, who was accused of having aided in hundreds of thousands of gassing murders at the Treblinka Camp. He was eventually deported to Israel, where a huge show trial was staged against him. This trial backfired on the orthodoxy, and led to the collapse of the orthodox Treblinka narrative, which has since been upheld only by censorship and government bayonets, meaning penal law outlawing dissent. Demjanjuk was acquitted, got his U.S. citizenship back, but the OSI went after him again, managed to have his citizenship revoked once more, and had him deported, this time to the perfectionist Germans, who made sure to leave no loophole open for Demjanjuk. They sentenced him to five years' imprisonment simply for allegedly having been present at the Sobibór Camp. This claim, denied by Demjanjuk, was based on a false ID card forged by the Soviet Union. (See the entry on John Demjanjuk for details.)

Other prominent cases of OSI persecutions include those of Feodor Federenko, Veralian Trifa and Andrije Artuković. The low-profile case of Martin Bartesch is perhaps the most interesting, because the OSI lost this case due to the skilled assistance Bartesch received from a competent lawyer. In this lawyer's article on how he won this case for Bartesch, he details how, in Bartesch's case,
- the OSI granted access to the pertinent files only after having been sued;
- they issued press releases claiming that Bartesch was a mass murderer of tens of thousands, although they had no evidence to support this claim;
- only when sued, did the OSI start searching for incriminating evidence;
- this search only uncovered exonerating evidence;
- this exonerating evidence was not disclosed to the defendant;
- distorted or incorrect translations were used in an attempt to frame the defendant;
- the OSI refused to retract the false charges against Bartesch when proven untrue;
- the OSI collected the names of citizens who wrote letters or protest to their elected officials,
- and the OSI considered taking administrative action against them, which is nothing short of government terrorism.

The temporary existence of the Office of Special Investigations shows the power of the orthodox Holocaust narrative. The fact that the OSI felt compelled to prosecute cases such as Martin Bartesch's shows that they had no real criminals to pursue. (For more details, see Allen 2000.)

The OSI was disbanded in 2010, and its staff integrated into another branch of the FBI.

OHLENDORF, OTTO

Otto Ohlendorf (4 Feb. 1907 – 7 June 1951), SS *Gruppenführer*, was head of Office III (SD-Inland, Internal Security Service) of the Reich Security Main Office (*Reichssicherheitshauptamt*). Just prior to the war against the Soviet Union, he was appointed head of *Einsatzgruppe* D, a position he held for a year.

Otto Ohlendorf

This group operated in the southern region of the temporarily German-occupied Soviet Union (Bessarabia, southern Ukraine, Crimea, Caucasus).

Ohlendorf's various postwar affidavits and testimonies during the Nuremberg International Military Tribunal and the "*Einsatzgruppen* Case" of the U.S. Nuremberg Military Tribunals are the mainstay upon which the orthodox dogma is based – that the *Einsatzgruppen* received a Hitler Order for the wholesale slaughter of Jews on the territory of the Soviet Union prior to the war against that country. However, during his extended investigations of this complex of alleged war crimes, German prosecutor Alfred Streim found out that Ohlendorf had convinced most of his fellow defendants to assume a line of defense that seemed most promising in skirting personal responsibility for the mass executions they were accused of: blame it all on a non-existing "*Führer* Order." This didn't work out as planned, though, as he and 13 of his 21 co-defendants were sentenced to death anyway. As a result, however, the historical record is contaminated with trial statements which are inconsistent with one another, and are not backed up by historical facts (see Jäckel/Rohwer, pp. 107-119; Earl 2009, pp. 182f.; Mattogno 2022c, pp. 132-137).

After the war, Ohlendorf surrendered to British forces in northern Germany. He was brought to London, where he was repeatedly interrogated in the infamous London Cage torture center. After seven weeks of unknown treatment, he admitted responsibility for the mass execution of 80,000 Jews in Russia. On 18 October 1945, he was transferred into U.S. custody at Landsberg prison, where he remained until his execution on 7 June 1951.

At the Nuremberg *Einsatzgruppen* Trial, Ohlendorf accepted responsibility for at least 90,000 victims of mass shootings carried out by *Einsatzgruppe* D, while he was in charge of that unit. While there is plenty of documental evidence to support this, this documentation is highly problematic, as a detailed analysis has shown (see Mattogno 2022c in general).

Ohlendorf's statements about the alleged use of

homicidal gas vans are even more problematic. He claimed, for instance, that Himmler presumably issued an order that only men should be executed by shooting, whereas women and children should only be murdered in gas vans, to spare them the horror of being shot in masses. However, this claim is neither backed up by any document nor by any other witness. Quite to the contrary, all witnesses to the alleged use of gas vans claim that men, women and children were killed in them indiscriminately.

When asked about any specific details of the gas vans, Ohlendorf couldn't answer, as he didn't know a thing about them: not how the gas was turned on, not whether they had windows. He answered this question with, "That is possible" – which is absurd, because truck cargo boxes don't come with windows.

He knew, however, that a physician once accompanied him in such a van to verify and then write a report that the victims were killed without them ever becoming aware of what was happening. Imagine hot, smoking, stinking, choking exhaust gases spewing into the enclosed space you are in, and you don't notice what happens, and agree to fall asleep peacefully. This is not realistic. Ohlendorf made up that physician and his report, and it goes without saying that there is no trace of either. Had Ohlendorf really accompanied the physician on that trip, he would have known how that van worked and how it looked. Ohlendorf's claim that only 15 or 25-30 people fit into that vehicle is at the extreme lower end of all witness claims. He moreover asserted that he refused to enforce Himmler's order by allowing his men *not* to use the vans. He insisted that they were used only a few times, leading only to a few hundred gas-van victims. This is rather incomprehensible, considering the efforts made to design, improve and construct the vehicles.

In contrast to this, the Just Document specifically states that 97,000 people had been successfully processed in those vans by June 1942. So who used them? Unless, of course, that document is as false as Ohlendorf's statements – which it is.

Ohlendorf's only source of information in this matter were the few documents he was shown by his prosecutors after the war, particular the Becker Document, which he was asked to authenticate twice. He falsely claimed that Becker was the constructor of the vans. However, Becker was merely a technician who is said to have made some repairs on them, and to have suggested improvements. Ohlendorf moreover asserted that Becker had always been in charge of the gas vans, meaning that they were never Ohlendorf's responsibility. However, if these vehicles existed, then the *Einsatzgruppen* were in charge of them, and so was Ohlendorf as head of *Einsatzgruppe* D. This was another one of Ohlendorf's failed defense strategies to confirm the legally unchallengeable claims in an attempt to assuage the court, but to deny any cooperation and responsibility.

(For Ohlendorf's various postwar statements in these matters see *IMT*, Vol. 4, pp. 322-324, 332-334; Document 2620-PS, *IMT* Vol. 31, pp. 39-41 (German), *NMT*, Vol. 4, pp. 205-207 (English), and his statements *ibid.*, pp. 301f.)

OHRDRUF

At the military training ground near the German town of Ohrdruf, a forced-labor camp was established in November 1944. Due to Germany's rapid collapse at that time, the camp never had a chance of developing any proper infrastructure. Therefore, living conditions were atrocious, death rates catastrophic. As U.S. troops approached, the camp was evacuated to the nearby Buchenwald Camp. Many inmates unable to keep up were allegedly shot along the way.

Most famous in this regard is a set of photographs showing General Dwight D. Eisenhower with other generals inspecting a small pyre with the remains of incompletely burned bodies.

The Ohrdruf training ground is furthermore the location of a suspected first attempt of German forces to test a nuclear bomb. The device is said to have been successfully tested in March of 1945. However, since the intensity of the blast had been severely underestimated, most military observers and the experimenters were killed in the process, together with many inmates in the nearby Ohrdruf Camp.

The Americans probably got wind of this disaster, and tried using it during the International Military Tribunal to their advantage. Evidently for the sake of military secrecy, they rebranded and relocated the event, thus making it difficult to recognize what it really referred to. They accused the Germans of having used an atomic bomb, not in Ohrdruf but near Auschwitz, and not as a test with hundreds or thousands of accidental victims among forced laborers, but as a means of instant extermination of 20,000 Jews. Here are the words of U.S. Chief Prosecutor Jackson when cross-examining Albert Speer, the Third Reich's Minister of Armament, who must have

Dwight D. Eisenhower inspecting a small cremation pyre at the Ohrdruf Camp with remains of incompletely burned victims of Germany's calamitous collapse.

known about the German atom bomb (*IMT*, Vol. 16, pp. 529f.):

> *"And certain experiments were also conducted and certain researches conducted in atomic energy, were they not? […] Now, I have certain information, which was placed in my hands, of an experiment which was carried out near Auschwitz […]. The purpose of the experiment was to find a quick and complete way of destroying people without the delay and trouble of shooting and gassing and burning, as it had been carried out […]. A village, a small village was provisionally erected, with temporary structures, and in it approximately 20,000 Jews were put. By means of this newly invented weapon of destruction* [atomic bomb], *these 20,000 people were eradicated almost instantaneously, and in such a way that there was no trace left of them;"*

Speer lied and pleaded ignorance of any such weapon being developed by Germany. (For more on the disastrous German atom-bomb test, see Karlsch 2005; Karlsch/Petermann 2007.)

OLÈRE, DAVID

David Olère was deported to Auschwitz in March 1943 and was employed there by the SS to paint portraits for them. He claimed that he lived in the attic of Crematorium III. Although he prepared some rather accurate architectural drawings of this building, they also include invisible features, such as the smoke ducts. He could have known their shape and position only from blueprints, which were probably provided to him by the Soviets after the war.

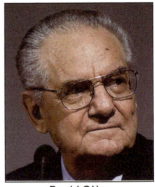

David Olère

Olére is most famous for a series of paintings allegedly depicting various scenes of the claimed extermination process at Auschwitz Birkenau. However, some of them clearly depict purely imaginary scenes, such as an SS ogre eating a dead girl, or oversized crematorium chimneys spewing flames and enormous amounts of smoke into the sky. Flames could not have come out of these crematorium chimneys, and air photos show that they emitted very little smoke, if any.

Some of his paintings do not even pretend to depict reality by the theme chosen, but an artist's interpretation of it, enriched with symbols, using lots of "poetic license" – which is to say: exaggerations and inventions.

In one drawing, he depicted how the members of the so-called *Sonderkommando* dragged corpses from the gas chamber with its heavy, bank-safe-like door straight to the cremation furnaces. However, the rooms claimed to have served as a homicidal gas chambers did not border on the furnace room in any of the Birkenau crematoria. Furthermore, all rooms claimed to have served as homicidal gas chambers only had primitive doors made of wooden boards. (See the entry on gastight doors.)

In another drawing, he shows the furnaces in Crematoria II and III in Birkenau close-up. He has doubled the size of the muffle doors in order to accommodate the many witness statements of multiple corpses pushed into the muffle at once. He has one bare-chested worker push a stretcher with several bodies on it into the muffle, which has flames coming out of it. That may be witness fantasy, but flames do not come out of a cremation muffle; working with a naked upper body in front of a glowing hot furnace is very bad advice; and the stretcher would have tipped down into the muffle, as its load was far heavier than the inmate holding the stretcher. In other words, this entire scenario is simply impossible – as were the claims of many a witness who Olére tried to give an artist's voice here.

One might think that Olére simply believed those witnesses whose tales he captured on canvas. But consider the tale he himself told mainstream histo-

"The Ogre of Birkenau," by David Olère.

rian Jean-Claude Pressac (1989, p. 554):

> "What can we say about former Krematorium III Sonderkommando member David Olère coolly telling me in 1981 that the SS made sausages of human flesh, except that he was still living in the nightmare that had been imposed on him and recounted anything that came into his head, […]"

By all accounts, Olére was simply another megalomaniac liar.

(For more details, see Rudolf 2023, pp. 462-465; see also Mattogno 2016f, pp. 90-94.)

OPEN-AIR INCINERATIONS
Fundamentals

Funeral fires on ceremonial pyres were common in Europe until the Christian Church banned this practice. In other parts of the world, where the Christian Church had little or no influence, the ritual burning of a deceased person remained quite common, most prominently in India. But even in Europe, burning dead bodies was practiced in times of mass deaths, such as epidemics or particularly during war time. The Second World War was no exception. In particular in various places where mass death occurred under German control, the resulting bodies are said to have been burned mostly on pyres, either on the flat ground or in pits and trenches.

The following table lists several German wartime camps plus the claimed crime scenes of the *Einsatzgruppen*, where a large number of bodies is said to have been burned on pyres, along with the point in time when these incinerations are said to have begun, if we follow the orthodox narrative:

Location/Unit	Claimed start of mass-grave exhumation and pyre cremation
Chełmno	summer 1942
Auschwitz	late September 1942
Sobibór	October 1942
Belzec	January 1943
Majdanek	February 1943
Treblinka	April 1943
Einsatzgruppen	July 1943

These outdoor cremations are said to have been motivated in some cases by hygienic and sanitary concerns (groundwater pollution; Auschwitz) or by esthetic concerns (stench; Chełmno), but in most if not all cases primarily by an attempt to erase the traces of mass crimes, if we follow the orthodox narrative.

In all the cases listed, the bodies of mass casualties or mass murder were first buried in mass graves, but presumably on orders of Heinrich Himmler, they all had to be exhumed again and burned. However, no documental trace of such a Himmler order has ever been found. It is attested to only by witness claims of low credibility (such as that by Rudolf Höss). To the contrary, a letter written by Himmler on 20 November 1942 has been preserved which clearly specifies that the bodies of deceased Jews have to be *either* cremated *or* buried. Hence, still in late 1942 no Himmler order existed to exhume and cremate all buried bodies (see Mattogno 2022c, p. 450). Therefore, none of the exhumation and cremation actions started prior to this date can be based on a general Himmler order. If any such order has ever been issued, one would furthermore expect it to have been implemented everywhere more or less at the same time, but this is absolutely not what we see.

Technologies

The biggest challenge when trying to combust a body is to raise its temperature to a point where its combustible components can ignite. The biggest impediment for this is the natural water content, which is about ⅔ of the mass of a human body. Most of this water has to evaporate first before tissue temperature can be raised to a point where it will combust.

The biggest enemy of open-air incineration is heat loss of any fire due to convection and radiation. This can be counteracted by surrounding the fire with insulated, heat-reflecting floors, walls and a ceiling, and ideally by extracting the heat contained in the smoke gases and using it to heat up air/oxygen fed into the fire for combustion. This is ultimately what properly designed cremation furnaces do. However, there are multiple stages to reach this technological endpoint. Energetically speaking, the worst open-air incineration is one that is conducted on a plain flat surface. The more a fire is surrounded by walls, the more its heat gets preserved. Hence, an efficient pyre is located in a pit or trench rather than on the flat soil. The closer the walls are together, the better. Therefore, a narrow and long, rectangular trench is better than a square-shaped one of the same surface area.

Abundant experience with funeral pyres in India, as well as scientifically evaluated experiences during various cattle epidemics, in particular the major hoof-and-mouth epidemic among British livestock in 2001, have led to some relatively reliable data, regarding:
- How much fuel is needed to cremate a body of a certain mass on open-air cremation pyres.
- Which is the best way of arranging open-air incineration pyres in case of mass cremations of hundreds or even thousands of bodies.
- What are the space and time requirements in such cases.

Structure

According to this data, a single-row pyre up to 2.5 m wide is required, so that air can reach in from both sides, and the pyre can be built and later maintained from both sides (stoking, refueling etc.). Fuel is to be placed at the bottom, with the bodies to be incinerated at the top, so that heat and flames rising from the fuel get used optimally. The longer the distance from the edge to the center of the pyre, the worse it will be supplied with oxygen, thus burning more slowly and unevenly.

The total height of a pyre should not exceed some 2 m (about 6 feet), resulting in a layer of fuel at the bottom and few layers of human corpses on top. If stacked higher, it becomes increasingly difficult to build such a pyre without technical equipment. Furthermore, the risk that the pile topples over increases considerably, for instance if the pyre burns unevenly, or any frozen ground melts and thus gives way unevenly.

Photo of a pyre built to burn livestock carcasses during the 2001 hoof-and-mouth epidemic in the UK. Note the protective clothes worn by the worker lighting the fire.

Outdoor livestock carcass cremation in the UK in 2001, seen from the air. Pit, excavated soil, massive destruction of vegetation and topsoil around the pits – nothing of that kind can be seen on any of the air photos of Auschwitz.

Outdoor livestock carcass cremation in the UK in 2001, seen from the air. The pyres which allegedly burned at Auschwitz, Belzec, Sobibór and Treblinka would have dwarfed fires like this and would have blanketed the entire area in smoke. Nothing of that kind can be seen on any of the air photos of Auschwitz.

If not wearing fireproof clothing, a safe distance of some 50 m minimum must be kept from a burning fire (similar to house or forest fires). If another pyre is operating next to a burning one, that distance needs to be increased to allow maneuvering room.

Time and Effort

It usually takes at least one day for a large cremation pyre to burn down. However, embers in the ashes keep glowing for up to a week or two. Hence, if the ashes are to be further processed (crushed), then it is necessary to wait for one to two weeks for everything to completely cool down. (Dousing with water would speed up cooling, but would make the frequently claimed ash-processing with sieves impossible.)

For example, the incineration of 800 British sheep required some 100 soldiers plus trucks and other equipment to move fuel and carcasses (such as backhoes or excavators). Without such equipment, considerably more men would be needed.

Once the pyres are lit, approaching them is possible only with protective clothes as worn by fire fighters.

Environmental Impact

Large outdoor cremation operations have a considerable impact on the environment. Two effects are of concern in the present context (see the illustrations):
– Moving topsoil to accommodate the pyres, transporting and arranging carcasses and fuel, as well as maintaining the fire and disposing of the cremation leftovers tear up the soil in large areas around the pyres.
– The fires themselves create huge smoke plumes which, depending on prevailing winds, can cover large areas of the sky.

Fuel

Data vary on the fuel necessary to cremate a corpse with the equivalent mass of an average human body. In terms of wood, most values given range from 100 to 200 kg of *dry* (seasoned) wood. The type of wood is also a factor, as hard woods like oak and maple have higher energy contents than soft woods, such as pine or spruce. Thus, results vary depending on the different pyre layouts and the different kinds of fuels used. If *freshly cut* wood is used instead, the amount required easily doubles, due to the high water content of fresh wood. Assuming 250 kg of fresh (green) wood per body is thus realistic. Self-immolating bodies are not part of the scientific literature, as none have ever been discovered during single-body or large-scale cremations.

A 50-year-old spruce forest usually yields some 500 solid cubic meters of wood per hectare (100 m × 100 m, a little more than two American football fields). This amounts to about 450 metric tons of wood. Hence, a square kilometer of such a forest contains some 45,000 metric tons of wood, and a square mile some 116,550 metric tons of wood.

An average prisoner is rated at being able to cut some 0.63 metric tons of fresh wood per workday. This value can be used to calculate, how many inmate lumberjacks it takes to cut a certain amount of wood within a given period of time. The entry on lumberjacks gives an overview of the firewood that would have been needed to burn the number of corpses alleged by witnesses, or by the orthodox narrative for various claimed Holocaust crime scenes. As an example, the next section discusses some claims made about outdoor cremations at the Auschwitz Camp.

(For details on open-air incinerations, see Mattogno 2016b, esp. pp. 60-63, 128-133; Graf/Kues/Mattogno 2020, pp. 138-157; Mattogno/Kues/Graf 2015, pp. 1226-1328.)

Holocaust Scenarios

Based upon the data resulting from large-scale animal cremations outdoors, it can be deduced that an optimally designed pyre using dry wood can be loaded with some 8 to 10 human corpses per running meter, or 4 to 5 bodies when using fresh wood. For instance, a pyre 20 m long and 2 m wide using dry wood could accommodate some 200 corpses (see Mattogno 2016b, pp. 134f.).

Former Auschwitz inmate Stanisław Jankowski, who gave 20 m × 2 m as the dimensions of the pyres he claims to have seen, insisted, however, that these pyres accommodated 2,000 bodies, which means that they would have been not 2 meters, but 20 meters high (when using dry wood) – a physical impossibility. When using fresh wood, the wood alone would have stacked up to almost 20 meters. The pit data claimed by former Auschwitz inmate Joshuah Rosenblum are similarly detached from reality. In addition, he and other Auschwitz inmates described the pyres as having been 5, 6, 8, 10, even 15 meters wide, which would have made it difficult to build them, impossible to maintain their centers, and inefficient to burn (see the table).

This is even truer for the alleged depth of the pits

Properties of Claimed Auschwitz Cremation Pits									
Witness	Pits	Length	Width	Depth	Location	Bodies per pit	Time	Wood*	Height†
Charles Bendel	3	12 m	6 m	1.5 m	near Crematorium V	333	1 hour	83 t	1.8 m
Shaul Chasan	1	–	–	4 m	near "Bunker 2"	–	–		
Szlama Dragon	5	25 m	6 m	3 m	near Crematorium V	1,000	1 day	250 t	2.6 m
Stanisław Jankowski	2	20 m	2 m	2 m	near Crematorium V	2,000	–	500 t	19.4 m
Henryk Mandelbaum	-	30-35 m	15 m	–	near Crematorium V	1,500-1,800	1-2 days	375-450 t	1.1-1.3 m
Filip Müller	5	40-50 m	8 m	2 m	near Crematorium V	1,200	5-6 hours	300 t	1.2 m
Filip Müller	4	–	–	–	near "Bunker 2"				
Miklós Nyiszli	2	50 m	6 m	3 m	near "Bunker 2"	2,500	1 day	625 t	3.2 m
Dov Paisikovic	2	30 m	6-10 m	–	near "Bunker 2"	–	–		
Joshuah Rosenblum	-	10 m	5 m	2 m	unspecified	2,000	2-3 hours	500 t	15.5 m
Arnošt Rosin‡	-	30 m	15 m	–	unspecified	–	–		
Henryk Tauber	4-5	–	–	–	near Crematorium V	> 400	2 days	100 t	
Shlomo Venezia	1	–	–	–	near "Bunker 2"				

Source: Mattogno 2016b, p. 28. * Fresh wood required, at 250 kg per body. † Stacking height just for the fresh wood, at 0.9 kg/m³, and a packing density of 1.4., calculated for the largest pit area indicated. ‡ Together with Czesław Mordowicz.

in which these pyres were allegedly placed: 1.5 to 4 meters, depending on the witness. With the groundwater standing close to the surface at Birkenau, any pit deeper than a meter was in acute danger of filling up with water, thus preventing any fire.

But independent of the groundwater level, building a pyre in a wide pit wouldn't have led to much of a gain in efficiency, but it certainly would have complicated the building, maintenance and clearing of such pyres, hence it would have made no sense at all.

The time allegedly required for building, burning and clearing out a pyre is commonly given as several hours, a day or at most two days, with the ashes being sifted through large sieves, in search of large unburned objects to be ground down or further burned. An extreme outlier in this regard is Charles Bendel, who gave a ludicrously short time of just one hour to process such a pyre.

Considering that it would have taken a week or more for a large pyre to cool down to the point when its ashes could be handled this way, these witness claims prove that they originate from fantasy rather than reality. (For more on ashes, see Mattogno 2016b, pp. 63-65.)

For more details on open-air incinerations at the various claimed Holocaust crime scenes, see the links in the initial table of this entry, as well as the entry on lumberjacks.

OPERATION "HARVEST FESTIVAL"

The orthodoxy insists that on 3 and 4 November 1943, all remaining Jews in the Trawniki and Poniatowa forced-labor camps, as well as in the Majdanek Concentration Camp, were murdered. Some 42,000 to 43,000 persons are said to have been shot and buried in mass graves on these two days, 17,000 to 18,000 of them in Majdanek. But then, the bodies were exhumed right away and burned on gigantic pyres over the next 50 days.

No document exists relating to this alleged event. The head of occupied Poland, Hans Frank, does not mention it in his extensive diary. When giving a speech during a meeting with Frank a couple weeks after the alleged event, Himmler says no word about it either. Odilo Globocnik stated in an undated document of that time that the workers of several labor camps had been evacuated and transferred. Several German police units noted in their activity diaries that they were involved in a major special operation in the Lublin area.

There is no proof that the term "Harvest Festival" has ever been used as a code word for anything during the Third Reich. The timing is off as well, because Harvest Festival (*Erntedankfest*) is a German secular holiday celebrating a year's grain and produce harvest on the first Sunday of October (not November).

As the war progressed, Germany's manpower situation became increasingly desperate. The more men were taken out of the production process to die at the various fronts, the more they needed to be replaced with whatever forced laborers could be mustered.

In the same vein, Himmler and his subordinates issued ever-more urgent orders to reduced camp mortality, preserve or improve all camp inmates' health and thus ability to work, and to integrate even modestly sick and handicapped inmates into the production process. Particularly relevant is an order by the head of all concentration and labor camps, Oswald Pohl, head of the SS's Economic and Administrative Main Office (*Wirtschafts- und Verwaltungshauptamt*). On 26 October 1943, he sent an order to the commandants of all concentration camps and their forced-labor subcamps. Therefore, this order was also addressed to the head of the camps at Majdanek, Trawniki and Poniatowa. It states:

"Thanks to the expansion and consolidation of the past 2 years, the concentration camps have become a factor of vital importance in German arms production. [...]

Now [...] all measures taken by the commandants [...] and physicians must work towards keeping the inmates healthy and fit.

Not out of a false sense of sentimentality, but because we need them with their physical abilities intact – because they must contribute to the German people winning a great victory – we must take good care of their health and well-being.

I propose as our first goal: no more than 10% of all inmates at a time may be unable to work due to illness. By everyone responsible working together, this goal must be attained.

This requires:

1) proper and practical diet,
2) proper and practical clothing,
3) making full use of all natural means for preserving health,
4) avoiding all unnecessary strain and expenditure of energy not directly required for work,
5) productivity bonuses. [...]"

In complete contravention to this order, the orthodoxy insists that, just eight days later, the three camp commandants of Majdanek, Trawniki and Poniatowa, with the help of various SS forces, rounded up all the Jews in these camps – whose work was absolutely crucial for the German war effort – and executed them all.

The orthodox narrative has its roots in reports of the Polish underground, although they wrote of 10,000 victims (later increased to 13,000), and dated the execution on the 5th of November.

No mass graves with at least 17,000 victims existed at the Majdanek Camp, nor graves with 15,000 bodies in Poniatowa or 8,000 in Trawniki. Hence, they must have been burned without leaving a trace – so the orthodoxy asserts, as they cannot concede that the witnesses they rely on can be profoundly wrong. However, the Majdanek Camp is in plain sight of the city of Lublin. Therefore, there should have been thousands of witnesses to this inevitably long-lasting, stinking, smoking conflagration of an outdoor cremation operation erasing the traces of 17,000 bodies. But there are none. The Polish resistance also reported nothing to that effect.

This didn't prevent the Polish judiciary from convincing Erich Mussfeldt, the former head of the Majdanek crematorium, to write down a lengthy confession about it all, after the Americans had softened him up in their torture center at the former Dachau Camp, and then extradited him to the Poles for further processing. Here is what Mussfeldt claimed in his confessions:

– First, three 100-m long pits, zig-zag in shape, were dug by inmates during the three days prior to the shooting. However, zig-zag shape makes no sense for mass graves, but makes sense for infantry fighting trenches. Many of those are visible around the camp's perimeter on an air photo taken in September 1944. This is probably the origin of that story.

– Then, Mussfeldt was forced to watch – eleven hours long – how "more than 17,000" victims were shot next to those pits, then dumped into them. However, the only reason to claim that he was forced to watch this alleged massacre is so he could satisfy the Poles demand that he was a witness.

– To drown out the shooting, loud marches and dancing music was played. However, music cannot drown out mass shootings going on for 11 hours. It can only attract even more attention. Tens of thousands of Poles living in the vicinity would have wondered what dance party was unfolding there, and would have gathered to join the fun…

– Some 300 Jews left alive sorted clothes left behind by the naked victims, while others covered the pits with soil. Two days later, Mussfeldt had 20 Russians (probably PoWs) assigned to him to burn the victims. However, at this point in time, the so-called *Aktion* 1005 is said to have been in full swing everywhere in German-controlled areas. This was the alleged order to exhume all bodies in mass graves and burn them. If those in charge at Majdanek were even marginally competent, no pits would have been dug ever, and no soil used to cover the murdered victims. After all, the plan must have been all along to burn the victims on pyres straight away.

– These 20 Russians collected wood, built pyres with it at the empty end of the pits, pulled any gold teeth from the corpses before putting them on a pyre, then burned it down. Once a pyre had burned out and the ashes cooled down, the ashes were taken out of the pit, and the bones ground with a "gasoline-powered mill." The bone powder was put into paper bags, taken away with cars, and used as soil fertilizer. This lasted until just before Christmas, hence some 50 days.

All these tasks would have been impossible to accomplish by just 20 Russians within 50 days. To make the point, let's just focus on the firewood needed, which the Russians "collected." With 250 kg of green wood needed to cremate one body during open-air incinerations, these 20 PoWs had to chop at least 4,250 tons of fresh wood in neighboring forests. This would have required the felling of all trees growing in a 50-year-old spruce forest covering some 9.4 hectares of land, or some 21 American football fields.

An average prisoner is rated at being able to cut some 0.63 metric tons of fresh wood per workday. If the last pyre was getting built five days prior to the operation ending, then these 20 inmates had 45 days to chop up wood, if they did nothing else. That would have amounted to some 567 tons of fresh wood, hence only some 13% of what would have been needed. To cut the required amount of wood within 45 days would have required a work force of some 150 dedicated lumberjacks. Hence, these 20 inmates would not have taken 45 days to get the wood needed, but almost a year, hence until several months after the conquest of the area by the Soviets. And this completely ignores the time and manpower needed to extract gold teeth from the corpses, build all the pyres required, burn them down, extract the resulting ashes, grind down the bones, and spread the ashes…

Furthermore, grinding the bones to dust would have been another impossible task. Outdoor pyres do not reduce corpses to mere ashes and bones. Considerable parts of a body burn only incompletely, and so does the firewood. These partly charred, mixed remains of flesh and wood cannot be ground to dust in mills. Moreover, we are talking about hundreds of metric tons of ashes. These would not have been filled into paper bags and driven around in cars, but loaded onto dump trucks and hauled away.

This all demonstrates that Mussfeldt's testimony was cooked up in the witch's cauldron of Polish post-war propaganda, with no connection to reality.

The Polish newspaper-in-exile *Dziennik Polski*, printed in England, published the following report on 20 November 1943:

"25,000 Jews were transferred from Majdanek to Cracow, where they were quartered in hundreds of recently constructed barracks. Probably these Jews will have to work in the German factories which have recently been transferred to the Cracow district."

And as mainstream historian Raul Hilberg noted, the number of Jewish forced laborers deployed in the armaments industries of the General Government *increased* from October 1943 to January 1944 from 22,444 to 26,296!

This explains what really happened.
(For more details, see Graf/Mattogno 2012, pp. 207-228.)

Operation Reinhardt → *Aktion Reinhardt*

ORANIENBURG

Oranienburg is a town north-northwest of Berlin. It was the location of a small prison facility functioning as a concentration camp between March 1933 and summer 1934, when it was dissolved. A new camp on the town's outskirts, called Sachsenhausen, was established in 1936. Since 1938, Oranienburg was also the seat of the SS's Concentration Camp Inspectorate headed by Richard Glücks. It was housed in a building adjacent to the Sachsenhausen Camp.

order, to exterminate Jews → **Hitler Order**
OSI → **Office of Special Investigations**

OSTROVSKY, LEONID

Leonid Ostrovsky was a Ukrainian Jew interned in the Syretsky Camp, 5 km from Kiev. On 16 August 1943, he was taken from there to Babi Yar, a place where tens of thousands of Jews are said to have been shot and buried by the Germans in mass graves in late September 1941 (see the entry on Babi Yar). He was interrogated by the NKGB on 12 November 1943 about his alleged experiences at Babi Yar.

Among other things, he stated that he and other slave-labor inmates were put in chains some 50-60 cm long, and had to exhume mass graves and burn the extracted bodies on pyres built on a stone platform measuring 30 × 40 meters. On an iron grid placed on rails, a layer of wood was placed, then two rows of corpses with the heads pointing outwards, and these were then covered with another layer of wood. Such a pyre was 2 to 2.5 meters high and contained 2,500-3,000 bodies.

However, this results in 1,250 to 1,500 bodies in

one row of a pyre that could not have been longer than 40 meters. This means that 31 to 38 bodies were placed on each running meter of the pyre. With 40 cm body width and 20 cm body height, that layer of bodies would have been up to 3 meters high.

Considering that some 250 kg of freshly cut wood is required to burn one average human corpse, to burn this many corpses per running meter would have required up to almost ten metric tons of wood. Fresh wood has a density of roughly 0.9 tons per m³, and when stacked on a pyre, the gaps make up some 40% of the space (for air and flames to go through). Therefore, ten metric tons of wood on a pyre fill a volume of some 15 cubic meters. Assuming a surface of 2 m² for each running meter of the pyre, this means that the stacked wood alone would have been 7.5 meters high, and the total pyre thus up to 10 meters and more – not 2 to 2.5 m as claimed by the witness. Such a huge pyre could have been built only with cranes. Once lit, it inevitably would have burned unevenly, hence would have toppled over and spilled burning wood and corpses all over the place.

Furthermore, placing wood on top of the corpses would have been a complete waste of everything, as most heat would have escaped upwards. Hence, this certainly would not have been done.

Ostrovsky asserted that a total of 25-30 pyres with 2,500-3,000 bodies each were built and burned down, so a total of some 62,500 to 90,000 victims. The initial number of 100 slave-labor inmates was increased to 321 "at the beginning of September."

Cremating an average human body during open-air incinerations requires some 250 kg of freshly cut wood. Cremating 62,500 bodies thus requires some 15,625 metric tons of wood. This would have required the felling of all trees growing in a 50-year-old spruce forest covering almost 35 hectares of land, or some 78 American football fields. An average prisoner is rated at being able to cut some 0.63 metric tons of fresh wood per workday. To cut this amount of wood within five weeks (35 days) that this operation supposedly lasted would have required a work force of some 700 dedicated lumberjacks just to cut the wood. Ostrovsky claims that his unit initially consisted only of 100, then of 321 inmates, all busy digging out mass graves, extracting bodies, building pyres, and according to other testimonies also sifting through ashes, scattering the ashes and refilling the graves with soil. Ostrovsky says nothing about where the firewood came from.

(For more details, see the entry on Babi Yar, as well as Mattogno 2022c, pp. 530f., and 550-563.)

OSTROWSKI COMPANY

The Ostrowski Company operated a factory at the Polish city of Koło, some 7 km northwest of the Chełmno Camp. After the war, a damaged moving truck of the German truck manufacturer Magirus, once operated by the moving company "Otto Koehn Spedition," was discovered on the Ostrowski factory grounds which several witnesses claimed to have been a "gas van." However, an investigation by Polish judge Władysław Bednarz established that this vehicle was *not* a "gas van." Still, photos taken by Bednarz in the context of his investigations were later shown by mainstream historians, such as Gerald Fleming and Christopher Browning, as proof for the existence of gas vans. (See Alvarez 2023, pp. 33-39, 151, 159, 165-171, 358.)

An ordinary damaged moving truck parked on the factory grounds of the Ostrowski Company was falsely identified by "witnesses" as a "gas van" presumably used to kill inmates at the Chełmno Camp. Gullible journalists and orthodox scholars have repeated this gas-van nonsense ever since.

Oswiecim → **Auschwitz**
outdoor cremations → **Open-Air Incinerations**

P

PACKING DENSITY, INSIDE GAS CHAMBER

Principles

How many people can stand on a surface area of one square meter (some 10 square feet, or a square 3'3" on a side)? Assuming that there are children in the mix, a figure of ten people seems physically possible – barely. The skeptical reader is invited to lay down some masking tape on the floor: a single square, 3'3" on a side, and see how many people can stand in that square.

The situation changes dramatically, if we consider a large crowd of naked strangers, of both genders, uncooperative and scared, who are told to take a shower together, such that they must line up extremely densely – breasts against shoulder blades, bellies against buttocks, genitals against genitals, shoulders against shoulders. No one could believe this is for taking a shower, so they will simply not cooperate. Screaming at them and threatening violence, or even beating them or shooting them will not work but rather trigger a panic in that room with unforeseeable consequences.

Packing people tightly into a given space requires that they can understand instructions, that they are told what the goal is, that they are willing to cooperate, and that they all have the discipline to follow orders. None of it is a given in any of the orthodox scenarios. The Jews came from all over Europe, and many if not most may not have understood what they were told already due to the language barriers. But then, if they did understand it, they were told a lie, as the given goal was presumably to take a shower, which means exactly the opposite of lining up tightly together.

Auschwitz

Take the case of the underground Morgue #1 of Crematoria II and III at Auschwitz Birkenau, for which we have blueprints showing their size, and the most witness accounts ever made for any homicidal gas-chamber claim. The room was 7 meters wide and 30 meters long. If we assume the average person to be half a meter wide and a quarter meter deep (25 cm), then physically we could fill the room as shown in the graphic, when packing them chest to back, shoulder to shoulder.

This amounts to 14 persons in a row, with 120 rows in total, resulting in 1,680 people, or 8 persons per square meter. This can be considered the realistic physical maximum of what can be achieved. However, considering that the intended victims would not have been told anything, let alone why they had to line up that way, they therefore would not have cooperated in achieving such a packing density. Thus, we may assume that *half* of that density, hence 4 people per square meter, is already optimistic. It may therefore be stated that anyone claiming that more than 1,000 people (4.75 people per m²) were crammed into this room is exaggerating.

The following table shows the claims of several prominent Birkenau witnesses, regarding how many people were allegedly packed into Morgue #1 (the alleged "gas chamber") of Crematoria II or III.

The conclusion is inescapable: Nearly all witnesses have exaggerated the number of people allegedly gassed in one batch, at times in an extreme way. It is a typical "conversion of evidence" on a lie. Exaggerating the claimed batch size of gassings clearly supports equally fantastic and exaggerated overall death-toll figures for Auschwitz.

The situation is not different for other gas-chamber claims, although there the situation is not as clear as the above example, because for most of them we lack material and documental evidence as to the size of the claimed gas chambers. However, some witnesses have made more-or-less-detailed statements both about how many people were gassed per chamber and per batch, and what the room's size was. This

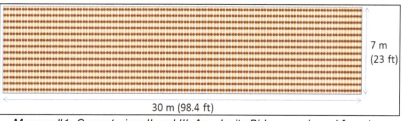

Morgue #1, Crematorium II and III, Auschwitz-Birkenau, viewed from top, packed full of people represented as dark brown dots (heads) and light brown base (trunk).

Witness	4,000 (19/m²)	3,000 (14.3/m²)	2,500 (11.9/m²)	2,000 (9.5/m²)	1,500 (7.1/m²)	1000 (4.8/m²)	500 (2.4/m²)
Daniel Bennahmias		•					
Pery Broad	•						
Shaul Chasan			•				
Stanisław Chybiński		2,800					
Leon Cohen				•			
Josef Erber		•					
David Fliamenbaum				•			
Chaim Frosch				•			
Dario Gabai		•	•				
Yaakov Gabai				•			
Salmen Gradowski			•				
Jeannette Kaufmann				•			
Hermine Kranz		•					
Michał Kula			•	•	•		
Erich Kulka				•			
Henryk Mandelbaum		•					
Hans Münch		•					
Marcel Nadsari		•					
Miklos Nyiszli		•		•			
Dov Paisikovic		•					
Aaron Pilo		•					
Regina Plucer						•	
Fritz Putzker				•			
Deszö Schwarz					•		
Roman Sompolinski							•
Soviet Report 26/2		•	•	•			
Henryk Tauber	•						
Morris Venezia		•					
Shlomo Venezia					1,800		
Rudolf Vrba				•			

Table title: CLAIMED PACKING DENSITY OF VICTIMS IN THE UNDERGROUND MORGUE #1 OF CREMATORIA II AND III AT AUSCHWITZ-BIRKENAU

is true for the two alleged makeshift facilities just outside the Auschwitz-Birkenau Camp commonly referred to as the "bunkers" of Auschwitz, and for some of the claimed gas chambers of the camps at Belzec and Treblinka. In these cases, when it comes to the size of the related claimed gas chambers, we depend on either what each witness has claimed, or what the orthodoxy has ordained to be "true."

In some cases, witnesses have invented figures for the size of the chamber and the people packed into them. For example, Szlama Dragon gave exact sizes of the so-called bunkers of Auschwitz – albeit contradicting material evidence for Bunker 2 – as well as the number of people per batch killed in them, which results in impossible packing densities of 20 to 25 people per m². For one of the alleged bunkers of Auschwitz (probably Bunker 1), Arnošt Rosin claimed a packing density of 12 and 19 per m². For an unknown chamber at some facility in Auschwitz, Charles S. Bendel had 1,000 people in a room of barely 40 or 50 m² (again 20 to 25 people per m²), although no such room ever existed there. Stanisław Jankowski claimed that 1,500-2,000 people were crammed into the larger chamber of Crematoria IV and V. This room had roughly 100 m², which would have resulted in a packing density of 15 to 20 people per m².

Belzec
Kurt Gerstein claimed an even more impossible

packing density of 28-32 persons per m² for the alleged gas chambers at the Belzec Camp.

Treblinka

As to the claimed Treblinka gas chambers, Abe Kon asserted that 600 people were pressed into an alleged room size of 6 m × 6 m, hence an impossible 16.7 people per m².

Jankiel Wiernik's figure for the Treblinka Camp was 400 to 450 people on (5m×5m=) 25 m² per chamber in the old building, hence 18 to 20 people per m², and 1,000 to 1,200 people on (7m×7m=) 49 m² per chamber in the new building, hence 20 to 24.5 people per m².

Lucjan Puchała asserted that 700 victims went into each Treblinka chamber, but he gave no room size. If we take what the orthodoxy claims (32 m² per room for the new building with larger chambers), then this results in a density of 22 people per square meter (or 14 for Wiernik's claimed 49 m²).

Aleksander Kudlik's figure for the Treblinka Camp, given Wiernik's claimed chamber size, was at least physically possible, although not much more realistic: 5,000 people in all ten chambers of some 49 m² each, hence only 10 people per m². If we take the orthodoxy's claim of 32 m², however, this value increases to an impossible 15.6 people per m².

Elias Rosenberg stated that 400 were squeezed into the initial, smaller chambers, which measured 4 m × 4 m, hence 16 m², if we take the orthodoxy's claims. That would have resulted in an impossible packing density of 25/m². For the new gas-chamber building, Rosenberg claimed a capacity of 12,000 people. According to orthodox claims, that building contained 10 chambers of 32 m² each. Hence, Rosenberg's victim count would have resulting in an impossible (and record-breaking) packing density of 37.5 people per m².

PAISIKOVIC, DOV

Dov Paisikovic (1 April 1924 – 1988) was a Jew from Hungary deported to Auschwitz, where he arrived on 31 May 1944. He claims to have been a member of the so-called *Sonderkommando*. Only the frenzy of the investigations leading to the Frankfurt Auschwitz show trial motivated Paisikovic to come forward with his testimony. His first affidavit was recorded on 17 October 1963 in Vienna. Seven days later, he was interrogated specifically for that trial, and on 8 October 1964, he testified in Frankfurt. In August 1964, he wrote a long report for the files of the Auschwitz Museum. The following list sums up the more-peculiar of Paisikovic's claims:

Dov Paisikovic

– For the alleged makeshift gassing facility outside the Birkenau Camp, usually called "Bunker 2," he used the term "Bunker V," which was coined by Höss, indicating that Paisikovic had read Höss's memoirs.
– For Paisikovic, the victims undressed outside, if at all, while other witnesses have the orthodoxy conclude that there were several undressing barracks nearby, which Paisikovic does not mention at all.
– Paisikovic's statement for the Auschwitz Museum is accompanied by four sketches of this "bunker." This and his description of the facility (three equally sized parallel rooms for 300 people) contradict the description and sketches drawn by the other key witness for the bunkers, Szlama Dragon (four unequally sized parallel rooms for 2,000 to 2,500 people). Both Paisikovic's and Dragon's sketches and descriptions radically contradict the foundation walls of this alleged building extant to this day (seven irregularly sized and arranged rooms).
– SS *Hauptscharführer* Moll allegedly came in a white uniform – although no SS man had such a uniform.
– The corpses he had to drag to a burning pit were bloated, which was not an effect of the gas, as he might have insinuated, but of these corpses having died several days earlier.
– According to his Vienna statement, the burning pit, 6 m wide and 50 m long, was ablaze, yet Paisikovic and his fellow inmates had no trouble dragging more corpses to it and throwing them onto this burning inferno without getting burned themselves. However, in his statement for the Auschwitz Museum, the pit he dragged bodies to measured 30 m × 10 m and was not yet on fire.
– The capacity of the burning pits near "Bunker V" were practically unlimited – although air photos of that time clearly show the absence of any large pits and of any smoke in the claimed area.

- 3,000 victims were crammed into Morgue #1 of Crematorium II (& III), the alleged homicidal gas chamber – an impossible packing density of 14.5 people per square meter in this room of 210 m² (per his Vienna statement; in his statement for the Auschwitz Museum, he claimed 2,000).
- For Paisikovic, Zyklon B was poured into this morgue/gas chamber through two roof openings into a large surface behind a net surrounding two concrete support pillars. The orthodoxy has it, however, that there were four wire-mesh Zyklon-B introduction columns separate from the concrete support columns.
- A gassing in this gas chamber lasted only 3 to 4 minutes – an impossibly short time (…or maybe it lasted 5 to 20 min., per his Frankfurt testimony.)
- Due to the tight space, dead people kept standing upright – which is physically impossible.
- This chamber was ventilated only for a quarter of an hour before the door was opened – again an impossibly short time that could not have removed all the poison gas from this room. He later doubled that time in his statement to the Auschwitz Museum. Still, with a room densely packed with corpses, that would not have been enough either.
- The ventilator fans were set in the side walls. In fact, the side walls only had ventilation openings. The fans were located in the building's attic.
- The crematorium's 15 furnaces (=muffles) burned 3,000 victims within 12 hours, meaning one body every 3.6 minutes! Paisikovic even says so: "about 4 minutes." In his statement for the Auschwitz Museum, he changed that to 2,000 bodies in 15 hours, with 2-3 bodies loaded into each muffle, which is still only 6¾ minutes per body, or some 20 minutes for a load of three (…or maybe the capacity was 3,000 in 24 hours, per his Frankfurt testimony, which is 7.2 minutes per body). However, the Birkenau furnaces were designed to burn one body within one hour.
- Two or three SS men monitored the work in the furnace room from another room through a window – but there was no window anywhere inside that building.
- After the mass-murder of the Hungarian Jews was over, all Hungarian *Sonderkommando* members were killed – of course except for Paisikovic, due to a miracle, like all other surviving Hungarian Jews claiming to have been members.
- Paisikovic insisted that, "once the furnace was burning, the bodies themselves fed the fire," so no fuel was needed. However, self-immolating bodies do not exist. The furnaces of Crematoria II and III needed at least on average 20 kg of coke per body under ideal conditions.
- In his 1964 statement for the Auschwitz Museum, he claimed that "Mengele and a Jewish inmate of Hungarian origin [M. Nyiszli] carried out various experiments on the dead and the living." This indicates that Paisikovic was aware of, and influenced by, Miklós Nyiszli's book about Auschwitz.

For more details on this witness, see Mattogno 2016f, pp. 109-113; 2021d, pp. 135-160.

Paneriai → Ponary

PANKOV, VASSILY

Vassily Pankov was a Ukrainian auxiliary presumably deployed as a guard at the Sobibór Camp. After the war, he was arrested for this. In his interrogation of 18 October 1950 by Soviet authorities, he was made to describe even the Buchenwald Camp as an extermination camp. According to Pankov, the gassing facility at Sobibór consisted of six chambers, and the engine supplying the asphyxiating exhaust gas was a diesel motor, with the execution lasting "an hour or more." However, diesel-engine exhaust gas is not suitable for mass murder, as it is barely toxic. The reference to a diesel engine is clearly an echo from the 1943 Soviet show trials at Krasnodar and Kharkov, where gas vans, allegedly killing with diesel-exhaust gases, played a major role.

(See the entry on Sobibór for more details, as well as Graf/Kues/Mattogno 2020, pp. 111f., 158; Mattogno 2021e, p. 223.)

PECHERSKY, ALEXANDER

Alexander Pechersky (22 Feb. 1909 – 19 Jan. 1990), a Soviet-soldier of the Red Army, ended up in German captivity in 1941. After an extended stay at a labor camp in Minsk, he ended up at the Sobibór Camp in September of 1943, where he organized a successful prisoner uprising just three

Alexander Pechersky

weeks later, on 14 October. He therefore is one of the stars of orthodox "Holocaust" history and the protagonist of a number of movies about the uprising.

In 1945, a report about his experiences while in German captivity was published in the Soviet Union, with an extended version of it appearing in 1946 in Yiddish titled *Revolt in Sobibór*. Pechersky's report is full of outrageous lies, the most striking of which are:

- He claimed that some other inmate told him that every day (or every other day in the extended version) 2,000 deportees were exterminated, with the camp already having existed for nearly a year and a half, which would amount to (500 days × 1,000 or 2,000 =) at least half a million, a number he elsewhere explicitly claims as the total death toll. This stands against some 200,000 victims claimed by today's orthodoxy. Moreover, trains going to Sobibór are rather well-documented, and there were only relatively few trains going to Sobibór in 1943 – none between 21 July and 14 September, and only a handful after Pechersky's arrival. Therefore, either he was told bold lies by his co-inmates, or he unscrupulously invented things.
- He claimed to have heard from a fellow inmate that the bath (evidently only one room) was equipped with "faucets for hot and cold water" and even with a "basin to wash in." However, the orthodoxy insists that those gas chambers were plain rooms with no accoutrements.
- Mass murder at Sobibór was presumably carried out with some bizarre "thick dark substance" coming down spiraling from holes in the roof of the death chamber (his 1945 manuscript has here simply "black gas"). However, mainstream historians insist that it was done using engine-exhaust gases.
- The gassing was observed by an SS man through a roof window. That is rejected by the orthodoxy as false.
- After the murder, the floors opened, and the bodies were discharged into carts below, which brought them to mass graves. According to the current orthodox narrative, however, no collapsible floors with carts underneath existed. The corpses were instead taken out of the chamber manually, sideways through a normal door.
- When he was interrogated again in 1961, probably in the context of the Eichmann Trial, he sanitized his account by eliminating everything not in line with the orthodox narrative – except for the wash basins, which he kept.
- Whenever people were led into the death chamber, a gaggle of 300 geese kept in the camp were made to honk and shriek loudly, so the victims' cries could not be heard.
- Pechersky befriended an 18-year-old German Jewish girl who spoke only German and Dutch and was kept alive for some inscrutable reason. They allegedly had extensive conversations in private, although Pechersky only spoke Russian. Therefore, all these conversations are made up as well.
- After his escape from Sobibór, Pechersky learned of a German camp nearby "where people were turned into soap."
- Pechersky told his tale of how the uprising unfolded, with all SS guards behaving friendly, naïve, unsuspecting, trusting and relaxed before getting butchered one by one by the scheming inmates. The SS men's claimed behavior is inconceivable if they were indeed guarding an extermination camp, in which no inmate could be trusted (and vice versa no guard), unless they were *not* guarding an extermination camp.
- Pechersky claimed that every night the guards had to hand in the clip of five cartridges which came with the rifle each of them had been issued. In a real extermination camp, however, where an inmate revolt had to be expected at any time, the camp administration would have made sure that all guards remained constantly armed to the teeth.

The last point can be complemented by a statement made by the former police captain Erich Wullbrandt in Braunschweig, Germany, in 1961. According to him, some of the Jews who had escaped during the revolt returned *voluntarily* to the camp the next night. Had Sobibór been an extermination camp, that would have been utterly inconceivable.

(See the entry on Sobibór for more details, as well as Graf/Kues/Mattogno 2020, pp. 69f., 84-93; Mattogno 2021e, pp. 82-84.)

PEER, MOSHE

Moshe Peer was a French Jew who, at the age of 9, was arrested and, together with his family and many other Jews from France, deported to Auschwitz. While his mother perished there, he and the rest of his family were transferred to the Bergen-Belsen Camp toward the end of the war, where they all survived. In an interview published on 5 August 1993 in the Montreal newspaper *The Gazette*, Peer declared

>
>
> THE GAZETTE, MONTREAL, THURSDAY, AUGUST 5, 1993
>
> ## Surviving the horror
> ### Author recounts experiences in Nazi concentration camp
>
> **KAREN SEIDMAN**
> THE GAZETTE
>
> ST. LAURENT – As an 11-year-old boy held captive at the Bergen-Belsen concentration camp during World War II, Moshe Peer was sent to the gas chamber at least six times.
>
> Each time he survived, watching with horror as many of the women and children gassed with him collapsed and died.
>
> To this day, Peer doesn't know how he was able to survive.
>
> "Maybe children resist better, I don't know," he said in an interview last week.
>
> **Spent 19 years on book**
>
> Now 60, Peer has spent the last 19 years writing a first-person account of the horror he witnessed at Bergen-Belsen. On Sunday, he spoke to about 300 young adults at the Petah Tikva Sephardic Congregation in St. Laurent about his book and his experience as a Holocaust survivor.
>
> The gathering was part of the synagogue's Shabbaton 93, which brought together young adults from across North America for a cultural and social experience.
>
> Called Inoubliable Bergen-Belsen (Unforgettable Bergen-Belsen), Peer wrote the book to make the reader feel like a witness at the scene.
>
> But he admits he can never recreate for anyone the living hell he experienced.
>
> "The condition in the camp is indescribable," Peer said. "You can't bring home the horror."
>
> In 1942, at age 9, Peer and his younger brother and sister were arrested by police in their homeland of France. His mother was sent to Auschwitz and never returned.
>
> Peer and his siblings were sent to Bergen-Belsen two years later.
>
> He recalls the separation from his parents as excruciating. But surviving the horrors of the camp quickly became a priority.
>
> "There were pieces of corpses lying around and there were bodies lying there, some alive and some dead," Peer recalled.
>
> **Peer** "Some went mad"
>
> "Bergen-Belsen was worse than Auschwitz because there people were gassed right away so they didn't suffer for a long time.
>
> "But at Bergen-Belsen people stayed months and months until they died – they suffered for a long period of time."
>
> Peer said Russian prisoners were kept in an open-air camp "like stallions" and were given no food or water. "Some people went mad with hunger and turned to cannibalism," Peer said.
>
> Peer's days began with a roll call of the numbered prisoners. This could last as long as five hours, while their captors calculated how many prisoners had died. Anyone who fell over during the roll call was beaten on the spot.
>
> After roll call, the prisoners returned to their barracks, where they were given a tiny piece of bread and some colored water.
>
> Peer and his siblings – who all survived – were cared for at the camp by two women, whom Peer has unsuccessfully tried to find.
>
> Children being children, they did play, sometimes chasing each other around the barracks. But there would always be some who were too sick or weak to get up.
>
> **Reunited with father**
>
> After the war, Peer was reunited with his father in Paris and the family moved to Israel. Peer's four children were born in Israel, but after serving in the Israeli army in a number of wars, Peer moved to Montreal in 1974.
>
> Even 49 years later, Peer is still haunted by his concentration-camp experience and still finds his memories keep him awake at night.
>
> But what he is most bitter about is the way the rest of world stood by and let the Holocaust happen.
>
> "No one told the Germans not to do it. They had the permission of the world," he said.

Karen Seidman, "Surviving the horror: Author recounts experiences in Nazi concentration camp," The Gazette, Montreal, 5. August 1993.

that as a boy he survived no fewer than six (!) gassings in the gas chamber of the Bergen-Belsen Camp:

> "As an 11-year-old boy held captive at the Bergen-Belsen concentration camp during World War II, Moshe Peer was sent to the gas chamber at least six times. Each time he survived, watching with horror as many of the women and children gassed with him collapsed and died. To this day, Peer doesn't know how he was able to survive.
>
> 'Maybe children resist better, I don't know,' he said in an interview last week."

The reason why he survived the gassings is very simple: No homicidal gas chamber ever existed at the Bergen-Belsen Camp, and no historian has ever claimed otherwise. Peer made it all up, all six of the alleged gassings.

Peer also claimed about the Bergen-Belsen Camp:

> "'There were pieces of corpses lying around and there were bodies lying there, some alive and some dead,' Peer recalls."

It is true that, during the final months of the Bergen-Belsen Camp's existence, dead and dying inmates were lying around everywhere as a result of a typhus epidemic that had gotten completely out of control due to Allied bombing raids having destroyed Germany's infrastructure. This made it impossible to supply anything to the camps or anywhere else, for that matter: food and water, medicine for the sick, fuel for the cremation furnace. But Peer's claim that "pieces of corpses" were lying around is pushing it too far. No one was dismembering corpses there.

Peer is a typical example of a witness undermining the entire orthodox narrative by demonstrating the fraudulent anecdotal nature it rests upon. The truth is hidden in the undeniable facts: Moshe Peer was nine when he arrived at Auschwitz, together with "his younger brother and sister," so they were not older than eight and seven, respectively. Clearly, if small children were sent to the gas chambers immediately upon arrival at Auschwitz, as the orthodox narrative wants us to believe, then these three children wouldn't have survived one day in that camp. But as we see, they all survived, and Auschwitz wasn't even the worst part of their experience, as he himself said: "Bergen-Belsen was worse than Auschwitz." Since he arrived at Bergen-Belsen during that camp's nightmarish final months, his statement is absolutely true, but it has nothing to do with homicidal gas chambers. Had there been such gas chambers in operation at Auschwitz, this article would never have been written, because Peer would not have survived his time at Auschwitz to tell his lies after the war.

PFANNENSTIEL, WILHELM

Wilhelm Pfannenstiel

Wilhelm Pfannenstiel (12 Feb. 1890 – 1 Nov. 1982), SS *Standartenführer*, was professor for hygiene at the University of Marburg. After the war, Kurt Gerstein claimed in his various statements that Pfannenstiel had accompanied him on a trip to visit the alleged extermination camps at Belzec and Treblinka. Although the destination of that trip was allegedly a secret, Pfannenstiel came along anyhow, "more by accident," as Gerstein wrote. Although what Gerstein was about to witness in Belzec and Treblinka was allegedly an extreme secret that no outsider was to witness, the outsider Pfannenstiel was allowed to tag along to witness it all anyway, or so Gerstein claimed. (See the entry about him for details)

As preposterous as Gerstein's various statements are, the French took them seriously. Since they had driven Gerstein to suicide and couldn't prosecute him anymore, they initiated proceedings against Pfannenstiel instead as being co-responsible for the alleged extermination policy. He was arrested and interrogated in preparation for the I.G. Farben Trial, and kept in Allied custody until 1950. The interrogation protocol shows that initially he insisted to have learned only later about gassings, but then both Pfannenstiel and his interrogator started regurgitating Gerstein's nonsense, as if it were a routine matter that everyone was familiar with – evidently because the interrogating prosecutor knew Gerstein's text, and he must have informed Pfannenstiel.

Pfannenstiel managed to wriggle his way out of Allied attempts to nail him for Gerstein's tall tales, but then, after the West-German judiciary took over in 1949, things got more serious. In 1950, he was interrogated as a suspect again, but due to his cooperation and claim that he was only an accidental observer – true to Gerstein's claims – he managed to switch his role to that of a witness for the prosecution the next time the issue came up in 1959. During the West-German Bełżec show trial of 1965, he was transformed into an important witness, the official guarantor of the "truth" of Gerstein's collection of delusions, much to the benefit of the Holocaust orthodoxy, who had no leg to stand on regarding Belzec. In gratitude for Pfannenstiel's services, three proceedings against him were shelved, and the first official German publication of Gerstein's report left out any reference to him.

In private, however, Pfannenstiel expressed what he really thought. In 1963, French Holocaust skeptic Paul Rassinier wrote him a letter, in which he explained his suspicion that Gerstein's report was neither true nor authentic, and that it had been drafted by the two U.S. officers who had first interrogated him in southwest Germany. Pfannenstiel minced no words in his response letter of 3 August 1963:

"Your assumptions regarding the genesis of his [Gerstein's] report, this most incredible piece of trash in which 'poetry' far outweighs truth, and also about his death [suicide], are in my opinion quite correct."

Pfannenstiel also explained that Gerstein's use of his name in this "trash" had caused him serious trouble.

In later testimonies, when trying to put Gerstein's "trash" in his own words, as was expected by the West-German judiciary, Pfannenstiel added his own set of contradictions and absurdities to the story, thus demonstrating that a dense web of lies simply cannot be straightened out. For instance, where Gerstein had spoken of 6,700 deportees, of whom 1,450 arrived dead at Belzec, Pfannenstiel spoke of 500, then later of 300 to 500 deportees, only "some" of whom arrived dead – or later, none at all.

Gerstein's mission, he insisted at one point, was *not* to switch the execution method from exhaust gas to hydrogen cyanide, as Gerstein had stated, but merely to disinfest a large quantity of clothes. Furthermore, he declared that Gerstein had been to Lublin and Belzec several times before, all quite in contrast to Gerstein's tale.

Pfannenstiel stated on one occasion that he had come along on Gerstein's trip for curiosity's sake; in a later testimony, he said that Globocnik had suggested his presence as a professor of hygiene, only to change that later again as his own suggestion to Globocnik; or maybe he was invited by Christian Wirth to observe a gassing, as he stated later. Or he went along so he could send a report to Berlin, as surely Hitler must have been unaware of what was going on, thus assuming the role which Gerstein had assigned to himself in his report: the knight in shining armor trying to rescue the Jews.

The gassing engine was either a 1,100-HP diesel motor set up outdoors on a platform, or a 10-HP motor setup inside the building. Neither fits the orthodox tale.

The gassing victims were either buried in mass graves, or first partly burned with some flammable liquid and then buried – while the orthodoxy has all the corpses burned to ashes.

In the face of Gerstein's untrustworthiness as a witness, Pfannenstiel's task was to give Gerstein's claims a credibility makeover by eliminating its outrageous exaggerations, which Pfannenstiel tried hard to achieve. Today, some members of the orthodoxy consider Pfannenstiel's testimony more important than Gerstein's, although in reality, Pfannenstiel's version only added more contradictions to this collection of nonsense.

(For more details, see the entry on Kurt Gerstein and Mattogno 2004a, pp. 52-62.)

PHANTOM EXTERMINATION CAMPS

According to some sources, certain German wartime camps are said to have had facilities for the mass murder of inmates, such as homicidal gas chambers, but all historians without exception reject these claims as false, based either on false rumors, distorted hearsay, misunderstandings or outright black-propaganda lies. These camps, some of which have been completely invented, include (see the entry for each camp for more details):
– Bergen-Belsen (false gas-chamber claims)
– Buchenwald (false gas-chamber claims)
– Flossenbürg (false gas-chamber claims)
– Gross-Rosen (false gas-chamber claims)
– Kosów Podlaski (invented camp)
– Lviv (invented camp)
– Mogilev (false gas-chamber claims)
– Nordhausen (false massacre claims)
– Pinsk (invented camp)
– Trawniki (false gas-chamber claims)
– Wolzek (invented camp)

PHENOL

In the past, the chemical phenol has been a medical and instrument disinfectant used in hospitals all over the world. It was also used by the inmate infirmary of the Auschwitz Camp for this purpose. The camp's documentation contains several orders of phenol by employees of the infirmary (see Mattogno 2023, Part 1, pp. 140, 194, 249, 264, 282).

The orthodoxy claims that this phenol was used to kill severely ill inmates with injections into the heart. This is based on document forgeries by Auschwitz inmate resistance groups, and on misrepresentations and inventions by Polish historians, primarily Danuta Czech. See the entry on lethal injections for more details.

Nowadays, phenol has been replaced in most cases by other, more efficient disinfectants.

PIAZZA, BRUNO

Bruno Piazza was an Italian Jew deported to Auschwitz at the end of July 1944. In a 1956 brochure, he claimed that he experienced a homicidal gassing at Auschwitz carried out inside a barracks that had 20 showers on the ceiling. Then some clerk wearing a mask entered the building, sprinkled potassium-cyanide powder onto the floor, "turned on the shower, left, closed the door, and after ten minutes we were all dead, asphyxiated." But as a dead man walking, or perhaps as a zombie, he managed to come home to Italy and write this brochure to tell us that this powder-shower system had replaced the previous method of ejecting cyanide-gas cylinders into the chamber. This was allegedly unsafe because sometimes the cylinders didn't break on impact, requiring the procedure to be repeated four or five times. None of this nonsense has ever been taken seriously by anyone. (For more details, see Mattogno 2021, pp. 348f.)

PILECKI, WITHOLD

Withold Pilecki (13 May 1901 – 25 May 1948) was a lieutenant in the Polish Clandestine Army in German-occupied Poland. As such, he was arrested on 19 September 1940 and interned at Auschwitz under the name Tadeusz Serafiński. Pilecki organized a Polish resistance group in that camp. He claimed to have escaped from Auschwitz on 27 April 1943, after which he wrote a report summarizing his alleged knowledge. In it, we read the following pertinent claims:

Withold Pilecki

- Pilecki listed all kinds of inmate numbers – admitted, shot, gassed, died of diseases, still present – which are highly inaccurate, if not to say freely invented.
- He claimed that up to August 1942, some 800,000 inmates had been gassed in Brzezinka [=Birkenau] at the Rajsko Camp, and that this number had climbed to over 1.5 million by March 1943. These numbers are preposterous even from an orthodox point of view. Moreover, for Pilecki, Birkenau was the gassing facility which was located at the Rajsko Camp; but in reality, Rajsko was a village to the southwest of Auschwitz that, even in the eyes of the orthodoxy, had nothing to do with exterminations.
- He claimed that even non-Jewish Czechs, Germans and others were gassed on arrival, which is preposterous nonsense even from an orthodox point of view.
- Pilecki asserted that inmates suffering from typhus, even those already recovering from it, were gassed in August 1942, even though the documents clearly show that the camp authorities tried everything to nurse typhus patients back to health.
- He claimed that, when mass graves had to be exhumed due to the risk of polluting the drinking water (which is correct), cranes were used for that purpose, which is an unprecedented and imaginary idea.

Pilecki claimed to have let himself get caught on purpose, so he would get inside the camp in order to collect information and transmit it to his outside contacts. Yet instead of conveying any accurate information, he merely repeated wild guesses and exaggerations, propaganda clichés and outright nonsense. He evidently knew

- nothing of the alleged gassings in the Main Camp's crematorium;
- nothing about the gas chambers' locations, features or modes of operation;
- nothing specific about the crematoria, other than mentioning the term;
- nothing about the two claimed gassing "bunkers";
- nothing specific about the open-air incinerations, other than mentioning non-existing cranes.

Pilecki also retold the story of the alleged first gassing at Auschwitz, but got that wrong, too, as for him this took place in just one prison cell of the penal bunker (basement of Block 11, Main Camp). The largest cell in that basement has just over 12 square meters, in which several hundred Soviet PoW were allegedly pressed, which would have been physically impossible. Pilecki also asserted that a commission watched the gassing with gas masks. However, the orthodoxy's tale insists that all cells or even the entire basement were used for that gassing, and that no one watched it.

(For more details, see Mattogno 2021, pp. 159-162.)

PILLER, WALTER

SS *Hauptscharführer* Walter Piller was the deputy commandant of the Chełmno Camp in 1944. Toward the end of the war, he was captured by the Soviets. After some time of appropriate treatment in their captivity, Piller signed a deposition. He stated in it that the extermination of Jews deported from the Lodz Ghetto started in mid-May and ended in mid-August of 1944. In some 36 trains – three trains per week – a total of roughly 25,000 Jews were sent to Chełmno to be killed there. These figures all collide with the orthodoxy's narrative, which knows only of ten trains on ten consecutive days from late June until early July.

Walter Piller

Piller stated moreover that the gas van's killing mechanism was operated by the driver opening a valve from the driver cabin during transit. This allowed some undefined gas to enter the cargo box and kill all inside within two to three minutes. This is also at odds with the orthodox narrative, which insists that the gas van's mechanism consisted of a simple hose connecting the exhaust pipe to the cargo box. This connection had to be made from the *outside*, and *before* the vehicle was driven. Doing this during transit was impossible. There was moreover no valve, and the gas used was not some mystical fast-active poison gas, but simply exhaust gas that killed within 20 minutes if produced by a gasoline engine – or not at all if coming from a diesel engine.

Hence, even from the orthodox perspective, Piller's coerced confession is full of typical Soviet propaganda lies and hyperbole. It also collides with the documented fate of the Jews from the Lodz Ghetto.

(For more details, see the entry on the Chełmno Camp, on gas vans as well as Mattogno 2017, pp. 59f.; Alvarez 2023, pp. 149-151.)

PILO, AARON

Aaron Pilo was a Greek Jew who was interned at Auschwitz from January 1943 to January 1945, where he claimed to have worked inside the crematoria. In June 1945, he signed a statement, in which he claimed the following, among other things:

– Each of the crematoria could cremate 3,000 bodies a day. However, each muffle could cremate only one corpse per hour, hence some 20 per day (leaving four hours to shut down, clean and reheat the hearths). At 46 muffles, that yields a theoretical maximum of 920 corpses daily for *all* crematoria, rather than 12,000.
– During his two years in Auschwitz, five million corpses were cremated in the crematoria. This is a million more even than the outrageous Soviet four-million propaganda figure.
– Up to 3,000 people fit into a gas chamber, which is an impossible packing density of more than 14 people per square meter in the largest claimed gas chamber, Morgue #1 of Crematoria II and III.
– A gassing lasted 3 minutes, which is absurdly short and physically impossible.
– The victims' hair was used to produce hats, because that's what Germany's military needed to win the war.
– The corpses were cremated in the crematoria by pouring gasoline over them, then tossing them into the fire. Here, the witness confounded stories told about how bodies allegedly were burned on pyres with the cremation procedure in furnaces.

This witness was merely regurgitating camp rumors and atrocity claims, but evidently had never worked in a crematorium. (For more details, see Mattogno 2021d, pp. 227-229.)

PILUNOV, STEFAN

Stefan Pilunov, a Soviet citizen from the village of Prisna near the Belorussia city Mogilev, was arrested in July 1943 for partisan activity, and held in a prison until 4 October of that year. On that day, he claims to have been deployed by his German captors in the exhumation of various regional mass graves and the cremation of the victims they contained.

On 20 May 1944, he signed a very long statement typed up at the office of the chief of staff of the Belorussian partisan movement. In it, he claimed to have been involved in exhuming and burning some 48,000 bodies from 4 October to some unspecified day in November 1943 in the vicinity of Mogilev. However, German wartime documents speak of a total of "only" 6,434 execution victims in this area, and the maximum orthodox claim sits at around 10,000.

His detailed description of the alleged cremation pyres is completely nonsensical and technically impossible: They consisted of a set of two parallel ditches, 7 to 8 meters long and 2 m apart, intersected by a second such set running perpendicular to it. (See his own illustration.) The ditches served to feed air into the pyres built on top of these ditches.

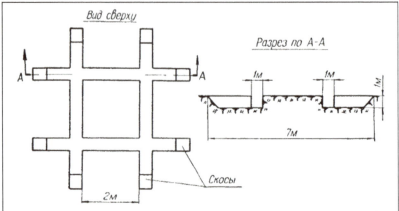

Structure of a "furnace" installation according to Stefan Pilunov: two sets or parallel, 1-m wide and deep ditches intersecting another at a rectangle. 20 layers of wood and bodies were allegedly piled up on top of the ditches up to 10 meters high.

Pilunov asserted that 20 alternating layers of firewood and bodies were piled up to a height of 8 to 10 meters. Since the base of each pyre was only maybe 2 meters wide, the stack would inevitably have collapsed well before the height of 8 meters was ever reached, and it certainly would have collapsed when set ablaze.

At a height of 10 meters, one layer of firewood and bodies would have been only half a meter thick. A little less than one cubic meter of firewood would have allowed only for the cremation of about three corpses per running meter in each layer. With these figures, the claimed number of cremations in the time frame alleged would not have been possible under the circumstances claimed by Pilunov.

Pilunov claimed that only 35 inmates were assigned to chopping firewood, while some 170 inmates were continually sent to Mogilev and nearby villages to procure boards, sticks, coal, pitch and other fuels. There were not enough German guards to keep all these inmates – running all over the region – under control. None of them ever tried escaping. This story cannot be true, all the more so, since these inmates were "bearers of the secret," and the Germans would not have risked their escape.

An average prisoner is rated at being able to cut some 0.63 metric tons of fresh wood per workday. Hence, within the 16 days allotted for clearing out the first set of mass graves containing some 25,000 to 35,000 bodies, the 35 wood choppers could have chopped some 310 tons of green wood. With 250 kg of green wood needed to cremate one body during open-air incinerations, this wood was good for cremating some 1,400 bodies, hence only some 5% of what was allegedly burned. Cremating 30,000 bodies would have required some 7,500 metric tons of wood. This would have required the felling of all trees growing in a 50-year-old spruce forest covering some 17 hectares of land, or some 37 American football fields. To cut this amount of wood within 16 days that this operation supposedly lasted would have required a work force of some 744 dedicated lumberjacks just to cut the wood. Hence, the 35 inmates would not have taken 16 days to get the wood needed, but rather 340 days or almost a year.

This testimony relates to one of many events claimed to have been part of the alleged German clean-up operation which the orthodoxy calls *Aktion 1005*. It shows that, if a lying witness is given incentives and the liberty to ramble on, they will inevitably expose themselves by absurd stories and preposterous claims. Pilunov's statement is a typical expression of fantastic Soviet propaganda.

In another part of his testimony, Pilunov also claimed to have spent a night sleeping with other inmates in a "gas van" – rather unlikely – which he described as a 4-m wide vehicle. However, since the maximum permissible width of road vehicles in Germany is 2.55 m, no road vehicle 4 m wide would ever have been manufactured. His description of two gas distribution boxes on either side of the vehicle, fed from the outside with engine-exhaust gas through two *rubber* hoses, is in stark contrast to what the orthodoxy claims these vans looked like. (One metal hose fed gas through a simple hole in the floor's center; see the entry on gas vans). Moreover, a rubber hose would not have withstood the heat of the exhaust gasses. In other words, Pilunov invented or imagined things.

Pilunov claimed that he was shot at the end of his activities, but was only wounded and unconscious. He awoke while lying on a burning pyre (!), from which he claimed to have succeeded fleeing without getting burned or being noticed by anyone.

When Pilunov was interrogated by German court officials in 1975, he had his story adjusted to resemble the orthodox narrative by building his pyres on rails over ditches rather than simple logs put across a crazy set of zigzagging ditches. He also reduced the pyres' height to four meters, which is still twice as high as would have been manageable.

(For more details, see Mattogno 2022c, pp. 357f., 616-629.)

PINSK

On 20 September 1942, the Yiddish-language periodical *Oif der Vach* (*On Guard*) published an article titled "The Jews of Warsaw Are Killed in Treblinka." The author claimed that Jews were being killed by gas or electrocution in three camps: Belzec, Treblinka and, for the Jews from western Belorussia, another one in the vicinity of the western Belorussian city of Pinsk. (See Arad 1987, pp. 244-246.)

All historians agree, however, that no such camp with any mass-murder facility ever existed in or near the city of Pinsk. This phantom extermination camp was the figment of the author's imagination, or if he had "sources," then they were nothing but black propaganda.

PINTER, STEPHEN F.

Stephen Pinter was an Austrian who immigrated to

America in 1906 at the age of 17. He obtained U.S. citizenship in 1924, and after the end of the Second World War, he applied with the U.S. War Department to become an investigative judge and prosecutor during the Allied war-crime trials in Germany. He got the job and started his duty in early 1946 at the U.S. War Crimes Commission at Dachau. His task there was to investigate events at the Flossenbürg Camp, and he eventually participated as a prosecutor during the respective trial. After that trial he changed to Salzburg, where he became Chief Defense Counsel for all war-crime trials conducted in Austria. In the years after the end of those trials, he made several public statements which clearly show a dedication to the truth. Here are several pertinent excerpts. (For details and sources, see Schwensen 2012):

> "I was in Dachau for 17 months after the war, as a U.S. War Department Attorney, and can state that there was no gas chamber at Dachau. […] Nor was there a gas chamber in any of the concentration camps in Germany."
>
> "I had nothing to do with Mauthausen. However, since I took some months investigating Flossenbürg and all the outcamps connected therewith, while stationed at Dachau, I can talk about those."
>
> "[The Flossenbürg Camp had] neither a gas chamber nor a mass shooting site."
>
> "[During the existence of the camp,] fewer than 300 persons died, by executions or due to other reasons."
>
> "As far as I could find out in six post-war years in Germany and Austria, a number of Jews were killed, but the number of one million was certainly never reached."
>
> "In general, I wrote many years ago to our local daily newspaper, that the allegation of the extermination of the Jewish race was grossly exaggerated, that I had many Jewish clients who had lived in Germany, Poland and other countries at Hitler's time and for whom I collected hundreds of thousands of dollars, thus getting their stories firsthand and could state that the SIX MILLION story was a myth."
>
> "While I did my best to represent the real and decent justice and to prevent a justice of hate, there were a number of persons who repeatedly brought in false or unfounded accusations against the German prisoners, and who, by means of obviously perjured witnesses gained successes before the military courts, which did not accord with the real facts. As a result of such miscarriages of justice, many were unfortunately sentenced although not guilty, and some of them were executed. Of the great trials in Dachau it was especially the Malmedy Trial and the Mauthausen and Buchenwald Concentration Camp Trials which became – during my stay in Dachau but without any involvement on my part in the trials – infamous due to their malfeasances."

pit-burning → **Open-Air Incinerations**

PLAN, TO EXTERMINATE THE JEWS

Any plan allegedly contrived aiming at the extermination of Europe's Jews is necessarily linked to a Hitler order to initiate such an extermination. Since there is no trace of such an order (see the entry on the Hitler Order), it is unsurprising that no documental trace of any plan has ever been found either.

The Holocaust, in its orthodox version, is an event that is said to have lasted more than three years (from mid-1941 to late 1944), encompassed almost an entire continent, and caused at least six million claimed victims. How could it possibly be perceived that such a vast undertaking was implemented without any plan?

U.S.-Jewish political scientist and historian Raul Hilberg, who during his lifetime was considered the world's leading orthodox Holocaust scholar, tried to explain how this vast project unfolded without an order, a plan or even without a budget (De Wan 1983):

> "But what began in 1941 was a process of destruction [of the Jews] *not planned in advance, not organized centrally by any agency. There was no blueprint and there was no budget for destructive measures. They* [these measures] *were taken step by step, one step at a time. Thus came about not so much a plan being carried out, but an incredible meeting of minds, a consensus mind reading by a far-flung* [German] *bureaucracy."*

Hence, Hilberg tried to explain this conundrum by resorting to telepathy. The absurdity here speaks for itself.

In lack of any wartime documents containing anything resembling a plan, interrogators, prosecutors and judges of various postwar judiciaries as well as historians have tried to explain the path along which the extermination of the Jews is said to have evolved. In doing so, they evidently neither followed an order, nor did they have a plan to present some coherent narrative as to how it supposedly transpired. As a result, their narrative is an incoherent, chaotic mess. The following outline of the orthodox attempts at explaining the evolution of the Holocaust is not based on wartime documents, physical traces or forensic findings, but exclusively and entirely on postwar anecdotes, hearsay, rumors and conjectures.

Regarding Auschwitz, the orthodoxy relies on postwar statements by former camp commandant Rudolf Höss. After prolonged torture, Höss "confessed" that he had received a verbal order from Himmler in June 1941. According to this, Hitler demanded the total extermination of all Jews, and Auschwitz was to be turned into an extermination machine to this effect. Thereafter, Adolf Eichmann was charged with finding a murder method, but he failed with this task. Luckily, Höss's deputy Karl Fritzsch, spontaneously and without having been asked to do so, came up with the idea of using Zyklon B.

On 3 July 1941, the Auschwitz Camp's construction office received two articles written by DEGESCH CEO Gerhard Peters, which described in detail sophisticated Zyklon-B circulation systems developed by the DEGESCH Company for fumigations. With a few alterations, this system could have been used for mass homicides. Yet instead of paying any attention to these articles, Fritzsch allegedly decided *two months later*, in early September, to simply dump Zyklon B into some basement rooms full of people, with no way of retrieving the Zyklon-B pellets, and with no ventilation system to clear the fumes afterwards. (See the entry on the first gassing at Auschwitz.)

The next steps in the Auschwitz gassing narrative were all *unplanned* improvisation as well: The first gassing at the old crematorium in the Auschwitz Main Camp a few weeks later was spontaneous and improvised: quickly hack holes through the roof of the crematorium's morgue while the victims were already waiting, dump Zyklon B on their heads and forget it, while the ventilation system ordered for that building was *never* installed (see the section "Propaganda History," subsection "Crematorium I" in the entry on the Auschwitz Main Camp).

The conversion of two old farmhouses outside the Birkenau Camp in the first half of 1942 into *makeshift* gassing facilities was also improvised: dump Zyklon B and forget it, with *no* ventilation system (see the entry on the bunkers of Birkenau).

Even the claimed late adaptations of the four new crematorium buildings at Birkenau in late 1942/early 1943, so they could serve homicidal purposes, were made with little or no forethought or planning (see Mattogno 2019). In fact, the alleged Zyklon-B introduction holes of Crematoria II and III are even said to have been hacked through the finished, thick reinforced concrete roofs with jack hammers (see the entry on Zyklon-B introduction devices). Certainly, none of this was planned in advance – if it ever happened in the first place.

Parallel to this constant bungling, the camp's headquarters started negotiations with a civilian company in July 1942 to build 19 DEGESCH circulation fumigation systems – to be installed in the camp's reception building for *disinfesting* inmate clothes, not for homicide! There is neither any documental nor any anecdotal trace that anything similar to such a system was ever considered to be used for homicidal gassings. (On the Peters articles at Auschwitz and the plans to build 19 disinfestation chambers, see Mattogno 2019, pp. 115f.)

The situation is even more convoluted when it comes to the alleged gas vans. Here, the orthodox narrative relies on a postwar fable told by Erich von dem Bach-Zelewski about an execution of 100 partisans, which Himmler allegedly attended. Shocked by the cruelty of the procedure, Himmler supposedly ordered a method to be devised which would be easier for the stressed German executioners. Although von dem Bach incredibly claimed that the new method used afterwards was blowing up people with explosives, historians take this non-event as the initiation of developing the so-called gas vans.

Here, the orthodox narrative splits. One strand claims that the murder method used at Germany's euthanasia centers served as a model: bottled carbon-monoxide gas. Such a bottle was allegedly hitched to a trailer pulled by a tractor in order to kill people locked up in the trailer. The other strand claims that the murder method was accidentally discovered by Arthur Nebe, in 1941 head of Germany's Criminal Police. When driving home drunk one night, he allegedly almost killed himself by leaving the car running in his garage – hence he realized that car exhaust gasses can kill. However, this "planned" method is based on nothing but a rumor (see the entry on Albert Widmann).

Next, Germany's high-tech research lab at the nation's top-notch Institute of Criminological Technology made some tests with truck exhaust gasses, but came up with no useful results (or so Albert Widmann claimed). Nevertheless, 30 trucks equipped with no-useful-results diesel engines were then ordered for the sake of exhaust-induced mass murder. All this, even though diesel exhaust is useless for such a purpose, which is the meaning of "no useful results." And all this, while Germany was mass-producing producer-gas devices by the tens of thousands every month, which were widely known to have the perfect potential of serving as gas-mass-murder machines. But those were never used. Clearly, there was no methodical thinking behind any of this.

The matter gets even more muddled when turning to the "*Aktion Reinhardt*" camps: Belzec, Chełmno, Sobibór, Treblinka. All of them started operating long after Auschwitz had allegedly received its order to exterminate Jews, and had "discovered" the best method during the "first gassing" in early September 1941: Zyklon B. Yet none of these other camps used the Auschwitz Camp's "research and development achievements." The boss of these four camps, Odilo Globocnik, did not ask Höss for any advice on how to plan this, and he did not plan and coordinate any efforts of "his" four camps to come up with an effective solution either. Rather, all these camps bungled about with their own method: Chełmno allegedly received two or three "gas vans" of mixed makes and models in late 1941; Belzec and Treblinka each presumably used exhaust gasses from a diesel engine incapable of gassing anyone, while Sobibór is said to have used exhaust gas from a gasoline engine. None of these camps' commandants learned from Auschwitz, because in Höss's anachronistic narrative, Treblinka was in operation (using engine exhaust gases) already long *before* June 1941. Therefore, Höss claimed to have learned from Treblinka *not* to use inefficient engine exhaust. But this is, of course, nonsense, as Treblinka became operational only in July 1942, more than a year *after* Höss supposedly received Himmler's order.

The climax of unplanned bungling was reached in the summer of 1943, when a makeshift homicidal gas chamber is said to have been set up at the Natzweiler Camp. Its claimed killing method is extremely primitive and physically impossible. If these claims were to be taken at face value, all they prove is that no plan in the entire German realm can have existed that late into the war to mass murder people in gas chambers.

This tangled web of inconsistent muddling is what today's historians claim, *after* they have streamlined their narrative and have culled from it all the claims that tell an even more disparate tale. The original, comprehensive narrative of all these camps is in fact a jumbled mixture of the most bizarre murder methods allegedly used. (See the section "Changing Murder Methods" in the entry on homicidal gas chambers, as well as the entries for each camp mentioned here for more details.)

The situation is no different with the *Einsatzgruppen*, as is explained in detail in the section "Extermination Order" of the entry dedicated to these units. No trace exists of any plan ever contrived, or order ever issued to the *Einsatzgruppen*, to systematically exterminate the Jews in the Soviet Union. When mass executions happened, Alfred Rosenberg's office, the formal German chief of all German-occupied Soviet territories, prohibited them, stating that no order or document exists implementing a policy of wanton annihilation. (See the entry on Alfred Rosenberg.) The one *Einsatzgruppen* commander who claimed otherwise after the war, Otto Ohlendorf, devised this lie as a (failed) defense strategy. (See the entry on Otto Ohlendorf.)

In sum: There was no plan to implement the "Final Solution" in terms of the physical extermination of the Jews, because no such solution was envisioned or implemented.

The best indicator for this is the story of the Majdanek Camp. After the camp's occupation by the Soviets in July 1944, it was claimed that *seven* homicidal gas chambers existed there. They were allegedly used to assist in killing the camp's initially claimed *two million* victims. By the year 2005, this propaganda image had been downsized in several steps. Currently, only *two* homicidal gas chambers are claimed, and the death toll is said to have been around *78,000* – less than 4% of the original claim.

The only plan visible in all this is the systematic, yet uncoordinated creation of atrocity tales, no matter how far-fetched. In view of documental and physical evidence, these tales had to be downsized, lest orthodox historians lose any remaining credibility.

PLUCER, REGINA

Regina Plucer was a Polish Jewess who was interned at the Auschwitz Camp from August 1943 until January 1945. On 11 May 1945, hence not even four months after leaving Auschwitz, she signed an affidavit in preparation for the Bergen-Belsen show trial. She asserted in it, among other things, that she had been deployed in dismantling Crematoria II and/or III. In that context, she claimed that *Sonderkommando* members told her how the gas chambers and cre-

mation furnaces had worked, which means that she had only hearsay information:
- Victims were often tipped from a truck down a chute. However, there was no access for trucks to the entry having a chute, and the chute was not right at the door, so no truck could have tipped anyone down the chute.
- The gas chamber could hold about a thousand persons ($4.8/m^2$). This is one of the very rare realistic assertions regarding the packing density of victims in the alleged gas chamber.
- She erroneously located the furnace room directly over Morgue #2 (the alleged undressing room), although there were no structures above either of the morgues.
- She claimed that there were 15 separate furnaces rather than the actual five furnaces with three muffles each.
- The corpses were allegedly loaded onto carts running on rails, and loaded from the carts into the furnaces. While that was the original design, it was installed only in Crematorium II for a short while, but then removed and replaced with simple stretchers. Birkenau *Sonderkommando* members still alive in late 1944 would not have described the device as the method used to introduce corpses into the furnaces. But Plucer may have seen the rails in the floor of Crematorium II and extrapolated from there.
- The furnaces were allegedly wood-fired – when indeed they were coke-fired.
- Poison powder was poured into the chamber through ten small chimneys – while there were none at all, yet the orthodoxy insists on four of them per chamber.
- On Plucer's instructions, a plan of Crematorium II was drawn, including the basement with the alleged undressing room and gas chamber. However, she aligned them side by side, separated by a wall, rather than in a rectangular fashion, connected by a hallway and vestibule. The rest of the plan is similarly invented and in stark contradiction to the actual layout.

Plucer's enormous blunders can only be explained by assuming that either she was *not* a member of the demolition squad, received false information from *Sonderkommando* members, or simply signed a false deposition. (For more details, see Mattogno 2021, pp. 357-361.)

PODCHLEBNIK, MICHAŁ

Michał Podchlebnik

Michał Podchlebnik was a Polish Jew who, during his interrogation by Judge Bednarz on 9 June 1945, claimed to have been deported to the Chełmno Camp in late December 1941 or early January 1942, depending on which of his statements we believe, and escaped from there after just a few days. He is one of only three Chełmno inmates who have testified about their alleged experiences. The other two are Szymon Srebrnik and Mieczysław Żurawski.

Here are some of the peculiar claims he made in them:
- The victims of gas-van asphyxiations allegedly looked normal. However, asphyxiation by carbon-monoxide poisoning would have resulted in corpses that would have had a very striking, distinctive pinkish-reddish complexion, something no real witness could have missed or forgotten.
- The victims were persuaded to climb into the gas van by being told that they were taking a shower in it, and they were even given towels and soap, which Podchlebnik had to collect after the deed. No sane SS man would have wasted any soap and towels on such a fool's errand of trying to convince inmates that they will take a shower inside a van's cargo box. And in any case, no one takes towels into a shower.
- When the van's door was opened, dark smoke came out. However, lethal gasoline engines merely produce light, bluish smoke, while Diesel engines can produce dark smoke, but are not lethal within realistic timeframes.
- On opening the van door, the Germans ran away from the vehicle, presumably in fear of the gas inside. That would never have happened, because the gas inside the cargo box would not have been more dangerous for people standing outside than any exhaust pipe of a running vehicle.
- Podchlebnik identified a third gas van that allegedly was out of order, standing in the camp yard with a wheel missing. Interestingly, that describes a photo of a damaged moving truck at the Ostrowski factory in Koło, which was shown to all witnesses interviewed by Judge Bednarz. Some of them identified it as one of the alleged gas vans, even though that vehicle was *not* a gas van at all,

as Judge Bednarz himself concluded.
- Instead of alarming the world about what he allegedly had witnessed, Podchlebnik remained totally silent for more than three years.

(For more details, see Alvarez 2023, pp. 160-164, 173f.; Mattogno 2017, pp. 67-69.)

PODCHLEBNIK, SALOMON

Salomon Podchlebnik was an inmate of the Sobibór Camp. In a concise deposition of 6 December 1945, he claimed that inmates at Sobibór were killed with an unspecified gas in one gas chamber, resulting in half a million victims. The orthodoxy insists, however, that there were several gas chambers, and that only half as many victims or even less died in the camp.

(See the entry on Sobibór for more details, as well as Mattogno 2021e, p. 77.)

POHL, OSWALD

Oswald Pohl (30 June 1892 – 7 June 1951), SS *Obergruppenführer*, headed the SS offices that, in early 1942, were consolidated as the SS's Economic and Administrative Main Office (*Wirtschafts- und Verwaltungshauptamt*). This office was directly subordinate to Heinrich Himmler as the *Reichsführer* SS. It handled all financial and administrative matters concerning the SS and its vast network of forced-labor industries and labor as well as concentration camps. One of Pohl's main tasks during the war was to maximize the labor output in quantity and quality that was coming out of the slave-labor force held in the Third Reich's ever-expanding network of concentration and labor camps.

The Holocaust orthodoxy constructs an insurmountable contradiction between Pohl's attempt to maximize the labor output of Germany's camp system on the one hand, and Himmler's alleged order to exterminate Europe's Jews on the other.

There is no trace in the documents that there was a conflict between Pohl and his superiors, though. To the contrary, Pohl and Himmler were in full agreement about what really mattered: maximized labor output.

For instance, on 30 April 1942, at a time when the three alleged extermination camps Auschwitz, Belzec and Sobibór are said to have commenced their mass extermination of Jews, Pohl reported to Himmler that "[t]he war has brought about a visible structural change in the concentration camps and their tasks regarding the employment of inmates. [...] The primary emphasis has shifted to the economic side. The total mobilization of inmate labor, first for wartime tasks (increase of armaments) and then for peacetime tasks, is moving ever more to the forefront." (*IMT*, Vol. 38, p. 364.) In his response, Himmler agreed. (*NMT*, Vol. 5, p. 302.)

Five months later, on 16 September 1942, when mass extermination at the Treblinka Camp supposedly was in full swing, Pohl reported to Himmler that all prisoners of the Reich were to be conscripted for armaments production, for which purpose the Jews destined for eastern migration "will have to interrupt their journey and work at armaments production." A little more than a year after that, in October 1943, Pohl wrote to all concentration camp commandants that "prison labor is very significant. It is vitally important that all measures be taken by the commandants, leaders of information services and physicians to ensure the maintenance of health and the capacity of prisoners to work." This was to be achieved by giving them sufficient nutritious food, proper clothing, natural measures for health and hygiene, rewards for good performances, and by avoiding unnecessary exertions. He repeated this again in a circular to all camp commandants on 26 December 1943: "All measures of the commanders have to focus on the health and productivity of the inmates." (For details, see Rudolf 2023, pp. 170-173).

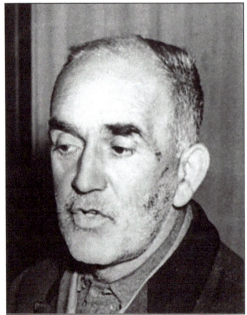

Oswald Pohl in Nuremberg 1947, with scabbed fresh wounds all over his left cheek from torture.

The orthodox claim that there was a conflict between Pohl trying to exploit inmates while Adolf Eichmann supposedly tried to ship them all to extermination camps to have them murdered there, assumes that Himmler was giving each of his subordinates conflicting and opposite orders. This is not based on documents but on postwar "confessions," and here primarily on those made by Rudolf Höss, the former commandant of the Auschwitz Camp. However, his postwar confessions, initiated by massive torture by his captors, are characterized by insurmountable internal contradictions and absurdities, and they are refuted by wartime documents. (For more details on this, see Mattogno 2020b, pp. 191-195.)

While Oswald Pohl was awaiting his own trial at Nuremberg (the so-called Pohl Case), he was softened up by his British captors at their torture center at Bad Nenndorf, where he was made to sign an affidavit. Here is what Pohl later reported about his treatment there:

> "In the locked and guarded cell, my hand fetters were removed neither by day nor by night, not even while eating or when relieving myself. Indeed, at night, while I was lying on the cot with my hands tied, I was tied to the pole of the cot with a second set of fetters, as a result of which I could not move and hence could not sleep. [...] Going back to my cell was like running the gauntlet, during which I fell several times, hitting the wall really hard, after guards had tripped me. [...]
> Finally, as if by command, all guards – there were some 8 to 10 people in the cell – pounced on me, pulled me up and pummeled me in blind rage, although I was fettered and thus defenseless. Blows rained down on my head, and they kicked all body parts of mine. Struggling to remain standing, I staggered from one corner to another, until I collapsed unconsciously after a massive blow or kick into my stomach. [...] During this brutal mistreatment, I lost a molar and an incisor. At 7 am the next morning, fettered as I was, I was brought to Nuremberg in a car." (Cf. Rudolf 2023, pp. 402-404.)

With methods like this, one can get almost any man to confess and consent to just about anything. Hence, it is unsurprising that Pohl did not contradict the extermination claims during his own trial, although he insisted that he was legally innocent, because he "never participated in measures of force against the Jews, nor approved of them, nor supported them knowingly." (*NMT*, Vol. 5, esp. pp. 664-676, 931-937, here p. 932; Pohl 1950, p. 43.)

Since the claimed extermination of the Jews by the Third Reich had been turned into a dogma that could not be challenged, Pohl's trial was an utter farce. This can already be gleaned from the fact that the prosecution opened its case by pulling out the atrocity lies of soap having been made from the fat of murdered victims, and their ashes used as fertilizers (*NMT*, Vol. 5, p. 253). The judges compelled Pohl to confess that he "knew" via leading questions rather than asking him the usual open-ended questions. Here are a few examples of these leading questions (*ibid.*, pp. 665, 670):

> "Q. Were you in charge of the concentration camps while this [extermination] *program was being carried out by RSHA?* [*Reichssicherheitshauptamt*, Germany's Department of Homeland Security...]
> Q. Well, were they [the gas chambers] *constructed while you were in charge?* [...]
> Q. Did you see any gas chambers when you were there? [...]
> Q. You knew they [the gas chambers] *were there.* [...]
> Q. And when you saw them and knew that Jews were being exterminated, you were in charge of that concentration camp? [...]
> Q. You knew that the transports were becoming bigger and people were coming in and took more space than the crematorium to kill them. You knew that, didn't you?"

It is true that, if an extermination policy had been in place, Pohl must have known about it. But none of the wartime documents that he wrote or came across in his office hinted in any way at such a policy, contrary to what the judges and the prosecution insinuated. Pohl's testimony about this consists of a string of self-contradictory statements in the style of "yes, I knew, but no, I didn't." All he claimed to have known revolved around Auschwitz, yet what he said in this regard repeatedly referred to Rudolf Höss, and once even to a special order Höss supposedly received from Himmler. This clearly indicates that Pohl's knowledge did not originate from wartime experiences, but from the "confessions" which the British had extracted from Höss via torture, and which had been introduced during the Nuremberg International Military Tribunal, together with Höss's live perjured testimony, as one of the most "convincing" pieces of evidence.

Today, the orthodoxy likes to present the "confessions" by Höss and Pohl as a convincing case of the "convergence of evidence", although the first was extracted by torture and is full of anti-historical nonsense, and the latter was extracted both by mistreatment and by suggestive interrogation techniques, and is contaminated by Höss's fraudulent statements.

POLAND

Poland had three roles within the context of the Holocaust:
1. Crime Scene
2. Victim
3. Propagandist

The last role is discussed in detail in the section on Poland of the entry on propaganda, so it will not be covered here.

Crime Scene

All the so-called extermination camps were located on what was legitimately Polish territory. They had the following Jewish death tolls, if we follow the orthodox narrative:
- Auschwitz – ca. 1,000,000 Jewish victims
- Treblinka – ca. 800,000 Jewish victims
- Belzec – ca. 434,000 Jewish victims
- Sobibór – ca. 200,000 Jewish victims
- Chełmno – ca. 150,000 Jewish victims
- Majdanek – ca. 80,000 victims, only some of which were Jews

Hence, the claimed death toll of these camps amounted to some 2.6 million Jewish victims. If we add to this the deaths in the many Polish ghettos, which are difficult to quantify, then Poland was the location where half of the six million victims perished who are claimed by the orthodoxy.

It needs to be stressed that the camps listed above were not *Polish* camps. They were German camps on Polish soil.

Victim

Majdanek is today considered by the orthodoxy mainly as a labor camp, with exterminations only playing a minor role. The camp's documents on inmate mortality show, that some 80% of all deceased prisoners were Jews of mixed origin, many of them from Poland. The orthodoxy posits additional Jewish victims of mass murder during the so-called Operation "Harvest Festival." During that claimed event, some 18,000 Jews are said to have been shot within two days in early November 1943. (For more details on this, see the entry dedicated to it.). The total death toll of Jews at Majdanek, as currently claimed by the orthodoxy, is just below 60,000, but it is not clear, how many of them were of Polish origin. We'll assume half of them, for argument's sake.

Most Jews deported to Auschwitz came from other European countries, such as Belgium, Czechia ("Protectorate"), France, Germany and Austria, Greece, Hungary, the Netherlands and Slovakia. However, some 190,000 Polish Jews were also deported to that camp, with 150,000 of them presumably killed on arrival.

Some 115,000 non-Polish Jews mainly from Germany and Austria, Czechia, Slovakia and the Baltics were deported to Sobibór. To all the other camps, mainly Polish Jews were deported and reportedly killed.

If we tally up the orthodoxy's claimed death toll of Polish Jews in these camps, we obtain:

Camp	Polish Jewish Victims
Auschwitz	ca. 150,000
Treblinka	ca. 750,000
Belzec	ca. 400,000
Sobibór	ca. 85,000
Chełmno	ca. 150,000
Majdanek	ca. 30,000
Total	ca. 1,565,000

To this total needs to be added any access mortality incurred in the many ghettos set up in numerous Polish towns and cities. These ghetto casualties are difficult to determine, since documented data on this seems to be very rare. (See the entry on ghettos for more details.)

Demography

The only orthodox study on Poland's Jewish population losses during the Second World War concluded that some 1,800,000 Polish Jews died in the Holocaust (Benz 1991, p. 495). This is in line with the above figures.

Demographic studies of the Jewish population in Poland gets complicated by several factors. First, Poland's borders changed drastically during and after the war. In effect, the entire country was moved westward by several hundred kilometers. The provinces in the east, annexed from the Soviet Union in 1921, were lost again, while Poland annexed in the west the German provinces of southern East Prussia, Silesia and eastern Pomerania.

Second, the last Polish census prior to the war was conducted only in 1931, at which point 3.1 million Poles registered as Jewish. Between the two world wars, the Polish state was a radically nationalist entity pursuing a policy of ethnic pressure against any minority it considered "Unpolish." Life was made increasingly uncomfortable if not impossible for Germans, Jews, Ukrainians, Lithuanians and (Belo)Russians by way of various persecutorial measures and acts.

As a result, Poland experienced a constant exodus of those minorities, Jews included. Mainstream sources report that some 100,000 Jews left Poland every year throughout the 1930s. These were mainly young adults migrating west and overseas. Hence, the fertility of Polish Jewry, already lower than the Polish average due to a higher-than-average urbanization, shrank considerably, probably reaching the point of zero growth in the later 1930s. Hence, when the war started, Polish Jewry may have shrunk down to just 2.5 million or even less. A little more than two thirds of them, or some 1.8 million, lived in the western and central parts of Poland that were eventually occupied by German forces.

Third, when the war with Germany broke out, some 100,000 Polish Jews fled southeast to Romania, while up to a million Jews fled east, where they were eventually overrun by the Red Army, who picked up most of these refugees and deported them to Siberia. Some 200,000 Jews are estimated to have died *en route*, while only 157,500 are said to have returned to Poland after the war. Western Jewish support organizations claimed during the war that they knew of 630,000 Polish Jews deported to Siberia which they tried to support. Hence, a total death toll of these deported Polish Jews of up to two thirds of a million is quite possible. Under any circumstances, these Jews were no longer within the reach of any anti-Jewish measures by the German occupational forces. Hence, when the Germans occupied their part of Poland, there may not have been more than a million Jews left.

Fourth, the Germans were very generous as to who they considered to be a Jew. Even if a person did not consider himself a Jew, if he had at least one Jewish parent, he was likely to be treated as a Jew by the Germans. With that generous definition, the Germans would have found more Jews than results from any census.

Fifth, there is rough consensus about how many Jews were registered as present in postwar Poland: some 200,000 to 240,000. But that does not necessarily mean that any difference between postwar and prewar figures died or were killed. In fact, displaced Polish Jews had little incentive to stay in a country that had proven in peacetime to have been similarly anti-Jewish in attitude, as was Hitler's Germany. Hence, large numbers of Polish Jews left Poland whenever they could, and migrated first west to Germany. There, they were lodged for months and sometimes years in one of the many large displaced-person camps. From there, most moved on to countries of better prospects, such as France, the UK, USA, and Palestine/Israel. This migration movement was largely undocumented during the first postwar years, and hence absolute numbers are almost impossible to come by.

The reliability of any of these data is so uncertain, and error margins too large, to base any reasonable conclusion on it regarding how many Polish Jews died in the hands of the German occupants. However, we must keep in mind that the German forces ultimately deported some 1.5 million Polish Jews – in their definition – to the various camps in Poland, as stated above. Hence, the question as to the actual death toll is better addressed by investigating what happened in those camps. Were the Jews there killed on arrival? Or were some, if not most of them deported farther east? And if a large-scale deportation of Polish Jews into the temporarily German-occupied Soviet territories occurred, as many wartime documents suggest (see the entry on resettlement), then the question to address is: What happened to the Jews deported east?

Some may have been executed by the *Einsatzgruppen*. However, these units' total documented death toll, most of them Soviet Jews, precludes any large-scale executions of Polish Jews. Many deported Polish Jews might have joined Soviet partisan groups. Some may have starved to death, died of diseases, or gotten killed as civilian collateral casualties of the ongoing hostilities. Again others may have been overrun by the Red Army, who may have left them alone, may have executed them as collaborators, or may have deported them to Siberian labor camps. With Stalin's Iron Curtain going down in Eastern Europe, there is no way of knowing for certain – and we ultimately might never know.

(For more details, see Rudolf 2019, pp. 187-189; Sanning 2023, pp. 19-44.)

POLEVOY, BORIS

Boris Nikolaevich Polevoy (aka Kampov; 17 March 1908 – 12 July 1981) was a Soviet journalist writing primarily for Soviet Russia's leading newspaper *Pravda*. His métier was similar to Ilya Ehrenburg's: glorifying communism and the Soviet Union, and as Pravda's official war correspondent during the war, exaggerating and inventing atrocity tales about the enemy and spreading them most effectively. (See Heddesheimer 2002 for more details.)

Polevoy was among the Soviet troops who entered the abandoned Auschwitz Camp on 27 January 1945. Here are some of the claims he made about that camp in his two first reports of 29 January and 2 February (for details, see Mattogno 2021, pp. 294f.):

Boris Nikolaevich Polevoy

- The eastern part of the camp had hundreds of mass graves containing several hundreds of bodies of murder victims each. In fact, the four mass graves that once contained probably between ten and twenty thousand typhus victims were located in the west of the camp.
- The camp had a crematorium almost 500 m long, equipped with shaft furnaces, in which corpses burned within 8 minutes. The actual crematoria buildings were some 50 m long, and they had normal-sized coke-fired cremation furnaces burning one corpse per muffle within an hour.
- Another building had metallic floors, in which victims were killed with high-voltage current. The floor opened, the corpses fell onto conveyor belts slowly moving to the shaft furnaces, where they were burned; the bones passed through rolling mills, and the resulting powder was used to fertilize the camp's gardens. All this is pure mendacious fantasy.
- Special mobile devices existed for killing children. Not even the most dogmatic orthodox historian has ever come up with anything to support that claim.

Mainstream historian Robert Jan van Pelt stooped to justify Polevoy's lies, while also acknowledging they belong to the "category of myth" (see Mattogno 2023b, pp. 80-82).

POLISH UNDERGROUND REPORTS

During the German occupation of Poland between 1939 and 1944, the Polish Government-in-Exile in London managed to organize a well-functioning shadow government inside Poland working completely underground. To one degree or another, it could count on the support of almost the entire Polish population. This underground government had informants almost everywhere.

Apart from active acts of resistance and sabotage, two of the most important tasks of the various branches of this shadow government were, first, to gather intelligence about what was happening in the country and to report it to London; and second, to spread propaganda aiming at lifting the spirit of the Polish resistance movement, hardening the resilience and anti-German stance of Poland's allies in East and West, and undermining any efforts of the occupational authorities to stabilize their rule. This of course included black propaganda, as in every war: exaggerate and invent losses the enemy suffers, and atrocities they supposedly committed.

The reports by the Polish underground sent to their government in London reflect all these aspects. Where claims and data can be verified by other documents, it shows that the Polish underground was indeed well informed about anything of significance happening inside Poland, including the territories Germany had temporarily annexed.

However, atrocity propaganda spread about many camps also show their false nature by their disparate, often contradictory or simply absurd nature which, when compared with reliable sources, turn out to be freely invented.

The Polish underground movement spread its tentacles also inside the various German labor and concentration camps, where it stayed in close contact with the resistance movements established among the inmates. In Auschwitz, for instance, the inmate resistance movement prided itself in having informants and collaborators in most every office and department of the camp authorities.

Since the Germans depended on inmates doing most of the work even in their offices, they could hide nothing from the resistance. Information flow between the camp-internal resistance and the underground outside was facilitated by corrupt German guards as well as privileged inmates permitted to leave the camp and work outside its fenced-in area.

The vast documentation about Auschwitz permits us to either verify or refute most claims made in the Polish underground reports sent to London. Some show that the resistance movement knew indeed very well what was really going on inside the camp. Others indicate that those writing these reports were not merely interested in informing their government in London – as well as its host, the British government. They were also in the business of supplying fuel and ammunition for black propaganda.

(For more details on this, see the sections on "Propaganda History" in the entries of the camps Auschwitz Main Camp, Belzec, Birkenau, Chełmno, Majdanek, Sobibór and Treblinka; see particularly on Auschwitz: Mattogno 2021, pp. 105-289).

PONARY (PANERIAI)

Ponary is the Polish name for the Lithuanian town Paneriai, which today is a mere district of Lithuanian's capital Vilnius. Between 1921 and 1939, the town was part of Poland, hence the name. During the two-year occupation by the Soviets from 1939 to 1941, a construction project was initiated in a forest outside of town for several oil-storage tanks. When German forces moved in in June 1941, only several circular pits had been finished, some with concrete or stone sidewalls.

The orthodoxy has it that German forces used these pits as mass graves for murdered Jews from the Vilnius area, and also for Soviet PoWs and Polish civilians. A total of somewhere between 70,000 and 100,000 victims are supposed to have been buried there, most of them Jews. This death toll makes this Holocaust crime scene comparable to Babi Yar outside of Kiev, although it is far less known.

There is only one contemporary witness report about these alleged mass executions: A certain A. Blyazer claimed in 1944 to have survived the shooting by jumping into the pit alive and getting covered by corpses. He later climbed out from beneath layers of bodies. In 1943, he was arrested again and assigned to exhuming and burning the bodies buried in those pits.

No mass shooting at this site is mentioned in the *Einsatzgruppen* reports. However, German documents report a total of some 24,300 persons killed in the Vilnius area. Furthermore, "several round-shaped burial sites about 30 meters in circumference" located in the Paneriai Forest are mentioned in a 1942 letter of the Healthcare Administration of Vilnius County in response to a request from the local district commissar to list and described the state of all mass graves in the area, as was compulsory throughout the Eastern European territories temporarily occupied by German forces. The letter neither specified the number of graves nor how many victims of which background were buried in them.

There exists moreover a set of photographs of these oil-tank pits showing many dozens, if not hundreds of people herded into them. (See the illustrations.) These photos were evidently taken by Germans or Lithuanian collaborators, who were obvi-

These two photos are said to show the execution of Jews at the Paneriai execution site. However, no actual executions can be seen on these photos. Hence, it is not clear at all what was documented with these photos.

ously not prevented from photographing this scene. It is unclear who the people gathered in those pits were and what their fate was, as the photographs do not show any actual shootings or victims of executions. The orthodoxy claims that the persons shown in those photos were Jews about to be executed.

The orthodoxy has it that, within the so-called *Aktion* 1005, the corpses buried in Paneriai were exhumed and burned on pyres starting in late 1943, and lasting until early July 1944, just before the area was reconquered by the Red Army.

When the Soviets occupied the area in July 1944, a commission of the Red Army inspected the grounds of the alleged burial site. Without any excavations, they asserted already at this point that 100,000 victims had been killed and buried there. A little later, the Soviets formed two investigative commissions, one by the terror organization NKGB, the other by an unspecified Soviet authority. They interviewed several witnesses who claimed to have been involved in the Germans' attempt at erasing the traces of their claimed crimes. Among these witnesses were most prominently Yuri Farber, A. Blyazer, Matvey Zaydel and Szloma Gol (see their respective entries).

These witnesses claimed to have been forced to exhume and burn between 56,000 and 100,000 bodies from December 1943 or January 1944 until April or May 1944. The cremation technique they described, in particular the size of the pyres they claimed to have built, exposes their tales as physically impossible. It becomes feasible only if downgraded by a factor of five or ten, if not more.

The Soviets also conducted some forensic investigations. Five circular pits were excavated, plus one long ditch. All in all, 515 corpses were exhumed and examined. An unspecified amount of ashes and scattered bones were allegedly encountered in the pits and the adjacent forest. From these impressions, the commission extrapolated that "no less than one hundred thousand" had been killed at that site. Photos taken show innocuous circular ditches with stone-lined walls. A few photos show individual corpses or at most a few dozen, but none shows hundreds of them.

Three witnesses claimed to have escaped from the pit they were forced to live in by digging a tunnel through the local sandy soil using their bare hands or with a spoon, propping up the tunnel's sand walls and roof with wooden posts and boards they made themselves, and lighting the tunnel with electric bulbs, using wires and electricity they got from who-knows where.

In 2016, a team of geological researchers claimed to have located this escape tunnel using ground-penetrating radar and electric resistance measurements. The tunnel is presumably some 35 meters long. (See Fleur 2016.) Excavations were scheduled for later. Such excavations should be less likely to find traces of a tunnel, which would have mostly collapsed and filled with sand over time, but more likely hundreds of wooden poles and boards once used to prop up the tunnel, as the witnesses have claimed. These would have been essential in the loose, sandy soil of that area. Such wooden objects also would have shown up on ground-penetrating radar scans, although they were not mentioned by the researchers. As far as can be established, neither any verifiable data of this research were ever published, nor were any excava-

The Ghetto Fighters' House Archives insist that this was the location at the Paneriai mass-extermination site, where the Jewish slave laborers were kept during their exhumation and cremation activities within the framework of Aktion 1005.

tions ever undertaken.

If we follow the witnesses' claims, the Paneriai site would have been smoking continually, day and night, between January and April 1944, if not even until July. Except for a brief claim in one of the Soviet reports that a local resident named Edward Ostrovski saw fire between October 1943 and July 1944, there is no contemporary source verifying that these huge cremations took place: no documents, no photographs, no other testimonies of locals.

(See also the accounts by Yuri Farber, A. Blyazer, Matvey Zaydel and Szloma Gol; for more details, see Mattogno 2022c, pp. 669-694.)

population statistics → **Demography, Jewish**
Posen speeches → **Himmler Speeches**

POSWOLSKI, HENRYK

Henryk Poswolski was a Polish Jew deported from the Warsaw Ghetto to the Treblinka Camp in January 1943, where he was employed as a bricklayer and stoker. However, he was not working at the camp's extermination sector, which was physically and optically cordoned off from the rest of the camp. (What he was stoking, then, remains a mystery.) Therefore, he had no access to it, and no first-hand knowledge about it. His hearsay story includes the following claims:

- The homicidal gas chambers even had washbasins installed to fool the victims. This is a unique claim that makes no sense, unless those basins actually worked.
- Two of the gas chambers had collapsible floors. "Under the floor passed carts with which the corpses were carried away." This claim, usually connected with the Sobibór Camp, is unique for Treblinka, technically extremely challenging and thus unlikely, completely unfounded, and rejected by all historians, orthodox or heterodox.
- A Diesel engine first created a vacuum, then introduced engine-exhaust gases. However, diesel exhaust is unsuited for mass murder, and creating a vacuum in a brick-and-mortar building is technically impossible (the external pressure would crush the walls), hence most certainly was not done.
- The bodies were burned using not wood, but a "certain white powder" as an evidently magical flame accelerant.
- Himmler visited the camp in March 1943, ordering that all buried corpses be burned. In fact, there is no trace of Himmler ever visiting the Treblinka Camp.

This is yet another example of why testimonies from hearsay should never be permitted, either in courts of law or in historiography. (For more details, see Mattogno 2021e, pp. 159f.)

PRADEL, FRIEDRICH

Friedrich Pradel (16 April 1901 – 24 Sept. 1978), SS *Sturmbannführer*, was head of Subdepartment II D 3a of Germany's Department of Homeland Security (*Reichssicherheitshauptamt*), which dealt with the Security Police's motor pool. As such, he is said to have organized the procurement of trucks that, according to his specifications, were allegedly changed into homicidal gas vans.

Together with his subordinate Harry Wentritt, who is said to have been the mechanic of this subdepartment who made the changes to the vehicles, he was put on trial in West Germany in 1966. At the end of it, he was sentenced to seven years imprisonment for aiding in the murder of at least 6,000 persons (hence 2.3 days per life taken). During this trial, other Germans testified who are said to have been involved in either maintaining, using or testing these vehicles. For this reason, this should have been the trial during which all uncertainties about these vehicles should have been settled.

However, we instead find a hodgepodge of mutually contradicting statements, and a court procedure that was one of the most outrageous in the history of West Germany:

- The main defendant Pradel was arrested in 1961 and was kept in pre-trial detention for five years before the trial started. This in itself amounts to coercion.
- The affidavit of another defendant was read out as evidence, although this affidavit was unsigned, and the defendant had committed suicide during his prolonged pre-trial detention.
- Each time the court faced conflicting testimonies, it didn't rule *in dubio pro reo* (if in doubt, rule for the defendant), but *pro dogma*.
- Two witnesses testified that they had sent two gas vans with leaky cargo boxes back to Berlin (to Wentritt) for repairs to make them airtight again. (Wentritt denied this.) However, gas-van cargo boxes could not function if airtight, hence repairing leaks was pointless. These witnesses did not report their experiences, but a myth created by a fabricated document said to have been written by

August Becker, an alleged inspector of gas vans, which was used as evidence by the court.
- Harry Wentritt described the way he connected the vans' exhaust system to the cargo box. However, this contradicts the orthodox narrative on how it was done, and it is technically absurd. (See the entry on Harry Wentritt.)
- Two chemists testified about tests on a gas van's exhaust for its suitability to kill. German engineers knew which type of engines produced exhaust gases suitable to kill. There was no need to test this. However, the Saurer trucks allegedly used had diesel engines, whose exhaust gases were unsuitable for homicides. That would have been known as well. Hence, these chemists' testimonies were a charade.
- During pretrial detention, Pradel claimed that he was ordered by his superior Walter Rauff to construct the gas vans in September 1941, and that he realized that this was part of the ordered mass extermination of the Jews. During the trial, however, he denied ever having had any knowledge that the vans were to be used to kill Jews (but the court did not believe him). However, the orthodoxy insists that, by September 1941, no gas vans had been conceived yet, and no decision for the extermination of the Jews made either. (This decision is usually dated to late October 1941.)
- The court had at its disposal the documentation of the Gaubschat Company showing the truck's features, which made them unsuitable for homicide. Yet the court misrepresented them in a way to make the story of gas vans credible.

This trial shows how malleable human memory is, if subjected to a long time of exposure to manipulative information and traumatizing pressure and coercion. These defendants' and witnesses' assertion that, yes, gas vans existed, can only be compared to medieval witch trial testimonies, in which doomed defendants admitted the existence of the devil and his minions.
(For more details, see Alvarez 2023, pp. 211-219.)

PRODUCER GAS

The early era of industrialization was an era of coal and coke. Steam machines were driven by coke and coal fires, homes were heated with them, food was cooked with them, and an entire industry evolved around producing coke from coal and using the byproduct – "coal gas" or "city gas" – to provide heating, cooking and lighting gas for entire towns and cities. However, a large fraction of city gas is carbon monoxide (CO), which is highly lethal to warm-blooded animals. Accidental deaths and suicides with this gas were quite common.

Exterminators recognized early on that mice and rats could be gassed using the ubiquitous city gas, but the procedure was unsafe for humans. In the early 1900s, the German medical professors Bernhard Nocht and Gustav Giemsa developed a fumigation method using CO that did not used piped city gas, but rather a separate device that produced gas rich in CO on demand in a defined manner. These devices were called producer-gas generators, and the fumigation method thus developed was called the Nocht-Giemsa method. Their device burned coke with limited amounts of oxygen, thus producing a gas with some 5% of CO. However, since insects are not sensitive to CO, this method was only suitable to kill warm-blooded pests, such as mice and rats. Before, during and after World War One, it was a very common method to combat these types of vermin in freight ships and storage facilities in harbors.

When Germany and her allies were cut off from foreign oil supplies by the Allied naval blockade during World War Two, producer-gas generators became an important technology for the Axis powers in Europe. These devices could be fired with wood, coal or coke, and could be tweaked to contain as much as 35% of CO. Such a fuel gas was perfectly capable of driving Germany's entire civilian transportation sector and also her military vehicle fleet, making her war machine largely independent of oil.

In an effort to accelerate the transition from liquid fuel to this type of gaseous fuel, the German government issued decree after decree, making the switch compulsory for a growing part of Germany's vehicle manufactures. Producer-gas generators were mass-

The Imbert-Generator was the most widespread producer-gas generator of the Third Reich, here in mass production on an assembly line in Cologne 1943.

produced by the hundreds of thousands. The technology was actively promoted by the highest quarters, including Adolf Hitler, Hermann Göring and Albert Speer. Hence, they all knew that Germany had hundreds of thousands of poison-gas generators everywhere.

In fact, during the war, Germany was a country built on carbon-monoxide technology in general, not just for propulsion. Large chemical factories existed, and new ones were built, which turned coal into a type of producer gas, again rich in CO, which was converted to several basic chemicals (such as methanol) needed for synthesizing more complex chemicals, such as artificial rubber.

The amount of CO produced in Germany during the war years to drive its vehicle fleet and to feed its vast chemical factories would have sufficed to kill the entire world population many times over. This transition to an economy built on coal turned hundreds of thousands of vehicles into potentially highly lethal gas vans, since their *fuel gas* – but *not* their *exhaust gas* – was extremely lethal. In addition, this toxic fuel gas could easily be ventilated, since it doesn't adhere to anything and doesn't dissolve in anything – quite in contrast to the rare and expensive hydrogen cyanide.

Therefore, when the so-called "Final Solution" was reaching its peak in 1942 and 1943, Germany had tens of thousands of engineers and mechanics familiar with this lethal-gas technology, hundreds of thousands of drivers capable of operating these devices, and an equal number of these poison-gas devices present literally everywhere, with no limitation on fuel.

Yet no one has ever claimed that this technology was used to kill even one single person.

(For details, see Kalthoff/Werner 1998, pp. 31-36; Rudolf 2019, pp. 463-467).

German wartime Henschel truck with Imbert producer-gas generator behind the driver's cabin.

German trucks "Opel Blitz," mass-produced during World War Two with producer-gas generators (behind the driver's cabin, passenger side).

PRONICHEVA, DINA

Dina Pronicheva was a Ukrainian Jew from Kiev who claimed, in at least 12 statements made between the 1940s and 1960, that she survived the mass shooting of Jews by Germans at the ravine of Babi Yar in Kiev on 29 September 1941.

According to her various testimonies, the Jews were driven to Babi Yar, surrounded everywhere by a dense row of Germans and auxiliaries with rifles, clubs and sticks. They had to undress at the top of the ravine, approach the edge of the ravine at one spot, and were shot there by machine-gun fire from the opposite side, falling dead or wounded into the ravine.

Machine-gun fire from the other side of the ravine, up to 100 meters away, would have been very inaccurate. Lots of ammunition would have been wasted this way, and stray bullets could have hit any of the guards. Furthermore, if 33,771 persons were all shot at one spot of the ravine's edge, they all would have been lying on one big heap that eventually would have reached the ravine's edge. Hence, someone had to drag away those corpses and spread them out in the ravine while all this wild machine-gun shooting was allegedly happening.

Pronicheva's account contradicts the current orthodox narrative, according to which the victims had to walk down into the ravine, then walk on the wobbly surface of wounded and

Dina Pronicheva

dead victims already lying on the ground to a spot pointed out to them. There, they had to lay face down on the already executed victims below them, and then got shot at close range with a bullet from a submachine gun into the nape of their neck.

The photos taken by German military photographer Johannes Hähle show that people had deposited large amounts of clothes and personal belongings at the bottom of a ravine, not at the top. However, there are no executed people visible on these photos, or any other traces of a massacre. (See the entry on Johannes Hähle.)

In other words: It cannot have happened. Pronicheva lied.

(For more details, see the entry on Babi Yar, as well as Mattogno 2022c, pp. 569-579.)

PROPAGANDA
Introduction

The term originates from the Latin word *propagare*, to propagate, and did not initially have any nefarious connotation. It simply meant the dissemination of information, with no implication that this information may be inaccurate or untrue. The shift in the term's meaning is a result of spreading disinformation through mass media with the intention of swaying public opinion, which became prevalent during the age of the World Wars and the subsequent Cold War, when radio and TV as well as mass-printed tabloids and booklets became widely consumed.

The only major power using disinforming propaganda during the First World War was the United Kingdom. Considering the success this propaganda had in stirring up public opinion in the Entente countries against Germany, and thus stabilizing their crumbling war efforts since 1915, all major countries subsequently created departments for psychological warfare aiming at winning support among their own population for their political efforts, while at once trying to subvert the unity and resistance of perceived enemy populations.

Accusations of planned or perpetrated mass atrocities have always been the main weapon of wartime propaganda, as they stir up one's own population against a portrayed enemy, and "justify" extreme measures against him. This type of propaganda dehumanizes the enemy in the eyes of your own soldiers, which are thus emotionally prepared to commit their own mass atrocities against the enemy – ironically in an attempt to prevent or avenge the enemy's (alleged) mass atrocities. Hence, it is fair to say that, to a large degree, mass-atrocity propaganda is geared toward creating mass atrocities.

Since World War Two was the most atrocious war ever fought in the history of mankind, it is safe to assume that mass-atrocity propaganda was also used by all sides to a degree never seen before or since. Anything else would be naïve to assume. The claimed events making up the Holocaust are among the most prominent mass-atrocities claimed to have occurred during World War Two. Therefore, investigating the role of propaganda in shaping the initial, as well as the current, narrative is a worthwhile endeavor. In fact, ignoring propaganda's role would be an inexcusable omission. Nevertheless, orthodox Holocaust historians systematically ignore or downplay the pivotal role which propaganda has played in our current understanding of this event.

The following sections will explore, in alphabetical order, each major country's propaganda efforts in the creation of the Holocaust narrative, with an additional section on Jewish contributions to it, as well as – and in contrast to all this – a section on Germany's involvement in mass-atrocity propaganda.

Czechoslovakia

During the Second World War, neither the "Protectorate" (occupied Czechia) nor Slovakia were locations of any major mass-murder events within the Holocaust. As such, there is no reason to include this country in this entry. However, one court case tried in communist Czechoslovakia in 1962 sheds a revealing light on the coercive methods used in Eastern Bloc countries to force witnesses to testify as the prosecution expected them to.

In 1962, Czechoslovakia's judiciary sentenced Ladislav Niznansky *in absentia* to death for allegedly having murdered 164 people in Slovakia during World War II. But Niznansky had fled to West Germany after the war, and that country refused to extradite him or recognize Communist kangaroo trials as legitimate proceedings. In 2001, the German judiciary changed its mind, reopened the case, and launched a criminal investigation against Niznansky. However, the witnesses who had testified in 1962 against Niznansky, had lost their fear of their country's judiciary, and revealed the methods used in 1962 to extract false testimonies from them. Here is the report by Germany's mainstream newsmagazine *Focus* (9 February 2004):

> "*One of the witnesses involved in the 1962 case stated that he was threatened by an investigator*

'with a pistol.' A second witness testified that he had incriminated Niznansky 'under psychological and physical duress.' Jan Holbus, another witness for the prosecution back in 1962, declared during his interrogation in 2001 that he was threatened that he 'will leave the room with his feet first,' if he does not testify as the prosecution expects him to."

This is the only known case where an Eastern Bloc court case about alleged German war crimes was reopened after the collapse of the Eastern Bloc. It stands to reason that the methods used by Soviet and Polish investigators in the immediate postwar years were at least as bad as this. It is also likely that similar methods were used by Eastern-Bloc authorities to coach witnesses slated to testify during West-German court proceedings (see the section on Poland). This would explain the astounding "convergence of evidence" of so many witness testimonies in so many lies, such as consistently exaggerated death toll figures, inflated cremation capacities (see the entry on cremation propaganda), and the repetition of proven lies, such as large-scale open-air incinerations at Auschwitz in the summer of 1944.

France

Since France was an occupied country until mid-/late 1944, she could not contribute to Allied propaganda efforts. The area of Germany which was eventually assigned as France's occupation zone in the southwest of Germany did not contain any major camp of notorious repute. Furthermore, the invading U.S. troops did not find anything in the labor camps they occupied which would have lent itself to any atrocity propaganda. Therefore, there was little of any substance onto which any Holocaust propaganda could be based.

The one minor exception was the small camp near the Alsatian village of Natzweiler. However, even in this regard, French involvement was minor. The camp's long-standing commandant Josef Kramer was captured by the British at Bergen-Belsen. After the British had softened him up with their customary torture, some French investigator helped extract a "confession" about one minor and truly unique alleged homicidal gassing. However, evidently not in the loop as to how such a gassing was supposed to have been carried out, the French had Kramer made up a story which is so outlandish that it threatens to undermine the entire homicidal gassing narrative. This is true in particular for Auschwitz-Birkenau, where Kramer was commandant in 1944 at a time of alleged large-scale mass gassings. If gassings happened there in the way the orthodoxy claims, Kramer would have known how to tell a credible tale. But he was evidently just as oblivious as the French interrogators.

Considering the French's negligible contribution to Germany's defeat, they might have suffered from an inferiority complex, which they tried to compensate for by outdoing the other Allies with their own atrocity tales. An indicator for this is an official French government report on German concentration camps, of which they had almost no first-hand knowledge. While the Soviets had claimed four million victims for the Auschwitz Camp they conquered, the French doubled this number in their report (eight million; Aroneanu 1945, pp. 7, 196), and they claimed a total of 26 million victims of all National-Socialist means of mass murder and persecution (*ibid.*, p. 197).

The other noteworthy propaganda contribution to the orthodox Holocaust narrative consists of the various statements by Kurt Gerstein, which he supposedly made voluntarily to the French occupational powers at his hometown. His statements were in fact "voluntary" to such a degree that he eventually committed suicide. Whether the preposterous nonsense exuded by Gerstein was the fruit of his own (sick) mind, or foisted upon him by the French's interrogation methods, must unfortunately remain an open question.

Gerstein's texts are the basis upon which the tall tale of the Belzec extermination camp was erected. This tale, in turn, formed the pattern used to create similar narratives for the Treblinka and Sobibór camps. While Gerstein's narrative was supported and believed by orthodox historians for many decades, they have mostly abandoned him by now as an untrustworthy witness. The basic features of his tales, however, have developed a life of their own, hanging in mid-air without any support. They are propped up only by the fanaticism of the believers, and by threats of social persecution and penal prosecution against the rest of us.

During the Nuremberg International Military Tribunal, the French not only introduced one of Gerstein's texts (1553-PS, *IMT*, Vol. 6, pp. 332-364), but also other propaganda claims, some of which are patently recognizable as preposterous lies, such as the claim that at "Auschwitz the most beautiful women were set apart, artificially inseminated, and then gassed." The French chief prosecutor followed this up with claims that at the Natzweiler Camp, "women were gassed while German doctors observed their reactions through a peephole," and execution happened there also by gas vans (*IMT*, Vol. 5, pp. 403f.). Today, none of it is taken seriously anymore, even by orthodox historians.

Germany

The first country during the Second World War to engage in mass-atrocity propaganda was Hitler's Germany. As German troops advanced into Poland in early September 1939, the Polish military and Polish civilians started pogroms against the German minority in northwestern Poland (the "Corridor"). While these massacres were real, the death toll later published by Goebbels's propaganda ministry were inflated in an attempt to make the German invasion look like a rescue operation.

Ironically, Goebbels's position as minister of propaganda did not mean that he could not be trusted; in fact, *precisely the opposite*: he understood that propaganda cannot be effective unless it is, by and large, true. This was acknowledged decades ago by prominent French scholar Jacques Ellul in his monumental work *Propaganda* (1962), and specifically with respect to Goebbels. Ellul refers to "Goebbels's insistence that facts to be disseminated must be accurate" (p. 53), adding that Goebbels "wore the title of Big Liar [...] and yet he never stopped battling for propaganda to be as accurate as possible. He preferred being cynical and brutal to being caught in a lie." Ellul continues:

> "He was always the first to announce disastrous events or difficult situations, without hiding anything. The result was a general belief, between 1939 and 1942, that German communiqués not only were more concise, clearer, and less cluttered, but were more truthful than Allied communiqués – and furthermore, that the Germans published all the news two or three days before the Allies. All this is so true that pinning the title of Big Liar on Goebbels must be considered quite a propaganda success."

The only other major German propaganda campaign involving mass atrocities revolved around their discoveries of the mass slaughter of dissidents and other prisoners in the Soviet Union, as they advanced into Soviet Russia in June 1941. Before the Soviets retreated from their western cities, they systematically killed all the inmates in all prisons, which to a large degree contained dissidents, hence people who would potentially collaborate with the Germans. However, none of the German reports about these events were invented, and not much of it, if anything, was exaggerated either.

This German anti-Bolshevist campaign really took off only in early 1943 with the discovery of the mass graves near Katyn, where more than 4,000 Polish officers had been shot and buried by the Soviets. However, the death-toll figure spread in that context (and later also about similar mass graves near Vinnitsa) was established by an independent, international group of forensic experts, and it was very accurate. In fact, the Germans never found all the mass graves of Stalin's Polish victims, which numbered more than 20,000. Therefore, the German atrocity propaganda revolving around Katyn and Vinnitsa actually *understated* the true dimension of this Soviet massacre.

After the war, both East and West Germany became part of the general Holocaust propaganda machine. East Germany followed the general Eastern-Bloc pattern of staging show trials that were unconvincing even for most orthodox historians. West Germany, however, went on a much more sophisticated and ultimately very successful path of harnessing its judiciary to rig the historical record.

At the beginning there was starvation and poverty in devastated postwar West Germany. Germany's destroyed economy had trouble getting off the ground in the late 1940s and early 1950s. It was encountering fierce opposition, mainly by Jewish pressure groups and Israel itself, to conclude trade deals and financial agreements on the international market. Hence, Germany struck a deal with Israel in 1952: Germany pays reparations for "the Holocaust," implying that its historical veracity is officially recognized, and Israel and World Jewry will refrain from impeding Germany's rise from the ashes. (For more on this, see the entry on compensation.)

From there on, Germany's government, in unison with many foreign and domestic pressure groups, pushed for the prosecution of suspects presumably involved in the perpetration of "Holocaust" crimes:

– Unwilling investigators, who realized the phony nature of the accusations, were ordered to initiate prosecutions anyway (see the entry on Adolf Rögner).
– Juries were cajoled into agreeing to guilty verdicts, even though they wanted to acquit (see the entry on Karl Wolff).

- Trials that had already been settled by the Allies after the war, or by Israel, and which had ended in amnesties or acquittals, were reopened and brought to merciless guilty verdicts (see the entries on Ilse Koch and John Demjanjuk.)
- An institution was set up whose sole purpose was to prepare prosecutions of suspects of "Holocaust" crimes: The *Zentrale Stelle*. This office systematically manipulated witnesses in order to make sure that the orthodox Holocaust narrative got cast in stone within German case law (see the entry on the *Zentrale Stelle*).
- The statute of limitations allowing the prosecution of murder was repeatedly extended, only to be completely lifted eventually, for the sole reason of allowing the continued prosecution of suspected Third-Reich murders. (See Rudolf 2019, pp. 118f.)
- Until 1994, anyone contesting the orthodox narrative was threatened with prosecution for insulting the witnesses, disparaging the commemoration of dead victims, and stirring up racial hatred against Jews. In 1994, dissent as such was made a crime of "denial," no matter its style or form, and courts were allowed to ban defense lawyers from speaking a single word in court, if they recalcitrantly tried to argue in favor of a defendant's historical claims. In 1998, it was even declared a crime to file motions during a trial aiming at introducing evidence which contests the orthodox narrative. (See Rudolf 2019, pp. pp. 20-29.)
- After 70 years of case law to the contrary, Germany's supreme court decided in 2016 that anyone can be prosecuted for accessory to murder who in any way contributed to the operation of any Third-Reich organization or facility allegedly involved in murder. This allowed for the prosecution of any German involved in anything official and/or military in nature during the Third Reich (see the entry on John Demjanjuk).

Poland

Ethnic conflicts rarely existed in Europe prior to the French Revolution and the Napoleonic wars. Citizenship, passports, border controls, official languages, ethnic or national allegiances were all but unknown. If there were wars, they were usually due to religious conflicts, or because some king or duke tried to extend their realm, always at the cost of the local populace.

The situation was drastically different after the Napoleonic Wars. Europe became increasingly defined by ethnicities and nation states. The Polish people were largely dominated by Russia, and to a minor degree by Prussia. During that time, the Poles developed a historic myth of national martyrdom, in which their ancestral homelands in the West were conquered by Germans in violent wars. The resident Polish population was either forcefully Germanized, ethnically cleansed or simply murdered. None of it is true, though. The only area which was conquered in wars by German knights with subsequent subjugation of the local nobility was West and East Prussia – plus later the area today covered by the Baltic countries. Affected by this were mostly not Slavs, but the Baltic tribes of the Prussians, Lithuanians, Latvians and Estonians. Neither of them was forcefully Germanized, ethnically cleansed or killed. This happened in the 12th and 13th century, and the nobleman who had *asked* for the German knights to help him subjugate the indomitable Prussian heathens was none other than the Polish king of that time. Over the next centuries, the Prussian population Germanized itself, without any pressure from anyone. In contrast to this, the German settlement activities in Silesia and Pomerania over the centuries have been completely peaceful. The newly arriving Germans simply were economically more adept and outbred the Poles.

After the First World War, Polish hyper-nationalism took over and tried to gain back the allegedly unjustly lost territories in the West by forcefully Polonizing, ethnically cleansing or outright murdering the century-old German population in West Prussia and East Upper Silesia. The inevitable conflict between Germans and Poles resulted in the outbreak of World War II.

Once Poland was defeated, the Polish underground developed a new myth of Polish martyrdom. This time it was based on real acts of persecution and terror by the occupational powers, although not all stories reported were true. In fact, much was highly exaggerated, because it aimed at stirring up Poland's Western allies, in particular London, whence the Polish Government in Exile had fled.

Initial reports on alleged atrocities committed at Auschwitz claimed Polish and Soviet-Russian victims. Once it had become clear that Polish minorities in the UK and USA had little political sway, hence the suffering of Poles attracted little attention there, tactics changed by putting Jewish victims in the center of attention. Wartime reports by the Polish underground about massacres presumably committed in the various concentration and alleged extermination camps on Polish prewar soil are the core around which all later narratives crystalized. Their importance can hardly be overestimated.

Towards and after the end of the war, reestablished Polish authorities collaborated closely with Soviet military authorities in forming investigative commissions. Based on the rigged findings of these Stalinist commissions, Polish authorities subsequently conducted numerous show trials against various German defendants. Among the most prominent are:
- The Lublin trial against six former guards of the Majdanek Camp (27 November to 2 December 1944). At that trial, the absurdly high death toll of 1.7 million victims was claimed.
- The Warsaw trial against former commandant of the Auschwitz Camp Rudolf Höss (11 to 29 March 1947). At that trial, the absurdly high death toll of four million victims was claimed, three million of them Poles.
- The Krakow trial against 40 former staff members of the Auschwitz Camp, where all the absurdities of the Höss Trial were repeated (24 November to 22 December 1947).

The findings presented during these and similar trials formed the basis upon which each camp's narrative was erected. In the case of Auschwitz, this was the starting point for the creation of the world's most visited and psychologically most powerful museum. (See the entry on the Auschwitz Museum.)

While the Warsaw and Krakow Trials were getting prepared, the Nuremberg International Military Tribunal took place. Although no Polish official took part in the trial, several documents prepared by Polish authorities got submitted. Among them was a lengthy report on the Treblinka Camp, according to which mass murder there was committed with hot-steam chambers. (See Document 3311-PS, *IMT*, Vol. 32, pp. 153-158). Another Polish document claimed that murder at Treblinka happened in "gas chambers, by steam and electric current" (USSR-93; see Mattogno/Graf 2023, pp. 50-62, esp. p. 62). These self-evident and preposterous propaganda claims of steam and electric murder at Treblinka have haunted orthodox historians ever since, who usually prefer to hide this from their readers.

Concurrent with these proceedings between late 1944 and late 1947, Poland was expelling, mass-murdering and force-Polonizing millions of Germans in southern East Prussia, West Prussia, Pomerania and Silesia. This was the largest ethnic cleansing of recorded history. These territories had been "given" to the Poles by the victorious Allies, with a blank check to do whatever they wanted with the hapless Germans. The Poles wasted no time to make their wildest dreams of reconquest of "their" lost western territories come true. But how could this genocide be justified?

With the Holocaust, of course. Any claim of German atrocities was welcomed to bolster Polish claims to rightful compensation by vast territories. In order to secure these spoils of war, Germany needed to be made to swallow completely the Polish narrative. This initiated stage two of the Polish propaganda campaign: make the German judiciary come to similar conclusions as the Polish judiciary, despite the terrible, Stalinist reputation of those Polish trials. Here is the way it was implemented:
- The International Auschwitz Committee, a communist propaganda organization headquartered in Krakow, Poland, lobbied to open criminal investigations in West Germany against Wilhelm Boger, a former employee at the Political Department of the Auschwitz Concentration Camp.
- Former inmates in contact with the International Auschwitz Committee were encouraged to file criminal complaints against former Auschwitz staff members.
- Parallel to this, the Auschwitz State Museum wrote a day-by-day account of what the Polish-communist authorities wanted the world to believe happened in the Auschwitz Camp. This chronicle was based to a large degree on the findings "established" by the aforementioned show trials.
- This streamlined account was immediately also published in a German translation, although there was only one possible reader for it: the German judiciary.
- Furthermore, the chronicle created by the Auschwitz Museum was then used to "instruct" Polish witnesses before traveling to the big German Frankfurt Auschwitz Trial. This ensured that all witnesses delivered a coherent story in line with the official narrative.
- The witnesses were accompanied to West Germany and monitored at all times by Polish secret-service officials, even inside the court room while testifying.
- Under massive pressure by the world's media, the

German judiciary completely swallowed everything they were fed by Warsaw.

It was the continuation of the war by means of psychological warfare. It was what the Germans call "*Raubsicherungspolitik*" – literally Robbery-Securing Policy, a policy designed to secure the spoils of history's greatest robbery ever, the annexation of East Germany by Poland, and the ethnic cleansing of its German population.

Unfortunately, it worked. The Frankfurt Auschwitz Trial was a watershed event in German history. After it, a deluge of similar trials followed, continuing well into the 21st Century, held against 80, 90 and 100-year-old geriatrics.

Branded with a perpetual guilt complex, the once-proud German nation has turned into a featureless mass of pathetic, self-flagellating individuals who agree that all that was done *to them* during and after the war – carpet bombing, mass murder of "disarmed enemy forces," mass deportations to Siberia, ethnic cleansing, starvation policies, dismantling of Germany's industrial equipment, robbery of its patents – was a just punishment for all the crimes allegedly committed *during* the war, in particular during the so-called Holocaust.

(For more on this, see Mattogno 2021, pp. 103-289; 2022b, pp. 7-22; as well as entries on camps on Polish [pre- and postwar] soil: Auschwitz, Belzec, Chełmno, Majdanek, Sobibór, Treblinka.)

Serbia

The Semlin Camp (also called Sajmište Camp) was the only location of significance in Serbia within the framework of the Holocaust. Some 7,000 Jews are said to have been killed there in early 1942 using gas vans. Their bodies were later allegedly exhumed and tracelessly burned within the framework of *Aktion 1005*. Hence, there is not only no trace of that crime, but also no trace that the crime's traces were eradicated. (See the entry on Semlin for more details.)

After all Jews had been murdered (or transferred elsewhere), the camp was converted to a detention and labor camp for political prisoners and partisans.

At the turn of 1944/45, the communist Yugoslav government, dominated by Serbs, formed a war-crimes commission. Among other things, they exhumed two mass graves near the Semlin Camp, where victims of the detention camp were supposedly buried, who are said to have died mainly due to starvation, diseases and exhaustion.

Original documents of the commission indicate that some 11,000 bodies were exhumed. However, in its report, the commission wrote that the mass graves contained 40,000 bodies. While the camp records show that exactly 23,637 inmates were ever detained there, the commission claimed that some 80,000 inmates had been incarcerated. These numbers were evidently inflated for propaganda reasons, because the commission's main purpose was to create evidence in order, "to justify Yugoslavia's claim for reparations," as orthodox historian Jovan Byford put it (Byford 2010, p. 25). Unfortunately, this shows the untrustworthiness of any of the commission's documents. Even the claimed number of 11,000 bodies found, which today's orthodox historians take at face value, may be dubious.

If the Germans really went to great lengths in order to destroy the remains of some 7,000 Jewish victims, why did they leave behind the other 11,000 victims? After all, these 11,000 bodies were a much bigger indictment of their crimes, quantitatively speaking, than the 7,000 Jewish victims.

The issue gets compounded by witness claims of gas-van murders at the Banjica Camp in Serbia, where exclusively non-Jewish Serbs were held (mostly dissidents and partisans). Orthodox historians reject those claims as based on rumors, hearsay and overzealous propaganda, presumably recognizable by the witness statements' inconsistencies and disparate nature. Yet the same is true for witness statements about gas vans allegedly deployed elsewhere (and any other execution-chamber mass-murder claim, for that matter). The only difference between the Banjica gas-van claims and all the others is that the claimed victims were Gentiles. This is the deeper cause why they get rejected by the orthodoxy. Preserving the Jewish exclusivity to their martyrdom demands the rejection of testimony claiming exclusively non-Jewish victims.

(For more details on this, see Alvarez 2023, pp. 22f.; 249-257.)

Soviet Union

The most blatant propaganda efforts, easily recognizable as such and thus also the least effective in the long run, were made by the Soviet Union. Orthodox historians recognize the systematic nature of torture by the Soviet judiciary, and the grotesque show-trial nature of trials during Stalin's reign. However, this has never stopped them from using and taking seriously the multitude of claims made by the Soviets. While the dimensions of the crimes claimed may have been inflated, the core of the claim is still true, they assert.

Soviet propaganda started right after the Soviets had won the battle of Stalingrad in early 1943, with the Germans for the first time retreating – in this case from the Caucasus region to avoid getting cut off after the fall of Stalingrad. Krasnodar is the largest city near the Caucasus mountains. The Germans retreated hastily, leaving it largely intact. This city thus became the stage of the first Soviet show trial focusing on alleged German mass atrocities.

The Soviet indictments written in February 1943 against eleven Soviet citizens accused them of having collaborated with the Germans. However, during the trial itself, the alleged German atrocities were on center stage, rather than the defendant's own alleged misdeeds. The German invaders were accused of mass hangings, shootings and asphyxiations in so-called "murder vans." Here, the legend of the "gas vans" was born, an execution weapon invented by the Soviet NKVD before the war, but then blamed in 1943 on the Germans. (See the entry on the gas vans.)

The resulting show trial in July 1943 was turned into a media spectacle by the Soviets, who used this show primarily to send a clear message to their own populace: Collaborate with the Germans, and you will be killed! The show trial was also used to spread counter-propaganda against the German exploitation of their discovery of the Katyn mass graves containing some 4,000 bodies. Hence, the Soviets topped this by claiming 7,000 victims of German atrocities.

After the Germans lost their last offensive battle in the East at Kursk in late August 1943, the Germans retreated steadily. The Ukrainian city of Kharkov was reconquered by the Soviets in late August. The next major propaganda show was staged here in December of 1943, this time with one Soviet collaborator and three captured German soldiers in the dock. Softened up with torture, they all enthusiastically embraced and confirmed the prosecution's atrocity claims. Among them was the charge that the German occupiers had killed some 30,000 Soviet citizens in and around Kharkov, many of them again in gas vans. Here as during the Krasnodar Trial, it was repeatedly asserted that these gas vans were equipped with Diesel engines – whose exhaust gases, however, were unable to kill as claimed. (For more details, see the entries on Krasnodar and Kharkov, on gas vans, as well as Alvarez 2023, pp. 111-129.)

When the Soviets conquered the first major German concentration camp in July 1944 – Majdanek –

Soviet propaganda poster of World War Two.

the Soviet propaganda machinery went in overdrive, inflating the camp's death toll by a factor of almost 50, and conjuring up homicidal gas chambers in every corner of the camp. (See the entry on Majdanek for more details.) Those propaganda lies later backfired when the orthodoxy had to make major admissions as to the mendacity of these Soviet claims, thus undermining the credibility of the entire orthodox Holocaust narrative.

Two months after conquering Majdanek, the Soviets captured the Klooga Camp in Estonia. After the huge Majdanek propaganda success, achieved to no small degree with gruesome photos of skeletons in front of a furnace, the Klooga "liberators" evidently felt under pressure to produce some similar visual material in support of yet another claimed German massacre. Hence, they staged photos showing piled-up tree trunks with people on and in between them. Unfortunately for them, these photos clearly demonstrate that these people were living actors used to stage an invented scene that could be used, and subsequently was used, for propaganda purposes. (See the entry on the Klooga Camp for more details.)

Throughout the war, Soviet domestic newspapers were publishing plenty of war propaganda depicting the Germans as bestial monsters who deserve to be slain wherever they are found. Some of these items were also published in the English-language newspaper *Soviet War News*. One of the most prominent and inflammatory contributors was Ilya Ehrenburg. In a contribution of the edition of 22 December 1944, Ehrenburg announced that the Germans had annihilated six million Jews. This was six months *before* the end of the war. (See Hoffmann 2001, pp. 189, 402f.)

A month later, on 27 January 1945, the Soviets conquered their ultimate propaganda prize: the Auschwitz Camp. Their subsequent absurd propaganda campaign about four million victims – killed by asphyxiation and electrocution, then transported via conveyor belts to a shaft furnace half a kilometer long – is described in the entry on Birkenau. After interrogating numerous camp inmates, the Soviets formed a combined Polish-Soviet investigative commission which wrote a fake report on the cremation capacity of the Auschwitz crematoria. It was rigged in such a way that the preordained result of four million victims was "confirmed" at that propaganda end as well. (For details on this, see Mattogno 2003d; Mattogno/Deana, Part 1, pp. 337-339.) After that, the Soviets handed over the Auschwitz Camp to the Poles, who continued this type of Auschwitz propaganda along similar lines.

During the International Military Tribunal at Nuremberg, the Soviet chief prosecutor Smirnov outdid all other Allies with a long rampage of preposterous atrocity claims. The entire Volume 7 of the proceedings is full of them. Here are some examples (all page numbers refer to *IMT*, Vol. 7):

– bashing people's brains in with a pedal-triggered brain-bashing machine while listening to the radio (pp. 376f.);
– gassing Soviet PoWs in a quarry (p. 388);
– killing PoWs during frost by turning them into ice statues (p. 433);
– Jewish children used by Hitler-Youth for target practice (pp. 447f.);
– mass murder with hot steam and electrocutions at Treblinka (Nuremberg Document USSR-93; Smirnov left out that passage when quoting from the document, pp. 477f.; see the section on Poland in this entry);
– an SS father skeet shooting babies thrown into the air while his 9-year old daughter applauds and shrieks: "Papa, do it again; do it again, Papa!" (p. 451);
– filling the mouths of victims with cement to prevent them from singing patriotic or communist songs (p. 475);
– forcing prisoners to lick stairs clean, and collect garbage with their lips (p. 491);
– killing people with poisoned soft drinks (p. 570);
– electrocution at Belzec (pp. 576f., Belzec misspelled as Belsen);
– mass murder by tree cutting: forcing people to climb trees, then cutting the trees down (p. 582);
– killing 840,000 Soviet PoWs at Sachsenhausen, and burning the bodies in four portable furnaces (p. 586);
– soap production from human fat (USSR-393, pp. 597-600);
– For more details on the USSR's role in spreading Holocaust propaganda via the IMT, see Carlos Porter's book *Made in Russia: The Holocaust*.

Right in the middle of the IMT, the Soviet Union conducted yet another show trial, this time in Leningrad from 28 December 1945 until 4 January 1946. Seven German officers were accused, convicted and executed (= murdered) by the Soviets for allegedly having participated in the Katyn Massacre of more than 4,000 Polish officers. This crime, committed by Soviets on Stalin's order, was "proven" to have been committed by the Germans instead by way of a Soviet forensic commission headed by Nikolai Burdenko. The Soviets had the gall to introduce this report as evidence during the IMT (USSR-054; *IMT*, Vol. 39, pp. 290-332). This shows the almost unfathomable magnitude of mendacity that was driving the Soviets.

Burdenko was involved in many more forensic investigations of mass graves in the Soviet Union allegedly containing the victims of German mass atrocities. The trustworthiness of these reports is just as low as that of Burdenko's Katyn Report, as none of them were ever verified by independent experts. (See the entry on *Aktion* 1005 for details.) It is quite possible that the Soviet Union took this opportunity to pin numerous mass graves, containing some of the 20+ million victims of decades of Lenin's and Stalin's terror on the Germans, just as Burdenko tried with Katyn – although here he ultimately failed. The forensic report by independent researchers organized by Germany in 1943 prevailed.

When the Nuremberg show trials were over, the world entered a new war, the Cold War. Rather than keeping alleged German atrocities on center stage, each side wanted to win "their" Germans as potential cannon fodder in a future hot war of NATO against the Warsaw Pact. In addition, the Soviets always deemphasized that the victims were Jews, speaking simply of Soviet citizens instead. With the violent birth of the State of Israel, the Soviet Union took sides against the Jews and with the Arabs. Moreover, Stalin planned to turn against the Jews with a planned show trial, which was to lead to a mass deportation of people who happened to be Jews. Only Stalin's death prevented it.

As a consequence of this development, much material collected against the Germans was not published for quite a while. For example, the big propaganda tome *The Black Book* by Ilya Ehrenburg and Vasily Grossman, announced with big fanfare in late 1944 and containing many more absurd and exaggerated atrocity claims against the Third Reich, was shelved, and so was the pile of expert reports on exhumed mass graves throughout the Soviet Union, authored by Burdenko and his ilk.

These old materials were pulled out the drawer, however, when the United States established a special department within the FBI in 1979. This Office of Special Investigations (OSI) was tasked with collecting evidence against European immigrants accused of having been involved in claimed German atrocities. Once such an individual was found, the O.S.I. litigated to have his citizenship revoked, and if successful, have him deported to other countries for further prosecution. (See the entry on the OSI for details.)

The Soviet Union took advantage of this invitation to meddle in internal U.S. affairs by submitting to the OSI incriminating material, much of it based on false witness testimonies and forged documents. The Soviet Union targeted with this primarily immigrants in the U.S. with a Ukrainian background. The goal was to damage the reputation of nationalist Ukrainian groups and individuals by bringing them into context of National-Socialist atrocities. This was to undermine the legitimacy of the Ukrainian independence movement.

Hence, Ehrenburg's *Black Book* was finally published in 1981. A collection of "expert reports" by Burdenko and his ilk about alleged *Nazi Crimes in the Ukraine*(!) saw the light of day in 1987 (Denisov/Changuli). It is no accident that this happened right around the time of the showdown in Israel of the OSI's most infamous witch-hunt victim, the Ukrainian John Demjanjuk.

United Kingdom

The United Kingdom was the country with the most experience in atrocity propaganda, as they were the only ones who had institutionalized this already during the First World War. Their approach to this during the Second World War was no different. The department in charge of psychological warfare was called Political Warfare Executive. They devised lies spread through numerous channels which aimed at undermining the enemy's morale, boosting the morale of Allied forces, and increasing animosities of occupied civilian populations against the Axis powers.

Most of the claimed mass-murder events are said to have occurred on Polish soil, and as such, reports by the Polish underground were crucial to understand what was going on in that country. Since the Polish Government in Exile was located in London, and almost all support for the Polish underground was organized by London, the British government was at all times familiar with reports going in and coming out of Poland, speaking of mass gassings and other mass murder activities.

In contrast to all other Allied governments, the Brits were in the enviable situation of having cracked the SS's radio encryption code between January 1942 and January 1943. Hence, the British managed to intercept and decipher all radio traffic between German concentration camps and their Oranienburg headquarters (see the entry on British Radio Intercepts). Therefore, they knew that there was no trace of any extermination policy in these intercepts, no trace of any homicidal gassing, and that the Poles were exaggerating the numbers of deported, incarcerated, perished and murdered victims.

To hide that they knew better, and also because it served their purpose of vilifying the Germans, the British nevertheless spread this type of Polish propaganda through their media channels. However, when it came to official communications, they inevitably revealed a bit of the truth.

In August 1943, Poland's government-in-exile lobbied the British and American governments to issue a public statement condemning "German terror in Poland." A draft for such a statement included references to mass execution in gas chambers. That is where Britain's psychological warfare experts stepped on the brake, vetoing this with clear words, and succeeded in getting all these references removed. Victor Cavendish-Bentinck, the Chairman of the Allied Joint Intelligence Committee, stated in this regard:

"In my opinion it is incorrect to describe Polish information regarding German atrocities as

'trustworthy'. The Poles, and to a far greater extent the Jews, tend to exaggerate German atrocities in order to stoke us up. They seem to have succeeded.

Mr Allen and myself have both followed German atrocities quite closely. [This is the hint at radio intercepts.] *I do not believe that there is any evidence which would be accepted in a Law Court that* Polish *children have been killed on the spot by Germans when their parents were being deported to work in Germany, nor that* Polish *children have been sold to German settlers.*

As regards putting Poles to death in gas chambers, I do not believe that there is any evidence that this has been done. There have been many stories to this effect, and we have played them up in PWE rumours without believing that they had any foundation. At any rate there is far less evidence than exists for the mass murder of Polish officers by the Russians at Katyn. On the other hand, we do know that the Germans are out to destroy Jews of any age unless they are fit for manual labour.

I think that we weaken our case against the Germans by publicly giving credence to atrocity stories for which we have no evidence. These mass executions in gas chambers remind me of the stories of employment of human corpses during the last war for the manufacture of fat, which was a grotesque lie and led to the true stories of German atrocities being brushed aside as being mere propaganda."

(For details on this, see Ritchie 2017.)

As described in the Section on British contributions to the propaganda history of the Birkenau Camp, this knowledge of gas-chamber claims being atrocity lies did not stop the British from spreading these false claims wherever they saw fit.

When the Red Army was about to enter Central Europe, mass atrocities were expected by everyone. In order to distract from them and to make these expected excesses "understandable," the British government upped the ante in early 1944. On 29 February 1944, the British Ministry of "Information" – Goebbels was at least honest and called his department the Propaganda Ministry – circulated a memo to the British Clergy and to the BBC stating (Rozek 1958, pp. 209f.):

"We know how the Red Army behaved in Poland in 1920 and in Finland, Estonia, Latvia, Galicia and Bessarabia only recently.

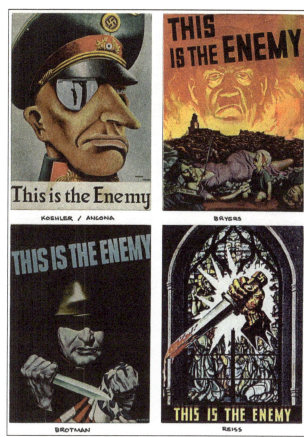

Anti-German Propaganda posters of World War Two.

We must, therefore, take into account how the Red Army will certainly behave when it overruns Central Europe. […]

Experience has shown that the best distraction is atrocity propaganda directed against the enemy. Unfortunately the public is no longer so susceptible as in the days of the 'Corpse Factory,' and the 'Mutilated Belgian Babies,' and the 'Crucified Canadians.' [On this, see Ponsonby 1971]

Your cooperation is therefore earnestly sought to distract public attention from the doings of the Red Army by your wholehearted support of various charges against the Germans and Japanese which have been and will be put into circulation by the Ministry."

The British became serious about Holocaust propaganda only after the war, when they extracted "confessions" from many former SS men with bestial torture (see the section on the UK in the entry on torture, as well as the entries on Bad Nenndorf, Hans Aumeier, Josef Kramer, Oswald Pohl and Rudolf Höss). They furthermore collected mendacious and vengeful "survivor" testimonies in preparation for their Bergen-Belsen Trial about events that allegedly unfolded at the Auschwitz, Bergen-Belsen and

Natzweiler Camps, their show trial against leading staff members of the Zyklon-B company Tesch & Stabenow, and finally their show trial about the Neuengamme Camp. (For more details, see the respective entries, as well as the section on British propaganda to the propaganda history of the Birkenau Camp.)

British files on the radio intercepts and on the systematic torture of German captives after the war were released only around the year 2000. Other files are reportedly still kept under lock and key. It stands to reason that they contain secrets which are even more devastating for orthodox historiography.

United States

Initially, U.S.-American contributions to Holocaust propaganda seem to have been largely limited to propagating the claims that came from London, both from the Polish government in exile, and from the common campaigns coordinated by the Allied Joint Intelligence Committee. (See the sections on Poland and the UK.) Still in the summer of 1943, on advice by their better-informed British allies, the U.S. government abstained from making gas-chamber claims in official statements.

This policy was definitely abandoned after the Vrba-Wetzler Report had gained considerable attention. This report in English translation and the writings by three other authors were then combined by the U.S. War Refugee Board into one report. This was published on 25 November 1944. (For more details, see the entry on the War Refugee Board Report.)

As U.S. troops entered Germany, Eisenhower's Psychological Warfare Division (PWD) came with a plan. As U.S. troops entered the Buchenwald Camp, they swiftly set up a table with ghoulish specimens claimed to have been made of murdered camp inmates, such as soap, a table lamp, two shrunken heads, tattooed skin etc. Townspeople were forced to file by this exhibit, while PWD actors gave mendacious explanations about these altogether fake items. The scene was recorded on film, and is shown to this day as "evidence" for National-Socialist atrocities. (See Irebodd 2009, and the entries on soap, shrunken heads and lampshades, of human skin, for more details.)

When U.S. troops entered any of the hundreds of cities their bomber fleets had destroyed, no cameras were ever rolling, and if anything was recorded, it vanished into some archives. The devastation the Allies' genocidal air warfare had wreaked, and the heaps of corpses they had produced, needed to be hidden from the world. However, when they entered German Camps, which inevitably fared even worse than the civilian population living around them, cameras were rolling in expectation of gruesome scenes. So did U.S. troops when entering Dachau. Every dead person they found, so they claimed, was a victim of German bestial atrocities, when in fact they all were victims of the end of a war in which the greatest butchers won.

Two propaganda movies were produced by the U.S. Psychological Warfare Division using film footage taken in liberated camps. One titled *The Nazi Concentration Camps* shows falsely labelled scenes from the camps at Bergen-Belsen, Nordhausen and Dachau, among others. It was used to manipulate the defendants and the judges during the International Military Tribunal (*IMT*, Vol. 2, pp. 431-434; transcript in Vol. 30, pp. 462-472; see the entries on the camps mentioned).

The other, titled *Todesmühlen* (*Death Mills*), shows similar scenes with misleading or outright mendacious narrations. This film was shown to the German civilian population in an attempt at "re-education" by means of psychological shock-and-awe exposure to alleged National-Socialist atrocities.

The biggest impact of U.S. psychological warfare against a prostrate Germany was achieved by organizing the International Military Tribunal (IMT), run by the four victorious Allied powers, albeit with U.S. staff at the helm, and the subsequent Nuremberg Military Tribunals (NMT), run only by the U.S. Especially the IMT was a huge propaganda success because it looked respectable on its façade, yet had been firmly rigged beforehand with various measures to ensure the desired outcome. With the accused Germans not having any fair chance at mounting an effective defense, this Tribunal went down as a precedent in the history of international law holding leaders accountable for their acts in international courts – although only the leaders of the *vanquished* nations. (See the entries on the IMT and the NMT for details.)

One of the various measures taken to ensure the IMT's and NMT's success was the IMT's obligation, by its statute, to blindly accept as true any report or court decision made by any of the Allied nations. Running up to the IMT, all nations had created court decisions by conducting show trials of a despicable nature. The U.S. was no exception to this. They held a series of show trials at Dachau, which were characterized by serial torture of German defendants (see the entry on torture), and a hysterical courtroom atmosphere where witnesses levied any imaginable accusations against any and all defendants. (See the entry on the Dachau Trials.)

News of these travesties of justice eventually reached the U.S., and investigations were launched to look into this (see the entry on Edward van Roden). This, together with the first fits of the nascent Cold War, led to an about-face of the U.S. government in the late 1940s. They lost all interest in Holocaust propaganda, and amnestied many of the German convicts they hadn't killed (yet).

Another about-face occurred in 1979, after the "Holocaust" had become a pseudo-religious fetish before which every Western politician has to kneel. That year, the U.S. government created a special branch of the FBI tasked with hunting alleged World-War-II war criminals of the former Axis powers living in the U.S., with the aim to deport them. (*Allied* war criminals were never prosecuted.) Among other cases, this office also created the Demjanjuk Case, which turned into the biggest Holocaust propaganda campaign since the Eichmann Trial, although it eventually backfired. (For more details, see the entries on the Office of Special Investigations and John Demjanjuk.)

Jewish Contributions

Pre-war anti-National-Socialist atrocity propaganda was almost exclusively Jewish in nature. It started already in early 1933, with Jewish organizations and media (such as the Jewish-owned *New York Times*) spreading invented reports about Jews being massacred in Germany, when in fact no such thing was happening at all. To this day, some fanatical Jews take this mendacious propaganda of their own ancestors at face value. (See for example Lipstadt 1986.)

During and after the war, Jews as the primary targets of National-Socialist persecution inevitably played a major role as witnesses to any crimes said to have occurred, and their lobby organizations and media outlets played a major role in disseminating these accounts.

While Stalin drastically reduced the number of influential Jews in the Soviet Union in the 1930s, that influence grew again after the outbreak of the German-Soviet war for obvious reasons. Ilya Ehrenburg and Vasily Grossman, two of the most influential Soviet anti-German propagandists, are two prominent examples for this.

While Jews inexorably played a major role as witnesses during Polish investigations and trials, they were not major contributors in conducting the investigations, staging the subsequent show trials, and exploiting the results in decades to come by writing propagandistic accounts of the various former German wartime camps located in Poland. Polish – and also Czech and Serbian – hyper-nationalism searching for justifications of ethnically cleansing millions of Germans from their century-old homeland needed no Jewish helping hand to find enough motivation in order to distort and forge the historical record.

There is some evidence showing that several of the interrogating and torturing staff members of the British occupational forces in Germany were German-speaking Jews, often recent immigrants to the UK who had fled from the Third Reich. (For example, some of Rudolf Höss's tormentors, and an interrogator for the Tesch Trial.)

The U.S.'s War Refugee Board was Henry Morgenthau's brainchild, and it was this organization which started official U.S. gas-chamber propaganda.

When it comes to the staff that controlled the U.S. postwar trials in Germany – whether in Dachau or later in Nuremberg – it is best to quote one of the leading U.S. prosecutors during the International Military Tribunal, Thomas Dodd. In a private letter to his wife on 20 September 1945, he wrote about the composition of the legal staff running the IMT behind the scenes (Dodd 2007, p. 135):

"You know I have despised anti-Semitism. You know how strongly I feel toward those who preach intolerance of any kind. With that knowledge, you will understand when I tell you that this staff is about seventy-five percent Jewish.

Now, my point is that the Jews should stay away from this trial – for their own sake. For – mark this well – the charge of a war for the Jews is still being made, and in the post-war years it will be made again and again.

The too large percentage of Jewish men and women here will be cited as proof of this charge. Sometimes it seems that the Jews will never learn about these things. They seem intent on bringing new difficulties down on their own heads."

Julius Streicher reportedly cried out moments before being hanged at Nuremberg: "Purimfest!" Whatever else he might have gotten wrong, he got this right.

One of the most-important watershed events in Holocaust propaganda was the show trial against

Adolf Eichmann – held and organized by the Jewish state of Israel.

Many of the most-prominent orthodox historians and promotors of the orthodox Holocaust narrative are Jewish:

Jean Ancel
Yitzak Arad
Hannah Arendt
Yehuda Bauer
Michael Berenbaum
Randolph Braham
Richard Breitman
Lucy Dawidowicz
Alexander Donat
Gerald Fleming
Martin Gilbert
Daniel J. Goldhagen
Richard G. Green
Alex Grobman
Israel Gutman
Raul Hilberg
Serge Klarsfeld
Shmuel Krakowski
Claude Lanzmann
Walter Laqueur
Deborah Lipstadt
Arno J. Mayer
Fritjof Meyer
Peter Novick
Robert van Pelt
Léon Poliakov
Gerald Reitlinger
Robert Rozett
Jules Schelvis
Julius H. Schoeps
Shmuel Spector
Pierre Vidal-Naquet
Georges Wellers
Elie Wiesel
Simon Wiesenthal
Efraim Zuroff

One may add to this most of the 208 contributors to Gutman's 1990 *Encyclopedia of the Holocaust*, many of whom have not been listed here, to round off this image.

An important part of propaganda is also the suppression of any dissident voice. While governments ultimately pass censorship laws, it is primarily Jewish pressure groups who have been pushing hardest for the censorship and punishment of all those who disagree with the orthodox Holocaust narrative.

Protectorate → **Czechia**
Prussian blue → **Iron Blue**

PUCHAŁA, LUCJAN

Lucjan Puchała was a Polish railway worker at Małkinia Station near Treblinka until June 1942, and then at the construction of the track from Treblinka Station to the sand pit near the Treblinka I Labor Camp. Necessarily from pure hearsay, he reported, among other things:

– There were 8 brick-and-cement gas chambers for 700 victims per chamber, hence together 3,200 victims. The orthodoxy insists, however, that there were initially only three chambers in a wooden building, with ten more in a brick-and-cement building added later. According to German court decisions, the room size was allegedly just 16 m² for the old and 32 m² for the new chambers. Squeezing 700 people into each would have resulted in an impossible packing density of either 44 or 22 people per square meter.

– Mass graves measuring "several dozen meters in length," 15 m deep and 10 m wide, were dug with excavators. That is three times as deep as most other claims, and refuted by archeological research, as there is no spot in the camp area showing soil disturbances going that deep.

– He claims to have observed from the gravel pit near the labor camp Treblinka I, several miles away, with forests in between and no hills anywhere, what was going on at the Treblinka II Camp. Why would anyone believe that?

– Once filled, the mass graves were cemented over. That is a unique claim which would have drastically complicated exhuming the graves later. In other words: it didn't happen.

– Cremating corpses began in the fall of 1942, but on a large scale only in winter "after Himmler's visit." This claimed timing is somewhat off the orthodox narrative, as Himmler's visit with subsequent cremations is usually claimed for March 1943. But since there is no trace of any Himmler visit ever happening in this context, all this is mere rumor mongering anyhow.

This is yet another example of why testimonies from hearsay should never be permitted, either in courts of law or in historiography. (For more details, see Mattogno 2021e, pp. 165f.)

PUTZKER, FRITZ

Fritz Putzker was a Jew from Vienna who passed through several camps, among them Auschwitz and Birkenau, where he arrived on 23 February 1943. He was deployed in this camp for nine months as a foreman in the workshops of the Lenz Corporation. Probably in 1945, he wrote a report, in which we read, among other things, that for some inscrutable reasons he managed to be present during homicidal gassings in all the crematorium types of Birkenau. Interjecting polemics into his account such as "Oh you blood hounds!", he claimed the following, among other things:

– Between 5-6 million people were killed in Birkenau from 1942 until its final evacuation. And this does not even cover the camp's entire history.

– The gas murder, allegedly carried out at 40 to 60 degrees Celsius(!), lasted 3 minutes, which is im-

possibly fast.
- In the two smaller crematoria, the murder lasted 6 to 8 minutes. This is still too short a time for a facility with no equipment to evaporate and dissipate the poison.
- An SS man "kept on jumping on the body of pregnant women until the birth literally protruded."
- For Putzker, Bunker V was not a makeshift gassing facility just outside the Birkenau Camp (usually called Bunker 2), but merely a funeral pyre.

Putzker's text is accompanied by two drawings of the two types of crematoria, which assign a maximum gas-chamber capacity of 2,000 victims to the larger of both facilities (which would result in a packing density of some 9.5 people/m², which is rather unrealistic). Neither of these drawings have the slightest resemblance with reality, highlighting the purely imaginary nature of his testimony. This is also confirmed by the cremation capacity he claims on those drawings: 3 to 4 bodies per muffle, and a total daily capacity per crematorium of 5,000 to 8,000 bodies, whereas the real theoretical maximum capacity stood at 300 bodies for the larger (II and III) and 160 bodies for the smaller crematoria (IV and V).

(For more details, see Mattogno 2021, pp. 363-366, 487f.)

pyres → Open-Air Incinerations

Q

QUAKERNACK, WALTER

Walter Quakernack (9 July 1907 – 11 Oct. 1946), SS *Oberscharführer*, was a mid-level employee at the Political Department of the Auschwitz Camp. He was mentioned by several witnesses, all of whom lack any credibility. Stanisław Jankowski constructed a fantastic tale involving Quakernack and another SS man being seduced by a Jewess doing a strip-tease in the undressing room, upon which she grabbed the other SS man's pistol and shot him – but missed Quakernack. Henryk Tauber mentioned him a few times as a member of the Political Department overseeing the Crematoria, and Tauber has him kill a fellow crematorium worker. In his 1979 book, Filip Müller plagiarized Jankowski's Holo-porn scene, and turned Quakernack into one of the main villains of Auschwitz involved in gassings and many other atrocities. With witnesses like this, Quakernack was sentenced to death in Belsen by a British kangaroo court, and subsequently executed.

Walter Quakernack

(For details, see the entries on the witnesses mentioned, and the index entries for Quakernack in Mattogno 2022e&d.)

R

RABINOWICZ, JAKUB

Jakub Rabinowicz was a Treblinka inmate who managed to escape from the camp probably in early September 1942. Later that month, his testimony was recorded by the Jewish underground movement of the Warsaw Ghetto. The extant fragment of it does not contain any reference to extermination facilities or killing methods, but it does mention a diesel engine used to create electricity for the camp. Other surviving documents from the ghetto make reference to Rabinowicz's testimony. One of them states that mass murder at Treblinka was carried out with steam, while another claims "gas, steam, electricity" as the murder methods. In other words, either Rabinowicz didn't know, or those referring to his statements didn't report it properly. (For more details, see Mattogno 2021e, pp. 121f.)

radio intercepts → **British Radio Intercepts**

RAJCHMAN, CHIL

Chil Rajchman

Chil Rajchman (aka Henryk or Ye(c)hiel Reichman(n), 14 June 1914 – 7 May 2004) was a Polish Jew who was deported to the Treblinka Camp on 10 October 1942, from which he escaped after an inmate uprising on 2 August 1943. Still during the war, he presumably wrote down his experiences in Yiddish, which were then rewritten by a poet named Nachum Bomze. His version is the only one that survived and was later translated and published in various languages (English see Rajchman 2011). Rajchman was also interrogated by a Polish investigative commission on 12 October 1945, and he testified in U.S. proceedings leading to the extradition of John Demjanjuk, as well as during the Demjanjuk show trial itself. Finally, the United States Holocaust Memorial Museum conducted an interview with him in December 1988.

Here are some of the more peculiar claims by Rajchman:

- First, the air was sucked out of the gas chambers through thick pipes, then gas coming from an unspecified engine flowed into the chambers through showerheads. Once the "Germans conducted an experiment" by only creating a vacuum, but not adding any gas. After 48 hours, some victims were still alive. However, creating a vacuum in a brick-and-mortar building is technically impossible (the external pressure would crush the walls), hence most certainly was not done. It was also useless, since a hermetically sealed room packed tightly with people has sufficient oxygen only for a few hours at best. After 48 hours, no one could have been alive.
- In the smaller gas chambers (three according to his Polish interview), victims simply looked like they had fallen asleep peacefully. Yet being gassed with hot, stinking, smoking exhaust gasses would have allowed no one to sleep peacefully.
- In the larger gas chambers – described in his Polish interview as ten rooms each measuring 6 m × 6 m – the victims' faces had turned completely black, while "their bellies were bloated and colored blue." This is toxicological nonsense. While hot exhaust gases can lead to burns, these color the skin red, not black or blue. Carbon monoxide, the most-lethal ingredient in engine-exhaust gases, results in pink, even cherry-red discolorations. This shows that Rajchman (and/or Bomze) had never seen victims of engine-exhaust gassings.
- The mass graves were some ten meters deep, which surely is an exaggeration, considering the difficulties that would have been associated with such a depth, not least with intruding groundwater.
- The total surface area covered by the graves he claimed would have been larger than the area of the camp where he claimed these graves were located.
- The mass graves allegedly contained some 1.5 million corpses – twice as many bodies as Jews were ever deported to that camp.
- He claimed that 10,000 (or 15,000) people were killed at Treblinka daily from his arrival until mid-December of 1942. Hence, during just two

months of his stay in the camp, some 600,000 to 900,000 people were killed, although documents show that only some 300,000 were deported there during that time.

– Starting in January 1943 (although the orthodoxy insists on March), exhumed corpses were put on a grate made of railway tracks 30 m long and 1.5 m wide and a half (or one and a half) meters off the ground. 2,500 bodies were placed on it, hence 83 per running meter. This is 20 times more than is possible as demonstrated by practical experiences during real-world open-air incinerations (4 to 5 corpses per running meter when using fresh wood as fuel). If placing three corpses per running meter in one layer of, say, 20 cm height, the pile would be (83/m÷3/m×0.2m=) five and a half meters high, not 2 meters, as Rajchman claimed. A pile one and a half meters wide and five and a half meters high would surely be unstable and topple over, particularly if set aflame and then inevitably burning unevenly.

– Fuel was added underneath the grate only after piling up the corpses! This is preposterous nonsense. In fact, in his Polish interview, he claimed that the corpses piled up on raised rails were simply lit from below.

– As fuel, they used "dry branches" in order to set the corpses on fire. Once ablaze, they evidently burned by themselves, yet the myth of self-immolating bodies is just that. Moreover, there would not have been enough space underneath the grates to add the actual firewood needed to burn the claimed load. In fact, only a few percent of the actual wood required could have been placed there.

– Since the Germans allegedly planned in 1943 (after Stalingrad!) to conquer Britain, they initiated plans to build a special incinerator in Treblinka for the British Jews. Such absurdity requires no comment.

– Last and best, Rajchman told this tale:

"At one time we put up a roast beside a large grave, into which more than 250,000 corpses had been thrown. The roast was loaded as usual and lit in the evening. There was a strong wind, and the fire burned so intensely, that it spread to the large opened grave. The blood from a quarter of a million human beings went up in flames and burned until the evening of the following day.

All of the leading camp staff came to take a look at this wonder. They marveled at this fantastic fire. The blood rose to the surface of the ground and ignited like fuel."

Is it necessary to point out that blood, which is 90% water, is in no way comparable to gasoline?

(For more details, see Kues 2010; Mattogno 2021e, pp. 157f.)

RAJGRODZKI, JERZY

Jerzy Rajgrodzki was deported to the Treblinka Camp on 12 September 1942, and escaped during the prisoner uprising on 2 August 1943. On an unspecified date, he wrote a lengthy report on his stay at the camp, which was published in 1958. He described the alleged Treblinka gas chambers, presumably operated with engine-exhaust gas, similar, but less detailed, to the way Jankiel Wiernik had described them in his 1944 booklet. Wiernik's booklet, whose tale was plagiarized by various authors and witnesses (such as Abraham Goldfarb), may also have been known to Rajgrodzki. He added some unique features to it which are not part of the common lore accepted by the orthodoxy, such as peepholes in the gas-chamber doors, an execution time of one hour, showers at the ceiling, and the conversion of Treblinka's first three-gas-chamber execution building into a workshop.

He claimed to have worked at removing corpses from the gas chambers a few times. He asserted that the victims lay dead in the chamber piled up to a height of five feet. Let's assume that on average seven people can lie on a surface of four square meters (six side-by-side, and one crosswise). The height of a human body lying down is on average at most 20 cm. To reach a stacking height of five feet (ca. 160 cm), this requires roughly eight layers. Hence, 56 people would be lying stacked up in this cubicle on four square meters. Standing up, this would result in a packing density of 14 people per square meter, which is not realistic, to say the least.

Rajgrodzki moreover told the tale of a young Jew helping to operate the gas-chamber engine. However, it is rather unlikely that a Jew was an accomplice of the mass murder of his fellow Jews. Supposedly, this Jew was later married – evidently to a deported Jewess while in the camp, for else, how would he know? And why would he mention it, if it hadn't been a memorable camp event? This may be an echo of the tall tale told by SS judge Konrad Morgen in his testimony at the Nuremberg International Military Tribunal of Jews won over by the SS to exterminate their brethren, and of a lavish Jewish wedding inside one of the *Aktion Reinhardt* Camps (of which Treblinka was one).

(For more details, see Mattogno 2021e, pp. 191f.)

RAJSKO

Rajsko is a village some 5 miles southwest of the city of Auschwitz. Most of its population was deported/resettled in 1941/42. The Hygiene Institute of the Waffen SS established its "Sanitary and Bacteriological Testing Station Southeast" there in 1943 ("*Hygienisch-bakteriologische Untersuchungsstelle Südost der Waffen-SS*"). It served primarily to conduct experiments on a number of vaccines in development, among them some against typhus. Furthermore, this institute analyzed thousands of blood and stool samples of Auschwitz inmates who had contracted typhus and had been admitted to the camp hospital. They were allowed to leave the typhus ward only once the typhus bacterium had been demonstrably cleared from their system. The files from this testing station have survived. These are altogether 151 volumes, which contain some 110,000 laboratory tests, among other things. These documents, now stored in the archives of the Auschwitz Museum, demonstrate that thousands of Auschwitz inmates were treated for the disease over extended periods of time and with no efforts spared. This is a resounding refutation of the myth that seriously sick inmates, unfit for labor, were killed as useless eaters. (For more information, see Rudolf 2019, pp. 152-154, 308.)

RAJZMAN, SAMUEL (SHMUEL)

Samuel Rajzman

Samuel Rajzman (1904 – 1979) was a Polish accountant who was deported from the Warsaw Ghetto to the Treblinka Camp in late September 1942 – or maybe in August of that year, according to his testimony at the Nuremberg International Military Tribunal (*IMT*, Vol. 8, p. 325). He managed to escape from that camp on 2 August 1943 during the inmate uprising, hence he was in the camp for over ten months.

A year later, Rajzman wrote a 16-page report about the camp, and in September 1944 he was questioned by a Soviet, and on 9 October 1945 by a Polish investigator. He testified briefly during the IMT in late February 1946. Also in 1946, he composed another essay, and he furthermore gave a recorded interview in 1950, neither of which contain any particulars about the claimed murder facilities, other than that they were gas chambers. He did not appear during any of the later trials where the Treblinka Camp was the focus of attention.

Here are some of the more peculiar claims made by Rajzman. As he himself asserted at one point, his knowledge is to a large degree based on stories heard from a man who himself was reporting things from hearsay. Evidently, ten months presence in the camp offered him no opportunity to discover anything firsthand. Hence, we are dealing here with a typical Chinese-whisper chain of rumors:

– Initially, victims were killed by pumping out the air from the chambers. Creating a vacuum in a brick-and-mortar building is technically impossible (the external pressure would crush the walls), hence this most certainly was not done.
– Later, the victims were killed with chlorine gas and Zyklon B. Engine-exhaust gases, the orthodoxy's current paradigm, were never mentioned by Rajzman.
– People were at times burned alive on pyres, so that "desperate lamentation sounded from the fire." Cremation had already begun when he arrived (August/September 1942), although the orthodoxy insists on March 1943 as the starting point of open-air incinerations.
– During his Polish interrogation, he asserted that, during the year he was at the camp, 25,000 Jewish slave-laborers died or were murdered, which is an absurdly high figure, meaning that the entire staff of some 800 slave laborers had to be replaced on average almost every ten days.
– Rajzman asserted that Heinrich Himmler visited the Treblinka Camp in February 1943 for an inspection. However, there is no evidence suggesting that Himmler ever visited Treblinka.
– At the Nuremberg Trial, he asserted that on average "ten to twelve thousand persons daily" were killed at Treblinka, which would amount to 3.65 million within the year of his presence. However, in his 1946 essay (and similar in his Soviet interview) he increased that to 25,000 persons per day – or an astonishing 9.1 million in a year! The protocol of his Soviet interview has a detailed list of victims that he claims the camp resistance recorded. Hence, this should be first-hand material,

not hearsay rumor-mongering. However, these numbers result in a total death toll of 2,775,000. Compare all this to today's orthodox figure of some 800,000 victims.
- According to his IMT testimony, cutting the women's hair before gassing lasted only five minutes. That would have worked only if there had been as many barbers with shears as there were women to be processed.
- During the IMT, he also claimed that the Germans planned to increase the number of gas chambers at Treblinka to 25 in order to exterminate other nationalities.

Rajzman's various testimonies are characterized by their lack of details, which is prudent considering that he was reporting only from double-hearsay. Wherever he conveys details, he is pitifully wrong, even if we take the orthodox narrative as the yardstick.

(For details, see Mattogno/Graf 2023, pp. 67-69, 96, 141; Mattogno 2021e, pp. 139-141, 151-154.)

RASCHER, SIEGMUND

Siegmund Rascher (12 Feb. 1909 – 26 April 1945), a *Luftwaffe* Major, was a physician who conducted often-lethal freezing and low-pressure experiments on concentration-camp inmates at the Dachau Camp. In 1944, he and his wife were arrested for kidnapping babies while falsely claiming them to be Mrs. Rascher's natural-born children. For this, both were executed shortly before the end of the war without ever facing formal charges, let alone a trial.

Siegmund Rascher

Rascher's relevance for the Holocaust is a 1942 letter he wrote to Himmler requesting to be allowed to test newly developed war gases in facilities at that time under construction inside the Dachau Camp. The orthodoxy claims that this is a smoking gun pointing at plans to build a homicidal gas chamber at the Dachau Camp. However, the only functional gas chambers in existence at Dachau are four Zyklon-B disinfestation chambers used for fumigating clothes.

Although there are plenty of documents proving Rascher's freezing and low-pressure experiments, no documents on any gas experiments exist. Only one witness has ever claimed to have experienced an experimental gassing: the Czech physician and former Dachau inmate Franz Blaha. However, his credibility is questionable, as an analysis of his testimony reveals.

(For more details, see the entries on Dachau and Franz Blaha, as well as Mattogno 2022a, pp. 14-20.)

RASSINIER, PAUL

Paul Rassinier (18 March 1906 – 28 July 1967) was a French high-school teacher. Born in Bermont, France, Rassinier joined the French Communist Party in 1922, at the age of only 16. In the course of time, however, Rassinier turned to pacifism and opposed the nationalization of private property advocated by the

Paul Rassinier

Communists, which is why he was expelled from the party in 1932. He joined the Federation of the Socialist Party two years later. In this party, too, he advocated his pacifism, which tended, among other things, to seek an understanding with Germany rather than a warlike conflict. From 1933 to 1943, Rassinier taught history at the Collège d'enseignement général in Belfort.

Immediately after the occupation of France by German troops, he helped establish the non-Communist resistance group Libération-Nord, where he tried to implement his policy of renouncing violence. In this context, he published an underground newspaper titled *La Quatrième Republique* (*The Fourth Republic*).

In 1940, due to anti-Jewish measures by the occupying regime, Rassinier began to provide false papers to Jews who wanted to flee France so that they could travel to Switzerland without problems. As a result of this activity, he was arrested by the Gestapo on 30 November 1943, and deported to the Buchenwald Camp. From April 1944 until his liberation by U.S. troops in April 1945, he had to help build German "retaliatory weapons" (*V-Waffen*) in the Dora subcamp under terrible conditions.

After the war, Rassinier, who was severely disabled due to his time in German concentration camps, joined the French Socialist Party and became involved in the leadership of the Belfort party district. As replacement of a deceased member of parliament, he occupied a seat in the French parliament in the fall of 1946, but lost it in the elections held shortly thereafter. Because of his resistance activities during the war, he received the French Gold Medal of Recognition and the highest award of the resistance movement, the High Red Rosette.

Because of his principle of nonviolence, he opposed the violent "purges" of former collaborators ("*épurations*") carried out in postwar France, which made him unpopular among many opinion leaders in France, especially the spiteful Communists.

The contrast between what he himself had experienced in the Buchenwald and Dora Camps, and what some other survivors published about these camps, made him a critic of survivor literature. On the one hand, he criticized that this literature concealed the fact that prisoners who collaborated with the SS ran the internal operations of the concentration camps, and that many of these prisoner functionaries, and not the SS, had been responsible for certain abuses and atrocities in the camps. On the other hand, Rassinier denounced as false claims that mass exterminations by means of gas chambers had taken place at Buchenwald Camp, since, in his experience, there was no homicidal gas chamber at the Buchenwald Camp – a fact confirmed today by all historians.

His more autobiographical approach, which characterizes his first book *Ulysses's Lie* (a merger of his two French books *Passage de la ligne* and *Le mensonge d'Ulysse*) as well as *What Now, Ulysses?* was complemented by his later works, which expanded his personal experiences to a more holistic-historical approach, in which the phenomenon of German concentration camps is examined in a broader, more general context. However, these works were written by a man with very limited means and no access to archival resources, and at a time when historical knowledge about these issues was just starting to evolve. Therefore, these non-autobiographical books are outdated today and should themselves be seen as objects of history rather than history books.

Today, Rassinier is rightly considered the "Father of Holocaust Revisionism," as he was the first to critically scrutinize the mainstream narrative, systematically apply the technique of source criticism to witness accounts on the Holocaust, and express his disbelief in a German extermination policy in general, and the existence of homicidal gas chambers in particular. His book on his personal experiences in two German camps – *Ulysses's Lie* – remains an important standard to assess the credibility of other witness accounts in this matter.

Works by Rassinier
- *Passage de la ligne*, La Librairie française, Paris, 1948.
- *Le mensonge d'Ulysse*, La Librairie française, Paris, 1950.
- *Ulysse trahi par les siens*, La Librairie Française, Paris, 1961.
- *Le véritable procés Eichmann ou les vainquers incorrigibles*, Les Sept Couleurs, Paris, 1962.
- *Le drame des juifs européens*, Paris, 1964.
- *L'opération vicaire*, La Table Ronde, Paris, 1965.
- *The Real Eichmann Trial or The Incorrigible Victors*, Institute for Historical Review, Torrance, 1976.
- *Debunking the Genocide Myth*, The Noontide Press, Torrance, CA, 1978.
- *The Holocaust Story and the Lies of Ulysses*, 2nd ed., Institute for Historical Review, New Port Beach, 1990.
- *Ulysses's Lie*, Castle Hill Publishers, Dallastown, PA, 2022.

RAUFF, WALTER

Walter Rauff

Walter Rauff (19 June 1906 – 14 May 1984), SS *Standartenführer*, headed Office II D of Germany's Reich Security Main Office (*Reichssicherheitshauptamt*) since November 1940, which was dealing with technical matters. Subdepartment 3a of this office dealt with the Security Police's motor pool and was headed by Friedrich Pradel. This office supposedly was in charge of supplying the *Einsatzgruppen* behind the Eastern front with so-called gas vans.

Toward the end of the war, Rauff ended up in U.S. captivity in Italy, where he was asked to confirm the authenticity of the Becker Document allegedly sent to him in May 1942. He complied by writing a handwritten note across a copy of it, and by signing a brief English affidavit asserting the same, and specifying that he knew nothing more about these vehicles, neither their number nor how many people were killed in them (*IMT*, Vol. 30, pp. 256-258). He even mislabeled the manufacturer of the vehicles' chassis (Saurer, Vienna) as the manufacturer of the gas vans located in Berlin. However, it was the Berlin Gaubschat Company that manufactured the cargo boxes allegedly misused for executing people.

During later interviews while in safe Chilean exile in the 1970s – Pinochet refused to extradite him – he revealed that he learned only after the war about a *Führer* order to exterminate the Jews:

> "*While I got to know after the war that there was a so-called Führer order, the content of which was the liquidation of the Jews for racial reasons, I cannot remember that during the war it had ever been said that there was such an order. Of the existence of such an order, I should have been informed for my activity in Tunis, because there were many Jews there who even worked for us voluntarily without anything happening to them.*"

When asked more specifically about the "gas vans," Rauff repeated that he could not recall how and when all this came about. He asserted that at some point he saw two of these gas vans standing around, and he "somehow" even "learned that the gas vans were used for the execution of sentences and for the killing of Jews." Hence, the person centrally responsible for the deployment of these gas vans – or so the orthodox narrative goes – could remember almost nothing about the gas vans, and he only accidentally learned that they were used for killing Jews, maybe only after the war.

Since Rauff was safe in Chile and had nothing to fear, he agreed to this interview with a German prosecutor. Rauff was therefore probably sincere with his answers. This demonstrates that he could not distinguish anymore between what he knew during the war and what he learned later. However, if he had indeed been in charge of deploying these vans following extermination orders from higher up, then he almost certainly would have remembered.

(For more details, see Alvarez 2023, esp. pp. 134-138.)

RAVENSBRÜCK

In May of 1939, a concentration camp for women was established near the town of Ravensbrück, some 90 km north of Berlin. It entered the stage of Holocaust historiography only after the war, when former inmates claimed during several show trials staged by the British that homicidal gas chambers had been built in that camp in February 1945 on Himmler's order, so that sick inmates could be killed. Subsequently, either some 1,500, 2,300+ or up to 3,000 inmates were killed that way, depending on which witness one is inclined to believe (if any).

There is no documental or material trace for such a facility. Its existence was "confirmed" by former members of the camp staff only after they had been softened up by the British with their customary torture.

The absurdly late construction of this alleged gas chamber contains the refutation of this false claim:
- In late 1944, the Bergen-Belsen Camp was turned into a collection camp for sick detainees from other camps, meaning there was no order to kill sick inmates.
- By late 1944, Himmler negotiated with the Swedish Red Cross and the World Jewish Congress behind Hitler's back about saving camp inmates. The negotiations resulted in the *liberation* of 7,800 female detainees from Ravensbrück before the end of the war. Claims that Himmler at once gave orders to kill all sick Ravensbrück inmates are preposterous.
- In Auschwitz, the crematoria were being destroyed in fall of 1944 – presumably to erase traces, but in fact to prevent the Soviets from abusing them for their propaganda. Hence, new gas chambers would *never* have been built right under the nose of the invading Allied armies as late as February 1945!
- When the Germans evacuated the Auschwitz Camp in January 1945 – which was supposedly an extermination camp – they did *not* kill sick inmates unable to walk, but simply left them behind.
- When the Auschwitz Camp was evacuated, almost 5,000 female inmates, plus some Auschwitz staff members, were transferred to Ravensbrück, bringing with them rumors and propaganda tales of gas chambers. It is hardly a coincidence that this is also the time when gas-chamber rumors started to circulate at Ravensbrück.
- In February 1945, Germany's infrastructure had totally collapsed. Almost nothing could be obtained for the various camps – fuel, water, food, medicine – and most certainly not construction material, machinery, and experts skilled at building a homicidal gas chamber.
- At that point, every German knew that the war was lost and coming to an end soon. In such a sit-

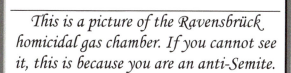

This is a picture of the Ravensbrück homicidal gas chamber. If you cannot see it, this is because you are an anti-Semite.

uation, no one would have even tried building a mass-atrocity facility that could be used only briefly – the claim is for just three weeks.
- The claimed victims – 1,500 or 2,500, depending on the witness – disappeared tracelessly, because they were all cremated. However, there wouldn't have been any fuel to cremate them, because in February/March/April of 1945 no one anywhere in Germany had any fuel. The country was completely shut down.
- Orthodox historians claim that Himmler ordered in the fall of 1944 that all exterminations must stop. (See the entry on Kurt Becher.) How does that fit with a new order to start such activities again in February 1945?

Few of the testimonies describing the alleged gas chamber(s) or the gassing procedure contain any details that would make it possible to critique them. Everything is superficial, and when it comes to former inmates, their claims are evidently based on hearsay and rumor. Former inmate Irma Trksakova, for instance, claimed she had learned from an inmate who allegedly "was able to escape" from the gas chamber [sic]:

> "It was a rather small room, whose cracks were plugged with blankets [sic!]. The SS men threw gas bombs [sic!] into the chamber; some women were only stunned; they were then cremated in this condition [sic!]."

All claims about homicidal gas chambers, no matter how contradictory, senseless, and cliché-laden, are taken at face value and rubber-stamped as "true" by orthodox historians regarding their core content: that gas chamber(s) existed.

In the case of gas-chamber claims at Flossenbürg, Buchenwald and Bergen-Belsen, orthodox historians agree that those are wrong; that no homicidal gas chambers existed there. Yet the only difference between those cases and Ravensbrück is that for Ravensbrück we have a slightly larger quantity of claims. But the sheer number of claims, whether small or large, does not mean that impossible things can happen.

The British interrogators not only falsified the historical record with regard to the alleged homicidal gas chamber, but they also exaggerated the camps death toll, as was done with almost all German camps. While orthodox historians today claim that 28,000 inmates died in Ravensbrück, the British set that number at 92,000.

(For more details, see Mattogno 2016e, pp. 180-197.)

RAZGONAYEV, MIKHAIL

Mikhail Razgonayev was a Ukrainian auxiliary who served at the Sobibór Camp as a guard from beginning to end. After the war, he was arrested for this by the Soviets. During his interrogation on 20-21 September 1948, Razgonayev described the gas-chamber facility as a stone/concrete building with a corridor on one side and four gas chambers along the other. Each chamber had two hermetically closing doors, one from the corridor, the other to the outside to extract the bodies. An engine just outside the building supplied exhaust gas, which was piped into the chambers through showerheads. Before people entered the chambers, "everyone would be given a piece of soap." The latter would have happened only if those rooms really were shower rooms.

Of all early witness statements, Razgonayev's description is the only one that comes very close to what the orthodoxy would later ordain to be the truth. However, they posit that, until late 1942, the Sobibór Camp had only a building with three gas chambers in a row, which was then enlarged with another set of three chambers, making it six. Razgonayev mentioned nothing about an enlargement of the gassing facility. Furthermore, the building ruins found at the camp, which the orthodoxy claims to have been the gas-chamber facility, had eight rooms, not three, four or six.

(See the entry on Sobibór for more details, as well as Graf/Kues/Mattogno 2020, pp. 101f., 283.)

RED CROSS

Since the Geneva Convention of 1929 only covered prisoners of war, the Third-Reich authorities consistently denied the International Committee of the Red Cross (ICRC) access to its concentration camps. This changed only toward the end of the war, when the German authorities realized that they could no longer maintain the camps due to Germany's collapsing infrastructure. At that point, they allowed representatives of the Red Cross to enter the camps in order to organize and supervise relief efforts for the inmates, and prepare handing over the camps to Allied forces.

ICRC representatives managed to get access to the Auschwitz Main Camp in 1944, but only in order to contact British PoWs held in that camp. They were not allowed to enter the Birkenau Camp, where exterminations are said to have been going on at that time. Evidently, they were unable to get confirmation for extermination claims.

The ICRC was also allowed to inspect the Theresienstadt Ghetto, and its report about that Jewish town was rather favorable. This causes ire and critique to this day from the orthodoxy, claiming that the ICRC got bamboozled by an SS propaganda show.

In the ICRC's detailed report about the fate of the Jews in Hungary after the German occupation of that country in early 1944, they mysteriously omitted any mention of the mass deportations taking place between May and July of that year. This has caused some to doubt the veracity of these events, although there is plenty of original wartime documentation substantiating that it happened.

After the war, the ICRC published a massive three-volume report on its activities during the war, with a main focus on victims of German persecutions. As has to be expected for a report written during an atmosphere of general postwar anti-German hysteria, the report contains general remarks about an alleged German policy of extermination toward the Jews. However, none of the specific activities the ICRC engaged in revealed any specifics about an ongoing extermination program. The 1,600 pages of the ICRC's report never hint at any homicidal gas chambers.

In their report on the liberation of the Dachau Camp by U.S. troops, the ICRC omitted the fact that the Americans executed all German guards and camp officials. That German victims of mass atrocities didn't seem to matter much to the ICRC can also be gleaned from the fact that no ICRC report ever addressed the mass atrocities committed against German civilians in Eastern and Central Europe at war's end or afterwards. Some twelve million Germans were ethnically cleansed from these regions, and more than two million of them died in the process. Yet the ICRC never addressed this with a single word. The same is true with all the looting, mass arrests, mass rape, mass deportations, continued trade blockade, intentional starvation policies and industrial plundering going on after the war until 1948. The ICRC turned a blind eye to it all.

The ICRC got involved, however, in tracing the victims of National-Socialist persecution by managing the International Tracing Service set up in central West Germany after the war's end – because the Allied victorious powers set it up that way. There was no interest in tracing the millions upon millions of German victims of Allied bombings, ethnic cleansing, automatic arrests, mass deportations, postwar starvation policies etc.

The ICRC claims to have been a neutral organization. However, their consistent ignoring of atrocities committed against German civilians proves this to be a myth. On the other hand, their consistent failure to find confirmation for any extermination policy carried out in German wartime camps reveals another myth.

(For more details, see the index entries on "Red Cross" in Butz 2015; Kollerstrom 2023, pp. 223f.)

REDER, RUDOLF

Rudolf Reder (aka Roman Robak, 4 April 1881 – 6 Oct. 1977) was a Polish Jew from Lviv who was deported to the Belzec Camp in July or August 1942 at age 61 – which should have been his death sentence. But he miraculously was selected to live and work there as a stove mechanic for four months

Rudolf Reder

before managing to escape. Currently, nine texts by Reder are known in which he describes what he claims to have experienced at that camp (depositions, interviews, testimonies and one booklet). Reder is considered the only (self-proclaimed) former inmate of the Belzec Camp who made significant statements about this camp. Apart from the highly unreliable postwar statements by the former SS man Kurt Gerstein and later trial statements of defendants and SS witnesses during the 1965 West-German Belzec show trial (including Wilhelm Pfannenstiel), Reder's texts are the only sources of information stemming from the immediate postwar period that historians have on events allegedly unfolding at Belzec.

A critical analysis of Reder's nine texts shows that they contradict one another in many respects. The following list is limited to the most strident examples of contradictions and to the more peculiar of Reder's claims:

- Reder claimed that the trains he arrived in had 50 cars, which would make it some 500 to 600 meters long. He claimed that the entire train drove into the camp on a spur that ended at the camp's center. However, the spur ran along the camp's western fence and was only some 260 meters long, allowing only half of his train to enter it.
- He claimed that the camp covered an area of one square kilometer, and that the forest around it had been cut down to a radius of three kilometers, when in fact the camp wasn't even a tenth of this size, and air photos show that the forest around it had not been cut down. Only some of it nearby had been thinned out.
- Although Reder claimed that, as a stove repair man, he could move freely around the entire camp and saw everything, he never mentioned any of the camp's essential facilities, such as the inmate infirmary, latrines, washrooms and showers for guards and inmates, the motor pool with the garage, and the Diesel engine driving the camp's electricity generator (although he mentions the use of electricity).
- Reder's various descriptions of the camp's layout and the way deportees were "processed" are highly contradictory, and they do not agree with what the orthodoxy claims about it. But in Reder's later statements, his description began to approach the official narrative, clearly indicating where his knowledge came from.
- Reder had Jews from all over Europe arrive at Belzec, although only Jews from Poland were deported there.
- He claimed that, on average, 10,000 to 20,000 deportees arrived daily during his four-months stay, which would result in 1.2 to 2.4 million deportees, although only just over 400,000 Jews were ever deported to Belzec in total.
- 1.2 to 2.4 million wasn't enough, though, because he estimated the total number of Jews killed during his 4-months stay at 3 million.
- Because the victims were packed so tightly into the gas chambers, "the corpses were standing upright" after the execution, which is physically impossible.
- Reder claimed that he was once asked to service the gasoline engine driving the killing mechanism. He describes it well: the exhaust gasses were vented directly to the outside and were *not* used to kill. There was never any odor when the chambers were opened. The engine drove a complex system of drive wheels and compressors, connected to the chambers with glass tubes. Only during the investigations for the German Belzec show trial did he adjust his tale to fit the orthodox narrative.
- There were allegedly 30 mass graves measuring 100 m × 25 m × 15 m. Assuming sloping walls, this would amount to some 20,000 m³ for each, and 600,000 m³ for all. These graves were either dug manually or by a machine, or manually with a machine carrying away the dug-out sand. But archeological research has demonstrated that in total only some 20,000 m³ of soil were ever disturbed in the camp area or its immediate vicinity, some of it by wild diggings of locals after the war.
- Reder claimed that "thick blood burst out of the pits and flooded the whole surface," as if the blood of dead victims could explode out of their bodies and eject out of graves like geysers.
- To boost the importance of his narrative, Reder claimed that Himmler visited the camp either in October or November 1942, although there is no trace of Himmler ever having set foot in that camp.
- In a camp where the old, sick and weak were allegedly constantly killed, the 61-year-old Reder, who toward the end was emaciated, weak and full of wounds, miraculously survived for four months.
- Reder told his story of how he managed to escape six times, each time with drastic contradictions to the others.

Reder's testimonies also have blatant contradictions to Kurt Gerstein's delusional musings. Historian Michael Tregenza, the orthodoxy's expert on Belzec, therefore concluded that both testimonies are unreli-

able.
(For more on this, see Mattogno 2021b, esp. pp. 7-88, 147-170.)

Reichman(n), Ye(c)hiel or Henryk → Rajchman, Chil

REICHSSICHERHEITSHAUPTAMT

The Third Reich's term *Reichssicherheitshauptamt* (RSHA) translates to Imperial National or simply Homeland Security Main Office. It was established in 1939 and merged Germany's police forces (Gestapo and ordinary police) and the SS intelligence-gathering service *Sicherheitsdienst* (Security Service) into one governmental body. This office was directly subordinate to the Chief of the German Police Heinrich Himmler. The head of this office was Reinhardt Heydrich until his assassination on 4 June 1942. The post remained unoccupied, hence headed directly by Himmler himself, until 30 January 1943, when Ernst Kaltenbrunner took over and kept this position until the end of the war.

RELIGION, HOLOCAUST AS

For many centuries, it was dangerous to state in public that God does not exist, that Jesus is not God's son, that he was not born of a virgin, and that he did not rise to the heavens. Today, saying these things is trivial. However, a similar reaction to what was earned for these statements back then is received today when stating in public that there were no gas chambers, far less than six million Jews died, and that there was no plan to exterminate them,

The old-time religions are no longer a taboo. They have been replaced by a new religion that is kept sacred by a large majority – if not consciously, then at least as a well-trained reflex due to massive societal conditioning. This new religion has all the hallmarks of a fully developed religion, except for one feature: It has no God. It knows no absolute good, no absolute love. It knows only evil:

– Monotheism = Thou shalt not abhor any other genocide as much as, and next to, the Jewish. The Holocaust is unique.
– Devil Incarnate = Adolf Hitler.
– Witches, sorcerers, wizards and warlocks = the evil Nazis.
– Absolute Evil = viral, eliminatory anti-Semitism.
– Golgotha = Auschwitz is the million-fold Jewish Golgotha. The sacrifice of the Christ-god at Calvary has been eclipsed by the suffering of the Jewish people at Auschwitz.
– The Martyrs = Jews who died in the Holocaust.
– The Saints = Holocaust survivors. "Because survivors are now revered as secular saints, one doesn't dare question them. Preposterous statements pass without comment." – Norman Finkelstein (2000, p. 82).
– The Beatified = the Righteous of the Nations, Gentiles who helped Jews survive to become saints.
– Infallibility = Jewish Holocaust witnesses and orthodox scholars always speak the truth, and if they accidentally get it wrong, it was an honest mistake caused by the Nazis having confused them.
– Holy Trinitarian Dogma = the three untouchable tenets of the holy teachings: a plan to exterminate, gas chambers to implement it, and six million Jewish victims as a result.
– Belief in Miracles = belief in the plan to exterminate European Jews despite the complete, total absence of any documental evidence whatsoever; belief in a weapon of mass destruction whose *primary characteristic* is its physical impossibility; and belief in the traceless disappearance of millions of bodies.
– Original Sin = the guilt of what the perpetrators did, and the rest of the world allowed to happen to God's Chosen People.
– Sin = any doubt in the Holy Dogma, or the Infallibility, or the Uniqueness.
– Heresy = those who openly declare their disbelieve, or dare to deny or even refute the Holy Dogma are ethically damned, excluded from society, denied civil rights, economically ruined, and ultimately thrown into jail, if not outright attacked and lynched.
– Redemption = accomplished by the ceaseless flow of money from anyone who can be framed as guilty or insufficiently respectful to Israel and/or Jewish pressure groups.
– Holy Sites = Holocaust crime scenes, such as the gas chambers of Auschwitz, Majdanek, Dachau, Neuengamme, Sachsenhausen; the killing fields of the extermination camps, such as Chełmno, Belzec, Sobibór, Treblinka; or the (imagined) mass graves at Babi Yar.
– Holy Shrines = Holocaust Memorial sites and museums.
– Holy Relics = the shoes, hair, teeth, rings, suitcases left behind by the deportees.

- Holy Warriors = Nazi Hunters, such as Simon Wiesenthal, Fritz Bauer, Gideon Hausner.
- Prophets = Jewish pseudo-intellectuals spreading meaningless and unverifiable nonsense, such as Elie Wiesel, Claude Lanzmann and Gitta Sereny.
- High Priests = those teaching the world what to believe, such as Deborah Lipstadt, Robert Jan van Pelt, Yitzak Arad, Michael Berenbaum, Serge Klarsfeld and Raul Hilberg.
- The One Commandment = this religion does not have *Ten* Commandments, but only one Prime Directive: Thou shalt prevent a future Holocaust by all means necessary.

> "The Holocaust became the new Western religion. Unfortunately, it is the most sinister religion known to man. It is a license to kill, to flatten, to nuke, to wipe, to rape, to loot and to ethnically cleanse. It made vengeance and revenge into a Western value. However, far more disconcerting is the fact that it robs humanity of its heritage, it is there to stop us from looking into our past with dignity. Holocaust religion robs humanity of its humanism." —Gilad Atzmon

RENARD, JEAN-PAUL

Jean-Paul Renard was a French priest who was deported to the Buchenwald Camp in 1942. After the war, a collection of poems by him was published titled *Chaines et lumières* (*Chains and Lights*). In an appendix to his own work, he wrote about his experience at Buchenwald, where we read:

> "I saw going into the showers thousands and thousands of persons over whom poured out, instead of a liquid, asphyxiating gases.
> I saw those who were unfit for work injected in the heart."

When confronted about the false gas-chamber claim by French historian Paul Rassinier in 1947, Renard responded:

> "Right, but that's only a figure of speech... and since those things existed somewhere, it is of no importance."

If that is every witness's attitude, then truth doesn't matter anywhere, because it did or may happen somewhere or at some point...
(See Rassinier 2022, pp. 146f.)

reparations → Compensation

RESETTLEMENT
Resettlement in Documents

National-Socialist Germany wanted its Jews to leave the country. Great efforts were made both to put Jews under all kinds of social, legal and economic pressure, making life miserable for them in Germany, and to give them incentives in case they emigrated. But when the war broke out, there were less and less options to do so.

On 25 November 1939, German officials wrote the first draft of what was later called the "*Generalplan Ost*," which aimed at Germanizing the territories annexed from Poland by resettling Poles living there in the remaining occupied Polish territories, and by resettling the Jews of Germany (including Austria, the Sudetenland, the Protectorate and annexed parts of western Poland) into those territories as well. The plan followed directives from two months earlier by Reinhardt Heydrich, chief of Germany's Department of Homeland Security (*Reichssicherheitshauptamt*). One of them envisioned the creation of a Jewish reservation in eastern Poland, but that never materialized.

In early 1940, German officials proposed to their then-Soviet ally to deport the German and Polish Jews to western Ukraine and/or to the "Autonomous Jewish Region Birobidzhan" in eastern Siberia. The Soviets turned down that request.

On 24 June 1940, Heydrich asked the German minister of foreign affairs to be informed of any ministerial meetings concerning the "final solution of the Jewish question," explaining that Hermann Göring had put him in charge in 1939 to carry out the Jewish emigration, but since the problem had now grown manifold due to the large amount of Polish Jews under German control, it could no longer be solved by emigration. He concluded:

> "Thus, a final solution on a territorial basis will impose itself."

This project of some kind of forced resettlement resulted in the foreign ministry developing the Madagascar Plan after the defeat of France, meaning the resettlement of all Jews under German control to the French colony Madagascar, rather than to Palestine. (See this entry for details.) However, since Britain never lost control of the high seas, and with the United States entering the war in late 1941, the prospects of creating and populating a Jewish colony overseas were eventually recognized as unrealistic.

With hopes for a peace treaty fading in the summer of 1940, plans were devised to concentrate the

Jews in an area around the Polish town of Nisko. This Nisko Plan was massively opposed by Hans Frank, governor of the General Government, which was the official name of occupied Poland. Frank managed to talk Hitler into stopping the deportation of more Jews into the already overburdened General Government.

When the war against the Soviet Union resulted in huge initial territorial gains for Germany in the second half of 1941, new perspectives opened up with the option of deporting and resettling Europe's Jews in the East instead. The first suggestion to that effect was proposed in late August 1941 by an employee at the German embassy in Paris, who suggested "moving the Jews into the eastern territories." A month later, Goebbels noted in his diary, that the Jews in the East "would all be deported to the camps [...] set up by the Bolsheviks," and that he hoped for the Berlin Jews to be moved to the East as well.

On 28 September 1941, Hitler ordered the deportation of the remaining Jews in Germany and the Protectorate, first to the territories annexed from Poland, then "further east next spring."

On 13 October 1941, Hans Frank and Alfred Rosenberg discussed deporting the Jewish population in Poland "into the occupied eastern territories," but shelved the plan for the future.

On 23 October 1941, Himmler stopped all Jewish emigration, effective immediately, and the deportation of western Jews began, with the first batch slated to go to Minsk and Riga.

The new policy of deporting Jews to the east was announced during the infamous Wannsee Conference on 20 January 1942. In its protocol, we read:

"In the meantime, the Reichsführer-SS and Head of the German Police [i.e. Himmler] *has forbidden any further emigration of Jews in view of the dangers posed by emigration in wartime and the looming possibilities in the East.*
III. As a further possible solution, and with the appropriate prior authorization by the Führer, emigration has now been replaced by evacuation to the East. This operation should be regarded only as a provisional option, though in view of the coming final solution of the Jewish question it is already supplying practical experience of vital importance."

Hence, on Hitler's orders, emigration was replaced by evacuation/resettlement/expulsion to the occupied territories in the East, but only as a temporary solution while awaiting a definitive solution of this issue after the war, something Hitler had asserted repeatedly.

The intention of the Third Reich leaders to "solve" the Jewish problem only after the war results also from many other documents, such as the so-called "Brown File" drafted by Rosenberg on 20 June 1941, which was later integrated into the "Green File" of September of 1942. We read there:

"All measures regarding to the Jewish question in the occupied territories in the East must be taken from the point of view that the Jewish question will be solved in a general way for the whole of Europe after the war. [...] Any kind of purely vexatious actions [against Jews], *being unworthy of a German, are to be abstained from."*

The Madagascar Plan was apparently abandoned on 10 February 1942, although Goebbels continued to speak of it in his diary as a viable option into March of that year. Instead, the Germans increasingly favored deportations to the German-occupied Soviet territories. Another important document, the Luther memorandum of August 1942, underscores that change, repeating with reference to the Wannsee Conference "that the *Führer* had now approved the evacuation of the Jews to the East," with a step-by-step process of first deporting them to the General Government, then on to the occupied eastern territories as soon as this became possible.

On 23 November 1942, Himmler said in a speech that the Jews had been removed from Germany to the East, where they were working on roads, railways etc.

In a report of 14 December 1942, a German ministerial department head summarized the implemented policy toward the Jews by writing that a "gradual cleansing of Jews from the Reich by their deportation to the East" had been implemented.

After Stalingrad, the string of documents talking about resettlements in the East subsided. This was largely because of the necessity of using all hands on deck. For the Jews, this meant that they were soon no longer resettled, but primarily deported to slave-labor camps. As the fronts crept up to Germany's borders, more and more Jews were deported back into Germany to work there.
(For more on this see Graf/Kues/Mattogno 2020, pp. 204-221.)

The Reality of Resettlements

There are no German wartime documents indicating that the Jews deported to the east were slated for mass murder, or were killed along the way in extermination camps. That doesn't stop orthodox historians from asserting that these exterminations took place anyway, pointing to anecdotal evidence by former deportees and "confessions" by German officials mostly during show-trial proceedings toward the end and after the war. They also claim that there is no evidence supporting the claim that these resettlements actually took place.

But this is where they are wrong. Sifting systematically through a plethora of wartime sources, Swedish historian Thomas Kues managed to find a long string of documents and media reports from during the war, demonstrating that thousands upon thousands of Jews were indeed deported to the temporarily German-occupied eastern territories. These sources are neatly listed and explained in the following publications, freely accessible to anyone who cares to look:

- Kues, "Evidence for the Presence of 'Gassed' Jews in the Occupied Eastern Territories," Parts 1 through 3," 2010a&b, 2011c.
- Graf/Kues/Mattogno 2020, pp. 291-374.
- Mattogno/Kues/Graf 2015, Part 1, pp. 561-703.

RINGELBLUM, EMMANUEL

Emmanuel Ringelblum (21 Nov. 1900 – 10? March 1944) was a Polish Jew who was forced to live in the Warsaw Ghetto during World War II. He organized an intelligence-gathering organization in the Ghetto named "*Oneg Szabat*." It gathered documents and recorded witness testimonies, among them some from individuals who claimed to have escaped from the Treblinka and Chełmno camps. Ringelblum managed to leave the ghetto just prior to the uprising, but was discovered in March 1944 and presumably executed shortly afterwards.

Emmanuel Ringelblum

Some of the documentation created by Ringelblum was discovered in the ruins of Warsaw after the war. Although damaged, most of the material discovered was salvaged, and is now known as the Ringelblum Archives. In the context of the Holocaust, of special interest are recorded testimonies, and chronicle entries allegedly based on testimonies, dealing with the alleged extermination camps Belzec, Chełmno, Sobibór and Treblinka. They show the rumor mill at work, spreading wildly disparate nonsense about these camps, even from an orthodox point of view.

(For more details, see the section "Propaganda History" of the entries on Belzec, Chełmno, Sobibór and Treblinka.)

Ringelblum Archives → **Ringelblum, Emmanuel**

ROGERIE, ANDRÉ

André Rogerie

André Rogerie (25 Dec. 1921 – 1 May 2014) was a member of the French resistance who got arrested in July 1943 and sent to various camps. He arrived at Auschwitz on 14 April 1944 via the Majdanek Camp. He remained at the camp until its evacuation on 18 January 1945. Back home he wrote a set of memoirs first published in 1946 and reprinted in 1988, in which he included camp rumors. Here are the relevant points from his terse text:

- The showerheads inside the gas chamber sprayed gas instead of water – although the showerheads were part of real water showers, while the orthodoxy falsely claims they were fake showers not exuding anything, because the poison gas was allegedly introduced through separate (non-existing) Zyklon-B introduction devices.
- The victims' bodies were cremated in electrical furnaces – when in fact all cremation furnaces were fired with coke.
- The ashes were used to enrich the infertile soil of Germany – while the orthodoxy insists that they were simply dumped into the rivers Sola and Vistula.

Rogerie's brief account simply repeats clichés learned through the camps' Chinese-whisper rumor mill. (For more details, see Mattogno 2021, pp. 392f.)

RÖGNER, ADOLF

Adolf Rögner was an incorrigible, pathological liar with multiple convictions for swindling, forgery and perjury, both before and after the war. Because of his status as "incorrigible," he spent time as a criminal at the Auschwitz Camp, where he was deployed as an inmate electrician. After the war, he was convicted again for similar offenses. While in prison, he stayed in contact with a former co-inmate of his, Hermann Langbein, head of the International Auschwitz Committee. Rögner hoarded publications and unpublished documents on all matters concerning Auschwitz and other wartime camps, and from his prison cell, he started pressing hundreds of criminal charges against a long list of former members of the Auschwitz Camp's staff. On inquiry by the Ministry of Justice of the German State Baden-Württemberg as to what was going on, the public prosecutor in charge of handling Rögner's case wrote that Rögner's criminal record showed

> "that as prosecution witness in trials against concentration camp personnel, Rögner has obviously lied for reasons of hatred and revenge.
>
> Rögner was therefore sentenced to a prison term of 3 years and 6 months for false accusations, false testimonies while not under oath, and perjury. […] In addition, Rögner's right to testify as a witness or expert in a trial has been revoked permanently."

The prosecutor described Rögner as a "vindictive psychopath" and a "self-contradicting pathological professional criminal," while Rögner described himself as a staunch communist who planned to move to Krakow in communist Poland, then the seat of the International Auschwitz Committee. He prided himself to have been instrumental in getting "many a Nazi" executed after the war with his testimonies, and that he had succeeded in starting the investigations which eventually led to the infamous Frankfurt Auschwitz show trial. Once Langbein found out about the investigation triggered by Rögner, he jumped on the bandwagon and offered his committee's assistance. Rögner was also the first witness testifying during that trial, thus setting the standards for this travesty of justice.

Here is a brief list of absurdities extracted from Rögner's demented claims:

– He made concrete accusations against 1,400 to 1,600 people, approximately 160 of whom were allegedly known to him by name. Almost all of them were probably taken from books and documents he had hoarded, which underscores Rögner's real career: a professional (dis)informer and perjuring false witness.
– Rögner claimed to have hidden behind a tree at the Auschwitz railway ramp, from where he claims to have seen how Wilhelm Boger, an investigator at the Auschwitz Camp's internal Gestapo unit, beat a girl unconscious, ripped her clothes off, then "drew his pistol and shot the girl once each in the left and right breast. Then he stuck the pistol barrel in the girl's genitals and fired one more shot." Apart from no other witness confirming this, the problem is that there were no trees anywhere near that ramp.
– Rögner accused another member of the camp gestapo, Walter Quakernack, to have tortured "inmates by crucifixion, stabbing the testicles with steel needles, and burning tampons in the vagina." This one and the previous example are nothing more than made-up Holocaust pornography invented by a sexually deprived, sick and perverted mind.
– Rögner claimed to have witnessed 30 other individual murders, all committed by Boger, in similar or even more sadistic ways. He also claimed to have witnessed acts of torture committed by Boger "without being noticed, through keyholes or windows." Peeping Tom Rögner never got caught spying around like this, of course.
– He alleged that the smallest children of arriving prisoners were thrown on a big pile, from where they were tossed in a truck, and then thrown alive into roaring cremation furnaces. Usually, however, this cliché involves throwing them into flaming pits of fire, not into furnaces.
– He stated that arriving children became so desperate on the ramp because of the brutality of the SS people that they hugged the legs of the SS men – and were then shot by them. That's not how children react to brutal people. Like everyone else, they try to get away from them and seek shelter with anyone else.

Rögner prided himself for having been a member of the camp's inmate resistance, together with other personalities such as Hermann Langbein and Bruno Baum, who even had the support of some SS men, such as Richard Böck. Studying these men's entries gives an idea what their main activity consisted of: spreading atrocity propaganda about what was going on at Auschwitz. But Rögner clearly went over the top with his frenzy. However, the investigating prosecutor's qualms in pursuing this case were brushed aside by orders from the highest political levels of West Germany, who saw themselves under massive international pressure – among them many Jewish organizations – to stage a show trial on Auschwitz. (For more details, see Rudolf 2003a-c; 2004c, p. 328;

2023, pp. 383-386, 423, 473.)

ROMANIA

Romania never deported any Jews to German camps, but when reconquering Moldova and Transnistria from the Soviet Union in 1941 with German help, pogroms against the local Jews broke out. The Jews were suspected by the Romanians and locals that they had collaborated with the Stalinist occupants. The Romanian authorities exacerbated the situation by deporting tens of thousands of Moldovan Jews east of the Dnester River, dumping them there in German-controlled territory. This led to a prolonged conflict with the German armed forces controlling some of these areas who did not want to be burdened with these homeless and jobless Jews. The ultimate death toll of this tragedy is unknown, but figures ranged from several thousand to over 100,000. (See the entry on Jewish demography for a broader perspective.)

ROSENBERG, ALFRED

Alfred Rosenberg

Alfred Rosenberg was born on 12 January 1893 to ethnic-German parents in Reval (today's Tallinn), Estonia. He went on to study architecture and engineering in Moscow, eventually earning a PhD in early 1918. Following the Russian and Bolshevist Revolutions of 1917 and 1918, he moved to Munich, Germany. In January 1919, eight months prior to Adolf Hitler, Rosenberg joined the small German Workers' Party (DAP), which was the precursor to the NSDAP, or "Nazi" party. In 1920, Rosenberg published the first two of his many books: *Immorality in the Talmud*, and *The Track of the Jew through the Ages*.

By 1929, Rosenberg had established what would become the "Institute for the Study of the Jewish Question," which analyzed negative Jewish influences in Germany and Europe. In 1930, he was appointed Reichstag Deputy; that was also the year that he published the first edition of his main work, *The Myth of the 20th Century*. When Hitler and the NSDAP assumed power in early 1933, Rosenberg was named head of the foreign political office. The next year, Hitler appointed him "cultural and educational leader" of the new Reich. By the end of the decade, Rosenberg was widely recognized as the chief ideologist of National Socialism. That being so, we will closely scrutinize the historical record he left behind.

Rosenberg voiced his opinion on how to handle the "Jewish question" on numerous occasions. During a press conference on 28 March 1941, Rosenberg stated that, for Europe, "the Jewish problem will only be solved when the last Jew has left the European continent." Just four days later, on 2 April 1941, he wrote a memorandum in which he suggested to weaken Russian imperialism by way of "a complete destruction of the Bolshevik Jewish governmental administration," among other things. In another memorandum of 29 April, he stated:

> "The Jewish question requires a general treatment, the temporary provisional solution of which must be determined (compulsory labor for Jews, ghettoization, etc.)"

On 7 May of that year, when Rosenberg had been slated to become the head of the upcoming Ministry for the Occupied Eastern Territories, he wrote instructions for his future subordinate Reich commissars. In this document, he repeated this goal:

> "The Jewish Question will undergo a decisive solution by the establishment of ghettos or labor columns."

On 20 June 1941, two days before the Germany's invasion of the Soviet Union, Rosenberg mentioned during a meeting of leaders of the Party and the German armed forces that an area around Minsk, the capital of Belorussia, will be set aside as a reservation for "undesirables," which probably referred primarily to Jews (Irving 1977, p. 271).

On 17 July 1941, some three weeks after Germany's invasion of the Soviet Union, Rosenberg was appointed head of the Ministry for the Occupied Eastern Territories, covering the areas that were to be captured from the Soviets in 1941 and 1942. However, his ministry had no police authority, which Himmler reserved for himself. Further undermining his position was the fact that Rosenberg's subordinates, Reich commissars Hinrich Lohse (for the northeastern territories) and Erich Koch (for Ukraine and Caucasus), were appointed by Hitler, and could not be dismissed by Rosenberg. Hence, these commissars insisted on reporting directly to Hitler rather than taking orders from Rosenberg.

As a result, Rosenberg had little direct impact on the German policy toward the Jews in the East, which was dominated by Himmler's forces. Rosenberg's moderate, conciliatory policies toward Russians, Ukrainians and other ethnic groups in the east were frequently undermined, especially by Koch. (On this, see his testimony and that of Hans Heinrich Lammers, Hitler's head of the Reich Chancellery, during the *IMT*, Vol. 11, pp. 47, 118, 478-484, 491f., 504-508.)

Once in office, Rosenberg implemented the policy he had announced earlier with a decree on 16 August 1941 that subjected all Jews in the Eastern Territories between 14 and 60 years of age to forced labor. On 18 November 1941, Rosenberg held a press conference, during which he stated that the Jews in the East eventually will be either shoved "over the Ural Mountains" to Siberia, or else eradicated in some other way.

Parallel to Rosenberg's effort to conscript Jews as forced laborers mainly in war industries, some of Himmler's forces in the East had other ideas. Wild mass executions were reported, which Lohse promptly prohibited. Himmler's Department for Homeland Security (*Reichssicherheitshauptamt*, RSHA) complained to Rosenberg's office about this interference in SS and police matters. In reaction to this, and evidently clueless, Rosenberg's office asked Lohse on 31 October what was going on.

Lohse responded on 15 November by writing that nothing in the existing orders and decrees points at killing off all Jews. Hence, executing them all, irrespective of their ability to work, seemed unjustifiable. He then asked whether the RSHA's intervention "is to be taken as an order to the effect that all Jews in the East are to be liquidated?" The response by Rosenberg's office to this question was non-committal, referring instead to some unknown oral communications.

However, the policy Rosenberg's office pursued with respect to the Jews did not change. In fact, while the above exchange was going on between Rosenberg's and Lohse's office, other communications were exchanged between them. On 9 November, Lohse's office urgently requested to suspend further transports with Jews, since the local camps "must be relocated much further east." This referred to labor camps right behind the front, doing important road-construction work in logistical support of Germany's advancing armies. On 13 November, Rosenberg's office responded to Lohse's telegram, agreeing that the Jews on these trains were "to be sent further East"; hence the camps in Riga and Minsk were only temporary measures.

This string of documents continued, including the Wannsee Protocol of early 1942, which also talks about sending the Jews East in labor columns doing road-construction work.

In the summer of 1942, with the evacuation of tens of thousands of Polish Jews from the Warsaw Ghetto in full swing, the receiving locations in the East were completely overwhelmed. In a desperate reaction to this, Wilhelm Kube, general commissar for Belorussia, complained to his superior Lohse on 31 July 1942 (and later also to Rosenberg directly), indicating that they had been executing tens of thousands of Jews in the area to prevent them from supporting the partisans. However, new transports of Jews were constantly arriving, making it impossible to pacify the region, evidently because these Jews ended up joining the partisans, too. Therefore, Kube threatened that they would henceforth execute all Jews arriving in unannounced transports, evidently rather than accommodating them. After some back and forth, Kube was made to shut up and accept and accommodate the incoming Jewish transports as "new residents" anyhow.

All this points to a general policy of deportation, resettlement and forced-labor deployment in the East, with a lot of interspersed massacres. Rosenberg must have been aware of the latter.

Rosenberg was apprehended after the war and put on trial at the Nuremberg International Military Tribunal as a "major war criminal." He was charged with ideologically preparing the German people for war and anti-Semitic measures, and with influencing foreign governments to become pro-National Socialist, among other things. In the context of the Holocaust, the various letters from his office and from Kube and Lohse mentioned earlier were introduced as evidence showing that he must have known that Jews were being massacred in the East, and that he agreed with these measures.

Reacting to these accusations, Rosenberg stated on 16 April 1946 (*IMT*, Vol. 11, p. 502):

"[R]*egarding shootings of saboteurs and also shootings of Jews, pogroms by the local population in the Baltic States and in the Ukraine, I took as occurrences of this war. I heard that in Kiev a large number of Jews had been shot, but that the greater part of the Jews had left Kiev; and the sum of these reports showed me, it is true, terrible harshness, especially some reports from the prison camps.*

But that there was an order for the individual annihilation of the entire Jewry, I could not assume; and if, in our polemics, the extermination of Jewry was also talked about, I must say that this word [extermination], *of course, must make a frightful impression in view of the testimonies we think are available now. But under conditions prevailing then, it was not interpreted as an individual extermination, as an individual annihilation of millions of Jews. I must also say that even the British Prime Minister, in an official speech in the House of Commons on 23 or 26 September 1943, spoke of the extermination in root and branch of Prussianism and of National Socialism. I happened to read these words from this speech. However, I did not assume that in saying this he meant the shooting of all Prussian officers and National Socialists."*

Thus, he clearly distinguished between the "extermination" of a collective (Jewry) in terms of disbanding it, and the murder ("individual annihilation") of a person or persons; the former does not entail the latter.

When cross-examined the next day, a lengthy exchange between him and U.S. Prosecutor Thomas Dodd ensued, during which Rosenberg again insisted that destroying a concept or ideology – Jewry – does not equate with murdering all Jews (*ibid.*, pp. 553-556).

While admitting massacres in the east, Rosenberg kept insisting that wholesale systematic slaughter in extermination facilities specifically built for this purpose had been inconceivable to him (*ibid.*, p. 515):

"[…W]hat has been testified to here the other day [by Rudolf Höss about Auschwitz on 15 April, one day earlier]*, I considered simply impossible and I would not have believed it even if Heinrich Himmler himself had related it to me. There are things which, even to me, appear beyond the humanly possible."*

In a "closing statement" written in Nuremberg on 31 August 1946, Rosenberg stated:

"The thought of a physical extermination of Slavs and Jews, i.e. the actual genocide, never crossed my mind, let alone that I propagated it in any way. I was of the opinion that the existing Jewish question had to be solved by creating minority rights, emigration or by settling the Jews in a national territory over a period of decades."

Prolific as Rosenberg was, he put ink on paper even while imprisoned in Nuremberg. In a typescript he wrote, among other things:

"I did not consider a literal interpretation of the expression 'annihilation' or 'extermination' to be humanly possible. I took the shootings in the East, of which I had been informed, as a necessary measure in the suppression of communist resistance, and also as local violations without assuming a really deliberate Fuehrer order. Reports from the Moscow radio station I put aside as propaganda."

Unsurprisingly, all this explanation came to naught in a trial that had a foregone conclusion. Rosenberg was found guilty, sentenced to death, and hanged in 1946. He was 53 years of age, and left behind a wife and young daughter.

Following his execution, the U.S. government took possession of many of Rosenberg's personal items, including a series of some 400 individual sheets marked "handwritten diary notes," covering the years 1934 to 1944. This "diary" remained filed away until 2012, when the US Holocaust Memorial Museum acquired the originals and made them public. Notably, the diary itself remains untranslated into English. One can review the hand-written originals online, or read commentary on them in English, but no full transcription in English (or any language) exists. This is almost certainly because these notes provide no substantiation for the conventional Holocaust story, and indeed have almost no reference to Jews at all. Undoubtedly, the Holocaust orthodoxy was sorely disappointed by the contents, and have sought to limit the damage to their own preferred view of events.

(For more details, see Mattogno 2022c, pp. 147-152, 325-337; Dalton 2020a.)

ROSENBERG, ELIYAHU

Eliyahu (also Ela, Elias) Rosenberg was a Polish Jew deported to the Treblinka Camp on 20 August 1942. He made a deposition in front of the Historical Commission of Warsaw, probably in 1945, which was recorded in very bad French and is barely comprehensible. It only

Eliyahu Rosenberg

mentions in passing that he had to drag corpses out of a gas chamber to a mass grave, but mentions no specifics at all.

Some two years later, in December 1947, probably after having read accounts from other former inmates, foremost that of Jankiel Wiernik, Rosenberg signed a 12-page statement in German, which now included more details about the gas chambers.

Rosenberg also testified during the Jerusalem show trial against John Demjanjuk. However, it is entirely focused on the defendant rather than providing any details about the alleged killing procedure. The only noteworthy claim in it is his assertion that Ivan the Terrible (which he claimed John Demjanjuk to have been) tried to force him into having sex with the dead bodies of gassed women – which is another example of made-up Holocaust pornography invented by a sick mind. (See the entry on Adolf Rögner for more examples.)

Here are some highlights from Rosenberg's 1947 depositions:
- Killing with the exhaust of a single Diesel engine, with 35 minutes for the last victim to die, verified by listening at the door until all was quiet. However, diesel exhaust is unable to kill anyone within 35 minutes.
- In the roof, there was a small window used by a man to control the gas supply. This is a unique claim. It is unclear how a man operating the diesel engine *inside* the building could control the engine, while looking evidently from *outside* the building through a window in the roof (or maybe through three windows, one for each chamber).
- Four hundred people were squeezed into one chamber of the first gas-chamber building – which according to the orthodoxy measured 4 m × 4 m, hence 16 m², resulting in an impossible packing density of 25/m².
- The tightly packed victims could not fall down, hence kept standing after death – which is physically impossible.
- In March 1943, new gas chambers were built, with room for up to 12,000 people. However, the orthodoxy insists that those chambers were built starting in October/November 1942. They supposedly contained 10 chambers of 32 m² each. Therefore, Rosenberg's victim count would have resulted in an impossible packing density of 37.5 people per m².

In this testimony, Rosenberg closely matched claims made by Jankiel Wiernik in his 1944 booklet, probably known to Rosenberg, regarding the number of gas chambers inside the old and new gassing facilities, as well as their gassing capacities. Rosenberg also incorporated Wiernik's idea of windows in the roof, although he changed their purpose.

(For more on Rosenberg, see Mattogno 2021e, pp. 187-190; Mattogno/Graf 2023, pp. 170f.)

Rosenberg, Walter → **Vrba, Rudolf**

ROSENBLAT, HERMAN

Herman Rosenblat (1929 – 5 Feb. 2015) was a Polish Jew who was deported from the Warsaw Ghetto to a subcamp of the Buchenwald Camp, then shortly before the war's end to the Theresienstadt Ghetto, where he was liberated.

Herman Rosenblat

Having gotten into serious financial difficulties in the 1990s, he decided to write down his wartime experiences and spice them up with inventions, such as that his current wife, as a little girl, gave him apples through the camp fence. The book titled, *Angel at the Fence*, and the movie rights to it, promised to rake in millions, thus solving Rosenblat's financial woes. Oprah Winfrey featured him prominently twice on her show, boosting his fame and thus sales prospects.

Mainstream researchers quickly found out, however, that his wife had never been anywhere near the camp where Rosenblat had been incarcerated during the war. Other aspects of his tales were considered false as well, such as Rosenblat's claim that he was scheduled to be gassed at the Theresienstadt Ghetto on 10 May 1945, and survived only because he was liberated a few hours before that. However, this ghetto had been handed over to the International Red Cross on 1 May, and no one has ever claimed that there was a homicidal gas chamber at Theresienstadt Ghetto, nor is there any other evidence to suggest there was.

When the truth emerged, Rosenblat's original book contracts were cancelled, yet not his contract to produce a movie. He eventually admitted having invented his love story, but insisted that, although the story existed only in his mind, he still believed it:

"*'I wanted to bring happiness to people,' he said.*

'I brought hope to a lot of people. My motivation was to make good in this world.'" (Bone 2008) Because this fake story is so beautiful after all – the world wants to be deceived – it appeared as a book a short while later, under a different title, a "novel" presumably based on Rosenblat's memoirs (Holt 2009).

(For more details, see Sherman 2008; Vice 2014a&b; and various articles published by the magazine *New Republic* at https://newrepublic.com/search?q=Rosenblat. For a remarkable 2009 interview with Rosenblat on *ABC News*, see www.dailymotion.com/video/x2qusht.)

ROSENBLUM, JOSHUAH

Joshuah Rosenblum, born in 1923, was a Polish Jew who was arrested in May 1941 and sent to the Sosnowice Transit Camp, and then to Wiesau. After working with about 300 Jews on a highway construction project about 125 km from Berlin, he was transferred to Klettendorf, near Breslau, from where he fled. Arrested by the German police in March 1944, he was interned in Auschwitz-Birkenau. After his liberation, he eventually immigrated to Israel.

Rosenblum made his first statement about Auschwitz in 1970 in Israel, hence it is probably infested with knowledge acquired later. In 1996, Rosenblum was moreover interviewed by German historian Barbara Siebert. Here are some pertinent points from Rosenblum's statements:

– At the start of a mass gassing in Crematorium IV and V, an SS man poured Zyklon B from a can into the room through two small windows. Yet in reality, those small openings were equipped with iron bars whose gaps were smaller than the width of a Zyklon-B can, which therefore could not have been emptied out into the room through those windows.
– Because the SS made the victims suffer, the *Sonderkommando* Jews decided to prepare their fellow Jews for the killing themselves, to treat them nicely, and not to tell them anything about their impending fate. But this is absurd: are we to thank those Jewish commandos for being nice, or condemn them for aiding the killers?
– These crematoria each presumably could burn about 800 bodies in 24 hours, although their maximum theoretical daily capacity was only some 160 bodies.
– Four corpses were allegedly thrown into each muffle every 10 minutes, meaning 24 bodies per hour. That would amount to 3,840 bodies per 20-hour working day, not 800. However, each cremation muffle was designed only for one corpse each, and could cremate only one body per hour.
– Pits measuring 2 m deep, 10 m long and 5 m wide were dug, in which 2,000 bodies were allegedly burned within 2 to 3 hours. However, burning down a huge cremation pyre during open-air incineration takes at least a day. Furthermore, at a packing density of 6 bodies per running meter and a height of 20 cm per body layer, this pyre would have been $(2{,}000\div10\text{m}\div6/\text{m}\times0.2\text{m}=)$ 6.67 meter high. Add to this a minimum of a similar stacking height of fuel wood needed, and the height of the pyre reaches 13 meters and more. How exactly was that pyre built and prevented from toppling over? And how was groundwater prevented from accumulating in the pits?
– When burning corpses in pits, "in order to save gasoline – the corpses could also be doused with human fat, which flowed into a pit at a deeper spot. We poured the human fat with buckets onto the people who were supposed to burn faster." Yet highly combustible fat burns on contact with fire or embers, hence could not flow anywhere. Also, gasoline was most certainly not use to burn corpses, as it was a scarce commodity during the war, and because it can char a body only superficially when poured onto it.
– From May 1944 until October 1944, the "fires burned incessantly – day and night." Air photos show, however, that no large-scale fires were burning in or around Auschwitz-Birkenau during that time.
– Victims were shot lying down next to the blazing pit – with the executor inevitably getting burned to a crisp in the process.
– Rosenblum claimed that the shot at the pit's edge often was not fatal, so the victims ran around inside the burning pit screaming, begging to get shot dead. But if they had to lie down to get shot, how did they end up inside the pit running around? However, if a victim had indeed gotten alive into the blazing inferno, the inhaled hot air and flames would have singed the lungs quickly, rendering any screaming and running around impossible.

(For more details, see Mattogno 2021d, pp. 222-227.)

ROSENBLUM, MORITZ

Moritz Rosenblum was arrested in Łódź on 16 December 1940 at age 22. He was admitted to a forced-labor camp near Frankfurt on Oder, from where he was transferred to Auschwitz in December 1942. On 26 May 1945, he made a deposition, in which he claimed to have seen a homicidal gassing on his arrival at Auschwitz.

The problems begin with the start of his story, because no transport arrived at Auschwitz with any inmates from Frankfurt on Oder or its vicinity during the entire month of December 1942.

He claimed that, due to an injured leg, he was selected on arrival to get gassed. He was then led to the "bathhouse" – meaning the homicidal gas chamber, which at that time could have been only one of the bunkers, the claimed makeshift facilities with several homicidal gas chambers each, located well outside the camp's perimeter. Contrary to all other accounts and the orthodoxy's narrative, he claims that there was then a second selection right by the bathhouse where any skilled men among the doomed were fished out. As a welder, Rosenblum got lucky, despite his bad leg.

He was then taken outside (probably the undressing hut) onto a square in the open where they had to undress and then get tattooed, which means that this must have occurred right next to the bathhouse. However, it is inconceivable that they were made to undress *outside* the undressing hut, when they were not even slated for gassing. Were they supposed to run back to the camp naked, carrying their clothes? Moreover, the place where people got their inmate-registration number tattooed into the forearms was the admissions building inside the Birkenau Camp (Construction Sector BIb). This sector also had a facility with an undressing room, an inmate shower and sauna, a dressing room, and a clothing disinfestation chamber operating with Zyklon B. This building is probably the origin of Rosenblum's confused story.

He wants to have seen how three SS officers came in a car, wore rubber gloves, and poured out five or six cans into an opening of the alleged gas chamber (in singular, although each bunker is said to have had several). Only a few minutes later, everything was silent, which would have been an impossibly short execution time. Then, several SS men presumably put on respirators and went into the gas chamber, staying in there for five minutes, after which inmates went in – evidently without respirators or gas masks – and started dragging out the corpses, which would have killed them, too.

The orthodox narrative allows for at least a short ventilation time before the inmates went in, although such a facility, packed tightly with many bodies and without any forced ventilation, would have taken many hours if not days to air out completely, allowing access without gas masks. Furthermore, no one else has ever claimed that SS men entered the claimed gas chamber for five minutes. In order to do what, exactly? Risk their lives?

(For more details, see Mattogno 2022e, pp. 183-185.)

ROSENTHAL, MARYLA

Maryla Rosenthal was a German Jewess who was deported to Auschwitz, where she was deployed as a secretary in the typing pool of the Political Department, hence the camp's Gestapo. She was one of the first witnesses interviewed in the course of the investigations against Wilhelm Boger,

Maryla Rosenthal

which ultimately expanded and became the infamous Frankfurt Auschwitz show trial. During her first interview, Mrs. Rosenthal was unable to confirm the accusations against her former boss or to confirm the general allegations of cruelties in Auschwitz. Among other things, Mrs. Rosenthal asserted that Boger had been a polite boss, both to her and her former colleagues at the typing pool, helping her out with food and clothes on occasion. She felt no hatred for Jews coming from him.

Mrs. Rosenthal then reported the manner in which the other women in the Political Department gossiped in the toilet and exchanged the latest camp talk, which she regarded with skepticism and kept her distance from. She heard talk about Boger committing massacres, but she insisted that she never saw him agitated or any other evidence supporting these rumors.

Needless to say, that didn't sit well with the prosecution who was looking for incriminating evidence, not exonerating ones. Hence, she was interviewed again. This time, she was confronted with the accusations made by other former inmates, which is clearly a manipulative interviewing technique. But she didn't budge, insisting that she had no memory of cruelties happening, either because her memory was no good, or because maybe her experience in Auschwitz "was simply too much for me. I could not grasp and process what I saw and heard there." In other words, they pulled out the *deus ex machina* called "suppressed memory," a phony theory used by Freudian psychiatric manipulators trying to talk clients into believing horror stories of their past, claiming that they subconsciously suppress recollections due to the trauma suffered. As was proven by many studies, this technique of reviving alleged suppressed memory only leads to the implantation of false memories. In fact, Mrs. Rosenthal's attitude – her positive description of Boger, her return to Germany because she didn't like Israel, and her use of the term "colleagues" in reference to her fellow-inmates – indicate that she was *not* traumatized by events in Auschwitz.

On the other hand, Mrs. Rosenthal recounted how witnesses met in Frankfurt, accommodated by associations of former camp inmates, such as Hermann Langbein's International Auschwitz Committee, who allowed witnesses to gather and exchange stories, thus exposing them to manipulative influences. Mrs. Rosenthal was stunned by what her former colleagues claimed they still remembered. She, on the contrary, resisted the implantation of false memories.

> "As I said before, I cannot remember that. I want to emphasize that I have not the slightest interest in protecting anybody. But on the other hand, I cannot say what I do not know."

The abnormality of Mrs. Rosenthal's testimony – the only clearly exonerating testimony among all the testimonies of former secretaries of the political department at Auschwitz – is generally recognized in the relevant literature. It is explained away by orthodox Holocaust historians, as well as by the Frankfurt Jury Court, with the claim that Mrs. Rosenthal must have suppressed the horrible side of her experiences, wiping them out of her memory entirely, relegating it all entirely to her subconscious mind.

In the end, Mrs. Rosenthal's testimony was not considered exonerating during the Frankfurt Auschwitz show trial, but, rather, as incriminating! According to the Frankfurt judges, the atrocities in Auschwitz were so horrible that Mrs. Rosenthal was so "traumatized" that she lost all recollection of these same atrocities, and that she was completely intimidated because she could no longer trust her own memory at all. By this logic, one can turn just about any exonerating testimony into an incriminating one. This turns all logic of evaluating evidence and of determining the truth on its head. With that approach, once a thesis has been postulated, it can no longer be refuted, as every exonerating testimony can be interpreted as incriminating. This is the logic of a true witch trial.

In reality, Mrs. Rosenthal was the only witness among those former typists who did not succumb to the false-memory syndrome, resisting the massive pressure to remember what no normal person would remember after 15 or even 20 years and more.
(For details, see Rudolf 2023, pp. 368-371; 2004b.)

ROSIN, ARNOŠT

Arnošt Rosin

Arnošt Rosin (born in 2013) was deported to Auschwitz from Slovakia on 17 April 1942. He escaped from the camp on 27 May 1944 together with Czesław Mordowicz. They both wrote a report together, which was added to the so-called War Refugee Board Report, whose main component is a lengthy report authored by Alfred Wetzler and Rudolf Vrba. However, Rosin's and Mordowicz's essay was added not as an independent account, but as a sequel to Wetzler's and Vrba's text. It is a brief chronicle of alleged events without further information on the alleged extermination techniques. In particular, it does not mention the alleged bunkers of Birkenau, a topic also neglected by Wetzler and Vrba. The report furthermore does not claim that Rosin had been a member of the *Sonderkommando*, yet merely repeats hearsay information from them.

One specific claim allegedly learned from the *Sonderkommando* is an invented inspection of Birkenau's Crematorium II by Himmler in mid-May 1944, just at the start of the deportation of the Hungarian Jews. Another invented, rather puerile fairy tale allegedly learned from the *Sonderkommando* is the claimed inspection of the Auschwitz Camp and of Birkenau's Crematorium II by a committee of four Dutch Jews, who wrote a report describing the conditions at Auschwitz in favorable terms, but who then unfortunately ended up getting killed when entering the crematorium. Needless to say, there is no trace of any of this happening, nor is it conceivable that the German authorities would have agreed to an inspection by a "committee of Jews."

Rosin's contribution to this report also claims that, during the deportation of Hungarian Jews to Auschwitz, "4 pits about 30 meters long and 15 meters wide" were burning day and night near Birkenau Camp, making the camp's cremation capacity "almost unlimited." However, air photos show that no huge burning and smoking pits existed during that time.

In later testimonies, in order to be able to describe things in more detail, Rosin depicted himself suddenly as a member of the *Sonderkommando*, which is simply a postwar invention to be able to testify in court. Rosin testified during the Polish show trials against former Auschwitz camp commandant Rudolf Höss and against other members of the Auschwitz Camp's former staff. Rosin stated, among other things:

– Because freshly dug mass graves had filled up with water, pumps were brought, and the three top officials of the camp themselves, Höss among them, pumped out the water with the help of others. No camp commandant would be present, let alone help, to do such menial work. This was clearly a lie meant to frame the defendant.
– Rosin described the facilities where mass murder supposedly occurred in April 1942, when he claimed to have started working there. This would have been the so-called Bunker 1, but his description of it and its start of operation (sometime in May 1942) do not match the orthodox account. For Rosin, the facility allegedly had only one chamber measuring 4 m × 4 m, or maybe 5 m × 5 m, yet 300 persons were forced into it, resulting in an impossible packing density between 12 and 19 persons per square meter. The orthodoxy insists, however, that this phantom facility measured some 15 m × 6 m, had *two* gas chambers, and started operations in late March 1942.
– Himmler's crematorium inspection from mid-May 1944 was shifted by Rosin to February 1943, on occasion of the first claimed gassing in Crematorium II, and Poland's governor general Hans Frank was present as well, which is a unique claim. This change makes Rosin's story align better with other witness statements, but even the orthodoxy agrees that these stories are all false, hence made up.
– Rosin stated that all inmates of the *Sonderkommando* were eventually killed on special orders from Höss. Again, this was a lie to frame Höss. But if all *Sonderkommando* members were killed, and he was one of them, how did he manage to survive? He doesn't say, but it probably doesn't matter, since his membership and all tales based on it are pure inventions.

(For more details, see Mattogno 2021, pp. 329-335.)

SACHSENHAUSEN

Sachsenhausen is the name of a district of the city of Oranienburg, some 12 miles north of Berlin. The SS had their headquarters in Oranienburg. In July 1936, a concentration camp was erected right next to the headquarters and named after that city district.

Orthodox sources state that some 600 inmates died in the camp through 1939. The camp's documentation, found by the Soviets when they occupied it, gives the following data:
- On 1 January 1940, the camp had 12,187 inmates.
- Between January 1940 and April 1945:
  - 120,009 inmates were admitted,
  - 8,571 inmates were released,
  - 69,084 transferred to other camps,
  - 19,900 died of diseases, injuries etc.
  - 675 were executed
  - 391 escaped,
  - 1,089 were handed over to local police units
  - 1,125 were transferred or released without further information.

Although the Soviet had access to that data, this didn't stop them from inventing or spreading wildly exaggerated mass-murder claims.

Sachsenhausen entered the history of the orthodox Holocaust narrative on 15 April 1945, when Willi Feiler, a former Sachsenhausen inmate, wrote an affidavit for British investigators. In it, he claimed, among other things, that a gas chamber was built at the camp in the fall of 1943 in a separate building, able to asphyxiate 500 persons at once by piping Zyklon gas through 500 shower fixtures. After the execution, so Feiler claimed, the entire floor folded downward, discharging the victims into four moveable cremation furnaces. It goes without saying that nothing remotely close to this ever existed or would have functioned.

Two weeks later, Ludwig Schmidt, another former Sachsenhausen inmate, gave his perspective on this tale for the British by claiming that gassings at Sachsenhausen were carried out not in a chamber, but in a vehicle that brought the victims from the barracks straight to the crematorium. Although Schmidt claimed to have cleaned the vehicle several times, he couldn't figure out how it worked (probably because it didn't work), and he assumed that the engine somehow sucked off the oxygen.

The British were eager to find evidence that gassings of inmates at Sachsenhausen were carried out using Zyklon B, because they were preparing a show trial against the managers of a company involved in distributing Zyklon B (see the entry on Bruno Tesch and Tesch & Stabenow).

In that context, they secured another affidavit by the former Sachsenhausen inmate Wilhelm Soerensen on 14 January 46, but it did not help their cause. Soerensen claimed that, when he arrived in January 1943, two homicidal gas chambers already existed in the camp. One of them measured 8 m × 8 m. Executions were carried out in these two chambers by an SS man, standing in the open doorway, shooting over the heads of the victims a projectile 8 cm long and 3 cm in diameter. This projectile "burst over the heads of the prisoners," killing everyone within 2 to 3 minutes, except for the SS man, who closed the door without anyone trying to get out with him.

Soerensen claimed that a third gas chamber was built inside the crematorium building in March or April 1943. This chamber had "wash basins, shower baths, clothes pegs and benches around the walls." The lethal fumes were allegedly "pumped in through the shower-bath pipes." Of course, none of it was helpful for the British to rig their case against Bruno Tesch and his co-defendants during the Tesch Trial.

The real masters over the future Sachsenhausen Camp propaganda were not the British, however, but the Soviets, who eventually staged the show trial for it.

On the day the German Wehrmacht surrendered the second time (9 May 1945), a former communist camp inmate named Koehlen wrote a report for the Soviets, in which he listed thousands of sick inmates having been either shot or gassed in "gas cells," without giving any specifics. In total, he claimed that more than 20,000 inmates had been killed in the camp mainly by executions. While the number is close to the actual death toll, the camp's records show that most of the casualties were due to "natural" deaths, not executions.

Considering that death-toll claims of millions had become common among Germany's accusers, the Soviets covered up what they knew to be the truth, and replaced it with absurd figures extracted from one unfortunate SS man who had fallen into Soviet captivity on 2 May 1945: On 20 June 1945, Paul Waldmann, who served as a driver at the Sachsenhausen Camp motor pool from 1936 until December 1941, signed an affidavit, which the Soviets submitted as "evidence" during the Nuremberg International Military Tribunal.

In his "confession," Waldmann claimed, among many other things, that 840,000 Soviet PoWs had been killed at the Sachsenhausen Camp, and that their bodies were tracelessly destroyed in four moveable crematoria transported on trailers (see *IMT*, Vol. 7, p. 586). He also described how the SS had installed in that camp a brain-bashing machine triggered by a pedal, which served to execute inmates conveyor-belt style (*ibid.*, pp. 376f.).

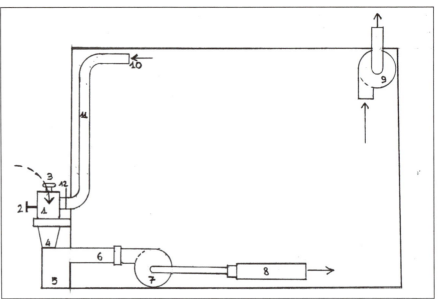

Schematic drawing of the technical equipment once contained in the delousing chamber at the Sachsenhausen Camp, following the drawing contained in the Soviet expert report. Compare this with the DEGESCH circulation system (entry on fumigation gas chamber; © Carlo Mattogno.)
1: Box to hold the Zyklon B can. 2: Lever to puncture the can. 3: Lid. 4: Funnel. 5: Box to catch falling Zyklon-B pellets. 6: Feeder pipe from can opener to fan. 7: Circulation fan. 8: Circulation exit pipe. 9: Exhaust fan. 10-12: Circulation entry pipe.

From 23 October to 1 November 1947, the Soviets finally conducted their Stalinist show trial in Berlin against 15 former staff members of the Sachsenhausen Camp, among them the former commandant Anton Kaindl. This Soviet kangaroo court acted under the premise that the National-Socialist regime had followed "a plan for the mass extermination" not just of political opponents, but of people in general. Sachsenhausen Camp was one of the many camps which were allegedly established to carry out this plan. To implement this plan, it supposedly received a homicidal gas chamber in March 1943, according to Kaindl's tall tale. During that trial, the defendants enthusiastically embraced and confirmed all the Soviet allegations, no matter how hairbrained. Kaindl even claimed that Gestapo chief Heinrich Müller gave him the order on 1 February 1945 to completely destroy the entire camp "by artillery fire and air attack or by gassing." Incredibly, orthodox historians take the results of that trial seriously. (See the entry on Anton Kaindl for details.)

A major blunder in the orchestration of this show trial was the expert report which the Soviets compiled of the alleged homicidal gas chamber allegedly located in the camp's hygiene building: Their description accurately depicts a DEGESCH circulation fumigation chamber. Every camp's hygienic building had such a facility, because delousing inmate clothes was one of the main purposes of a hygienic building. Even the tiny size of the room – 2.75 m × 3 m – confirms this impression, all the more so, since such a small cubicle most certainly would not have been planned for the *mass* extermination of humans.

After the war, the Sachsenhausen Camp served as one of Communist East Germany's worst concentration camps for the incarceration of anti-communist dissidents and other recalcitrant Germans. Its conditions were at least as bad as under National-Socialist rule. The camp was finally closed in 1952, at which point the hygiene building was torn down that allegedly contained the homicidal gas chamber – or probably just the fumigation chamber – and the brain-bashing device.

If this building indeed had contained genuine material evidence for any execution device, the Communist East German authorities certainly would have maintained the building and turned it into the center piece, the crown jewel, of the museum which was subsequently established there. But they did not preserve anything, because there wasn't anything to preserve.

Interestingly, Gerhart Schirmer, a German PoW

Section of the ruins of the torn-down hygiene/crematorium building at the Sachsenhausen Camp (1998). 1: fumigation chamber; 2: undressing room; 3: garage.

who, after the war, was briefly incarcerated at the Sachsenhausen Camp under Soviet rule, stated in a 1992 publication:

> "In any case, together with other prisoners I personally had the 'fun' of installing a gas chamber and shooting facility in the Russian camp at Oranienburg (Sachsenhausen), which did not exist until then." (Schirmer 1992, pp. 49f.)

If true, that mock facility was probably removed later, when the camp was turned into a concentration camp for political prisoners of Communist East Germany, as they had no use for such mock facilities, or so one would hope. At any rate, there is neither documental nor material proof for Schirmer's claim either.

Schirmer was prosecuted for this statement for stirring up the German people. None of the other witnesses making inflammatory and demonstrably false claims regarding Sachsenhausen or any other German wartime camp was ever prosecuted, because only statements potentially exonerating Germany are illegal, no matter whether they are inflammatory or not, or demonstrably true or not.

(For more details, see Schwensen 2011, 2012a, 2014; Jansson 2014a; Mattogno 2023d; 2016e, pp. 150-180; 2022, pp. 119-143; Rudolf 2023, pp. 75-78.)

SACKAR, JOSEF

Josef Sackar was deported from Greece to Auschwitz, where he arrived on 11 April 1944. He testified about his alleged experiences only in the 1980s when interviewed by Israeli historian Gideon Greif. His interview is therefore inevitably contaminated with elements picked up during some 40 years of exposure to a one-sided narrative.

In this interview, he claimed that, after three weeks of quarantine, he was assigned to a *Sonderkommando* and ended up working inside Crematorium III. Here are some of the more peculiar claims from Sackar's interview:

– Although he wasn't slated to work at the open-air incineration pit, where murdered Jews were supposedly burned, on the first day of his work he was shown one anyway, so he could get used to the sight – and become familiar with the greatest and darkest secret of the Third Reich, so that he could boast about it later.
– He called the pits "bunkers," although the orthodoxy insists that this term was supposedly reserved for the phantom makeshift gassing facilities just outside the Birkenau Camp. Sackar, however, had no knowledge of such a facility.
– When the Jews from Hungary arrived starting in the second half of May 1944, many large cremation pits were used to burn murdered Jews, since the cremation furnaces were supposedly overwhelmed. However, air photos from that time show that there were no burning and smoking cremation pits at or near Birkenau.
– A gassing inside Crematorium III's gas chamber took only half an hour, after which the doors were opened, meaning that this time included the ventilation of the room, which is physically impossible, as it would have taken hours to clear the room of poisonous

Josef Sackar

vapors.
- Ventilation was done not by a powerful ventilation system, of which Sackar knew nothing, but simply by opening the lids covering the Zyklon-B introduction devices (wire-mesh columns).
- He claims that on occasion 20,000 people were cremated daily at Auschwitz, which is technically impossible, as all Birkenau crematoria together had a theoretical maximum daily capacity of 920 bodies, not 20,000, and large-scale open-air incinerations simply didn't happen, as air photos prove.

(For more details, see Mattogno 2022e, pp. 23-30.)

SADOWSKA, RAJZLA

Rajzla Sadowska was a Polish Jew deported to Auschwitz. During the investigations leading up to the Frankfurt Auschwitz show trial, she testified that at one point while at Auschwitz, she suffered such a serious work-related accident that she could not work anymore. She feared "selection" and then gassing, but instead she was taken to the camp hospital until she made a recovery. Then the infamous Dr. Mengele conducted very painful experiments on her, after which she was hobbled, yet instead of getting gassed now, she was again nursed back to health. No one ever asked her for any proof of her injuries. After the war, she immigrated to Israel, but quickly decided the climate in Israel wasn't to her liking, so she moved to Germany instead, which shows how deeply traumatized she was by the horrific things perpetrated by Hitler's Germany.

This testimony is a typical and rather common example of an inmate trying to turn a positive, exonerating experience of healthcare provided at Auschwitz into an incriminating one, throwing in horror clichés about Josef Mengele for good measure, which are all untrue.

(For more details, see Rudolf 2023, pp. 490f.)

Sajmište → Semlin

SAUNAS

Saunas (steam baths) are a Finish invention to boost the human immune system by alternating exposure to high heat and humidity to let the sweat wash out skin impurities, with cold showers followed by dips into cold-water pools afterwards. This method spread to Germany during World War II, and from there to the entire world.

The SS recognized the health benefits of saunas early on, and integrated them into the hygiene facilities for its troops, but then also for inmates in various concentration camps. In Auschwitz Birkenau, for instance, a sauna was built both for the guards, and also for the inmates. The latter was built inside the shower and disinfestation building BW 5b (see illustration).

Imagine what inmates must have thought of this device, meaning those who rarely or never had seen *a shower*, let alone a sauna, in their lives. Former Auschwitz inmates Erich Kulka and Ota Kraus wrote this about the sauna at Birkenau in their book *Die Todesfabrik* (*The Death Factory*, Kraus/Kulka 1958, pp. 47f.):

"Even without specialist knowledge, anyone will recognize that the Nazi doctors constantly committed crimes against humanity in the concentration camps. We cannot forget the SS officer, a doctor, who resided in Birkenau at the beginning of 1943. His little hobby-horse was the 'Finnish sauna.'

This bath, in Birkenau, consisted of two rooms, separated from each other which could be hermetically sealed off from each other by means of a door.

The inmates had to undress in the corridor and give up their clothing and underclothing for delousing.

In the first room was a gigantic brick furnace, in which large stones were brought to white heat over a period of several hours before the beginning of the bath. Against the wall opposite the fur-

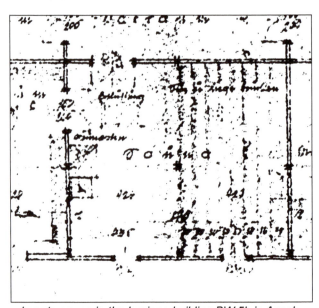

Inmate sauna in the hygiene building BW 5b in Auschwitz Birkenau. Section enlargement of a German wartime construction blueprint. (Pressac 1989, p. 57).

nace was an extremely primitive bench, arranged in steps, reaching almost to the ceiling.

The naked inmates had to sit on these benches, as closely together as they could. One sat next to the other, the healthy ones pressed next to the sick ones, many of whom had infectious skin eruptions.

Then the heated stones were doused with water. As a result of the heat, the emaciated, sick, ruined bodies of the inmates began to sweat heavily. The new arrivals, who had to climb to the highest benches, sweated most of all. Sweat, mixed with dirt and pus from suppurating sores, ran down in streams.

When a few had already begun to lose consciousness, the hermetically-sealed door was opened to the second room, in which the naked inmates were driven under ice-cold showers with shouting and the blows of truncheons by the inmate trustees."

To anybody who had never seen a sauna, and who was prepared to believe the worst about the Germans, this luxury installation naturally appeared as an instrument of torture. In some cases, it may even have given rise to the rumor that people were killed by the Germans in steam chambers, as has been alleged for the Treblinka Camp (see that entry).

This example shows how beneficial health measures introduced by the Germans were misconstrued into instruments of torture by ignorant and/or malicious witnesses.

SAURER COMPANY

For many decades, the Swiss Saurer Company was leading in the development of truck Diesel engines. They furthermore had branches in Austria and France. By the time the Second World War broke out, the Swiss and Austrian branches equipped their trucks exclusively with Diesel engines, while the French branch phased out the last gasoline-engine trucks in 1941.

In 1942, the transportation department of the Reich Security Main Office ordered 30 Saurer truck chassis with the aim of having the Berlin Gaubschat Company equip them with cargo boxes for an unspecified purpose. The Holocaust orthodoxy claims that these cargo boxes were designed or retrofitted to serve as mobile homicidal gas chambers, the so-called gas vans. It is safe to say, however, that these Saurer vehicles had Diesel engines, because had the goal been to deploy gasoline engines, other makes and models would have been much easier to purchase than Saurer gasoline trucks, who at that point in time might have been available only here and there as second-hand vehicles or in overstocked inventories (of which there were few during the war, if any). Diesel exhaust gas, however, is unsuitable for mass murder due to its low carbon-monoxide content. (For more details, see Alvarez 2023, p. 28.)

SCHELLEKES, MAURICE

Maurice Schellekes wrote a brief report in Israel in 1981, almost 40 years after his claimed experiences at Auschwitz, hence inevitably contaminated with elements picked up during those decades. He even mentioned that events at Auschwitz have been described "in so many papers and books" that they need not be repeated. His motivation to write something anyhow was his feeling that he had to defend himself against arguments proffered by Holocaust skeptics. He referred specifically to Thies Christophersen's brochure *The Auschwitz Lie*. However, Schellekes's text is so superficial and full of platitudes that it is worthless as a historical source. He insisted that he saw everything that was going on, but he described things as if he knew nothing specific about them.

He wrote that, from mid-August 1942, he was assigned to the *Sonderkommando* and had the ghastly task of burying thousands of corpses in mass graves, allegedly victims of mass gassings. However, at that time, the typhus epidemic at Auschwitz and Birkenau reached its peak, with many hundreds of victims daily, most of whom were initially buried in mass graves due to a lack of cremation capacity. The situation was so out of control that creating additional corpses by mass murder would have been logistically impossible in the late summer and fall of 1942, so this can safely be ruled out. Hence, what Schellekes describes is, if true, probably related to the burial of typhus victims. Burying hundreds and thousands of dead bodies was surely a horrific task, no matter how the victims had died. This much must be granted him.

After a month of this work, his *Sonderkommando* assignment ended – probably because from late September 1942, corpses were no longer buried, because they threatened to poison the drinking water. They were burned on pyres instead. Schellekes, however, didn't know that context. He then underwent his next selection. As a carrier of the holiest of all of the Third Reich's secret, we would expect him to have been killed, but instead he was allowed for the rest of his time in Auschwitz to be a normal inmate with normal work assignments at the Main Camp and in Birkenau, where he was able and allowed to spread his knowledge among hundreds and thousands of his co-inmates, obviously because his German captors knew that there was nothing secret or problematic about his knowledge.

Demonstrating typical Jewish chutzpah, Schelleckes ended his text by admonishing Holocaust skeptics: "How dare they!" But of course, the same could be said, with vastly greater force, of the hundreds of false and lying Holocaust witnesses.

(For more details, see Mattogno 2022e, pp. 176-179.)

SCHELVIS, JULES

Jules Schelvis

Jules Schelvis was a Dutch Jew who was deported to the Sobibór Camp on 1 June 1943. As he stated in a deposition in Amsterdam on 21 January 1946, this camp served as a transit camp for him: After he had arrived there, he was selected to join a group of 80 deportees who, after three hours, were transferred to Trawniki, and from there to Dorohucza for a labor assignment. He moreover found out about the alleged extermination activities at the Sobibór Camp only through the stories of an acquaintance who had escaped from the camp.

Despite his clear and unequivocal experience, he later became the most prolific orthodox historian of the Sobibór Camp, *denying* its role as a transit camp. Instead, he tried hard to force the massive body of contradictory and evidently false, if not to say mendacious, witness statements into the prevailing orthodox narrative.

(See the entry on Sobibór for more details, as well as Schelvis 2007; Graf/Kues/Mattogno 2020, pp. 41, 48-56, and *passim*; Mattogno 2021e, p. 80.)

SCHINDLER'S LIST, MOVIE

The 1993 movie *Schindler's List*, directed by Jewish-American director Steven Spielberg, is loosely based on Thomas Keneally's novel *Schindler's Arc*. The imprint of the 1982 edition of this book states:

> *"This book is a work of fiction. Names, places, and incidents are either products of the author's imagination or are used fictitiously. Any resemblance to actual events or locales or persons, living or dead, is entirely coincidental."*

This remark was removed in later editions. Over the years, orthodox historians have pointed out that the story line of both Keneally's book and Spielberg's movie are massively distorted. Spielberg openly admitted that he deliberately shot his movie in black and white and created unsteady camera effects to suggest it is a documentary of its time.

According to the movie, the German commandant Amon Göth of the Plaszow Camp randomly shot prisoners from his home balcony overlooking

Invented scene in Spielberg's movie Schindler's List, *showing corpses transported on a conveyor belt into a blazing pit.*

the camp. According to air photos made at that time, however, the commandant's home was situated at the foot of a rise, with the camp itself located on top of this rise. Hence the scene depicted in the movie was physically impossible.

In another movie scene, a conveyor belt is seen transporting corpses toward a burning fire in a pit, dumping them into the blaze (see the illustration). While such a scenario may show what many people came to expect when it comes to the Holocaust – with the orthodox narrative speaking incessantly about a highly industrialized, conveyor-belt style mass extermination – such a device has never been attested to by anyone.

The fact that Amon Göth was arrested and prosecuted by the SS-internal court system during the war is of course not mentioned in the movie.

(For more details, see Rudolf 2019, pp. 253f.)

SCHWARZ, DESZÖ

Deszö Schwarz was an Austrian Jew deported to Auschwitz in late 1943. He spent two months in quarantine. He made an undated deposition at Nuremberg that received the document number NO-2310. In it, Schwarz stated that Birkenau had four identical crematoria, each with underground "gassing bunkers," even though that was true only for two of them (Crematoria II and III). They supposedly had a capacity of up to 1,500 persons. He moreover claimed a fifth execution site where victims were killed with a shot into the neck, then thrown into a flaming pit.

Schwarz made another, more detailed deposition on 26 December 1957 in Vienna (Wiener Library, Cat. No. 105927, Ref. 1656/3/8/764). We read there that, during the first night of his arrival at Auschwitz in late 1943, he claims to have witnessed how inmates selected for death were brought to the edge of a pit in which a fire raged day and night. They were shot and fell into the fire. Children were thrown in alive. Camp Commandant Josef Kramer relished the sight, slapping his thighs in delight. However, if we follow the orthodox narrative, there were no cremation pits active at that time. They are said to have started only in May 1944 with the influx of Hungarian Jews, yet air photos refute even that claim.

Furthermore, Kramer became commandant of the Birkenau Camp only in May 1944, and most certainly would not have attended mass killings at imaginary fire pits, even if they had existed. Moreover, anyone standing at the edge of a blazing pit would soon burn himself, including any SS men executing people there. Furthermore, the orthodoxy has it that, between May and July 1944, cremation pits were located behind Crematorium V and outside of the camp's perimeter near Bunker 2. Since Schwarz was admitted for two months to the quarantine section on arrival, which was far away from both claimed pit locations, how could he possibly have seen what was happening there on his first day at the camp?

Although Schwarz never worked in or near any of the crematoria, he knew that the gassing victims were brought from the gas chamber on carts to the furnaces, which is reminiscent of the false claims made in the War Refugee Board Report. No crematorium in Birkenau had carts going from any alleged gas chamber to the furnaces.

Schwarz moreover calculated that, between January 1944 and October 1944 alone, some 3 million people were gassed at Auschwitz – versus about 580,000 on the orthodox view. Needless to say, he was neither a reliable nor a trustworthy witness.

SCHWARZBART, IGNACY

Ignacy Schwarzbart was a member of the Polish National Council. He reworded and spread reports received by the Polish government in exile in London from the Polish underground about mass executions at the Belzec Camp using electrocution chambers, which is rejected as untrue by all histori-

Ignacy Schwarzbart

ans today. Schwarzbart's reports were subsequently spread by major Jewish media outlets, such as the *Jewish Telegraphic Agency* and *The New York Times*. Schwarzbart's text was used by the Polish agent and black propagandist Jan Karski to further elaborate on the theme.

(For more details, see Mattogno 2004a, pp. 12-14; 2021e, pp. 25f.)

SCHWELA, SIEGFRIED

Siegfried Schwela (3 May 1905 – 10 May 1942), SS *Hauptsturmführer*, was a camp physician at Auschwitz from August 1941. He became the garrison physician of that camp on 21 March 1942. Under his healthcare leadership, sanitary and health conditions in the camp deteriorated to such a degree that in particular typhus became rampant not only among the inmates, but also among the SS staff. Schwela himself contracted the disease and died of it on 10 May 1942. He was replaced by Kurt Uhlenbrock, who also contracted typhus, and barely managed to survive. His successor was Eduard Wirths, who pushed through with the Berlin authorities the necessary sanitary and healthcare measures to combat and eventually resolve the catastrophic sanitary and health conditions, in particular at the Birkenau Camp.

SEHN, JAN

In the years 1945 through 1947, Jan Sehn (22 April 1909 – 12 Dec. 1965) was a Polish investigative judge and a member of the Polish Central Commission for the Investigation of German Crimes in Poland. He took over the investigations concerning events at the former Auschwitz camp complex from the Soviets in the spring of 1945. His team interrogated numerous witnesses and scoured through the more than one hundred thousand pages of documents the German camp authorities had left behind. Of particular importance was the almost complete documentation of the Central Construction Office of the Waffen SS Auschwitz. This office had been in charge of building and maintaining the camp in its entirety.

Sehn was charged with assisting the Polish prosecution in preparing the upcoming two Stalinist show trials against former camp commandant Rudolf Höss on the one hand, and against several former lower-ranking camp officials on the other. From the vast documentation, and with the help of Polish engineer Roman Dawidowski, Sehn cherry-picked ambivalent documents that included terms such as "gas," "gastight," and "gas chamber," or "*sonder*" and "*spezial*" (meaning "separate" or "special"), ripped them out of their documental and historical context, and misrepresented them as circumstantial evidence allegedly proving that homicidal gas chambers existed at the former camp, and had been used for mass murder.

Jan Sehn

Their long list of misinterpreted innocuous documents was rediscovered in the 1980s by French researcher Jean-Claude Pressac. He plagiarized Sehn's and Dawidowski's work without mentioning them, and rebranded their misrepresented pieces of evidence as "criminal traces." Then he added a few more items he had found to this mendacious list, and used them in an attempt to bolster the orthodox Auschwitz narrative. A few years later, Jewish-Dutch historian Robert Jan van Pelt plagiarized Pressac's work, without mentioning him, and presented it as his research result.

Jan Sehn and all his followers ignored and hid from the courts, from the defense and from the public that the vast extant Auschwitz documentation actually proves the exact opposite of their narrative: terms such as "gas chamber" refer to disinfestation gas chambers meant to *save* inmate lives, not kill them. Furthermore, the camp authorities had gone to great lengths and enormous efforts and expenses in their desperate attempts at improving living conditions and thus survival chances for all inmates. (See the section "Documented History" of the entry on the Birkenau Camp and on healthcare for details.)

Sehn consistently sought to defend and promote the propagandistic paradigm that the Soviets had created with their initial investigations at the camp. Before Sehn began his work, a mixed Polish-Soviet "expert commission" had "determined" that the Auschwitz crematoria had the capacity to cremate four million bodies – and indeed did so. This way, this mock commission confirmed the camp's preordained death toll of four million. One member of this four-member Polish-Soviet commission was Sehn's right-hand man Roman

Witness Claims on Cremation Capacity of Birkenau Crematoria

Witness	Daily Capacity
Reality	ca. 1,000
S. Dragon	10,000-12,000
	11,350
H. Mandelbaum	*38,800*
H. Tauber (Soviet)	*11,600*
H. Tauber (Polish)	*7,800*
D. Fliamenbaum	*8,830*
S. Jankowski	8,000
M. Nyiszli	20,000/*9,930*
D. Paisikovic (Austria)	*18,400*/*41,400*
D. Paisikovic (Germany)	*9,460*
J. Rosenblum	36,000/*26,490*
F. Müller	10,000/*9,930*
J. Sackar	20,000
D. Gabai	8,590/*8,830*
L. Cohen	*9,200*
R. Höss	7,000
E. Mussfeldt	6,620
Soviet experts	9,000/*9,530*
R. Dawidowski	8,000/*11,470*
J. Sehn	12,000/*8,830*

Roman typeface: explicitly stated; *italic typeface*: calculated from other data given by the witness.

Dawidowski.

Many of the witnesses interviewed by Sehn also confirmed the camp's preordained death toll. They either did so explicitly or by claiming absurdly inflated deportation numbers, gassing and/or cremation capacities that resulted in the expected casualty figures (see the table). This "convergence of evidence" on the same lie proves the orchestrated nature of all these witness testimonies. (See in this regard also the entry on cremation propaganda.)

Jan Sehn was supposed to testify about his "findings" in late 1965 during the Frankfurt Auschwitz show trial. However, he suddenly died in his Frankfurt hotel room before he could testify.

(For more details, see Mattogno 2019, esp. pp. 288, 513-523.)

SEIDENWURM WRZOS, MARY

Mary Seidenwurm Wrzos was a Polish Jewess who claims to have been incarcerated at the Majdanek Camp during the war. After the war, she emigrated to Sweden, where a book about her alleged experiences was published in 1945 in Stockholm titled *De dödsdömda vittnar* (*The Doomed Bear Witness*, edited by Gunhild and Einar Tegen). We read in it:

> "*We walked three kilometers from the labor camp in Lublin to the actual concentration camp [Majdanek], under guard by heavily armed SS men. We were taken to subterranean rooms that were very conveniently furbished. Each of us received a clothes hanger to put our things on. The shoes had to be properly tied together.*
>
> *We went into the 'shower room' completely naked, carrying only a towel and a piece of soap. I immediately noticed that the doors were made of unusually thick iron. Since I did not push myself forward, it happened that I was the last to step inside the gas chamber. I looked at the ceiling. Besides the usual showerheads, I could see three large black holes. Now I knew where I was! The heavy iron door began to close, but slowly, very slowly. And about at the same time, gas began to pour out of the three large black holes!*
>
> *With supernatural power I began to bang on the door, which had still not closed completely. 'I am a German, I am a German camp police, I am a German transport guard'. I yelled these words over and over, and at the same time, I beat on the door like crazy. It began to open, but very slowly. Blood was dripping from my forehead, from my arms, from my knees. I lay there, all my weight put against the door, panting for air, while it slowly opened before me (it seemed to take an eternity). My whole body was covered in cold sweat. I am going to suffocate. Then the door is opened. Men wearing gas masks pull me out through the narrow opening. I hear a couple shots fired at the women who try to get past me. Air. Air. At last air. Everything is spinning. Then I lose consciousness.*
>
> *When I woke up, the female German-Jewish Kapo stood before me. She helped me up and put me in order. (Everything had taken less than half a minute.) When I looked at myself in the mirror the next day, I saw that I had a gray stripe of hair on the left side.*"

Unfortunately, no underground room existed at Majdanek, none of the claimed homicidal gas chambers is said to have had fake showerheads, none of them had three large black holes, none of the gasses allegedly used would have shown an effect within half a minute, and none would have led to bleeding foreheads, arms and knees, let alone grey streaks of hair. The witness also fails to tell us what the reaction of the SS was when they discovered that she wasn't a German guard after all. Apparently, they let it slide. Finally, inmates were issued towels and soap only when actually taking a shower, which is probably the real background of her story.

SELF-IMMOLATING BODIES

After several cases were reported where the bodies of deceased individuals had slowly burned to a large degree, investigations into the phenomenon have revealed that, under highly unusual circumstances, large parts of a human body can indeed burn almost to ashes without any fuel. These cases are usually initiated by small fires such as candles setting aflame some fabric, usually cotton, which subsequently acts like a wick, slowly melting and burning subcutaneous fat deposits. The heat produced can be enough to slowly evaporate the body's water, thus enabling also the remaining tissues made of fat and protein to burn. This phenomenon requires a body with sufficient fat content, meaning an overweight or obese person. This procedure takes many hours and burns only the trunk plus, in highly obese cases, also fat-rich parts of the extremities, but usually not the lower extremities (lower arms and legs, feet and hands) which have less fat content (Nickell/Fischer 1984; Nickell 1998).

It goes without saying that this is not a way to turn

human bodies into ashes swiftly and completely. In particular, it would not have worked with the millions of Jews deported to German camps, most of whom had lived a life of deprivation to the point of starvation for months if not years. Overweight or even obese individuals were rare among them.

Nevertheless, there are many witnesses to the claimed National-Socialist mass murder of the Jews who insisted that the victims' bodies were burned to ashes with little or no fuel, either in crematoria or on pyres. Experiences with large-scale outdoor combustions of culled livestock have shown, however, that cremation without fuel is a far-fetched illusion (see the entry for open-air incinerations). Furthermore, more than a century of scientific and historical data on millions of cremations in crematoria has equally shown that burning the human body in such devices requires considerable amounts of fuel – again with the exception of obese individuals.

Among the witnesses having made false claims about self-immolating human bodies are:

- Paul Blobel
- Leon Cohen
- Eliezer Eisenschmidt
- Leon Finkelsztein
- Yaakov Gabai
- Richard Glazar
- Stanisław Jankowski
- Stanisław Kon
- Olga Lengyel
- Maurice Lequeux
- Kurt Marcus
- Konrad Morgen
- Marcel Nadsari
- Ludwik Nagraba
- Dov Paisikovic
- Chil Rajchman
- Jean-François Steiner
- Franz Suchomel
- Franz Süss
- Jerzy Tabeau
- Henryk Tauber
- (M. Vaillant-Couturier)
- Shlomo Venezia
- Szyja Warszawski
- Jankiel Wiernik

This "convergence of evidence" on the same lie proves the copy-cat and/or orchestrated nature of these witness testimonies.

SEMLIN

According to the orthodox narrative, some 7,000 Serbian Jews are said to have been killed by German occupational forces in early 1942 in the Semlin Camp in Serbia, which is called Sajmište Camp by the Serbs. These murders are said to have been committed using a gas van that was specifically transported to that camp from Germany with two dedicated drivers. The bodies of the murdered victims were later allegedly exhumed and tracelessly burned within the framework of *Aktion* 1005.

The only witness who ever testified about this exhumation and cremation activity in front of Yugoslavian officials is a certain Momčilo Damjanović. However, his testimony contains numerous preposterous claims that make the witness untrustworthy. (See the entry on this witness).

In the fall of 1941, with partisan activities in Serbia escalating, the German authorities decided to crack down on the partisans by imposing extremely harsh reprisal shooting ratios of 100 executions of hostages for every German soldier or civilian killed in Serbia. Next to Serbian civilians held in prisons for various reasons, male Jews were picked as the primary victims of these reprisal shootings. Jewish women, children and the elderly were to be arrested and held in the Semlin Camp. On 2 October 1941, German foreign minister Ribbentrop cabled to Belgrade with respect to these women, children and the elderly:

"As soon as the technical means exist for the complete solution of the Jewish question, the Jews will be deported on the waterway [i.e., the Danube] *to the reception camps in the east."*

No document is known which indicates that this instruction was ever revised or rescinded.

The Semlin Camp is not mentioned in any document connected with gas vans. A photostat copy (white on black) of a telegram exists, speaking of a Saurer truck being transferred to Berlin for repairs from Belgrade after completion of a "special order." This document was presented as evidence for the deployment of a gas van in Serbia already during the International Military Tribunal (Document PS-501, in the set together with the so-called August Becker Document). But since Saurer trucks all had diesel engines, and because diesel exhaust gas is not lethal, this cannot have been a homicidal gas van.

The German court that put the writer of this telegram on trial in 1953 saw that differently, however. They strictly followed the path of what the Nuremberg Allied tribunals had "established." Therefore, former SS *Oberführer* and Colonel of the Police Dr. Emanuel Schäfer, who was the superior of the men running the Semlin Camp, never had a realistic chance of defense. Two more trials held some 15 years later – one against the camp commandant Herbert Andorfer, the other against a former camp guard – followed the deep rut established by earlier trials. In none of these trials was any question ever asked as to how exhaust gas from a diesel engine could possibly kill. None of the suspicious features of the documents used *ad nauseam* to "prove" the existence and use of gas vans was ever addressed either. They were probably not even noticed by the prosecution, the judges or any of the defense lawyers. They all simply believed – or wanted to believe.

One witness, by the way, could even see things that didn't exist, even from an orthodox point of view: During the Jerusalem Eichmann Trial, one witness claimed that the Jews in the Semlin Camp were murdered in stationary gas chambers rather than a gas vas.

(For more details on this, see the entries on gas vans, August Becker, Gaubschat Company, Saurer Company, and also Alvarez 2023, pp. 22f., 148, 185-188, 225-227, 249-257.)

Serbia → Yugoslavia

SHANGHAI (CHINA)

Within the context of the Holocaust, wartime Shanghai played a role as a temporary safe haven and transit stopover for some 20,000 Jews fleeing Europe and the Soviet Union in the 1930s. The reason for this is that Shanghai did not require any visas for Jews to enter and stay in the city.

SHEFTEL, YORAM

After John Demjanjuk's first defense lawyer, Dov Eitan, had been assassinated the day before Demjanjuk's appeal trial before the Jerusalem Court of Appeals was to start, Demjanjuk's second lawyer Yoram Sheftel was attacked during Eitan's funeral: someone threw acid into his face which almost made him blind (Sheftel 1994, pp. 243-263).

Yoram Sheftel

SHOES OF DEPORTEES

Both the Auschwitz Museum and the Majdanek Museum have an exhibit on display showing what are said to be the shoes of former camp inmates. (See the illustrations.)

The shoes of Majdanek used to be piled up in a barracks, where the Soviets photographed them in the summer of 1944. They presented these photographs as evidence for mass murder committed at Majdanek. The shoes in the Auschwitz show case consist merely of one layer put on an inclined plane to give the false impression that this is a large pile of shoes. These, too, are presented as evidence for mass murder at Auschwitz, although these shoes' origin is completely unknown and undocumented.

A pile of shoes, in and of itself, proves nothing but the fact that someone has put them there. If it were otherwise, any collection of old clothes and shoes for charities would prove mass murder of the former owners.

As numerous wartime documents show, the SS operated a huge clothing and shoe manufacturing and recycling operation at Majdanek. Among other things, worn-out or damaged shoes and clothes from Germany's armed forces, as well as clothing and shoes of inmates admitted to various camps, were all sent to Majdanek for further processing. Right opposite of where the Soviets found the shoe storage at Majdanek is the camp's shoemaker workshop (*Schumacher-Werkstätte*), and it is even labelled as such. The fact was later recognized by orthodox historians, although they still insist that many if not most of the former owners of the clothes and shoes sent to Maj-

Showcase at the Auschwitz Museum, showing a layer of old shoes on an inclined plane, giving the false impression of being a pile.

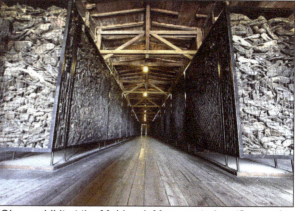
Shoe exhibit at the Majdanek Museum today. (Some of it was destroyed in a 2010 fire.)

danek were murdered.

Most notably, the Majdanek Museum displays to this day at their infamous shoe-storage building a sign at the entrance stating that these shoes belonged "to victims of 'Operation Reinhardt.'" According to the orthodox Holocaust narrative, *Aktion Reinhardt* was the code name for the wholesale slaughter of European Jews by National-Socialist Germany. (See the entry on *Aktion Reinhardt*.)

It goes without saying that it is not possible to determine the fate of an item's former owner by staring at the item in devotion. This is possible only by assessing anecdotal, documental, material and forensic evidence.

(For more information, see Rudolf 2023, pp. 18-21.)

shortwave delousing → **Microwave Delousing**

SHOW TRIALS

Calling a legal proceeding a "show trial" amounts to accusing the involved judiciary of not playing by the rules of a fair trial. The degree of unfairness can vary, of course. The following are some of the features that distinguish show trials from normal, fair trials. The more of them are that are present, the more a trial has the characteristics of a show trial. The following list of key features of show trials includes a brief discussion of the degree to which these features are typically given for trials against alleged perpetrators of claimed Holocaust crimes, or of historical dissidents challenging the mainstream narrative in countries where this is a criminal offense (see the "Penal Law" section of the entry on censorship):

– *The crime as such, which in some cases is invented or exaggerated, cannot be challenged, or only with great obstacles.* As the entries on absurd claims, exaggerated death tolls, cremation propaganda and many individual witnesses demonstrate, claims about the Holocaust have been partially invented and at times greatly exaggerated. Furthermore, ever since and including the Allied postwar trials, the Holocaust, with many of its claimed constituent crimes, has been legally undeniable and incontestable in many countries. Even in the U.S., the court dealing with the Mermelstein case decided that the use of homicidal gas chambers at Auschwitz cannot be contested. The "reality" of Holocaust claims is said to be as self-evident as the fact that water doesn't flow uphill. (Although that is circular logic, because we define uphill as the direction in which water doesn't flow.)

– *The alleged crimes are described as extraordinarily evil.* The Holocaust is frequently referred to as the worst crime in the history of mankind, the nadir of absolute evil. Challenging the veracity of Holocaust claims in turn is equated with violating the world's holiest of all taboos. There is no heresy worse than contesting that "it" happened the way that the orthodoxy claims it did.

– *The indictment contains polemical and/or political expressions.* Defendants accused of perpetrating Holocaust crimes are frequently depicted as assistants of the devil incarnate, Adolf Hitler. Scholars trying to revise the lopsided historical image are called by media and judiciary the worst names our society has at its disposal: deniers, anti-Semites, Nazis, racists…

– *During the trial, the acts investigated are forced into an overarching ideological framework of alleged moral or historical evil.* During trials against alleged perpetrators, it is common legal practice not to focus primarily on the defendant's deeds, but first to paint a grand image of unique and unparalleled National-Socialist atrocities, in which the defendant's acts are portrayed as a more-or-less important cogwheel in the machinery of unimaginable terror. Any attempt to portray events in a more differentiated way is seen as a despicable and in some countries even illegal act of "minimizing" or "trivializing" the Holocaust.

– *The judges are subjected to significant political and public pressure to sentence the defendants.* Especially during Israeli trials (against Adolf Eichmann and John Demjanjuk) and during West-German proceedings against alleged NS perpetrators, public and political expectations were massive to see the defendants convicted and sentenced severely. Whenever a defendant was acquitted or punished only mildly, harsh criticism was sure to follow. See the entry on Karl Wolff to learn, how even juries were pressured to secure convictions. So far, only one case is known where judges decided to convict a historical dissident mildly, granting him honorable motives in trying to defend his nation (Günter Deckert, Germany). This caused a media uproar which led to this judge, Dr. Rainer Orlet, having to retire early to avoid prosecution.

– *The defendants/victims are unpopular individu-*

als, usually political or ideological dissidents. There is no political ideology more despised than National Socialism. Any defendant accused of participation in claimed Holocaust crimes is inevitably linked to that ideology. Most were even members of the party or one of its affiliated organizations. Historical dissidents on this topic are also regularly depicted as adherents of this most-nefarious of all ideologies, although that is not even true in most cases.
– *The aim is to deter and discipline adherents and sympathizers of the targeted political or ideological group.* After the war, the aim clearly was to utterly destroy the targeted political groups – National Socialism as an ideology and its organizations as their manifestation – to destroy their reputation for all eternity, and to deter anyone from developing any sympathy for them. This goal has not changed to this day, and the judiciary is misused to achieve it. This is not to say that combating totalitarian or dictatorial ideologies isn't a legitimate objective. However, abusing the judiciary to achieve political or ideological objectives is clearly wrong.
– *One-sided media attention serves to publicly prejudge, denigrate and humiliate the defendants.* One of the first things the Allies did after the war was to ensure that no media outlet existed in Europe that could present arguments of the other side. Total censorship came down over Europe. Only one side of the story has ever been published during trials against alleged Holocaust perpetrators, and with great sensationalism. The Holocaust narrative that media outlets are allowed to tell is today enshrined by law in many European countries, in Israel, Australia and Canada. Amazon, Google, YouTube, Ingram Content Group, and other major players on the Internet and in the distribution of media items have joined the club of total censorship of dissident viewpoints. As a result, the mainstream media can spread their one-sided and mendacious stories with impunity and without anyone correcting or complementing them. Dissidents, in particular those on trial, have been and are portrayed by the mainstream media as vile individuals deserving the utmost contempt and punishment. The mainstream media ferociously demand the destruction of free speech, so they can solidify their monopoly over the public mind.
– *Principles of the rule of law are disregarded, in particular by curtailing the rights of the defense.* The Allied postwar trials had a legal framework that made it practically impossible for the defendants to muster any kind of efficient defense. First, new laws were applied retro-actively. Next, anything witnesses for the prosecution claimed was considered true until proven otherwise. Claims in reports filed by the prosecution were incontestable. Defense lawyers could not speak in private with their clients. Access to the prosecution's files were severely limited or not granted at all. But the worst was yet to come: when dissidents started challenging the taboo in the 1980s and 1990s, new case law was created in some countries (such as Germany) that declared it a crime to introduce any evidence challenging the taboo, and a new law allows – in fact, obligates – the court to muzzle defense lawyers if they dare challenge the taboo orally during the proceedings.
– *Testimonies of alleged victims, often presented in an emotional way, receive precedent over other, more reliable types of evidence, such as documents, material evidence and expert testimonies, although testimonies of parties who have a vested interest are notoriously highly unreliable.* The sad truth is that not a single defense lawyer, let alone judge or prosecutor, in any of the hundreds of trials dealing with Holocaust crimes, ever asked for the introduction of documental or physical evidence that may clarify whether the purported crimes did indeed occur, or whether certain claims about them were physically possible. Furthermore, no trace of a murder victim was ever found or forensically investigated, and no trace of a murder weapon was ever found or subjected to a forensic investigation. (With two known exceptions: the Vienna Auschwitz trial against Walter Dejaco and Fritz Ertl, where an expert witness was asked to interpret crematorium blueprints – see the entry on Walter Dejaco – and one trial in Australia, where the court initiated the exhumation of a mass grave; see the section "Forensic Findings" of the entry on the *Einsatzgruppen*). No normal murder trial could even begin without some trace of the victims and weapons, and could certainly never obtain a conviction. The first trials where the defense tried introducing such evidence were the trials against Holocaust dissident Ernst Zün-

del. After this, several other trials against historical dissidents have followed suit. However, the main outcome of this was not the unbiased evaluation of the evidence offered, but an increase in persecution of the dissidents daring to challenge the taboo, foremost directed against expert witnesses attempting to show that certain Holocaust claims can be refuted with documental and material evidence.

– *Confessions and witness testimonies are obtained by illegal means (manipulation, suggestion, bribery, pressure, coercion, torture etc.).* Toward the end of the war and in subsequent years, all Allied occupational forces systematically used torture and other extortion methods to obtain "confessions" from incarcerated defendants, and "survivor" organizations used their leverage over food rations and lodging options to pressure "survivors" into complicity with their scheme of writing a one-sided history. Later, prosecutors and "survivor" organization collaborated in compiling dossiers on certain crime complexes containing detailed "information" on all potential perpetrators and their claimed crimes, which were sent to witnesses, so they could learn what they were expected to "know."

– *The harsh verdict is at times disproportionate to the claimed crime.* There is no punishment harsh enough for mass murder, so this cannot apply. However, in recent years, even mere bureaucrats in administrative positions, not involved in any murderous activities, were prosecuted and punished. It is argued that they must have known what is now considered "self-evident," hence they must have known that they were aiding in mass murder. And even if not, lack of knowledge is not permitted as a defense. On the other hand, there is no parallel in the history of mankind to what has happened primarily in Europe after the war: an entire civilization decided to prescribe the writing of history by penal law and mercilessly imprison those who voice dissident points of view, with cumulative prison terms that may exceed 10 years – for writing controversial but peaceful texts about history. The world hasn't seen such perfidy since the medieval Inquisition.

In conclusion, almost every single trial ever held against any alleged Holocaust perpetrator, and every single trial ever staged against any Holocaust dissident, has been a show trial. There may be variations as to the degree of show-trial character, but all trials fulfilled most of the above-listed criteria.

The one exception from that rule was the previously mentioned Vienna Auschwitz trial of 1972 against Dejaco and Ertl. There, the judges asked for an expert report to verify whether the blueprints of the crematoria provided by the Auschwitz Museum show any indication that these buildings contained homicidal gas chambers, or if not, whether the rooms claimed to have been such gas chambers could conceivably have been converted to serve such a purpose.

Even skilled judges are incompetent as historians, and many, if not most, verdicts ever handed down in this matter have later been demonstrated to be grossly inaccurate, if not outright wrong. History cannot and must not be written by court decisions.

SHOWERS
Fake Showers

Many witnesses claimed that the victims of homicidal gassings were told by SS men or their helpers that, in order to be admitted to the camp, they needed to have their clothes laundered and disinfested, and they themselves had to take a shower. This, it is frequently claimed, was a deception, so the victims would remain calm, would willingly get undressed, and would more or less voluntarily enter the homicidal gas chamber. To make that deception credible, the victims are often said to have been handed towels and soap when walking into the shower room/gas chamber, and the alleged homicidal gas chambers were presumably fitted with items making them look like shower rooms – foremost with dummy showerheads that were not connected to anything, or that were actually connected to some poison-gas supply rather than water.

The issuance of towels and soap, however, most certainly would never have happened, considering the mess it would have created and the effort necessary to retrieve and clean these items afterwards. In addition, no one takes towels into a shower. (See the entry on Towels, Soap, Toothbrushes inside Gas Chambers.)

The Crematoria II and III at Auschwitz are a prime example for this. One of their underground morgues is said to have been misused as a homicidal gas chamber, and many witnesses claimed that they had in their ceiling (fake) showerheads meant to deceive the victims. Some even claimed that these showerheads were used to introduce the poison gas rather than water.

Real Showers

In order to prevent the introduction and spread of disease, any inmate admitted or transferred to a German wartime camp had to undergo a hygienic routine prescribed by camp orders. The inmates had to go into a hygienic building featuring disinfestation and often also laundry facilities, undressing and dressing rooms, and an inmate shower. There they had to undress, hand over their clothes, then go into a shower room – where soap was provided – and take a shower. After that, they went out the other side into a separate dressing room, where towels may have been provided, and where they were given disinfested and laundered inmate/prison clothes. In addition, most inmates were then placed into a quarantine section of the camp for several weeks, to make sure they did not carry any infectious diseases.

A very similar procedure was followed when inmates were transferred away from a camp. Before being transported, they again had to undergo this procedure and then remain isolated from the rest of the camp until their transport took them away. This was to ensure that the inmate did not introduce any infectious diseases to his new destination.

(On hygienic measures at Auschwitz, see Rudolf 2020, pp. 76-90, as well as the many entries about disinfestation and disinfection in Mattogno 2023, Part 1.)

Crematoria II and III at Auschwitz-Birkenau fit nicely into that scenario. There is a plethora of wartime documents showing that real inmate showers were installed in both basements of these facilities as a makeshift measure to increase the available showers in the camp while the large disinfestation and shower facility – called *Zentralsauna* – was being built. These basement showers were to use the heat permanently produced by the waste incinerator which was located in the chimney wing of both buildings. Therefore, the showers in these basements were *not* fake, but real, and inmates going in there really took showers of warm water. However, that may have happened only for a short period of time, because these showers were probably taken out of use toward the end of 1943, after the *Zentralsauna* had become operational. From that point onward, the inmate workers in these crematoria marveled about the reason why no-longer functioning showerheads were located in a room which, when they saw that place, was only used to store corpses (which is, after all, the primary function of a morgue).
(For more details on the real showers, see Mattogno 2019, pp. 134-142.)

False Gas-Shower Claims

Some witnesses have claimed that showerheads were actually used to feed poison gas into the claimed homicidal gas chambers. In cases where Zyklon B is said to have been used for the murder, this would have been technically very challenging, as this product – liquid hydrogen cyanide soaked on gypsum pellets – was not a gas under pressure, and therefore could not have been fed into a pipe as such. The orthodox narrative has it that murder with Zyklon B happened simply by Zyklon B's gypsum pellets getting poured into the gas chamber through some opening – either on the floor or into some column. (See the entry on Zyklon-B introduction devices.)

In other cases, such as the use of bottled, pressurized gas (such as carbon monoxide) or gas from internal combustion engines, piping gas through showerheads would have been technically feasible, but is usually rejected by the orthodoxy as untrue. Simple pipes with a single opening in the wall per chamber are said to have been used.

Here is a list of some of the witnesses who have falsely claimed that the gas came out of showerheads:

Auschwitz
 – Ada Bimko
 – Chaim Engel
 – Jeannette Kaufmann
 – Sofia Kaufmann Schafranov
 – Imre Kertész
 – Leo Laptos
 – Pelagia Lewińska
 – Bruno Piazza (water showers used to develop gas from powder on the floor)
 – Resistance writings of 29 August 1942 and of late 1942/early 1943
 – André Rogerie
 – Jerzy Tabeau
 – Siegfried van den Bergh
 – Alfred Wetzler
 – letter from an anonymous escaped inmate published by the Polish underground in August 1942 (see Mattogno 2021, p. 124)
 – tale from an anonymous French worker published by a French underground paper in May 1944 (see

Mattogno 2021, pp. 191f.)

Other Camps
- Abraham Bomba (Treblinka)
- Abraham Krzepicki (Treblinka)
- Chil Rajchman (Treblinka)
- Willi Feiler (Sachsenhausen)
- Wilhelm Soerensen (Sachsenhausen)
- Saartje Wijnberg (Sobibór)

This "convergence of evidence" on the same lie proves the copy-cat or orchestrated nature of these witness testimonies.

SHRUNKEN HEADS, MYTH OF

At the Buchenwald Camp shortly after its occupation by U.S. American troops in April 1945, the U.S. Armed Forces' Psychological Warfare Division (PWD) set up a table displaying items meant to prove National-Socialist atrocities. For "educational" purposes, the local population was forced to walk by this table and hear a U.S. official in uniform explain to them what they were seeing.

Among the items displayed were pieces of skin with drawings, allegedly consisting of tattooed human skin, a lampshade, and also two shrunken heads.

One of these shrunken heads was presented during the Nuremberg International Military Tribunal (IMT) as evidence of the "pathological Nazi culture" (*IMT*, Vol. 3, p. 516). The official U.S. Army report coming with this head claimed:

> "There I also saw the shrunken heads of two young Poles who had been hanged for having relations with German girls. The heads were the size of a fist, and the hair and the marks of the rope were still there."

How anyone could deduce this story from glancing at a set of shrunken heads mounted on little pedestals is beyond comprehension.

A photograph of these two shrunken heads shows, however, that both heads' skin is of dark complexion, hence they are not from ethnic central Europeans. Furthermore, both faces clearly show remnants of war paint, as is used by indigenous peoples of the Americas. They are also the only ethnic groups worldwide who have developed a "pathological culture" of shrinking the heads of killed enemy warriors.

Therefore, these are most likely shrunken heads from two South- or Central-American indigenous warriors. They were probably found by a European or North-American anthropologist, colonist or conqueror, who brought them back either to Europe or North America. There they were mounted on pedestals and were either part of a private collection or became an exhibit at some anthropological museum. They were taken from this collection by individuals of the U.S. PWD, and added to the horror collection of the Buchenwald re-education table.

After the IMT was over, the two heads disappeared tracelessly and have not been seen since. That alone is very indicative.

(For more details, see Rudolf 2023, pp. 94-98; Irebodd 2008, 2009.)

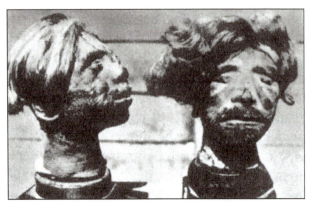

Shrunken heads, allegedly of some victim of National-Socialist atrocities. However, these faces have a dark complexion and clear signs of war paint as used by indigenous peoples of the Americas.

SILBERSCHEIN, ABRAHAM

Abraham Silberschein

Abraham Silberschein was a member of the Polish parliament, a delegate of the World Jewish Congress and a member of the Committee for Assistance to the Suffering Jews in the Occupied Countries. As such, he collected witness testimonies about the alleged extermination of Jews in occupied Poland, which he published in Geneva in 1944 in a multi-volume series under the German title *Die Judenausrottung in Polen* (*The Extermination of the Jews in Poland*). The series contains statements by Jerzy Tabeau on Auschwitz as well as various texts on Belzec, Sobibór and Treblinka without mentioning any author. Silberschein also possessed a version of the report by Alfred Wetzler and Rudolf Vrba, which forms the core of the so-called War Refugee Board Report. This version is now stored at the Yad

Vashem Archives.

Here are some peculiar claims in Silberschein's texts about Belzec:
- Victims were killed by electrocution with an electric oven. However, the orthodoxy insists that murder occurred at Belzec with engine-exhaust gases.
- The victims' body fat was drained, and special camp factories turned it into soap and shoe polish.
- Hospitals were built to drain the blood of Jewish children. Even the most fanatical orthodox historians consider that claim to be untrue.

Here are some more peculiar claims in Silberschein's texts about Treblinka:
- The extermination building consisted of an undressing room, a shower room, a dressing room, plus an experimental gas chamber that was connected to a furnace room, from which a railway led to the "cemetery." However, the orthodox narrative has it that the gassing facility had neither an undressing nor a dressing room, that there was no furnace or furnace room anywhere at Treblinka, and that no rail connected the gas-chamber building with the mass graves.
- Arriving inmates first took a bath, then waited in holding cells. But eventually, they were brought from there to the "gas and furnace chambers," where they were *steamed* to death with *water vapor*. The orthodoxy insists, however, that there was no shower and no waiting time for arriving inmates, but that they were gassed right on arrival with Diesel-exhaust gases – which are unsuitable for mass murder. What would have been the purpose of going to great length in giving thousands of deportees a warm shower, if they were to be killed soon anyway?
- An orchestra had to play music during executions, with the musicians being killed after every gassing batch, to be replaced with new musicians. This is ludicrous.

Silberschein's books reflect one of the earliest impressions of the claimed mass murder in these four camps, allegedly originating from survivors who had just escaped these hellish places and whose memories were still fresh and not yet contaminated with stories later spread through media and survivor associations. Yet still, the stories were all dead wrong, even compared to today's orthodox narrative.

SIMPSON, GORDON

Gordon Simpson (30 Oct. 1894 – 13 February 1987) was a justice of the Supreme Court of Texas from January 1945 until September 1949. Together with Edward van Roden, at that time Chief of U.S. Military Justice in Europe, Simpson was appointed in 1948 to an extraordinary commission. This commission was charged with investigating claims that German inmates in U.S. custody at Dachau had been physically abused. Simpson and van Roden concluded in their report that such abuse had indeed been pervasive and severe. (See the entries on Edward van Roden, and the section "United States" of the entry on torture.)

Gordon Simpson

SIX MILLION (JEWISH VICTIMS)
Importance

The alleged Six Million Jewish fatalities is the single most important number of the Holocaust, and one of the most consequential statistics in all of history. It appears everywhere that we hear about the Holocaust. The US Holocaust Memorial Museum website writes:

> "The Holocaust was the systematic, bureaucratic, state-sponsored persecution and murder of approximately six million Jews."

The official Israeli institute Yad Vashem says:

> "The Holocaust was the murder of approximately six million Jews by the Nazis and their collaborators."

Orthodox historians are extremely confident of this number; as Jacob Robinson writes (1976, p. 281):

> "There can be no doubt as to the accuracy of the estimated figure of some six million victims."

Walter Laqueur's *Holocaust Encyclopedia* concurs (Laqueur/Baumel-Schwartz 2001, p. 139):

> "The round figure of 6 million admits of no serious doubt."

Clearly, much stands or falls on this single number, which has been called repeatedly a symbolic figure.

Six Million before the Holocaust

So, we have an obvious question: Where did the infamous figure of Six Million come from in the first place? One would naturally presume it to be impossible to calculate the death toll in the midst of a raging world war. Even in the immediate aftermath, we would know little for certain. It turns out that the world was told of Six Million Jewish victims not only in the immediate aftermath of the war, but *during* the war, at the *start* of the war, and even *before* the war – in fact, *decades before the war*. The seemingly impossible history of the Six Million constitutes a fascinating subtext to the larger Holocaust narrative.

One can find reference to "6 million" and "Jews" in newspapers dating from decades ago, even more than a century. In 1850, the *Christian Spectator* cited a total of "6,000,000 Jews" in the world; in 1870, *The New York Times* (*NYT*) followed suit; in 1889, the *NYT* reported that Six Million Jews "were all in a state of political bondage"; and in 1891, they referred to "six million persecuted and miserable wretches."

By 1900, the Zionist movement was gaining strength and was anxious to encourage "suffering" Jews to move to Palestine. That year, the *NYT* quoted activist Stephen Wise as saying that, in Europe, "There are 6,000,000 living, bleeding, suffering arguments in favor of Zionism." In 1901, the *Chicago Daily Tribune* reported on the "hopeless condition" of the "six million Jews in Russia." In 1905, Zionists began to fret that "Russia, with its 6,000,000 Jews," wasn't promoting emigration.

Soon thereafter, World War I began. We then begin to read in the *NYT* of the plight of "more than 6,000,000 Jews who live within the war zone." The next month carried more reports of the eternally damned, "of whom more than 6,000,000 are in the very heart of the war zone"; they were consequently "subjected to every manner of suffering and sorrow," and all Americans were called upon to help. In 1916, we read that "the world is silent" despite the fact that "nearly six million Jews are ruined, in the greatest moral and material misery." A year later, Rabbi Samuel Schulman exclaimed that "six millions of Jews are living in lands where they are oppressed, exploited, crushed, and robbed of every inalienable human right." In May of 1917, we hear that "six million Jews – half the Jews of the world – are calling to you for help."

By late 1918, the war was nearing its end. Did we have Six Million Jewish fatalities? No. Somehow, they all managed to survive. Instead of attending their funerals, we were then called upon to aid their recovery: "Six million souls will need help to resume normal life when war is ended," writes the *NYT*.

One might have thought that this would have been the end of the stories of the Six Million. It was not. The infamous number simply shifted to a new region. In September of 1919, we find that it was now the *Ukrainian* and *Polish* Jews who were subject to misery; "6,000,000 are in peril." We are further horrified to read that "the population of 6,000,000 souls in Ukrania and in Poland... are going to be completely exterminated." Naturally, this was "the paramount issue of the present day." Once again, Six Million Jews under threat of extermination.

The trend continued for years, too numerous to elaborate. References include the following:
– "unbelievable poverty, starvation and disease [for] about 6,000,000 souls, or half the Jewish population of the earth" (1919).
– "typhus menaced 6,000,000 Jews of Europe" (1920).
– "hunger, cold rags, desolation, disease, death – six million human beings without food, shelter, clothing" (1920).
– "Russia's 6,000,000 Jews are facing extermination by massacre" – again! (1921).
– "over 6,000,000" Russian Jews "neglected" (1924).

Six Million during the Holocaust

This brings us to the Nazi era, where the Six Million appeared once again – and long before World War II. The first reference came just two months after Hitler assumed power in January 1933. The *NYT* reported on a "Hitler protest" vote by some local New York government officials. Rabbi Stephen Wise issued an appeal: "[We are] now active in relief and reconstruction work in Eastern Europe where 6,000,000 Jews are involved." Three years later, in 1936, we read in the London *Times* of "6,000,000 unwanted unfortunate" Jews, and of "these 6,000,000 people without a future." On that same day, the *NYT* reported on a speech by British Zionist Chaim Weizmann, who "dwelt first on the tragedy of at least 6,000,000 'superfluous' Jews in Poland, Germany, Austria." In February 1937, we hear that "five to six million Jews in Europe are facing expulsion or direst poverty."

Such references continued on through 1938 and 1939. War began in September of that year, and anti-Nazi propaganda accelerated. In mid-1940, the *NYT* quoted Nahum Goldmann:

"Six million Jews are doomed to destruction if the victory of the Nazis should be final."

This was still at least one full year before Hitler allegedly decided to begin his program of Jewish mass murder – according to orthodox experts. How could Goldmann have known what was to come?

In January of 1942, we read that Heinrich Himmler "has uprooted approximately 6,000,000 human beings" and shipped them to occupied Poland. By mid-1942, it was "a vast slaughterhouse for Jews" in Europe; one million were reported dead, and the remainder of the "6,000,000 to 7,000,000" at risk. The sad tale continued throughout the war years:
- Hitler intends "the extermination of some 6,000,000 [Jewish] persons in the territories over which [his] rule has been extended" (London *Times*, 1943).
- "Save doomed Jews," said Rabbi Hertz; the world "has done very little to secure even the freedom to live for 6,000,000 of their Jewish fellow men."
- Two million are dead, "and the four million left to kill are being killed, according to plan."

Then came the first definitive claim – in January of 1945, four months before the end of the war: "6,000,000 Jews Dead." Jacob Lestchinsky claimed that the prewar population of 9.5 million had been reduced to 3.5 million. In May 1945, we read something of an official declaration from Lord Wright of the UN War Crimes commission:

"It has, however, been calculated that in all about six million Jews were deliberately slaughtered in [gas chambers] *and other ways."*

Calculated by whom? On what basis? And using what hard evidence? He did not say.

Thus we see that the Six Million has an impressive legacy. Traditional historians often emphasize that the figure came from the Germans at the Nuremberg trial that began in November 1945 – which is true. A minor functionary, Wilhelm Höttl, testified to this number early in the proceedings. Historians like to portray this as a kind of dramatic revelation, and as "official confirmation" of the number – which is a ridiculous claim. As we have seen, the number had been known, discussed and anticipated for decades. And even then, in late 1945, no one had taken the smallest of steps to actually confirm such an estimate. It was pure hearsay, based on decades of propaganda, most from Jewish sources.

(For specific dates and page numbers, see Dalton 2020; Heddesheimer 2017.)

More than Six Million

After the war, the U.S. military government in occupied Germany created a documentary movie title *Death Mills*. It showed a sequence of horrific footages taken after the occupation of several German wartime camps. It was shown to the German civilian population in order to further the Allies' goal of "reeducation." The narrator never speaks about the religious background of the victims, but claims that all German camps were "death mills," and collectively some 20 million people were murdered in them. This number has since popped up on occasion, and even figures higher than that – up to 26 million – can be found in media and literature, albeit without specifying their religious or ethnic affiliation.

In subsequent decades, scholars and journalists alike spread the claim that, in addition to some six million Jews, other victim groups also were victims of the Holocaust, adding further millions to the total. For instance, leading German public prosecutor Adalbert Rückerl mentioned in 1968 that eight million non-Jews also fell victim to National-Socialist mass murder, making it a total of 14 million.

Simon Wiesenthal persistently spread the claim that, in addition to six million Jews, some five million non-Jews also died during the Holocaust. He has been attacked by numerous Jewish scholars for this, who claim that the five-million non-Jewish death-toll figure is unfounded and untrue. Wiesenthal has defended his invented 5-million claim by explaining that he wanted a number large enough to attract the attention of non-Jews to the Holocaust, but not larger than the actual number of Jewish victims, in order to maintain their primacy in the pecking order of victims and martyrs. (See Scott 2017; Rudolf 2023, pp. 15-18).

The "other" victim groups consists of Gypsies, homosexual men, Jehovah's Witnesses, and Poles, as well as the Slavic peoples in general. As the entries for these groups explain, mass-murder claims with vastly inflated victim numbers have been thoroughly debunked, in many cases even by orthodox scholars. This kind of revisionism and down-grading of mass-murder claims is quite acceptable to, and welcome by, orthodox scholars, as this preserves the primacy of Jewish victimhood.

Demography

Holocaust skeptics were the first to publish a detailed demographic study about Jewish losses during World War Two. In his 1983 study *The Dissolution of Eastern European Jewry*, Walter Sanning analyzed global changes in Jewish population, albeit relying in part on possibly questionable journalistic sources. He concluded that many Jews had died during the war but most due to causes unrelated to mass murder; only some 300,000 additional deaths could not be explained by ordinary causes.

The orthodoxy countered this study with a collection of essays published in 1991 in a German book titled *Dimension des Völkermords* (*Dimension of Genocide*), which was never translated into any other language (see Benz 1991). In this study, the overall Jewish death toll was calculated as follows: First, for every country that was at some point under German influence, the Jewish population figures from the last pre-war census and from the first postwar census were established. Then, the death toll was established by deducting the pre-war figure from the postwar number, with minor adjustments here and there. But this had the effect of wrongly counting several categories of "missing Jews," including:
 – Jews who died fighting as partisans or soldiers
 – Jews deported by Stalin to parts of the Soviet Union
 – Jews who fled the warzone
 – Jews who voluntarily emigrated (such as to Israel or the U.S.)

All these "Jewish losses" were counted as Holocaust victims.

Furthermore, this book's authors, who each investigated one country, did not coordinate their work well, if at all. Since the borders of many European countries changed drastically before, during and after the war, everyone should have agreed first what borders to pick, but that was not done. In the end, they counted at least 1.5 million missing Jews twice because of this flawed approach.

After all the rigging and maximizing of their demographic data, they concluded, unsurprisingly:

> "The bottom line indicates a minimum of 5.29 and a maximum of just over 6 million [Jewish victims]." (Benz 1991, p. 17)

And they add, in all seriousness:

> "Of course, the purpose of this project also was not to prove any pre-set figure ('six million') […]." (Ibid., p. 20)

But this is a laughable claim, at best.

(For a detailed comparison of Sanning's and Benz's books, see Rudolf 2019, pp. 175-206.)

SKARŻYŃSKI, KAZIMIERZ

Kazimierz Skarżyński was a Pole living in the village of Wólka Okrąglik near the Treblinka Camp who testified twice in front of a Soviet investigative commission about the Treblinka Camp, once on 22 August 1944, and then again one day later.

In his first deposition, he claimed to know from Jews incarcerated at Treblinka that Jews were killed "in hermetically sealed chambers […] by pumping out the air." However, creating a vacuum in a brick-and-mortar building is technically impossible (the external pressure would crush the walls), hence most certainly was not done.

In his second deposition, evidently cajoled by the Soviet investigators, he removed the reference to vacuum chambers and merely stated that Jews were killed "in a special chamber." This resembles the testimonies of Abe Kon. (See Mattogno 2021e, pp. 137f.)

skin, human, used for objects → **Lampshades**

SLOVAKIA

The German and Slovak government agreed in early 1942 that Germany would take all of Slovakia's Jews in return for a certain payment. During the first phase in March and April, only Jews fit for labor were deported to the labor camps of Majdanek and Auschwitz. Starting in late April 1942, everyone was deported, including entire families. Those fit for work were admitted into the Majdanek or Auschwitz camps, whereas the rest was sent on to various camps and ghettos, and since late May 1942 also directly to Sobibór for moving them further east.

When in July 1942 military necessities did not allow sending deportation trains with civilians east, everyone was sent to Auschwitz, with some deportees not getting registered in the camp, either because they had been taken off elsewhere or were continuing their journey. The orthodoxy insists that they were gassed on arrival, though. During these 1942 deportations, altogether not quite 48,000 Jews were deported from Slovakia.

A second wave of deportations occurred in September 1944, after the brief German occupation of Slovakia. Some 13,000 to 14,000 are said to have been deported within a few months. Some 7,000 to 8,000 of them presumably ended up at Auschwitz, while the rest was deported to German labor camps, such as Ravensbrück and Sachsenhausen.

In total, some 61,000 – 62,000 Jews were deported from Slovakia during the war. (See the entry on Jewish demography for a broader perspective.)

SOAP, FROM JEWISH CORPSES

Many a witness has claimed that the bodies of Holocaust victims were processed, and their body fat was used to manufacture soap and other fat-based products, such as lubricants for machinery. Such rumors started circulating in Poland in the summer of 1942 in connection with the deportation of the Jews from the Warsaw Ghetto. These rumors made their way to Jewish groups in neutral Switzerland, and from there to the U.S. government, who forwarded that "information" to the Vatican. In September 1942, Stephen Wise, Chairman of the World Jewish Congress, wrote a report about it, and the Jewish-owned *New York Times* quoted him on 26 November 1942. Already six days earlier, Heinrich Himmler reacted to Wise's memorandum, ordering Gestapo chief Heinrich Müller to investigate the matter and to make absolutely sure that the bodies of deceased Jews are either buried or cremated, "and that nothing else can happen to these bodies at any location." In other words: as soon as these rumors received public attention, the highest German authorities gave orders that explicitly prohibited the use of deceased Jews for anything.

It goes without saying that this did not stop the rumor mill. It was moreover fanned by the Allies, who actively invented and spread rumors to that effect. For instance, the British Political Warfare Executive claimed in one of its black-propaganda campaigns that the amputated limbs of German soldiers were processed to make soap from their fat content. The Polish underground helped out, too. In June 1944, an anonymous Pole made a deposition in Stockholm claiming that at Auschwitz the bodies of gassed Jews were turned into grease, then shipped off in packages labeled "Auschwitz Lubricant Factory."

One claim frequently made in this context is that German pieces of soap bore the imprint RJF, allegedly standing for "*Reines Juden Fett*" – pure Jewish fat. In fact, during the war, Germany had an agency in charge of organizing and rationing the supplies of industrial greases and lubricants, called <u>R</u>eichsamt für <u>I</u>ndustrielle <u>F</u>ettversorgung (Reich Office for Industrial Fat Supply), abbreviated RIF. This was the text imprinted on their soap, not RJF.

During the Nuremberg International Military Tribunal, the rumors of human fat turned into soap received the seal of official "truth" when the Soviets presented pieces of soap as evidence claiming that the fat which was the base ingredient of this product came from Jews who died in mass killings. The claim was supported by an affidavit claiming that a certain Professor Rudolf Spanner at the Anatomical Institute in Danzig had turned the fat of dead people into soap. This charge was echoed by the verdict as follows (*IMT*, Vol. 1, p. 252):

> "*After cremation* [of the victims of mass murder] *the ashes were used for fertilizer, and in some instances attempts were made to utilize the fat from the bodies of the victims in the commercial manufacture of soap.*"

Today, however, no mainstream historian supports the thesis anymore that any attempt was ever made to turn the fat of deceased or murdered inmates into soap or any other related product.

However, this Professor Dr. Rudolf Spanner from Danzig really did exist, and 60 years later, the pieces of soap presented by the Soviets were analyzed. The conclusion was that they were produced either from human or from pig fat. When Dr. Spanner was interrogated in 1947/48, he explained the harmless origin of this primitive soap from the anatomical institute, created as a natural byproduct of the legitimate and perfectly legal processing of corpses donated to his institute for research and education. After this interview, his case was shelved. This underscores the mendacity with which the Soviets had presented their

Soap, allegedly from human fat, Soviet "evidence" during the Nuremberg Military Tribunal.

pieces of evidence at Nuremberg.

None of this can stop the real believer though: In an article in the Israeli newspaper *Haaretz International* dated 11 February 2005, Jewish journalist Amiram Barkat reported about "Soap said made from Jews in Holocaust found in Israel."

Here is a brief list of witnesses or their mouthpieces who repeated the false soap rumors as their own "knowledge":
– Rachel Auerbach
– four distinguished university professors: Berthold Epstein, Prague; Bruno Fischer, Prague; Henri Limousin, Clermont-Ferrand; and Géza Mansfeld, Budapest
– Olga Lengyel
– Konrad Morgen
– Alexander Pechersky
– Abraham Silberschein
– Simon Wiesenthal

This "convergence of evidence" on the same lie proves the copy-cat or orchestrated nature of these witness testimonies.

(For more details, see Weber 1991; Mattogno 2023b, pp. 23-31; 2022c, pp. 448-451; Rudolf 2023, pp. 90-93.)

soap, inside gas chamber → **Towels**

SOBIBÓR
Documented History

Wartime documents concerning Sobibór are very rare, but the few that do exist do not corroborate the orthodox narrative.

Chronologically the first of these few documents is a telegram sent by Hans Höfle to the SS headquarters in Berlin on 11 January 1943, which was intercepted and deciphered by the British (see the entry on Hans Höfle). From this document we learn that, by the end of 1942, 101,370 Jews had arrived at "S", which probably stands for Sobibór. The message contains no indications regarding the fate of the deportees.

The next extant document dates from 5 July 1943. It is an order by SS chief Heinrich Himmler to Oswald Pohl, the head of the SS's Economic Administrative Main Office (SS-*Wirtschafts- und Verwaltungshauptamt*), stating:

> "The Sobibór transit camp, located in the Lublin district, is to be converted into a concentration camp. A dismantling unit for captured enemy munitions is to be set up in the concentration camp."

In Gutman's 1990 *Encyclopedia of the Holocaust*, Israeli historian Yitzhak Arad lied about this document by changing the unequivocal term "transit camp" used by Himmler into "extermination camp":

> "On 5 July 1943, Himmler ordered Sobibór to be closed as an extermination camp and transformed into a concentration camp." (Gutman 1990, p. 1377)

On 15 July 1943, in his reply to Himmler, Pohl suggested *not* to convert the "Sobibór transit camp in the Lublin district", because dismantling seized enemy munitions could be done without such a measure. Therefore, Pohl also referred to Sobibór as a transit camp.

Several German wartime documents mention an inmate uprising with subsequent mass escape from Sobibór on 14 October 1943. A day after the event, the commander of the Lublin security police stated in a telex that the inmates overpowered the guards and killed at least nine SS men and two foreign auxiliaries. Some 300 inmates had escaped, while those who didn't manage to flee were either shot or detained inside the camp. After the local SS staff had been either killed or proven incompetent, camp security afterwards was taken over by military police and Wehrmacht units, who were also searching for the fugitives.

A later document dated 17 March 1944 gives a summary of the event, and states that one SS officer and 10 SS NCOs were killed by inmates on that day.

Propaganda History

On 1 July 1942, the *Polish Fortnightly Review*, published by the Polish government in British exile, contained an article which mentioned that the "majority of the Jews of Lublin were carried off over a period of several days to the locality of Sobibór, near Włodawa, where they were all murdered with gas, machine-guns and even by being bayoneted."

In early July, Jewish chroniclers inside the Warsaw Ghetto (Emmanuel Ringelblum's group) received news that Jews were being deported to a place called Sobibór. Rumors had it that this was another death camp like the one at Bełżec.

A report published on 7 September 1942 in the *Polish Fortnightly Review* briefly mentioned that "a new camp of tortures had been set up in Sobibór." The newspaper *Rzeczpospolita Polska* had a similarly terse remark on 19 November 1942 by simply stating that the Sobibór Camp was "temporarily not in operation but is being enlarged." A first generic references to the murder method used at Treblinka, Bełżec and Sobibór – "murdered, probably with gases" – is contained in an official report of the Polish Government in Exile dated 23 December 1942.

Throughout the year 1943, Polish underground periodicals and government reports repeatedly mentioned Sobibór very briefly as a death camp where most of the Jews deported there were murdered, but they gave no specifics. Hence, practically nothing was known about Sobibór.

A text written in 1945 by the Polish War Crimes Office does not contain any specifics either, other than the assertion that Jews had been murdered there. Although it was known that several hundred Jews had escaped from the camp in 1943, evidently none of them had given any useful specifics about the camp either. This situation had barely changed when the Polish government submitted its report to the Nuremberg International Military Tribunal (IMT). At least we learn from it that "thousands upon thousands of Jews were deported and killed in gas chambers." During the IMT, the Soviet prosecutor merely mentioned Sobibór (misspelled as Sobibur in the transcript) in passing as a camp of large-scale exterminations (*IMT*, Vol. 7, p. 576).

Witness statements by former Sobibór inmates recorded during the early years after the war paint a peculiar image of the murder method allegedly used at that camp. This image is somewhat consistent, as the following table shows, which summarizes key features of these testimonies. This is complemented by the rather late account of Ya'akov Biskovitz (1961).

The table's first column contains the witness's name and the date when the testimony was recorded or published; the second column lists the claimed murder method; the third indicates how the executioners monitored the murder; and the fourth lists any auxiliary mechanical means.

While many of these witnesses disagree on various other issues, it is safe to say that, when it comes to the core of the claims, gas-chamber mass murder at Sobibór was committed primarily using chlorine gas; that the procedure was observed through windows in the roof; and most of all, that the gas chamber(s) had a collapsible floor allowing the discharge of the victims' corpses into carts in the basement underneath. This is also reflected by Jewish and Polish summaries of these accounts of 1946.

Another common feature of most witness statements is the claim that they could not see or easily find out what was going on in the part of the camp where the extermination supposedly took place. This is referred to as Camp III or Sector III. This area was supposedly cordoned off, and entering it was forbidden to inmates living and working in other camp areas.

For orthodox historians, the almost unanimous insistence of most Jewish witnesses on these bizarre and extremely unlikely collapsing floors with carts underneath poses a serious problem. They explain it away by blaming this "misinformation" on the fact that these inmates could not see what was going on in that part of the camp, hence relied on rumors and hearsay. However, that cannot be true either, because:

– Several witnesses claimed that they had been informed by inmates in Camp III verbally or in writing about what transpired there: Moshe Bahir and Ber Freiberg, plus Stanisław Szmajzner (who had inmates killed with Zyklon B).
– During the Eichmann Trial, Ber Freiberg claimed to have worked in Camp III next to the gas chamber, shaving thousands of naked women – although this might have been mere sexual fantasy, because in earlier testimonies he had said he had no access to Camp III.
– Another witness had even claimed to have helped build the gas chamber, so he *must* have known – but that witness had built an electrocution chamber (Srul Fajgielbaum).

As in the case of the Treblinka Camp, it took again the radical intervention of a Polish investigative judge to put an end to this testimonial anarchy. Facing this wall of ludicrous witness statements inconsistent with what was claimed, or rather ordained, for other similar camps such as Belzec and Treblinka, Polish investigative judge Zdzisław Łukaszkiewicz decided in 1947 to ditch all witness accounts on Sobibór and to rewrite history from scratch. He decreed *ex cathedra* that mass murder at Sobibór occurred using engine-exhaust gases. No more chlorine, Zyklon B or electrocution; no more roof windows; and no more collapsing floors with carts beneath. Łukaszkiewicz simply copied the claims for the Belzec Camp, which he had described in a chapter just prior to writing about Sobibór. This was to become the pattern around which all subsequent official statements and scholarly publications on Sobibór would coalesce.

In stark contrast to all these Jewish testimonies

Witness	Method	Observation	Mechanics
Ber(isch) Freiberg 10 Aug. 44, 27 Jul. 45	electric machine, filling gas tanks, chlorine	roof window	floors open, discharge bodies into carts below
Leon Feldhendler 1944	chlorine and other gases	–	–
Zelda Metz 1944/45?	chlorine	little window	floors open, discharge bodies into carts below
Josef Trajtag 10 October 1945	gas		floors open, discharge bodies into carts below
Srul Fajgielbaum 5 November 1945	electric current	–	–
S. Podchlebnik 6 December 1945	gas	–	–
Icek Lichtmann 18 December 1945	gas	–	floors open, discharge bodies into carts below
Ursula Stern 1945	gas through showers	–	floors open, discharge bodies
Chaim Engel 19 July 1946	gas through showers	–	floors open, discharge bodies
Salomea Hanel 1945	chlorine	–	–
Saartje Wijnberg 22 June 1946	gas through showers	–	floors open, discharge bodies into carts below
Alexander Pechersky 1946 (book)	a thick dark substance, spiraling from vents	roof window	floors open, discharge bodies into carts below
Hella Felenbaum-Weiss, 1946?	chlorine	–	killed while in trains during transit
Moshe Bahir 1950	gas through showers	little roof window	floors open, discharge bodies into carts below
Ya'akov Biskovitz 5 June 1961	–	–	floors open, discharge bodies into carts below

stand statements made during and a few years after the war by Ukrainians, who either escaped from Sobibór or who were later accused by the Soviet judiciary of having not just collaborated with the Germans, which was already treason worth the death penalty; they were accused of having served as auxiliary forces at the Sobibór Camp, hence having played a crucial role in the claimed murder of hundreds of thousands of Jews. One can imagine what methods were used to make these prisoners "confess."

The earliest testimony was recorded by a Soviet partisan unit. It is allegedly from an unnamed Ukrainian who was a Sobibór guard, but fled and joined Soviet partisans in 1943. The report describes a building with eight rooms, each holding 500 people. Gas from an engine was used to kill within 5-10 minutes. The bodies were then taken to a pyre, were placed on rails in sets of 1,000-1,500 people, and then, a "small fire" was lit underneath, upon which the corpses caught fire and burned all by themselves. Since the self-immolation of human corpses is physically impossible, it undermines this report's credibility.

After the war, Stalin's war against partisans fighting for Ukraine's independence continued – also in the courtrooms. A show trial was prepared against Ukrainians accused of helping the Germans run their "death camps." One Ukrainian arrested and charged in that context was Mikhail Razgonayev. During his interrogation on 20-21 September 1948, Razgonayev described the gas-chamber facility as a stone/concrete building with a corridor on one side and four gas chambers along the other. Each chamber had two hermetically closing doors, one from the corridor, the other to the outside to extract the bodies. An engine just outside the building supplied exhaust gas, which was piped into the chambers through showerheads. Except for the showerheads and the number of chambers, this version was close to what Łukaszkiewicz had decreed a year earlier.

Another unlucky Ukrainian auxiliary interrogated by the Soviets while in prison was Vassily Pankov. In his interrogation of 18 October 1950, he was made to described even the Buchenwald Camp as a death camp, which points at the methods used to extract his statement. According to Pankov, the gassing facility at Sobibór consisted of six gas chambers, and the engine supplying the asphyxiating exhaust gas was a diesel motor, with the execution lasting "an hour or more."

Evidently, the Soviets had been informed by Łukaszkiewicz's paper on how the mass murder was supposed to have been conducted at Sobibór, and they added their own spin with references to the evil German-invented diesel motor, as they had done during their 1943 show trials at Krasnodar and Kharkov (see the entries on gas vans and these two cities).

Equipped with testimonies like this, the Soviet Union conducted three propaganda show trials against former Ukrainian camp guards of Sobibór in the 1950s and 1960s. Except for one, all defendants were sentenced to death and executed.

In 1950, West Germany conducted two trials against defendants accused of having committed atrocities at the Sobibór Camp. The stated goal of Germany's trials against suspected war criminals was always to show the world that Germany had learned its lesson and was repentant – among other things by mercilessly lashing out against those accused of atrocities. Anything witnesses for the prosecution claimed was considered true, whereas anything the defendants claimed was deemed a lie, if it contradicted the charges. Rigged this way, the affirmation of the orthodox narrative was assured, and that was all that mattered – not so much whether the defendants were sentenced or acquitted. During these two trials, neither the witnesses nor the defendants gave any description of the alleged mass-murder weapon, and the judges showed no interest in elucidating the matter either.

This deliberate ignorance changed only with the 1965/66 Sobibór Trial at Hagen, West Germany, with twelve defendants. Many defendants cooperated with the prosecution and court by giving descriptions of the alleged mass-murder facility along the line of what was already "known" at that time. Five of them were acquitted as a result. Erich Fuchs even described the engine used as "a heavy Russian gasoline engine (probably a tank or tractor engine) of

Death-Toll Propaganda

Victim numbers claimed for the Sobibór Camp	
2,500,000	Samet Mottel
2,000,000	Zelda Metz, Stanisław Szmajzner
1,000,000	Nachman Blumental, Moshe Bahir
800,000	Chaim Engel and S. Engel-Wijnberg
600,000	Yuri Suhl
500,000	I. Ehrenburg/V. Grossman, A. Pechersky
350,000	Erich Bauer
300,000	Léon Poliakov
250,000	*Encyclopedia of the Holocaust*, Wolfgang Scheffler
200,000	Raul Hilberg
170,000	Jules Schelvis
110,000	Karl Frenzel, 1987
50,000 – 70,000	Karl Frenzel, 1966
30,000 – 35,000	Jean-Claude Pressac
25,000 – 30,000	Hubert Gomerski, 1950

at least 200 HP (V-engine, 8 cylinders, water-cooled)." As a thank you, he received only four years in prison for having aided in the murder of 79,000 persons. That is 26.6 minutes for every life taken. Other defendants had similar cheap verdicts. Only one defendant received a life-term but was released early. Erich Bauer, in prison for life after his 1950 trial, tried in vain to score points by drawing camp maps and gas-chamber plans.

Despite considerable contradictions between the defendant's statements, the Hagen District Court described the gas-chamber facilities, operated with engine-exhaust gas, as follows:

1. An earlier building on a concrete platform, a corridor and three chambers off to one side, each 4 m × 4 m in size, with two air-raid shelter doors, one from the corridor, the other for extracting the bodies.
2. A solid later building, replacing the old building, had twice the number of chambers of the same size as the old chambers.

Finally, the second show trial against John Demjanjuk was staged in Munich between 2009 and 2011 for his alleged role as a guard of that camp. The trial did not yield any new insights into Sobibór.

Today, most orthodox scholars by and large follow the narrative developed by the Hagen Court, which followed the false lead of Łukaszkiewicz's "history."

Forensic Findings

The first forensic investigations at Sobibór were carried out by The Central Commission of Inquiry into German Crimes in Poland in 1945 and 1946. Soil mixed with ashes and human remains was discovered in what was assumed to be former mass graves, and rubble of a building was located which witnesses identified as the "gas chamber." Neither the volume of the graves nor the possible quantity of ashes and human remains in them was determined.

In 1960, it was decided to turn the former campgrounds into a memorial. In that context, the site with the building foundations claimed to have been the gas chamber was covered with asphalt, and a memorial was erected nearby.

Forty years later, a second forensic investigation was launched, which was to last some 16 years. By that time, the location of the alleged gas chamber had been forgotten, and no one seems to have consulted the archives about the 1945/46 findings and the 1960 memorial plans either. Hence, it took almost 14 years, and the removal of the memorial's roads and parking lots, to rediscover the foundation walls and other traces of the building labeled "gas chamber." This discovery was declared sensational, although nothing about these building traces points at the purpose this structure once served.

During that thorough investigation, a network of core samples was taken in a dense gridwork pattern to identify not only building ruins, but also areas of disturbed soil pointing at former mass graves. All in all, a maximum of some 15,050 m³ of disturbed soil was located. Leaving the top half meter as a soil cover, the effective volume for mass graves could have been a little over 13,000 m³.

The orthodoxy currently claims that some 80,000 corpses were buried at Sobibór by October 1942. Afterwards, new victims were allegedly burned right away on pyres. Burying 80,000 bodies in some 13,000+ m³ results in a quite reasonable packing density of roughly six bodies per cubic meter. Hence, the orthodoxy's claims in this regard are physically possible.

However, if considering the number of corpses that are said to have been burned between October 1942 and October 1943 – meaning all the victims killed at Sobibór – and therefore the firewood needed for this, the situation changes. Experiences with large-scale open-air incinerations have shown that some 250 kg of fresh wood are needed for the outdoor cremation of one average human body.

Unfortunately, it is rather unclear how many victims in total were allegedly killed and thus burned, as there is no agreement among the orthodoxy in this regard (see the death-toll table). Taking the number given by Gutman's 1990 and Rozett's/Spector's 2000 *Encyclopedias of the Holocaust* – 250,000 victims – results in the need for some 62,500 metric tons of green wood.

Hence, the camp needed a formidable collection of resources: space for the many huge pyres; the manpower needed to exhume the bodies; manpower to fell, transport and chop thousands of trees; manpower to build and maintain the pyres; and manpower to extract and scatter the ashes.

The maximum number of inmates – claimed by any witness – who were deployed at Sobibór to cut trees and bring them to the camp as firewood was 40. Data based on experience with forced laborers such as PoWs shows that they could fell not quite ⅔ of a metric ton of trees per day. This makes some 26 tons of wood for 40 inmates per day. To cut 62,500 metric tons would have taken them some 2,480 days of un-

Drone photo of archaeological digs in the area of the former Sobibór Camp, with labels added by the German news magazine Der Spiegel *(Hecking 2014). There is no physical or documental evidence supporting the claim that the unearthed foundation walls belonged to a homicidal-gas-chamber building.*

Characteristics of Mass Graves and Mass Cremations at Sobibór		
	CLAIMED	FOUND
no. of corpses	170,000 to 2.5 million	scattered remains
space required (@ 6 bodies/m³)	28,330 to 416,700 m³	at most 13,000 m³
claimed cremation time	October 1942 – October 1943, ca. 365 days	
corpses cremated	466 to 6,850 per day	
green wood needed (@ 250 kg/body)	116 to 1,710 metric tons per day	
total green wood needed	42,500 to 625,000 metric tons	

interrupted work, which is almost seven years. Alternatively, to get the work done in time, it would have required 272 dedicated lumberjacks.

Add to this the fact that the Polish forests were tightly managed by the German occupational forces as precious resources for lumber and fuel. Hence, the SS couldn't send droves of inmates to adjacent forests and cut them down without getting permission to do so. Of course, there is no documental or material trace of any such massive tree-felling activity having been applied for, been granted, let alone occurred. Air photos taken of the Sobibór area by German reconnaissance planes in 1944 show no areas denuded of trees in the camp's vicinity either.

None of it has left a trace, either in witness statements, or in documents, or in the material and forensic record. Thus, we can say with confidence that none of it happened.

Current Orthodox Narrative

The current orthodox narrative about Sobibór is the result of the forgery perpetrated by Judge Łukaszkiewicz. He replaced the early narrative – dominated by many witness accounts about chlorine gas-chambers with roof windows and collapsible floors – with a narrative copied straight from the script developed for the Belzec Camp.

The Belzec narrative, in turn, had been the result of a similar manipulation, which consisted of splitting the camp's history into two phases: an early phase with a small, wooden gas-chamber facility, and a late phase with a larger, brick-and-concrete facility. This was done not because there was evidence for it, but because the few witnesses for that camp contradicted one another as to the nature of the gassing facility. The orthodoxy therefore decided to "explain" that contradiction by splitting the camp's history into two phases (see the entry on Belzec for details).

Although early testimonies don't yield any trace for two different phases in the Sobibór Camp's history either, that did not stop the orthodoxy from forcing a "consistency" between Belzec and Sobibór in this regard as well by simply declaring it a fact. That allowed them also to "explain" the contradictions among various testimonies as to the nature of the alleged gassing facility, although in this case, the many contradicting claims about the alleged mass-murder facility would require splitting the camp's history into several dozen phases, not just two. Furthermore, most of them would have to have existed parallel in time, perhaps in parallel Holocaust universes.

Nowadays, witness testimonies recorded decades after the war are used to support this thesis of two camp phases. However, at that late a point in time, the split-personality dogma of all *Aktion Reinhardt* Camps had already become a dogma known and thus parroted by many witnesses.

There is one event in Sobibór's history about which everyone agrees that it is true and real: the inmate uprising of 14 October 1943, with the subsequent escape of some 300 inmates. However, during that camp-wide inmate uprising, only such inmates escaped and survived who had been in those sectors of the camp that did *not* contain any mass-murder facilities.

Here we need to pause. The orthodoxy claims that Sobibór's primary objective was to mass murder hundreds of thousands of deportees. Therefore, it is only logical that most of the work that had to be done in that camp would have been connected with that mass murder. Here are the tasks allegedly done:
– cutting the hair of thousands of inmates;
– removing precious-metal tooth fillings after the execution;
– hauling the victims out of the chambers;
– exhuming bodies still lying in older mass graves;
– felling huge numbers of trees;
– hauling the trees into the camp;
– debranching and sawing or chopping them to manageable firewood sizes;
– building large pyres with firewood and corpses;
– maintaining the fires;
– clearing the burned-down pyres;

- sifting through large amounts of ashes in search of unburned pieces;
- putting unburned remains back onto a pyre;
- disposing of the ashes.

Therefore, if the orthodox narrative were true, by far the largest number of inmates in that camp would have been employed in that very mass-murder sector, the so-called Sector III. Furthermore, these inmates also should have had the highest motivation for an uprising, for obvious reasons. Hence, when a revolt broke out, it had to be expected that it mainly encompassed exactly these inmates. In consequence, most escapees and survivors, and thus witnesses, also should have consisted of these inmates.

In addition, these inmates would have had the strongest motivation to tell their tale, as they were the ones who had seen all the claimed horrors. Judicial authorities also would have had strong motives to locate and interrogate these witnesses, as they were the ones with first-hand knowledge.

However, we find the *exact opposite* to be true: not a single witness is known who claimed to have been employed in that elusive sector.

Using Occam's Razor, the simplest explanation
- for the invisibility of events unfolding in Sector III;
- for the systematically false claims about the alleged gas-chambers by self-proclaimed hearsay witnesses asserting to have received their information through "secret" messages from inmates in Sector III;
- and for the total lack of any survivor, let alone witness, from that sector,

is the simple fact that Sector III never existed.

Finally, there is plenty of anecdotal, material and documental evidence indicating that many Jews deported to Sobibór ended up elsewhere and very much alive. One of the most prominent among them is orthodox Sobibór historian Jules Schelvis, who was deported to Sobibór himself as a young man. At Sobibór, he was assigned to a labor group and transferred elsewhere. For him, Sobibór was a simple transit camp, as it was for thousands upon thousands of other Jewish deportees.

(For more details on the Sobibór Camp, see Graf/Kues/Mattogno 2020; Mattogno 2021e, pp. 215-236, 273-295; see also the entry on resettlement with further references.)

SOMPOLINSKI, ROMAN

Roman Sompolinski

Roman Sompolinski was a Polish Jew who was arrested in 1939 and, after staying at various camps, ended up in Auschwitz at the end of 1943, where he claims to have worked inside Crematorium II as a member of the *Sonderkommando* from December 1943 until February 1944. From Auschwitz he was transferred to Bergen-Belsen in December 1944. Here are some peculiar claims regarding Auschwitz from an affidavit he signed on 24 May 1945 for the Belsen Trial:

- Although all other *Sonderkommando* members were killed after six months, he "escaped this fate because I contracted typhus and was removed to hospital." The orthodox narrative has it, though, that inmates becoming seriously ill were even more likely to be killed. Sompolinski was nursed back to health because the Germans cared, and they evidently did not see him as a dangerous carrier of secrets.
- Before entering the gas chamber, the victims were given towels and soap. This most certainly would never have happened, considering the mess it would have created and the effort necessary to retrieve and clean these items afterwards. In addition, no one takes towels into a shower.
- Once the victims were inside the alleged gas chamber, an SS man in a control room underneath the "bathroom" turned on the gas. There was no room underneath any of the rooms claimed to have been homicidal gas chambers. Furthermore, the orthodox narrative has it that the gas was not "turned on" – this requires gas under pressure – but rather Zyklon B were pellets thrown through some opening into the chambers.
- The victims' screams were drowned "by a brass band playing outside," and a radio inside. This is a unique claim requiring no further comment.
- Death occurred within 3-5 minutes, which is impossibly fast for a room without forced evaporation and dissipation of the gas.
- The bodies were put on a chute, so they dropped into "a subterranean room adjacent to the crematorium ovens." However, in Crematorium II, the

ground-floor furnace room was one level *up* from the underground morgue presumably misused as a homicidal gas chamber.
– From the chute, eight bodies were transferred to a tipper trolley on rails, which was wheeled to the furnaces. This story is reminiscent of the War Refugee Board Report, but it is still untrue. In fact, in Crematorium II, corpses were brought upstairs by a rickety makeshift freight elevator.
– Corpses burned to ashes within about three minutes. This is the world record in lying about the Auschwitz cremation capacity. The actual cremation time was one entire hour.

Had Sompolinski really worked inside this building for three months, he would have gotten the layout and equipment at least nearly right. But his description is completely made up, as is the rest of his tall extermination tale. (For more details, see Mattogno 2021, pp. 311-315.)

Sonderaktion, Sonderbehandlung → **Special Treatment**

SONDERKOMMANDO

Sonderkommando is a German term meaning "special unit" or "special squad." It is used to this day in German military and police forces to denote units that have been assigned special tasks outside of routine duties. This was also the case during the Second World War.

Many of the subunits of the *Einsatzgruppen* operating in the rear of the German army in the temporarily occupied Soviet Union were called *Sonderkommandos*. The units which, according to orthodox historians, tried erasing the traces of mass graves presumably created by the *Einsatzgruppen* within the context of the alleged *Aktion* 1005, were also called *Sonderkommandos*. (See the entry on *Aktion* 1005.)

The most-common usage of the term *Sonderkommando* in the orthodox Holocaust narrative relates to the Auschwitz Camp. Many former Auschwitz detainees used this term to refer to inmates, usually of Jewish denomination, who were tasked to do the claimed gruesome extermination work:
– assist deportees slated for gassing to get undressed;
– make them enter the gas chambers;
– after the gassing, drag the corpses out of the gas chamber;
– break out any precious-metal tooth fillings, and search body orifices for hidden valuables;
– bring the corpses to mass graves, furnaces or burning pits;
– bury the corpses in mass graves, and later exhume them again;
– push bodies into furnaces, and fuel the furnace hearths;
– build pyres and maintain the fires;
– sift through ashes for valuables, and also for unburned remains, to either crush them or throw them back into the fire;
– dispatch of the ashes.

Many witnesses – among them many former Auschwitz inmates who claimed to have been a member of this *Sonderkommando* – claimed that these inmates were treated preferably by the SS as an incentive and reward for the work they were doing. On the other hand, as "carriers of a terrible secret," these inmates are said to have been housed separately from all other inmates, and kept in isolation, so they could not bear witness to other inmates. (See the 1944 Vrba-Wetzler Report, part of the War Refugee Board Report, as an early example.)

Many self-proclaimed former *Sonderkommando* members also claimed that these units were killed by the SS on a regular basis in order to eliminate dangerous witnesses, although they disagree on the particulars. The most prominent witness in this regard is Miklós Nyiszli. He asserted that each *Sonderkommando* was killed after four months, and that the first *Sonderkommando* was already formed in 1940. However, even orthodox historians confirm that this is not true, because the first such unit was supposedly formed only sometime in 1942, and there was no predetermined schedule for liquidating *Sonderkommandos*. They claim this because the various witness statements in this regard vary wildly, making it impossible to discern any pattern.

Other former self-proclaimed members of the *Sonderkommando* who made concrete claims about periodical eliminations of this unit were:
– Charles Bendel: every few months.
– Daniel Bennahmias: 2-6 months.
– André Lettich: every three or four months.
– Josef Sackar: every six months.
– Roman Sompolinski: about 6 months.
– Henryk Tauber: after a few months.
– Shlomo Venezia: four months.

Filip Müller stated that *Sonderkommando* members were killed on occasion, but he insisted that no definite pattern existed. Other witnesses spoke of irregular eliminations of some or all members of the *Son-*

derkommando (Henryk Mandelbaum; Ludwik Nagraba; Dov Paisikovic; Joshuah Rosenblum).

Original wartime documents prove that the term *Sonderkommando* was used by the Auschwitz camp administration for numerous inmate labor squads, among them:
- *Sonderkommando* Birkenau BW 20: inmate electrician squad at the camp's power plant;
- *Sonderkommando* pest control;
- *Sonderkommando* Reinhardt: women's unit assigned to sorting clothes;
- *Sonderkommando* Zeppelin: outside unit based in Breslau;
- *Sonderkommando* I & II: units warehousing inmates' personal effects;
- *Sonderkommando* construction depot: unit at the construction-depot warehouse;
- *Sonderkommando* Dwory: unit working in the village of Dwory (10 km east of Auschwitz);
- *Sonderkommando* Buna: unit working at the Monowitz I.G. Farben plant;
- *Sonderkommando* clothing workshops: unit producing clothing;
- *Sonderkommando* DAW: unit employed by the SS enterprise *Deutsche Ausrüstungswerke* (German Equipment Works);
- *Sonderkommando* "Sola-Hütte": inmate squad running this SS vacation resort;

Other documents refer to *Sonderkommandos* formed for temporary tasks, such as certain construction projects.

Interestingly, *none* of these documents refer to a *Sonderkommando* employed at any of the crematoria. There are no extant documents on mass graves, pyres or homicidal gas chambers. Camp documents dealing with the crematoria staff give those units numbers, and if they are named, they are simply called crematorium stokers (*Heizer Krematorium*). Hence, in the camp's bureaucracy, these units were not considered special.

Here is a long list of former Auschwitz inmates who survived the war and either proclaimed (here linked), or were otherwise identified, to have been a member of the so-called *Sonderkommando*. This list proves that the members of the alleged *Sonderkommandos* were never killed, because they were not considered by the SS to have been "carriers of a terrible secret":

– Aba/Abo	– Szaja Gertner	– Waclaw Lipka	– Sava
– Alfred Aboav	– Tew(v)el Gis(s)er	– Aharon Lubowitsch	– Maurice Schellekes
– Jan Agrestowski	– Simon Gotland	– Gabriel Malinski	– Sol Schindel
– André Balbin	– Salmen Gradowski	– Henryk Mandelbaum	– Moritz/Max Schwarz
– Fredy Bauer	– Saul Hazan	– Mikusz	– Jacob Sender (Zander)
– Berko/Berl Becker	– Erko Hejblum	– Emanuel Mittelman	– Bernhard A. Sokal
– Charles Bendel	– Samuel Hejblum	– Moses Mizrahi	– Roman Sompolinski
– Daniel Bennahmias	– Chaim Herman	– Mieczyslaw Morawa	– Jankiel Sosnowski
– Maurice Benroubi	– Joseph Ilczuk	– Moryc	– Milan Spanik
– Wladyslaw Biskup	– Stanisław Jankowski	– Filip Müller	– Franz Süss
– Baruch Blum	– Sigmund Jurkowski	– Marcel Nadsari	– Serge Szawinski
– Milton Buki	– Samij Karolinskij	– Ludwik Nagraba	– Rachmin(l) Szulklaper
– Shaul Chasan	– David Karvat	– David Nencel	– Henryk Tauber
– Zawek/Zauwel Chrzan	– Morris Kesselmann	– Simon Neumann	– Judel Toper
– Leon Cohen	– Mosiek (van) Kleib	– Ajzik Nowik	– Simon Umschweif
– Moszek Cy(Zi)zner	– Pepo Kolias	– Miklós Nyiszli	– George van Ryk
– Abraham Dragon	– Shlojme Laj(ei)zer	– Roman Obydzinski	– Morris Venezia
– Szlama Dragon	– David Lea	– David Olère	– Shlomo Venezia
– Yishayahu Isaïe Ehrlich	– Aron Lej(i)bowicz	– Dov Paisikovic	– J(Y)ank(ie)l Weinkranz
– Eliezer Eisenschmidt	– Szmul Lejbowicz	– Aaron Pilo	– Moszek Weinkranz
– Louis Welfke Fink(el)	– Lemko	– Lemke/Chaïm Pliszko	– Joseph Weiss
– Moshe Fry(ie)dman(n)	– André Lettich	– Otto Pressburger	– Eliezer Leon Welbel
– Dario Gabai	– Moshe Levi	– Joshuah Rosenblum	– Moshe Wygnanski
– Yaakov Gabai	– Henry Levy	– Felix Rosenthal	– Shlomo Maki Yohanan
– Moshé Garbarz	– Salmen Lewenthal	– Arnost Rosin	– Jakob Zy(Si)lberberg
– Michel Gelbert	– Nathan/Nysel Lewin	– Josef Sackar	

This list is certainly not complete. Many of these persons claimed to have worked in the *Sonderkommando* for many months, if not years. To judge the trustworthiness of those who claimed to have been a member, one should read the assessment of their testimonies in their respective entries in this encyclopedia. The result is devastating.

Consider that, at its peak in the summer of 1944, 900 inmates were working at the Auschwitz crematoria in day and night shifts. Since inmates died and escaped, were transferred and released, and rotated to other assignments, several thousand inmates will have worked at one time or another in those facilities. Many of them will have survived. All of them could have testified after the war, but most of them probably did not.

We need to keep in mind that a catastrophic tragedy was unfolding at Auschwitz in 1942/43. A devastating typhus epidemic caused thousands of inmates to die every month. The old crematorium at the Main Camp was overwhelmed by this, and it even had to be taken out of operation for some two months in late spring and summer of 1942. Thousands of typhus victims could not be cremated, so they were buried in mass graves. With the local groundwater standing near the surface, these graves threatened to poison the region's drinking water. Therefore, the graves had to be emptied again, and the bodies burned on pyres, until the crematoria could handle the number of victims, which the typhus epidemic kept causing well into 1943. (See the section "Documented History" of the entry on the Birkenau Camp for details.)

Someone had to do all this gruesome work, and it wasn't the SS. Many former inmates involved in this horrific work may not have understood what was going on, and may have misinterpreted it in light of rumors and (post)war propaganda. Others did understand, but were unlikely to go on record with what they experienced. Many simply wanted to forget, while others realized that their memories did not match what society expected them to remember, so they decided to stay out of trouble by keeping it to themselves.

It required a mean-spirited, vindictive, attention-seeking or profit-oriented mindset, indifferent to truth and accuracy, to twist this tragedy into a horror scenario by adding homicidal gas chambers and mass gassings. How many of such individuals were among the thousands of inmates who did the described horrible work? The answer lies in the assessment of the testimonies of the persons listed above.

The term *Sonderkommando* was later also used for inmate units who are said to have performed, at other camps, similar tasks as those listed at the beginning of this entry.

(For more details on the usage of the term *Sonderkommando*, see Mattogno 2016b, pp. 141-149; 2016d, pp. 111-114; 2020, pp. 127-132; 2020a, pp. 252-264; 2022c, pp. 37-39; for details on the testimonies of self-proclaimed former *Sonderkommando* members, see the entry for each, as well as Mattogno 2020a, 2021, 2021d, 2022d, 2022e; see also www.sonderkommando.info.)

SOURCE CRITICISM

The modern method of source criticism was developed in the mid-1800s by German historian Leopold von Ranke, but it is in general applicable to all fields of academic inquiry. More generally expressed, it should be called "evidence criticism." It is based on the observation that evidence needs to be evaluated as to its reliability, accuracy and authenticity, and those who created, maintained or interpreted the evidence need to be evaluated for their trustworthiness.

Authenticity

This criterion concerns documents and material evidence. The question to ask is: Is this piece of evidence really what it appears to be? The aim is to expose outright forgeries and items that have been tampered with. The tools to assess this are mostly forensic in nature, but for written documents, linguistics is also important. Experts are required to accurately interpret forensic testing results, or to do linguistic assessments.

Trustworthiness

The trustworthiness of an expert witness depends on his skills, on his track record, and on any potential bias that may lead to unconscious or deliberate misinterpretation of data. This is true for any witness. Describing an event accurately is a skill not equally shared by all; reporting only some facts but hiding others – or telling outright lies – in pursuit of some aim, plagues most witness accounts on politically or emotionally loaded issues. If such behavior can be demonstrated, it seriously undermines a witness's trustworthiness, and hence the credibility of anything he or she may claim.

Ability to Know

The first question to ask about any witness claim is: Was the witness in a position to know? Many Holocaust survivors reported deportation figures, mass-grave contents, cremation capacities and total death tolls, although very few, if any, were ever in a position to know. Answering this pivotal question can serve to expose witnesses who claim to report first-hand knowledge, but instead are dishonest conveyors of hearsay or rumors.

Logics

Claims must adhere to basic logical rules. This includes that a person cannot be in several places at the same time, and that events cannot unfold anachronistically (that is, out of proper time sequence). For example, a witness cannot be truthful who describes a homicidal gassing by giving information that would have required him to have observed it at once from outside the gassing building, from inside the gassing building, and even from inside the gas chamber. Other witnesses claimed to have experienced events at times when they simply could not have happened, such as encountering Josef Mengele at Auschwitz when he wasn't yet deployed there. (See the entry on Mengele.)

Physically Possible

Any claim that is physically impossible cannot be true. In the present case, this includes for instance physically impossible packing densities of people jammed into alleged gas chambers; claims of bodies burning without fuel; flames shooting out of chimneys; blood geysers; and liquid fat collected from burning bodies, to name but a few. (See the respective entries.)

Internal and External Consistency

A true account cannot contain self-contradicting claims. It also cannot contradict facts established otherwise, especially those established by evidence of higher credibility. For example, if hundreds of witnesses claim that sick people were murdered at the Auschwitz Camp, but hundreds of wartime camp documents demonstrate that huge healthcare efforts were made for all inmates, who were systematically treated and cured, then the documents take precedent over the testimonies, unless it can be otherwise demonstrated that the documents' contents are wrong. (See the section on "Auschwitz" of the entry on "Healthcare.")

Or take the claim by many witnesses that huge pyres were constantly burning at Auschwitz-Birkenau in the spring and summer of 1944. One single air photo taken at the claimed peak of this alleged activity suffices to refute all witnesses. (See the section on "Auschwitz" of the entry on "Air Photos.")

Independence

A claim usually becomes more credible, the more sources confirm it. This requires, however, that all these sources report it from first-hand knowledge and without any other influence. However, if many sources converge in claims that can be demonstrated to be false, then this proves that these reports cannot be based on first-hand experience. It reveals that all these sources were exposed to identical or similar false information, and hence are not independent. Furthermore, such a convergence on untrue claims demonstrates that none of these witnesses are trustworthy reporters of actual events. (See the entry on "Convergence of Evidence.")

Impartial Assessment

When scrutinizing evidence in this sense, it is critically important to apply objective criteria consistently. This is necessary to avoid introducing a bias that can lead to the rejection or acceptance of evidence not based on their objective value, but on the subjective value for the agenda of the person assessing the evidence.

For instance, ever since the end of World War Two, judicial authorities have always only looked for evidence supporting the prevailing Holocaust narrative. Witness accounts and documents were only superficially assessed for their authenticity and credibility. This "source criticism" merely aimed at weeding out (and hiding) the blatantly absurd and impossible. The main focus, however, was on finding seemingly credible evidence that confirmed a preordained narrative. (See the entries on the International Military Tribunal, on Auschwitz Trials, Belzec Trial, Bergen-Belsen Trials, Majdanek Trials, Show Trials, John Demjanjuk, Gottfried Weise and Karl Wolff.)

Mainstream historians also tend to pick those passages from selected documents and witness testimony that support their narrative, while failing to evaluate all pertinent pieces of evidence in their totality, and according to all rules laid out above. (See Mattogno 2016e, 2019, 2020, 2021c for examples.)

Importance of Source Criticism

In the context of the Holocaust, most evidence adduced to prove claims of mass murder is anecdotal in nature, which includes witness accounts of alleged victims, bystanders and perpetrators. Moreover, many of these accounts were made in an atmosphere of war and postwar propaganda bordering at times on mass hysteria, and leading to various degrees of witness duress. While the hysterical atmosphere subsided as time passed, duress has only shifted in nature – away from massive physical threats and abuses (see the entry on torture) to threats of societal persecution and criminal prosecution.

This was accompanied by a wide variety of incentives for any witness willing to confirm what judicial authorities and sensationalistic media wanted to hear, no matter whether it was true or not.

In other words, there has never been a case in history in which giving false testimony was more tempting and more rewarding than with the Holocaust. Correspondingly, there has also never been a case for which source criticism was more important than this one.

Outlawing Source Criticism

In Western societies, critically assessing the value of survivor testimony is considered a sacrilege, as the survivors are perceived by many as saints and martyrs. (See the entry on "Religion, Holocaust as.") In many countries, foremost in Europe, it can even be a crime to expose as unreliable, inaccurate or untrue the story of a survivor – or any other evidence adduced to support the orthodox Holocaust narrative. Such an act is said to denigrate the commemoration of those who died in the Holocaust, and it presumably incites to hatred against the Holocaust's victim groups. (See the entry on "Censorship.")

In consequence, the very act of source criticism itself is threatened with criminal prosecution in those countries. However, without source criticism, the writing of history becomes impossible, and deteriorates to the writing of mere historical novels.

Repercussions of Source Criticism

The devastating effect of the orthodoxy's failure to apply uncompromising source criticism to the evidentiary basis of the orthodox Holocaust narrative can be gleaned from almost every entry in this work. Already in 1988, when skeptical scholars had only begun evaluating the historical record, French mainstream historian and camp survivor Michel de

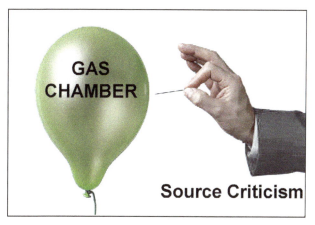

Boüard realized that professional source criticism would ultimately spell doom for the orthodox Holocaust narrative. (See the entry on him.) French mainstream historian Jean-Claude Pressac expressed it similarly some 10 years later (Igounet 2000, pp. 651f.):

"On the one hand, resentment and vindictiveness [of the survivors] have gained the upper hand over reconciliation, and therefore memory the upper hand over history. On the other hand, the communist stranglehold on the most important leadership positions in the camps, the formation of associations after the liberation under communist control, as well as the fifty-year-long creation of a 'people's democratic' [=communist] history of the camps has led to […] the clumsy anti-fascist language. Shoddiness, exaggeration, omission and lies are the hallmarks of most accounts from this era. The unanimous and irrevocable discrediting which has afflicted the communist writings must inevitably have consequences for the depiction of life in the concentration camps, which is spoiled by the communist idea, and thus must finish it off.

Can this development be reverted? It is too late. A general correction is factually and humanely impossible. […] And new documents will unavoidably turn up and will overthrow the official certainties more and more. The current view of the world of the [National-Socialist] camps, though triumphant, is doomed. What of it can be salvaged? Only little. Puffing up the universe of the concentration camps amounts to squaring the circle and to turning black into white. […T]he pain has been exploited and turned into hard cash: decorations, pensions, careers, political influence. […]

Of all these events, […] only those will prevail

whose reality is ascertained [by source criticism]. *The others are assigned to the trash can of history."*

(See also the entry on Evidence.)

SOVIET UNION

Introduction

The Soviet Union played four roles within the context of the Holocaust:
1. Crime Scene
2. Victim
3. Perpetrator
4. Propagandist

The last role is discussed in detail in the section on the Soviet Union of the entry on propaganda, so it will not be covered here.

Anti-Bolshevism was one of the four main motives of National-Socialist enmity toward Jews. As described in the section on "Motives for National-Socialist anti-Judaism" of our entry on Motives, it was one of the major driving forces behind ruthless National-Socialist attitudes and actions toward Jews living in the Soviet Union. (See that entry for more details.)

Crime Scene

Between late 1941 and late 1942, German authorities deported many Jews from western and central European countries to various locations in the temporarily German-occupied Soviet Union. If we follow the orthodox narrative, many if not most of them were killed there by the *Einsatzgruppen* and associated units. In particular the camp Maly Trostenets near Minsk (capital of Belorussia), and the prison at Fort IX near Kaunas (Lithuania) deserve to be mentioned in this context. Thousands of deported Jews are said to have been executed there. (See the entries on these topics for more details.)

Victim

While many foreign Jews deported to the east became the target of German units, Jews living inside the Soviet Union were the primary target of the *Einsatzgruppen* and associated units. If they were executed, this happened primarily by way of mass shootings, but poisoning in so-called gas vans is also claimed. (See that entry for more details).

Orthodox estimates of the death toll inflicted by these events range from just under a million up to three million. German wartime documents speak of some 750,000 victims, but their reliability is questionable. (For more on this, see the entry on the *Einsatzgruppen*.) Furthermore, this number includes the execution of Jews deported into the Soviet Union from other countries.

Perpetrator

When war broke out between Germany and Poland on 1 September 1939, many Jews tried fleeing from the invading German army, who had the reputation of not being very kind to Jewish folks. Jewish contemporaneous sources report that between 500,000 and one million Jews fled east into the parts of Poland that were occupied by the Soviets a short while later. Unwelcome as they were, the majority of these displaced Polish Jews were promptly deported to Siberia. Jewish relief organizations reported during that time that they tried helping up to 630,000 Polish Jews in Siberian labor camps who actually made it there alive. (See Sanning 2023, pp. 37-44.)

When war broke out between Germany and the Soviet Union in June 1941, the same flight reflex set in with Soviet Jews, who anticipated the German forces to invade with the wrath and anger of counter-revolutionary radicals. The reports of the *Einsatzgruppen* are full of references to towns and cities across the temporarily German-occupied Soviet Union whose Jewish population had to a large degree fled or been evacuated, or rather deported, along with large parts of the population considered crucial to the war effort. Many of these fleeing, evacuated or deported individuals also ended up in mostly Siberian labor camps, where they were put to work for the overall war effort.

Estimates of the number of Jews deported during that wave range into the millions. However, the German reports on fleeing and deported Jews were not based on statistical evaluation of their own census data compared with the data the Soviets created before they left. Rather, the Germans relied to no small degree on what the local populace told them about how many Jews there were before and how many there were then. Those local collaborators may have told the Germans what they thought the Germans wanted to hear.

On 25 October 1941, Hitler said during one of his private dinners (see the entry on Adolf Hitler):

"It is good if the terror precedes us that we are exterminating Jewry."

That reputation led to a massive flight of the Jews, which in turn saved the Germans a lot of trouble of having to deal with them one way or another. Hence, the Germans *wanted* to hear that the Jews were running. And so, they heard it. This is a typical case of confirmation bias. Hence, in the end, we do not know exactly how many Baltic and Soviet Jews "got away." But close to a million or more is very well possible.

(For more details, see Mattogno 2022c, pp. 166-177; Sanning 2023, pp. 64-103.)

The survival rate of the Polish Jews deported to Siberia in 1939 and 1940, at a time when there was no war with Germany yet, was dismal, as for all inmates in the GULag. Some 200,000 Jews are estimated to have died *en route*. Some 157,500 are said to have returned to Poland after the war. If 200,000 died before arriving, 630,000 were cared for after arriving, and 157,500 returned back home, then (200,000 + 630,000 − 157,500 =) some 670,000 Polish Jews disappeared on the way to or in Siberia, because Stalin had decided so.

The fate of the Soviet Jews and other pivotal persons who fled or were deported away starting in June 1941, may have been better than the fate of the deported Polish Jews, because the former were needed for the larger war effort. However, considering the generally awful living condition in Soviet Russia during the war, the attrition rate among them will also have been considerable. (For more details, see Sanning 2023, pages 103-106.).

These losses of Jewish lives are tragic, but they are strictly speaking not victims of the National-Socialist Holocaust. They are, in a sense, the victims of Stalin's own Holocaust.

Demography
The only orthodox study trying to determine the Soviet Union's Jewish population losses during the Second World War concluded that almost three million Soviet Jews died in the Holocaust. This number was basically determined by subtracting the number of Jews who reported themselves as Jews during the first postwar census – some two million – from those of the last prewar census – some five million (Benz 1991, pp. 499-560).

Hence, there were several reasons for a reduction in the official Jewish population in the Soviet Union, none of which have anything to do with "the Holocaust," and yet they are counted as Holocaust victims anyway. These reasons include: Stalin's various deportation victims; Jewish soldiers and partisans killed in action; victims of diseases; collateral victims of war; natural excess of deaths over births; religious conversions or simple refusal to register as a Jew; as well as any emigration during and after the war.

Already during Stalin's reign, the Soviet Union had turned against its Jewish citizens by way of purges and mass deportations. The postwar Soviet Union became strongly opposed to Zionism and the Jewish state, taking sides with the Arab nations in both wars against Israel. Hence, it was not wise for a Jew in the radically atheistic, anti-Zionist Soviet Union to register himself as a Jew in any census. Therefore, the Jewish population figures of some two million in various Soviet postwar censuses may not have reflected reality at all.

Once the Soviet Union allowed the emigration of its Jews to Israel, and even more so after the Soviet Union collapsed in 1991, the number of Jews presumably living in the Soviet Union suddenly rose drastically, from three to four to five million. At least this is what Jewish pressure groups claimed, who had an interest in as many Jews wanting to emigrate as possible. Moreover, many Russians may suddenly have discovered some Jewish relative, real or invented, and used them to escape. Hence, these numbers must be viewed with equal skepticism. (For more on this, see Rudolf 2019, pp. 189-193.)

SPANNER, RUDOLF

Rudolf Spanner was a professor of human anatomy at the university of Danzig until 1946. Primitive soap cakes confiscated at his institute were submitted during the Nuremberg International Military Tribunal by the Soviets as proof that the Germans turned the bodies of murdered camp inmates into soap. It turned out that these pieces of soap had a completely harmless background that has nothing to do with processing deceased or murdered camp inmates. The investigations initiated against Spanner were shelved when the innocuous nature of this soap was established. (For more, see the entry on Soap, from Jewish Corpses.)

Rudolf Spanner

SPECIAL TREATMENT
General Usage in German Wartime Documents
The German term *Sonderbehandlung* (special treat-

ment) and other related terms, such as *Sonderaktion* (special operation) and *Sondermaßnahme* (special measure) appear on numerous occasions in original German wartime documents.

In a general context of the Second World War, German documents containing the term "special treatment" could have both beneficial as well as detrimental implications. In the latter case, the term was sometimes used as a euphemism for executions or murder. Some of these documents were introduced as such during the Nuremberg International Military Tribunal (Documents NO-905, 1944-PS, 3040-PS). However, these have nothing to do with Jews as such. Document 3040-PS, for instance, ordered that serious crimes ought to be punished with special treatment, to be carried out "with the noose" (*IMT*, Vol. 31, pp. 500-512, here pp. 505-507).

In his Nuremberg testimony, Ernst Kaltenbrunner, the last chief of Germany's Department of Homeland Security (*Reichssicherheitshauptamt*, RSHA), stated that the term "special treatment" usually referred to "a death sentence, not imposed by a public court but by an order by Himmler" (*IMT*, Vol. 11, p. 336). In this regard, Document 3040-PS states that special treatment, meaning execution, needed to be approved by the RSHA (*IMT*, Vol. 31, p. 505), while Document NO-905 discusses responsibilities when deciding such applications.

Examples for beneficial meanings of that term are:
- the exemption from resettlement of minorities friendly to the Germans (660-PS);
- the preferential treatment of Ukrainian women who can be Germanized and who were to be employed as household helpers in Germany (025-PS);
- the gentler treatment of eastern populations in contrast to a tough military attitude (1024-PS);
- release from imprisonment (1193-PS);
- better food supplies for Baltic and Ruthenian people (EC-126);
- Germany's concentration-camp regulations stipulated that "inmates of honor" (usually high-ranking politicians of occupied countries) had to be "treated specially," meaning they were privyleged.

This last example was confirmed Kaltenbrunner during his Nuremberg testimony, according to which "special treatment" for captured dignitaries of hostile countries meant lodging in luxury hotels with regal service (*IMT*, Vol. 11, pp. 338f.).

Euthanasia

The "mercy" killing of severely mentally disabled patients during the Third Reich – called Program 14 f 13 by the German bureaucracy – was temporarily extended during the war to encompass also permanently severely disabled patients in Germany's wartime camps, and as such referred to on occasion as "special treatment." However, a manpower shortage gradually changed that attitude. An order to all camp commandants dated 26 March 1942 specified that "every inmate worker must be maintained for the camp" (1151-PS). A little more than a year later, on 27 April 1943, Himmler ordered that frailness and physical infirmity can no longer be reasons for such special treatment (NO-1007):

"The Reichsführer SS and Head of the German Police has decided in principle that in the future only mentally ill prisoners may be processed by the medical boards created for Program 14 f 13.

All other prisoners unfit for work [...] are in principle exempt from this program. Bedridden prisoners should be assigned work that they can perform in bed."

This implies, of course, that up to then inmates physically unfit for work were not in principle exempt from getting culled like injured cattle, if a medical board had decided so. However, camp documents show that euthanasia decisions, while not rare, were not made in large masses. (See Mattogno 2016a, pp. 88-91.)

Special Treatment of Jews

Particularly pervasive is the term "special treatment" in documents connected with the Third Reich's treatment of the Jews. However, in most cases, this term did not mean execution. The richest documentation in this regard has been preserved for the Auschwitz Camp. These documents, however, never mention mass killings. The orthodoxy asserts that code words were used for this, such as "special treatment," "special measures," "special actions," etc. But a thorough study of hundreds of documents containing these buzz word shows that all of them, without exception, find an innocuous explanation, if seen in their proper documental and historical context. (For details on this, see Mattogno 2016a & 2016d).

The starting point is that every deportation of Jews from their point of origin via Auschwitz, either to forced-labor deployments or to resettlements, was called "special operation" (*Sonderaktion*). In fact, the Third Reich's way of treating the Jews differently than anyone else was called "special treatment." Hence, anything in connection with Jews could and often did receive the term "special" attached to it, because the Jews were not normal concentration-camp inmates, who were usually criminals, PoWs or regime opponents. That did not imply per se that a document having that term refers to something murderous.

Another large complex of Auschwitz documents containing "special" terms stand in connection with large construction efforts to improve the hygienic, sanitary and healthcare situation at Auschwitz. (See the entries on Eduard Wirths and Birkenau for details.) These were "special (construction) measures" meant to save inmate lives. They stood in connection with "Implementation of Special Treatment" of the Jews, as a detailed project description for the construction of the Birkenau Camp states. However, the only building in that project description that is explicitly designated for "special treatment" is the large inmate shower and disinfestation facility, later nicknamed *Zentralsauna*. This building served to save lives as well, not take them. The crematoria, where the orthodoxy insists "special treatment" through mass gassing occurred, do not carry any "special" term in this project description. (See the illustration.)

A series of documents shows that certain inmates were marked with "SB" in registries. The orthodoxy insists that these inmates had been selected as unfit for work in order to get killed. However, a close analysis of these and other documents shows that this cannot be true. Foremost, many documents prove that sick inmates were regularly registered in many documents without any sign of them getting killed, and many documents prove that the camp authorities usually spared no efforts to cure sick inmates, and even to care for many who were incurable.

Other cases of the innocuous use of "special" terms are distorted in a ludicrous way by some orthodox historians to "prove" homicide. Here is the most-striking example: Around Christmas and New Year of 1942/43, the Auschwitz Camp was still on lockdown due to the raging typhus epidemic. As a consequence, not even the almost 1,000 civilians working in that camp were allowed to go on holiday leave. When they learned about this in mid-December, they organized a camp-wide strike. In reaction, the camp Gestapo interrogated all civilian workers to find out what the issue was and how to solve it. They called this a "special operation [*Sonderaktion*] for security reasons encompassing all civilian workers."

One orthodox historian, following the dogma that "special" terms mean murder, decided that the Gestapo started killing these civilian workers to break their strike. But this was not so, as later documents prove. First, the strike was resolved by granting these

"Project: PoW Camp Auschwitz (Implementation of Special Treatment)". Auschwitz Camp, document of the Central Construction Office, dated 29 October 1942. Here page 5 (cropped at the bottom): Entry 13b) contains the cost estimate for the four crematoria with morgues, furnaces, ventilation systems and chimneys (but no gas chambers), with no use of any "special" term. Entry 16a) contains the cost estimate for the inmate shower and disinfestation facility, later nickname Zentralsauna, here labeled as "Disinfestation facility, for special treatment" ("Entwesungsanlage für Sonderbehandlung").

civilians a two-week vacation over the holidays. And second, the day after the "special action" was over, all civilian workers happily reported back to work. (See Mattogno 2016d, pp. 98f., for details of this case; see Mattogno 2016a and 2016d in general for more details on this special topic.)

SPEER, ALBERT

Albert Speer (19 March 1905 – 1 Sept. 1981) was Germany's Minister of Armaments and War Production from 8 February 1942 until 30 April 1945. He was indicted during the Nuremberg International Military Tribunal for his extended use of forced laborer in the Third Reich's various construction and armament projects that he managed. He was sentenced to 20 years' imprisonment for it.

Albert Speer

Throughout his life and in his two autobiographies, titled *Inside the Third Reich: Memoirs* (1970) and *Spandau: The Secret Diaries* (1976), he has denied having had any knowledge of an extermination program of the Jews. From his governmental position, he organized, funded and allocated material for the construction and expansion of concentration camps, including foremost Auschwitz. Hence, if a "Final Solution" in terms of a wholesale slaughter in gas chambers was implemented at Auschwitz, it is inconceivable that Speer did not know about it.

However, as the vast documentation about Auschwitz proves incontrovertibly, there is no trace of such a program being implemented. Quite the contrary, the massive construction and expansion works undertaken at that camp from 1942 onward aimed at drastically improving the hygienic, sanitary and healthcare situation for all inmates. (See the entries on Auschwitz Main Camp and Birkenau.)

On the other hand, Speer must have been aware of a general eliminatory attitude among the SS toward the Jews, because he attended one of Himmler's most infamous speeches, in which the latter minced few words as to what he wanted his listeners to believe about the fate of the Jews. During that speech of 6 October 1943 in front of the political elite of the Third Reich, Himmler even addressed Speer a few times personally. (See the entry on Himmler speeches.)

Hence, Speer was correct to some degree, but he also suffered from selective memory.

SPRINGER, ELISA

Elisa Springer (12 Feb. 1918 – 19 Sept. 2004) was an Austrian Jewess who married an Italian and moved to Italy in 1940, living under a false identity. She was betrayed in 1944, arrested and deported to Auschwitz, arriving there in early August. After three months she was transferred to the Bergen-Belsen Camp.

Elisa Springer

She went public with her story only in 1997 with the publication of her autobiographical story. She claimed in it that "the gas chambers and furnaces" in Bergen-Belsen were put into operation after Josef Kramer had become camp commandant there (Springer 1997, p. 88). However, there was never a homicidal gas chamber conceived or planned, let alone built and put in operation at the Bergen-Belsen Camp, and the camp had only *one* furnace, which went into operation long before Kramer was transferred to that camp in late 1944. Together with Moshe Peer, Elisa Springer is among the few witnesses who have made up bold lies about alleged homicidal gas chambers the in Bergen-Belsen Camp.

SREBRNIK, SZYMON

Szymon Srebrnik (10 April 1930 – 16 Aug. 2006) was a Polish Jew who, during an interview with Judge Bednarz on 29 June 1945, claimed that at age 13 he was arrested with his mother and taken to the Chełmno Camp. He is one of only three Chełmno inmates who have testified about their alleged experiences. The other two are Michał Podchlebnik and Mieczysław Żurawski.

Szymon Srebrnik

Srebrnik was interrogated about his experiences for the first time in late June 1945, at age 15, by Polish investigating judge Władysław Bednarz. A year later, he made a deposition for the Central Commission for Jewish History. Fifteen years later, he testified during the Eichmann show trial in Jerusalem, a few years after that at the German Chełmno show trial at Bonn, and finally he was interviewed by Claude Lanzmann for his 1985 documentary *Shoah*. Here are the main peculiarities of his various testimonies:

- In 1945, he claimed to have arrived at Chełmno in March 1944, but during the Eichmann Trial, he claimed that he arrived there in the summer of 1943, or maybe closer to 1944. Either way, the orthodoxy insists that the Chełmno Camp was inactive between April 1943 and April 1944, so neither of Srebrnik's dating was possible.
- Had Chełmno really been an extermination camp where everyone was killed more-or-less on arrival, with only a few strong, healthy and young men kept as slaves to fell trees, chop them up, dig mass graves, haul corpses, arrange pyres, crush cremation remains, then no boy of age 13 would have survived. Yet Srebrnik claims to have done all these jobs for about a year at age 13/14.
- Srebrnik even claimed that, as a 13/14-year-old boy, he won long jumping and racing contests against other – grown-up – inmates
- He made frequent row-boat trips together with SS men, singing Polish folk tunes and Prussian military songs together.
- The first job he allegedly had to do was removing the rubble of a destroyed house. In the debris, they found "skulls, hands and legs," allegedly the remnants of Jews who had been locked up inside the house, and were then killed by blowing up the premise. This would have been a ludicrously inefficient way of killing people.
- With each interrogation, he claimed a higher death toll for the camp: in his 1945 interview, he claimed that a total of 15,000 Jews had been killed in 1944 at Chełmno. During the 1961 Eichmann Trial, this grew to 1,000 to 1,200 victims daily for 9 months straight, or more than 300,000 just for 1944. During the interview with Claude Lanzmann, the daily death toll had grown to 2,000, which results in 540,000 victims for 9 months. The orthodoxy insists, however, that less than 10,000 victims were killed there in 1944.
- When Judge Bednarz showed a photo of a derelict Magirus truck on the grounds of the Ostrowski Company, Srebrnik enthusiastically recognized and identified this vehicle as one of the gas vans allegedly used at Chełmno. Yet that truck was an ordinary moving truck, as Bednarz's report on that truck showed.
- Srebrnik claimed that some Jews, when tending the pyres, suddenly caught fire and died in the flames themselves, which he called "instances of unintended self-incineration." While one would suffer serious burns when working without protective clothes near large-scale fires, no person ever would catch fire and burn to ashes.
- In his 1945 deposition, he told a tale how a co-inmate had to throw his gassed sister into the fire, where she suddenly came back to life and cursed him shouting, "You murderer, why are you throwing me into the furnace? I'm still alive." No one can breathe while inside a blaze, let alone shout at anyone. So, during the Eichmann Trial, he dropped the claim that his sister came back to life…
- During his interview with Lanzmann, Srebrnik topped the story of the flame-resuscitated sister by claiming that an entire load of Jews presumably gassed in a gas van came back to life, but they were thrown into the fire by Srebrnik and his colleagues anyhow, alive, without offering resistance. "They could feel the fire burn them."
- When the camp was dissolved, he claimed that he was executed with a shot into the neck, but the bullet exited through his mouth and tip of the nose without killing him. If that were so, it would have caused serious damage to the front of his upper jaw, destroying his incisors in the process. Yet all photos of him show no serious scarring above his upper lip or lower nose, and he also had all his teeth. (During the Eichmann trial, a little scar he had on his nose was no longer caused by a bullet but by some glass sliver.)
- Wounded as he allegedly was, he heroically broke both headlights of the SS's car illuminating the scene. No one noticed the noise this lengthy and violent process would have caused, and no one noticed the sudden darkness either, so he managed to run away into the darkness. In later statements, he no longer claimed that, though…
- He explained to Lanzmann how he coped:
  "When I saw all that, it didn't affect me. […] I was only 13 years old and all I'd ever seen until I came here were dead bodies. Maybe I didn't understand."

It is more likely, however, that he wasn't affected by all he claims to have experienced because it was all a figment of the imagination.

(For more details, see Alvarez 2011; 2023, pp. 158-160, 171-173; Mattogno 2017, pp. 63-67).

STAHLECKER, WALTER

At the beginning of Germany's invasion of the Soviet Union, Walter Stahlecker (10 Oct. 1900 – 23 March 1942), SS *Brigadeführer*, was the head of *Einsatzgruppe* A operating in the Baltics and northern Russia. He is the author of two extended reports on the activities of his *Einsatzgruppe*, the so-called Stahlecker Reports. Stahlecker died as a result of a partisan attack. (For more details, see the entry on the *Einsatzgruppen* and on the Stahlecker Reports.)

Walter Stahlecker

STAHLECKER REPORTS

During his time as commander of *Einsatzgruppe* A since Germany's invasion of the Soviet Union, SS *Brigadeführer* Walter Stahlecker compiled two extended reports on the structure, personnel and activities of his task force. The first of these so-called Stahlecker Reports covers events and activities since the outbreak of hostilities until and including 15 October 1941. It has 143 pages plus 18 appendices with together 78 pages, hence a total of 221 pages. The second report covers events and activities from 16 October 1941 until 31 January 1942. This report is even longer, with its 228 pages of text plus 19 appendices.

Only very small parts of these reports deal with executions. Among other issues, the latter document reported on the civil population's morale; politics and administration; propaganda; cultural areas; ethnicity; public health; Jews; church; economic policy; food situation; agriculture; industry and trade; resistance movements. Further elaborating on these issues were appendices about ethnicity and churches in Belorussia; religious denominations in Latvia and Estonia; religious life in Estonia; minimum wage and existential minimum; social insurance; age distribution in Latvia; livestock in Lithuania, Latvia and Estonia; types of crops in Latvia and Estonia; employment situation in trade and industry in Latvia.

These reports testify to the vast research and data-gathering activities Stahlecker's unit unfolded. It shows that the men doing this work and compiling their results were highly educated people rather than a gang of brutish thugs.

On the other hand, the death toll claimed in these reports is truly staggering. The second "Stahlecker Report" lists a total of 143,774 victims of all causes for Lithuania (executions, pogroms etc.). Of the 4,500 Jews who had lived in Estonia in early 1940, this reports states, only some 2,000 stayed behind when the war with Germany began, while some 2,500 fled or were evacuated. Of the remaining 2,000 Jews, none were left on 31 January 1942. A map appended to the report lists as executed (see the illustration):

Estonia:	963
Latvia:	35,238
Lithuania:	136,421

Since Stahlecker died in late March of 1942 after a partisan attack, he did not compile any later reports such as these, and his successors evidently did not have the intention or resources to follow in Stahlecker's ambitious footsteps. However, there are other summary documents created by the *Einsatzgruppen* which testify to a similar diversity of activities. (For more details, see Mattogno 2022c as well as the entry on the *Einsatzgruppen*.)

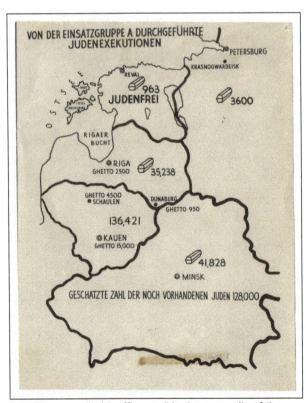

The so-called "coffin map" in the appendix of the second Stanlecker Report.

STANDING UPRIGHT, DEAD GASSING VICTIMS

Numerous witnesses have claimed to have been present when an alleged homicidal gas chamber at a German wartime camp was opened after a mass execution using poison gas. Many of them have described that the packing density of the victims inside the gas chamber was so high that there was no room for the dead victims to fall over, so most or all of them kept standing upright even after death.

The frequently claimed packing densities of ten persons per square meter and more are not only unlikely or even impossible, but they could also not explain why the dead would keep standing upright. Even if the upper bodies of people squeezed into a room are packed tightly together – an act that requires discipline and voluntary cooperation – there is enough room for the legs to fold, hence for the bodies to slump down and tilt any which way. Note also that the human body does not go stiff from inhaling hydrogen cyanide (the active ingredient in Zyklon B) or carbon monoxide (the most-lethal component of engine-exhaust gases). Furthermore, it takes hours for *rigor mortis* to set in, meaning the stiffening of muscles after death. Therefore, the tale of people standing upright in their death is a myth.

Here is a list of witnesses who have made statements to this effect, displaying a "convergence of evidence" on a lie:
– Pery Broad
– Milton Buki
– Shaul Chasan
– Dario Gabai
– Kurt Gerstein
– Abraham Goldfarb
– Maurice Lequeux
– Henryk Mandelbaum
– Filip Müller
– Dov Paisikovic
– Rudolf Reder
– Elias Rosenberg
– Karl Schluch (Belzec Trial)
– Morris Venezia

STANEK, FRANCISZEK

Franciszek Stanek was a Polish employee at the Auschwitz railway station during the war. He was interrogated by the Soviets on 3 March 1945, during which he helped fill in the information gap caused by the lack of documents on transports by claiming vastly exaggerated numbers of deportation trains arriving at Auschwitz:
– 150 transports in 1942 with a total of 190,000-200,000 deportees.
– 360 transports in 1943 with a total of 720,000 deportees.
– 1,500 transports in 1944 with a total of approximately four million people!

He arrived at a total of some five million deportees, allowing the Soviets to claim four million victims. This is a clear case of the forced "convergence of evidence" on a lie by an evidently orchestrated testimony. (For more details, see Mattogno 2021, pp. 304f.)

STANGL, FRANZ

Franz Stangl

Franz Stangl (26 March 1908 – 28 June 1971), SS *Hauptsturmführer* at war's end, worked various positions within the so-called Euthanasia Program from early 1940 until March 1942. After this, he was transferred to *Aktion Reinhardt*. He served as commandant of the Sobibór Camp from 28 April until 28 August 1942, when he was transferred to Treblinka as this camp's second commandant. After the inmate uprising in Treblinka in August 1943, the camp was closed down, and Stangl and the remaining SS staff transferred to Triest, Italy, to fight partisans.

After the war, he eventually emigrated to Brazil, where he was arrested in 1967 and extradited to Germany. In 1970, he was put on trial in Düsseldorf as the only defendant in Germany's second Treblinka Show Trial. After the orthodox narrative of Treblinka had been cast incontestably into legal stone during the first Düsseldorf Treblinka Trial in 1964/65, with Kurt Franz as one of the defendants, Stangl's trial outcome was predetermined. Fifty witnesses testified during this trial, most of which had already testified seven years earlier during the first Düsseldorf Treblinka Trial. Their trustworthiness, or the lack thereof, can be assessed by the critical analysis of their testimonies as summarized in the respective entries. (See the section "Treblinka" of the entry on witnesses.)

As in all other Holocaust show trials, the Düsseldorf court – defense lawyer, prosecutor, judges – did nothing to determine how such a huge mass murder with complete erasure of its traces would have been possible, technically speaking. No one was interested in finding traces of the murder weapon, of the murder victims, or the means with which they were made to disappear.

Stangl was sentence to imprisonment for life for the murder of at least 400,000 Jews. Undeterred, he filed an appeal with the delusion that he would be acquitted ultimately, and walk out as a free man.

In her 1974 book *Into That Darkness*, British journalist Gitta Sereny claimed that she had extended interviews with Stangl after his conviction. She claimed that, during these unrecorded interviews, he confessed the correctness of the orthodox view – while his appeal claiming innocence was pending. However, Sereny wrote all the passages of Stangl's alleged confession in such as style as to make it difficult if not impossible to discern whether Stangl was really confessing, or whether Sereny was only using his ambiguous words to garnish her interpretation of it. Furthermore, there is nothing in this "confession" that confirms any fact, let alone any detail as to how the mass murder was committed, and how the 800,000 bodies were tracelessly eliminated. Confronted about all this by another journalist, Sereny admitted that Stangl had *not* confessed, but that she had used the book as a literary device to make him look like he did.

By sheer coincidence, Stangl died the day after his last interview with Sereny.

(For more details, see Mattogno/Graf 2023, pp. 30-32.)

STARK, HANS

Hans Stark (14 June 1921 – 29 March 1991), SS *Oberscharführer*, served at the Auschwitz Camp from Christmas 1940 to November 1942, with an extended furlough from Christmas 1941 until the end of March 1942. In June 1941, he joined the Political Department. In preparation of the Frankfurt Auschwitz show trial, he was interrogated on 23 April 1959. During the trial itself, he also took the stand. Here are some of Stark's peculiar claims:

Hans Stark

- Stark claimed that the alleged gas chamber inside Crematorium I had just one door looking like an air-raid-shelter door, but the morgue had two doors, none of which looked like an air-raid-shelter door. Such a door was installed only when the building was converted to an air-raid-shelter in 1944, when Stark had left the camp. Hence, he was reporting the situation as it has been shown since 1947 to tourists.
- He insisted that the roof had two round openings of some 35 cm diameter, although the orthodoxy insists that there were (and are again) four square openings measuring some 50 cm × 50 cm.
- Stark's statements during his pre-trial deposition and during his trial testimony about a gassing, in which he claimed to have directly participated, are contradictory. The gassing concerned either "200–250 Jews" or "150 or 200 […] Jews and Poles"; the victims were gassed either for being Jews, including children, or because they were "people that had been sentenced to death by a court-martial," but definitely without any children.
- Once the Zyklon B had been dumped onto the people inside, it took only "a few minutes" for all to be quiet (hence unconscious). Yet the poison absorbed in the Zyklon-B gypsum pellets evaporates and dissipates only slowly, so it would have taken at least ten, if not twenty minutes for all victims to collapse unconscious.
- After some 10–15 minutes, the room was allegedly opened, but it would have taken hours to ventilate a room where Zyklon pellets keep emitting the poison for at least another hour.
- Stark reported about homicidal gassings in two wooden houses erected in early 1942 close to the railway ramp at Birkenau. However, Stark was not even present in that camp in early 1942, the railway ramp at Birkenau was built only in 1944, and such wooden gassing houses near that or any other railway ramp are completely unheard of.
- When shown photos taken in 1944 of Jews arriving at the Birkenau railway ramp, he confirmed that this shows the situation as he knew it. However, the ramp shown on those photos didn't exist during Stark's time at the camp.

Stark admitted that he was a lavish consumer of Auschwitz literature, hence we are dealing here with a clear case of false memory syndrome.

(For more details, see Mattogno 2016c, pp. 67-

71.)

STEINER, JEAN-FRANÇOIS

Jean-François Steiner (born 17 Feb. 1938) is a French-Jewish author who in 1966 published a novel, to some degree ghostwritten by Gilles Perrault, which is allegedly based on statements of former inmates of the Treblinka Camp. In spite of it being presented as fiction, it was initially nevertheless highly praised by the orthodoxy and was very successful in France, but also with its German and English translations.

The most-glaring untrue claims about the Treblinka Camp concern the alleged mass cremation of the victims of the purported mass murder. It tells the tale of how the "specialist in the cremation of bodies" Herbert Floss found out about self-immolating bodies, and how to make use of that discovery to burn the bodies that resisted cremation:

> "all the bodies did not burn at the same rate; there were good bodies and bad bodies, fire-resistant bodies and inflammable bodies. The art consisted in using the good ones to burn the bad ones."

The mountain of human corpses piled upon the grate was ignited with small campfires lit underneath. Once the corpses had caught fire, the entire pyre soon became a gigantic inferno:

> "The bodies burst into flames. [...] The spectacle had an infernal quality [...]. Floss beamed. This fire was the finest day of his life. [...] An extraordinary party began. [...] ten times the men raised their arms, each time shouting 'Heil Hitler.' [...] The party lasted until the funeral pyre was entirely consumed. After the toasts came the songs, savage and cruel, songs of hatred, songs of fury, songs of glory to Germany the eternal."

After a later change of mind, even one of the most dogmatic orthodox Holocaust scholars, the French Jew Pierre Vidal-Naquet, re-categorized Steiner's anti-German hate fest as "sub-literature" tending towards sadism. (For more details, see Mattogno/Graf 2023, pp. 27-29.)

STERN, URSULA

Ursula Stern was an inmate of the Sobibór Camp. According to a deposition summarized and published by the Dutch Red Cross, Stern claimed that there was one gas chamber at this camp into which the gas was fed through showerheads. After the murder, the floors opened, and the bodies were discharged into a space below.

Her claims are rejected as false by the orthodoxy, who insists on several gas chambers, into which engine-exhaust gas was fed through pipes rather than showerheads. These chambers did not have collapsible floors either. The corpses were instead taken out of the chamber manually, sideways through a normal door.

(See the entry on Sobibór for more details, as well as Graf/Kues/Mattogno 2020, pp. 70, 109; Mattogno 2021e, p. 75.)

STEYUK, YAKOV

Yakov Steyuk was a Ukrainian Jew interned in the Syretsky Camp, 5 km from Kiev. On 18 August 1943, he was taken from there to Babi Yar, a place where tens of thousands of Jews are said to have been shot and buried by the Germans in mass graves in late September 1941 (see the entry on Babi Yar). He was interrogated by the NKGB on 12 and 15 November 1943 about his alleged experiences at Babi Yar.

Among other things, Steyuk stated that he and 100 other slave-labor inmates were put in chains, had to exhume mass graves, and burn the extracted bodies on pyres. He claimed that the pyres they built consisted of several layers of wood and bodies, reaching the height of four meters, and containing about 5,000 corpses each. Later he specified that a pyre had about *20 layers*(!) of alternating wood and bodies.

Let's assume that a running meter of a pyre two meters wide can accommodate four corpses. Each corpse requires 250 kg of freshly cut wood (see open-air incinerations). The density of green wood is roughly 0.9 tons per m^3, and its stacking density on a pyre is 1.4 (40% for air and flames to go through). This means that the wood required to burn just one layer of corpses stacks up to a height of some 0.75 meters. Adding the body layer gets us to roughly a meter. Twenty such layers result in a pyre 20 meters high. It would have been impossible to build such a pyre, and also impossible to burn it down without it collapsing and spilling burning wood and corpses all over the place.

Steyuk asserted that at least ten such pyres were burned, hence a total of some 50,000 bodies. In the second interview, Steyuk first said he doesn't know how many bodies there were exhumed and burned in total, but when pressed for a number, he stated that there had been some 45,000 bodies.

When interrogated again in 1980 by the KGB, he now "remembered" that each pyre contained 2,000 bodies and was only 3 meters high; that there were up to sixty of them; that the slave-labor work force was increased to 325; that the total death toll amounted to 100,000 victims; that the evil SS officer running the show was called Topaide; and that the Germans also used gas vans to kill people. This late enrichment of his "memory," bringing it in line with other similarly groomed testimonies, evidently resulted from coaching sessions he had with Soviet authorities, whose investigative commission had invented the SS man Topaide and the use of gas vans in their 1944 expert report on Babi Yar.

With 250 kg of freshly cut wood needed to cremate one body on a pyre, cremating 50,000 or 100,000 bodies would have required some 12,500 to 25,000 metric tons of wood. An average prisoner is rated at being able to cut some 0.63 metric tons of fresh wood per workday. To cut this amount of wood within five weeks (35 days) that this operation supposedly lasted would have required a work force of some 567 to 1,134 dedicated lumberjacks just to cut the wood. Steyuk claimed initially that his unit consisted only of 100 inmates, all busy digging out mass graves, extracting bodies, building pyres, and – as other witnesses claimed – moreover sifting through ashes, scattering the ashes and refilling the graves with soil. Steyuk says nothing about where the firewood came from.

(For more details, see the entry on Babi Yar, as well as Mattogno 2022c, pp. 531-533, and 550-563.)

STRAWCZYŃSKI, OSKAR

Oskar Strawczyński was a Polish Jew deported to the Treblinka Camp, where he claims to have arrived on 5 October 1942. He was interviewed about his experiences on 7 October 1945. His knowledge about the claimed exterminations occurring at that camp are all from hearsay:

> *"From the accounts of Hersz Jabłkowski, who was a blacksmith and came from Stoczek Węgrowski, I know what the gas chambers looked like."* – Jabłkowski allegedly helped build the gas-chamber facility.

- Strawczyński stated that there here were four concrete chambers measuring 3 m × 3 m – while the orthodoxy insists on three wooden (4 m × 4 m) or ten concrete chambers (8 m × 4 m).
- He didn't know how the killing was done, but assumed either vacuum or exhaust gases.
- He claimed that during the first 130 days of the camp's operation, three trains with 60 cars each packed with 100 people, arrived every day and were exterminated at the camp. This amounts to some 2,340,000 victims – as opposed to the some 800,000 claimed by the orthodoxy.

Erroneous hearsay information, unfounded speculations and exaggerated death-toll claims are the hallmarks of this testimony that isn't worth the paper it is written on. A book co-authored with another self-proclaimed Treblinka survivor, Israel Cymlich, appeared in 2007 with the title *Escaping Hell in Treblinka*. Sixty years of exposure to massively memory-manipulating influences (see the entry on false-memory syndrome) certainly did not make his claims – or Cymlich's first-time claims – on alleged exterminations more relevant or reliable.

(See Mattogno 2021e, pp. 138, 156f.)

STREICHER, JULIUS

Julius Streicher

Julius Streicher (12 Feb. 1885 – 16 Oct. 1946), a German newspaper publisher and National-Socialist politician, is most famous for his tabloid newspaper *Der Stürmer* – which translates to "The Striker" or "The Attacker." This periodical is today most-renowned for its radical and at times vulgar anti-Jewish articles and cartoons. To this day, these cartoons epitomize National-Socialist anti-Judaism. However, Streicher's sledge-hammer rhetoric was looked down upon by many leading personalities of the Third Reich. When he used his newspaper to attack other National Socialists, he was declared unfit for leadership by the Party Court, and was eventually stripped of all his positions. The only exception was his position as *Gauleiter* of Frankonia, which he had held since 1925. But even in this role he was limited to the formal title from 1940 on.

Streicher's influence on the Holocaust is limited to his paper's drastic anti-Jewish stance. During the Nuremberg International Military Tribunal (IMT), he was charged exactly for that.

Of interest in the present context is the way Streicher was treated while in U.S. custody in Nuremberg. He testified in court on 26 April 1946. In the transcript of the IMT published in 1947, we read how he first summarized his life, then explained how he first met Hitler during a 3-hour speech, and how he was proud to have handed over his own movement to Hitler. He mentioned that in 1940 he was given a "leave of absence," which no doubt referred to the fact that he had factually been stripped of all positions within the National-Socialist state. Asked why he had been dismissed from a teaching position, he denied any wrongdoing of indecency. Then, a short while later, the transcript mentions him lashing out against a witness who had testified before him, for which he was reprimanded by the court after a complaint by U.S. prosecutor Justice Jackson (*IMT*, Vol. 12, pp. 309-311).

According to a journalist who was reporting daily on the IMT for the London *Times*, events unfolded somewhat differently, though. In an article published the next day under the headline "Streicher Opens His Case," we read how Streicher recounted his first encounter with Hitler (*The Times*, 27 April 1946, p. 3):

"'*He* [Hitler] *had been speaking for three hours and was drenched in perspiration.* […]'

Streicher said that he had been charged with handing over his anti-Jewish movement to Hitler. 'Yes!' said Streicher, 'I am proud of it. For 20 years I have spoken at meetings every week, to thousands of people.'

Raising his voice to a shrill cry, he declared that after he found himself in allied captivity, he was kept for four days in a cell without clothes. 'I was made to kiss negroes' feet. I was whipped. I had to drink saliva,' he declared.

He paused for breath, and then screamed: 'My mouth was forced open with a piece of wood, and then I was spat on. When I asked for a drink of water I was taken to a latrine and told, 'Drink.' These are the sort of things the Gestapo has been blamed for.'

Saying that 'allegations on my honour' were false, he denied seducing a woman schoolteacher in France. Speaking of his place in the counsels of the Nazi Party, he said he was the only unpaid Gauleiter in the Reich.

Then he ejaculated suddenly: 'The witness Gisevius was a traitor' (Dr. Hans Gisevius, who ended his evidence earlier in the day).

Mr. Justice Jackson, the chief United States prosecutor, protested, saying that no question had been put to Streicher to which that observation could be an answer. He asked Lord Justice Lawrence to admonish Streicher.

Lord Justice Lawrence (to Streicher). 'You have no right to comment on the evidence of a previous witness, and certainly no right to call a witness a traitor.'"

Therefore, we know that Streicher had complained during his testimony about having been tortured in captivity, and we know that this entire passage was deleted from the published record. This proves that the judges at the IMT colluded with the prosecution to remove anything from this transcript that shines a bad light on these proceedings. What else has been deleted or altered? We will never know. This episode undermines the credibility of the entire IMT record. Was Streicher tortured, and the IMT officials lied about it by deleting this passage off the record? Or was Streicher the liar by making false claims?

Streicher wrote a detailed account of his treatment in U.S. captivity, which eventually made it into the hands of German mainstream historian Werner Maser. The many verifiable details in this account make it a credible testimony, Maser later opined.

For his "crime" of anti-Jewish journalism, Streicher was sentenced to death and executed by hanging on 16 October 1946. Virulent, aggressive anti-Judaism was a capital offense.

(For more details, see Dalton 2020a; Irving 1996, pp. 51f.; Stimely 1984; see also the entry on torture.)

STRUMMER, ADELE

Adele "Deli" Strummer (née Aufrichtig, 2 May 1922 – 25 July 2016) was an Austrian Jewess who was deported to Theresienstadt in 1943, then a while later for eight days to Auschwitz, from where she was sent to a labor-subcamp of the Flossenbürg Camp. Toward the end of the war, she was evacuated to the Mauthausen Camp, where she was liberated by U.S. troops. She eventually emigrated to the U.S., where she had a successful career as a gynecologist.

Starting in 1980, she toured as a speaker telling her story as a "survivor." In 1988, she self-published a book titled *A Personal Reflection of the Holocaust*. When an extended version of it was to be turned into a movie in the late 1990s, scholars noticed differences between the script and the book. After some digging, they revealed a series of untruths Strummer had been telling her audiences for years:

– As the year of her deportation to Theresienstadt she gave 1941, rather than 1943.
– She claimed to have been in Auschwitz for nine months, when in fact she was there only for eight days.
– She claimed to have been at the Bergen-Belsen

Camp, which was completely false.
- She claimed that she entered a homicidal gas chamber five times, but came out alive, because the guards "turned on the water instead of the gas." She probably took real showers and converted them later, as a dramatic effect for her audiences, into attempts at gassing her.
- On 5 May 1945, the day the Mauthausen Camp was liberated, she was allegedly lined up with other inmates to be gassed. She was walking toward the gas chamber doors as the American knights in shining armor rode into the camp rescuing her. The problem is that the SS had left the camps two days earlier, and that the camp was self-governed by inmates when U.S. troops arrived. Moreover, if we take the orthodox narrative for granted, homicidal gassing supposedly stopped in late 1944 on Himmler's order, or so Kurt Becher claimed in a perjurious affidavit after the war. However, there is no physical trace of any homicidal gas chamber ever having existed at that Mauthausen Camp. The facility presented as such was a real shower room.
- She claimed her husband died in the Holocaust, when in fact he survived, and she divorced him in 1947. In fact, he was still alive while she was touring the country.

Adele Strummer had no children and never remarried. After her medical career ended, her way out of loneliness and lack of purpose was by finding a new passion: creating a large crowd of admiring followers – her new family – by manipulating gullible audiences with her passionate yet mendacious speeches. Unsuspecting school children were her preferred targets, as she explained:

> "Children really listen to me, they cling to me. I have over 200,000 children."

Substitute children. However, after falling from grace, she lost them all. Ironically, her maiden name – Aufrichtig – is German for "sincere," "candid."
(For more, see Copeland 2000; Vice 2014a&b.)

Struthof → Natzweiler

STUTTHOF

Just one day after the outbreak of open hostilities between Germany and Poland, the German authorities established a detention camp near the town of Stutthof in the region of the "Free City of Danzig" meant to contain anti-German Polish political activists. This region had been separated from Germany after the First World War and was formally subject to the supervision of the League of Nations. However, ever since the end of the First World War, Poland had tried to gain total control of it with several repressive and provocative measures. This was one of the main reasons for the German-Polish conflict.

Since 1941, the Stutthof Camp also served as a "labor education camp" for individuals who had violated their labor contracts in any way. In 1942, the camp officially obtained the status of a concentration camp, with the aim to serve the surrounding farms as a forced-labor pool.

Extant documents show that the main purpose of the Stutthof Camp during the later phase of the war was systematic data gathering of concentration-camp inmates in order to deploy them more efficiently in Germany's economy. Hence, Stutthof had been turned into a large labor reservoir and distribution hub for forced laborers for the German war economy. Hence, large transports of Jews were coming into Stutthof, and they left the camp as well.

Within the context of the Holocaust, this camp becomes interesting as we enter the year 1944, when its prisoner population increased drastically due to the massive influx of Jewish inmates who were transferred from the Baltic countries, as well as from Hungary and Poland via Auschwitz.

The orthodox Polish narrative, which was clearly molded by Stalinist war propaganda, has it that in 1944 the camp was converted into an "auxiliary extermination camp" in order to support the mass murder allegedly simultaneously unfolding at Auschwitz. However, instead of killing its Jews, it is well-documented that, from July 1944, thousands of Jews were transferred from Stutthof to other concentration camps in central and west Germany. Two transports with some 2,000 inmates were even sent *to* Auschwitz. They consisted mainly of women with children who had been evacuated from the Baltic countries. Hence, if Stutthof was an "auxiliary extermination camp," it did a terrible job.

Claims about the existence of a homicidal gas chamber at Stutthof rest on shaky ground:
1. No documents exist supporting the claim that a homicidal gas chamber existed at the Stutthof Camp, or that any such gassings occurred.
2. Although no physical evidence exists for that claim either, it cannot be ruled out categorically that the camp's Zyklon-B fumigation chamber, a small building of just 8.5 m × 3.5 m, was used as a homicidal gas chamber.

3. However, this building could be observed by all inmates. Considering that between 20 and 50 inmates were released from Stutthof every day, even including the time period during which homicidal gassings are said to have been carried out, these alleged gas murders would have become known everywhere fast.
4. The extermination claims are linked to claims about the local crematorium's cremation capacity, which was grotesquely exaggerated by these witnesses, throwing an unfavorable light onto their trustworthiness.
5. Claims about the number of victims, their ethnic and religious affiliation, as well as the dates of these gassings are contradictory, very vague and contain at times obvious propaganda. Some witnesses even claimed that inmates were gassed in narrow-gauge railway cars.

Stutthof Camp, Zyklon-B fumigation chamber, mendaciously rebranded by the Stuffhof Museum as a homicidal gas chamber (komora gazowa). In the background, a railway cart presumably also used for homicidal gassings.

While these are not conclusive arguments *against* claims about homicidal gassings, the evidence offered to support these claims isn't convincing either.

In the wider Holocaust context, the Stutthof Camp is significant less for its alleged homicidal gassings than for the inmate transfers from and to this camp starting in the summer of 1944. These transfers have far-reaching repercussions on the entire orthodox Holocaust narrative.

Beginning in late June 1944, large transports of Jews arrived at Stutthof, mainly either from the Baltic countries or from the Auschwitz Camp. The first set was the result of the Red Army advancing into these countries, leading to the evacuation of all sorts of camps in that area, while the second set consisted of Jews from Hungary and the Lodz Ghetto, for whom Auschwitz had only been a transit camp.

These transports seriously undermine the orthodox extermination narrative for two reasons:
1. Some of the inmates from the Baltic countries were German Jews. According to the orthodox narrative, however, these Jews are said to have been murdered on arrival in those Baltic camps several years earlier. The data about the Stutthof Camp prove that at least some of them were not murdered.
2. If we follow the orthodox narrative, the vast majority of Hungarian Jews deported to Auschwitz since May 1944, as well as the Jews deported to Auschwitz from the Lodz Ghetto in August 1944, are said to have been murdered on arrival without having been registered. The data about the Stutthof Camp prove, however, that at least some of

Stutthof Camp, inside view of the Zyklon-B fumigation chamber, with intense blue wall stains of Iron Blue, caused by exposure to hydrogen-cyanide gas.

these unregistered Jews (23,566, to be precise) were not murdered on arrival but were transferred to other camps as forced laborers.

It is unlikely that all Jews from the Baltic countries, Hungary and Lodz who were transited through Auschwitz in the summer of 1944 eventually ended up in Stutthof. After all, Stutthof was only a relatively small camp, and only one among many others. It stands to reason that many more Jews were sent elsewhere as well, of whom orthodox historians assume that they were murdered at Auschwitz.

For instance, it has been demonstrated that at least 79,200 of the Hungarian Jews deported to Auschwitz in the spring and summer of 1944, who were *not* registered there, were transferred to other camps. The orthodoxy insists, however, that not getting registered at Auschwitz meant immediate death in its gas chambers. This is evidently untrue. Had the Germans intended to kill those Jews, they wouldn't have put them on a merry-go-round, crisscrossing Eastern Europe through numerous camps, but would have finished them off, once they laid their hands on them. Stutthof therefore also demonstrates that the orthodox conjecture about the mass murder of inmates who were not registered on arrival at Auschwitz is untenable.

The highest registration number assigned to a Stutthof inmate is 105,302, issued on 17 January 1945. A few days later, evacuation transports started. Hence this number is probably close to the maximum number of inmates who were incarcerated at Stutthof altogether. A thorough study of the camp's various records shows that some 26,100 inmates died during the camp's entire existence. More than half of them died in the final months of the war, from November 1944 on, when Germany's collapsing infrastructure made it impossible, particularly in the east, to provide camps with anything they needed. A typhus epidemic, combined with starvation, dismal hygienic conditions and no possible medical care, were the main cause of these late fatalities.

Orthodox Polish historians have added to the documented number of deceased inmates some 39,000 more victims, thus reaching a death toll of 65,000. These additional victims were allegedly killed in the camp's fumigation/homicidal gas chamber. However, there is no documental or material trace of these inmates ever having existed, let alone being murdered this way or any other way.

(For more details on this, see Graf/Mattogno 2016.)

SUCHOMEL, FRANZ

Franz Suchomel (3 Dec. 1907 – 18 Dec. 1979), SS *Unterscharführer*, became a photographer at the Hadamar euthanasia institution in March 1941. In August, he was transferred to the Treblinka Camp, were he confiscated and inventoried the property brought in by Jewish deportees. In October 1943, he was briefly posted to the Sobibór Camp while its operations were suspended. He was put on trial in Düsseldorf, Germany, in 1965 for his involvement in the alleged activities at Treblinka. He was ultimately sentenced to six years imprisonment for aiding in mass murder.

Franz Suchomel

Suchomel spoke out only almost 40 years after the event, after he had served his prison term and was then interviewed by Claude Lanzmann for his movie *Shoah*. Lanzmann later revealed how he persuaded alleged German perpetrators to agree to an interview with him: He created a fake ID and fake academic credentials for himself, invented a research association he claimed to work for that didn't exist, forged letterheads of an institution that did exist, and paid every single one of the alleged perpetrators 3,000 deutschmarks for their interview (worth some 6,000 US dollars in 2023), plus had them sign an agreement not to reveal this fact.

However, in an article published by *The New York Times* on 20 October 1985 (p. H-17), Lanzmann claimed that the interview with Suchomel was filmed against Suchomel's wish and without his knowledge with a camera hidden in a bag. But throughout the interview, the camera follows the actors repeatedly, and Suchomel looks into the camera on occasion when explaining things. The camera even follows his pointer stick in close-up motions across a large camp map when Suchomel explains things. It is evident from this that Suchomel knew that he was being recorded and where the camera was, and that someone made the camera move all the time, which would not have been possible, had the camera been hidden in a bag standing still somewhere nearby. Therefore, the entire interview was a charade.

Suchomel's statements include three claims in particular which render his entire testimony even more suspicious:

1. He insisted that, when the Germans decided to exhume some 700,000 corpses buried in mass graves, their Jewish work slaves "preferred to be shot rather than work there." Considering that these work slaves are said to have been witnesses of the mass murder of their brethren by the Germans and their auxiliaries, and that they were certain to be killed sooner or later as well, such a reaction is the only one conceivable. However, this is not what the mainstream narrative tells us, which insists that the Jewish slave laborers didn't resist or even actively helped the Germans mass murder their brethren and eliminate the traces of this heinous crime. Suchomel had more common sense than all orthodox scholars together, though, so he changed the story line by claiming that the German perpetrators had to do the exhumation and cremation work themselves. Lanzmann

didn't believe that and tried to correct Suchomel, but Suchomel insisted: "In that case, the Germans had to lend a hand." Imagine a few dozen German SS men excavating 700,000 corpses, then building 700 huge pyres for a thousand corpses each – all by themselves and within just four months! An impossible task, for sure.

2. Suchomel claimed that people were constantly shot at the edge of burning pits, and that the victims realized what was going on only after they had reached the pits. Yet any SS man standing at the edge of a blazing pit constantly shooting people would have been badly burned. Furthermore, the deportees slated for getting shot inevitably heard from the distance that people were constantly getting shot, and the flames and smoke of a blazing fire cannot be hidden either, so how would the SS have succeeded in making them walk up to this spot that was unapproachable for anyone already due to its heat? Another impossible task.

3. In Suchomel's story, the corpses thrown into the blazing fire pits burned almost without any fuel: "With rubbish, paper and gasoline, people burn very well." Yet the self-immolation of human corpses is a myth far removed from reality. In fact, open-air incinerations of human corpses require huge amounts of fuel. Some garbage and paper, lit with gasoline, may be suitable to light and kindle proper fuel such as wood and coke, but would not do much of anything to veritable mountains of corpses.

For Suchomel, the impossible and surreal was real. (For more details, see Beaulieu 2003.)

SUŁKOWSKI, JAN

Jan Sułkowski was a Polish Jew who claimed to have been interned at the Treblinka Camp. He claimed in a postwar deposition published in 1948 that one way of murdering Jews at the camp consisted of forcing them to climb up a "death bridge," a scaffold built for that purpose, then shoot them down as target practice. This testimony is unique and has been swept under the carpet by the orthodoxy. (For more details, see Mattogno/Graf 2023, pp. 26f.)

SURVIVORS

Psychology

In Western societies, Holocaust survivors are revered as martyrs and saints. Challenging their claims is a sacrilege; in fact, it can even be a crime in many countries. Survivors have joined their own organizations, and are supported by both NGOs and by many governments to pursue their various financial, political and societal interests. They are encouraged to share their stories among themselves and with others during gatherings, media appearances, film and literature. However, where critique and scrutiny are stifled or even outlawed, while hyperbole and drama get rewarded, truthfulness gets trampled underfoot.

After decades of these dynamics, many survivors have forgotten their true experiences in the ghettoes and camps. They increasingly and at times unconsciously replaced them with group fantasies of martyrdom and with horror fairy tales as they have been spread since the outbreak of the war by all means available to Western societies. There is no topic in the history of mankind where the pressure to remember certain things is anywhere near as intense as when it comes to the Holocaust. Decades of memory-altering, unchecked and unopposed, one-sided propaganda on all channels of society have made the false-memory syndrome a common occurrence among Holocaust survivors. Egomaniacs, braggarts, liars and cheats have been rewarded, while moderate, honest, sincere individuals have been pushed to the sidelines or suppressed altogether.

Already before it started, a looming Holocaust became a very important aspect of Jewish identity. (See the section "Six Million before the Holocaust" of the entry on six million.) Today, the Holocaust reigns supreme as Jewry's main pillar of self-understanding. Hence, the role of the survivor has never been much about telling what really happened, but rather about telling a tale that can serve as the founding myth of modern post-Holocaust Jewry in general and Israel in particular.

(See Garaudy 2000; Finkelstein 2000, 2005; Rudolf 2023, pp. 149f.; Dalton 2020, pp. 282-286.)

Demography

According to information from the Israel-based official organization Amcha, which devotes all its activities to caring for Holocaust survivors, 834,000 to 960,000 Holocaust survivors were still alive in the summer of 1997. The same organization defines a "Holocaust survivor" as

"any Jew who lived in a country at the time when it was: – under Nazi regime; – under Nazi occupation; – under regime of Nazi collaborators as well as any Jew who fled due to the above regime or occupation."

In 2001, Sergio DellaPergola, a professor at the Hebrew University in Jerusalem, determined that the number of Holocaust survivors had *increased* to 1,092,000 at that time. This amounted to an annual growth rate of some 50,000 Holocaust survivors, which is clearly ludicrous; in reality, the numbers are rapidly approaching zero.

According to the data provided by Amcha, roughly $^1/_3$ of all Holocaust survivors still alive in 1997 were so-called "child survivors," meaning they were 16 years or younger at the end of the war. This data can be applied to the known life-expectancy data available for a people that had a similarly terrible experience during the war – the Germans. Calculating back to how many Holocaust survivors must have been alive right at the end of the war for there to be roughly a million left in 2000, it turns out that one has to start with at least 4.3 million. If one were to assume that the Jews had a worse wartime experience than the Germans, hence the average survivor was in worse shape at war's end than the average German – which many scholars tend to assume – then there must have been at least some 5 million Jewish Holocaust survivors in 1945.

The inflationary definition of "Holocaust survivor" by Amcha and other scholars such as DellaPergola means that some 8 million Jews were affected by the Holocaust, although many never ended up under National-Socialist rule due to emigration, flight or (Soviet) deportation.

Hence, the maximum number of Jewish population reduction during "the Holocaust" amounts to some three million Jews. This includes all Jews who became victims of Stalinist mass deportations and slave-labor camps, of regular combat (as soldiers or civilians casualties of war) as well as irregular combat (partisans), of non-German pogroms, natural excess of deaths over births, etc. In effect, the maximum possible number of the actual Jewish death toll of the Holocaust is probably closer to two million. But this is an upper limit; most Holocaust skeptics estimate an actual Jewish death toll under one million, and perhaps as low as 500,000.

Based on numbers provided by the New York-based Holocaust Claims Conference, only some 200,000 survivors were still alive in 2023. By definition, every one of these survivors was 78 years old or older at that point.

However, one should be aware that published numbers of Holocaust survivors are likely manipulated due to its financial implications for Jewish organizations who have better fund-raising results when claiming higher survivor numbers in need of support.

(For more details on survivor statistics, see Rudolf 2019, pp. 202-204.)

SÜSS, FRANZ

Franz Süss (or Szüsz, born 12 April 1902) was a Slovak Jew deported to Auschwitz in late May 1942, where he claims to have been assigned to the *Sonderkommando*. He made a deposition in 1964, the protocol of which was filed in Israel at the Yad Vashem Archives. Süss's account is one of the very few which give an idea regarding the actual origins and tasks of the *Sonderkommando*. Here are the main takeaways from his account:

– In late May/early June 1942, the *Sonderkommando* had the sole task of burying the bodies of inmates who had died of "natural" causes (disease, starvation, deprivation). The daily death toll he mentioned – 200 to 300 – is not quite twice the recorded mortality during that time.
– He mentioned a daily death toll of 400 to 600 inmates when the typhus epidemic broke out due to catastrophic hygienic conditions at Birkenau (in July/August 1942), which is all true, except for his figures, which were not daily averages but rather peak values in August 1942.
– The victims were buried in four large mass graves some 10 meters wide (correct). The length Süss indicated (400 m) is four times the length visible on air photos, and the depths he indicated (3 m) is probably twice as deep as would have been possible. He described how the pits filled with groundwater (correct), which had to be pumped off.
– He mentioned some 60,000 typhus victims buried in these graves, which were exhumed and burned starting in October 1942. The actual number is probably closer to 10,000 to 20,000, though, but the fact and the month are fairly accurate.
– Süss knew absolutely nothing about the so-called "bunkers." He wrote only from hearsay about some gassing experiments, presumably done in some barracks rather than a converted farmhouse, but insisted that no mass gassings happened while he worked there.
– Süss mentioned intensified deportations around the time the typhus epidemic broke out, which is indeed true: There were twice as many deportees in August 1942 than during June and July of that

year. He insisted, however, that all arrivals were accommodated in barracks "built at a furious pace," and that no mass gassing happened at that time:

> "The people died a so-called natural death, that is, they were beaten to death, and most of them starved to death. Less calories, plus work. The result is always death."

Süss eventually contracted typhus himself, but rather than getting killed as a severely sick and dangerous witness unfit for work, he was nursed back to health, because he was evidently no carrier of any secrets. Once out of the hospital, he became a clerk in some office, and evidently lost touch with his former *Sonderkommando* colleagues, which he then declared summarily murdered without having any first-hand knowledge of it, evidently merely following the orthodox narrative. At that point of his deposition, Süss switched from his own experiences to hearsay, even saying so expressly. What follows is filled with common black-propaganda clichés, such as:

– He "heard" about a Himmler visit to one of the new crematoria. However, there is no trace of such a visit, which even orthodox scholars reject as a mere rumor.
– "Allegedly" Eichmann visited for the same reason. The same is true for this claimed visit as well.
– Süss "heard" about a clerk gathering valuables from inmates "who was actually walled in" – how bizarre!
– Süss had to throw in the obligatory name Mengele for good measure, whose statement about a mass selection in the infirmary he "heard" himself.
– Every inmate unfit for work was gassed at Auschwitz in 1942 to 1943, even German inmates! Except for the good *Sonderkommando* Jew Süss, of course. Such outrageous nonsense is rejected by every historian.
– The crematoria allegedly had a capacity between 20,000 and 24,000 a day, plus an unlimited additional capacity in open-air incineration pits. However, the Birkenau crematoria altogether only had a theoretical maximum capacity of 920 bodies per day.
– To cremate the corpses on a pyre during open-air incinerations, it was enough to set them afire with some gasoline, and "later everything burned automatically." However, self-immolating corpses simply do not exist. They require a lot of fuel to burn to ashes, particularly on outdoor pyres.

This testimony underscores once more why depositions from hearsay must be disregarded by both judiciary and academia. (For more details, see Mattogno 2022e, pp. 149f., 169-175.)

SWIMMING POOL

Attentive observers have noted items or facilities at the so-called death camps that seem entirely inappropriate, and which in fact suggest a much-more benign usage of those camps. The brothel at the Auschwitz Main Camp is one such item, and the "zoo" at Treblinka is another. Then we have the barber shop, dentist, and shoemaker at Belzec, and the dentist, carpenter, and painter's shop at Sobibór. Such luxuries naturally belie the "death camp" image that is commonly promoted. Orthodox scholars claim that such things were strictly for SS and officer use, but still, they are remarkably odd amenities for such camps.

One of the strangest such objects is perhaps the swimming pool at Auschwitz Main Camp. It is a large rectangular pool, about 30 m long by 5 m wide, located at the rear-center of the camp, within sight of the main road. By all appearances, it was an actual swimming pool: it has entry/exit ladders at both ends; three low diving blocks at both ends; and a 3-m high block at one end (with the diving board missing today).

Around the year 2000, museum officials added a revealing sign at the pool that reads: "Fire brigade reservoir built in the form of a swimming pool, probably in early 1944." Clearly, Polish museum officials were worried about the "look" of a swimming pool at the most notorious death camp in history, so they concocted an excuse: it was really a fire-water reservoir, but "disguised" by the SS to look like a pool – in the same way that those gas chambers were allegedly disguised to look like ordinary shower rooms (which they were). Unlike the showers, there is no obvious reason to disguise a water reservoir – unless it was to make the inmates feel like they had been interned in some kind of vacation resort, and thus to make no trouble as they were being herded off to the gas chambers. Clearly, this is an absurd proposition.

Another issue is the alleged creation of the pool in "early 1944." We recall that the camp was opened in May 1940, and was allegedly functioning as a mass-gassing facility for two full years at that point. It seems very odd that camp managers did not see the need for a fire reservoir until "early 1944."

Worse still, there was a 2007 film made about the pool, called *Swimming in Auschwitz*, telling the story of six teenage Jewesses at the camp (incredibly, they all survived). For them, the pool was clearly... *a swimming pool*. Here is a quotation from the film's website:

> *"The film's title derives from its most powerful story. Marching through the camp on a particularly hot August day, the group passed by a swimming pool kept for Nazi officers. For one of the women, this sight was just too tempting. To the shock of the rest of the group, she jumped in the pool and swam from one end to the other."*

Someone obviously forgot to inform the girls that this was really a fire reservoir; of course, the museum sign was not yet posted in 1944. Furthermore, the "August" must have been August of 1944, which was just at the end of the deadliest sustained gassing activities at the camp: up to 200,000 Jews gassed per month, allegedly. One would think that, under such perilous conditions, teenage girls would hardly risk swimming in the SS pool; that would have meant a sure trip to the gas chambers. Yet one did, and they paid no price at all.

Furthermore, few people know that there are a series of smaller pools at Birkenau. These are squarer in design, and lack ladders or diving blocks. The sloped sides clearly indicate that these were in fact fire reservoirs, unlike the one in Auschwitz.

Finally, there is a credible witness testimony from right after the war, elucidating what this pool was all about. During the war, Marc Klein, a French-Jewish biology professor from Strasbourg, was arrested in his hometown in 1944, and incarcerated at the Auschwitz Main Camp for a while. Right after the war, he described in his memoirs how inmates in this camp managed to pursue various activities. Among them were also water-ball games, which selected inmates played "in the outdoor pool that had been built by inmates within the camp." Many other inmates stood around the pool and cheered on the water athletes. (See the entry on Marc Klein for details.)

From late 1943, Auschwitz camp authorities implemented air-raid protection measures inside and outside the camp. This included air-raid shelters and fire-extinguishing water reservoirs. In the Birkenau

Inmate swimming pool inside the Auschwitz Main Camp, with three starting blocks at both ends, and a block for a three-meter diving board (the board no longer exists). This is German-quality work, as it holds the water to this day. Photos taken in 1997, before the Auschwitz Museum added a sign mendaciously stating that this is a "fire brigade reservoir built in the form of a swimming pool." Top: Inmate accommodation blocks in the background. Bottom: camp wall with watchtower in the background.

Camp, a series of smaller pools were set up that served exclusively this purpose. At the Main Camp, however, the camp officials evidently took a combined approach, merging the necessity of a fire-extinguishing pool with the usefulness of a swimming pool. Documents show that the camp administration had been ordered from Berlin to offer all kinds of privileges to those inmates who behaved, cooperated, and had good work ethics. It stands to reason that many spare-time activities – swimming in the pool included – were offered as incentives to implement this policy. This is standard practice in prisons around the world.

While documents about the planning and construction of the pool must have been abundant during its creation, none seem to have survived. Considering that the documentation for almost all the rest of the camp's construction activities is virtually complete, this raises the suspicion that someone tried to hide from the world the benign nature of this pool, and the benign intentions of the camp administration in building it.

SZAJN-LEWIN, EUGENIA

Eugenia Szajn-Lewin (1909 – 1944) was a Jewish journalist who lived in the Warsaw Ghetto and kept a diary of important events during this time. She was killed during the Warsaw uprising in 1944. On the rumors circulating about Treblinka, she wrote in her diary in late 1942 (Szajn-Lewin, pp. 83f.):

> "The worst thing is death in Treblinka. By now, all know of Treblinka. There they cook people alive. They know by now that Bigan has escaped from Treblinka. […]
>
> He [Bigan] *will build halls like the ones in Treblinka. Everything will be modern: the boilers that are heated by current, the steam-gas in there, the floor movable and sloping. 'There I will drive in the Germans, all naked. Many, many Germans, so that every corner is made use of, every centimeter.' And from the boilers the gaseous steam is conducted through the pipes, the boilers are red, and the steam... a hellish boiling bath. Four minutes suffice, then the floor flap automatically drops down, and the slimy mass of red, curled bodies flows away into the cesspit. And finished, the pits are simply filled with chlorine, and there is no more trace of what was once alive. 'All this lasts only seven minutes, you hear me?'"*

However, the orthodoxy insists that mass murder in the Treblinka Camp was committed using Diesel-engine exhaust; the facility's floors were not collapsible (a claim more frequently associated with the Sobibór Camp); and the corpses had to be hand-carried from the gas chambers to the mass graves. No "Bigan" who escaped from Treblinka is known, and if someone really escaped from there and brought news from what was going on at Treblinka, why was this news so terribly distorted?

SZENDE, STEFAN

Stefan Szende

Stefan (István) Szende (10 April 1901 – 5 May 1985) was a bilingual Austro-Hungarian Jew who started a moderate political career in Berlin as a Socialist just prior to Hitler's ascension to power. He was eventually arrested in late 1933 for continuing a socialist party, then tried and sentenced to two years imprisonment for this "offense." After his release, he was first in Czech and then in Swedish exile, where he started a career as an author. In 1944, his book titled *The Last Jew in Poland* was published first in Swedish, and a year later also in English and German. The book is about the claimed extermination of Polish Jewry, although it is unknown what Szende's sources were. Judging by its contents – he refers to Poles who have heard stories of unknown Jews who escaped from Belzec – Szende at best relied on Polish underground reports which had reached Sweden.

On the Bełżec Camp, his book contains the following peculiar claims (see Szende 1944, pp. 263-265; Szende/Folkmann, pp. 159-161):

– Five million people were slated to be killed on *Führer*'s order, all of them evidently at Belzec. However, no such *Führer* order has ever been located.
– The Germans, as highly talented people, had highly efficient engineers of death. Put in charge by the Gestapo, after months of planning and constructing, they solved the technical problems involved in the mass slaughter of millions with the latest modern technical means. That needs to be expected if it were true, but there is no trace of any inventing, planning, constructing, testing of any highly efficient solution, and certainly no modern one.

- The result of this huge engineering effort was the scientific slaughter-house at Belzec: a facility occupying "an area almost five miles across." Actually, the camp itself was only some 250 meters across, not even a sixth of a mile. The largest size ever claimed by a witness for a Belzec extermination building is 100 m × 100 m (Rudolf Reder), but all other anecdotal evidence points at much smaller facilities.
- Trains with Jews drove into a tunnel beneath the execution building. No such thing ever existed.
- After disembarking and getting undressed – although later, the Jews allegedly were put naked into the train to save time – the victims

    "were herded into a great hall capable of holding several thousand people. This hall had no windows and its flooring was of metal. Once the Jews were all inside, the floor of this hall sank like a lift into a great tank of water which lay below it until the Jews were up to their waists in water. Then a powerful electric current was sent into the metal flooring and within a few seconds all the Jews, thousands at a time, were dead.

    The metal flooring then rose again, and the water drained away. The corpses of the slaughtered Jews were now heaped all over the floor. A different current was then switched on and the metal flooring rapidly became red hot, so that the corpses were incinerated as in a crematorium and only ash was left.

    The floor was then tipped up and the ashes slid out into prepared receptacles."
- On certain days, 20 to 30 trains loaded with 3,000 to 5,000 Jews each were processed, hence between 60,000 and 150,000 people per day!

This is totally at odds with the current mainstream narrative. The orthodoxy currently claims that the Belzec Camp first had a wooden shack with three small gas chambers, then a larger, ill-defined one made of brick and concrete. Execution was supposedly carried out by feeding engine-exhaust gasses of Diesel engine into the rooms (if we believe the pathological liar Kurt Gerstein), even though Diesel-engine exhaust gases are unsuitable for mass murder. Furthermore, the orthodoxy insists that there was no electricity involved in neither the killing nor the cremation. The latter supposedly occurred on huge pyres in open-air incinerations.

(For more details, see the entry about the Belzec Camp.)

SZLAMEK REPORT

The so-called Szlamek Report is a text written in 1942 by Jewish underground fighters of the Warsaw Ghetto, and deposited there in the ghetto's unofficial archive, where it was found after the war. The text describes in diary form alleged experiences made at the Chełmno Camp during a fictitious inmate's stay there for ten days. Some orthodox scholars attribute the text to a certain Jakov Grojanowski, others to a certain Szlojme Fajner. But the text itself only has the name "Szlamek" on it.

(For more details, see the entry on the Chełmno Camp, as well as Mattogno 2017, pp. 51-59.)

SZMAJZNER, STANISŁAW

Stanisław Szmajzner

Stanisław Szmajzner was an inmate of the Sobibór Camp. In 1966, he was interrogated by the German judiciary, when he claimed that exhaust gases were used at Sobibór only initially for mass gassing, but were later replaced with Zyklon B. He elaborated more on this in his 1968 Portuguese book titled *Inferno em Sobibór*. He claimed in it that he had received secret notes from a friend who worked in the camp's extermination sector that is said to have been cordoned off and invisible from the sector where Szmajzner worked and lived. These notes described what was unfolding there.

According to this, the single gas chamber with just one door was filled with the exhaust gas of a diesel engine. However, diesel-engine exhaust gas is not suitable for mass murder, as it is barely toxic. As if aware of this, Szmajzner's friend told him that the diesel engine was eventually replaced with a system using Zyklon B, and that the roof window used to observe the killing was then also used to throw in the Zyklon B. Since one chamber was not enough, another of the same designed was then erected.

Szmajzner's claims are rejected as false by the orthodoxy, who insists on *several* gas chambers in one building; on no observation windows in the roof; and on the continual use of engine-exhaust gases, which is commonly claimed to have come from a gasoline engine.

Szmajzner makes several other peculiar claims in his book, among them:
- After an 18-year-old Jew was appointed foreman of all Jews working in the camp's extermination sector, he turned into "a real German, even a staunch defender of Nazism," believing that all Jews needed to be eradicated, thus executing his tasks with more sadism than the Germans.
- The total death toll of the Sobibór Camp reached nearly two million, versus orthodox estimates of around 200,000.
- The forest unit chopping wood for the pyres all day long received only a piece of bread per day as food. With that, they would have quit working within a day or two due to exhaustion.
- The German Jews deported to Sobibór kept admiring their *Führer* Adolf, and worked hard to please him.

Most of this outrageous nonsense needs no comment, except for the claimed total death toll, which is roughly ten times higher than what the orthodoxy currently asserts.

(See the entry on Sobibór for more details, as well as Graf/Kues/Mattogno 2020, pp. 29-31, 61, 72, 83f., 109; Mattogno 2021e, p. 91.)

SZPERLING, HENIKE

In 1947, the "eyewitness account" of Henike Szperling about his stay at the Treblinka Camp was published in a Jewish historical journal. Szperling claimed to have been deported there in September 1942. He was deployed in the part of the camp where no extermination activities occurred, working in a unit sorting clothes. On 2 August 1943, he escaped during a prisoner uprising.

Szperling knew only from hearsay what was allegedly going on in the invisible extermination area, where no one was allowed to go. He did not describe the killing method or the facilities, only that inmates were pushed into a "bath of the dead," which he also called "bath chambers." He claimed that bodies were eventually burned rather than buried, but the technique he described is not only at odds with the current orthodox narrative, it is also technically impossible: instead of first building a pyre of fuel and corpses in alternating layers, then setting it ablaze, he insisted that flammable material was thrown into a pit and set on fire; only when this pyre was ablaze, were layers of corpses and additional wood thrown into the flames. But the heat of the blazing fire would have prevented anyone from approaching it, let alone working near it. (For more details, see Mattogno 2021e, pp. 186f.)

T

TABEAU, JERZY

Jerzy Tabeau (born Wesołowski, 18 Dec. 1918 – 11 May 2002) was a Polish medical student who joined the Polish underground army in 1939. He was arrested in March 1942 and sent to Auschwitz Main Camp, where he fell ill with pneumonia but was nursed back to health in the inmate infirmary. After that, he became a male nurse, in which role he contracted typhus. Although again seriously sick and unfit for labor, he again got nursed back to health.

Jerzy Tabeau

He claimed to have escaped the camp in late November 1943, and around the turn of 1943/1944, he wrote a report on his alleged experiences at Auschwitz, which was published in August 1944 in Abraham Silberschein's series *The Extermination of the Jews in Poland*. In November 1944, an English translation was included in the War Refugee Board Report, with the author wrongly given as an anonymous "Polish major." The passages on extermination claims about Auschwitz contain the following peculiar claims about the so-called "bunkers" (although he didn't use that term):

- Special gas chambers were built near the Birkenau Camp into which gas was supplied through valves opening and closing hermetically. However, the orthodoxy has it that these buildings already existed and were merely adapted with minor changes. Also, the gas was supposedly introduced through hatches in the wall, not through valves.
- The doomed inmates were driven to this building without escorts, because the facility was allegedly inside the camp. However, both "bunkers" are said to have been outside the camp, and an armed escort would have been very much needed.
- Everyone received a towel and soap when entering the gas chamber. This most certainly would never have happened, considering the mess it would have created and the effort necessary to retrieve and clean these items afterwards. In addition, no one takes towels into a shower.
- An SS man threw hydrogen-cyanide bombs through the valves into the chamber. No such thing as hydrogen-cyanide bombs existed. The orthodoxy has it that Zyklon-B pellets were poured through hatches.
- After only 10 minutes, the doors were opened, and a special unit carried away the bodies. Ten minutes, however, was not even enough time for everyone to die, let alone to air out the space. Since Zyklon B releases its poison for an hour or two, depending on the ambient temperature, and because this alleged facility presumably had no ventilation system, the poison content inside the room still would have been rising when the doors were allegedly opened, endangering and eventually killing anyone who dared enter the facility for heavy labor.
- Bodies placed in mass graves had to be exhumed in late 1942 and their remains burned. This much is true, as those corpses, buried into the groundwater, threatened to poison the region's drinking water. However, these were the corpses of the raging typhus epidemic, not mass-murder victims, as Tabeau claimed.
- The subsequent open-air incineration of the decomposing bodies was allegedly done by simply drenching the piled-up bodies with gasoline. However, gasoline would have been useful only for igniting some solid fuel, such as wood or coke, but Tabeau does not mention this – implying that those corpses, once lit, underwent self-immolation. But that is a myth, because lots of solid fuel would have had to be put underneath those piles of bodies for them to be cremated on open-air incinerations.

Jerzy Tabeau was admitted to the Auschwitz Main Camp, where he spent his time at the inmate infirmary. He therefore had no first-hand knowledge of anything going on inside or outside the Birkenau Camp, nor did he claim he had. Whatever his sources of "information" were, they were very evidently extremely inaccurate even by orthodox standards – if he didn't make up the whole story himself. His physically impossible claims about one of the alleged "bunkers" – facilities that never existed in reality – are mere reflections of an evolving pattern of atrocity propaganda developed and spread by the various Auschwitz resistance groups, to which Tabeau, as a former member of the Polish partisan army, probably had good contacts. (For more details, see Mattogno 2021, pp. 144-148).

TAUBER, HENRYK

Henryk Tauber (aka Fuchsbrunner; 8 July 1917 – 3 Jan. 2000) was a Polish Jew sent to the Auschwitz Camp in November 1942. He claimed to have been assigned to the *Sonderkommando* and worked as a furnace stoker first at the Main Camp's crematorium, then in Crematorium II at the Birkenau Camp.

Henryk Tauber

Tauber made three depositions right after the war, with the first of them occurring in late February 1945 in front of a Soviet commission. His next deposition was end of May 1945 in front of Polish investigative judge Jan Sehn. Another much shorter deposition was filed with the Jewish Historical Commission of Krakow also in 1945. Tauber was prudent enough not to testify anymore in later years.

After other key witnesses for the alleged extermination activities at Auschwitz had been exposed as untrustworthy, such as Rudolf Höss, Miklós Nyiszli, Charles Bendel and Filip Müller, Henryk Tauber's testimony gained in importance with the orthodoxy. They were impressed by Tauber's accurate description of Crematorium II, where he claimed to have worked for more than a year. Due to his current importance to prop up the orthodox Auschwitz narrative, his testimonies are examined here in more detail.

When it comes to describing architectural features of Crematorium II, Tauber's statements are indeed fairly accurate, meaning that he probably really worked in that building for some time. It is also possible that, in order to refresh his memory, he was shown some documents and blueprints from the former camp administration's archives, which the Soviets had found untouched when capturing Auschwitz a month earlier.

Tauber becomes untrustworthy, however, when he delves into technical and historical issues, such as when describing the furnaces capacities, the alleged gassing procedure, and certain claimed events. Here are the pertinent claims emphasizing this assessment:

– He claimed that the first homicidal gassing at Crematorium II involved 4,000 victims jammed into a space of 210 m², hence an impossible packing density of more than 19 people per square meters.
– He asserted that, in March and April 1943, Dr. Josef Mengele brought Zyklon B in a Red-Cross vehicle to Crematorium II for homicidal gassings. However, Mengele was assigned to Auschwitz only on 30 May 1943.
– Tauber exaggerated the operating temperatures of the furnaces, which according to instruction manuals was to be between 800 and 1,000 °C, while Tauber, who as an inmate hardly had any means to determine furnace temperatures properly, set it to 1,200 to 1,500 °C in his first interview. That may have been a result of the Soviets influencing him, who, in an expert report on the Majdanek furnaces of August 1944, had made a similar false claim in order to exaggerate the Majdanek furnaces' capacity. (Graf/Mattogno 2012, pp. 112-114.)
– Tauber claimed that four to five bodies were simultaneously cremated in one muffle. This claim is physically and thermo-technically impossible. The Auschwitz muffles were designed to cremate only one body at a time. The muffle doors were too small to introduce more than two corpses at once, the muffle walls and the coke hearth could not provide enough heat to maintain operating temperature, and four or five corpses would have impeded the air flow in the muffle.
– Tauber's claim for the average time it took to cremate one body was contradictory, but ranged between 5 and 18 minutes, when in fact the cremation of a single body took about one hour.
– Tauber asserted that they pushed in two corpses at once, then a second set of two corpses, which had to be done quickly before the arms and legs of the first pair of corpses began to rise from the heat. However, dead people cannot raise their arms and legs, and neither can heat, which burns muscles, but does not contract them in a coordinated fashion defying gravity. This statement resembles that of Szlama Dragon in this regard and shows a "convergence of evidence" for orchestrated lies.

- Placing a second pair of bodies on top of one pair already lying on the muffle grate would have required tipping the 45-cm-wide stretcher steeply upward to get it on top of the two corpses already in that muffle. This would have meant hitting the muffle vault, where it is 45 cm wide, with the stretcher's end rather than being able to insert it fully to unload the next two corpses – which might have slid backwards and off the stretcher with such an inclination.
- The number of daily cremations claimed by Tauber for Crematorium II – on average 2,500 – would have been impossible also, because the freight elevator in that building had a capacity of only five corpses. To get 2,500 bodies into the furnace room, that elevator had to do 500 uninterrupted round trips. For a 20-hour workday, that would amount to just 2 minutes and 24 seconds for each round trip, including the loading and unloading of these bodies.
- Tauber claimed that, if a load of bodies was burning badly, they added "a woman's corpse […] to speed up the burning process." Any load of multiple bodies would have burned "badly" initially due to the huge amount of water that needed to be evaporated, no matter the gender. Adding another corpse to an already overfilled muffle would have made matters worse. Humans are not combustion material. They do not self-immolate. However, that didn't stop Tauber from claiming this four times: Fuel was only needed to ignite the bodies, which then burned all by themselves. He even saw fat dripping from the bodies down into the ash box, where it ignited and burned the bodies. However, in a glowing furnace, fat burns off where it reaches a surface. It has no chance of running and dripping anywhere.
- In order to draw the attention of Allied bomber pilots flying by, Tauber claimed that they placed up to eight emaciated corpses into a muffle, "so that a larger fire came out of the chimney, and the airmen became aware of it." However, flames cannot shoot out of crematorium chimneys, and most certainly not from burning emaciated, hence fat-less bodies. Furthermore, it would have been utterly impossible to insert eight bodies into one muffle, emaciated or not.
- Tauber claimed that, starting in May 1944, huge open-air incineration pits were dug and gigantic pyres set ablaze at Birkenau. However, air photos of that time and area show that no such gigantic pits of fires ever existed.
- He asserted that fat exuding from the corpses burning in open-air incineration pits percolated to the pits' bottom, flowed along channels and collected in even deeper collection pits, from where it was scooped out and poured back onto the corpses to fuel the fire. However, fat cannot collect and flow along the bottom of a blazing pit. It ignites where it reaches the surface. Furthermore, with the high groundwater level at Birkenau, the deep collection pits would have filled with water, not fat. In addition, standing next to a blazing fire to collect boiling fat from a deep pit would have led to the scooper getting severe burns.
- Tauber relates that, once a gigantic outdoor pyre was ablaze, more corpses were thrown in. However, with such a blaze causing severe burns to anyone approaching it, we must assume that they used catapults to sling the corpses onto the blazing pyre from a safe distance.
- He claimed that the alleged gas chamber's ventilation system was turned on only *after* the door had been opened. That would have happened only if everyone involved was suicidal, the SS members included.
- Although he did not work at Crematoria IV and V, he asserts that Zyklon B was introduced in the claimed gas chambers of these facilities by pouring Zyklon B cans out through hatches, which he correctly described as having been protected by iron bars. However, these hatches, the frames and shutters of which have survived, were so small that any iron bar placed in them would have made the opening too narrow to stick a Zyklon-B can through that opening. Therefore, no Zyklon-B can could ever be poured out through these hatches.

There are more inconsistencies and historical falsehoods contained in Tauber's testimonies, including atrocity tales containing their own refutation, for instance the story of a *Sonderkommando* man who, because he "was dawdling at work," was allegedly chased into a pit with boiling human fat at one of the outdoor pyres…

These detailed highlights suffice to show that Tauber, just like Nyiszli, Bendel, Müller and many other self-proclaimed *Sonderkommando* members, is untrustworthy when it comes to claims about alleged extermination activities at Auschwitz. (For more details, see Mattogno 2022d, pp. 9-49, 74-114.)

TESCH & STABENOW

Tesch & Stabenow (Testa) was a pest-control company headquartered in Hamburg, Germany, established in 1924. They used a broad variety of methods and techniques. One chemical used was Zyklon B with its active ingredient hydrogen cyanide. Bruno Tesch had been involved in the development of Zyklon B, but the DEGESCH (*Deutsche Gesellschaft für Schädlingsbekämpfung*, German Association for Pest Control) held the patents to it. Tesch & Stabenow received the exclusive license to distribute Zyklon B to all clients east of the River Elbe. To the West, the Frankfurt company Heerd & Lingler (HeLi) had an exclusive license.

Between September and November 1945, the British conducted a major show trial in their zone of occupation about crimes presumably committed by former SS camp officials of the Bergen-Belsen and Auschwitz camps. Most defendants were severely tortured during pre-trial detention, and former camp inmates were encouraged to let their rage and lust for revenge run free. The trial ended with the foregone conclusion of proving that mass murder with Zyklon B had been committed at Auschwitz. (See the entry on the Bergen-Belsen Trials.)

With Zyklon-B gassings "proven" in court, this claim could no longer be challenged by the defense in other trials. The British next turned against the responsible managers of Tesch & Stabenow for allegedly having delivered Zyklon B to Auschwitz and other camps while knowing that it was mainly used to kill inmates.

During the trial's preparation, the British interrogator, the Jew Anton Freud – a grandson of Sigmund Freud – used threats and lies in his attempts to get company employees to confess to things they insisted were untrue. He grossly misrepresented Auschwitz as a small camp with no need for huge Zyklon-B deliveries for pest control. However, the exact opposite was true: Auschwitz was an order of magnitude larger, and its long-lasting typhus epidemic orders of magnitude worse, than any other German wartime camp. Therefore, Testa's Zyklon-B supplies were perfectly justified and explicable with innocuous circumstances.

The judges sided with the torturing, threatening, lying and misrepresenting prosecution. They sentenced Dr. Tesch and his right-hand man Karl Weinbacher to death and had them both executed in what was a clear-cut case of judicial murder, mainly prepared and arranged by Anton Freud.

(For more details, see Mattogno 2022, pp. 17-41; 147-202.)

TESCH, BRUNO

Bruno Tesch

Bruno Tesch (14 Aug. 1890 – 16 May 1946) was a German businessman and owner of the pest-control company Tesch & Stabenow. He was indicted and put on a show trial by the British for his company's massive sales of Zyklon B to the SS, and especially to the Auschwitz Camp. Based on false testimonies and misrepresented documental evidence, Tesch was eventually sentenced to death and executed. This was a clear-cut case of judicial murder.

(For more details, see the entry on Tesch & Stabenow.)

THERESIENSTADT

In November 1941, the entire northern Czech town of Theresienstadt (Terezin in Czech) was turned into a ghetto for Czech and elderly German Jews, as well as privileged German Jews, among them Jewish luminaries and many decorated veterans of the First World War and their families. Later, deportees from other countries arrived there as well. Over the years, many of the ghetto inhabitants were transferred to other camps, among them most prominently Auschwitz.

The orthodox narrative has it that the Theresienstadt Jews arriving at Auschwitz were either gassed on arrival or at a later date. However, a detailed analysis of the sources of these assertions reveals that they are based on rumors and unreliable witness reports (József Cyrankiewicz, Ota Kraus, Erich Kulka, Leib Langfus, Otto Wolken). They are usually either unconfirmed by any documents, or are even refuted by them.

(For more details, see Mattogno 2022b, pp. 177f., 215-218, 257, 266-271.)

Former Theresienstadt inmate Herman Rosenblat claimed in 2008 that a homicidal gas chamber existed at the Theresienstadt Ghetto. However, his entire wartime memoirs were exposed as a fraud even before they were published. (See the entry on him.)

THILO, HEINZ

Heinz Thilo (8 Oct. 1911 – 13 May 1945), SS *Hauptsturmführer*, was a German physician who, in July 1942, was assigned as troop and camp physician to the Auschwitz Camp. After the end of the war, he committed suicide. Johann P. Kremer quoted Thilo in his diary as having called Auschwitz the "anus mundi" – ass of the world.

TOOLS, OF MASS MURDER

If we take witness statements at face value, then we have to conclude that an astonishingly wide array of murder weapons is said to have been used for the mass murder of victims during the Holocaust. Apart from the obvious ones, such as simple starvation and disease to let people die from neglect, and bullets used during executions by units such as the *Einsatzgruppen*, there are many others, which deserve more attention. Many of these claimed weapons are unique to the Holocaust.

In most murder cases, the crime is divided into two acts: first the actual murder, and then an attempt to erase the traces of the crime – here mainly the means and methods to destroy the victims' corpses.

Murder Weapons

The claimed murder weapons fall into four main categories:
1. Bullets. Shootings are said to have been the primary execution method used by the *Einsatzgruppen*.
2. Gas Vans. These were presumably used by the *Einsatzgruppen*, as well as at the Semlin Camp in Serbia and at the Chełmno Camp.
3. Execution chambers. These come with a wide variety of claimed murder methods, which hint at a severe lack of coordination and a chaotic approach during the so-called Holocaust:
   - Gasoline-engine exhaust: currently claimed for the Sobibór Camp, but some sources also attribute it to the camps at Belzec and Treblinka.
   - Diesel-engine exhaust: currently claimed for the camps at Belzec and Treblinka, but some sources also attribute it to the Sobibór Camp. Furthermore, several sources claim or imply that diesel-engine exhaust gases were also used by the so-called gas vans.
   - Vacuum: this method of pumping the air out of a room, thus suffocating everyone inside, has been claimed by witnesses for the camps at Treblinka and Belzec, and rarer also for Auschwitz, but only as a first stage before adding toxic gases. This method has been abandoned by the orthodoxy, and is usually shamefully covered up and hidden from their readers.
   - Chlorine: this method was frequently claimed for the Sobibór Camp, and also implied by Franz Blaha for Dachau. This method has also been abandoned by the orthodoxy, and is usually again covered up and hidden from their readers.
   - War gases (such as mustard gas): this method has been claimed for the Auschwitz Camp in early reports of the Polish underground. This method has been abandoned by the orthodoxy, and is covered up and hidden from their readers.
   - High-voltage electricity: This method has been claimed for Auschwitz, Belzec, Sobibór and Treblinka. This method has been abandoned by the orthodoxy, and is covered up and hidden from their readers.
   - Cyanide powder, mixed with water or an unknown liquid: this method is claimed for the Natzweiler Camp, and Bruno Piazza insisted that a version of it was also used at the Auschwitz Camp.
   - Zyklon B: This method has been claimed for Auschwitz, Dachau, Gusen, Majdanek, Mauthausen, Neuengamme, Ravensbrück, Sachsenhausen, Stutthof. Since Zyklon B was the most-commonly used insecticide in wartime Germany, most camps were supplied with it for reasons of pest control. Hence, it cannot surprise that claims of homicide with this product sprung up almost everywhere. One witness – Stanisław Szmajzner – claimed the use of Zyklon B for Sobibór, allegedly replacing engine exhaust gas, but no one takes him seriously.
   - Steam: This claimed method is unique and also common for early witness claims about the Treblinka Camp. It may have been based on a steam disinfestation device. This method has been abandoned by the orthodoxy, and is covered up and hidden from their readers.
   - Bottled carbon monoxide: this method is claimed for the earliest iteration of gas vans, as well as for the Majdanek Camp. It is said to have been copied from experiences learned during Germany's euthanasia killings. These were presumably carried out using bottled carbon monoxide.

- A "dark substance": this claim is unique for the Sobibór Camp, made by only one witness, albeit an important one: Alexander Pechersky. This method has been abandoned by the orthodoxy, and is covered up and hidden from their readers.
4. There are a number of rather peculiar murder weapons claimed by very few or even single witnesses, most of which are not taken seriously by anyone. Orthodox historians sweep these claims under the rug, as embarrassing indicators of witnesses carried away by mental or emotional disturbances. However, these wild claims are not necessarily wilder than the ones listed earlier:
   - Air hammer (pneumatic hammer): this method was claimed for the Auschwitz Camp in early reports of the Polish underground. (See the section on "Polish wartime propaganda" in the entry on Birkenau.)
   - Tree felling: this was a method claimed by a Soviet prosecutor during the Nuremberg International Military Tribunal (*IMT*, Vol. 7, p. 582).
   - Explosives: this method was claimed by Albert Widmann for a single, failed set of experiments, and by Erich von dem Bach-Zelewski, stating that this method replaced shootings for the *Einsatzgruppen*.
   - Chlorinated or quick lime: this method was claimed by Jan Karski for the Belzec Camp, or rather for trains going there; a message of the Polish underground transferred that method over to Treblinka. Three former Treblinka inmates incorporated this rumor in their postwar testimonies (Leon Finkelsztein, Abraham Goldfarb, Szyja Warszawski). A certain Mieczysław Sekiewicz imagined it for the Chełmno Camp, yet without trains: inmates placed in a pit were showered with water, then with boiling quick lime.
   - A death bridge: this method – shooting people down from a scaffold as target practice – was claimed by Jan Sułkowski for the Treblinka Camp.
   - Tarp-covered gassing trenches: This make-shift gassing "solution" was claimed by Otto Wolken.
   - Portable, quick-assembly gas chamber: This gassing porta potty was claimed by Adolf Eichmann.

More of these and similar anecdotal aberrations are listed in the entry on Absurd Claims.

Tools to Erase Murder Traces

The tools to erase the traces of the crime, in terms of making the victims vanish, come in three forms:
1. Cremation furnaces, commonly with vastly exaggerated claims regarding their capacity. (See the section "Furnace Cremations" of the entry on cremation propaganda). Such furnaces should be expected to have existed foremost at the pure extermination camps at Belzec, Chełmno, Sobibór and Treblinka, with together almost two million claimed victims. However, none of these camps had any crematoria. While Chełmno had a primitive field furnace, it was totally unsuited for the gargantuan claimed task.
2. Open-air incineration on pyres, also commonly with vastly exaggerated claims regarding their capacity, and also with implicit or explicit claims of self-immolating bodies in need of no fuel, burning all by themselves. (See the section "Open-Air Incinerations" of the entry on cremation propaganda, as well as the entry on lumberjacks.). These pyres are said to have been used in the camps at Auschwitz, Belzec, Chełmno, Maly Trostinets, Semlin, Sobibór and Treblinka. Furthermore, within the context of the so-called *Aktion* 1005, such pyres are said to have been used in hundreds if not thousands of locations in the temporarily German-occupied Soviet Union while burning the *Einsatzgruppen*'s victims.
3. Explosives. This method of "destroying" the bodies of deceased or killed inmates was claimed by Rudolf Höss, which is one of the many reasons why his various testimonies have a low degree of credibility. Vladimir Davydov mentioned explosives as a corpse-removal technique.

toothbrushes → **Towels**

TOPF & SÖHNE

The company J.A. Topf & Söhne (Topf & Sons) of Erfurt, Germany, was established in 1878 with a focus on brewery equipment (malting plants). Prior to World War One, Topf & Sons expanded into the field of furnace manufacture. By the 1920, Topf & Sons had successfully expanded into the field of steam boilers, but they also manufactured other firing equipment, such as exhaust-heat recuperators, forced-draft devices, chimney constructions, industrial furnaces of all kinds, and cremation furnaces. Up to the beginning of the Second World War, Topf & Sons expanded rapidly.

From 1878 to 1934, Topf's Furnace Construction Department manufactured about 30,000 furnaces of all types and 3,710 varying sets of brewery equipment.

Kurt Prüfer

On the eve of the First World War, Topf & Sons built their first cremation furnaces. Their market share in this field grew steadily, until they became Germany's dominant cremation-furnace manufacturer at the outbreak of World War II. They also expanded into other fields of engineering, such as heating, ventilation, pest-control and disinfestation equipment.

Cremation furnaces designed and built by Topf were erected in several concentration camps of the Third Reich, among them most prominently all furnaces at the Auschwitz Camp, but also furnaces at the Gusen, Buchenwald and Mauthausen camps. (For details on these furnaces, see the respective section in the entry on crematoria.)

In early March 1946, four of Topf's leading engineers were arrested by the Soviet occupational forces in Central Germany and repeatedly interrogated, first in Berlin, then in Moscow: Kurt Prüfer (cremation, waste incineration), Karl Schultze (heating and ventilation), Fritz Sander (boiler and furnace construction) and Gustav Braun (head of the project department). Sander died during the interrogations, while the others were sentenced to extended prison terms. Prüfer died in Soviet captivity in 1952, while Schultze and Braun were amnestied and released in 1955 after the Soviet Union had established diplomatic relations with West Germany.

Prüfer and Schultze, who both had been involved in the design and construction of the Topf cremation furnaces, were both asked during their interrogations, how many corpses could be cremated at Auschwitz in one crematorium in one hour. Despite the heavy duress that their Soviet captivity must have put on them, both Topf engineers stated independently that their furnaces could cremate one body in each muffle per hour. This is in agreement with documented and engineering data.

The Topf Company was nationalized by the East German communist authorities in 1948, and renamed twice. It had its sole focus on malting equipment and grain storage. In 1951, the former owner of Topf & Sons relocated to Wiesbaden, West Germany, where he reestablished the company, with a focus on cremation furnaces. The company went on a steady decline and was dissolved in 1963.

Topf & Sons is seen by the orthodoxy as one of the most prominent German companies that profited from "the Holocaust" by providing the SS with the means required to erase the traces of its mass-murder activities, and by providing ventilation equipment for the alleged homicidal gas chambers at Auschwitz. However, a realistic look into the actual design of the ventilation equipment and cremation furnaces that Topf produced and installed shows that there was nothing criminal about these devices.

(For more information, see the entries on ventilation and on crematoria, as well as Mattogno/Deana, Part 1, esp. pp. 163-168, 312f.)

TORTURE
Soviet Union

Soviet Russia is infamous for its systematic mistreatment, torture and murder of millions of prisoners from all walks of life already prior to the war with Germany. The legal standing of prisoners certainly did not improve with the outbreak of hostilities, and reached a fever pitch toward the end of the conflict. The treatment that German prisoners (or those helping the Germans) received in Soviet captivity can be gleaned from the behavior of the defendants during the Soviet show trials in Krasnodar and Kharkov. As was typical for Soviet show trials prior to the war, the defendants behaved as if they were fanaticized prosecutors, enthusiastically embracing any accusation made against them, using the same ideological polemics as their detractors, and demanding harsh punishments for themselves, while behaving like pre-programmed automatons. (See Bourtman 2008 for an assessment of the Krasnodar trial.)

Some cases of Soviet physical torture have come to light. For example, Karlheinz Pintsch, adjutant to Rudolf Hess, was tortured for months by the KGB in Moscow, and a certain Jupp Aschenbrenner was tortured to make him "confess" allegations relating to the use of gas vans behind the eastern front. The use of outright physical abuse to achieve the mindless compliance in show trials does not seem to have been systematic, however. As Alexandr Solzhenitsyn has described in detail in his trilogy *Gulag Archipelago* (1974, vol. 1), the main method used in Stalin's Soviet Union in order to break a prisoner's will and make him comply with whatever was asked of him was sleep deprivation, commonly carried out by sticking prisoners naked into an unheated, moist stand-up cell of such a small floor area that it was impossible to sit down, let alone lay down in it. This torture method leaves no physical traces but breaks down everyone eventually.

Since the Soviet Union never let anyone investigate the conditions in its interrogation centers, there is little direct evidence pointing at systematic torture of prisoners who later became defendants or testified during Soviet show trials, but the behavior of the defendants can only be explained by systematic and massive abuse.

Poland

Little is known about the detention and interrogation conditions in postwar Poland. However, we need to consider that it was a Stalinist country that was in the process of genocidally cleansing everything German from its territory. In his book *An Eye for an Eye*, John Sack has described this genocidal atmosphere of vengeance, where German civilians in Polish detention were systematically abused and deprived of life's essentials, and many dying as a result. While the defendants of the Polish postwar show trials were apparently treated somewhat better, their meek and compliant behavior in court, even when faced with evidently untrue or even absurd charges, indicates that they had been psychologically worn down in some way. The only account we have about detention conditions stems from Rudolf Höss, who mentioned that the abuse and deprivations he had to suffer from guards and co-inmates in Polish prison wore him down and almost finished him off (Höss 1959, p. 195).

United States (Occupational Forces Germany)

After several German and American defense attorneys involved in U.S. trials against Germans in occupied Germany complained that their clients and other defendants and witnesses had been systematically tortured in U.S. detention and interrogation centers, several official U.S. commissions investigated some of these claims in 1949. However, these committees were accused by U.S. civil-rights organizations of being merely symbolic fig-leaves for the U.S. Army and for politics alike, since they had served to cover up the true extent of the scandal.

One particularly dedicated investigator at that time was Senator Joseph McCarthy, active as an observer sent by the U.S. Senate. He resigned his post after two weeks and gave a moving speech before the U.S. Senate in protest against the collaboration between investigative committee members and the U.S. Armed Forces during the cover-up of the scandal. His detailed list of abuses inflicted upon German defendants in U.S. captivity is horrifying (McCarthy 1949).

Another investigation led by Edward van Roden, of former U.S. Chief of Military Justice, and Gordon Simpson, judge at the Texas Supreme Court, described conditions during the U.S. postwar trials held in Dachau in detail, listing the following abuses inflicted by U.S. investigators on German prisoners, among others (Roden 1949):
– beatings and brutal kickings;
– knocking out teeth and breaking jaws;
– mock trials with sham death sentences, followed with false promises of acquittal when signing confessions;
– solitary confinement with no contact to anyone;
– all but two of the 139 cases had their testicles injured beyond repair;
– unsigned affidavits of prisoners driven into suicide by torture were used as evidence anyway.

Considering the abuses inflicted by U.S. investigators on prisoners in Iraq (Abu Ghraib) and in Guantanamo Bay, we see a pattern, almost a U.S.-American tradition.

United Kingdom

In 2005, the British authorities released archival documents from hitherto undisclosed internal investigations showing that, during and after the war, Germans in British captivity had been systematically mistreated in veritable torture centers both in Germany and Britain. In London, the British had set up the so-called "London Cage," a secret torture center where German prisoners, concealed from the Red Cross, were beaten, deprived of sleep, held in stress positions for days at a time, threatened with execution or with unnecessary surgery, starved and hair ripped out.

Another such facility, "Camp 020," kept prisoners in either total light or total dark for days at a time, subjected them to mock executions, or left them naked for months at a time.

Of greatest concern in all this, apart from the humanitarian abuses, was the fact that

"[A]fter the war, interrogators switched from ex-

tracting military intelligence to securing convictions for war crimes. Of 3,573 prisoners who passed through [the Cage], more than 1,000 were persuaded to sign a confession or give a witness statement for use in war crimes prosecutions." (Cobain 2012)

Historian Stephen Howe summed up the situation (Howe 2012):

"a horribly repetitive picture […] of British governments and their agents using systematic brutality […] and then lying about it all."

Suffice it to say that virtually any statement, on any topic, could be obtained from the captive Germans under such conditions.

Worse still were interrogation centers set up in the British occupation zone in postwar Germany, most infamous among them a prison in Bad Nenndorf, some 15 km west of Hanover. Prisoners there were systematically beaten, exposed to extreme cold, starved and tortured using specific torture devices.

Many a prominent German wartime official went through that torture center and was treated with these methods to soften them up and make them cooperative and confessing, among them Rudolf Höss, the former commandant of the Auschwitz Camp, and Oswald Pohl, head of the Economic and Administrative Main Office, which was in charge of the German wartime camps. Both have described their torture. In Höss's case, the massive three-day torture he suffered right after his arrest was confirmed in detail and with pride by his tormentors decades later.

August Eigruber, former *Gauleiter* of Austria, was mutilated and castrated after the war. Josef Kramer, last commandant of the Bergen-Belsen Camp, as well as other SS men and women, were tortured until they begged to be allowed to die (Belgion 1949, pp. 80f., 90). The British journalist Alan Moorehead reported how he was allowed to see prisoners in such a British torture center (Connolly 1953, pp. 105f.):

"The man was lying in his blood on the floor, a massive figure with a heavy head and bedraggled beard […] 'Why don't you kill me?' he whispered. 'Why don't you kill me? I cannot stand it anymore.' The same phrases dribbled out of his lips over and over again. 'He's been saying that all morning, the dirty bastard,' the sergeant said."

Assessment

Even West Germany's official top "Nazi hunter" of the 1970s and 1980s, public prosecutor Adalbert Rückerl, recognized that during the Allied postwar trials, confessions of defendants were used that had been obtained "sometimes under the worst possible physical and psychological pressure."

Official documents, acts, reports, or other records by any authority or commission of any Allied country that was based on this kind of "evidence" were then considered "facts of common knowledge." According to Article 21 of the London Agreement defining the legal framework of the Nuremberg postwar trials, such "facts of common knowledge" were incontestable, hence could not be challenged by the defense. In this manner, clearly inadmissible evidence was admitted through the backdoor that had been obtained systematically by all occupying powers involved with barbaric methods. This is one important aspect of the "evidence" on which most "Holocaust" accusations rest.

(For more details, see Rudolf 2023, pp. 401-404, 406-408.)

TOWELS, SOAP, TOOTHBRUSHES INSIDE GAS CHAMBERS

A common thread running through many witness testimonies about homicidal gassings in German wartime camps is the claim that the perpetrators applied a ruse: telling their victims that, for hygienic and health reasons, they would have to take a shower before being admitted to a camp or before being transferred elsewhere. To make that lie sound credible, witnesses claim that the alleged gas chambers were equipped with items making them look like shower rooms, such as showerheads on the ceiling and in some cases even faucets, sinks and mirrors on the walls (see the entries on Sofia Litwinska, Alexander Pechersky, Henryk Poswolski, and the statement by Wilhelm Soerensen quoted in the entry on Sachsenhausen).

It is an undisputed fact that inmates who were really admitted to a wartime camp routinely were subjected to hygienic procedures in order to prevent the spread of diseases. (See the entry on showers for details.)

However, any perpetrator planning to mass murder hundreds or even thousands of victims in a gas chamber would never have issued each of them a towel and a piece of soap, hence hundreds or even thousands of towels and pieces of soap with each batch. First of all, no one takes towels into a communal shower, where they would only get wet and dirty. If a deception was planned, stacks of towels would have been merely shown to inmates in the undressing room before walking into the "shower room," with the explanation given, that, once they step out of that shower room, each one of them gets a towel to dry off. Adding a thousand towels to a thousand bodies to be killed with poison gas would have caused a logistical nightmare for the murderers: The fabric of the towels soaks up poison gas, making it even more difficult to ventilate the place later. After the deed, a thousand poison-soaked towels, soiled with all the body fluids panicking people release in their death throes, needed to be collected and laundered (and the ripped ones discarded), before they could be given to the next batch of alleged victims.

It is even worse with the claimed pieces of soap, which would all have ended up on the floor, trampled upon by two thousand panicking feet, mixed up with the already-mentioned body fluids. Little if any of it could have been recovered. It would have been a waste of soap on a large scale. In other words: it certainly never happened.

Here is a list of witnesses who claimed otherwise, demonstrating how cross-fertilization of many witnesses' minds with rumors and clichés leads to a "convergence of evidence" on a lie:
 – Ada Bimko
 – David Fliamenbaum
 – Gyula Gál
 – Szaja Gertner
 – Bruno Israel
 – Sofia Kaufmann Schafranov
 – Imre Kertész (soap only)
 – Hermine Kranz
 – Olga Lengyel
 – André Lettich
 – Mordecai Lichtenstein
 – Sofia Litwinska (with mirrors on the wall)
 – Henryk Mandelbaum (he even has toothbrushes handed out to the victims)
 – Kurt Marcus (his chamber was equipped with towel holders, soap dishes and bathroom mats)
 – Hans Münch
 – Narcyz Tadeusz Obrycki
 – Isaac Egon Ochshorn
 – Michał Podchlebnik
 – Resistance reports of August 1942, late 1942/early 1943 and May 1944
 – Mary Seidenwurm Wrzos
 – Roman Sompolinski
 – Jerzy Tabeau
 – Rudolf Vrba/Alfred Wetzler, and Wetzler separately (with soap dishes)

This "convergence of evidence" on the same lie proves the copy-cat or orchestrated nature of these witness testimonies.

Tracing Service → **International Tracing Service, Arolsen**

TRAJTAG, JOSEF

Josef Trajtag was an inmate of the Sobibór Camp. In a deposition of 10 October 1945, he reported from hearsay that Sobibór had one gas chamber, where an unspecified gas was used for killings. After the murder, the floors opened, and the bodies were discharged into carts below, which brought them to mass graves.

His claims are rejected as false by the orthodoxy, who insists on several gas chambers, which did not have collapsible floors with carts underneath. The corpses were instead taken out of the chamber manually, sideways through a normal door.

(See the entry on Sobibór for more details, as well as Mattogno 2021e, pp. 75f.)

TRANSIT CAMPS

In the context of the Third Reich, the term "transit camp" refers to camps that were not designed or equipped to accommodate inmates for an extended period of time. They served merely to send them on to other locations after a brief stop-over. This stop-over may have included issuing of food and some hygienic procedures (showers, disinfestation). Some concentration camps had sections which served as transit subcamps. Inmates were housed there only for a brief time, often without being officially admitted to the camp (registered), after which they were sent off to some other destination.

Closely related to transit camps were "collection camps," where prisoners from a region were collected and then, usually already after only a short while, sent on to more permanent camps (labor, PoW and concentration camps).

Belzec, Chełmno, Sobibór, Treblinka

The four camps at Belzec, Chełmno, Sobibór and Treblinka are a special case. None of them were designed or equipped to accommodate large numbers of inmates for an extended period of time. However, it is well established that large numbers of inmates were sent to these camps. The best evidence for this is the so-called Höfle telegram, which list the number of inmates who arrived at Chełmno, Sobibór and Treblinka, and also at the Majdanek Camp by the end of 1942 (see the entry for Hans Höfle):

Location	Jews arrived by end of 1942
Majdanek	24,733
Belzec	434,508
Sobibór	101,370
Treblinka	713,555
Total	1,274,166

The number of Jews arriving at the Chełmno Camp can be gleaned from the so-called Korherr Report, which lists for early 1943 a total of 145,301 Jews which had been "transited through" the Warthegau (see the entry on Richard Korherr). Warthegau was the wartime German name for an area of annexed western Poland. The only "camp" located in this area was Chełmno. This means that Korherr believed Chełmno to have served as a transit camp. In fact, it was not a camp at all; it was a mere building staffed by an SS unit with several transport vehicles (alleged to have been gas vans).

The orthodox narrative has it that most inmates arriving at transit camps were killed on arrival in execution chambers (or gas vans). The problematic nature of this claim can be gleaned from the entry for each of these camps in this encyclopedia: neither the documental nor the material evidence supports that claim, and the anecdotal evidence is full of contradictions, impossibilities and absurdities.

The few extant documents about these camps indicate that they were transit camps, indeed:
– In a letter exchange between Heinrich Himmler and Oswald Pohl, both refer to Sobibór as a transit camp. (See the entry on Sobibór.)
– Belzec is referred to in one document as the outermost border station from where Jews "cross the border [to the East] and never return to the Government General [occupied Poland]." (See the entry on Belzec.)

The background of this is that Belzec, Sobibór and Treblinka were located near the demarcation line between German- and Soviet-occupied Poland (see Illustration). No train could continue travelling much further east from these camps, because the Soviet railway system starting east of it used broad-gauge railway tracks, while the rest of Europe had the narrower standard gauge. Hence, any traveler going east – or coming from the east going west – had to change trains along this line. If these three camps were transit camps for Jews on their forced journey east, the main purpose would have been to change trains from normal to broad gauge – and vice versa on the way back.

Rumors of allegedly fake shower baths (Sobibór) and presumably murderous steam chambers (Treblinka) could be explained with actual disinfestation measures implemented in those camps. Documents about the construction of large sanitary facilities at Treblinka point in that direction. Even Kurt Gerstein's bizarre story about his visit at Belzec could find an explanation: after all, Gerstein was one of the SS's leading experts on *hygiene*, and he visited the Majdanek, Belzec and Treblinka Camps together with Wilhelm Pfannenstiel, who was a professor at, and director of, the *Hygienic* Institute at the University of Marburg, and also the *hygienic* adviser to the Waffen-SS. It is plain to see that this journey, if it occurred at all, was about implementing hygienic measures. Extermination camps had no need for hygienic measures.

Supporting this is a large body of evidence demonstrating that thousands of Jews ended up fur-

Location of six National-Socialist camps generally referred to as "extermination camps": Chełmno, Treblinka, Sobibór, Majdanek, Belzec and Auschwitz. (Zentner 1982, p. 522)

ther east indeed. (See the entry on resettlement for more details). There is also some interesting anecdotal evidence supporting the transit-camp notion. For instance, Polish black-propagandist Jan Karski, who claims to have entered the Belzec Camp during the war, stated in a 1987 interview that, in his opinion, "Belzec was a transit camp." Former Auschwitz inmate Abraham Cykert reported that he had been transited through the Belzec Camp.

The most prolific orthodox chronicler of the Sobibór Camp, Jules Schelvis, was himself transited through the Sobibór Camp with other inmates, ending up some place else on a labor assignment. Other anecdotal evidence shows likewise that, starting in September 1943, numerous railway transports with Jews were sent from Minsk westward via the Sobibór Camp, which in these instances served indeed as a transit camp. (See the entry on Maly Trostinets for details).

Several Holocaust survivors reported in interviews conducted by various orthodox Holocaust institutions that they had been transited through the Treblinka Camp together with hundreds of other inmates (see the entry on Treblinka, as well as Hunt 2014).

This shows that Treblinka and Sobibór served indeed as a transit camp for many inmates. Therefore, they must have had the infrastructure to fulfill this function.

Auschwitz

The Auschwitz Camp was initially thought of as a mere transit camp, before plans were eventually upgraded to a full-fledged concentration camp.

When some 400,000 Hungarian Jews were deported in 1944, the orthodoxy has it that almost all of them were killed on arrival, since there is no record of them getting registered in the camp. However, air photos taken of the Auschwitz Camp at that time prove irrefutably that the orthodox narrative of a mass murder of unprecedented scale is untrue.

Many of these Hungarian Jews were indeed deported *via* Auschwitz, but not with the final destination Auschwitz. At that time, large parts of the Auschwitz-Birkenau Camp were turned into a transit camp for these Jews, foremost in the hospital section, Camp Sector III, which was still under construction. In July of 1944, Birkenau had one of its older, completed sectors rededicated to serve as a transit camp for Jewesses deported from Hungary. After a quarantine, they got eventually transferred to other labor and concentration camps throughout Germany.

Documents show that, of the Jews deported from Hungary, almost 130,000 (30%) were transited through Birkenau and ended up in other camps (see the entries on Birkenau and on Hungary). Other documents show that thousands of Jews deported from Hungary and from Lodz to Birkenau ended up at the Stutthof Camp, proving once more that Birkenau was indeed a transit camp for tens, if not hundreds of thousands of Jews, rather than an extermination camp. The lack of documental evidence for the fate of the other Hungarian Jews does not prove that they were murdered. It merely proves that documents of their final destinations were either lost or destroyed, or have not yet been discovered.

(For more details on this, see the entries on Hungary and Lodz Ghetto, as well as Mattogno 2010, 2023c; Rudolf 2023, pp. 290-295.)

TRAWNIKI

Trawniki was a forced-labor camp located half way between the Belzec and Sobibór Camp. It was established in the fall of 1941. Some 20,000 Jewish inmates are said to have passed through this camp. The camp also served as a training facility for SS men, among them Soviet PoWs, most of them Ukrainians, who volunteered to serve as guards in various German camps.

In the fall of 1943, 10,000 Jewish inmates of the Trawniki Camp were relocated to other camps during a major operation of relocating SS-owned and operated companies together with their Jewish labor force. The orthodoxy has dubbed this Operation "Harvest Festival," claiming that all these Jews (plus many more from the Majdanek Camp), were killed. (See the related entries for more information.)

No historian claims that any mass murder using execution facilities took place in the Trawniki Camp. There is neither material, documental nor anecdotal evidence to support such a claim. However, that did not stop Polish and Jewish groups from claiming otherwise anyway.

Between April and June 1942, Polish underground sources spread the "information" that Jews were being killed in masses at Trawniki using toxic gases in gas chambers, after which the victims' bodies were burned in a primitive crematorium. This was presented to the public as the "truth" by the Polish government in its London exile in July of 1942. Jewish sources, such as the *Jewish Telegraphic Agency*, repeated that disinformation in 1942 and 1943.

This phantom extermination camp is a creation of black-propaganda sources.

(For more information, see Mattogno 2021e, pp. 94-97.)

TREBLINKA
Documented History

As with Belzec and Sobibór, very few documents about Treblinka have surfaced after the war, but they allow us to draw a rough image of this camp's history.

There were actually two camps at Treblinka. The first, later called Treblinka I, was a mere labor camp near a gravel pit. It was officially established by ordinance of the Governor of the Warsaw District dated 15 November 1941. The order to construct the camp, in which its purpose is also stated, was published on 16 December 1941 in the occupational government's Official Gazette for the Warsaw District. The mining of gravel from the pits near Treblinka I was managed by a "SS Special Unit Treblinka," which ran a formal company whose name translates to "German Earth and Rock Works, Inc., Gravel Works Treblinka."

Treblinka II was some 2 km away from Treblinka I. It was established in the first half of 1942. One document relating to this is a labor certificate about building a railway spur from the main line up to the camp. It was issued by Central Construction Office of the Waffen-SS and Police Warsaw on 1 June 1942, and was valid for 15 days. The names of two German companies involved in constructing the camp are known. Also known are several documents from June and July 1942 that deal with the procurement of construction material for the expansion of the Treblinka Camp, hence for setting up Treblinka II. These documents list 1,300 meters of electric cables, 90 light bulbs and other lighting fixtures, but most importantly large quantities of water pipes (at least 160 m) and many pipe fittings, as well as fixtures needed to extract large amounts of water from a well. These items were evidently needed to build a sanitary installation of a significant size.

In what follows, if there is no qualifier, the terms Treblinka and Treblinka Camp refer to the Treblinka II Camp, hence the alleged extermination camp.

Numerous wartime documents confirm the deportation of Jews from the Warsaw Ghetto to Treblinka. Among them are railway schedules showing that a train went every day from Warsaw to Treblinka, returning empty. Another document shows that each train contained 5,000 Jews, and yet another that, between 22 July and 3 October 1942, 310,322 Jews were "removed" from the ghetto. The 22nd of July is therefore also the date when the Treblinka Camp is said to have started operating.

There are numerous documents regarding the organization of these "resettlement" transports, as they were officially called. On 21 August 1942, one month into the evacuation of the Jews from the Warsaw Ghetto, the responsible Higher-SS leader reported to Goebbels on the deportations. He told Goebbels that the Jews are now "established in the East." (See the entry on Joseph Goebbels.)

Finally, there is a telegram sent by Hans Höfle to the SS headquarters in Berlin on 11 January 1943, which was intercepted and deciphered by the British (see the entry on Hans Höfle). It states that, by the end of 1942, 713,555 Jews had arrived at "T", which probably stands for Treblinka. The message contains no indications regarding the fate of the deportees.

There are also a few documents dealing with transports of Jews from the Warsaw Ghetto which evidently went through Treblinka and ended up in the German-occupied eastern territories of the Soviet Union.

In 1943, the German authorities started relocating tens of thousands of Jews from the Warsaw Ghetto who were employed by companies important to the war effort, to local concentration and labor camps. The companies were relocated as well, so these Jews could keep working for them. The Jews resisted that relocation, leading to the famous uprising of the Warsaw Ghetto, starting on 19 April 1943 and lasting until 16 May 1943.

Jews arrested during that uprising were either executed or sent to Treblinka, presumably to be eliminated there according to the Stroop Report, which summarized the events of the ghetto uprising from a German point of view. However, there are numerous witness accounts of Jews stating that, during the ghetto uprising, hundreds upon hundreds of Jews were deported from the Warsaw Ghetto through Treblinka to other camps, or sometimes directly to other camps. Several orthodox studies show in fact that tens of thousands of these uprising Jews were sent to other camps, among them primarily Majdanek. Many of the respective trains transited through Treblinka.

The Jews of the Białystok Ghetto suffered not quite as harsh a fate when that ghetto was dissolved in August of 1943. Eventually, some 25,000 Jews

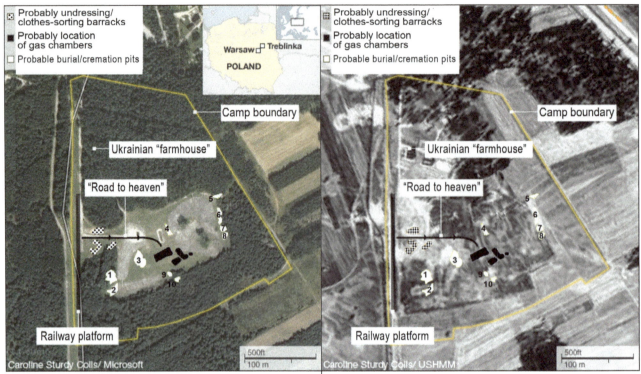

Air photo of the former Treblinka Camp, taken in 2012 by a team of British archeologists lead by Dr. Caroline Sturdy Colls. The labels are theirs, and the term "probable" indicates that they haven't found any clear-cut traces of anything.

Air photo of the former Treblinka Camp, taken in November 1944, with the same camp border line, markings and labels added as in the left photo by Sturdy Colls.

were deported to Treblinka, and orthodox historians have shown that most of them ended up in Majdanek, while others were sent to Auschwitz. Therefore, these deportees were all merely transited through Treblinka.

Propaganda History

Starting in late May 1942 and stretching into mid-July 1942, several reports of the Polish underground reported that Jews were deported in masses to Treblinka, where they were massacred by either getting buried alive, clubbed to death, shot or gassed. However, the camp was still under construction at that time, and Jews were deported to Treblinka only starting on 22 July 1942.

Only a month after deportations of Jews from the Warsaw Ghetto to Treblinka began, the Polish underground press started reporting about it. Claims of mass murder, committed with a wide variety of conflicting killing methods, point to the propaganda purpose of these messages. Several early stories mentioned mobile gas chambers that could be moved over pits, where the dead bodies they contained were then dumped through some tipping mechanism.

The report of 8 September 1942 switched from mobile gas *chambers* to mobile gassing *victims*: it claimed that a convenient gas with a delayed effect was used which allowed the evidently cooperative victims to walk to their mass graves and fall into them before dying.

The author of an article published in the Yiddish periodical *Oif der Vach* (*On Guard*) dated 20 September 1942 wasn't sure whether the Jews at Treblinka were gassed or electrocuted, but he was certain that, after the murder was completed, the room's floor opened up and discharged the bodies "into a machine." This rumor reflects false stories spread about the Sobibór Camp. The article also claimed that two more such camps existed: one in Belzec, and the other "in the vicinity of Pinsk," which is totally made up.

A Polish underground report of 5 October 1942 reports about a "20 HP internal-combustion engine, which is in operation around the clock," hence evidently driving an electricity generator. However, the engine's fuel had been mixed with some "toxic fluids," resulting in toxic exhaust gases used to kill the Jews. The report claimed a death toll of 320,000 Jews already by the end of August 1942 (that is, after just six weeks of operation), at which point only a little over 200,000 Jews had been deported to Treblinka.

Chroniclers of the Warsaw Ghetto (Emmanuel Ringelblum's group) noted in late September 1942 that ordinary steam was used for mass murder at Treblinka. On 9 October 1942, they rumored that a "giant electric chair" – probably some huge electrocution facility – was used there to kill ten thousand Jews and Poles a day. Not even a week later, these chroniclers noted about Treblinka: "Method of killing: gas, steam, electricity." It's good practice to cover all bases.

A report of mid-October 1942 claimed that Jews from the Warsaw Ghetto were sent to Treblinka and Bełżec Camps in trains sprinkled with chlorine and lime – a fable clearly inspired by Jan Karski's black-propaganda rumors about mass murder by chlorinated-lime trains. Once they had arrived at the camps, the surviving Jews were supposedly murdered in a gas chamber. However, no Jews from the Warsaw Ghetto were ever deported to Belzec.

Several underground reports of October and November 1942 asserted that Jews deported to Treblinka were killed in gas chambers, without giving any specifics. One of the reports claiming to be an eyewitness story states that the gassing victims had a "bluish color." However, carbon-monoxide gassing victims look distinctly reddish-pink, not bluish. The story was accompanied by a completely invented camp map.

On 25 November 1942, *The New York Times* published their first mention of the camp. They gave no details, other than to say that people shipped there were "mass-murdered" (p. 10). But this had the effect of bringing attention to the camp to a wide public audience.

A telegram dated 4 December 1942 from the Jewish Agency in Tel Aviv to the World Jewish Congress in New York claimed that Jews at Treblinka were either killed by pumping out the air or with some poison gas.

A Polish underground report sent to London on 31 March 1943 asserted that Treblinka was equipped "probably" with 100 (!) gas chambers. Another report sent with the same batch stated that three murder methods were used at Treblinka: Initially, the deportees were shot with machine guns, then they were steamed in steaming chambers, and finally they were killed during transit in Jan-Karski-style trains with floors covered with quicklime.

A Polish underground report of late April 1943, essentially repeated a month later, claimed that 15,000 Jews were murdered in Treblinka every day in an unspecified gas chamber. Their corpses were initially buried, but later, they used "corrosive acids so strong that the body together with the bones becomes shapeless and gets reduced to dust." This is clearly fantasy-fiction.

On 25 June 1943, *The New York Times* reported that trainloads of Bulgarian Jews were being transported "to Treblinka camp, where the gas chambers can handle as many as 7,000 executions daily" (p. 4).

An alleged witness account of August 1943 mentioned "eight barracks built for 7,000 men," but then, only one building "was flooded with gas."

In November 1943, Marek Ptakowski mentioned "electric furnace engines" which had produced three million victims in just half a year. However, murder was carried out either by machine-gun fire, by burning in electric furnaces, by gas chambers, or by killing them directly in the trains, which entered "a huge hall, from where they returned full of corpses."

A Polish underground report of 8 September 1943 mentions the inmate uprising of 2 August 1943. Orthodox historians assume that some 100 inmates managed to escape during that event, hence some 100 eyewitnesses, which should have been able to provide detailed, consistent and more or less identical descriptions on the alleged mass-murder method used at Treblinka. However, after that mass escape, the same more-or-less-senseless stories continued to circulate, with a focus on extermination by water vapor.

All the claimed killing systems mentioned above occurred sporadically and very briefly in the various reports about Treblinka. The killing method mentioned most often and described in detail was steam. It occurred for the first time in an account by the witness Jakub Rabinowicz in the second half of September 1942. It became the prevailing "truth" two months later, when the Warsaw Ghetto's underground movement composed a long article dated 15 November 1942 that contained a very detailed description of the Treblinka Camp and its operations. It mentions a gas-chamber building killing with steam that consisted of ten chambers, each 35 square meters large, five each on both sides of a 3-m-wide corridor. A diesel motor is claimed to have provided the camp with electricity. By the time the report was written, the camp allegedly had already two million Jewish victims.

This report was sent to the Polish government in exile in London in early 1943. An English translation titled "Treblinka. Official Report Submitted to the Polish Government" appeared in 1943 in the anthology *The Black Book of Polish Jewry*. Since this was the Polish government's official position, but also because it was said to be based on an eyewitness account and was very detailed, it was considered reliable, was widely disseminated, and was promptly echoed by subsequent reports and accounts too numerous to mention here.

Most of these reports were the work of journalists and propagandists, not of first-hand witnesses. Although they claimed to rely on witness accounts, these are never named. That changed after the Treblinka region had been conquered by the Red Army. Soon thereafter, Soviet and Polish commissions were set up and started interviewing survivors, railway employees and local residents.

The Soviets were the first to set up a commission. As a summary of the testimonies they collected – among them prominently Jankiel Wiernik's 1944 book – the commission wrote on 24 August 1944 that every victim was "given soap, a towel and underclothing" on the way to the "bath." However, this was not claimed by any witness. It is moreover safe to say that no sane executioner would have issued those items to thousands of people about to be killed, but only if they were about to take a shower and get fresh clothes afterwards.

If we follow the Soviet report, the execution facility allegedly "consisted of 12 chambers, each 6 × 6 m in size. 400 to 500 people were driven at a time into one chamber," which would have resulted in an unlikely packing density of 11 to 14 people per square meter. The execution was carried out by a machine that "pumped the air out of the room." Hence execution by vacuum. These claims were allegedly based on statements by the witnesses Abe Kon, Hejnoch Brener and Samuel Rajzman. However, creating a vacuum in a brick-and-mortar building is technically impossible (the external pressure would crush the walls), hence most certainly was not done. As a death toll, the report claimed three million victims, four times more than is currently claimed by the orthodoxy.

On 11 September 1944, the Soviet press agency TASS released a press release that deviated somewhat from the commission report. It mentioned an initial three-chamber facility, plus a later eight-chamber facility, operated with an unnamed gas rather than vacuum, and with observation windows in the door.

On 15 September 1944, a mixed Polish-Soviet commission issued a report summarizing its findings. It claimed that the camp's gas-chamber facility had three rooms. Initially, victims were killed by "pumping the air out of rooms by means of a small car motor," but later, unnamed chemicals were used instead. The chambers had roof windows for observations, a feature commonly claimed by witnesses about the Sobibór execution facility.

Also in September of 1944, during the Soviet investigations into Treblinka, Soviet-Jewish propagandist Vasily Grossman visited the area. Afterwards, he wrote a long article titled "Treblinka Hell," which was later published by various outlets. It repeated the claims made by Jankiel Wiernik in his June 1944 essay, including the 3-million death-toll claim, but as a second murder method, it also mentioned "pumping the air out of the chambers with special pumps."

Rachel Auerbach created her own version of Treblinka in a 1946 article, by mostly relying on Jankiel Wiernik's script. However, she added a few absurd claims, such as self-immolating bodies, blood as an excellent fuel, and fat extracted from burning bodies. (See the entry dedicated to her.)

More witnesses were interrogated during the Polish investigations in preparation of the show trial against Ludwig Fischer, the German wartime governor of the Warsaw District (17 December 1946 to 3 March 1947).

Testimonies of identified witnesses recorded in the years 1942 through 1946, when memories were still fresh, unadulterated and most reliable – or so one should think – are listed in the following table. The date given after the name in the first column indicates when the respective deposition was made.

Witness	Claimed Murder Method	Miscellaneous Claims
Dawid Nowodowski / 18 August 1942	no mass murder claimed	–
Jakub Rabinowicz / 2nd half Sept. 1942	no method stated/steam/ gas, steam, electricity	diesel electricity generator
Abraham Krzepicki / Oct./Nov. 1942?	chlorine?	–
Abraham Krzepicki / after 26 Dec. 1942	gas, coming from pipes on the roof	saw normal shower room; built crematorium building
Jankiel Wiernik / September 1943?	chlorine	

Witness	Claimed Murder Method	Miscellaneous Claims
Jankiel Wiernik (?) / November 1943	initially machine guns later unspecified gas chambers	3 million victims
Jankiel Wiernik / 6 June 1944	exhaust gas from Soviet tank-engine as electricity generator	yellow corpses; millions of victims; plagiarized map
Jankiel Wiernik / 4 January 1947	unspecified gas in chambers	2.5 million victims by Feb 1943, self-immolating corpses
Samuel Rajzman / 28 July 1944	initially vacuum later toxic gas	10 chambers, 700-800 people each; 2,774,000 casualties
Samuel Rajzman / August 1944	initially vacuum later gas	–
Samuel Rajzman / 26 September 1944	initially vacuum later chlorine or Zyklon B	–
Abe Kon / 17 August 1944	vacuum	12 chambers, 6 m × 6 m each 400 persons/m²
Abe Kon / 22 August 1944	gas ("turned on")	12 chambers, 6 m × 6 m each 400 persons/m²
Abe Kon / 9 October 1945	vacuum	12 chambers
Hejnoch Brener / 17 August 1944	no method stated	5,000 victims per batch
Hejnoch Brener / 9 October 1945	vacuum	–
Stanisław Kon / 18 August 1944	no method stated	3 million victims total
Stanisław Kon / 18 August 1944	initially machine guns later vacuum or exhaust gas	fireproof excavator dumped bodies on burning pyres
Kazimierz Skarżyński / 22 August 1944	vacuum	–
Kazimierz Skarżyński / 23 August 1944	no method stated	"special chamber"
Abraham Goldfarb / 21 September 1944	1st facility: engine gas; 2nd facility: first chlorinated lime, then engine gas	1st facility: tractor engine for both gassing and electricity
Abraham Goldfarb / 1986?	gas chamber	dead victims standing upright chlorinated lime in trains
Oskar Berger / 1945	initially machine guns, later gas	–
Eugeniusz Turowski / 7 October 1945	initially machine guns later gas chambers	ventilators in gas chambers and under cremation grates
Oskar Strawczyński / 7 October 1945	vacuum or engine exhaust gas	–
Henryk Poswolski / 9 October 1945	after air evacuation, introduction of diesel exhaust gas	collapsible floors with cart underneath
Szyja Warszawski / 9 October 1945	first chlorine, then engine-exhaust gas	chlorinated lime in trains self-immolating bodies
Aleksander Kudlik / 10 October 1945	after air evacuation, introduction of exhaust gas	–
Aron Czechowicz / 11 October 1945	liquid poured through roof chimneys, while engine runs	–
Henryk Reichman / 12 October 1945	after air evacuation, introduction of exhaust gas	victims black and blue self-immolating bodies
Silvia Kersch / 12 December 1945	burned alive in 4 big furnaces	4 tall chimneys
Leon Finkelsztein / 28 December 1945	engine-exhaust gas on engine failure, chlorine	chlorinated lime in trains self-immolating bodies
Samuel Willenberg / 1945	no method stated	"chambers"
Samuel Willenberg / 1986	diesel-engine exhaust gases from Soviet tank engine	
Szymon Goldberg / 1946	after air evacuation, introduction of car exhaust gas; ether; chlorine	
Jan Sułkowski / 1948	execution from a death bridge	

Whereas propaganda messages of the Polish-Jewish underground during the war primarily claimed that mass murder at Treblinka was committed with steam, wartime and immediate-postwar witnesses have two main foci: vacuum and engine-exhaust gas, with the latter gaining the upper hand as time went on. But there are always many other claimed methods, and several witnesses couldn't agree on a method, or claimed diverging methods throughout the camp's history. Again others changed their mind regarding the claimed murder method within just a few days, when interviewed again. One witness even flip-flopped twice (Abe Kon).

A detailed analysis of all these witness statements (see their respective entries) shows that the chaotic image created by the above table only gives the tip of the iceberg of the random chaos reigning among these testimonies in almost every regard. Most witnesses admit that they are reporting only from hearsay. The nature of the claims by many of those witnesses who do not openly admit that their knowledge is from hearsay at best – or who assert first-hand knowledge – suggests that they reported from hearsay as well.

Notably, the one witness who should definitely have first-hand knowledge – the camp mechanic Eugeniusz Turowski, who claims to have repaired gas-chamber equipment on several occasions – stated that he could not give any specifics at all.

While this testimonial chaos was still brewing and churning, the propagandists gearing up for the Nuremberg International Military Tribunal had a problem: what claims should they submit? The Soviets submitted with their Document USSR-93 the claim that murder at Treblinka had been committed "in gas chambers, by steam and electric current." The Polish government decided to stick to what they had published in their report of 15 November 1942, meaning the Treblinka victims were steamed to death like lobsters (Document PS-3311).

This Polish government report of 15 November 1942 is of central importance for writing the history of the Treblinka Camp, because of its early date, its detailed description, its "authoritativeness" as an official government statement, and because it had been plagiarized and thus spread by other victims repeating its features (Wiernik, Goldfarb). However, its embarrassing insistence on steam chambers has orthodox historians resort to blatant forgeries to hide this fact from their readers. Yitzhak Arad, for instance, who contributed the entry on Treblinka to Gutman's 1990 *Encyclopedia of the Holocaust*, discusses this Polish report in his 1987 book, yet writes four times that the report is about *gas* chambers, when in fact it is about *steam* chambers (Arad 1987, pp. 354f.).

It took the radical intervention of a Polish investigative judge to put an end to this testimonial anarchy. Zdzisław Łukaszkiewicz decided in 1946 to ditch all witness statements on Treblinka that contain anything else but engine-exhaust gases, and to write a cleansed version of Treblinka's history. No more steam, vacuum, chlorine, chlorinated lime, electrocution, ether, toxic fluids or fuel additives, mobile gas chambers and delayed-action gases and whatever else had been claimed over the past four years. Łukaszkiewicz mainly took Wiernik's later version of the tale, which aligned nicely with the version he had already cobbled together for the Belzec Camp, and dropped all the rest.

And that is essentially what the world has been stuck with ever since.

Later witness accounts, such as that by Eliyahu Rosenberg, followed this pattern, probably more influenced by Wiernik's account, published in several languages and well-known among the survivor communities, rather than by Łukaszkiewicz's report. Early orthodox holocaust historians, such as Léon Poliakov (1951) and Gerald Reitlinger (1953), gladly followed in Łukaszkiewicz's footsteps by simply copying over to Treblinka (and also Sobibór) what Kurt Gerstein had claimed for the Belzec Camp: diesel-engine exhaust gasses had been used, period. It matters not that Gerstein has been totally discredited as a witness in the meantime. (Wiernik never mentioned the type of engine.)

The propaganda image painted by historians was cast in stone during two West-German show trials against defendants who had done duty at the Treblinka Camp. Both took place at Düsseldorf. The first, lasting from October 1964 to September 1965, saw ten defendants, among them Kurt Franz. He was sentenced to life imprisonment for the collective murder of 300,000 persons and for several individual murders. The second Treblinka trial, which took place from May to December 1970, had only one defendant: the second Treblinka commandant Franz Stangl. He was sentenced to life imprisonment for contributing to the murder of at least 400,000 Jews, but he died before the verdict came into effect.

While more than 100 witnesses had been interrogated for the first trial, this number went down to some 50 for the second trial. At that point in time, more than 20 years after the alleged events – and most importantly after the Eichmann Trial – the witness accounts were probably contaminated with the propaganda incessantly spread around the globe. However, neither the pre-trial investigators nor the judges did anything to find out what the sources of a witness's knowledge were. In fact, the procedures of West Germany's judicial office called *Zentrale Stelle*, which was spearheading the pre-trial investigations, made sure that witnesses' memories were *systematically* contaminated with what the investigators already thought they "knew" about Treblinka and every defendant. (See the entry on the *Zentrale Stelle*.)

Furthermore, the Düsseldorf court had orthodox historians Helmut Krausnick (1964) and Wolfgang Scheffler (1971) testify as "experts" about the camp's history. Both orthodox historians repeated what they had learned from sources, such as Łukaszkiewicz's rigged report, and earlier accounts by their colleagues, such as Poliakov, Reitlinger and Raul Hilberg. None of them made the effort to go to the early sources as laid out in the above table.

Cornered this way, the defendants made the only smart choice open to them: they were cooperative with investigators, prosecutors and judges, confirmed what was considered to be true already anyway, didn't contradict what orthodox historians claimed, yet at the same time tried to minimize as much as possible their own responsibility and contribution for what allegedly happened.

Within such a framework, no one asked questions about the ability of diesel-engine exhaust gases to kill; about traces of the murder victims, their mass graves and the alleged huge cremation pyres; or about the feasibility of burning 700,000 bodies within a short period of time on open-air incineration pyres.

The entire absurdity of this procedure became glaringly apparent during the Jerusalem show trial against John Demjanjuk, who was accused of having assisted in the mass murder of Jews at Treblinka as a Ukrainian auxiliary. When that case was reviewed by Israel's Supreme Court, it threw out the entire case because all witness testimonies were considered unreliable, and all witnesses untrustworthy. But virtually the same witnesses had testified with the same stories at Düsseldorf.

Yet the propaganda image invented by Polish wartime propagandists, plagiarized by Wiernik, given official approval by Łukaszkiewicz, and cast in legal stone by German judges, stands to this day – protected in many countries by the threat of imprisonment for anyone who disagrees.

Forensic Findings

Three sets of forensic investigations were carried out on the grounds of the former Treblinka Camp:

Soviet Investigations

On 22 and 23 August 1944, a Soviet commission carried out an inspection of the Treblinka Labor Camp, where they found 13 individual graves and two mass graves with together a little over 300 bodies in a claimed grave volume of some 250 m³ – or just over one body per cubic meter. The Treblinka Death Camp was also inspected, but no excavations were carried out. Based on witness accounts and the superficial visibility of ashes and bone fragments on the campgrounds, the commission concluded that

"the cremation of people has been determined beyond a doubt. The extent of the extermination of human beings was monstrous: about three million."

Polish Investigations

On 6 November 1945, a combined Jewish-Polish commission headed by Judge Łukaszkiewicz visited the former Treblinka campgrounds. They discovered that it had been devastated by wild diggings as well as by numerous explosions of bombs and artillery shells. These were created by the local populace and Soviet soldiers in search of gold and jewelry. They left behind a moonscape with uncounted craters up to 6 meters deep and 25 meters in diameter, and scattered human remains and garbage.

Between 9 and 13 November 1945, Judge Łukaszkiewicz supervised a series of excavations on the former campgrounds. While they found scattered human remains in a few places, they did not locate any mass graves or large volumes of soil mixed with ashes or human remains.

On 9 and 10 August 1946, Judge Łukaszkiewicz searched for mass graves in the area of the labor camp Treblinka I. His findings were quantitatively similar to the Soviet investigation mentioned above.

Therefore, Łukaszkiewicz's investigations were a complete failure. Although he conducted excavations at the spot where the witness Samuel Rajzman had claimed a mass grave was located, nothing was discovered. Another dig at a location pointed out by witnesses to be the place where the two alleged gassing facilities once were encountered merely "undisturbed layers of earth." The amount of burned and unburned human remains found was miniscule compared to the magnitude of slaughter claimed.

Hence, neither the Soviets nor the Poles uncovered even the slightest scrap of proof that Treblinka II, the alleged extermination camp, was the location of any kind of mass murder. However, the Soviets did not dig at all, and the Poles only in a few places.

British Investigations

This was to change when a British team of forensic archeologist started investigating the campgrounds starting in 2011. The use of modern non-invasive technologies promised new results: ground-penetrating radar is capable of locating solid objects underground and disturbed layers of soil, while LIDAR can detect subtle changes in ground elevations from the air, which can be associated with subsiding mass graves.

Considering the havoc that wild grave diggers, exploding munitions and also the Polish excavations of 1945 must have left behind in the ground, some disturbed soil had to be found. But the amount of disturbed soil discovered in no way matches the volume of mass graves that was expected.

The orthodoxy claims that some 764,000 bodies were buried at Treblinka before the incineration of corpses was started. The British investigations only located a disturbed-soil volume of some 15,600 m³. Taking the top 50 cm off as a grave cover, this leaves some 14,300 m³ to bury corpses. If the bodies were as densely packed as in the mass graves discovered at the Treblinka I Camp (only a little more than a body per cubic meter), then only some 14,300 bodies were buried there. If we increase that packing density to an unheard-of extreme value of 10 bodies per cubic meter, then some 143,000 could have been buried there.

However, some of that disturbed volume resulted from the trenches dug by Łukaszkiewicz only containing undisturbed layers of soil, and quite a few of the bomb craters and wild digs of the immediate postwar time undoubtedly also turned otherwise undisturbed soil into disturbed soil.

No matter how we turn it, if we follow the currently available data, there was no room to bury at least (764,000 – 143,000 =) 621,000 corpses. Where did these corpses go?

Death-Toll Propaganda

Victim numbers claimed for Treblinka
(For references not given here, see Rudolf 2023, p. 257)

3,000,000	V. Grossman, J. Wiernik, Soviet Commission 1944
2,774,000	Samuel Rajzman
1,582,000	Historian Ryszard Czarkowski
1,200,000	Franciszek Ząbeki
1,074,000	Rachel Auerbach
974,000	Historian Frank Golczewski
912,000	Historian Manfred Burba
900,000	Historian Wolfgang Scheffler
881,390	Historian Yitzhak Arad
870,000	*Encyclopedia of the Holocaust* (Gutman 1990, p. 1486)
800,000	Zdzisław Łukaszkiewicz
781,000	Soviet Prosecutor Smirnov (*IMT*, Vol. 8, p. 330)
750,000	Historians Raul Hilberg, Stanisław Wojtczak
≥ 700,000	Historians Helmuth Krausnick, Uwe D. Adam
200,000 – 250,000	Historian Jean-Claude Pressac

Other Forensic Considerations

Diesel-engine exhaust gas is unable to kill within the time frame claimed. Hence, unfit for the claimed job was Treblinka's murder weapon – which the orthodoxy decided upon only after Łukaszkiewicz's manipulation of the historical record, and after early orthodox historians' decision to cast claimed features of the Belzec Camp onto the Treblinka Camp.

The orthodoxy's narrative regarding the incineration of killed inmates at Treblinka would have created formidable logistical challenges for the perpetrators and their assistants. All the corpses claimed had to be burned with open-air incinerations on huge pyres, since the camp had no cremation furnaces. The table shows some data about the claimed events.

The wood needed to cremate these corpses had to come from local forests, which would have led to large swaths of land around the camp getting denuded of any trees, but that evidently didn't happen. The space requirement for the many huge pyres, and the manpower needed to exhume the bodies; fell, transport and chop tens or even hundreds of thousands of trees; build and maintain the pyres; extract and scatter the ashes, would have been formidable.

According to the current orthodox narrative, at least some 700,000 bodies had to be burned at Treblinka. For this, some 175,000 metric tons of green wood would have been needed. The maximum number of inmates, claimed by any witness, who were deployed at Treblinka to cut trees and bring it to the camp as firewood was 100. Data based on experience

Characteristics of Mass Graves and Mass Cremations at Treblinka		
	CLAIMED	FOUND
no. of corpses	700,000 to 3 million	scattered remains
space required (@ 6 bodies/m³)	116,700 to 500,000 m³	at most 14,500 m³
claimed cremation time	April – July 1943, ca. 122 days	
corpses cremated	5,700 to 24,600 per day	
green wood needed (@ 250 kg/body)	1,430 to 6,150 metric tons per day	
total green wood needed	175,000 to 750,000 metric tons	

with forced laborers such as PoWs shows that they could fell some 0.63 metric tons of trees per day. This makes some 63 tons of wood for 100 inmates per day. To cut some 175,000 metric tons would have taken them some 2,778 days of uninterrupted work, which is more than seven and a half years (!) – while they had only some 122 days to do it. Alternatively, to get the work done in time, it would have required 2,277 (!) dedicated lumberjacks.

Add to this the fact that the Polish forests were tightly managed by the German occupational forces as precious resources for lumber and fuel. Hence, the SS couldn't send droves of inmates to adjacent forests and cut them down without getting permission to do so. Of course, there is no documental or material trace of any such massive tree-felling activity having been applied for, been granted, let alone occurred. Air photos taken of the Treblinka area by German reconnaissance planes in 1944 show no areas denuded of trees in the camp's vicinity either.

None of it has left a trace: neither in witness statements, nor in documents, nor in the material and forensic record. In fact, if witnesses talk about details of the cremation of corpses, their claims are often ludicrous beyond belief: stories of self-immolating bodies abound among them. (See the entries for Leon Finkelsztein, Richard Glazar, Stanisław Kon, Chil Rajchman, Jean-François Steiner, Franz Suchomel, Szyja Warszawski and Jankiel Wiernik).

(For more details, see Mattogno/Graf 2023, pp. 77-89, 137-154; Mattogno 2021e, pp. 237-269, 273-295; Rudolf 2023, pp. 256-282.)

Current Orthodox Narrative

The current orthodox narrative follows largely the lines of the West-German verdicts of 1965 and 1971, which in turn are mainly based on Jankiel Wiernik's 1944 booklet, although there are a few modifications.

According to this, the camp started operating with the first transport trains arriving from the Warsaw Ghetto on 23 July 1942. At this point, only one gas-chamber facility made of wood existed, which had three gas chambers in a row, each measuring 4 m × 4 m (rather than Wiernik's 5 m × 5 m). A fourth room, an engine room, contained a diesel engine from a Soviet tank (probably a T-34, which had a diesel engine and was very common). Its exhaust gas was piped into the rooms and killed within half an hour. However, diesel-engine exhaust gas is not lethal in the timeframe considered, and no engine of a captured Soviet tank would have been used, because it would have been difficult to obtain, to transport, to install, to maintain and to get eventually needed spare parts.

Due to an alleged lack of gassing capacity, a new, solidly built gas-chamber facility made of bricks and concrete was constructed between August/September to October/November 1942. It had two times five chambers on either side of a corridor, each with a surface area of 8 m × 4 m (rather than Wiernik's 7 m × 7 m). The old building was kept, so that the gas-chamber capacity, measured in room surface area, grew from initially 46 m² to 368 m², hence by a factor of eight.

The claim that a new building was needed is refuted by the transportation data. Orthodox historian Yitzhak Arad has asserted that, by the end of October 1942, 694,000 Jews had already been murdered in Treblinka's old gas chambers. After that month, "only" another 187,390 had to be deported (Arad 1987, pp. 392-397). The ratio of the killings in the time intervals up to the end of October 1942 and after that is therefore 1:0.27. In other words, the need for gassing capacity shrank to almost a quarter, while the capacity increased eight-fold. Hence, if the original three small gas chambers were used at 100% capacity up to the end of October 1942, from there on, with the new chambers added, they were used only at less than 4% of their capacity!

So, why did the Polish report of 15 November 1942, and later also Wiernik and others, insist on more, larger gas chambers? It is rather simple: Three gas chambers were simply not monstrous enough. The demonic nature of the Germans had to be undergirded with ever-escalating atrocity claims. After all, Wiernik needed to accommodate 3 million victims, not "just" 700,000.

The next event in Treblinka's history is the claimed visit by Heinrich Himmler in March 1943. During that visit, he allegedly ordered that burials needed to stop, and that all buried victims had be exhumed and cremated on pyres. However, there is no trace in the documental record that such a visit ever happened. In fact, Himmler's alleged exhumation-cremation order is said to have been issued for each claimed camp at a different point in time. This indicates that there could not have been any plan or logic behind this, pointing at the random nature of these claims. (See the entry on open-air incinerations for details.) Still, based on this phantom event, huge cremations allegedly started in late March/early April 1943, and lasted four months, until the end of July 1943. The logistical challenges would have been insurmountable, as described in the section on "Other Forensic Considerations." It simply cannot have happened, particularly not as described by many witnesses.

The one event in Treblinka's history about which everyone agrees that it is true and real is the inmate uprising of 2 August 1943 with the subsequent escape of 100 to 200 inmates. It is striking, however, that most inmates who later testified claimed to have had no direct knowledge of the alleged exterminations, because they were not members of the inmate teams working in Treblinka's extermination sector, which was allegedly strictly cordoned off and inaccessible to all other inmates.

Here we need to pause. The orthodoxy claims that Treblinka's primary objective was to mass murder hundreds of thousands of deportees. Therefore, it is only logical that most of the work that had to be done in that camp would have related to that mass murder. Here are the tasks allegedly done:
– cutting the hair of thousands of inmates;
– removing precious-metal tooth fillings after the execution;
– hauling the victims out of the chambers;
– exhuming bodies still lying in older mass graves;
– felling huge numbers of trees;
– hauling the trees into the camp;
– debranch and sawing and/or chopping them to manageable firewood sizes;
– building large pyres with firewood and corpses;
– maintaining the fires;
– clearing the burned-down pyres;
– sifting through large amounts of ashes in search of unburned pieces;
– putting unburned remains back onto a pyre;
– disposing of the ashes.

Therefore, if the orthodox narrative were true, by far the largest number of inmates in that camp would have been employed in that very mass-murder sector. Furthermore, these inmates also should have had the highest motivation for an uprising for obvious reasons. Hence, when a revolt broke out, it had to be expected that it foremost encompassed exactly these inmates. In consequence, most escapees and survivors, and thus witnesses, also should have consisted of these inmates.

In addition, these inmates would have had the strongest motivation to tell their tale, as they were the ones who had seen all the claimed horrors. Judicial authorities also would have had strong motives to locate and interrogate these witnesses, as they were the ones with first-hand knowledge.

However, we find the exact opposite to be true: most witnesses claimed to have had no direct knowledge of what transpired in that extermination sector. And many of those who gave the impression of first-hand experiences made statements so outlandish that we must conclude that they, too, had no first-hand knowledge.

Using Occam's Razor, the simplest explanation
– for the invisibility of events unfolding in Treblinka's extermination sector, as claimed by numerous witnesses;
– for the systematically false claims about the alleged gas-chambers in Treblinka's extermination sector;
– and for the scarcity of alleged survivors from that sector,

is the simple fact that Treblinka's extermination sector never existed.

(For more on Treblinka, see Mattogno/Graf 2023; Mattogno 2021e; Mattogno/Kues/Graf 2015.)

trenches → Open-Air Incinerations

TRUBAKOV, ZIAMA

Ziama Trubakov was a Ukrainian Jew interned in the Syretsky Camp, 5 km from Kiev. On 18 August 1943, he was taken from there to Babi Yar, a place where tens of thousands of Jews are said to have been shot and buried by the Germans in mass graves in late September 1941 (see the entry on Babi Yar). Trubakov evidently was interviewed about his alleged experiences for the first time more than 20 years after the event by German court officials on 14 February 1967. Thirteen years after that, in 1980, Trubakov was interrogated in the Soviet Union, but not by court officials, yet by the KGB.

Among other things, Trubakov stated that he and other slave-labor inmates had to exhume mass graves and burn the extracted bodies on pyres. One such pyre was built on a platform measuring 10 m × 10 m. Between 2,000 and 2,500 bodies were placed on it in layers, alternating with layers of wood, reaching a height of 2.5 to 3 meters. He asserted moreover that a total of about 125,000 bodies were burned this way. His team of slave laborers was eventually increased to encompass 320 people.

He insisted that the pyres initially smoked heavily, but then burned without smoking, while "at the bottom, from under the ash pan, a thick black mass flowed to a specially adapted pit and then was buried." However, there is no way a large pyre using freshly cut wood could burn without smoking heavily. Furthermore, it is absolutely inconceivable how burning corpses in a hot blaze could lead to a black mass flowing anywhere. These claims are utterly bizarre.

On the pyre described by Trubakov, some 20 to 25 bodies would have been placed per square meter. With some 250 kg of freshly cut wood needed to burn one body, this would have amounted to 5 to 6.25 metric tons of wood. Fresh wood has a density of roughly 0.9 tons per m^3, and when stacked on a pyre, the gaps make up some 40% of the space (for air and flames to go through). Therefore, 5 to 6.25 metric tons of wood on a surface of one square meter stack up to a height of some 8 to 10 meters. Add to this the 20 to 25 bodies. This means that the pyres described by Trubakov would have been at least ten meters high, not 2.5 to 3 m. Such a huge pyre could have been built only with cranes. Once lit, it inevitably would have burned unevenly, hence would have toppled over, spilling burning wood and corpses all over the place.

Trubakov claimed that, after the pyres had burned down, unburned bones were ground down, the cremation remains sifted through sieves, and the powder scattered. However, wood-fired pyres burn unevenly and leave behind lots of unburned wood pieces, charcoal, and incompletely burned body parts, not just ashes and bones (80% of leftovers would have been from wood, not corpses). Incompletely burned wood and human remains could not have been ground. Any sieve would have clogged with the first load. Moreover, any occasional rainfall would have rendered any burned-out pyre into a moist heap of highly alkaline, corrosive slush that could not have been processed at all. If 125,000 bodies were burned, then several thousand metric tons of cremation leftovers had to be processed. Just this job would have required hundreds of men to complete in time.

Cremating an average human body during open-air incinerations requires some 250 kg of freshly cut wood. Cremating 125,000 bodies thus requires some 31,250 metric tons of wood. This would have required the felling of all trees growing in a 50-year-old spruce forest covering almost 70 hectares of land, or some 156 American football fields. An average prisoner is rated at being able to cut some 0.63 metric tons of fresh wood per workday. To cut this amount of wood within five weeks (35 days) that this operation supposedly lasted would have required a work force of some 1,417 dedicated lumberjacks just to cut the wood. Trubakov claimed that his unit consisted only of 320 inmates, all busy digging out mass graves, extracting bodies, building pyres, crushing bones, sifting through ashes, scattering the ashes and refilling the graves with soil. Trubakov says nothing about where the firewood came from.

In his KGB interview on 28 May 1980, Trubakov added a few details he had "forgotten" in 1967, such as that all inmates had been shackled, that the evil SS officer running the show was called Topaide. This person was invented in 1944 by the Soviet commission investigating the alleged events at Babi Yar. These little details hint at the actual source of his "information."

(For more details, see the entry on Babi Yar, as well as Mattogno 2022c, pp. 538, and 550-563.)

TURNER, HARALD

Harald Turner (8 Oct. 1891 – 9 March 1947), SS *Gruppenführer*, was SS commander in German-occupied Serbia during the war. Because he was trying to come to an agreement with the Serbs to gain their support for the German occupational policy, he was considered as too soft on the Serbs. As a result, the anti-Serbian hardliner August Meyzner was appointed as head of the local SS units in early 1942, which seriously undermined Turner's position. After the war, Turner was extradited to communist Yugoslavia, put on a show trial, sentenced to death and executed.

In the context of the Holocaust, the only item of

relevance is a letter Turner is said to have written on 11 April 1942 and addressed to SS General Karl Wolff, who was chief of Himmler's personal staff. This letter has several very peculiar features, some of which are:
- It is written on letter-size paper (8.5"×11"), which did and still does not exist in Europe. It is an exclusively U.S.-American (and Canadian) paper format.
- The letter's contents make no sense. Turner talks in cryptic terms about some foiled Wehrmacht intrigue centered around him yet directed against Himmler and the SS in general and in fact against the entire German "corps of tenured civil servants" (*Beamtenschaft*) – but no such grand Wehrmacht conspiracy is known to historians, nor does it make any sense to encompass all of Germany's tenured civil servants.
- Turner speaks of Jewish officers held as PoWs, who might find out about their Jewish relatives having been killed in Serbia, which then could somehow affect the well-being of German PoWs in Canada. First, there were no "Jewish officers" held in German PoW camps. Next, if any of the officers in German PoW camps were Jews, they surely did not have Serbian relatives in Serbian camps which Turner, according to this letter, was about to kill with "delousing vans." Finally, it is utterly incomprehensible what the few German PoWs in Canada had to do with any of this.
- The letter is riddled with very bad German, to the point of being almost incomprehensible, and its punctuation is erratic. Turner had a PhD in law and wrote very good German with proper punctuation, as other genuine letters show. Hence, this letter was not written or dictated by him.
- Some of the very bad German expressions sound just fine when translated literally into English. The peculiar remark about German PoWs in Canada allegedly affected by this makes sense only from the perspective of some Canadian, which fits the spelling of this country's name in this letter: Canada instead of the German way: Kanada.
- The writer of this letter faked a "rune SS" by superimposing a set of double slashes on a dash and adding another set of double slashes a three-quarter line lower: ⫽. This has never been seen in any document. As other letters written by Turner show, he had at his disposal a typewriter with proper SS runes. But even if not, then a simple double-SS was perfectly acceptable. Somebody clearly tried to fake something here.

The orthodoxy insists that this letter identifies the term "delousing" as a euphemism or "code word" for homicidal gassings, so that here the expression "delousing van" really meant "gas van." However, no other wartime document uses the term "delousing van" as a reference to a homicidal gas van. Furthermore, Turner was not only soft on the Serbs, but also on the Jews, as is shown by his attempt to prevent the execution of 1,500 male Jews as hostages. The letter analyzed here gives the opposite impression, however, and is therefore not just out of style but also out of character.

(For more details, see Alvarez 2023, pp. 89-94, 345-348.)

TUROWSKI, EUGENIUSZ

Eugeniusz Turowski was a Polish Jew who was deported to the Treblinka Camp on 5 September 1942. He was interviewed by Polish judge Łukaszkiewicz on 7 October 1945. At the camp, he was assigned to the machine shops, where he helped build, repair and maintain that camp's various machines and mechanical devices until the uprising on 2 August 1943. If that were the case, however, he should be the one man in the camp who should have known exactly how the gas chamber functioned. Yet he had no idea how the murder was committed. While he did not know what he should have known, he knew a lot of things that did not exist:
- He was told that the first Jews arrived at Treblinka in June 1942, although the camp opened only at the end of July 1942. Initially, arriving inmates were allegedly killed with machine guns, because the execution chambers weren't ready yet. Imagine the panic among the deportees, how they start running chaotically, and how stray bullets are whizzing by everyone – deportees, guards, auxiliaries and SS men. Still, both the wrong starting date and the machine-gunning claim were made by another Treblinka survivor, Stanisław Kon, who was interviewed by Polish judge Łukaszkiewicz on that same day. This is a clear case of "convergence of evidence" on a lie. Oskar Berger also claimed this early starting date combined with machine-gun killings.
- Turowski claimed to have repaired devices from the gas chambers, among them especially ventilators, although the orthodox narrative has it that these facilities had no ventilators. And indeed, had gassing with engine exhaust occurred, venti-

lators would have been superfluous, as a simple airing out would do the trick. A fan for a real communal shower room would have made sense, though.
- A few lines later, Turowski mentions fans used to blow air under the open-air incineration grates. Considering the enormous heat of such large pyres, these fans must have been fire-proof. They also would have been useless, as natural convection would have done the fanning trick just fine. Moreover, the orthodoxy insists that no one else has ever heard of such fans.
- His claims about how and when cremations started are also out of sync with the mainstream narrative.

Like so many other witnesses, Turowski took local rumors and seasoned them with his own anachronistic and fanciful stories as he saw fit. (For more details, see Mattogno 2021e, pp. 163f.; https://zapisyterroru.pl/.)

TYPHUS

Typhus fevers are a group of diseases caused by bacteria that are transmitted by parasitic insects, such as fleas, lice and chiggers. In the context of the Holocaust, epidemic typhus is relevant. Epidemic typhus is also sometimes called European, classic, or louse-borne typhus, as well as jail fever. The disease is caused by the bacteria *rickettsia prowazekii*. It was discovered in 1910 by Howard Ricketts and in 1913 by Stanislaus Prowazek. It is a micro-organism found in the intestines and salivary glands of infected lice.

Body louse.

Whereas typhus is the term commonly used in English to refer to all diseases caused by various rickettsia bacteria, the German term for epidemic typhus is *"Fleckfieber."* This German term's literal translation into English – "spotted fever" – is used in the English language for a different disease, the Rocky Mountain Spotted Fever, which is transferred by ticks.

The symptoms of epidemic typhus are high fever, obstruction of the throat, rapid breathing, coughing, body and muscle aches, vomiting and nausea. Dehydration and a rapid loss of body weight compound the disease. Most important in this context is a marked psychosis at the peak of the illness, an inces-

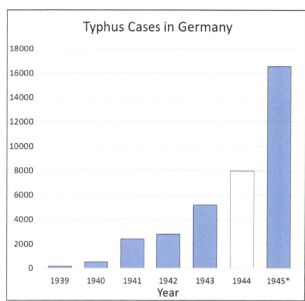
Typhus cases in Germany as officially recorded and published by the German civilian authorities (1939 through 1943) and as encountered by U.S. troops in their zone of occupation (1945). No data is available for 1944. The numbers for the years 1939 through 1943 do not include typhus cases in German labor or concentration camps, otherwise those numbers would be vastly higher.

sant state of delirium. The word typhus actually comes from the Greek word "τυφος" meaning stupor, referring to the frenzy developed by the sick. It results in nightmarish delusions which, if not treated therapeutically, can mislead cured patients to think that their deluded imaginations were real experiences.

During World War II, German authorities desperately tried finding an efficient vaccination against the disease, among them by experimenting with new vaccine candidates on concentration-camp inmates. These experiments were ultimately unsuccessful. To this day, there is no vaccination against this disease.

Epidemic typhus has been endemic in eastern Europe for centuries, and has caused repeated epidemic outbreaks, causing the death of thousands and even millions. During times of war, typhus and dysentery killed more people in Europe than did wounds inflicted by armed conflict. Typhus was extinct in Germany by the late 1800s, but it returned during World War I through the eastern front, claiming thousands of lives among German soldiers. Drastic measures to disinfest soldier's clothes were implemented.

The same scenario unfolded again during World War II, intensely exacerbated by the many overcrowded labor, concentration and PoW camps with insufficient sanitary and hygienic facilities. Disastrous outbreaks of the disease in camps such as Auschwitz (1942/43) and Bergen-Belsen (late 1944/45) caused tens of thousands of inmates to lose their lives. Massive attempts were made to suppress the disease with improved sanitary camp facilities and lice-killing insecticides such as Zyklon B and DDT, as well as other techniques, such as hot-air and microwave disinfestation. However, these measures collapsed at war's end, when no supplies reached the camps anymore due to Germany's destroyed production and transport infrastructure.

These attempts at staving off this disease were subverted by Polish partisans who *deliberately* spread lice infested with this disease throughout occupied Poland. This type of illegal biological warfare against the German occupants may have been one reason why the German camp authorities at Auschwitz and in other camps never got the disease fully under control. The primary victims of this Polish warfare were camp inmates, hence probably their own compatriots. The piles of dead typhus victims were then used after the war as propaganda material to accuse the Germans of a policy of extermination against their prisoners.

Extract from a report of the Polish underground army to the to the Allies' Combined Chiefs of Staff dated 7 September 1943: "3. Activities of retaliation [...] Typhoid-fever microbes and typhoid-fever lice: in a few hundred cases." Since typhoid fever is caused by a type of salmonella bacterium spread through food and water, while epidemic typhus is spread by lice, this is clearly a bad translation. Lice spread typhus, not typhoid fever.

Some preposterous eyewitness accounts about alleged experiences at camps such as Auschwitz may be partly explained by nightmarish fantasies which accompany the disease. Tens of thousands of inmates contracted the disease there, and many of them ultimately survived it due to German medical care. Of course, none of them received any therapy afterwards to process their psychotic delusions.

(For more details, see Humm 2004; Rudolf 2004a; 2020, pp. 68-70; 2023, pp. 374-376.)

U

UHLENBROCK, KURT

Kurt Uhlenbrock (2 March 1908 – 7 Aug. 1992), SS *Sturmbannführer*, was a German physician serving in an SS armored infantry division until 7 August 1942, when he was transferred to the Auschwitz Camp as garrison physician. His primary task was to combat the typhus epidemic which had gotten out of control there and had killed the previous garrison physician Siegfried Schwela on 10 May 1942. However, Uhlenbrock contracted typhus himself relatively quickly, got seriously sick, and barely survived. He was replaced while sick by Eduard Wirths on 4 September 1942, and left Auschwitz for good on 2 October 1942.

UKRAINE

Ukraine had four roles within the context of the Holocaust:
1. Perpetrator
2. Crime Scene
3. Victim
4. Propaganda Podium

Perpetrator
The Ukrainian people suffered incredible hardships during the Bolshevist revolution and even more so under the subsequent Stalinist rule, in particular during the Holodomor. Most Ukrainians were probably keenly aware of the predominance of people with a Jewish background among their oppressors.

For these reasons, in the eyes of most non-Jewish Ukrainians, the Germans came as liberators from both Soviet and Jewish oppression. Many of them did not wait for German armed forces to show up, but started pogroms as the Soviets retreated. Others were eager helpers of whatever the Germans planned to do with the Soviets and the Jews. They were more than willing to start pogroms or even lend assistance during executions.

Many volunteered to guard prison, PoW, labor and concentration camps. Based on numerous witness testimonies, the orthodox narrative has it even that Ukrainian helpers, so-called Trawnikis (derived from the Trawniki training camp), played a crucial role among those who are said to have run the so-called extermination camps.

Crime Scene
Not just one, but two *Einsatzgruppen* – C and D – were active in Ukraine. The most infamous crime scene associated with these units is on the outskirts of Ukraine's capital Kiev: Babi Yar. The Janowska Road Camp near Lviv is also among the better-known places connected with the Holocaust.

Victim
The *Einsatzgruppen*'s ranked death-toll list includes several entries for Ukrainian locations:

Location	Victims
Kiev	33,776
Kamenets-Podolsky	23,600
Nikolayev, Kherson	22,467
Rovno	15,240
Dnepropetrovsk	10,350
Simferopol	10,300
Odessa	10,000
Lviv	8,154
Zhitomir	4,843

Ukraine was completely occupied by Germany, and many parts of it for a long time. This put all of Ukraine's remaining Jews in mortal danger, and many paid with their life for the wrath of the revolution's victims,' and their foreign masters' lust for revenge. (For the complete list, see the section "Documented History" of the entry on the *Einsatzgruppen*.)

Propaganda Podium
At war's end, Ukraine was turned into a podium for anti-German and anti-Ukrainian propaganda spread by Stalinist show trials and mock investigative commissions. The most famous of these show trials was staged in late 1943 in Kharkov. The most prominent collection of Soviet forensic investigations into alleged German atrocities is titled *Nazi Crimes in the Ukraine*. It was published in an English translation right after the hysterical climax of the Jerusalem show trial against the exiled Ukrainian John Demjanjuk (Denisov/Changuli 1987; to grasp their propaganda content, see the section "Soviet Propaganda Claims" of the entry on *Aktion* 1005).

In more recent times, French Priest Patrick Desbois turned the search for mass graves into a public spectacle, thus drawing media attention to the killing fields of Ukraine. However, he focused only on those graves which presumably contain Jewish bodies, with perhaps a total of many tens of thousands, up to a few hundred thousand victims. These may all be wartime victims of the Germans and their collaborators (see Mattogno 2015a). However, there has never been any comparable media spectacle for the many millions of non-Jewish Ukrainians who were victims of the Soviets and their collaborators from the prewar and postwar periods. This double-standard is hard to reconcile with known facts.

ultra-shortwave delousing → **Microwave Delousing**

UTHGENANNT, OTTO

Otto Uthgenannt (born 1935) was a German claiming to have been incarcerated at the Buchenwald Camp. For years he traveled throughout Germany, telling school students his stories of suffering – until a German newspaper exposed him as a notorious, previously convicted forger and fraudster. Germany's Jewish newspaper pointed out the core problem:

Otto Uthgenannt

> "[German-Jewish] *Historian Julius Schoeps* [...] *said: 'Such cases are getting more frequent.'* [...] The *pattern works as follows: 'By being a victim, I gain new friends who don't question me.' It is precisely the monstrosity of the Nazi terror which almost prohibits asking critical questions when someone tells about his suffering."*

In fact, Jewish lobby groups have always been at the forefront of those demanding the persecution and prosecution of anyone who dares scrutinize "survivor" testimony and expose false witnesses. Any failure of critical inquiry is due to their own efforts.
(For sources, see Rudolf 2023, pp. 438f.)

V

VAILLANT-COUTURIER, MARIE-CLAUDE

Marie-Claude Vaillant-Couturier

Marie-Claude Vaillant-Couturier (née Vogel; 3 Nov. 1912 – 11 Dec. 1996) was a communist member of the French resistance against the German occupation during World War II. She was arrested on 9 February 1942 by the French police, and on 24 January 1943 deported to Auschwitz-Birkenau. She arrived there three days later and was initially assigned to earthworks, but was later deployed at the inmate infirmary due to her knowledge of German. She joined the inmates' communist-dominated camp resistance involved in spreading atrocity propaganda. In August 1945, she was transferred to the woman's camp at Ravensbrück.

In 1945, she had her alleged camp experiences published in a brochure titled *Auschwitz*, in which she also described – necessarily from hearsay – the presumed gassing procedure. On 28 January 1946, she testified at the Nuremberg International Military Tribunal. As her hearsay sources, she claimed a little French girl assigned to undressing infants in a crematorium – in itself a unique claim – and unspecified *Sonderkommando* members. The pertinent and peculiar claims of her accounts include:

- During homicidal gassings, gas capsules were thrown through an opening in the ceiling. However, the orthodoxy has it that Zyklon-B pellets were poured into Zyklon-B introduction devices built into openings in the roof.
- The killing with gas took five minutes for women and three for men. However, in a facility without means to accelerate the evaporation of the liquid poison from the carrier material, and its dissipation into the large room, such short execution times are physically impossible.
- She personally saw immense flames escaping from the crematorium chimneys, although such a phenomenon is technically impossible with coke-fired crematoria.
- It took only "a few minutes" to turn people into ashes, although it took an hour to cremate one body in the Auschwitz crematoria.
- There were allegedly eight cremation furnaces at Auschwitz, when in fact the Birkenau Camp had four crematoria with together 12 furnaces with 46 muffles total.
- Ditches for open-air incineration of corpses were filled with dry branches soaked in a flammable liquid. They were set on fire, and only then were corpses or living children thrown into them. However, some dry branches would not have done the job. Large stakes of wood would have been needed, since the self-immolation of bodies is a mere myth. However, if she meant huge stacks of wood set ablaze, then the resulting fire would not have allowed anyone to approach it. Bodies thrown in afterwards would have had to be tossed with catapults from a safe distance.
- The gas-chamber doors were supposedly opened 5 or 7 minutes after the start of the execution, hence without prior ventilation. However, ventilation was obligatory and would have taken many hours.
- Without further comment: The SS had a spanking machine to punish naughty inmates (*IMT*, Vol. 6, p. 213):

    "One of the most usual punishments was 50 blows with a stick on the loins. They were administered with a machine which I saw, a swinging apparatus manipulated by an SS."

It is a bad idea to let mortal enemies – here Communists versus National Socialists – testify against each other, for we are unlikely to hear the truth. (For more details, see Mattogno 2021, pp. 374f.)

VAN DEN BERGH, SIEGFRIED

Siegfried van den Bergh was an Auschwitz inmate who, right after the war, wrote his war memoirs. Regarding mass murder at Auschwitz, he made the following peculiar claims:

- Poison gas was emitted into the gas chamber through showerheads. However, the product allegedly used at Auschwitz, Zyklon B, contains liquid hydrogen cyanide absorbed on gypsum pel-

lets. The liquid poison evaporates slowly, and the developing gas is not under pressure, hence cannot be ducted through pipework
- The victims allegedly died immediately. However, since the gas evaporated and spread out slowly in the absence of any means to heat and dissipate the toxic fumes, no instant murder would have been possible.
- The gas-chamber floor opened, so that the bodies fell into carts below, which brought them to the cremation furnaces. However, no opening-floor mechanism with carts beneath ever existed at Auschwitz (or anywhere else).
- Flames many meters long came out of the chimneys. However, with the smoke and chimney ducts together almost 30 m long, no flames could have come out of the chimneys.

(For more details, see Mattogno 2021, pp. 295f.)

VAN HERWAARDEN, MARIA

Maria van Herwaarden was a young German woman who was incarcerated at Auschwitz and Birkenau from December 1942 to January 1945 for having had a sexual relationship with a Polish man. She testified as a witness for the defense during the Second Zündel Trial in Toronto in 1988.

Already on the way to Auschwitz, she stated, rumors spread that they would be gassed on arrival. Hence, during the admission procedure at Auschwitz, after having been shaved, van Herwaarden was "terribly scared" when entering the shower room because "they said gas would be coming from the top, but it was only water."

During her stay at the camp, van Herwaarden used the camp's sauna facility twice.

Van Herwaarden insisted that Jewish inmates at Birkenau were treated the same way as other prisoners.

When she became seriously ill, she was admitted to the infirmary and was nursed back to health.

She estimated that the smoking chimneys she saw were some 5 km away from the camp. This is roughly the distance from the Birkenau Camp to the Buna Factory of the I.G. Farbenindustrie, near the town of Monowitz. A lot of coke was burned there to generate electricity and produce process gas.

Whereas she saw many prisoners die in the camp from diseases, and several commit suicide, she never saw any prisoners killed. She was unaware as to how these dead inmates were disposed of, and could not remember seeing a crematorium. During the time she was at Auschwitz, she asserted that she saw nothing that pointed at a mass murder of Jews. While gassing rumors were bandied about at the camp, she personally never saw anything of the sort.

(For more details, see Kulaszka 2019, pp. 277-279.)

VAN RODEN, EDWARD L.

Edward van Roden

Edward van Roden (1892-1973) was a Pennsylvania judge who served on a special postwar committee (The Simpson Commission) to investigate possible prisoner abuse and torture by Americans against captive Germans.

Among the many war crimes of World War Two was the Malmedy Massacre of 17 December 1944. During the Battle of the Bulge, some 120 US soldiers were captured and (allegedly) executed by a Waffen-SS group. In mid-1946, and as part of the postwar Dachau Trials, American prosecutors tried 74 German officers and soldiers for the murders. Eventually, 43 of them were sentenced to death by hanging.

During the trial, several defendants complained about torture and duress of various kinds. Later, about a year and a half after the trial, almost all defendants issued affidavits, complaining of abuse and rescinding their earlier confessions. As a result, U.S. Secretary of the Army Kenneth Royall created the Simpson Commission in mid-1948, which was tasked with investigating these claims. As stated, van Roden was a member of that commission. He traveled with chair Gordon Simpson to Munich in order to investigate the matter.

While there, van Roden was appalled by what he heard, both from the remaining living Germans and from the American prosecutorial team. Upon returning to the U.S., van Roden began to speak out publicly regarding his findings, eventually releasing an article titled "American atrocities in Germany" (*The Progressive*, Feb. 1949, pp. 21f.). The article included several shocking assertions. It opens thusly:

"American investigators at the U. S. Court in Dachau, Germany, used the following methods to obtain confessions: Beatings and brutal kickings. Knocking out teeth and breaking jaws. Mock tri-

als. Solitary confinement. Posturing as priests. Very limited rations. Spiritual deprivation. Promises of acquittal."

Van Roden worried that, if unpunished, these abuses "would be a blot on the American conscience for eternity," so reprehensible were they.

At issue was the behavior of the American prosecution team. Though van Roden did not mention it, this team, like most at Nuremberg and Dachau, were heavily Jewish. The Malmedy team included Burton Ellis, Paul Shumacker, William Perl, Morris Ellowitz, Herbert Strong, and Harry Thon, along with a certain Kirschbaum, a Steiner, and a Rosenthal. The legal advisor was Col. A. H. Rosenfeld.

Van Roden elaborated on the process:

"The American prohibition of hear-say evidence had been suspended. Second and third-hand testimony was admitted, although the Judge Advocate General warned against the value of hearsay evidence, especially when it was obtained, as this was, two or three years after the act. Lt. Col. Ellis and Lt. Perl of the Prosecution pleaded that it was difficult to obtain competent evidence. Perl told the court, 'We had a tough case to crack and we had to use persuasive methods.' He admitted to the court that the persuasive methods included various 'expedients, including some violence and mock trials.' He further told the court that the cases rested on statements obtained by such methods."

Here, Jewish prosecutors Ellis and Perl admitted that they used "persuasive methods" to obtain desired results. Van Roden continued:

"Our investigators [Ellis, Perl et al.] would put a black hood over the accused's head and then punch him in the face with brass knuckles, kick him, and beat him with rubber hose. Many of the German defendants had teeth knocked out. Some had their jaws broken. All but two of the Germans, in the 139 cases we investigated, had been kicked in the testicles beyond repair. This was Standard Operating Procedure with American investigators. Perl admitted use of mock trials and persuasive methods including violence and said the court was free to decide the weight to be attached to evidence thus received. But it all went in."

Those who studied the Nuremberg Military Tribunals will concur that such torture was indeed "standard operating procedure" for the Americans.

Also troubling to van Roden were the mock trials, often with a religious theme:

"Sometimes a prisoner who refused to sign was led into a dimly lit room, where a group of civilian investigators, wearing U. S. Army uniforms, were seated around a black table with a crucifix in the center and two candles burning, one on each side. 'You will now have your American trial,' the defendant was told. The sham court passed a sham sentence of death. Then the accused was told, 'You will hang in a few days, as soon as the general approves this sentence: but in the meantime, sign this confession and we can get you acquitted.' Some still wouldn't sign. We were shocked by the crucifix being used so mockingly.

In another case, a bogus Catholic priest (actually an investigator) entered the cell of one of the defendants, heard his confession, gave him absolution, and then gave him a little friendly tip: 'Sign whatever the investigators ask you to sign. It will get you your freedom. Even though it's false, I can give you absolution now in advance for the lie you'd tell.'"

Such revelations by a respected American judge cast doubt on virtually all postwar confessions, including gassings of Jews, numbers killed, and alleged views of Hitler, Himmler, and other higher-ups.

VEIL, SIMONE

Simone Veil

Simone Jacob, whose last name changed to Veil after marrying, was a young Jewish woman from France who was deported to Auschwitz in April 1944. When Polish historian Danuta Czech wrote the first edition of her *Auschwitz Chronicle*, she reported that not a single woman of the transport with which Ms. Jacob arrived at Auschwitz had been registered there. Hence, Mrs. Czech jumped to the unproven conclusion that all these women had been gassed. Hence, Ms. Jacob had been gassed on arrival as well.

In 1979, Simone Veil, née Jacob, became the first president of the newly created European Parliament.

In the second edition of her *Auschwitz Chronicle* of 1989/1990, Danuta Czech corrected this and other similar errors. She had now found 223 women from that transport who had been registered after all. Unable to learn from past mistakes, she declared that those about whose fate she had no information were "killed in the gas chambers" – with not a shred of evidence to back this up.

When the writings of French Holocaust skeptic Dr. Robert Faurisson attracted a lot of public attention in the early 1980s in France, Mrs. Veil stated the following regarding the skeptics' claim on the lack of credible evidence for the existence of homicidal gas chambers at Auschwitz:

> "Everyone knows that the Nazis destroyed these gas chambers and systematically eradicated all the witnesses."

This statement is false for two reasons: First, because some claimed homicidal gas chambers are said to have survived. Second, many witnesses who claimed to have seen homicidal gas chambers survived and testified during and after the war. This is demonstrated by the long yet still-incomplete list of witnesses in the present work. However, an analysis of these accounts also reveals their unprecedented unreliability.

Simone Veil's statement is moreover a logical fallacy. If a claim cannot be demonstrated to be true because of a lack of evidence, then the claim is simply not true. Claiming that all evidence was destroyed in turn requires evidence that this claim is true. Hence, Mrs. Veil tried to rescue her primary thesis – homicidal gas chambers existed – by supporting it with an auxiliary hypothesis – all evidence was destroyed. This auxiliary hypothesis immunizes the primary thesis from any attempt at refuting it, and is thus impermissible. If such an argument were allowed, then any claim, no matter how insane, would have to be true, if accompanied by claims that all evidence for its veracity has been destroyed.

(For more information, see Rudolf 2019, pp. 130-131, 181f., fn 36.)

VENEZIA, MORRIS

Morris Venezia

Morris (Maurice) Venezia (25 Feb. 1921 – 2 Sept. 2013) was an Italian Jew deported from Greece to Auschwitz, where he arrived on 11 April 1944 together with his brother Shlomo Venezia, among others. In contrast to his brother, he never elaborated in public in great detail what he claimed to have experienced while at Auschwitz. However, in 1996, he was interviewed by the University of Southern California's Shoah Foundation for almost four hours. He claimed that he was made to cut off the hair from the heads of dead women inside a large room of Crematorium II and/or III, but later worked on cremating bodies. His tale of what he experienced in that crematorium is full of internal and external contradictions, as well as technical impossibilities:

- He claimed that he worked as a member of the *Sonderkommando* in Crematorium III only for a short while. He then decided to hide each day when having to go to work, as he refused to do this work of extracting bodies from the gas chamber and cremating them in the furnaces. But then he insisted that he experienced the destruction of the Hungarian Jews (May-July 1944), the *Sonderkommando* revolt (October 1944) and the dismantling of the crematoria (November/December 1944) all while working at Crematorium III. Hence, he neither ever "hid" to avoid working, nor would the SS let him do it anyway.
- He asserted that he had no way of getting in contact with Jewish victims entering the crematorium to be gassed, but he described how they undressed, how the women reacted when seeing the naked men, how they entered the gas chamber, how the door was closed behind them, and how the victims screamed inside, for which he must have been present, which he said he was. Hence, he was in contact with these victims at all points of the process.
- He stated that the naked women walking to the gas chamber started screaming when seeing the naked men going there as well. However, either men and women were strictly separated in different crematoria, unable to see one another, or they undressed all together in the same room. There were no separate undressing rooms for different genders in these buildings. Therefore, the women could not *suddenly* see the group of naked men approaching.
- He affirmed multiple times that 3,000 inmates were packed into the underground gas chamber of Crematorium III. At 210 m², this amounts to a physically impossible packing density of 14.3 persons per m².
- When asked to describe the gas chamber, he merely said that "there is nothing to describe; it

was an empty room." However, that room had seven concrete pillars and, if we follow the orthodox narrative, four conspicuous Zyklon-B introduction devices. Venezia simply didn't know what to say, due to a profound lack of knowledge.
- He insisted that the gassing took only 3 to 4 minutes. This is technical nonsense, as gassings in much-better equipped U.S. execution gas chambers took on average ten minutes. At Auschwitz, they would have taken considerably longer than that. (See the entry on Zyklon B for details.)
- He claimed that ventilation was "nothing," as it went swiftly. However, the ventilation system installed was designed for morgues, not for gas chambers. It would have taken a long time to ventilate a room like this. (See the entry on ventilation for details.)
- He asserted that, when the doors were opened, the victims were still standing, because they were packed like sardines, hence could not fall over. Only their heads slumped. However, a packing density needed to achieve such an effect is physically impossible with people walking into a room.
- He stated that, after the gassing, they pulled out *all* the victims' teeth, because "at that time, everybody used to have golden teeth," which is blatant nonsense.
- He proclaimed that it took 15-20 minutes to burn a load of three bodies in a furnace of Crematorium III. However, the Auschwitz furnaces could burn only one body per muffle at a time within one hour. (See the Auschwitz section of the entry on crematoria for details.)
- He affirmed that, during the deportation of the Jews from Hungary, trenches with wood fires were always burning. Into these conflagrations, they would throw bodies that the crematoria could not process. However, air photos of that time prove that no such burning trenches existed. Furthermore, approaching such a blaze to throw in more bodies would have been possible only with heat-protective clothes, or catapults would have had to be used from a safe distance.
- He conveyed the tale how one of his cousins was trapped in the burning Crematorium IV during the Auschwitz *Sonderkommando* revolt on 7 October 1944. Trying to escape from the fire, he went to the upper floor, hiding in a bathroom. Eventually, the floor burned through, and he fell to the ground floor. However, that building had no upper floor.

None of what Morris Venezia told us about the extermination events presumably unfolding in the crematoria can be true. Each time he was asked for details or concrete data, his complete ignorance was exposed.

(See the interview at youtu.be/P-IinMCbdJA.)

VENEZIA, SHLOMO

Shlomo Venezia (29 Dec. 1923 – 1 Oct. 2012) was an Italian Jew deported from Greece to Auschwitz, where he arrived on 11 April 1944 together with his brother Morris Venezia and five other notorious false witnesses: Josef Sackar, Yaakov Gabai, Shaul Chasan, Leon Cohen and Daniel Bennahmias.

Shlomo Venezia

After three weeks of quarantine, Venezia was supposedly assigned to the so-called *Sonderkommando* of Birkenau Crematorium III (but also to that of Crematorium II and briefly to that of Bunker 2…).

After 50 years of contaminating his memories with ubiquitous mainstream Holocaust themes and tropes, he finally decided to make public statements about his alleged experiences by granting an interview in 1995. Six years later, he made a written deposition, followed by another interview in January 2002. Five years after that, he had his own book published that expanded on the theme even more. And last but not least, a hitherto-unpublished statement of his appeared in 2010.

Here are some of the peculiar claims Venezia made in his various statements, some of which were "aided" by mainstream historian Marcello Pezzetti, which probably means that they were brought in line with the orthodox narrative:
- He claimed that he and some 320 other inmates were selected on arrival. He can neither have counted this nor remembered it for so long – Venezia's cousin Yaakov Gabai "remembered" 700 selectees, And indeed, the number "accidentally" matches that printed in the orthodoxy's standard chronology of the camp (Czech 1990, p. 609).
- He claimed that bodies of deceased inmates were brought to a morgue in Birkenau's quarantine sector, where they were allegedly left to rot for two or three weeks. However, there was no morgue in that camp sector, and several documents show

that corpses were picked up twice a day throughout the camp and brought to the crematoria's morgues. In fact, Venezia uses the official German term for the basement morgues of Crematoria II and III – *Leichenkeller*. However, these supposedly served as undressing rooms and gas chambers. But if corpses were brought there for storage, then which rooms served the extermination purposes?

– When he claimed to have started working at Crematorium III, a "palisade three meters high" allegedly surrounded the building. However, a photo from the so-called *Auschwitz Album*, taken by SS men on occasion of the arrival of a train with Jews deported from Hungary (hence a little later than Venezia's first day at work – this photo is reproduced in Venezia's book) shows that this building had no palisade around it at all. However, Filip Müller mentioned this palisade in his account, which may be Venezia's source.

– According to his book, when weeding the yard of Crematorium II on his first day of work, Venezia noticed "a window" on eye level, peeked through it, and saw corpses piled up. However, this building had 47 windows on eye level.

– In his 2002 interview, however, he claimed that, on the first day of work, he was granted the privilege to work at the so-called "Bunker 2" for just one day, so he could witness a gassing and tell the world about it later. However, the orthodoxy insists that Bunker 2 was re-activated only with the arrival of transports from Hungary starting on 17 May 1944, hence several weeks after Venezia's alleged first day at work.

– To accomplish the gassing, an SS man dropped a box of "stuff" through a hatch, and ten minutes later, "the door" (singular) was opened. However, the mainstream narrative has it that *pellets* from a can of stuff (Zyklon B) were *poured* through *five* hatches, and *four* doors were opened afterwards. Incidentally, Venezia's wrong description matches a similarly flawed drawing by David Olère, which is reproduced in Venezia's book – another case of cross-pollination into the "convergence of evidence" on a lie.

– The imaginary gassing at Bunker 2 lasted only ten minutes. However, ten minutes is too short to kill people with Zyklon B without any means to accelerate the evaporation of the liquid poison from the carrier material and the dissipation into a large room.

– After the gassing, the doors were opened, and Venezia and his colleagues had to drag out the corpses right away. However, entering a room for heavy labor in which Zyklon B granules, poured among the victims, was still releasing its poison, would have been fatal in the long run without gas masks and protective clothes. Airing out such a place for many hours if not days would have been mandatory.

– The gassing victims' bodies were thrown onto a huge burning pit. However, with such a blaze causing severe burns to anyone approaching it, they must have used catapults to sling the corpses onto the blazing pyre from a safe distance.

– Corpses in open-air incineration pits burned all by themselves due to their body fat, which Venezia and his colleagues had to collect and pour back onto the burning pyre. However, the self-immolation of human bodies is a myth, and no fat from burning corpses can accumulate anywhere, let alone be collected, as it burns the instant it reaches a corpse's surface.

– The very few things Venezia says about Crematoria II and III are wrong: During a gassing, he and a colleague helped an SS man pour Zyklon B into "a manhole" on the morgue's roof. Therefore, Venezia helped mass-murder his fellow Jews! This runs contrary to the orthodox narrative, which has exclusively SS men doing that job, and there were supposedly four Zyklon-B introduction devices, not one manhole, through

Auschwitz-Birkenau; inmates deported from Hungary, probably in late May or June 1944, walking from the train westbound along the railway ramp, passing between Crematoria II and III. Crematorium III is visible in the background – with no obstruction by a palisade or anything similar. Photo taken from The Auschwitz Album *(Meier/Klarsfeld 1989).*

which the poison was allegedly poured. In reality, however, there weren't any openings in that roof at all.
- There were allegedly fake showerheads on the ceiling of the gas chamber. However, documents clearly show that these showers were real functioning showers.
- The gas-chamber door presumably looked like that of a walk-in fridge. However, all doors at Birkenau were made of wooden boards held together by iron bands and were manufactured by inmates in the camp's carpentry shop. Venezia may have taken that false description from another drawing by David Olère.
- Venezia insisted that SS men never wore any gas masks at the crematorium – that's because there never was any gas…
- He mentioned Josef Mengele's "Hungarian-Jewish physician assistant," which is a clear reference to Miklós Nyiszli. This indicates that Venezia was aware of, and influenced by, Nyiszli's book about Auschwitz.
- Like Miklós Nyiszli and his plagiarizer Filip Müller, Venezia insisted that the gas was "thrown on the ground" of the gas chamber, which was occupied by up to 1,700 people. The evaporating gas filled the chamber like water – from the bottom to the top. Consequently, the victims, in an attempt to reach higher layers with non-poisonous air, climbed "on top of each other until even the last one died." However, the active ingredient of Zyklon B, hydrogen cyanide, is insignificantly lighter than air and invisible. Hence, no such scene would have occurred. This proves that Venezia has never seen a real homicidal gassing with Zyklon B, and that he has plagiarized this scene either from Nyiszli and/or from Müller. In addition, the orthodoxy claims that Zyklon B wasn't thrown on the ground, but rather that it was retrievable via certain Zyklon-B introduction devices.
- When it comes to how corpses were dragged out of the gas chamber and to the furnaces, Venezia expressly refers to two drawings by David Olère as printed in his book. Other scenes Venezia describes are also evidently inspired by Olère's drawings printed in his book.
- Inspired by Nyiszli's invented story of a young woman who came out of the gas chamber alive, Venezia invented a similar scene. In his tale, the sole gassing survivor was a breast-feeding baby, allegedly kept alive, quote, "by the force of the suction at her mother's breast," unquote – which is pure nonsense.
- Two to three bodies were cremated in each muffle at once within 20 minutes. However, the cremation of one body took roughly an hour. Furthermore, had they managed to stuff three corpses into a muffle designed only for one body, it would have taken three times as long if not longer to cremate them. Hence, Venezia exaggerated the cremation capacity by a factor of nine. The same technically impossible data were mentioned by Nyiszli: three bodies per muffle within 20 minutes. However, Venezia contradicted himself on this topic numerous times.
- Venezia personally saw flames escaping from the crematorium chimneys, although such a phenomenon is technically impossible with coke-fired crematoria.

As can be seen, Venezia included almost all the false rumors and clichés about the extermination activities claimed for Auschwitz in order to beef up his story, including the untrue claim, evidently also copied from Nyiszly, that the members of the *Sonderkommando* were killed every four months to eliminate dangerous carriers of secrets – except for Venezia and his brother, of course.

Venezia's late narrative has gained much atten-

"Bunker 2." Drawn by David Olère in 1945, showing just one door and one window/hatch. (Klarsfeld 1989, p. 34)

tion worldwide. His book has been translated into 23 languages, including Arabic, Farsi (Persian) and Marathi (a language spoken in India). It has been hailed by the orthodoxy as the latest and one of most convincing stories yet about the gas chambers at Auschwitz, although it is mostly a regurgitation of invented themes spread by David Olère, Miklós Nyiszli and Filip Müller.

(For more details, see Mattogno 2022e, pp. 101-131.)

VENTILATION
Principles

By "ventilating" an enclosed space, we refer here to replacing old, stale or contaminated air with fresh, uncontaminated air. In an ideal scenario of a cuboid space (room), fresh air would be pushed in along the entire surface area of one end of the room, and stale air would be taken out along the entire surface area at the opposite end. With a laminar air flow, hence without any turbulence, a complete replacement of the entire air would happen after a fresh air volume equivalent of the room's volume has been pushed in. However, such an ideal setup does not exist in reality. Air inlets and outlets never cover the entire surface area of a wall, inlets and outlets are not always located at opposite ends of a room, and turbulences always happen. In fact, since the quantities and locations of inlets and outlets are never ideal, air turbulences are even necessary, so that air in areas that are not located along straight lines from inlets to outlets, is replaced as well.

A turbulent exchange of stale air with fresh air requires much more time to achieve a complete replacement of all air, since some of the fresh air inevitably gets expelled together with stale air. In cases of perfect mixing of fresh air with stale air, pushing in one complete room volume of fresh air leads to only some 2/3 of the stale air getting expelled, together with some 1/3 of fresh air. This partial reduction of remaining stale air continues with every new air exchange, so the fraction of stale air still in the room decreases exponentially with time. Of course, perfect mixing does not always happen either, so there will be areas in the room where the scenario is closer to a laminar air flow – along straight lines between inlet and outlet – and areas where mixing is occurring only slowly – in pockets distant from any air inlet and outlet. In the latter regions, the reduction of stale air is even slower.

In this context, it matters little whether "stale air" means merely a reduced amount of oxygen, or the presence of unpleasant smells, high humidity, aerosols or some toxic component.

Fumigations/Disinfestations

Any enclosed space can be disinfested with a gaseous chemical that is toxic to the targeted infesting organism. Wartime instructions issued by DEGESCH, the company that held the patent for Zyklon B, indicate that buildings disinfested with Zyklon B can be aired out with natural draft (without giving a time), once all windows and doors are opened, and provided that the premise is not tightly filled with objects (see Leuchter *et al.* 2017, p. 84). Wartime instructions issued by German authorities during the war stipulated that buildings disinfested with Zyklon B which do not have a forced (mechanical) ventilation ought to be air out for at least 20 hours (Nuremberg Document NI-9912, see Rudolf 2016, pp. 122f.).

A dedicated fumigation gas chamber usually has some ventilation system accelerating the airing-out process, either by sucking out the room's air with a fan, replacing it with air coming through a door, for example (which, when using a disinfestant toxic to humans, can be dangerous in the case of fan failure or opposing wind conditions), or by installing two

Auschwitz-Birkenau, inmates shower and disinfestation facility BW 5b, here the wing with the Zyklon-B fumigation chamber. Note the two openings for two air-extraction fans (now removed). Enlarged in the inset. (Photo of 1991.)

fans, one of which extracts air, while the other feeds in fresh air. Under optimal conditions, these fans are located at opposite ends of the room.

In German wartime camps, we find examples of dedicated Zyklon-B-fumigation gas chambers of a more rudimentary nature without mechanical ventilation (for instance at the Stutthof Camp, see Graf/Mattogno 2016, pp. 117-124), or with just one or two air-extraction fans set in one wall (at the Auschwitz Main Camp and at Birkenau, respectively, see Mattogno 2016f, pp. 240f.). Ventilating these facilities would have taken many hours before they could be entered without protective gear.

Furthermore, professionally designed Zyklon-B fumigation gas chambers existed, such as the DE-GESCH circulation chambers. These devices had powerful blowers that sucked in and extracted a volume of fresh air equal to the chamber's volume within less than a minute, hence going through more than 60 complete air exchanges per hour, allowing for a swift ventilation in much less than an hour, even if the chamber was stuffed with fumigated objects (see Rudolf 2023, pp. 127f.). Four such systems were installed at the Dachau Camp, where they are exhibited to this day.

Morgues

Every morgue, no matter the place and time of its existence, needs an efficient ventilation system to prevent the smell of rotting corpses from filling the place. A classic standard work on German architectural norms stipulates that a morgue requires a minimum of five air exchanges per hour and 10 during intensive use, such as in cases of war, natural disasters or epidemics.

Epidemics caused by the effects of war were exactly what Germany's wartime camps were facing. Hence, the ventilation systems planned and installed inside the morgues of the Birkenau Crematoria II and III had a capacity at the upper end of this range (see Rudolf 2016, pp. 173-176):
– Morgue #1 (the alleged homicidal gas chamber) had a capacity of 9.5 air exchanges per hour.
– Morgue #2 (the alleged undressing rooms) had 11 air exchanges per hour.

There were other systems in those buildings with higher capacities:
– The system serving the ground-level work area of the physician (dissecting room, laying-out room, washroom) had a capacity of some 10 air exchanges per hour.

Auschwitz Main Camp, Block 3. Round opening covered by a metal lid, which housed the air-extraction fan for the Zyklon-B fumigation chamber located on the second floor of the building. Enlarged in the inset. (Photo of 1992).

– The furnace room's ventilation system had a capacity of 9.7 air exchanges per hour.

We see that all systems were designed to have roughly 10 air exchanges per hour, hence at the upper end of architectural recommendations, as is to be expected.

Note that the room presumably misused as a homicidal gas chamber had a system that was *not* significantly different from all the other rooms, indicating that it was *not* planned to serve a sinister purpose. This design had been planned since the inception of that building in late 1941, hence at a time when even the orthodoxy agrees that no plans existed to misuse the facilities for mass homicide. This change in the room's purpose supposedly occurred sometime late 1942, but it did not result in an increase in the ventilation capacity of Morgue #1. This means that, from a technical point of view, its planned function did not change. (See Rudolf 2023, pp. 127f.; Mattogno/Poggi.)

Little documents have survived indicating what ventilation systems, if any, were installed in Crematoria IV and V in Birkenau. Evidently no such system was ever ordered or installed for Crematorium IV. A system ordered for Crematorium V seems to have been either never installed or only toward the summer of 1944. The drawing showing its design has been lost, so it is not clear which rooms were to be serviced with this system, which makes calculating a capacity speculative (See Mattogno 2019, pp. 156-158).

The morgue of the old crematorium at the Auschwitz Main Camp, which supposedly served as a homicidal gas chamber on an unknown number of occasions between late 1941 and early 1942, was never equipped with a proper ventilation system. In late 1940, the Topf Company had offered a system for the morgue providing for 20 air exchanges per hour. The camp authorities ordered a re-designed system in mid-March 1941, but since the delivery time was long, a makeshift solution was implemented connecting the morgue to the smoke duct of one of the two cremation furnaces next door, thus using the chimney's draft to suck out air from the morgue. This system worked so badly that it was decided in June 1941 to add fans in the building's roof, which were installed in early fall of 1941. The exact design is unknown, as no description or drawing has been preserved, but it has nothing to do with homicide, as the planning period (early June 1941) is well before any decision was allegedly made to commit mass murder at Auschwitz, let alone to convert this morgue for that purpose.

The proper ventilation system was delivered in late 1941, but by late 1942, at a time when the homicidal gassings claimed by the orthodoxy for this facility had allegedly ceased, it had still not been installed. Hence, that morgue never had a properly functioning ventilation system during the time span when it was supposedly misused for homicidal gassings. Furthermore, the camp authorities evidently saw no reason to install the delivered system at a time when they were allegedly misusing this room for mass homicide with toxic gases. This indicates that no homicidal gassing ever occurred in that room. (See Mattogno 2016f, pp. 17-23.)

Homicidal Gassings

Real-world data about the ventilation of homicidal gas chambers can be gleaned from the hydrogen-cyanide gas chamber systems once used in some U.S. states for capital punishment. After an execution, the chamber's powerful ventilation system carried out numerous air exchanges within fifteen minutes, after which the chamber was entered with protective gear to remove the victim. The fan was left running until the next day to ensure that any residues of the toxic gas were removed. (See Leuchter *et al.* 2017, p. 205.)

The necessity and technology of ventilating any claimed German wartime mass-execution chambers would have depended on the toxic gas claimed to have been used.

In the case of engine-exhaust gasses, as claimed for the gas vans as well as for stationary chambers at the camps at Belzec, Sobibór and Treblinka, mechanical ventilation systems would not have been required, because the exhaust gases allegedly used were not highly toxic: diesel-engine exhaust gases were not lethal in the short run at all, and gasoline-engine exhaust gases would have required extended exposures to full concentrations to have an effect. Therefore, natural ventilation by simply opening doors at both ends of a room filled with such gases would have swiftly rendered the air in such rooms non-lethal under any circumstances. Since the lethal component of exhaust gases – carbon monoxide – is not water soluble and thus does not accumulate on wet bodies, a large pile of entangled bodies, though slowing air movement down, would not have caused a major challenge, as the amount of exhaust fumes lingering between corpses would not have been enough to kill anyone when moving a body.

The situation is drastically different when using Zyklon B, meaning hydrogen cyanide, however, as is claimed for the camps at Auschwitz Main Camp, Birkenau, Stutthof, and also Majdanek (at least claimed in the past), as well as a string of minor

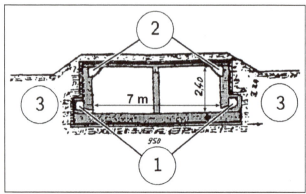

Auschwitz-Birkenau, construction blueprint of Crematorium II + III, cross section through Morgue #1 (alleged homicidal gas chamber); numbers added: 1: air-extraction ducts; 2: air-intake ducts; 3: soil.

events claimed in western camps (see the entry on homicidal gas chambers). Hydrogen cyanide is much more toxic than carbon monoxide, and it is also highly water soluble, making it accumulate on moist surfaces. This results in much longer ventilation times, and thus the need for powerful mechanical ventilation systems.

The scenario of hundreds or thousands of humans tightly packed into an execution chamber leads to complications comparable to fumigations of moist laundry and clothes that greatly exacerbate the difficult ventilation challenge:
- During fumigations, clothes and linens are put on hangers on fumigation racks, hence they hang loosely. Consequently, fresh air can freely flow around and through them, facilitating the venting process. However, air cannot move freely around and through a large pile of collapsed humans lying on top of each other. In fact, ventilating the air around and underneath those victims becomes almost impossible.
- During fumigations, air temperatures were kept warm, in part to make sure that the clothes and linens are dry, so that no gas gets absorbed in any humidity. However, human skin is by definition moist, and even more so when under stress in a struggle for life and death, not to mention any bodily fluids released in the ensuing panic. Therefore, a large pile of dead humans, moist for numerous reasons, would have absorbed considerable quantities of hydrogen cyanide, further prolonging any ventilation process.

For these reasons, the minimum duration for a successful ventilation of a fumigated premise mentioned in German wartime instructions – 20 hours if not more – would have applied most certainly to any mass gassing in large rooms that did not have any mechanical ventilation equipment. In fact, considering the knowledge and skills of German experts on fumigations with Zyklon B as demonstrated by the forced-ventilated fumigation chambers built in many wartime camps, it is inconceivable that any mass-execution chamber applying Zyklon B ever would have been built without a powerful mechanical ventilation system. Any claims to the contrary can be safely dismissed as wartime propaganda.

Furthermore, any claim that such mass-execution rooms not equipped with mechanical ventilation systems were entered instantly or within 10, 20 or 30 minutes of opening the room's doors and/or windows merely serves to highlight the physically impossible propaganda nature of these claims.

In the case of Auschwitz, this applies to homicidal gassing claims in the so-called bunkers of Birkenau, in Crematorium IV, and any such gassings in Crematorium V before the summer of 1944, none of which are said to have had any ventilation systems. To make matters worse, Zyklon B is said to have been poured amongst the inmates in these facilities, releasing its poison slowly for at least an hour, and perhaps up to two hours, depending on ambient conditions. Hence, no ventilation success could have been achieved *at all* before all hydrogen cyanide had evaporated.

Although Morgue #1 of Crematoria II and III in Birkenau, the alleged homicidal gas chamber, had a ventilation system, it was clearly planned and designed for a morgue, not for homicidal gassings. It was moreover badly designed, as air intake and outlet were located on the same wall, only some 2 m apart, so that fresh air blown in through the inlets near the ceiling was to a large degree sucked out again through the outlets near the floor rather than flowing across the 7-meter-wide room to the outlets on the other side. Hence, air in the center of that room was poorly ventilated.

Using an unheated basement room with inevitably cool and moist walls for gassings with Zyklon B is a very bad idea, since cool and moist walls absorb large quantities of the poison. When aired out, the walls then slowly release the absorbed poison, slowing the ventilation process. Moreover, the air-extraction openings in these rooms were located at floor level, where dead bodies would have obstructed them at least partly, further slowing the ventilation process. (See Mattogno/Poggi.)

A successful ventilation in these rooms would have depended on whether the applied Zyklon B could be removed after the gassing, which depends on the nature of the Zyklon-B introduction device claimed for this room (see this entry). Without the ability to remove the poison, successful ventilation would have lasted several hours. In case Zyklon B could be removed, the duration could be reduced to maybe an hour, although pockets of gas would have persisted among the piles of bodies. Claims that the doors were opened only minutes after the execution and that the bodies were removed right away are simply false.

Vernichtung → Extirpation
VHF delousing → Microwave Delousing

VOSS, PETER

Peter Voss, allegedly born on 18 December 1897 in Flensburg, Germany, is said to have been an SS *Oberscharführer* deployed at the Auschwitz Camp. However, there does not seem to exist any documentation about the presence or activity of a person with that name at that camp.

Voss is mentioned (with spelling varieties) as a cruel SS boss of the Birkenau crematoria by several witnesses, among them Henryk Tauber, Stanisław Jankowski, Henryk Mandelbaum and Filip Müller. (See the entries on these witnesses to assess their trustworthiness; see also the entries on Erich Mussfeldt and Otto Moll.)

The postwar fate of this Peter Voss, if he existed, is equally unknown.

VRBA, RUDOLF

Rudolf Vrba (born as Walter Rosenberg, 11 Sept. 1924 – 27 March 2006) was a Slovakian Jew deported to the Majdanek Camp on 14 June 1942, and 16 days later, on 30 June, transferred to the Auschwitz Camp. Initially, he was employed at the inmate property warehouse of the Main Camp, sorting and registering the property which inmates brought along. Later, he served as a clerk in a section of Construction Sector II in Birkenau. He claims to have been involved in the camp's clandestine resistance movement.

Rudolf Vrba

On 7 April 1944, he managed to escape together with Alfred Wetzler. They reached Slovakia, where their stories were typed up in a report that was first published in a German translation in Switzerland on 17 May 1944. Together with two other reports of three other escapees (Jerzy Tabeau, Czesław Mordowicz, Arnošt Rosin), the Vrba-Wetzler Report was published in English translations by the U.S. government as the so-called War Refugee Board Report. As such, the story told by Vrba and Wetzler about what was happening at Auschwitz was made known all over the world. Hence, the impact and thus the importance of this report for the formation of the orthodox Auschwitz narrative can hardly be overestimated.

Riding the Holocaust-propaganda wave triggered by the Eichmann Trial in 1961, a series of stories by Vrba was published in the British newspaper *Daily Herald*. Two years later, this series appeared as a book titled *I Cannot Forgive*, although it was at least partly ghostwritten by the journalist Alan Bestic. Vrba testified during the Frankfurt Auschwitz show trial, and was interviewed by Claude Lanzmann for the documentary *Shoah*, although it does not contain any specific claims about the alleged extermination at Auschwitz or any information on how he has received information about it. His last testimony was during the First Zündel Trial in 1985 in Toronto, Canada.

Here are some of the most pertinent and peculiar claims made by Vrba in his report co-authored with Wetzler and in his book:

– A drawing attached to the report allegedly shows the layout of Crematoria II and III, which the text explains in more detail. However, it is all wrong:
  1. In their drawing, the furnace room shows nine furnaces with four muffles each arranged in a semi-circle around a chimney, when in reality there were five furnaces with three muffles each arranged in a straight line, at a good distance from the chimney.
  2. In their drawing, the two morgues (alleged undressing room and gas chamber) are on the same level as the furnace room, all arranged in a straight line. In reality, the furnace room was on ground level, the two morgues in the basement, arranged in a rectangle and linked via a hallway and vestibule.
  3. In their drawing, the gas chamber was linked to the furnace room with a set of rails, upon which carts filled with corpses were driven to the furnaces. In reality, a freight elevator transported bodies from the basement upstairs.
– The report claims that victims were issued towels and soap before entering the gas chamber. This most certainly would never have happened, considering the mess it would have created and the effort necessary to retrieve and clean these items afterwards. In addition, no one takes towels into a shower.
– The report claims that three bodies were cremated in a muffle at once within 90 minutes. However, adding several corpses into a muffle designed to burn one body in one hour would not have been possible already due to the small introduction door, and would have lasted much longer than 90 minutes.

- In total, Crematoria II and III each could allegedly cremate 2,000 corpses per day (which was also the claimed capacity of the undressing room). This stands in contrast to the actual theoretical maximum of some 300 bodies per day. Unhappy with this "low" cremation capacity compared to other survivor claims, Vrba doubled that to 4,000 per day in his 1963 book.
- The gas was poured into the room through "three traps," while the orthodoxy insists on four Zyklon-B introduction devices.
- The time required for the gassing was only three minutes. However, in a facility without means to accelerate the evaporation of the liquid poison from the carrier material (Zyklon B) and the dissipation into the large room, such short execution times are physically impossible.
- Vrba claimed to have seen, counted and memorized the data of all transports of Jews that arrived at Auschwitz during his time at the camp, so that he could write the data down once he had escaped. Thus, a list in the report, which was admitted as Document L-002 at the Nuremberg International Military Tribunal (IMT, Vol. 37, p. 433), sums up the total numbers of inmates from every affected European country, who were allegedly gassed at Auschwitz between April 1942 and April 1944, resulting in a total of 1,765,000 victims. However, according to wartime documents analyzed by mainstream historians, in that same period, only a little over 500,000 Jews were deported to Auschwitz, not all of whom are said to have been gassed.
- In 1961, Vrba claimed that, according to his calculations, some 2,500,000 people were murdered at Auschwitz within three years – as opposed to the current orthodox figure of roughly a million for the entire camp's existence.
- Vrba's references to transports allegedly gassed and the bodies burned on pyres are not compatible with the documented or even the orthodox chronology. At the time this is said to have occurred (early 1942), open-air incinerations weren't said to have commenced yet (they started in September 1942). Moreover, all deportees of transports he mentioned that arrived prior to July 1942 were registered and admitted to the camp, so there were no gassings at all.
- The utterly wrong description of the crematoria proves that Wetzler and Vrba had not received any information in this regard, hence cannot have been in contact with any inmate working in those facilities, or if they were in touch with any such person, Vrba and Wetzler evidently never asked for a description, hence weren't interested in facts. Instead, their whole description was invented from scratch, either by Vrba on his own accord or by the camp's resistance movement, evidently without any input from crematorium workers. Yet Vrba claimed repeatedly that Sonderkommando members were the source of his information, and several survivors later claimed that crematorium workers had been in close contact with the resistance movement. One of them later even confirmed what Vrba had written in his book, that he had provided the data and even a floor plan of the crematorium to Vrba: the plagiarizer Filip Müller. In fact, several people involved in this plot told different, mutually contradictory stories about who gave what information to whom. None of them tell the truth. This story was made up from scratch, and everybody wanted a piece of the fame built on this lie, adding more layers of mendacity to the story.
- Although there is no evidence that Adolf Eichmann had ever been to Auschwitz, he is featured prominently in Vrba's 1961 series of articles published opportunistically on occasion of Eichmann's trial in Jerusalem. Vrba falsely stated that Eichmann visited the camp in 1942 and again on occasion of the inauguration of the first Birkenau

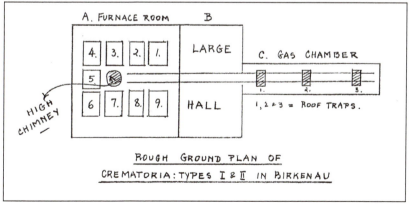

Rudolf Vrba's freely invented floor-plan sketch of Crematoria II and III, as published with the War Refugee Board Report. Compare this layout with the real layout as shown in the illustrations contained in the Auschwitz-Birkenau section of the entry on crematoria.

Crematorium in early 1943, celebrating this event together with Himmler and his entourage. Both are completely invented stories.
- In the 1961 series of articles, Vrba promoted himself to a member of the Sonderkommando allegedly involved in exhuming the corpses of 20,000 Soviet PoWs – although only 12,000 Soviet PoWs ever reached Auschwitz.
- While he had no specific knowledge of the alleged murders at the so-called "bunkers" before 1961, in that year he promoted himself to a member of the Sonderkommando working there as well.
- Vrba saw an open-air incineration trench "half a mile long and 30 yards wide" being dug at Auschwitz, which is preposterous nonsense.

In his 1963 book *I Cannot Forgive*, Vrba ratcheted up his mendacity one more notch, circulating black propaganda and entangling himself in contradictions:
- Synchronized with Wetzler's identical change in his 1964 book *What Dante Didn't See*, Vrba also increased the cremation capacity by reducing the time it allegedly took to cremate three corpses from 90 minutes (1944) to 20 minutes.
- He claimed that he saw with his own eyes that Himmler visited Auschwitz in January 1943, who came to witness the gassing of not 8,000 Jews as in his 1944 report, but of only 3,000.
- The corpses were no longer hauled to the furnaces in carts on rails, but in special lifts (plural, although there was only one in each crematorium).
- The inmate labor force exhuming mass graves grew from 200 to 1,400 inmates.

(For more details, see Mattogno 2021, pp. 217-243.)

Compared to his report, articles and book, Vrba's interview with Claude Lanzmann for the documentary *Shoah* is outright boring, as it contains no concrete claims about any alleged extermination activities. It centers mostly around Vrba's story on how he tried to warn the inmates of the Theresienstadt Family Camp within Birkenau about their allegedly impending annihilation, as well as a detailed retelling of his escape and how his and Wetzler's report came to be and was spread around the world. Interestingly, he did not claim that the information contained in his report was based on information he had received from *Sonderkommando* members. (Lanzmann 1985; Interview transcript at U.S. Holocaust Memorial Museum, reference RG-60.5016.)

There is an interesting footnote to the Lanzmann interview. In his book *Pietà,* Swedish Professor Georg Klein, a Jew originally from Hungary and as such himself a "Holocaust survivor," told of a conversation he had with Rudolf Vrba in 1987. Klein reports about persecutions during the war, but that he had no knowledge of mass exterminations at the time. During his conversation with Klein, Vrba mentioned that he was once asked whether the horrible things he described in Lanzmann's documentary *Shoah* were really true. Vrba answered that he didn't know because he was *only an actor reciting his lines*. In his book, Klein wrote that he will never forget Vrba's sardonic smile when retelling this exchange (Klein 1992, pp. 133f.).

Vrba's final undoing occurred during the First Zündel Trial in 1985. During his testimony, Vrba once more insisted on the accuracy of his memory regarding the data he had provided in his 1944 report. However, when he was confronted with the inaccuracies and contradictions in his report and his book during cross-examination, he admitted several times to having used "poetic license" in his book. During re-examination, the prosecutor then asked Vrba:

"*Have you used poetic license in your testimony?*"

Vrba denied it, so the prosecutor asked him how he came up with his (false) figure of 1.765 million gassing victims, and Vrba went on a longwinded "explanation," trying again to justify his lies. The prosecutor left it at that. Vrba never testified publicly again after that.

(See the exchange in Rudolf 2020b, pp. 287f.)

Vrba-Wetzler Report → War Refugee Board Report

WAEL, MONIQUE DE

Monique de Wael

Monique de Wael (born 12 May 1937) is a Belgian Catholic who lost her parents during the Second World War. They had been arrested and deported by the German occupational forces for resistance activities, and never returned home. In 1988, de Wael immigrated to the U.S., where she wrote a book under the pen name Misha Defonseca titled *Misha: A Mémoire of the Holocaust Years*. She claimed that this was her wartime autobiography. The story line has her living with wolves during a part of her journey to Ukraine and back during the war, in a futile search for her deported parents. In 2008, the book was turned into a movie titled *Surviving with the Wolves*. This attracted the attention of Serge Aroles, a French scientist whose passion is debunking stories of children raised by wolves. Aroles discovered that de Wael lived with her grandparents and attended school during the years she claimed to have traveled through Europe. De Wael eventually admitted the hoax, yet insisted that her story "has been my reality." This is yet another case of a false witness. (For details, see "A pack of…"; Daniel 2008.)

WANNSEE CONFERENCE

During the year 1941, it became clear to Germany's top officials that there would be no peace in the West. Therefore, any plans to force Jews out of Europe to some overseas region, as was suggested with the so-called Madagascar Plan, became increasingly unlikely. On the other hand, Germany's initial successes during its invasion of the Soviet Union opened new perspectives of deporting Jews into those newly conquered regions. Therefore, the Third Reich's plans for a Final Territorial Solution shifted from Madagascar to territories in eastern Europe.

First steps in this regard were discussed during a meeting of higher party echelons at a mansion in the Wannsee District of Berlin, which later became known as the Wannsee Conference. It had originally been scheduled for 9 December 1941, but due to America's entry into the war, it was rescheduled for 20 January 1942. We know of the contents of this conference thanks to several participants who testified about it after the war, and due to the so-called Wannsee Protocol, a document which is said to contain the meeting's minutes.

If we follow this document, Reinhardt Heydrich was both the organizer and the main speaker at that conference. The protocol starts with a summary of measures taken by the German government up to the fall of 1941 in order to expedite the emigration of Jews from the German sphere of influence. Next, it explains that deportation to the east has replaced the policy of emigration. The Protocol lists the number of Jews in Europe. Strangely, it even contains countries where Germany had no influence at all: England, Ireland, Turkey, Portugal, Sweden, Switzerland and Spain. Furthermore, many figures listed are highly inflated.

The Protocol next deals briefly with how deportations from some of these countries could be implemented. A long section deals with the question of whether, and under which circumstances, so-called "half-Jews" and "quarter-Jews" are to be deported, and what is to happen with children from marriages between Jews and non-Jews or between persons of "mixed blood."

In connection with deportations to the east, it states that Jews will henceforth be put to work constructing roads on their migration to the east, which will result in a reduction of their total number due to a natural selection process effected by the harsh conditions. It then addresses what to do with the Jews who will survive these harsh conditions:

> "The possibly finally remaining leftover, since it will undoubtedly consist of the most resistant portion, will have to be treated accordingly, because it is the product of natural selection and, on their release, has to be regarded as a seed of a new Jewish revival (see the experience of history.)"

This is the only ambivalent passage in this protocol. The orthodoxy interprets it to mean that surviving Jews will not be released, but treated by simply killing them off. However, the protocol speaks of "natural" selection at the end of this forced-labor project during this forced migration to the east. Nothing is said here about any murder during that process. Only when this project is over, and possibly after the end of the war, the question of some kind of "special treatment" arises. What that might imply is not dealt with in the protocol, for that was obviously an issue of the distant future. The text moreover states clearly that these Jews *have to be* regarded as a seed of a Jewish revival *on* their release. It does not say that the Jews *would be* a seed of a Jewish revival *if* released.

In fact, the Third Reich was not opposed to a Jewish revival. Prior to the outbreak of war with the Soviet Union, numerous projects existed in Germany geared toward facilitating a new beginning of Jews *after* they had emigrated from the German sphere of influence (see the entry on emigration). Several documents indicate that plans existed for the time after the war to get the Jews out of Europe for a new beginning. This evidently makes sense only if this "remaining leftover" was still there at war's end.

There is not a word in this protocol about whether, when or how Jews were supposed to be exterminated. Hence, Yehuda Bauer, professor at the Hebrew University in Jerusalem, explained in 1992:

"The public still repeats, time after time, the silly story that at Wannsee the extermination of the Jews was arrived at."

However, that does not stop mainstream media to repeat that false assertion. Orthodox historians insist instead that the decision to murder the European Jews had already been made earlier. The Wannsee Conference's function was merely to coordinate the efforts of various government branches to organize and implement that decision. However, the protocol's contents only point at coordination with regard to deportation and forced labor, not extermination. In addition, there is no trace of a Hitler order for an extermination, and the orthodox narrative of how the Holocaust allegedly unfolded – in a chaotic and anarchistic fashion – points to there not having been any plan or coordination at all. (See the entry on Plan, to Exterminate the Jews.)

A second Wannsee Conference took place on 6 March 1942, during which issues left open at the first conference were discussed. They centered around whether forced sterilization and forced divorces

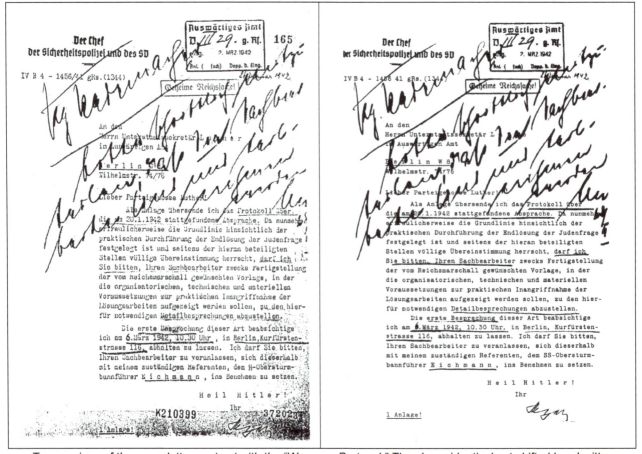

Two versions of the cover letter sent out with the "Wannsee Protocol." They have identical yet shifted handwritten remarks, on text typed on different typewriters. One or both of them are forgeries.

should be implemented for certain Jews or their spouses who were unwilling to emigrate or get deported. This meeting's protocol also merely refers to evacuations and settlements, but not to murder. However, even discussion about forced sterilization remained purely on paper. No program of forced sterilization was ever pursued.

The Wannsee Conference was not held in a vacuum. In fact, there are several documents by German high-level politicians and bureaucrats created around the time of this conference which discuss the matters involved. All of them speak about deportation, evacuation and resettlement. Not even one of them has the slightest reference to any plans of extermination.

For a formal critique of the protocol created during the Wannsee Conference, see the next entry.

(For more details, see Mattogno 2022c, pp. 95-103; Rudolf 2023, pp. 128-132.)

WANNSEE PROTOCOL

Several scholars have raised doubts about the authenticity of the so-called Wannsee Protocol. This document is alleged to have been written by Adolf Eichmann after the so-called Wannsee Conference of 20 January 1942. For a discussion of the contents of the Wannsee Conference as laid out in its protocol, see the previous entry.

The point of departure for claims that this protocol may be a forgery is the fact that the person who claimed to have discovered this document – Robert Kempner – reproduced a copy of it in one of his books. However, the version published by Kempner is different than the one which today is claimed to be the original. Furthermore, several participants of the conference testified after the war that the content of the alleged protocol was incorrect, because quite a lot was missing which had been discussed, while things were mentioned which had not been topics of the meeting.

Others have pointed out many stylistic and formal errors. A central point of contention is the use of the runic ᛋᛋ symbol, which had its own key on official typewriters of the Third Reich. The only extant copy of this protocol claims to be the 16th copy of 30 copies altogether. However, this 16th copy exists in at least *five* different versions, some with a normal "SS" and some with a runic-formed "ᛋᛋ." All these versions show some minor deviations in the text as listed in the table. At best, only one of them can be authentic; all other copies are not.

The cover letter belonging to the "Wannsee Protocol" likewise exists in two versions, one with normal "SS" and one with runic-formed "ᛋᛋ." Here, though, the situation is even more unmistakable: not only was an attempt made to leave the typewritten area unaltered, but the handwritten notes of some official, which are found on the version with the normal SS key, have been copied onto the second ver-

Summary of deviations, compared with version A, of various versions of the 16th copy of the "Wannsee Protocol."

A Kempner version		D Poliakov-Wulf version	F Ludwigsburg version I	G Ludwigsburg version II	H Staatsarchiv version
Text	Line				
Schöngarth	025	Schoengarth	Schoengarth	Schoengarth	Schoengarth
diesen Gegner	058	diese Gegner	diese Gegner	diesen Gegner	diesen Gegner
30.1.1933	102	3o.Januar 1933	3o.Januar 1933	3o 1.1933	30.1.1933
15.3.1938	102	15.März 1938	15.März 1938	15.3 1938	15.3.1938
15.3.1939	104	15.März 1939	15.März 1939	15.3.1939 -	15.3.1939
1/4 Million	199	1/2 Million	1/2 Million	1/4 Million	1/4 Million
sollen nun im Zuge	209	sollen im Zuge	sollen im Zuge	sollen im Zuge	sollen im Zuge
wird	273	hat	hat	hat	hat
irgendwelche Lebensgebieten	319	irgendwelchen Gebieten(Lebens)	irgendwelchen Gebieten(Lebens)	irgendwelchen Lebensgebieten	irgendwelchen Lebensgebieten
des Verbleibens im Reich	336	für das Verbleiben im Reich	für das Verbleiben im Reich	des Verbleibens im Reich	des Verbleibens im Reich
Deutschen	365	deutschblütigen	deutschblütigen	deutschen	deutschen
Deutschen	382	Deutschblütigen	Deutschblütigen	Deutschen	Deutschen
und Mischlingen 1. Grades	388	und Mischlingen 2. Grades	und Mischlingen 2. Grades	und Mischlingen 1. Grades	und Mischlingen 1. Grades
Mischehen- und Mischlingsfragen	410	Mischehen-Mischlingsfragen	Mischehen-Mischlingsfragen	Mischehen- und Mischlingsfragen	Mischehen- und Mischlingsfragen

sion with runic-formed "⚡⚡" symbols. But the forgers did not manage to completely erase all traces of the old typewritten text. Some of these traces are still there. Compared with the first version, the identical handwriting has also slipped a few millimeters with respect to the machine text. The forgery is plainly obvious and recognizable to anyone. The proof of the forgery, at least of one version of the cover letter, has thus been furnished for a long time now.

For now, we can only be mystified about the reasons for these manipulations. After all, the protocol's contents do not prove that the Third Reich was planning to exterminate the Jews, as the previous entry shows; indeed, quite the contrary.
(For more details, see Rudolf 2023, pp. 132-135.)

WAR REFUGEE BOARD REPORT

The War Refugee Board was an organization established by Roosevelt in January 1944. It was the result of Secretary of the Treasury Henry Morgenthau lobbying for an official government agency assisting minorities, in particular Jews, persecuted by the Third Reich. This would have been within the area of responsibility of the State Department. Morgenthau pushed the U.S. administration to officially recognized that the Third Reich was pursuing a policy of mass extermination against the Jews, in particular by means of gas chambers. The U.S. State Department was reluctant to follow Morgenthau with this, not the least because Anglo-American intelligence could not confirm gas-chamber and mass-murder rumors. As late as August 1943, the Chairman of the Allied Joint Intelligence Committee had strongly recommended not mentioning anything to this effect in a public declaration. (See the entry Propaganda, section "United Kingdom.")

This reluctance to accept the echoes of their own propaganda as true was washed away in July 1944 at the latest, when the Red Army conquered the Majdanek Camp. The subsequent Soviet and Polish gas-chamber and mass-extermination propaganda set an example to be repeated when other camps were captured.

In November 1944, the War Refugee Board collected three essays written by five Auschwitz escapees. With a few editorial changes, they published these texts together as one report, the so-called War Refugee Board Report (WRB Report). It is also sometimes misleadingly called the "Auschwitz Protocols," although it is not a protocol of anything. These texts allegedly confirm that Auschwitz was an extermination center where Jews were being mass murdered in gas chambers using Zyklon B. The three contributing sets of refugees were:

– Jerzy Wesołowski, who later assumed the name Jerzy Tabeau. He escaped from Auschwitz in late November 1943, and wrote his essay at the turn of 1943/1944. It was included in the WRB Report anonymously as written by a "Polish major."
– Alfred Wetzler and Walter Rosenberg, who escaped on 7 April 1944, and wrote their essay in May 1944. After his escape from Auschwitz, Rosenberg had assumed the pseudonym Rudolf Vrba, which he kept for the rest of his life.
– Czesław Mordowicz and Arnošt Rosin, who escaped on 27 May 1944. Their text was not fully included in the WRP report, but only its main parts as a sequel to Wetzler's and Vrba's text.

For a critique of these three texts, see the entries of Jerzy Tabeau, Rudolf Vrba and Arnošt Rosin.

With the WRB Report, the U.S. government officially adopted the orthodox Auschwitz narrative as spread since 1942 by the Auschwitz Camp's underground movement.

WARSAW GHETTO

Jewish ghettos are not an invention of wartime Germany, nor the deplorable conditions found in some of them during wartimes. It demonstrates calloused indifference, at best, to force people to live in close quarters with insufficient food supplies and inadequate medical care and sanitary installations, as was the case in the Warsaw Ghetto and many other similar wartime ghettos. The suffering and loss of human life resulting from this was tragic. But it was not a deliberate, systematic policy of mass extermination that led to this, which is why the details of this ghetto and others like it will not be covered in detail in this encyclopedia.

The Polish underground had spread black propaganda since early 1942 claiming that the German occupational forces in Poland and elsewhere implemented a policy of total physical extermination of the Jews. Beginning in July 1942, hundreds of thousands of Jews from the Warsaw Ghetto were being deported, most of them via the Treblinka Camp. Reports coming back to the ghetto indicated that Jews were being killed there by various means, when in fact they were generally being transited through to other destinations further east. (See the entry on Treblinka for details.)

Jewish leaders in the Warsaw Ghetto therefore

decided to fight back. They started an uprising on 19 April 1943. It was put down brutally by German armed forces, for the most part within a few days, but skirmishes carried on until mid-May. Jews who survived were again generally deported via Treblinka. While the immediate victims of this uprising represent a tragic loss of life, armed resistance against an occupational force during a war has always been, and will always be, met with force.

Because the ghetto uprising was not part of a premeditated, systematic mass extermination, it will not be covered here in detail. The fate of the survivors deported via Treblinka, however, is very much of interest, and is dealt with in the entry about Treblinka.

It is difficult to establish the death toll caused by all the events occurring in this ghetto. It is not even known exactly how many Jews passed through the ghetto. Orthodox sources for this vary between 400,000 and 600,000. (Friedman 1954, p. 79: 420,000 to 500,000; Corni 2003, p. 195: 400,000. Dean 2010, p. 342: "some 450,000"; Longerich 2010, p. 167: 410,000 to 590,000.) Daily death tolls also vary greatly, ranging from 100+ per day claimed by orthodox scholars to 10,000 daily (!) reported by *The New York Times* on 7 February 1943, although that may have included those deported from the ghetto. The sources by which orthodox scholars determine day-to-day deaths in the ghetto are rather questionable. Much needs to be researched before anything safe can be stated about this. (For details, see Dalton 2020, pp. 83-89.)

There is one media item which links the Warsaw Ghetto with a premeditated, systematic, even industrialized plan to exterminate the Jews, however. The Polish monthly periodical *Wieś i Miasto* (*Village and City*) published the following news in November 1943 (Vol. IV, No. 7, p. 7):

> "In the area of the former Warsaw Ghetto, the Germans built gas chambers, which went into operation for the first time on 17 October of this year [1943]. Since then, they have been killing ten [sic] people a day there."

All historians agree, however, that no such puny homicidal gas chamber ever existed in the area of the former Warsaw Ghetto. This was simply black propaganda. For the propagandists, no tragedy is heartbreaking enough to stop them from sullying its commemoration with some pernicious lie.

WARSZAWSKI, SZYJA

Szyja Warszawski was a Polish Jew deported to Treblinka on 23 July 1942 from Kielce. He was interviewed by a Polish investigator on 9 October 1945. Here are some of his pertinent claims:

- Deportees were killed in the trains in transit with chlorine (probably meaning chlorinated lime) sprinkled in the railway cars. This is a clear echo of the black propaganda spread by Jan Karski, and also claimed by Abraham Goldfarb and Leon Finkelsztein.
- Working as a carpenter in the vicinity of the "chambers," he saw four concrete chambers – rather than three wooden ones, as the orthodox narrative has it.
- The murder was initially carried out with chlorine, and only after a month or so was a motor added, "installed next to the chambers in a special wooden room," whose exhaust gases were used. A new building with ten chambers twice the size was added later.
- Warszawski claimed that, after some experiments, the Germans found a way of building a cremation grate, underneath which "a fire was lit and corpses were thrown on top with a dredger; once the corpses caught fire, they continued to burn." However, self-immolating bodies do not exist. Leon Finkelsztein copied this nonsense from Warszawski.

(See Mattogno 2021e, pp. 164f.; https://zapisyterroru.pl/.)

WATT, DONALD

During World War Two, Donald Watt (10 Aug. 1918 – 29 May 2000) was an Australian soldier. In 1995, Watt published his memoirs, titled *Stoker*. He claimed in it that he had been incarcerated at the Auschwitz Camp, where he was allegedly assigned to the *Sonderkommando* serving as a cremation furnace stoker.

Due to its many claims not in agreement with the orthodox narrative of what transpired at Auschwitz and how the crematoria and gas chambers allegedly function, skepticism was soon voiced by mainstream scholars from leading orthodox institutions, such as Yad Vashem, the Auschwitz Museum and the U.S. Holocaust Memorial Museum. Watt's memoirs were ultimately exposed as fake by German-Australian mainstream historian Konrad Kwiet in 1997. (See Kwiet 1997.)

weapons, of mass murder → Tools

WEDDING RINGS

For years, the United States Holocaust Memorial Museum has posted this image on the encyclopedia section of their website, currently (March 2023) with the following explanation:

> "Wedding rings taken from prisoners. The rings were found near the Buchenwald concentration camp following liberation by US Army soldiers. Germany, May 1945."

Note that these objects all look alike. They have the same shape and the same size. Wedding rings, however, come in all kinds of sizes, fitting different-size fingers, and they come in many different styles, colors (= different precious-metal alloys), shapes, and many of them with jewels embedded. (See the second image.)

The first photo, taken by the U.S. Army, shows industrial clippings of metal tubes of a constant diameter, probably scrap metal from some production line that was cutting tubes to a certain length. The photo is part of the U.S. psychological warfare department's operations framing the German nation with horrible crimes committed by presenting false evidence, such as these rings, lampshades allegedly made of human skin, soap made of the fat of concentration-camp victims, and shrunken heads from murdered camp inmates.

Top: Propaganda Image of the U.S. Army of May 1945, claiming to depict collection of wedding rings found at the Buchenwald Camp. (https://encyclopedia.ushmm.org/content/en/photo/wedding-rings)

Right: Random collection of real wedding rings.

WEISE, GOTTFRIED

Gottfried Weise (11 March 1921 – 1 March 2000), SS *Unterscharführer*, was deployed at the inmate property administration at the Auschwitz Camp from May 1944. Between 1986 and 1988, Weise was tried and sentenced for five cases of murder allegedly committed during his time at Auschwitz.

The case of Gottfried Weise is the only legal case against an alleged perpetrator within the so-called Holocaust where the defense decided to go all in and let skeptical scholars (revisionists) help them all the way. It did not change the outcome of the trial, but it made it possible to document the show-trial nature of this type of trial.

The basic characteristics are:
– Once a (often Jewish) "Holocaust survivor" has claimed a crime, it is considered an incontrovertible fact.
– Evidence offered to refute the crime is rejected by the court, because the court is interested only in evidence that can elucidate the already-established fact that there was a crime.
– Consequently, criminal proceedings merely serve the purpose of establishing the dimension of the

Gottfried Weise

claimed crime, naming the culprits and meting out the punishment they presumably deserve. For a detailed documentation of this case, see Rudolf 2019, pp. 141-173.

WEISS, JANDA

Janda Weiss was a 14-year-old teenager deported from the Theresienstadt Ghetto to Auschwitz in May 1944. After the war, he made a deposition which was printed in a U.S. compendium on the Buchenwald Camp. Here are some of Weiss's peculiar statements:

- On arrival, he saw "horrible tongues of flame coming out of" the crematorium chimney. However, the Birkenau coke-fired crematoria could not emit flames from their chimneys.
- He claimed that "it was well known that every transport was gassed after six months." The orthodoxy insists, however, that, starting in July 1942, individuals deemed unfit for labor were selected from each transport and killed instantly, the rest admitted to the camp.
- Only the strongest men and women were sorted out, the rest gassed. And Janda Weiss, at age 14, claims to have been among the strongest of this transport.
- Paying tribute to the cliché, the ineluctable Dr. Mengele allegedly did the initial selection, and the one for the *Sonderkommando* assignments. However, on arrival, no inmate could have known the identity of any SS men.
- He visited the barracks of the *Sonderkommando* members, where he found out "about the horrors of the crematorium." However, the orthodoxy has it that this unit was isolated from the rest of the camp, hence could not be "visited." Furthermore, considering that all camp sectors were surrounded by barbed wire fences, walking around visiting people was simply no option in general.
- Old people were allegedly dumped from trucks into burning trenches while still alive. However, the heat of the blaze would have set the truck on fire if such a procedure had been tried.
- He claimed to have later worked in the crematorium as a *Sonderkommando* member, so he must have had first-hand knowledge, but he claimed that the undressing room was "in front of the gas chamber." That description fits for no claimed facility, though.
- People were allegedly asked to put their "shoes into the cubbyholes," meaning there were large shoe-storage shelves. This is a unique claim and flies in the face of the orthodox narrative.
- Inside the gas chamber "were three columns for the ventilators, through which the gas poured in." However, the ventilators were placed in the building's attic, and the orthodoxy has it that there were *four* Zyklon-B introduction devices in the alleged homicidal gas chambers of Crematorium II and III.
- "Small children were thrown in[to the gas chamber] through a window." However, that basement room had no windows.
- "The lungs of the victims slowly burst." The poison allegedly used – hydrogen cyanide – has no such effect.
- The killing lasted about "three minutes." However, in a facility without means to accelerate the evaporation of the liquid poison from the carrier material (Zyklon B) and the dissipation into the large room, such short execution times are physically impossible.
- The chamber was opened right after the killing was over. However, the presence of poison gas in this room would have required a lengthy ventilation time.
- If the cremation furnaces could not keep up, surplus corpses were thrown into fire trenches. However, with such a blaze causing severe burns to anyone approaching it, it must be assumed that they used catapults to sling the corpses onto the blazing pyre from a safe distance. Furthermore, air photos prove that no such open-incineration trenches existed at that time.
- "Once it happened that a victim crawled out of a burning trench." Not likely.
- "Once Moll put a naked woman in the trench and shot her in the genitals." This is Holo-porn. Weiss evidently had some unsatisfied sexual issues.
- "On another occasion he [Moll] arranged twelve women who were lined up behind each other in a row, […]. Then he mercilessly shot through them all with a single bullet." Not possible.
- "He [Moll] hanged a man up by his hands and shot him until his arms were torn through; then he hanged him up by the feet and repeated the process." Possible only with a huge waste of ammunition, which can be ruled out.
- Weiss also repeated a Chinese-whisper story, retold in variations by many, of a Jewess dancing naked in front of SS men, then taking one of their guns and shooting them. Again, this is yet more Holo-porn.

Whatever the motive of a 14-year-old teenager were to tell these outrageous lies, the problem really is not so much his lurid fantasy, but grownups who take that at face value and print it as "evidence" in a book. (See Janda Weiss's statement in Hackett 1995, pp. 349f.)

WEISSMANDL, MICHAEL DOV

Michael Dov Weissmand(e)l (25 Oct. 1903 – 29 Nov. 1957) was a Slovakian Rabbi who was summoned to meet the Slovakian Jews Rudolf Vrba and Alfred Wetzler after their escape from Birkenau. Weissmandel was either hoodwinked by Vrba and Wetzler to believe their mendacious propaganda story about Auschwitz, or else he even helped create its contents. Once the report had been typed up, Weissmandel helped distribute it. He used this occasion to appeal to the Allies in a letter of 16 May 1944 to bomb the Auschwitz Camp, asking them why they are "silent about this slaughter, in which some six million Jews have been murdered thus far, and in which tens of thousands are now being murdered every day?" This was one day before the arrival of the first mass-deportation trains carrying Hungarian Jews to Auschwitz. This letter is one of the earliest references to six million victims of the Holocaust during the final phase of the Second World War. (See Heddesheimer 2017, p. 12; Mattogno 2021, p. 221; Vrba-Lanzmann interview transcript, USHMM, RG-60.5016.)

Michael Dov Weissmandl

WELICZKER, LEON

Leon Weliczker (aka Leon Wells, 10 March 1925 – 19 Dec. 2009) was a Jew from Lviv who, after the German invasion of the Soviet Union, lived initially at the Lvov Ghetto, but at age 18 was transferred to the Janowska Forced-Labor Camp. After the war, he studied first in Gleiwitz (Polish: Gliwice), then in Munich, graduating with a PhD in engineering. He later emigrated to the United States, where he changed his last name to Wells.

In 1944, he deposited a witness statement in the Soviet Union about his alleged work from 15 June 1943 until 20 November 1943 in a "death brigade" at the outskirts of the western Ukrainian city of Lviv. Some excerpts of notes he wrote down during the war were published in an edited version in a 1946 book, whose translated title is *The Death Brigade*. It is the most-important source for the alleged eradication of mass graves near Lviv within the context of what today's orthodoxy calls *Aktion* 1005. Here are several peculiar claims made by Weliczker:

Leon Weliczker

– At age sixteen/seventeen, he was rounded up on four occasions to be shot with all the other Jews in his group, but he managed to escape every time. He then ended up in the Janowska Labor Camp near Lviv, escaped from there as well, and was finally assigned to the "death brigade," but again managed to flee. While everyone else got killed, he miraculously escaped six times as the sole survivor.

– In his 1944 statement, Weliczker claimed that his death brigade exhumed and burned 310,000 bodies from mass graves near the Janowska Labor Camp, which even orthodox historians consider inflated by a factor of three. In his book, he claims to quote from a diary he kept while working in the death brigade. These diary entries only mention a total of some 30,000 exhumed and cremated bodies. Asked during his testimony at the Eichmann Trial how many bodies his unit burned, he repeated the first figure: "A few hundred thousand."

– Although right at the city's edge, no contemporary photographs, documents or testimonies exist of this alleged enormous cremation activity presumably lasting eleven weeks.

– Weliczker described an absurd and physically impossible cremation technique: a large area of wooden logs (7 m × 7 m) was set on fire – with an olive-oil squirting machine! After the pyre was ablaze, Weliczker and his co-inmates brought corpses on stretchers, climbed with them on a wooden platform next to the fire, and threw the bodies into the fire. A stoker stood next to the pyre stoking the fire. If bodies were thrown in wrongly, the inmates had to climb into the fire, pull the bodies out, and throw them in properly.

This absurd story fails on several points: olive oil was virtually unknown, very rare and very expensive in Central and Eastern Europe during the war; furthermore, although olive oil can burn if sprayed in a fine mist, it generally it is not flammable, and certainly would never be used to ignite something; the wooden platforms would have caught fire; the stoker would have burned himself; the inmates would have gotten severe burns; those climbing in to get bodies out would never have gotten out themselves. Weliczker made it up from beginning to end, with no truth to it whatsoever. He claimed that normal pyres with alternating layers of wood and bodies were built later, and ignited only once properly built, but he abstains from giving any data about those pyres.

– Cremating an average human body during open-air incinerations requires some 250 kg of freshly cut wood. Cremating 300,000 bodies thus requires some 75,000 metric tons of wood. This would have required the felling of all trees growing in a 50-year-old spruce forest covering almost 167 hectares of land, or some 374 American football fields. An average prisoner is rated at being able to cut some 0.63 metric tons of fresh wood per workday. To cut this amount of wood within the six month (160 days) he claimed to have worked on that project would have required a work force of some 750 dedicated lumberjacks just to cut the wood. According to Weliczker's account, all the members of his unit were busy digging out mass graves, extracting bodies, building pyres, sifting through ashes, scattering the ashes, refilling the graves with soil, and planting them with grass seeds and saplings. He says nothing about where the firewood came from.

– Weliczker claimed that all cremation ashes were sifted through fine flour-type sieves to find bones fragments and metal objects (gold teeth). Bone fragments were either pulverized (manually with wooden pestles, or in a bone mill), or burned again. However, wood-fired pyres burn unevenly and leave behind lots of unburned wood pieces, charcoal, and incompletely burned body parts, not just ashes (80% of which would have been wood ash). Those remains could not have been crushed or ground down in ball mills. If 100,000 bodies were processed, as the orthodoxy claims, then several thousand metric tons of ashes had to be processed this way by a few dozen inmates within a few months – in small flour sieves that would have clogged with the first load. Moreover, any occasional rainfall would have rendered any burned-out pyre into a moist heap of highly alkaline, corrosive slush that could not have been processed at all. Hence, Weliczker's tale is pure fantasy.

– The ball mill allegedly used to grind up bones has turned out to have been a road-building device to crush gravel. Since most inmates from the Janowska Camp were deployed in building roads, this is what this machine was used for. (See the entry on bone mill.)

– He asserted that the empty graves were filled up, and grass was planted, making the grave indistinguishable from surrounding areas within weeks. As every garden owner knows, freshly sown patches of grass are distinguishable from old-grass areas for years. Furthermore, unless heavy machinery is used to compact filled-in soil – which Weliczker does not mention – the soil filled into pits several meters deep will subside considerably within weeks, turning them into very easily distinguishable depressions.

– Weliczker mentioned several other locations where his death brigade allegedly unearthed bodies. These bodies were allegedly put into refrigeration trucks and driven to the Janowska Camp for burning. For several locations mentioned by Weliczker, no events resulting in mass graves are known. The use of refrigeration trucks, commonly used to transport perishable food items, to transport decomposing corpses of mass-murder victims is highly unlikely, to say the least.

Orthodox historian Thomas Sandkühler wrote about Weliczker's book:

"Weliczker's shocking notes have only little probative value."

However, because there are no other informative sources for the alleged exhumation and cremation activities near Lviv, Weliczker's ludicrous novel is the mainstay upon which almost the entire load of the orthodox narrative of these alleged events rests.

(For other, far-less informative witnesses, see the entries on Abraham Beer, Heinrich Chamaides, Moische Korn and David Manusevich; for more details on Weliczker, see Mattogno 2021c, pp. 489-513.)

Wells, Leon → **Weliczker, Leon**

WENNERSTRUM, CHARLES F.

Charles F. Wennerstrum (11 Oct. 1889 – 1 June 1986) was a U.S. American lawyer who served on the Iowa Supreme Court from 1941 to 1958. After the Second World War, he was the presiding judge of the Nuremberg Tribunal in Case 7 against several German generals in the so-called "Hostage Case." Although he only experienced the prosecution's mild excesses in the courtroom, he published the following devastating opinion on these proceedings immediately following the judgment (Foust 1948):

Charles F. Wennerstrum

> "If I had known seven months ago what I know today, I would never have come here.
>
> Obviously, the victor in any war is not the best judge of the war crime guilt. […] The prosecution has failed to maintain objectivity aloof from vindictiveness, aloof from personal ambitions for convictions. It has failed to strive to lay down precedents which might help the world to avoid future wars. The entire atmosphere here is unwholesome. […] Lawyers, clerks, interpreters and researchers were employed who became Americans only in recent years [mostly emigrated Jews], whose backgrounds were embedded in Europe's hatreds and prejudices. The trials were to have convinced the Germans of the guilt of their leaders. They convinced the Germans merely that their leaders lost the war to tough conquerors.
>
> Most of the evidence in the trials was documentary, selected from the large tonnage of captured records. The selection was made by the prosecution. The defense had access only to those documents which the prosecution considered material to the case. […]
>
> Also abhorrent to the American sense of justice is the prosecution's reliance upon self-incriminating statements made by the defendants while prisoners for more than two and a half years, and repeated interrogation without presence of counsel. Two and one-half years of confinement is a form of duress in itself.
>
> The lack of appeal leaves me with a feeling that justice has been denied.
>
> […] The German people should receive more information about the trials and the German defendants should receive the right to appeal to the United Nations."

WENTRITT, HARRY

Harry Wentritt was a mechanic at the motor pool administration of Germany's Security Police, which was Subdepartment II D 3a of Germany's Department of Homeland Security (*Reichssicherheitshauptamt*). In 1966, together with his superior Friedrich Pradel, he stood trial for allegedly having made mechanical changes to a set of trucks in 1941/42, turning them into homicidal gas vans. He should have been the one person perfectly able to describe exactly how these vehicles functioned and what type of engine they used.

However, in all his statements, he said nothing about the type of engine used (gasoline or diesel). When it comes to the way the exhaust gases were introduced into the cargo box, he described a technically absurd and nonfunctional method: He claimed that a piece from the van's exhaust pipe was cut out, and a T-piece inserted instead. This was then used to attach a metal hose to an opening cut into the cargo box's floor.

A truck's exhaust pipe does not extend all the way to the back of the truck but usually ends half way on one side. Connecting it to a hole in the center of the cargo box would certainly be possible with a metal hose, but inserting a T-piece makes no sense at all. Any exhaust pipe ends in the open. If it is too long, simply cut it short. Otherwise, connect it to the opening in question as needed. There is no point in cutting a piece out from the middle of the pipe, then reconnect the trailing end of it with a T-piece. Furthermore, a simple T-piece would have foiled the purpose of redirecting the gas, because the gas, following the path of least resistance, would have escaped from the tailpipe into the open rather than flowing into the enclosed cargo box. Piping the gas into the box would have required the closure of the other exit of the T-piece. But since this trailing end of the exhaust pipe was not needed, the entire exercise is futile. A simple elbow pipe redirecting the end of the exhaust pipe toward the opening in the floor would have done the trick.

Two other witnesses have made similarly foolish statements years before Wentritt. Maybe Wentritt learned this nonsense from reading their accounts. (See the entries on Bronisław Falborski and Johann

Hassler.)

Wentritt ended up serving three years for his alleged contribution to the creation of the gas vans. It was deemed served with the time he had spent in pre-trial detention. Hence, he walked away as a free man.

(For more details, see Alvarez 2023, pp. 211-219.)

WERNER, KURT

During the war, Kurt Werner was a member of *Sonderkommando* 4a, which was part of *Einsatzgruppe* C. On 28 May 1964, he made a deposition during West-German investigations on the alleged mass shooting of Kiev Jews at Babi Yar. He claimed to have been one of 12 men who were doing the shootings. He said nothing about whether the Jews were dressed or naked, and if the latter, then where they had left their clothes.

Werner stated that, at the beginning of the operation, he and his fellow gunmen had to go to the bottom of the ravine. Then, the victims were led down the slopes of the ravine towards them. The Jews had to lie face down on the ground, where they were shot in the back of the neck. The following Jews had to lie down on the bodies of those previously shot.

This version is in stark contrast to claims by witnesses who were interrogated by the NKGB after the German retreat from Kiev. These witnesses insisted that the victims were either shot while standing at the upper edge of the ravine, then falling down into the ravine dead or wounded; or they had to run along the ravine and were shot while running, by men standing at the ravine's edge. Children were tossed alive into the ravine.

(For more details, see the entry on Babi Yar, as well as Mattogno 2022c, p. 573.)

Wesołowski, Jerzy → Tabeau, Jerzy

WETZLER, ALFRED

Alfred Wetzler (10 May 1918 – 8 Feb. 1988) was a Slovakian Jew who was deported to Auschwitz on 13 April 1942, where he became a clerk in one of the Birkenau camp sections. He managed to escape from Birkenau together with Rudolf Vrba on 7 April 1944. Once they both reached Slovakia, they co-authored the so-called Vrba-Wetzler Report, an extract of which eventually became the main part of the U.S. War Refugee Board Report. (For more details on this report, see the entry on Rudolf Vrba.)

In later writings, Wetzler added additional layers of lies to the mendacious Vrba-Wetzler Report. Among them are the following peculiar claims:

Alfred Wetzler

– In 1945, Wetzler published a paraphrased version of the Vrba-Wetzler Report with the indicative title *Auschwitz: The Tomb of Four Million People*, a number he repeated three times through the text. The four-million death-toll figure was invented by the Soviets on occupying Auschwitz, to dwarf their 1.5-million death-toll figure claimed for the Majdanek Camp, which they had conquered 5 months earlier. This figure has been debunked by orthodox historians as vastly exaggerated. Wetzler repeated that false figure in early 1946 when questioned by a prosecutor, insisting that, of the 4 million victims, 2.5 million were Jews.

– In late 1963, Wetzler wrote a deposition for the Auschwitz Museum in which he claimed that the (false) statistical data included in the 1944 report was also based on notes brought along, something Vrba had denied all along, insisting instead that all was based on his "excellent" memory. Wetzler also claimed that some Soviet PoW had given them a hand-drawn floor plan of the crematorium, thus contradicting Filip Müller, who had claimed this drawing as his own.

In 1964, a book by Wetzler was published under the pen name Jozef Lánik titled *What Dante Didn't See*. With it, Wetzler dug himself even deeper into his mendacious hole. Here are some pertinent examples:

– He expanded on several pages on the false story of Himmler's visit to Birkenau on the occasion of the inauguration of Crematorium II (with 2,000 victims rather than the 8,000 of the 1944 report). In this context he wrote about a window in a steel door of the gas chamber, through which peaked "Himmler, medical professors from Berlin, Hamburg, Münster, representatives of various companies," etc. The problem is that the entire event is freely invented, and that there were no steel doors at Auschwitz.

– Wetzler claimed that the gas was poured into the ventilators, and that, inside the gas chamber, "tiny crystals are pouring out of the showers." That was no accident as he repeated that claim four more times. However, the orthodoxy has it that the poison-gas gypsum pellets were poured into some Zyklon-B introduction devices. These "crystals" would only have clogged up pipes and showerheads without having any effect. Furthermore, the ventilators of this room were located in the building's attic, with the ventilation openings and ducts placed along the basement room's side walls.

– Wetzler claimed that Engineer Prüfer, from the Erfurt company Topf & Sons, had built the gas chamber. In fact, Prüfer only supervised the erection of the Topf *cremation furnaces* in all of the Auschwitz crematoria.

– Wetzler claimed that a second, larger gas chamber existed underneath the one inspected by Himmler and his entourage. No such thing existed.

– He claimed that Himmler insisted that soap dishes should be provided, and that more towels and soap ought to be handed out. This most certainly would never have happened, considering the mess it would have created and the effort necessary to retrieve and clean these items afterwards. In addition, no one takes towels into a shower.

– Synchronized with Vrba's identical change in his 1963 book *I Cannot forgive*, Wetzler also increased the cremation capacity by reducing the time it allegedly took to cremate three corpses from 90 minutes (1944) to 20 minutes. In reality, it took them one hour to cremate one body.

– The total capacity of the crematoria grew from 6,000 corpses per day in 1944 to "6,000, 7,000, 8,000, and now perhaps even 10,000 corpses," while the actual theoretical maximum capacity was 920 bodies per day.

– He reduced the total death toll to three million, although that's still three times today's orthodox figure. He even wrote that this number was included "at the end of the [1944] report," but that's a lie, too.

For even more details about this crucially important Auschwitz liar, see the entry on Rudolf Vrba with more details about the Vrba-Wetzler Report, as well as Mattogno's analysis in Mattogno 2021, pp. 234-238.

WIDMANN, ALBERT

Albert Widmann (8 June 1912 – 24 Dec. 1986), SS *Sturmbannführer*, was a German PhD chemist who in 1940 became the head of the section of analytical chemistry at the German Institute for Criminological Technology in Berlin (*Kriminaltechnisches Institut*, KTI). Right at the beginning of the Third Reich's euthanasia action, Widmann is said to have received verbal orders from Arthur Nebe, then head of the Reich Police Department for Criminal Investigations (*Reichskriminalpolizeiamt*), to find a suitable poisonous chemical with which to kill severely mentally disabled patients. Widmann recommended bottled carbon monoxide.

In late 1941, Widmann is said to have been involved in the development of "gas vans." In this context, Widmann spread a rumor on how this alleged murder method was "discovered." It starts out with a preposterous rumor that Widmann's boss Nebe had the idea of using engine-exhaust gases because he once accidentally gassed himself this way, which is most certainly untrue (see the entry on Arthur Nebe for more). Next, instead of using the vast research and experimental resources available to them in their institute in peaceful Berlin and at the various mental institutions in Germany, Nebe and Widmann allegedly picked up 400 kg of explosives somewhere and several meters of metal hoses, then drove 1,000 km with this load to Minsk near the Russian-German front, of all places, in order to do some experiments there with patients of a mental asylum.

The first experiment they are said to have conducted allegedly consisted of putting several mental patients into a shed, then blowing it up with some of the explosives they had brought along. Why it took an experiment to verify that people surrounded by explosive get killed when the explosives detonate is an unsolved mystery. It goes without saying that the results of that experiment were unsatisfactory as well, because body parts "whirled through the air and got stuck in the trees," as Germany's news magazine *Der Spiegel* quoted Widmann's trial statement. This conclusion did not require any experiment either, because any moderately intelligent person can predict that blowing up people with explosives leads to body parts and organs being thrown all around. Cleaning up this mess was neither an easy nor a pleasant job (Widmann also mentioned the crater that needed filling in…), so this murder method was abandoned. (Note that Erich von dem Bach-Zelewski made similar postwar claims, and that Rudolf Höss, the former commandant of the Auschwitz Camp, stated after the war that Paul Blobel had tried to make corpses disappear(!) by blowing them up. See the two entries on explosives.)

This story was invented by Widmann himself during an interrogation conducted in 1960. It contains more absurd claims about how they got the explosives. We therefore may assume that he was taking his interrogators for a ride. During his trial, Widmann repeated this nonsense. The court believed him unquestioningly, and the media spread the gory news. No one exercised the least degree of critical thinking, which is what nearly always happens when Holocaust atrocity claims are involved.

This was not the end of this tragicomedy, though. After they realized that dynamite was not the ideal murder weapon, they presumably connected the exhaust pipe of their car to a tube inserted into the wall of one room of a mental institution, using some of the metal hoses they had brought along. The first attempt didn't work, so they had a second vehicle, this time a truck, also connected to the room through a second tube. Now there was success; all patients locked up in the room eventually died. During his interrogation leading up to his trial, Widmann was confronted with seemingly corroborating evidence for this alleged gassing in a mental asylum: He was shown four photographs showing a scene that he later described. However, later research has shown that these photos were stills from staged footage recorded for a U.S. propaganda documentary for the Nuremberg International Military Tribunal (see Schwensen 2013). Hence, nothing of what Widmann testified had any relation to real-world events.

If Widmann really developed, in 1939, the murder method for euthanasia killings in German's mental institutions, and if those had been working very reliably for two years by late 1941, then why did Widmann have to travel 1,000 km east to try some insane methods to find out how best to kill mental patients there? Even Widmann's interrogator in preparation of his trial was doubtful, as he asked him whether such a single experiment would have justified such a journey. If bottled carbon-monoxide gas wasn't good enough, experiments with other methods, such as engine exhaust or generator gas, could have easily been done in Berlin. Additionally, at the time of the Minsk trip, some early version of "gas vans" were allegedly already in use, if we believe the orthodox narrative, so Widmann's tale is not just absurd, but also anachronistic.

Widmann also confirmed that he was involved in testing the efficiency of a new set of "gas vans" equipped by the Berlin Gaubschat Company. However, when reading Widmann's testimony in this regard, the disorganization, ridiculous incompetence and gross carelessness of all involved is striking. He also insisted that his tests "did not have a useful result," which is difficult to believe – unless he tried getting toxic fumes out of a diesel engine. Of course, this cannot but yield useless results, as

Jankiel Wiernik

diesel exhaust is rather harmless. That's a trivial statement in the world of engine-fume toxicology, and was certainly known to Germany's top toxicologists, so they would never have tried testing a diesel truck's exhaust gases for mass-murder in the first place. In other words: Widmann describes things that would not have happened in the real world.

Widmann also spread the lie that the crematorium chimney of a hospital emitted "5 m high flames," although that was technically impossible. He claimed to have been asked for advice as to how such chimney fires can be prevented. No hospital administrator in his right mind would ask an analytical chemist about issues of cremation technology, though. This case highlights once more that Widmann was making up wild stories on whatever topic he was talking about – perhaps consciously, as a sign that he was being interrogated under duress.

(For more details, see Alvarez 2023, pp. 219-225.)

WIERNIK, JANKIEL (YANKIEL)

Jankiel Wiernik (1889 – 1972) was a Polish Jew who was deported from the Warsaw Ghetto to the Treblinka Camp on 23 August 1942. He escaped from there during the inmate uprising on 2 August 1943. On 6 June 1944, a text written by Wiernik titled *A Year in Treblinka* was sent by a Pole linked to the propaganda branch of the Polish underground government to the Polish Government-in-Exile in London. The text was published both in Polish and in an English translation that same year. An almost identical typewritten text of 22 pages with the same title, and also a separate 3-page manuscript, have made their way into an Israeli archive. This manuscript is probably Wiernik's earliest texts, and the typewritten text may have been the basis for the published texts.

Wiernik was furthermore interviewed on 12 October 1946 by Polish judge Łukaszkiewicz, and he testified during a Polish show trial against Ludwig Fischer, the German wartime governor of the Warsaw District, on 4 January 1947. Here are some pertinent claims made by Wiernick in his texts:

- According to his manuscript, the killing was carried out using *chlorine*. In his later typed text, he claimed instead that mass murder occurred by feeding in the exhaust gas of a Soviet tank engine that served as an electricity generator for the camp. Of course, it would have had to run uninterruptedly in that case. Moreover, for such a task, a dedicated diesel engine would have been used, for which spare parts were available, but most certainly not the engine of a captured Soviet tank. It would have been much more difficult to obtain, to transport, to install and to rig to a dynamo, let alone to repair due to the lack of spare parts. Hence, there certainly was no Soviet tank engine driving anything. However, the exhaust of a diesel engine would not have been lethal in the time claimed.
- The three chambers of the old building measuring 5 m × 5 m held 450 and 500 people each, which would have resulted in an impossible packing density of 18 to 20 people per square meter. The ten chambers in the new building measured 7 m × 7 m and held 1,000 to 1,200 people each, which would have resulted in an impossible packing density of 20 to 24.5 people per square meter.
- The killing took some 25 minutes – which could have been achieved only with a gasoline engine, but not with any diesel electricity generator.
- The gassing victims looked yellow, although the victims of carbon-monoxide poisoning look decidedly reddish-pink.
- 10,000 to 15,000 people were gassed every day when he arrived, which was stepped up to 20,000 daily when the ten additional chambers were in service – which for a year's worth of operation would have resulted in some 3.5 to 5.5 million victims for even the lower arrival numbers.
- Wiernik claimed during his 1947 trial testimony that 2.5 million victims had been buried already by February 1943 in the Treblinka Camp – more than three times what the orthodoxy currently claims as the camp's total death toll.
- Wiernik insisted that Heinrich Himmler visited the Treblinka Camp around February 1943, at which point he "gave the order to exhume and burn all the corpses." However, there is no evidence suggesting that Himmler ever visited Treblinka.
- Wiernik furthermore asserted that exhumed corpses were simply piled on pyres and lit – evidently with no fuel whatsoever. In fact, in his book, he wrote:

    "It turned out that bodies of women burned more easily than those of men. Accordingly, the bodies of women were used for kindling the fires." (Donat 1979, p. 170)

    However, self-immolating corpses simply do not exist.
- To top it all, during his 1947 trial testimony, he stated:

    "On these [cremation] *piles were stacked three thousand or more old, young, men, women, pregnant women. Everything was engulfed in flames, and the bellies burst open at this high temperature and the babies jumped out alive."*

Interestingly, another text by an unnamed author exists that was published in late November 1943 in the Polish newspaper *Kraj* (*Country*). It has very similar contents to Wiernik's text, hence might be an earlier draft of his later account. The article claims that initially inmates at Treblinka were machine-gunned, because the gas chambers had yet to be built. That is rather unlikely, though, because machine guns are notoriously difficult to aim and make bullets fly all over the place. The text says nothing about the killing method applied in the gas chambers.

A November 1942 report of the resistance movement inside the Warsaw Ghetto demonstrates that Wiernik is a profane plagiarizer. To his published Polish text, Wiernik added a map which he copied from this 1942 report. Wiernik kept the map's title, legend and even the numbering of objects shown in it, which is explained in the 1942 report, but not in Wiernik's text. It is all in there: the old building with three chambers, the new with ten larger chambers. He only replaced the false rumor of steam chambers of the 1942 report with the false claim of tank-engine-exhaust chambers.

(For more details, see the entry on Treblinka, as well as Mattogno/Graf 2023, pp. 70-74; Mattogno 2021e, pp. 124-129, 148-151; Mattogno/Kues/Graf 2015, pp. 784-798; https://zapisyterroru.pl/.)

WIESEL, ELIE

Elie (Eliezer) Wiesel (30 Sept. 1928 – 2 July 2016) was a Romanian-born Jew who claimed to have been deported in May 1944 to Auschwitz at age 15 with his entire family, including his 50-year-old father, from what was then Hungary. When the Auschwitz Camp was evacuated, Wiesel claimed that he and his father Shlomo Wiesel decided to join the Germans retreating west. The Wiesels eventually ended up at the Buchenwald Camp, where Elie's father died shortly before the camp was liberated by U.S. troops on 11 April 1945.

Elie Wiesel

The problem with this story is that admission records of both the Auschwitz and the Buchenwald Camps show only the admission of an *Abraham* Wiesel, born in 1900, hence *44* years old in 1944, and a *Lazar* Wiesel, born 4 Sept. 1913, hence *31* years old in 1944, too old to be Elie or to be accidentally confused with him. Abraham Wiesel was six years younger than Shlomo Wiesel's claimed age, and the first names don't match. There is no trace in any German camp record of any man with the last name Wiesel or similar who was born in or around 1928. Therefore, Elie Wiesel was probably neither ever in Auschwitz nor in Buchenwald, and Abraham Wiesel may also not have been Elie's father.

After the war, Wiesel first lived as an orphan in France, and later immigrated to the United State. Not too long after the war, Wiesel wrote an allegedly autobiographical text in Yiddish about his experiences in Auschwitz and Buchenwald, titled *Un di velt hot geshvign* (*And the World Remained Silent*), which was published in Argentina in 1956. An adapted French translation of it was eventually radically rewritten by French author François Mauriac, to live up to his literary expectations, and published in 1958 with the title *La Nuit* (*Night*). Translations in all major and many minor languages followed in subsequent decades. The book has become required reading for students at many high schools, colleges and universities around the globe, and is probably one of the most influential Holocaust texts.

The text has numerous false claims that radically undermine the credibility of its author, among them for example (based on the original French edition; other translations have been cleansed of some of this nonsense):

– Wiesel claimed that they were deported in early June 1944 and arrived in Auschwitz in April 1944 – yes, he traveled backward in time! The admission records for Abraham and Lazar Wiesel in Auschwitz show 24 May 1944.

– Wiesel claimed that, in the cattle car crammed full of frightened and suffering Jews on their way to Auschwitz, the young orthodox Jews in the car had a sex orgy. That passage, based on a young man's perverted sexual fantasy but certainly not on reality, was censored out in all foreign and also all later French translations.

– Wiesel wrote how the inmates locked up in the railway cattle car could see flames spewing out of large chimneys into the black of the night, as the train was approaching the Birkenau Camp. However, no flames can come out of crematorium chimneys whose furnaces are fired with coke.

– Wiesel followed the cliché that every Auschwitz inmate, he and his father included, was selected by Dr. Josef Mengele, whom he described as a "typical SS officer, cruel face, […] and a monocle," which is the opposite of Mengele's complexion, who wore no glasses and looked rather friendly.

– After passing the initial Mengele selection on the railway ramp, Wiesel and his father kept on walking, when they saw nearby two large fire pits. Into one of them, a truck dumped living babies, and the other, larger one was meant for adults. However, air photos of exactly that time show no such burning pits anywhere in the area, and even the orthodoxy agrees that no burning pit was located anywhere near the railway platform, so Wiesel described something that everyone agrees didn't exist.

– During his entire text, Wiesel never used the term "gas chamber," but only the word "crematorium." This annoyed the translator of the German edition so much that he replaced all instances of "crematorium" with "gas chamber," including two cases in the section about the Buchenwald Camp, where everyone agrees no homicidal gas chamber existed.

– Wiesel described the hanging of a child, suffering because its low weight didn't break its neck when the stool was pulled. Scholars agree that children were not sentenced to death and killed like that at Auschwitz. It is an allegorical scene.

– On 18 January 1945, when the Auschwitz Camp was evacuated, sick or injured inmates who had difficulties walking were given the choice to either stay and wait for the Soviets, or leave with the retreating Germans. Elie wrote that, after some contemplation with his father, and in spite of rumors that those left behind might get executed – a risk that was even higher when they left with the Germans – they decided anyway to leave with the Germans rather than wait for the Soviet liberators. Here is how U.S. engineer Fritz Berg described this pivotal decision:

> *"The choices that were made here in January 1945 are enormously important. In the entire history of Jewish suffering at the hands of gentiles, what moment in time could possibly be more dramatic than this precious moment when Jews could choose between, on the one hand, liberation by the Soviets with the chances to tell the whole world about the evil 'Nazis' and to help bring about their defeat – and the other choice of going with the 'Nazi' mass murderers and to continue working for them and to help preserve their evil regime. […]*
>
> *The momentous choice brings Shakespeare's Hamlet to mind:*
>
> *'To remain, or not to remain; that is the question:' to remain and be liberated by Soviet troops and risk their slings and rifles in order to tell the whole world about the outrageous 'Nazis' – or, take arms and feet against a sea of cold and darkness in order to collaborate with the very same outrageous 'Nazis.' Oh what heartache – ay, there's the rub! Thus conscience does make cowards of us all."*

– Of the 100 inmates traveling on a train to Buchenwald, Wiesel claimed that only 12 survived (88% death rate), although the original records show that the death rate was only about 2%.

Elie Wiesel left Auschwitz with his German captors, because he knew that the truth about Auschwitz was nowhere near what he later wrote in *Night*, this novel disguised as an autobiography written by a disturbed mind filled with hate and a lust for revenge. This novel may have been his first act of systematic lying, but it wasn't his last, as Warren Routledge has thoroughly documented in his critical biography of Elie Wiesel. (For more details, see Desjardins 2012; Routledge 2020; Rudolf 2023, pp. 477-480.)

WIESENTHAL, SIMON

Simon Wiesenthal (31 Dec. 1908 – 20 Sept. 2005) was a Galician Jew (today's western Ukraine) whose wartime history is unclear, because he has made conflicting statements about it. At one point, he claimed to have been slated for a mass execution with thousands of other Jews, but at the very moment, when it was his turn to get shot, his name was miraculously called out by someone, and he was led away. This unlikely turn has caused skepticism even among mainstream historians, calling Wiesenthal's description of the event "apocryphal" (see Walters 2009, pp. 85f.)

Simon Wiesenthal

He claimed in one text that he joined the anti-German and anti-Ukrainian pro-Stalinist partisans in late 1943, but was caught by the Germans in June of 1944, leading to the miraculous shooting story just mentioned; in another account, he simply stated that he was in hiding during that time, which is probably the truth. After an ordeal of westward evacuation, he ended up at the Mauthausen Camp, where he was liberated.

After the war, he remained in Austria and instantly started collecting information on alleged National-Socialist war criminals with the aim of bringing them to justice. He quickly gained the support of U.S. occupational authorities, and after the creation of Israel, he closely cooperated with that state's secret services. In 1960, he officially became a Mossad agent, drawing a monthly salary from them. As Israeli author Tom Segev writes in his 2010 biography of Wiesenthal, he had an ambivalent relationship to the truth. As a true Mossad agent, spreading information and disinformation was all part of the game. The "truth" was clearly subordinated to political purposes.

Although Wiesenthal could contribute nothing to the orthodox Holocaust narrative as a witness, he used his influence to spread information and disinformation about what happened to the Jews in Europe during World War II. For instance, in 1946, he published a brochure on the Mauthausen Camp mainly containing his own sketches trying to depict the horrors of this camp. One drawing allegedly depicts three inmates bound to posts and brutally put to death by the Germans. However, he copied this picture from a photo that had appeared in *Life* magazine in 1945 showing the execution of three German spies in December 1944. In his brochure, Wiesenthal also made use of the phony "confession" allegedly extorted from Mauthausen commandant Franz Ziereis by former inmates while Ziereis was bleeding to death.

For years, Wiesenthal has repeatedly spread the false claim that the fat of murdered Jews was used to manufacture soap. He also spread the false story, invented by Stefan Szende in 1944, that people were killed with electrocution at Belzec.

Wiesenthal did not hesitate to invent "Nazi criminals" either, as the case of Polish-born Chicago man Frank Walus proves. Wiesenthal framed him as a Gestapo agent who committed atrocities in Poland during the war. However, during an extended court case, Walus proved that he had been working on a German farm all through the war and was never in Poland, let alone committed any crimes there.

Much of Wiesenthal's claim to fame as a "Nazi Hunter" is smoke and mirrors, although he certainly also had his successes. He moreover provided considerable assistance toward organizing witnesses testifying against individuals accused of having committed war crimes. Furthermore, with his dis/information services, he surely also influenced the testimony of many witnesses – but certainly not toward being more truthful.

Another lingering legacy of Wiesenthal is the claim that the Holocaust had not six million victims, but 11 million. However, he made up that figure without having any basis for it, as quite a few mainstream scholars have complained over the decades. Wiesenthal wanted to sell the Holocaust to the gentiles, and in order to pique their interest, he threw in five million non-Jewish victims, just a million short of the claimed Jewish death toll of six million, in order to ensure Jewish victimhood supremacy. Again, truth was relegated to the back bench.

(For more details, see Weber 1995b, Rudolf 2023, pp. 15-17, 73; Segev 2010.)

WIJNBERG, SAARTJE

Saartje Wijnberg was the wife of Chaim Engel, and also an inmate of the Sobibór Camp. In three depositions of 22 June and 19 July 1946 as well as 29 August 1949, she claimed that the gas was fed into the gas chamber(s) through showerheads, and that, after the murder, the floors opened, and the bodies were discharged into carts below, which brought them to mass graves. The deposition signed together with her husband (19 July 1946) speaks of gas chambers, while her own ones mention only one chamber. In her mutual deposition with her husband, she also claimed a death toll of some 800,000 victims for the camp.

All these claims are rejected as false by the orthodoxy. According to their narrative, the gas was fed through pipes rather than showerheads. These chambers did not have collapsible floors with carts underneath either. The corpses were instead taken out of the chamber manually, sideways through a normal door. Furthermore, only about a quarter million victims are said to have died in the camp.

(See the entry on Sobibór for more details, as well as Graf/Kues/Mattogno 2020, p. 109; Mattogno 2021e, pp. 81f.)

WILLENBERG, SAMUEL

Samuel Willenberg (16 Feb. 1923 – 19 Feb. 2016) was a Polish Jew who was deported from the Opatów Ghetto to Treblinka on 20 October 1942. According to his memoirs, he was employed there first at sorting inmate property, then for other activities, such as weaving branches into fences to hide the camp's events from the outside world. He managed to escape from that camp during the inmate uprising on 2 August 1943.

Samuel Willenberg

After the war, he briefly served in the Polish army, and in 1950, he emigrated to Israel. In 1945, he penned a 30-page account of his experiences at Treblinka, titled "I Survived Treblinka." However, it contains no reference to any extermination procedure, but merely states:

"After the performance of their workday, these people were directed naked to the chambers."

What "chambers" means is left to the reader's speculation.

Enticed by the hysterical atmosphere of the Jerusalem show trial against John Demjanjuk in the mid-1980s, Willenberg expanded on that theme by writing an entire book about his time at the Treblinka Camp titled *Revolt in Treblinka* (1986 in Hebrew, and 1989 in Polish) and *Surviving Treblinka* (the 1989 U.S. edition). In this book, he elaborated in detail about the things he evidently was unaware of in 1945. The remarks he added in this regard, however, are evidently based either on Holocaust literature of the time and/or on media reports and witness statements made in the context of the Demjanjuk Trial. In a "convergence of evidence" of false claims, Willenberg agreed with all these sources that people were killed with exhaust gasses from a Soviet tank's diesel engine. Unfortunately for Willenberg, diesel-engine exhaust gasses are utterly unsuited for mass murder. Furthermore, no Soviet captured tank engine would ever have been considered, let alone used for any such task, because it would have been difficult to obtain, to transport, to install, to maintain, to repair, and to run. (See the entry on the Treblinka Camp for more details.)

Willenberg's texts are among the least-informative sources on the extermination procedure allegedly used at Treblinka. His testimonies indicate that there simply wasn't anything to remember and report about any mass-extermination technique. (For more details, see Mattogno 2021e, pp. 130-132.)

wire-mesh columns (for use with Zyklon) → Zyklon-b Introduction Devices

WIRTH, CHRISTIAN

Christian Wirth (24 Nov. 1885 – 26 May 1944), SS *Sturmbannführer*, was a German police officer who was assigned to supervise euthanasia killings in German mental institutions in late 1939. In late 1941, he was assigned to head the Belzec Camp. In August 1942, he became inspector of the *Aktion Reinhardt* camps. After this operation was terminated in 1943, he was assigned to an anti-partisan unit in northern Italy in late 1943, where he was killed by partisans in May 1944.

Christian Wirth

There is very little documentation about Wirth's actual activities. His activities as commandant of the Belzec Camp are obscure, because we only have the two extremely unreliable testimonies of Kurt Gerstein and Rudolf Reder from the immediate postwar period. While Reder did not even mention Wirth, Gerstein described him as "a frail and small man," when in fact he was tall and broad-shouldered. We furthermore have several brief references to Wirth as a brutal, calloused man, made decades after the war by defendants in West-German trials about crimes allegedly committed at the Belzec, Sobibór and Treblinka camps. It stands to reason, however, that those defendants used Wirth as a conveniently dead scapegoat who couldn't respond to his accusers. Hence, their terse statements must be viewed with skepticism as well.

(For some details, see the index entries for C. Wirth in Mattogno 2004a, 2021b&e, Mattogno/Graf 2023, Graf/Kues/Mattogno 2020.)

WIRTHS, EDUARD

Eduard Wirths (4 Sept. 1909 – 20 Sept. 1945), SS *Obersturmbannführer*, served as a German army physician in Norway and in the Soviet Union. After suffering a heart attack in early 1942, he was posted to the Dachau Camp for special training, then served briefly as garrison physician at the Neuengamme Camp starting in July 1942. In early September 1942, he was transferred to the Auschwitz Camp. His main task was to get the typhus epidemic under control that had been ravaging the camp since June/July 1942, killing one of Wirths's predecessors (Siegfried Schwela) and rendering another unfit for duty for a long time (Kurt Uhlenbrock).

Eduard Wirths

Upon discovering the catastrophic sanitary, hygienic and medical conditions at Auschwitz, Wirths urged and quickly convinced the Berlin authorities to take drastic measures with a huge special-construction program meant to remedy the situation. The program, which cost hundreds of millions of dollars in today's currency, included installing proper toilet, wash, shower and delousing facilities, improving the camp's drainage system, building a wastewater treatment plant, and expanding the Birkenau Camp to include a huge hospital section with more than 100 barracks for the treatment of sick and injured inmates.

His efforts were eventually successful in suppressing the typhus epidemic and other dangerous diseases, which gained him the admiration of the camp inmates – among them Hermann Langbein, who later became one of the most virulent orthodox Auschwitz propagandists. In a 1943 Christmas card for Wirths, Langbein, an influential inmate functionary at the time, wrote that Wirths had saved the lives of 93,000 inmates with his efforts, and that all Auschwitz inmates wished that he stayed with them for the next year. This praise by inmates finds a parallel in the praise Wirths received several times from his superiors for his unrelenting lobbying for the camp inmates' welfare and wellbeing. That was his job, he did it well, and he was lauded by all sides for it.

As garrison physician, Wirths was in charge of all supplies of Zyklon B, and he had major influence on construction plans for anything involving medicine, sanitation and hygiene, including the crematoria.

The orthodoxy claims that the four crematoria at Birkenau were originally planned only as facilities to hygienically dispose of deceased inmates, but that these plans were changed in late 1942 to make these buildings serve primarily as mass-murder weapons using Zyklon B. At that time,
- Dr. Eduard Wirths was the head over Zyklon B supplies and all accessories, such as hydrogen-cyanide test kits, gas masks, filters etc.
- He decided which Auschwitz physician had to be on duty during inmate selections at the railway ramp or in the inmate infirmaries inside the camp.
- He defined the criteria according to which what type of inmate was to be selected for which fate.
- He was one of the persons in charge of planning the functionality of the crematoria – which is significant, given that Wirths's office and laboratory were located in Crematorium II beginning February 1943.

Therefore, after camp commandant Rudolf Höss, Dr. Wirths would have been the second person in charge, bearing primary responsibility for the claimed mass murder of some one million Jews at Auschwitz using Zyklon B and other claimed murder methods (such as phenol injections). The camp's inmate functionaries, foremost Hermann Langbein – who was Wirths's secretary – would have been keenly aware of this. It is thus incomprehensible that Langbein or any other inmate of influence would have written the above-mentioned Christmas card in 1943, if by that time some half a million inmates had been killed under Wirths's control and supervision.

The documentation on Wirths's activities at Auschwitz is comprehensive, and all of it is exclusively benign and in the best interest of the inmates.

After the war, Dr. Wirths was arrested by the Allies and charged with the murder of four million inmates. It is unknown what they did to him while he was in their custody, but it was enough for him to commit suicide after a few days in prison – at age 36. (For many more details, see Mattogno 2016a, esp. pp. 219-276; 2016d.)

WIRTSCHAFTS- UND VERWALTUNGSHAUPTAMT

The Third Reich's department named *Wirtschafts- und Verwaltungshauptamt* (WVHA) translates to Economic and Administrative Main Office. It was established in 1942 by merging two previously independent offices of the SS. The WVHA was directly subordinate to Heinrich Himmler as the *Reichsführer* SS. This office handled all financial and administrative matters concerning the SS and its vast network of forced-labor industries and labor as well as concentration camps. Head of the WVHA was Oswald Pohl until the end of the war.

WISLICENY, DIETER

Dieter Wisliceny (13 Jan. 1911 – 4 May 1948) SS *Hauptsturmführer*, was one of Adolf Eichmann's deputies at the office at Germany's Department of Homeland Security (*Reichssicherheitshauptamt*) dealing with the so-called "Jewish question." As such, he was involved in the ghettoization and eventual deportation of Jews from several eastern European countries.

Dieter Wisliceny

Together with Wilhelm Höttl, Wisliceny was instrumental in "establishing" for the Nuremberg International Military Tribunal (IMT) that six million Jews had died as a result of National-Socialist persecution and extermination policy, although Wisliceny only confirmed five million victims.

After the war, Wisliceny was arrested for his involvement in mass deportations of Jews. He testified for the prosecution during the IMT. Asked about how many Jews were killed during the "Final Solution," Wisliceny claimed that Eichmann had talked about four, sometimes even five million Jews subjected to the "Final Solution," but that he does not know how many of them survived. In other words, the number of Jews included in the "Final Solution" did not necessarily mean they had been killed. After all, deportation, not murder, was Eichmann's and Wisliceny's job. What happened to the Jews at their destinations was, strictly speaking, none of their business. However, when asked whether Eichmann, during their last meeting in February 1945, had said anything about the number of Jews actually *killed*, Wisliceny stated (*IMT*, Vol. 4, p. 371):

> "He said he would leap laughing into the grave because the feeling that he had 5 million people on his conscience would be for him a source of extraordinary satisfaction."

Eichmann, however, denied this during his own trial at Jerusalem in 1961 (Aschenauer 1980, pp. 460f., 473ff., 494).

While Höttl was rewarded for his collaboration with the Allies in cementing the six-million death-toll figure by never being subject to any prosecution, Wisliceny was extradited to Stalinist Czechoslovakia, put on a show trial, sentenced to death and executed; he was 37.

WITCH TRIALS

Modern-day trials staged against alleged perpetrators or deniers of claimed Holocaust crimes have many characteristics which put them into the same category as medieval witch trials. The table below lists some of the pertinent characteristics of witch trials, and how they compare with trials against claimed

Comparison of Various Types of Modern-Day Trials with Medieval Witch Trials			
Witch-Trial Characteristic	NS Trial	Denier Trial	Normal Trial
Crimes sometimes from the realm of the supernatural.	Rarely	Nothing supernatural	Nothing supernatural
Torture and abuse was initially used to extract confessions, but rarely needed anymore in later decades and centuries, although always threatened.	Torture was common in immediate postwar years, but absent in later years.	No torture	No torture
The sentence was either death by excruciating methods or acquittal.	Death sentences were the rule in immediate postwar years, but sentences were differentiated later.	Differentiated, but often harsh sentences for peaceful thoughtcrimes.	Differentiated sentences.
The defense on occasion challenged witness testimony and demanded material evidence, although rarely with success.	The defense very rarely challenged witness testimony and almost never demanded material evidence.	The defense regularly tries to challenge witness testimony and to offer material evidence.	The defense regularly challenges witness testimony and demands material evidence.
The crime committed is considered particularly heinous, atrocious and unique.	The crime committed is considered particularly heinous, atrocious and unique (for "deniers" on an intellectual level).		No extraordinary assessment for crimes.
The prosecution and its witnesses have fool's freedom, can claim whatever they please, and will rarely get in trouble even if caught lying.	The prosecution and its witnesses have fool's freedom, can claim whatever they please, and won't get in trouble even if caught lying. In trials against dissidents, prosecutors often don't have to prove anything, as all claims are self-evident.		Prosecution witnesses risk prosecution for perjury.
The defense is almost completely paralyzed, exonerating evidence is often rejected.	The defense is almost completely paralyzed; offering exonerating evidence is either always rejected, or in some countries even illegal and a new criminal offense.		The defense is not impeded.
The underlying facts (devil and witchcraft exist) are considered self-evident, no longer in need of proof, and cannot be challenged.	The underlying facts (Holocaust, 6 million, gas chambers, a plan) are considered self-evident, no longer in need of proof, and cannot be challenged.		All aspects can be challenged.
Denial of the existence of the devil and of witchcraft is considered the greatest heresy of the time.	Contesting the Holocaust or any of its essential aspects is considered the greatest heresy of the time.		Contesting the claimed crime is perfectly legitimate.
Many similar testimonies were seen as a "convergence of evidence"; contradictions and impossibilities in decisive details were ignored.	Many similar testimonies are seen as a "convergence of evidence"; contradictions and impossibilities in decisive details are ignored.		There are rarely many testimonies, and they are usually contested where needed.

National-Socialist perpetrators and against those contesting the reality of these crimes or their dimension.

(For more details, see Rudolf 2019, pp. 120f.)

WITNESSES

Although a claim cannot be evidence of its own truth, claims made by people asserting to have witnessed something in connection with the Holocaust are very often taken at face value by most people, if the claim supports the orthodox narrative. It is therefore very important to subject these claims to a thorough source criticism to verify their veracity. (See the entry on source criticism.)

This entry contains several lists – alphabetically organized by the claimed crime location or complex – with the names of witnesses who have testified about the given crime location or complex. Many of them are included in this encyclopedia with a critical assessment of their assertions.

For a list of false witnesses who never were at the claimed locations at the asserted time, see that entry.

Aktion 1005
  Adametz, Gerhard
  Amiel, Szymon
  Beer, Abraham
  Berlyant, Semen
  Blobel, Paul
  Blyazer, A.
  Brodsky, Isaak
  Budnik, David
  Chamaides, Heinrich
  Damjanović, Momčilo
  Davydov, Vladimir
  Doliner, Iosif
  Edelman, Salman
  Faitelson, Alex
  Farber, Yuri
  Gol, Szloma
  Kaper, Yakov
  Korn, Moische
  Kuklia, Vladislav
  Manusevich, David
  Ostrovsky, Leonid
  Pilunov, Stefan
  Steyuk, Yakov
  Trubakov, Ziama
  Weliczker, Leon
  Zaydel, Matvey

Auschwitz
  Aumeier, Hans (SS)
  Bacon, Yehuda
  Bard-Nomberg, Helena
  Baum, Bruno
  Behr, Emil
  Bendel, Charles S.
  Bennahmias, Daniel
  Benroubi, Maurice
  Bialek, Regina
  Bily, Henry
  Bimko, Ada
  Böck, Richard (SS)
  Boger, Wilhelm (SS)
  Broad, Pery S. (SS)
  Buki, Milton
  Chasan, Shaul
  Christophersen, Thies (SS)
  Chybiński, Stanisław
  Cohen, Leon
  Cykert, Abraham
  Cyrankiewicz, Jozef
  Dejaco, Walter (SS)
  Dibowski, Wilhelm
  Długoborski, Wácław
  Dragon, Abraham
  Dragon, Szlama
  Eisenschmidt, Eliezer
  Epstein, Berthold
  Fabian, Bela
  Farkas, Henry
  Fischer, Bruno
  Fischer, Horst (SS)
  Fliamenbaum, David
  Franke-Gricksch, Alfred (SS)
  Frankl, Viktor
  Friedman, Arnold
  Fries, Jakob
  Frosch, Chaim
  Gabai, Dario
  Gabai, Yaakov
  Gál, Gyula
  Garbarz, Moshé
  Gertner, Szaja
  Grabner, Maximilian (SS)
  Gradowski, Salmen
  Gröning, Oskar (SS)
  Grüner, Miklós
  Gulba, Franciszek
  Herman, Chaim
  Höss, Rudolf (SS)
  Jankowski, Stanisław
  Kaduk, Oswald (SS)
  Karolinskij, Samij
  Karvat, David
  Kaufmann Schafranov, Sofia
  Kaufmann, Jeannette
  Kertész, Imre
  Klehr, Josef (SS)
  Klein, Marc
  Kranz, Hermine
  Kraus, Ota
  Kremer, Johann Paul (SS)
  Kula, Michał
  Kulka, Erich
  Langbein, Hermann
  Langfus, Leib
  Laptos, Leo
  Lea, David
  Lengyel, Olga
  Lequeux, Maurice
  Lettich, André
  Levi, Primo
  Lévy, Robert
  Lewental, Salmen
  Lewińska, Pelagia
  Lichtenstein, Mordecai
  Limousin, Henri
  Litwinska, Sofia
  Mandelbaum, Henryk
  Mansfeld, Géza
  Marcus, Kurt
  Mermelstein, Melvin
  Müller, Filip
  Münch, Hans (SS)
  Mussfeldt, Erich (SS)
  Nadsari, Marcel
  Nagraba, Ludwik
  Nahon, Marco

Nyiszli, Miklos
Obrycki, Narcyz Tadeusz
Ochshorn, Isaac Egon
Olère, David
Paisikovic, Dov
Piazza, Bruno
Pilecki, Withold
Pilo, Aaron
Plucer, Regina
Putzker, Fritz
Rogerie, André
Rögner, Adolf
Rosenblum, Joshuah
Rosenblum, Moritz
Rosenthal, Maryla
Rosin, Arnošt
Sackar, Josef
Sadowska, Rajzla
Schellekes, Maurice
Schwarz, Deszö
Sompolinski, Roman
Stanek, Franciszek
Stark, Hans (SS)
Süss, Franz
Tabeau, Jerzy
Tauber, Henryk
Vaillant-Couturier, Marie-Claude
Venezia, Morris
Venezia, Shlomo
Vrba, Rudolf
Weiss, Janda
Wetzler, Alfred
Wiesel, Elie
Wirths, Eduard (SS)
Wohlfahrt, Wilhelm
Wolken, Otto
Złobnicki, Adam

Belzec
　Cykert, Abraham
　Fuchs, Erich (SS)
　Gerstein, Kurt (SS)
　Gley, Heinrich (SS)
　Hirszman, Chaim
　Jührs, Robert (SS)
　Karski, Jan
　Kozak, Stanisław
　Oberhauser, Josef (SS)
　Pfannenstiel, Wilhelm (SS)
　Reder, Rudolf
　Schluch, Karl (SS)

Szende, Stefan
Unverhau, Heinrich (SS)

Bergen-Belsen
　Barton, Russell
　Peer, Moshe
　Springer, Elisa

Buchenwald
　Hénocque, Georges
　Rassinier, Paul
　Renard, Jean-Paul
　Rosenblat, Herman

Chełmno
　Burmeister, Walter (SS)
　Falborski, Bronisław
　Grojanowski, Jakov
　Israel, Bruno
　Piller, Walter (SS)
　Podchlebnik, Michał
　Sekiewicz, Mieczysław
　Srebrnik, Szymon
　Żurawski, Mieczysław

Dachau
　Blaha, Franz

Einsatzgruppen
　Bach-Zelewski, Erich von dem (SS)
　Höfer, Fritz (SS)
　Ohlendorf, Otto (SS)
　Pronicheva, Dina
　Werner, Kurt (SS)

Flossenbürg
　Friedman, Arnold

Gas Vans
　Becker, August (SS)
　Burmeister, Walter (SS)
　Falborski, Bronisław
　Hassler, Johann (SS)
　Ohlendorf, Otto (SS)
　Pilunov, Stefan
　Rauff, Walter (SS)
　Widmann, Albert (SS)

Gross-Rosen
　Ochshorn, Isaac Egon

Holocaust (general)
　Becher, Kurt (SS)
　Eichmann, Adolf (SS)
　Frank, Hans (SS)
　Göring, Hermann (SS)
　Höfle, Hans (SS)
　Höttl, Wilhelm (SS)
　Korherr, Richard (SS)
　Larson, Charles
　Morgen, Konrad (SS)
　Pinter, Stephen F.
　Rosenberg, Alfred (SS)
　Wisliceny, Dieter (SS)

Majdanek
　Denisow, Piotr
　Grocher, Mietek
　Mussfeldt, Erich (SS)
　Seidenwurm Wrzos, Mary

Mauthausen
　Maršálek, Hans

Mogilev
　Bach-Zelewski, Erich von dem (SS)

Natzweiler
　Kramer, Josef
　Weydert, Georg

Neuengamme
　Bagrowsky, Steffan
　Bahr, Wilhelm (SS)
　Bösch, Ernst
　Brandenburger, Otto
　Bruns, August
　Cäsar, Ernst
　Christensen, Walter
　Dingeldein, Ernst
　Edler, Ernst
　Erdmann, Hermann (SS)
　Filsinger, Walter (SS)
　Gondzik, Ewald
　Groß, Hans
　Händler, Josef
　Hoffmann, Emil
　Hoffmann, Günther
　Hottenbacher, Karl
　Kilbinger, Otto
　Krause, Franz

Lüdke, Albin
Ludwig, Bruno
Lütkemeyer, Albert (SS)
Merten, Georg
Motz, Eugeniusz
Mueller, Wilhelm
Müller, Michael
Pauly, Max (SS)
Poot, Theodor
Roding, Werner
Roehl, Karl
Saalwächter, Ernst
Schultz, Friedrich
Schwerger, Heinrich
Struck, Hermann
Szafrański, Zygmunt
Tamsen, Friedrich
Wackernagel, Günther
Winter, Anton
Witt, Hans Christian (SS)
Witt, Karl
Zuleger, Eduard
Zwinscher, Willy

Plazow
  Göth, Amon (SS)

Ravensbrück
  Neudeck, Ruth
  Percival Karl Treite (SS)
  Rudroff, Anni
  Schwarzhuber, Josef (SS)
  Suhren, Fritz (SS)
  Trksakova, Irma
  Woźniakówna, Michalina

Sachsenhausen
  Feiler, Willi
  Kaindl, Anton (SS)
  Schmidt, Ludwig
  Soerensen, Wilhelm
  Waldmann, Paul (SS)

Semlin
  Damjanović, Momčilo

Sobibór
  Bahir, Moshe
  Barbl, Heinrich (SS)
  Bauer, Erich (SS)
  Biskovitz, Ya'akov
  Blatt, Thomas Toivi
  Bolender, Kurt (SS)
  Danilchenko, Ignat (SS aid)
  Engel, Chaim
  Engel-Wijnberg, Selma
  Fajgielbaum, Srul
  Feldhendler, Leon
  Felenbaum-Weiss, Hella
  Freiberg, Ber (Dov)
  Fuchs, Erich (SS)
  Gomerski, Hubert (SS)
  Hanel, Salomea
  Hödl, Franz (SS)
  Ittner, Alfred (SS)
  Lambert, Erwin (SS)
  Lerer, Samuel
  Lerner, Leon
  Lichtman, Eda
  Lichtmann, Icek
  Metz, Zelda
  Mottel, Samet
  Pankov, Vassily (SS aid)
  Pechersky, Alexander
  Podchlebnik, Salomon
  Razgonayev, Mikhail (SS aid)
  Schelvis, Jules
  Schütt, Hans-Heinz (SS)
  Stangl, Franz (SS)
  Stern, Ursula
  Szmajzner, Stanisław
  Trajtag, Josef
  Unverhau, Heinrich (SS)
  Wagner, Gustav (SS)
  Wijnberg, Saartje

Treblinka
  Auerbach, Rachel
  Berger, Oskar
  Bomba, Abraham
  Buchholcowa, Janina
  Chomka, Władysław
  Czechowicz, Aron
  Finkelsztein, Leon
  Franz, Kurt (SS)
  Glazar, Richard
  Goldberg, Szymon
  Goldfarb, Abraham I.
  Gray, Martin
  Kersch, Silvia
  Kon, Abe
  Kon, Stanisław
  Krzepicki, Abraham
  Kudlik, Aleksander
  Lesky, Simcha
  Nowodowski, Dawid
  Poswolski, Henryk
  Puchała, Lucjan
  Rabinowicz, Jakub
  Rajchman, Chil
  Rajgrodzki, Jerzy
  Rajzman, Samuel (Shmuel)
  Rosenberg, Eliyahu
  Skarżyński, Kazimierz
  Stangl, Franz (SS)
  Strawczyński, Oskar
  Suchomel, Franz (SS)
  Sułkowski, Jan
  Szajn-Lewin, Eugenia
  Szperling, Henike
  Turowski, Eugeniusz
  Warszawski, Szyja
  Wiernik, Jankiel (Yankiel)
  Willenberg, Samuel
  Ząbecki, Franciszek

WITNESSES AGAINST MASS MURDER

Witnesses who were at a certain location at a time for which some kind of mass-murder activity has been claimed, but who could *not* confirm having seen any evidence of it, can rightfully be called witnesses *against* mass murder. Most of them explained that they found out about this alleged mass murder only after the war, due to the pervasive propaganda campaign unleashed after Germany's defeat.

Holocaust "survivors" who insist that they did not know or experience anything confirming the orthodox narrative on mass exterminations are usually ignored by Western societies. After all, if they missed the most important action of their lifetime, who would be interested in their story? As the case of

Maryla Rosenthal demonstrates, sometimes these witnesses are put under enormous pressure to "remember" what everyone expects them to. If they insist too stubbornly that it did not happen, they themselves can become a target of societal persecution, and in many countries even of criminal prosecution.

Under these circumstances, it is not surprising that cases of "survivors" insisting that they did not know are rarely reported, and never became the attention focus of either media or judicial authorities.

And yet, some conspicuous cases have come to light. The following incomplete list contains the names of former camp inmates who have made statements to this effect, and who are featured in this encyclopedia:
- Emil Behr (Auschwitz)
- Wilhelm Dibowski (Auschwitz)
- Jakob Fries (Auschwitz)
- Georg Klein (Auschwitz; see entry on R. Vrba)
- Stanisław Kozak (Belzec)
- Primo Levi (Auschwitz)
- Dawid Nowodowski (Treblinka)
- Maryla Rosenthal (Auschwitz)
- Rajzla Sadowska (Auschwitz)
- Jules Schelvis (Sobibór)
- Franz Süss (Auschwitz)
- Maria Van Herwaarden (Auschwitz)

To be completed.

WOHLFAHRT, WILHELM

Wilhelm Wohlfahrt, a Pole living in Warsaw, was incarcerated in the Auschwitz Camp on 8 January 1942. In March of that year, he was assigned to the camp's Construction Office, where he was employed as a surveyor who was permitted to leave the camp area to do his job. This is even confirmed by extant camp documents. He testified during the trial against former camp commandant Rudolf Höss.

In a brief passage during that statement, he spoke of having seen from a distance of 400 to 500 meters, through his surveying instruments, how bodies were being loaded onto carts near what he called the "little red house" near the Birkenau Camp (which refers to Bunker 1). He did not describe anything about the building or any mass-murder procedure, only that he saw bodies. He located this alleged facility somewhat farther away from the camp than the orthodoxy claims today, but that may be incidental.

Wohlfahrt briefly described "Bunker 2" (which he called "little white house") as a building with four evenly dimensioned gas chambers of some 4 by 7-8 m in size, each of some 30 m², hence a total of some 120 m². This is the only feature he mentioned that can be checked against other witness claims and reality. The orthodoxy's narrative is largely based on Szlama Dragon's postwar statements. However, Dragon insisted on four *unevenly* sized rooms, all with the same length, but with varying widths in a ration of roughly 12:7:4:2.5. Another witness, Dov Paisikovic, has claimed three equally sized rooms. They all made it up, however, because the foundation walls of a former building, which the orthodoxy claims are the ruins of "Bunker 2," still exist today. It shows seven irregularly sized and arranged rooms.

(For more details, see Mattogno 2016f, pp. 106-108.)

WOLFF, KARL

Karl Wolff

Karl Wolff (13 May 1900 – 17 July 1984), SS *Obergruppenführer*, was Heinrich Himmler's chief of staff and his liaison officer to Adolf Hitler. As such, he had access to all the material crossing Himmler's desk. Toward the end of the war, on Himmler's initiative, Wolff negotiated an early surrender of the German forces in Italy to the U.S. Forces. Probably as a reward for this, Wolff did not get prosecuted by the Allies. However, the West-German authorities were not a part of this background deal, so in 1962, they started prosecuting Wolff for his alleged involvement in the deportation of 300,000 Italian Jews.

The case that unfolded at the Munich Jury Court in 1964 did not quite go the way the prosecution and the powers behind it had planned. Wolff steadfastly insisted that he knew nothing about any systematic exterminations happening during the war. The prosecution's case rested entirely on circumstantial evidence. Some 90 witnesses testified, but only three of them incriminated Wolff. While the three professional judges, bending to political pressure, were ready to sentence Wolff anyway, the six jury members were not.

Deliberations behind closed doors went on for

eight days, during which the professional judges pointed out the political dimension of the case, since the entire world was watching and expecting a merciless guilty verdict. The slim majority of just one jury member eventually agreed to a 15-year prison term, but only after they had been promised that Wolff would be pardoned and released from prison after a year or two.

However, when one of the jury members, Norbert Kellnberger, found out in 1969 that Wolff was still in prison, he started stirring things up, and eventually managed to get Wolff released in 1971 "for health reasons." Kellnberger went public with this story in 1974, which was picked up and reported by some German media.

This case shows how postwar trials against alleged National-Socialist perpetrators bear all the hallmarks of show trials: the alleged crime itself cannot be challenge, and guilty verdicts for the claimed perpetrators are foregone conclusions, a few exceptions here and there notwithstanding.
(For more details on this, see Rudolf 2023, pp. 425f.)

WOLKEN, OTTO

Otto Wolken (27 April 1903 – 1 Feb. 1975), was an Austrian Jew and physician deported to Auschwitz on 20 June 1943. From October 1943, he was deployed as an inmate physician and later also as main clerk in the outpatient clinic of the Birkenau quarantine camp. In that function, he furtively transcribed various German documents and created some of his own (the best-known is the so-called "Quarantine List").

At war's end, he was interrogated twice by Polish investigative judge Jan Sehn in preparation for the trials against former camp commandant Rudolf Höss and against members of the Auschwitz Camp's staff. During those interrogations, Wolken handed over his transcribed lists and other documents he had prepared while at Auschwitz. His testimony and his documents were considered so important by the Polish judiciary that they fill an entire dedicated binder of the trial material (Volume 6 of the Höss Trial). Next to Höss, Wolken is one of the key witnesses on which Polish historian Danuta Czech relied when writing her "definitive" orthodox chronology of the Auschwitz Camp.

Two sets of Wolken's documents are of importance: His "Daily Reports", and the already mentioned "Quarantine List." The "Daily Reports" are records Wolken kept in his own notebooks of inmates coming and leaving the quarantine camp. However, his numbers are largely inconsistent, but more importantly, each time a substantial number of inmates was transferred from the quarantine camp elsewhere, Wolken insists that they were killed in gas chambers. He had no first-hand knowledge of it, though, since his perspective from the quarantine camp was necessarily limited to what was going on in his sector, which was only a very small part of the entire Birkenau Camp.

Otto Wolken

The "Quarantine List" is even more interesting and revealing, because we have two versions of it: Wolken's original handwritten list, and a list typed by the Polish judiciary. In this list, Wolken entered the number of inmates admitted to the Birkenau quarantine camp (Camp Sector BIIa) from 24 October 1943 to 3 November 1944. While on the first several pages of his handwritten original list, the Block No. is listed where those admitted inmates were lodged, that column was replaced in the typewritten version with one saying "gassed." In other words: when Wolken wrote those lists during the war, he evidently knew nothing about gassings, but when he worked together with the Polish authorities to put his documents to good use against his former captures, they all colluded to manipulate his original material into something it does not say. It's a clear-cut case of document forgery.

Furthermore, while Wolken could have known how many deportees were admitted to his sector, he could not know the total number of deportees, and thus just as little the number of deportees *not* admitted to the camp, hence allegedly gassed according to the current orthodox narrative. He claims to have found out about the total number of deportees from members of those transports who ended up in his sector. But how could *they* have known this?

Wolken's mendacity also shows through in his testimony, which has the following peculiar claims:
– He claimed to have been sent to the gas chamber on arrival at Auschwitz with all the rest of his transport, but that he was saved because the morgue (aka gas chamber) happened to have been

full of bodies.
- True to the false cliché, Wolken claimed that selections were usually made by Dr. Mengele.
- He claimed that 700,000 Hungarian Jews were deported to Auschwitz, of whom 600,000 were gassed. However, only a little more than 400,000 Jews were deported from Hungary, and air photos show that the claimed mass-extermination of Jews deported from Hungary simply did not happen.
- Around the same time of the deportation of Hungarian Jews, 350,000 Jews from various ghettos were allegedly also deported to Auschwitz, 300,000 of whom were supposedly gassed. However, even if we follow the orthodox narrative, the only major deportation to Auschwitz of Jews from ghettos in that time frame came in July and August 1944 from the Lodz Ghetto and comprised only a maximum of 70,000 Jews.
- Wolken claimed that *Sonderkommandos* repeatedly refused to do their work, as a result of which the entire unit was gassed and burned. However, the orthodox narrative knows nothing of repeated mutinies, and rejects the claim that these units were repeatedly killed.
- Wolken dated the one *Sonderkommando* mutiny that is document to have occurred to 21 September 1944, but it actually happened on 7 October 1944.
- He admitted knowing of gassings only from hearsay, but considers it to be true because he himself saw cans of Zyklon B – after the delousing of inmate huts!
- Wolken claimed that on the day Himmler visited Auschwitz, on 17 July 1942, no inmate was allowed to be seen dead, so none died, which proves that the SS had the dying under their deliberate control. First, Wolken wasn't in the camp at that time, so could not have known. Furthermore, this claim isn't even true, as the typhus epidemic raging in the camp did not listen to orders issued by the SS. In July 1942, 4,403 deceased inmates were registered, most of them victims of the typhus epidemic, hence 142 on average every day.
- Just as with most everything else, he knew of killings with phenol injections also only from hearsay.
- Wolken's testimony is full of claims, all from hearsay, about alleged experiments with female private parts, but he insisted to know first-hand that women never received any underwear in the camp and had to walk around almost naked. Even orthodox historians agree that the latter claim is preposterous nonsense. That man had some serious sexual deprivation issues.
- Wolken insisted that the Soviet claim of four million Auschwitz victims was only marginally off the mark, because his figures allegedly demonstrate that "only" 3.5 million plus a few others died at Auschwitz. Contrast this to today's orthodox death-toll figure of roughly one million.
- And here is Wolken's most-absurd claim, made in a statement for the 1947 Warsaw trial against former Auschwitz camp commandant Rudolf Höss:

> "Ditches were dug and covered with canvas, serving as provisional gas chambers."

Wolken's testimony is a hodgepodge of hearsay, rumors and clichés, mixed with Polish and Soviet propaganda that he was more than eager to integrate and confirm with his statements. The documents he produced are very questionable historical sources, in particular when it comes to claims about allegedly gassed inmates, of whose existence, let alone fate, he could not have had any reliable knowledge.

(For more details, see Mattogno 2023b, p. 20; 2022b, pp. 35-40.)

WOLZEK

Rudolf Höss, the former commandant of the Auschwitz Camp, was captured by the British just before midnight on 11 March 1946. They subsequently tortured him uninterruptedly for three days. After this, they had him write a confession about his alleged leading involvement in the extermination of the Jews. His handwritten confession was transcribed, and while doing so, the text was enhanced, and Höss was made to sign that enhanced version. One passage not included in the original manuscript reads as follows:

> "In June 1941 I was summoned to Himmler in Berlin where he basically told me the following. The Fuehrer has ordered the solution of the Jewish question in Europe. Several so-called extermination camps already exist in the General Government (BELZEK near RAVA RUSKA eastern Poland, TREBLINKA near MALINA [Malkinia] on the River BUG, and WOLZEK near LUBLIN)."

The problem with this passage is that no camp by the name Wolzek or anything similar ever existed. There is also no town by that name. The third alleged extermination camp whose name should be there, if we follow the orthodox narrative, is Sobibór, which was located some 80 km east of Lublin.

One might assume that this invented name slipped in because, after three days of sleep deprivation and torture, Höss was capable of writing and saying anything, just to make the torture stop. However, this was no accident at all, because Höss did not correct this wrong name when discussing these three camps during an interrogation on 4 April 1946, and then expressly repeated this list of alleged extermination camps in an affidavit written after that interrogation on 5 April 1946;

> "I was ordered to establish extermination facilities at Auschwitz in June 1941. At that time, there were already in the general government three other extermination camps; Belzek, Treblinka and Wolzek."

He confirmed the correctness of that list under oath during his IMT testimony on 15 April 1946 (*IMT*, Vol. 11, p. 417), and repeated it once more in an affidavit of 20 May 1946:

> "The older extermination camps Belsen [Belzec], Treblinka and Wolzek had used monoxide gas."

Höss cannot plead lack of knowledge of the various camps existing in the Third Reich either. He was not only one of the longest serving and highest-ranking camp commandants, but he was actually promoted to the Inspectorate of Concentration Camps in late 1943. As such, it was his duty to supervise *all* the camps. Therefore, he was very well familiar with all the names and locations of all camps, and all the problems they had, because that was his job from late 1943 onward.

It stands to reason that this was not an accident. Höss may well have included this fake name of a phantom camp repeatedly for a reason. And for those willing to see, the reason seems obvious: To show the world that his testimony was coerced nonsense. That is, it may have been Höss's message in a bottle, slipped out into the world without his tormentors noticing, containing the simple message that what he was saying was not true. If so, then the message has been received and understood.

Once Höss was extradited to Poland, he couldn't use this ruse anymore, as the Polish investigators, in contrast to the rather clueless Brits, knew very well that no such thing as Wolzek ever existed. Hence, in his text written while in a Polish prison, Höss duly substituted Wolzek with Sobibór. This would then imply that some of the information contained in his account written in Poland was something spoon-fed to him by his Polish captors. And this indeed is what an analysis of Höss's text suggests.

(For more details, see the entry on Rudolf Höss, and Mattogno 2020b, esp. pp. 195-197.)

wood gas → Producer Gas, Carbon Monoxide

Y

YAD VASHEM

The Yad Vashem World Holocaust Remembrance Center in Jerusalem is the most important site of the orthodox Holocaust ideology, second only perhaps to Auschwitz itself. The Center runs a museum, a research center, and an online Holocaust encyclopedia. But the most ambitious project of this institution is the attempt to identify all victims of the Holocaust by name and with as much of their personal background as possible.

In contrast to the database by the International Tracing Service (ITS), Yad Vashem enables visitors to tally the Holocaust victims listed in their database. As of early 2023, they listed 5,388,746 victims as murdered, and another 2,017,240 victims in the undefined category "others." If they died, too, and are counted as Holocaust victims, then the total is already higher than seven million.

However, the reliability and relevance of the information contained in this database is very low for several reasons:

– The number is inflated: It includes not just people who were murdered, but also people who died as a result of armed resistance, who perished up to six months after the liberation (until the end of October 1945) as well as Jews who died during flight, evacuation and deportation from the advancing German armies. For example, the database contains thousands of Holocaust victims who allegedly died in Siberia or in Moscow.
– Submissions are unverified and unverifiable: Anyone can submit claims about Holocaust-related deaths of family members, relatives, friends, acquaintances or neighbors. Case in point: When someone submitted a photo of Joseph Goebbels's wife with invented data as a Holocaust victim, she got promptly listed in the database – until the prank was revealed. Hence, most submissions are not and cannot be verified.
– Mass dumps: Entire groups of Jews from certain villages, towns and ghettos with their fate largely unknown were collectively entered as "presumably murdered."
– Double and multiple entries: When millions of people submit claimed data about millions of people they consider missing from a pool of only millions of people, then inevitably names get submitted twice, thrice, even multifold. This sometimes occurs with different ways of spelling a name, which makes such multiple entries difficult to detect.
– Survivors included: The database includes both names of people allegedly murdered and those who survived. Unless submitted persons can be demonstrated to have survived, they are considered murdered or missing. Hence, many of those listed as "murdered" may actually have survived.

This method is the opposite of that applied by the ITS. While the latter lists victims as deceased only if documental proof is available, Yad Vashem lists any submission as a murder case, unless the person affected can be shown to have survived. This ensures a maximum number of Holocaust victims.

(For more details, see Rudolf 2023, pp. 43-46; Kollerstrom 2023, pp. 96f.)

YUGOSLAVIA

Yugoslavia was dismembered during the Second World War: It consisted of German-aligned Croatia, German-occupied Serbia and areas temporarily occupied/annexed by neighboring countries. In the present context, we focus on Serbia and Croatia. (See the entry on Jewish demography for a broader perspective.)

Serbia

In July 1941, a major uprising occurred in Serbia, which the German forces managed to quell only with draconian reprisal measures, during which 100 hostages were shot for every killed German soldier. Next to communists, partisans and Serb nationalists, almost all Serbian Jewish males were held as hostages. In the end, almost all of these Jewish men were executed in reprisal killings. Some 7,000 women, children and the elderly were kept in the Semlin Camp near Belgrade. Documents indicate that they were slated for deportation, but the orthodoxy insists that they were murdered using a gas van. (See the entry on Semlin for details.)

Croatia

About 39,000 Jews are believed to have lived on the

territory which was short-lived wartime Croatia. Some 6,200 of them were deported in two batches of transports, the first with some 5,000 individuals in the second half of 1942, and a second batch in May 1943. Only some 1,700 of these Jews were shipped to Auschwitz, the rest evidently to various destinations in Germany. The fate of the other Jewish inmates is unclear, but is closely linked to the events that unfolded at the Jasenovac Camp. Only a minority of the inmates of that camp were Jews, but the general death toll for this camp ranges wildly, and both documental and forensic evidence is scant, such that no reliable estimate can be developed. (See the entry on Jasenovac for details.)

Z

ZĄBECKI, FRANCISZEK

Franciszek Ząbecki was a Polish railway worker employed at Treblinka Station from May 1941 as a rail traffic controller. He was interrogated on 21 December 1945 by Polish judge Zdzisław Łukaszkiewicz. Ząbecki claimed that he managed to salvage some German documents on rail transports to Treblinka, and that he handed them over to Łukaszkiewicz. In 1946, Łukaszkiewicz published image reproductions of three such documents without reference to Ząbecki, but they provide no useful information. (See Mattogno 2021e, p. 167.)

ZAYDEL, MATVEY

Matvey Zaydel (aka Motle Zaidl), a Jew from Vilnius, Lithuania, was interrogated by a Soviet commission, whose report is undated, but probably dates from 1946. According to this report, Zaydel claimed to have been arrested by German forces in October 1943. From December 1943 until April 1944, he was forced to exhume and burn corpses from mass graves near a Vilnius suburb called Ponary. He escaped from there at an unknown date and under unknown circumstances.

However, in a much-later interview for Claude Lanzmann's documentary *Shoah* sometime in the early 1980s, Zaydel plagiarized the tale told by Yuri Farber about a sophisticated escape tunnel, fitted with support poles and electric lighting. (See the entry on Farber.) If we follow Zaydel, they dug that tunnel into the sandy soil mainly with a tablespoon. Since Zaydel's statements made during the *Shoah* interview, and the concurrent statements by his alleged former co-inmate Itzhak Dugin, are evidently polluted with "knowledge" gained after the war, it is worthless as evidence, hence will be ignored here.

In his 1946 interview, Zaydel claimed to have been involved in preparing firewood and burning corpses. He asserted that the pyres were built by having a layer of firewood, then a layer of 100 corpses, and so on, until the pyre contained 2,000 or even 3,000 bodies. This would amount to some 20 to 30 layers.

Cremating an average human body during open-air incinerations requires some 250 kg of freshly cut wood. With such pyres, a layer that is as wide as the bodies are tall can accommodate some four to five bodies per meter. Hence, Zaydel's pyre would have been some 20-25 m long. One hundred bodies require some 25 tons of freshly cut wood. The density of green wood is roughly 0.9 tons per m^3, and its stacking density on a pyre is 1.4 (40% for air and flames to go through). This means that the wood required to burn 100 bodies would have had a volume of some 40 m^3. Spread out over a pyre 25 m long and 2 m wide, this wood would have stacked up to a height of some 0.8 meters, and together with the corpses to about 1 meter. A pyre with 20 or 30 such layers would have been 20 to 30 meters high. Of course, a pyre two meters wide can never be 20 or 30 meters high. It would collapse at a shorter height already. While the shape of the pyre can be changed (for instance 7 m × 7 m, as other witnesses claimed, although that makes it much more difficult to build, burn and dispose later), this would not affect the height.

Zaydel claimed that, within five months, 80 to 90 thousand corpses were processed this way. Cremating 80,000 bodies requires some 20,000 metric tons of wood. This would have required the felling of all trees growing in a 50-year-old spruce forest covering almost 45 hectares of land, or some 100 American football fields. An average prisoner is rated at being able to cut some 0.63 metric tons of fresh wood per workday. To cut this amount of wood within five months (150 days) would have required some 211 dedicated lumberjacks doing nothing else but felling and cutting up trees. Zaydel does not indicate how many inmates were in his unit. Other testimonies about the claimed Ponary mass graves indicate that their unit had no more than 80 inmates, with most if not all of them busy digging out mass graves, extracting bodies, building pyres, sifting through ashes, crushing bones, and scattering the resulting powder. There were nowhere near 200 lumberjacks in that unit.

If Zaydel's tale has any real background, it would have been on a much smaller order of magnitude than what he claims.

This testimony relates to one of many events claimed to have been part of the alleged German clean-up operation which the orthodoxy calls *Aktion*

1005. The above exposition demonstrates that Zaydel's scenario is detached from reality. Its claimed dimensions cannot be based on experience, but on mere propaganda, imagination and delusion. (See also the similar accounts by Yuri Farber, A. Blyazer and Szloma Gol; for more details, see Mattogno 2022c, pp. 679f., 683-688.)

ZENTRALE STELLE

Under (West) German law, a district attorney's office can investigate a crime only if either the crime location or the residence of a suspect is located in its area of jurisdiction. Since many claimed National-Socialist crimes were committed outside of Germany, and because the residence of many suspected perpetrators was either unknown, scattered around Germany or in a foreign country, it proved to be challenging to find any German DA office to put in charge of certain investigations.

In addition to this, local investigators frequently proved unwilling to pursue certain complaints, as it was clear that many witness claims were inconsistent, improbable or outright absurd. (See the entry on Adolf Rögner.) Furthermore, much supportive material was submitted by untrustworthy government agencies of Eastern-Bloc countries with a very transparent agenda to destabilize West Germany or damage the country's reputation by inflating or inventing National-Socialist crimes and claiming continuity between the Third Reich and West Germany.

To circumvent these problems, the German authorities established in late 1958 a Central Office of State Justice Administrations for the Investigation of National-Socialist Crimes (*Zentrale Stelle der Landesjustizverwaltungen zur Aufklärung nationalsozialistischer Verbrechen* – or *Zentrale Stelle* [Central Office] for short). This office was staffed with ideologically "reliable" investigators, meaning individuals who would not question the veracity of incriminating claims, whether made by witnesses, published in books and media, "established" during Allied postwar show trials, or submitted by any foreign government agency.

To this end, this Central Office cooperated closely with law-enforcement agencies in Israel and communist Eastern-Bloc countries, as well as with various organizations of former camp inmates – most of which were inevitably dominated by Jews and communists, who had formed the majority of wartime camp inmates. In order to get the expected information from witnesses, it has been reported that "second-degree coercions" were employed, meaning threats of various kinds in case of non-compliance with an interrogator's expectations.

The most scandalous aspect of the Central Office's activities were the case files they compiled about certain crime complexes. These so-called "criminals' dossiers" were made available to all potential witnesses, and to domestic and foreign investigative bodies for the purpose of further dissemination to witnesses. In these dossiers, all supposed perpetrators were listed along with their photographs both from the time these dossiers were compiled and from National-Socialist times, and a description of the crimes imputed to them – as well as such crimes as *might* have taken place, but for which witnesses and/or clues to the identity of the perpetrators were still lacking. In an introduction, the potential witnesses were asked to keep this blatant and illegal manipulation of witness memories confidential, lest the defense might find out about it and scuttle the entire case. Then, the potential witnesses were asked to assign the criminals to the crimes and to add other crimes which might be missing from the dossier.

With this approach, the German judiciary made sure that the orthodox narrative about the Holocaust – as defined mainly by Allied postwar show trials, organizations of former inmates, communist Eastern-Bloc countries and by Israel – would enter German case law as incontrovertible historical "truth." Contesting this judicially ordained "truth" was then made a criminal offense in Germany.

Despite the war ending nearly 80 years ago, the Central Office is still in operation. According to the group's website (as of late 2023), they are still abiding by a 2015 resolution to operate "as long as there exist prosecution tasks to fulfill"; the end of this process is "not yet foreseeable."

(For more details, see the section of Germany in the entry on propaganda, as well as Rudolf 2015; 2023, pp. 421-424.)

ZENTRALSAUNA, AUSCHWITZ BIRKENAU

Shortly after plans were developed to set up a large PoW camp west of Auschwitz near the village of Brzezinka (Birkenau), these plans included a large facility containing inmate showers and disinfestation devices for inmate clothes. A map showing an early stage of the camp from late March 1942 shows an outline of this building where it was eventually erected.

Auschwitz-Birkenau, Building 32, the camp's inmate shower and disinfestation facility, the so-called Zentralsauna *(1998).*

A detailed project description for the Birkenau Camp dated 28 October 1942 and titled "Construction Project: Auschwitz Prisoner-of-War Camp (Implementation of Special Treatment)" lists this building on page 5 as a

"*disinfestation facility*
1. for special treatment. […]
2. for the guard troops."

This was the only building that was associated with "special treatment" in that project description. (See the illustration in the entry on "Special Treatment."). Since disinfestation for guard troops was the second purpose of that facility, "for special treatment" undoubtedly referred to inmates. At that time, Birkenau was repurposed from a PoW camp to serve the "Implementation of Special Treatment" instead. Hence, the camp served as a central hub either for the forced-labor deployment of deported Jews, or for their deportation further east.

According to the orthodox narrative, the term "special treatment" was a euphemism for the wholesale slaughter of Jews in the crematoria's gas chambers. However, the project description entry for the Birkenau crematoria does *not* contain the term "special treatment" or anything similar, unlike the disinfestation facility in the very next line. This document shows, therefore, that no association between this term and the crematoria existed. In reality, this term was *exclusively* associated with the *life-saving* shower and fumigation facility.

This building later received the identification number BW 32, and was nicknamed "*Zentralsauna,*" although it did not contain any sauna. It was equipped with large undressing and dressing halls, a room with 50 warm-water showers, and four large hot-air disinfestation autoclaves. The two coke furnaces and boiler system used to generate the hot air were built underground. Since the groundwater level in Birkenau stood close to the surface, constructing this facility's basement required that the groundwater seeping in was continually pumped off. Static calculations for this building only began in March 1943, and it became operational only by the end of 1943, being officially handed over to the camp administration on 22 January 1944.

From the fall of 1942 onward, the Birkenau Camp had two other large inmate shower and disinfestation facilities (BW 5a and BW 5b). These even had a sauna each, which is probably where the nickname of the new planned building came from. However, these buildings had only two badly designed large Zyklon-B fumigation rooms, each called a "gas chamber" in the blueprints. They operated rather inefficiently and probably also ineffectively. One of them was later remodeled to contain several smaller hot-air disinfestation chambers rather than one large Zyklon-B room. Notably, no one has ever claimed that inmates were killed in these fumigation "gas chambers."

Delays in the *Zentralsauna*'s construction were one reason why hygienic conditions in the Birkenau Camp improved only slowly in

Two hot-air disinfestation autoclaves inside the Zentralsauna *(1998).*

1943. At the end of 1943, the *Zentralsauna* became operational: shortly thereafter, the first microwave disinfestation unit was deployed at Auschwitz, and in spring 1944, the first deliveries of DDT (German name: Lauseto) arrived at Auschwitz, finally improving the camp's hygienic and sanitary conditions to a level where mortality finally dropped to low levels. This, unfortunately, occurred near the end of the war, when the national situation became catastrophic, and therefore camp conditions once again declined.

(For details, see documents quoted in Mattogno 2023, pp. 90f., 177f., 240, 258, 263f., 341, 349, 354, 358, 387.)

ZIEREIS, FRANZ

Franz Ziereis (13 Aug. 1905 – 24 May 1945), SS *Sturmbannführer*, was the commandant of the Mauthausen Camp from 1939 until the end of the war. He fled on May 3 and tried hiding in his hunting lodge in the Alps, but was discovered there and, when trying to flee, was shot and badly wounded. He was then apparently incarcerated for a short time but died in custody.

Franz Ziereis

Two documents exist whose authors claim them to be summaries of an interrogation presumably carried out with Ziereis while he was slowly bleeding to death. None of them have his signature, and their contents are so absurd that it boggles the mind how any of it could have been taken seriously. Yet still, one of them, an affidavit by the former Mauthausen inmate Hans Maršálek, got accepted into evidence at the Nuremberg International Military Tribunal. Since these documents' contents cannot be attributed to Ziereis, they will not be discussed here. See the entry on Hans Maršálek for more details.

ŻŁOBNICKI, ADAM

Adam Żłobnicki was a Pole who has incarcerated at the Auschwitz Camp during the war. When the Polish authorities established the Auschwitz Museum, Żłobnicki was hired as a guard.

When French Holocaust skeptic Robert Faurisson raised serious doubts in 1979/1980 about the authenticity of the alleged homicidal gas chamber inside the old crematorium at the Auschwitz Main Camp, the Auschwitz Museum started collecting witness statements in order to bolster its narrative.

One central issue in this context are the four Zyklon-B introduction shafts present in today's roof of that building, which are said to have allowed dumping that poisonous product on victims locked in the building's morgue. Museum officials have always insisted that these opening were added after the war when the building was "reconstructed" to make it look like it allegedly did when it supposedly served as a homicidal gassing facility. They also insist that those new openings added by them were put in the identical place where the old, original holes had been, allegedly once visible in the ceiling as former holes patched up with cement. However, museum authorities had to admit that there is no evidence whatsoever about the condition of this building upon them taking charge of it in 1946, and that no records were kept as to the "reconstruction" of this building either.

In order to shore up their claim that the new introduction holes were put in the place where the old ones had been, which was challenged by disbelievers, they did not interview any of the architects, engineers or workers involved in that "reconstruction," but interviewed the museum guard Adam Żłobnicki, although he had not involved in those reconstruction efforts. Żłobnicki promptly "confirmed" the museum's claims and added that little brick chimneys were built around the new holes. This is wrong, however, as the new holes only received some crude wooden boards forming a primitive shaft. Four brick chimneys are located elsewhere on that roof. Two large ones served to ventilate the furnace room since its inception in 1941, and two small ones ventilated the air-raid protection shelters included in that building in 1944. This shows that Żłobnicki mistook what he saw for something else entirely.

That the long-term, loyal museum employee Żłobnicki lied can be seen from two facts:
1. Traces of any former Zyklon-B introduction holes in the ceiling of the former morgue of the Main Camp's crematorium would have been the *most important* material evidence which the Polish authorities could present when preparing their cases against former camp commandant Rudolf Höss and the former members of the Auschwitz Camp's staff. Huge efforts were made to collect all kinds of material, forensic and documental evidence in preparation for these two trials. Missing

among them, however, are any photos or testimonies proving that these traces in the ceiling ever existed. Therefore, we must presume that they did not exist.
2. The location of today's holes in the ceiling of what the museum presents as a homicidal gas chamber has been chosen to make them evenly distributed in the room *as it exists today*. However, that room was only created by the Poles *after the war* during their "reconstruction," making a number of mistakes in the process. The original morgue (aka gas chamber) had been converted in 1944 by the Germans into an air-raid shelter by adding a new entrance with a vestibule (air lock), and by adding several sturdy separation walls. When doing their "reconstruction" after the war, the museum did *not* remove that new entrance with vestibule, and when knocking down the air-raid shelter's sturdy separation walls, they knocked down one separation wall too many, including one which used to separate the morgue from the washroom next door. By so doing, they created a room *longer* than it was when it served as a morgue, and it became asymmetrical due to the vestibule around the air-raid shelter's entrance. The arrangement of the new introduction holes reflects both changes: they evenly cover the length of this new room and even accommodate that vestibule. Hence, they were clearly a product of this flawed "reconstruction," not of a re-opening of traces of old holes.

Złobnicki lied, and so did and do the Auschwitz Museum officials; they still lie about this to this day. To make matters worse, the original state of this roof was *primary* evidence to confirm or refute the alleged crime of mass murder by gas. By claiming that they destroyed that evidence without keeping or creating any records of the original state, the museum authorities have admitted that *they* committed a crime back in 1946/47 during their botched "reconstruction": tampering with the key evidence of a claimed crime scene of alleged mass murder. Hence, the Auschwitz Museum is a criminal organization, and Złobnicki was an accomplice in their attempt to hide their crimes. It remains to be seen if any Museum officials will ever be brought to justice.
(For more details, see Mattogno 2020, pp. 15-24.)

ZÜNDEL TRIALS

In 1983, the German immigrant to Canada Ernst Zündel, a confessing admirer of Adolf Hitler, was charged in a Canadian court for knowingly spreading false news about the Holocaust. This offense allegedly had been committed by Zündel when he sold a 1974 brochure contesting the orthodox Holocaust narrative.

With the help of a French expert for the critique of documents and testimonies, Dr. Robert Faurisson, and with the assistance of a courageous defense lawyer, Douglas Christie, Zündel subsequently mounted his best defense effort. The trial took place in Toronto from 7 January until 27 February 1985. The case attracted huge media attention in Canada and the U.S.

Due to errors of law, a retrial was ordered on appeal, which took place between 18 January and 13 May 1988. Although this second trial did not attract as much attention as the first, it had a far bigger impact, due to the fact that both the only expert on execution technologies, the U.S.-American Fred Leuchter, and world-renowned British historian David Irving testified on behalf of the defendant. Both subsequently became the target of vicious attacks in an attempt to destroy their reputations and careers. However, the genie was out of the bottle, and it caught the attention of many skeptics; they subsequently turned a further scrutinizing eye on the historical record.

Although Zündel was initially sentenced to a nine-months prison term – for "hate-mongering," as the judge expressed it – Canada's Supreme Court declared as unconstitutional the law under which Zündel had been prosecuted, thus acquitting him of all charges. (For more details, see Kulaszka 2019; Rudolf 2020b; Zündel 2022.)

In 2022, Canada's parliament passed a bill outlawing views diverging from the orthodox Holocaust narrative. It threatens every dissident with up to two years imprisonment. So far, Canada's Supreme Court has not (yet) declared this law unconstitutional.

ŻURAWSKI, MIECZYSŁAW

Mieczysław Żurawski was one of only three former inmates of the Chełmno Camp who testified after the war about the alleged events unfolding there. His statement of 31 July 1945 does not contain quite as much information as those of the other two testifying inmates (Szymon Srebrnik and Michał Podchlebnik). Żurawski also testified during the 1961 Eichmann Trial and the 1963 Chełmno Trial in West Germany. He claimed to have been deported from the Lodz Ghetto to Chełmno in 1944, together with some

7,000 to 10,000 other Jews. His testimony is the mainstay upon which the orthodoxy's claim rests that the Chełmno Camp had a second phase of extermination activities in 1944, after its buildings had been demolished in 1943.

Existing documents show that some 7,000 Jews fit for work were indeed evacuated from the Lodz Ghetto in July 1944, including a certain "Mordka Zorawski." However, there is no documental proof that these evacuation transports went to Chełmno. All extant documental evidence suggests that these skilled and experienced workers from the Lodz Ghetto were transferred to other worksites in Germany. This served to remove them from the advancing Red Army. (See the entry on the Lodz Ghetto.) Żurawski described the two gas vans allegedly used to murder inmates at the Chełmno Camp in generic terms, but did not know any details, such as the van's make or how exactly the "gas" was turned on. He claimed an impossibly short execution time (four minutes), and asserted that the victims located near the entry of the exhaust gasses were burned with their skin peeling off, although second- or third-degree burns due to hot gases do not result in the skin peeling off from the underlying tissue.

Żurawski's credibility sinks even lower due to his claim that the field furnace presumably used at Chełmno to cremate corpses took only 15 minutes to burn all the corpses piled up in it, although in reality this would have taken many hours.

Żurawski admitted to knowing only from hearsay about the story of someone throwing his own sister into the flames while still alive. This tall tale was told by Srebrnik about his own sister, and shows the cross-pollination among these witnesses, thus creating a fraudulent "convergence of evidence." Not satisfied with this story, Żurawski topped this off by inventing a whole string of similar alleged events of people thrown alive into the furnace.

Żurawski's story of his escape is another false tale, which even the interrogating judge Bednarz realized: Żurawski claimed that he fought his German captors with a knife and managed to run away. However, he had earlier claimed that all inmates' ankles had been shackled with a short steel chain at all times, disabling them from walking fast, let alone running. When asked by the judge how he managed to get rid of that chain, Żurawski simply claimed that he cut a link of his steel chain with a "large tailor's scissors." Unlikely, to say the least.

When Judge Bednarz showed Żurawski a photo of a dilapidated truck on the Ostrowski factory grounds in the Polish town of Koło – which was (mis)identified by the other witnesses as "the" gas van – Żurawski refused to go along with that story and stated instead that this was a disinfestation van. That wasn't true either, as it was a simple moving van, as Bednarz himself concluded in a report written after investigating the truck.

Żurawski also testified during the Jerusalem Eichmann Trial, where his Polish testimony was used as a pattern to mold the "new" testimony, while leaving out the evident nonsense. However, Żurawski added another absurd claim to his roster of nonsense by insisting that the Germans at Chełmno had a target-practice game with their rifles consisting of lining up inmates, putting bottles on their heads, then either hitting the bottle or… the head.

In Jerusalem, Żurawski tried to remedy his *faux pas* on the mis-identification of the gas van at Koło by insisting that, when the Chełmno Camp was dissolved, the gas vans were taken to Koło (meaning the Ostrowski factory grounds). How he could have known that remains a mystery, since he claimed to have run away before the camp's dissolution.

(For more details, see Alvarez 2023, pp. 164-166, 174; Mattogno 2017, pp. 62f.)

ZYKLON B
History

One of the most efficient methods to fight lice and thereby to contain and eliminate typhus – and to kill other vermin like grain beetles, fleas, cockroaches, termites, mice, rats and many more as well – is their poisoning with highly volatile hydrogen cyanide.

Liquid hydrogen cyanide has a short shelf life and is extremely dangerous when handled incorrectly. Therefore, the *in-situ* development of gaseous hydrogen cyanide by pouring a strong acid (usually semi-diluted sulfuric acid) onto a highly soluble cyanide powder (such as sodium or potassium cyanide) was used instead until a few years after the First World War. However, numerous accidents resulted in research efforts to produce a safer method. This resulted in the development of "Zyklon" by German chemists, which was a mixture of a highly irritating liquid with a liquid cyanide component (methyl cyanoformate). Due to the irritant, it was considered safe, hence it was sold so liberally in the early 1920s that accidents occurred again, leading to the ban of all cyanide products for pest control in Germany in July 1922.

In September of 1922, the German Association for Pest Control (*Deutsche Gesellschaft für Schädlingsbekämpfung*, DEGESCH) was granted the exclusive right to develop and use cyanide-based pest-control chemicals in Germany. Around the same time, DEGESCH developed a superior substitute product for Zyklon, called "Zyklon B," which was liquid hydrogen cyanide mixed with a chemical stabilizer and a teargas (as a warning agent) absorbed on diatomaceous earth. A little later, this chemical mixture was also sold absorbed on wood-fiber disks, and in the 1930s, diatomaceous earth was replaced by gypsum pellets as the carrier material, which, unlike diatomaceous earth, did not tend to compact during storage and transport, thus keeping its liquid-absorbing properties.

By the advent of Word War Two, almost all Zyklon B sold in Europe consisted of the gypsum type, called "Erco." This product was packed in tin cans measuring 15.4 cm in diameter and of various heights, depending on the can's cyanide contents. DEGESCH distributed cans containing 200, 500, 1,000 and 1,500 g of liquid hydrogen cyanide, with the carrier material weighing roughly twice that amount. Hence, a 1-kg-can of Zyklon B contained 1 kg of hydrogen cyanide, plus some 2 kg of gypsum pellets.

While the stabilizer was legally required as an additive to prevent the possibility of violent polymerizations, the warning agent was not required. In fact, it was argued by some that the warning agent was misleading, since it evaporated and dissipated much slower than the almost odorless hydrogen cyanide. Hence, anyone relying on noticing the irritant before assuming that they were at risk would have been in serious danger.

As the war progressed, the producers of Zyklon B had growing difficulties obtaining any irritant, as chemical factories producing it were a main target of Allied bombers, or they suffered war-related shortages. In addition, chemical irritants weren't high on anyone's priority lists. As a result, Zyklon B without irritants was the preferred option, in particular for non-civilian customers who did not use the chemical in the potential presence of civilians, such as the Wehrmacht and the SS. The orthodoxy's occasional claim that this proves homicidal intent is unfounded.

To this day, 100 years after its invention, Zyklon B continues to play a role in the battle against pests.

Evaporation Characteristics

The hydrogen cyanide absorbed by the Zyklon-B gypsum pellets evaporates rather slowly. If the pellets are dispersed (meaning not piled up) and humidity in the air is low, this process lasts roughly two hours at room temperature. This is intentional, since in many civilian applications, the person spreading out the pellets must retreat safely afterwards, and because small leaks in the typical treated building make it desirable that some hydrogen cyanide continues to be released over time, compensating for these losses.

When assessing testimonies reporting homicidal gassings with Zyklon B, two issues are of prime importance: first, the claimed duration of the execution, and second, the claimed duration of the subsequent ventilation.

1. Duration of the execution. In contrast to executions in U.S. execution gas chambers, where hydrogen-cyanide vapors are developed instantly in full force and right beneath the victim by pouring semi-diluted sulfuric acid into a bowl of potassium cya-

Zyklon-B cans with the grey gypsum granules (trade name Erco) which once were soaked in hydrogen cyanide; Yad Vashem exhibit.
(Photo by Adam Jones; commons.wikimedia.org)

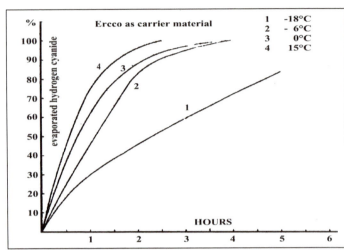

Evaporation rate of hydrogen cyanide from the Erco carrier material (gypsum with some starch) at various temperatures, low relative humidity and fine distribution.

nide (see the section on "U.S. Execution Gas Chambers" of the entry on homicidal gas chamber), Zyklon B thrown into a room full of people will take much longer, as the gas develops slowly and must dissipate throughout a larger room. While a room tightly filled with (naked) people may reach air temperatures around 30°C, its relative humidity will certainly be close to or right at 100%. While the former helps to speed up the evaporation initially, the latter will lead to humidity condensing on the gypsum pellets, resulting in the evaporation process slowing down to a crawl, since hydrogen cyanide is extremely soluble in water.

Therefore, it must be assumed that any kind of homicide using Zyklon B would be considerably slower than U.S. executions, which on average lasted some ten minutes, but could take up to almost twenty minutes. Therefore, any reported execution time less than 20 minutes is certainly wrong. In fact, since the goal was to kill every victim – even the toughest one standing in a corner far away from where the Zyklon happens to be – this process almost certainly took even longer than that. Had the Zyklon B not been spread out among the victims but kept piled up in some device with no fan dissipating the vapors, as is claimed for some Zyklon-B introduction devices, the execution process would have been delayed even more due to the piled-up nature of the pellets kept away from the inmates' movements and body heat.

2. Ventilation time. No ventilation of a room containing Zyklon B can be successful unless either the Zyklon-B pellets have been removed or all the hydrogen cyanide in them has evaporated. For only two claimed homicidal gas chambers, some witnesses have claimed devices that allowed for the removal of the Zyklon-B pellets from the gas chamber (Crematoria II and III at Auschwitz; see the entry on Zyklon-B introduction devices). In all other cases, the Zyklon B is said to have been sprinkled loosely among the victims. In that case, even the strongest ventilation system would not have succeeded in rendering such a room safe for access until at least an hour, and perhaps two, after the introduction of Zyklon B.

Zyklon Deliveries

Many German concentration camps received copious deliveries of Zyklon B; these were used in disinfestation facilities (rooms or "chambers") for clothing, linens, and personal items, and in order to disinfest camp facilities, ranging from inmate and guard lodgings to storage and administration facilities. In the camps listed in the following table, Zyklon B is also said to have been misused for mass homicide. In fact, however, there is no solid evidence for any of these claims that even a single person was killed with Zyklon B. See the entries for these camps for more details on this.

In general, there was no noticeable difference in the amounts of Zyklon B ordered by camps where mass murder using this product is said to have occurred versus other camps where no such crimes have been reported, such as Buchenwald or Bergen-Belsen. Therefore, the simple fact that any camp received Zyklon B by no means proves that it was misused for murder, as Allied prosecutors wrongly claimed during various postwar trials.

Auschwitz was by far the camp which received the largest amounts of Zyklon B, but it was also the camp with by far the largest number of inmate lodging buildings and other camp facilities in need of disinfestation. Furthermore, it was the one camp where louse and flee infestation reached cataclysmic dimensions, and thus underwent a massive deployment

CAMP	CLAIMED NO. OF VICTIMS
Auschwitz	ca. 1,000,000
Dachau	a handful, if any
Gusen	several hundred
Majdanek	a few thousand, if any
Mauthausen	several thousand
Neuengamme	a few hundred
Ravensbrück	up to 3,000
Sachsenhausen	several thousand
Stutthof	several thousand

of all kinds of methods – heat, steam, chemicals (such as DDT) and advanced technologies (such as microwave delousing devices) – to combat these carriers of devastating epidemics. Therefore, the camp's extraordinary size and the dramatic dimension of its fateful epidemics explain perfectly well the large Zyklon B deliveries to this camp.

(For more details, see Kalthoff/Werner 1998; Leipprand 2008; Rudolf 2020, pp. 70-85, 236-240; Mattogno 2019, pp. 444-453; 2021a, pp. 71-83.)

ZYKLON-B INTRODUCTION DEVICES

Several German wartime camps are said to have had homicidal gas chambers in which Zyklon B was used for mass murder (see the entry on Zyklon B). For most of them, the way Zyklon B is said to have been introduced is uncontested. The situation is different for the claimed homicidal gas chambers at Auschwitz, and here in particular for the morgues (aka gas chambers) of Crematoria II and III at Auschwitz-Birkenau. The following list pertains to this very room. It has in the first column the source of a claim (person or organization), then the claimed type of testimony, with "1" meaning first-hand, so the witness claims to have seen it him-/herself, and "2" meaning second- or third-hand, meaning hearsay. Because these testimonies are the least reliable in principle, they are rendered in grey in order to de-emphasize them. The subsequent columns contain various ways and methods by which the poison is said to have been introduced, with a simple fat dot • where it applies, or a brief description for a variation of the given method:

- *poured into room*: The Zyklon-B pellets were poured into the room through holes in the roof on top or in between the inmates, without any additional devices.
- *piped into room*: Not Zyklon B, but hydrogen-cyanide gas was piped in as indicated.
- *container thrown in*: Not Zyklon B pellets, but a container with some form of the gas was thrown in, to burst or explode open on impact.
- *pipe/sheet-metal column*: Zyklon-B pellets were poured into columns made of perforated sheet metal.
- *wire-mesh column*: Zyklon-B pellets were poured into columns made of various layers of wire-mesh.

As each entry for these witnesses demonstrate, all their testimonies are filled with exaggerations, inventions, impossible claims and distortions. Hence, none of these witnesses are trustworthy. Therefore, there is no reason to give any of the claimed methods of introducing Zyklon B precedence over the others. Even more so since there exists no material or documental trace for *any* Zyklon-B introduction device or method. Furthermore, detailed investigations of the ruins of Morgue #1 of Crematorium II have demonstrated that the holes claimed by many to have been used to throw in Zyklon B (or to attach any claimed introduction devices, columns or pillars) did not exist during the war.

The holes which can be found in the collapsed roof of this morgue were hacked in after it had been completed, and most likely after it had been blown up at the war's end. By the time these roofs were cast (early 1943), there either had been a plan in place for a long time to exterminate the Jews, or there was no such plan. If a plan existed, these buildings would have been planned accordingly, with predefined holes when the roofs were cast. Since no such holes exist, there was no plan to have such holes. Hence, there was no plan to exterminate Jews as it is claimed today.

Since the turn of the millennium, after decades of indifference regarding the many contradictory claims in this regard, the orthodoxy has come to a consensus that the wire-mesh columns described in detail by Michał Kula, and in a similar, yet less detailed way also by Henryk Tauber and Josef Sackar, were the device used, and that all other witnesses erred or lied. The reason for this decision is that Kula's devices would have allowed the removal of Zyklon B pellets from the columns. This, in turn, would have allowed a faster ventilation of the alleged gas chamber, which is a pivotal requirement for the credibility of frequent claims that the gas-chamber doors were opened a short while after the end of the execution.

All these witnesses missed the pivotal point of a hypothetical device meant to facilitate the mass execution of people locked up in the claimed room: its *primary* feature would have been the rapid evaporation of the gas and its fast dissipation into the entire room. In fact, German DEGESCH experts had developed such a device as part of their circulation fumigation chambers, such as were installed at Dachau. The Auschwitz camp authorities received a detailed description of this device, and filed it away in their archives. They then ordered 19 of them – for the disinfestation chambers planned for the Main Camp's reception building (although they were never delivered and eventually replaced by a microwave disinfestation device; see this entry). However, nothing was ever done to use or adapt this advanced and rather simple technology for any homicidal gassings.

While Kula's device would have allowed the removal of the Zyklon B pellets, and thus accelerated the clearing of the gas, it would have introduced other serious problems with the execution: the

Witness	type	poured in	piped in	container thrown in	pipe/sheet-metal column	wire-mesh column
C.S. Bendel	1				●	
R. Bialek	1		floor drain	bombs		
A. Bimko	1		showers			
S. Chasan	1					open bottom
S. Chybiński	2		lower air ducts			
L. Cohen	1				●	
S. Dragon	1				●	
H. Fischer	1	●				
D. Fliamenbaum	1	●				
Franke-Gricksch	1				pillars	
Y. Gabai	1	barred glass window			pipes	
S. Gertner	1	window				
J. Kaufmann	2		showers			
S. Kaufmann	2		showers			
I. Kertész	2		showers			
M. Kula	1					●
E. Kulka	2				pillars	
M. Lequeux	2					grated column
S. Lewental	1	upper doors				
P. Lewińska	2		showers			
M. Lichtenstein	2	1 hatch				
S. Litwinska	1		windows			
H. Mandelbaum	1		windows			screen columns*
K. Marcus	2	onto net				
F. Müller	1				scattering spiral	
M. Nyiszli	1				●	
M. Nadsari	1	●				
M. Nahon	2			bomb thru window		
N.T. Obrycki	2			cartridge		
I.E. Ochshorn	1			bombs		
D. Paisikovic	1					net around concrete columns
B. Piazza	1/2	CN powder on floor (1)†		cylinders (2)		
A. Pilo	1	●				
R. Plucer	1	10 chimneys				
F. Putzker	1	gas doors				
A. Rogerie	2		showers			
J. Sackar	1					●
R. Sompolinski	1		turned on			
J. Tabeau	2			bombs		
H. Tauber	1					●
M.C. Vaillant-C.	2			capsules		
J. Weiss	1				3 fan columns	
A. Wetzler	2	thru showers				
Vrba/Wetzler	2	3 traps				
S. Venezia	1	1 manhole				

* after gassing, gas release continued, hence pellets not retrievable.
† gas activated by turning on water showers.

Zyklon-B pellets inside the claimed 3-layered columns would have been kept away from the victims' body heat, and would have been kept lumped together in the narrow, 15-mm gap between the two layers of the inner, removable column as described by Kula. Thus, humidity in this moist basement room would have quickly condensed on the gypsum granules, slowing the gas's evaporation to a crawl (see the entry on Zyklon B). The moist gypsum pellets moreover would have become gooey, sticking together and to the claimed wire mesh, making it difficult to clean the device later.

What makes this claim farcical is the orthodoxy's assertion that, when the SS built these buildings, they completely *forgot* to include the four Zyklon-B-introduction holes in the roof (or holes to house any claimed device). Only once the thick reinforced concrete roof had been cast in January 1943, isolated with a layer of tar and then covered with a cement screed – at a point when the extermination of the Jews is said to have been going on already for almost a year – did someone realize that they had forgotten the most essential element for the alleged mass-murder facility: *the roof holes*. Hence, someone allegedly came with a jack hammer and ruined the roof, including its layer of isolating tar plus the cement screed protecting it, in order to create the needed holes.

The entire claimed project was a fool's errand. No architect or camp leadership would ever have allowed four holes to be brutally knocked through this basement room's massive reinforced concrete roof, which would have severely compromised the roof's integrity and would have led to considerable rainwater leaks and damage.

Instead, any competent engineer would have used the room's air-intake duct to serve the desired purpose. This duct was accessible from the building's inside, for instance in the attic near the fresh-air intake chimney that went out through the roof. This duct could have been equipped easily with a heating coil to preheat the air; or some warm air from the nearby crematorium chimney could have been diverted for this purpose. In the stream of this preheated air, a wire-mesh basket, inserted into the duct behind some port, could have been filled with Zyklon-B pellets. This way, the warm air would have evaporated the gas swiftly, and carried it evenly into the basement through the many outlets along both

Hole in the shattered roof of Morgue #1 of Crematorium II at Auschwitz-Birkenau. It was created after the war by Polish investigators to gain access to the morgue's interior, because the entry area had collapsed after the building had been dynamited by the Germans before retreating from Auschwitz. Note that the roof's rebars were only bent back, but not removed. (Photo of 1997.)

long sides of the room, rapidly dissipating the gas everywhere. Once done after some 20 minutes or so, the basket with the pellets could have been removed, and the room could have been ventilated using the same duct. Such a system would have been cheap, effective, fast, and non-destructive.

Cheaper and easier still would have been the installation in the crematorium's attic of a producer-gas generator fueled with wood. These devices, which produced a highly toxic gas with some 20-30% carbon monoxide, were mass-produced during the war and were available literally everywhere. Its lethal producer gas could have been fed into the morgue's air intake shaft. That solution would have been cheaper in every regard, and ventilation of the morgue afterwards would have been greatly simplified, since producer gas does not adhere to anything or dissolve in anything, quite in contrast to Zyklon B's hydrogen cyanide.

Knocking holes through a thick concrete roof in order to install some unusable wire-mesh devices would never have happened, and as the lack of any material and documental traces shows, it never happened. The only plausible and logical conclusion is that no such mass-gassing scheme was ever planned or implemented at Auschwitz.

(For more details, see Rudolf 2023, pp. 217-227; Rudolf 2020, pp. 132-162; Rudolf/Mattogno 2017, pp. 291-407.)

Bibliography

- "A pack of...?". *Science*, March 14, 2008, Vol. 319, No. 5869, p. 1467.
- Adam, Uwe Dietrich. "Les chambres à gaz," in: Colloque de l'Ecole des Hautes Etudes en Sciences Sociales (ed.), *L'Allemagne nazie et le génocide juif*, Gallimard-Le Seuil, Paris, 1985, pp. 236-261.
- Allen, Andrew 2000. "The Office of Special Investigations and the Holocaust Myth," *The Revisionist*, Codoh Series, No. 3, 2000.
- Allen, Martin 2005. *Himmler's Secret War: The Covert Peace Negotiations of Heinrich Himmler*, Da Capo Press, Boston, 2005.
- Alvarez, Santiago 2011. "Lanzmann's 'Shoah' Witness Simon Srebnik," *Inconvenient History*, Vol. 3, No. 1, 2011; http://inconvenienthistory.com/3/1/3139.
- Alvarez, Santiago 2023. *The Gas Vans: A Critical Investigation*, 2nd ed., Castle Hill Publishers, Bargoed, UK, 2023.
- Alvarez, Santiago 2023a. "The Seventh Gas Chamber of Majdanek," *Inconvenient History*, Vol. 15, No. 1, 2023; http://inconvenienthistory.com/15/1/8208.
- Arad, Yitzhak 1987. *Belzec, Sobibor, Treblinka. The Operation Reinhard Death Camps*, Indiana University Press, Bloomington/Indianapolis, 1987.
- Arad, Yitzhak 2009. *The Holocaust in the Soviet Union*. University of Nebraska Press, Lincoln/Yad Vashem, Jerusalem, 2009.
- Aroneanu, Eugène. *Documents pour servir à l'histoire de la guerre: Camps de concentration*, Office français d'édition, 1945.
- Aschenauer, Rudolf 1980. *Ich, Adolf Eichmann*, Druffel, Leoni, 1980.
- Aynat, Enrique 2023. "The Death Books of Auschwitz: Statistical Data on the Mortality of Jews Deported from France to Auschwitz in 1942," *Inconvenient History*, Vol. 15, No. 2, 2023; https://inconvenienthistory.com/15/2/8215.
- Badcock, James. "How Spanish Nazi Victim Enric Marco Was Exposed as Impostor", *BBC News*, 5 May 2015; https://bbc.co.uk/news/world-europe-32582420.
- Barton, Russell. "Belsen," in: *History of the Second World War*, No. 109, 1975, pp. 3025-3029.
- Bartrop, Paul, Michael Dickerman (eds.), *The Holocaust: An Encyclopedia and Document Collection*, ABC-CLIO, Santa Barbara, Cal., 2017.
- Bauer, Yehuda 1994. *Jews for Sale? Nazi-Jewish Negotiations, 1933-1945*, Yale University Press, New Haven, 1994.
- Baum, Bruno 1949. *Widerstand in Auschwitz*, Kongress-Verlag, Berlin, 1949.
- BBC 2013. *Auschwitz: Inside the Nazi State*, BBC/Furneaux & Edgar Productions, 2013; https://vimeo.com/120776242.
- BBC 2013a. *Treblinka: Inside Hitler's Secret Death Camp*, BBC/Furneaux & Edgar Productions, 2013; https://vimeo.com/120776242; Smithsonian, "Treblinka: Hitler's Killing Machine"; www.smithsonianchannel.com/shows/treblinka-hitlers-killing-machine/0/3403868.
- Beaulieu, Jean-Francois. "Holocaust Movie *Shoah* Exposed as Propaganda," *The Revisionist*, Vol. 1, No. 2, 2003, pp. 166-168.
- Bednarz, Władysław 1946. "The Extermination Camp at Chełmno (Kulmhof)," in: *Central Commission for Investigation of German Crimes in Poland*, Vol. I, Warsaw, 1946.
- Belgion, Montgomery. *Victor's Justice*, Regnery, Hinsdale, IL, 1949.
- Benz, Wolfgang. *Dimension des Völkermords*, Oldenbourg, Munich, 1991.
- Berenbaum, Michael 1993. *The World Must Know*. Little, Brown & Co., New York, 1993.
- Berg, Friedrich P. 1986. "Zyklon B and the German Delousing Chambers," *Journal of Historical Review*, Vol. 7, No. 1, 1986, pp. 73-94.
- Berg, Friedrich P. 1988. "Typhus and the Jews," *Journal of Historical Review*, Vol. 8, No. 4, No. 1988, pp. 433-481.
- Berg, Friedrich P. 2003. "Poison Gas über alles," *The Revisionist*, Vol. 1, No. 1, No. 2003, pp. 37-47.
- Bezwinska, Jadwiga, Danuta Czech 1984 (eds.). *KL Auschwitz Seen by the SS*, H. Fertig, New York, 1984.
- Billig, Joseph. *La solution finale de la question juive*, Beate Klarsfeld, Paris, 1977.
- Bily, Henry. "Mon histoire extraordinaire," *Le Déporté pour la liberté*, No. 461f., October – November 1991.
- Bischoff, Erich. *The Book of the Shulchan Aruch*, Clemens & Blair, Ann Arbor, MI, 2023: German original: *Das Buch vom Schulchan aruch*, Hammer Verlag, Leipzig, 1929.
- Bjorklund, David F. (ed.). *False-Memory Creation in Children and Adults: Theory, Research, and Implications*, Lawrence Erlbaum Ass., Mahwah, NJ, 2000.
- Black, Edwin. *The Transfer Agreement: The Untold Story of the Secret Agreement between the Third Reich and Jewish Palestine*, Macmillan, New York, 1984.

- Bode, Christian. *Zur Geschichte der Gerichtlichen Medizin an der Universität Jena im Zeitraum von 1901 bis 1945*, Dissertation, Universität Jena, 2007.
- Bone, James. "Herman Rosenblat's Holocaust memoir of love is exposed as a hoax," *The Times*, December 29, 2008; www.timesonline.co.uk/tol/news/world/us_and_americas/article5409220.ece.
- Bourtman, Ilya. "'Blood for Blood, Death for Death': The Soviet Military Tribunal in Krasnodar, 1943," *Holocaust and Genocide Studies*, Vol. 22, No. 2, 2008, pp. 246-265.
- Brauburger, Stefan, Andreas Sulzer. *Hitlers Geheimwaffen-Chef: Die zwei Leben Hans Kammlers*, ZDF, documentary, Mainz, Germany, 17 June 2019.
- Brechtken, Magnus. *Madagaskar für die Juden. Antisemitische Idee und politische Praxis 1885-1945*, Studien zur Zeitgeschichte, Vol. 53, 2nd ed., Oldenbourg, Munich, 1998.
- Brentar, Jerome A. "My Campaign for Justice for John Demjanjuk," *The Journal of Historical Review*, Vol. 13, No. 6, 1993, pp. 2-8.
- Brugioni, Dino, Robert Poirier. *The Holocaust Revisited: A Retrospective Analysis of Auschwitz-Birkenau Extermination Complex*, Central Intelligent Agency, Washington, D.C., 1979.
- Buchanan, Pat. "'Ivan the Terrible' – More Doubts," *New York Post*, 17 March 1990, p. 26.
- Butz, Arthur R. 2015. *The Hoax of the Twentieth Century*, Historical Review Press, Brighton, UK, 1976; 4th edition, Castle Hill Publishers, Uckfield, 2015.
- Byford, Jovan. "'Shortly afterwards, we heard the sound of the gas van.' Survivor Testimony, and the Writing of History," *History & Memory*, Vol. 22, No. 1, 2010, pp. 5-47.
- Cercas, Javier, *The Impostor*, MacLehose Press, London, 2018.
- Christianson, Scott. *The Last Gasp: The Rise and Fall of the American Gas Chamber*, University of California Press, Berkeley, CA, 2010.
- Cobain, Ian 2005a. "Revealed: UK wartime torture camp" & "The secrets of the London cage," *The Guardian*, 12 Nov. 2005; www.theguardian.com/uk/2005/nov/12/topstories3.secondworldwar; www.theguardian.com/uk/2005/nov/12/secondworldwar.world.
- Cobain, Ian 2005b. "The interrogation camp that turned prisoners into living skeletons," *The Guardian*, 17 Dec. 2005; www.theguardian.com/uk/2005/dec/17/secondworldwar.topstories3.
- Cobain, Ian 2012. "How Britain tortured Nazi POWs", *Daily Mail*, 26 October 2012.
- Cobain, Ian 2013. *Cruel Britannia: A Secret History of Torture*, Portobello Books, London, 2013.
- Cohen, Leon. *From Greece to Birkenau: The Crematoria Workers' Uprising*. The Salonika Jewry Research Center, Tel-Aviv/Jerusalem, 1996.
- Connolly, Cyril (ed.). *The Golden Horizon,* Weidenfels & Nicholson, London, 1953.
- Copeland, Libby. "Survivor: When Deli Strummer, symbol of the Holocaust, was caught stretching the truth, it raised a hard question: How much suffering is enough?", *The Washington Post*, 24 Sept. 2000, p. F01.
- Corni, Gustavo 2003. *Hitler's Ghettos*. Oxford University Press, Oxford, 2003.
- Cox, Cyrus. *Auschwitz: Forensically Examined*, Castle Hill Publishers, Uckfield, 2019.
- Curilla, Wolfgang. *Die deutsche Ordnungspolizei und der Holocaust im Baltikum und in Weissrussland 1941-1944*. Ferdinand Schöningh, Paderborn, 2006.
- Czech, Danuta 1990. *Auschwitz Chronicle*, 1939-1945, H. Holt, New York, 1990 (German edition: *Kalendarium der Ereignisse im Konzentrationslager Auschwitz-Birkenau 1939-1945*, Rowohlt, Reinbek, 1989).
- Dalton, Thomas 2019. *Goebbels on the Jews*, Castle Hill Publishers, Uckfield, 2019.
- Dalton, Thomas 2020. *Debating the Holocaust: A New Look at Both Sides*, 4th ed., Castle Hill Publishers, Uckfield, 2020.
- Dalton, Thomas 2020a. *Streicher, Rosenberg, and the Jews: The Nuremberg Transcripts*, Castle Hill Publishers, Uckfield, 2020.
- Dalton, Thomas 2021. "Jasenovac Unmasked," *Inconvenient History*, Vol. 13, No. 4, 2021; www.InconvenientHistory.com/13/4/8046.
- Dalton, Thomas 2023. *Hitler on the Jews*, 2nd ed., Castle Hill Publishers, Bargoed, UK, 2023.
- Daniel, Jane. *Bestseller! The $33 Million Verdict, the 20-Year Hoax, the Truth behind the Headlines*, Laughing Gull Press, Gloucester, MA, 2008.
- De Wan, George. "The Holocaust in Perspective," *Newsday*, Long Island, New York, Feb. 23, 1983, p. II/3.
- Dean, Martin. "Ghettos," in: Peter Hayes, John K. Roth (eds.), *The Oxford Handbook of Holocaust Studies*, Oxford University Press, Oxford, 2010.
- Defonseca, Misha. *Misha: A Mémoire of the Holocaust Years*, Mt. Ivy Press, Bluebell, PA, 1997.
- Demant, Ebbo. *"Direkt von der Rampe weg..."*: *Drei Täter geben zu Protokoll*, Rowohlt, Reinbek, 1979.
- Denisov, Vladmir N., Gleb I. Changuli (eds.). *Nazi Crimes in the Ukraine*, Naukova Dumka Publishers, Kiev, 1987.

- Desbois, Patrick 2009. *The Holocaust by Bullets: A Priest's Journey to Uncover the Truth Behind the Murder of 1.5 Million Jews*, Palgrave Macmillan, New York, 2009.
- Desjardins, Daniel D. "Night. A Review," *Inconvenient History*, Vol. 4, No. 2, 2012; https://inconvenienthistory.com/4/2/3178.
- Dimont, Max. *Jews, God and History*, New American Library, New York, 1962.
- Dineen, Tana. *Manufacturing Victims: What the Psychology Industry Is Doing to People*, R. Davies, Montréal, 1996.
- Dirks, Christian 2006. *Die Verbrechen der Anderen: Auschwitz und der Auschwitz-Prozess der DDR. Das Verfahren gegen den KZ-Arzt Dr. Horst Fischer*, Schöningh, Paderborn, 2006.
- Dirks, Christian 2011. "'Vergangenheitsbewältigung' in der DDR: Zur Rezeption des Prozesses gegen den KZ-Arzt Dr. Horst Fischer 1966 in Ost-Berlin." In: Jörg Osterloh, Clemens Vollnhals (eds.), *NS-Prozesse und deutsche Öffentlichkeit: Besatzungszeit, frühe Bundesrepublik und DDR*, Vandenhoeck & Ruprecht, Göttingen, 2012.
- Długoborski, Wácław, Franciszek Piper (eds.). *Auschwitz 1940-1945: Central Issues in the History of the Camp*, Auschwitz-Birkenau State Museum, Oświęcim, 2000.
- Dodd, Christopher. *Letters from Nuremberg*, Crown, New York, 2007.
- Donat, Alexander (ed.). *The Death Camp Treblinka*, Holocaust Library, New York, 1979.
- Earl, Hilary. *The Nuremberg SS-Einsatzgruppen Trial 1945-1958*, Cambridge University Press, Cambridge, 2009.
- Ehrenburg, Ilya, Vasily Grossman 1981 (eds.). *The Black Book*. Holocaust Library, New York, 1981.
- Ellul, Jacques. *Propaganda: The Formation of Men's Attitude*. Knopf, New York, 1962.
- Faculté des lettres de l'Université de Strasbourg (ed.). *De l'Université aux camps de concentration. Témoignages strasbourgeois*, 2nd ed., Belles-Lettres, Paris 1954 (1st ed. 1947).
- Faurisson, Robert 1980. *Mémoire en défense*, La Vieille Taupe, Paris 1980.
- Faurisson, Robert 1981. "Confessions of SS Men who were at Auschwitz," *Journal of Historical Review*, Vol. 2, No. 2, 1981, pp. 103-136.
- Faurisson, Robert 1982. "Is the Diary of Anne Frank Genuine?," *Journal of Historical Review*, Vol. 3, No. 2, 1982, pp. 147-209.
- Faurisson, Robert 1983. "Les tricheries de l'Album d'Auschwitz," 10 Dec. 1983; aaargh.vho.http/fran/archFaur/1980-1985/RF831209.html.
- Faurisson, Robert 1985. *Is the Diary of Anne Frank Genuine?*, IHR, Torrance, 1985.
- Faurisson, Robert 1991. Book review of *Auschwitz: Technique and operation of the gas chambers*, part 1, *Journal of Historical Review*, Vol. 11, No. 1, 1991, pp. 25-66.
- Faurisson, Robert 1992. "Le faux témoignage d'Henry Bily," *Revue d'Histoire Révisionniste*, Vol. 6, 1992, pp. 190-194.
- Faurisson, Robert 1999. *Écrits révisionnistes*, 4 vols., publ. by author, Vichy 1999; 2nd ed. 2004.
- Faurisson, Robert 2001. "The Auschwitz I Swimming Pool," 20 July 2001; https://robert-faurisson.com/history/the-Auschwitz-i-swimming-pool/.
- Faurisson, Robert 2003. "How many deaths at Auschwitz?," *The Revisionist*, Vol. 1, No. 1, 2003, pp. 17-23.
- Fest, Joachim C. 1975. *Hitler*, Vintage Books, New York, 1975.
- Fest, Joachim C. 1973. *Hitler: Eine Biographie*, Ullstein, Frankfurt/Main, 1973.
- Finkelstein, Norman G. 2000. *The Holocaust Industry: Reflections of the Exploitation of Jewish Suffering*, Verso, London/New York 2000.
- Finkelstein, Norman G. 2005. *Beyond Chutzpah. On the Misuse of Anti-Semitism and the Abuse of History*, University of California Press, Berkeley 2005.
- Fleur, Nicholas. "Escape Tunnel Dug by Hand Is Found at Holocaust Massacre Site," *The New York Time*, 29 June 2016, www.nytimes.com/2016/06/29/science/holocaust-ponar-tunnel-lithuania.html.
- Floerchinger, Jane. "Concentration Camp Conditions Killed Most Inmates, Doctor Says," *The Wichita Eagle*, 1 April 1980, p. 4C.
- Foust, Hal. "Nazi Trial Judge Rips 'Injustice,'" *Chicago Tribune*, 23 Feb. 1948.
- Fréjafon, Georges-Louis. *Bergen-Belsen: Bagne sanatorium*, Librairie Valois, Paris, 1947 (©1945).
- Friedman, Arnold 1972. *Death Was Our Destiny*, Vantage Press, New York, 1972.
- Friedman, Filip 1946. *To jest Oświęcim!* Krakow, 1945. English: *This Was Oświęcim: The Story of a Murder Camp*, The United Jewish Relief Appeal, London, 1946.
- Friedman, Philip 1954. "The Jewish Ghettos of the Nazi Era," *Jewish Social Studies*, Vol. 16, 1954, pp. 61-88.
- Fritsch, Theodor. *Handbuch zur Judenfrage*, 31st ed., Hammer-Verlag, Leipzig, 1932.
- Ganzfried, Daniel. *…alias Wilkomirski. Die Holocaust-Travestie*, Jüdische Verlagsanstalt, Berlin 2002.
- Garaudy, Roger. *The Founding Myths of Modern Israel*, Institute for Historical Review, Costa Mesa, 2000.
- Gärtner, Michael, Werner Rademacher (=Willy Wallwey). "Ground Water in the Area of the PoW Camp Birkenau," *The Revisionist*, Vol. 1, No. 1, 2003, pp. 3-12.

- Gassner, Ludwig. "Verkehrshygiene und Schädlingsbekämpfung," *Gesundheits-Ingenieur*, Vol. 66, No. 15, 1943, pp. 174ff.
- Gilbert, Martin. *Auschwitz and the Allies*, Holt, Rinehart and Winston, New York 1981.
- Gilbert, S. "The Use of Diesel Engines Underground in British Coal Mines," *The Mining Engineer* (GB), Vol. 133, June 1974, pp. 395-406.
- Glazar, Richard. *Trap with a Green Fence*, Northwestern University Press, Evanston, IL, 1995.
- Goldstein, Eleanor, Kevin Farmer (eds.). *True Stories of False Memories*, Social Issues Resources, Boca Raton, FL, 1993.
- Goshen, Seev 1981. "Eichmann und die Nisko-Aktion im Oktober 1939," in: *Vierteljahrshefte für Zeitgeschichte*, Vol. 29, No. 1, January 1981, pp. 74-96.
- Grabher, Michael. *Irmfried Eberl: "Euthanasie"-Arzt und Kommandant von Treblinka*, Europäischer Verlag der Wissenschaft, Frankfurt/Main, 2006.
- Grabitz, Helge. *NS-Prozesse – Psychogramme der Beteiligten*, 2nd ed., C.F. Müller, Heidelberg, 1986.
- Graf, Jürgen 2019. *Auschwitz: Eyewitness Reports and Perpetrator Confessions of the Holocaust: 30 Gas-Chamber Witnesses Scrutinized*, Castle Hill Publishers, Uckfield, 2019.
- Graf, Jürgen, Carlo Mattogno 2012. *Concentration Camp Majdanek*, 3rd ed., The Barnes Review, Washington, D.C., 2012. (Original German edition: *KL Majdanek*, Castle Hill Publishers, Hastings, 1998.)
- Graf, Jürgen, Carlo Mattogno 2016. *Concentration Camp Stutthof*, 4th ed., Castle Hill Publishers, Uckfield, 2016.
- Graf, Jürgen, Thomas Kues, Carlo Mattogno. *Sobibór: Holocaust Propaganda and Reality*, 2nd ed., Castle Hill Publishers, Uckfield, 2020.
- Greif, Gideon 2005. *We Wept without Tears: Interviews with Jewish Survivors of the Auschwitz Sonderkommando*. Yale University Press, New Haven, 2005.
- Grigorenko, Piotr. *Erinnerungen*, Bertelsmann, Munich 1981; English: Petr G. Grigorenko, *Memoirs*, Norton, New York 1982.
- Grüner, Nikolaus Michael (Miklós). *Stolen Identity: Auschwitz Number A-7713*, self-published, Stockholm 2007.
- Gutman, Israel 1990 (ed.). *Encyclopedia of the Holocaust*, Yad Vashem, Jerusalem/MacMillan, New York, 1990.
- Hackett, David A. (ed.). *The Buchenwald Report*, Westview Press, Boulder/San Francisco/Oxford, 1995.
- Hecking, Claus 2014. "Recovering the Lost History of Sobibór", *Der Spiegel*, 26 Sept. 2014; www.spiegel.de/international/zeitgeist/the-archeological-excavations-that-led-to-the-gas-chambers-of-sobibor-a-993733.html.
- Heddesheimer, Don 2002. "'Nothing Has Been Invented:' The War Journalism of Boris Polevoy," *Journal of Historical Review*, Vol. 21, No. 1, 2002, pp. 23-38.
- Heddesheimer, Don 2017. *The First Holocaust: The Surprising Origin of the Six-Million Figure,* 4th ed., Castle Hill Publishers, Uckfield 2017.
- Heliotis, Panagiotis. "The Manuscripts of Marcel Nadjari," in: *Inconvenient History*, Vol. 10. No. 2, 2018; www.inconvenienthistory.com/10/2/5461.
- Henderson, Y., H. W. Haggard. *Noxious Gases*, Reinhold Publishing, New York, 1943.
- Hénocque, Georges. *Les Antres de la Bête: Fresnes, Buchenwald, Dachau*, Durassie & Co., Paris, 1947.
- Hess, Rudolf. Speech held on 14 May 1935, at the German-Swedish Association at Stockholm; Rudolf Hess Association, Documentation No. 9, Planegg; http://unglaublichkeiten.net/lager/Rudolf-Hess-Rede-Stockholm-1935.pdf.
- Heyne, Johannes 2018. "British Torture at Bad Nenndorf," *Inconvenient History*, Vol. 10, No. 3, 2018; www.inconvenienthistory.com/10/3/5924.
- Hilberg, Raul 1961/1985/2003. *The Destruction of the European Jews*, Quadrangle Books, Chicago 1961; 2nd ed., Holmes & Meyer, New York 1985; 3rd ed., Yale University Press, New Haven, CT, 2003.
- Hinsley, F.H. *British Intelligence in World War Two*, Her Majesty's Stationery Office, London, 1981.
- Hoffmann, Joachim. *Stalin's War of Extermination 1941-1945*, Theses & Dissertations Press, Capshaw, AL, 2001.
- Holland, M. "The Horrors of Belsen," *Sunday Herald Sun* (Melbourne, Australia), 22 Jan. 1995, p. 93; M. Holland, "Man Who Uncovered the Horror of Belsen," *Sunday Times* (Perth, W. Australia), 5 Feb. 1995, p. 2.
- Holming, Göran. "Himmler's Order to Stop the Gassing of the Jews," *Inconvenient History*, Vol. 15, No. 2, 2023; www.inconvenienthistory.com/15/2/958.
- Holstein, Bernard (=Brougham). *Stolen Soul: A True Story of Courage and Survival*, University of Western Australia Press, Perth 2004.
- Holt, Penelope. *The Apple: Based on the Herman Rosenblat Holocaust Memoir*, York House Press, Ryebrook, NY, 2009.
- Höss, Rudolf. *Commandant of Auschwitz: The Autobiography of Rudolf Hoess*, The World Publishing Company, Cleveland/New York, 1959.
- Howe, Stephen. "Review of *Cruel Britannia*," *Independent*, UK, 24 November 2012.

- Hrabar, Roman. Zofia Tokarz, Jacek Wilczur, *The Fate of Polish Children During the Last War*, Interpress, Warsaw, 1981.
- Humm, Otto. "Typhus – The Phantom Disease," *The Revisionist*, Vol. 2, No. 1, 2004, pp. 84-88.
- Hunt, Eric 2014. *The Treblinka Archeology Hoax*, 20th Century Hoax, Phoenix, AZ, 2014.
- Igounet, Valérie 2000. *Histoire du négationnisme en France*, Editions du Seuil, Paris, 2000.
- International Military Tribunal. *Trial of the Major War Criminals* (IMT), Nuremberg 1947; http://avalon.law.yale.edu/subject_menus/imt.asp.
- Irebodd, Dean 2008. "Nazi Shrunken Heads," documentary, 2008; www.HolocaustHandbooks.com.
- Irebodd, Dean 2009. "Buchenwald: A Dumb-Dumb Portrayal of Evil," documentary, 2nd ed., 2009; www.HolocaustHandbooks.com.
- Irebodd, Dean 2023. "The CIA During World War II", documentary, 2023; https://odysee.com/@Denierbud:0/ciaduringworldwar2:1.
- Irving, David 1977. *Hitler's War*, Hodder & Stoughton, London, 1977.
- Irving, David 1991. *Hitler's War*, Focal Point, London, 1991.
- Irving, David 1996. *Nuremberg: The Last Battle*, Focal Point, London, 1996.
- Isacovici, Salomón, Juan Manuel Rodríguez 1990. *A7393, hombre de cenizas*, Diana, México City, 1990; English: *Man of Ashes*, University of Nebraska Press, Lincoln, 1999.
- Jäckel, Eberhard, Jürgen Rohwer (eds.). *Der Mord an den Juden im Zweiten Weltkrieg*, Fischer Verlag, Frankfurt/Main, 1987.
- Jackson, Nigel. "John Demjanjuk: The Man More Sinned Against," *Inconvenient History*, Vol. 4, No. 2, 2012; www.inconvenienthistory.com/4/2/3177.
- Jansen, Hans. *Der Madagaskar-Plan. Die beabsichtigte Deportation der europäischen Juden nach Madagaskar*, Herbig, Munich, 1997.
- Jansson, Friedrich 2014. "Jan Karski's Visit to Belzec: A Reassessment," *Inconvenient History*, Vol. 6, No. 4, 2014; www.inconvenienthistory.com/6/4/3336.
- Jansson, Friedrich 2014a. "The Origin of the Soviet Report on the 'Next-Generation' Homicidal Gas Chamber at Sachsenhausen," *Inconvenient History*, Vol. 6, No. 4, 2014; https://inconvenienthistory.com/6/4/3341.
- Jansson, Friedrich 2015. "Aspects of the Tesch Trial," *Inconvenient History*, Vol. 7, No. 1, 2015; www.inconvenienthistory.com/7/1/3357.
- Jastrzębska, Halina, "Maurerschule w Auschwitz," in: *Zeszyty Oświęcimskie*. Wydawnictwo Państwowego Muzeum Auschwitz-Birkenau w Oświęcimiu, Vol. 24, 2008, pp. 263-299.
- Kalthoff, Jürgen, Martin Werner. *Die Händler des Zyklon B*, VSA-Verlag, Hamburg, 1998.
- Karlsch, Rainer. *Hitlers Bombe: Die geheime Geschichte der deutschen Kernwaffenversuche*, Deutsche Verlags-Anstalt, Munich, 2005.
- Karlsch, Rainer, Heiko Petermann (eds.). *Für und wider "Hitlers Bombe": Studien zur Atomforschung in Deutschland*, Waxmann, Münster 2007.
- Karski, Jan. *Story of a Secret State*, Houghton Mifflin, Boston, 1944.
- Kaufmann, Sylvain, *Le livre de la mémoire: Au-delà de l'enfer*, Jean-Claude Lattès, Paris, 1992.
- Kertész, Imre. *Fatelessness*, Vintage Anchor, New York, 2004.
- Klarsfeld, Serge 1978. *Le Mémorial de la Déportation des Juifs de France*, Klarsfeld, Paris 1978; English: *Memorial to the Jews deported from France 1942-1944*, Beate Klarsfeld Foundation, New York, 1983.
- Klarsfeld, Serge 1989 (ed.), *David Olère: A Painter in the Sonderkommando at Auschwitz*, The Beate Klarsfeld Foundation, New York, 1989.
- Klee, Ernst, Willi Dressen. *Schöne Zeiten*, S. Fischer, Frankfurt, 1988; English: *The Good Old Days*, Free Press, New York, 1991.
- Klein, Georg 1989/1992. *Pietà*, Bonniers, Stockholm, 1989; English: MIT Press, Cambridge, Mass., 1992.
- Klein, Marc 1946. "Observations et réflexions sur les camps de concentration nazis," *Revue d'Études germaniques*, No. 3, 1946, pp. 244-275; www.phdn.org/histgen/Auschwitz/klein-obs46.html.
- Kogon, Eugen, Hermann Langbein, Adalbert Rückerl *et al.* 1993 (eds.). *Nazi Mass Murder: A Documentary History of the Use of Poison Gas*, Yale Univ. Press, New Haven, 1993.
- Kollerstrom, Nicholas 2014. "The 'Ministry of Truth' at Britain's National Archives: The Attempt to Discredit Martin Allen," *Inconvenient History*, Vol. 6, No. 2, 2014; www.inconvenienthistory.com/6/2/3296.
- Kollerstrom, Nicholas 2023. *Breaking the Spell: The Holocaust, Myth & Reality*, 6th ed., Castle Hill Publishers, Uckfield, 2023.
- Kosinski, Jerzy. *The Painted Bird*, Houghton Mifflin, Boston, 1965.
- Kraus, Ota, Erich Kulka 1958. *Die Todesfabrik*, Kongress-Verlag, East-Berlin, 1958.
- Kraus, Ota, Erich Kulka 1966. *The Death Factory: Document on Auschwitz*, Pergamon Press, Oxford, 1966.

- Kraus, Ota, Erich Schön [Erich Kulka]. *Továrna na smrt*. Čin, Prague, 1946.
- Krausnick, Helmut, Hans-Heinrich Wilhelm. *Die Truppe des Weltanschauungskrieges: Die Einsatzgruppen der Sicherheitspolizei und des SD 1938-1942*, Deutsche Verlags-Anstalt, Stuttgart, 1981.
- Kues, Thomas 2009. "Tree-felling at Treblinka," *Inconvenient History*, Vol. 1, No. 2, 2009; www.inconvenienthistory.com/1/2/1912.
- Kues, Thomas 2010. "Chil Rajchman's Treblinka Memoirs," Inconvenient History, Vol. 2, No. 1, 2010; www.inconvenienthistory.com/2/1/1916.
- Kues, Thomas 2010a. "Evidence for the Presence of 'Gassed' Jews in the Occupied Eastern Territories, Part 1," *Inconvenient History*, Vol. 2, No. 2, 2010; www.inconvenienthistory.com/2/2/3111.
- Kues, Thomas 2010b. "Evidence for the Presence of 'Gassed' Jews in the Occupied Eastern Territories, Part 2," *Inconvenient History*, Vol. 2, No. 4, 2010; www.inconvenienthistory.com/2/4/3127.
- Kues, Thomas 2011a. "The Maly Trostenets 'Extermination Camp': A Preliminary Historiographical Survey, Part 1," *Inconvenient History*, Vol. 3, No. 1, 2011; www.inconvenienthistory.com/2/4/3141.
- Kues, Thomas 2011b. "The Maly Trostenets 'Extermination Camp': A Preliminary Historiographical Survey, Part 1," *Inconvenient History*, Vol. 3, No. 2, 2011; www.inconvenienthistory.com/2/4/3147.
- Kues, Thomas 2011c. "Evidence for the Presence of 'Gassed' Jews in the Occupied Eastern Territories, Part 3," *Inconvenient History*, Vol. 3, No. 4, 2011; www.inconvenienthistory.com/3/4/3166.
- Kulaszka, Barbara (ed.). *The Second Zündel Trial: Excerpts from the Court Transcript of the Canadian "False News" Trial of Ernst Zündel, 1988*, Castle Hill Publishers, Uckfield, 2019.
- Kulischer, Eugene M. *The Displacement of Population in Europe*. Published by the International Labour Office, Montreal, 1943.
- Kwiet, Konrad 1997. "Anzac and Auschwitz: The unbelievable story of Donald Watt," *Patterns of Prejudice*, Vol. 31, No. 4, 1997, pp. 53-60.
- Langbein, Hermann 1995. *Menschen in Auschwitz*, Europaverlag, Vienna, 1995: English edition: *The People of Auschwitz*, Univ. of North Carolina, Chapel Hill, 2004.
- Langer, Lawrence L., *The Afterdeath of the Holocaust*, Palgrave Macmillan, Cham, 2021.
- Lanzmann, Claude 1985. *Shoah*, Pantheon Books, New York 1985; available as VHS video, DVD and on YouTube.
- Laqueur, Walter, Judith Baumel-Schwartz 2001 (eds.). *The Holocaust Encyclopedia*, Yale University Press, New Haven, 2001.
- Laqueur, Walter. *The Terrible Secret*, Little, Brown & Co, Boston 1980; 2nd ed., H. Holt, New York, 1998.
- Lebailly, Jacques. "Interview with Michel De Boüard on the 'Thesis of Nantes'," *Journal of Historical Review*, Vol. 8. No. 3, 1988, pp. 381-384.
- Leide, Henry. *Auschwitz und Staatssicherheit: Strafverfolgung, Propaganda und Geheimhaltung in der DDR*, Bundesbeauftragter für die Unterlagen des Staatssicherheitsdienstes der ehemaligen DDR, Berlin, 2019.
- Leipprand, Horst. *Das Handelsprodukt Zyklon B: Eigenschaften, Produktion, Verkauf, Handhabung*. Self-published, Mannheim, 2008.
- Lengyel, Olga. *I Survived Hitler's Ovens*, Avon, New York, 1947.
- Leuchter, Fred A., Robert Faurisson, Germar Rudolf. *The Leuchter Reports: Critical Edition*, 5th ed., Castle Hill Publishers, Uckfield, 2017.
- Levi, Primo 1947/1966/1984. *Se questo è un uomo*, Einaudi, Turin, 1966/1984 (De Silva, Turin 1947); English: *If this is a Man*, Penguin, Harmondsworth/New York, 1979.
- Levi, Primo 1986. *Survival in Auschwitz*, Summit Books, New York, 1986.
- Lewy, Günther 2001. *The Nazi Persecution of the Gypsies*, Oxford University Press, Oxford/NewYork, 2001.
- Lipstadt, Deborah E. 1986. *Beyond Belief: The American Press and the Coming of the Holocaust 1933-1945*, The Free Press, New York, 1986.
- Loftus, Elizabeth 1994. *The Myth of Repressed Memory*, St. Martin's Press, New York, 1994.
- Loftus, Elizabeth 1997. "Creating False Memories," *Scientific American*, Vol. 277, No. 3, 1997, pp. 70-75; https://staff.washington.edu/eloftus/Articles/sciam.htm.
- Loftus, Elizabeth 2003. "Award for Distinguished Scientific Applications of Psychology," *American Psychologist*, Vol. 58, No. 11, 2003, pp. 864-873.
- Longerich, Peter. *Holocaust: The Nazi Persecution and Murder of the Jews*, Oxford University Press, Oxford, 2010.
- Lüftl, Walter 2003 (as Werner Rademacher). "Engineer's Deathbed Confession: We Built Morgues, not Gas Chambers," *The Revisionist*, Vol. 2, No. 3, 2003, pp. 296f.
- Lüftl, Walter 2004. "1972: A Somewhat Different Auschwitz Trial," *The Revisionist*, Vol. 2, No. 3, 2004, pp. 294f.
- Mächler, Stefan. *Der Fall Wilkomirski*, Pendo, Zürich 2000; English: *The Wilkomirski Affair*, Schocken Books, New York, 2001.
- Madden, Catherine, Jim Kelly. "Holocaust man's claims queried," *The Sunday Times* (Perth), 31 Oct. 2004.

- Margry, Karel. "The Katyn Massacre," in: *After the Battle*, Vol. 92, 1996, pp. 1-33.
- Mark, Jonathan. "Memory Plays Tricks About Mengele," *The Times of Israel*, 7 April 2020; https://jewish-week.timesofisrael.com/memory-plays-tricks-about-mengele/ (accessed April 10, 2020).
- Maršálek, Hans. *Die Geschichte des Konzentrationslagers Mauthausen*, Österreichische Lagergemeinschaft Mauthausen, Vienna, 1980.
- Mason, Alpheus T. *Harlan Fiske Stone: Pillar of the Law*, Viking, New York, 1956.
- Mattogno, Carlo 1988. "The Myth of the Extermination of the Jews Part II," *The Journal of Historical Review*, Vol. 8, No. 3, 1988, pp. 261-302.
- Mattogno, Carlo 1988a. *Medico ad Auschwitz: Anatomia di un falso*. Edizioni La Sfinge, Parma, 1988.
- Mattogno, Carlo 1989. "The First Gassing at Auschwitz: Genesis of a Myth," *The Journal of Historical Review*, Vol. 9, No. 2, 1989, pp. 193-222.
- Mattogno, Carlo 1990. "Two false testimonies from Auschwitz," *The Journal of Historical Review*, Vol. 10, No. 1, 1990, pp. 25-47.
- Mattogno, Carlo 1990a. "Auschwitz: A Case of Plagiarism," *Journal of Historical Review*, Vol. 10 No. 1, 1990, pp. 5-24.
- Mattogno, Carlo 1990b. "Jean-Claude Pressac and the War Refugee Board Report," *Journal of Historical Review*, Vol. 10 No. 4, 1990, pp. 461-486.
- Mattogno, Carlo 2003a. "Open-Air Incinerations in Auschwitz: Rumor or Reality?," *The Revisionist*, Vol. 1, No. 1, 2003, pp. 14-17.
- Mattogno, Carlo 2003c. "The 'Gassing' of Gypsies in Auschwitz on August 2, 1944," *The Revisionist*, Vol. 1, No. 3, 2003, pp. 330-332.
- Mattogno, Carlo 2003d. "The Four Million Figure of Auschwitz: Origin, Revisions and Consequences," *The Revisionist*, Vol. 1, No. 4, 2003, pp. 387-392, 393-399.
- Mattogno, Carlo 2004a. *Bełżec in Propaganda, Testimonies, Archeological Research, and History*, Theses & Dissertations Press, Chicago, 2004.
- Mattogno, Carlo 2004b. "Flames and Smoke from the Chimneys of Crematories," *The Revisionist*, Vol. 2, No. 1, 2004, pp. 73-78.
- Mattogno, Carlo 2004c. "The Morgues of the Crematories at Birkenau in the Light of Documents," *The Revisionist*, Vol. 2, No. 3, 2004, pp. 271-294.
- Mattogno, Carlo 2010. "Origins and Functions of the Birkenau Camp," *Inconvenient History*, Vol. 2, No. 2, 2010; www.inconvenienthistory.com/2/2/3113.
- Mattogno, Carlo 2012. "Christian Gerlach and the 'Extermination Camp' at Mogilev," *Inconvenient History*, Vol. 4, No. 2, 2012; https://inconvenienthistory.com/4/2/3183.
- Mattogno, Carlo 2014. "Gypsy Holocaust? The Gypsies under the National Socialist Regime," *Inconvenient History*, Vol. 6, No. 1, 2014; https://inconvenienthistory.com/6/1/3239.
- Mattogno, Carlo 2014a. "The Recovery of Human Fat in the Cremation Pits," in: *Inconvenient History*, Vol. 6, No. 3, 2014; https://inconvenienthistory.com/6/3/3332.
- Mattogno, Carlo 2015. *The Central Construction Office of the Waffen-SS and Police Auschwitz. Organization, Responsibilities, Activities*, 2nd ed., Castle Hill Publishers, Uckfield, 2015.
- Mattogno, Carlo 2015a. "Patrick Desbois and the 'Mass Graves' of Jews in Ukraine," *Inconvenient History*, Vol. 7, No. 3, 2015; www.inconvenienthistory.com/7/3/3433.
- Mattogno, Carlo 2016a. *Healthcare in Auschwitz: Medical Care and Special Treatment of Registered Inmates*, Castle Hill Publishers, Uckfield, 2016.
- Mattogno, Carlo 2016b. *Auschwitz: Open-Air Incinerations*, 2nd ed., Castle Hill Publishers, Uckfield, 2016.
- Mattogno, Carlo 2016c. *Auschwitz: Crematorium I and the Alleged Homicidal Gassings*, 2nd ed., Castle Hill Publishers, Uckfield, 2016.
- Mattogno, Carlo 2016d. *Special Treatment in Auschwitz: Origin and Meaning of a Term*, 2nd ed., Castle Hill Publishers, Uckfield, 2016.
- Mattogno, Carlo 2016e. *Inside the Gas Chambers: The Extermination of Mainstream Holocaust Historiography*, 2nd ed., Castle Hill Publishers, Uckfield, 2016.
- Mattogno, Carlo 2016f. *Debunking the Bunkers of Auschwitz: Black Propaganda versus History*, Castle Hill Publishers, Uckfield, 2016.
- Mattogno, Carlo 2017. *The Chełmno Camp in History and Propaganda Chelmno: History and Propaganda*, 2nd ed., Castle Hill Publishers, Uckfield, 2017.
- Mattogno, Carlo 2019. *The Real Case for Auschwitz: Robert van Pelt's Evidence from the Irving Trial Critically Reviewed*, 2nd ed., Castle Hill Publishers, Uckfield, 2019.

- Mattogno, Carlo 2020. *Curated Lies: The Auschwitz Museum's Misrepresentations, Distortions and Deceptions*, 2nd ed., Castle Hill Publishers, Uckfield, 2020.
- Mattogno, Carlo 2020a. *An Auschwitz Doctor's Eyewitness Account: The Bestselling Tall Tales of Dr. Mengele's Assistant Analyzed*, 2nd ed., Castle Hill Publishers, Uckfield, 2020.
- Mattogno, Carlo 2020b. *Commandant of Auschwitz: Rudolf Höss, His Torture and His Forced Confessions*, Castle Hill Publishers, Uckfield, 2020.
- Mattogno, Carlo 2021. *The Making of the Auschwitz Myth: Auschwitz in British Intercepts, Polish Underground Reports and Postwar Testimonies (1941-1947). On the Genesis and Development of the Gas-Chamber Lore*, 2nd ed., Castle Hill Publishers, Uckfield, 2021.
- Mattogno, Carlo 2021a. *Deliveries of Coke, Wood and Zyklon B to Auschwitz: Neither Proof nor Trace for the Holocaust*, Castle Hill Publishers, Uckfield, 2021.
- Mattogno, Carlo 2021b. *Rudolf Reder versus Kurt Gerstein: Two False Testimonies on the Bełżec Camp Analyzed*, 2nd ed., Castle Hill Publishers, Uckfield, 2021.
- Mattogno, Carlo 2021c. *Bungled: "The Destruction of the European Jews": Raul Hilberg's Failure to Prove National-Socialist "Killing Centers." His Misrepresented Sources and Flawed Methods*, Castle Hill Publishers, Uckfield, 2021.
- Mattogno, Carlo 2021d. *Sonderkommando Auschwitz I: Nine Eyewitness Testimonies Analyzed*, Castle Hill Publishers, Uckfield, 2021.
- Mattogno, Carlo 2021e. *The "Operation Reinhardt" Camps Treblinka, Sobibór, Bełżec: Black Propaganda, Archeological Research, Expected Material Evidence*, Castle Hill Publishers, Uckfield, 2021.
- Mattogno, Carlo 2022. *The Neuengamme and Sachsenhausen Gas Chambers: With a Focus on British Investigations for the Tesch Trial*, Castle Hill Publishers, Bargoed, 2022.
- Mattogno, Carlo 2022a. *The Dachau Gas Chamber: Documents, Testimonies, Material Evidence*, Castle Hill Publishers, Bargoed, 2022.
- Mattogno, Carlo 2022b. *Mis-Chronicling Auschwitz: Danuta Czech's Flawed Methods, Lies and Deceptions in Her "Auschwitz Chronicle"*, Castle Hill Publishers, Dallastown, PA, 2022.
- Mattogno, Carlo 2022c. *The Einsatzgruppen in the Occupied Eastern Territories*, 2 vols., 2nd ed., Castle Hill Publishers, Uckfield, 2022.
- Mattogno, Carlo 2022d. *Sonderkommando Auschwitz II: The False Testimonies by Henryk Tauber and Szlama Dragon*, Castle Hill Publishers, Dallastown, PA, 2022.
- Mattogno, Carlo 2022e. *Sonderkommando Auschwitz III: They Wept Crocodile Tears. A Critical Analysis of Late Witness Testimonies*, Castle Hill Publishers, Uckfield, 2022.
- Mattogno, Carlo 2022f. *Auschwitz: The First Gassing. Rumor and Reality*, 4th ed., Castle Hill Publishers, Dallastown, PA, 2022.
- Mattogno, Carlo 2023. *The Real Auschwitz Chronicle*, 2 volumes, Castle Hill Publishers, Bargoed, 2023.
- Mattogno, Carlo 2023a. "The Ghetto of Lodz in Holocaust Propaganda: The Clearing of the Lodz Ghetto and Deportations to Auschwitz (August 1944)," *Inconvenient History*, Vol. 15, No. 2, 2023; www.InconvenientHistory.com/15/2/8213.
- Mattogno, Carlo 2023b. *A Three-Quarter Century of Propaganda. Origins, Development and Decline of the "Gas Chamber" Propaganda Lie*, 2nd ed., Castle Hill Publishers, Bargoed, UK, 2018.
- Mattogno, Carlo 2023c. *Politics of Slave Labor: The Fate of the Jews Deported from Hungary and the Lodz Ghetto in 1944*, Castle Hill Publishers, Bargoed, UK, 2023 (in preparation).
- Mattogno, Carlo 2023d. "Sachsenhausen Concentration Camp: Occupancy Reports and 'Extermination Operations' 1940 to 1945," *Inconvenient History*, Vol. 15, No. 2, 2023; https://inconvenienthistory.com/15/2/8216.
- Mattogno, Carlo, Franco Deana. *The Cremation Furnaces of Auschwitz: A Technical and Historical Study*, 2nd ed., Castle Hill Publishers, Uckfield, 2021.
- Mattogno, Carlo, Jürgen Graf. *Treblinka: Extermination Camp or Transit Camp*, 4th ed., Castle Hill Publishers, Bargoed, UK, 2023.
- Mattogno, Carlo, Guiseppe Poggi. "The Ventilation Systems of Crematoria II and III in Birkenau", *Inconvenient History*, Vol. 9, No. 3, 2017; www.inconvenienthistory.com/9/3/4888.
- Mattogno, Carlo, Thomas Kues, Jürgen Graf. *The "Extermination Camps" of "Aktion Reinhardt": An Analysis and Refutation of Factitious "Evidence," Deceptions and Flawed Argumentation of the "Holocaust Controversies" Bloggers*, 2nd ed., Castle Hill Publishers, Uckfield, 2015.
- Mauriello, Christoper. *Forced Confrontation*, Lexington Books, Lanham, 2017.
- Mayer, Arno J. *Why Did the Heavens Not Darken?* Pantheon, New York, 1988 (1990).
- McCallum, John D. *Crime Doctor: Dr. Charles P. Larson, World's Foremost Medical-Detective, Reports from His Crime File*, Writing Works, Mercer Island, Wash., 1978.

- McCarthy, Joseph. Speech before the U.S. Senate, *Congressional Record – Senate*, No. 134, 26 July 1949, pp. 10397ff.
- McNamara, B.P. *The Toxicity of Hydrocyanic Acid Vapors in Man*, Edgewood Arsenal Technical Report EB-TR-76023, Department of the Army, Headquarters, Edgewood Arsenal, Aberdeen Proving Ground, Maryland, August 1976; www.dtic.mil/cgi-bin/GetTRDoc?AD=ADA028501 (accessed on 17 Oct. 2016).
- Meier, Lili, Serge Klarsfeld (eds.), *The Auschwitz Album*, Beatle Klarsfeld Foundation, New York, 1989.
- Miller, Francis T. *A History of World War II*, John C. Winston, Philadelphia, 1945.
- Morsch, Günter, Bertrand Perz (eds.). *Neue Studien zu nationalsozialistischen Massentötungen durch Giftgas*, Metropol Verlag, Berlin, 2011.
- Müller, Filip 1979. *Eyewitness Auschwitz: Three Years in the Gas Chambers*, Stein and Day, New York, 1979.
- Müller, Otward 2004. "Sinti and Roma – Yarns, Legends, and Facts," *The Revisionist*, Vol. 2, No. 3, 2004, pp. 254-259.
- Naumann, Bernd. *Auschwitz*, Athenäum-Verlag, Frankfurt 1965; English: Auschwitz, Pall Mall Press, London, 1966.
- Neumann, Robert. *Aufstieg und Untergang des 3. Reiches*, Verlag Kurt Desch, Munich, 1961.
- Nickell, Joe, John F. Fischer. "Spontaneous Human Combustion," *The Fire and Arson Investigator*, Vol. 34, No. 3, 1984, pp. 4-11; *ibid.*, Vol. 34, No. 6, 1984, pp. 3-8.
- Nickell, Joe. "Fiery Tales That Spontaneously Destruct," *Skeptical Inquirer*, Vol. 22, No. 2, 1998; www.csicop.org/si/show/fiery_tales_that_spontaneously_destruct.
- Nicosia, Francis R. *The Third Reich and the Palestine Question*, I.B. Tauris, London, 1985.
- Noakes, Jeremy, Geoffrey Pridham (eds.). *Nazism: A History in Documents and Eyewitness Accounts 1919-1945*, Schocken Books, New York, 1988.
- O'Keefe, Theodore J. 1994. "'Best Witness': Mel Mermelstein, Auschwitz and the IHR," *Journal of Historical Review*, Vol. 14, No. 1, 1994, pp. 25-32.
- O'Keefe, Theodore J. 1997. "History and Memory: Mel Mermelstein's 'Eyewitness' Evidence," *Journal of Historical Review*, Vol. 16, No. 4, 1997, pp. 2-13.
- O'Keefe, Theodore J. 2001. "Was Holocaust Survivor Viktor Frankl Gassed at Auschwitz?," *Journal of Historical Review*, Vol. 20, No. 5+6, 2001, pp. 10f.
- O'Neil, Robin. "Bełżec: A Reassessment of the Number of Victims," *East European Jewish Affairs*, Vol. 29, Nos. 1-2, 1999.
- Ofshe, Richard. *Making Monsters: False Memories, Psychotherapy, and Sexual Hysteria*, 3rd ed., University of California Press, Berkeley, CA, 1996.
- Pattle, R. E., H. Strech, F. Burgess, K. Sinclair, J.A.G. Edginton. "The Toxicity of Fumes from Diesel Engine under Four Different Running Conditions," *British Journal of Industrial Medicine*, Vol. 14, 1957, pp. 47-55; www.vho.org/GB/c/FPB/ToxDiesel.html.
- Pelt, Robert J. van 2002. *The Case for Auschwitz: Evidence from the Irving Trial*, Indiana University Press, Bloomington/Indianapolis, 2002.
- Perry, J. H. *Chemical Engineer's Handbook*, Wilmington, Delaware, 1949.
- Peters, Gerhard 1938. "Eine moderne Eisenbahn-Entwesungsanlage," *Anzeiger für Schädlingskunde*, Vol. 14, No. 8, 1938, pp. 98f.
- Phillips, Raymond (ed.). *Trial of Josef Kramer and Forty-Four Others (The Belsen Trial)*. William Hodge and Company, Limited. London, Edinburgh, Glasgow, 1949.
- Piper, Michael C. 1994. *Best Witness: The Mel Mermelstein Affair and the Triumph of Historical Revisionism*, Center for Historical Review, Washington, D.C., 1994.
- Plantin, Jean, "The Myth of Flames Rising from Crematoria Chimneys," *Inconvenient History*, Vol. 15, No. 4, 2023; www.inconvenienthistory.com/15/4/8229.
- Pohl, Oswald. *Credo: Mein Weg zu Gott*, A. Girnth, Landshut 1950.
- Poliakov, Léon 1951/1979. *Bréviare de la haine: Le IIIe Reich et les Juifs*, Calmann-Lévy, Paris, 1951/1979.
- Ponsonby, Arthur. *Falsehood in War-time, Containing an Assortment of Lies Calculated throughout the Nations during the Great War*, Garland, New York, 1971.
- Porter, Carlos W. *Made in Russia: The Holocaust*, Historical Review Press, Brighton, 1988.
- Pressac, Jean-Claude 1985. *The Struthof Album*, The Beate Klarsfeld Foundation, New York, 1985.
- Pressac, Jean-Claude 1989. *Auschwitz: Technique and Operation of the Gas Chambers*, Beate Klarsfeld Foundation, New York, 1989.
- Pressac, Jean-Claude 1993. *Les crématoires d'Auschwitz. La machinerie du meurtre de masse*, Éditions du CNRS, Paris, 1993.
- Pressac, Jean-Claude 1994. *Die Krematorien von Auschwitz. Die Technik des Massenmordes*, Munich, Piper, 1994.
- Rajchman, Chil 2011. *Treblinka. A Survivor's Memory 1942–1943*, MacLehose Press, London, 2011.

- Rassinier, Paul 2022. *Ulysses's Lie*, Castle Hill Publishers, Dallastown, PA, 2022.
- Redaction. "Mise au point," *Le déporté pour la liberté*, no. 463, December 1991 – January 1992, p. 5.
- Reitlinger, Gerald 1953/1961/1987. *The Final Solution*, various editions: 1st, Vallentine & Mitchell, London 1953; 2nd ed., A.S. Barnes, New York, 1961; 3rd ed., Jason Aronson, Northvale, NJ, 1987.
- Renk, Brian 1991. "The Franke-Gricksch 'Resettlement Action Report': Anatomy of a Fabrication," *The Journal of Historical Review*, Vol. 11, No. 3, 1991, pp. 261-279.
- Ritchie, Andy. "Britain's Rumor Factory," *Inconvenient History*, Vol. 9, No. 2, 2017; www.inconvenienthistory.com/9/2/4269.
- Robinson, Jacob 1976. "The Holocaust." In: Israel Gutman, Livia Rothkirchen (eds.), *The Catastrophe of European Jewry*, Yad Vashem, Jerusalem, 1976.
- Roden, Edward Leroy van. "American Atrocities in Germany," *The Progressive*, February 1949, pp. 21f.; www.historiography-project.com/clippings/1949/02/american-atrocities-in-germany.html.
- Roginskij, Arsenij B., Frank Drauschk, Anna Kaminsky. *"Erschossen in Moskau": Die deutschen Opfer des Stalinismus auf dem Moskauer Friedhof Donskoje 1950-1953*, Metropol, Berlin, 2006.
- Roques, Henri. *The Confessions of Kurt Gerstein*, Institute for Historical Review, Costa Mesa, CA, 1989.
- Rothfels, Hans. "Augenzeugenbericht zu den Massenvergasungen," *Vierteljahrshefte für Zeitgeschichte*, Vol. 1, No. 2, 1953, pp. 177-194.
- Routledge, Warren B. *Elie Wiesel, Saint of the Holocaust: A Critical Biography*, Castle Hill Publishers, Uckfield, 2020.
- Rozek, Edward J. *Allied Wartime Diplomacy*, John Wiley & Sons, New York, 1958.
- Rozett, Robert, Shmuel Spector (eds.). *Encyclopedia of the Holocaust*. Yad Vashem, Jerusalem/Facts on File, New York, 2000.
- Rückerl, Adalbert 1984. *NS-Verbrechen vor Gericht*, 2nd ed., C.F. Müller, Heidelberg, 1984.
- Rudolf, Germar 2003a. "From the Records of the Frankfurt Auschwitz Trial, Part 1" *The Revisionist*, Vol. 1, No. 1, 2003, pp. 115-118.
- Rudolf, Germar 2003b. "From the Records of the Frankfurt Auschwitz Trial. Part 2," *The Revisionist*, Vol. 1, No. 2, 2003, pp. 235-238.
- Rudolf, Germar 2003c. "From the Records of the Frankfurt Auschwitz Trial, Part 3," *The Revisionist*, Vol. 1, No. 3, 2003, pp. 352-358.
- Rudolf, Germar 2003d. "From the Records of the Frankfurt Auschwitz Trial, Part 4," *The Revisionist*, Vol. 1, No. 4, 2003, pp. 468-472.
- Rudolf, Germar 2004a. "Aspects of Biological Warfare During World War II," *The Revisionist*, Vol. 2, No. 1, 2004, pp. 88-90.
- Rudolf, Germar 2004b. "From the Records of the Frankfurt Auschwitz Trial, Part 5," *The Revisionist*, Vol. 2, No. 2, 2004, pp. 219-223.
- Rudolf, Germar 2004c. "From the Records of the Frankfurt Auschwitz Trial. Part 6," *The Revisionist*, Vol. 2, No. 3, 2004, pp. 327-330.
- Rudolf, Germar 2005. "From the Records of the Frankfurt Auschwitz Trial. Part 8," *The Revisionist*, Vol. 3, No. 2, 2005, pp. 189-196.
- Rudolf, Germar 2015. "How Postwar German Authorities Orchestrated Witness Statements in Nazi Crime Cases," *Inconvenient History*, Vol. 7, No. 2, 2015; www.inconvenienthistory.com/7/2/3432.
- Rudolf, Germar 2016 (ed.). *Auschwitz: Plain Facts*, 2nd ed., Castle Hill Publishers, Uckfield, 2016.
- Rudolf, Germar 2017. *Probing the Holocaust: The Horror Explained*, documentary, Castle Hill Publishers, Uckfield, 2017; www.HolocaustHandbooks.com.
- Rudolf, Germar 2019 (ed.). *Dissecting the Holocaust*, 3rd ed., Castle Hill Publishers, Uckfield, 2019.
- Rudolf, Germar 2019a. *Auschwitz: Technique and Operation of the Gas Chambers: An Introduction and Update to Jean-Claude Pressac's Magnum Opus*, Castle Hill Publishers, Uckfield, 2019.
- Rudolf, Germar 2019b. "How Danuta Czech Invented 100,000 Gassing Victims," *Inconvenient History*, Vol. 11, No. 1, 2019; www.inconvenienthistory.com/11/1/6509/.
- Rudolf, Germar 2020. *The Chemistry of Auschwitz: The Technology and Toxicology of Zyklon B and the Gas Chambers – A Crime Scene Investigation*, 2nd ed., Castle Hill Publishers, Uckfield, 2020.
- Rudolf, Germar (ed.) 2020a. *Air-Photo Evidence: World War Two Photos of Alleged Mass Murder Sites Analyzed*, 6th ed., Castle Hill Publishers, Uckfield, 2020.
- Rudolf, Germar 2020b (ed.). *The First Zündel Trial: The Court Transcript of the Canadian "False News" Trial of Ernst Zündel, 1985*, Castle Hill Publishers, Uckfield, 2020.
- Rudolf, Germar 2020c. "The Thin Internal Walls of Krematorium I at Auschwitz," *Inconvenient History*, Vol. 12, No. 2, 2020; www.inconvenienthistory.com/12/2/7298. .

- Rudolf, Germar 2023. *Lectures on the Holocaust: Controversial Issues Cross-Examined,* 4th ed., Castle Hill Publishers, Bargoed, 2023.
- Rudolf, Germar 2023a. *The Day Amazon Murder Free Speech,* 3rd ed., Castle Hill Publishers, Bargoed, 2023.
- Rudolf, Germar 2023b. "Auschwitz Doctor Hans Münch Interviewed," *Inconvenient History,* Vol. 15, No. 2, 2023; http://inconvenienthistory.com/15/2/8213.
- Rudolf, Germar, Carlo Mattogno. *Auschwitz Lies,* 4th ed.., Castle Hill Publishers, Uckfield, 2017.
- Rudolf, Germar, Ernst Böhm. *Garrison and Headquarters Orders of the Auschwitz Concentration Camp: A Critically Commented Selection,* Castle Hill Publishers, Uckfield, 2020.
- Sack, John 1993/1995. *An Eye for an Eye,* Basic Books, New York, 1993.
- Sanning, Walter N. (=Wilhelm Niederreiter). *The Dissolution of Eastern European Jewry,* 3rd ed., Castle Hill Publishers, Bargoed, 2023.
- Schelvis, Jules. *Sobibór: A History of a Nazi Death Camp,* Berg Publishers, Oxford, 2007.
- Schepers, Elmar, "Viktor Emil Frankl in Auschwitz," *Inconvenient History,* Vol. 15, No. 3, 2023; https://inconvenienthistory.com/15/3/8221.
- Schirmer, Gerhart. *Sachsenhausen – Workuta,* Grabert, Tübingen, 1992.
- Schirmer-Vowinckel, Ilse. "On the Fate of Gypsies in the Third Reich," *The Revisionist,* Vol. 2, No. 3, 2004, pp. 331-333.
- Schirra, Bruno. "Die Erinnerung der Täter," *Spiegel,* 40/1998, pp. 90ff.; www.spiegel.de/spiegel/print/d-8001833.html.
- Schwarz, Solomon M. *Jews in the Soviet Union,* Syracuse Univ. Press., Syracuse, 1951.
- Schwensen, Klaus 2011. "The Report of the Soviet Extraordinary State Commission on the Sachsenhausen Concentration Camp. The Genesis of a Propaganda Project," *Inconvenient History,* Vol. 3, No. 4, 2011; https://inconvenienthistory.com/3/4/3160.
- Schwensen, Klaus 2012. "Stephen F. Pinter: An Early Revisionist," *Inconvenient History,* Vol. 4, No. 1, 2012, http://inconvenienthistory.com/4/1/3175.
- Schwensen, Klaus 2012a. "The Number of Victims of Sachsenhausen Concentration Camp (1936-1945)," *Inconvenient History,* Vol. 4, No. 3, 2012; https://inconvenienthistory.com/4/3/3184.
- Schwensen, Klaus 2013. "The Three Photographs of an Alleged Gas Van," *Inconvenient History,* Vol. 5, No. 1, 2013; www.inconvenienthistory.com/5/1/3203.
- Schwensen, Klaus 2013a. "The Bone Mill of Lemberg," in: *Inconvenient History,* Vol. 5, No. 3, 2013, pp. 297-332; www.inconvenienthistory.com/5/3/3220.
- Schwensen, Klaus 2014. "The 'Report on Concentration Camp Sachsenhausen' (Prisoner's Report) of 12 June 1945," *Inconvenient History,* Vol. 6. No. 3, 2014; https://inconvenienthistory.com/6/3/3333.
- Scott, Hadding 2016. "The Joseph Hirt Story," 2 July 2016; https://codoh.com/library/document/the-joseph-hirt-story/.
- Scott, Hadding 2017. "Anti-Gentiles Deny the 5 Million," 23 February 2017; https://codoh.com/library/document/anti-gentiles-deny-the-5-million/.
- Segev, Tom 2010. *Simon Wiesenthal: The Life and Legends,* Doubleday, New York, 2010.
- Sereny, Gitta. *Into that Darkness,* Mc Graw-Hill, New York, 1974.
- Setkiewicz, Piotr 2011. "Zaopatrzenie materiałowe krematoriów i komór gazowych Auschwitz: koks, drewno, cyklon," in: *Studia nad dziejami obozów konzentracyjnych w okupowanej Polsce,* Państwowe Muzeum Auschwitz-Birkenau, Auschwitz, 2011.
- Shahak, Israel. *Jewish History, Jewish Religion,* Pluto Press, London, 1994.
- Shahak, Israel. Norton Mezvinsky, *Jewish Fundamentalism in Israel,* Pluto Press, London, 1998.
- Shapiro, Henry. "Prints Volume on Atrocities against Jews", *Youngstown Vindicator* (Ohio), 27 Nov. 1944.
- Sheftel, Yoram. *The Demjanjuk Affair: The Rise and Fall of the Show Trial,* Victor Gollancz, London, 1994.
- Sherman, Gabriel. "The Greatest Love Story Ever Sold," *The New Republic,* 25 Dec. 2008; https://newrepublic.com/article/61006/the-greatest-love-story-ever-sold.
- Shermer, Michael, Alex Grobman. *Denying History: Who Says the Holocaust Never Happened and Why Do They Say it?,* University of California, Berkeley, Los Angeles, London, 2000.
- Shirer, William. *The Rise and Fall of the Third Reich,* Fawcett Crest, New York, 1960.
- Singer, Melissa. "Holocaust 'memoir' withdrawn," *Australian Jewish News,* 6 Nov. 2004.
- Skorczewski, Dawn. "What is the Story? Two Sonderkommando Interviews in the USC Shoah Foundation Archive", 6 Oct. 2015, https://sfi.usc.edu/news/2015/10?page=2.
- Sloan, James P. *Jerzy Kosinski: A Biography,* Plume, New York, 1997.
- Smith, Arthur L. *Die "Hexe von Buchenwald": Der Fall Ilse Koch,* Böhlau, Cologne, 1983.

- Smith, Bradley F., Agnes F. Peterson (eds.). *Heinrich Himmler. Geheimreden 1933 bis 1945 und andere Ansprachen*, Propyläen, Frankfurt/Main, 1974.
- Solzhenitsyn, Aleksandr. *The Gulag Archipelago*, 3 vols., Harper & Row, New York, 1974-1978.
- Speer, Albert 1970. *Inside the Third Reich: Memoirs*, Macmillan, New York, 1970.
- Speer, Albert 1976. *Spandau: The Secret Diaries*, Macmillan, New York, 1976.
- Springer, Elisa 1997. *Il silenzio dei vivi. All'ombra di Auschwitz, un racconto di morte e di risurrezione*, Marsilio Editore, Venice, 1997.
- Springer, Markus. "The New Face of the 'Holocaust,'" *The Revisionist*, Vol. 2, No. 3, 2004, pp. 297-300.
- St. George, George. *The Road to Babyi-Yar*, Spearman, London, 1967.
- Staatliches Museum Auschwitz-Birkenau (ed.). *Die Sterbebücher von Auschwitz*, Saur, Munich, 1995.
- Stäglich, Wilhelm 1986/2015. *The Auschwitz Myth: A Judge Looks at the Evidence*, Institute for Historical Review, Newport Beach, CA, 1986; 3rd ed., Castle Hill Publishers, Uckfield, 2015.
- State of Israel. *The Trial of Adolf Eichmann. Record of Proceedings in the District Court of Jerusalem*. Jerusalem, 1993.
- Steiner, Jean-François. *Treblinka*, Stalling, Oldenburg 1966; English: Simon and Schuster, New York 1967.
- Stiftung Niedersächsische Gedenkstätten (ed.). *Bergen-Belsen Wehrmacht POW Camp, 1940-1945, Concentration camp, 1943-1945, Displaced persons camp, 1945-1950*, Wallstein, Göttingen, 2010.
- Stimely, Keith. "The Torture of Julius Streicher," *Journal of Historical Review*, Vol. 5, No. 1, 1984, pp. 106-119.
- Suzuki, Ikuo. *Unmasking Anne Frank: Her Famous Diary Exposed as a Literary Fraud*: Clemens & Blair, Ann Arbor, MI, 2022.
- Szajn-Lewin, Eugenia. *Aufzeichnungen aus dem Warschauer Ghetto*, Reclam Verlag, Leipzig, 1994.
- Szende, Stefan, Adolf Folkmann. *The Promise Hitler Kept*, V. Gollancz, London/Roy, New York, 1945.
- Szende, Stefan. *Den siste juden från Polen*, Bonnier, Stockholm, 1944.
- Taft, Robert A. *The Papers of Robert A. Taft*. Vol. 3: 1945-1948, Kent State University Press, Kent, Ohio, 2003.
- Tarter, Donald E. "Peenemünde and Los Alamos – Two Studies" in: Graham Hollister-Short, Frank A.J.L. James (eds.), *History of Technology*, Vol. 14, Mansell, London 1992, pp. 150-170; reprinted in *The Journal of Historical Review*, Vol. 19, No. 4, 2000, pp. 34-48.
- Tegen, Gunhild, Tegen, Einar (eds.). *De dödsdömda vittna: Enquêtesvar och intervjuer*, Wahlström & Widstrand, Stockholm, 1945.
- Toland, John. *Adolf Hitler*, Doubleday, New York, 1976.
- Townsend, Gregory. "Structure and Management," in: Luc Reydams, Jan Wouters, Cedric Ryngaert (eds.), *International Prosecutors*, Oxford University Press, Oxford 2012.
- Tremlett, Giles. "Spain's Concentration Camp Hero Is Exposed as a Fraud," *The Guardian*, 12. May 2005; https://theguardian.com/world/2005/may/12/secondworldwar.spain.
- Treue, Wilhelm 1955. "Hitlers Denkschrift zum Vierjahresplan 1936," *Vierteljahrshefte für Zeitgeschichte*, Vol. 3, No. 2, 1955, pp. 184-210.
- Treue, Wilhelm 1958. "Rede Hitlers vor der deutschen Presse," *Vierteljahrshefte für Zeitgeschichte*, Vol. 6, No. 2, 1958, pp. 175-191.
- *Trials of War Criminals before the Nuremberg Military Tribunals under Control Council Law. No. 10* (NMT), 15 vols., U.S. Government Printing Office, Washington, D.C., 1949-1953; www.loc.gov/rr/frd/Military_Law/NTs_war-criminals.html.
- Vice, Sue 2014a. "Translating the Self: False Holocaust Testimony," *Translation and Literature*, Vol. 23, No. 2, 2014, pp. 197-209.
- Vice, Sue 2014b. "False and Embellished Holocaust Testimony," in: *Textual Deceptions: False Memoirs and Literary Hoaxes in the Contemporay Era*, Edinburgh Univ. Press, Edinburgh, 2014.
- Volodarsky, Boris. *The KGB's Poison Factory: From Lenin to Litvinenko*, Frontline Books, London, 2009.
- von Knieriem, August. *Nürnberg. Rechtliche und menschliche Probleme*, Klett, Stuttgart, 1953.
- Voslensky, Michael S. *Das Geheime wird offenbar: Moskauer Archive erzählen*, Langen Müller, Munich, 1995.
- Walters, Guy 2009. *Hunting Evil: The Nazi War Criminals Who Escaped and the Quest to Bring Them to Justice*, Broadway Books, New York, 2009.
- Walters, Guy 2011. "The curious case of the 'break into Auschwitz'," *New Statesman*, 17 November 2011; https://newstatesman.com/culture/2011/11/avey-book-holocaust-Auschwitz.
- Walters, Guy 2013. "Could there be anything more twisted than these Holocaust fantasies? How more and more people are making up memoirs about witnessing Nazi crimes," *Daily Mail*, 21 June 2013; https://dailymail.co.uk/news/article-23. .
- Weber, Mark 1982. "Declaration of Mark Edward Weber," *Journal of Historical Review*, Vol. 3, No. 1, 1982, pp. 31-51.

- Weber, Mark 1986. "Buchenwald: Legend and Reality," *Journal of Historical Review*, Vol. 7, No. 4, 1986, pp. 405-417.
- Weber, Mark 1991. "Jewish Soap," *Journal of Historical Review*, Vol. 11, No. 2, 1991, pp. 217-227.
- Weber, Mark 1995a. "Bergen-Belsen Camp: The Suppressed Story," *Journal of Historical Review*, Vol. 15, No. 3, 1995, pp. 23-30.
- Weber, Mark 1995b. "Simon Wiesenthal: Fraudulent 'Nazi Hunter'," *Journal of Historical Review*, Vol. 15, No. 4, 1995, pp. 8-26.
- Weber, Mark 1998. "Holocaust Survivor Memoir Exposed as Fraud," *Journal of Historical Review*, Vol. 17, No. 5, 1998, pp. 15f.
- Weber, Mark 1999. "High Frequency Delousing Facilities at Auschwitz," *Journal of Historical Review*, Vol. 18, No. 3, 1999, pp. 4-12.
- Weckert, Ingrid 1991. *Flashpoint: Kristallnacht 1938: Instigators, Victims and Beneficiaries*, Institute for Historical Review, Costa Mesa, Cal., 1991.
- Weckert, Ingrid 2016. *Jewish Emigration from the Third Reich*, 2nd ed., Castle Hill Publishers, Uckfield, 2016.
- Weindling, Paul. *Epidemics and Genocide in Eastern Europe, 1890-1945*, Oxford University Press, Oxford/New York, 2000.
- Werner, Steffen. *The Second Babylonian Captivity*, Castle Hill Publishers, Uckfield, 2019.
- Wickoff, Jack. "The Myth of the Extermination of Homosexuals by the Third Reich," *Inconvenient History*, Vol. 15, No. 2, 2023; https://inconvenienthistory.com/15/2/8217.
- Wiesel, Elie 1960. *Night*, Hill and Wang, New York, 1960.
- Wilkomirski, Binjamin. *Fragments. Memories of a Wartime Childhood*, Schocken Books, New York, 1996.
- Willenberg, Samuel. *Revolt in Treblinka*, Żydówski Instytut Historyczny, Warsaw, 1989.
- Winter, Peter. "Oskar Groening Trial Dissolves into Farce," 21 July 2015; https://peterwinterwriting.blogspot.com/2015/07/oskar-groening-trial-dissolves-into.html.
- Yeager, Carolyn 2010. "Denis Avey: The Man Who Would Be Righteous," 16 March 2010; https://codoh.com/library/document/denis-avey-the-man-who-would-be-righteous/.
- Yeager, Carolyn 2011. "The Case against Denis Avey, the BBC, and the British Government," 18 April 2011; https://codoh.com/library/document/the-case-against-denis-avey-the-bbc-and-the/ .
- Zentner, Christian. *Der große Bildatlas zur Weltgeschichte*, Unipart, Stuttgart, 1982.
- Zimmermann, Michael 1989. *Verfolgt, vertrieben, vernichtet: Die nationalsozialistische Vernichtungspolitik gegen Sinti und Roma*, Klartext-Verlag, Essen 1989.
- Zimmermann, Michael 1996. *Rassenutopie und Genozid: Die nationalsozialistische "Lösung der Zigeunerfrage,"* Christians, Hamburg, 1996.
- Zündel, Ernst. *The Holocaust on Trial: The Second Trial against Ernst Zündel 1988*, 2nd ed., Castle Hill Publishers, Dallastown, PA, 2022.
- Zuroff, Efraim. *Occupation Nazi-Hunter: The Continuing Search for the Perpetrators of the Holocaust*, KTAV, Hoboken, NJ, 1994.

Index of Names

— A —
Aba/Abo: 502
Aboav, Alfred: 502
Achamer-Pifrader, Humbert: 166
Adam, Uwe Dietrich: 229, 548
Adametz, Gerhard: 20, 21, 55, 56, 339, 591
Adelsberger, Lucie: 200
Adenauer, Konrad: 120
Agrestowski, Jan: 502
Alderman, Sidney: 287
Allen, Andrew: 398
Allen, Martin: 255
Altstotter, Josef: 392
Alvarez, Santiago: 65, 105, 114, 155, 190, 225, 251, 309, 318, 347, 350, 360, 389, 407, 418, 424, 432, 439, 440, 456, 477, 483, 511, 552, 581, 583, 606
Amiel, Szymon: 28, 29, 79, 123, 163, 193, 304, 339, 591
Ancel, Jean: 446
Andorfer, Herbert: 482
Arad, Yitzhak: 100, 172, 419, 446, 461, 494, 546, 548, 549
Arendt, Hannah: 446
Arlt: 354
Aroles, Serge: 571
Aroneanu, Eugène: 33, 329, 435
Artuković, Andrije: 398
Asch, Sholem: 232
Aschenauer, Rudolf: 590
Aschenbrenner, Jupp: 535
Auerbach, Rachel: 29, 30, 183, 320, 494, 544, 548, 593
Aumeier, Hans: 30, 42, 49, 213, 443, 591
Avey, Denis: 51, 192
Aynat, Enrique: 204

— B —
Bach-Zelewski, Erich von dem: 14, 57, 166, 183, 224, 258, 368, 388, 421, 534, 582, 592
Bacon, Yehuda: 57, 58, 200, 591
Badcock, James: 357
Baer, Richard: 335
Bagrowsky, Steffan: 592
Bahir, Moshe: 59, 495-497, 593
Bahr, Wilhelm: 592
Balbin, André: 502
Banach, Ludwik: 281
Barbl, Heinrich: 593
Bard-Nomberg, Helena: 60, 61, 591
Barkat, Amiram: 494
Bartel, Erwin: 42, 61
Bartelmas, Adolf: 200
Bartesch, Martin: 398
Barton, Russell: 61, 75, 76, 592
Bartrop, Paul: 12, 14
Baskind, Ber: 61
Bauer, Erich: 497, 593
Bauer, Fredy: 502

Bauer, Fritz: 208, 461
Bauer, Yehuda: 32, 33, 62, 186, 446, 572
Baum, Bruno: 41, 62, 65, 464, 591
Baumel-Schwartz, Judith: 11, 14, 114, 224, 489
Beaulieu, Jean-Francois: 521
Becher, Kurt: 14, 47, 62, 246, 255, 275, 280, 284, 302, 457, 518, 592
Becker, August: 63-65, 223, 225, 270, 399, 432, 455, 482, 483, 592
Becker, Berko/Berl: 502
Bednarz, Władysław: 65, 104, 113-115, 123, 292, 407, 423, 510, 511, 606
Beer, Abraham: 65, 298, 579, 591
Behr, Emil: 65, 591, 594
Belgion, Montgomery: 317, 537
Bendel, Charles S.: 72, 77, 128, 194, 200, 244, 257, 272, 365, 368, 393, 404, 410, 501, 502, 530, 531, 591, 610
Bennahmias, Daniel: 73, 410, 501, 502, 561, 591
Benroubi, Maurice: 73, 74, 502, 591
Benz, Wolfgang: 152, 153, 154, 426, 492, 507
Berenbaum, Michael: 264, 446, 461
Berg, Friedrich P.: 156, 216, 586
Berg, Isai Davidovich: 74, 223
Berger, Oskar: 77, 123, 313, 545, 552, 593
Berlyant, Semen: 21, 54, 77, 78, 91, 339, 591
Bernays, Murray: 287
Bestic, Alan: 568
Bezwinska, Jadwiga: 98, 99
Bialek, Regina: 20, 77, 78, 177, 365, 591, 610
Biddle, Francis: 287
Bierkamp, Walter: 166
Billig, Joseph: 186
Bily, Henry: 79, 591
Bimko, Ada: 77, 79, 200, 272, 487, 538, 591, 610
Bischoff, Erich: 377
Biskovitz, Ya'akov: 89, 495, 496, 593
Biskup, Wladyslaw: 502
Bjorklund, David F.: 191
Black, Edwin: 176
Blaha, Franz: 90, 144, 145, 454, 533, 592
Blatt, Thomas: 90, 593
Blobel, Paul: 14, 23, 24, 26, 56, 91, 150, 183, 255, 278, 371, 482, 582, 591
Blum, Baruch: 502
Blumental, Nachman: 497
Blyazer, A.: 92, 194, 236, 339, 429-431, 591, 602
Bock, Ludwig: 92, 93, 352, 353
Böck, Richard: 20, 93, 94, 464, 591
Bode, Christian: 326
Boger, Wilhelm: 94, 98, 209, 438, 464, 470, 471, 591

Böhm, Ernst: 40
Böhme, Horst: 166
Bolender, Kurt: 593
Bomba, Abraham: 95, 488, 593
Bomze, Nachum: 451
Bone, James: 469
Bormann, Martin: 286, 289
Bösch, Ernst: 592
Boüard, Michel de: 96, 505
Bourtman, Ilya: 223, 309, 318, 535
Brack, Viktor: 178
Braham, Randolph: 446
Brandenburger, Otto: 592
Brandt, Karl: 392
Brauburger, Stefan: 303
Braun, Gustav: 535
Brechtken, Magnus: 342
Breitman, Richard: 57, 368, 446
Breitwieser, Arthur: 49, 198, 209
Brener, Hejnoch: 97, 183, 544, 545
Brentar, Jerome A.: 152
Broad, Pery S.: 42, 45, 76, 98, 99, 123, 128, 200, 209, 239, 278, 281, 410, 513, 591
Brodsky, Isaak: 21, 54, 91, 99, 100, 339, 591
Brougham, Bernard: see Holstein, Bernhard
Browning, Christopher: 407
Brudno, Walter: 287
Brugioni, Dino: 22
Bruns, August: 592
Buber-Neumann, Margarete: 200
Buchanan, Pat: 151
Buchholcowa, Janina: 101, 593
Budnik, David: 21, 54, 91, 101, 102, 339, 591
Bühler, Josef: 206
Buki, Milton: 102, 103, 281, 365, 502, 513, 591
Bulawko, Henry: 200
Burba, Manfred: 548
Burdenko, Nikolai N.: 353, 441, 442
Burmeister, Walter: 104, 105, 113, 116, 592
Buszko, Jozef: 47
Butz, Arthur R.: 272, 281, 458
Byford, Jovan: 439

— C —
Cäsar, Ernst: 592
Caspesius, Victor: 209
Cavendish-Bentinck, Victor: 442
Cercas, Javier: 357
Chamaides, Heinrich: 96, 110, 111, 298, 315, 339, 357, 579, 591
Changuli, Gleb I.: 442, 555
Chasan, Shaul: 23, 111, 112, 218, 244, 404, 410, 502, 513, 561, 591, 610
Chomka, Władysław: 116, 593
Christensen, Walter: 592
Christianson, Scott: 273
Christie, Douglas: 605

Christophersen, Thies: 116, 477, 591
Chrzan, Zawek/Zauwel: 502
Churchill, Winston: 34
Chybiński, Stanisław: 84, 87, 117, 128, 410, 591, 610
Clay, Lucius D.: 325
Cobain, Ian: 58, 59, 338, 537
Cohen, Leon: 118, 128, 194, 218, 244, 365, 410, 480, 482, 502, 561, 591, 610
Connolly, Cyril: 537
Copeland, Libby: 518
Corni, Gustavo: 231, 232, 575
Corry, Joe: 126, 192
Costello, Paddy: 329
Cox, Cyrus: 23
Curilla, Wolfgang: 172
Cykert, Abraham: 140, 540, 591, 592
Cymlich, Israel: 516
Cyrankiewicz, Jozef: 62, 140, 532, 591
Czarkowski, Ryszard: 548
Czech, Danuta: 45-47, 98, 99, 104, 140, 141, 197, 201, 208, 210, 240, 247, 323, 331, 337, 338, 371, 379, 416, 559, 561, 595
Czechowicz, Aron: 141, 545, 593

— D —
Dalton, Thomas: 23, 182, 187, 232, 235, 261, 272, 273, 299, 360, 467, 491, 517, 521, 575
Daluege, Kurt: 147, 175, 254
Damjanović, Momčilo: 147, 148, 339, 482, 591, 593
Daniel, Jane: 571
Danilchenko, Ignat: 593
Darwin, Charles: 377
Davydov, Vladimir: 20, 21, 54, 91, 148, 149, 183, 266, 339, 534, 591
Dawidowicz, Lucy: 33, 348, 446
Dawidowski, Roman: 49, 85, 88, 128, 138, 149, 480, 481
De Wan, George: 261, 420
Dean, Martin: 231, 575
Deana, Franco: 89, 122, 129, 131, 132, 134, 137, 138, 149, 200, 441, 535
Debrise, Gilbert: 200
Deckert, Günter: 93, 484
Defonseca, Misha: see Wael, Monique de
Dejaco, Walter: 49, 50, 88, 150, 485, 486, 591
DellaPergola, Sergio: 522
Demant, Ebbo: 177, 301, 309
Demjanjuk, John: 151, 152, 155, 164, 174, 211, 236, 397, 437, 442, 445, 451, 468, 483, 484, 497, 504, 547, 555, 587
Denisov, Vladmir N.: 442, 555
Denisow, Piotr: 155, 592
Desbois, Patrick: 173
Desjardins, Daniel D.: 586
Dibowski, Wilhelm: 155, 591, 594
Dickerman, Michael: 12, 14
Dimont, Max: 76
Dineen, Tana: 191
Dingeldein, Ernst: 592

Dirks, Christian: 199
Długoborski, Wácław: 33, 47, 156, 591
Dodd, Christopher: 287, 445
Dodd, Thomas J.: 238, 287, 445, 467
Doessekker, Bruno: 157, 191, 192, 307
Doliner, Iosif: 21, 54, 91, 157, 158, 339, 591
Donat, Alexander (ed.): 30, 446, 584
Dönitz, Karl: 13, 285, 286
Dragon, Abraham: 158-160, 174, 502, 591
Dragon, Szlama: 87, 104, 123, 128, 158-160, 174, 194, 244, 365, 368, 404, 410, 411, 480, 502, 530, 591, 594, 610
Dressen, Willi: 311, 312
Dubin, Gerhard: 88, 150
Dugin, Itzhak: 160, 601
Dwork, Deborah: 157

— E —
Earl, Hilary: 398
Eberl, Irmfried: 163
Edelman, Salman: 28, 29, 79, 163, 193, 591
Edler, Ernst: 592
Ehrenburg, Ilya: 67, 163, 243, 427, 441, 442, 445, 497
Ehrlich, Yishayahu Isaïe: 502
Ehrlinger, Erich: 166
Eichmann, Adolf: 20, 33, 57, 62, 89, 114, 163, 164, 176, 210, 230, 253, 255, 264, 274, 275, 277, 279, 280, 281, 304, 323, 391, 413, 421, 424, 445, 446, 455, 483, 484, 495, 510, 511, 523, 534, 547, 568, 569, 573, 578, 589, 590, 592, 606
Eigruber, August: 537
Einstein, Albert: 13
Eisenhower, Dwight D.: 101, 285, 399, 400, 444
Eisenschmidt, Eliezer: 174, 194, 200, 218, 482, 502, 591
Eitan, Dov: 174, 483
Ellis, Burton: 559
Ellowitz, Morris: 559
Ellul, Jacques: 436
Engel, Chaim: 177, 487, 496, 497, 587, 593
Epstein, Berthold: 23, 87, 177, 194, 198, 336, 356, 365, 494, 591
Epstein, Hedy: 287
Erber, Josef: 102, 177, 410
Erdmann, Hermann: 592
Ertl, Fritz: 49, 50, 88, 150, 177, 485, 486

— F —
Fabian, Bela: 128, 189, 200, 591
Fabre, René: 388
Faitelson, Alex: 189, 190, 194, 202, 203, 591
Fajgielbaum, Srul: 183, 190, 495, 496, 593
Fajner, Szlojme: 242, 526
Falborski, Bronisław: 113, 123, 190, 580, 592

Farber, Yuri: 29, 92, 123, 193, 194, 235, 236, 339, 430, 431, 591, 601, 602
Farkas, Henrik: 194, 591
Farmer, Kevin: 191
Faurisson, Robert: 33, 38, 79, 151, 205, 272, 309, 320, 388, 560, 604, 605
Federenko, Feodor: 398
Feiler, Willi: 473, 488, 593
Feinsilber, Alter: see Jankowski, Stanisław
Feldhendler, Leon: 90, 195, 496, 593
Felenbaum-Weiss, Hella: 195, 496, 593
Fénelon, Fania: 200
Ferencz, Benjamin: 287
Fest, Joachim C.: 260, 261
Filsinger, Walter: 592
Fink(el), Louis Welfke: 502
Finkelstein, Norman G.: 121, 155, 157, 460, 521
Finkelsztein, Leon: 196, 197, 237, 482, 534, 545, 549, 575, 593
Fischer, Bruno: 177, 194, 198, 494, 591
Fischer, Horst: 49, 50, 199, 369, 591, 610
Fischer, John F.: 481
Fischer, Ludwig: 544, 584
Fleming, Gerald: 407, 446
Fleming, Ian: 126
Fleur, Nicholas: 430
Fliamenbaum, David: 128, 201, 410, 480, 538, 591, 610
Flick, Friedrich: 392
Floerchinger, Jane: 328
Florstedt, Hermann: 201, 352
Floss, Herbert: 515
Foust, Hal: 580
Frank, Anne: 204, 205
Frank, Edith: 205
Frank, Hans: 14, 206, 207, 264, 284, 286, 404, 462, 472, 592
Frank, Margot: 205
Frank, Otto: 205
Franke-Gricksch, Alfred: 28, 207, 591, 610
Frankl, Viktor: 200, 210, 591
Franz, Kurt: 210, 211, 513, 546, 593
Freiberg, Ber: 211, 495, 496, 593
Freitag, Helmut: 379, 393
Fréjafon, Georges-Louis: 317
Frenzel, Karl: 497
Freud, Anton: 532
Freud, Sigmund: 532
Frick, Wilhelm: 286
Friedman, Arnold: 19, 177, 200, 202, 211, 212, 591, 592
Friedman, Filip: 20, 33, 195
Friedman, Philip: 231, 575
Fries, Jakob: 212, 591, 594
Fritsch, Theodor: 377
Fritzsch, Karl: 213, 274, 275, 277, 421
Fritzsche, Hans: 286
Frosch, Chaim: 23, 200, 213, 410, 591
Fry(ie)dman(n), Moshe/Moniek: 502
Fuchs, Wilhelm: 166
Fuchs, Erich: 497, 592, 593
Fuchsbrunner, Henryk: see Tauber, Henryk

Funk, Walther: 286

— G —
Gabai, Dario: 128, 217, 410, 480, 502, 513, 591
Gabai, Yaakov: 20, 128, 217-219, 410, 482, 502, 561, 591, 610
Gál, Gyula: 87, 219, 538, 591
Galilei, Galileo: 319
Gallo, Max: 241
Ganzfried, Daniel: 157
Garaudy, Roger: 521
Garbarz, Moshé: 219, 220, 230, 502, 591
Gärtner, Michael: 245
Gassner, Ludwig: 215
Geiger: 281
Gelbert, Michel: 502
Gelpern, Dmitrii: 189
Gerlach, Christian: 57, 354, 368
Germański, Aleksander: 281
Gerstein, Kurt: 14, 20, 67, 68, 70, 71, 96, 227-230, 272, 410, 415, 416, 435, 459, 513, 526, 539, 546, 588, 592
Gertner, Szaja: 230, 502, 538, 591, 610
Giemsa, Gustav: 214, 432
Gilbert, Gustav: 287
Gilbert, Martin: 73, 446
Gilbert, S.: 156
Gis(s)er, Tew(v)el/Zeiwel: 502
Gisevius, Hans: 517
Glass, Kurt: 19
Glazar, Richard: 232, 233, 482, 549, 593
Gley, Heinrich: 592
Globocnik, Odilo: 27, 65, 225, 226, 228, 229, 233, 255, 263, 264, 275, 404, 416, 422
Glücks, Richard: 16, 196, 233, 234, 254, 255, 264, 284, 302, 359, 363, 406
Godzieszewski, Czeslaw: 316
Goebbels, Joseph: 139, 184, 186, 187, 227, 234, 235, 257, 264, 284, 341, 436, 443, 462, 541, 599
Goetz, Cecilia: 287
Gol, Szloma: 92, 193, 194, 235, 236, 339, 430, 431, 591, 602
Golczewski, Frank: 548
Goldberg, Szymon: 236, 545, 593
Goldensohn, Leon: 287
Goldfarb, Abraham I.: 196, 236, 237, 238, 452, 513, 534, 545, 546, 575, 593
Goldhagen, Daniel J.: 171, 172, 446
Goldman, Ari L.: 19
Goldmann, Nahum: 490, 491
Goldstein, Eleanor: 191
Gomerski, Hubert: 497, 593
Gondzik, Ewald: 592
Goodman, Ralph: 287
Gorbacheva, Nadezhda T.: 54
Gorce, Nelly: 200
Göring, Hermann: 28, 176, 195, 238, 239, 253, 254, 264, 272, 278, 284, 286, 289, 433, 461, 592
Goshen, Seev: 391

Göth, Amon: 14, 239, 478, 479, 593
Gotland, Simon: 502
Grabher, Michael: 163
Grabitz, Helge: 211
Grabner, Maximilian: 42, 49, 61, 99, 102, 239, 240, 326, 591
Gradowski, Salmen: 240, 410, 502, 591
Graf, Jürgen: 28, 30, 59, 74, 80, 90, 99, 108, 112, 131, 156, 177, 179, 182, 195, 211, 220, 226, 233, 236, 243, 250, 254, 255, 257, 261-263, 273, 312, 313, 315, 338, 342, 349, 350, 352, 353, 366, 383, 403, 406, 412, 413, 438, 454, 458, 462, 463, 468, 478, 500, 514, 515, 520, 521, 527, 530, 549, 550, 565, 584, 587, 588
Gray, Martin: 192, 241, 593
Green, Richard G.: 446
Greif, Gideon: 118, 158, 160, 174, 217-219, 323, 475
Greifelt, Ulrich: 392
Griffith-Jones., Mervyn: 287
Grigorenko, Piotr: 223
Grobman, Alex: 264, 446
Grocher, Mietek: 177, 242, 592
Grojanowski, Jakov: 113, 242, 526, 592
Gröning, Oskar: 242, 243, 591
Groß, Hans: 592
Grossman, Vasily: 67, 163, 183, 243, 442, 445, 497, 544, 548
Grünberg, Isak: 354
Grüner, Nikolaus Michael (Miklós): 245, 591
Grynszpan, Herschel: 139, 140
Gulba, Franciszek: 245, 246, 591
Gutman, Israel: 11-14, 23, 33, 47, 70, 71, 115, 157, 224, 280, 281, 311, 312, 348, 390, 446, 494, 498, 546, 548

— H —
Haber, Fritz: 150
Hackett, David A.: 578
Hähle, Johannes: 53, 54, 57, 249, 250, 262, 434
Händler, Josef: 592
Hanel, Salomea: 250, 496, 593
Hartl, Albert: 230, 231
Hassler, Johann: 251, 581, 592
Hausner, Gideon: 461
Hazan, Saul: 502
Hecking, Claus: 498
Heddesheimer, Don: 164, 378, 427, 491, 578
Heftler, Nadine: 200
Hejblum, Erko: 502
Hejblum, Samuel: 502
Heliotis, Panagiotis: 385
Hencke: 281
Henderson, Y.: 107
Hénocque, Georges: 101, 252, 592
Herman, Chaim: 252, 502, 591
Hertz, Joseph: 491
Hess, Rudolf: 186, 286, 535
Heydrich, Reinhardt: 27, 28, 147, 176, 195, 206, 238, 253-255, 259, 260, 264, 284, 295, 302, 359, 390, 460, 461, 571

Heyne, Johannes: 58
Hilberg, Raul: 33, 120, 172, 231, 261, 348, 406, 420, 446, 461, 497, 547, 548
Himmler, Heinrich: 16, 23-27, 45-47, 57, 59, 62-64, 71, 72, 80, 81, 123, 143, 147, 166, 178, 183, 184, 186, 196, 224-226, 228, 229, 234, 235, 246, 253-261, 264, 274-277, 279, 280, 284, 302, 313-315, 317, 341, 342, 344, 356, 359, 361, 362, 366, 367, 388, 396, 399, 401, 404, 421, 422, 424, 425, 431, 446, 453, 454, 456, 457, 459, 460, 462, 465-467, 471, 472, 491, 493, 494, 508, 510, 518, 523, 539, 550, 552, 559, 570, 581, 582, 584, 589, 594, 596
Hingst, Marie Sophie: 192
Hinsley, F.H.: 97
Hirszman, Chaim: 258, 592
Hirt, Joseph: 192, 258, 365
Hitchcock, Alfred: 76
Hitler, Adolf: 13, 16, 19, 50, 60, 62, 98, 119, 120, 139, 152, 171, 174-176, 178, 184-187, 196, 205, 206, 223, 226, 228, 229, 234, 238, 241, 254, 255, 257-262, 264, 275, 276, 284-287, 302, 308, 314, 315, 317, 328, 341, 347, 373-376, 398, 416, 420, 421, 427, 433, 436, 441, 456, 460, 462, 465, 466, 476, 484, 490, 491, 506, 515, 517, 525, 527, 559, 572, 594, 605
Hochhuth, Rolf: 228
Höcker, Karl-Friedrich: 209, 353
Hödl, Franz: 593
Höfer, Fritz: 54, 262, 263, 592
Hoffmann, Emil: 592
Hoffmann, Günther: 592
Hoffmann, Joachim: 163, 441
Höfle, Hans: 28, 65, 66, 69, 98, 263, 275, 314, 494, 538, 541, 592
Holbus, Jan: 435
Holland, M.: 76, 126, 319
Holming, Göran: 62
Holstein, Bernhard: 192, 273
Holstein, Denise: 200
Holt, Penelope: 469
Höss, Rudolf: 20, 24, 41, 42, 45, 46, 49, 77, 85, 86, 91, 122, 128, 138, 149, 150, 158, 183, 194, 197, 198, 213, 239, 240, 255, 261, 264, 266, 274-279, 284, 297, 302, 316, 321, 326, 355, 357, 369, 371, 379, 381, 385, 401, 411, 421, 422, 425, 438, 443, 445, 467, 472, 480, 530, 534, 536, 537, 582, 589, 591, 594-597, 604
Hössler, Franz: 76, 150, 278, 279
Hottenbacher, Karl: 592
Höttl, Wilhelm: 164, 279, 491, 589, 590, 592
Howe, Stephen: 537
Hrabar, Roman: 76
Hubert, Morris: 19
Humm, Otto: 554
Hunt, Eric: 540

— I —
Icek, Lichtmann: 593
Igounet, Valérie: 505
Ilczuk, Joseph: 502
Irebodd, Dean: 101, 238, 325, 444, 488
Irving, David: 123, 260, 262, 290, 517, 605
Isacovici, Salomón: 291, 292
Israel, Bruno: 114, 292, 538, 592
Ittner, Alfred: 593

— J —
Jabłkowski, Hersz: 516
Jäckel, Eberhard: 398
Jackson, Nigel: 152
Jackson, Robert H.: 284-287, 289, 399, 517
Jacob, Lili: see Meier, Lili (née Jacob)
Jacob, Simone: see Veil, Simone
Jäger, Karl: 167, 168, 202, 203, 295, 296, 297
Jankowski, Stanisław: 42, 128, 194, 244, 247, 297, 298, 365, 368, 379, 403, 404, 410, 449, 480, 482, 502, 568, 591
Jansen, Hans: 342
Jansson, Friedrich: 99, 305, 475
Jastrzębska, Halina: 201
Jeckeln, Friedrich: 166
Jodl, Alfred: 286
Jones, Adam: 607
Jost, Heinz: 166
Jührs, Robert: 592
Jurkowsk, Sigmund: 502
Just, Willy: 64, 112, 115, 223, 225, 399

— K —
Kaduk, Oswald: 200, 209, 301, 591
Kahn, Annette: 200
Kaindl, Anton: 301, 302, 474, 593
Kaiser, Magdolna: 192
Kalb, C.: 201
Kallmeyer, Helmut: 179
Kaltenbrunner, Ernst: 14, 62, 264, 286, 302, 359, 460, 508
Kalthoff, Jürgen: 150, 433, 609
Kammler, Hans: 278, 302, 303
Kaper, Yakov: 21, 54, 91, 303, 304, 339, 591
Kaplan, Benjamin: 287
Kaplan, William: 287
Karasik, Avraham: 79, 304, 339
Karlsch, Rainer: 400
Karolinskij, Samij: 304, 502, 591
Karski, Jan: 14, 66, 196, 237, 304, 305, 479, 534, 540, 543, 575, 592
Karvat, David: 305, 502, 591
Kaskowiak, Stanisław: see Jankowski, Stanisław
Kaufmann Schafranov, Sofia: 306, 487, 538, 591, 610
Kaufmann, Jeannette: 77, 128, 306, 410, 487, 591, 610
Kaufmann, Sylvain: 201
Keitel, Wilhelm: 286
Kellnberger, Norbert: 595
Kelly, Jim: 273

Kempner, Robert: 287, 573
Keneally, Thomas: 478
Kersch, Silvia: 307, 545, 593
Kertész, Imre: 307, 487, 538, 591, 610
Kesselmann, Morris/Moniek: 502
Kielar, Wiesław: 281
Kilbinger, Otto: 592
Kirschbaum: 559
Klarsfeld, Serge: 203, 446, 461, 562, 563
Klee, Ernst: 311, 312
Klehr, Josef: 209, 281, 309, 331, 591
Kleib, Mosiek (van): 502
Klein, Georg: 570, 594
Klein, Marc: 309, 310, 524, 591
Koch, Erich: 465, 466
Koch, Ilse: 19, 118, 309, 312, 325, 326, 371, 437
Koch, Karl-Otto: 19, 312, 325, 352
Koczy, Rosemarie: 192
Koehlen: 473
Kogon, Eugen: 118
Kolias, Pepo: 502
Kollerstrom, Nicholas: 39, 98, 255, 273, 290, 328, 458, 599
Kon, Abe: 183, 312, 313, 411, 492, 544, 545, 546, 593
Kon, Stanisław: 77, 123, 257, 313, 482, 545, 549, 552, 593
Korherr, Richard: 14, 50, 112, 176, 177, 227, 263, 313-315, 539, 592
Korn, Moische: 96, 110, 298, 315, 339, 357, 579, 591
Kosinski, Jerzy: 192, 315, 316
Kotov: 318
Kozak, Stanisław: 68, 70, 316, 592, 594
Krakowski, Shmuel: 47, 151, 446
Kramer, Josef: 14, 23, 49, 76, 77, 316, 317, 387, 388, 435, 443, 479, 510, 537, 592
Kranz, Hermine: 77, 317, 318, 365, 410, 538, 591
Kranz, Tomasz: 348
Krauch, Karl: 392
Kraus, Ota: 128, 318, 322, 323, 476, 532, 591
Krause, Franz: 592
Krausnick, Helmut: 172, 547, 548
Krebsbach, Eduard: 363
Kremer, Johann Paul: 49, 319, 533, 591
Kremer, Tibère: 33
Krupp von Bohlen und Halbach, Gustav: 286
Krupp, Alfried: 392
Krzepicki, Abraham: 29, 320, 488, 544, 593
Kube, Wilhelm: 466
Kudlik, Aleksander: 183, 320, 411, 545, 593
Kues, Thomas: 23, 28, 59, 80, 90, 108, 112, 177, 179, 182, 195, 211, 226, 233, 250, 254, 257, 261-263, 273, 315, 338, 342, 354, 366, 403, 412, 413, 452, 458, 462, 463, 478, 500, 515, 527, 550, 584, 587, 588
Kuklia, Vladislav: 21, 54, 91, 320, 321, 339, 591

Kula, Michał: 58, 278, 281, 321, 322, 336, 396, 410, 591, 609, 610
Kulaszka, Barbara: 61, 75, 76, 129, 558, 605
Kulischer, Eugene M.: 206
Kulka, Erich: 128, 217, 318, 322, 323, 410, 476, 532, 591, 610
Kurant, Tadeusz: 281
Kuśmierczak, Michał: 67
Kwiet, Konrad: 575

— L —
Lächert, Hildegard: 92
Lagarde, Paul de: 341
Laj(ei)zer, Shlojme: 502
Lambert, Erwin: 593
Lammers, Hans: 260, 466
Langbein, Hermann: 19, 41, 62, 208, 326, 335, 464, 471, 588, 589, 591
Langfus, Leib: 327, 333, 334, 532, 591
Lánik, Jozef: see Wetzler, Alfred
Lansky, Lev: 354
Lanzmann, Claude: 95, 114, 160, 190, 379, 446, 461, 511, 520, 568, 570, 578, 601
Laptos, Leo: 327, 487, 591
Laqueur, Walter: 11, 14, 114, 224, 304, 446, 489
Larson, Charles: 268, 328, 592
Laternser, Hans: 209
Lauterpacht, Hersh: 287
Lawrence, Geoffrey: 287, 517
Lea, David: 328, 502, 591
Lebailly, Jacques: 96
Leide, Henry: 199
Leipprand, Horst: 609
Lej(i)bowicz, Aron: 502
Lejbowicz, Szmul: 502
Lemkin, Raphael: 287
Lemko: 502
Lenard, Philipp: 12
Lengyel, Olga: 23, 128, 328, 329, 482, 494, 538, 591
Lenin, Vladimir Ulyanov: 119, 441
Lequeux, Maurice: 23, 123, 128, 329, 330, 482, 513, 591, 610
Lerer, Samuel: 593
Lerner, Leon: 330, 593
Lesky, Simcha: 330, 593
Lestchinsky, Jacob: 491
Lettich, André: 128, 331, 332, 501, 502, 538, 591
Leuchter, Fred A.: 88, 89, 145, 251, 273, 349, 564, 566, 605
Levi, Moshe: 502
Levi, Primo: 14, 201, 252, 332, 333, 369, 591, 594
Levin, Meyer: 205
Levy, Henry: 502
Lévy, Robert: 23, 333, 591
Lewental, Salmen: 23, 327, 333, 334, 591, 610
Lewenthal, Salmen: 502
Lewin, Nathan/Nysel: 502
Lewinkopf, Jozef: see Kosinski, Jerzy
Lewińska, Pelagia: 23, 200, 334, 487, 591, 610

Lewy, Günther: 246, 247
Ley, Robert: 286
Lichtenstein, Mordecai: 123, 183, 335, 538, 591, 610
Lichtman, Eda: 593
Lichtmann, Icek: 335, 496
Liebehenschel, Arthur: 14, 49, 335, 336
Limousin, Henri: 177, 194, 336, 494, 591
Lipka, Waclaw: 502
Lipstadt, Deborah E.: 123, 157, 445, 446, 461
List, Wilhelm: 392
Litwinska, Sofia: 77, 177, 322, 336, 365, 537, 538, 591, 610
Loftus, Elizabeth: 191
Lohse, Hinrich: 465, 466
Longerich, Peter: 231, 575
Louria, Renée: 201
Lubowitsch, Aharon/Arcik: 502
Lüdke, Albin: 593
Ludwig, Bruno: 593
Lüftl, Walter: 151, 372
Łukaszkiewicz, Zdzisław: 77, 97, 123, 196, 313, 338, 348, 495, 497, 499, 546-548, 552, 583, 601
Luther, Martin (politician): 16, 196, 462
Luther, Martin (reformer): 377
Lütkemeyer, Albert: 593

— M —
Mächler, Stefan: 157
Madden, Catherine: 273
Majlech, Michal: see Buki, Milton
Malinski, Gabriel: 502
Mandelbaum, Henryk: 23, 87, 128, 195, 257, 354-356, 365, 404, 410, 480, 502, 513, 538, 568, 591, 610
Mańkowski, Bronisław: 190
Mansfeld, Géza: 177, 194, 356, 494, 591
Manusevich, David: 96, 110, 230, 298, 315, 339, 356, 357, 579, 591
Maous, Françoise: 201
Marco, Enric: 192, 357
Marcus, David: 287
Marcus, Kurt: 19, 23, 128, 195, 230, 244, 357, 482, 538, 591, 610
Maremukha, Andrei I.: 53
Margry, Karel: 173
Mark, Bernard: 240
Mark, Jonathan: 365
Markiewicz, Jan: 88
Maršálek, Hans: 250, 302, 326, 359, 360, 363, 592, 604
Maser, Werner: 517
Mason, Alpheus T.: 289
Mattogno, Carlo: passim
Mauriac, François: 585
Mauriello, Christopher: 391
Maxwell-Fyfe, David: 287
Mayer, Arno J.: 262, 446
McCallum, John D.: 328
McCarthy, Joseph: 536
McNamara, B.P.: 282
Meier, Lili (née Jacob): 34, 562
Mende, Alfred: 192

Mengele, Josef: 72, 78, 102, 118, 159, 177, 258, 298, 318, 336, 355, 364, 365, 381, 394, 412, 476, 504, 523, 530, 563, 577, 585, 596
Menthon, François de: 287
Mermelstein, Melvin: 365, 366, 484, 591
Merten, Georg: 593
Metz, Zelda: 366, 496, 497, 593
Meyer, Ernst: 77
Meyer, Fritjof: 33, 446
Meyzner, August: 551
Mezvinsky, Norton: 377
Michelet, Edmond: 201
Mieczyslaw Grajewski: see Gray, Martin
Mikusz: 502
Milch, Erhard: 392
Miller, Francis T.: 76
Millu, Liana: 201
Mirbach: 281
Mittelman, Emanuel/Manni: 502
Mizrahi, Moses: 502
Moll, Otto: 368, 369, 411, 568, 577
Molotov, Vyacheslav: 53
Moorehead, Alan: 537
Morawa, Mieczyslaw: 502
Mordowicz, Czesław: 369, 370, 404, 471, 568, 574
Morgen, Konrad: 19, 123, 312, 325, 369-371, 452, 482, 494, 592
Morgenthau, Henry: 445, 574
Morsch, Günter: 156
Moryc: 502
Mottel, Samet: 378, 497, 593
Motz, Eugeniusz: 593
Mueller, Wilhelm: 593
Mulka, Robert: 209
Müller, Filip: 19, 23, 42, 128, 178, 195, 200, 244, 272, 281, 322, 323, 365, 368, 378-381, 393, 404, 449, 480, 501, 502, 513, 530, 531, 562, 563, 564, 568, 569, 581, 591, 610
Müller, Heinrich: 257, 301, 359, 474, 493
Müller, Michael: 593
Müller, Otward: 247
Müller, Paul: 149
Münch, Hans: 49, 381, 382, 410, 538, 591
Mussfeldt, Erich: 49, 128, 155, 382, 383, 405, 406, 480, 568, 591, 592
Mylius, Karin: 192

— N —
Nadsari, Marcel: 385, 410, 482, 502, 591, 610
Nagraba, Ludwik: 128, 385, 386, 482, 502, 591
Nahon, Marco: 20, 386, 591, 610
Naumann, Bernd: 99
Naumann, Erich: 166
Nebe, Arthur: 166, 178, 224, 274, 388, 389, 421, 582
Nencel, David: 502
Neudeck, Ruth: 593
Neumann, Robert: 229

Neumann, Simon: 502
Newman, Randolph: 287
Nickell, Joe: 481
Nicosia, Francis R.: 176
Nikitchenko, Iona: 287
Nivromont, Pierre: 201
Niznansky, Ladislav: 434, 435
Noakes, Jeremy: 262
Nocht, Bernhard: 214, 432
Nowik, Ajzik: 502
Nowodowski, Dawid: 391, 544, 593, 594
Nyiszli, Miklos: 19, 23, 58, 72, 79, 128, 200, 244, 272, 332, 337, 365, 379, 393, 394, 404, 410, 412, 480, 501, 502, 530, 531, 563, 564, 592, 610

— O —
O'Keefe, Theodore J.: 210, 366
Oberhauser, Josef: 68, 71, 72, 395, 592
Obrycki, Narcyz Tadeusz: 123, 128, 395, 538, 592, 610
Obydzinski, Roman: 502
Ochshorn, Isaac Egon: 20, 243, 257, 396, 538, 592, 610
Ofshe, Richard: 191
Ohlendorf, Otto: 14, 166, 171, 284, 392, 398, 399, 422, 592
Olère, David: 19, 200, 381, 400, 401, 502, 562-564, 592
Oppenheimer, Robert: 126
Orlet, Rainer: 484
Ostrovski, Edward: 431
Ostrovsky, Leonid: 21, 54, 91, 339, 406, 407, 591
Owens, Jesse: 258

— P —
Paisikovic, Dov: 23, 128, 159, 365, 381, 404, 410-412, 480, 482, 502, 513, 592, 594, 610
Palitzsch, Gerhard: 198
Pankov, Vassily: 412, 497, 593
Panzinger, Friedrich: 166
Pattle, R.E.: 156
Pauly, Max: 593
Pechersky, Alexander: 14, 183, 412, 413, 494, 496, 497, 534, 537, 593
Peer, Moshe: 19, 76, 178, 413, 414, 415, 510, 592
Pegov, Vladimir Y.: 200
Perl, William: 559
Perrault, Gilles: 515
Perry, J.H.: 99, 194
Perz, Bertrand: 156
Peters, Gerhard: 150, 214, 421
Peterson, Agnes F.: 256
Petko, Anany S.: 200
Pezzetti, Marcello: 561
Pfannenstiel, Wilhelm: 71, 227-229, 415, 416, 459, 539, 592
Phillips, Raymond: 77, 278, 316, 317
Piaskowski, Jozef: 190
Piazza, Bruno: 416, 487, 533, 592, 610
Pilecki, Withold: 84, 331, 417, 592
Piller, Walter: 113, 116, 417, 418, 592
Pilo, Aaron: 128, 410, 418, 502, 592,

610
Pilunov, Stefan: 339, 368, 418, 419, 591, 592
Pinochet, Augusto: 456
Pinter, Stephen F.: 201, 419, 592
Pintsch, Karlheinz: 535
Piper, Franciszek: 33, 47, 88, 156
Piper, Michael C.: 366
Plantin, Jean: 200
Pliszko, Lemke/Chaïm: 502
Plucer, Regina: 77, 410, 422, 423, 592, 610
Podchlebnik, Michał: 113, 114, 423, 424, 510, 538, 592, 605
Podchlebnik, Salomon: 424, 496, 593
Poggi, Guiseppe: 565, 567
Pohl, Oswald: 14, 16, 58, 62, 123, 196, 255, 264, 284, 302, 323, 359, 392, 404, 424, 425, 443, 494, 537, 539, 589
Poirier, Robert: 22
Pol Pot: 119, 378
Polevoy, Boris: 87, 183, 427, 428
Poliakov, Léon: 33, 229, 446, 497, 546, 547, 573
Ponsonby, Arthur: 443
Poot, Theodor: 593
Porter, Carlos W.: 441
Poswolski, Henryk: 183, 196, 257, 431, 537, 545, 593
Pradel, Friedrich: 63, 64, 431, 432, 455, 580
Pressac, Jean-Claude: 33, 45-47, 73, 98, 123, 135, 138, 349, 387, 401, 476, 480, 497, 505, 548
Pressburger, Otto: 502
Pridham, Geoffrey: 262
Pronicheva, Dina: 54, 433, 434, 592
Prüfer, Kurt: 128, 535, 582
Prützmann, Hans-Adolf: 166
Ptakowski, Marek: 543
Puchała, Lucjan: 257, 411, 446, 593
Putzker, Fritz: 128, 410, 446, 447, 592, 610

— Q —
Quakernack, Walter: 77, 449, 464

— R —
Rabinowicz, Jakub: 183, 451, 543, 544, 593
Rademacher, Franz: 341
Rademacher, Werner: 245
Raeder, Erich: 286
Rajca, Czesław: 348
Rajchman, Chil: 183, 230, 451, 452, 482, 488, 549, 593
Rajgrodzki, Jerzy: 452, 593
Rajzman, Samuel (Shmuel): 183, 257, 453, 454, 544, 545, 547, 548, 593
Ramler, Siegfried: 287
Rasch, Otto: 166
Rascher, Siegmund: 90, 143, 274, 454
Rassinier, Paul: 251, 272, 391, 415, 454, 455, 461, 592
Rauff, Walter: 14, 63, 432, 455, 456, 592

Razgonayev, Mikhail: 457, 496, 593
Reder, Rudolf: 20, 68-71, 230, 257, 458, 459, 513, 526, 588, 592
Reichel: 281
Reinhardt, Fritz: 27
Reitlinger, Gerald: 32, 33, 446, 546, 547
Renard, Jean-Paul: 101, 461, 592
Renk, Brian: 207
Resnais, Alain: 347
Ricketts, Howard T.: 553
Riefenstahl, Leni: 13
Rieger, Jürgen: 93
Ringelblum, Emmanuel: 66, 112, 113, 463, 494, 543
Ritchie, Andy: 443
Robinson, Jacob: 489
Roding, Werner: 593
Rodríguez, Juan Manuel: 291
Roehl, Karl: 593
Rogerie, André: 463, 487, 592, 610
Roginskij, Arsenij B.: 207
Rögner, Adolf: 65, 93, 94, 208, 326, 436, 463, 464, 468, 592, 602
Röhm, Ernst: 13
Rohwer, Jürgen: 398
Roman Robak: see Reder, Rudolf
Roosevelt, Eleanor: 258
Roosevelt, Franklin D.: 258, 284, 287, 574
Roques, Henri: 96, 228, 272
Rosenberg, Alfred: 14, 185, 187, 206, 284, 286, 422, 462, 465-467, 592
Rosenberg, Eliyahu: 411, 467, 468, 513, 546, 593
Rosenberg, Walter: see Vrba, Rudolf
Rosenblat, Herman: 468, 469, 532, 592
Rosenblum, Joshuah: 23, 128, 195, 244, 403, 404, 469, 480, 502, 592
Rosenblum, Moritz: 470, 592
Rosenfeld, A. H.: 559
Rosenman, Samuel: 287
Rosenthal: 559
Rosenthal, Felix: 502
Rosenthal, Maryla: 94, 209, 470, 471, 592, 594
Rosin, Arnošt: 23, 86, 257, 369, 404, 410, 471, 472, 502, 568, 574, 592
Rothfels, Hans: 228
Routledge, Warren B.: 245, 586
Royall, Kenneth: 558
Rozek, Edward J.: 443
Rozett, Robert: 11-14, 47, 224, 347, 348, 390, 446, 498
Rublee, George: 175
Rückerl, Adalbert: 69, 365, 491, 537
Rudel, Hans-Ulrich: 12
Rudenko, Roman: 287
Rudolf, Germar: 19, 23, 33, 39, 40, 56, 62, 63, 65, 70, 76, 85, 86, 88, 89, 92-94, 99, 103, 108, 109, 123, 126, 136, 139-141, 145, 147, 152, 155, 156, 164, 174, 179, 191, 199, 204, 206, 210, 212-214, 216, 222, 227, 238, 239, 250, 252, 255, 257, 273, 279, 281, 282, 290, 291, 301, 312, 320, 322, 326, 327, 350, 360, 361, 367, 378, 381, 391, 401, 424, 425, 427, 433, 437, 453, 464, 471, 475, 476, 479, 484, 487, 488, 491, 492, 494, 507, 521, 522, 537, 540, 548, 549, 554, 556, 560, 564, 565, 570, 573, 574, 577, 586, 587, 591, 595, 599, 602, 605, 609, 611
Rudolph, Arthur: 397
Rudroff, Anni: 593
Rühl, Felix: 64

— S —
Saalwächter, Ernst: 593
Sack, John: 536
Sackar, Josef: 23, 128, 218, 475, 476, 480, 501, 502, 561, 592, 609, 610
Sadowska, Rajzla: 365, 476, 592, 594
Sander, Fritz: 535
Sandkühler, Thomas: 579
Sanning, Walter N.: 152, 153, 154, 272, 427, 492, 506, 507
Sauckel, Fritz: 286
Sava: 502
Schacht, Hjalmar: 286
Schäfer, Emanuel: 482
Scheffler, Wolfgang: 497, 547, 548
Schelewna Schier, Rozalja: 67
Schellekes, Maurice: 477, 502, 592
Schelvis, Jules: 446, 478, 497, 500, 540, 593, 594
Schepers, Elmar: 210
Schindel, Sol: 502
Schirmer, Gerhart: 474, 475
Schirmer-Vowinckel, Ilse: 247
Schirra, Bruno: 382
Schluch, Karl: 71, 513, 592
Schmidt, Ludwig: 473, 593
Schoeps, Julius H.: 446, 556
Schön, Erich: see Kulka, Erich
Schulman, Samuel: 185, 490
Schultz, Friedrich: 593
Schultze, Karl: 128, 535
Schütt, Hans-Heinz: 593
Schwarz, Deszö: 23, 410, 479, 592
Schwarz, Moritz/Max: 502
Schwarz, Solomon M.: 172
Schwarzbart, Ignacy: 66, 305, 479
Schwarzhuber, Josef: 593
Schwela, Siegfried: 479, 555, 588
Schwensen, Klaus: 96, 420, 475, 583
Schwerger, Heinrich: 593
Scott, Hadding: 258, 491
Seetzen, Heinz: 166
Segev, Tom: 586, 587
Sehn, Jan: 49, 85, 88, 104, 122, 123, 128, 138, 149, 158, 197, 480, 481, 530, 595
Seibert, Wolfgang: 192
Seidenwurm Wrzos, Mary: 178, 481, 538, 592
Sekiewicz, Mieczysław: 114, 534, 592
Sender (Zander), Jacob: 502
Sereny, Gitta: 230, 241, 461, 514
Setkiewicz, Piotr: 150
Seyss-Inquart, Arthur: 286
Shahak, Israel: 377
Shapiro, Henry: 243
Shawcross, Hartley: 287

Sheftel, Yoram: 174, 483
Sher, Neal: 397
Sherman, Gabriel: 469
Shermer, Michael: 264
Shirer, William: 261
Shorrock, Judy: 273
Shulevitz, Judith: 157
Shumacker, Paul: 559
Siebert, Barbara: 469
Siedlecka, Johanna: 316
Silberschein, Abraham: 67, 183, 488, 489, 494, 529
Simpson, Gordon: 146, 368, 489, 536, 558
Singer, Melissa: 273
Skarżyński, Kazimierz: 183, 492, 545, 593
Skorczewski, Dawn: 217
Sloan, James P.: 316
Smirnov, Lev N.: 441, 548
Smith, Arthur L.: 312, 325, 326
Smith, Bradley F.: 256
Smith, Bradley R.: 366
Soerensen, Wilhelm: 473, 488, 537, 593
Sokal, Bernhard Abraham: 502
Solzhenitsyn, Aleksandr: 535
Sompolinski, Roman: 77, 128, 410, 500-502, 538, 592, 610
Sonnenfeldt, Richard: 287
Sosnowski, Jankiel: 502
Spanik, Milan: 502
Spanner, Rudolf: 493, 507
Spector, Shmuel: 11-14, 47, 224, 347, 348, 390, 446, 498
Speer, Albert: 255, 286, 399, 400, 433, 510
Spielberg, Steven: 239, 478
Spörl, Axel: 192
Springer, Elisa: 76, 201, 510, 592
Springer, Markus: 307
Srebrnik, Szymon: 114, 423, 510, 511, 592, 605, 606
St. George, George: 311, 312
Stäglich, Wilhelm: 272
Stahlecker, Walter: 60, 166, 167, 171, 295, 296, 512
Stalin, Joseph Jughashvili: 60, 86, 89, 119, 163, 165, 227, 243, 284, 326, 362, 378, 427, 436, 439, 441, 442, 445, 492, 496, 507, 535
Stanek, Franciszek: 88, 123, 513, 592
Stangl, Franz: 14, 163, 210, 513, 514, 546, 593
Stark, Hans: 42, 61, 209, 379, 514, 592
Steinberg, Paul: 201
Steiner: 559
Steiner, Jean-François: 482, 515, 549
Steinmeyer, Heinrich: 58
Steinmeyer, Marie: 58
Stern, Ursula: 496, 515, 593
Steyuk, Yakov: 21, 54, 91, 339, 515, 516, 591
Stimely, Keith: 517
Straka, Georges: 201
Strawczyński, Oskar: 183, 516, 545, 593
Streicher, Julius: 286, 289, 445, 516, 517
Streim, Alfred: 398
Strong, Herbert: 559
Stroop, Jürgen: 541
Struck, Hermann: 593
Strummer, Adele: 517, 518
Sturdy Colls, Caroline: 347, 542
Suchomel, Franz: 482, 520, 521, 549, 593
Suhren, Fritz: 593
Suhl, Yuri: 497
Sułkowski, Jan: 521, 534, 545, 593
Sulzer, Andreas: 303
Süss, Franz: 128, 257, 365, 482, 502, 522, 523, 592, 594
Susskind, David: 33
Suzuki, Ikuo: 205
Szafrański, Zygmunt: 593
Szajn-Lewin, Eugenia: 183, 525, 593
Szawinski, Serge: 502
Szende, Stefan: 67, 183, 525, 587, 592
Szmajzner, Stanisław: 495, 497, 526, 527, 533, 593
Szperling, Henike: 527, 593
Szulklaper, Rachmin(l): 502

— T —
Tabeau, Jerzy: 20, 86, 482, 487, 488, 529, 538, 568, 574, 592, 610
Tadeusz Serafiński: see Pilecki, Withold
Taft, Robert A.: 289
Tamsen, Friedrich: 593
Tarter, Donald E.: 397
Tauber, Henryk: 23, 58, 87, 123, 128, 138, 160, 195, 200, 365, 368, 404, 410, 449, 480, 482, 501, 502, 530, 531, 568, 592, 609, 610
Taylor, Telford: 287
Tegen, Einar: 481
Tegen, Gunhild: 481
Tesch, Bruno: 86, 99, 353, 389, 445, 473, 532
Thilo, Heinz: 319, 533
Thomas, Max: 166
Thon, Harry: 559
Tillion, Germaine: 201
Toland, John: 312, 325, 371
Toper, Judel: 502
Toulouse-Lautrec, Béatrice de: 201
Townsend, Gregory: 287
Trajtag, Josef: 496, 538, 593
Tregenza, Michael: 68, 69, 459
Treite, Percival K.: 593
Tremlett, Giles: 357
Treue, Wilhelm: 186
Trifa, Veralian: 398
Trksakova, Irma: 457, 593
Trubakov, Ziama: 21, 54, 91, 101, 339, 550, 551, 591
Truman, Harry S.: 284
Tudjman, Franjo: 299
Türk, Richard: 66
Turner, Harald: 223, 270, 551, 552
Turowski, Eugeniusz: 77, 123, 313, 545, 546, 552, 553, 593

— U —
Uhlenbrock, Kurt: 480, 555, 588
Umschweif, Simon: 502
Unverhau, Heinrich: 592, 593
Uthgenannt, Otto: 192, 556

— V —
Vabres, Henri de: 287
Vaillant-Couturier, Marie-Claude: 19, 200, 482, 557, 592
van den Bergh, Siegfried: 200, 487, 557
van Herwaarden, Maria: 558
van Pelt, Robert J.: 123, 281, 428, 446, 461, 480
van Roden, Edward L.: 146, 368, 445, 489, 536, 558, 559
van Ryk, George: 502
Veesenmayer, Edmund: 279, 280
Veil, Simone: 559, 560
Venezia, Morris: 23, 128, 410, 502, 513, 560, 561, 563, 592
Venezia, Shlomo: 123, 128, 195, 200, 365, 404, 410, 482, 501, 502, 560-563, 592, 610
Vice, Sue: 192, 286, 307, 469, 518
Vidal-Naquet, Pierre: 446, 515
Volodarsky, Boris: 223
vom Rath, Ernst: 139
von Braun, Wernher: 303, 397
von Knieriem, August: 290
von Leeb, Wilhelm: 392
von Neurath, Konstantin: 286
von Papen, Franz: 286
von Prowazek, Stanislaus J.M.: 553
von Ribbentrop, Joachim: 195, 253, 286
von Schirach, Baldur: 287
von Thadden, Eberhard: 279, 280
von Weizsäcker, Ernst: 392
Voslensky, Michael S.: 74, 223
Voss, Peter: 568
Vrba, Rudolf: 32-34, 72, 86, 87, 117, 128, 192, 194, 212, 257, 272, 332, 410, 444, 471, 488, 501, 538, 568, 569, 570, 574, 578, 581, 582, 592, 594, 610

— W —
Wachendorff, Irena: 192
Wackernagel, Günther: 593
Wael, Monique de: 192, 571
Wagner, Gustav: 593
Wagner, Horst: 280
Waldmann, Paul: 474, 593
Walsh, William: 287
Walters, Guy: 51, 126, 586
Walus, Frank: 587
Warszawski, Szyja: 237, 482, 534, 545, 549, 575, 593
Wartenberg, Hannah: 287
Watt, Donald: 192, 575
Weber, Józef: 281
Weber, Mark: 75, 76, 101, 157, 366, 367, 494, 587
Weckert, Ingrid: 139, 176
Weinbacher, Karl: 532
Weindling, Paul: 150
Weinkranz, J(Y)ank(ie)l: 502

Weinkranz, Moszek: 502
Weise, Gottfried: 504, 576
Weiss, Janda: 23, 58, 157, 200, 365, 502, 577, 578, 592, 610
Weissmandl, Michael Dov: 578
Weizmann, Chaim: 490
Welbel, Eliezer Leon: 502
Weliczker, Leon: 96, 111, 298, 315, 339, 578, 579, 591
Wellers, Georges: 33, 446
Wells, Leon: see Weliczker, Leon
Wennerstrum, Charles F.: 289, 580
Wentritt, Harry: 65, 431, 432, 580, 581
Werner, Kurt: 54, 263, 581, 592
Werner, Martin: 150, 433, 609
Werner, Steffen: 261
Wesołowski, Jerzy: see Tabeau, Jerzy
Wetzler, Alfred: 34, 72, 86, 87, 117, 128, 192, 194, 257, 272, 332, 444, 471, 487, 488, 501, 538, 568-570, 574, 578, 581, 582, 592, 610
Weydert, Georg: 592
Wheeler-Bennett, John: 287
Wickoff, Jack: 276
Widmann, Albert: 183, 200, 388, 389, 421, 422, 534, 582, 583, 592
Wiernik, Jankiel (Yankiel): 237, 257, 320, 338, 411, 452, 468, 482, 544-549, 583, 584, 593
Wiesel, Abraham: 245, 585
Wiesel, Elie: 14, 23, 200, 230, 245, 271, 307, 316, 365, 446, 461, 584-586, 592
Wiesel, Lazar: 245, 585
Wiesel, Shlomo: 245, 585
Wiesenthal, Simon: 14, 68, 446, 461, 491, 494, 586, 587
Wijnberg, Saartje: 488, 496, 497, 587, 593
Wilhelm, Hans-Heinrich: 94, 172
Wilkomirski, Binjamin: see Doessekker, Bruno
Willenberg, Samuel: 123, 233, 545, 587, 588, 593
Willson, Laurel Rose: 192
Winfrey, Oprah: 468
Winter, Anton: 593
Winter, Peter: 243
Wirth, Christian: 71, 228, 229, 255, 275, 370, 371, 388, 416, 588
Wirths, Eduard: 81, 139, 199, 252, 302, 326, 364, 372, 480, 509, 555, 588, 589, 592
Wise, Stephen: 490, 493
Wisliceny, Dieter: 14, 164, 279, 281, 589, 590, 592
Wissberg: 281
Witt, Hans Christian: 593
Witt, Karl: 593
Wohlfahrt, Wilhelm: 592, 594
Wohlthat, Helmuth: 175, 176
Wojtczak, Stanisław: 548
Wolff, Karl: 71, 436, 484, 504, 552, 594, 595
Wolken, Otto: 20, 41, 192, 247, 365, 532, 534, 592, 595, 596
Wolman, Jakub: 247
Wolny, Jan: 281
Woźniakówna, Michalina: 593
Wulf, Joseph: 573
Wullbrandt, Erich: 413
Wygnanski, Moshe: 502

— Y —

Yeager, Carolyn: 51
Yohanan, Shlomo Maki: 502

— Z —

Ząbecki, Franciszek: 593, 601
Ząbeki, Franciszek: 548
Zaretskaya, Mira: 354
Zaydel, Matvey: 92, 161, 193, 194, 236, 339, 430, 431, 591, 601, 602
Zedong, Mao: 271, 378
Zentner, Christian: 539
Ziereis, Franz: 250, 359, 363, 586, 604
Zimmermann, Michael: 246
Żłobnicki, Adam: 44, 592, 604, 605
Zuleger, Eduard: 593
Zündel, Ernst: 117, 120, 212, 261, 272, 349, 486, 558, 568, 570, 605
Żurawski, Mieczysław: 114, 123, 423, 510, 592, 605, 606
Zuroff, Efraim: 365, 446
Zwinscher, Willy: 593
Zy(Si)lberberg, Jakob/Yankl: 502